ADVENTURES
IN ENGLISH LITERATURE

The ADVENTURES IN LITERATURE Program

ADVENTURES FOR READERS: BOOK ONE
Teacher's Manual
Tests
Reading/Writing Workshop A

ADVENTURES FOR READERS: BOOK TWO
Teacher's Manual
Tests
Reading/Writing Workshop B

ADVENTURES IN READING
Teacher's Manual
Tests
Reading/Writing Workshop C

ADVENTURES IN APPRECIATION
Teacher's Manual
Tests
Reading/Writing Workshop D

ADVENTURES IN AMERICAN LITERATURE
Teacher's Manual
Tests

ADVENTURES IN ENGLISH LITERATURE
Teacher's Manual
Tests

CURRICULUM AND WRITING

Leopold Damrosch
University of Virginia
Charlottesville, Virginia

Leonard F. Dean
Formerly of New York University
New York, New York

William Keach
Rutgers University
New Brunswick, New Jersey

Gerald Levin
University of Akron
Akron, Ohio

The Mall in St. James's Park by Thomas Gainsborough.
Copyright, the Frick Collection, New York

ADVENTURES
IN ENGLISH LITERATURE

HERITAGE EDITION REVISED

HBJ Harcourt Brace Jovanovich, Publishers
Orlando New York Chicago San Diego Atlanta Dallas

Acknowledgments

For permission to reprint copyrighted material, grateful
acknowledgment is made to the following sources:

Curtis Brown Associates, Ltd.: "Mermaid, Dragon,
Fiend" from *Collected Poems* by Robert Graves. Copyright 1938 by Robert Graves.

Jonathan Cape Ltd.: "Naming of Parts" from *A Map of
Verona* by Henry Reed.

The Devin-Adair Company: "The Wild Goat's Kid" from
The Stories of Liam O'Flaherty by Liam O'Flaherty.
Copyright © 1956 by The Devin-Adair Company.

*Dodd, Mead & Company, Inc. and McClelland and
Stewart Limited:* "The Soldier" and an excerpt from
"Peace" from *The Collected Poems of Rupert Brooke* by
Rupert Brooke. Copyright 1915 by Dodd, Mead & Com-
pany, Inc.; renewed 1943 by Edward Marsh.

*Dodd, Mead & Company, Inc. and The Society of
Authors for The Estate of George Bernard Shaw:* "Pygmalion" by Bernard Shaw. Copyright 1913, 1914, 1916,
1930, 1941, 1944 by George Bernard Shaw; renewed 1957
by The Public Trustee as Executor of The Estate of
George Bernard Shaw.

*Doubleday & Company, Inc., A. P. Watt, The Executors
of The Estate of W. Somerset Maugham and William
Heinemann Ltd.:* "The Verger" from *Cosmopolitans* by
W. Somerset Maugham. Copyright 1929 by W. Somerset
Maugham. Published in Britain by William Heinemann
in *Collected Short Stories of W. Somerset Maugham.*

Faber and Faber Ltd.: "The Sunlight on the Garden" and
"The Wiper" from *The Collected Poems of Louis
MacNeice* by Louis MacNeice. "Days" from *The Whit-
sun Weddings* by Philip Larkin.

Faber and Faber Ltd., and Farrar, Straus & Giroux, Inc.:
"On the Move" from *Selected Poems 1950–1975* by
Thom Gunn. Copyright © 1957, 1958, 1961, 1967, 1971,
1973, 1974, 1975, 1976, 1979 by Thom Gunn. Published
in Britain in *The Sense of Movement.*

Harcourt Brace Jovanovich, Inc.: Notes for "Macbeth"
from *Adventures in English Literature,* Classic Edition,
edited by Paul McCormick, Winifred Post, Quentin
Anderson, et al. Copyright © 1963, 1968, 1973 by
Harcourt Brace Jovanovich, Inc. From *Mrs. Dalloway* by
Virginia Woolf. From the Instructor's Manual to Accom-
pany *Literature: Structure, Sound and Sense* by Laurence
Perrine. From Introduction to "Songs of Innocence" from
English Romantic Writers, edited by David Perkins.
"Kings and Queens of England" slightly abridged from
Ancient and Medieval England by J. R. Lander. Copy-
right © 1973 by Harcourt Brace Jovanovich, Inc.

*Harcourt Brace Jovanovich, Inc. and Edward Arnold
(Publishers) Ltd.:* "Notes on the English Character" from
Abinger Harvest by E. M. Forster. Copyright 1936; re-
newed 1964 by E. M. Forster.

Harcourt Brace Jovanovich, Inc. and Jonathan Cape Ltd.:
"The Sniper" from *Spring Sowing* by Liam O'Flaherty.
Published in Britain in *The Short Stories of Liam
O'Flaherty.*

*Harcourt Brace Jovanovich, Inc. and Faber and Faber
Ltd.:* "Preludes" and "The Hollow Men" from *Complete
Poems 1909–1962* by T. S. Eliot. Copyright 1936 by
Harcourt Brace Jovanovich, Inc.; renewed © 1963, 1964
by T. S. Eliot. From "Little Gidding" from *Four Quartets*
by T. S. Eliot.

*Harcourt Brace Jovanovich, Inc., A. M. Heath & Com-
pany Ltd. and The Estate of Sonia Brownwell Orwell
and Martin Secker & Warburg Ltd.:* "Shooting an Ele-
phant" from *Shooting an Elephant and Other Essays* by
George Orwell. Copyright 1945, 1946, 1949, 1950 by
Sonia Brownwell Orwell; renewed 1973, 1974 by Sonia
Orwell. From "The Lion and the Unicorn" from *The
Orwell Reader* by George Orwell.

*Harcourt Brace Jovanovich, Inc., The Hogarth Press Ltd.
and The Author's Literary Estate:* From "1940—Tuesday, September 10th" from *A Writer's Diary* by Virginia
Woolf. "The New Dress" from *The Haunted House and*

Critical Readers

Contents

See page xv for the contents of *Reading and Writing About Literature*

The Restoration and Eighteenth Century

The Twentieth Century 673

*Reading and Writing
About Literature* 919

The Middle Ages
449–1485

The Anglo-Saxon Period
449–1066

THE GERMANIC INVASIONS

Very little is known about the Britons, a Celtic people who were the original inhabitants of Britain. They were conquered by the Romans in the first century A.D. and became a part of the Roman Empire. Evidence of this occupation exists in familiar place names ending in *-caster* or *-chester*, a local version of the Latin word for "camp," *castra*. Around the year 410, when the Roman legions were required at home to protect the capital, the peoples of Britain were left unprotected and fell prey to raiding and looting from their neighbors on the Continent.

According to tradition, it was in 449 that the first band of people from the great North German plain crossed the North Sea to Britain and settled in what is now the county of Kent. They were Jutes, from the peninsula of Jutland in Denmark, and they were the first of many Germanic invaders. Following the Jutes came Angles and Saxons. The Britons were no match for the invaders, but they did not retreat to the mountains and moors without a struggle. The legendary King Arthur may have been the leader of the Celtic people who were driven into Wales.

These Germanic tribes brought with them a common language, the ancestor of our present-day English, called Old English or Anglo-Saxon. Together they created the Anglo-Saxon England ("Angle-land") that lasted until 1066, when the Normans led by William, Duke of Normandy, successfully invaded and conquered the country.

During the Anglo-Saxon period, England was not the unified country it is today. Most of this time the land was divided into separate kingdoms, the most important of which were Kent, Northumbria, Mercia, and Wessex. During the last two centuries of this period, the Anglo-Saxons were compelled to organize themselves to resist further invasions from the Vikings, or Norsemen, whom they called "Danes." King Alfred of Wessex (871–899) was able to unite his people and to force the Danes to the northeast part of England. Anglo-Saxon England was born in warfare, remained an essentially military society, and came to an end in 1066 because of the superior strategy of another military power—the Normans.

King Arthur Tapestry (detail)

Ionian Cross

The Venerable Bede (detail)

449   500   **Anglo-Saxon Kings**   600

King Arthur? 510?–600?   Iona monastery founded 563   Augustine's mission 597

Danish invasion 787   Book of Kells 700's   Venerable Bede 673–735   Caedmon of Whitby c. 670

700

800

Alfred the Great 871–899   *Beowulf* 700?

Anglo-Saxon Chronicle 892   Edward the Confessor 1042–1066   Norman Conquest 1066

900   1000   **1066**

Page from the *Beowulf* manuscript

Page from the Book of Kells

Edward the Confessor (detail), Wilton Diptych

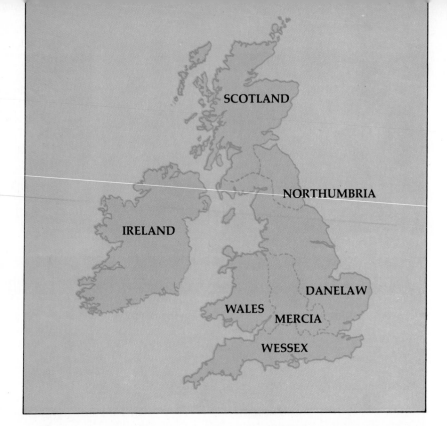

The British Isles in the time of King Alfred.

ANGLO-SAXON CIVILIZATION

Although the Anglo-Saxons frequently fought with one another, they had a great deal in common. Besides a common language base they shared a heroic ideal and set of traditional heroes. They admired men of outstanding courage, whatever tribe they came from. Loyalty to the leader and the tribe and fierce personal valor were considered necessary for the survival of all. Persons of rank were received with grave courtesy, whatever their tribe or people. The ruler was supposed to be generous to those who were loyal, and the followers, in return for this generosity, were to remain loyal. Everyone was aware of the shortness of life and the passing away of all things. Everything was thought to be determined by an impersonal, irresistible fate. Therefore, all competed zealously for fame, the only thing that lasted.

Anglo-Saxon society was comparatively well-developed, branching out from the family unit to the clan and tribe and then to the kingdom. While the Anglo-Saxons easily developed great loyalty to their chosen leaders, they had a natural tendency toward what we should call now a democratic habit of mind—that is, they liked to hold meetings in which people could openly express what they thought and felt.

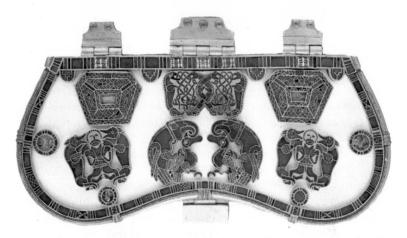

Purse-lid decorated with gold, garnets, and millefiori glass, Sutton Hoo Ship Burial (c. 625). Courtesy, British Museum

Although it is widely known that the Anglo-Saxons were hardy and brave, it is not generally realized that they had a highly developed feeling for beauty. They had a passion for fine ornament, and they produced many beautiful pieces, such as brooches and bracelets of exquisite design and workmanship. They were in fact a more artistic and poetic people than their Norman conquerors, who were essentially soldiers and administrators. The Anglo-Saxons also had vigorous minds. They had men of great learning such as the Venerable Bede (see page 22). By the end of the period we are studying, learning in England was so admired on the Continent that it was natural for European rulers to send to England for teachers.

One aspect of Anglo-Saxon civilization that survives in our daily lives is the names of certain weekdays. The names of these days are derived from the names of old Anglo-Saxon gods: Tuesday from *Tiw*, the god of war; Wednesday from *Woden*, the chief Teutonic god; Thursday from *Thor*, the god of thunder; and Friday from *Frigga*, goddess of the home. Even many basic American traditions in law, conduct, outlook, language, and literature are a legacy from the Anglo-Saxons.

Ornamental boss from a scabbard or sheath, Sutton Hoo. Courtesy, British Museum

THE ESTABLISHMENT OF CHRISTIANITY

Christianity came early to Britain. In A.D. 314 a bishop of London attended the church council at Arles in France. The spread of Christianity was strengthened by missionaries from the Continent. The most famous of these, Saint Augustine, came in 597 and established a monastery at Canterbury. He became the first Archbishop of Canterbury. The Archbishops of Canterbury came to be regarded as the "Primates" of England, or the highest ecclesiastical authority.

In 664 there was a synod at Whitby Abbey, a famous monastery for men and women under the leadership of the Abbess Hilda. She was also spiritual director of the pious Caedmon, the first English religious poet, whose life by Bede is included in this unit (page 23). This synod united the English church with Roman Christianity. The church began to draw the island kingdoms together and encouraged ties, intellectual and commercial, with the rest of Europe.

Cruciform page, Lindisfarne Gospels (c. 700), Cotton MS. Nero D.IV, fol. 26V.
Courtesy, British Library

ANGLO-SAXON LITERATURE

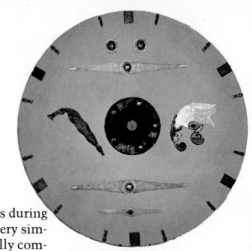

> And sometimes a proud old soldier
> Who had heard songs of the ancient heroes
> And could sing them all through, story after story,
> Would weave a net of words for Beowulf's
> Victory, tying the knot of his verses
> Smoothly, swiftly, into place with a poet's
> Quick skill, singing his new song aloud
> While he shaped it . . .

Reconstruction of a shield, Sutton Hoo. Courtesy, British Museum

This is how the *Beowulf* poet describes the singing of songs during his day. In fact, what is described in these lines is probably very similar to the circumstances under which the poem was originally composed. Anglo-Saxon poetry was an oral art. Poems were not written down until a much later period. Poems were sung, frequently to the accompaniment of a harp. Poets recited well-known poems from memory and at times created new ones. The professional poet, or *scop*, had a very important function in this society. He was the memory and historian of the tribe. It was he who remembered the important heroes, the kings, the important battles, and the folklore of the tribe. The oral nature of the poetry probably necessitated a strong beat and alliteration. These poetic devices not only aided the memory, they were the necessary raw materials for free invention. New songs, such as the one that the soldier sings in the passage above, were made out of old matter.

The two most important traditions of Anglo-Saxon poetry were the heroic tradition and the elegiac tradition, which mourns the passing of earlier, better times. Onto these traditions were grafted Christian beliefs, which gradually replaced pagan ones. Of the 30,000 lines of Anglo-Saxon poetry that remain to us, the most important single poem is the epic *Beowulf*. Of the great elegiac lyrics, the personal, dramatic "Seafarer" is a good example. It may be that the poems to have survived are the ones that appealed to the monks who finally committed them to writing. There are, however, some light and witty riddles in the early manuscripts that may call this theory into question. To the Anglo-Saxon, the riddle was an intellectual exercise. What do you think is the subject of this one?

> I'm prized by men, in the meadows I'm found,
> Gathered on hill-sides, and hunted in groves;
> From dale and from down, by day I am brought.
> Airy wings carry me, cunningly store me,
> Hoarding me safe. Yet soon men take me;
> Drained into vats, I'm dangerous grown.
> I tie up my victim, and trip him, and throw him;

Often I floor a foolish old churl.
Who wrestles with me, and rashly would measure
His strength against mine, will straightway find himself
Flung to the ground, flat on his back,
Unless he leave his folly in time,
Put from his senses and power of speech,
Robbed of his might, bereft of his mind,
Of his hands and feet. Now find me my name,
Who can blind and enslave men so upon earth,
And bring fools low in broad daylight.

The churchmen who wrote verse generally wrote in Latin, though occasionally they included lines in English. (It was from their imitation of church hymns in Latin that the gradual introduction of rhyme into English verse developed.) The earlier prose writers and chroniclers among the Anglo-Saxon churchmen also wrote in Latin. The greatest of these was known as the Venerable Bede (673–735), the most learned and industrious writer of the whole period, author of *A History of the English Church and People* (731), an excellent historical authority of its time. As a historian, Bede is rightly regarded as "the father of English history." Nearly two centuries later, Alfred the Great, the ablest and most remarkable of all English kings, not only became the patron of scholars and educators but also turned author and translator himself after delivering his kingdom from the Danes. Anglo-Saxon prose and history owe most to his influence and his example. Rather than use Latin, as had been the custom, Alfred promoted use of written English and was responsible for the initiation of the *Anglo-Saxon Chronicle*, the first historical record to be kept in English. The briefest study of Alfred's reign makes nonsense of any idea of the Anglo-Saxons as drunken oafs existing in a "Dark Age." Alfred maintained diplomatic relations with all neighboring kings and princes, sent frequent embassies to Rome, corresponded with the Patriarch of Jerusalem, and may even, as we are told, have sent a mission as far as India. He also formulated a code of law and founded the first English "public schools." A truly great man, Alfred did much to educate a society that, with its social organization and laws, its letters and arts, was far from being barbarous, but, indeed, made an enduring contribution to our civilization.

Note: The dates given throughout after the names of kings and rulers are the dates of their reigns; those after the names of literary and other historical figures are birth and death dates.

The geography of *Beowulf.*
Redrawn after F. Klaeber,
Beowulf

from **Beowulf** *Translated by Burton Raffel*

English literature begins with *Beowulf.* It is England's heroic epic, a proper beginning for a national literature, but it belongs to everyone because it is profoundly human. The poem shapes and interprets materials connected with the tribes from northern Europe, the Angles, Saxons, and Jutes, who invaded England after the Romans left in the fifth century. Their tribal history is in the poem. It is remote, even monstrous, and yet familiar: "keeping the bloody feud/Alive . . . and paying the living / For one crime only with another" (lines 68–72). It is a history of festering pride, loud talk, and drunken violence, of spies, bloody borders, and raids. But against this dark background the poem presents another kind of history. It is a history in which a stranger comes openly to help rather than covertly to kill and loot, in which eating and drinking and speaking and gift-giving are natural ceremonies uniting young and old, in which heroic strength is wise and generous. It is a history of ideal possibilities.

The only surviving manuscript of *Beowulf* dates from around 1000, but the work itself was probably composed sometime during the eighth century. The poem, which recounts the exploits of third- or fourth-century Geats and Danes (see map above), is doubtless based on earlier unwritten stories that had been passed from generation to generation by word of mouth. The Anglo-Saxons of Britain shared a common group of heroes with other Germanic peoples, and the hero Beowulf certainly has his origins in an earlier, pagan era. The author of the written version that has come down to us seems to have been a Christian. The language of this version is Old English. The translation you will read in Modern English is by the poet Burton Raffel.

Beowulf, like all epic poems, is about a hero who is leader of his people. The action is extraordinary, the hero larger than life. The diction is stately and many of its scenes — the banquet, the battle, the boast, the voyage, and the funeral — are traditional. The general tone of the poem is somber, owing to a vision of evil in the world, a belief in the power of Fate (*Wyrd* is the Old English word for it) to rule human destiny, and resignation to the certainty of death.

The first selection begins during a banquet given by the Danish king, Hrothgar (hrŏth′gär) in a new mead-hall called Herot, to commemorate his victories. The mead-hall (or banqueting-hall) is so called because of a popular drink, mead, a fermented liquor made of water, honey, malt, and yeast, which was drunk at banquets and celebrations. Herot is also intended to be a place of peace and community. It is a symbol of the loyalty and interdependence of the lord and his faithful warriors. However, Fate has the monster Grendel in store for the Danes.

Page from the *Beowulf* manuscript (c. 1000), Cotton MS. Vitellius A.XV, fol. 140r. Courtesy, British Library

The Coming of Grendel

A powerful monster, living down
In the darkness, growled in pain, impatient
As day after day the music rang
Loud in that hall,° the harp's rejoicing
Call and the poet's clear songs, sung   5
Of the ancient beginnings of us all, recalling
The Almighty making the earth, shaping
These beautiful plains marked off by oceans,
Then proudly setting the sun and moon
To glow across the land and light it;   10
The corners of the earth were made lovely with trees
And leaves, made quick with life, with each
Of the nations who now move on its face. And then
As now warriors sang of their pleasure:
So Hrothgar's men lived happy in his hall   15
Till the monster stirred, that demon, that fiend,
Grendel, who haunted the moors, the wild
Marshes, and made his home in a hell
Not hell but earth. He was spawned in that slime,
Conceived by a pair of those monsters born   20
Of Cain,° murderous creatures banished
By God, punished forever for the crime
Of Abel's death. The Almighty drove
Those demons out, and their exile was bitter,
Shut away from men; they split   25
Into a thousand forms of evil—spirits
And fiends, goblins, monsters, giants,
A brood forever opposing the Lord's
Will, and again and again defeated.

Then, when darkness had dropped, Grendel   30
Went up to Herot, wondering what the warriors
Would do in that hall when their drinking was done.
He found them sprawled in sleep, suspecting
Nothing, their dreams undisturbed. The monster's
Thoughts were as quick as his greed or his claws: 35
He slipped through the door and there in the silence
Snatched up thirty men, smashed them
Unknowing in their beds and ran out with their bodies,
The blood dripping behind him, back
To his lair, delighted with his night's slaughter.   40

---

4. **hall:** Herot. 21. **Cain:** Cain, the son of Adam and Eve, was cursed by God for slaying his brother Abel. There was a tradition that Cain sired a family of monsters. See the Biblical story in Genesis 4.

At daybreak, with the sun's first light, they saw
How well he had worked, and in that gray morning
Broke their long feast with tears and laments
For the dead. Hrothgar, their lord, sat joyless
In Herot, a mighty prince mourning   45
The fate of his lost friends and companions,
Knowing by its tracks that some demon had torn
His followers apart. He wept, fearing
The beginning might not be the end. And that night
Grendel came again, so set   50
On murder that no crime could ever be enough,
No savage assault quench his lust
For evil. Then each warrior tried
To escape him, searched for rest in different
Beds, as far from Herot as they could find,   55
Seeing how Grendel hunted when they slept.
Distance was safety; the only survivors
Were those who fled him. Hate had triumphed.
   So Grendel ruled, fought with the righteous,
One against many, and won; so Herot   60
Stood empty, and stayed deserted for years,
Twelve winters of grief for Hrothgar, king
Of the Danes, sorrow heaped at his door
By hell-forged hands. His misery leaped
The seas, was told and sung in all   65
Men's ears: how Grendel's hatred began,
How the monster relished his savage war
On the Danes, keeping the bloody feud
Alive, seeking no peace, offering
No truce, accepting no settlement, no price   70
In gold or land, and paying the living
For one crime only with another. No one
Waited for reparation from his plundering claws:
That shadow of death hunted in the darkness,
Stalked Hrothgar's warriors, old   75
And young, lying in waiting, hidden
In mist, invisibly following them from the edge
Of the marsh, always there, unseen.
   So mankind's enemy continued his crimes,
Killing as often as he could, coming   80
Alone, bloodthirsty and horrible. Though he lived
In Herot, when the night hid him, he never
Dared to touch king Hrothgar's glorious
Throne, protected by God — God,
Whose love Grendel could not know. But Hrothgar's   85
Heart was bent. The best and most noble
Of his council debated remedies, sat

Gold buckle with inter-
lace pattern, Sutton Hoo.
Courtesy, British Museum

In secret sessions, talking of terror
And wondering what the bravest of warriors could do.
And sometimes they sacrificed to the old stone gods.   90
Made heathen vows, hoping for Hell's
Support, the Devil's guidance in driving
Their affliction off. That was their way,
And the heathen's only hope, Hell
Always in their hearts, knowing neither God   95
Nor His passing as He walks through our world, the Lord
Of Heaven and earth; their ears could not hear
His praise nor know His glory. Let them
Beware, those who are thrust into danger,
Clutched at by trouble, yet can carry no solace   100
In their hearts, cannot hope to be better! Hail
To those who will rise to God, drop off
Their dead bodies and seek our Father's peace!

   So the living sorrow of Healfdane's son°
Simmered, bitter and fresh, and no wisdom   105
Or strength could break it: that agony hung
On king and people alike, harsh
And unending, violent and cruel, and evil.
   In his far-off home Beowulf, Higlac's°
Follower and the strongest of the Geats—greater   110
And stronger than anyone anywhere in this world—
Heard how Grendel filled nights with horror
And quickly commanded a boat fitted out,
Proclaiming that he'd go to that famous king,
Would sail across the sea to Hrothgar,   115
Now when help was needed. None
Of the wise ones regretted his going, much
As he was loved by the Geats: the omens were good,

---

104. **Healfdane's son** (hā′ălf-dĕn-nə): Hrothgar. The word means "half-dane." Healfdane's mother was a foreigner.   109. **Higlac** (hĭg′ə-lăk): king of the Geats. He is
Beowulf's feudal lord and his uncle.

And they urged the adventure on. So Beowulf
Chose the mightiest men he could find,   120
The bravest and best of the Geats, fourteen
In all, and led them down to their boat;
He knew the sea, would point the prow
Straight to that distant Danish shore.

The Coming of Beowulf

When he reaches the Danish shore, Beowulf explains his mission to the
alert watchman, who receives him courteously, posts a guard to protect
his ship, and leads him and his men to Herot. There he is welcomed by
the noble Wulfgar and presented to King Hrothgar.

Then Wulfgar went to the door and addressed   125
The waiting seafarers with soldier's words:
  "My lord, the great king of the Danes, commands me
To tell you that he knows of your noble birth
And that having come to him from over the open
Sea you have come bravely and are welcome.   130
Now go to him as you are, in your armor and helmets,
But leave your battle-shields here, and your spears,
Let them lie waiting for the promises your words
May make."
          Beowulf arose, with his men
Around him, ordering a few to remain
With their weapons, leading the others quickly
Along under Herot's steep roof into Hrothgar's
Presence. Standing on that prince's own hearth,
Helmeted, the silvery metal of his mail shirt
Gleaming with a smith's high art, he greeted
The Danes' great lord:
                    "Hail, Hrothgar!
Higlac is my cousin° and my king; the days
Of my youth have been filled with glory. Now Grendel's
Name has echoed in our land: sailors
Have brought us stories of Herot, the best   145
Of all mead-halls, deserted and useless when the moon
Hangs in skies the sun had lit,
Light and life fleeing together.
My people have said, the wisest, most knowing

Reconstructed helmet
with gilt-bronze orna-
ment, Sutton Hoo.
Courtesy, British Museum

142. **cousin:** a general term for a relative.

And best of them, that my duty was to go to the Danes'　　150
Great king. They have seen my strength for themselves,
Have watched me rise from the darkness of war,
Dripping with my enemies' blood. I drove
Five great giants into chains, chased
All of that race from the earth. I swam　　155
In the blackness of night, hunting monsters
Out of the ocean, and killing them one
By one; death was my errand and the fate
They had earned. Now Grendel and I are called
Together, and I've come. Grant me, then,　　160
Lord and protector of this noble place,
A single request! I have come so far,
O shelterer of warriors and your people's loved friend,
That this one favor you should not refuse me—
That I, alone and with the help of my men,　　165
May purge all evil from this hall. I have heard,
Too, that the monster's scorn of men
Is so great that he needs no weapons and fears none.
Nor will I. My lord Higlac
Might think less of me if I let my sword　　170
Go where my feet were afraid to, if I hid
Behind some broad linden° shield: my hands
Alone shall fight for me, struggle for life
Against the monster. God must decide
Who will be given to death's cold grip.　　175
Grendel's plan, I think, will be
What it has been before, to invade this hall
And gorge his belly with our bodies. If he can,
If he can. And I think, if my time will have come,
There'll be nothing to mourn over, no corpse to prepare　　180
For its grave: Grendel will carry our bloody
Flesh to the moors, crunch on our bones
And smear torn scraps of our skin on the walls
Of his den. No, I expect no Danes
Will fret about sewing our shrouds, if he wins.　　185
And if death does take me, send the hammered
Mail of my armor to Higlac, return
The inheritance I had from Hrethel, and he
From Wayland.° Fate will unwind as it must!"

　　Then Hrothgar's men gave places to the Geats,　　190
Yielded benches to the brave visitors

---

172. **linden:** Beowulf's shield is made of linden wood, a very sturdy wood similar
to North American basswood.　189. **Wayland** (wā′lănd): a blacksmith celebrated in
many surviving Germanic poems. His workmanship was of the finest, and only
aristocrats could afford it.

And led them to the feast. The keeper of the mead
Came carrying out the carved flasks,
And poured that bright sweetness. A poet
Sang, from time to time, in a clear   195
Pure voice. Danes and visiting Geats
Celebrated as one, drank and rejoiced.

   There was the sound of laughter, and the cheerful clanking
Of cups, and pleasant words. Then Welthow,
Hrothgar's gold-ringed° queen, greeted   200
The warriors; a noble woman who knew
What was right, she raised a flowing cup
To Hrothgar first, holding it high
For the lord of the Danes to drink, wishing him
Joy in that feast. The famous king   205
Drank with pleasure and blessed their banquet.
Then Welthow went from warrior to warrior,
Pouring a portion from the jeweled cup
For each, till the bracelet-wearing queen
Had carried the mead-cup among them and it was Beowulf's   210
Turn to be served. She saluted the Geats'
Great prince, thanked God for answering her prayers,
For allowing her hands the happy duty
Of offering mead to a hero who would help
Her afflicted people. He drank what she poured,   215
Edgetho's brave son, then assured the Danish
Queen that his heart was firm and his hands
Ready:
     "When we crossed the sea, my comrades
And I, I already knew that all
My purpose was this: to win the good will   220
Of your people or die in battle, pressed
In Grendel's fierce grip. Let me live in greatness
And courage, or here in this hall welcome
My death!"
       Welthow was pleased with his words,
His bright-tongued boasts; she carried them back   225
To her lord, walked nobly across to his side.
   The feast went on, laughter and music
And the brave words of warriors celebrating
Their delight. . . .

---

200. **gold-ringed:** wearing gold bracelets.

Reconstructed drinking
horns and maple bottle,
Sutton Hoo.
Courtesy British Museum

The Battle with Grendel

After the banquet the Danes retire for the night, but Beowulf and his followers stay on in Herot as they have requested. Beowulf renews his promise to
fight without a weapon and pretends to sleep. His followers take the places
of Hrothgar's men and settle down for the night.

> Out from the marsh, from the foot of misty   230
> Hills and bogs, bearing God's hatred,
> Grendel came, hoping to kill
> Anyone he could trap on this trip to high Herot.
> He moved quickly through the cloudy night,
> Up from his swampland, sliding silently   235
> Toward that gold-shining hall. He had visited Hrothgar's
> Home before, knew the way—
> But never, before nor after that night,
> Found Herot defended so firmly, his reception
> So harsh. He journeyed, forever joyless,   240
> Straight to the door, then snapped it open,
> Tore its iron fasteners with a touch
> And rushed angrily over the threshold.
> He strode quickly across the inlaid
> Floor, snarling and fierce: his eyes   245
> Gleamed in the darkness, burned with a gruesome
> Light. Then he stopped, seeing the hall
> Crowded with sleeping warriors, stuffed
> With rows of young soldiers resting together.
> And his heart laughed, he relished the sight,   250
> Intended to tear the life from those bodies
> By morning; the monster's mind was hot
> With the thought of food and the feasting his belly
> Would soon know. But fate, that night, intended
> Grendel to gnaw the broken bones   255
> Of his last human supper. Human
> Eyes were watching his evil steps,
> Waiting to see his swift hard claws.

Grendel snatched at the first Geat
He came to, ripped him apart, cut   260
His body to bits with powerful jaws,
Drank the blood from his veins and bolted
Him down, hands and feet; death
And Grendel's great teeth came together,
Snapping life shut. Then he stepped to another   265
Still body, clutched at Beowulf with his claws,
Grasped at a strong-hearted wakeful sleeper
—And was instantly seized himself, claws
Bent back as Beowulf leaned up on one arm.
    That shepherd of evil, guardian of crime,   270
Knew at once that nowhere on earth
Had he met a man whose hands were harder;
His mind was flooded with fear—but nothing
Could take his talons and himself from that tight
Hard grip. Grendel's one thought was to run   275
From Beowulf, flee back to his marsh and hide there:
This was a different Herot than the hall he had emptied.
But Higlac's follower remembered his final
Boast and, standing erect, stopped
The monster's flight, fastened those claws   280
In his fists till they cracked, clutched Grendel
Closer. The infamous killer fought
For his freedom, wanting no flesh but retreat,
Desiring nothing but escape; his claws
Had been caught, he was trapped. That trip to Herot   285
Was a miserable journey for the writhing monster!
    The high hall rang, its roof boards swayed,
And Danes shook with terror. Down
The aisles the battle swept, angry
And wild. Herot trembled, wonderfully   290
Built to withstand the blows, the struggling
Great bodies beating at its beautiful walls;
Shaped and fastened with iron, inside
And out, artfully worked, the building
Stood firm. Its benches rattled, fell   295
To the floor, gold-covered boards grating
As Grendel and Beowulf battled across them.
Hrothgar's wise men had fashioned Herot
To stand forever; only fire,
They had planned, could shatter what such skill had put   300
Together, swallow in hot flames such splendor
Of ivory and iron and wood. Suddenly
The sounds changed, the Danes started
In new terror, cowering in their beds as the terrible
Screams of the Almighty's enemy sang   305

In the darkness, the horrible shrieks of pain
And defeat, the tears torn out of Grendel's
Taut throat, hell's captive caught in the arms
Of him who of all the men on earth
Was the strongest.

                That mighty protector of men
Meant to hold the monster till its life
Leaped out, knowing the fiend was no use
To anyone in Denmark. All of Beowulf's
Band had jumped from their beds, ancestral
Swords raised and ready, determined
To protect their prince if they could. Their courage
Was great but all wasted: they could hack at Grendel
From every side, trying to open
A path for his evil soul, but their points
Could not hurt him, the sharpest and hardest iron   320
Could not scratch at his skin, for that sin-stained demon
Had bewitched all men's weapons, laid spells
That blunted every mortal man's blade.
And yet his time had come, his days
Were over, his death near; down   325
To hell he would go, swept groaning and helpless
To the waiting hands of still worse fiends.
Now he discovered—once the afflictor
Of men, tormentor of their days—what it meant
To feud with Almighty God: Grendel   330
Saw that his strength was deserting him, his claws
Bound fast, Higlac's brave follower tearing at
His hands. The monster's hatred rose higher,
But his power had gone. He twisted in pain,
And the bleeding sinews deep in his shoulder   335
Snapped, muscle and bone split
And broke. The battle was over, Beowulf
Had been granted new glory: Grendel escaped,
But wounded as he was could flee to his den,
His miserable hole at the bottom of the marsh,   340
Only to die, to wait for the end
Of all his days. And after that bloody
Combat the Danes laughed with delight.
He who had come to them from across the sea,
Bold and strong-minded, had driven affliction   345
Off, purged Herot clean. He was happy,
Now, with that night's fierce work; the Danes
Had been served as he'd boasted he'd serve them; Beowulf,
A prince of the Geats, had killed Grendel,
Ended the grief, the sorrow, the suffering   350

A Celtic hanging bowl,
Sutton Hoo.
Courtesy, British Museum

Forced on Hrothgar's helpless people
By a bloodthirsty fiend. No Dane doubted
The victory, for the proof, hanging high
From the rafters where Beowulf had hung it, was the monster's
Arm, claw and shoulder and all.   355

   And then, in the morning, crowds surrounded
Herot, warriors coming to that hall
From faraway lands, princes and leaders
Of men hurrying to behold the monster's
Great staggering tracks. They gaped with no sense   360
Of sorrow, felt no regret for his suffering,
Went tracing his bloody footprints, his beaten
And lonely flight, to the edge of the lake
Where he'd dragged his corpselike way, doomed
And already weary of his vanishing life.   365
The water was bloody, steaming and boiling
In horrible pounding waves, heat
Sucked from his magic veins; but the swirling
Surf had covered his death, hidden
Deep in murky darkness his miserable   370
End, as hell opened to receive him.
   Then old and young rejoiced, turned back
From that happy pilgrimage, mounted their hardhooved
Horses, high-spirited stallions, and rode them
Slowly toward Herot again, retelling   375
Beowulf's bravery as they jogged along.
And over and over they swore that nowhere
On earth or under the spreading sky
Or between the seas, neither south nor north,
Was there a warrior worthier to rule over men.   380
(But no one meant Beowulf's praise to belittle
Hrothgar, their kind and gracious king!)
   And sometimes, when the path ran straight and clear,
They would let their horses race, red
And brown and pale yellow backs streaming   385
Down the road. And sometimes a proud old soldier
Who had heard songs of the ancient heroes
And could sing them all through, story after story,
Would weave a net of words for Beowulf's
Victory, tying the knot of his verses°   390
Smoothly, swiftly, into place with a poet's
Quick skill, singing his new song aloud
While he shaped it. . . .

389–390. **Would weave . . . verses:** The poet compares the composing of a song to
the weaving of a tapestry.

FOR STUDY AND DISCUSSION

1. What do you think Grendel represents? With what aspects of nature is he associated? How does Grendel's world contrast with that of Herot?

2. Besides being exciting, how is the battle with Grendel a representation of good against evil? What is the significance of Beowulf's meeting Grendel alone and unarmed?

3. The warriors who follow Grendel's footprints to the lake have no sense of sorrow, feel no regret for Grendel's suffering. How did you respond to him after he was wounded? How do you think the poet wanted you to respond? Point out specific lines that support your answer.

4. In what ways does *Beowulf* illustrate the following Anglo-Saxon ideals of conduct: (a) allegiance to lord and king; (b) love of glory as the ruling motive of every noble life; and (c) belief in the inevitability of fate?

CHARACTERISTICS OF ANGLO-SAXON POETRY

Anglo-Saxon poetry had a strong oral tradition behind it. The poems were memorized rather than written and were recited by *scops*, wandering poets who chanted their poems in the mead halls of kings and nobles.

Anglo-Saxon poetry does not rhyme, but the poems have very strong rhythms, suitable for chanting. The rhythm of a line depends primarily on the number of *beats*, or accented syllables. Each line has four beats. The number of unaccented syllables in a line may vary. Some lines may be long and others short. Each line has a strong pause, or *caesura* (sĭ-zhoͦor'ə), after the second beat. Each line is divided into two parts, each with two beats.

Alliteration is used to bind together the two halves of a line. One or more accented syllables in the first half of a line almost always alliterate with one or more accented syllables in the second half.

If the jingle about Old King Cole were put into Anglo-Saxon verse form, it might sound like this:

Cole was the King; he was keen and merry;
Mirthful he was, with minstrels in mead-hall.
He called for his cup; he called for his pipe.
His fiddlers were three, and fine was their
  trilling.

Another characteristic of Anglo-Saxon poetry is the use of *kennings*. A kenning is a metaphorical phrase or compound word used instead of the name of a person or thing. For example, Grendel is called the "shepherd of evil" (line 270). Kennings are closely related to riddles. What might the following kennings refer to: "the whale-road"; "the sea-paths"; "God's bright beacon"; and "Heaven's high arch"?

FOR COMPOSITION

1. Epic heroes usually exemplify the character traits most admired by their societies. What qualities are most admired by Beowulf's society? Write a short essay on the ideal king and warrior, citing evidence from the poem.

2. Every generation has had its heroes who reflect the general character of their society. Discuss the similarities and differences in the concept of the hero in Anglo-Saxon times and today. What do these differences reveal about the change in morals and values? What do they reveal about continuity in our morals and values?

3. Dragons - mythical monsters short paper

4. Fairy tale, myth or fable short epic

Bede
673–735

Bede, the Venerable, was the earliest historian of England and the earliest important prose writer. He was a contemporary of the unknown author of *Beowulf.* Bede, who was a monk, was known in his own day as a man of great scholarship and learning. His books were read and copied all over Europe. The title "Venerable" was added to his name in recognition of his reputation for wisdom, humility, and scholarship. He seems to have traveled little and spent most of his life, beginning at the age of seven, at the monastery of Jarrow.

Bede's *History of the English Church and People* was originally written in Latin. However, the translation into Old English, undertaken in the reign of King Alfred the Great, became a classic and helped the people of the emerging English nation to take pride in their past. The *History* itself is more than a chronicle of events. It also contains legends, lives of saints, local traditions, and stories. One can get a fairly accurate picture of the daily life of the people from Bede's history.

"Caedmon of Whitby," the selection included here, tells of a miraculous event in the life of a man many people consider to be the first English religious poet. Caedmon was taken into Whitby Abbey in Northumbria when it was governed by its founder, St. Hilda (658–680), and so his Hymn dates from that period. He may have been the first to use the old heroic verse forms for exclusively religious subjects.

An early scribe thought to be Venerable Bede, from an illuminated manuscript, Add. 39943, F. 2.
Courtesy, British Library

from A History of the English Church and People

Translated by Leo Sherley-Price

Caedmon of Whitby

In this monastery of [Whitby] lived a brother singularly gifted by God's grace. So skillful was he in composing religious and devotional songs that, when any passage of Scripture was explained to him by interpreters, he could quickly turn it into delightful and moving poetry in his own English tongue. These verses of his have stirred the hearts of many folk to despise the world and aspire to heavenly things. Others after him tried to compose religious poems in English, but none could compare with him; for he did not acquire the art of poetry from men or through any human teacher but received it as a free gift from God. For this reason he could never compose any frivolous or profane verses; but only such as had a religious theme fell fittingly from his devout lips. He had followed a secular occupation until well advanced in years without ever learning anything about poetry. Indeed it sometimes happened at a feast that all the guests in turn would be invited to sing and entertain the company; then, when he saw the harp coming his way, he would get up from table and go home.

On one such occasion he had left the house in which the entertainment was being held and went out to the stable, where it was his duty that night to look after the beasts. There when the time came he settled down to sleep. Suddenly in a dream he saw a man standing beside him who called him by name. "Caedmon," he said, "sing me a song." "I don't know how to sing," he replied. "It is because I cannot sing that I left the feast and came here." The man who addressed him then said: "But you shall sing to me." "What should I sing about?" he replied. "Sing about the Creation of all things," the other answered. And Caedmon immediately began to sing verses in praise of God the Creator that he had never heard before, and their theme ran thus:

> Praise we the Fashioner now of Heaven's fabric,
> The majesty of his might and his mind's wisdom,
> Work of the world-warden, worker of all wonders,
> How he the Lord of Glory everlasting,
> Wrought first for the race of men Heaven as a rooftree,
> Then made he Middle Earth to be their mansion.

This is the general sense, but not the actual words that Caedmon sang in his dream; for verses, however masterly, cannot be translated literally from one language into another without losing much of their beauty and dignity. When Caedmon awoke, he remembered everything that he had sung in his dream, and soon added more verses in the same style to a song truly worthy of God.

Early in the morning he went to his superior, the reeve,[1] and told him about this gift that he had received. The reeve took him before the abbess,[2] who ordered him to give an

---

1. **reeve:** the manager of an estate; here the steward in charge of the monastery.
2. **abbess:** the superior of a monastery for nuns and monks.

account of his dream and repeat the verses in the presence of many learned men, so that a decision might be reached by common consent as to their quality and origin. All of them agreed that Caedmon's gift had been given him by our Lord. And they explained to him a passage of Scriptural history or doctrine and asked him to render it into verse if he could. He promised to do this, and returned next morning with excellent verses as they had ordered him. The abbess was delighted that God had given such grace to the man, and advised him to abandon secular life and adopt the monastic state.[3] And when she had admitted him into the Community as a brother, she ordered him to be instructed in the events of sacred history. So Caedmon stored up in his memory all that he learned, and like one of the clean animals chewing the cud, turned it into such melodious verse that his delightful renderings turned his instructors into auditors. He sang of the Creation of the world, the origin of the human race, and the whole story of Genesis. He sang of Israel's exodus from Egypt, the entry into the Promised Land, and many other events of Scriptural history. He sang of the Lord's Incarnation, Passion, Resurrection, and Ascension into Heaven, the coming of the Holy Spirit, and the teaching of the apostles. He also made many poems on the terrors of the Last Judgment, the horrible pains of Hell, and the joys of the Kingdom of Heaven. In addition to these, he composed several others on the blessings and judgments of God, by which he sought to turn his hearers from delight in wickedness and to inspire them to love and do good. For Caedmon was a deeply religious man, who humbly submitted to regular discipline and hotly rebuked all who tried to follow another course. And so he crowned his life with a happy end.

---

3. **monastic state:** Caedmon was originally a lay brother attached to the monastery. Here the abbess is inviting him to become a full-fledged member of the monastery by taking special vows and participating in the singing of the choir.

FOR STUDY AND DISCUSSION

1. The story of Caedmon has perennial appeal as an account of lowliness exalted. Where else may one find this theme? Bear in mind that Caedmon had his dream in a stable.

2. Why were the learned men convinced that Caedmon had received his gift from God?

3. Bede, who wrote in Latin, explains that he can give only the "sense" of the poem that Caedmon sang (in Anglo-Saxon) for the person who appeared to him in his sleep. Bede explains that "verses, however masterly, cannot be translated literally from one language into another without losing much of their beauty and dignity." Do you agree? Why or why not?

The Seafarer   *Translated by Burton Raffel*

"The Seafarer," an anonymous poem of uncertain date, was found in the so-called *Exeter Book*, one of the four important collections of Anglo-Saxon poetry that have survived. The poem is lyrical and elegiac. The speaker of the poem, an old sailor, speaks of the terror and the wonder he feels for the sea.

The poem conjures up what going to sea in an open, high-prowed ship must have been like in Anglo-Saxon days. The Irish Sea and the North Sea waters were very different from the tranquil, warm waters of the Mediterranean Sea, which had been the waterway of the Greeks and the Romans.

Because of the importance of the sea to an island people, British poetry is frequently concerned with the sea, and the images and feelings expressed in "The Seafarer" recur in many later poems.

This tale is true, and mine. It tells
How the sea took me, swept me back
And forth in sorrow and fear and pain,
Showed me suffering in a hundred ships,
In a thousand ports, and in me. It tells   5
Of smashing surf when I sweated in the cold
Of an anxious watch, perched in the bow
As it dashed under cliffs. My feet were cast
In icy bands, bound with frost,
With frozen chains, and hardship groaned   10
Around my heart. Hunger tore
At my sea-weary soul. No man sheltered
On the quiet fairness of earth can feel
How wretched I was, drifting through winter
On an ice-cold sea, whirled in sorrow,   15
Alone in a world blown clear of love,
Hung with icicles. The hailstorms flew.
The only sound was the roaring sea,
The freezing waves. The song of the swan
Might serve for pleasure, the cry of the sea-fowl,   20
The death-noise of birds instead of laughter,
The mewing of gulls instead of mead.
Storms beat on the rocky cliffs and were echoed
By icy-feathered terns and the eagle's screams;
No kinsman could offer comfort there,   25
To a soul left drowning in desolation.
         And who could believe, knowing but
The passion of cities, swelled proud with wine
And no taste of misfortune, how often, how wearily,
I put myself back on the paths of the sea.   30
Night would blacken; it would snow from the north;
Frost bound the earth and hail would fall,

The coldest seeds. And how my heart
Would begin to beat, knowing once more
The salt waves tossing and the towering sea!   35
The time for journeys would come and my soul
Called me eagerly out, sent me over
The horizon, seeking foreigners' homes.
          But there isn't a man on earth so proud,
So born to greatness, so bold with his youth,   40
Grown so brave, or so graced by God,
That he feels no fear as the sails unfurl,
Wondering what Fate has willed and will do.
No harps ring in his heart, no rewards,
No passion for women, no worldly pleasures,   45
Nothing, only the ocean's heave;
But longing wraps itself around him.
Orchards blossom, the towns bloom,
Fields grow lovely as the world springs fresh,
And all these admonish that willing mind   50
Leaping to journeys, always set
In thoughts traveling on a quickening tide.
So summer's sentinel, the cuckoo, sings
In his murmuring voice, and our hearts mourn
As he urges. Who could understand,   55
In ignorant ease, what we others suffer
As the paths of exile stretch endlessly on?
          And yet my heart wanders away,
My soul roams with the sea, the whales'
Home, wandering to the widest corners   60
Of the world, returning ravenous with desire,
Flying solitary, screaming, exciting me
To the open ocean, breaking oaths
On the curve of a wave.
                    Thus the joys of God
Are fervent with life, where life itself   65
Fades quickly into the earth. The wealth
Of the world neither reaches to Heaven nor remains.
No man has ever faced the dawn
Certain which of Fate's three threats
Would fall: illness, or age, or an enemy's   70
Sword, snatching the life from his soul.
The praise the living pour on the dead
Flowers from reputation: plant
An earthly life of profit reaped
Even from hatred and rancor, of bravery   75
Flung in the devil's face, and death
Can only bring you earthly praise
And a song to celebrate a place

With the angels, life eternally blessed
In the hosts of Heaven. The days are gone   80
When the kingdoms of earth flourished in glory;
Now there are no rulers, no emperors,
No givers of gold, as once there were,
When wonderful things were worked among them
And they lived in lordly magnificence.   85
Those powers have vanished, those pleasures are dead.
The weakest survives and the world continues,
Kept spinning by toil. All glory is tarnished.
The world's honor ages and shrinks,
Bent like the men who mold it. Their faces   90
Blanch as time advances, their beards
Wither and they mourn the memory of friends.
The sons of princes, sown in the dust.
The soul stripped of its flesh knows nothing
Of sweetness or sour, feels no pain,   95
Bends neither its hand nor its brain. A brother
Opens his palms and pours down gold
On his kinsman's grave, strewing his coffin
With treasures intended for Heaven, but nothing
Golden shakes the wrath of God   100
For a soul overflowing with sin, and nothing
Hidden on earth rises to Heaven.
                We all fear God. He turns the earth,
He set it swinging firmly in space,
Gave life to the world and light to the sky.   105
Death leaps at the fools who forget their God.
He who lives humbly has angels from Heaven
To carry him courage and strength and belief.
A man must conquer pride, not kill it,
Be firm with his fellows, chaste for himself,   110
Treat all the world as the world deserves,
With love or with hate but never with harm,
Though an enemy seek to scorch him in hell,
Or set the flames of a funeral pyre
Under his lord. Fate is stronger   115
And God mightier than any man's mind.
Our thoughts should turn to where our home is,
Consider the ways of coming there,
Then strive for sure permission for us
To rise to that eternal joy,   120
That life born in the love of God
And the hope of Heaven. Praise the Holy
Grace of Him who honored us,
Eternal, unchanging creator of earth. Amen.

FOR STUDY AND DISCUSSION

1. The first 64 lines express contrasting feelings about seafaring. What are those feelings? How do they change with the seasons?

2. The transitional sentence, lines 64–66, connects seafaring with religion. What sets of ideas is the poet trying to compress into this sentence? How, if at all, are they related to the feelings about seafaring in the opening section?

3. Lines 80–103 contrast the dismal present with the glorious past. What are the main points of the contrast?

4. What are the meanings of "home" in line 117? What kind of "seafaring" does the poet finally advocate?

5. Some critics consider this poem a kind of dialogue or conversation between two opposing attitudes. Imagine the poem as a conversation between two speakers. Which lines would be spoken by each one? Give line numbers. Try giving each speaker a name to characterize the attitude expressed.

FOR COMPOSITION

In a short essay compare the speaker of this poem and his attitudes toward fate and the sea with Beowulf and his attitudes. How does the elegiac tone of this poem compare with the heroic tone of *Beowulf?*

A Viking ship known as the Oseberg Ship.
© University Museum of National Antiquities, Oslo, Norway

The Old English Period

Language existed long before written literature. We cannot trace English, or any other language, to its ultimate origin, because this origin is buried far back in the prehistoric past of the human race.

We can, however, trace the history of English as far back as a language that scholars call "Indo-European," which was spoken five or six thousand years ago by a group of tribes who lived somewhere in Europe or in the western part of Asia. Well before 2000 B.C., this group began to break up. One branch migrated as far as India; other branches found their way to Asia Minor, to Greece, to Italy, and to northern and western Europe. Once the various branches were geographically separated, the form of the language spoken by each branch gradually changed. By the beginning of the first century A.D., the original Indo-European tongue had evolved into more than a dozen distinctly different languages, among them Sanskrit, Greek, Latin, and Germanic. Latin later evolved into the group of modern languages that includes Italian, French, and Spanish. Germanic evolved into the group of languages that includes German, Dutch, Swedish, and English.

The history of English as a separate language begins in the middle of the fifth century A.D., when the Angles, Saxons, and Jutes invaded Britain. The invaders brought with them their own language, a dialect of Germanic. This dialect, which soon came to be designated as "Angleish," or English, was the ancestor of our present-day language. The invaders also brought with them their own alphabet, which consisted of a set of characters called runes. The runic alphabet was used for carving inscriptions on materials like wood and stone. Except for these carvings, however, not much use was made of writing. Written records were not kept; stories, legends, and poems were passed along orally from generation to generation. Most of the knowledge we have of Old English, therefore, is based on manuscripts that were written fairly late in the Anglo-Saxon period by monks who used the Latin alphabet for writing English.

An Old English inscription in the runic alphabet is a complete mystery to most of us today. Later forms of writing, like that in the sample from the *Beowulf* manuscript reproduced on page 10, also seem to represent a strange language. Even printing in our modern alphabet a passage in Old English would not help very much to clarify its meaning, although you would be able to recognize a few words and you could probably guess at the meanings of many others. Look, for example, at the following passage from *Beowulf*. Beneath the Old English is a word-for-word translation in Modern English. A modern poetic translation of the same passage appears on page 19, beginning with line 338.

Scolde Grendel thonan
Should Grendel thence
feorhseoc fleon under fenhleothu
life-sick flee under fen-slopes
secean wynleas wic. Wiste the geornor
seek joyless dwelling. Knew he more surely
thæt his aldres wæs ende gegongen,
that his life's was end reached
dogora dægrim.
days' day-number.

The literal sense of this is, "Thence Grendel, dying, had to flee through the bogs and seek his joyless dwelling. He knew surely that his life's end was reached, [his allotted] number of days."

A number of the Old English words in this passage are the same, or nearly the same, as their modern equivalents—for instance, *under, thæt, his, wæs, ende*. In fact, although many other languages have contributed words to present-day English, the basic words that we use most often are usually part of the native English stock. Such words include most of our prepositions, like *under, to, for, from, with;* most of our connectives, like *that, and, where, or;* most of our pronouns, like *his, I, we, your;* and many of our common nouns and verbs.

The grammar of present-day English is also closely related to that of Old English. For instance, our verbs still have many of the same tense formations that they had in Old English: *was* and *were* are still past-tense forms of the verb *be,* just as *wæs* and *wære* were past-tense forms in Old English. And word order in Modern English tends to follow the same patterns that were used in Old English: a preposition precedes its object, a subject usually precedes its verb, an appositive usually follows the word with which it is in apposition. In fact, the contributions that other languages have made to English have usually not affected the basic structure of the language very much, but have merely supplied new words that can be fitted into English sentence patterns.

During the Anglo-Saxon period, there were three other languages that made contributions to the English vocabulary. The first was the language spoken by the Celtic population of Britain. The Celts retreated before the Anglo-Saxon invaders but left behind them a number of Celtic place names and geographical terms, including *Kent, York, Thames, Dover,* and *Avon.* A second language that contributed words to Old English was Latin. After the Anglo-Saxons had been converted to Christianity, they adopted many Christian terms from Latin, including *altar, disciple, mass, nun,* and *shrine.* A number of words related to education and learning, such as *school, verse, paper,* and *title,* were also taken over from Latin during this period, as were some everyday words like *plant, mat,* and *box.* The third influential language was Old Norse, the language of the Danish invaders who settled in the northern part of England. The names of about six hundred towns in northern England still end in *-by,* from the Old Norse *byr* ("town"), and the same word is preserved in *bylaw.* Most of the words that the Danes contributed to our language are everyday terms like *add, fellow, guess, kindle, leg, loose, lug, nag, raise, sky,* and *window.*

For six hundred years English was an isolated language. In subsequent chapters you will see how the English language widened in scope and eventually spread throughout the globe.

FOR STUDY AND DISCUSSION

1. The words listed below have been part of the English language for over a thousand years. Using an unabridged dictionary or a college dictionary, find out which words are native English terms and which ones entered Old English from Celtic, Latin, or Old Norse:

after	drink	mother	scrap
crag	egg	noon	temple

2. During the Anglo-Saxon period, people in the northern part of England often adopted an Old Norse word in place of an Old English word that had the same meaning, while people in southern England usually continued to use the Old English term. In some cases both words have survived as part of our language. Following are four pairs of this kind. Look up the words in each pair in a dictionary and find out which is the native English term and which the Old Norse term:

no, nay	skill, craft
sick, ill	skin, hide

The Medieval Period
1066–1485

THE NORMAN CONQUEST

The Battle of Hastings (redrawn) from the Bayeaux Tapestry (c. 1077).
The Mansell Collection

The official history of the Medieval period begins in 1066 with the Battle of Hastings in which Harold, the king of England, was defeated by William "the Conqueror," Duke of Normandy. William invaded England to support his claim that he had been promised the succession to the English throne. The coming of the Normans to England was not another hit-and-run raid, but a full-fledged invasion and occupation. The occupation was imposed systematically and can be described in modern terms. There was an inventory and seizure of property. Martial law was put into effect. A strong central government was set up with lines of authority clearly defined. William was an efficient and ruthless soldier and an able administrator. With his followers, many of whom were adventurers and soldiers of fortune, he was soon able to conquer the whole country. He reigned for twenty-one years, and the succession was assured at his death.

The Normans—a name derived from "Northman"—were in large part descended from the Vikings who had seized and then remained in northwestern France, which became known as Normandy. After

Murder of
Thomas à Becket (detail),
from an
illuminated manuscript,
Harley MS. 5102, f. 32.
Courtesy, British Library

more than a hundred years in France, the Normans had adopted many French customs and had their own variation of the French language, Norman-French. They were a curious people: superb soldiers, excellent administrators and lawyers, great borrowers and adapters, but lacking inventiveness and original ideas. Even the architecture and the ambitious building in stone that they introduced into England originated in northern Italy. It used to be assumed that the Norman conquerors "civilized" the defeated Anglo-Saxons, but in some respects, notably in their more democratic system of government and in their crafts and designs, the Anglo-Saxons were more advanced than the Normans. William was able to subdue the whole land partly because he could adopt and use the institutions of the highly centralized and stable Anglo-Saxon government.

The dual kingdoms of England and Normandy established by William became the most powerful force in Europe. William's descendants greatly increased their land holdings in Europe, either through marriage or by conquest. The Norman kings of England spent much of their time across the English Channel, fighting for their French territories, and later administering their Continental kingdoms. The court, of course, accompanied the king. It is a tribute to the stability of the kingdom and its management that one of its kings, Richard "the Lion-Hearted," could spend all but five months of his ten years' reign outside of his English kingdom.

The Norman and Anglo-Saxon elements were gradually fused into a national English character, neither predominately Norman nor Anglo-Saxon but a subtle blend of both. After losing their own rulers, the Anglo-Saxons adapted to Norman ways. Many found that they could raise their station through the Church or through the court, and began to mingle with their Norman overlords. One prominent example is that of Thomas à Becket, who became Henry II's Lord Chancellor and later Archbishop of Canterbury.

Arms of William I and
Henry I (drawing).
Radio Times Hulton
Picture Library

LAND AND THE FEUDAL SYSTEM

Since most of the great Anglo-Saxon landowners were wiped out by the invasion, William had a great deal of land at his disposal. Retaining much himself, the rest he granted to those who had fought faithfully with him. The year 1066 brought the largest change of land ownership in the history of England. William felt that the land of England was his by right of conquest and that he was free to deed land to his vassals by royal charter, expecting obedience and service in return. Thus, William introduced into England the feudal system as it was practiced on the Continent.

Feudalism was a complicated system of landholding. Nobody owned land independently but only as a vassal of an overlord, who in turn owed allegiance either to some great noble or to the king. The system was really an elaborate chain of loyalties, with rent, so to speak, paid principally in military service to the overlord.

The grants William gave were mainly the estates of certain Anglo-Saxons who had died at the Conquest. The boundaries of these estates were frequently vague, and the first twenty years of Norman rule saw many disputes about property. Therefore, in 1086, William had a complete inventory of all property drawn up in the very important *Domesday Book* (sometimes called *Doomsday*), the book of judgments. It listed all the landowners and showed the extent of their claims. The *Anglo-Saxon Chronicle*, a history written by monks hostile to William, says of this great inventory, "It is a shame to tell though he thought no shame to do it. So very narrowly he caused it to be traced out that there was not one single hide or yard of land, not even an ox, nor a cow, nor a swine, that was not set down in writing." This was an administrative feat without equal anyplace else in Europe. Taxes in England could now be based on real property—previously, there had been a uniform tax for all.

THE MEDIEVAL CHURCH

Roughly from the eleventh to the fifteenth century, the people of Western Europe belonged to one homogeneous society with a common culture and a common set of beliefs. The single institution that did most to promote this unity was the Medieval Church. This institution crossed physical boundaries and differences in language. Latin, the language of the Church, became the language of all educated persons. Despite fierce national loyalty, every person was also responsible to the Church. No matter what kingdoms, dukedoms, principalities, or free cities people belonged to, they were all also sons and daughters of the Church, the Christian commonwealth of Europe.

The Church grew and prospered during the period and continued to be the dominant force in preserving and transmitting culture — in teaching, writing, and translating, and in copying, collecting, and distributing manuscripts. It was Europe's chief publisher, librarian, and teacher. Its scholars and philosophers moved freely from university to university and from one country to another. In England, its abbeys and monasteries were not only the main centers of learning and the arts in the period before the founding of Oxford and Cambridge universities in the thirteenth century, but, as economically self-sufficient units, they were also often immense farms, places where all manner of handicrafts were taught and practiced.

MEDIEVAL LIFE

Most people lived in the country and were attached to a feudal manor. There they worked their own fields and the lands of the lord of the manor, to whom they owed their allegiance. As the period progressed, however, farming became less important than herding. The wool produced by English sheep was considered preferable to that of almost any other part of Europe. It became profitable, therefore, to turn cornfields into pasture land for sheep. By the end of the thirteenth century, there were probably as many as fifteen or eighteen million sheep in England — four or five for every person. This economic development greatly altered the daily life of the common people. Instead of farmers, many people became herders, but also a large percentage of the population became involved in the wool industry. Cottages became small mills involved in carding and combing, spinning and weaving — some even in dyeing the finished cloth. The common people now paid what they owed their overlords from their wages rather than in farm labor.

Earlier, some large towns and cities had grown up, mainly in the south and related to the court. London is an example. But the widespread production of wool and woolen fabric, and its wide-scale exportation, encouraged the growth of cities in the north. More and more people began to live in towns and cities rather than on manors. A whole new class of merchants grew up. Many became immensely rich, and through favors to the court many of them entered the gentry; some, even the nobility. These populous centers, far from the influence of the French court, developed native forms of literature, songs and ballads, and a native drama with a good deal of color and pageantry.

The first people to form guilds (societies to regulate prices and standards) were the merchants. Later the cottage workers also formed guilds to assure fair wages and prices and good standards of material

The Bayeaux Tapestry (detail), The Battle of Hastings

The Murder of Thomas à Becket

1066   **Norman Rule 1066–1154**   **1100**   **Plantagenet**

Kings 1154–1399

Norman
Conquest 1066

Doomsday Book
1086

Crusades begin
1096

Murder of Thomas à
Becket 1170

Geoffrey Chaucer
1340–1400

Hundred Years' War
1337–1453

Magna Carta 1215

1300   **1200**

House of Lancaster

First Parliament 1265

Sir Thomas Malory ? –1471

*Sir Gawain and the
Green Knight* 1300's

Wars of the Roses
1455–1485

Caxton's printing
press 1476

1399–1461   **1400**   **House of York 1461–1485**   **1485**

Seddon Portrait of Chaucer (detail)

Sir Gawain and the Lady

The Knight, Caxton's *Canterbury Tales*

Time Line   35

A castle, from
*Très Riches Heures du Duc
de Berry,* (illumination),
Chantilly Musée, Conde MS.
Giraudon

and workmanship. The guild system encouraged a kind of extended family life. A master dyer would often have living with him several apprentices and also journeymen, men who had passed their apprenticeship and were in training to be masters themselves.

With prosperity and a simultaneous growth in population, the English turned to other kinds of work. This is the period of the great English cathedrals, Winchester and Lincoln, Salisbury and Durham. It is hard to believe the labor that went into the construction of these cathedrals—often over a period of several hundred years. (Yorkminster was begun as a Norman church in 1070 and was not completed until 1472.) Guilds were founded for many of these workers: stonecutters and masons, carpenters and woodcarvers, glass blowers and stainers. Much of the communal life of the city centered around these magnificent monuments, where, among other things, the first English dramas were performed.

Life in the Middle Ages was austere in many ways. There were few of the comforts and conveniences we take for granted. Travel was difficult and often dangerous. Food (lacking sugar and potatoes and many other things), even for the rich, probably offered little variety. Since there was no way to preserve or refrigerate food, sometimes a lot had to be eaten quickly while it was in season. Winters brought a very limited and unwholesome diet for most people. The countryside, however, and to some extent the towns were probably fresh, colorful, and beautiful without the smoke of modern industrial factories. Also, the dress of the period seems to have been bright and varied, as evidenced by the paintings of the time: great lords in sumptuous attire and their retinues in colorful livery; even the guild members, in clothing characteristic of their trades.

ENGLISH LAW

In the twelfth century, Richard Fitzneal, an English cleric, wrote, "When William the Conqueror had subdued the whole island, and by terrible examples had tamed the minds of the rebels, he decided to place the government of the people on a written basis and subject them to the rules of law." There had been written documents under Anglo-Saxon kings, but not all of them were easily available or centrally based. One of William's innovations was to institute written public documents for most government actions.

Even more important in the development of England's present-day system of laws was the notion of common law that took root during this period. The term common law refers to law that is common to the whole country and all its people, in contrast to kinds of law applying only to certain classes of persons. It developed as society itself developed, based not on legal statutes but on custom and usage.

One significant law that came into effect during this period was the law of primogeniture, which gave the firstborn son exclusive right to inherit his father's titles, lands, and estates. It is still the rule in England today.

During the early part of this period, matters of law were still settled by what were called *ordeals*. People's innocence or guilt was settled by setting them tasks, and if they were successful at them, they were judged innocent. Disputes between two people were also settled by ordeals, such as the personal combat central to *Sir Gawain and the Green Knight*. In 1215 Pope Innocent III declared that the ordeal system was "irrational." Without the sanction of the Church, secular governments had to find a suitable replacement for ordeals. Gradually, in England, people who were indicted were asked to abide by the judgment of their neighbors. In this way, the very important jury system came into being.

In 1215, a group of angry barons forced King John (1199–1216) to sign an agreement called the *Magna Carta,* or Great Charter. Although the charter originally had mainly to do with taxes levied by the king, it firmly established that levies must be made with the consent of the barons. In retrospect, the charter has come to seem much more important than merely limiting the king's taxing powers. In it we can see foreshadowed the right of trial by jury, *habeas corpus,* or the right not to be illegally detained, and the beginnings of representative government in Parliament.

The capture of Alexandria (detail), MS. Franc. 1584.
Bibliothèque Nationale, Paris

THE CRUSADES

In spite of the treasured memory of great heroes like King Richard "the Lion-Hearted," the history of the Crusades makes dismal reading. The first Crusade was proclaimed in 1095 by Pope Urban II. Other Crusades followed in 1191, 1202, 1217, and 1270. Each Crusade began in high hope, in a genuine desire to rescue Jerusalem from the Turks, but most ended squalidly in raiding, looting, and a tangle of power politics. Still, in the end, Western Europe gained much from these expeditions to the Near East. Christian Europe was exposed to Arabic culture—especially mathematics and medicine. Commercial and intellectual horizons were greatly broadened, and both knowledge and all manners of refinements in living were brought back from the East. It was the Crusades too, even though they ended so badly, that encouraged the ideal of true knightly behavior known as *chivalry*.

Today we use the term *chivalrous* to describe the conduct of well-mannered and sensitive men toward women, but the medieval idea of chivalry, though it included the relations between the sexes, went far beyond this. It sought, with the aid of the Church, to make the knightly warrior as devout and tenderhearted off the battlefield as he was bold and fearless on it. The bloodstained, ferocious history of the Crusades suggests that chivalry was an ideal rather than an actual code of conduct. It was, however, of considerable importance in literature, where it was joined to the companion idea of *romance*.

THE HUNDRED YEARS' WAR

It took about two hundred and fifty years for Normans and Saxons to merge their individual identities into one English nation. Unfortunately for both England and France, the English monarchy never voluntarily relinquished its hold on its French possessions. As a result, there were numerous costly wars in France, culminating in the series of wars now known as the "Hundred Years' War" (1337–1453). Although in the end driven from France, England won many a famous victory in these wars, thanks largely to the terrible longbows of the English infantry. Used by the English from the time of Edward I (1272–1307) onward, these six-foot bows, with yard-long arrows capable of piercing a knight's armor, were among the most effective weapons known to Western Europe in the late Middle Ages. In fact, the longbows—together with gunpowder, another new element in European warfare—eventually did much to end the Middle Ages by making knights and castles less effective in warfare.

THE WARS OF THE ROSES

In 1348 England was struck by the Black Death, the first of a series of plagues that killed more than a third of the population. The scarcity of labor caused by the plagues was the death knell of feudalism. In 1381, inflamed by repressive laws and burdensome taxes and encouraged by the teachings of the religious reformer John Wycliffe, the peasants rose in bloody revolt. The revolt was put down harshly, but economic and social unrest continued. Then, hard on the heels of the Hundred Years' War, came the so-called Wars of the Roses (1455–1485), a civil war between the House of York, whose emblem was the white rose, and the House of Lancaster, symbolized by a red rose. When in 1485 Henry VII succeeded Richard III and united the feuding families through marriage, he ended the wars and founded the Tudor line. With Henry's accession, the real Middle Ages vanished.

MEDIEVAL LITERATURE: THE ROMANCE

The form of literature much favored by the Anglo-Normans was the *romance*. Medieval romance consisted largely of tales of chivalry to which were added a love interest and all sorts of wonders and marvels—fairy enchantments, giants, dragons, wizards, and sorceresses.

The medieval concept of romantic love came from France. Indeed the first English romances—verse, and later prose tales relating the quests knights undertook for their ladies—were translations from the French. These romantic tales came from three principal sources—Britain (the story of King Arthur and his knights), France (the court of Charlemagne), and Rome (classical stories such as the conquest of Troy). In the famous legends of King Arthur and his Knights of the Round Table, collected and retold by Sir Thomas Malory in his *Morte d'Arthur*, chivalry and romance play equal parts.

King Arthur's Britain is based on Celtic folklore and has almost no historical basis. The Round Table is not the usual military and political alliance, but an ideal aristocratic brotherhood. Its knights ride forth to realize themselves through individual feats of arms and acts of courtesy. Their adventures are often novel and unexpected, but they are alike in illustrating the chivalric ideals of honor, courage, courtesy, and service to women. The finest verse romance in English, *Sir Gawain and the Green Knight*, is about one of the knights at Arthur's court.

GEOFFREY CHAUCER

The first truly great figure in English literature was Geoffrey Chaucer (1340?–1400). Although ready to traffic in the fashionable romance of the day, he obviously was quite skeptical about it, being as sharply realistic as a modern novelist in much of his work. Because Chaucer is so far removed from us, and his manner and language, especially in the original Middle English, seem so quaint, we can easily underestimate this astonishing man. He was not only a great poet and a fine storyteller but also the first of the poker-faced humorists. There is just a twinkle in his eye as he gravely, often ironically, adds one descriptive stroke to another, never failing, if we are alert, to make his points. This man, whether moving as a diplomat from one royal court to another or lounging about an innyard among people, missed nothing. And his greatest work belongs not to romance but to poetic and humorous realism. With Chaucer, the writer is no longer anonymous but emerges in all the variety and subtlety of an impressive individual.

Chaucer Reading
(frontispiece),
CCCC MS. 61.
Masters and Fellows of
Corpus Christi College,
Cambridge

FOLK POETRY AND THE DRAMA

From the common people of early England and Scotland came
ballads—songs not written down but recited and sung in innumerable alehouses and at thousands of firesides. This folk poetry
flourished in the fourteenth and fifteenth centuries, but it was not

until the middle of the eighteenth century that it was carefully collected and published. Through the German poet Herder, who had a passion for folk poetry, these English and Scottish ballads came to influence the whole German Romantic movement and then later, the English Romantic poets. But most of them originally belong, as their themes and settings suggest, to the later Middle Ages, to whose unknown wandering minstrels many future generations of poets were enormously indebted.

The popular drama reached a tremendous height in the Elizabethan Age, but its origins are in the Middle Ages. During the frequent holiday times celebrating religious festivals, the trade guilds entertained the crowd with miracle plays—rough dramatizations of Biblical stories performed on large wagons or on platforms erected in marketplaces or innyards. As a rule the wicked characters in these plays, including the Devil himself, were played as comic characters, thereby creating a tradition of popular comedy that the Elizabethan dramatists followed. It was all very rough-and-ready, but in these humble performances there was already stirring the glorious theater of Shakespeare.

Toward the end of the Middle Ages in England, during the dark troubled times of the fifteenth century, the miracle plays gave place to the morality plays. These plays, although presented in the same way as the miracle plays, tended to be elaborate and sophisticated dramatic allegories in which characters representing various virtues and vices confronted one another. The most famous of the morality plays, and one still often performed in many countries, was *Everyman*. Although this play was not English in origin, a thoroughly English adaptation of it soon became very popular. Even during the present century this play has been performed in the English theater fairly often.

English literature owes a great deal to the Middle Ages. In this period a great many literary forms had their origin. The High, or Gothic, Middle Ages, best represented now by their glorious cathedrals, have always haunted the imagination of the more poetic English writers with a bright and gaily colored vision of cavalcades of knights, squires, minstrels, pages, pilgrims, crusaders, troubadours, monks, scholars, and fine ladies in hilltop castles. But the real secret of the appeal of this period at its best does not lie in its romantic picturesqueness, enchanting though that may be. It comes from the fact that during these years Western civilization—restless, inventive, aggressive, troubled—achieved an elaborately organized way of life completely contained within a common religion.

Early English and Scottish Ballads

The ballads of early England and Scotland, known today as *popular, traditional,* or *folk* ballads, arose in medieval times—mostly in the fifteenth century—from the traditions of the common people. Because they were passed on from generation to generation by word of mouth and not set down in writing for several centuries, it is impossible to trace the identity of their original authors or to ascertain which of the many variations was the original version.

Few of the English and Scottish folk ballads were printed before the eighteenth century. It was *Reliques of Ancient English Poetry,* the collection of ballads published by Bishop Thomas Percy in 1765, that gave impetus to an interest in these old ballads that persists to this day. Since the publication of Percy's collection, others have been inspired to make their own collections. The Scottish poet and novelist Sir Walter Scott, among others, went to the English-Scottish border region to write down—from the dictation of the border people who were still singing them—the various versions of many of these old songs.

The subject matter of the folk ballads stemmed from the everyday life of the common folk. The most popular themes, often tragic ones, were disappointed love, jealousy, revenge, sudden disaster, and deeds of adventure and daring. Many of the usual devices of telling a story are evident in the old ballads. The narrative is simple and direct. A single incident is related in dramatic fashion, with only slight attention paid to characterization and description. Little or no background introduction is given and the story is developed largely through dialogue, the narrative often hinted at rather than told in detail. Sometimes the reader must guess what happens between stanzas or who is speaking in certain stanzas.

Another device commonly used in ballads is the *refrain,* in which the last line or two of each stanza are repeated, thus adding an effective note of emphasis or suspense and contributing to the ballad's melody and rhythmic flow. Sometimes *incremental repetition* is used: that is, the repetition of a previous line or lines but with a slight variation each time, which advances the story stanza by stanza.

Above all, the ballads are musical in nature. They were meant to be sung, one voice carrying the main part of the stanza, with the rest of the group joining in on the refrain. Since the French word for ballad once meant *to dance,* it is likely that people also danced to the old ballad rhythms.

Sir Patrick Spens

The king sits in Dumferling° toune,
  Drinking the blude-reid wine:
"O whar will I get a skilly° skipper,
  To sail this new schip of mine?"

O up and spak an eldern knicht,°   5
  Sat at the kings richt kne:
"Sir Patrick Spens is the best sailor,
  That ever sailed the se."

The king has written a braid° letter,
  And sealed it wi his hand,   10
And sent it to Sir Patrick Spens,
  Was walking on the strand.

The first line that Sir Patrick red,
  A loud lauch lauched he;
The next line that Sir Patrick red,   15
  The teir blinded his ee.°

"O wha is this has don this deid,
  And told the king o' me,
To send us out at this time o' the yeir,
  To sail upon the se!   20

"Mak ready, mak ready, my mirry men
    all,
  Our guid schip sails the morne."
"Now, ever alake,° my master deir,
  I feir a deadlie storme.

"I saw the new moone late yestreen,   25
  Wi' the auld moone in hir arme,
And if we gang to se, master,
  I feir we'll cum to harme."

O laith,° laith wer our guid Scots lords
  To weet their cork-heild schoone;°   30
Bot lang owre° a' the play was playd,
  They wat their hats aboone.°

O lang, lang may their ladies sit,
  Wi their fans into their hand;
Before they se Sir Patrick Spens   35
  Cum sailing to the strand.

And lang, lang may their maidens sit,
  Wi their gold kems° in their hair,
All waiting for their ain deir loves,
  For thame they'll se na mair.   40

Haf owre,° haf owre to Aberdour,°
  'Tis fiftie fadom deip,
And thair lies guid Sir Patrick Spens,
  Wi the Scots lords at his feit.

29. **laith:** loath, unwilling. 30. **cork-heild schoone:** cork-heeled shoes. 31. **owre:** ere, before. 32. **They . . . aboone:** Their hats floated above them. 38. **kems:** combs. 41. **Haf owre:** half over, halfway. **Aberdour:** a small town near Edinburgh.

1. **Dumferling** (dŭm-fûr′lĭng): a town near Edinburgh, now Dunfermline. 3. **skilly:** skillful. 5. **eldern knicht:** older knight. 9. **braid:** on a broad sheet, or long. 16. **ee:** eye. 23. **alake:** alack, alas.

Bonnie George Campbell

For centuries the frontiers between Scotland and England were the scene of frequent clashes between the people of both countries. A number of ballads known as border ballads deal with the tragic consequences of these border feuds. The following ballad tells of one man who set out for battle and never returned.

In some versions of the ballad, the hero is called Bonnie James Campbell. Note the ironic contrast of the last two stanzas of the poem.

High upon Highlands,°
  And low upon Tay,°
Bonnie George Campbell
  Rode out on a day.

He saddled, he bridled,   5
  And gallant rode he,
And hame cam° his guid horse,
  But never cam he.

Out cam his mother dear,
  Greeting fu sair,°   10
And out cam his bonnie bride,
  Riving° her hair.

"The meadow lies green,
  The corn is unshorn,
But Bonnie George Campbell   15
  Will never return."

Saddled and bridled
  And booted rode he,
A plume in his helmet,
  A sword at his knee.   20

But toom° cam his saddle,
  All bloody to see,
Oh, hame cam his guid horse,
  But never cam he!

Medieval knight (woodcut).
New York Public Library, Print Room

---

1. **Highlands:** northern part of Scotland.   2. **Tay:** the largest river in Scotland.   7. **hame cam:** home came.   10. **Greeting fu sair:** weeping full sore.   12. **Riving:** tearing.   21. **toom:** empty.

Bonny Barbara Allan

As is the case with so many ballads, the constant telling and retelling of this tragic love song has resulted in a great variety of versions. Ninety-two variations of this popular ballad have found their way into the folklore of Virginia alone. In some of these versions the hero's name varies. In some versions, Barbara dies repentant, in others not. The version given here is considered as close to the original Scottish story as any others that are known.

It was in and about the Martinmas
    time,°
  When the green leaves were a-falling,
That Sir John Graeme, in the West
    Country,
  Fell in love with Barbara Allan.

He sent his men down through the
    town   5
  To the place where she was dwelling:
"O haste and come to my master dear,
  Gin° ye be Barbara Allan."

O hooly,° hooly rose she up,
  To the place where he was lying,   10
And when she drew the curtain by,
  "Young man, I think you're dying."

"O it's I'm sick, and very, very sick,
  And it's a' for Barbara Allan";
"O the better for me ye's never be,   15
  Though your heart's blood were a-
    spilling.

"O dinna ye mind,° young man," said
  she,
  "When the red wine ye were fillin',
That ye made the healths gae round
  and round,
  And slighted Barbara Allan?"   20

He turned his face unto the wall,
  And death was with him dealing;
"Adieu, adieu, my dear friends all,
  And be kind to Barbara Allan."

And slowly, slowly raise she up,   25
  And slowly, slowly left him,
And, sighing, said she could not stay,
  Since death of life had reft him.

She had not gane a mile but twa,°
  When she heard the dead-bell ringing, 30
And every jow° that the dead-bell geid,°
  It cried, "Woe to Barbara Allan!"

"O mother, mother, make my bed!
  O make it saft and narrow!
Since my love died for me today,   35
  I'll die for him tomorrow."

They buried her in the old churchyard,
  And Sir John's grave was nigh her.
And from his heart grew a red, red rose,
  And from her heart a brier.   40

They grew to the top o' the old church
  wall,
  Till they could grow no higher,
Until they tied a true love's knot—
  The red rose and the brier.

---

1. **Martinmas time:** November 11. 8. **Gin:** if.
9. **hooly:** slowly. 17. **dinna ye mind:** don't you remember.

29. **not . . . twa:** gone only two miles. 31. **jow:** stroke. **geid:** gave.

Get Up and Bar the Door

It fell about the Martinmas time,
  And a gay time it was then,
When our goodwife got puddings to
    make,
  She's boild them in the pan.

The wind sae cauld blew south and
    north.   5
  And blew into the floor;
Quoth our goodman to our goodwife,
  "Gae out and bar the door."

"My hand is in my hussyfskap,°
  Goodman, as ye may see;   10
An it should nae be barrd this hundred
    year,
  It's no be barrd for me."°

They made a paction° tween them twa.
  They made it firm and sure.
That the first word whaeer° shoud
    speak,   15
  Shoud rise and bar the door.

Then by there came two gentlemen,
  At twelve o'clock at night,
And they could neither see house nor
    hall,
  Nor coal nor candlelight.   20

"Now whether is this a rich man's
    house,
  Or whether it is a poor?"°
But neer a word wad ane o' them°
    speak,
  For barring of the door.

And first they° ate the white puddings, 25
  And then they ate the black:
Tho muckle° thought the goodwife to
    hersel,
  Yet neer a word she spake.

Then said the one unto the other,
  "Here, man, tak ye my knife;   30
Do ye tak aff the auld man's beard,
  And I'll kiss the goodwife."

"But there's nae water° in the house,
  And what shall we do than?"
"What ails ye at the pudding broo,°   35
  That boils into° the pan?"

O up then started our goodman,
  An angry man was he:
"Will ye kiss my wife before my een,
  And scad° me wi pudding bree?"°   40

Then up and started our goodwife,
  Gied three skips on the floor:
"Goodman, you've spoken the fore-
    most word;
  Get up and bar the door."

---

25. **they**: the strangers. 27. **muckle**: much. 33. **water**: probably to scald the beard in order to scrape it off. 35. **"What . . . broo**: "What's the matter with using the pudding water?" 36. **into**: in. 40. **scad**: scald. **bree**: broth, liquor.

---

9. **hussyfskap**: household duties. 11–12. **An . . . me.":** "The door will not be barred in a hundred years if I have to bar it." 13. **paction**: agreement. 15. **whaeer**: whoever. 21–22. **"Now . . . poor?":** The strangers ask this question. 23. **them**: the man and his wife.

FOR STUDY AND DISCUSSION

Sir Patrick Spens

1. The demands of duty is a common literary theme. Sir Patrick Spens does his duty even though he is certain it will lead to his death. Explain his reaction to the King's letter in lines 13–16.
2. What role does a superstitious belief in evil omens play in "Sir Patrick Spens"?
3. Some versions of this ballad tell of the storm at sea in which Sir Patrick and his crew perished. This version does not. Instead, the poem shifts at line 29 to a lament for the lost sailors. What do you think about this shift? Would anything be gained by continuing the narrative? At what point in the narrative are you first aware that the ballad will end tragically?
4. What irony lies in the remark that the Scots nobles were reluctant to wet their fancy shoes? What is the tone of the last line?

Bonnie George Campbell

1. Ballads often make use of dramatic contrasts to underscore theme. What is the implied contrast with the abundant grain fields in lines 13–14? What is the effect of this contrast?
2. Would the poem be more or less effective if the circumstances of Bonnie George Campbell's death were revealed? Explain.

Bonny Barbara Allan

1. What reason does Barbara give for her apparent coldness at Sir John's bedside? Does the ballad ask us to take sides in this lovers' quarrel?
2. In what way do Barbara and Sir John play the same role in the poem? Could you argue that they are united in death?

Get Up and Bar the Door

To establish a basically comic situation and complicate it with even more ludicrous developments is a popular device in comedy. How is this device used in the ballad?

THE FOLK BALLAD

Unlike the literary ballads written by poets such as Sir Walter Scott and Samuel Taylor Coleridge, the old folk ballads were the "popular songs" of their day. As such, their form was simple and regular and thus fairly easy to remember in performance. The typical ballad stanza consists of four lines — that is, a *quatrain* — with eight syllables in the first and third lines and six syllables in the shorter second and fourth lines. The clear and definite beat of the ballad stanza makes it readily adaptable to all types of stories. The meter is usually iambic, meaning that, as is shown in the stanza quoted below, the stress in each line falls on every other syllable. (An iamb is a metrical foot consisting of an unaccented syllable followed by an accented one.) Unlike the alliterative verse of the Anglo-Saxon period, the ballad rhymes, with the rhyme usually appearing in the second and fourth lines of each stanza, as is shown here.

> The wind sae cauld blew south and north,
>   And blew into the *floor;*
> Quoth our goodman to our goodwife,
>   "Gae out and bar the *door.*"

The metrical simplicity of the ballad matches the simplicity of its language. Although code language is sometimes used (for example, asking that one's bed be made "soft and narrow" means that the speaker is dying), the language of the ballads is usually direct and straightforward. So too is the ballad's narrative, despite the use of understatement, abrupt transitions, and tantalizing clues that often make it necessary for the reader to puzzle out who is speaking in a given stanza and what has happened between stanzas.

FOR COMPOSITION

1. The job of a newspaper reporter is to present only the facts. Write a reporter's version of the story of Sir Patrick Spens. Then compare this version with the ballad, pointing out what the ballad conveys that the newspaper version does not.
2. If there are collections of British and American folk ballads in your library, write a composition in which you compare several versions of "Bonny Barbara Allan." Describe changes that have been made in the American versions and defend the version that you think is most effective.

Geoffrey Chaucer
1340?-1400

Geoffrey Chaucer, The Seddon Portrait.
Houghton Library, Harvard University

To William Caxton, England's first printer, Geoffrey Chaucer was "the worshipful father and first founder and embellisher of ornate eloquence in our English." Perceptive as this praise was in its time, today Chaucer is acclaimed not only as "the father of English poetry" but also as the father of English fiction – in short, as the father of English literature. In addition, we are indebted to him for the most vivid contemporary description of fourteenth-century England.

A man of affairs as well as a man of letters, Chaucer's development as the one was closely paralleled by his development as the other. Born into a family that belonged to the rising middle class, he obtained through his father, a successful wine merchant, a position as page in a household closely associated with the court of King Edward III. His mastery of Latin, French, and Italian, in addition to equipping him for diplomatic and civil service, also enabled him to translate literary works in all three languages, an important factor in his development as a writer.

A court favorite, Chaucer rose quickly in the world. Before he was twenty he served as a soldier in France and, upon being captured, was ransomed by his king. Thereafter, throughout his life, he served his country loyally – as courtier, diplomat, civil administrator, and translator. Entrusted with important and delicate diplomatic missions, he traveled on several occasions to France and Italy, and his journeys abroad played an important role in his literary and intellectual development. Subsequently, he served as Comptroller of Customs for the Port of London; Member of Parliament; Justice of the Peace; Clerk of the Works at Westminster Abbey, the Tower of London, and elsewhere; and finally as a sub-forester of one of the king's forests. He was, in fact, a highly valued public servant and was fortunate to enjoy for most of his life the patronage of the influential John of Gaunt, Duke of Lancaster and uncle of King Richard II. During his long public career, he became acquainted with the most important men of his day – diplomats and rulers as well as writers. At his death, his reputation as a man of affairs and his genius as a poet were well established. Today, in the history of English literature, Chaucer's name stands second only to that of Shakespeare.

One of Chaucer's most important contributions to English literature is his development of the resources of the English language for literary purposes. In his day, English was still considered primarily a rough peasant language. England's Norman rulers had introduced French to England, and this language was still spoken in court circles and by the aristocracy. Church Latin was used in the monasteries, the centers of learning, and was still at the command of the educated. Although earlier poets had written in a primitive English, there was very little English literature beyond the range of traditional and anonymous ballads. When he began to write, therefore, Chaucer had to proceed by trial and error, taking his models at first from French and Italian sources and feeling his way toward a full use of his native tongue. Chaucer himself spoke late Middle English, the London speech of his day. By using this language instead of the more fashionable French for his poetry, he added tremendously to its prestige and set an example that was followed thereafter.

As a writer, Chaucer was extremely prolific. In his early short lyrics and longer works such as *The Book of the Duchess,* we see the influence of the French poetry of his day. Later, in works such as *Parliament of Fowls* and *Troilus and Criseyde,* his writing reflected the influence of the Italian masters Dante, Petrarch, and Boccaccio. By 1386, when he began *The Canterbury Tales,* his most ambitious work, he had become master of his craft.

For *The Canterbury Tales* Chaucer used the structural device of the frame story, a popular one used in the thousand and one tales of *The Arabian Nights' Entertainment* and the one hundred tales of Boccaccio's *Decameron.* As the frame around which to group his tales, Chaucer chose a springtime pilgrimage to Canterbury Cathedral, the site of the splendid shrine of St. Thomas à Becket, who had been murdered there two centuries before. In Chaucer's day it was customary throughout Europe for members of all classes to travel to religious shrines to seek miraculous cures, to gain remission of their sins, or simply to satisfy their wanderlust. In England the pilgrimage to Canterbury was by far the most popular, and to this day traces of the old "pilgrims' way" still persist.

Chaucer's choice of frame for *The Canterbury Tales,* in addition to giving equal scope to his talents as narrator, philosopher, dramatist, and observer, had several other advantages. By using the device of a journey, it was possible to bring together quite naturally persons of varied occupations and diverse social rank, a rarity in medieval society. Thus Chaucer was able to present in his work a cross-section of medieval society, drawing his characters from the three most important groups of his day—feudal, ecclesiastical, and urban. The characters who are members of the feudal system are related to the land: these are the Knight, the Squire, the Yeoman, the Franklin, the Reeve, the Miller, and the Plowman. Those in the ecclesiastical order represent individuals belonging to the medieval church: the Parson, the Summoner, the Monk, the Prioress, the Friar, the Pardoner, and the Student. The other pilgrims are professional and mercantile laymen from the fast-growing towns of Chaucer's day: the Physician, the Lawyer, the Manciple, the Merchant, the Shipman, the tradesmen, the Cook, the Wife of Bath (a clothmaker), and the Innkeeper.

Chaucer's plan for *The Canterbury Tales* was an ambitious one. Each pilgrim was to tell two stories on the way to Canterbury and two on the return journey to London. The poet died, however, before this plan was realized and, instead of the proposed one hundred twenty-four stories, he wrote only twenty-four. The portion of the work that was completed, however, is a masterpiece of vivid and realistic writing. Setting his work in his own time, he established a realistic style of writing that was to persist for centuries. Chaucer's descriptions of the pilgrims in his *Prologue* are considered by historians as our best picture of life in fourteenth-century England. In these portraits Chaucer's own background and temperament are reflected. A man of the world, large-minded, humane, tolerant, and amused by his fellow human beings, he shows a profound understanding of human motivation, and comments—sometimes seriously, sometimes humorously—both on his characters and on some of the most critical social problems of his day. His tone ranges from comic to ironic to satirical, but always he reveals himself as a genial and warm-hearted person who has sympathy for his fellow human beings.

Though *The Canterbury Tales* is often referred to as the first collection of short stories in English literature, these stories, unlike the modern short story, are written in poetry rather than in prose. In the *Prologue,* Chaucer experimented with rhymed pairs of five-beat iambic lines, a verse form known as the heroic couplet and popularized three centuries later by John Dryden and Alexander Pope. Chaucer's style in *The Canterbury Tales* is remarkably flexible; for he had by this time thrown off the stiff conventions of his earlier French and Italian sources. His prose, like his vocabulary, is easy and informal. Although he was always an amateur who never wrote for pay or publication, Chaucer achieved in *The Canterbury Tales* the deceptive ease that is the hallmark of the professional.

Chaucer died in 1400 and was buried in Westminster Abbey. He was the first English poet to be buried in what has come to be known as the Poets' Corner.

The Prologue to
The Canterbury Tales

Translated by Nevill Coghill

Entering the world of Geoffrey Chaucer through *The Canterbury Tales* is rather like standing in front of a splendid medieval painting or Florentine fresco. Painted in bright colors against a glowing background, the Knight, the Prioress, the Monk, the Pardoner, the Wife of Bath, and the rest of the Canterbury pilgrims move in perpetual sunlight, like processional figures winding uphill into the blue distance. In the *Prologue* to his masterpiece, Chaucer, with a brisk flourish, paints the setting of his story and then proceeds to introduce his cast of characters, from the Knight to the Host of the Tabard Inn. In his role as narrator, Chaucer maintains throughout an air of personal detachment; his appreciation of the individuality of his characters affords an honest and objective account of each of them. Indeed, at times it is difficult to determine whether he intends to commend or reprimand, so well does he blend satire with faint praise. In this broad panorama of human nature, the poet reveals what is base, noble, and essentially human in all people.

Note that the first forty-two lines of the *Prologue* are given in the original Middle English, with a Modern English translation by Nevill Coghill following them. As you read, notice the similarities between the two forms of the language.

In reading Chaucer's *Prologue* in the original Middle English, remember that you are, after all, reading English and that most of Chaucer's words either have not changed in spelling or are close enough to their modern equivalents to cause little or no trouble. Most of the consonants are pronounced just as we do those in modern English. Pronounce every syllable in a word, even when it appears to be our modern silent *e* (marked in the original Middle English with two dots over the *e*). Thus, the word *croppës* is pronounced in two syllables as *crop-pess*.

Once you try reading the *Prologue* aloud, you will soon become accustomed to Middle English. You will find it much less like a foreign tongue and more like an oddly musical form of your own language—which, of course, it is. You will also discover that the sense will come more easily as you more closely approximate the sound.

The Franklin (detail),
Ellesmere Manuscript.
The Huntington Library

Whan that° Aprill with his shourës sootë°   When sweet
The droghte of March hath percëd to the rootë
And bathëd every veyne in swich licour°   such liquid
Of which vertu° engendrëd is the flour,   By power of which
Whan Zephirus eek° with his sweetë breeth   5 also
Inspirëd hath in every holt° and heeth°   wood heath
The tendrë croppës,° and the yongë sonnë   shoots
Hath in the Ram his half cours y-ronnë,
And smalë fowelës maken° melodyë   birds make
That slepen al the nyght with open eyë,   10
So priketh hem° Nature in hir corages,°   stirs them their hearts
Than longen° folk to goon° on pilgrymages,   Then long go
And palmeres° for to seken° straungë strondës,° pilgrims seek strands
To fernë halwës kouthe° in sondry londës.   distant shrines known
And specially, from every shirës endë   15
Of Engelond, to Caunterbury they wendë,
The holy, blisful martir for to sekë
That hem hath holpen° whan that they were seekë.° helped sick
 Bifel° that in that sesoun on a day   It befell
In Southwerk at the Tabard, as I lay   20
Redy to wenden on my pilgrymagë
To Caunterbury with ful devout coragë,°   heart
At nyght was come into that hostelryë
Wel nyne-and-twenty in a compaignyë
Of sondry folk by aventure y-fallë°   25 chance fallen
In felaweshipe, and pilgrymes were they allë
That toward Caunterbury wolden° rydë.   intended to
The chambrës and the stablës weren wydë,°   spacious
And wel we weren esëd attë bestë°;   entertained at the best
And shortly, whan the sonnë was to restë,   30
So hadde I spoken with hem everichon°   every one
That I was of hir° felaweshipe anon;   their
And madë forward° erly for to rysë   (we) made agreement
To take oure wey ther-as° I yow devysë.°   where tell
 But nathelees,° whil I have tyme and space, 35 nevertheless
Er that° I ferther in this tale pace,°   Before pass
Me thynketh it° acordant to resoun   It seems to me
To telle yow al the condicioun
Of ech of hem° so as it semed me,   them
And whiche they weren, and of what degree,   40
And eek° in what array that they were inne;   also
And at a knyght than wol I first bigynne.

When in April the sweet showers fall
And pierce the drought of March to the root, and all
The veins are bathed in liquor of such power
As brings about the engendering of the flower,
When also Zephyrus° with his sweet breath   5
Exhales an air in every grove and heath
Upon the tender shoots, and the young sun
His half-course in the sign of the Ram° has run,
And the small fowl are making melody
That sleep away the night with open eye   10
(So nature pricks them and their heart engages)
Then people long to go on pilgrimages
And palmers° long to seek the stranger strands
Of far-off saints, hallowed in sundry lands,
And specially, from every shire's end   15
In England, down to Canterbury they wend
To seek the holy blissful martyr,° quick
To give his help to them when they were sick.
    It happened in that season that one day
In Southwark,° at The Tabard, as I lay   20
Ready to go on pilgrimage and start
For Canterbury, most devout at heart,
At night there came into that hostelry
Some nine and twenty in a company
Of sundry folk happening then to fall   25
In fellowship, and they were pilgrims all
That towards Canterbury meant to ride.
The rooms and stables of the inn were wide;
They made us easy, all was of the best.
And shortly, when the sun had gone to rest,   30
By speaking to them all upon the trip
I soon was one of them in fellowship
And promised to rise early and take the way
To Canterbury, as you heard me say.
    But nonetheless, while I have time and space,   35
Before my story takes a further pace,
It seems a reasonable thing to say
What their condition was, the full array
Of each of them, as it appeared to me
According to profession and degree,   40
And what apparel they were riding in;
And at a Knight I therefore will begin.

Chaucer (detail),
Ellesmere MS.
The Huntington Library,
San Marino, Ca.

---

5. **Zephyrus:** (zĕf′ər-əs) the west wind. 8. **Ram:** Aries, the first of the twelve
signs of the zodiac. The date is April 11, 1387. 13. **palmers:** pilgrims who visited
the Holy Land and wore two crossed palms to indicate that they had done so.
17. **martyr:** Thomas à Becket, Archbishop of Canterbury, martyred in 1170.
20. **Southwark** (sŭth′ərk): a borough of London.

There was a *Knight*, a most distinguished man,
Who from the day on which he first began
To ride abroad had followed chivalry,   45
Truth, honor, generousness and courtesy.
He had done nobly in his sovereign's war
And ridden into battle, no man more,
As well in Christian as in heathen places,
And ever honored for his noble graces.   50
   When we took Alexandria,° he was there.
He often sat at table in the chair
Of honor, above all nations, when in Prussia.
In Lithuania he had ridden, and Russia,
No Christian man so often, of his rank.   55
When, in Granada, Algeciras sank
Under assault, he had been there, and in
North Africa, raiding Benamarin;
In Anatolia he had been as well
And fought when Ayas and Attalia fell,   60
For all along the Mediterranean coast
He had embarked with many a noble host.
He was of sovereign value in all eyes.
And though so much distinguished, he was wise
And in his bearing modest as a maid.   65
He never yet a boorish thing had said
In all his life to any, come what might;
He was a true, a perfect gentle-knight.
   Speaking of his equipment, he possessed
Fine horses, but he was not gaily dressed.   70

The Knight (woodcut), Caxton's edition of
The Canterbury Tales (c. 1484).

---

51. **Alexandria:** The Knight had engaged in campaigns that spanned the Continent
from Spain to Asia Minor, from the Baltic Sea to North Africa.

He wore a fustian° tunic stained and dark
With smudges where his armor had left mark;
Just home from service, he had joined our ranks
To do his pilgrimage and render thanks.

He had his son with him, a fine young *Squire*,   75
A lover and cadet, a lad of fire
With locks as curly as if they had been pressed.
He was some twenty years of age, I guessed.
In stature he was of a moderate length,
With wonderful agility and strength.   80
He'd seen some service with the cavalry
In Flanders and Artois and Picardy°
And had done valiantly in little space
Of time, in hope to win his lady's grace.
He was embroidered like a meadow bright   85
And full of freshest flowers, red and white.
Singing he was, or fluting all the day;
He was as fresh as is the month of May.
Short was his gown, the sleeves were long and wide;
He knew the way to sit a horse and ride.   90
He could make songs and poems and recite,
Knew how to joust and dance, to draw and write.
He loved so hotly that till dawn grew pale
He slept as little as a nightingale.
Courteous he was, lowly and serviceable,   95
And carved to serve his father at the table.

There was a *Yeoman* with him at his side,
No other servant; so he chose to ride.
This Yeoman wore a coat and hood of green,
And peacock-feathered arrows, bright and keen   100
And neatly sheathed, hung at his belt the while
—For he could dress his gear in yeoman style,
His arrows never drooped their feathers low—
And in his hand he bore a mighty bow.
His head was like a nut, his face was brown.   105
He knew the whole of woodcraft up and down.
A saucy brace° was on his arm to ward
It from the bow-string, and a shield and sword
Hung at one side, and at the other slipped
A jaunty dirk,° spear-sharp and well-equipped.   110

---

71. **fustian:** coarse cloth of cotton and linen.   82. **Flanders . . . Picardy:** places on
the north coast of the Continent.   107. **brace:** bracelet.   110. **dirk:** a short,
straight dagger.

A medal of Saint Christopher° he wore
Of shining silver on his breast, and bore
A hunting-horn, well slung and burnished clean,
That dangled from a baldric° of bright green.
He was a proper forester, I guess.   115

    There also was a *Nun*, a Prioress,
Her way of smiling very simple and coy.
Her greatest oath was only "By Saint Loy!"°
And she was known as Madam Eglantyne.
And well she sang a service,° with a fine   120
Intoning through her nose, as was most seemly,
And she spoke daintily in French, extremely,
After the school of Stratford-atte-Bowe;°
French in the Paris style she did not know.
At meat her manners were well taught withal;   125
No morsel from her lips did she let fall,
Nor dipped her fingers in the sauce too deep;
But she could carry a morsel up and keep
The smallest drop from falling on her breast.
For courtliness she had a special zest,   130
And she would wipe her upper lip so clean
That not a trace of grease was to be seen
Upon the cup when she had drunk; to eat,
She reached a hand sedately for the meat.
She certainly was very entertaining,   135
Pleasant and friendly in her ways, and straining
To counterfeit a courtly kind of grace,
A stately bearing fitting to her place,
And to seem dignified in all her dealings.
As for her sympathies and tender feelings,   140
She was so charitably solicitous
She used to weep if she but saw a mouse
Caught in a trap, if it were dead or bleeding.
And she had little dogs she would be feeding
With roasted flesh, or milk, or fine white bread.   145
And bitterly she wept if one were dead
Or someone took a stick and made it smart;
She was all sentiment and tender heart.
Her veil was gathered in a seemly way,
Her nose was elegant, her eyes glass-gray;   150

---

111. **Saint Christopher:** patron of travelers and foresters. 114. **baldric:** a belt worn
over one shoulder and across the chest and back to support a sword. 118. **Saint
Loy:** courtly and talented seventh-century French saint. 120. **service:** Nuns
chanted the daily prayers or services. 123. **Stratford-atte-Bowe:** A Benedictine
nunnery near London.

Her mouth was very small, but soft and red,
Her forehead, certainly, was fair of spread,
Almost a span° across the brows, I own;
She was indeed by no means undergrown.
Her cloak, I noticed, had a graceful charm.   155
She wore a coral trinket on her arm,
A set of beads, the gaudies° tricked in green,
Whence hung a golden brooch of brightest sheen
On which there first was graven a crowned *A*,
And lower, *Amor vincit omnia.*°   160
    Another *Nun,* the chaplain at her cell,
Was riding with her, and *three Priests*° as well.

    A *Monk* there was, one of the finest sort
Who rode the country; hunting was his sport.
A manly man, to be an Abbot able;   165
Many a dainty horse he had in stable.
His bridle, when he rode, a man might hear
Jingling in a whistling wind as clear,
Aye, and as loud as does the chapel bell
Where my lord Monk was Prior of the cell.   170
The Rule of good Saint Benet or Saint Maur°
As old and strict he tended to ignore;
He let go by the things of yesterday
And took the modern world's more spacious way.
He did not rate that text at a plucked hen   175
Which says that hunters are not holy men
And that a monk uncloistered is a mere
Fish out of water, flapping on the pier,
That is to say a monk out of his cloister.
That was a text he held not worth an oyster;   180
And I agreed and said his views were sound;
Was he to study till his head went round
Poring over books in cloisters? Must he toil
As Austin° bade and till the very soil?
Was he to leave the world upon the shelf?   185
Let Austin have his labor to himself.

The Nun's Priest (detail),
Ellesmere MS.
The Huntington Library

---

153. **span:** nine inches.   157. **gaudies:** Every gaud, the eleventh bead on a rosary, or set of prayer beads, was larger than the rest. These were for praying the paternoster, or the Lord's Prayer. These gauds were colored green.   160. *Amor vincit
omnia:* "Love conquers all" in Latin.   162. **three Priests:** Only one priest is mentioned again, and the count of "nine and twenty" (line 24) allows for only one.
171. **The Rule . . . Saint Maur:** Saint Benedict wrote a set of regulations for his
monasteries. Nunneries used this rule as well. Benet is a French version of his
name and Maur is French for Maurice, one of his disciples.   184. **Austin:** English
version of Saint Augustine's name. This early bishop of Hippo in North Africa was
critical of monks' laziness.

This Monk was therefore a good man to horse;
Greyhounds he had, as swift as birds, to course.
Hunting a hare or riding at a fence
Was all his fun, he spared for no expense.   190
I saw his sleeves were garnished at the hand
With fine gray fur, the finest in the land,
And on his hood, to fasten it at his chin
He had a wrought-gold cunningly fashioned pin;
Into a lover's knot it seemed to pass.   195
His head was bald and shone like looking-glass;
So did his face, as if it had been greased.
He was a fat and personable priest;
His prominent eyeballs never seemed to settle.
They glittered like the flames beneath a kettle;   200
Supple his boots, his horse in fine condition.
He was a prelate fit for exhibition,
He was not pale like a tormented soul.
He liked a fat swan best, and roasted whole.
His palfrey° was as brown as is a berry.   205

There was a *Friar*, a wanton° one and merry,
A Limiter,° a very festive fellow.
In all Four Orders° there was none so mellow
So glib with gallant phrase and well-turned speech.
He'd fixed up many a marriage, giving each   210
Of his young women what he could afford her.
He was a noble pillar to his Order.
Highly beloved and intimate was he
With County folk within his boundary,
And city dames of honor and possessions;   215
For he was qualified to hear confessions,
Or so he said, with more than priestly scope
He had a special license from the Pope.
Sweetly he heard his penitents at shrift°
With pleasant absolution, for a gift.   220
He was an easy man in penance-giving
Where he could hope to make a decent living;
It's a sure sign whenever gifts are given
To a poor Order that a man's well shriven,
And should he give enough he knew in verity   225
The penitent repented in sincerity.
For many a fellow is so hard of heart

---

205. **palfrey:** saddle horse.   206. **wanton:** jolly.   207. **Limiter:** a begging friar who
was given a district to beg in.   208. **Four Orders:** There were four orders of begging friars: Dominicans, Franciscans, Carmelites, and Austin friars.   219. **shrift:**
confession to a priest.

He cannot weep, for all his inward smart.
Therefore instead of weeping and of prayer
One should give silver for a poor Friar's care. 230
He kept his tippet° stuffed with pins for curls,
And pocket-knives, to give to pretty girls.
And certainly his voice was gay and sturdy,
For he sang well and played the hurdy-gurdy.°
At sing-songs he was champion of the hour. 235
His neck was whiter than a lily-flower
But strong enough to butt a bruiser down.
He knew the taverns well in every town
And every innkeeper and barmaid too
Better than lepers, beggars and that crew, 240
For in so eminent a man as he
It was not fitting with the dignity
Of his position, dealing with a scum
Of wretched lepers; nothing good can come
Of dealings with the slum-and-gutter dwellers, 245
But only with the rich and victual-sellers.
But anywhere a profit might accrue
Courteous he was and lowly of service too.
Natural gifts like his were hard to match.
He was the finest beggar of his batch, 250
And, for his begging-district, payed a rent;
His brethren did no poaching where he went.
For though a widow mightn't have a shoe,
So pleasant was his holy how-d'ye-do
He got his farthing from her just the same 255
Before he left, and so his income came
To more than he laid out. And how he romped,
Just like a puppy! He was ever prompt
To arbitrate disputes on settling days
(For a small fee) in many helpful ways, 260
Not then appearing as your cloistered scholar
With threadbare habit hardly worth a dollar,
But much more like a Doctor or a Pope.
Of double-worsted was the semi-cope°
Upon his shoulders, and the swelling fold 265
About him, like a bell about its mold
When it is casting, rounded out his dress.
He lisped a little out of wantonness°
To make his English sweet upon his tongue.
When he had played his harp, or having sung, 270

---

231. **tippet:** a long, hanging hood. 234. **hurdy-gurdy:** a lutelike instrument played by cranking a wheel. 264. **semi-cope:** cape. 268. **wantonness:** here, affectation.

His eyes would twinkle in his head as bright
As any star upon a frosty night.
This worthy's name was Hubert, it appeared.

There was a *Merchant* with a forking beard
And motley dress; high on his horse he sat,   275
Upon his head a Flemish beaver hat
And on his feet daintily buckled boots.
He told of his opinions and pursuits
In solemn tones, and how he never lost.
The sea should be kept free at any cost   280
(He thought) upon the Harwich–Holland range,
He was expert at currency exchange.
This estimable Merchant so had set
His wits to work, none knew he was in debt,
He was so stately in negotiation,   285
Loan, bargain and commercial obligation.
He was an excellent fellow all the same;
To tell the truth I do not know his name.

An *Oxford Cleric,* still a student though,
One who had taken logic long ago,   290
Was there; his horse was thinner than a rake,
And he was not too fat, I undertake,
But had a hollow look, a sober stare;
The thread upon his overcoat was bare.
He had found no preferment in the church   295
And he was too unworldly to make search
For secular employment. By his bed
He preferred having twenty books in red
And black, of Aristotle's° philosophy,
To having fine clothes, fiddle or psaltery.°   300
Though a philosopher, as I have told,
He had not found the stone for making gold.
Whatever money from his friends he took
He spent on learning or another book
And prayed for them most earnestly, returning   305
Thanks to them thus for paying for his learning.
His only care was study, and indeed
He never spoke a word more than was need,
Formal at that, respectful in the extreme,
Short, to the point, and lofty in his theme.   310
The thought of moral virtue filled his speech
And he would gladly learn, and gladly teach.

---

299. **Aristotle** (ăr′ĭs-tŏt′l): Greek philosopher (384–322 B.C.), regarded by medieval
scholars as the highest authority on all matters of learning.   300. **psaltery** (sôl′tə-
rē): an ancient stringed instrument.

A *Sergeant at the Law* who paid his calls,
Wary and wise, for clients at St. Paul's°
There also was, of noted excellence.   315
Discreet he was, a man to reverence,
Or so he seemed, his sayings were so wise.
He often had been Justice of Assize
By letters patent, and in full commission.
His fame and learning and his high position   320
Had won him many a robe and many a fee.
There was no such conveyancer° as he;
All was fee-simple° to his strong digestion,
Not one conveyance could be called in question.
Nowhere there was so busy a man as he;   325
But was less busy than he seemed to be.
He knew of every judgment, case and crime
Recorded, ever since King William's time.
He could dictate defenses or draft deeds;
No one could pinch a comma from his screeds,°   330
And he knew every statute off by rote.
He wore a homely parti-colored coat
Girt with a silken belt of pin-stripe stuff;
Of his appearance I have said enough.

There was a *Franklin*° with him, it appeared;   335
White as a daisy-petal was his beard.
A sanguine man, high-colored and benign,
He loved a morning sop of cake in wine.
He lived for pleasure and had always done,
For he was Epicurus'° very son,   340
In whose opinion sensual delight
Was the one true felicity in sight.
As noted as Saint Julian° was for bounty
He made his household free to all the County.
His bread, his ale were finest of the fine   345
And no one had a better stock of wine.
His house was never short of bake-meat pies,
Of fish and flesh, and these in such supplies
It positively snowed with meat and drink
And all the dainties that a man could think.   350
According to the seasons of the year
Changes of dish were ordered to appear.

---

314. **St. Paul's:** London cathedral located near the Inns of Court. Lawyers met outside it to discuss their cases out of court.   322. **conveyancer:** one who draws up legal papers for the transfer of property.   323. **fee-simple:** unrestricted ownership.
330. **screeds:** long, tiresome documents.   335. **Franklin:** landowner.   340. **Epicurus** (ĕp′ĭ-kyŏŏr′əs): a Greek philosopher (342?–370 B.C.), who taught that happiness is the goal of life.   343. **Saint Julian:** a saint known for his hospitality.

He kept fat partridges in coops, beyond,
Many a bream and pike were in his pond.
Woe to the cook whose sauces had no sting   355
Or who was unprepared in anything!
And in his hall a table stood arrayed
And ready all day long, with places laid.
As Justice at the Sessions° none stood higher;
He often had been Member for the Shire.   360
A dagger and a little purse of silk
Hung at his girdle, white as morning milk.
As Sheriff he checked audit, every entry.
He was a model among landed gentry.

　　A *Haberdasher*, a *Dyer*, a *Carpenter*,   365
A *Weaver* and a *Carpet-maker* were
Among our ranks, all in the livery
Of one impressive guild-fraternity.
They were so trim and fresh their gear would pass
For new. Their knives were not tricked out with brass   370
But wrought with purest silver, which avouches
A like display on girdles and on pouches.
Each seemed a worthy burgess,° fit to grace
A guild-hall with a seat upon the dais.
Their wisdom would have justified a plan   375
To make each one of them an alderman;
They had the capital and revenue,
Besides their wives declared it was their due.
And if they did not think so, then they ought;
To be called "Madam" is a glorious thought,   380
And so is going to church and being seen
Having your mantle carried like a queen.

　　They had a *Cook* with them who stood alone
For boiling chicken with a marrow-bone,
Sharp flavoring-powder and a spice for savor.   385
He could distinguish London ale by flavor,
And he could roast and seethe and broil and fry,
Make good thick soup and bake a tasty pie.
But what a pity—so it seemed to me,
That he should have an ulcer on his knee.   390
As for blancmange,° he made it with the best.

---

359. **Sessions:** a term during which court is in session.   373. **burgess:** an alderman.   391. **blancmange** (blə-mänj′): in Chaucer's day, a sweet, creamy dish made
with chicken. Its name comes from French words meaning "white" and "eat."

There was a *Skipper* hailing from far west;
He came from Dartmouth, so I understood.
He rode a farmer's horse as best he could,
In a woolen gown that reached his knee.   395
A dagger on a lanyard° falling free
Hung from his neck under his arm and down.
The summer heat had tanned his color brown,
And certainly he was an excellent fellow.
Many a draft of vintage, red and yellow,   400
He'd drawn at Bordeaux, while the trader snored.
The nicer rules of conscience he ignored.
If, when he fought, the enemy vessel sank,
He sent his prisoners home; they walked the plank.
As for his skill in reckoning his tides,   405
Currents and many another risk besides,
Moons, harbors, pilots, he had such dispatch
That none from Hull to Carthage was his match.
Hardy he was, prudent in undertaking;
His beard in many a tempest had its shaking,   410
And he knew all the havens as they were
From Gotland to the Cape of Finisterre,°
And every creek in Brittany and Spain;
The barge he owned was called the *Maudelayne*.

A *Doctor* too emerged as we proceeded;   415
No one alive could talk as well as he did
On points of medicine and of surgery,
For, being grounded in astronomy,
He watched his patient's favorable star
And, by his Natural Magic, knew what are   420
The lucky hours and planetary degrees
For making charms and magic effigies.
The cause of every malady you'd got
He knew, and whether dry, cold, moist or hot;°
He knew their seat, their humor and condition.   425
He was a perfect practicing physician.
These causes being known for what they were,
He gave the man his medicine then and there.
All his apothecaries in a tribe
Were ready with the drugs he would prescribe   430
And each made money from the other's guile;
They had been friendly for a goodish while.
In his own diet he observed some measure;

---

396. **lanyard:** a loose rope around the neck. 412. **From Gotland . . . Finisterre:**
from Sweden to the tip of Spain. 424. **He knew . . . or hot:** The body was thought
to be composed of equal parts of four elements, any imbalance of which would
cause illness.

There were no superfluities for pleasure,
Only digestives, nutritives and such.   435
He did not read the Bible very much.
In blood-red garments, slashed with bluish-gray
And lined with taffeta, he rode his way;
Yet he was rather close as to expenses
And kept the gold he won in pestilences.   440
Gold stimulates the heart, or so we're told.
He therefore had a special love of gold.

   A worthy *woman* from beside *Bath* city
Was with us, somewhat deaf, which was a pity.
In making cloth she showed so great a bent   445
She bettered those of Ypres and of Ghent.°
In all the parish not a dame dared stir
Towards the altar steps in front of her,
And if indeed they did, so wrath was she
As to be quite put out of charity.   450
Her kerchiefs were of finely woven ground;
I dared have sworn they weighed a good ten pound,
The ones she wore on Sunday, on her head.
Her hose were of the finest scarlet red
And gartered tight; her shoes were soft and new.   455
Bold was her face, handsome, and red in hue.
A worthy woman all her life, what's more
She'd had five husbands, all at the church door,
Apart from other company in youth;
No need just now to speak of that, forsooth.   460
And she had thrice been to Jerusalem,
Seen many strange rivers and passed over them;
She'd been to Rome and also to Boulogne,
Saint James of Compostella and Cologne,°
And she was skilled in wandering by the way.   465
She had gap-teeth, set widely, truth to say.
Easily on an ambling horse she sat
Well wimpled° up, and on her head a hat
As broad as is a buckler or a shield;
She had a flowing mantle that concealed   470
Large hips, her heels spurred sharply under that.
In company she liked to laugh and chat
And knew the remedies for love's mischances,
An art in which she knew the oldest dances.

The Wife of Bath (detail),
Ellesmere MS.
The Huntington Library

---

446. **Ypres** (ē′pr) **and of Ghent** (gĕnt): centers of the famous Flemish wool trade.
463–464. **She'd . . . Cologne:** four famous shrines in Europe. At Cologne's cathedral the bones of the Magi could be seen.   468. **wimpled:** wearing a scarf around the head, neck, and chin.

A holy-minded man of good renown   475
There was, and poor, the *Parson* to a town,
Yet he was rich in holy thought and work.
He also was a learned man, a clerk,
Who truly knew Christ's gospel and would preach it
Devoutly to parishioners, and teach it.   480
Benign and wonderfully diligent,
And patient when adversity was sent
(For so he proved in great adversity)
He much disliked extorting tithe° or fee,
Nay rather he preferred beyond a doubt   485
Giving to poor parishioners round about
From his own goods and Easter offerings.
He found sufficiency in little things.
Wide was his parish, with houses far asunder,
Yet he neglected not in rain or thunder,   490
In sickness or in grief, to pay a call
On the remotest, whether great or small,
Upon his feet, and in his hand a stave.°
This noble example to his sheep he gave,
First following the word before he taught it,   495
And it was from the gospel he had caught it.
This little proverb he would add thereto
That if gold rust, what then will iron do?
For if a priest be foul in whom we trust
No wonder that a common man should rust.   500
The true example that a priest should give
Is one of cleanness, how the sheep should live.
He did not set his benefice to hire°
And leave his sheep encumbered in the mire
Or run to London to earn easy bread   505
By singing masses for the wealthy dead,
Or find some Brotherhood and get enrolled.
He stayed at home and watched over his fold
So that no wolf should make the sheep miscarry.
He was a shepherd and no mercenary.   510
Holy and virtuous he was, but then
Never contemptuous of sinful men,
Never disdainful, never too proud or fine,
But was discreet in teaching and benign.
His business was to show a fair behavior   515
And draw men thus to Heaven and their Savior,
Unless indeed a man were obstinate;
And such, whether of high or low estate,

---

484. **tithe:** a church tax consisting of one tenth of one's income.   493. **stave:**
staff.   503. **benefice to hire:** pay someone else to do his parish duties.

He put to sharp rebuke to say the least.
I think there never was a better priest.   520
He sought no pomp or glory in his dealings,
No scrupulosity had spiced his feelings,
Christ and His twelve apostles and their lore
He taught, but followed it himself before.

There was a *Plowman* with him there, his brother   525
Many a load of dung one time or other
He must have carted through the morning dew.
He was an honest worker, good and true,
Living in peace and perfect charity,
And, as the gospel bade him, so did he,   530
Loving God best with all his heart and mind
And then his neighbor as himself, repined
At no misfortune, slacked for no content,
For steadily about his work he went
To thrash his corn, to dig or to manure   535
Or make a ditch; and he would help the poor
For love of Christ and never take a penny
If he could help it, and, as prompt as any,
He paid his tithes in full when they were due
On what he owned, and on his earnings too.   540
He wore a tabard° smock and rode a mare.

There was a *Reeve,*° also a *Miller,* there,
A College *Manciple*° from the Inns of Court,
A papal *Pardoner*° and, in close consort,
A Church-Court *Summoner,*° riding at a trot,   545
And finally myself—that was the lot.

The *Miller* was a chap of sixteen stone,
A great stout fellow big in brawn and bone.
He did well out of them, for he could go
And win the ram at any wrestling show.   550
Broad, knotty and short-shouldered, he would boast
He could heave any door off hinge and post,
Or take a run and break it with his head.
His beard, like any sow or fox, was red
And broad as well, as though it were a spade;   555
And, at its very tip, his nose displayed
A wart on which there stood a tuft of hair
Red as the bristles in an old sow's ear.

---

541. **tabard:** a short jacket.   542. **Reeve:** steward of a manor.   543. **Manciple:**
purchasing agent.   544. **Pardoner:** one who has the authority to sell pardons and
indulgences.   545. **Summoner:** one whose job is to summon sinners to church
courts.

The Miller (detail),
Ellesmere MS.
The Huntington Library

His nostrils were as black as they were wide.
He had a sword and buckler at his side, 560
His mighty mouth was like a furnace door.
A wrangler and buffoon, he had a store
Of tavern stories, filthy in the main.
His was a master-hand at stealing grain.
He felt it with his thumb and thus he knew 565
Its quality and took three times his due—
A thumb of gold, by God, to gauge an oat!
He wore a hood of blue and a white coat.
He liked to play his bagpipes up and down
And that was how he brought us out of town. 570

The *Manciple* came from the Inner Temple;
All caterers might follow his example
In buying victuals; he was never rash
Whether he bought on credit or paid cash.
He used to watch the market most precisely 575
And got in first, and so he did quite nicely.
Now isn't it a marvel of God's grace
That an illiterate fellow can outpace
The wisdom of a heap of learned men?
His masters—he had more than thirty then— 580
All versed in the abstrusest legal knowledge,
Could have produced a dozen from their College
Fit to be stewards in land and rents and game
To any Peer in England you could name,
And show him how to live on what he had 585
Debt-free (unless of course the Peer were mad)
Or be as frugal as he might desire,
And they were fit to help about the Shire
In any legal case there was to try;
And yet this Manciple could wipe their eye. 590

The *Reeve* was old and choleric and thin;
His beard was shaven closely to the skin,
His shorn hair came abruptly to a stop
Above his ears, and he was docked on top
Just like a priest in front; his legs were lean, 595
Like sticks they were, no calf was to be seen.
He kept his bins and garners very trim;
No auditor could gain a point on him.
And he could judge by watching drought and rain
The yield he might expect from seed and grain. 600
His master's sheep, his animals and hens,
Pigs, horses, dairies, stores and cattle pens
Were wholly trusted to his government.
And he was under contract to present

The accounts, right from his master's earliest years. 605
No one had ever caught him in arrears.
No bailiff, serf or herdsman dared to kick,
He knew their dodges, knew their every trick;
Feared like the plague he was, by those beneath.
He had a lovely dwelling on a heath, 610
Shadowed in green by trees above the sward.
A better hand at bargains than his lord,
He had grown rich and had a store of treasure
Well tucked away, yet out it came to pleasure
His lord with subtle loans or gifts of goods, 615
To earn his thanks and even coats and hoods.
When young he'd learnt a useful trade and still
He was a carpenter of first-rate skill.
The stallion-cob he rode at a slow trot
Was dapple-gray and bore the name of Scot. 620
He wore an overcoat of bluish shade
And rather long; he had a rusty blade
Slung at his side. He came, as I heard tell,
From Norfolk, near a place called Baldeswell.
His coat was tucked under his belt and splayed. 625
He rode the hindmost of our cavalcade.

There was a *Summoner* with us in the place
Who had a fire-red cherubinish face.°
Black, scabby brows he had, and a thin beard.
Children were afraid when he appeared. 630
No quicksilver, lead ointments, tartar creams,
Boracic, no, nor brimstone, so it seems,
Could make a salve that had the power to bite,
Clean up or cure his whelks° of knobby white
Or purge the pimples sitting on his cheeks. 635
Garlic he loved, and onions too, and leeks,
And drinking strong red wine till all was hazy.
Then he would shout and jabber as if crazy,
And wouldn't speak a word except in Latin
When he was drunk, such tags as he was pat in; 640
He only had a few, say two or three,
That he had mugged up out of some decree;
No wonder, for he heard them every day.
And, as you know, a man can teach a jay
To call out "Walter" better than the Pope. 645
But had you tried to test his wits and grope
For more, you'd have found nothing in the bag.
Then "*Questio quid juris*"° was his tag.

---

628. **Who . . . face:** In medieval art, angels' faces were painted red. 634. **whelks:**
pimples. 648. ***Questio quid juris:*** "The question is, what is the law."

He was a gentle varlet° and a kind one,
No better fellow if you went to find one.   650
He wore a garland set upon his head
Large as the holly-bush upon a stake
Outside an ale-house, and he had a cake,
A round one, which it was his joke to wield
As if it were intended for a shield.   655

  He and a gentle *Pardoner* rode together,
A bird from Charing Cross of the same feather,
Just back from visiting the Court of Rome.
He loudly sang "Come hither, love, come home!"
The Summoner sang deep seconds to this song.   660
No trumpet ever sounded half so strong.
This Pardoner had hair as yellow as wax,
Hanging down smoothly like a hank of flax.
In driblets fell his locks behind his head
Down to his shoulders which they overspread;   665
Thinly they fell, like rat-tails, one by one.
He wore no hood upon his head, for fun;
The hood inside his wallet had been stowed,
He aimed at riding in the latest mode;
But for a little cap his head was bare   670
And he had bulging eyeballs, like a hare.
He'd sewed a holy relic on his cap;
His wallet lay before him on his lap,
Brimful of pardons come from Rome all hot.
He had the same small voice a goat has got.   675
His chin no beard had harbored, nor would harbor,
Smoother than ever chin was left by barber.
I judge he was a gelding, or a mare.
As to his trade, from Berwick down to Ware
There was no pardoner of equal grace,   680
For in his trunk he had a pillowcase
Which he asserted was Our Lady's veil.
He said he had a gobbet° of the sail
Saint Peter had the time when he made bold
To walk the waves, till Jesu Christ took hold.   685
He had a cross of metal set with stones
And, in a glass, a rubble of pigs' bones.
And with these relics, any time he found
Some poor up-country parson to astound,
On one short day, in money down, he drew   690
More than the parson in a month or two,
And by his flatteries and prevarication

---

649. **varlet:** scoundrel, knave.   683. **gobbet:** fragment.

Made monkeys of the priest and congregation.
But still to do him justice first and last
In church he was a noble ecclesiast. 695
How well he read a lesson or told a story!
But best of all he sang an Offertory,
For well he knew that when that song was sung
He'd have to preach and tune his honey-tongue
And (well he could) win silver from the crowd. 700
That's why he sang so merrily and loud.

   Now I have told you shortly, in a clause,
The rank, the array, the number and the cause
Of our assembly in this company
In Southwark, at that high-class hostelry 705
Known as The Tabard, close beside The Bell.
And now the time has come for me to tell
How we behaved that evening; I'll begin
After we had alighted at the inn,
Then I'll report our journey, stage by stage, 710
All the remainder of our pilgrimage.
But first I beg of you, in courtesy,
Not to condemn me as unmannerly
If I speak plainly and with no concealings
And give account of all their words and dealings, 715
Using their very phrases as they fell.
For certainly, as you all know so well,
He who repeats a tale after a man
Is bound to say, as nearly as he can,
Each single word, if he remembers it, 720
However rudely spoken or unfit,
Or else the tale he tells will be untrue,
The things invented and the phrases new.
He may not flinch although it were his brother,
If he says one word he must say the other. 725
And Christ Himself spoke broad in Holy Writ,
And as you know there's nothing there unfit,
And Plato says, for those with power to read,
"The word should be as cousin to the deed."
Further I beg you to forgive it me 730
If I neglect the order and degree
And what is due to rank in what I've planned.
I'm short of wit as you will understand.
   Our *Host*° gave us great welcome; everyone
Was given a place and supper was begun. 735

---

734. **Host:** The Host has been almost certainly identified as Harry Bailly, who had an inn at Southwark in Chaucer's time.

He served the finest victuals you could think,
The wine was strong and we were glad to drink.
A very striking man our Host withal,
And fit to be a marshal in a hall.
His eyes were bright, his girth a little wide;   740
There is no finer burgess in Cheapside.°
Bold in his speech, yet wise and full of tact,
There was no manly attribute he lacked,
What's more he was a merry-hearted man.
After our meal he jokingly began   745
To talk of sport, and, among other things
After we'd settled up our reckonings,
He said as follows: "Truly, gentlemen,
You're very welcome and I can't think when
—Upon my word I'm telling you no lie—   750
I've seen a gathering here that looked so spry,
No, not this year, as in this tavern now.
I'd think you up some fun if I knew how.
And, as it happens, a thought has just occurred
And it will cost you nothing, on my word.   755
You're off to Canterbury—well, Godspeed!
Blessed Saint Thomas answer to your need!
And I don't doubt, before the journey's done
You mean to while the time in tales and fun.
Indeed, there's little pleasure for your bones   760
Riding along and all as dumb as stones.
So let me then propose for your enjoyment,
Just as I said, a suitable employment.
And if my notion suits and you agree
And promise to submit yourselves to me   765
Playing your parts exactly as I say
Tomorrow as you ride along the way,
Then by my father's soul (and he is dead)
If you don't like it you can have my head!
Hold up your hands, and not another word."   770
    Well, our consent of course was not deferred,
It seemed not worth a serious debate;
We all agreed to it at any rate
And bade him issue what commands he would.
"My lords," he said, "now listen for your good,   775
And please don't treat my notion with disdain.
This is the point. I'll make it short and plain.
Each one of you shall help to make things slip
By telling two stories on the outward trip

---

741. **Cheapside:** a district of London.

To Canterbury, that's what I intend, 780
And, on the homeward way to journey's end
Another two, tales from the days of old;
And then the man whose story is best told,
That is to say who gives the fullest measure
Of good morality and general pleasure, 785
He shall be given a supper, paid by all,
Here in this tavern, in this very hall,
When we come back again from Canterbury.
And in the hope to keep you bright and merry
I'll go along with you myself and ride 790
All at my own expense and serve as guide.
I'll be the judge, and those who won't obey
Shall pay for what we spend upon the way.
Now if you all agree to what you've heard
Tell me at once without another word, 795
And I will make arrangements early for it."
    Of course we all agreed, in fact we swore it
Delightedly, and made entreaty too
That he should act as he proposed to do,
Become our Governor in short, and be 800
Judge of our tales and general referee,
And set the supper at a certain price.
We promised to be ruled by his advice
Come high, come low; unanimously thus
We set him up in judgment over us. 805
More wine was fetched, the business being done;
We drank it off and up went everyone
To bed without a moment of delay.
    Early next morning at the spring of day
Up rose our Host and roused us like a cock, 810
Gathering us together in a flock,
And off we rode at slightly faster pace
Than walking to St. Thomas' watering-place;°
And there our Host drew up, began to ease
His horse, and said, "Now, listen if you please, 815
My lords! Remember what you promised me.
If evensong and matins will agree°
Let's see who shall be first to tell a tale.
And as I hope to drink good wine and ale
I'll be your judge. The rebel who disobeys, 820
However much the journey costs, he pays.
Now draw for cut and then we can depart;
The man who draws the shortest cut shall start."

---

813. **St. Thomas' watering-place:** a resort less than two miles from the Tabard Inn.
817. **If evensong . . . agree:** If you feel this morning as you did last night.

FOR STUDY AND DISCUSSION

1. Studying Chaucer's character sketches reveals his ability to depict not only a type—a person typical of his or her class and occupation—but an individual as well. One method Chaucer uses to individualize his characters is to describe their physical appearance. How do Chaucer's descriptions of the external appearance of the pilgrims reveal or suggest their inner nature?

2. The eighteenth-century English poet William Blake remarked, "Every age is a Canterbury pilgrimage; we all pass on, each sustaining one or other of these characters." In this statement Blake notes that the various types of characters in Chaucer's *Prologue* are to be found in every society. What modern equivalents of the Merchant and the Oxford Student can you suggest? Describe them. Do the characteristics of any of the other pilgrims suggest any contemporary figures, even though they might belong to a different profession?

3. Chaucer is a great satirist, though he is almost never bitter when he pokes fun at the foibles and weaknesses of people. Point out examples of Chaucer's genial satire in the *Prologue*. Find also evidence of those characteristics he admires in people.

4. In describing his characters, Chaucer also discloses a good deal about himself. In which passages does he reveal his tolerance? His sense of humor? His keen observation and love of nature?

Canterbury Pilgrims (woodcut).
The Mansell Collection

SIMILES

Chaucer makes use of a number of striking comparisons to enhance his description of the pilgrims. For example, in these lines, the Friar's eyes are compared to stars:

> His eyes would twinkle in his head as bright
> As any star upon a frosty night.
>
> (271–272)

A comparison of this kind is known as a *simile*. A simile is a figure of speech based on a comparison between two things that are essentially unlike. In a simile, a word of comparison such as *like* or *as* is always used.

What similes are used in these lines about the Pardoner?

> This Pardoner had hair as yellow as wax,
> Hanging down smoothly like a hank of flax.
> In driblets fell his locks behind his head
> Down to his shoulders which they overspread;
> Thinly they fell, like rat-tails, one by one.
>
> (662–666)

Why are these comparisons effective?

Find other similes in the *Prologue*. Explain why these figures of speech are more imaginative and convey an idea more vividly than a literal expression might.

FOR COMPOSITION

1. Compare the Monk and the Parson, using specific examples to support your general points about their personalities, abilities, and so on.

2. Using Chaucer's methods, write a character sketch about a type of person found in modern society. You may wish to describe a doctor, a lawyer, an industrialist, a teacher, an actor, or someone else. Write your sketch in either prose or verse.

from The Pardoner's Tale

After the Knight begins the pilgrims' game of storytelling by telling a grace-ful tale of courtly love, a chivalric theme entirely appropriate to its narrator, the Miller, the Reeve, the Prioress, Chaucer himself—each of the pilgrims in turn—tells his or her tale. The stories related by the pilgrims present an extended revelation of their characters and serve to confirm Chaucer's por-trayal of them in the *Prologue.* These tales shed much light on medieval thought and conduct, and most of them leave the reader with some moral, maxim, or timeless piece of wisdom.

Finally it is the Pardoner's turn to entertain the company. He launches into a sermon using as his text: *"Radix malorum est cupiditas,"* or "Greed is the root of all evil." Illustrating his text with an *exemplum,* or illustrative anecdote, he tells the story of three roisterers, which follows below.

The Pardoner (detail),
Ellesmere MS.
The Huntington Library

It's of three rioters I have to tell
Who long before the morning service bell°
Were sitting in a tavern for a drink.
And as they sat, they heard the hand-bell clink
Before a coffin going to the grave;   5
One of them called the little tavern-knave°
And said "Go and find out at once—look spry!—
Whose corpse is in that coffin passing by;
And see you get the name correctly too."
"Sir," said the boy, "no need, I promise you;   10
Two hours before you came here I was told.
He was a friend of yours in days of old,
And suddenly, last night, the man was slain,
Upon his bench, face up, dead drunk again.
There came a privy thief, they call him Death,   15
Who kills us all round here, and in a breath
He speared him through the heart, he never stirred.
And then Death went his way without a word.
He's killed a thousand in the present plague,°
And, sir, it doesn't do to be too vague   20
If you should meet him; you had best be wary.
Be on your guard with such an adversary,
Be primed to meet him everywhere you go,
That's what my mother said. It's all I know."

---

2. **morning service bell:** sometime between the hours of 6:00 and 9:00 A.M.
6. **tavern-knave:** a serving boy.   19. **plague:** the Black Death, which killed almost half the population of England in 1348 and 1349.

The publican joined in with, "By Saint Mary,   25
What the child says is right; you'd best be wary,
This very year he killed, in a large village
A mile away, man, woman, serf at tillage,°
Page in the household, children—all there were.
Yes, I imagine that he lives round there.   30
It's well to be prepared in these alarms,
He might do you dishonor." "Huh, God's arms!"
The rioter said, "Is he so fierce to meet?
I'll search for him, by Jesus, street by street.
God's blessed bones! I'll register a vow!   35
Here, chaps! The three of us together now,
Hold up your hands, like me, and we'll be brothers
In this affair, and each defend the others,
And we will kill this traitor Death, I say!
Away with him as he has made away   40
With all our friends. God's dignity! To-night!"
  They made their bargain, swore with appetite,
These three, to live and die for one another
As brother-born might swear to his born brother.
And up they started in their drunken rage   45
And made towards this village which the page
And publican had spoken of before.
Many and grisly were the oaths they swore,
Tearing Christ's blessed body to a shred;°
"If we can only catch him, Death is dead!"   50
  When they had gone not fully half a mile,
Just as they were about to cross a stile,
They came upon a very poor old man
Who humbly greeted them and thus began,
"God look to you, my lords, and give you quiet!"   55
To which the proudest of these men of riot
Gave back the answer, "What, old fool? Give place!
Why are you all wrapped up except your face?
Why live so long? Isn't it time to die?"
  The old, old fellow looked him in the eye   60
And said, "Because I never yet have found,
Though I have walked to India, searching round
Village and city on my pilgrimage,
One who would change his youth to have my age.
And so my age is mine and must be still   65
Upon me, for such time as God may will.
  "Not even Death, alas, will take my life;
So, like a wretched prisoner at strife

---

28. **tillage:** plowing. 49. **Tearing . . . shred:** In swearing, they used expressions
such as "God's arms" (line 32) and "God's blessed bones" (line 35).

Within himself, I walk alone and wait
About the earth, which is my mother's gate,   70
Knock-knocking with my staff from night to noon
And crying, 'Mother, open to me soon!
Look at me, mother, won't you let me in?
See how I wither, flesh and blood and skin!
Alas! When will these bones be laid to rest?   75
Mother, I would exchange—for that were best—
The wardrobe in my chamber, standing there
So long, for yours! Aye, for a shirt of hair°
To wrap me in!' She has refused her grace,
Whence comes the pallor of my withered face.   80
    "But it dishonored you when you began
To speak so roughly, sir, to an old man,
Unless he had injured you in word or deed.
It says in holy writ, as you may read,
'Thou shalt rise up before the hoary head   85
And honor it.' And therefore be it said
'Do no more harm to an old man than you,
Being now young, would have another do
When you are old'—if you should live till then.
And so may God be with you, gentlemen,   90
For I must go whither I have to go."
    "By God," the gambler said, "you shan't do so,
You don't get off so easy, by Saint John!
I heard you mention, just a moment gone,
A certain traitor Death who singles out   95
And kills the fine young fellows hereabout.
And you're his spy, by God! You wait a bit.
Say where he is or you shall pay for it,
By God and by the Holy Sacrament!
I say you've joined together by consent.   100
To kill us younger folk, you thieving swine!"
    "Well, sirs," he said, "If it be your design
To find out Death, turn up this crooked way
Towards that grove, I left him there today
Under a tree, and there you'll find him waiting.   105
He isn't one to hide for all your prating.
You see that oak? He won't be far to find.
And God protect you that redeemed mankind,
Aye, and amend you!" Thus that ancient man.
    At once the three young rioters began   110
To run, and reached the tree, and there they found
A pile of golden florins° on the ground,
New-coined, eight bushels of them as they thought.

---

78. **shirt of hair:** here, a shroud.   112. **florins:** gold coins.

No longer was it Death those fellows sought,
For they were all so thrilled to see the sight,   115
The florins were so beautiful and bright,
That down they sat beside the precious pile.
The wickedest spoke first after a while.
"Brothers," he said, "you listen to what I say.
I'm pretty sharp although I joke away.   120
It's clear that Fortune has bestowed this treasure
To let us live in jollity and pleasure.
Light come, light go! We'll spend it as we ought.
God's precious dignity! Who would have thought
This morning was to be our lucky day?   125
    "If one could only get the gold away,
Back to my house, or else to yours, perhaps—
For as you know, the gold is ours, chaps—
We'd all be at the top of fortune, hey?
But certainly it can't be done by day.   130
People would call us robbers—a strong gang,
So our own property would make us hang.
No, we must bring this treasure back by night
Some prudent way, and keep it out of sight.
And so as a solution I propose   135
We draw for lots and see the way it goes,
The one who draws the longest, lucky man,
Shall run to town as quickly as he can
To fetch us bread and wine—but keep things dark—
While two remain in hiding here to mark   140
Our heap of treasure. If there's no delay,
When night comes down we'll carry it away,
All three of us, wherever we have planned."
    He gathered lots and hid them in his hand
Bidding them draw for where the luck should fall.   145
It fell upon the youngest of them all,
And off he ran at once towards the town.
    As soon as he had gone the first sat down
And thus began a parley° with the other:
"You know that you can trust me as a brother;   150
Now let me tell you where your profit lies;
You know our friend has gone to get supplies
And here's a lot of gold that is to be
Divided equally amongst us three.
Nevertheless, if I could shape things thus   155
So that we shared it out—the two of us—
Wouldn't you take it as a friendly turn?"
    "But how?" the other said with some concern,

---

149. **parley:** discussion.

"Because he knows the gold's with me and you;
What can we tell him? What are we to do?"   160
   "Is it a bargain," said the first, "or no?
For I can tell you in a word or so
What's to be done to bring the thing about."
"Trust me," the other said, "you needn't doubt
My word. I won't betray you, I'll be true."   165
   "Well," said his friend, "you see that we are two,
And two are twice as powerful as one.
Now look; when he comes back, get up in fun
To have a wrestle; then, as you attack,
I'll up and put my dagger through his back   170
While you and he are struggling, as in game;
Then draw your dagger too and do the same.
Then all this money will be ours to spend,
Divided equally of course, dear friend.
Then we can gratify our lusts and fill   175
The day with dicing at our own sweet will."
Thus these two miscreants° agreed to slay
The third and youngest, as you heard me say.
   The youngest, as he ran towards the town,
Kept running over, rolling up and down   180
Within his heart the beauty of those bright
New florins, saying, "Lord, to think I might
Have all that treasure to myself alone!
Could there be anyone beneath the throne
Of God so happy as I then should be?"   185
   And so the Fiend,° our common enemy,
Was given power to put it in his thought
That there was always poison to be bought,
And that with poison he could kill his friends.
To men in such a state the Devil sends   190
Thoughts of this kind, and has a full permission
To lure them on to sorrow and perdition;°
For this young man was utterly content
To kill them both and never to repent.
   And on he ran, he had no thought to tarry,   195
Came to the town, found an apothecary
And said, "Sell me some poison if you will,
I have a lot of rats I want to kill
And there's a polecat too about my yard
That takes my chickens and it hits me hard;   200
But I'll get even, as is only right,
With vermin that destroy a man by night."

---

177. **miscreants** (mĭs'krē-ənts): villains. 186. **Fiend:** Satan, the devil.
192. **perdition:** damnation.

The chemist answered, "I've a preparation
Which you shall have, and by my soul's salvation
If any living creature eat or drink   205
A mouthful, ere he has the time to think,
Though he took less than makes a grain of wheat,
You'll see him fall down dying at your feet;
Yes, die he must, and in so short a while
You'd hardly have the time to walk a mile,   210
The poison is so strong, you understand."
     This cursed fellow grabbed into his hand
The box of poison and away he ran
Into a neighboring street, and found a man
Who lent him three large bottles. He withdrew   215
And deftly poured the poison into two.
He kept the third one clean, as well he might,
For his own drink, meaning to work all night
Stacking the gold and carrying it away.
And when this rioter, this devil's clay,   220
Had filled his bottles up with wine, all three,
Back to rejoin his comrades sauntered he.
     Why make a sermon of it? Why waste breath?
Exactly in the way they'd planned his death
They fell on him and slew him, two to one.   225
Then said the first of them when this was done,
"Now for a drink. Sit down and let's be merry,
For later on there'll be the corpse to bury."
And, as it happened, reaching for a sup,
He took a bottle full of poison up   230
And drank; and his companion, nothing loth,
Drank from it also, and they perished both.
     There is, in Avicenna's long relation°
Concerning poison and its operation,
Trust me, no ghastlier section to transcend   235
What these two wretches suffered at their end.
Thus these two murderers received their due,
So did the treacherous young poisoner too.

Dance of Death, Lübeck
(engraving) Anon. German.
Public Library, Print Room

---

233. **Avicenna's long relation:** Avicenna (ăv'ə-sĕn'ə) was an Arab physician (980–
1037) who wrote a book on medicines with a chapter on poisons.

FOR STUDY AND DISCUSSION

1. The fact that we meet the rioters drinking in a tavern in the early morning does not bode well for their future. What other vices do they exhibit?

2. The tavern-knave and the publican, or tavern-keeper, advise the rioters to be wary of Death. How do the three men ignore this advice?

3. When the three men vow "to live and die for one another," they imply that they are willing to sacrifice themselves for the common good. What is ironic about this vow?

4. A key figure in the narrative is the old man whom the comrades meet on the road. He himself cannot die, but he knows where Death is to be found. Why do you think Chaucer brings him into the tale? What might he symbolize?

5. A good short story is a graphic narrative that achieves its effects through swiftness and compression. In what ways is "The Pardoner's Tale" like a good short story?

FOR COMPOSITION

Medieval writers recognized "The Pardoner's Tale" as an *exemplum*, a tale inserted into a sermon to illustrate a moral. In this case, the moral is, of course, "Greed is the root of all evil."

Write your own exemplum, a tale illustrating a common saying such as "A stitch in time saves nine," or "A fool and his money are soon parted." Remember while you are writing that much of the effectiveness of an exemplum depends on a good choice of details.

Joust Before the King (Arthur?) (illumination), Douce MS. 383.
The Bodleian Library

Sir Thomas Malory

?–1471

Thomas Malory wrote *Morte d'Arthur* ("Death of Arthur") in a prison cell. The charges against him ranged from extortion, robbery, and cattle rustling, to "waylaying the Duke of Buckingham." It is possible, however, that few of the crimes were real. He was, after all, a Lancastrian in a time of Yorkist ascendancy, and the law is ever a ready weapon to those in power. In fact, in 1468 when two general amnesties were declared by King Edward IV, Malory, unlike the other prisoners in jail at the time, was not set free. This may indicate that Malory had been singled out as a particular enemy by the Crown because of his opposing role in the Wars of the Roses.

Born around 1400, Malory left his family's seat in Warwickshire and entered upon a distinguished career. He fought in the Hundred Years' War and was elected to Parliament in 1445. It was during the days of civil disorder that preceded the Wars of the Roses that his fortune took a downward course from which it never recovered. Malory apparently tried to regain land that was rightfully his, and was arrested and indicted on a wide variety of offenses, which appear to have been committed during 1451 and 1452. Although he pleaded not guilty to all charges brought against him and his actual guilt is in doubt, Malory was far from a peaceful, law-abiding citizen and very much a part of the turbulent times in which he lived. He once engineered an escape from prison by swimming across a moat and, together with a band of followers, terrorized a nearby abbey for two days. It is thought that he was serving a twenty-year prison term when he wrote *Morte d'Arthur* and that he remained in jail until his death in 1471, one year after completing his great work. Malory's literary achievement was the compilation, arrangement, and rewriting from the original Latin, French, and English sources of the tales of King Arthur and the Knights of his Round Table. These he linked together under the title *Morte d'Arthur,* a work that stands as the last great collection of medieval romances.

Malory was fortunate to have been a contemporary of William Caxton, author, translator, editor, and the man who introduced printing into England. The debt of English literature to Caxton is immeasurable. Over a hundred books are known to have been printed and sometimes translated in his shop, among them *The Canterbury Tales* and *Morte d'Arthur.* Caxton first published the latter in 1485, adding a preface that provided historical background to the legend of King Arthur.

Morte d'Arthur, a faithful representation of chivalric ideas and medieval life and thought, has inspired later writers to treat the same theme. Malory's serious approach to the romantic world of gentle knights and fair ladies, however, stands in direct contrast to the lighter treatment of this theme in books such as *A Connecticut Yankee in King Arthur's Court* by Mark Twain, *Galahad* by John Erskine, and *The Once and Future King* by T. H. White.

from Morte d'Arthur

While there are no contemporary records to prove the truth of the Arthurian legends, the many ancient songs and stories celebrating the reign of Arthur suggest that such a man truly existed. However, although in his preface to *Morte d'Arthur,* William Caxton offered to skeptics what he considered proof of Arthur's existence, the real King Arthur remains shrouded in mystery, and it can be assumed only that he was a Celtic chieftain of the sixth century, known for his wisdom and courage.

Early sources indicate that King Arthur and his knights—Galahad, Gawain, and the others—were not originally the romantic figures that appear in Malory's story. These heroes came into Norman minstrelsy from twelfth-century poetic accounts. In these tales Arthur and his Celtic earls were rough heroes in the epic tradition of *Beowulf*. As time passed, however, an enormous body of chivalric romance grew up around them, and the rude Celtic heroes became marvelously refined. Every circumstance of their lives was embellished with ceremony. Arthur's exploits were enlarged, a round table was established for his counsel, and to his circle of knights a French knight was added, the renowned Launcelot.

Morte d'Arthur was written in a time of transition. The feudal order was dying. By the time Malory began writing his story, soldiers were fighting with gunpowder, a middle class of tradesmen was arising, and the practices of chivalry were being superseded by a new aristocratic code. Malory, in a desire to escape the disorder and uneasiness of his day, tried to recapture lost ideals of the romantic past as recounted in his tale of noble kings, adventurous knights, and damsels in distress.

Malory's tale begins with the mysterious birth of Arthur and ends with his equally mysterious death. The central concern is with the adventures of Arthur and his famous Knights of the Round Table—a group dedicated to the ideal of moral and spiritual perfection afforded by the union of the knightly code of courage and loyalty and the monastic code of chastity and purity. The knights fight many battles and win much glory, all of which is a credit to the name of King Arthur.

Near the end of the story, however, the tide of good fortune turns. Launcelot falls in love with Arthur's queen, Guinevere, and the lady returns his love. One by one the other knights become discontented, selfish, or disillusioned. Thus weakened, the kingdom is attacked by force under Sir Mordred, Arthur's treacherous nephew, and ultimately it goes down in defeat. Arthur is borne away on a barge by three mysterious ladies of Avalon.

In the following account young Arthur, guided by his faithful companion Merlin, the court magician, receives his sword Excalibur from the Lady of the Lake. Because the various legends of King Arthur arose at different points in time, it is not unusual to find many contradictory episodes in Malory's story. For example, elsewhere in *Morte d'Arthur* Arthur receives his sword as a boy when one day he pulls it from a block of stone, thus proving his right to rule England.

The following selection, told in Malory's simple and distinctive prose though modernized in spelling, relates an incident that occurred when Arthur was a young man and still in the initial stages of proving himself the epitome of the chivalric ideal. The aura of romance and mystery that is so characteristic of the medieval period is in full evidence here.

Sword of Henry, Prince of Wales.
The Wallace Collection

How Arthur Fought with King Pellinore and How Merlin Saved Arthur's Life, and Arthur by the Mean of Merlin Gat His Sword Excalibur.

Then on the day there came in the court a squire on horseback, leading a knight before him wounded to the death, and told him how there was a knight in the forest had reared up a pavilion[1] by a well and hath slain my master, a good knight, his name was Miles; wherefore I beseech you that my master may be buried, and that some knight may revenge my master's death. Then the noise was great of that knight's death in the court, and every man said his advice. Then came Griflet that was but a squire, and he was but young, of the age of the king Arthur, so he besought the king for all his service that he had done him to give the order of knighthood.

Thou art full young and tender of age, said Arthur, for to take so high an order on thee.

Sir, said Griflet, I beseech you to make me knight.

Sir, said Merlin, it were great pity to lose Griflet, for he will be a passing[2] good man when he is of age, abiding with you the term of his life. And if he adventure his body with yonder knight at the fountain, it is in great peril if ever he come again, for he[3] is one of the best knights of the world, and the strongest man of arms.

Well,[4] said Arthur.

So at the desire of Griflet, the king made him knight.

Now, said Arthur unto Sir Griflet, sith[5] I have made you knight thou might give me a gift.

What ye will, said Griflet.

Thou shalt promise me by the faith of thy body, when thou hast jousted with the knight at the fountain, whether it fall[6] ye be on foot or on horseback, that right so ye shall come again unto me without making any more debate.

I will promise you, said Griflet, as you desire. Then took Griflet his horse in great haste, and dressed his shield[7] and took a spear in his hand, and so he rode a great wallop till he came to the fountain, and thereby he saw a rich pavilion, and thereby under a cloth stood a fair horse well saddled and bridled, and on a tree a shield of divers colors and a great spear. Then Griflet smote on the shield with the butt of his spear, that the shield fell down to the ground.

With that the knight came out of the pavilion and said, Fair knight, why smote ye down my shield?

For[8] I will joust with you, said Griflet.

It is better ye do not, said the knight, for ye are but young, and late made knight, and your might is nothing to mine.

As for that, said Griflet, I will joust with you.

That is me loath, said the knight, but sith I must needs, I will dress me thereto.

Of whence be ye? said the knight.

Sir, I am of Arthur's court.

So the two knights ran together that Griflet's spear all to-shivered; and therewithal he smote Griflet through the shield and the left side and brake the spear, and the truncheon[9] stuck in his body, that horse and knight fell down.

When the knight saw him lie so on the ground, he alighted, and was passing heavy,[10] for he weened[11] he had slain him, and then he

---

1. **pavilion:** (pə-vĭl′yən): a tent.
2. **passing:** exceedingly.
3. **he:** the knight at the fountain.
4. **Well:** It is well, or so be it. Arthur is replying to Griflet's request, not to Merlin.
5. **sith:** since.

6. **fall:** happen.
7. **dressed his shield:** took up his shield in position for combat.
8. **For:** because.
9. **truncheon** (trŭn′chən): spear shaft.
10. **passing heavy:** exceedingly grieved; weighed down with sorrow.
11. **weened:** supposed.

unlaced his helm and gat him wind, and so with the truncheon he set him on his horse, and so betook him to God,[12] and said he had a mighty heart, and if he might live he would prove a passing good knight. And so Sir Griflet rode to the court, where great dole[13] was made for him. But through good leeches[14] he was healed and saved.

Then King Arthur was passingly wroth for the hurt of Sir Griflet. And so he commanded a privy man of his chamber that ere it be day his best horse and armor, with all that longeth[15] unto his person, be without the city or tomorrow day.[16] Right so on tomorrow day he met with his man and his horse, and so mounted up and dressed his shield and took his spear, and bade his chamberlain tarry there till he came again. And so Arthur rode a soft pace till it was day, and then was he ware of three churls[17] chasing Merlin, and would have slain him. Then the king rode unto them, and bade them: Flee, churls! Then were they afeard when they saw a knight, and fled. O Merlin, said Arthur, here hadst thou been slain for all thy crafts[18] had I not been.

Nay, said Merlin, not so, for I could save myself an[19] I would: and thou art more near thy death than I am, for thou goest to the deathward, an God be not thy friend.

So as they went thus talking they came to the fountain, and the rich pavilion there by it. Then King Arthur was ware where sat a knight armed in a chair.

Sir knight, said Arthur, for what cause abidest thou here, that there may be no knight ride this way but if he joust with thee? I rede thee leave[20] that custom, said Arthur.

This custom, said the knight, have I used and will use maugre[21] who saith nay, and who is grieved with my custom let him amend it that will.

I will amend it, said Arthur.

I shall defend[22] thee, said the knight. Anon[23] he took his horse and dressed his shield and took a spear, and they met so hard either in other's shields, that all to-shivered their spears. Therewith anon Arthur pulled out his sword.

Nay, not so, said the knight; it is fairer, said the knight, that we run more together with sharp spears.

I will well, said Arthur, an I had any more spears.

I have enow, said the knight; so there came a squire and brought two good spears, and Arthur chose one and he another; so they spurred their horses and came together with all their mights, that either brake their spears to their hands. Then Arthur set hand on his sword.

Nay, said the knight, ye shall do better; ye are a passing good jouster as ever I met withal, and for the love of the high order of knighthood let us joust once again.

I assent me, said Arthur.

Anon there were brought two great spears, and every knight gat a spear, and therewith they ran together that Arthur's spear all to-shivered. But the other knight hit him so hard in the midst of the shield that horse and man fell to the earth, and therewith Arthur was eager and pulled out his sword and said, I will assay[24] thee, sir knight, on foot, for I have lost the honor on horseback. Then the knight alighted and dressed his shield unto Arthur. And there began a strong battle with many

---

12. **betook him to God:** left him to the care of God.
13. **dole:** grieving.
14. **leeches:** doctors.
15. **longeth:** belongs.
16. **without . . . day:** outside the city before daylight tomorrow.
17. **churls:** peasants.
18. **crafts:** magic arts.
19. **an:** if.
20. **rede thee leave:** advise you to give up.

21. **maugre** (mô′gər): in spite of.
22. **defend:** prohibit, prevent.
23. **Anon:** at once.
24. **assay** (ă-sā′): test, try.

great strokes, and so hewed with their swords that the cantels[25] flew in the fields. So at the last they smote together that both their swords met even together. But the sword of the knight smote King Arthur's sword in two pieces, wherefore he was heavy.

Then said the knight unto Arthur, Thou art in danger whether me list to save thee or slay thee, and but thou yield thee as overcome and recreant,[26] thou shalt die.

As for death, said King Arthur, welcome be it when it cometh, but to yield me unto thee as recreant I had liefer die than to be so shamed. And therewithal the king leapt unto Pellinore,[27] and took him by the middle and threw him down, and raced off[28] his helm. When the knight felt that, he was adread, and anon he brought Arthur unto him, for he was a passing big man of might, and raced off his helm and would have smitten off his head.

Then came Merlin and said, Knight, hold thy hand, for an thou slay that knight thou puttest this realm in the greatest damage that ever was realm: for this knight is a man of more worship than thou wotest of.[29]

Why, who is he? said the knight.

It is King Arthur.

Then would he have slain him for dread of his wrath, and heaved up his sword, and therewith Merlin cast an enchantment to the knight, that he fell to the earth in a great sleep. Then Merlin took up King Arthur and rode forth on the knight's horse.

Alas! said Arthur, what hast thou done, Merlin? Hast thou slain this good knight by thy crafts? There liveth not so worshipful a knight as he was; I had liefer than the stint of my land a year that he were alive.[30]

Care ye not, said Merlin, for he is wholer than ye; for he is but asleep, and will awake within three hours. I told you, said Merlin, what a knight he was: here had ye been slain had I not been.

Right so the king and he departed, and went unto an hermit that was a good man and a great leech. So the hermit searched all his wounds and gave him good salves; so the king was there three days, and then were his wounds well amended that he might ride and go, and so departed. And as they rode, Arthur said, I have no sword.

No force,[31] said Merlin, hereby is a sword that shall be yours, an I may.

So they rode till they came to a lake, the which was a fair water and broad, and in the midst of the lake Arthur was ware of an armed cloth in white samite,[32] that held a fair sword in that hand.

Lo! said Merlin, yonder is that sword that I spake of. With that they saw a damsel going upon the lake.

What damsel is that? said Arthur.

That is the Lady of the Lake, said Merlin; and within that lake is a rock, and therein is as fair a place as any on earth, and richly beseen;[33] and this damsel will come to you anon, and then speak ye fair to her that she will give you that sword. Anon withal came the damsel unto Arthur, and saluted him, and he her again.

Damsel, said Arthur, what sword is that, that yonder the arm holdeth above the water? I would it were mine, for I have no sword.

Sir Arthur, king, said the damsel, that sword is mine, and if ye will give me a gift when I ask it you, ye shall have it.

---

25. **cantels** (kăn'təlz): pieces of fragments cut or sliced off, presumably from their shields.
26. **but . . . recreant** (rĕk'rē-ənt): unless you admit that you are defeated and a coward.
27. **Pellinore:** the knight of the fountain.
28. **raced off:** tore off.
29. **more . . . wotest of:** more importance than you know.
30. **liefer . . . alive:** I would rather have him alive than have a year's income from my land.

31. **No force:** no matter.
32. **samite** (să'mīt): heavy silk, interwoven with gold and silver.
33. **beseen:** decorated.

By my faith, said Arthur, I will give you what gift ye will ask.

Well! said the damsel, go ye into yonder barge, and row yourself to the sword, and take it and the scabbard with you, and I will ask my gift when I see my time. So Sir Arthur and Merlin alighted and tied their horses to two trees, and so they went into the ship, and when they came to the sword that the hand held, Sir Arthur took it up by the handles and took it with him, and the arm and the hand went under the water. And so they came unto the land and rode forth.

Then Sir Arthur looked on the sword and liked it passing well.

Whether[34] liketh you better, said Merlin, the sword or the scabbard?

Me liketh better the sword, said Arthur.

Ye are more unwise, said Merlin, for the scabbard is worth ten of the sword, for whiles ye have the scabbard upon you, ye shall never lose no blood, be ye never so sore wounded; therefore keep well the scabbard always with you. So they came unto Carlion,[35] whereof his knights were passing glad. And when they heard of his adventures, they marveled that he would jeopard[36] his person so, alone. But all men of worship said it was merry to be under such a chieftain that would put his person in adventure as other poor knights did.

---

34. **Whether:** which.
35. **Carlion:** Arthur's residence, which has been identified with the modern town of Caerleon in southwest England.
36. **jeopard** (jĕp'ərd): risk.

FOR STUDY AND DISCUSSION

1. Merlin describes Pellinore as one of the best knights in the world and the strongest, so it is not surprising that if anyone could defeat Arthur it would be he. What other evidence is there that Arthur's defeat at his hands does not diminish Arthur's own stature as hero and leader?
2. Chaucer describes the Knight in *The Canterbury Tales* as fearless in battle, but meek and courteous otherwise. How does Arthur measure up to this standard of chivalry?
3. Beowulf and Arthur represent ideals of heroism and leadership in their respective societies. What similarities and differences do you find in the two epic heroes?

LANGUAGE AND VOCABULARY

In *The Canterbury Tales* and *Morte d'Arthur* we have two vivid examples of the intermingling of Norman-French and Anglo-Saxon. In Chaucer we find graceful and courtly French terms such as *chivalrye, sovereyn,* and *gentil* set in direct contrast to more basic everyday words of the Anglo-Saxon language such as *coppe, eek, londes, ech,* and *yong.* In *Morte d'Arthur,* words such as *wroth, ween,* and *wotest* seem quite harsh beside French words such as *pavilion* and *chamberlain.*

Meanings, like customs, vary according to time, place, and situation. Today, changes in meaning take different forms. Words may become generalized and extended, or specialized and restricted. Thus, a mill today is no longer just a place to grind grain, but a place to make things by any process; corn no longer refers to all grains, and in the United States refers only to maize. Then too, words may take on positive or negative connotations and meanings so that *churl,* once defined as "peasant," now refers to a rude and surly person. The following list of words of French derivation is taken from the works of Chaucer and Malory. Using your dictionary for reference, explain the change in meaning that has taken place in each word since its original use in Old French. Which type of change does each represent?

adventure	charity	jeopardy
assay	company	recreant
bachelor	gentle	sanguine

from **Sir Gawain and the Green Knight**

Translated by Burton Raffel

This remarkable poem, which exists in only one manuscript (now in the British Museum), was written at the time of Chaucer but was lost and then rediscovered and published in 1839. We have no idea who the author was, but we know from the dialect he wrote in that he was not a Londoner. It is thought that he was a northerner. By general agreement, this poem is the best of all the English medieval romances, and it surpasses in greatness all other poetry of this period except that of Chaucer. Its writer was familiar with aristocratic life and was probably himself a gentleman attached to an aristocratic household. The poem continues the alliterative device of an earlier period. It is written in what the present translator calls *strophes* (rather than stanzas) of unequal length. Each strophe ends with a "bob and a wheel." A *bob* is a short line of one, two, or three syllables followed by a *wheel,* or four rhymed lines. Except for the bob and wheel, each line has four stressed syllables with a variable number of unstressed ones.

The story begins during a wonderful Christmas-season party at King Arthur's court in Camelot. The young king, always reluctant to eat before the day's adventure has appeared, is still standing by his place when in rides the gigantic Green Knight armed with only a huge ax. He offers to submit to a blow from the ax if he can return the blow a year and a day hence. Sir Gawain, the best of knights, accepts the challenge and chops off the head of the stranger, who thereupon coolly picks up his own head, mounts his horse, reaffirms the bargain, and rides away.

Camelot is a sober place the following November when Sir Gawain arms and prays and sets out on his perhaps fatal mission. After weeks of cold and lonely questing through the giant-haunted wilds of north Wales, he suddenly comes upon a splendid castle, where he is warmly received by the lord of the castle and his lady. When he is assured that the Green Knight and his chapel are nearby, Sir Gawain is glad to join the Christmas-season party which is in progress. For the next three mornings his host, the lord of the castle, goes hunting, and Sir Gawain is visited by the lord's beautiful young wife, who woos him with increasing ardor. It is agreed that in the evening Sir Gawain and his host will exchange the fruits of the day. Gawain keeps the pledge and exchanges one kiss for a deer, two kisses for a boar, and three kisses for a fox; but he does not reveal that the lady has also persuaded him to accept a love token, a magic green girdle that will protect the wearer from any harm. On the appointed day Sir Gawain sets out to keep his promise, with a servant of his host as guide. The guide urges him to give up his foolhardy mission and promises never to betray him, but Sir Gawain rejects the proposal, and rides on alone. He is ready to meet the fate that he accepted, for the honor of King Arthur and the Knights of the Round Table. But he does take the expediency of wearing his magic green girdle to protect himself from the murderous, seemingly invincible green monster that he must meet.

A Medieval feast, from *Très Riches Heures du Duc de Berry*, Chantilly Musée.
Giraudon

Then he spurred Gringolet° down the path,
Across a slope, beside a grove,
Riding a rough road to the valley
Below. Then he looked about. It seemed wild,
No sign of shelter anywhere, nothing   5
But steep hills on every side,
Gnarled crags with huge rocks,
Crags scratching at the sky! He stopped,
Pulled back on the reins, held Gringolet ready
While he stared this way and that, seeking   10
The chapel. He saw nothing—except
A queer kind of mound, in a glade
Close by, a rounded knoll near a stream,
Set right on the bank, beside the brook:
And that water bubbled as though it were boiling!   15
He sent Gringolet forward, stopped
Near the mound, dismounted and tied his horse
To a lime tree, looping the reins on a branch.
Then he walked closer, walked around
The knoll, trying to think what it was.   20
He saw holes at the end and the sides,
Saw patches of grass growing everywhere,
And only an old cave inside—
A hole—a crevice in a crag: he couldn't
              Tell.   25
    "My Lord, My Lord," said that courteous knight,
    "Can this be the chapel? At midnight,
    Here, the devils of hell
    Could pray their prayer quite well!

"By Jesus, it's lonely here: this chapel   30
Is ugly, gruesome, all overgrown.
But a good place for the green knight,
He could serve the devil properly here,
By Christ, it's Satan who struck me with this meeting,
I feel it! He's sent me here to destroy me.   35
What an evil church: may destruction end it!
The most cursèd chapel I've ever come to!"
His helmet on his head, spear in his hand,
He climbed across to its rough roof—
Then heard, from a high hill, on a boulder,   40
Beyond the brook, a violent noise—
What! It clattered on the cliff, as if
To split it, like a grindstone grinding a scythe.

---

1. **Gringolet:** Gawain's horse.

What! It whirred like water at a mill.
What! It rushed and it rang, and it sang   45
Miserably. "That's meant for me," said Gawain,
"A kind of greeting. By Christ, I'll greet him
                    Better.
        God's will be done—'Alas, alas!'—
        What good is wailing? It never   50
        Helps; I'll never gasp,
        Though my life will be severed."

Then he raised his voice, calling out loud:
"Who lives in this place? who's here as he promised
To be? Gawain is walking right   55
On your roof. If you want him, come to him quickly,
Now or never, let's have it done with."
"Just wait," said someone up over his head,
"What you're waiting to have, you'll have in a hurry."
But he stayed where he was, working that wheel   60
With a whirring roar. Then he stopped, and stepped
Down across a crag, came

Sir Gawain visited by the Lady of the Castle (English, c. 1400),
MS. Cotton Nero A.X., art 3, fol. 125r.
Courtesy, British Library

Through a hole, whirling a fierce weapon,
A long-bladed battle-ax, sharpened for the stroke,
Its massive blade bent to the shaft,   65
Filed like a knife, on a grindstone four feet
Wide; a leather strap hung at
Its length; and the green man looked as he'd looked
At the start, his skin and his beard and his face.
Except that he skipped like a dancer, setting   70
His ax handle on stones and leaping along.
At the brook, to keep dry, he leaned on the handle
And hopped across, and hurried to Gawain,
Grim on a broad battlefield covered
                                    With snow.   75
         And Gawain waited,
         Not bowing low;
         And the green man said: "You came:
         I can trust you now.

"Be careful, Gawain! You're welcome," the green man   80
Went on, "here in my home, you've made
A difficult journey, and you came on time,
You've kept your faith. Now keep the rest:
A year ago I gave you your chance;
Today the turn is mine. We're completely   85
Alone, in this valley; no one can come
Between us, however fiercely we fight.
Take off your helmet, and take my ax stroke.
Hold yourself still, as I did when you slashed
My head from my shoulders with a single blow."   90
"By God," said Gawain, "may the Holy Ghost
Grant me the power to begrudge you nothing.
Keep to the bargain, swing just once,
And I'll stand still, and you'll do exactly
                                    As you please."   95
         And he bent his neck, leaned
         Forward; the white flesh gleamed.
         He tried to seem
         Fearless, but his knees

Were weak. And the green man got ready, lifted   100
That huge ax in both his hands,
Swung it up with all his strength,
And pretended to swing straight at his neck.
If he'd hurled it down as he swung it high
Gawain would have been dead forever.   105
But the knight looked to the side, and saw it
Coming, glittering as it fell to his throat,

And he pulled his shoulders back, just a bit,
And the green man jerked the blade away,
And poured a host of proud words on that prince: 110
"Gawain? You can't be Gawain, his name
Is too noble, he's never afraid, nowhere
On earth—and you, you flinch in advance!
I've heard nothing about Gawain the coward.
And I, did I flinch, fellow, when you swung   115
At my neck? I never spoke a word.
My head fell, and I never flinched.
And you, before it can happen your heart
Is quaking. Who doubts that I'm the better
                  Man?"   120
    "I flinched," said Gawain,
    "I won't again.
    And this much is plain:
    My head, if it falls, won't talk in my hands.

"But get it done, let it be over.   125
Bring me my fate, and bring it quickly.
I'll stand like a stone: on my word of honor
My neck will be still till your stroke comes to it."
"Have at you, then!" he cried, and heaved it
Up, and glared as fierce as a madman.   130
He swung it sharply, but not at his neck,
Held it back, before it could hurt him.
And Gawain waited, stood like a stone,
Or the stump of a tree tied to the ground
By a hundred tangled roots. And the green man   135
Laughed and told him, gaily: "I take it
You're ready, now, and it's time to strike.
Let Arthur's knighthood save your neck,
That noble rank protect you, if it can."
And Gawain replied, angry and ashamed: 140
"May the better man strike. You talk too long:
Perhaps you've frightened yourself with these threats?"
"Ah well," said the green man, "you've turned so brave
That I need to delay no longer. Your time
                  Is now."   145
    He took up a stance,
    And his face scowled,
    And to Gawain his chances
    Of living seemed scant.

He swung his weapon swiftly up,   150
And down, the blade toward the bare flesh;
And he struck hard, but hurt him only

With a nick, that snipped the skin. The edge
Grazed Gawain's white neck, and bright
Blood shot from his shoulder to the ground,   155
And as soon as he saw that gleam on the snow
He leaped forward a spear-length or more,
Throwing his helmet furiously into place,
Jerking his shield around in front of him,
Drawing his sword, and speaking fiercely—   160
Never since his mother bore him had he known
Half the happiness he suddenly felt:
"Stop, green man! Don't swing again!
I've taken a single stroke, and stood still for it:
No more, or else I'll repay you in kind   165
—Believe me, fellow, I'll pay you fully
                          And well.
            You've had your stroke,
            And one was all
            We agreed to, in Arthur's hall.   170
            And so, sir, stop, halt!"

The green man stood listening, leaning on his ax
(It was upside down, he rested on the blade),
And watching the knight, how bravely he waited,
How unafraid, armed and ready,   175
Standing alert. And he liked what he saw.
And then he spoke, with a cheerful, booming
Voice, addressing Gawain: "Warrior,
Soldier, no need to be fierce, now.
No one's used you badly, shown you   180
Discourtesy; what was done was what we agreed:
I owed you a stroke, I've paid you a stroke:
I release you from any and all obligations.
Perhaps, if my hands were quicker, I could have
Dealt you a better blow, and done harm.   185
I pretended one stroke, a threat, a joke,
But left you whole; I had the right,
Because of our other agreement, in my castle;
You kept it faithfully, performed like an honest
Man, gave me everything you got.   190
Except that you kissed my wife: I swung
For that reason—but you gave me back her kisses.
So all you got, for that, was a puff
                    Of air:
            An honest man   195
            Need never fear.
            But still, the third day, there
            In my castle, you failed—and you felt that, here.

"That belt you're wearing: it's mine, my wife
Gave it to you—I know it all, knight,   200
The kisses you took, and gave, and all
You did, and how she tempted you: everything.
For I planned it all, to test you—and truly,
Not many better men have walked
This earth, been worth as much—like a pearl   205
To a pea, compared to other knights.
But you failed a little, lost good faith
—Not a beautiful belt, or in lust,
But for love of your life. I can hardly blame you."
And Gawain stood silent, stood a long time,   210
So burdened with grief that his heart shuddered:
His blood ran like fire in his face,
He winced for shame at the green man's words.
And finally he found words of his own:
"A curse on cowardice and a curse on greed!   215
They shatter chivalry, their vice destroys
Virtue." Then he loosened the belt, unfastened it,
And grimly threw it to the green man. "There!
Take the faithless thing, may it rot!
Fear of your blow taught me cowardice,   220
Brought me to greed, took me from myself
And the goodness, the faith, that belong to knighthood.
I'm false, now, forever afraid
Of bad faith and treachery: may trouble, may sorrow
       Come to them!   225
   Oh knight: I humbly confess
   My faults: bless me
   With the chance to atone.
   "I'll try to sin less."

Then the green man laughed, and courteously explained: 230
"The damage you did me is cured, it's gone.
You stand confessed so clean, you took
Such plain penance at the point of my ax,
That I hold you cleansed, as pure in heart
As if from your birth to this day you'd never   235
Sinned! And Gawain, I give you this belt,
As green as my gown. Remember your challenge,
Here, as you walk your way among knights
And princes, keep this token for chivalrous
Men to know your adventure at the green   240
Chapel. And now, in this New Year, come
To my castle again, and we'll finish this festival
       With good cheer."

FOR STUDY AND DISCUSSION

1. Along with the threat of the ax, Gawain has to withstand the taunts of the Green Knight. What taunts does Gawain use in return? Describe Gawain's probable feelings at this point in the story.
2. What is Gawain's immediate reaction after his neck has been nicked? What evidence can you find that Gawain is really brave?
3. What is the Green Knight's attitude toward knighthood and the chivalric code? How does this attitude enter into the tone of the conclusion?

FOR COMPOSITION

In a brief composition, tell what you learned from the selections in this unit about the literature, the customs and society, and the ideals and beliefs of the Middle Ages.

Head of King Arthur (detail),
from Nicholas Bataille, *The Nine Heroes Tapestries*
The Metropolitan Museum of Art, Cloisters Collection

Sir Gawain and the Green Knight 95

The Middle English Period

A great deal happened to our language between the time of *Beowulf* and the time of *The Canterbury Tales*. If you compare the lines in Old English that are printed on page 29 with the selection in Chaucer's Middle English on page 52, you will see that Chaucer's language is on the whole understandable to a modern reader—whereas the Old English lines are incomprehensible, except for a few scattered words.

The differences between Old English and the English of Chaucer's time were a result of changes in both the grammatical system and the vocabulary of the language. The most noticeable change in the grammatical system was the disappearance of most grammatical endings on words. As an example, look at the various forms of the expression "the day" in Old English and in Chaucer's English.

Old English

	Singular		*Plural*	
Nominative	se	dæg	tha	dagas
Accusative	thone	dæg	tha	dagas
Genitive	thæs	dæges	thara	daga
Dative	thæm	dæge	thæm	dagum
Instrumental	thy	dæge	thæm	dagum

Middle English

	Singular	*Plural*
Nominative, Accusative	the day	the dayes
Genitive	the dayes	

A glance at the listing above shows that in Middle English the system of grammatical endings became greatly simplified. We do not know exactly why the Old English grammatical endings changed or disappeared. One reason, however, was probably the tendency in spoken English to hurry over unaccented syllables, leaving out unimportant sounds.

From the point of view of language historians, it is these grammatical changes that mark the division between Old English and Middle English. The Norman Conquest did not have a direct influence on these changes: they had begun to take place about a century before the Conquest, and they were essentially complete within about a century after it.

The Conquest did, however, have a great influence on the changes in vocabulary that took place during the Middle English period. The Normans brought the French language into England; and, by the close of the Middle English period, more than ten thousand French words had been assimilated into English.

The rate of borrowing was slow at first. During the first two centuries following the Conquest, French remained the language of the Norman rulers and English the language of the common people. The two groups did not intermingle to any great extent. Only about nine hundred French words are known to have made their way into English during this time, and many of those words were of the kind that people of the humbler classes would be likely to learn from their masters—words like *dame, sir, noble,* and *servant.*

The overwhelming flow of French words into English began about the middle of the thirteenth century. Political ties between England and Normandy were cut at this time, and the Normans who stayed in England began to consider themselves English. Most of them learned English and began using it in their daily affairs. Landowners, government officials, judges, and lawyers gradually began to conduct their transactions in English instead of French. In changing to English from French, however, they continued to employ a great many French terms.

Some of these were terms for which there were no exact equivalents in English—for instance, governmental terms such as *parliament, council,* and *mayor.* But many of the other terms introduced from French at this time were commonplace words like *people, city, village, air, river, carry, join, move,* and *push.* Of course, there were already words in English to express these ideas. What happened to the native vocabulary when this flood of French words poured into the language? Sometimes a French word completely replaced the English word. French *people,* for instance, soon replaced English *leod.* Very often, however, the words from both languages continued in use. We thus have French *city* along with the native English *borough,* French *village* along with the native English *town,* and so forth.

Although French was the chief language from which Middle English derived new words, it was not the only one. Churchmen and scholars of the period continued to borrow words from Latin, just as their Anglo-Saxon predecessors had done. Another source of new words was opened when trade sprang up between England and the Low Countries during the late Middle Ages. A number of our commercial terms—for instance, *freight* and *mart*—were borrowed from Dutch or Flemish at this time.

One extremely significant development that took place in Middle English was the gradual adoption of a standard written language. During the early part of the period, there was no such thing as "standard English": people wrote in their own local dialects and spelled according to their own pronunciations. From about 1400 on, however, people in all parts of England tended to make their written English conform to the usage of the London dialect. Local differences continued to exist in the spoken language, but they practically disappeared from written English.

The passages by Chaucer (page 52) and Malory (pages 83–86) represent the London dialect of Middle English at somewhat different historical stages. The ballads on pages 44–47 are not in Middle English (Middle English versions no longer exist), but in a dialect directly descended from the Middle English dialect of northern England and southern Scotland. Although this dialect is still spoken in parts of Scotland, it is rarely used today as a written language. English-speaking people the world over now write the standard language that developed from the London dialect of Chaucer's day.

If a group of Americans were transported to the London of Chaucer's day, they would find it impossible either to make themselves understood or to understand what was said to them. The reason for this is that English pronunciation changed greatly between Chaucer's time and Shakespeare's. The changes were so extensive that Middle English and Modern English sound like two different languages. The changes were the result of what is called the Great Vowel Shift.

The most important changes involved the pronunciation of vowel sounds. In Middle English—as in Latin and in most modern foreign languages that are written in the Latin alphabet—the letter *a* represented the sound *ah,* while a long *e* sounded like our long *a,* and long *i* and *y* like our long *e.* A long *o* was always pronounced *oh,* and a long *u* (often spelled *ou*) was *oo.* Thus the Middle English pronunciation of *care* might sound to us like *car; sheep* would sound to us like *shape; my* would sound like *me; to* would sound like *toe;* and *south* would sound like *sooth.* During the fifteenth and sixteenth centuries, however, the pronunciation of all the long vowel sounds gradually shifted. By Shakespeare's time most of the long vowels had acquired the values that they still have today.

FOR STUDY AND DISCUSSION

1. As we have seen, Middle English often borrowed a French word for which there was already a corresponding word in English. In such cases, it frequently happened that one of the two words continued to be used in a general sense while the other developed a more limited or specialized meaning. Look up the following pairs of words in an unabridged dictionary or a college dictionary. Which word in each pair came from French, and which from Old English? Which is the more general word in each pair, and which is more limited?

anoint	deem	house
smear	judge	mansion

2. Because of the tendency of learned men to borrow words from Latin, Middle English sometimes acquired not only a French equivalent but also a Latin equivalent for a native English term. In cases where all three words have remained in use, sometimes the Latin word has continued to sound a little more bookish or high-flown than the other two. In the following sets of synonyms, one word in each set entered Middle English from Old English, one entered from French, and one entered directly from Latin. Using a dictionary, find out the language from which each word came into Middle English. For these sets, do you think it is true that the Latin word seems more high-flown than the other two? Explain.

belief, credo, faith   royal, kingly, regal

Queen Elizabeth I,
The Ditchley Portrait, by
Marcus Gheeraerts, the Younger
(c. 1592).
National Portrait Gallery, London

The Renaissance
1485–1660

THE RENAISSANCE IN EUROPE

The period of European history and culture traditionally known as the Renaissance began in Italy during the fourteenth century and extended, in England at least, past the middle of the seventeenth century. Renaissance means "rebirth" — the "rebirth" of those intellectual and artistic energies that characterized ancient Greek and Roman civilization, and with this the awakening of a whole range of new interests in human beings and the world they lived in. Of course Renaissance, like other very broad historical terms, must not be understood too literally. People in the Middle Ages were not entirely ignorant of those aspects of Greek and Roman culture supposedly "reborn" during the Renaissance. Historians have taught us not to think of the Middle Ages as the "Dark Ages" anymore. But it is true that in the Renaissance people came to take a revitalized interest in Greek and Roman civilization and often thought of their own times as a return to the glorious achievements of classical antiquity. "I anticipate the approach of a golden age," wrote Erasmus of Rotterdam, the great Dutch thinker who exerted a strong influence in England at the beginning of the sixteenth century: "I am led to a confident hope that not only morality and Christian piety, but also a genuine and purer literature, may come to renewed life or greater splendor." It is this spirit of excited and hopeful renewal that, more than anything else, justifies our calling this period the Renaissance.

The Renaissance had its origins in Italy, in the writing of Petrarch (1304–1374) and Boccaccio (1313–1375), in the painting of Giotto (1266?–1337?), in the architecture of Brunelleschi (1377?–1446), and in the sculpture of Donatello (1386?–1466). The fifteenth century saw the culmination of the Renaissance in Italy. The city of Florence, in particular, established itself at this time as a focal point of intellectual trends and artistic accomplishments that we think of as essentially Renaissance. Scholars and educators who called themselves Humanists began to emphasize the capacities of the human mind and the achievements of human culture, in contrast to the medieval emphasis on God and contempt for the things of this world. Under the encouragement of its most famous ruler, Lorenzo de' Medici (1449–1492), himself a student of classical antiquity and a very fine poet, the goals of Renaissance Humanism were pursued with unrivaled intensity. The visual arts flourished as never before: both Leonardo da Vinci (1452–1519) and Michelangelo (1475–1564) began their careers in the Florence of Lorenzo the Magnificent, as he was called. Gradually this fervor of intellectual and artistic excitement spread northward to other European countries — to France, to Germany, to the Low Countries, and lastly to England. All these countries had their own native literary and artistic traditions, and it would be wrong to see the progress of the Renaissance in northern

Europe as a matter of totally Italian influence. But Italy was the origin, and it was mainly to Italy that later Renaissance writers and artists looked for inspiration.

The Renaissance was not only a period of new artistic and intellectual enterprise but also a time of territorial exploration and discovery. Lorenzo de' Medici died in 1492 – but most of us are more familiar with 1492 as the year in which Christopher Columbus reached the New World. Columbus was but one of many adventurous seamen whose voyages of discovery dramatically expanded the world that Europeans had previously known. The expansion was not merely geographical. These voyages marked the first stages of national colonizing and commercial ventures that would eventually establish complex economic and political links between Europe and both Asia and the Americas. It is perhaps in this respect, more than in any other, that the Renaissance was the beginning of the modern world.

THE RENAISSANCE IN ENGLAND: HENRY VIII AND ELIZABETH I

There is considerable truth in the observation that England was slow to participate in the European Renaissance. The reasons for this are largely political. During the fifteenth century, the great period of the Renaissance in Italy, England experienced terrible internal turmoil and instability. With the two dominant aristocratic houses, the Yorks and the Lancasters, battling each other for the throne in the Wars of the Roses (1455–1485), the country was hardly in a condition to respond to the new artistic and intellectual currents. The printing of books from movable type, one of the most significant and far-reaching of all Renaissance inventions, had only just been introduced into England when Henry Tudor, Earl of Richmond, defeated the Yorkist King Richard III at Bosworth Field in 1485 and was crowned King Henry VII (1485–1509). With the establishment of the Tudor dynasty, which was to rule the country for more than a century, England began to move toward the stability and confidence necessary for sustained artistic achievement.

But the progress of the Renaissance in England was to be slow and fitful. Henry VIII came to the throne when his father died in 1509. A willful and audacious man, Henry VIII (1509–1547) saw himself mainly as a powerful political leader. But he was aware of what the Renaissance had achieved in Europe, and he wanted also to be thought of as an enlightened Renaissance prince. Erasmus spoke of Henry VIII in just this way, and indeed under Henry's rule Erasmus'

Sir Thomas Wyatt (detail), Holbein

Henry VIII (detail), Holbein

Sir Thomas More (detail), Holbein

1485   **Henry VII 1485–1509**   **1500**   **Henry VIII 1509–1547**

Columbus reaches America 1492   Cabot's exploration 1497   Sir Thomas Wyatt 1503–1542   More's *Utopia* 1516

Macbeth 1606   England and Scotland under one king 1603   *Romeo and Juliet* composed 1594

James I 1603–1625   **1600**

Founding of Jamestown 1607   Globe Theater 1599   Spanish Armada 1588

John Milton 1608–1674   Shakespeare's *Sonnets* 1609   King James Bible 1611   *Collected Works of Ben Jonson* 1616

John Donne (detail)

Defeat of the Spanish Armada

Globe Theater from Hollar's View of London

Edmund Spenser (detail)

Elizabeth I (detail), Marcus Gheeraerts, the Younger

Ben Jonson

1520

Edward VI 1547–1553

Mary I 1553–1558

Luther and Reformation 1517
Earl of Surrey 1517?–1547

Sonnet form introduced
1527

Church of England
1534

Edmund Spenser
1552–1599

Marlowe's *Doctor Faustus*
1587

John Donne
1572–1631

William Shakespeare
1564–1616

Elizabeth I 1558–1603

Voyage of Francis Drake
1577–1580

Ben Jonson
1572–1637

Francis Bacon
1561–1626

First Folio of Shakespeare's
Plays 1623

Donne's *Songs and Sonnets*
1633

Milton's *Poems*
1645

Charles I 1625–1649

Puritan Commonwealth 1649–1660

1660

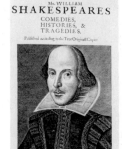

Frontispiece (detail)

First Folio, 1623

Charles I (detail), A. Van Dyke

Milton as a young man (detail)

Henry VIII by Hans Holbein.
Stichting Collectie Thyssen-Bornemisza, Lugano

friend, Sir Thomas More (1478–1535), became the center of an active and brilliant circle of English Humanists. More's *Utopia* (1516) may be thought of as the first literary masterpiece of the English Renaissance. At Henry VIII's court two gifted poets, Sir Thomas Wyatt (1503–1542) and Henry Howard, Earl of Surrey (1517?–1547), were writing poems based on their exploration of Italian models. These beginnings of an English literary Renaissance coincided, however, with the emergence of religious and historical forces that would once again disrupt literary and artistic progress.

By the beginning of the sixteenth century, the movement of religious protest against the authority and corruption of the Roman Catholic Church had been simmering for several years. This movement, known as the Protestant Reformation, was fiercely accelerated in 1517 when Martin Luther nailed to the door of a church in Wittenberg, Germany, his famous Ninety-five Theses, declaring his objections to certain long-standing abuses in the Church. The Protestant Reformation deeply altered the course of the Renaissance in England. Henry VIII had always presented himself as a loyal champion of the Roman Catholic Church, and there was no religious motive for England to align itself with the Protestant revolt against the Pope and Rome. There were, however, political and personal motives. Henry VIII's first wife, Catherine of Aragon, had not produced a male heir to the throne. When Henry asked for a divorce, the Pope refused. Henry not only defied the Pope and remarried — he also declared himself Supreme Head of the Church in England (also known as the Anglican Church).

The long-range consequences of England's break with Rome and Catholicism were profound. England came to have a new and more independent national identity. But there were more immediate consequences of Henry VIII's decision. When Sir Thomas More opposed Henry's divorce and refused to swear oaths of allegiance to him as Supreme Head of the English church, he was imprisoned and executed: the leading figure of the early Renaissance in England was sacrificed to what the king saw as political necessity. More's death remains a haunting reminder of the way in which the cultural and artistic spirit of the Renaissance was savagely subordinated to the drive for dynastic power and authority.

On the death of Henry VIII in 1547, the cause of the Reformation in England was advanced under the rule of his nine-year-old son, Edward VI, who was guided in all governmental affairs by a council of senior officials. But when the boy king died prematurely in 1553, the crown fell to his older sister Mary (1553–1558), the offspring of Henry VIII's marriage to Catherine of Aragon. Mary was half Spanish and a devout Catholic. She became the wife of Philip II of Spain and instituted a reign of terror against English Protestants in an attempt to return England to Catholic authority. The reign of "Bloody Mary" posed a double threat to England's developing national identity because Spain, the country of her mother and her husband, had emerged as the dominant and most imperialistic power in sixteenth-century Europe. But Mary died after only five years on the throne, and her half-sister Elizabeth, Henry VIII's daughter by his second wife, Anne Boleyn, became queen. Elizabeth I (1558–1603), only twenty-five when she came to the throne, was to lead her country forward again in the direction of the strong national unity and triumphant cultural achievement begun, however imperfectly, by her father.

Elizabeth had a sharp intellect and an excellent Renaissance education. Her tutor, Roger Ascham (1515–1568), became a leading figure in the second generation of English Humanists. An accomplished

Elizabeth I
by Nicholas Hilliard.
Walker Art Gallery,
Liverpool

linguist and poet herself, Elizabeth was ideally equipped to encourage those literary and artistic developments that would finally allow the Renaissance in England to grow and flourish. Fortunately, she was also an extremely clever diplomat and a shrewd, at times even ruthless, politician. England was still beset by internal tension between Protestants and Catholics, and by the external threat of Spanish imperialism. Elizabeth promoted peace and prosperity by steering a moderate religious course between Protestant extremism and capitulation to Catholicism, and by directing the country's precarious financial affairs with realistic ingenuity. In foreign affairs she became the wonder of her age. England had not been a leader in exploring the New World, but by the second half of the sixteenth century, daring English seamen, most notably Sir Francis Drake

(1540?–1596), had begun to prey upon Spanish ships returning with wealth from America and Asia. Though ostensibly privateering ventures outside the Queen's control, these raids on Spanish shipping brought much-needed funds into Elizabeth's treasury. (Drake was knighted in 1580 for returning from the Pacific with a million pounds in booty.) The raids were in fact an unacknowledged war against Spain, England's major foreign enemy. Only Elizabeth's skillful diplomacy prevented open and potentially disastrous war from breaking out. She played France off against Spain; she used her unmarried status as a way of securing the support of countries that saw either greater power or greater vulnerability for themselves in the prospect of the English Queen's marrying a foreign nobleman.

Spanish frustration could not be contained indefinitely, however, and in 1588 the Spanish Armada, the strongest naval force of the age, sailed against England. But the smaller and more maneuverable English ships sent the Armada back in ignoble defeat, aided by a timely storm that helped scatter and destroy the Spanish fleet. The storm was afterward interpreted as an act of divine intervention on England's behalf. The victory over the Armada marked the culmination of Elizabeth's authority in a country that had become, in less than a century, one of the most powerful in the world.

The Spanish Armada, Anon.
The Bettmann Archive

ELIZABETHAN LITERARY ACHIEVEMENT

As Elizabeth led England through difficult times toward increasing national confidence, her court in London became the center of an exuberant literary culture that was "Renaissance" in the fullest sense of that term. Many individuals of talent came to the court either to contribute what they could to the government, to distinguish themselves artistically, or both. In the late 1570's two writers of real genius, Sir Philip Sidney (1554–1586) and Edmund Spenser (1552–1599), emerged to bring the promising developments of sixteenth-century English poetry to triumphant fruition. Sidney and Spenser were close friends, and in their literary discussions they talked about how to reform English poetry to make it the equal of that produced in Italy and France. Sidney was for his contemporaries a living embodiment of the ideal Renaissance gentleman, notable as much for his political ideas, his military prowess, and his personal charm as he was for his literary ability. Like most Elizabethan aristocrats, Sidney wrote for a private circle of friends. Very little of his work was published until after his tragically early death in 1586. Spenser, on the other hand, saw himself as a professional man of letters, a scholar-poet who would seek to rival in English the greatest works of his classical, medieval, and Renaissance predecessors. Spenser's masterpiece, a vast yet only partly completed allegorical epic called *The Faerie Queene* (1590, 1596), is dedicated to Queen Elizabeth. This work both celebrates and assesses the values and achievements of her reign.

The greatest and most distinctive achievement of Elizabethan literature is the drama. In contrast to the poetry we have just been surveying, Elizabethan drama had its origins as much in native folk culture and popular entertainment as in the sophisticated, aristocratic world of literary circles and the court. There was a strong tradition of popular religious drama in medieval England: mystery and miracle plays, and later, morality plays. By the end of the fifteenth century, plays with nonreligious plots and characters also began to appear, although most of these interludes, as they were called, were written for private performances at aristocratic banquets and other festive occasions. Toward the middle of the sixteenth century, writers educated at the universities of Oxford and Cambridge began to produce plays influenced by their study of classical dramatic theory and practice. But the best of these plays still contained elements of the native dramatic tradition—scenes of broad provincial comedy, for example. We may say, then, that the glorious dramatic work of later Elizabethan drama, of William Shakespeare (1564–1616) and his contemporaries, grew from a fusion of native English and classical traditions. This fusion is deeply characteristic of the Elizabethan Renaissance as a whole.

The triumph of Elizabethan drama is to a large degree the triumph of dramatically spoken English—of the English language in its capacity to create a full and immediate sense of a fictional or theatrical situation. From the beginning of the century, English writers had displayed a special flare for using language dramatically. The best poems of Wyatt, like the best poems of Sidney and John Donne (1572–1631), are dramatic to a degree that distinguishes them from Italian or French Renaissance poetry. Acknowledging the central importance of dramatic language in the English literary Renaissance as a whole helps us comprehend the remarkable achievement of Elizabethan drama.

The plays of Shakespeare and his contemporaries are perfect vehicles for realizing the richness and flexibility of the English language at a crucial stage in its development. They are so in part because of the particular requirements of the Elizabethan theater. By modern standards Elizabethan stagecraft—sets, costumes, atmospheric effects (sound and lighting)—was rudimentary and sketchy: the world of the play had to be created in the minds of the audience through the spoken word. When Shakespeare opens *Henry V* by asking the audience to "Piece out our imperfections with your thoughts," to "Think when we talk of horses that you see them/Printing their proud hoofs i' the receiving earth," he is calling attention directly to something that Elizabethan playgoers were indirectly asked to do all the time. Elizabethan audiences had to use their imaginations with characters as well: all women's parts were played by boys. Fortunately, the Elizabethan theater seems to have been blessed with remarkable actors capable of projecting the magnificent verse of Shakespeare or Christopher Marlowe (1564–1593) or Ben Jonson (1572–1637) with convincing subtlety and with astonishing speed. Many long Elizabethan plays normally cut for modern production were presented in their entirety without straining the audience's involvement. The "stars" of the Elizabethan stage, men like Edward Alleyn and Richard Burbage, were incomparable speakers of dramatic verse. Shakespeare himself was an actor as well as a playwright (he took the part of the ghost in *Hamlet*), a fact we should remember in responding to his astonishing ability to engage our minds and emotions by commanding the full resources of the English language.

The first public theater in London was erected in Shoreditch, an area just outside the city limits, in 1576. Others, including the Globe, the home theater of Shakespeare's company, were soon built in Southwark across the river Thames. To think of Elizabethan audiences crowding into these theaters for afternoon performances of Shakespeare and Marlowe is to think of the loud, dirty, bustling, endlessly

Costume design for
a court masque by
Inigo Jones.
The Mansell Collection

energetic city of London itself. London had grown enormously since Chaucer's time, when it had a population of around 50,000. By 1563, five years into Elizabeth's reign, it had doubled in size; in 1605, two years after her death, it had a population of 224, 275. All sorts of people contributed to this rapid growth: there was a growing middle class of merchants and shopkeepers, adding to and thriving on a fiercely expanding economy; there were sea captains and sailors of every nationality; there were skilled artisans and apprentices, still organized in many cases into the sixteenth-century descendants of their medieval guilds; and there were the boisterous commonfolk, scratching out an existence one way or another in this teeming city. Indications are that all these classes made up the theater audiences. Members of the nobility might be given a special seat right on stage; witty, sophisticated young law students from the Inns of Court might be among those who would have bought a seat under the roofs in the gallery; a motley collection of less well-off or less particular playgoers would fill the "pit" to eat, drink, hiss, catcall, and applaud the great lines in their own way. It is easy to see why one of the first steps taken by the government when the plague struck London in 1593–1594 was to close the public theaters. Of course, they were soon opened again by popular demand.

London in 1616 (detail, engraving) by John Vischer.
Courtesy, The British Museum

ELIZABETHAN TASTE AND ATTITUDES

Elizabethan attitudes toward literature and art, and toward life in general, were a peculiar combination of old and new, of attachments to the medieval past and anticipations of a more modern outlook. It is helpful to know something about these attitudes in order to adjust our own responses to writings that are, after all, products of English culture four hundred years ago. The most striking feature of Elizabethan artistic taste is a delight in elaborate pattern and complicated ornament and artifice. For us the word *artificial* carries a negative meaning. It designates those aspects of human conduct or of our material surroundings that are unreal or insincere, and we oppose it to the positive word *natural*. But for the Elizabethans, *artificial* is a word of praise, a positive extension of the word *art* itself. It designates that which is made by human skill and ingenuity, that which adds to and improves upon the order found in the natural world. Elizabethan love of the artificial, the patterned, and the ornamental appears in every aspect of life: in the fantastically decorated gowns we see in the portraits of Queen Elizabeth; in the intricate designs of Elizabethan buildings and gardens; in musical forms such as the madrigal, where as many as twelve different vocal parts or lines may be combined to form a bewildering texture; in poetic forms like the sonnet or the sestina, with their complicated rhyming and rhetorical patterns. In literature this delight in the "artificial" was both abstract and functional. It was abstract in that Elizabethans enjoyed following verbal patterns with their eyes and their ears much as we might enjoy a design woven in cloth or a repeated tune or rhythmic beat in a piece of music. It was functional in that to the Elizabethan mind, verbal patterning and arrangement were essential means of expressing the true order of the mental and material universe.

To appreciate this last point, we need to know something about what has been aptly called the Elizabethan World Picture. Elizabethans saw the world as a vast, unified, hierarchical order, or "Great Chain of Being," created by God. Every existing being or thing was ranked within a category in the chain. The categories were ranked by the attributes of their members, from the lowest group—all matter and no spirit—to the highest group—all spirit and no matter. Thus, inanimate things were at the bottom of the chain. Above were the plant and animal kingdoms. Human beings, akin to animals biologically but possessing souls and free will, were at the midpoint of the chain. Humans could choose to become either "a little lower than the angels" (the next group up the ladder) or depraved (animallike). As each group had its place in the chain, so each member had its place within the group. The lion was considered the highest ranking member of the animal kingdom, the oyster the lowest. Metals ranged from gold down to lead, and the plant kingdom was headed by the rose. This perfect order allowed for the doctrine of correspondences: each member of a group corresponded to same-ranking members of other groups. Thus gold, the most valuable of minerals, could be equated with the oak (greatest of trees) or with the sun (first among stars). The lion (head of the animals) could represent a king or queen (head of a nation), and a rose could represent God. Because any one of these could evoke one or all of the others, Elizabethan writers had at hand a wealth of symbolic relationships, references, and allusions. This view of a coherent, harmonious universe had held sway since the Middle Ages, and during the next century it would undergo substantial questioning and alteration. Some late Elizabethan writers were already beginning to suggest that there were aspects of experience that could not be accounted for adequately in terms of the old "World Picture." But most Elizabethans accepted it, if not naively and literally, at least as a system that provided a language—a repository of images, metaphors, analogies—for communicating life's infinite, and usually meaningful, variety.

THE JACOBEAN ERA (1603–1625) TRANSITION TO A NEW AND TUMULTUOUS CENTURY

On the surface the final years of Queen Elizabeth's reign were a time of confidence and security. After the victory over the Armada, something like a public cult had developed around the personage of the Virgin Queen, or Gloriana, as the poets often called her. When Spenser addressed her at the beginning of his *Faerie Queene* as "Goddess heavenly bright,/Mirror of grace and Majesty divine,/Great Lady of the greatest Isle," he was expressing an ideal most of his countrymen held to the end of Elizabeth's life. True, there was a certain unreality in praising the chaste beauty of an unmarried woman in her sixties. True, too, was the unsettling fact that Elizabeth had faced a serious rebellion led by the Earl of Essex in the final years of the century. She also had to contend with a House of Commons increasingly reluctant to provide sufficient tax revenues for the running of government. But Elizabeth maintained control through all of this. With her death in 1603, the Tudor dynasty came to an end. She was succeeded by her cousin, James Stuart, already King of Scotland and the son of Elizabeth's former archenemy, Mary, Queen of Scots. James I ruled his kingdom of Scotland together with that of England until 1625, and the period of his reign is known as the Jacobean Era. (Jacobean comes from *Jacobaeus*, a Latin form of the name James.)

The reign of James I initiated a time of deep religious and political unrest in England. It was as if the turbulent energies in English society that Elizabeth had managed to contain and harness had grown too intense for the old order and for the abilities of James, a morose, pedantic man who possessed none of Elizabeth's instinct for practical politics. We can perceive the emerging religious unrest when we recall that during James's reign the first group of English Puritans, strict Protestants who wished to "purify" the Church of England, came to America because they did not feel free to practice their dissenting beliefs in England. Political ferment was reflected in the House of Commons, which asserted its growing power against the Crown and also gained the support of the people by refusing to vote taxes.

In the early part of the seventeenth century, even deeper philosophical and intellectual changes were beginning to undermine faith in the older Elizabethan world view. The forerunners of modern astronomy, Copernicus (1473–1543) and Galileo (1564–1642), had argued that the sun, not the earth, was at the center of the universe, and that there might even be a plurality or infinity of worlds. These and other early scientific investigations called into question the very basis of the divinely ordered, hierarchical universe. Most people rejected the new discoveries and clung to their old ideas, but not without being disturbed by the dawning of a new age of scientific thought.

CIVIL WAR, THE PROTECTORATE, AND THE RESTORATION (1625–1660)

When James I's son Charles ascended the throne in 1625, England was well on its way to civil war. As we have already seen, the causes were both religious and political. The days were long past when Elizabeth had steered a course of moderation and compromise between Protestant extremism and lingering loyalty to Catholicism. By the second quarter of the seventeenth century, the Puritan movement had developed into a powerful enemy of the Anglican establishment. When Charles I (1625–1649), following James, attempted to crack down on organized religious protest, he met with violent opposition. In Parliament, the lawyers and landlords who controlled the House of Commons withheld more and more funds from the executive functions of government. Charles responded by trying to rule without the support of Parliament, through his chief supporters and agents in the Church (Archbishop William Laud) and the army (Thomas Wentworth, Earl of Strafford), in what amounted to a government of royal absolutism. But the strategy was doomed to failure: dissatisfaction in the country was too virulent; Parliament had grown too strong and was determined to call the king and his supporters to account. Laud and Wentworth were imprisoned and executed. As Parliament set about voting wholesale reforms of both church and state, Charles left London and established his army at Nottingham. By August of 1642, England was in the throes of open civil war.

The king's supporters, many of them carefree, long-haired reckless young "Cavaliers" from families of country gentry, were no match militarily for the Parliamentary forces, made up primarily of grimly determined Puritans who wore their hair cropped off severely and were therefore known as "Roundheads." Oliver Cromwell (1599–1658), commander of the Parliamentary forces, had molded his men into a fearless and disciplined New Model Army (known as "Ironsides"), which fought all the more fiercely because it saw itself as the agent of God's vengeance and punishment. By the beginning of 1649, the royalist forces had been defeated and King Charles himself was a prisoner. The more radical element in Parliament was determined to have the king executed. To achieve this, they managed to expel those more moderate members who found the idea of killing the king repugnant, however determined they may have been in their political opposition to him. Charles I was tried as an enemy of the English people by a Parliament reduced to about fifty of its most extreme and vindictive members, and on January 30, 1649, he was beheaded. Andrew Marvell (1621–1678), perhaps the subtlest poet of the seventeenth century and himself a minor figure in Cromwell's government, later evoked this terrible moment in "An Horatian Ode upon Cromwell's Return to Ireland":

> That thence the Royal Actor borne,
> The tragic scaffold might adorn;
>   While round the armèd bands
>   Did clap their bloody hands.
> (lines 53–56)

After a brief period of confusion when the Rump Parliament, as it was called, tried to govern on its own, Cromwell took the power of government into his own hands and established what he called the Protectorate (1653–1658). This was in effect a military dictatorship, and it was not to endure for very long. Cromwell died in 1658, and those who were unhappy began to establish contacts with Charles I's eldest son, who had set up a government in exile in Paris. By 1660 the English people had had enough of harsh Puritan rule, and Charles II (1660–1685) returned in what we call the "Restoration" of the monarchy. A new Parliament was elected, and England returned to the form of government it had known before the war.

English society, however, had been deeply altered by the Civil War and the experience of Cromwell's Protectorate. Although loyal to Charles II, Parliament had a new sense of its importance in directing the affairs of the country. In general the old authoritarian and hierarchical pattern of Elizabethan and Jacobean England was reconstituted along looser, more tolerant lines. Religiously and politically, England had more than ever before become a country of multiplicity and diversity. The Anglican Church and the monarchy had been restored to prominence, but never again would these institutions dominate English life as they had done, or as they had tried to do, before the Civil War.

LITERATURE IN A CENTURY OF CHANGE AND UNCERTAINTY

After the extravagant achievements of Elizabethan literature, we might anticipate a certain falling off in a century so beset by social disruption and intellectual change. But in fact the literature of seventeenth-century England is every bit as vital as that of the previous century, and its vitality springs, both directly and indirectly, from the disruption and change we have just been surveying. Although much has been made of the ways in which seventeenth-century literature differs from Elizabethan literature, we should not exaggerate the differences. Many Elizabethan writers, including Shakespeare, produced their finest work under James I. And writers whom we tend to think of as central to the new century, such as Donne, began their careers at the height of Elizabeth's reign. The Elizabethan literary heritage was extremely important for the seventeenth century, and some of the most significant developments represent extensions of rather than reactions against Elizabethan practice. Yet seventeenth-century writers were confronted with problems of conflicting values and expressions that the Elizabethans had only begun to imagine. The literature of this century is great mainly for the resourcefulness with which it contends with those problems.

In drama, the early decades of the seventeenth century saw a continuation of the boundless creativity of the Elizabethan stage. True, in much Jacobean drama a darker and more disturbing image of life appears: themes of violence, madness, and corruption come to the fore. But in the best plays of John Marston (1575?–1634), John Webster (1580?–1625?), Cyril Tourneur (1575?–1626), Thomas Middleton (1570?–1627), and others, these themes are projected in language of audacious, daring brilliance. Ben Jonson, the greatest Jacobean playwright after Shakespeare, produced satirical comedies that fused classical learning with earthy fun. He also devised elaborate courtly masques—lavish and spectacular entertainments that combined music, song, dance, and splendid costuming. The theaters were closed in 1642 at the beginning of the Civil War, and of course

Cromwell, with his Puritan belief in the sinfulness of such public entertainment, kept them closed during the Protectorate. With the return of Charles II in 1660, drama flourished again, but in new modes strongly influenced by the French theater.

Without too much oversimplification, we may understand the poetry of the first half of the seventeenth century as the expression of two main styles or approaches. The first is that of the "metaphysical poets," a term coined by Samuel Johnson in the eighteenth century to refer to these writers' use of difficult, highly intellectualized images often drawn from Scholastic philosophy or metaphysics. The metaphysical poets are also referred to as the School of Donne, after the most important explorer of this style. Metaphysical poetry extends the Elizabethan love of intricate verbal artifice and feeling for dramatic voice and situation along new stylistic lines. The metaphysical poem is more argumentive in tone; its language is more colloquial; its meter is usually varied, irregular, even deliberately rough and harsh; it often depends, as Dr. Johnson observed, on "a combination of dissimilar images, or discovery of occult [hidden] resemblances in things apparently unlike." Metaphysical poetry seems to confront the disruptions and strains in the intellectual and religious life of the seventeenth century by incorporating these elements directly into the verbal drama of the poem.

The second major style or approach in early seventeenth-century poetry was classical and conservative. This poetry subjected experience to the discipline and restraint of reason, of classical form, of meticulous craftmanship. Ben Jonson was the chief practitioner of this style, and we often refer to his immediate followers as the School of Jonson or, referring more specifically to the group of young poets who took up Jonson's neoclassical standards, as the "Sons of Ben" or the "Tribe of Ben." While Jonson's own poetic goals were clarity, efficiency, and purity of expression, the Sons of Ben were on the whole less exacting and serious. Many of their poems are light, witty, and elegant, yet they retain that Jonsonian emphasis on fineness and precision of form. We call these writers—Robert Herrick (1591–1674), John Suckling (1609–1642), Richard Lovelace (1618–1657)—the "Cavalier" poets. Suckling and Lovelace were real Cavaliers, wealthy if rather ineffectual members of Charles I's army. Their poems display an effortless, aristocratic nonchalance. The entire Jonsonian tradition, including its Cavalier segment, provided the main basis for post-Restoration poetry in the age of John Dryden and Alexander Pope.

The seventeenth century is a magnificent period for English prose. Elizabethan prose had its splendid moments—in Sir Philip Sidney's sophisticated, idealizing pastoral romance, the *Arcadia*; in Thomas

Nashe's raucous, energetic, realistic prose fiction; in Richard Hooker's majestic defense of Anglican doctrine, *Of the Laws of Ecclesiastical Polity*. But in the seventeenth century English prose really came into its own. In the area of scientific and philosophical inquiry, Sir Francis Bacon (1561–1626) began in his *Essays* to move away from the elaborate, complicated sentences of Elizabethan prose and to develop a manner more succinct, informal, and pithy. As an age of intense religious controversy, the seventeenth century produced a number of great preachers. The prose of John Donne and Lancelot Andrewes (1555–1626) reflects the fact that their sermons were meant to be dazzling public performances, intellectually impressive and emotionally gripping. Seventeenth-century prose is richly varied, and it would be misleading to try to categorize it too neatly. In fact two of the greatest prose writers have to be thought of as eccentrics. Robert Burton (1577–1640), in *The Anatomy of Melancholy* (1621), sets forth his curious, encyclopedic, far-fetched learning in sentences that constantly startle and unsettle the reader with their seemingly improvised structure and quirky wordplay. Sir Thomas Browne (1606–1682), on the other hand, orchestrates sentences of great eloquence and fantastic metaphorical complexity in works such as *Religio Medici* ("A Doctor's Faith," 1643) and *Hydrotaphia* ("Urn Burial," 1658).

One monument of seventeenth-century prose deserves to be singled out for special attention. This is the translation of the Bible organized and sponsored by James I and known as the Authorized or King James Version (1611). The language of this book, the work of many translators, is so familiar to us that we are often unaware of just how moving it can be in a literary sense. Until the end of the nineteenth century, most fine prose in English was to some degree indebted to it. Of all the works of the later seventeenth century, *The Pilgrim's Progress* (1678) by John Bunyan (1628–1688) is perhaps the best example of what a powerfully effective model the prose of the King James Version provided. It is interesting that a century of such violent religious strife should have given us an English Bible of such permanent appeal.

We may conclude by reflecting briefly on the awesome figure of John Milton (1608–1674), whose writing embraces so much of what is vital in the literature not only of the seventeenth century, but of the entire Reniassance in England. Milton's sheer range is staggering. He wrote some of the finest sonnets, *the* finest pastoral elegy (*Lycidas*), and *the* most successful epic poem (*Paradise Lost*) in all of English literature. At its best, his prose is as powerful as any produced in a century of splendid prose. The principal argument of his best prose work, the *Areopagitica* (ăr′ē-ŏp′ə-jĭt′ĭ-kə), that books

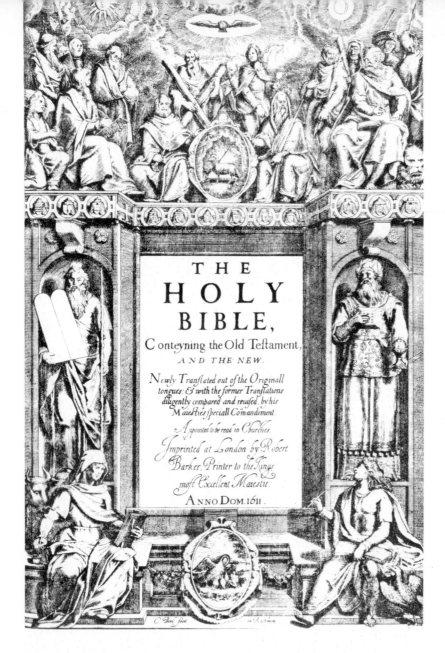

The King James Bible,
1611 (frontispiece).
Folger Shakespeare Library

must be printed freely without the restrictions of licensing or censorship, is central to the seventeenth-century spirit of controversy and intellectual expansion. His professed aim in *Paradise Lost*, to pursue "Things unattempted yet in prose or rhyme" and to "justify the ways of God to men," puts a soaring, daring Renaissance artistic enterprise at the service of the most essential need of a country torn apart by religious uncertainty and dispute. Milton traditionally marks the end of the English Renaissance—a rewarding and challenging culmination of all that had gone before.

The Elizabethan Age
Lyrics of the Early Renaissance

Sir Thomas Wyatt
1503–1542

Sir Thomas Wyatt is generally thought of today as the most interesting lyric poet of the first half of the sixteenth century. The Elizabethans preferred Wyatt's slightly younger contemporary Henry Howard, Earl of Surrey (1517?–1547), because his poems were smoother and more perfectly finished. But twentieth-century readers have seen that Wyatt's somewhat rougher verse can be full of dramatic energy and personal expressiveness.

Wyatt was a courtier and diplomat for Henry VIII for most of his life. He went on a number of diplomatic missions to Spain, France, and Italy, where he became familiar with European Renaissance poetry. Much of his best poetry is concerned with adapting European poetry forms and ideas to English poetry. He frequently translated and imitated the sonnets of the great fourteenth-century Italian poet Petrarch (1304–1374), and is usually credited with introducing the fourteen-line sonnet into English. But he also wrote wonderful lyrics in the native English song tradition. What distinguishes Wyatt's best work in both the Italian and the English lyric traditions is his dramatic capacity, his ability to create the sense of a genuine speaking voice giving expression to a convincing human situation. Most love poetry of the early Renaissance was concerned with a single basic situation: a lover has been rejected by a beautiful but cold and disdainful woman, and he pours out his longing and frustration in a series of elaborate comparisons or images. Wyatt takes over this situation from Petrarch and the Italian poets, but his handling of it is often distinctively fresh, and sometimes witty and ironic.

As a member of Henry VIII's court, Wyatt had more to do than write love poetry. Life at court was risky and unpredictable: one moment a man would find himself in the king's favor; the next moment

Thomas Wyatt (drawing) by Hans Holbein.
Copyright Reserved by Her Majesty, The Queen

he would be in danger of losing his reputation, or even his life. It is thought that as a young man Wyatt may have been involved with Anne Boleyn, whom Henry married after his divorce from Catherine of Aragon. One can imagine the riskiness of this situation for Wyatt. On two later occasions Wyatt was arrested and imprisoned for conduct that displeased Henry. But both times he was eventually pardoned. Near the end of his life, he retired for a time to his home in his native Kent, from which he wrote a satirical verse letter on the follies of court life.

My Galley Chargèd° with Forgetfulness

My galley chargèd with forgetfulness
  Through sharp seas, in winter night doth pass
  'Tween rock and rock; and eke° mine enemy°, alas,
  That is my lord steereth with cruelness.
And every oar a thought in readiness,   5
  As though that death were light in such a case.
  An endless wind doth tear the sail apace
  Of forcèd sighs and trusty fearfulness.
A rain of tears, a cloud of dark disdain,
  Hath done the wearied cords° great hinderance,   10
  Wreathed with error and eke with ignorance.
The stars° be hid that led me to this pain
  Drowned is reason that should me consort,°
  And I remain despairing of the port.

°**Chargèd:** laden, weighed down. 3. **eke:** also. **mine enemy:** either the speaker's passion or Cupid, god of love. 10. **cords:** rigging ropes. 12. **stars:** figuratively, the eyes of the woman who has rejected the speaker's love. 13. **consort:** accompany; a term used for a companion ship.

Whoso List to Hunt

Whoso list° to hunt, I know where is an hind,°
  But as for me, alas, I may no more:
  The vain travail hath wearied me so sore.
  I am of them that farthest cometh behind;
Yet may I by no means my wearied mind   5
  Draw from the deer: but as she fleeth afore,
  Fainting I follow. I leave off therefore,
  Since in a net I seek to hold the wind.
Who list her hunt, I put him out of doubt,
  As well as I may spend his time in vain: 10
  And graven with diamonds, in letters plain
There is written her fair neck round about:
  "*Noli me tangere,*° for Caesar's I am;
  And wild for to hold, though I seem tame."

---

1. **Whoso list:** whoever cares, whoever wants. **hind:** a doe. 13, *Noli me tangere:* "Don't touch me," from the Latin of John 20:17; presumably referring to Anne Boleyn, in whom Henry VIII had already taken an interest.

My Galley Chargèd with Forgetfulness

1. This poem is a fairly close translation by Wyatt of an Italian sonnet by Petrarch, in which an unhappy lover compares his emotional state to a ship lost on a stormy sea. What particular aspects of the sea and the ship does the poem focus on? What aspects of the speaker's emotional state do the images of ship and sea correspond to?

2. Wyatt's poem is about emotions out of control. Yet he expresses this idea through a sonnet, which is a tightly structured poetic form. How does Wyatt use the structure of the sonnet to control and organize the emotions in the poem? Does this high degree of organization make the poem more, or less, effective? Give reasons to support your answer.

Whoso List to Hunt

What reason is there in this poem to think that the speaker is a lover trying to discourage himself from pursuing an unavailable woman, and not simply a hunter who has given up following a wild deer? If the deer is really a woman, what impression of her does the poem create? Who is "Caesar" in line 13?

The Sonnet

In modern usage the word *sonnet* refers to a fourteen-line poem written in iambic pentameter (each line contains ten syllables, five of which are usually stressed). The word *sonnet* comes from the Italian *sonetto*, which means "little sound" or "little song." The sonnet originated in Italy in the thirteenth century. In the fourteenth century Petrarch produced what was to become the most important group of sonnets in European literature. His great sequence of 366 lyrics, containing 317 true sonnets, is addressed to a woman named Laura, whom Petrarch loved but with whom he was never able to establish a close relationship. Throughout the fifteenth and sixteenth centuries Petrarch remained the dominant influence in Renaissance lyric poetry, particularly in the sonnet.

The Italian sonnet was introduced into English poetry by Wyatt. His contemporary Henry Howard, Earl of Surrey, was also an innovative sonnet writer in the time of Henry VIII. The sonnets of Wyatt and Surrey were widely known to later sixteenth-century poets through a collection published in 1557 called *Tottel's Miscellany*.

During the Elizabethan period the sonnet really came into its own. Sidney's *Astrophel and Stella*, the first great sonnet sequence in English, was written about 1582 and published in 1591. It started a vogue for sonnet cycles in England which continued right through the end of the century. Producing a sonnet cycle became the fashionable thing to do for an aspiring writer. Other important Elizabethan sonnet cycles were written by Sidney's friend and biographer Fulke Greville, and by Samuel Daniel, Michael Drayton, Spenser, and Shakespeare.

The central theme in these sonnet cycles was the love of the poet for a beautiful but unattainable woman. The convention governing the relationship between the poet and his lady was inflexible. She was the "cruel fair" whose favors her servant sought endlessly but hopelessly. Her moods created the weather. A brightening glance, for example, was a good omen but not entirely trustworthy, because eyes as "rising suns" could change instantly to eyes as "stars," in which case they were capable of emitting "angry sparks." Then again, while the lady's eyes were alternately suns or stars, her hair was almost invariably "gold wires"; her cheeks, "roses"; her lips, "cherries"; and her teeth, "orient pearls." The love lyrics addressed to her were not necessarily addressed to a living person. It was small matter whether the lady did or did not exist in fact. Very often these love poems were addressed to a small circle of congenial spirits — fellow poets, wits, ladies of fashion — whom the poet wished to amuse. The way to impress this company was to exhibit special ingenuity in devising new variations on the old theme or in polishing one's work to an impressively high gloss. The reproach that such poetry is "insincere" would have astonished any Elizabethan. The rules were there with all the weighty authority of tradition behind them, and they were there to be followed. To depart from them would be as incomprehensible as if a chess player were to propose a change of rules to his opponent in order that he "might express himself better."

There are two main types of sonnets:

1. The "Italian" or "Petrarchan" sonnet. This type of sonnet has a rhyme scheme which divides the poem into an octave (the first 8 lines) and a sestet (the last six lines). Using letters of the alphabet to represent words that rhyme, the usual rhyme scheme of the octave may be represented as *abbaabba*. Sometimes the scheme is *abababab*. The sestet may rhyme in various ways: *cdecde*, for example, or *cdcdcd*. The shift from octave to sestet is often a point of dramatic change in the Italian sonnet. We sometimes call this shift the turn or *volta* (an Italian word meaning "turn"). In the original Italian form, the sestet almost never ends with a rhyming pair, or couplet. But English poets, from Wyatt on through Sidney and John Donne, tend to prefer a final couplet.

2. The "English" or "Shakespearean" sonnet. In this form the lines are organized into three groups of alternating rhymes plus a final couplet. The four-line groups are called quatrains. The rhyme scheme, then, is usually *abab cdcd efef gg*. Although this type of sonnet is often called "Shakespearean," it was actually developed by Henry Howard, the Earl of Surrey, many years before Shakespeare used it.

A third type of sonnet, the "Spenserian," is less important historically than the Petrarchan and Shakespearean forms. But it is characteristic of Spenser to have invented his own sonnet form with complicated interlocking rhymes: *abab bcbc cdcd ee.* We may note the similarity to the nine-line stanza that Spenser invented for his epic poem, *The Faerie Queene: ababbcbcc.*

All these facts about different sonnet forms are important only if they help us experience and talk about the meaning of specific poems. It may seem strange to us that Elizabethan writers would have wanted to express themselves in a form so strictly controlled and predetermined. But for the Elizabethans the intricate pattern of the sonnet had an intrinsic beauty, pleasurable to contemplate in the way that an abstract design in a piece of cloth or carpet is pleasurable to look at. They would also have valued the sonnet pattern as a challenge to their skill as poets. Most important, however, the Elizabethans would have thought of the formal demands of the sonnet not simply as restrictions or limitations, but as expressive resources—as structural features that give shape, emphasis, and organization to what is said.

As readers, we need to be alert to these expressive resources of sonnet form. We should consider questions like the following: How does a poet use rhymes and rhyme scheme to reinforce what the poem says? How does a poet take advantage of the turn from octave to sestet, or the shift from one quatrain to another? How does the final couplet function? How do the patterns created by rhyme relate to other patterns created by grammar, word order, the positioning or grouping of images, or the movement of logical argument? When we learn to read with questions like these in mind, sonnets become interesting because of, rather than in spite of, their strict form.

Edmund Spenser
1552-1599

Edmund Spenser (detail, engraving) by
John Guyse.
National Portrait Gallery, London

Because his influence on later poets was considerable, Spenser is often referred to as "the poet's
poet." He is generally acknowledged to be the
greatest nondramatic poet of the Elizabethan Age.

Spenser was born and educated in London. He attended Cambridge University as a "sizar," a student who received payment toward his college expenses for performing certain useful duties.
Spenser's career as a poet began at Cambridge,
where he became friendly with other young writers
interested in applying the forms and standards of
classical poetry to English poetry. He left Cambridge in 1576 and took a series of positions in the
service of prominent English noblemen, including
the Earl of Leicester, Queen Elizabeth's favorite.
While he was attached to Leicester, Spenser came
to be friends with Sir Philip Sidney, and during the
late 1570's they often met to discuss literature and
to read each other's poetry.

In 1579 Spenser dedicated to Sidney his first
major work, a series of pastoral poems arranged according to the months of the year and called *The
Shepherd's Calendar.* Soon after its publication, he
went to Ireland as an assistant to Lord Grey of Wilton, who was Lord Deputy of Ireland. He lived
there for the rest of his life, carrying out his administrative duties and working on the grand poetic projects he had laid out for himself. Spenser returned to London twice. His first visit, in 1589,
was inspired by Sir Walter Raleigh, who visited
Spenser in Ireland and encouraged him to go to
London and publish the completed portions of a
vast epic poem he was writing called *The Faerie
Queen.* Written in a deliberately archaic style, this
magnificent poem uses myths and legends from
England's rich medieval past to sum up the values
and achievements of the entire Elizabethan Age.
The first three books of *The Faerie Queene,* each
one more than five thousand lines long, were published in 1590, and Spenser was soon recognized as
England's greatest poet. During the 1590's he continued to work on *The Faerie Queene* (he planned
eventually to publish twelve, perhaps even twenty-
four, books in all!) and to write many other kinds of
poems. In 1596 three additional books of *The
Faerie Queene* appeared. But Spenser never received the secure position at Elizabeth's court that
he longed for. The queen had awarded him an
annual pension of fifty pounds in 1591, but nothing
more substantial was offered.

Spenser's last few years in Ireland were darkened
by an insurrection against English rule there. His
estate, Kilcolman, was sacked by Irish rebels, and
he had to return to London, where he died on
January 13, 1599. He was buried near Chaucer, his
great medieval forerunner, in Westminster Abbey.

The poems printed here show Spenser's style as a
lyric poet. They come from a sequence of sonnets
called *Amoretti* ("little Cupids" or "little love
poems"), published in 1595. The sequence as a whole
may be based on Spenser's courtship of Elizabeth
Boyle, who became his second wife in the summer
of 1594. Spenser is much less dramatic, much more
formal and stately, than Wyatt or Sidney. The sonnet form he invented, based on an intricate pattern
of interlocking rhymes, contributes to his highly
formal, undramatic approach to the lyric.

from **The Faerie Queene**

Spenser's masterpiece, *The Faerie Queene*, is written in a stanza of the poet's own invention, ever since called the Spenserian stanza. It consists of eight lines in iambic pentameter and a ninth line, an alexandrine, containing an additional foot. Thus the last line contains two more syllables than the other lines. Here is stanza 41 from Book I, Canto I, a famous description of the House of Morpheus (sleep).

Rhyme scheme

a	And more, to lulle him in his slumber soft,
b	A trickling streame from high rock tumbling downe,
a	And ever-drizzling raine upon the loft.°
b	Mixt with a murmuring winde, much like the sowne
b	Of swarming Bees, did cast him in a swowne:°
c	No other noyse, nor peoples troublous cryes,
b	As still are wont t'annoy the wallèd towne,
c	Might there be heard: but carelesse Quiet lyes,
c	Wrapt in eternall silence farre from enemyes.

3. **upon the loft:** upon the roof.   5. **swowne:** swoon, fainting spell.

Sonnet 26

Rhyme scheme°

a	Sweet is the rose, but grows upon a briar;	
b	Sweet is the juniper, but sharp his bough,°	
a	Sweet is the eglantine, but pricketh near;	
b	Sweet is the fir bloom, but his branch is rough;	
b	Sweet is the cypress, but his rind is tough;	5
c	Sweet is the nut, but bitter is his pill;°	
b	Sweet is the broom flower, but yet sour enough;	
c	And sweet is moly,° but his root is ill.	
c	So every sweet with sour is tempered still,°	
d	That maketh it be coveted the more:	10
c	For easy things, that may be got at will,	
d	Most sorts of men do set but little store.	
e	Why then should I account of little pain,	
e	That endless pleasure shall unto me gain!	

Rhyme scheme: For a note on the Spenserian sonnet, see page 123.   2. **his bough:** In the sixteenth century, *his* was used where today we use *its*. *Bough* was probably pronounced to rhyme with *rough* in medieval times, to which Spenser likes to refer.   6. **pill:** center or core.   8. **moly:** an herb with white blossoms and a black root.   9. **still:** always.

Sonnet 67

Like as a huntsman after weary chase,
Seeing the game from him escaped away,
Sits down to rest him in some shady place,
With panting hounds, beguilèd of their prey:
So, after long pursuit and vain assay,°   5
When I all weary had the chase forsook,
The gentle deer returned the selfsame way,
Thinking to quench her thirst at the next brook.
There she, beholding me with milder look,
Sought not to fly, but fearless still did bide,   10
Till I in hand her yet half trembling took,
And with her own good will her firmly tied.
   Strange thing, me seemed, to see a beast so wild
   So goodly won, with her own will beguiled.

5. **assay:** attempt.

Sonnet 75

One day I wrote her name upon the strand,°
But came the waves and washed it away;
Again I wrote it with a second hand,
But came the tide, and made my pains his prey.
"Vain man," said she, "that dost in vain assay   5
A mortal thing so to immortalize!
For I myself shall like to this decay,
And eke° my name be wiped out likewise."
"Not so," quod I, "let baser things devise
To die in dust, but you shall live by fame: 10
My verse your virtues rare shall eternize,
And in the heavens write your glorious name;
Where, whenas death shall all the world subdue,
Our love shall live, and later life renew."

1. **strand:** beach. 8. **eke:** also.

Sonnet 79

Men call you fair, and you do credit° it,
For that yourself you daily such do see;
But the true fair, that is the gentle wit
And virtuous mind, is much more praised of me.
For all the rest, however fair it be,   5
Shall turn to naught and lose that glorious hue;
But only that is permanent and free
From frail corruption that doth flesh ensue,°
That is true beauty; that doth argue you
To be divine and born of heavenly seed;   10
Derived from that fair Spirit, from whom all true
And perfect beauty did at first proceed:
He only fair, and what he fair hath made;
All other fair, like flowers, untimely fade.

---

1. **credit:** believe.   8. **ensue:** outlast.

FOR STUDY AND DISCUSSION

Sonnet 26
Shakespeare's King Henry IV says, "Out of this nettle, danger, we pluck the flower, safety." What similar thought does this sonnet express? By what device does Spenser develop his idea? In the closing couplet what does Spenser mean by "little pain" and by "endless pleasure"?

Sonnet 67
In this sonnet Spenser uses the same basic comparison that Wyatt uses in "Whoso List to Hunt." What is this comparison? Why does the deer behold the speaker "with milder look" in line 9? What does the speaker mean when he says he captured the deer "with her own good will"? What is the speaker's attitude at the end of the poem?

Sonnet 75
How does the poet propose to make his love's virtues live on? Define the different senses in which the word *vain* is used (line 5).

Sonnet 79
What is the difference between Spenser's use of "fair" in line 1 and his use of "true fair" in line 3? The word *fair* occurs seven times in this sonnet. Comment on its probable meaning in each of these seven contexts. To whom does "he" (line 13) refer? What does the poet feel is "true beauty"?

FOR COMPOSITION

Wyatt's "Whoso List to Hunt" and Spenser's "Sonnet 67" make use of the same metaphorical idea—that of the hunter who has momentarily given up pursuing a deer—for different expressive purposes. Write a paper comparing Wyatt's and Spenser's different handling of this idea. How is the speaker's attitude to the deer developed in each poem? How does each poet treat the ideas of wildness and tameness? What do the specific differences suggest about the view of love conveyed in each poem? Is representing a woman as a gentle but wild animal appropriate or inappropriate?

Sir Philip Sidney
1554–1586

Sir Philip Sidney, Anon.
National Portrait Gallery, London

To many of his contemporaries, Sidney was an embodiment of the ideal Renaissance man and courtier. Spenser addressed him in the dedication to *The Shepherd's Calendar* (1579) as "the noble and vertuous gentleman most worthy of all titles both of learning and chivalry." When he died prematurely in 1586 at age thirty-two, the entire country mourned his loss.

Sidney came from a prominent aristocratic family who lived in Kent (also the native county of Sir Thomas Wyatt). His uncle was Robert Dudley, Earl of Leicester, Spenser's employer and Elizabeth's favorite. He attended Oxford University, but left without taking a degree to complete his education by traveling in Europe. Coming from such a well-connected English family, Sidney was introduced to many famous writers, educators, and heads of state on his travels. He also saw firsthand the terrible religious conflict between Protestants and Catholics, which erupted in such disasters as the massacre of French Protestants on Saint Bartholomew's Day in 1572. Sidney returned to England passionately committed to the Protestant cause. He had also learned of the main literary and artistic developments of the late Renaissance in Italy, France, and northern Europe.

Back in England, Sidney assumed the roles of courtier, diplomat, and casual man of letters. His deepest interests were political and religious. Writing and discussing poetry were for him private and informal, not professional, activities. At the country estate of his sister, Mary, Countess of Pembroke, he began his long pastoral romance in prose, with interspersed poems, called *Arcadia.* Sometime during the early 1580's Sidney wrote a long essay called *The Defense of Poesy*, which is the finest piece of Elizabethan literary criticism we have and a classic in the history of criticism. His *Defense*, provoked by an extremist Puritan attack against poetry and plays, rises far above the immediate controversy and addresses itself to the universal values of imaginative literature.

Sidney's contribution to lyric poetry was enormous. About 1582 he wrote a sonnet sequence called *Astrophel and Stella* (the names mean "Star-lover and Star") modeled on the sonnet sequences of Petrarch and other Italian and French poets of the Renaissance. This series of 108 sonnets reflects an actual autobiographical situation—Sidney's love for and eventual engagement to Penelope Devereux. The engagement didn't work out, and she eventually married Lord Rich. Penelope Devereux is unquestionably identified with the Stella of the sonnet sequence, and in some sonnets there are puns on her married name ("Hath no misfortune but that Rich she is").

Astrophel and Stella is the first fully developed sonnet sequence in English. Sidney's approach to the individual sonnet and to the cycle as a whole is intensely dramatic. Astrophel is concerned not just with his love for Stella, but with the difficulty of giving convincing poetic expression to that love. Through the interplay of argument and feeling in *Astrophel and Stella*, Sidney develops both an analysis and a demonstration of how to write subtly and impressively about love. Sidney's sonnet cycle was the chief inspiration for many other such cycles in the 1590's. Two of the best-known sonnets in this sequence have been chosen for inclusion here.

Although a brilliant and sophisticated love poet, Sidney was also a man of deep moral conviction. He died fighting for the Dutch Protestants against the Spanish at Zutphen in 1586.

Sonnet 31

With how sad steps, O Moon, thou climb'st the skies!
How silently, and with how wan a face!
What, may it be that even in heavenly place
That busy archer° his sharp arrows tries?
Sure, if that long-with-love-acquainted eyes   5
Can judge of love, thou feel'st a lover's case.
I read it in thy looks; thy languished grace,
To me, that feel the like, thy state descries.°
Then, even of fellowship, O Moon, tell me,
Is constant love deemed there but want of wit?°   10
Are beauties there as proud as here they be?
Do they above love to be loved, and yet
Those lovers scorn whom that love doth possess?
Do they call virtue there ungratefulness?

---

4. **busy archer:** Cupid, god of love.   8. **descries:** betrays, makes known.   10. **wit:** intelligence, good sense.

Sonnet 39

Come, Sleep! O Sleep, the certain knot of peace,
The baiting place° of wit, the balm of woe,
The poor man's wealth, the prisoner's release,
The indifferent judge between the high and low;
With shield of proof shield me from out of the prease°   5
Of those fierce darts Despair at me doth throw:
O make in me those civil wars to cease;
I will good tribute pay, if thou do so.
Take thou of me smooth pillows, sweetest bed.
A chamber deaf to noise and blind to light,   10
A rosy garland and a weary head:
And if these things, as being thine by right,
Move not thy heavy grace, thou shalt in me,
Livelier than elsewhere, Stella's image see.

---

2. **baiting place:** place of refreshment.   5. **prease:** crowd.

FOR STUDY AND DISCUSSION

Sonnet 31

1. *Personification* is a figure of speech in which something nonhuman is given human qualities. In this sonnet, how does Sidney personify the moon? Why does the moon climb the sky with "sad steps" (line 1)?

2. In what sense are the moon's eyes "long-with-love-acquainted"? Rephrase in your own words the question asked in lines 12–13. What is the tone of the poem?

Sonnet 39

1. What does the speaker ask of sleep in this sonnet? "The poor man's wealth" is an apparent contradiction. How do you explain this phrase? Why is it effective in this context?

2. Why is sleep "the indifferent judge"? What "civil wars" take place within the speaker?

3. Both sonnets are examples of the poetic device called *apostrophe,* in which an absent person, place, or abstraction is addressed as though it were alive and present. How do Sidney's sonnets fit this definition?

FOR COMPOSITION

Reread the sonnets of Spenser and Sidney. Of these two poets, which do you think has a more realistic approach to his subject matter? In your discussion, consider each poet's use of imagery, personification, and tone.

A courtly sonneteer (miniature) by Nicholas Hilliard.
Victoria and Albert Museum, Crown Copyright

Christopher Marlowe
1564–1593
Sir Walter Raleigh
1552–1618

Sir Walter Raleigh, Anon.
National Portrait Gallery, London

Christopher Marlowe was born in the cathedral town of Canterbury, in the same year as Shakespeare. In 1580 he went to Cambridge University on a scholarship usually given to students preparing for the ministry. But Marlowe never entered the ministry. Instead he wrote plays, and he became the most exciting Elizabethan dramatist of the late 1580's, before Shakespeare's talent had begun to be fully realized. He also became a figure notorious for, among other things, spying and brawling. In 1593, before he had reached his thirtieth birthday, he was stabbed to death at an inn. Some say the stabbing occurred in an argument over the bill, but others think that Marlowe was killed because of his involvement in undercover political intrigue. Marlowe's gifts as a poet may have exceeded his dramatic talent, for he left unfinished at his death one of the finest narrative poems of the Elizabethan Renaissance, *Hero and Leander*.

Sir Walter Raleigh is known to us all as a founder of Virginia and as the man who introduced tobacco into Europe. Yet his talents were enormously varied. He was a soldier, explorer, and colonizer, but also a courtier, poet, philosopher, and historian. He had a good deal in common with Marlowe. Both were reckless, free-thinking men who eventually came to violent ends. Raleigh became a favorite of Queen Elizabeth in the 1580's. When the Queen discovered his secret marriage in 1592 to Elizabeth Throckmorton, one of her maids of honor, she had him imprisoned for a time in the Tower of London. But in a few years he won his way back into favor through his military exploits and his expeditions to South America. Raleigh's fortunes rose to new heights. They fell drastically in 1603, however, when James I came to the throne. Convinced that Raleigh was part of a plot to bar his accession, James had him imprisoned until 1616. In that year he was released to make one last voyage to South America. The expedition failed miserably and ran afoul of the Spanish. When he returned to England, Raleigh was executed on the charges of treason for which he origi-

nally had been imprisoned. Cool and self-possessed to the end, Raleigh seems to have written one of his best poems, "The Author's Epitaph, Made by Himself," the night before he died. On the scaffold he is reported to have smiled as he ran his finger along the edge of the ax and said: "This is a sharp medicine, but it is a physician for all diseases."

The poems by Marlowe and Raleigh which appear on page 132 are good examples of how mistaken it is to assume that the speaker of a poem is necessarily the author. Marlowe the man is no more the "Passionate Shepherd" of the first poem than Raleigh is the "Nymph" of the second. Both poets are working here with traditional roles or voices from pastoral literature—literature that uses shepherds and an idealized rustic landscape to explore indirectly a whole range of ideas and themes. We might describe the voice of Raleigh's nymph as "antipastoral," but that too is part of the pastoral tradition in the larger sense. Raleigh would have been the first to appreciate the fact that the view of life expressed by his nymph is as conventional, and perhaps in its way as incomplete, as that expressed by Marlowe's shepherd.

The Passionate Shepherd to His Love

Christopher Marlowe

Come live with me and be my love,
And we will all the pleasures prove°
That hills and valleys, dales and fields,
Or woods or steepy mountain yields.

And we will sit upon the rocks,
Seeing the shepherds feed their flocks,
By shallow rivers, to whose falls
Melodious birds sing madrigals.

And I will make thee beds of roses,
And a thousand fragrant posies,
A cap of flowers, and a kirtle°
Embroidered all with leaves of myrtle;

A gown made of the finest wool,
Which from our pretty lambs we pull;
Fair linèd slippers for the cold,
With buckles of the purest gold;

A belt of straw and ivy buds
With coral clasps and amber studs;
And if these pleasures may thee move,
Come live with me and be my love.

The shepherd swains shall dance and sing
For thy delight each May morning;
If these delights thy mind may move,
Then live with me and be my love.

---

2. **prove:** experience.   11. **kirtle:** skirt.

The Nymph's Reply to the Shepherd

Sir Walter Raleigh

If all the world and love were young,
And truth in every shepherd's tongue,
These pretty pleasures might me move
To live with thee and be thy love.

Time drives the flocks from field to fold,   5
When rivers rage, and rocks grow cold;
And Philomel° becometh dumb;
The rest complains of cares to come.

The flowers do fade, and wanton fields
To wayward Winter reckoning yields;   10
A honey tongue, a heart of gall,
Is fancy's spring, but sorrow's fall.

Thy gowns, thy shoes, thy beds of roses,
Thy cap, thy kirtle, and thy posies,
Soon break, soon wither, soon forgotten,   15
In folly ripe, in reason rotten.

Thy belt of straw and ivy buds,
Thy coral clasps and amber studs,
All these in me no means can move
To come to thee and be thy love.   20

But could youth last, and love still breed,
Had joys no date,° nor age no need,
Then these delights my mind might move
To live with thee and be thy love.

---

7. **Philomel:** the nightingale.   22. **date:** ending.

A burning lover (miniature) by
Nicholas Hilliard.
Victoria and Albert Museum, Crown Copyright

FOR STUDY AND DISCUSSION

The Passionate Shepherd to His Love

1. What does the shepherd in Marlowe's poem offer his love to make his world sound attractive and desirable? What things does he offer her that he cannot possibly provide?

2. Notice that lines 19 and 20 at the end of the fifth stanza in Marlowe's poem almost repeat the poem's opening lines. What effect is created by this near repetition? Instead of ending with this refrain-like repetition, the shepherd goes on for another stanza. Does the promise of the final stanza add anything new to the promises made earlier? If so, what does it add?

The Nymph's Reply to the Shepherd

1. What assumption made by Marlowe's shepherd does Raleigh's nymph begin by attacking? How does she follow up this attack?

2. As in Marlowe's poem, lines 19 and 20 of the fifth stanza of Raleigh's poem sound like a summarizing refrain. Yet the nymph, like the shepherd, goes on for an additional stanza. Why does this last stanza begin with "But"? How are lines 19 and 20 transformed in lines 23 and 24? Describe the change in attitude in the last stanza, and how it affects your evaluation of the nymph's reply.

FOR DRAMATIZATION

Imagine how you could dramatize the exchange between Marlowe's "Passionate Shepherd" and Raleigh's "Nymph." What would each figure look like? In what tone of voice would they speak? Can you translate the debate between shepherd and nymph into modern terms? (Remember to allow for the fact that the shepherd and nymph are traditional literary types, and that neither of them is quite as confident of his or her view at the end of the poem as at the beginning.)

William Shakespeare
1564–1616

William Shakespeare, The Chandos Portrait
(detail), attributed to R. Burbage or J. Taylor.
National Portrait Gallery, London

It is natural that we should be curious about the life of a writer who is almost unanimously considered to be the greatest figure of English literature. Fortunately, more facts are known about Shakespeare than about most Elizabethan playwrights. We know that he was born in Stratford-on-Avon in April (probably on the 23rd), 1564, and that his father, John, was a fairly prominent citizen of the town who eventually became an alderman and bailiff. Shakespeare was presumably educated at the local school in Stratford. He never attended a university. In 1582 he married Anne Hathaway. They had a daughter in 1583, and twins, a boy and a girl, in 1585. After this there is no factual information for seven years, but we know that by 1592 he was in London working as an actor and a play-

wright, for in this year he was attacked in writing by a resentful rival.

In 1593 the London theaters were closed because of an outbreak of the plague, and Shakespeare, temporarily out of work, needed the support of a private patron. He got such support from the Earl of Southampton, a wealthy young nobleman to whom Shakespeare dedicated two rather long narrative poems: *Venus and Adonis* (1593) and *The Rape of Lucrece* (1594). When the theaters reopened, Shakespeare became a member of the most successful company of actors in London, the Lord Chamberlain's Men. He became a shareholder in this company and its principal playwright. By 1597, Shakespeare had prospered sufficiently to be able to buy a fine house back home in Stratford. In 1599 Shakespeare's company built the famous Globe Theater, where most of his best-known plays were performed. Queen Elizabeth often summoned the Lord Chamberlain's Men to put on private performances for her at court. When James I came to the throne in 1603, he took over the Lord Chamberlain's Men as his own acting company and renamed them The King's Men. By this time Shakespeare's status as the greatest dramatist of his day was securely established.

It is not possible to know exactly when Shakespeare wrote each of his thirty-seven plays. We know when most of the plays were first published, but an Elizabethan playwright would have been much more concerned with getting his plays performed than with seeing them in print, and the date of composition may have preceded the date of publication by several years. Still, scholars have tried to date the plays by poring over what evidence there is both inside and outside the text, and their hypotheses provide a reasonable basis for considering the development of Shakespeare's art. He began, it seems, by writing comedies (*The Comedy of Errors, Love's Labor's Lost*) and plays based on English history (the three *Henry VI* plays, *Richard III*). His first tragedy, *Titus Andronicus*, was written about 1593 or 1594. *Romeo and Juliet* came between 1594 and 1596, along with the finest of his early comedies, *A Midsummer Night's Dream*. *The Merchant of Venice* was written about 1597, *Julius Caesar* about 1599. Just before the turn of the century, Shakespeare wrote a small group of marvelous romantic comedies: *Much Ado About Nothing, As You Like It*, and *Twelfth Night*. Then, with the dawning of the new century, came the

Anne Hathaway's Cottage, Shottery.
Shakespeare Birthplace Trust, Stratford-on-Avon, England

period of the great tragedies: *Hamlet* (1600–1601), *Othello* (1603–1604), *King Lear* and *Macbeth* (1605–1606), *Antony and Cleopatra* (1606–1607), and *Coriolanus* (1607–1609). Shakespeare's last plays, apart from a final dramatization of English history in *Henry VIII*, are often called the "romances" because of their freely imaginative settings and themes and because they do not fit readily into established molds of comedy or tragedy. The greatest of these are *The Winter's Tale* (1610–1611) and *The Tempest* (1611).

Shakespeare seems to have retired to Stratford about 1610, though he continued to write for the London stage. He had made considerable money from his career as an actor, playwright, and company shareholder. He invested substantially in Stratford real estate and he led the life of a prominent and respected citizen. He died on April 23, 1616 (probably his fifty-second birthday), and was buried in the local church. Seven years after his death, some of his friends and fellow actors collected and published an edition of thirty-six of the plays in one large volume—the famous First Folio (1623).

Shakespeare's Sonnets

Shakespeare's sonnets were published in 1609, but most of them were written much earlier, probably in the 1590's, when Sidney's *Astrophel and Stella* established the vogue of the Elizabethan sonnet cycle. There are 154 sonnets in all, and together they suggest a "story," although the exact details of that "story" are elusive and mysterious. The first 126 sonnets are addressed mainly to a young man of great beauty and promise. The speaker expresses his affection and admiration for the young man, urges him to marry and perpetuate his virtues through children, and warns him about the destructive power of time, age, and moral weakness. Sonnets 78–86 of this group are concerned with a rival poet who has also addressed poems to the young man. Sonnets 127–152 are addressed to a lady with dark hair, eyes, and complexion. Both the speaker and the young man seem to be involved with her romantically.

There has always been much speculation about the biographical meaning of the "story" of Shakespeare's sonnets, but no one has ever produced a convincing theory connecting it with the facts of Shakespeare's life. The situations and relationships suggested in the sonnets are best understood as the fictional means through which Shakespeare explores universal questions about time and death, about beauty and moral integrity, about love, and about poetry itself.

Sonnet 18

Rhyme scheme

a	Shall I compare thee to a summer's day?
b	Thou art more lovely and more temperate.
a	Rough winds do shake the darling buds of May,
b	And summer's lease hath all too short a date.°
c	Sometime too hot the eye of heaven shines, 5
d	And often is his gold complexion dimmed.
c	And every fair from fair sometime declines,
d	By chance or nature's changing course untrimmed.°
e	But thy eternal summer shall not fade,
f	Nor lose possession of that fair thou owest,° 10
e	Nor shall Death brag thou wander'st in his shade
f	When in eternal lines to time thou grow'st.
g	So long as men can breathe, or eyes can see,
g	So long lives this, and this gives life to thee.

---

4. **date:** duration of a lease.   8. **untrimmed:** shorn of its beauty.   10. **owest:** ownest.

Sonnet 29

When in disgrace with fortune and men's eyes
I all alone beweep my outcast state,°
And trouble deaf Heaven with my bootless° cries,
And look upon myself and curse my fate,
Wishing me like to one more rich in hope,   5
Featured like him,° like him with friends possessed,
Desiring this man's art and that man's scope,
With what I most enjoy contented least—
Yet in these thoughts myself almost despising,
Haply I think on thee, and then my state,   10
Like to the lark at break of day arising
From sullen earth, sings hymns at Heaven's gate.
   For thy sweet love remembered such wealth brings
   That then I scorn to change my state with kings.

---

2. **state**: condition.   3. **bootless**: futile.   6. **like him**: like another.

Sonnet 30

When to the sessions° of sweet silent thought.
I summon up remembrance of things past,
I sigh the lack of many a thing I sought,
And with old woes new wail° my dear time's waste.
Then can I drown an eye, unused to flow,   5
For precious friends hid in death's dateless° night,
And weep afresh love's long since canceled woe,
And moan the expense° of many a vanished sight.
Then can I grieve at grievances foregone,°
And heavily from woe to woe tell o'er°   10
The sad account of forebemoanèd moan,
Which I new-pay as if not paid before.
   But if the while I think on thee, dear friend,
   All losses are restored and sorrows end.

---

1. **sessions**: sittings of a law court. Note the metaphoric relation to "summon,"
"canceled," "grievances," and so on.   4. **new wail**: lament anew.   6. **dateless**:
without end.   8. **expense**: loss.   9. **foregone**: long past.   10. **tell o'er**: count up,
examine.

Sonnet 73

fall in
fall

twilight

fire
dying
embers

That time of year thou mayst in me behold
When yellow leaves, or none, or few, do hang
Upon those boughs which shake against the cold,
Bare ruined choirs° where late the sweet birds sang.
In me thou see'st the twilight of such day   5
As after sunset fadeth in the west,
Which by and by black night doth take away,
Death's second self, that seals up all in rest.
In me thou see'st the glowing of such fire,
That on the ashes of his youth doth lie   10
As the deathbed whereon it must expire,
Consumed with that which it was nourished by.°
   This thou perceivest, which makes thy love more strong,
   To love that well which thou must leave ere long.

---

4. **choirs:** *Choir* refers to the part of a church where services are held, here used metaphorically. 12. **Consumed . . . by:** choked by the ashes of the wood that fueled its flame.

Sonnet 116

Let me not to the marriage of true minds
Admit impediments.° Love is not love
Which alters when it alteration finds,
Or bends with the remover to remove.
Oh no! It is an ever-fixèd mark   5
That looks on tempests and is never shaken.
It is the star° to every wandering bark,°
Whose worth's unknown, although his° height be taken.
Love's not Time's fool, though rosy lips and cheeks
Within his bending sickle's compass come.   10
Love alters not with his brief hours and weeks,
But bears it out even to the edge of doom.°
   If this be error and upon me proved,
   I never writ, nor no man ever loved.

---

2. **impediments:** reasons for not allowing a marriage to proceed. 7. **star:** the North Star, by which sailors are guided at sea. **bark:** a ship. 8. **his:** its; in lines 10 and 11, *his* refers to Time. 12. **doom:** Judgment Day.

Sonnet 130

My mistress' eyes are nothing like the sun,
Coral is far more red than her lips' red.
If snow be white, why then her breasts are dun,
If hairs be wires, black wires grow on her head.
I have seen roses damasked,° red and white,　　　　　　　5
But no such roses see I in her cheeks.
And in some perfumes is there more delight
Than in the breath that from my mistress reeks.°
I love to hear her speak, yet well I know
That music hath a far more pleasing sound.　　　　　　10
I grant I never saw a goddess go,°
My mistress, when she walks, treads on the ground.
　　And yet, by Heaven, I think my love as rare
　　As any she belied with false compare.

5. **damasked:** variegated.　8. **reeks:** emanates from.　11. **go:** walk.

FOR STUDY AND DISCUSSION

1. In Sonnet 18 what is the relationship in lines 1–8 between the young man's loveliness and temperateness and that of a "summer's day"? What is the relationship in lines 9–12 between the young man's "eternal summer" and the "eternal lines" of the speaker's verse? In what sense can the speaker make the young man eternal through poetry?
2. In Sonnet 29 what two moods are contrasted? What kinds of men does the speaker say he envies? What causes his change of mood in the last few lines of the poem? Judging from the reference in lines 11–12 of Sonnet 29, what would you say the lark symbolizes?
3. Compare the shift in mood in Sonnet 30 with that in Sonnet 29. Where does the shift take place in Sonnet 30? What is the effect of altering the placement of the shift? Has the speaker in Sonnet 30 been more or less successful in overcoming his unhappiness than in Sonnet 29? Give reasons to support your answer.
4. The images in Sonnet 73 are considered particularly effective. How do the three principal images introduced in the three quatrains relate to the mood and theme of the poem? Each of these images is followed by an additional metaphor. Explain the appropriateness of each metaphor to the principal image of the quatrain and to the poem as a whole.
5. In Sonnet 116, what is the meaning of line 13? In the second quatrain to what is true love compared? How does the image of Time in the third quatrain relate to the theme of the poem?
6. Sonnet 130 has been called "anti-Petrarchan" because the speaker celebrates his mistress as the opposite of the ladies idealized in most Renaissance love poetry. What is the lady of this poem like? What elements of comedy can you find in the poem?

FOR COMPOSITION

Spenser
Sidney
Donne Milton

1. After reading at least four sonnets written by poets other than Shakespeare, write an essay in which you compare several of them to one or more by Shakespeare. In your essay, say whether the Shakespeare sonnet is more or less pleasing or effective than the others. Use direct quotations to support your argument.
2. Try to write a sonnet in the Shakespearean pattern. When you have finished your poem, write a short paragraph in which you discuss the special difficulties you encountered in using this form.

Songs from Shakespeare's Plays

The Elizabethan period was a great age of English music and song. Musical training was part of every gentleman's education. Even Englishmen who had no formal musical training could take great delight in the many forms of popular music—in street songs, folk songs, and ballads. Singing was a vital part of Elizabethan culture at all levels. It is hardly surprising, then, that Shakespeare included all sorts of songs, from the most formal and elegant to the simplest and most popular, in his plays.

Shakespeare uses songs in his plays for many purposes. Sometimes songs set or contribute to the atmosphere of a scene. Sometimes they function almost as soliloquies for the expression of private thoughts and feelings. Sometimes they serve as part of a celebration or festivity. Sometimes, as in the songs sung by the Fool in *King Lear*, apparently simple and even nonsensical songs touch upon the deepest themes of the play. Although Shakespeare's songs should ultimately be read or heard in the context of the plays they come from, they can be, and always have been, appreciated in their own right as isolated lyric expressions.

The original printed versions of Shakespeare's plays do not contain the music to which the words of Shakespeare's songs would have been sung. But there is reason to believe that at least some of the musical settings traditionally used in performances of the plays derive from the original ones. Students with musical training may find it interesting to look up the musical settings of the songs printed here. It is only when we hear these songs sung that they come fully alive.

Tell Me Where Is Fancy° Bred?

In *The Merchant of Venice* (Act Three, Scene 2), this song is sung while Bassanio tries to choose among the caskets of gold, silver, and lead. If he chooses correctly, he will win Portia for his wife. The opening lines rhyme with *lead,* intending perhaps to give Bassanio a hint.

Tell me where is fancy bred,
Or in the heart or in the head?
How begot, how nourishèd?
   Reply, reply.
It is engendered in the eyes,   5
With gazing fed, and fancy dies
In the cradle where it lies.
   Let us all ring fancy's knell.
   I'll begin it.—Ding, dong, bell.
Ding, dong, bell.   10

° **Fancy:** love.

These songs from *As You Like It* are sung by Amiens, a follower of the banished Duke. The first song (Act Two, Scene 5) comments on the happy life of retreat led in the Forest of Arden. The second (Act Two, Scene 7) contrasts nature's harshness with human ingratitude.

Under the Greenwood Tree

Under the greenwood tree
Who loves to lie with me,
And turn his merry note
Unto the sweet bird's throat,°
Come hither, come hither, come hither.   5
   Here shall he see
   No enemy
But winter and rough weather.

Who doth ambition shun,
And loves to live i' the sun,   10
Seeking the food he eats,
And pleased with what he gets,
Come hither, come hither, come hither.
   Here shall he see
   No enemy   15
But winter and rough weather.

3–4. **And turn . . . throat:** and harmonize his happy song with that of the birds.

Blow, Blow, Thou Winter Wind

Blow, blow, thou winter wind.
Thou art not so unkind
  As man's ingratitude.
Thy tooth is not so keen,
Because thou art not seen,   5
  Although thy breath be rude.
Heigh-ho! Sing, heigh-ho! unto the green holly.
Most friendship is feigning, most loving mere folly.
  Then, heigh-ho, the holly!
   This life is most jolly.   10

Freeze, freeze, thou bitter sky,
That dost not bite so nigh
  As benefits forgot.
Though thou the waters warp,°
Thy sting is not so sharp   15
  As friend remembered not.
Heigh-ho! Sing, heigh-ho! unto the green holly.
Most friendship is feigning, most loving mere folly.
  Then, heigh-ho, the holly!
   This life is most jolly.   20

---

14. **warp:** freeze.

It Was a Lover and His Lass

This third song from *As You Like It* is sung for the wedding of Audrey, "a country wench," and Touchstone (Act Five, Scene 3). It is sung by a young page on the day before the wedding.

It was a lover and his lass,
   With a hey, and a ho, and a hey nonino,
That o'er the green cornfield did pass
   In the springtime, the only pretty ringtime,°
When birds do sing, hey ding a ding, ding.   5
Sweet lovers love the spring.

Between the acres of the rye,
   With a hey, and a ho, and a hey nonino,
These pretty country folks would lie,
   In the springtime, the only pretty ringtime,   10
When birds do sing, hey ding a ding, ding.
Sweet lovers love the spring.

This carol they began that hour,
   With a hey, and a ho, and a hey nonino,
How that a life was but a flower   15
   In the springtime, the only pretty ringtime,
When birds do sing, hey ding a ding, ding.
Sweet lovers love the spring.

And therefore take the present time,
   With a hey, and a ho, and a hey nonino,   20
For love is crownèd with the prime
   In the springtime, the only pretty ringtime,
When birds do sing, hey ding a ding, ding.
Sweet lovers love the spring.

---

4. **ringtime:** the season for exchanging rings (during courtship).

Fear No More the Heat o' the Sun

This song is from *Cymbeline* (Act Four, Scene 2). It is a lament for the heroine Imogen, who is supposed dead.

Fear no more the heat o' the sun,
  Nor the furious winter's rages.
Thou thy worldly task hast done,
  Home art gone and ta'en thy wages.
Golden lads and girls all must,   5
As° chimney sweepers, come to dust.
Fear no more the frown o' the great.
  Thou art past the tyrant's stroke.
Care no more to clothe and eat.
  To thee the reed is as the oak.   10
The scepter, learning, physic,° must
All follow this and come to dust.

Fear no more the lightning flash,
  Nor the all-dreaded thunderstone.°
Fear not slander, censure rash.   15
  Thou hast finished joy and moan.
All lovers young, all lovers must
Consign to thee and come to dust.
No exorciser harm thee!
Nor no witchcraft charm thee!   20
Ghost unlaid forbear thee!°
Nothing ill come near thee!
Quiet consummation have,
And renownèd be thy grave!

6. **as:** like. 11. **scepter, learning, physic:** kings, scholars, doctors.

14. **thunderstone:** In Elizabethan times meteorites were thought to be the cause of thunder. 21. **forbear thee:** leave thee alone.

FOR STUDY AND DISCUSSION

1. Several of these songs are about the natural world at a particular season of the year. What words and phrases does Shakespeare use to create the feeling of these particular seasons? What characteristic human activities does he mention in connection with the seasons? Contrast one of the songs about spring with the song about winter.
2. In "Under the Greenwood Tree," "Blow, Blow, Thou Winter Wind," and "Fear No More the Heat o' the Sun," Shakespeare deals with a relationship to nature on the one hand and to sophisticated society and worldly ambition on the other. How is this contrast developed in each of the three poems? From what perspective or point of view are the contrasts presented?
3. All of these songs except one have a *refrain*—a phrase, line, or group of lines repeated in the course of a song, sometimes with slight changes. Look carefully at the refrains in each of Shakespeare's songs printed here. In what sense may they be said to function as condensations of the main themes in the songs as a whole?

FOR COMPOSITION

1. Shakespeare's songs are often not as simple as they seem. In "Tell Me Where Is Fancy Bred?" for example, what answer is given to the question posed at the beginning? Is the question really answered? How do the "eyes" relate to the "heart" and the "head" respectively? What does it mean to "ring fancy's knell"? Does the song itself successfully perform this feat? Explain your answers in a brief essay.
2. All these songs contain an element of sadness or seriousness. Pick out these elements, and show how they relate to the mood of each song as a whole. "It Was a Lover and His Lass" may seem to lack an element of sadness or seriousness, but think about line 15, "How that a life was but a flower," or about the word *only* in the repeated phrase "springtime, the only pretty ringtime." In what sense do these lines and phrases carry a double meaning? Discuss your findings in a brief essay.

Shakespeare's Theater

As physical structures, the London theaters in which Shakespeare's plays were performed reflect the development of English drama during the course of the sixteenth century. Early in the century, companies of actors traveled about the country performing their plays wherever they could hope to find an audience. Some companies were maintained by individual noblemen for their private entertainment, but even these groups were allowed to "tour" when their services were not immediately required by their masters. Since there were as yet no public theaters, touring actors would set up a platform in an enclosed innyard. Spectators could then watch the plays either from the windows of the inn or from the ground.

The Elizabethan audiences at plays held on these temporary innyard stages were frequently rowdy. All sorts of shady activities went on among the crowds, particularly in London. So in 1574 the Common Council of London required that all places where plays were held be licensed. It was probably to evade the restrictions of this new law, and also to establish a more satisfactory place for putting on plays, that a company known as the Earl of Leicester's Men, led by the great actor Richard Burbage, built the first theater in London in 1576, just outside the city walls. The structure was called, simply, "the Theater." It was made of wood, and it probably resembled the arrangements of the innyards where plays were previously performed. It would have been open to the sky, except for roofed galleries on three sides, and there would have been a large platform jutting out into the middle of the enclosure. All performances were held during the day—there was no artificial lighting. The Theater must have been a great success, because other similar structures were soon put up nearby and across the Thames in Southwark, an area of London notorious for its bull-baiting and bear-baiting pits. In 1599 the famous Globe Theater, where most of Shakespeare's plays were performed, was erected in this area.

What we know about the Globe and other Elizabethan theaters comes from surviving drawings and construction contracts, and from stage directions in the plays themselves. There was, as we have said, an open enclosure where the "groundlings" could stand for a penny, surrounded by roofed galleries on all sides. The stage, a raised platform projecting into the enclosure, would have been at least partially covered with a roof supported by two pillars at the front. Two doors on either side of the stage led back to a dressing room. Below the stage was an area used by musicians and sound-effects men, and occasionally by actors playing the parts of ghosts or spirits who would ascend or descend by means of trap doors. Directly behind the main stage was a recessed inner stage, called the "inner below," either closed off by a curtain or opened up for the presentation of scenes where an indoor or enclosed atmosphere was required. Above the main stage was an area known as the "upper stage" or the "inner above," provided by the continuation of the roofed gallery above the stage. Sometimes spectators occupied this area, but more often than not it was used as part of the stage—as Juliet's bedroom, perhaps, or as the wall of Macbeth's castle. A balcony probably extended out for a few feet from this "upper stage."

Interior of the Swan Theater (drawing, 1596) by John DeWitt.
Courtesy, British Museum

The dimensions of Elizabethan theaters were not large. It has been estimated that the outside diameter of the Globe was 86 feet; its height about 33 feet; its open yard about 56 feet across. The Fortune, a square theater modeled on the Globe, was to have been 80 feet outside and 55 feet inside, with a stage 43 feet broad. Yet these modest-sized theaters could accommodate relatively large audiences: proba-

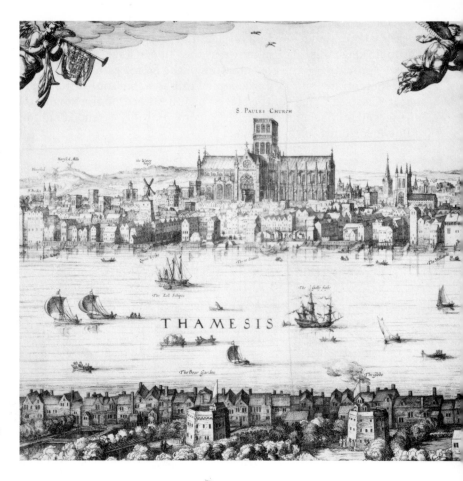

View of London (engraving, 1616) by John Vischer, showing Old St. Paul's Cathedral on the North Bank and The Globe Theater on the South Bank.
Courtesy, British Museum

bly about eight hundred standing in the yard, and as many as fifteen hundred seated in the roofed galleries.

There was no curtain across the front of the main stage. Scenes began or ended when actors came on or left the stage. Although costumes were often rich and elaborate, by modern standards sets were simple and rudimentary, as were atmospheric effects. "Scenery" as we know it today was hardly used at all. One of the pillars supporting the roof of the stage might serve as a tree, or even as the wall of a building. Much that is accomplished in the modern theater through the technology of stagecraft depended in the Elizabethan theater almost entirely on language.

Elizabethan audiences were much more accustomed than we are to using their imaginations to fill out what the playwright could only suggest verbally. And here we must keep in mind the intimacy of the theater in Shakespeare's day, with its modest dimensions and its

absence of a main curtain controlling the access of the audience to the stage. Elizabethan audiences were much closer, physically and imaginatively, to the immediate details of the performance. Elizabethan actors, on the other hand, would have been more closely in touch with the immediate reactions of their audience. This intimacy between actors and audience made possible subtle effects of voice and gesture. It also meant that the audience's disapproval would have been very palpably communicated—whether in the form of a crude snarl from a "groundling" who might just as soon have gone to the bear-baiting, or in the form of a more mannerly sneer from a clever young gallant seated in the gallery.

Although it may seem primitive and quaint to us today, the Elizabethan theater provided a lively, flexible, intimate environment for the splendid drama written during this period. It is always useful to remember the basic features of Shakespeare's theater when reading his plays.

The Tragedy of *Macbeth*

Shakespeare's *Macbeth* presents the most familiar of all tragic patterns: the rise and fall of a powerful but flawed man. The story comes from an account of eleventh-century Scottish history which Shakespeare found in Holinshed's *Chronicles,* the most popular book of British history in his day. Shakespeare transforms Holinshed's rather crude narrative of treachery, murder, political rebellion, and revenge into a tensely structured tragic action. The course and pace of this action are determined by a complex interplay between the internal desires and fears of the main characters and the external forces of circumstance and fate.

Macbeth was probably the last of Shakespeare's four great tragedies to be written—it follows *Hamlet, Othello,* and *King Lear.* It may have been written for a specific performance before James I at Hampton Court Palace in 1606. The company of which Shakespeare was a member, you will recall, had been taken over by James I in 1603 and renamed The King's Men. Even more specifically, James I was King of Scotland when he came to the English throne, and his family, the Stuarts, claimed descent from a line of Scottish kings that went all the way back to Banquo. The very positive characterization of Banquo in the play, and the prophetic procession in Act Four, Scene 1, showing the eight future kings descendent from Banquo, would certainly have flattered King James, the ninth Stuart monarch. But the power of Shakespeare's play goes far beyond its immediate historical significance. Like all great tragedies, *Macbeth* offers us a timeless image of the human will struggling against forces, including those of the mind itself, which are beyond its ultimate control.

Macbeth has always been a success on the stage, partly because of its ingeniously suspenseful construction, partly because of its ominous, brooding atmosphere, and partly because of the brilliantly conceived roles of Macbeth and Lady Macbeth. Great actors from all periods in the history of English theater have triumphed in Macbeth's "Tomorrow, and tomorrow, and tomorrow" speech, and in Lady Macbeth's sleepwalking scene shortly before she dies. Both characters combine qualities of good and of evil, of strength and of weakness. And in a sense both grow in self-awareness even as they become more desperately enmeshed in the consequences of their evil actions. The theatrical power of Shakespeare's skill in characterization is nowhere more convincingly displayed than in *Macbeth.*

Macbeth

Dramatis Personae

Duncan, King of Scotland
Malcolm ⎫ his sons
Donalbain ⎭
Macbeth ⎫ generals of the
Banquo ⎭ King's army
Macduff ⎫
Lennox ⎪
Ross ⎪ noblemen of
Menteith ⎪ Scotland
Angus ⎪
Caithness ⎭
Lady Macbeth
Lady Macduff
Gentlewoman attending
  on Lady Macbeth

Hecate, goddess of witchcraft
Three Witches
Fleance, son of Banquo
Siward, Earl of Northumberland,
  general of the English forces
Young Siward, his son
Seyton, an officer attending
  on Macbeth
Boy, son of Macduff
An English Doctor
A Scottish Doctor
A Sergeant
A Porter
An Old Man
Apparitions

Lords, Gentlemen, Officers, Soldiers, Murderers, Attendants, and Messengers

Setting: Scotland and England, the eleventh century.

Act One

Scene 1

[*A desert place. Thunder and lightning. Enter three* Witches.]

First Witch. When shall we three meet again
    In thunder, lightning, or in rain?
Second Witch. When the hurly-burly's done,
    When the battle's lost and won.
Third Witch. That will be ere the set of sun.   5
First Witch. Where the place?
Second Witch.   Upon the heath.
Third Witch. There to meet with Macbeth.
First Witch. I come, Graymalkin!°
All. Paddock° calls. Anon°
    Fair is foul, and foul is fair: 10
    Hover through the fog and filthy air.   [*Exeunt.*]

---

8. **Graymalkin:** cat. 9. **Paddock:** toad. According to the superstition of the times, witches used the cat and the toad as helpers. **Anon:** at once.

Scene 2

[*A camp near Forres.° Alarum° within. Enter* Duncan, Malcolm, Donalbain, Lennox, *with*
Attendants, *meeting a bleeding* Sergeant.]

Duncan. What bloody man is that? He can report,
    As seemeth by his plight, of the revolt
    The newest state.
Malcolm.   This is the sergeant
    Who like a good and hardy soldier fought
    'Gainst my captivity. Hail, brave friend!   5
    Say to the king the knowledge of the broil°
    As thou didst leave it.
Sergeant.   Doubtful it stood.
    As two spent swimmers, that do cling together
    And choke° their art. The merciless Macdonwald—
    Worthy to be a rebel, for to that   10
    The multiplying villainies of nature
    Do swarm upon him—from the western isles
    Of kerns and gallowglasses° is supplied;
    And fortune, on his damnèd quarrel smiling,
    Showed° like a rebel's wench. But all's too weak;   15
    For brave Macbeth—well he deserves that name—
    Disdaining fortune, with his brandished steel,
    Which smoked with bloody execution,
    Like valor's minion° carvèd out his passage
    Till he faced the slave;   20
    Which ne'er shook hands, nor bade farewell to him,
    Till he unseamed him° from the nave to the chaps,
    And fixed his head upon our battlements.
Duncan. O valiant cousin! worthy gentleman!
Sergeant. As whence the sun 'gins his reflection°   25
    Shipwrecking storms and direful thunders break,
    So from that spring whence comfort seemed to come
    Discomfort swells. Mark, king of Scotland, mark:
    No sooner justice had with valor armed
    Compelled these skipping kerns to trust their heels,   30
    But the Norweyan° lord, surveying vantage,
    With furbished arms and new supplies of men
    Began a fresh assault.

Stage Directions (S.D.). **Forres** (fôr′ĭs): a town in northeast Scotland, site of King Duncan's palace. **Alarum:** a trumpet call offstage. 6. **broil:** battle. 9. **choke:** render useless. 13. **kerns and gallowglasses:** light-armed, undisciplined soldiers and better-trained, more heavily armed soldiers. 15. **Showed:** appeared. 19. **minion:** favorite. 22. **unseamed him:** split him open. 25. **'gins . . . reflection:** rises. 31. **Norweyan** (nôr-wā′yən): Norwegian.

[handwritten marginal note: It seemed as though things were going well, they turned bad.]

Duncan.   Dismayed not this
   Our captains, Macbeth and Banquo?
Sergeant.   Yes;   35
   As° sparrows eagles, or the hare the lion.
   If I say sooth,° I must report they were
   As cannons overcharged with double cracks,° so they
   Doubly redoubled strokes upon the foe.
   Except they meant to bathe in reeking wounds,
   Or memorize another Golgotha,°   40
   I cannot tell.
   But I am faint, my gashes cry for help.
Duncan. So well thy words become thee as thy wounds;
   They smack of honor both. Go get him surgeons.

                                   [*Exit* Sergeant, *attended.*]

   Who comes here?

                       [*Enter* Ross.]

Malcolm.   The worthy thane° of Ross.   45
Lennox. What a haste looks through his eyes! So should he look
   That seems to speak things strange.
Ross.   God save the king!
Duncan. Whence camest thou, worthy thane?
Ross.   From Fife, great king;
   Where the Norweyan banners flout the sky
   And fan our people cold. Norway himself,   50
   With terrible numbers,
   Assisted by that most disloyal traitor,
   The thane of Cawdor,° began a dismal conflict;
   Till that Bellona's bridegroom,° lapped in proof,°
   Confronted him with self-comparisons,   55
   Point against point rebellious, arm 'gainst arm,
   Curbing his lavish° spirit; and, to conclude,
   The victory fell on us.
Duncan.   Great happiness!
Ross.   That now
   Sweno, the Norways' king, craves composition;°
   Nor would we deign him burial of his men   60
   Till he disbursèd at Saint Colme's inch°
   Ten thousand dollars to our general use.

---

35. **As:** no more than.   36. **sooth:** truth.   37. **cracks:** charges.   40. **memorize . . . Golgotha** (gŏl'gə-thə): make the
place as memorable for slaughter as Golgotha, where Christ was crucified.   45. **thane:** a Scottish title of rank similar to the English earl.   53. **Cawdor** (kô'dər).   54. **Bellona's bridegroom:** Macbeth, a great soldier, is called the mate
of Bellona, the Roman war goddess.   **lapped in proof:** dressed in armor.   57. **lavish:** insolent.   59. **composition:**
terms of peace.   61. **Saint Colme's inch:** island near Edinburgh (now called Inchcolm).

Duncan. No more that thane of Cawdor shall deceive
　　Our bosom interest.° Go pronounce his present° death,
　　And with his former title greet Macbeth.　　　　　　　　　　　65
Ross. I'll see it done.
Duncan. What he hath lost, noble Macbeth hath won.　　　　　[*Exeunt.*]

Scene 3

　　　　　[*A heath near Forres. Thunder. Enter the three* Witches.]

First Witch. Where hast thou been, sister?
Second Witch. Killing swine.°
Third Witch. Sister, where thou?
First Witch. A sailor's wife had chestnuts in her lap,
　　And munched, and munched, and munched. "Give me," quoth I.　　5
　　"Aroint thee,° witch!" the rump-fed ronyon° cries.
　　Her husband's to Aleppo° gone, master o' the *Tiger;*
　　But in a sieve° I'll thither sail,
　　And, like a rat without a tail,
　　I'll do, I'll do, and I'll do.　　　　　　　　　　　　　　　10
Second Witch. I'll give thee a wind.
First Witch. Thou'rt kind.
Third Witch. And I another.
First Witch. I myself have all the other,
　　And the very ports they blow,　　　　　　　　　　　　　15
　　All the quarters that they know
　　I' the shipman's card.°
　　I will drain him dry as hay;
　　Sleep shall neither night nor day
　　Hang upon his penthouse lid;°　　　　　　　　　　　　20
　　He shall live a man forbid.°
　　Weary se'nnights° nine times nine
　　Shall he dwindle, peak,° and pine;
　　Though his bark cannot be lost,
　　Yet it shall be tempest-tost.　　　　　　　　　　　　　25
　　Look what I have.
Second Witch. Show me, show me.
First Witch. Here I have a pilot's thumb,
　　Wrecked as homeward he did come.　　　　　　[*Drum within.*]

---

64. **bosom interest:** vital concerns.　**present:** immediate.
　2. **Killing swine:** Witches were commonly accused of killing their neighbors' pigs.　6. **Aroint thee:** be off!　**ron-yon:** mangy creature.　7. **Aleppo:** trading center in Syria.　8. **sieve:** In the Scottish witchcraft trials of 1592, witches confessed to sailing in sieves.　17. **card:** compass.　20. **penthouse lid:** eyelid; literally, the slanted roof of a shed.　21. **forbid:** accursed.　22. **se'nnights:** weeks.　23. **peak:** grow thin.

Third Witch. A drum, a drum! 30
    Macbeth doth come.
All. The weird sisters, hand in hand,
    Posters° of the sea and land,
    Thus do go about, about;
    Thrice to thine and thrice to mine 35
    And thrice again, to make up nine.
    Peace! the charm's wound up.

---

33. **Posters:** quick riders.

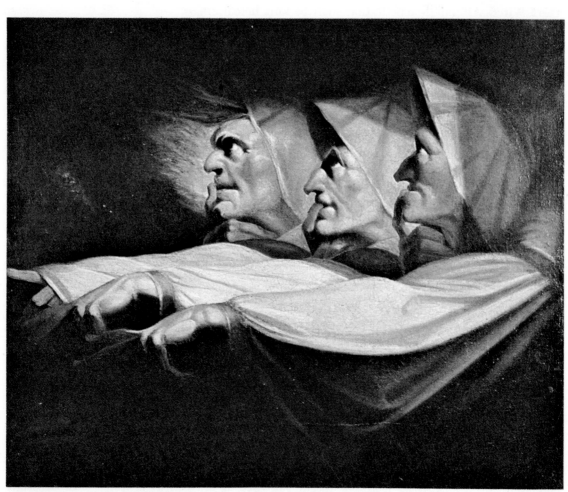

The Weird Sisters by Henry Fuseli.
Governors of the Royal Shakespeare Theater, Stratford-on-Avon

[*Enter* Macbeth *and* Banquo.]

Macbeth. So foul and fair a day I have not seen.
Banquo. How far is 't called to Forres? What are these
    So withered and so wild in their attire, 40
    That look not like the inhabitants o' the earth,
    And yet are on 't? Live you? or are you aught
    That man may question? You seem to understand me,
    By each at once her choppy° finger laying
    Upon her skinny lips. You should° be women, 45
    And yet your beards forbid me to interpret
    That you are so.
Macbeth.   Speak, if you can. What are you?
First Witch. All hail, Macbeth! hail to thee, thane of Glamis!°
Second Witch. All hail, Macbeth! hail to thee, thane of Cawdor!
Third Witch. All hail, Macbeth, that shalt be king hereafter! 50
Banquo. Good sir, why do you start, and seem to fear
    Things that do sound so fair? I' the name of truth,
    Are ye fantastical,° or that indeed
    Which outwardly ye show? My noble partner
    You greet with present grace and great prediction 55
    Of noble having° and of royal hope,
    That he seems rapt° withal; to me you speak not.
    If you can look into the seeds of time,
    And say which grain will grow and which will not,
    Speak then to me, who neither beg nor fear 60
    Your favors nor your hate.
First Witch. Hail!
Second Witch. Hail!
Third Witch. Hail!
First Witch. Lesser than Macbeth, and greater. 65
Second Witch. Not so happy,° yet much happier.
Third Witch. Thou shalt get kings, though thou be none;
    So all hail, Macbeth and Banquo!
First Witch. Banquo and Macbeth, all hail!
Macbeth. Stay, you imperfect speakers, tell me more. 70
    By Sinel's° death I know I am thane of Glamis;
    But how of Cawdor? The thane of Cawdor lives,
    A prosperous gentleman; and to be king
    Stands not within the prospect of belief,
    No more than to be Cawdor. Say from whence 75
    You owe this strange intelligence, or why
    Upon this blasted heath you stop our way
    With such prophetic greeting? Speak, I charge you.   [*Witches* vanish.]

---

44. **choppy:** chapped. 45. **should:** must. 48. **Glamis:** pronounced in two syllables in the play, but pronounced *glämz* in Modern English. 53. **fantastical:** creatures of the imagination. 56. **having:** possessions. 57. **rapt:** in a trance. 66. **happy:** fortunate. 71. **Sinel's** (sī'nəlz): Macbeth's father.

Banquo. The earth hath bubbles, as the water has,
  And these are of them. Whither are they vanished?   80
Macbeth. Into the air; and what seemed corporal° melted
  As breath into the wind. Would they had stayed!
Banquo. Were such things here as we do speak about?
  Or have we eaten on the insane root°
  That takes the reason prisoner?   85
Macbeth. Your children shall be kings.
Banquo.   You shall be king.
Macbeth. And thane of Cawdor too: went it not so?
Banquo. To the selfsame tune and words. Who's here?

[*Enter* Ross *and* Angus.]

Ross. The king hath happily received, Macbeth,
  The news of thy success; and when he reads   90
  Thy personal venture in the rebels' fight,
  His wonders and his praises do contend
  Which should be thine or his.° Silenced with that,
  In viewing o'er the rest o' the selfsame day,
  He finds thee in the stout Norweyan ranks,   95
  Nothing afeard of what thyself didst make,
  Strange images of death.° As thick as hail
  Came post° with post; and every one did bear
  Thy praises in his kingdom's great defense,
  And poured them down before him.
Angus.   We are sent   100
  To give thee from our royal master thanks;
  Only to herald thee into his sight,
  Not pay thee.
Ross. And, for an earnest° of a greater honor,
  He bade me, from him, call thee thane of Cawdor;   105
  In which addition,° hail, most worthy thane!
  For it is thine.
Banquo.   [*Aside*] What, can the devil speak true?
Macbeth. The thane of Cawdor lives; why do you dress me
  In borrowed robes?
Angus.   Who was the thane lives yet;
  But under heavy judgment bears that life   110
  Which he deserves to lose. Whether he was combined
  With those of Norway, or did line° the rebel
  With hidden help and vantage,° or that with both
  He labored in his country's wreck, I know not;

---

81. **corporal:** of bodily substance, real. 84. **insane root:** henbane or hemlock, supposed to cause madness. 93. **Which . . . his:** whether he should wonder at you or praise you. 96–97. **Nothing . . . death:** killing and not being afraid of being killed. 98. **post:** mounted messenger. 104. **earnest:** pledge. 106. **addition:** title. 112. **line:** support. 113. **vantage:** assistance.

But treasons capital,° confessed and proved,   115
Have overthrown him.
Macbeth.   [*Aside*] Glamis, and thane of Cawdor!
The greatest is behind.° [*To* Ross *and* Angus] Thanks for your pains.
[*To* Banquo] Do you not hope your children shall be kings,
When those that gave the thane of Cawdor to me
Promised no less to them?
Banquo.   That, trusted home,°   120
Might yet enkindle you unto° the crown,
Besides the thane of Cawdor. But 'tis strange;
And oftentimes, to win us to our harm,
The instruments of darkness tell us truths,
Win us with honest trifles, to betray 's   125
In deepest consequence.
Cousins, a word, I pray you.
Macbeth.   [*Aside*] Two truths are told,
As happy prologues to the swelling act
Of the imperial theme.°—I thank you, gentlemen.
[*Aside*] This supernatural soliciting   130
Cannot be ill, cannot be good. If ill,
Why hath it given me earnest of success,
Commencing in a truth? I am thane of Cawdor.
If good, why do I yield to that suggestion
Whose horrid image doth unfix my hair   135
And make my seated° heart knock at my ribs,
Against the use of nature?° Present fears
Are less than horrible imaginings;
My thought, whose murder yet is but fantastical,
Shakes so my single state° of man that function°   140
Is smothered in surmise;° and nothing is
But what is not.°
Banquo.   Look, how our partner's rapt.
Macbeth. [*Aside*] If chance will have me king, why, chance may crown me,
Without my stir.
Banquo.   New honors come upon him,
Like our strange° garments, cleave not to their mold   145
But with the aid of use.
Macbeth.   [*Aside*] Come what come may,
Time and the hour runs through the roughest day.
Banquo. Worthy Macbeth, we stay upon your leisure.
Macbeth. Give me your favor.° My dull brain was wrought
With things forgotten. Kind gentlemen, your pains   150

---

115. **capital:** deserving death.   117. **behind:** yet to come.   120. **home:** fully.   121. **enkindle . . . unto:** set afire your hopes for.   129. **imperial theme:** that Macbeth will be king.   136. **seated:** firmly imbedded.   137. **Against . . . nature:** in an unnatural way.   140. **single state:** Man was often regarded as a "microcosm," a miniature universe.   **function:** action.   141. **surmise:** imagination.   141–142. **nothing . . . not:** Nothing is real to me except my imaginings.   145. **strange:** new.   149. **Give . . . favor:** Forgive me.

Are registered° where every day I turn
The leaf to read them. Let us toward the king.
[*To* Banquo] Think upon what hath chanced, and, at more time,
The interim having weighed it,° let us speak
Our free hearts each to other.
Banquo.   Very gladly.   155
Macbeth. Till then, enough. Come, friends.   [*Exeunt.*]

Scene 4

[*Forres. The Palace. Flourish.*° Enter Duncan, Malcolm, Donalbain, Lennox, *and*
   Attendants.]

Duncan. Is execution done on Cawdor? Are not
   Those in commission yet returned?
Malcolm.   My liege,
   They are not yet come back. But I have spoke
   With one that saw him die; who did report
   That very frankly he confessed his treasons,   5
   Implored your highness' pardon and set forth
   A deep repentance. Nothing in his life
   Became him like the leaving it; he died
   As one that had been studied in his death
   To throw away the dearest thing he owned,   10
   As 'twere a careless trifle.
Duncan.   There's no art
   To find the mind's construction° in the face;
   He was a gentleman on whom I built
   An absolute trust.

             [*Enter* Macbeth, Banquo, Ross, *and* Angus.]

             O worthiest cousin!
   The sin of my ingratitude even now   15
   Was heavy on me. Thou art so far before
   That swiftest wing of recompense is slow
   To overtake thee. Would thou hadst less deserved,
   That the proportion both of thanks and payment
   Might have been mine!° Only I have left to say,   20
   More is thy due than more than all can pay.

he learned to die well dignified

---

151. **registered:** recorded (in my heart).   154. **The . . . it:** having considered it meanwhile.
  S.D. **Flourish:** trumpet fanfare.   12. **the . . . construction:** a person's character.   19–20. **That . . . mine:** that my
thanks might have exceeded the rewards you deserve.

Macbeth. The service and the loyalty I owe,
　　In doing it, pays itself. Your highness' part
　　Is to receive our duties; and our duties
　　Are to your throne and state, children and servants,　　　　　　25
　　Which do but what they should, by doing everything
　　Safe toward° your love and honor.
Duncan.　　　　　　　　　　　　Welcome hither;
　　I have begun to plant thee, and will labor
　　To make thee full of growing. Noble Banquo,
　　That hast no less deserved, nor must be known　　　　　　30
　　No less to have done so, let me infold thee
　　And hold thee to my heart.
Banquo.　　　　　　　　　There if I grow,
　　The harvest is your own.
Duncan.　　　　　　　　　My plenteous joys,
　　Wanton° in fullness, seek to hide themselves
　　In drops of sorrow. Sons, kinsmen, thanes,　　　　　　35
　　And you whose places are the nearest, know
　　We will establish our estate° upon
　　Our eldest, Malcolm, whom we name hereafter _Malcolm named heir to the throne_
　　The Prince of Cumberland; which honor must
　　Not unaccompanied invest him only,　　　　　　40
　　But signs of nobleness, like stars, shall shine
　　On all deservers. From hence to Inverness,°
　　And bind us further to you.
Macbeth. The rest is labor, which is not used for you.°
　　I'll be myself the harbinger and make joyful　　　　　　45
　　The hearing of my wife with your approach;
　　So humbly take my leave.
Duncan.　　　　　　　　　My worthy Cawdor!
Macbeth. [_Aside_] The Prince of Cumberland! That is a step _hamartia - the tragic flaw in the character that leads to downfall_
　　On which I must fall down, or else o'erleap,
　　For in my way it lies. Stars, hide your fires; _plots killing_
　　Let not light see my black and deep desires;　　　　　　50
　　The eye wink at° the hand; yet let that be,
　　Which the eye fears, when it is done, to see. [_Exit._]
Duncan. True, worthy Banquo; he is full so valiant,
　　And in his commendations I am fed;　　　　　　55
　　It is a banquet to me. Let's after him,
　　Whose care is gone before to bid us welcome.
　　It is a peerless kinsman.　　　　　　[_Flourish. Exeunt._]

Shows desire to be king

---

27. **Safe toward:** with sure regard for.　34. **Wanton:** unrestrained.　37. **We . . . estate:** I (here, as elsewhere, Duncan uses the royal "we") will make (Malcolm) the heir to my throne.　42. **Inverness:** Macbeth's castle.　44. **The . . . you:** Anything done for you is a pleasure.　52. **wink at:** be blind to.

Scene 5

[Inverness. Macbeth's castle. Enter Lady Macbeth, *reading a letter.]*

Lady Macbeth. "They met me in the day of success; and I have learned by the perfectest
report, they have more in them than mortal knowledge. When I burned in desire to
question them further, they made themselves air, into which they vanished. Whiles I
stood rapt in the wonder of it, came missives° from the king, who all-hailed me 'Thane
of Cawdor'; by which title, before, these weird sisters saluted me, and referred me to   5
the coming on of time with 'Hail, king that shalt be!' This have I thought good to
deliver thee, my dearest partner of greatness, that thou mightst not lose the dues of
rejoicing, by being ignorant of what greatness is promised thee. Lay it to thy heart, and
farewell."
　　Glamis thou art, and Cawdor; and shalt be   10
What thou art promised. Yet do I fear thy nature;
It is too full o' the milk of human kindness
To catch the nearest way. Thou wouldst be great;
Art not without ambition, but without
The illness° should attend it. What thou wouldst highly   15
That wouldst thou holily; wouldst not play false,
And yet wouldst wrongly win. Thou 'ldst have, great Glamis,
That which cries, "Thus thou must do, if thou have it";
And that which rather thou dost fear to do
Than wishest should be undone.° Hie thee hither,   20
That I may pour my spirits in thine ear,
And chastise with the valor of my tongue
All that impedes thee from the golden round,°
Which fate and metaphysical° aid doth seem
To have thee crowned withal.

[Enter a Messenger.]

　　　　　　　　　　　What is your tidings?   25
Messenger. The king comes here tonight.
Lady Macbeth.　　　　　　　　　　Thou 'rt mad to say it!
　　Is not thy master with him? who, were 't so,
Would have informed for preparation.
Messenger. So please you, it is true; our thane is coming.
　　One of my fellows had the speed of° him.   30
Who, almost dead for breath, had scarcely more
Than would make up his message.
Lady Macbeth.　　　　　　　　　Give him tending;
　　He brings great news.　　　　　　　　　　　　　　　*[Exit* Messenger.]
　　　　　　　　The raven himself is hoarse

---

4. **missives:** messengers.　15. **illness:** here, wickedness.　17–20. **Thou 'ldst . . . undone:** The thing that you want,
great Glamis, requires doing certain things to obtain it, things you are afraid to do, but, once done, you will not
want undone.　23. **golden round:** crown.　24. **metaphysical:** supernatural.　30. **had . . . of:** overtook.

That croaks the fatal entrance of Duncan
Under my battlements. Come, you spirits   35
That tend on mortal thoughts, unsex me here,
And fill me from the crown to the toe topfull
Of direst cruelty! make thick my blood;
Stop up the access and passage to remorse,
That no compunctious visitings of nature°   40
Shake my fell purpose, nor keep peace between
The effect and it! Come to my woman's breasts,
And take my milk for gall,° you murdering ministers,°
Wherever in your sightless° substances
You wait on nature's mischief! Come, thick night,   45
And pall° thee in the dunnest° smoke of hell,
That my keen knife see not the wound it makes,
Nor Heaven peep through the blanket of the dark,
To cry "Hold, hold!"

Give me courage & give her strength

                    [*Enter* Macbeth.]

          Great Glamis! worthy Cawdor!
Greater than both, by the all-hail hereafter!   50
Thy letters have transported me beyond
This ignorant present, and I feel now
The future in the instant.
Macbeth.   My dearest love,
  Duncan comes here tonight.
Lady Macbeth.   And when goes hence?
Macbeth. Tomorrow, as he purposes.
Lady Macbeth.   O, never   55
  Shall sun that morrow see!
  Your face, my thane, is as a book where men
  May read strange matters. To beguile° the time,
  Look like the time; bear welcome in your eye,
  Your hand, your tongue; look like the innocent flower,   60
  But be the serpent under 't. He that's coming
  Must be provided for; and you shall put
  This night's great business into my dispatch;
  Which shall to all our nights and days to come
  Give solely sovereign sway° and masterdom.   65
Macbeth. We will speak further.
Lady Macbeth.   Only look up clear;°
  To alter favor° ever is to fear.
  Leave all the rest to me.   [*Exeunt.*]

---

40. **compunctious . . . nature:** natural feelings of pity and remorse. 43. **gall:** bitterness. **murdering ministers:**
spirits of murder. 44. **sightless:** invisible. 46. **pall:** envelop as with a pall. **dunnest:** darkest. 58. **beguile:**
deceive. 65. **sovereign sway:** absolute power. 66. **look up clear:** look innocent. 67. **To . . . favor:** to change your
facial expression, that is, to show fear.

Scene 6

[*Before* Macbeth's *castle. Hautboys and torches.*° *Enter* Duncan, Malcolm, Donalbain, Banquo, Lennox, Macduff, Ross, Angus, *and* Attendants.]

Duncan. This castle hath a pleasant seat;° the air
    Nimbly and sweetly recommends itself
    Unto our gentle senses.
Banquo.   This guest of summer,
    The temple-haunting martlet,° does approve,°
    By his loved mansionry,° that the heaven's breath   5
    Smells wooingly here; no jutty, frieze,
    Buttress, nor coign of vantage,° but this bird
    Hath made his pendent bed and procreant cradle.°
    Where they most breed and haunt, I have observed,
    The air is delicate.

                [*Enter* Lady Macbeth.]

Duncan.   See, see, our honored hostess!   10
    The love that follows us sometimes is our trouble,
    Which still we thank as love. Herein I teach you
    How you shall bid God 'ild° us for your pains,
    And thank us for your trouble.
Lady Macbeth.   All our service
    In every point twice done and then done double   15
    Were poor and single business to contend
    Against those honors deep and broad wherewith
    Your majesty loads our house; for those of old,
    And the late dignities heaped up to them,
    We rest your hermits.°
Duncan.   Where's the thane of Cawdor?   20
    We coursed° him at the heels, and had a purpose
    To be his purveyor;° but he rides well;
    And his great love, sharp as his spur, hath holp° him
    To his home before us. Fair and noble hostess,
    We are your guest tonight.
Lady Macbeth.   Your servants ever   25
    Have theirs, themselves, and what is theirs in compt,°
    To make their audit at your highness' pleasure,
    Still° to return your own.

S.D. **Hautboys** (hō'boiz) **and torches:** The oboes announce the entrance of royalty; the torches indicate that it is night. 1. **seat:** location. 4. **martlet:** swallow, once a slang word for dupe—one who is easily deceived. **approve:** show. 5. **mansionry:** building. 7. **coign of vantage:** convenient corner. 8. **procreant** (prō'krē-ənt) **cradle:** where the young are hatched. 13. **God 'ild:** God reward. They should thank him for the trouble he causes them, since he is there because he loves them. 20. **rest ... hermits:** remain bound to pray for you, as hermits pray for a benefactor's soul. 21. **coursed:** chased. 22. **purveyor:** court official who goes ahead to arrange for the provisions for the king's table. 23. **holp:** helped. 26. **compt:** account. 28. **Still:** always.

Duncan.   Give me your hand;
  Conduct me to mine host. We love him highly,
  And shall continue our graces toward him.   30
  By your leave, hostess.   [*Exeunt.*]

Scene 7

[Macbeth's *castle. Hautboys and torches. Enter a* Sewer,° *and divers* Servants *with dishes
  and service, and pass over the stage. Then enter* Macbeth.]

Macbeth. If it were done when 'tis done, then 'twere well
  It were done quickly. If the assassination
  Could trammel up the consequence, and catch
  With his surcease success;° that but this blow
  Might be the be-all and the end-all here,   5
  But° here, upon this bank and shoal of time,
  We'd jump° the life to come. But in these cases
  We still have judgment here; that we but teach
  Bloody instructions, which, being taught, return
  To plague the inventor. This even-handed° justice   10
  Commends° the ingredients of our poisoned chalice°
  To our own lips. He's here in double trust;
  First, as I am his kinsman and his subject,
  Strong both against the deed; then, as his host,
  Who should against his murderer shut the door,   15
  Not bear the knife myself. Besides, this Duncan
  Hath borne his faculties° so meek, hath been
  So clear° in his great office, that his virtues
  Will plead like angels, trumpet-tongued, against
  The deep damnation of his taking-off;   20
  And pity, like a naked newborn babe,
  Striding the blast, or heaven's cherubin, horsed
  Upon the sightless couriers° of the air,
  Shall blow the horrid deed in every eye,
  That tears shall drown the wind. I have no spur   25
  To prick the sides of my intent, but only
  Vaulting ambition, which o'erleaps itself
  And falls on the other.°

[*Enter* Lady Macbeth.]

How now! What news?

S.D. **Sewer:** steward butler. 2–4. **If . . . success:** if only the murder would have no aftereffects, but be final and
successful with Duncan's death. 6. **But:** even. 7. **jump:** risk. 10. **even-handed:** impartial. 11. **Commends:** offers. **chalice:** cup. 17. **faculties:** powers. 18. **clear:** free from reproach. 23. **sightless couriers:** unseen messengers,
i.e., the winds. 28. **other:** i.e., the other side.

Lady Macbeth. He has almost supped. Why have you left the chamber?

Macbeth. Hath he asked for me?

Lady Macbeth.   Know you not he has?   30

Macbeth. We will proceed no further in this business.
He hath honored me of late; and I have bought
Golden opinions from all sorts of people,
Which would be worn now in their newest gloss,
Not cast aside so soon.

Lady Macbeth.   Was the hope drunk   35
Wherein you dressed yourself? Hath it slept since?
And wakes it now, to look so green and pale
At what it did so freely?° From this time
Such I account thy love. Art thou afeard
To be the same in thine own act and valor   40
As thou art in desire? Wouldst thou have that
Which thou esteem'st the ornament of life,°
And live a coward in thine own esteem,
Letting "I dare not" wait upon "I would,"
Like the poor cat i' the adage?°

Macbeth.   Prithee, peace!   45
I dare do all that may become a man;
Who dares do more is none.

Lady Macbeth.   What beast was 't, then,
That made you break° this enterprise to me?
When you durst do it, then you were a man;
And, to be more than what you were,° you would   50
Be so much more the man. Nor time nor place
Did then adhere,° and yet you would make both.
They have made themselves, and that their° fitness now
Does unmake you. I have given suck, and know
How tender 'tis to love the babe that milks me;   55
I would, while it was smiling in my face,
Have plucked my nipple from his boneless gums,
And dashed the brains out, had I so sworn as you
Have done to this.

Macbeth.   If we should fail?

Lady Macbeth.   We fail!
But screw your courage to the sticking-place   60
And we'll not fail. When Duncan is asleep—
Whereto the rather shall his day's hard journey
Soundly invite him—his two chamberlains
Will I with wine and wassail° so convince°

---

38. **freely:** without compulsion. 42. **ornament of life:** i.e., the crown. 45. **adage:** This refers to the old proverb,
"The cat would eat fish but would not wet her feet." 48. **break:** reveal. 50. **to . . . were:** that is, to be king. 52.
Did then adhere: was then suitable for the murder. 53. **that their:** their very. 64. **wassail:** carousing; boisterous
drinking and merrymaking. **convince:** overcome.

That memory, the warder of the brain,
Shall be a fume,° and the receipt of reason
A limbeck only.° When in swinish sleep
Their drenchèd natures lie as in a death,
What cannot you and I perform upon
The unguarded Duncan? What not put upon
His spongy officers, who shall bear the guilt
Of our great quell?°
Macbeth.   Bring forth men children only;
For thy undaunted mettle should compose
Nothing but males. Will it not be received,
When we have marked with blood those sleepy two
Of his own chamber and used their very daggers,
That they have done 't?
Lady Macbeth.   Who dares receive it other,
As we shall make our griefs and clamor roar
Upon his death?
Macbeth.   I am settled, and bend up°
Each corporal agent° to this terrible feat.
Away, and mock the time with fairest show;
False face must hide what the false heart doth know.   [*Exeunt.*]

65

70

75

80

---

66. **be a fume:** be confused by the fumes of drink. 66–67. **the receipt . . . only:** The part of the brain that reasons would become like a still (limbeck), distilling only confused thoughts. 72. **quell:** murder. 79. **bend up:** stretch tight. 80. **corporal agent:** bodily strength and power.

FOR STUDY AND DISCUSSION

1. Shakespeare opens the play with the witches conversing on the heath. What atmosphere and tone are created in this short opening scene? How does the line "Fair is foul, and foul is fair," later echoed in Scene 3, foreshadow the events of the entire act?

2. We first hear about Macbeth in Scene 2, through the speeches of the wounded sergeant as he reports to Duncan. What initial impression are we given of Macbeth? In what ways is this impression confirmed in Scene 3? In what ways is it not confirmed?

3. Macbeth and Banquo react differently to the witches and their predictions. Compare their reactions. How does the presence of Banquo in this act help create a sharper impression of Macbeth? In what ways is Banquo "lesser than Macbeth, and greater"?

4. Is there any evidence in this act that Macbeth had previously entertained the possibility of becoming king? If so, what does this indicate about the role the witches play in influencing Macbeth's thoughts and actions?

5. What are Lady Macbeth's reactions when she receives Macbeth's letter in Scene 5? How do her reactions compare with those of Macbeth earlier, when he hears the witches' prophecies and when he learns he has been made thane of Cawdor? What impression do you form of her character in the remaining scenes of this act?

6. Study carefully Macbeth's soliloquy at the beginning of Scene 7: "If it were done when 'tis done, then 'twere well / It were done quickly." What do we learn about Macbeth's state of mind from this speech? What is his conflict? How does he describe Duncan's character? What is the effect of Lady Macbeth's arguments?

7. Shakespeare ends Act One with Macbeth and Lady Macbeth plotting the murder of Duncan. How exactly do they plan to kill him? What is the dramatic effect of concluding the act by letting us see the murder plot as it crystallizes?

BLANK VERSE

Except for a few isolated prose passages, *Macbeth* is written in *blank verse,* which, introduced into English literature in the sixteenth century, was used in most Elizabethan dramas. Blank verse is unrhymed verse written in iambic pentameter. An *iamb* is one unstressed syllable followed by one stressed syllable, as in the words *tŏ dánce.* The term *pentameter* indicates that there are five feet, or beats, to a line. Note the following example from Act One of *Macbeth:*

Wĭll Í | wĭth wíne | ănd wássăil só | cŏnvínce
  1   2   3   4   5

Many lines are, of course, irregular and vary from this pattern. Some lines have only four strong stresses; others may have five stresses that are in an irregular order.

More than any other verse form, blank verse most closely reflects the natural, easy rhythms of English speech. Because of this and because of its fluency and flexibility, blank verse has always been a popular form. After Shakespeare and the Elizabethans, it was used by later poets such as Milton, Wordsworth, Tennyson, and Browning, and more recently by T. S. Eliot and Maxwell Anderson, who used a freer version of this meter in their poetic dramas.

Set design for *Macbeth,* Act Two, by Gordon Craig.
From *Towards a New Theatre,* by E. G. Craig (London/Dent), 1913

Act Two

Scene 1

[*Court of* Macbeth's *castle. Enter* Banquo, *and* Fleance° *bearing a torch before him.*]

Banquo. How goes the night, boy?
Fleance. The moon is down; I have not heard the clock.
Banquo. And she goes down at twelve.
Fleance.   I take 't, 'tis later, sir.
Banquo. Hold, take my sword. There's husbandry° in heaven;
    Their candles are all out. Take thee that° too.   5
    A heavy summons° lies like lead upon me,
    And yet I would not sleep. Merciful powers,
    Restrain in me the cursèd thoughts that nature
    Gives way to in repose!

[*Enter* Macbeth, *and a* Servant *with a torch.*]

                Give me my sword.
    Who's there?   10
Macbeth. A friend.
Banquo. What, sir, not yet at rest? The king's abed.
    He hath been in unusual pleasure, and
    Sent forth great largess to your offices.°
    This diamond he greets your wife withal,   15
    By the name of most kind hostess; and shut up°
    In measureless content.
Macbeth.   Being unprepared,
    Our will became the servant to defect;
    Which else should free have wrought.°
Banquo.   All's well.
    I dreamt last night of the three weird sisters: 20
    To you they have showed some truth.
Macbeth.   I think not of them;
    Yet, when we can entreat an hour to serve,
    We would spend it in some words upon that business,
    If you would grant the time.
Banquo.   At your kind'st leisure.
Macbeth. If you shall cleave to my consent, when 'tis,   25
    It shall make honor for you.

S.D. **Fleance** (flē-ăns). 4. **husbandry:** economy. 5. **that:** probably his sword belt. 6. **heavy summons:** great weariness. 14. **largess . . . offices:** gifts of money to the servant quarters. 16. **shut up:** retired to his room. 17–19. **Being . . . wrought:** Had we more warning of the king's visit, our hospitality would have been more lavish.

If I can still be loyal I will listen to you

Banquo.   So° I lose none
  In seeking to augment it, but still keep
  My bosom franchised° and allegiance° clear,
  I shall be counseled.°

Macbeth.   Good repose the while!

If I won't stain my honor I will be loyal

Banquo. Thanks, sir; the like to you!   [*Exeunt* Banquo *and* Fleance.]   30

Macbeth. Go bid thy mistress, when my drink is ready,
  She strike upon the bell. Get thee to bed.   [*Exit* Servant.]
  Is this a dagger which I see before me,
  The handle toward my hand? Come, let me clutch thee.
  I have thee not, and yet I see thee still.   35
  Art thou not, fatal vision, sensible°
  To feeling as to sight? or art thou but
  A dagger of the mind, a false creation,
  Proceeding from the heat-oppressèd brain?
  I see thee yet, in form as palpable°   40
  As this which now I draw.
  Thou marshal'st° me the way that I was going;
  And such an instrument I was to use.
  Mine eyes are made the fools o' the other senses,   — *he hallucinating*
  Or else worth all the rest; I see thee still,   45
  And on thy blade and dudgeon° gouts° of blood,
  Which was not so before. There's no such thing.
  It is the bloody business which informs°
  Thus to mine eyes. Now o'er the one half-world
  Nature seems dead, and wicked dreams abuse   50
  The curtained sleep! witchcraft celebrates
  Pale Hecate's° offerings, and withered murder,
  Alarumed by his sentinel, the wolf,
  Whose howl's his watch,° thus with his stealthy pace,
  With Tarquin's ravishing strides,° toward his design   55
  Moves like a ghost. Thou sure and firm-set earth,
  Hear not my steps, which way they walk, for fear
  Thy very stones prate of my whereabout,
  And take the present horror° from the time,
  Which now suits with° it. Whiles I threat, he lives;   60
  Words to the heat of deeds too cold breath gives.   [*A bell rings.*]
  I go, and it is done; the bell invites me.
  Hear it not, Duncan; for it is a knell
  That summons thee to heaven or to hell.   [*Exit.*]

on his way to murder duncan

---

26. **So:** so long as. 28. **bosom franchised:** conscience clear. **allegiance:** that is, to the king. 29. **counseled:** listen to your proposal. 36. **sensible:** tangible. 40. **palpable:** obvious. 42. **marshal'st:** leadest. 46. **dudgeon:** handle **gouts:** drops. 48. **informs:** creates forms. 52. **Hecate** (hĕk ′ə-tē): goddess of the underworld and of witchcraft, to whom the witches pledge allegiance. 54. **howl's . . . watch:** tells time by howling. 55. **Tarquin's . . . strides:** like Tarquin, son of a sixth-century Roman king. 59. **present horror:** the silence of midnight. 60. **suits with:** matches.

Scene 2

[*The same. Enter* Lady Macbeth.]

Lady Macbeth. That which hath made them drunk hath made me bold;
  What hath quenched them hath given me fire. Hark! Peace!
  It was the owl that shrieked, the fatal bellman,°
  Which gives the stern'st good night. He is about it.
  The doors are open; and the surfeited grooms°   5
  Do mock their charge with snores. I have drugged their possets,°
  That death and nature do contend about them,
  Whether they live or die.
Macbeth. [*Within*] Who's there? what, ho!
Lady Macbeth. Alack, I am afraid they have awaked,   10
  And 'tis not done. The attempt and not the deed
  Confounds° us. Hark! I laid their daggers ready;
  He could not miss 'em. Had he not resembled
  My father as he slept, I had done 't.

[*Enter* Macbeth.]

                    My husband!
Macbeth. I have done the deed. Didst thou not hear a noise?   15
Lady Macbeth. I heard the owl scream and the crickets cry.
  Did not you speak?
Macbeth.   When?
Lady Macbeth.   Now.
Macbeth.   As I descended?
Lady Macbeth. Aye.
Macbeth. Hark!
  Who lies i' the second chamber?
Lady Macbeth.   Donalbain.   20
Macbeth. This is a sorry sight.   [*Looking on his hands.*]
Lady Macbeth. A foolish thought, to say a sorry sight.
Macbeth. There's one did laugh in 's sleep, and one cried "Murder!"
  That they did wake each other. I stood and heard them;
  But they did say their prayers, and addressed them   25
  Again to sleep.
Lady Macbeth.   There are two lodged together.
Macbeth. One cried "God bless us!" and "Amen" the other,
  As they had seen me with these hangman's hands.
  Listening their fear, I could not say "Amen,"
  When they did say "God bless us!"

---

3. **fatal bellman:** At midnight on the night before an execution, a bellman rang a handbell outside the condemned man's cell, bidding him to repent his sins.   5. **surfeited grooms:** overfed servants.   6. **possets:** warm drinks, taken at bedtime.   12. **Confounds:** ruins.

Lady Macbeth.   Consider it not so deeply.   30
Macbeth. But wherefore could not I pronounce "Amen"?
   I had most need of blessing, and "Amen"
   Stuck in my throat.
Lady Macbeth.   These deeds must not be thought
   After these ways; so, it will make us mad.
Macbeth. Methought I heard a voice cry "Sleep no more!   35
   Macbeth does murder sleep," the innocent sleep,
   Sleep that knits up the raveled sleave° of care,
   The death of each day's life, sore labor's bath,
   Balm of hurt minds, great nature's second course,°
   Chief nourisher in life's feast——
Lady Macbeth.   What do you mean?   40
Macbeth. Still it cried "Sleep no more!" to all the house;
   "Glamis hath murdered sleep, and therefore Cawdor
   Shall sleep no more; Macbeth shall sleep no more."
Lady Macbeth. Who was it that thus cried? Why, worthy thane,
   You do unbend° your noble strength, to think   45
   So brainsickly of things. Go get some water,
   And wash this filthy witness from your hand.
   Why did you bring these daggers from the place?
   They must lie there; go carry them; and smear
   The sleepy grooms with blood.
Macbeth.   I'll go no more.   50
   I am afraid to think what I have done;
   Look on 't again I dare not.
Lady Macbeth.   Infirm of purpose!
   Give me the daggers. The sleeping and the dead
   Are but as pictures; 'tis the eye of childhood
   That fears a painted devil. If he do bleed,   55
   I'll gild the faces of the grooms withal;
   For it must seem their guilt.   [*Exit. Knocking within.*]
Macbeth.   Whence is that knocking?
   How is 't with me, when every noise appalls me?
   What hands are here? Ha! they pluck out mine eyes.
   Will all great Neptune's ocean wash this blood   60
   Clean from my hand? No, this my hand will rather
   The multitudinous seas incarnadine,°
   Making the green one red.

                    [*Reenter* Lady Macbeth.]

Lady Macbeth. My hands are of your color; but I shame
   To wear a heart so white. [*Knocking within*] I hear a knocking   65

— my hands are red w/ blood yet I didn't kill

---

37. **raveled sleave:** tangled skein, as of yarn.   39. **second course:** the main part of the feast.   45. **unbend:** relax.   62. **incarnadine** (in-kär′nə-dīn): make red.

At the south entry. Retire we to our chamber;
A little water clears us of this deed.
How easy is it, then! Your constancy°
Hath left you unattended. [*Knocking within*] Hark! more knocking.
Get on your nightgown, lest occasion call us,   70
And show us to be watchers. Be not lost
So poorly in your thoughts.
Macbeth. To know my deed, 'twere best not know myself. [*Knocking within*] *—guilt*
Wake Duncan with thy knocking! I would thou couldst!   [*Exeunt.*]

Scene 3

[*The same. Knocking within. Enter a* Porter.]

Porter.° Here's a knocking indeed! If a man were porter of hell gate, he should have old
turning the key.° [*Knocking within*] Knock, knock, knock! Who's there, i' the name of
Beelzebub?° Here's a farmer, that hanged himself on the expectation of plenty.° Come
in time; have napkins enow about you; here you'll sweat for 't. [*Knocking within*]
Knock, knock! Who's there, in the other devil's name? Faith, here's an equivocator,°   5
that could swear in both the scales against either scale; who committed treason
enough for God's sake, yet could not equivocate to heaven. O, come in, equivocator.
[*Knocking within*] Knock, knock, knock! Who's there? Faith, here's an English tailor
come hither, for stealing out of a French hose.° Come in, tailor; here you may roast
your goose.° [*Knocking within*] Knock, knock; never at quiet! What are you? But this   10
place is too cold for hell. I'll devil-porter it no further; I had thought to have let in some
of all professions that go the primrose way to the everlasting bonfire. [*Knocking
within*] Anon, anon! I pray you, remember the porter.   [*Opens the gate.*]

[*Enter* Macduff *and* Lennox.]

Kelly

Macduff. Was it so late, friend, ere you went to bed,
That you do lie so late?   15
Porter. Faith, sir, we were carousing till the second cock;° and drink, sir, is a great
provoker.
Macduff. I believe drink gave thee the lie last night.
Porter. That it did, sir, i' the very throat on me. But I requited him for his lie; and, I think,
being too strong for him, though he took up my legs sometime, yet I made a shift to   20
cast him.°
Macduff. Is thy master stirring?

[*Enter* Macbeth.]

---

68. **constancy:** firmness of purpose.
  1. The following speech is said by a drunken porter (a man who tends the castle gate). It is full of puns and jests that
refer to current happenings in Shakespeare's day. 1–2. **old . . . key:** grow old letting in so many damned souls. 3. **Beelzebub** (bē-ĕl′zə-bŭb): Satan's assistant. **expectation of plenty:** He hoarded grain in hopes that a bad harvest would raise
prices. 5. **equivocator:** liar. 9. **stealing . . . hose:** The tailor stole some cloth from the hose while making them. 10.
goose: tailor's pressing iron. 16. **second cock:** 3 A.M. 21. **cast him:** vomit.

Our knocking has awaked him; here he comes.
Lennox. Good morrow, noble sir.
Macbeth.   Good morrow, both.
Macduff. Is the king stirring, worthy thane?
Macbeth.   Not yet.   25
Macduff. He did command me to call timely on him.
  I have almost slipped the hour.
Macbeth.   I'll bring you to him.
Macduff. I know this is a joyful trouble to you;
  But yet 'tis one.
Macbeth. The labor we delight in physics° pain.   30
  This is the door.
Macduff.   I'll make so bold to call,
  For 'tis my limited service.°   [*Exit.*]
Lennox. Goes the king hence today?
Macbeth.   He does—he did appoint so.
Lennox. The night has been unruly: where we lay,
  Our chimneys were blown down; and, as they say,   35
  Lamentings heard i' the air; strange screams of death,
  And prophesying with accents terrible
  Of dire combustion° and confused events
  New hatched to the woeful time. The obscure bird°
  Clamored the livelong night; some say, the earth   40
  Was feverous and did shake.
Macbeth.   'Twas a rough night.
Lennox. My young remembrance cannot parallel — *I've never seen a nite like this*
  A fellow to it.

[*Reenter* Macduff.]

Macduff. O horror, horror, horror! Tongue nor heart
  Cannot conceive nor name thee!
Macbeth. ⎱
Lennox. ⎰   What's the matter?   45
Macduff. Confusion now hath made his masterpiece!
  Most sacrilegious murder hath broke ope
  The Lord's anointed temple,° and stole thence
  The life o' the building!
Macbeth.   What is 't you say? The life?
Lennox. Mean you his majesty?   50
Macduff. Approach the chamber, and destroy your sight
  With a new Gorgon.° Do not bid me speak;
  See, and then speak yourselves.   [*Exeunt* Macbeth *and* Lennox.]

---

30. **physics:** cures.   32. **limited service:** appointed duty.   38. **dire combustion:** terrible horror.   39. **obscure bird:** owl, obscure (meaning "dark") because the owl is a nocturnal bird.   48. **Lord's . . . temple:** the body of the king.   52. **Gorgon:** the snake-headed monster Medusa, so terrible to look upon that it turned those who saw it to stone.

Awake, awake!
Ring the alarum bell. Murder and treason!
Banquo and Donalbain! Malcolm! awake!   55
Shake off this downy sleep, death's counterfeit,
And look on death itself! Up, up, and see
The great doom's image!° Malcolm! Banquo!
As from your graves rise up, and walk like sprites,°
To countenance° this horror! Ring the bell.   [*Bell rings.*]   60

[*Enter* Lady Macbeth.]

Lady Macbeth. What's the business,
    That such a hideous trumpet calls to parley°
    The sleepers of the house? Speak, speak!
Macduff.   O gentle lady,
    'Tis not for you to hear what I can speak;
    The repetition, in a woman's ear,   65
    Would murder as it fell.

[*Enter* Banquo.]

               O Banquo, Banquo,
    Our royal master's murdered!
Lady Macbeth.   Woe, alas!
    What, in our house?
Banquo.   Too cruel anywhere.
    Dear Duff, I prithee, contradict thyself,
    And say it is not so.   70

[*Reenter* Macbeth *and* Lennox, *with* Ross.]

Macbeth. Had I but died an hour before this chance,°
    I had lived a blessèd time; for, from this instant,
    There's nothing serious in mortality.
    All is but toys:° renown and grace is dead;
    The wine of life is drawn, and the mere lees   75
    Is left this vault° to brag of.

[*Enter* Malcolm *and* Donalbain.]

Donalbain. What is amiss?
Macbeth.   You are, and do not know 't:
    The spring, the head, the fountain of your blood
    Is stopped; the very source of it is stopped.

---

58. **great . . . image:** Doomsday, the end of the world.   59. **sprites:** ghosts.   60. **countenance:** be in keeping with.   62.
parley: a conference of war.   71. **chance:** event.   74. **toys:** trifles.   76. **vault:** as used here, world.

Macduff. Your royal father's murdered.

Malcolm. O, by whom? 80

Lennox. Those of his chamber, as it seemed, had done 't.
Their hands and faces were all badged° with blood;
So were their daggers, which unwiped we found
Upon their pillows.
They stared, and were distracted; no man's life 85
Was to be trusted with them.

Macbeth. O, yet I do repent me of my fury,
That I did kill them.

Macduff. Wherefore did you so?

Macbeth. Who can be wise, amazed, temperate and furious,
Loyal and neutral, in a moment? No man. 90
The expedition° of my violent love
Outrun the pauser,° reason. Here lay Duncan,
His silver skin laced with his golden blood,
And his gashed stabs looked like a breach in nature
For ruin's wasteful entrance; there, the murderers, 95
Steeped in the colors of their trade, their daggers
Unmannerly breeched° with gore. Who could refrain,
That had a heart to love, and in that heart
Courage to make 's love known?

Lady Macbeth. Help me hence, ho! ~~fainted~~

Macduff. Look to the lady. 100

Malcolm. [*Aside to* Donalbain] Why do we hold our tongues,
That most may claim this argument for ours?

Donalbain. [*Aside to* Malcolm] What should be spoken here, where our fate,
Hid in an auger hole,° may rush, and seize us?
Let's away; 105
Our tears are not yet brewed.

Malcolm. [*Aside to* Donalbain] Nor our strong sorrow
Upon the foot of motion.°

Banquo. Look to the lady: [Lady Macbeth *is carried out.*]
And when we have our naked frailties hid,°
That suffer in exposure, let us meet,
And question this most bloody piece of work, 110
To know it further. Fears and scruples shake us.
In the great hand of God I stand; and thence
Against the undivulged pretense I fight
Of treasonous malice.°

Macduff. And so do I.

---

82. **badged:** marked: literally, wearing a badge as servants of murder. 91. **expedition:** hasty action. 92. **pauser:** restrainer. 97. **Unmannerly breeched:** covered with blood instead of their regular sheaths. 104. **augur hole:** a tiny hole, an improbable hiding place; that is, the smallest event may cause our downfall. 107. **Upon . . . motion:** is not yet moving. 108. **when . . . hid:** when we have put on our clothes. All but Macduff have come straight from bed. 113–114. **Against . . . malice:** I fight against the malicious treason which is not yet fully revealed.

All.   So all.

Macbeth. Let's briefly put on manly readiness,   115
  And meet i' the hall together.

All.   Well contented.

[Exeunt all but Malcolm *and* Donalbain.]

Malcolm. What will you do? Let's not consort with them;
  To show an unfelt sorrow is an office
  Which the false man does easy. I'll to England.

Donalbain. To Ireland, I; our separated fortune   120
  Shall keep us both the safer. Where we are,
  There's daggers in men's smiles. The near in blood,
  The nearer bloody.°

Malcolm.   This murderous shaft° that's shot
  Hath not yet lighted,° and our safest way
  Is to avoid the aim. Therefore, to horse;   125
  And let us not be dainty of leave-taking,
  But shift away. There's warrant in that theft
  Which steals itself, when there's no mercy left.°   *[Exeunt.]*

Because he's King's son — I'm next for crown + murder

Scene 4

[Outside Macbeth's *castle. Enter* Ross *and an* Old Man.]

Old Man. Threescore and ten I can remember well;
  Within the volume of which time I have seen
  Hours dreadful and things strange; but this sore night
  Hath trifled former knowings.

Ross.   Ah, good father,
  Thou seest, the heavens, as troubled with man's act,   5
  Threaten his bloody stage. By the clock, 'tis day,
  And yet dark night strangles the traveling lamp.°
  Is 't night's predominance, or the day's shame,
  That darkness does the face of earth entomb,
  When living light should kiss it?

Old Man.   'Tis unnatural,   10
  Even like the deed that's done. On Tuesday last,
  A falcon, towering in her pride of place,
  Was by a mousing owl hawked at and killed.

Ross. And Duncan's horses — a thing most strange and certain —
  Beauteous and swift, the minions of their race,   15
  Turned wild in nature, broke their stalls, flung out,
  Contending 'gainst obedience, as they would make
  War with mankind.

122–123. **The . . . bloody:** The nearer we are in blood relationship to Duncan, the more likely we are to be murdered.   **shaft:** arrow.   124. **lighted:** come down to earth.   127–128. **There's . . . left:** We are justified in stealing away in these merciless times.
   7. **traveling lamp:** sun.

Old Man.   'Tis said they eat each other.

Ross. They did so, to the amazement of mine eyes

    That looked upon 't. Here comes the good Macduff.   20

[Enter Macduff.]

    How goes the world, sir, now?

Macduff.   Why, see you not?

Ross. Is 't known who did this more than bloody deed?

Macduff. Those that Macbeth hath slain.

Ross.   Alas, the day!

    What good could they pretend?

Macduff.   They were suborned;°

    Malcolm and Donalbain, the king's two sons,   25

    Are stolen away and fled; which puts upon them

    Suspicion of the deed.

Ross.   'Gainst nature still!

    Thriftless ambition, that wilt ravin up°

    Thine own life's means! Then 'tis most like

    The sovereignty will fall upon Macbeth.   30

Macduff. He is already named, and gone to Scone°

    To be invested.

Ross.   Where is Duncan's body?

Macduff. Carried to Colmekill,°

    The sacred storehouse of his predecessors,

    And guardian of their bones.

Ross.   Will you to Scone?   35

Macduff. No, cousin, I'll to Fife.°

Ross.   Well, I will thither.

Macduff. Well, may you see things well done there. Adieu!

    Lest our old robes sit easier than our new!°

Ross. Farewell, father.

Old Man. God's benison° go with you; and with those   40

    That would make good of bad, and friends of foes!   *[Exeunt.]*

---

24. **suborned** (sə-bôrned'); bribed.   29. **ravin up:** devour greedily.   31. **Scone** (skōōn): where Scottish kings were crowned.   33. **Colmekill:** the ancient burying place of Scottish kings, now called Iona.   36. **Fife:** Macduff's castle 38. **Lest . . . new:** Macduff shows his misgivings about the future with Macbeth as king.   40. **benison:** blessing.

FOR STUDY AND DISCUSSION

1. An atmosphere of foreboding and horror is built up in Act Two. Much of the horror is implicit in Macbeth's famous "dagger" soliloquy in Scene 1 (lines 33–64). Why does Macbeth refer to the dagger as "fatal vision"? What does he mean by a "dagger of the mind"? What is suggested by having Macbeth experience a hallucination at this moment, just before the murder?

2. In Scene 2, after the murder of Duncan, Macbeth is troubled by voices he heard or thought he heard. Why could he not say "Amen" when a voice said, "God bless us!"? What is meant by "Macbeth does murder sleep"? Why won't Macbeth return to Duncan's room? How, on the other hand, does Lady Macbeth characterize the dead, in lines 53–55?

3. The symbols of blood and water are interwoven in lines 55–68 of Scene 2. What does each symbolize? How do the different attitudes of Macbeth and his wife to their bloodstained hands serve to point up the basic difference in their characters?

4. The porter's speech as he answers the knocking at the gate at the beginning of Scene 3 is one of the best-known examples in all Shakespeare of what is called "comic relief." Judging from this scene, what do you think "comic relief" means? What exactly is relieved by the porter's comic speech? What elements or images in the speech provide an extension of, rather than a contrast to, the atmosphere of the preceding scene?

5. The murder of Duncan provokes different thoughts and reactions in Macbeth's guests. After carefully rereading Scene 3, lines 68–128, describe the private thoughts of Banquo and Malcolm.

6. In Scene 4 there are several examples of dramatic irony in which situations are the tragic reverse of what the participants think. What is ironic about Macduff's replying to Ross's question "Those that Macbeth hath slain" (line 23)? What is ironic about Macduff's suspicion of Duncan's two sons, Malcolm and Donalbain?

7. What examples are there throughout Act Two of the effect upon nature of human deeds? In Scene 4 alone, what three strange and unnatural events are described that would instill the superstitious Elizabethan audience with a sense of foreboding?

Act Three

Scene 1

[*Forres. The palace. Enter* Banquo.]

Banquo. Thou hast it now: king, Cawdor, Glamis, all,
    As the weird women promised, and, I fear,
    Thou play'dst most foully for 't; yet it was said
    It should not stand in thy posterity,
    But that myself should be the root and father   5
    Of many kings. If there come truth from them—
    As upon thee, Macbeth, their speeches shine—
    Why, by the verities on thee made good,
    May they not be my oracles as well,
    And set me up in hope? But hush! no more.   10

[*Sennet*° *sounded. Enter* Macbeth, *as king,* Lady Macbeth, *as queen,* Lennox, Ross, Lords, Ladies, *and* Attendants.]

S.D. **Sennet:** trumpet fanfare announcing the approach of an important person.

Macbeth. Here's our chief guest.

Lady Macbeth.   If he had been forgotten,
  It had been as a gap in our great feast,
  And all-thing° unbecoming.

Macbeth. Tonight we hold a solemn supper,° sir,
  And I'll request your presence.

Banquo.   Let your highness   15
  Command upon me; to the which my duties
  Are with a most indissoluble tie
  For ever knit.

Macbeth. Ride you this afternoon?

Banquo. Aye, my good lord.   20

Macbeth. We should have else desired your good advice,
  Which still hath been both grave and prosperous,
  In this day's council; but we'll take tomorrow.
  Is 't far you ride?

Banquo. As far, my lord, as will fill up the time   25
  'Twixt this and supper. Go not my horse the better,
  I must become a borrower of the night
  For a dark hour or twain.

Macbeth.   Fail not our feast.

Banquo. My lord, I will not.

Macbeth. We hear, our bloody cousins are bestowed   30
  In England and in Ireland, not confessing
  Their cruel parricide, filling their hearers
  With strange invention. But of that tomorrow,
  When therewithal we shall have cause of state
  Craving us jointly.° Hie you to horse; adieu,   35
  Till you return at night. Goes Fleance with you?

Banquo. Aye, my good lord. Our time does call upon 's.°

Macbeth. I wish your horses swift and sure of foot;
  And so I do commend you to their backs.
  Farewell.   [*Exit* Banquo.] 40
  Let every man be master of his time
  Till seven at night. To make society
  The sweeter welcome, we will keep ourself
  Till suppertime alone; while° then, God be with you!
                    [*Exeunt all but* Macbeth *and an* Attendant.]
  Sirrah, a word with you: attend those men   45
  Our pleasure?

Attendant. They are, my lord, without the palace gate.

Macbeth. Bring them before us.   [*Exit* Attendant.]
                    To be thus° is nothing;
  But° to be safely thus. — Our fears in Banquo

---

13. **all-thing:** altogether.   14. **solemn supper:** ceremonious feast.   35. **Craving us jointly:** demanding the attention of
both of us.   37. **Our . . . upon 's:** Our business is urgent.   44. **while:** until.   48. **thus:** king.   49. **But:** unless.

Stick deep; and in his royalty of nature°   50
Reigns that which would be feared. 'Tis much he dares;
And to° that dauntless temper of his mind,
He hath a wisdom that doth guide his valor
To act in safety. There is none but he
Whose being I do fear; and, under him,   55
My Genius is rebuked,° as, it is said,
Mark Antony's was by Caesar. He chid the sisters
When first they put the name of king upon me,
And bade them speak to him; then prophetlike
They hailed him father to a line of kings.   60
Upon my head they placed a fruitless crown,
And put a barren scepter in my gripe,°
Thence to be wrenched with an unlineal hand,
No son of mine succeeding. If 't be so,
For Banquo's issue have I filed° my mind;   65
For them the gracious Duncan have I murdered;
Put rancors in the vessel of my peace
Only for them; and mine eternal jewel° — *soul to Devil*
Given to the common enemy of man,°
To make them kings — the seed° of Banquo kings!   70
Rather than so, come, Fate, into the list,
And champion me to the utterance!° Who's there?

[*Reenter* Attendant, *with two* Murderers.]

Now go to the door, and stay there till we call.   [*Exit* Attendant.]
Was it not yesterday we spoke together?
First Murderer. It was, so please your highness.
Macbeth.   Well then, now   75
Have you considered of my speeches? Know
That it was he in the times past which held you
So under fortune,° which you thought had been
Our innocent self. This I made good to you
In our last conference, passed in probation with° you,   80
How you were borne in hand,° how crossed, the instruments,
Who wrought with them, and all things else that might
To half a soul° and to a notion° crazed
Say "Thus did Banquo."
First Murderer.   You made it known to us.

---

50. **royalty of nature:** kingly nature.   52. **And to:** added to.   56. **My . . . rebuked:** My guardian spirit is cowed.   62. **gripe:** grip.   65. **filed:** defiled.   68. **eternal jewel:** immortal soul.   69. **common . . . man:** the Devil.   70. **seed:** descendants.   72. **champion . . . utterance:** fight me to the death.   77–78. **held . . . fortune:** was the cause of your bad fortune.   80. **passed . . . with:** proved to.   81. **borne in hand:** deceived.   83. **half a soul:** halfwit.   **notion:** mind.

Macbeth. I did so, and went further, which is now   85
    Our point of second meeting. Do you find
    Your patience so predominant in your nature
    That you can let this go? Are you so gospeled°
    To pray for this good man and for his issue,
    Whose heavy hand hath bowed you to the grave   90
    And beggered yours for ever?
First Murderer.   We are men, my liege.
Macbeth. Aye, in the catalog ye go for men;
    As hounds and greyhounds, mongrels, spaniels, curs,
    Shoughs,° water rugs,° and demiwolves, are clept°
    All by the name of dogs; the valued file°   95
    Distinguishes the swift, the slow, the subtle,
    The housekeeper, the hunter, every one
    According to the gift which bounteous nature
    Hath in him closed, whereby he does receive
    Particular addition,° from the bill   100
    That writes them all alike; and so of men.
    Now, if you have a station in the file,°
    Not i' the worst rank of manhood, say 't;
    And I will put that business in your bosoms,
    Whose execution takes your enemy off,   105
    Grapples you to the heart and love of us,
    Who wear our health but sickly in his life,
    Which in his death were perfect.°
Second Murderer.   I am one, my liege,
    Whom the vile blows and buffets of the world
    Have so incensed that I am reckless what   110
    I do to spite the world.
First Murderer.   And I another
    So weary with disasters, tugged with fortune,
    That I would set my life on any chance,
    To mend it, or be rid on 't.
Macbeth.   Both of you
    Know Banquo was your enemy,
Both Murderers.   True, my lord.   115
Macbeth. So is he mine; and in such bloody distance,°
    That every minute of his being thrusts
    Against my near'st of life;° and though I could
    With barefaced power sweep him from my sight
    And bid my will avouch° it, yet I must not,   120
    For certain friends that are both his and mine,

---

88. **gospeled:** ready to forgive. 94. **Shoughs** (shŭks): shaggy-haired dogs. **water rugs:** water spaniels. **clept:** called. 95. **valued file:** list of those valued. 100. **addition:** distinction (to set him apart from other dogs). 102. **file:** ranks. 107–108. **Who . . . perfect:** So long as Banquo lives, I am a sick man. 116. **distance:** disagreement. 118. **near'st of life:** inmost being, myself. 120. **avouch:** justify.

Whose loves I may not drop, but wail his fall°
Who I myself struck down; and thence it is,
That I to your assistance do make love,
Masking the business from the common eye   125
For sundry weighty reasons.
Second Murderer.   We shall, my lord,
Perform what you command us.
First Murderer.   Though our lives——
Macbeth. Your spirits shine through you. Within this hour at most
I will advise you where to plant yourselves;
Acquaint you with the perfect spy o' the time,°   130
The moment on 't; for 't must be done tonight,
And something° from the palace; always thought
That I require a clearness;° and with him—
To leave no rubs nor botches in the work—
Fleance his son, that keeps him company,   135
Whose absence is no less material to me
Than is his father's, must embrace the fate
Of that dark hour. Resolve yourselves apart;°
I'll come to you anon.
Both Murderers.   We are resolved, my lord.
Macbeth. I'll call upon you straight; abide within.   [*Exeunt* Murderers.]   140
It is concluded. Banquo, thy soul's flight,
If it find heaven, must find it out tonight.   [*Exit.*]

Scene 2

[*The palace. Enter* Lady Macbeth *and a* Servant.]

Lady Macbeth. Is Banquo gone from court?
Servant. Aye, madam, but returns again tonight.
Lady Macbeth. Say to the king, I would attend his leisure
For a few words.
Servant.   Madam, I will.   [*Exit.*]
Lady Macbeth.   Naught's had, all's spent,
Where our desire is got without content.   5
—'Tis safer to be that which we destroy
— Than by destruction dwell in doubtful joy.

[*Enter* Macbeth.]

How now, my lord! why do you keep alone,

---

122. **wail his fall:** Macbeth must pretend to bewail Banquo's death.   130. **the . . . time:** the exact moment.   132. **something:** some distance.   133. **require a clearness:** must remain above suspicion.   138. **Resolve . . . apart:** Make your own decision.

Of sorriest fancies your companions making,
Using those thoughts which should indeed have died   10
With them they think on? Things without all remedy
Should be without regard; what's done is done.
Macbeth. We have scotched° the snake, not killed it;
    She'll close° and be herself, whilst our poor malice
    Remains in danger of her former tooth.°   15
    But let the frame of things disjoint, both the worlds suffer,°
    Ere we will eat our meal in fear, and sleep
    In the affliction of these terrible dreams
    That shake us nightly. Better be with the dead,
    Whom we, to gain our peace, have sent to peace,   20
    Than on the torture of the mind to lie
    In restless ecstasy.° Duncan is in his grave;
    After life's fitful fever he sleeps well;
    Treason has done his worst; nor steel, nor poison,
    Malice domestic, foreign levy, nothing,   25
    Can touch him further.
Lady Macbeth.   Come on;
    Gentle my lord, sleek o'er your rugged looks;
    Be bright and jovial among your guests tonight.
Macbeth. So shall I, love; and so, I pray, be you.
    Let your remembrance apply to Banquo;
    Present him eminence,° both with eye and tongue;   30
    Unsafe the while, that° we
    Must lave° our honors in these flattering streams,
    And make our faces vizards° to our hearts,
    Disguising what they are.
Lady Macbeth.   You must leave this.   35
Macbeth. O, full of scorpions is my mind, dear wife!
    Thou know'st that Banquo, and his Fleance, lives.
Lady Macbeth. But in them nature's copy 's not eterne.°
Macbeth. There's comfort yet; they are assailable;
    Then be thou jocund; ere the bat hath flown   40
    His cloistered flight, ere to black Hecate's summons
    The shard-borne° beetle with his drowsy hums
    Hath rung night's yawning peal, there shall be done
    A deed of dreadful note.
Lady Macbeth.   What's to be done?
Macbeth. Be innocent of the knowledge, dearest chuck,°   45
    Till thou applaud the deed. Come, seeling° night,

[Handwritten note: He didn't tell Lady M about Banquo's murder]

[Handwritten note: — Hints of murder]

---

13. **scotched**: wounded.   14. **close**: heal.   15. **in . . . tooth**: in as much danger as before.   16. **But . . . suffer**: Let the universe fall to pieces, let both heaven and earth perish.   22. **ecstasy**: madness, mental agony.   31. **Present . . . eminence**: make much of him.   32. **Unsafe . . . that**: we are not safe as long as.   33. **lave**: wash.   34. **vizards** (vĭz'ərdz): masks.   38. **in . . . eterne**: They will not live forever.   42. **shard-borne**: borne aloft on scaly wings.   45. **chuck**: chick.   46. **seeling**: blinding. In falconry the eyelids of a hawk were sealed (sewn shut) in order to train it.

Scarf up the tender eye of pitiful day;
And with thy bloody and invisible hand
Cancel and tear to pieces that great bond°
Which keeps me pale! Light thickens, and the crow   50
Makes wing to the rooky° wood;
Good things of day begin to droop and drowse;
Whiles night's black agents to their preys do rouse.
Thou marvel'st at my words; but hold thee still;
Things bad begun make strong themselves by ill.   55
So, prithee, go with me.

If you start out doing something bad as you go on that character builds

[Exeunt.]

Scene 3

[*A park near the palace. Enter three* Murderers.]

First Murderer. But who did bid thee join with us?
Third Murderer.   Macbeth.
Second Murderer. He needs not our mistrust, since he delivers
    Our offices° and what we have to do
    To the direction just.°
First Murderer.   Then stand with us.
    The west yet glimmers with some streaks of day;   5
    Now spurs the lated traveler apace
    To gain the timely inn; and near approaches
    The subject of our watch.
Third Murderer.   Hark! I hear horses.
Banquo. [*Within*] Give us a light there, ho!
Second Murderer.   Then 'tis he; the rest
    That are within the note of expectation°   10
    Already are i' the court.
First Murderer.   His horses go about.°
Third Murderer. Almost a mile; but he does usually,
    So all men do, from hence to the palace gate
    Make it their walk.
Second Murderer.   A light, a light!

[*Enter* Banquo, *and* Fleance *with a torch.*]

Third Murderer.   'Tis he.
First Murderer. Stand to 't.   15

---

49. **great bond:** that which binds me; that is, Banquo's life.   51. **rooky:** full of rooks, or crows.
  3. **offices:** duties.   4. **direction just:** exact detail.   10. **note of expectation:** list of expected guests.   11. **His . . . about:** His horses have been taken to the stable.

Banquo. It will be rain tonight.

First Murderer.   Let it come down.   [*They set upon* Banquo.]

Banquo. O treachery! Fly, good Fleance, fly, fly, fly!
 Thou mayst revenge. O slave!   [*Dies.* Fleance *escapes.*]

Third Murderer. Who did strike out the light?

First Murderer.   Was 't not the way?

Third Murderer. There's but one down; the son is fled.

Second Murderer.   We have lost   20
 Best half of our affair.

First Murderer. Well, let's away, and say how much is done.   [*Exeunt.*]

Scene 4

[*Hall in the palace. A banquet prepared. Enter* Macbeth, Lady Macbeth, Ross, Lennox,
 Lords, *and* Attendants.]

Macbeth. You know your own degrees;° sit down. At first
 And last the hearty welcome.

Lords.   Thanks to your majesty.

Macbeth. Ourself will mingle with society,
 And play the humble host.
 Our hostess keeps her state,° but in best time   5
 We will require her welcome.

Lady Macbeth. Pronounce it for me, sir, to all our friends;
 For my heart speaks they are welcome.

[First Murderer *appears at the door.*]

Macbeth. See, they encounter thee with their hearts' thanks.
 Both sides are even; here I'll sit i' the midst;   10
 Be large in mirth; anon we'll drink a measure°
 The table round. [*Approaching the door*] There's blood upon thy face.

First Murderer. 'Tis Banquo's then.

Macbeth. 'Tis better thee without than he within.
 Is he dispatched?   15

First Murderer. My lord, his throat is cut; that I did for him.

Macbeth. Thou art the best o' the cutthroats: yet he's good
 That did the like for Fleance. If thou didst it,
 Thou art the nonpareil.°

First Murderer.   Most royal sir,
 Fleance is 'scaped.   20

Macbeth. Then comes my fit again. I had else been perfect,
 Whole as the marble, founded as the rock,
 As broad and general as the casing° air;

---

 1. **degrees:** ranks. At state banquets each guest was seated according to his rank.   5. **keeps . . . state:** sits on a throne apart.   11. **measure:** toast.   19. **nonpareil:** without equal.   23. **casing:** enclosing.

But now I am cabined, cribbed, confined, bound in
To saucy doubts and fears. But Banquo's safe?   25
First Murderer. Aye, my good lord; safe in a ditch he bides,
With twenty trenchèd gashes on his head,
The least a death to nature.°
Macbeth.   Thanks for that;
There the grown serpent lies; the worm° that's fled
Hath nature that in time will venom breed,   30
No teeth for the present. Get thee gone; tomorrow
We'll hear ourselves again.   [*Exit* Murderer.]
Lady Macbeth.   My royal lord,
You do not give the cheer. The feast is sold
That is not often vouched,° while 'tis amaking,
'Tis given with welcome. To feed were best at home;   35
From thence the sauce to meat is ceremony;°
Meeting were bare without it.
Macbeth.   Sweet remembrancer!
Now, good digestion wait on appetite,
And health on both!
Lennox.   May 't please your highness sit.

[*The* Ghost *of* Banquo *enters, and sits in* Macbeth's *place.*]

Macbeth. Here had we now our country's honor roofed,°   40
Were the graced person of our Banquo present;
Who may I rather challenge for unkindness
Than pity for mischance!°
Ross.   His absence, sir,
Lays blame upon his promise. Please 't your highness
To grace us with your royal company.   45
Macbeth. The table's full.
Lennox.   Here is a place reserved, sir.
Macbeth. Where?
Lennox. Here, my good lord. What is 't that moves your highness?
Macbeth. Which of you have done this?
Lords.   What, my good lord?
Macbeth. Thou canst not say I did it; never shake   50
Thy gory locks at me.
Ross. Gentlemen, rise; his highness is not well.
Lady Macbeth. Sit, worthy friends; my lord is often thus,
And hath been from his youth. Pray you, keep seat;

---

28. **nature:** natural life.   29. **worm:** little snake.   33–34. **The feast . . . vouched:** The feast at which guests are not made welcome is a mere bought dinner.   36. **From . . . ceremony:** When one is away from home, politeness or ceremony adds a pleasant flavor to the meal.   40. **our . . . roofed:** all the most honorable men in the country under our roof.   42–43. **Who . . . mischance:** That is, I'd rather believe that he is absent through discourtesy than because of some accident.

The fit is momentary; upon a thought°   55
He will again be well. If much you note him,
You shall offend him and extend his passion.
Feed, and regard him not. [*To* Macbeth] Are you a man?
Macbeth. Aye, and a bold one, that dare look on that
Which might appall the devil.
Lady Macbeth.   O proper stuff!   60
This is the very painting of your fear;
This is the air-drawn dagger which, you said,
Led you to Duncan. O, these flaws° and starts,
Impostors to true fear, would well become
A woman's story at a winter's fire,   65
Authorized° by her grandam. Shame itself!
Why do you make such faces? When all's done,
You look but on a stool.
Macbeth. Prithee, see there! behold! look! lo! how say you?
Why, what care I? If thou canst nod, speak too.   70
If charnel houses° and our graves must send
Those that we bury back, our monuments
Shall be the maws of kites.°   [Ghost *vanishes.*]
Lady Macbeth.   What, quite unmanned in folly?
Macbeth. If I stand here, I saw him.
Lady Macbeth.   Fie, for shame!
Macbeth. Blood hath been shed ere now, i' the olden time,   75
Ere humane statute purged the gentle weal;°
Aye, and since too, murders have been performed
Too terrible for the ear. The time has been,
That, when the brains were out, the man would die,
And there an end; but now they rise again,   80
With twenty mortal murders on their crowns,°
And push us from our stools. This is more strange
Than such a murder is.
Lady Macbeth.   My worthy lord,
Your noble friends do lack you.
Macbeth.   I do forget.
Do not muse at me, my most worthy friends;   85
I have a strange infirmity, which is nothing
To those that know me. Come, love and health to all;
Then I'll sit down. Give me some wine; fill full.
I drink to the general joy o' the whole table,
And to our dear friend Banquo, whom we miss;   90
Would he were here! to all, and him, we thirst,
And all to all.

---

55. **upon a thought:** in a moment.   63. **flaws:** literally, gusts of wind.   66. **Authorized:** vouched for.   71. **charnel houses:** places where human bones, dug up in making a new grave, were stored.   73. **maws of kites:** bellies of birds of prey.   76. **Ere . . . weal:** before humane laws civilized the state.   81. **crowns:** heads.

Lords. Our duties, and the pledge.

[*Reenter* Ghost.]

Macbeth. Avaunt!° and quit my sight! let the earth hide thee!
   Thy bones are marrowless, thy blood is cold;
   Thou hast no speculation° in those eyes   95
   Which thou dost glare with!
Lady Macbeth.   Think of this, good peers,
   But as a thing of custom; 'tis no other;
   Only it spoils the pleasure of the time.
Macbeth. What man dare, I dare.
   Approach thou like the rugged Russian bear,   100
   The armed rhinoceros, or the Hyrcan° tiger;
   Take any shape but that,° and my firm nerves
   Shall never tremble; or be alive again,
   And dare me to the desert° with my sword;
   If trembling I inhabit° then, protest me   105
   The baby of a girl. Hence, horrible shadow!
   Unreal mockery, hence!   [Ghost *vanishes*.]
                Why, so; being gone
   I am a man again. Pray you, sit still.
Lady Macbeth. You have displaced the mirth, broke the good meeting,
   With most admired° disorder.
Macbeth.   Can such things be,   110
   And overcome° us like a summer's cloud,
   Without our special wonder? You make me strange
   Even to the disposition that I owe,°
   When now I think you can behold such sights,
   And keep the natural ruby of your cheeks,   115
   When mine is blanched with fear.
Ross.   What sights, my lord?
Lady Macbeth. I pray you, speak not; he grows worse and worse;
   Question enrages him. At once, good night.
   Stand not upon the order of your going,°
   But go at once.
Lennox.   Good night; and better health   120
   Attend his majesty!
Lady Macbeth.   A kind good night to all!
             [*Exeunt all but* Macbeth *and* Lady Macbeth.]

---

93. **Avaunt** (ə-vônt′): Begone!   95. **speculation:** power of sight.   101. **Hyrcan** (hûr′kən): from Hyracania, an ancient Asian province south of the Caspian Sea.   102. **that:** that is Banquo's shape.   104. **desert:** a place where neither of us could escape.   105. **inhabit:** remain indoors.   110. **admired:** to be wondered at.   111. **overcome:** come over, overshadow.   113. **disposition . . . owe:** my own nature.   119. **Stand . . . going:** Do not wait to leave in order of rank.

Macbeth. It will have blood; they say, <u>blood will have blood.</u>
    Stones have been known to move and trees to speak;
    Augurs° and understood relations° have
    By maggot-pies and choughs and rooks brought forth
    The secret'st man of blood.° What is the night?   125
Lady Macbeth. Almost at odds with morning, which is which.
Macbeth. How say'st thou, that Macduff denies his person
    At our great bidding?
Lady Macbeth.   Did you send to him, sir?
Macbeth. I hear it by the way; but I will send.   130
    There's not a one of them but in his house
    I keep a servant fee'd.° I will tomorrow,
    And betimes I will, to the weird sisters.
    More shall they speak; for now I am bent° to know,
    By the worst means, the worst. For mine own good,   135
    All causes shall give way. I am in blood
    Stepped in so far that, should I wade no more,
    Returning were as tedious as go o'er.
    Strange things I have in head, that will to hand;
    Which must be acted ere they may be scanned.°   140
Lady Macbeth. You lack the season° of all natures, sleep.
Macbeth. Come, we'll to sleep. My strange and self-abuse
    Is the initiate fear° that wants hard use;
    We are yet but young in deed.   *[Exeunt.]*

Scene 5

    [A heath. Thunder. Enter the three Witches, *meeting* Hecate.]

First Witch. Why, how now, Hecate! you look angerly.
Hecate. Have I not reason, beldams° as you are,
    Saucy and overbold? How did you dare
    To trade and traffic with Macbeth
    In riddles and affairs of death;   5
    And I, the mistress of your charms,
    The close contriver° of all harms,
    Was never called to bear my part,
    Or show the glory of our art?
    And, which is worse, all you have done   10
    Hath been but for a wayward son,

---

124. **Augurs:** omens. **understood relations:** the relation between the omen and what it signifies.   126. **man of blood:** murderer.   132. **fee'd:** in my pay as a spy.   134. **bent:** eager.   140. **scanned:** examined: 141. **season:** that which keeps fresh.   143. **initiate fear:** novice's fear; that is, when I have more experience in murder, I shall not be troubled by ghosts.
    Many scholars believe that Scene 5 was not written by Shakespeare. The lines by Hecate in this scene and in Scene 1 of Act Four are not characteristic of Shakespeare's work.   2. **beldams:** hags.   7. **close contriver:** secret inventor.

Spiteful and wrathful, who, as others do,
Loves for his own ends, not for you.
But make amends now; get you gone,
And at the pit of Acheron°   15
Meet me i' the morning; thither he
Will come to know his destiny.
Your vessels and your spells provide,
Your charms and everything beside.
I am for the air; this night I'll spend   20
Unto a dismal and a fatal end;
Great business must be wrought ere noon.
Upon the corner of the moon
There hangs a vaporous drop profound;
I'll catch it ere it come to ground;   25
And that distilled by magic sleights°
Shall raise such artificial sprites°
As by the strength of their illusion
Shall draw him on to his confusion.°
He shall spurn fate, scorn death, and bear   30
His hopes 'bove wisdom, grace, and fear;
And you all know, security°
Is mortals' chiefest enemy. *MacBeth will fall when he feels secure*

[*Music and a song within:* "Come away, come away," *etc.*]

Hark! I am called; my little spirit, see,
Sits in a foggy cloud, and stays for me.   [*Exit.*]   35
First Witch. Come, let's make haste; she'll soon be back again. [*Exeunt.*]

Scene 6

[*Forres. The palace. Enter* Lennox *and another* Lord.]

Lennox. My former speeches have but hit your thoughts,
Which can interpret further;° only, I say,
Things have been strangely borne.° The gracious Duncan
Was pitied of Macbeth; marry, he was dead;
And the right-valiant Banquo walked too late;   5
Whom, you may say, if 't please you, Fleance killed,
For Fleance fled; men must not walk too late.
Who cannot want° the thought how monstrous
It was for Malcolm and for Donalbain

---

15. **Acheron** (ăk'ə-rŏn): hell; in Greek mythology, the river leading to Hades.   26. **sleights:** devices.   27. **artificial
sprites:** spirits created by magic.   29. **confusion:** destruction.   32. **security:** false sense of safety.
  2. **Which . . . further:** from which you can draw your own conclusions.   3. **borne:** managed.   8. **want:** be without.

To kill their gracious father? Damnèd fact! 10
How it did grieve Macbeth! Did he not straight
In pious rage the two delinquents tear,
That were the slaves of drink and thralls° of sleep?
Was not that nobly done? Aye, and wisely too; 15
For 'twould have angered any heart alive
To hear the men deny 't. So that, I say,
He has borne all things well; and I do think
That had he Duncan's sons under his key—
As, an 't please Heaven, he shall not—they should find
What 'twere to kill a father; so should Fleance. 20
But, peace! for from broad° words and 'cause he failed
His presence at the tyrant's feast, I hear
Macduff lives in disgrace. Sir, can you tell
Where he bestows himself?

Lord.　　　　　　　　The son of Duncan, *Since Macbeth has been*
From whom this tyrant holds the due of birth,° 25 *king people are insecure*
Lives in the English court, and is received
Of the most pious Edward with such grace
That the malevolence of fortune nothing
Takes from his high respect.° Thither Macduff
Is gone to pray the holy king, upon his aid 30
To wake Northumberland and warlike Siward;
That by the help of these—with Him above
To ratify the work—we may again
Give to our tables meat, sleep to our nights,
Free from our feasts and banquets bloody knives, 35
Do faithful homage and receive free honors;°
All which we pine for now; and this report
Hath so exasperate the king that he
Prepares for some attempt of war.

Lennox.　　　　　　　Sent he to Macduff?
Lord. He did; and with an absolute "Sir, not I," 40
The cloudy° messenger turns me his back,
And hums, as who should say, "You'll rue the time
That clogs° me with this answer."

Lennox.　　　　　　　And that well might
Advise him to a caution, to hold what distance
His wisdom can provide. Some holy angel 45
His message ere he come, that swift blessing
May soon return to this our suffering country *— Suspicious of Macbeth*
Under a hand accursed!

Lord.　　　　　　I'll send my prayers with him.　　　　*[Exeunt.]*

---

13. **thralls:** slaves.　21. **broad:** too free, unguarded.　25. **From . . . birth:** Malcolm's claim to the throne is withheld by Macbeth.　28-29. **That . . . respect:** In spite of his misfortunes, he is regarded with the utmost respect.　36. **free honors:** honors given to free men.　41. **cloudy:** surly.　43. **clogs:** burdens.

FOR STUDY AND DISCUSSION

1. In the opening speech of Act Three, Banquo muses on the witches' prophecies. Which have come true? Which give Banquo hope for the future? Why has Banquo remained silent when he believes that Macbeth has played "most foully" (line 3)?

2. In the opening conversation of Scene 1 (lines 11–40), there are several examples of dramatic irony. Pick out four separate instances and explain the irony of each.

3. How do Scenes 1 and 2 reveal a moral change in Macbeth? There is also a change in the relationship between Macbeth and his wife. What is the change and where is it most apparent? What does it reveal about Macbeth's moral state?

4. One of the great puzzles of the play is the appearance of the third murderer in Scene 3. Some authorities feel it is a messenger from Macbeth; some feel it is Macbeth himself; some feel it is a person who, either from friendship to Banquo's cause or at the witches' instigation, joins the murderers to assure Fleance's escape. Select one of these theories, or invent one of your own, and be ready to defend it.

5. In the banquet scene (Scene 4), what speeches by Macbeth seem to call forth Banquo's ghost? What is ironic about this timing? How does Lady Macbeth act to save Macbeth?

6. By the time of the banquet scene, Macbeth has taken the two major steps necessary for the achievement of his goal. This action and the simultaneous increase of tension are known technically as the *rising action* of the play. Rising action builds toward a *climax*, the dramatic highpoint, or point of greatest tension in the play. All action after the climax is referred to as the *falling action*, or resolution, of the play. Reread the banquet scene (Scene 4). Why is it the climax, or turning point, of *Macbeth*?

Act Four

Scene 1

[*A cavern. In the middle, a boiling caldron. Thunder. Enter the three* Witches.]

First Witch. Thrice the brinded° cat hath mewed.
Second Witch. Thrice and once the hedge pig whined.
Third Witch. Harpier° cries, "'Tis time, 'tis time."
First Witch. Round about the caldron go;
    In the poisoned entrails throw.   5
    Toad, that under cold stone
    Days and nights has thirty-one
    Sweltered venom sleeping got,
    Boil thou first i' the charmèd pot.
All. Double, double toil and trouble;   10
    Fire burn, and caldron bubble.
Second Witch. Fillet of a fenny snake,
    In the caldron boil and bake;
    Eye of newt and toe of frog,
    Wool of bat and tongue of dog,   15
    Adder's fork° and blindworm's° sting,
    Lizard's leg and howlet's wing,
    For a charm of powerful trouble,
    Like a hell broth boil and bubble.

---

1. **brinded:** striped.　3. **Harpier:** one of the spirits attending the witches.　16. **fork:** forked tongue.　**blindworm:** small, harmless, limbless lizard.

All. Double, double toil and trouble;   20
    Fire burn, and caldron bubble.
Third Witch. Scale of dragon, tooth of wolf,
    Witches' mummy, maw and gulf°
    Of the ravined° salt-sea shark,
    Root of hemlock digged i' the dark,   25
    Slivered in the moon's eclipse,
    Nose of Turk and Tartar's lips,
    Finger of birth-strangled babe
    Ditch-delivered by a drab,
    Make the gruel thick and slab;°   30
    Add thereto a tiger's chaudron,°
    For the ingredients of our caldron.
All. Double, double toil and trouble;
    Fire burn, and caldron bubble.
Second Witch. Cool it with a baboon's blood,   35
    Then the charm is firm and good.

[Enter Hecate, *to the other three* Witches.]

Hecate. O, well done! I commend your pains;
    And every one shall share i' the gains;
    And now about the caldron sing,
    Like elves and fairies in a ring,   40
    Enchanting all that you put in.

[Music and a song: "Black spirits," *etc.* Hecate *retires.*]

Second Witch. By the pricking of my thumbs,
    Something wicked this way comes.
        Open, locks,
        Whoever knocks!   45

[Enter Macbeth.]

Macbeth. How now, you secret, black, and midnight hags!
    What is 't you do?
All.   A deed without a name.
Macbeth. I conjure you, by that which you profess,°
    Howe'er you come to know it, answer me;
    Though you untie the winds and let them fight
    Against the churches; though the yesty° waves   50
    Confound and swallow navigation up;

---

23. **maw and gulf:** belly and gullet. 24. **ravined:** ravenous. 30. **slab:** like thick mud. 31. **chaudron:** entrails. 48. **that**
. . . **profess:** that is, witchcraft. 51. **yesty:** foaming.

Though bladed corn be lodged° and trees blown down;
Though castles topple on their warders' heads;
Though palaces and pyramids do slope   55
Their heads to their foundations; though the treasure
Of nature's germens° tumble all together,
Even till destruction sicken; answer me
To what I ask you.

First Witch.   Speak.

Second Witch.   Demand.

Third Witch.   We'll answer.

First Witch. Say, if thou 'dst rather hear it from our mouths,   60
Or from our masters'?

Macbeth.   Call 'em; let me see 'em.

---

53. **lodged:** beaten down.   57. **germens:** seeds.

Scene from *Macbeth* by George Cathermole, showing the apparition of
eight kings in Act Four.
Folger Shakespeare Library

First Witch. Pour in sow's blood, that hath eaten
    Her nine farrow;° grease that's sweaten
    From the murderer's gibbet° throw
    Into the flame.
All.   Come, high or low;   65
    Thyself and office° deftly show!

          [*Thunder.* First Apparition: *an armed* Head.°]

Macbeth. Tell me, thou unknown power——
First Witch.   He knows thy thought;
    Hear his speech, but say thou naught.
First Apparition. Macbeth! Macbeth! Macbeth! beware Macduff;
    Beware the thane of Fife. Dismiss me. Enough.   [*Descends.*] 70
Macbeth. Whate'er thou art, for thy good caution, thanks;
    Thou hast harped° my fear aright: but one word more——
First Witch. He will not be commanded: here's another,
    More potent than the first.

          [*Thunder.* Second Apparition: *a bloody* Child.°]

Second Apparition. Macbeth! Macbeth! Macbeth!   75
Macbeth. Had I three ears, I 'ld hear thee.
Second Apparition. Be bloody, bold, and resolute; laugh to scorn
    The power of man, for none of woman born
    Shall harm Macbeth.   [*Descends.*]
Macbeth. Then live, Macduff; what need I fear of thee?   80
    But yet I'll make assurance double sure,
    And take a bond of fate.° Thou shalt not live;
    That I may tell pale-hearted fear it lies,
    And sleep in spite of thunder.

    [*Thunder.* Third Apparition: *a* Child *crowned,*° *with a tree in his hand.*]

                    What is this
    That rises like the issue of a king,   85
    And wears upon his baby brow the round
    And top of sovereignty?°
All.   Listen, but speak not to 't.
Third Apparition. Be lion-mettled, proud; and take no care
    Who chafes, who frets, or where conspirers are.

---

63. **farrow:** young pigs.   64. **gibbet:** gallows on which the bodies of criminals were left hanging as a warning.   66. **office:** function. S.D. **an armed Head:** a symbol of Macduff. 72. **harped:** hit upon. S.D. **a bloody Child:** Macduff at birth. 82. **take . . . fate:** To be sure the prophecy is fulfilled, he will kill Macduff. S.D. **a Child crowned:** symbol of Malcolm. 87. **top of sovereignty:** crown.

mirror w/ 8 kings

Macbeth shall never vanquished be until
Great Birnam wood to high Dunsinane hill
Shall come against him.   *Macbeth safe until*
                                                               the forest walks up the 90
                                                               hill
                                                        [*Descends.*]
Macbeth.   That will never be.
Who can impress° the forest, bid the tree
Unfix his earth-bound root? Sweet bodements!° good!
Rebellion's head, rise never till the wood   95
Of Birnam rise, and our high-placed Macbeth
Shall live the lease of nature,° pay his breath
To time and mortal custom. Yet my heart
Throbs to know one thing: tell me, if your art
Can tell so much: shall Banquo's issue ever   100
Reign in this kingdom?
All.   Seek to know no more.
Macbeth. I will be satisfied; deny me this,
And an eternal curse fall on you! Let me know.
Why sinks that caldron? and what noise is this?   [*Hautboys.*]
First Witch. Show!   105
Second Witch. Show!
Third Witch. Show!
All. Show his eyes, and grieve his heart;
Come like shadows, so depart!

[*A show° of eight* Kings, *the last with a glass° in his hand;* Banquo's Ghost *following.*]

Macbeth. Thou art too like the spirit of Banquo; down!   110
Thy crown doth sear mine eyeballs. And thy hair,
Thou other gold-bound brow, is like the first.
A third is like the former. Filthy hags!
Why do you show me this? A fourth! Start, eyes!
What, will the line stretch out to the crack of doom?   115
Another yet! A seventh! I'll see no more.
And yet the eighth appears, who bears a glass
Which shows me many more; and some I see
That twofold balls and treble scepters° carry.
Horrible sight! Now, I see, 'tis true;   120
For the blood-boltered° Banquo smiles upon me,
And points at them for his.° [*Apparitions vanish.*] What, is this so?
First Witch. Aye, sir, all this is so; but why
Stands Macbeth thus amazedly?

---

93. **impress:** force into service.   94. **bodements:** prophecies.   97. **lease of nature:** his natural span of life.   S.D. **show:** a
dumb show—figures passing silently across the back of the stage.   **glass:** mirror.   119. **twofold . . . scepters:** insignia of
the kingdoms of England, Scotland, and Ireland, united in 1603 when Scotland's James VI (descended from Banquo)
became James I of England.   121. **blood-boltered:** his hair matted with blood.   122. **his:** that is, his descendants.

Come, sisters, cheer we up his sprites,°   125
And show the best of our delights.
I'll charm the air to give a sound,
While you perform your antic round;°
That this great king may kindly say,
Our duties did his welcome pay.   130

[*Music. The* Witches *dance, and then vanish with* Hecate.]

Macbeth. Where are they? Gone? Let this pernicious hour
Stand aye accursèd in the calendar!
Come in, without there!

[*Enter* Lennox.]

Lennox.   What's your grace's will?
Macbeth. Saw you the weird sisters?
Lennox.   No, my lord.
Macbeth. Came they not by you?
Lennox.   No indeed, my lord.   135
Macbeth. Infected be the air whereon they ride;
And damned all those that trust them! I did hear
The galloping of horse: who was 't came by?
Lennox. 'Tis two or three, my lord, that bring you word
Macduff is fled to England.
Macbeth.   Fled to England!   140
Lennox. Aye, my good lord.
Macbeth. Time, thou anticipatest my dread exploits;
The flighty purpose never is o'ertook
Unless the deed go with it.° From this moment   *do what he thinks*
The very firstlings of my heart shall be
The firstlings of my hand. And even now,   145
To crown my thoughts with acts, be it thought and done.
The castle of Macduff I will surprise;
Seize upon Fife; give to the edge o' the sword
His wife, and babes, and all unfortunate souls
That trace him in his line. No boasting like a fool;   150
This deed I'll do before this purpose cool.
But no more sights!—Where are these gentlemen?
Come, bring me where they are.

                    [*Exeunt.*]

---

125. **sprites:** spirits.   128. **antic round:** grotesque dance.   143–144. **The . . . it:** An impulsive plan is never fulfilled unless carried out at once.

Scene 2

[*Fife.* Macduff's *castle. Enter* Lady Macduff, *her* Son, *and* Ross.]

Lady Macduff. What had he done, to make him fly the land?
Ross. You must have patience, madam.
Lady Macduff. He had none;
    His flight was madness. When our actions do not,
    Our fears do make us traitors.
Ross. You know not
    Whether it was his wisdom or his fear.   5
Lady Macduff. Wisdom! to leave his wife, to leave his babes,
    His mansion and his titles° in a place
    From whence himself does fly? He loves us not;
    He wants the natural touch; for the poor wren,
    The most diminutive of birds, will fight,   10
    Her young ones in her nest, against the owl.
    All is the fear and nothing is the love;
    As little is the wisdom, where the flight
    So runs against all reason.
Ross. My dearest coz,°
    I pray you, school° yourself; but for your husband,   15
    He is noble, wise, judicious, and best knows
    The fits o' the season.° I dare not speak much further;
    But cruel are the times, when we are traitors
    And do not know ourselves, when we hold rumor
    From what we fear, yet know not what we fear,   20
    But float upon a wild and violent sea
    Each way and move.° I take my leave of you;
    Shall not be long but I'll be here again.
    Things at the worst will cease, or else climb upward
    To what they were before. [*To the boy*] My pretty cousin,   25
    Blessing upon you!
Lady Macduff. Fathered he is, and yet he's fatherless.
Ross. I am so much a fool, should I stay longer,
    It would be my disgrace and your discomfort.
    I take my leave at once.   [*Exit.*]
Lady Macduff. Sirrah, your father's dead;   30
    And what will you do now? How will you live?
Son. As birds do, mother.
Lady Macduff. What, with worms and flies?
Son. With what I get, I mean; and so do they.

---

7. **titles:** possessions.   14. **coz:** cousin.   15. **school:** discipline.   17. **fits . . . season:** disorders of the time.   22. **Each . . . move:** tossed this way and that, as a ship in a tempest.

Lady Macduff. Poor bird! thou 'ldst never fear the net nor lime,°
   The pitfall nor the gin.° 35
Son. Why should I, mother? Poor° birds they are not set for.
   My father is not dead, for all your saying.
Lady Macduff. Yes, he is dead. How wilt thou do for a father?
Son. Nay, how will you do for a husband?
Lady Macduff. Why, I can buy me twenty at any market. 40
Son. Then you'll buy 'em to sell again.
Lady Macduff. Thou speak'st with all thy wit; and yet, i' faith,
   With wit enough for thee.
Son. Was my father a traitor, mother?
Lady Macduff. Aye, that he was. 45
Son. What is a traitor?
Lady Macduff. Why, one that swears and lies.
Son. And be all traitors that do so?
Lady Macduff. Every one that does so is a traitor, and must be hanged.
Son. And must they all be hanged that swear and lie? 50
Lady Macduff. Every one.
Son. Who must hang them?
Lady Macduff. Why, the honest men.
Son. Then the liars and swearers are fools, for there are liars and swearers enow to beat the
   honest men and hang up them. 55
Lady Macduff. Now, God help thee, poor monkey! But how wilt thou do for a father?
Son. If he were dead, you 'ld weep for him; if you would not, it were a good sign that I
   should quickly have a new father.
Lady Macduff. Poor prattler, how thou talk'st!

[*Enter a* Messenger.]

Messenger. Bless you, fair dame! I am not to you known, 60
   Though in your state of honor I am perfect.°
   I doubt° some danger does approach you nearly.
   If you will take a homely° man's advice,
   Be not found here; hence, with your little ones.
   To fright you thus, methinks, I am too savage; 65
   To do worse to you were fell° cruelty,
   Which is too nigh your person. Heaven preserve you!
   I dare abide no longer. [*Exit.*]
Lady Macduff.   Whither should I fly?
   I have done no harm. But I remember now
   I am in this earthly world; where to do harm 70
   Is often laudable, to do good sometime
   Accounted dangerous folly. Why then, alas,

---

34. **lime:** birdlime, a sticky substance to trap small birds. 35. **gin:** trap. 36. **Poor:** worthless. 61. **in ... perfect:** I well
know you to be an honorable person. 62. **doubt:** suspect. 63. **homely:** simple. 66. **fell:** fierce.

Do I put up that womanly defense,
To say I have done no harm?

[*Enter* Murderers.]

                What are these faces?
First Murderer. Where is your husband?   75
Lady Macduff. I hope, in no place so unsanctified
   Where such as thou mayst find him.
First Murderer.   He's a traitor.
Son. Thou liest, thou shag-eared° villain!
First Murderer.   What, you egg!   [*Stabbing him.*]
   Young fry of treachery!
Son.   He has killed me, mother:
   Run away, I pray you!   [*Dies.*]   80

[*Exit* Lady Macduff, *crying "Murder!" Exeunt* Murderers, *following her.*]

Scene 3

[*England. Before the* King's *palace. Enter* Malcolm *and* Macduff.]

Malcolm. Let us seek out some desolate shade, and there
   Weep our sad bosoms empty.
Macduff.   Let us rather
   Hold fast the mortal° sword, and like good men
   Bestride our downfall'n birthdom.° Each new morn
   New widows howl, new orphans cry, new sorrows   5
   Strike heaven on the face, that it resounds
   As if it felt with Scotland and yelled out
   Like syllable of dolor.°
Malcolm.   What I believe, I'll wail,
   What know, believe, and what I can redress,
   As I shall find the time to friend,° I will.   10
   What you have spoke, it may be so perchance.
   This tyrant, whose sole° name blisters our tongues,
   Was once thought honest; you have loved him well;
   He hath not touched you yet. I am young; but something
   You may deserve of him through me, the wisdom   15
   To offer up a weak poor innocent lamb
   To appease an angry god.
Macduff. I am not treacherous.
Malcolm.   But Macbeth is.
   A good and virtuous nature may recoil

---

78. **shag-eared:** hairy-eared.
  3. **mortal:** deadly.   4. **birthdom:** native land.   8. **Like . . . dolor:** an anguished echo.   10. **to friend:** to be a friend.   12.
sole: very.

In an imperial charge.° But I shall crave your pardon; 20
That which you are my thoughts cannot transpose.°
Angels are bright still, thou the brightest° fell.
Though all things foul would wear the brows of grace,
Yet grace must still look so.°

Macduff.   I have lost my hopes.

Malcolm. Perchance even there where I did find my doubts. 25
Why in that rawness° left you wife and child,
Those precious motives, those strong knots of love,
Without leave-taking? I pray you,
Let not my jealousies° be your dishonors,
But mine own safeties.° You may be rightly just, 30
Whatever I shall think.

Macduff.   Bleed, bleed, poor country!
Great tyranny! lay thou thy basis sure,
For goodness dare not check thee; wear thou thy wrongs;
The title is affeered!° Fare thee well, lord;
I would not be the villain that thou think'st 35
For the whole space that's in the tyrant's grasp,
And the rich East to boot.

Malcolm.   Be not offended;
I speak not as in absolute fear of you.
I think our country sinks beneath the yoke;
It weeps, it bleeds; and each new day a gash 40
Is added to her wounds. I think withal
There would be hands uplifted in my right;
And here from gracious England have I offer
Of goodly thousands. But, for all this,
When I shall tread upon the tyrant's head, 45
Or wear it on my sword, yet my poor country
Shall have more vices than it had before,
More suffer and more sundry ways than ever,
By him that shall succeed.

Macduff.   What should he be?

Malcolm. It is myself I mean; in whom I know 50
All the particulars of vice so grafted
That, when they shall be opened, black Macbeth
Will seem as pure as snow, and the poor state
Esteem him as a lamb, being compared
With my confineless harms.

19–20. **recoil . . . charge:** commit a wicked deed at a king's command.   21. **transpose:** change.   22. **brightest:** Lucifer, the brightest angel.   24. **still look so:** still appear as goodness. Malcolm can't tell yet whether Macduff is to be trusted.   26. **rawness:** unprotected state.   29. **jealousies:** suspicions.   30. **safeties:** protection.   34. **affeered:** confirmed; that is, since goodness dares not oppose tyranny, tyranny's title or right to power is confirmed.

Macduff.   Not in the legions   55
Of horrid hell can come a devil more damned
In evils to top Macbeth.
Malcolm.   I grant him bloody,
Luxurious,° avaricious, false, deceitful,
Sudden, malicious, smacking of every sin
That has a name; but there's no bottom, none,   60
In my voluptuousness. Your wives, your daughters,
Your matrons and your maids, could not fill up
The cistern of my lust, and my desire
All continent impediments° would o'erbear
That did oppose my will. Better Macbeth   65
Than such an one to reign.
Macduff.   Boundless intemperance
In nature is a tyranny; it hath been
The untimely emptying of the happy throne
And fall of many kings. But fear not yet
To take upon you what is yours. You may   70
Convey your pleasures in a spacious plenty,°
And yet seem cold,° the time you may so hoodwink.
We have willing dames enough; there cannot be
That vulture in you, to devour so many
As will to greatness dedicate themselves,   75
Finding it so inclined.
Malcolm.   With this there grows
In my most ill-composed affection such
A staunchless° avarice that, were I king,
I should cut off the nobles for their lands,
Desire his jewels and this other's house;   80
And my more-having would be as a sauce
To make me hunger more, that I should forge
Quarrels unjust against the good and loyal,
Destroying them for wealth.
Macduff.   This avarice
Sticks deeper, grows with more pernicious root   85
Than summer-seeming° lust, and it hath been
The sword of° our slain kings. Yet do not fear;
Scotland hath foisons° to fill up your will,
Of your mere own.° All these are portable,°
With other graces weighed.   90
Malcolm. But I have none. The king-becoming graces,
As justice, verity, temperance, stableness,

---

58. **Luxurious:** lustful.   64. **continent impediments:** restraints.   71. **Convey . . . plenty:** find plenty of room in which to indulge your pleasures secretly.   72. **cold:** chaste.   78. **staunchless:** insatiable.   86. **summer-seeming:** fleeting, that which lasts like summer only for a season.   87. **The sword of:** that which has killed.   88. **foisons:** plenty.   89. **mere own:** own property.   **portable:** endurable.

Bounty, perseverance, mercy, lowliness,
Devotion, patience, courage, fortitude,
I have no relish of them, but abound
In the division of each several crime,
Acting it many ways. Nay, had I power, I should
Pour the sweet milk of concord into hell,
Uproar the universal peace, confound
All unity on earth.

Macduff.   O Scotland, Scotland!

Malcolm. If such a one be fit to govern, speak.
I am as I have spoken.

Macduff.   Fit to govern!
No, not to live. O nation miserable
With an untitled° tyrant bloody-sceptered,
When shalt thou see thy wholesome days again,
Since that the truest issue of thy throne°
By his own interdiction° stands accursed,
And does blaspheme his breed? Thy royal father
Was a most sainted king; the queen that bore thee,
Oftener upon her knees than on her feet,
Died every day she lived.° Fare thee well!
These evils thou repeat'st upon thyself
Have banished me from Scotland. O my breast,
Thy hope ends here!

Malcolm.   Macduff, this noble passion,
Child of integrity, hath from my soul
Wiped the black scruples, reconciled my thoughts
To thy good truth and honor. Devilish Macbeth
By many of these trains° hath sought to win me
Into his power, and modest wisdom plucks me
From overcredulous haste; but God above
Deal between thee and me! for even now
I put myself to thy direction, and
Unspeak mine own detraction,° here abjure
The taints and blames I laid upon myself,
For strangers to my nature. I am yet
Unknown to woman, never was forsworn,°
Scarcely have coveted what was mine own,
At no time broke my faith, would not betray
The devil to his fellow, and delight
No less in truth than life; my first false speaking
Was this upon myself. What I am truly,

_95_

_100_

_105_

_110_

_115_

_120_

_125_

_130_

---

104. **untitled:** having no right to the throne.   106. **truest . . . throne:** child of the true king.   107. **interdiction:** exclusion.   111. **Died . . . lived:** lived always in a state of grace, prepared for death.   118. **trains:** enticements.   123. **detraction:** slander.   126. **was forsworn:** broke my oath.

Is thine and my poor country's to command;
Whither indeed, before thy here-approach,
Old Siward,° with ten thousand warlike men,
Already at a point,° was setting forth.   135
Now we'll together; and the chance of goodness
Be like our warranted quarrel!° Why are you silent?
Macduff. Such welcome and unwelcome things at once
'Tis hard to reconcile.

[*Enter a* Doctor.]

Malcolm. Well; more anon.—Comes the king forth, I pray you?   140
Doctor. Aye, sir; there are a crew of wretched souls
That stay his cure;° their malady convinces
The great assay of art;° but at his touch—
Such sanctity hath Heaven given his hand—
They presently amend.
Malcolm.   I thank you, Doctor.   [*Exit* Doctor.] 145
Macduff. What's the disease he means?
Malcolm.   'Tis called the evil;°
A most miraculous work in this good king;
Which often, since my here-remain in England,
I have seen him do. How he solicits Heaven,
Himself best knows; but strangely visited people,   150
All swoln° and ulcerous, pitiful to the eye,
The mere° despair of surgery, he cures,
Hanging a golden stamp° about their necks,
Put on with holy prayers; and 'tis spoken,
To the succeeding royalty he leaves   155
The healing benediction. With this strange virtue,
He hath a heavenly gift of prophecy,
And sundry blessings hang about his throne,
That speak him full of grace.

"King" has power of God; whereas MacBeth turns people bad

[*Enter* Ross.]

Macduff.   See, who comes here?
Malcolm. My countryman; but yet I know him not.   160
Macduff. My ever-gentle° cousin, welcome hither.

---

134. **Siward** (Sē'wärd).   135. **at a point**: prepared for action.   136–137. **the chance . . . quarrel:** May our chance of success be as good as the outcome of our argument.   142. **stay his cure**: wait for him to heal them.   142–143. **convinces . . . art:** defeats the best efforts of medical skill.   146. **evil:** scrofula (skrŏf'yə-lə), a skin disease. Edward the Confessor reputedly healed sufferers by his saintly touch. The reference is made here as a compliment to James I, who, though at first reluctant to continue the practice of touching sufferers, finally yielded to the urgings of his English ministers.   151. **swoln:** swollen.   152. **mere:** utter.   153. **stamp:** medal.   161. **gentle:** noble.

Malcolm. I know him now. Good God, betimes° remove
    The means° that makes us strangers!
Ross.   Sir, amen.
Macduff. Stands Scotland where it did?
Ross.   Alas, poor country!
    Almost afraid to know itself. It cannot   165
    Be called our mother, but our grave; where nothing,
    But who knows nothing, is once seen to smile;
    Where sighs and groans and shrieks that rend the air
    Are made, not marked; where violent sorrow seems
    A modern ecstasy.° The dead man's knell   170
    Is there scarce asked for who;° and good men's lives
    Expire before the flowers in their caps,
    Dying or ere they sicken.
Macduff.   O, relation°
    Too nice,° and yet too true!
Malcolm.   What's the newest grief?
Ross. That of an hour's age doth hiss the speaker;°   175
    Each minute teems° a new one.
Macduff.   How does my wife?
Ross. Why, well.
Macduff.   And all my children?
Ross.   Well too.
Macduff. The tyrant has not battered at their peace?
Ross. No; they were well at peace when I did leave 'em.
Macduff. Be not a niggard of your speech; how goes 't?   180
Ross. When I came hither to transport the tidings,
    Which I have heavily borne, there ran a rumor
    Of many worthy fellows that were out;°
    Which was to my belief witnessed° the rather,
    For that I saw the tyrant's power afoot.   185
    Now is the time of help; your eye in Scotland
    Would create soldiers, make our women fight,
    To doff° their dire distresses.
Malcolm.   Be 't their comfort
    We are coming thither. Gracious England hath
    Lent us good Siward and ten thousand men;   190
    An older and a better soldier none
    That Christendom gives out.
Ross.   Would I could answer
    This comfort with the like! But I have words

---

162. **betimes:** soon. 163. **means:** that is, Malcolm's exile from Scotland. 170. **modern ecstasy:** a slight mental disturbance. 170–171. **The dead . . . who:** People can no longer keep track of Macbeth's victims. 173. **relation:** account. 174. **nice:** exact. 175. **That . . . speaker:** There are so many sorrows that a report only an hour old is hissed as stale news. 176. **teems:** gives birth to. 183. **out:** in rebellion. 184. **witnessed:** confirmed. 188. **doff:** put off.

That would be howled out in the desert air,
Where hearing should not latch° them.

Macduff.   What concern they?   195
The general cause? or is it a fee grief°
Due to some single breast?

Ross.   No mind that's honest
But in it shares some woe; though the main part
Pertains to you alone.

Macduff.   If it be mine,
Keep it not from me—quickly let me have it.   200

Ross. Let not your ears despise my tongue for ever,
Which shall possess them with the heaviest sound
That ever yet they heard.

Macduff.   Hum! I guess at it.

Ross. Your castle is surprised; your wife and babes
Savagely slaughtered: to relate the manner,   205
Were, on the quarry° of these murdered deer,
To add the death of you.

Malcolm.   Merciful Heaven!
What, man! ne'er pull your hat upon your brows;
Give sorrow words. The grief that does not speak
Whispers the o'erfraught° heart and bids it break.   210

Macduff. My children too?

Ross.   Wife, children, servants, all
That could be found.

Macduff.   And I must be from thence!
My wife killed too?

Ross.   I have said.

Malcolm.   Be comforted.
Let's make us medicines of our great revenge,
To cure this deadly grief.   215

Macduff. He has no children. All my pretty ones?
Did you say all? O hell kite! All?
What, all my pretty chickens and their dam
At one fell swoop?

Malcolm. Dispute it° like a man.

Macduff.   I shall do so;   220
But I must also feel it as a man.
I cannot but remember such things were,
That were most precious to me. Did Heaven look on,
And would not take their part? Sinful Macduff,
They were all struck for thee! Naught° that I am,   225
Not for their own demerits, but for mine,
Fell slaughter on their souls. Heaven rest them now!

---

195. **latch:** catch.   196. **fee grief:** a grief belonging to only one person.   206. **quarry:** heap of game slain in a hunt.   210. **o'erfraught:** overburdened.   220. **Dispute it:** Resist your grief.   225. **Naught:** worthless.

Malcolm. Be this the whetstone of your sword; let grief
    Convert to anger; blunt not the heart, enrage it.
Macduff. O, I could play the woman with mine eyes 230
    And braggart with my tongue! But, gentle heavens,
    Cut short all intermission; front to front°
    Bring thou this fiend of Scotland and myself;
    Within my sword's length set him; if he 'scape,
    Heaven forgive him too!
Malcolm.   This tune goes manly. 235
    Come, go we to the king; our power is ready;
    Our lack is nothing but our leave.° Macbeth
    Is ripe for shaking, and the powers above
    Put on their instruments.° Receive what cheer you may:
    The night is long that never finds the day.   [*Exeunt.*] 240

---

232. **front to front:** face to face.   237. **leave:** permission to go.   239. **Put . . . instruments:** encourage us as their agents.

FOR STUDY AND DISCUSSION

1. Hecate and the witches call up four separate apparitions for Macbeth. What are they? Why is Macbeth oblivious to the hidden meanings in the witches' prophecies? What occurrence in this scene deeply disturbs him? Why does the last king carry a looking glass? *more to come*

2. Why does Macbeth decide to murder Macduff's family? How does this decision differ from his decisions to murder Duncan and Banquo? *had good reason* What does this indicate about the development of Macbeth's character? *less motivation - no remorse*

3. Reread the conversation in Scene 2 between Lady Macduff and her son. What is Lady Macduff *thinks MacDuff is a traitor*

clever-fathe
like? What is her son like? How does this lively, intimate exchange affect our response to the brutal killing with which this scene ends?

4. In Scene 3, how does Malcolm describe himself to Macduff? Why does he misrepresent his character to Macduff? What aspects of his character here suggest that he will be a strong leader of the Scottish patriot forces against Macbeth?

5. Shakespeare's handling of the intensely emotional scene when Ross tells Macduff of the *suspense* murder of his wife and children is particularly masterful. How does Ross's behavior here build up the intensity of the moment? What does Malcolm say to try to help Macduff control his grief and redirect his emotions? *take it out on MacB*

doesn't come rite out w/ bad news

Resist grief like a man

Act Five

Scene 1

[*Dunsinane. Anteroom in the castle. Enter a* Doctor of Physic *and a* Waiting-Gentlewoman.]

Doctor. I have two nights watched with you, but can perceive no truth in your report. When was it she last walked?

Gentlewoman. Since his majesty went into the field,° I have seen her rise from her bed, throw her nightgown upon her, unlock her closet, take forth paper, fold it, write upon 't, read it, afterward seal it, and again return to bed; yet all this while in a most fast sleep. 5

Doctor. A great perturbation in nature, to receive at once the benefit of sleep, and do the effects of watching! In this slumbery agitation, besides her walking and other actual performances, what, at any time, have you heard her say?

Gentlewoman. That, sir, which I will not report after her. 10

Doctor. You may to me; and 'tis most meet you should.

Gentlewoman. Neither to you nor any one, having no witness to confirm my speech.

[*Enter* Lady Macbeth, *with a taper.*]

Lo you, here she comes! This is her very guise;° and, upon my life, fast asleep. Observe her; stand close.°

Doctor. How came she by that light? 15

Gentlewoman. Why, it stood by her; she has light by her continually; 'tis her command.

Doctor. You see, her eyes are open.

Gentlewoman. Aye, but their sense is shut.

Doctor. What is it she does now? Look, how she rubs her hands.

Gentlewoman. It is an accustomed action with her, to seem thus washing her hands. I have 20 known her continue in this a quarter of an hour.

Lady Macbeth. Yet here's a spot.

Doctor. Hark! She speaks. I will set down what comes from her, to satisfy my remembrance the more strongly.

Lady Macbeth. Out, damned spot! out, I say! — One: two: why, then 'tis time to do 't. — Hell 25 is murky! — Fie, my lord, fie! a soldier, and afeard? What need we fear who knows it, when none can call our power to account? — Yet who would have thought the old man to have had so much blood in him?

Doctor. Do you mark that?

Lady Macbeth. The thane of Fife had a wife; where is she now? — What, will these hands 30 ne'er be clean? — No more o' that, my lord, no more o' that; you mar all with this starting.

Doctor. Go to, go to; you have known what you should not.

---

3. **into the field:** out with the army.   13. **guise:** custom.   14. **close:** hidden.

Gentlewoman. She has spoke what she should not, I am sure of that; Heaven knows what she has known. 35

Lady Macbeth. Here's the smell of the blood still; all the perfumes of Arabia will not sweeten this little hand. Oh, oh, oh!

Doctor. What a sigh is there! The heart is sorely charged.°

Gentlewoman. I would not have such a heart in my bosom for the dignity of the whole body. 40

Doctor. Well, well, well——

Gentlewoman. Pray God it be, sir.

Doctor. This disease is beyond my practice; yet I have known those which have walked in their sleep who have died holily in their beds.

Lady Macbeth. Wash your hands, put on your nightgown; look not so pale. — I tell you yet 45 again, Banquo's buried; he cannot come out on 's grave.

Doctor. Even so?

Lady Macbeth. To bed, to bed! There's knocking at the gate. Come, come, come, come, give me your hand. What's done cannot be undone. — To bed, to bed, to bed! [*Exit.*]

Doctor. Will she go now to bed? 50

Sleepwalking - tells secrets about killings

Gentlewoman. Directly.

Doctor. Foul whisperings are abroad; unnatural deeds
Do breed unnatural troubles; infected minds
To their deaf pillows will discharge their secrets.
More needs she the divine than the physician. 55
God, God forgive us all! Look after her;
Remove from her the means of all annoyance,°
And still keep eyes upon her. So, good night;
My mind she has mated,° and amazed my sight.
I think, but dare not speak.

Gentlewoman.   Good night, good doctor.   [*Exeunt.*] 60

Scene 2

[*The country near Dunsinane. Drum and colors.° Enter* Menteith,° Caithness,° Angus, Lennox, *and* Soldiers.]

Menteith. The English power is near, led on by Malcolm,
His uncle Siward and the good Macduff.
Revenges burn in them; for their dear causes
Would to the bleeding and the grim alarm°
Excite the mortified° man. 5

Revenge his families death

Angus.   Near Birnam wood
Shall we well meet them; that way are they coming.

Caithness. Who knows if Donalbain be with his brother?

---

38. **charged:** burdened; oppressed with care.   57. **annoyance:** harm.   59. **mated:** confused.
  S.D. **Drum and colors:** a drummer and a soldier with a flag.   **Menteith** (mĕn-tēth′).   **Caithness** (kāth′nəs).   4. **alarm:** call to arms.   5. **mortified:** half dead.

Lennox. For certain, sir, he is not; I have a file
    Of all the gentry. There is Siward's son,
    And many unrough youths that even now   10
    Protest their first of manhood.°
Menteith.   What does the tyrant?
Caithness. Great Dunsinane he strongly fortifies.
    Some say he's mad; others that lesser hate him
    Do call it valiant fury; but, for certain,
    He cannot buckle his distempered cause   15
    Within the belt of rule.°
Angus.   Now does he feel
    His secret murders sticking on his hands;
    Now minutely° revolts upbraid his faith breach;
    Those he commands move only in command,
    Nothing in love. Now does he feel his title   20
    Hang loose about him, like a giant's robe
    Upon a dwarfish thief.
Menteith.   Who then shall blame
    His pestered° senses to recoil and start,
    When all that is within him does condemn
    Itself for being there?
Caithness.   Well, march we on,   25
    To give obedience where 'tis truly owed. —
    Meet we the medicine of the sickly weal,°
    And with him pour we in our country's purge
    Each drop of us. —
Lennox.   Or so much° as it needs,
    To dew° the sovereign flower° and drown the weeds.°   30
    Make we our march toward Birnam.   *[Exeunt, marching.]*

[handwritten annotations: "the people who follow him do so cuz they are commanded to do so. not big enough to wear a robe" / "not out of loyalty" / "Malcolm — common good of Scotland" / "give of ourselves totally"]

Scene 3

    [Dunsinane. A room in the castle. Enter Macbeth, Doctor, *and* Attendants.*]*

Macbeth. Bring me no reports; let them fly all;°
    Till Birnam wood remove to Dunsinane,
    I cannot taint° with fear. What's the boy Malcolm?
    Was he not born of woman? The spirits that know
    All mortal consequences° have pronounced me thus: 5
    "Fear not, Macbeth; no man that's born of woman

---

11. **Protest . . . manhood:** show that they have hardly reached manhood.   16. **Within . . . rule:** under control.   18. **minutely:** every minute.   **faith breach:** disloyalty.   23. **pestered:** troubled.   27. **medicine . . . weal:** the medicine (i.e., Malcolm and his party) that will heal the commonwealth.   30. **dew:** water.   **sovereign flower:** Malcolm.   **weeds:** Macbeth.
  1. **let . . . all:** let them all desert me.   3. **taint:** be infected.   5. **mortal consequences:** human fate.

Shall e'er have power upon thee." Then fly, false thanes,
And mingle with the English epicures!°
The mind I sway by and the heart I bear
Shall never sag with doubt nor shake with fear.   10

[*Enter a* Servant.]

The devil damn thee black, thou cream-faced loon!
Where got'st thou that goose look?
Servant. There is ten thousand——
Macbeth.   Geese, villain?
Servant.   Soldiers, sir.
Macbeth. Go, prick thy face, and over-red thy fear,
Thou lily-livered boy. What soldiers, patch?°   15
Death of thy soul? those linen° cheeks of thine
Are counselors to fear. What soldiers, whey-face?
Servant. The English force, so please you.
Macbeth. Take thy face hence.   [*Exit* Servant.]
                    Seyton!—I am sick at heart.
When I behold—Seyton, I say!—This push°   20
Will cheer me ever, or disseat me now.
I have lived long enough. My way of life
Is fall'n into the sear,° the yellow leaf;
And that which should accompany old age,
As honor, love, obedience, troops of friends,   25
I must not look to have; but, in their stead,
Curses, not loud but deep, mouth honor, breath,
Which the poor heart would fain deny, and dare not.
Seyton!

[*Enter* Seyton.]

Seyton. What is your gracious pleasure?
Macbeth.   What news more?   30
Seyton. All is confirmed, my lord, which was reported.
Macbeth. I'll fight till from my bones my flesh be hacked.
Give me my armor.
Seyton.   'Tis not needed yet.
Macbeth. I'll put it on.
Send out moe° horses; skirr° the country round;   35
Hang those that talk of fear. Give me mine armor.
How does your patient, doctor?
Doctor.   Not so sick, my lord,

---

8. **epicures:** gluttons, that is, not soldiers.   15. **patch:** fool.   16. **linen:** pale as linen.   20. **push:** attack.   23. **sear:** dry, withered.   35. **moe:** more.   **skirr:** scour.

As she is troubled with thick-coming fancies.
That keep her from her rest.

Macbeth. Cure her of that.
    Canst thou not minister to a mind diseased,   40
    Pluck from the memory a rooted sorrow,
    Raze out the written troubles of the brain
    And with some sweet oblivious antidote
    Cleanse the stuffed bosom of that perilous stuff
    Which weighs upon the heart?

Doctor. Therein the patient   45
    Must minister to himself.

Macbeth. Throw physic° to the dogs; I'll none of it.
    Come, put mine armor on; give me my staff.
    Seyton, send out. Doctor, the thanes fly from me.
    Come, sir, dispatch. If thou couldst, doctor, cast   50
    The water° of my land, find her disease,
    And purge it to a sound and pristine° health,
    I would applaud thee to the very echo.
    That should applaud again.—Pull 't off, I say.°—
    What rhubarb, senna, or what purgative drug,   55
    Would scour these English hence? Hear'st thou of them?

Doctor. Aye, my good lord; your royal preparation
    Makes us hear something.

Macbeth. Bring it after me.
    I will not be afraid of death and bane,
    Till Birnam forest come to Dunsinane.   60

Doctor. [*Aside*] Were I from Dunsinane away and clear,
    Profit again should hardly draw me here.   [*Exeunt.*]

Scene 4

[*Country near Birnam wood. Drum and colors. Enter* Malcolm, *old* Siward *and his* Son,
Macduff, Menteith, Caithness, Angus, Lennox, Ross, *and* Soldiers *marching.*]

Malcolm. Cousins, I hope the days are near at hand
    That chambers will be safe.°

Menteith. We doubt it nothing.

Siward. What wood is this before us?

Menteith. The wood of Birnam.

Malcolm. Let every soldier hew him down a bough
    And bear it before him; thereby shall we shadow°   *use as a shield* 5
    The numbers of our host and make discovery   *trees marching up hill*
    Err in report of us.

---

47. **physic:** medicine. 50–51. **cast . . . water:** diagnose the illness. 52. **pristine:** i.e., former. 54. **Pull . . . say:** Macbeth
orders Seyton to pull off part of his armor which has been put on wrong in his haste.
  2. **chambers . . . safe:** that is, a man will be safe in his own home. 5. **shadow:** conceal.

Soldiers.   It shall be done.
Siward. We learn no other but the confident tyrant
  Keeps still in Dunsinane, and will endure
  Our setting down° before 't.
Malcolm.   'Tis his main hope;   10
  For where there is advantage to be given,
  Both more or less have given him the revolt,°
  And none serve with him but constrainèd° things
  Whose hearts are absent too.
Macduff.   Let our just censures
  Attend the true event,° and put we on   15
  Industrious soldiership.
Siward.   The time approaches
  That will with due decision make us know
  What we shall say we have and what we owe.
  Thoughts speculative their unsure hopes relate,
  But certain issue strokes must arbitrate;°   20
  Toward which advance the war.   *[Exeunt, marching.]*

Scene 5

[Dunsinane. Within the castle. Enter Macbeth, Seyton, *and* Soldiers, *with drum and colors.]*

Macbeth. Hang out our banners on the outward walls;
  The cry is still "They come!" Our castle's strength
  Will laugh a siege to scorn; here let them lie
  Till famine and the ague° eat them up.
  Were they not forced° with those that should be ours,   5
  We might have met them dareful, beard to beard,
  And beat them backward home.   *[A cry of women within.]*
     What is that noise?
Seyton. It is the cry of women, my good lord.   *[Exit.]*
Macbeth. I have almost forgot the taste of fears.
  The time has been, my senses would have cooled   10
  To hear a night-shriek; and my fell of hair°
  Would at a dismal treatise° rouse and stir
  As life were in 't. I have supped full with horrors;
  Direness, familiar to my slaughterous thoughts,
  Cannot once start° me.

[Reenter Seyton.]

---

10. **setting down:** siege.   12. **Both . . . revolt:** Both the higher and lower classes ("more or less") have deserted Macbeth.   13. **constrainèd:** forced.   15. **Attend . . . event:** wait until the battle is over.   20. **arbitrate:** decide.
  4. **ague:** fever.   5. **forced:** reinforced.   11. **my . . . hair:** the hair on my scalp.   12. **dismal treatise:** gloomy story.   15. **start:** startle.

Wherefore was that cry? 15

Seyton. The queen, my lord, is dead.

Macbeth. She should have died hereafter;°
There would have been a time for such a word.
Tomorrow, and tomorrow, and tomorrow,
Creeps in this petty pace from day to day 20
To the last syllable of recorded time,
And all our yesterdays have lighted fools
The way to dusty death. Out, out, brief candle!
Life's but a walking shadow, a poor player
That struts and frets his hour upon the stage 25
And then is heard no more. It is a tale
Told by an idiot, full of sound and fury,
Signifying nothing.

[*Enter* Messenger.]

Thou comest to use thy tongue; thy story quickly.

Messenger. Gracious my lord, 30
I should report that which I say I saw,
But know not how to do it.

Macbeth.   Well, say, sir.

Messenger. As I did stand my watch upon the hill,
I looked toward Birnam, and anon, methought,
The wood began to move.

Macbeth.   Liar and slave! 35

Messenger. Let me endure your wrath, if 't be not so.
Within this three mile may you see it coming;
I say, a moving grove.

Macbeth.   If thou speak'st false,
Upon the next tree shalt thou hang alive,
Till famine cling° thee; if thy speech be sooth,° 40
I care not if thou dost for me as much.
I pull in resolution,° and begin
To doubt the equivocation° of the fiend
That lies like truth: "Fear not, till Birnam wood
Do come to Dunsinane." And now a wood 45
Comes toward Dunsinane. Arm, arm, and out!
If this which he avouches does appear,
There is nor flying hence nor tarrying here.
I 'gin to be aweary of the sun,
And wish the estate o' the world were now undone. 50
Ring the alarum bell! Blow, wind! come, wrack!°
At least we'll die with harness° on our back.   [*Exeunt.*]

---

17. **She . . . hereafter:** She would have died sometime.   40. **cling:** wither.   **sooth:** truth.   42. **resolution:** courage.   43.
equivocation: double talk.   51. **wrack:** wreck.   52. **harness:** armor.

Scene 6

[*Dunsinane. Before the castle. Drums and colors. Enter* Malcolm, *old* Siward, Macduff, *and their* Army, *with boughs.*]

Malcolm. Now near enough; your leavy° screens throw down,
 And show like those you are. You, worthy uncle,
 Shall, with my cousin, your right noble son,
 Lead our first battle. Worthy Macduff and we
 Shall take upon 's else remains to do,   5
 According to our order.
Siward.   Fare you well.
 Do we but find the tyrant's power tonight,
 Let us be beaten, if we cannot fight.
Macduff. Make all our trumpets speak; give them all breath,
 Those clamorous harbingers° of blood and death.   [*Exeunt.*]   10

Scene 7

[*Another part of the field. Alarums. Enter* Macbeth.]

Macbeth. They have tied me to a stake; I cannot fly,
 But, bearlike, I must fight the course.° What's he
 That was not born of woman? Such a one
 Am I to fear, or none.

[*Enter* Young Siward.]

Young Siward. What is thy name?
Macbeth.   Thou 'lt be afraid to hear it.   5
Young Siward. No; though thou call'st thyself a hotter name
 Than any is in Hell.
Macbeth.   My name's Macbeth.
Young Siward. The devil himself could not pronounce a title
 More hateful to mine ear.
Macbeth.   No, nor more fearful.
Young Siward. Thou liest, abhorrèd tyrant; with my sword   10
 I'll prove the lie thou speak'st.   [*They fight and* Young Siward *is slain.*]
Macbeth.   Thou wast born of woman.
 But swords I smile at, weapons laugh to scorn,
 Brandished by man that's of a woman born.   [*Exit.*]

[*Alarums. Enter* Macduff.]

---

1. **leavy:** leafy.   10. **harbingers:** messengers.
2. **But . . . course:** Like a bear chained to a stake and attacked by hounds, Macbeth must endure to the end.

Macduff. That way the noise is. Tyrant, show thy face!
    If thou be'st slain and with no stroke of mine,   15
    My wife and children's ghosts will haunt me still.
    I cannot strike at wretched kerns,° whose arms
    Are hired to bear their staves;° either thou, Macbeth,
    Or else my sword with an unbattered edge
    I sheathe again undeeded. There thou shouldst be;   20
    By this great clatter, one of greatest note
    Seems bruited.° Let me find him, fortune!
    And more I beg not.   *[Exit. Alarums.]*

[Enter Malcolm *and old* Siward.]

Siward. This way, my lord; the castle's gently rendered:°
    The tyrant's people on both sides do fight;   25
    The noble thanes do bravely in the war;
    The day almost itself professes yours,
    And little is to do.
Malcolm.   We have met with foes
    That strike beside us.°
Siward.   Enter, sir, the castle.   *[Exeunt. Alarums.]*

Scene 8

[Another part of the field. Enter Macbeth.]

Macbeth. Why should I play the Roman fool,° and die
    On mine own sword? Whiles I see lives, the gashes
    Do better upon them.

[Enter Macduff.]

Macduff.   Turn, hell-hound, turn!
Macbeth. Of all men else I have avoided thee.
    But get thee back; my soul is too much charged   5
    With blood of thine already.
Macduff.   I have no words;
    My voice is in my sword, thou bloodier villain
    Than terms can give thee out!   *[They fight.]*
Macbeth.   Thou losest labor;
    As easy mayst thou the intrenchant° air
    With thy keen sword impress° as make me bleed.   10

---

17. **kerns:** foot soldiers hired as mercenaries.   18. **staves:** spears.   22. **bruited:** revealed by the noise.   24. **gently rendered:** easily surrendered.   29. **beside us:** on our side.
    1. **play . . . fool:** like Brutus or Cassius, who committed suicide in the moment of defeat.   9. **intrenchant:** that cannot be cut.   10. **impress:** make a dent in.

Let fall thy blade on vulnerable crests;°
I bear a charmèd life, which must not yield
To one of woman born.
Macduff.   Despair thy charm;
And let the angel whom thou still hast served
Tell thee, Macduff was from his mother's womb   15
Untimely ripped.
Macbeth. Accursèd be that tongue that tells me so,
For it hath cowed my better part of man!
And be these juggling fiends no more believed,
That palter° with us in a double sense;   20
That keep the word of promise to our ear,
And break it to our hope. I'll not fight with thee.
Macduff. Then yield thee, coward,
And live to be the show and gaze o' the time.
We'll have thee, as our rarer monsters° are,   25
Painted upon a pole,° and underwrit,
"Here may you see the tyrant."
Macbeth.   I will not yield,
To kiss the ground before young Malcolm's feet,
And to be baited with the rabble's curse.
Though Birnam wood be come to Dunsinane,   30
And thou opposed, being of no woman born,
Yet I will try the last. Before my body
I throw my warlike shield. Lay on, Macduff,
And damned be him that first cries "Hold, enough!"

                                     [Exeunt, fighting. Alarums.]

[Retreat. Flourish. Enter, with drum and colors, Malcolm, *old* Siward, Ross, *the other*
   Thanes, *and* Soldiers.]

Malcolm. I would the friends we miss were safe arrived.   35
Siward. Some must go off;° and yet, by these I see,
So great a day as this is cheaply bought.
Malcolm. Macduff is missing, and your noble son.
Ross. Your son, my lord, has paid a soldier's debt.
He only lived but till he was a man;   40
The which no sooner had his prowess confirmed
In the unshrinking station° where he fought,
But like a man he died.
Siward.   Then he is dead?
Ross. Aye, and brought off the field. Your cause of sorrow

---

11. **vulnerable crests:** heads that can be wounded.   20. **palter:** juggle.   25. **monsters:** freaks.   26. **Painted . . . pole:** your
portrait painted on a placard and stuck on a pole.   36. **go off:** be killed in battle.   42. **unshrinking station:** standing firm
when he fought Macbeth.

Must not be measured by his worth, for then   45
   It hath no end.
Siward.   Had he his hurts before?°
Ross. Aye, on the front.
Siward.   Why then, God's soldier be he!
   Had I as many sons as I have hairs,   [*Flourish.*]
   I would not wish them to a fairer death.
   And so, his knell is knolled.
Malcolm.   He's worth more sorrow.   50
   And that I'll spend for him.
Siward.   He's worth no more.
   They say he parted well, and paid his score;
   And so, God be with him! Here comes newer comfort.

        [*Reenter* Macduff, *with* Macbeth's *head.*]

Macduff. Hail, king! for so thou art. Behold, where stands
   The usurper's cursèd head. The time is free.°   55
   I see thee compassed with thy kingdom's pearl,°
   That speak my salutation in their minds;
   Whose voices I desire aloud with mine:
   Hail, King of Scotland!
All.   Hail, King of Scotland!   [*Flourish.*]
Malcolm. We shall not spend a large expense of time   60
   Before we reckon with your several° loves,
   And make us even with you.° My thanes and kinsmen,
   Henceforth be earls, the first that ever Scotland
   In such an honor named. What's more to do,
   Which would be planted newly with the time,   65
   As calling home our exiled friends abroad
   That fled the snares of watchful tyranny;
   Producing forth the cruel ministers
   Of this dead butcher and his fiendlike queen,
   Who, as 'tis thought, by self and violent hands   70
   Took off her life; this, and what needful else
   That calls upon us, by the grace of Grace,
   We will perform in measure,° time, and place;
   So, thanks to all at once and to each one,
   Whom we invite to see us crowned at Scone.   [*Flourish. Exeunt.*]   75

---

46. **before:** in front. Because young Siward was wounded in front, his father knew that he died fighting, not fleeing.   55.
The . . . free: Liberty is restored.   56. **compassed . . . pearl:** surrounded by the noblest men in the kingdom.   61. **several:**
separate.   62. **make . . . you:** pay you what we owe.   73. **measure:** full measure.

FOR STUDY AND DISCUSSION

1. In Scene 1, the famous "sleepwalking scene," Lady Macbeth relives events that have taken place earlier in the play. In her ravings she skips from one event to another but she always returns to the same one. Of the three events she broods over, which troubles her most deeply? Why? Why is Lady Macbeth obsessed with the idea of washing her hands?

2. In Scene 3, reread lines 22–28, beginning, "I have lived long enough." What does this soliloquy tell us about Macbeth's state of mind on the eve of battle? What traditional comforts of old age does he realize will not be his? Which of Shakespeare's sonnets on pages 136–139 has a similar theme?

3. Macbeth's final word on the meaning of life is given in Scene 5, lines 19–28. How would you describe, in one word, the tone of this soliloquy? What are Macbeth's thoughts on life as expressed in lines 19–23? What specifically is the "brief candle" and what is its connection to "a poor player"? Why is it significant that this speech was written for an actor?

4. Macbeth is a brave soldier almost to the end. On what occasions in Act Five does Macbeth express his courage? Where does his courage momentarily fail him? Macbeth is sometimes cited as an example of "the villain as hero." Do you agree? Explain your answer.

5. The play concludes with a public oration by Malcolm, who is about to be crowned King of Scotland. What aspects of this speech make it an appropriate conclusion? Do we learn anything new in the speech?

6. Tragedy moves an audience to sympathy. If *Macbeth* were nothing but the story of an evil man and his violent crimes, it would not have the power to move us as it does. The central figure of the play is a tragic hero—a man of imagination and courage, with a fatal weakness, or tragic flaw, in his character. What is that flaw and how does it destroy him? Does Lady Macbeth share this flaw?

THE PLAY AS A WHOLE

1. Although Macbeth and Lady Macbeth possess a number of the same character traits, they also reveal many dissimilarities of character. Referring to specific lines or incidents throughout the play, compare and contrast the characters of Macbeth and his wife.

2. Analyze the character of one of the leading figures in *Macbeth* and show, by reference to specific lines in the play, the means whereby this person's character is revealed: through the reactions of others, through the person's own actions or conversations, or through soliloquies.

3. While the speeches of both Macbeth and Lady Macbeth are written in blank verse (see page 165), the poetic language in which they express their thoughts and feelings is quite different. Quoting passages from the play, analyze and compare the language used by Macbeth and his wife. How does Shakespeare individualize his characters through their language?

4. A frequent subject of debate is the question of just how much control the witches had over Macbeth's free will and his destiny. Present your own opinions on this argument, supporting your viewpoint with references to the play.

FOR COMPOSITION

1. In his closing speech, Malcolm refers to Macbeth and Lady Macbeth as "this dead butcher and his fiendlike queen." Are these adequate descriptions of Macbeth and his wife? Defend your answer, citing the strongest evidence from the play.

2. It can be argued that the characters of the first Thane of Cawdor, Duncan, Banquo, Lady Macbeth, and Macbeth all contain flaws which, to a greater or lesser degree, are the cause of their downfall. Referring to specific passages in the play, describe the flaws of each of these characters and explain why you think each character was or was not deserving of his or her fate.

Reading *Macbeth*

In reading *Macbeth*, or any other play, five factors demand special attention: theme, plot, characterization, diction, atmosphere.

The theme of *Macbeth* can be summed up in Macbeth's own words: "They say blood will have blood." *Macbeth* opens with a meeting of the three witches, a scene which creates an atmosphere of foreboding and introduces the evil powers which are about to tempt Macbeth to his ruin. After a scene showing King Duncan and his nobles receiving the report of Macbeth's victory in battle, the witches reappear, as they said they would, to meet Macbeth. When Macbeth enters with Banquo, the witches accost them and make their prophecies, to which Macbeth reacts strongly. Thereafter each scene arises out of what has gone before, and we, the spectators, become more and more involved in the story, until the inevitable downfall of Macbeth.

But plot depends on character: in life, events happen because people act according to their different natures. Unless a writer convinces us that a person is "real," we have little interest in him or her. In *Macbeth*, Shakespeare has concentrated all his skill in characterization in the two leading figures: Macbeth and Lady Macbeth. Before Macbeth appears, we hear of his great bravery in battle. In the next scene, when we first see him, we sense that he is vastly ambitious and so given to brooding that he becomes unconscious of what is happening around him. Two scenes later Lady Macbeth, commenting on his letter, gives us her view of her husband's nature—"too full o' the milk of human kindness." With that remark she convinces us that she herself is *not*. Macbeth is ambitious but somewhat scrupulous; he has evil desires but is too timid to play false—unless his wife forces him to it. Lady Macbeth, it seems obvious, is the stronger nature. In Scene 7 we see her work on her husband. Macbeth's soliloquy (lines 1–28) shows that he shrinks from the murder of Duncan; his wife, however, forces him into action with her taunt that he is a coward. Many other examples of skillful characterization abound in this play.

Diction, the language used by the characters, is a most important aspect of any play. *Macbeth* is full of the highest dramatic verse, especially in Macbeth's important speeches and soliloquies. A great dramatic speech joins a perfect union of sound, rhythm, and meaning to the individual speaker and the situation, thus enabling the audience to experience vicariously the character's feelings. A good example of a great dramatic speech is Macbeth's soliloquy (Act Three, Scene 1) as he awaits the murderers whom he has hired to kill Banquo. The speech begins on a level of calm, objective thought:

Banquo is dangerous, dauntless, and wise; he overshadows Macbeth; he even dared rebuke the weird sisters until they promised that he would be the father of a line of kings. With this prospect Macbeth's objectivity is overcome by passion; rational statement is replaced by the repetitions of emotional rhetoric: "for *Banquo*'s issue . . . for *them* . . . only for *them* . . . to make *them* kings" — until it rises into a final note, almost a cry, of desperation that he will dare fate to a fight to the finish.

A fifth factor demanding our attention is atmosphere, the way a dramatist persuades us to respond to and feel the mood of a scene. In *Macbeth* examples vary from the mood of a fine summer evening, with birds feeding their young in nests under the eaves as Duncan comes to Macbeth's castle, to the tense quiet of the scene where Lady Macbeth listens as Macbeth murders the King and then comes down the stairs, his hands sticky with blood. Stark monosyllables build up the atmosphere: "Did you not speak?" "When?" "Now." "As I descended?" "Aye." "Hark!" The world breaks in on this scene of horror when a sudden loud knocking interrupts the whisperings. The audience is now so tense that relief must be given. To this end, Shakespeare shifts suddenly to the drunken porter, who grumblingly pretends that he is the keeper of the gate of Hell and does not realize that he is so indeed.

Atmosphere is also created through the use of imagery, in some striking simile or metaphor. Three images are most significant in *Macbeth*: blood, water, and darkness. In listening to the play, we are seldom conscious of the use of these or any other images. Like the soft drumbeats in a symphony, however, the imagery affects our total response to the significance of the tragedy — but we hardly notice unless we are concentrating on the drummer.

Shakespeare's Imagery

Whether we think of Shakespeare's plays when we read them as literary works of art complete in themselves, or whether we think of them as being like blueprints or scores fully realized only in execution or performance, every aspect of Shakespearean drama depends ultimately on language. Plot, structure, character, atmosphere — all these come into being and take shape either through, or in direct relation to, the words Shakespeare wrote.

One of the most important dimensions of Shakespeare's language is *imagery*. Imagery is a broad term referring to all those forms of poetic language — metaphors, similes, symbols, passages of heightened natural description — through which a writer expands and deepens the basic literal meaning of what he says. Shakespeare's writing, like that of most of his contemporaries but to a finer degree, draws much of its life and power from imagery.

Shakespeare uses imagery to give individual speeches a richer and subtler range of meaning, and to establish verbal patterns and connections through the play as a whole. Consider, for example, Macbeth's short speech upon hearing from the doctor that it is Lady Macbeth's mind, not her body, that is ill:

> Cure her of that.
> Canst thou not minister to a mind diseased,
> Pluck from the memory a rooted sorrow,
> Raze out the written troubles of the brain,
> And with some sweet oblivious antidote
> Cleanse the stuffed bosom of that perilous stuff
> Which weighs upon the heart?
>
> (V, 3, 39–45)

Macbeth knows that Lady Macbeth's "disease" is mental rather than physical, but he talks about it all the same in vivid physical terms, as if by doing so he might make it easier to deal with. He refers to "sorrow" as something "rooted" in "the memory," as if it were a weed or other undesirable plant. In the next line the image changes: here he asserts that the "troubles of the brain" are "written," and he asks if the doctor can "raze out" ("erase") these troubles. In lines 43–45 the image shifts again: a troubled mind is like a stuffed up or congested body the doctor may "cleanse" with "some sweet oblivious antidote" or medicine. Elizabethans believed that emotional conditions were caused by the balance of certain fluids in the body, called "humors." Knowing this, one might take Macbeth's lines literally. But the doctor does not take them literally—his reply ("Therein the patient / Must minister to himself") shows that he realizes Macbeth has been speaking figuratively about a moral or spiritual condition. The speech ends subtly, with a phrase often used without any sense of its metaphorical qualities. But Macbeth's persistent presentation of thoughts and emotions in physical terms makes the image of that which "*weighs* upon the heart" come alive.

So far we have looked at the images of Macbeth's speech in isolation. But most of them belong to groups or "clusters" of images used repeatedly throughout the play. The plant image in the phrase "rooted sorrow" connects this line with many other references to plants in *Macbeth*: with Duncan's words to Macbeth in Act One, Scene 4, lines 28–29 ("I have begun to *plant* thee, and will labor / To make thee full of *growing*"); with Lady Macbeth's advice in Act One, Scene 5, line 60 ("look like the innocent *flower* . . ."); with

Banquo's speculation at the very beginning of Act Three ("yet it was said . . . / . . . that myself should be the *root* and father / Of many kings"); with Macbeth's famous lines in the soliloquy just before the speech we have been looking at ("My way of life / Is fall'n into the sear, the yellow *leaf*"). The image of cleansing later in the speech should make us think of all those references to washing and water in the play. We may recall in particular Lady Macbeth's "What, will these hands ne'er be clean" in the sleep-walking scene (Act Five, Scene 1, lines 30–31). The imagery of disease, which runs throughout this speech, also runs throughout the entirety of *Macbeth*. Shakespeare uses such groups of images to reinforce the main themes of his play. In the case of the plant imagery, it is the theme of evil growing out of good, and good growing out of evil. The imagery of washing and cleansing contributes to the theme of guilt; the imagery of disease, to the themes of unnatural evil and political disorder.

Imagery is also one of Shakespeare's main resources in the creation of character. From the point of view of his fellow countrymen, Macbeth is "bloody" from the beginning of the play until the end. We first hear about Macbeth from the wounded captain, who praises Macbeth's "brandished steel, / Which smoked with *bloody* execution" (Act One, Scene 2, lines 17–18). We last hear about him from Malcolm, who calls him "this dead *butcher*" (Act Five, Scene 8, line 69). From a more internal, private perspective, Macbeth first openly confesses his ambition to be king in images drawn from the theater:

> Two truths are told
> As happy *prologues* to the swelling *act*
> Of the imperial *theme.*
> > (I, 3, 127–129)

We can see just how far Macbeth has fallen, and yet how much he is still the Macbeth of Act One, if we compare the theatrical imagery here to that in the great Act Five soliloquy:

> Life's but a walking shadow, a poor *player*
> That struts and frets his hour upon the *stage*
> And then is heard no more.
> > (V, 5, 24–26)

The images of butchery and of acting in the theatrical sense help us see both the alteration and the continuity in Macbeth's character from Act One to Act Five. Other less important images help define Macbeth's character at a particular moment in the play. Near the end, for example, when he is surrounded by his enemies, Macbeth sees himself as a captured, taunted animal ("But bearlike I must fight the course," Act Five, Scene 7, line 2; "I will not yield / . . . to be baited with the rabble's curse," Act Five, Scene 8, lines 27–29).

Imagery may not be *the* key to Shakespeare's plays, as some later writers have claimed. But studying it is certainly one of the important ways we have of understanding the meaning and the beauty of his dramatic art.

FOR COMPOSITION

Several critics, particularly Caroline Spurgeon and Cleanth Brooks, have commented on "old clothes" imagery in *Macbeth*. Spurgeon notes: "The idea constantly recurs that Macbeth's new honors sit ill upon him, like a loose and badly fitting garment, belonging to someone else":

> Now does he feel his title
> Hang loose about him, like a giant's robe
> Upon a dwarfish thief.
> (V, 2, 20–22)

Brooks notes that "the series of garment metaphors which run through the play is paralleled by a series of masking or cloaking images":

> Come, thick night,
> And pall thee in the dunnest smoke of hell,
> That my keen knife see not the wound it makes,
> Nor Heaven peep through the blanket of the dark,
> To cry, "Hold, Hold!"
> (I, 5, 45–49)

1. Select several clothing images from *Macbeth* and explain their purpose. For example, do they reveal character, contribute to mood, or emphasize theme.

2. In *Macbeth*, the aura of darkness, deception, and horror that envelops the entire play is evoked by the imagery. Citing examples from the play, show how the dominant images of darkness, blood, nature, and the supernatural contribute to the atmosphere of this tragedy.

from On the Knocking at the Gate in *Macbeth*

Thomas De Quincey

One of the most famous interpretations of *Macbeth* appears in this essay by De Quincey, a nineteenth-century critic and essayist. At the opening of the essay, De Quincey reveals that he had always been puzzled by the effect of the knocking at the gate, which occurs in Act Two, Scenes 2 and 3, just after Duncan has been murdered: "The effect was that it reflected back upon the murderer a peculiar awfulness and a depth of solemnity." After long deliberation, De Quincey found an explanation for the extraordinary effect of this dramatic action.

. . . At length I solved it to my own satisfaction; and my solution is this: — Murder, in ordinary cases, where the sympathy is wholly directed to the case of the murdered person, is an incident of coarse and vulgar horror; and for this reason — that it flings the interest exclusively upon the natural but ignoble instinct by which we cleave to life: an instinct which, as being indispensable to the primal law of self-preservation, is the same in kind (though different in degree) amongst all living creatures. This instinct, therefore, because it annihilates all distinctions, and degrades the greatest of men to the level of "the poor beetle that we tread on," exhibits human nature in its most abject and humiliating attitude. Such an attitude would little suit the purposes of the poet. What then must he do? He must throw the interest on the murderer. Our sympathy must be with *him* (of course I mean a sympathy of comprehension, a sympathy by which we enter into his feelings, and are made to understand them — not a sympathy of pity or approbation). In the murdered person, all strife of thought, all flux and reflux of passion and of purpose, are crushed by one overwhelming panic; the fear of instant death smites him "with its petrific mace."[1] But in

the murderer, such a murderer as a poet will condescend to, there must be raging some great storm of passion — jealousy, ambition, vengeance, hatred — which will create a hell within him; and into this hell we are to look.

In *Macbeth,* for the sake of gratifying his own enormous and teeming faculty of creation, Shakespeare has introduced two murderers: and, as usual in his hands, they are remarkably discriminated: but — though in Macbeth the strife of mind is greater than in his wife, the tiger spirit not so awake, and his feelings caught chiefly by contagion from her — yet, as both were finally involved in the guilt of murder, the murderous mind of necessity is finally to be presumed in both. This was to be expressed; and, on its own account, as well as to make it a more proportionable antagonist to the unoffending nature of their victim, "the gracious Duncan," and adequately to expound "the deep damnation of his taking off," this was to be expressed with peculiar energy. We were to be made to feel that the human nature — *i.e.,* the divine nature of love and mercy, spread through the hearts of all creatures, and seldom utterly withdrawn from man — was gone, vanished, extinct, and that the fiendish nature had taken its place. And, as this effect is marvellously accomplished in the *dialogues* and *soliloquies* themselves, so it is finally con-

---

1. **petrific mace:** stone mace; an allusion to Milton's *Paradise Lost* (**X**, 294).

summated by the expedient under consideration; and it is to this that I now solicit the reader's attention. If the reader has ever witnessed a wife, daughter, or sister in a fainting fit, he may chance to have observed that the most affecting moment in such a spectacle is *that* in which a sigh and a stirring announce the recommencement of suspended life. Or, if the reader has ever been present in a vast metropolis on the day when some great national idol was carried in funeral pomp to his grave, and, chancing to walk near the course through which it passed, has felt powerfully, in the silence and desertion of the streets, and in the stagnation of ordinary business, the deep interest which at that moment was possessing the heart of man—if all at once he should hear the deathlike stillness broken up by the sound of wheels rattling away from the scene, and making known that the transitory vision was dissolved, he will be aware that at no moment was his sense of the complete suspension and pause in ordinary human concerns so full and affecting as at that moment when the suspension ceases, and the goings-on of human life are suddenly resumed. All action in any direction is best expounded, measured, and made apprehensible, by reaction. Now, apply this to the case in *Macbeth*. Here, as I have said, the retiring of the human heart and the entrance of the fiendish heart was to be expressed and made sensible. Another world has stepped in; and the murderers are taken out of the region of human things, human purposes, human desires. They are transfigured: Lady Macbeth is "unsexed"; Macbeth has forgot that he was born of woman; both are conformed to the image of devils; and the world of devils is suddenly revealed. But how shall this be conveyed and made palpable? In order that a new world may step in, this world must for a time disappear. The murderers and the murder must be insulated—cut off by an immeasurable gulf from the ordinary tide and succession of human affairs—locked up and sequestered in some deep recess; we must be made sensible that the world of ordinary life is suddenly arrested, laid asleep, tranced, racked into a dread armistice; time must be annihilated, relation to things without abolished; and all must pass self-withdrawn into a deep syncope[2] and suspension of earthly passion. Hence it is that, when the deed is done, when the work of darkness is perfect, then the world of darkness passes away like a pageantry in the clouds: the knocking at the gate is heard, and it makes known audibly that the reaction has commenced; the human has made its reflux upon the fiendish; the pulses of life are beginning to beat again, and the reestablishment of the goings-on of the world in which we live first makes us profoundly sensible of the awful parenthesis that had suspended them.

O mighty poet! Thy works are not as those of other men, simply and merely great works of art, but are also like the phenomena of nature, like the sun and the sea, the stars and the flowers, like frost and snow, rain and dew, hailstorm and thunder, which are to be studied with entire submission of our own faculties, and in the perfect faith that in them there can be no too much or too little, nothing useless or inert, but that, the farther we press in our discoveries, the more we shall see proofs of design and self-supporting arrangement where the careless eye had seen nothing but accident!

---

2. **syncope** (sĭn′kə-pē): unconsciousness.

FOR COMPOSITION

In a short essay analyze De Quincey's argument and tell why you agree or disagree with his interpretation.

Francis Bacon
1561–1626

Francis Bacon was a key figure in the transition from the intellectual world of the late Middle Ages to that of modern Europe. Though designated an Elizabethan, Bacon was, more precisely, the prophet of a new century, one characterized by its growing scientific spirit. He recognized his unique position, calling himself "the trumpeter of a new age." His career and character reveal him to be a man of various qualities. His critics agree: Alexander Pope called him "the wisest, brightest, and the meanest of mankind," while Ben Jonson declared him to be "one of the greatest men, and most worthy of admiration that had been in many ages."

Bacon's misfortune was to make a great name for himself by a rare combination of intellectual energy and worldly acumen, to be counted among the wise men of his time, and then, by a paradoxical twist, to find himself publicly disgraced. Born into an aristocratic family, he entered diplomatic service after two years at Cambridge University. He studied law and became a member of Parliament in 1584. During his service as a royal counsel under Queen Elizabeth, he incurred much ill feeling by helping to secure a conviction for treason against the Earl of Essex, whose patronage he had previously enjoyed. It was not until the reign of James I that he was able to achieve the status that he so eagerly sought. In a period of eleven years he advanced to the influential position of Lord Chancellor. In 1618, the same year, he was also raised to a barony. But his political success was short-lived. Three years later, he was brought before the House of Lords on charges of bribery. While he pleaded guilty, he denied that he had allowed "gifts" to influence his judicial decisions. In any case, he was thrown out of office, fined, and imprisoned. After two days in the Tower of London, Bacon was released and, retiring from public life, he thereafter gave himself over to literature and scientific experiment.

Lytton Strachey remarked that "Bacon's mind was universal in its comprehensiveness; there was nothing in the world of which he could not write." This was not an overstatement. Neither was the claim made by Bacon himself as a typical Renaissance scholar, "I have taken all knowledge to be my province." During the course of his lifetime he distinguished himself as a scholar in several fields and as a scientist, writer, and philosopher. His practical experience of the world also made him a great lawyer and a considerable statesman. As a philosopher he was greatly concerned with human beings' understanding of themselves and the world they live in. *The Advancement of Learning,* in which Bacon analyzed the various divisions of knowledge and considered the possible means of advancing them, epitomizes this concern as does his later great work *Novum Organum (The New Instrument),* in which he described the method by which knowledge could be universalized. Bacon's major contribution to modern science was his promotion of the inductive method of reasoning, which, exactly contrary to the deductive method used by medieval scholars, formulated generalizations only after close observation of facts.

But it was not only in science that Bacon broke new ground. When he published his first *Essays* in 1597, he became England's first essayist. Like Montaigne, whose *Essais* appeared almost twenty years before his own, Bacon wrote in the idiom of the classical scholar, undertaking in a more formal style than Montaigne's discussions of topics such as "Of Studies," "Of Travel," "Of Followers and Friends," and "Of Marriage and Single Life." The *Essays,* written in a powerful, direct, and compact style, are laden with quotations, metaphors, witticisms, and allusions which clearly mark them as the work of Francis Bacon. As a Renaissance scholar, Bacon wrote more often in Latin than he did in English, which perhaps accounts for the fact that his English style sometimes seems difficult or obscure to modern readers. But his commentaries are shrewd and often brilliant, and as apt today as when first written.

Of Studies

Studies serve for delight, for ornament, and for ability. Their chief use for delight is in privateness and retiring; for ornament, is in discourse; and for ability, is in the judgment and disposition of business. For expert men can execute, and perhaps judge of particulars, one by one; but the general counsels, and the plots and marshaling of affairs come best from those that are learned. To spend too much time in studies is sloth; to use them too much for ornament is affectation; to make judgment wholly by their rules is the humor of a scholar. They perfect nature, and are perfected by experience: for natural abilities are like natural plants, that need pruning by study; and studies themselves do give forth directions too much at large, except they be bounded in by experience. Crafty men contemn studies, simple men admire them, and wise men use them; for they teach not their own use; but that is a wisdom without them and above them, won by observation. Read not to contradict and confute, nor to believe and take for granted, nor to find talk and discourse, but to weigh and consider. Some books are to be tasted, others to be swallowed, and some few to be chewed and digested; that is, some books are to be read only in parts; others to be read, but not curiously;[1] and some few to be read wholly, and with diligence and attention. Some books also may be read by deputy, and extracts made of them by others; but that would[2] be only in the less important arguments and the meaner sort of books; else distilled books are, like common distilled waters,[3] flashy things. Reading maketh a full man; conference a ready man; and writing an exact man. And, therefore, if a man write little, he had need have a great memory; if he confer little, he had need have a present wit; and if he read little, he had need have much cunning, to seem to know that he doth not. Histories make men wise; poets, witty; the mathematics, subtile; natural philosophy, deep; moral, grave; logic and rhetoric, able to contend. *Abeunt studia in mores.*[4] Nay, there is no stond[5] or impediment in the wit but may be wrought out by fit studies, like as diseases of the body may have appropriate exercises. Bowling is good for the stone and reins,[6] shooting for the lungs and breast, gentle walking for the stomach, riding for the head, and the like. So if a man's wit be wandering, let him study the mathematics; for in demonstrations, if his wit be called away never so little, he must begin again. If his wit be not apt to distinguish or find differences, let him study the schoolmen; for they are *Cymini sectores.*[7] If he be not apt to beat over[8] matters, and to call up one thing to prove and illustrate another, let him study the lawyer's cases. So every defect of the mind may have a special receipt.[9]

---

1. **curiously:** carefully.

2. **would:** should.
3. **common distilled waters:** herbal home remedies.
4. *Abeunt . . . mores:* "Studies become manners of life" (Ovid, *Heroides* XV. 83).
5. **stond:** stoppage.
6. **stone and reins:** gallbladder and kidneys.
7. *Cymini sectores:* "hairsplitters" (literally, "dividers of cumin seed").
8. **beat over:** reason through.
9. **receipt:** prescription, remedy.

BACON'S STYLE

One of the characteristics of Bacon's style is his use of aphorisms. (An *aphorism* is a concise and pithy statement about experience.) Here is an example of the aphoristic style from Bacon's essay "Of Studies": "Reading maketh a full man; conference a ready man; and writing an exact man." Find other examples of the aphoristic style in Bacon's essay.

Bacon also makes use of parallel structure—the repetition of phrases that are similar in structure. The sentence beginning "Some books are to be tasted . . ." is an example of parallel structure. How is the metaphor in this sentence developed? What does Bacon do in the latter part of this sentence? What other parallel structures can you find in the essay?

FOR COMPOSITION

Although Bacon is the father of the English essay, his writing style is not the easy, personal one associated with later examples of that literary°form. Select from "Of Studies" two passages that are especially heavy or formal. Rewrite these passages in light, Modern English.

Essayes.

Religious Meditations.

Places of perswasion and disswasion.

Seene and allowed.

At London,
Printed for Humfrey Hooper, and are
to be sold at the blacke Beare
in Chauncery Lane.
1 5 9 7.

Bacon's *Essays,* first edition (frontispiece).
Culver Pictures

The King James Bible

In 1604, only a year after he had ascended the throne, King James I appointed fifty-four of England's most eminent scholars and churchmen to begin work on a new translation of the Bible. This entailed comparing the various English translations then in existence with the Latin Bibles of the Middle Ages as well as with the original Greek and Hebrew texts. Seven years later, in 1611, the Authorized, or King James, Version of the Holy Bible was completed. Often referred to as "the only classic ever created by a committee," its uniform excellence and beauty caused it from the start to be acknowledged as a masterpiece, an outstanding literary work whose great popularity persists to the present day.

The significance of the King James Bible lies not only in its own intrinsic merits but in the fact that it represents the culmination of many efforts throughout several centuries to provide English-speaking peoples with a Bible written in their own tongue. Throughout most of the Middle Ages, the Bible was written in Latin and was therefore inaccessible to most people. Though there were several early attempts to render small parts of the Scriptures into English, little of importance was achieved until late in the fourteenth century, when John Wycliffe and his followers produced the first complete transcription into English. This translation of 1382 succeeded in reaching a fair number of people, although the manuscripts were costly, representing as they did enormous amounts of meticulous handiwork.

With the advent of the Reformation, which spread throughout Europe early in the sixteenth century, came a new emphasis on the Bible as the ultimate authority on religious doctrine. Simultaneously, therefore, a need arose for English translations that would make the Bible available to a still larger number of people. It was William Tyndale, a leader of the English Reformation, who produced the first printed version of the New Testament in English. Determined to bring the Bible to all men, even "the boy that driveth the plow," Tyndale sacrificed his life to his mission. He printed his masterful translation of the New Testament in 1525 and then, despite the violent religious conflicts of his time, proceeded to translate the Old Testament. He never finished. Imprisoned for heresy in 1535, Tyndale was executed eighteen months later.

Various other English Bibles followed, among them Miles Coverdale's version (1535), based partly on Tyndale's translation, and the so-called Great Bible, which was prepared with Coverdale's supervision. Under the auspices of Henry VIII, the Great Bible in 1540 was finally established for use in the churches. It was not until the appearance of the King James Version in 1611, however, that there existed a simple, well-translated English Bible that was both authorized by the Church and generally accepted by the people.

The King James Bible was indisputably such a book. Produced with exacting care by the most distinguished scholars, written at a time when the English language was at its height, it has communicated eloquently with every age. Its simplicity, beauty, and vigor of language, its sheer poetry, has influenced both English and American literature immeasurably. As generations of readers have memorized it, quoted it, and woven its phrases into their speech, the King James Version has continued, after more than three centuries, to have a tremendous effect upon our language. Writers of both prose and poetry have consciously or unconsciously drawn upon it for vocabulary and imagery, the rhythm of a passage, or the shaping of a phrase.

Analyzing a sample from the King James Version will perhaps reveal something of its brilliant use of language. Here is an illustration from the Book of Psalms. In its Greek derivation *psalm* means "song"; the original Hebrew title means "praise." Such is the purpose of these poems.

Psalm 8

O Lord our Lord,
How excellent is thy name in all the earth!
Who hast set thy glory above the heavens.
Out of the mouths of babes and sucklings hast thou ordained
    strength because of thine enemies,
That thou mightest still the enemy and the avenger.   5
When I consider thy heavens, the work of thy fingers,
The moon and the stars, which thou hast ordained;
What is man, that thou art mindful of him?
And the son of man, that thou visitest him?
For thou hast made him a little lower than the angels,   10
And hast crowned him with glory and honor.
Thou madest him to have dominion over the works of thy
    hands;
Thou hast put all things under his feet:
All sheep and oxen,
Yea, and the beasts of the field;   15
The fowl of the air, and the fish of the sea,
And whatsoever passeth through the paths of the seas.
O Lord our Lord,
How excellent is thy name in all the earth!

Note first that the two opening lines are also used to conclude the poem. *Repetition* is one device that was frequently employed by King James's translators. *Parallelism*, another form of repetition, is found in phrases such as "the work of thy fingers" and "the works of thy hands"; "the fowl of the air, and the fish of the sea"; and in the psalmist's two questions. *Imagery* abounds in the awesome description of God, whose hands molded heaven and earth. *Comparison* is used to describe the relationship between God and man: God, whose glory is "above the heavens," and man who is "a little lower than the angels." Throughout, there is a perfect blend of language and content.

Psalm 8 is one of the many examples of the rich and varied use of language in the King James Version of the Bible. That this superb seventeenth-century translation has had so great an influence on subsequent English prose and poetry is easily appreciated.

from GENESIS, CHAPTERS 2–3

In the day that the Lord God made the earth and the heavens, and every plant of the field before it was in the earth, and every herb of the field before it grew (for the Lord God had not caused it to rain upon the earth, and there was not a man to till the ground) there went up a mist from the earth, and watered the whole face of the ground. And the Lord God formed man of the dust of the ground, and breathed into his nostrils the breath of life; and man became a living soul.

And the Lord God planted a garden eastward in Eden; and there he put the man whom he had formed. And out of the ground made the Lord God to grow every tree that is pleasant to the sight, and good for food; the tree of life also in the midst of the garden, and the tree of knowledge of good and evil.

And the Lord God took the man, and put him into the garden of Eden to dress it and to keep it. And the Lord God commanded the man, saying, "Of every tree of the garden thou mayest freely eat: but of the tree of the knowledge of good and evil, thou shalt not eat of it: for in the day that thou eatest thereof thou shalt surely die."

And the Lord God said,

"It is not good that the man should be alone; I will make him a help meet for him." And out of the ground the Lord God formed every beast of the field, and every fowl of the air; and brought them unto Adam to see what he would call them: and whatsoever Adam called every living creature, that was the name thereof. And Adam gave names to all cattle, and to the fowl of the air, and to every beast of the field; but for Adam there was not found a help meet for him.

And the Lord God caused a deep sleep to fall upon Adam, and he slept: and he took one of his ribs, and closed up the flesh instead thereof; and the rib, which the Lord God had taken from man, made he a woman, and brought her unto the man.

And Adam said,

"This is now bone of my bones,
  And flesh of my flesh:
  She shall be called Woman,
  Because she was taken out of Man."

Therefore shall a man leave his father and his mother, and shall cleave unto his wife:

and they shall be one flesh. And they were both naked, the man and his wife, and were not ashamed.

Now the serpent was more subtil than any beast of the field which the Lord God had made.

And he said unto the woman,

"Yea, hath God said, 'Ye shall not eat of every tree of the garden'?"

And the woman said unto the serpent,

"We may eat of the fruit of the trees of the garden: but of the fruit of the tree which is in the midst of the garden, God hath said, 'Ye shall not eat of it, neither shall ye touch it, lest ye die.' "

And the serpent said unto the woman,

"Ye shall not surely die: for God doth know that in the day ye eat thereof, then your eyes shall be opened, and ye shall be as gods, knowing good and evil."

And when the woman saw that the tree was good for food, and that it was pleasant to the eyes, and a tree to be desired to make one wise, she took of the fruit thereof, and did eat, and gave also unto her husband with her; and he did eat. And the eyes of them both were opened, and they knew that they were naked; and they sewed fig leaves together, and made themselves aprons.

And they heard the voice of the Lord God walking in the garden in the cool of the day: and Adam and his wife hid themselves from the presence of the Lord God amongst the trees of the garden.

And the Lord God called unto Adam, and said unto him,

"Where art thou?"

And he said,

"I heard thy voice in the garden, and I was afraid, because I was naked; and I hid myself."

And he said,

"Who told thee that thou wast naked? Hast thou eaten of the tree, whereof I commanded thee that thou shouldest not eat?"

And the man said,

"The woman whom thou gavest to be with me, she gave me of the tree, and I did eat."

And the Lord God said unto the woman, "What is this that thou hast done?"

And the woman said, "The serpent beguiled me, and I did eat."

And the Lord God said unto the serpent,

"Because thou hast done this,
Thou art cursed above all cattle,
And above every beast of the field;
Upon thy belly shalt thou go,
And dust shalt thou eat
All the days of thy life:

Expulsion from Paradise (detail, fresco) by Masaccio, Santa Maria del Carmine, Florence. Scala

And I will put enmity between thee and the woman,
And between thy seed and her seed;
It shall bruise thy head,
And thou shalt bruise his heel."

Unto the woman he said,

"I will greatly multiply thy sorrow and thy conception;
In sorrow thou shalt bring forth children;
And thy desire shall be to thy husband,
And he shall rule over thee."

And unto Adam he said,
"Because thou hast hearkened unto the voice of thy wife, and hast eaten of the tree, of which I commanded thee, saying, 'Thou shalt not eat of it':

"Cursed is the ground for thy sake;
In sorrow shalt thou eat of it all the days of thy life.
Thorns also and thistles shall it bring forth to thee;

And thou shalt eat the herb of the field;
In the sweat of thy face shalt thou eat bread,
Till thou return unto the ground;
For out of it wast thou taken:
For dust thou art,
And unto dust shalt thou return."

And Adam called his wife's name Eve; because she was the mother of all living. Unto Adam also and to his wife did the Lord God make coats of skins, and clothed them.

And the Lord God said, "Behold, the man is become as one of us, to know good and evil: and now, lest he put forth his hand, and take also of the tree of life, and eat, and live for ever—" therefore the Lord God sent him forth from the garden of Eden, to till the ground from whence he was taken. So he drove out the man; and he placed at the east of the garden of Eden Cherubims, and a flaming sword which turned every way, to keep the way of the tree of life.

from I CORINTHIANS, CHAPTER 13

Though I speak with the tongues of men and of angels, and have not charity, I am become as sounding brass, or a tinkling cymbal. And though I have the gift of prophecy, and understand all mysteries, and all knowledge; and though I have all faith, so that I could remove mountains, and have not charity, I am nothing. And though I bestow all my goods to feed the poor, and though I give my body to be burned, and have not charity, it profiteth me nothing. Charity suffereth long, and is kind; charity envieth not; charity vaunteth not itself, is not puffed up, doth not behave itself unseemly, seeketh not her own, is not easily provoked, thinketh no evil; rejoiceth not in iniquity, but rejoiceth in the truth; beareth all things, believeth all things, hopeth all things,

endureth all things. Charity never faileth: but whether there be prophecies, they shall fail; whether there be tongues, they shall cease; whether there be knowledge, it shall vanish away. For we know in part, and we prophesy in part. But when that which is perfect is come, then that which is in part shall be done away. When I was a child, I spoke as a child, I understood as a child, I thought as a child: but when I became a man, I put away childish things. For now we see through a glass, darkly; but then face to face: now I know in part; but then shall I know even as also I am known. And now abideth faith, hope, charity, these three; but the greatest of these is charity.

The Elizabethan Age

It may come as a surprise to learn that Shakespeare wrote in Modern English, since the language of the Elizabethan Age often seems antiquated and quite "unmodern" to twentieth-century readers. Nevertheless, Shakespeare's speech and our own have enough in common so that language historians consider that they both belong to the same stage in the history of English. If a group of twentieth-century Americans could be transported through time and space to the London of Shakespeare's day, they would find that they could communicate fairly easily with the people they would meet. They would feel that these people were speaking English with an unfamiliar accent, it is true, but their accent would not be much harder for Americans to understand than some of the present-day accents of the British Isles. (Some pure Elizabethan pronunciations are also preserved in local dialects in parts of the United States that were settled by the English during the sixteenth century.) The major reason for the similarity is the Great Vowel Shift, which occurred sometime in the fifteenth century. The vowel shift gave Modern English a new set of long vowel sounds—sounds that have persisted up to the present. This was the most important change in the language between Chaucer's time and Shakespeare's.

Another striking change was the disappearance of the final *e* sound at the ends of words. In Chaucer's verse the final *e* was often pronounced in words like *space, straunge* ("strange"), and *ende* ("end"). The tendency in spoken English to hurry over unaccented syllables, a tendency that seems always to have been present in the language, probably accounted for the dropping of these final *e*'s in

pronunciation. The same tendency probably also accounted for the fact that many other unaccented vowel sounds came to be reduced to the *uh* sound represented in dictionaries by the symbol "ə" (schwa).

English spelling, oddly enough, was not much affected by these great changes in pronunciation. As we discovered in studying the language of the Middle English period (pages 96–98), a standard written form of English came into use during the fifteenth century. Before that time, every writer's spelling had represented his own pronunciation, and spellings therefore had varied widely not only from one historical period to the next but also from one local dialect to the next. Once fairly standardized forms had come into use, though, scribes and clerks—who did most of the actual writing of Middle English documents—tended to adhere to the familiar spellings instead of respelling words according to their own pronunciation. The introduction of the printing press into England reinforced this tendency. The early printers often relied for their material on manuscripts that had been written by Middle English scribes, and a printer would simply set words into type the way he found them written in the manuscript. It thus happened that a great many Middle English spellings became permanently fixed in our language, despite the later changes in the pronunciation of the words.

This is why long *a, e, i, o,* and *u* usually stand for different sounds in Modern English than they do in all other languages that use the Latin alphabet. The same reason accounts for the presence of so many "silent letters" in English words. The *gh* in words like *night, slaughter,* and *freight* had been pronounced in

Middle English; as had the final *e* that ends so many words, and the initial *g* and *k* in words like *gnat* and *knob*.

Another change was in the structure of the language. The few inflected endings to words that Middle English had retained began to drop out. The endings for plurals and possessives are two notable exceptions. With the loss of inflective word endings, word order became even more important. The function of words in a sentence began to be indicated more and more by the use of prepositions to indicate "by" whom or "to" whom or "for" whom something was done. The Elizabethans experimented with the use of prepositions until they came up with the elaborate and efficient system we have today.

The Elizabethans continued to borrow words from other languages. Throughout the Middle Ages, educated individuals had usually preferred to use Latin for their serious writing. But now the English began to take a new pride in their native tongue, and they deliberately set out to use English in writing about all matters. To do this, they found they frequently had to borrow terms from Latin or Greek to express concepts for which there were no words in English. Many of our abstract terms entered the language this way—from Latin, words like *allusion, consolidate, education, esteem, exist, meditate;* from Greek, words like *synonymous, autocracy, catastrophe.* The languages of Continental Europe also continued to supply new words. The English who traveled abroad brought back news of Continental customs and fashions, introducing words like the French *vogue* and *mustache.* From Italy they brought back many words relating to architecture and music, like *piazza, sonata,* and *violin.* From Spaniards they acquired words relating to the exploration of the New World, such as *alligator, armadillo,* and *cocoa.* Spanish sailors and traders passed on some terms from American Indian languages, too, including *canoe, cannibal, hurricane,* and *tobacco.*

By about 1550, it had become so fashionable for writers to sprinkle their pages with foreign expressions that critics began to object strongly to "inkhorn terms" (Latin and Greek words) and "oversea language" (European words). Some of the words that the critics singled out for ridicule do sound strange to us today: *adminiculation* ("help"), *suppeditate* ("provide"), *splendidious.* But other terms that were attacked as being obscure and newfangled are now quite familiar to us: *celebrate, compatible, confidence, destitute, extol, inflate,* and *strenuous,* to name a few. Toward the end of the Elizabethan Age, writers grew more cautious about borrowing foreign words, but a great many of the new words that had already been introduced were on their way to becoming a permanent part of our language.

FOR STUDY AND DISCUSSION

1. Most Latin words that had entered English during the Anglo-Saxon period gradually changed in form and meaning as the centuries passed. Some of the same Latin words were "re-borrowed" early in the Modern English period, with their original Latin form and meaning. Look up the following two pairs of words in the dictionary, and find out which word in each pair was borrowed by Old English and which by Modern English. Which word is closer to the Latin word in form and meaning?

clerk, cleric   script, shrift

2. The change in pronunciation of long vowel sounds in the transition from Middle English to Modern English is known to language historians as the "Great Vowel Shift." Look up the Great Vowel Shift in Thomas Pyles's *The Origins and Development of the English Language* or Albert C. Baugh's *A History of the English Language* or in another book on language history, and prepare a brief explanation of the phonetic process involved.

The Jacobean Age

The Metaphysical Poets

John Donne and the seventeenth-century poets who wrote in a style inspired by or similar to his are called the metaphysical poets. This term was coined by Samuel Johnson, the great eighteenth-century critic, who was following a hint by John Dryden. Dryden had said that in his poems Donne "affects the metaphysics . . . and perplexes the minds of the fair sex with nice speculations of philosophy . . . ." (By "metaphysics," Dryden meant speculations on the basic principles governing the realms of knowledge and being.) Johnson followed up this idea by observing that the "metaphysical poets" were fond of displaying obscure and specialized learning in their poems. He went on to talk about the verbal wit with which this learning is expressed. In the poetry of Donne and his followers, Dr. Johnson found "a combination of dissimilar images, or discovery of occult resemblances in things apparently unlike . . . . The most heterogeneous ideas are yoked by violence together."

Neither Dryden nor Dr. Johnson liked the metaphysical poets. They thought that these writers were too concerned with showing how clever they were. After the eighteenth century, Donne and his followers went largely unread until the twentieth century. Through the influence of T. S. Eliot and other modern poets, the metaphysical poets were rediscovered. Many readers in the twentieth century have seen that the metaphysical poets' tendency to express themselves in elaborate intellectualized images (often called "conceits") and knotty arguments is a genuine attempt to confront the complications of life. And the "violence" or tension Dr. Johnson rightly perceived in the drawing together of dissimilar ideas can be seen as a source of positive expressive energy. The metaphysical poets make extensive use of paradox—an apparent contradiction which turns out on close inspection to yield a valuable perception. Their poems tend to be written in lines of unequal or varying length, and in rhythms that reflect the irregular and unpredictable movements of an active mind and of an informal speaking voice.

The metaphysical poets wrote both love poems and religious or meditative lyrics. The stylistic features just mentioned are characteristic of both categories of metaphysical verse. In fact one of the fascinating and often surprising things to observe in metaphysical poetry is the application of religious images and ideas to human love, and, vice versa, the application of language normally associated with human love to religious experience.

John Donne
1572–1631

John Donne as a melancholic lover, Anon.
Marquess of Lothian/National Galleries of Scotland

John Donne's life is usually thought of as having two very different and opposing phases. The first phase is typified in his witty, rakish, intellectually flashy love poems. In the second phase, he became a famous and eloquent preacher.

Born into a wealthy, distinguished Roman Catholic family, Donne was brilliant and well educated. In the early 1590's he went to study law at one of the Inns of Court, the great institutions for legal study in London. The sophisticated young Elizabethans with whom Donne associated at the Inns of Court were notorious for their wild extracurricular activities, and Donne's early love lyrics and satires, privately circulated among his fellow students, were much admired. Toward the end of the century, Donne began to make his way in the world, establishing a name for himself with his charm and brilliant intellect at the court of Queen Elizabeth. He also proved himself as a soldier and adventurer in expeditions with Sir Walter Raleigh and the Earl of Essex. In 1598 he was appointed private secretary to Sir Thomas Egerton, one of the highest officials in Elizabeth's government, and his prospects for advancement were bright.

But Donne's fortunes took a turn for the worse: in 1601 he secretly married the sixteen-year-old Ann More, Lady Egerton's niece. The marriage was discovered by Ann's father, who had Donne dismissed from office and imprisoned. This crisis brought on a period of great turmoil and uncertainty for Donne, but it eventually ushered in the second phase of his career, when he became the most famous preacher of his day. As a young man Donne had drifted away from the Roman Church. But during his troubled middle years, though he became increasingly concerned with religion, he did not join the Anglican Church. King James I recognized Donne's potential as a religious thinker and preacher, however, and in 1607 declared that if Donne expected any advancement or employment from him, it would have to be in the Church. Thus, partly because of external pressure and partly because of the changes in his own thinking, Donne decided to enter the ministry in 1615. His success was immediate and lasted until the end of his life.

From 1621 until his death he was Dean of St. Paul's Cathedral, the London center of the Church of England. A few weeks before he died he delivered his own funeral sermon, the final public performance of the most theatrical and spellbinding preacher of the age.

The transformation in Donne's life from clever love poet and courtier to eminent divine is certainly remarkable. But the links and continuities between the two phases are perhaps more significant than the differences. From the outset Donne's writing shows a mind that was restlessly energetic, highly individualistic, and essentially dramatic. Donne provokes his readers; he seems to challenge our minds to be as agile and as daring as his own. The sense of vivid immediacy in his writing, whether directed toward an uncooperative mistress in the love lyrics or toward a stern and mysterious God in the *Divine Meditations* (or "Holy Sonnets"), derives from his unrivaled ability to enact through language the urgency and complexity of thought and experience.

Song

Sweetest love, I do not go
  For weariness of thee,
Nor in hope the world can show
  A fitter love for me;
    But since that I   5
Must die at last, 'tis best
To use° myself in jest,
    Thus by feigned deaths° to die.

Yesternight the sun went hence,
  And yet is here today;   10
He hath no desire nor sense,
  Nor half so short a way;
    Then fear not me,
But believe that I shall make
Speedier journeys, since I take   15
    More wings and spurs than he.

O how feeble is man's power,
  That if good fortune fall,
Cannot add another hour,
  Nor a lost hour recall!   20
    But come bad chance,
And we join to it our strength,
And we teach it art and length,
    Itself o'er us to advance.

When thou sigh'st, thou sigh'st not wind,   25
  But sigh'st° my soul away;
When thou weep'st, unkindly kind,
  My life's blood doth decay:
    It cannot be
That thou lovest me as thou say'st,   30
If in thine my life thou waste,
    That art the best of me.

Let not thy divining heart
  Forethink me any ill;
Destiny may take thy part   35
  And may thy fears fulfill.
    But think that we
Are but turned aside to sleep:
They who one another keep
    Alive, ne'er parted be.   40

26. **sigh'st:** A sigh supposedly consumed a drop of the heart's blood.

7. **use:** condition. 8. **feigned deaths:** imagined deaths.

FOR STUDY AND DISCUSSION

1. Why does the speaker explain his parting as a pretended death?
2. A *paradox* is a statement or phrase that seems to contradict itself. In line 27 the speaker calls his love "unkindly kind." She is "kind" in weeping at their parting. What is "unkindly" about her sorrow?
3. In the final stanza how does the speaker suggest that those who love one another are never actually apart?

A Valediction: Forbidding Mourning

As virtuous men pass mildly away,
　And whisper to their souls, to go,
Whilst some of their sad friends do say,
　The breath goes now, and some say, no:

So let us melt, and make no noise,　　　　5
　No tear-floods, nor sigh-tempests move.
'Twere profanation° of our joys
　To tell the laity our love.

Moving of th' earth brings harms and fears,
　Men reckon what it did and meant,　　　10
But trepidation° of the spheres,
　Though greater far, is innocent.

Dull sublunary° lovers' love
　(Whose soul is sense) cannot admit
Absence, because it doth remove　　　　15
　Those things which elemented° it.

But we by a love, so much refined,
　That our selves know not what it is,
Inter-assurèd of the mind,
　Care less, eyes, lips, and hands to miss.

Our two souls therefore, which are one,
　Though I must go, endure not yet
A breach, but an expansion,
　Like gold to airy thinness beat.

If they be two, they are two so　　　　25
　As stiff twin compasses are two,
Thy soul the fixed foot, makes no show
　To move, but doth, if th'other do.

And though it in the center sit,
　Yet when the other far doth roam,　　30
It leans, and hearkens after it,
　And grows erect, as that comes home.

Such wilt thou be to me, who must
　Like the other foot, obliquely run;
Thy firmness makes my circle° just,　　35
　And makes me end, where I begun.

---

7. **profanation:** debasement, violation of that which is holy.
The speaker is thinking of the love he shares with his lady
as sacred, in contrast to the less elevated love of ordinary
people ("the laity"). 11. **trepidation:** literally, "shudder-
ing." The contrast is between this harmless heavenly motion and a more limited but sinister "moving of th' earth"
(line 9), that is, earthquakes. See Commentary. 13. **sublunary:** beneath the sphere of the moon, therefore subject to
constant change and imperfection. 16. **elemented:** composed.

---

35. **circle:** the symbol of perfection, because like
God and eternity, it has no beginning and no end.

COMMENTARY

According to Izaak Walton, the seventeenth-century biographer, Donne wrote this poem for his
wife on the eve of his departure for France in 1611.
Whether fact or legend, this idea of the poem's occasion puts us in touch with the special kind of
seriousness we find in the "Valediction" (literally,
a speech of parting or farewell). Travel across the
sea was much more dangerous and uncertain in
Donne's time than it is today. In urging himself
and his lady not to weep as they say goodbye,
Donne's speaker is confronting the possibility of a
final, as well as a temporary, separation.

　It may help you in reading this poem to know

that in the Renaissance, people thought of the universe as having the earth at its center. The other
heavenly bodies were located in concentric spheres
beyond the earth, with God and the angels surrounding and controlling the entire cosmic system.
All existence below the circle of the moon, including the earth, was changeable and imperfect. Beyond the circle of the moon the heavenly spheres
were thought to be perfect.

　In the "Valediction," the speaker defines and
celebrates a love that transcends the physical and
can therefore endure and even grow through separation. In doing so, he moves through a series of intellectually surprising images or comparisons.
After the first stanza, in which Donne's speaker

compares his parting from his lady to the parting of the soul from a virtuous man at death, two main types of comparative images are introduced. "So let us melt, and make no noise" (line 5) refers to the melting of precious metal by a goldsmith or alchemist (pure gold does not sputter when melted). This image is developed later in lines 15–24 and culminates in the idea of "gold to airy thinness beat" (the finest gold leaf is actually buoyant and will float in the air like a feather). The second stanza also introduces another category of comparative images, those referring to the motions or changes of the earth and cosmos. The tears and sighs of parting lovers are depicted with witty exaggeration as "tear-floods" and "sigh-tempests" (line 6). These references are extended in the "Moving of th' earth" and "trepidation of the spheres" in the next stanza, and in the mockery of "Dull sublunary" lovers in the fourth stanza.

As each image in the poem unfolds, the speaker's attitude shifts as he responds to what the image means to him. He may joke or exaggerate as people who are close to one another sometimes do when faced with a crisis. Or he may remind himself and his lady of the undeniable importance of physical contact even as he praises their ability to do without it. The poem concludes with the famous image of the "stiff twin compasses" (line 26). Donne uses the plural "compasses" because he is thinking of the two connected feet of the sort of instrument we use to draw circles in geometry. These feet are separated and inclined when a circle is being drawn. When the circle is completed, the feet can be straightened up and closed. Donne's comparison is based upon the idea of the circle as a symbol of perfection, but the language in the last three stanzas also reminds us of the concerns that make up an earthly human relationship.

Ark Royal, flagship of Sir Walter Raleigh.
The Mansell Collection

Holy Sonnets

These poems were written between 1609 and 1611, before Donne was ordained. Donne's sonnets are of the Italian form, with a clear shift at the volta, or turn, after the eighth line, and a marked change of tone in the sestet. The tone of Donne's octaves, usually passionate and dramatic, gives way to a quiet, devotional tone in the sestets.

Map of the world (1585), showing winds blowing from various corners on a round globe.
Culver Pictures

Holy Sonnet 4

At the round earth's imagined corners,° blow
Your trumpets, angels; and arise, arise
From death, you numberless infinities
Of souls, and to your scattered bodies go;
All whom the flood did, and fire shall, o'erthrow,   5
All whom war, dearth, age, agues,° tyrannies,
Despair, law, chance hath slain, and you whose eyes
Shall behold God, and never taste death's woe.°
But let them sleep, Lord, and me mourn a space;
For, if above all these, my sins abound,   10
'Tis late to ask abundance of Thy grace
When we are there. Here on this lowly ground,
Teach me how to repent; for that's as good
As if Thou hadst sealed my pardon with Thy blood.

---

1. **imagined corners:** Donne may be thinking here of old flat maps of the world, which often depicted angels blowing their trumpets from the four corners. (See also Revelation 7:1.) 6. **agues** (ā′gyo͞oz): fevers, caused by malaria. 7–8. **you . . . woe:** those who will be alive at the time of the Last Judgment (Luke 9:27).

Holy Sonnet 6

Death, be not proud, though some have called thee
Mighty and dreadful, for thou art not so;
For those whom thou think'st thou dost overthrow
Die not, poor Death, nor yet canst thou kill me.
From rest and sleep, which but thy pictures be,   5
Much pleasure; then from thee much more must flow,°
And soonest our best men with thee do go,
Rest of their bones, and soul's delivery.°
Thou art slave to fate, chance, kings, and desperate men,
And dost with poison, war, and sickness dwell,   10
And poppy° or charms can make us sleep as well
And better than thy stroke; why swell'st° thou then?
One short sleep past, we wake eternally
And death shall be no more; Death, thou shalt die.

5–6. **From rest . . . flow:** If we get pleasure from rest and sleep, which are but images of death, we should derive much more from death itself. 7–8. **And soonest . . . soul's delivery:** Our best men go with you to rest their bones and free their souls. 11. **poppy:** opium, a narcotic drug. 12. **swell'st:** that is, with pride.

Holy Sonnet 10

Batter my heart, three-personed God;° for, you
As yet but knock, breathe, shine, and seek to mend;
That I may rise, and stand, o'erthrow me, and bend
Your force, to break, blow, burn, and make me new.
I, like an usurped town, to another due,°   5
Labor to admit you, but oh, to no end,
Reason your viceroy° in me, me should defend,
But is captived, and proves weak or untrue,
Yet dearly I love you, and would be loved fain,
But am betrothed unto your enemy,   10
Divorce me, untie, or break that knot again,
Take me to you, imprison me, for I
Except you enthral° me, never shall be free,
Nor ever chaste, except you ravish me.

---

1. **three-personed God:** the Trinity: Father, Son, and Holy Ghost. 5. **to another due:** owing allegiance to another, the devil. 7. **viceroy:** deputy. Reason was thought to be the link with God. 13. **enthral:** enslave.

FOR STUDY AND DISCUSSION

1. Sonnet 4 is a meditation on the Last Judgment. To what "flood" and "fire" does the poet refer in line 5? In your own words, describe whatever differences you see (in tone, action, rhythm) between the octave and the sestet of the sonnet.

2. In Sonnet 6 the speaker personifies Death for the purpose of diminishing Death's power. What is the speaker's attitude toward his own confrontation with Death? In the sestet, how does the speaker characterize Death? Explain the paradox in the last two lines of the sonnet.

3. In Sonnet 10 the speaker pleads for God's intervention in his life. In the octave, what specifically is the speaker asking God to do? Explain the paradoxes of the last two lines.

DONNE'S POETIC STYLE

John Donne's sharp reaction against the decorum of Elizabethan love poetry is readily seen by comparing his poetic style with that of Elizabethan poets like Spenser, Sidney, and Marlowe (see pages 126–132). The Elizabethans praised and pined for distant and idealized ladies in gentle and courtly language. Donne, on the other hand, used an unconventional, straightforward, and often brusque style. And, instead of perpetuating what he felt was the trite blandness of the typical Elizabethan metaphor in which a lady was described as a "fair flower"—her lips rubies, her eyes sapphires, and her locks gold—Donne used striking images and the *metaphysical conceit,* a less ornamental but still often extravagant metaphor that points out an unusual parallel between what are usually highly dissimilar elements. A conceit typical of Donne's original and far more intellectual style is his comparison of himself lying sick in bed to a map which is being studied by his doctors ("Hymn to God, My God, in My Sickness"). The comparisons are original and apt, however unconventional by Elizabethan standards.

Also characteristic of Donne's style is his use of *paradox,* a statement apparently, though not necessarily, self-contradictory. Look again, for example, at line 27 of "Song," where a lady is referred to as being "unkindly kind." This is an example of paradox, though a special kind of paradox, a figure of speech called *oxymoron.* Taken from the Greek *oxys* meaning "sharp" and *moros* meaning "foolish," oxymoron is a short self-contradictory phrase (like "living death" or "beloved enemy") which suggests a paradox in a very few words.

What are the apparent paradoxes in "A Valediction: Forbidding Mourning"? In the phrase "break, blow, burn, and make me new" in Holy Sonnet 10?

FOR COMPOSITION

Select from this book or from your outside reading two poems, one by a sixteenth-century poet and typically Elizabethan, and the other by John Donne and typical of his innovative work. Explain how these two poets contrast as to attitude, content, and language.

Meditation 17

Nunc lento sonitu dicunt, Morieris.
(Now, this bell tolling softly for another,
says to me, Thou must die.)

Perchance he for whom this bell tolls may be so ill as that he knows not it tolls for him; and perchance I may think myself so much better than I am as that they who are about me and see my state may have caused it to toll for me, and I know not that.

The church is catholic, universal, so are all her actions; all that she does belongs to all. When she baptizes a child, that action concerns me; for that child is thereby connected to that body which is my head too, and ingrafted into that body whereof I am a member.[1] And when she buries a man, that action concerns me: all mankind is of one author, and is one volume. When one man dies, one chapter is not torn out of the book, but translated[2] into a better language; and every chapter must be so translated. God employs several translators; some pieces are translated by age, some by sickness, some by war, some by justice; but God's hand is in every translation, and his hand shall bind up all our scattered leaves again for that library where every book shall lie open to one another.

As therefore the bell that rings to a sermon calls not upon the preacher only but upon the congregation to come, so this bell calls us all; but how much more me who am brought so near the door by this sickness! There was a contention as far as a suit[3]—in which piety and dignity, religion and estimation,[4] were mingled—which of the religious orders should ring to prayers first in the morning; and it was determined that they should ring first that rose earliest.

If we understand aright the dignity of this bell that tolls for our evening prayer, we would be glad to make it ours by rising early, in that application, that it might be ours as well as his, whose indeed it is.

The bell doth toll for him that thinks it doth; and though it intermit again, yet from that minute that that occasion wrought upon him he is united to God.

Who casts not up his eye to the sun when it rises? but who takes off his eye from a comet when that breaks out? Who bends not his ear to any bell which upon any occasion rings? but who can remove it from that bell which is passing a piece of himself out of this world?

No man is an island entire of itself; every man is a piece of the continent, a part of the main.[5] If a clod be washed away by the sea, Europe is the less, as well as if a promontory were, as well as if a manor[6] of thy friend's or of thine own were. Any man's death diminishes me, because I am involved in mankind, and therefore never send to know for whom the bell tolls; it tolls for thee.

Neither can we call this a begging of misery or a borrowing of misery, as though we were not miserable enough of ourselves but must fetch in more from the next house, in taking upon us the misery of our neighbors. Truly it were an excusable covetousness if we did, for affliction is a treasure, and scarce any man hath enough of it. No man hath affliction enough that is not matured and ripened by it and made fit for God by that affliction.

If a man carry treasure in bullion or in a

---

1. **member:** of the church.
2. **translated:** carried across spiritually from one realm to another.
3. **suit:** lawsuit.
4. **estimation:** self-esteem.

5. **main:** mainland.
6. **manor:** estate.

wedge of gold and have none coined into current money, his treasure will not defray him as he travels. Tribulation is treasure in the nature of it, but it is not current money in the use of it, except we get nearer and nearer our home, heaven, by it. Another man may be sick too, and sick to death, and this affliction may lie in his bowels as gold in a mine and be of no use to him; but this bell that tells me of his affliction digs out and applies that gold to me, if by this consideration of another's danger I take mine own into contemplation, and so secure myself by making my recourse to my God, who is our only security.

FOR STUDY AND DISCUSSION

1. What bell is Donne referring to at the beginning of "Meditation 17"? What is the connection between the tolling of this bell and "the bell that rings to a sermon," or the "bell that tolls for our evening prayer"?

2. Donne builds up very carefully to the famous sentence: "No man is an island entire of itself; every man is a piece of the continent, a part of the main." What other images does he use in the Meditation to express the idea that human beings do not exist in isolation, that everyone is a part of common humanity? How is this idea related to the theme of the tolling of the bell, summarized in ". . . never send to know for whom the bell tolls; it tolls for thee"?

FOR COMPOSITION

Donne's "Meditation 17" achieves both unity and diversity by stating a single theme and illustrating it with a number of variations. Donne's main theme is the one Ernest Hemingway used as the title of his novel *For Whom the Bell Tolls*. Write a short essay in which you state Donne's main theme and his variations. How do the variations relate to the central theme?

George Herbert
1593–1633

Herbert is the most important of the metaphysical poets after Donne. He was born into an aristocratic Welsh family and educated at Cambridge University, where his distinguished career resulted in his being elected Public Orator of the University. Herbert was in a position to rise to high public office or to a prominent place at court. He decided instead to become a minister. In 1630 he accepted a position in a small village church at Bemerton, near Salisbury. Here he preached eloquent sermons to the farmers and villagers and devoted himself to the care of his rural congregation. His ministry at Bemerton lasted only three years: he died in 1633 and was mourned by parishioners intensely loyal to this learned, aristocratic man who had given up a life of fame and prominence to serve them.

Although a friend and in some respects a poetic follower of Donne, Herbert's poetry is quieter, more graceful, less obviously dazzling in its argument and imagery. Where Donne's religious verse is often full of doubt, anxiety, and nervous energy, Herbert's is full of resignation, humility, and wise obedience. Herbert frequently makes use of *emblematic images*—verbal pictures or figures with a long tradition of moral or religious meaning attached to them. His ability to make us appreciate the value imbedded in traditional symbolic figures of this kind is delicate and masterful. Herbert is constantly trying to make poetry into an appropriate vehicle for prayer and devotion. The fact that he sometimes doubts whether poetry can be an adequate way of communicating with God testifies to the integrity of his poetic efforts.

The two poems presented here are taken from *The Temple,* a volume arranged by Herbert himself and published shortly after his death in 1633.

Virtue

Sweet day, so cool, so calm, so bright,
The bridal of the earth and sky;
The dew shall weep thy fall tonight,
     For thou must die.

Sweet rose, whose hue angry and brave°   5
Bids the rash gazer wipe his eye;
Thy root is ever in its grave,
     And thou must die.

Sweet spring, full of sweet days and roses,
A box where sweets° compacted lie;   10
My music shows ye have your closes,°
     And all must die.

Only a sweet and virtuous soul,
Like seasoned timber, never gives;
But though the whole world turn to coal,°   15
     Then chiefly lives.

---

5. **angry and brave:** red (the color of anger) and brilliant.   10. **sweets:** perfumes.
11. **closes:** the concluding cadences of a piece of music.   15. **turn to coal:** turn to cinder and ash in the fires of the Last Judgment (see II Peter 3:10).

Easter Wings

Lord, who createdst man in wealth and store,°
  Though foolishly he lost the same,
    Decaying more and more,
      Till he became
        Most poor: 5
        With thee
      O let me rise
    As larks, harmoniously,
  And sing this day thy victories:
Then shall the fall further the flight in me.   10

My tender age in sorrow did begin:
  And still with sicknesses and shame
    Thou didst so punish sin,
      That I became
        Most thin.   15
        With thee
      Let me combine,
    And feel this day thy victory:
  For, if I imp° my wing on thine,
Affliction shall advance the flight in me.   20

---

1. **store:** abundance.   19. **imp:** In falconry, feathers were grafted onto a falcon's damaged wing to help it fly.

FOR STUDY AND DISCUSSION

Virtue

1. The first two stanzas of "Virtue" are devoted to the "Sweet day" and the "Sweet rose." How are these aspects of the natural world treated in the first two lines of these stanzas? In the last two lines? How does the imagery of the third stanza relate to that of the first and second stanzas?

2. What words or phrases in the first three stanzas suggest a personification of nature? How is the act of personification related to the theme of death?

3. In the final stanza of "Virtue," Herbert compares the "sweet and virtuous" soul to "seasoned timber." Why is this image an effective one for the soul? How is this image related to the images of the rose and the spring used earlier in the poem?

Easter Wings

1. How does the shape of the poem help express its meaning?

2. What "fall" is Herbert referring to in line 10? What is paradoxical about a fall furthering a flight?

Andrew Marvell
1621–1678

The facts of Marvell's life present a deceptively stable and unspectacular background for his subtle, enigmatic poetry. The son of a Puritan clergyman from the north of England, Marvell attended Hull Grammar School and then went on to Cambridge University. After graduating in 1638, he traveled in Europe for a number of years before returning to England. Around 1650 he took a position as tutor to the daughter of Sir Thomas Fairfax, Lord-General of Oliver Cromwell's Parliamentary army. Marvell was highly skilled in the classical languages, and in 1657 he was made an assistant to John Milton, Latin Secretary for the Puritan Commonwealth (Milton composed official government documents in the formal Latin still required in the seventeenth century). The idea of Marvell as Milton's assistant is richly suggestive, for their poetry is in many respects complementary. Themes that Milton takes up in his bold, uncompromising grand manner are touched upon in Marvell's poetry with a cool, sophisticated indirectness. After the Restoration, when Milton was faced with imprisonment and perhaps even execution, Marvell seems to have been instrumental in working behind the scenes to secure the great poet's freedom. In 1659 Marvell was elected Member of Parliament for his home town of Hull, which he continued to represent until his death in 1678.

Although usually grouped with the metaphysical poets, Marvell stands apart from Donne and his followers in some respects. His tone, which is often light, witty, and even playful, links him with the Cavalier poets. Metrically, he prefers the graceful swing of the four-beat line in couplet and quatrain to the uneven cadence and irregular stanza of the metaphysicals. Yet there is great depth in Marvell's poetry. Marvell has a wonderful way of presenting extraordinary experiences from more than one perspective, and of making us see the strangeness in experiences so familiar that we are likely to take them for granted. His attitude is that of a poised and curious observer whose seriousness is mixed with a delight in the play of his own mind.

All of Marvell's lyric poems were written by the early 1650's, although they were not published until 1681, when they seemed old-fashioned and out-of-date. After the Commonwealth period, Marvell turned to prose and satire. He, like Donne, was largely forgotten during the eighteenth century. Again, it was the modern poet T. S. Eliot who helped to revive his reputation. Eliot saw that Marvell's wit and magniloquence joined together the two great strands of seventeenth-century poetry.

The Garden

How vainly men themselves amaze°
To win the palm, the oak, or bays;°
And their uncessant labors see
Crowned from some single herb or tree:
Whose short and narrow-vergèd shade   5
Does prudently their toils upbraid;
While all flowers and all trees do close°
To weave the garlands of repose.

Fair Quiet, have I found thee here,
And Innocence, thy sister dear!   10
Mistaken long, I sought you then
In busy companies of men.
Your sacred plants, if here below,
Only among the plants will grow.
Society is all but rude,   15
To° this delicious solitude.

No white nor red° was ever seen
So amorous as this lovely green.
Fond lovers, cruel as their flame,
Cut in these trees their mistress' name: 20
Little, alas, they know or heed
How far these beauties hers exceed!
Fair trees, wheresoe'er your barks I
    wound,
No name shall but your own be found.

---

1. **amaze:** perplex. 2. **the palm, the oak, or bays:** crowns of victory for athletes, statesmen, and poets, respectively. 7. **close:** unite. 16. **To:** compared to. 17. **white nor red:** a lady's complexion, i.e., female beauty.

When we have run our passion's
    heat,°   25
Love hither makes his best retreat.°
The gods, that mortal beauty chase,
Still in a tree did end their race:
Apollo hunted Daphne so,
Only that she might laurel grow;   30
And Pan did after Syrinx speed,
Not as a nymph, but for a reed.°

What wondrous life in this I lead!
Ripe apples drop about my head;
The luscious clusters of the vine   35
Upon my mouth do crush their wine;
The nectarine and curious° peach
Into my hands themselves do reach;
Stumbling on melons, as I pass,
Ensnared with flowers, I fall on grass.   40

Meanwhile the mind from pleasure
    less°
Withdraws into its happiness;
The mind, that ocean° where each kind
Does straight its own resemblance
    find;
Yet it creates, transcending these,   45
Far other worlds and other seas,°
Annihilating all that's made
To a green thought in a green shade.°

Here at the fountain's sliding foot,
Or at some fruit-tree's mossy root,   50
Casting the body's vest aside,
My soul into the boughs does glide:
There, like a bird, it sits and sings,
Then whets° and combs its silver
    wings,
And, till prepared for longer flights,   55
Waves in its plumes the various light.°

Such was that happy garden-state,
While man there walked without a
    mate:
After a place so pure and sweet,
What other help could yet be meet!°   60
But 'twas beyond a mortal's share
To wander solitary there:
Two paradises 'twere in one
To live in paradise alone.

How well the skillful gardener drew,   65
Of flowers and herbs, this dial° new;
Where, from above, the milder sun
Does through a fragrant zodiac run;
And, as it works, the industrious bee
Computes its time° as well as we!   70
How could such sweet and wholesome
    hours
Be reckoned but with herbs and flowers!

---

25. **heat:** race.   26. **retreat:** in religious and military senses.   29–32. **Apollo . . . reed:** Apollo pursued Daphne, who escaped by turning into a laurel tree; Pan pursued Syrinx, who was transformed into a reed, from which he made his pipes.   37. **curious:** exquisite, rare.   41. **from pleasure less:** experiencing less pleasure in nature than the senses do (and so turning inward). 43. **ocean:** It was believed that the sea contained creatures resembling all of those on land. The implication is that the mind comprehends everything in the world.   45–46. **Yet . . . seas:** The imagination creates worlds that have no equivalent in the real world. 48. **green shade:** In the Renaissance the garden symbolized the contemplative life.

54. **whets:** preens.   56. **various light:** many-colored light (in contrast to the white light of eternity). 60. **meet:** suitable; in Genesis 2:18, God gives Adam a help meet, Eve.   66. **dial:** sundial. The implication is that the growth and decline of the garden records the passage of time.   70. **time:** a pun on the herb *thyme*, out of which bees make honey.

COMMENTARY

Gardens in Renaissance literature are usually places that invite us to delight in the pleasures of the senses. A garden is a special part of the natural world set aside and improved upon by human skill and ingenuity. All the delightful things in nature — flowers, fruits, shade trees, running brooks — are concentrated and perfected; all the unpleasant things are excluded. The garden is traditionally a favorite place of retreat from the concerns and uncertainties of the outside world. We enter the garden to relax, to indulge our senses of sight, smell, and hearing, and often to be alone with the person we love.

The garden of Marvell's poem seems at first to fit the traditional Renaissance version exactly. Having entered it, the speaker talks about how pointless are the struggles of the world he has left behind. He revels in the quiet coolness, and in a natural profusion so lush that it literally thrusts itself upon him. But what Marvell's speaker seems to enjoy more than anything else is solitude, and here the significance of the garden in this poem begins to veer away from that of the traditional paradise of sensory delights. The speaker scoffs at the "Fond lovers" (line 19) who have come to the garden together and have celebrated their affection by carving their names in the bark of the trees. He jests that he would carve the name of each tree into its bark, suggesting that his only loves are the oak, elm, and maple. He wants to escape from "passion's heat" (line 25). In lines 27–32 he says that when the ancient gods pursued maidens, their real goal was a vegetable love.

The climax of the poem comes in lines 41–48, when, even as his senses are being overwhelmed by the fruits of the garden, his mind "Withdraws into its happiness" (line 42). Marvell's garden is ultimately a paradise of the mind and the spirit, not of the senses. In lines 57–64, the speaker speculates that God originally created the Garden of Eden as just such a spiritual paradise. But the key element, as we have seen all along, is solitude. When man came to share the Garden of Eden with a mate, the speaker suggests, the possibility of temptation was too great. This reliance on and fondness for solitude is the most important characteristic of Marvell's speaker. It is a characteristic the poem asks us to think about carefully, and not simply to take for granted.

FOR STUDY AND DISCUSSION

1. What pleasures does the speaker find in the garden? Can they be found elsewhere? Judging from lines 15–16 and lines 61–64, what does the speaker seem to enjoy most in the garden?

2. Color, often used symbolically, is very important in "The Garden." In lines 17–24, what are the colors red and white associated with? How does the color green relate to red and white?

3. Look carefully at lines 33–40, where the speaker describes his enjoyment of the fruits. How do you interpret the last two lines of this stanza? How does this stanza relate to the Fall of Adam and Eve, alluded to in lines 57–64?

4. How is the mind described in lines 41–48? How can the mind both create and annihilate (lines 45–47)?

5. "The Garden" is one of the finest examples of pastoral poetry in the English language. What atmosphere does Marvell create in the poem? What is his attitude toward nature?

FOR COMPOSITION

Compare "The Garden" with Marlowe's "The Passionate Shepherd to His Love" (page 132). In what ways are these poems similar? In what ways different?

Henry Vaughan
1621–1695

Like George Herbert, whose poetry he greatly admired, Henry Vaughan was a Welshman. He studied at Oxford University but did not complete his degree. He then spent some time in London studying law. During the Civil War he fought with the Royalist forces of Charles I, and his earliest poems are written in the nonchalant, offhand manner of the Cavalier poets. Later in the 1640's Vaughan took up the study of medicine, and in 1647 he went back to his native Wales to set up practice. There he began to write poetry that was much more serious than his earlier verse. His most important volume, *Silex Scintillans,* was published in 1650. The title means "The Fiery Flint" and refers to the poet's own heart, which is imagined as a flint from which God has struck sparks of divine poetic inspiration. "I was deaf and dumb: a flint," Vaughan says to God at the beginning of the volume: "You launch your attack and shatter that boulder, my stony heart. . . . Look, its fragments are flashing at last to heaven and to you, and my cheeks are wet with tears wrung from flint."

Vaughan is the most mystical and emotional of all the metaphysical poets. His twin brother Thomas was an eccentric philosopher and practitioner of alchemy, and Henry himself was interested in occult relationships between the natural and spiritual worlds. In a century that was being increasingly dominated by scientific rationalism and materialism, Vaughan kept alive in his poems a sense of a spiritual dimension in nature, revealed in signs and symbols to which the rational mind is blind. Only God's divine inspiration can pierce through the veil that normally obscures earthly perception.

In "The Retreat," one of his finest poems, Vaughan imagines a state of pure spiritual existence prior to the individual's life on earth. Vaughan's speaker longs to return to early childhood, that moment of life when the individual has just left behind this condition of pure spiritual existence. The poem is a fascinating anticipation of William Wordsworth's famous "Ode on Intimations of Immortality from Recollections of Early Childhood," written more than one hundred fifty years later.

An Elizabethan musing by Sir Isaac Oliver, showing a figure who has withdrawn from the society of house and garden (in background) to a retreat with nature.

The Retreat

Happy those early days, when I
Shined in my angel-infancy!
Before I understood this place
Appointed for my second race,°
Or taught my soul to fancy aught   5
But a white, celestial thought;
When yet I had not walked above
A mile or two from my first love;
And looking back, at that short space,
Could see a glimpse of His bright face;   10
When on some gilded cloud or flower
My gazing soul would dwell an hour,
And in those weaker glories spy
Some shadows° of eternity;
Before I taught my tongue to wound   15
My conscience with a sinful sound,

Or had the black art to dispense
A several° sin to every sense,
But felt through all this fleshy dress
Bright shoots of everlastingness.   20
   O how I long to travel back,
And tread again that ancient track!
That I might once more reach that plain,
Where first I left my glorious train;°
From whence th' enlightened spirit sees   25
That shady city of palm trees.°
But ah! my soul with too much stay°
Is drunk, and staggers in the way!
Some men a forward motion love,
But I by backward steps would move;   30
And, when this dust falls to the urn,
In that state I came, return.°

---

4. **second race:** earthly existence; the first was in
heaven.   14. **shadows:** images.

18. **several:** different.   24. **train:** way of life.
26. **shady city of palm trees:** perhaps Paradise, or more
likely the New Jerusalem, the Heavenly City spoken of
in the Bible (Deuteronomy 34:1–4).   27. **stay:** delay.
32. **return:** and would return.

FOR STUDY AND DISCUSSION

Why do you think Henry Vaughan calls his poem
"The Retreat"? What does Vaughan mean by
"angel-infancy" (line 2)? By "my first love" (line
8)? To what state does he wish to return?

FOR COMPOSITION

Compare the different ideas of retreat explored in
Marvell's "The Garden" and Vaughan's "The Retreat." What do these different ideas of retreat and
solitude have in common?

The Tribe of Ben

Ben Jonson, the great poet and dramatist of the early seventeenth century, exerted a tremendous influence over the literary ideals and practices of his own age and of succeeding ages. In the latter part of his life, he assumed the role of literary celebrity and arbiter of taste. He had many friends and admirers among his contemporaries, but the most loyal were a group of younger writers who loved to meet, talk, and drink with Jonson at the Mermaid, the Old Devil Inn, and other London taverns frequented by literary types. Robert Herrick, Thomas Carew, Sir John Suckling—these are the best known of the young wits whom Jonson himself referred to as "The Tribe of Ben."

Jonson was a learned student of classical Latin poetry; his standards of verbal clarity, efficiency, and perfection were often demanding to the point of severity. But there is also a lighter, more informal, more personal side of Jonson's verse, and it was this side that came to be reflected most consistently in the poems written by the Tribe of Ben. Since some of these followers of Jonson were wealthy aristocrats and country gentlemen who fought on the side of King Charles I in the Civil War, they are also frequently called the Cavalier poets. Referring to the easy, seemingly casual style of Cavalier poetry, a modern critic once joked that it sounds as if it were written while falling off a horse. But the casualness is largely a carefully cultivated manner. Jonson's insistence on the hard work and craft of writing may be felt behind the best Cavalier poetry, with its polished lines and neatly turned phrases. This aspect of Jonson's legacy was to become extremely important in poetry in the age of John Dryden and Alexander Pope.

Ben Jonson
1572–1637

Ben Jonson is the most important dramatist of his age after Shakespeare, as we noted in the general introduction to the Renaissance. His stature as a poet is no less imposing. Even more than Donne, Jonson set an example for later poets that would have a lasting effect throughout the seventeenth and eighteenth centuries.

Unlike most of his followers in the "Tribe of Ben," Jonson did not come from a family of land and wealth. His father, a minister, died when Jonson was an infant, and he was adopted by a bricklayer. He managed to receive a good secondary education while growing up in London, but he never attended a university. Much of Jonson's immense learning was acquired through private reading and study. After working for a time as a bricklayer, he entered the army and fought in Flanders on the side of the Dutch Protestants in their struggle for independence from Spain. Returning to London around 1595, he went to work as an actor and playwright, and he was immediately successful. The major obstacle to his early literary career was a hot temper. He was once jailed for killing a fellow actor in a duel, and throughout his career he was embroiled in bitter literary disputes with other playwrights. Yet Jonson did grow mellower with age and increasing recognition. From 1605 on, Jonson produced masques for the court of James I— elaborate and expensive allegorical spectacles combining music, drama, and dance, and always culminating in a compliment to the king or the royal family. In 1616 James appointed Jonson poet laureate and granted him a comfortable pension. His death in 1637, only a few years after Charles I was faced with open rebellion, was mourned as the end of an era.

Jonson's poetry marks the serious beginning of that movement in English art, literature, and taste which we know as *neoclassicism*. Earlier Renaissance writers had of course studied the classical Greek and Latin authors, but Jonson made such study a much more systematic basis for his own art. He wrote in all the classical poetic forms except epic: epigram, satire, verse epistle, epitaph, ode. His lighter lyrics and songs, some of which are represented on pages 254–257, flow with an ease and a purity that come from Jonson's absolute mastery of rhythm and sound. They are the finest poems of their kind in English.

Ben Jonson (painting after A. Blyenberch), Anon. Granger Collection

On My First Son

Farewell, thou child of my right hand,° and joy;
　My sin was too much hope of thee, loved boy,
Seven years thou wert lent to me, and I thee pay,
　Exacted by thy fate, on the just day.°
O, could I lose all father° now! For why　　　　　　　　　5
　Will man lament the state he should envy?
To have so soon 'scaped world's and flesh's rage,
　And, if no other misery, yet age!
Rest in soft peace, and, asked, say here doth lie
　Ben Jonson his best piece of poetry;　　　　　　　　　10
For whose sake, henceforth, all his vows be such
　As what he loves may never like too much.

---

1. **child of my right hand:** The Hebrew name, Benjamin, means literally "son of
my right hand." Jonson's son died of the plague in 1603. 4. **on . . . day:** exactly
on the day. 5. **lose . . . father:** lose the feeling of being a father.

Song: To Celia

Drink to me only with thine eyes,
And I will pledge with mine;
Or leave a kiss but in the cup,
And I'll not look for wine.
The thirst that from the soul doth rise,　　　　　　　　　5
Doth ask a drink divine:
But might I of Jove's nectar sup,
I would not change for thine.

I sent thee late a rosy wreath,
Not so much honoring thee,　　　　　　　　　　　　　　10
As giving it a hope, that there
It could not withered be.
But thou thereon did'st only breathe,
And sent'st it back to me;
Since when it grows, and smells, I swear,　　　　　　　15
Not of itself, but thee.

To the Memory of My Beloved Master, William Shakespeare

To draw no envy, Shakespeare, on thy name,
Am I thus ample to thy book and fame;
While I confess thy writings to be such
As neither man nor muse can praise too much.
'Tis true, and all men's suffrage.° But these ways   5
Were not the paths I meant unto thy praise:
For silliest° ignorance on these may light,
Which, when it sounds at best, but echoes right;
Or blind affection, which doth ne'er advance
The truth, but gropes, and urgeth all by chance;   10
Or crafty malice might pretend this praise,
And think to ruin, where it seemed to raise . . .
But thou art proof against them, and, indeed,
Above the ill fortune of them, or the need.
I therefore will begin. Soul of the age!   15
The applause, delight, the wonder of our stage!
My Shakespeare, rise! I will not lodge thee by
Chaucer, or Spenser, or bid Beaumont° lie
A little further, to make thee a room.
Thou art a monument without a tomb,   20
And art alive still while thy book doth live
And we have wits to read and praise to give.
That I not mix thee so, my brain excuses,
I mean with great, but disproportioned Muses;
For if I thought my judgment were of years,   25
I should commit thee surely with thy peers,
And tell how far thou didst our Lyly outshine,
Or sporting Kyd, or Marlowe's° mighty line.
And though thou hadst small Latin and less Greek,
From thence to honor thee, I would not seek   30
For names; but call forth thundering Aeschylus,
Euripides, and Sophocles to us;
Pacuvius, Accius,° him of Cordova dead,°
To life again, to hear thy buskin° tread,
And shake a stage; or, when thy socks° were on,   35

---

5. **suffrage:** vote; decision.   7. **silliest:** simplest, most innocent.   18. **Beaumont:** Francis Beaumont, a dramatist and contemporary of Jonson and Shakespeare.   27–28. **Lyly, Kyd, Marlowe:** sixteenth-century English dramatists who influenced Shakespeare.   31–33. **Aeschylus . . . Accius:** classical Greek and Roman writers of tragedy.   33. **him . . . dead:** refers to Seneca.   34. **buskin:** a thick-soled shoe, worn by tragic actors.   35. **socks:** thin-soled shoes, worn by comic actors.

Leave thee alone for the comparison
Of all that insolent Greece or haughty Rome
Sent forth, or since did from their ashes come.
Triumph, my Britain, thou hast one to show
To whom all scenes of Europe homage owe.   40
He was not of an age, but for all time!
And all the Muses still were in their prime,
When, like Apollo, he came forth to warm
Our ears, or like a Mercury to charm.
Nature herself was proud of his designs   45
And joyed to wear the dressing of his lines,
Which were so richly spun, and woven so fit,
As, since, she will vouchsafe no other wit.
The merry Greek, tart Aristophanes,
Neat Terence, witty Plautus,° now not please,   50
But antiquated and deserted lie,
As they were not of Nature's family.
Yet must I not give Nature all; thy art,
My gentle Shakespeare, must enjoy a part.
For though the poet's matter nature be,   55
His art doth give the fashion; and, that he
Who casts to write a living line, must sweat
(Such as thine are) and strike the second heat
Upon the Muses' anvil, turn the same
(And himself with it) that he thinks to frame,   60
Or, for the laurel, he may gain a scorn;
For a good poet's made, as well as born.
And such wert thou! Look how the father's face
Lives in his issue; even so the race
Of Shakespeare's mind and manners brightly shines   65
In his well turnèd and true filèd° lines;
In each of which he seems to shake a lance,°
As brandished at the eyes of ignorance.
Sweet swan of Avon! what a sight it were
To see thee in our waters yet appear,   70
And make those flights upon the banks of Thames
That so did take Eliza and our James!°
But stay, I see thee in the hemisphere
Advanced, and made a constellation there!
Shine forth, thou Star of Poets, and with rage   75
Or influence, chide or cheer the drooping stage,
Which, since thy flight from hence, hath mourned like night,
And despairs day, but for thy volume's light.

49–50. **Aristophanes . . . Plautus:** classical Greek and Roman writers of comedy
admired by Jonson.   66. **filèd:** polished.   67. **shake a lance:** probably a pun on
Shakespeare's name.   72. **Eliza . . . James:** Queen Elizabeth I and King James I.
(Shakespeare's plays were performed for both.)

It Is Not Growing like a Tree

It is not growing like a tree
  In bulk, doth make man better be;
Or standing long an oak, three hundred year,
To fall a log at last, dry, bald, and sere:
     A lily of a day   5
      Is fairer far in May;
  Although it fall and die that night,
  It was the plant and flower of light.
In small proportions, we just beauties see,
And in short measures, life may perfect be.   10

Queen and Huntress

Queen and huntress, chaste and fair,
  Now the sun is laid to sleep,
Seated in thy silver chair,
  State in wonted manner keep:
    Hesperus° entreats thy light   5
    Goddess excellently bright.

Earth, let not thy envious shade
  Dare itself to interpose;
Cynthia's° shining orb was made
  Heaven to clear when day did close: 10
    Bless us then with wishèd sight,
    Goddess excellently bright.

Lay thy bow of pearl apart,
  And thy crystal-shining quiver;
Give unto the flying hart°   15
    Space to breathe, how short soever:
    Thou that mak'st a day of night—
    Goddess excellently bright.

The Chase of Diana (detail) by
Zampieri Domenico, Galleria Borghese, Rome.
Editorial Photocolor Archives

---

5. **Hesperus** (hĕs′pĕr-əs): the evening star. 9. **Cynthia:** another name for the
moon goddess, Diana. 15. **hart:** male deer. Diana was also goddess of the hunt.

FOR STUDY AND DISCUSSION

On My First Son

How would you describe the tone of this poem? What line tells you that Jonson considered his son his most perfect creation? Jonson says we should envy the dead and that death has a number of advantages. What might be his purpose in saying this?

Song: To Celia

How does the singer use the idea of drinking a cup of wine to compliment his lady? What object or experience provides the focus in the second stanza? What clever turn of thought provides the compliment at the end of the poem?

To the Memory of My Beloved Master

What does Jonson reveal about himself in his tribute to Shakespeare? In what specific ways does he describe Shakespeare's greatness as a poet and a dramatist?

It Is Not Growing like a Tree

In this poem is Jonson arguing that the lily is superior to the oak tree? Explain your answer. Without reference to trees and lilies, state Jonson's theme.

Queen and Huntress

This song is from the final masque in *Cynthia's Revels* (1600) in which Cynthia (Diana) symbolizes Queen Elizabeth. Diana was the classical goddess associated with chastity, with the moon, and with the hunt. What images in each stanza contribute to our sense of these attributes? What specific qualities do the images in the three stanzas have in common?

FOR COMPOSITION

1. "It Is Not Growing like a Tree" belongs to a tradition called "the good life," after a poem by the Roman poet Horace. Herbert's poem "Virtue" is another poem of the same type. Compare the good advice that each poet gives on how to live. Which do you think is the better advice?

2. Ben Jonson's tombstone in Westminster Abbey bears the legend "O Rare Ben Jonson." The five selections you have read make up only a tiny sampling of his work, but they do suggest the variety in which his genius expressed itself. Using direct quotations as illustrations, write a short essay showing why Jonson deserved to be called "rare."

Robert Herrick
1591–1674

Robert Herrick was the most demonstratively loyal of all the members of the "Tribe of Ben." He was not a country aristocrat, however—he came from the London middle class. His father was a goldsmith, and since he died shortly after the poet's birth, Herrick was apprenticed at an early age to his wealthy uncle, also a jeweler and goldsmith. He eventually went to study at Cambridge University, where he received his B.A. in 1617 and his M.A. in 1620. Herrick was ordained in 1623, but he did not accept a church position immediately. He was deeply attached to London, and he returned there to live the enjoyable life of fraternizing with Jonson and his circle. In 1629, however, the time came for him to assume a more responsible and independent existence. Somewhat reluctantly, he left London to become the rector of Dean Prior in Devonshire, a lovely rural county far in the southwest of England.

At first Herrick seems not to have enjoyed the life of a country parson, so far removed from the lively, sophisticated conversation at the Old Devil Inn. His poems suggest that he lived in his imagination the witty, urbane social existence he really longed for. But they also suggest that he eventually came to love the fresh Devonshire countryside, famous for strawberries, thick cream, and lovely west-country girls.

In 1647 Herrick was made to feel the effects of the Civil War. As an Anglican clergyman, he was ejected from his position as rector at Dean Prior. He had to return to London, and when he did so he took the opportunity of publishing the poems he had written under two titles: *Hesperides* for the secular poems, *Noble Numbers* for the religious poems. Both groups appeared in a single volume in 1648. But the country was in turmoil at this time over the trial and execution of Charles I, and not much was made of Herrick's poetry. He returned to his position at Dean Prior after the Restoration in 1660 and lived there until his death without ever publishing his poetry again.

All Herrick's poems are distinguished by their high degree of stylistic polish, their classical balance and sense of proportion, and their modesty of theme and argument. Herrick is not directly concerned with the deeper questions of life. He customarily takes up a light, even whimsical subject, and articulates his response to it with a delicate warmth and sureness of touch. The refinement of his poetic craftmanship inevitably reminds one of his early association with the art of the jeweler and the goldsmith. His best poems are like richly worked miniatures—they give us that special pleasure of contemplating the small thing done incomparably well.

To the Virgins, to Make Much of Time

Gather ye rosebuds while ye may,
  Old Time is still a-flying;
And this same flower that smiles today,
  Tomorrow will be dying.

The glorious lamp of heaven, the sun,   5
  The higher he's a-getting;
The sooner will his race be run,
  And nearer he's to setting.

That age is best which is the first,
  When youth and blood are warmer;   10
But being spent, the worse, and worst
  Times, still succeed the former.

Then be not coy, but use your time;
  And while ye may, go marry:
For having lost but once your prime,   15
  You may forever tarry.

An Ode for Him (Ben Jonson)

       Ah Ben!
     Say how, or when
    Shall we thy guests
  Meet at those lyric feasts,
     Made at the Sun,   5
  The Dog, the Triple Tun?°
Where we such clusters had,
As made us nobly wild, not mad;
  And yet each verse of thine
Outdid the meat, outdid the frolic wine.   10

       My Ben
   Or° come again:
   Or send to us,
  Thy wit's great overplus;
     But teach us yet   15
   Wisely to husband° it;
  Lest we that talent spend:
And having once brought to an end
  That precious stock, the store
Of such a wit the world should have no more.   20

5–6. **Sun, Dog, Triple Tun:** the names of taverns where Herrick used to associate with Jonson and the Tribe of Ben.   12. **Or:** either.   16. **husband:** conserve.

FOR STUDY AND DISCUSSION

To the Virgins, to Make Much of Time
The theme of this poem, "live for today," belongs to a tradition known as *carpe diem* (literally "seize the day") that was typically Cavalier. Which lines in this poem best summarize this theme? How do the symbols in this poem help convey this theme? What is the tone of the poem?

An Ode for Him
1. This is one of many tributes in verse paid by Herrick to Ben Jonson. What aspects of his friendship with Jonson does Herrick recall? In stanza 2, what danger does Herrick see in following Jonson's great example? How can Jonson himself help his followers contend with this danger?

2. Notice the shape of the stanzas. How does the movement from shorter to longer lines in each stanza control the pace and organization of thought in the poem?

FOR COMPOSITION

1. Do you think that the idea of "living for today" would have been popular during the Middle Ages? Why or why not? Do you think it is popular today? Write a short composition giving reasons for your answers.

2. "An Ode for Him," like Jonson's "Song: To Celia," depends upon exaggeration. Many compliments do. Try writing a thank-you note to a friend in which you compliment by exaggeration.

Sir John Suckling
1609–1642

Richard Lovelace
1618–1657

Suckling and Lovelace are the two names always associated with Cavalier poetry, and rightly so: both of them were in fact soldiers in the Cavalier army of Charles I. Before the Civil War, Sir John Suckling was already notorious at the court of Charles I as a gambler and a rake. When war broke out, he used his wealth and influence to raise a company of one hundred men, lavishly outfitted in scarlet coats and white doublets, to fight for the king. The troop was hopelessly ineffective. Later Suckling took part in a plot to rescue the leader of the Royalist army from imprisonment in the Tower of London. The plot was discovered, and Suckling had to flee England. He died in Paris a short time later, neglected and deprived of the great wealth he had once possessed.

Lovelace came from an old and wealthy Kentish family. With his good looks and elegant manners, he created quite a stir when he went to study at Oxford University. After Oxford he became a favorite courtier under King Charles and Queen Henrietta Maria. Naturally he was a staunch supporter of the king during the Civil War. Having been once imprisoned by the Parliamentary forces, he left England for a time to fight with the French army against the Spanish. When he returned to England he was again thrown into prison. Like Suckling, he lost all his wealth and land during this turbulent period. In 1657 he died in poverty at age thirty-nine.

The poems of Suckling and Lovelace epitomize what we think of as the Cavalier manner: witty, charming, graceful in a way that shows their poetic discipleship to Ben Jonson. Lovelace is on the whole more serious than "natural, easy Suckling," whose poems are sometimes merely suave verbal trifles. At its best the poetry of both Suckling and Lovelace is tinged with a slight element of desperation or melancholy—which may remind us that behind a façade of gallantry and elegance, their careless, aristocratic lives were crumbling away. Their poems are always concerned, in one way or another, with the passing of time.

The Constant Lover

Sir John Suckling

Out upon it! I have loved
    Three whole days together!
And am like to love three more,
    If it prove fair weather.

Time shall molt away his wings   5
    Ere he shall discover
In the whole wide world again
    Such a constant lover.

But the spite on 't is, no praise
    Is due at all to me: 10
Love with me had made no stays,
    Had it any been but she.

Had it any been but she,
    And that very face,
There had been at least ere this   15
    A dozen dozen in her place.

Why So Pale and Wan

Sir John Suckling

Why so pale and wan, fond lover?
   Prithee, why so pale?
Will, when looking well can't move her,
   Looking ill prevail?
   Prithee, why so pale?   5

Why so dull and mute, young sinner?
   Prithee, why so mute?
Will, when speaking well can't win her,
   Saying nothing do 't?
   Prithee, why so mute?   10

Quit, quit for shame! This will not move;
   This cannot take her.
If of herself she will not love,
   Nothing can make her:
   The devil take her!   15

To Althea,° from Prison

Richard Lovelace

When Love with unconfinèd wings
   Hovers within my gates,
And my divine Althea brings
   To whisper at the grates;
When I lie tangled in her hair   5
   And fettered to her eye,
The birds that wanton° in the air
   Know no such liberty.

When flowing cups run swiftly round
   With no allaying Thames,°   10
Our careless heads with roses bound,
   Our hearts with loyal flames;
When thirsty grief in wine we steep,
   When healths and draughts go free—
Fishes that tipple in the deep   15
   Know no such liberty.

When, like committed linnets,° I
   With shriller throat shall sing
The sweetness, mercy, majesty,
   And glories of my king;°   20
When I shall voice aloud how good
   He is, how great should be,
Enlargèd° winds, that curl the flood,
   Know no such liberty.

Stone walls do not a prison make,   25
   Nor iron bars a cage;
Minds innocent and quiet take
   That for an hermitage;°
If I have freedom in my love
   And in my soul am free,   30
Angels alone, that soar above,
   Enjoy such liberty.

°**Althea** (ăl-thē′ə). 7. **wanton** (wŏn′tən): play about.
9–10. **cups ... Thames:** wine undiluted with water
(from the river Thames). 17. **committed linnets:** caged
birds. 20. **my king:** Charles I, in whose service Lovelace was "committed" to prison. 23. **Enlargèd:** set free
or released. 27–28. **Minds ... hermitage:** Even a
prison may be suitable for quiet meditation.

To Lucasta, on Going to the Wars

Richard Lovelace

Tell me not, sweet, I am unkind,
   That from the nunnery
Of thy chaste breast and quiet mind
   To war and arms I fly.

True, a new mistress now I chase,   5
   The first foe in the field;
And with a stronger faith embrace
   A sword, a horse, a shield.

Yet this inconstancy is such
   As you too shall adore;   10
I could not love thee, dear, so much,
   Loved I not honor more.

FOR STUDY AND DISCUSSION

The Constant Lover

Suckling's speaker is bragging about the constancy of his love. How do we know that the speaker is consciously ironic? How does the speaker's attitude change in the third stanza, as he begins to compliment his lady? How are the wit and irony of the first two stanzas extended in the last stanza of the poem?

Why So Pale and Wan

The speaker of this poem is attempting to tease an unhappy lover out of his depression. What features of the stanzas give the poem a clever arrangement? What does the surprising ending of the poem suggest about the speaker's attitude?

To Althea, from Prison

In this poem what three kinds of liberty are described? Note in the first three stanzas the comparison with something in nature. In what ways is the choice appropriate for each stanza? How does the fourth stanza form a climax to the three stanzas that precede it?

To Lucasta, on Going to the Wars

Lovelace's poem depends upon the speaker's applying to warfare language normally used to describe love and courtship. Which words in the poem are transferred in this way? What does this entire process suggest about the speaker's attitude toward going to the wars? What do the last two lines of the poem mean?

FOR COMPOSITION

Lovelace and Suckling, considered by many as twin stereotypes of the Cavalier ideal, are sometimes also contrasted. The last stanza of "Why So Pale and Wan" and the last two lines of "To Lucasta, on Going to the Wars" are well-known lines of English poetry. Write a short essay in which you contrast the philosophies of the two poets as expressed in these lines.

George Wither

1621–1678

George Wither is remembered today as a writer of clear and sparkling pastoral poetry. His uncompromising character is evident both in his politics and in his poetry: his politics moved him from Royalist to Puritan; his poetry defied the age by harking back to Elizabethan traditions. He wrote poetry that was extremely popular in spite of its unfashionable pastoral content, and satirical political pamphlets that soon landed him in prison. The period of his best lyric writing ended in 1622 with the publication of *Fair Virtue, the Mistress of Philarete,* which includes "Shall I, Wasting in Despair." Thereafter Wither's growing immersion in Puritanism seemed to stifle his gift for poetry. Captured by the Royalists, he was saved from death only by the intervention of Sir John Denham, who claimed he saved Wither so that he himself would not be considered the worst poet in England! Not long after the Civil War, he lost his appointment under Cromwell "by declaring unto him [Cromwell] those truths which he was not willing to hear of." Later, Wither's pamphleteering resulted in another prison term. His poetic reputation waned during his lifetime only to be revived by Charles Lamb and others who admired the "virile lyricism" of his early poetry.

Shall I, Wasting in Despair

Shall I, wasting in despair,
Die, because a woman's fair?
Or make pale my cheeks with care,
'Cause another's rosy are?
Be she fairer than the day,   5
Or the flowery meads in May,
　　If she be not so to me,
　　What care I how fair she be?

Should my heart be grieved or pined,
'Cause I see a woman kind?   10
Or a well-disposèd nature
Joinèd with a lovely feature?
Be she meeker, kinder than
Turtle dove, or pelican,°
　　If she be not so to me,   15
　　What care I how kind she be?

Shall a woman's virtues move
Me to perish for her love?
Or her well-deserving known,
Make me quite forget mine own?   20
Be she with that goodness blest
Which may gain her name of best,
　　If she be not such to me,
　　What care I how good she be?

'Cause her fortune seems too high,   25
Shall I play the fool and die?
Those that bear a noble mind,
Where they want° of riches find,
Think, "What, with them, they would do
That, without them, dare to woo!"   30
　　And unless that mind I see,
　　What care I though great she be?

Great, or good, or kind, or fair,
I will ne'er the more despair!
If she love me (this believe!)   35
I will die, ere she shall grieve;
If she slight me when I woo,
I can scorn, and let her go;
　　For if she be not for me,
　　What care I for whom she be?   40

---

14. **pelican:** a bird which was believed to tear open its breast in order to feed its offspring with its own blood.

28. **want:** lack.

The Puritan Age

John Milton
1608–1674

Milton is the greatest writer of the seventeenth century, and one of the giants of English literature as a whole. In his life and literary career the two dominant historical movements of Renaissance and Reformation combine and receive their most intense and intelligent expression. He towers over his age as Shakespeare towers over the Elizabethan age, and as Chaucer towers over the medieval period.

Milton was born in London. His education began at St. Paul's School, where he showed from the beginning a prodigious talent for mastering the ancient languages and literatures: Greek, Latin, and Hebrew. He went on to distinguish himself at Cambridge University, where he graduated B.A. in 1629, M.A. in 1632. He might well have entered the ministry upon completing his formal studies. But Milton decided that he had still not fully equipped himself for the work he was capable of performing, and he retired for five years to his father's country house in Buckinghamshire, where he read virtually all there was to read of ancient and modern writing. His poetic compositions came only occasionally during this period of intense private study. In 1634 he wrote a masque called *Comus* at the request of an aristocratic family who lived nearby. In 1637 he wrote the finest pastoral elegy in English, *Lycidas*, to memorialize the tragic death of a Cambridge friend and classmate. But basically during this period Milton was preparing himself for more ambitious undertakings, in religion and politics as well as in poetry. In 1638 he left England to complete his education with two years of travel in Europe. When he returned home late in 1639, England was on the verge of civil war.

Milton was an ardent Puritan all his life. For him the heart of the Christian religion was the individual's relation to God. Each person had to be free to develop his or her own understanding of God's word through careful and dedicated study of the Bible. In his view, the Church of England still retained many of those rituals and institutions of au-

John Milton as a young man, Anon. (1629).
National Portrait Gallery, London

thority which were characteristic of Catholicism and which stood between the individual and God. These rituals and institutions were enforced by a hierarchy in both church and state, and ultimately by a king who ruled by divine right. For Milton and most of his fellow Puritans, the only true king was God, and the only true voice of authority was God's as he spoke to each individual Christian.

Given these religious and political convictions, it was inevitable that Milton would play an active role in public affairs during the Civil War and the Puritan Commonwealth. Soon after his return to England he began publishing pamphlets attacking the existing establishment of the Church of England. During the early years of the war his involvement in controversy had a more personal basis. Milton was married to Mary Powell in June, 1642.

Six weeks after the marriage she left to return to her parents, and for several years Milton issued pamphlets in which he argued that all Englishmen should have the right to get a divorce. Quite understandably, Milton gained the reputation of being a political radical during these years. When Charles I was executed in 1649, Milton defended the Puritan Parliament before European governments which were deeply distressed by the course of events in England. It was while he was engaged in this project that Milton went blind, doubtlessly due to the severe eyestrain brought on by ceaseless reading and Latin composition. But with the help of various scribes and secretaries, he was still able to perform his valuable services as Latin Secretary for Cromwell's government.

With the Restoration of the monarchy in 1660, Milton not only was confronted with the collapse of the cause to which he had given so much, but also was imprisoned and threatened with execution. Through the intervention of friends who carried some influence with the new royal government, Milton was let off with a fine and some loss of property. Shortly afterward, living in blindness and virtual seclusion from all but the members of his immediate family, Milton began his great Biblical epic, *Paradise Lost*. It was completed in 1667. With unprecedented daring and penetration, Milton draws out all the human and theological implications of the fall of Adam and Eve as it is told in the Old Testament. His aim is nothing less than to "justify the ways of God to men," and in doing so he never once flinches from the more mysterious or difficult of God's ways. For Milton, his role as a poet, not less than his role as a public servant, was a divine "calling." He was to be "God's English Poet": he felt that his verse originated in and was guided by the Holy Spirit. Milton places his command of the resources of Greek and Roman epic (Homer's *Iliad* and *Odyssey*, Virgil's *Aeneid*) at the service of his great Christian subject. *Paradise Lost* is written in blank verse (unrhymed lines of iambic pentameter), in a style combining the grand sonority and power of the classical epic with scrupulous subtlety and precision. It is the most fully achieved long poem in the English language. Before his death Milton published two other works on a grand scale: *Paradise Regained* and *Samson Agonistes*. Both appeared in 1671; neither is as successful as *Paradise Lost*.

On His Having Arrived at the Age of Twenty-Three

How soon hath Time, the subtle thief of youth,
  Stolen on his wing my three and twentieth year!
  My hasting days fly on with full career,
  But my late spring no bud or blossom° showeth.
Perhaps my semblance° might deceive° the truth,   5
  That I to manhood am arrived so near,
  And inward ripeness doth much less appear,
  That some more timely-happy spirits° endueth.°
Yet be it less or more, or soon or slow,
  It shall be still° in strictest measure even   10
  To that same lot, however mean or high,
Toward which Time leads me, and the will of Heaven;
  All is, if I have grace to use it so,
  As ever° in my great Taskmaster's eye.

---

4. **blossom:** poetry. 5. **semblance:** appearance. **deceive:** prove false. 8. **spirits:** people who at the same age seem more accomplished as poets. **endueth:** endoweth. 10. **still:** always. 14. **ever:** eternity.

On His Blindness

(handwritten: memorize — extra credit)

When I consider how my light is spent,
  Ere half my days, in this dark world and wide.
  And that one talent° which is death to hide
  Lodged with me useless, though my soul more bent
To serve therewith my Maker, and present   5
  My true account, lest he, returning, chide.
  "Doth God exact day labor, light denied?"
  I fondly° ask; but Patience, to prevent
That murmur, soon replies: "God doth not need
  Either man's work or his own gifts; who best   10
  Bear his mild yoke, they serve him best; his state
Is kingly—thousands° at his bidding speed
  And post o'er land and ocean without rest:
  They also serve who only stand and wait."

---

3. **talent:** a reference to the parable of the talents (Matthew 25:14–30) in which a servant is reprimanded for hiding his one talent, or coin, in the earth instead of putting it to good use. 8. **fondly:** foolishly. 12. **thousands:** of angels.

COMMENTARY

As a writer of sonnets Milton can be as bold and powerful on a small scale as he is in the epic dimensions of *Paradise Lost*. He was a devoted student of Italian literature, and he preferred the older Italian sonnet form of octave and sestet to the Shakespearean form of three quatrains and a couplet. The sonnets are also Milton's most personal poems. The two we have here commemorate key moments in a life of extraordinary creative ambition and self-discipline. In both of them we can see that combination of attitudes so typical of Milton: a proud individualism firmly subordinated to the will of God.

FOR STUDY AND DISCUSSION

On His Having Arrived at the Age of Twenty-Three

1. What images are applied to Time in the opening lines of the poem? How might the phrase "my late spring" in line 4 refer to Milton's talent? How is this idea extended in the phrase "inward ripeness" in line 7? What happens to Milton's worry about achievement and maturity in lines 9–14?
2. Some readers think that "All" at the beginning of line 13 refers to time; others think the word refers to Milton's talent or ability. Which interpretation do you prefer? Give reasons to support your preference.

On His Blindness

1. In what two senses is the word *talent* employed? Is Milton's talent in fact useless? Why is it "death" to hide it?
2. Do you think the word *wait* in the famous last line suggests mere submission to the fact that God has ordained Milton's blindness? Explain.

from **Paradise Lost**

Before deciding to write an epic poem on the Fall of Man, Milton had considered and rejected many other projects for long works, including a poem on the legends of King Arthur. He also sketched a drama on the Fall, "Adam Unparadised," but gave it up, perhaps because the span of the action of a tragedy was customarily limited to a single day. The great epic models of the day were Homer and Virgil, and Milton followed their pattern in many ways. (Staging a battle in Heaven, beginning his action in the middle—*in medias res*—and then telling the earlier part of the story through the reminiscences of his characters, furnishing an elaborate catalog of the princes among the fallen angels, are a few of these.) But the first few lines of *Paradise Lost* make us aware that the Book of Genesis is the controlling source of the poem. Here, as elsewhere in Milton, the broad reaches of classical tradition are subordinated to the Christian story, and are even more sharply limited by Milton's focus on what happens within the single mind. The very heart of the poem, is, after all, Adam's decision—that crucial misuse of reason and free will which explains the history of all generations to come. Aside from that action, Milton's agents are necessarily Satan and "the greater Man," He who redeems us from the consequences of Adam's action.

The following selection is from Book I, the opening of the poem. After stating his subject and invoking a Heavenly Muse, who may inspire him to deal with matters higher than those of classical epic, Milton tells of the situation of the fallen angels, what they first feel and how they first act in Hell. Generations of readers have found the most interesting character of Milton's poem to be Satan. The Romantics, who had a taste for lonely rebels, called Satan the "hero" of the poem. But Milton's largest intention is far from this. To "justify the ways of God to men" is not to apologize, but to make very plain to each reader how fatal, how irretrievable, are the actions of human beings, who are mortal and who have but one chance to follow the right path. Satan is secondary because he can never finally win or lose.

Of man's first disobedience, and the fruit
Of that forbidden tree, whose mortal taste
Brought death into the world, and all our woe,
With loss of Eden, till one greater Man°
Restore us, and regain the blissful seat,   5
Sing, Heavenly Muse,° that on the secret° top
Of Oreb, or of Sinai,° didst inspire
That shepherd, who first taught the chosen seed
In the beginning how the Heavens and Earth
Rose out of Chaos;° or if Sion hill°   10
Delight thee more, and Siloa's brook° that flowed
Fast by the oracle of God, I thence
Invoke thy aid to my adventurous song,
That with no middle flight intends to soar
Above the Aonian mount,° while it pursues   15
Things unattempted yet in prose or rhyme.
And chiefly thou, O Spirit,° that dost prefer
Before all temples the upright heart and pure,
Instruct me, for thou know'st; thou from the first
Wast present, and with mighty wings outspread   20
Dovelike sat'st brooding on the vast abyss
And mad'st it pregnant: what in me is dark
Illumine, what is low raise and support;
That to the highth° of this great argument
I may assert Eternal Providence,   25
And justify the ways of God to men.
    Say first, for Heaven hides nothing from thy view,
Nor the deep tract of Hell, say first what cause
Moved our grand° parents in that happy state,
Favored of Heaven so highly, to fall off   30
From their Creator, and transgress his will
For one restraint,° lords of the world besides?
Who first seduced them to that foul revolt?
The infernal Serpent; he it was, whose guile,

---

4. **one . . . Man:** Christ. 6. **Heavenly Muse:** Milton invokes Urania, the muse of
astronomy and sacred poetry, to help him compose his great epic. Milton associates her with the divine spirit that inspired "that shepherd," Moses, who received
the word of God and interpreted it for the Hebrews, "the chosen seed." **secret:**
remote, mysterious. 7. **Oreb . . . Sinai:** Horeb (hôr′ĕb) and Sinai (sī′nī′), alternate
names for the mountain on which God gave Moses the law. 9–10. **In . . . Chaos:**
The first five books of the Bible are ascribed to Moses. 10. **Sion hill:** one of the
hills of Jerusalem on which the temple was built. 11. **Siloa's brook:** a stream
near Sion Hill where stood the temple, "the oracle of God." 15. **Aonian mount:**
Mount Helicon in Greek mythology, home of the Muses. Milton refers to
his intention of writing on a theme greater than Greek poetry had attempted.
17. **Spirit:** divine inspiration. 24. **highth:** height. 29. **grand:** first. 32. **one re-**
straint: that they should not eat of the fruit of the tree of knowledge.

Stirred up with envy and revenge, deceived 35
The mother of mankind, what time his pride
Had cast him out from Heaven, with all his host
Of rebel angels, by whose aid aspiring
To set himself in glory above his peers,
He trusted to have equaled the Most High, 40
If he opposed; and with ambitious aim
Against the throne and monarchy of God,
Raised impious war in Heaven and battle proud
With vain attempt. Him the Almighty Power
Hurled headlong flaming from the ethereal sky 45
With hideous ruin and combustion down
To bottomless perdition, there to dwell
In adamantine° chains and penal fire,
Who durst defy the Omnipotent to arms.
Nine times the space that measures day and night 50
To mortal men, he with his horrid crew
Lay vanquished, rolling in the fiery gulf,
Confounded though immortal. But his doom
Reserved him to more wrath; for now the thought
Both of lost happiness and lasting pain 55
Torments him; round he throws his baleful eyes,
That witnessed° huge affliction and dismay
Mixed with obdúrate pride and steadfast hate.
At once as far as angels ken° he views
The dismal situation waste and wild: 60
A dungeon horrible on all sides round
As one great furnace flamed, yet from those flames
No light, but rather darkness visible
Served only to discover sights of woe,
Regions of sorrow, doleful shades, where peace 65
And rest can never dwell, hope never comes
That comes to all; but torture without end
Still urges,° and a fiery deluge, fed
With everburning sulphur unconsumed:
Such place Eternal Justice had prepared 70
For those rebellious, here their prison ordained
In utter darkness, and their portion set
As far removed from God and light of Heaven
As from the center thrice to the utmost pole.°
O how unlike the place from whence they fell! 75
There the companions of his fall, o'erwhelmed

---

48. **adamantine:** unbreakable, hard as a diamond.   57. **witnessed:** gave evidence
of.   59. **ken:** sight.   68. **Still urges:** always presses, afflicts.   74. **center . . . pole:**
three times the distance from the earth (center) to the furthest point in the universe.

Satan cast into Hell, from *Très Riches Heures du Duc de Berry*, Chantilly Musée,
Conde MS.
Giraudon

With floods and whirlwinds of tempestuous fire,
He soon discerns, and weltering by his side
One next himself in power, and next in crime,
Long after known in Palestine, and named   80
Beelzebub.° To whom the Archenemy,
And thence in Heaven called Satan, with bold words
Breaking the horrid silence thus began:
   "If thou beest he—but O how fallen! how changed
From him, who in the happy realms of light   85
Clothed with transcendent brightness didst outshine
Myriads though bright—if he whom mutual league,
United thoughts and counsels, equal hope
And hazard in the glorious enterprise,
Joined with me once, now misery hath joined   90
In equal ruin: into what pit thou seest
From what height fallen! so much the stronger proved
He with his thunder; and till then who knew
The force of those dire arms? Yet not for those,
Nor what the potent Victor in his rage   95
Can else inflict, do I repent or change,
Though changed in outward luster, that fixed mind
And high disdain, from sense of injured merit,
That with the Mightiest raised me to contend,
And to the fierce contention brought along   100
Innumerable force of spirits armed
That durst dislike his reign, and, me preferring,
His utmost power with adverse power opposed
In dubious battle on the plains of Heaven,
And shook his throne. What though the field be lost?   105
All is not lost; the unconquerable will,
And study of revenge, immortal hate,
And courage never to submit or yield:
And what is else not to be overcome?
That glory never shall his wrath or might   110
Extort from me. To bow and sue for grace
With suppliant knee, and deify his power
Who from the terror of this arm so late
Doubted° his empire, that were low indeed,
That were an ignominy and shame beneath   115
This downfall; since by fate the strength of gods
And this empyreal substance° cannot fail,

---

81. **Beelzebub** (bē-ĕl′zə-bŭb): the name given in this poem to the fallen angel next
in command to Satan. In other connections, the name is often used interchangeably with that of Satan. 114. **Doubted:** feared for. 117. **empyreal substance:**
Heaven, the empyrean, and its inhabitants were composed of an indestructible
substance.

Since through experience of this great event,
In arms not worse, in foresight much advanced,
We may with more successful hope resolve   120
To wage by force or guile eternal war
Irreconcilable to our grand Foe,
Who now triumphs, and in the excess of joy
Sole reigning holds the tyranny of Heaven."
    So spake the apostate Angel, though in pain,   125
Vaunting aloud, but racked with deep despair;
And him thus answered soon his bold compeer:°
    "O Prince, O Chief of many thronèd Powers,
That led the embattled Seraphim° to war
Under thy conduct, and in dreadful deeds   130
Fearless, endangered Heaven's perpetual King,
And put to proof his high supremacy,
Whether upheld by strength, or chance, or fate;
Too well I see and rue the dire event,
That with sad overthrow and foul defeat   135
Hath lost us Heaven, and all this mighty host
In horrible destruction laid thus low,
As far as gods and heavenly essences
Can perish: for the mind and spirit remains
Invincible, and vigor soon returns,   140
Though all our glory extinct, and happy state
Here swallowed up in endless misery.
But what if he our Conqueror (whom I now
Of force believe almighty, since no less
Than such could have o'erpowered such force as ours)   145
Have left us this our spirit and strength entire
Strongly to suffer and support our pains,
That we may so suffice his vengeful ire,
Or do him mightier service as his thralls
By right of war, whate'er his business be,   150
Here in the heart of Hell to work in fire,
Or do his errands in the gloomy deep?
What can it then avail, though yet we feel
Strength undiminished, or eternal being
To undergo eternal punishment?"   155
    Whereto with speedy words the Archfiend replied:
"Fallen Cherub, to be weak is miserable,
Doing or suffering:° but of this be sure,
To do aught good never will be our task,
But ever to do ill our sole delight,   160
As being the contrary to his high will

---

127. **compeer:** companion, equal.   129. **Seraphim** (sĕr'ə-fĭm): angels of the highest
rank.   158. **Doing or suffering:** whether active or passive.

Whom we resist. If then his providence
Out of our evil seek to bring forth good,
Our labor must be to pervert that end,
And out of good still° to find means of evil;   165
Which ofttimes may succeed, so as perhaps
Shall grieve him, if I fail° not, and disturb
His inmost counsels from their destined aim.
But see the angry Victor hath recalled
His ministers of vengeance and pursuit   170
Back to the gates of Heaven; the sulphurous hail
Shot after us in storm, o'erblown hath laid
The fiery surge, that from the precipice
Of Heaven received us falling, and the thunder,
Winged with red lightning and impetuous rage,   175
Perhaps hath spent his shafts, and ceases now
To bellow through the vast and boundless deep.
Let us not slip° the occasion, whether scorn
Or satiate° fury yield it from our Foe.
Seest thou yon dreary plain, forlorn and wild,   180
The seat of desolation, void of light,
Save what the glimmering of these livid flames
Casts pale and dreadful? Thither let us tend
From off the tossing of these fiery waves,
There rest, if any rest can harbor there,   185
And reassembling our afflicted powers,°
Consult how we may henceforth most offend
Our Enemy, our own loss how repair,
How overcome this dire calamity,
What reinforcement we may gain from hope,   190
If not, what resolution from despair."
    Thus Satan talking to his nearest mate
With head uplift above the wave, and eyes
That sparkling blazed; his other parts besides,
Prone on the flood, extended long and large,   195
Lay floating many a rood,° in bulk as huge
As whom the fables name of monstrous size,
Titanian or Earthborn, that warred on Jove,
Briareos or Typhon,° whom the den
By ancient Tarsus held, or that seabeast   200

---

165. **still:** always. 167. **fail:** mistake. 178. **slip:** lose. 179. **satiate** (sā'shē-āt): satisfied. 186. **afflicted powers:** overthrown forces. 196. **rood:** Milton conceived of
the angels as being enormous in size. A rood (rō͞od) is equal to seven or eight
yards. 198–199. **Titanian . . . Typhon:** the Titans and Giants ("Earthborn") were
often confused. Briareos (brī-ār'ē-əs), also called Briareus, was a hundred-handed
giant who helped Zeus (Jove) defeat the Titans. Typhon (tī'fən), a son of Earth, was
a hundred-headed serpent monster from Cilicia (sə-lĭsh'ə), near Tarsus, who attacked heaven and was imprisoned by Zeus.

Leviathan,° which God of all his works
Created hugest that swim the ocean stream:
Him haply slumbering on the Norway foam,
The pilot of some small night-foundered skiff,
Deeming some island, off, as seamen tell,   205
With fixèd anchor in his scaly rind
Moors by his side under the lee, while night
Invests the sea, and wishèd morn delays:
So stretched out huge in length the Archfiend lay
Chained on the burning lake; nor ever thence   210
Had risen or heaved his head, but that the will
And high permission of all-ruling Heaven
Left him at large to his own dark designs,
That with reiterated crimes he might
Heap on himself damnation, while he sought   215
Evil to others; and enraged might see
How all his malice served but to bring forth
Infinite goodness, grace and mercy shown
On man by him seduced, but on himself
Treble confusion, wrath and vengeance poured.   220
   Forthwith upright he rears from off the pool
His mighty stature; on each hand the flames
Driven backward slope their pointing spires, and rolled
In billows, leave in the midst a horrid vale.
Then with expanded wings he steers his flight   225
Aloft, incumbent° on the dusky air
That felt unusual weight, till on dry land
He lights, if it were land that ever burned
With solid, as the lake with liquid fire;
And such appeared in hue, as when the force   230
Of subterranean wind transports a hill
Torn from Pelorus,° or the shattered side
Of thundering Etna, whose combustible
And fueled entrails thence conceiving fire,
Sublimed° with mineral fury, aid the winds,   235
And leave a singèd bottom all involved°
With stench and smoke:° such resting found the sole
Of unblest feet. Him followed his next mate,
Both glorying to have scaped the Stygian° flood

---

201. **Leviathan** (lə-vī′ə-thən): a sea monster.   226. **incumbent:** lying.   232.
Pelorus (pə-lôr′əs): a cape in Sicily, now Faro.   235. **Sublimed:** sublimated, i.e.,
turned into vapor by heat and solidified by cooling.   236. **involved:** enveloped.
230–237. **as when . . . smoke:** an example of the extended simile Milton frequently uses to strengthen his pictures.   239. **Stygian** (stĭj′ē-ən): pertaining to the
river Styx, which, in Greek mythology, surrounded the abode of the dead. Satan
and Beelzebub, because they are of immortal substance, cannot die.

As gods, and by their own recovered strength,　　　　　　240
Not by the sufferance of supernal° power.
　　"Is this the region, this the soil, the clime,"
Said then the lost Archangel, "this the seat
That we must change for Heaven, this mournful gloom
For that celestial light? Be it so, since he　　　　　　245
Who now is sovran° can dispose and bid
What shall be right: farthest from him is best,
Whom reason hath equaled, force hath made supreme
Above his equals. Farewell, happy fields,
Where joy forever dwells! Hail, horrors! hail,　　　　　　250
Infernal world! and thou, profoundest Hell,
Receive thy new possessor; one who brings
A mind not to be changed by place or time.
The mind is its own place, and in itself
Can make a Heaven of Hell, a Hell of Heaven.　　　　　　255
What matter where, if I be still the same,
And what I should be, all but less than he
Whom thunder hath made greater? Here at least
We shall be free; the Almighty hath not built
Here for his envy, will not drive us hence:　　　　　　260
Here we may reign secure, and in my choice
To reign is worth ambition, though in Hell:
Better to reign in Hell than serve in Heaven."

---

241. **supernal:** heavenly.　246. **sovran:** sovereign.

Angel Binding the Dragon (watercolor) by William Blake, showing the "adamantine chains and penal fire."
Fogg Art Museum, Harvard University

COMMENTARY

> If then his providence
> Out of our evil seek to bring forth good,
> Our labor must be to pervert that end,
> And out of good still to find means of evil . . .
>
> (lines 162–165)

With these words Satan states the principle that must henceforth govern the behavior of the fallen angels. After he makes this announcement, the main action of the poem begins with Satan's determination to leave the brimstone lake on which he floats and seek the shore, "that ever burned / With solid, as the lake with liquid fire." In lines 192–241 Milton gives us for the first time a sense of physical scene, of creatures huge almost beyond imagination, and of a hell horrible indeed, but clearly most horrible because of what it contains, an erring will opposed to God. Satan addresses his new home:

> Hail, horrors! hail,
> Infernal world! and thou, profoundest Hell,
> Receive thy new possessor; one who brings
> A mind not to be changed by place or time.
> The mind is its own place, and in itself
> Can make a Heaven of Hell, a Hell of Heaven.
>
> (lines 250–255)

The words "The mind is its own place" may remind us of the "bottomless perdition" of line 47. Satan is damned by enclosing himself within his own mind, his own error. And this error is a "bottomless" one from which he cannot escape. Satan's claim (see line 248) that he has been overcome by nothing more than force, that his reason equals God's, is a terrible mistake.

FOR STUDY AND DISCUSSION

1. What does Milton tell us about his purpose in the opening 26 lines of the poem? To whom does Milton compare himself indirectly in line 8, when he refers to "That shepherd"? What are the implications of this comparison?
2. What provoked Satan to divert "our grand parents" from their original relationship to God? What was Satan attempting to do in Heaven before he was cast out?
3. Compare the attitudes of Beelzebub and Satan in their dialogue in Hell. What differences are there and why are these differences significant?
4. Why does Milton invest Satan with dignity and power?

FOR COMPOSITION

Make an argument for the proposition that in the passage from Book I, Hell is a state of mind. Construct an opposing argument for the proposition that it is a place. Base your assertions on evidence from the text. Present both arguments in an essay, then determine which is the stronger position.

The Language of *Paradise Lost*

Milton's first readers, like ourselves, found in his verse an unusual majesty and elevation. How is it secured? If you read aloud, as you must if you are to understand and enjoy Milton, you will soon find that particular words have taken on an extraordinary sonority and weight. Consider, for example, the following passage:

> . . . what in me is dark
> Illumine, what is low raise and support;
> That to the highth of this great argument
> I may assert Eternal Providence,
> And justify the ways of God to men.
>
> (lines 22–26)

In the phrasing "what in me is dark/Illumine," the word *illumine* seems for the first time to express fully what we always knew it meant, "to light up." It is hardly an accident that this is a word of Latin origin. Much of Milton's power with words comes from his intimate sense of the relation of their original meanings in Latin to their differently shaded meanings in English.

We may note that the word *argument,* which to our ears suggests a lively dispute, has more than one sense to give it weight here. We still employ it to mean the reasoned presentation of a case, a meaning here bound up with a sense with which we are unfamiliar—in which *argument* means the "content of a work." Milton is dealing with what, from his point of view, is the greatest possible argument: the story of the creation, fall, and promised redemption.

Milton makes skillful use of Latin sentence construction, which he carries over into English. Note that the first sixteen lines of Milton's epic make up a single sentence. The governing verb of that sentence occurs in the sixth line, beginning "Sing, Heavenly Muse." Milton builds the passage to a climax by delaying the use of the verb and placing a number of qualifications first.

A second quotation may be used to illustrate how plastic English sentence structure appears in Milton's hands:

> Him the Almighty Power
> Hurled headlong flaming from the ethereal sky
> With hideous ruin and combustion down
> To bottomless perdition, there to dwell
> In adamantine chains and penal fire,
> Who durst defy the Omnipotent to arms.
>
> (lines 44–49)

First of all, we notice that placing "Him" (Satan) before "Almighty Power" has the effect of focusing our attention on Satan and his fall (the placing of the pronoun as the chief stress in the line contributes to this). The word "Him" also introduces the succession of *h* sounds that includes "*h*urled *h*eadlong" in the second line and "*h*ideous" in the third. This succession would be flat if it were not interrupted by "Almighty Power."

The normal English order of this sentence would be something like this: The Almighty Power hurled Satan, who had dared to take arms against him, down to hell to live in chains and fire. In Milton's passage the relative clause introduced by "Who" comes at the very end, *after* we have had a chance to absorb the consequences of defying God. Through the exact placement and ordering of words, Milton creates the feeling of Satan's being hurled out of Heaven and falling that vast distance down to Hell. We may make a rough list of the elements of the sentence in this form:

Subject:	Almighty Power
Object:	Him (Satan)
Verb:	Hurled
How "hurled"?	Headlong
In what state?	Flaming
From whence?	Ethereal sky
Under what conditions?	With hideous ruin and combustion
In what direction?	Down
To what place (state)?	Perdition
Kind of perdition?	Bottomless
To do what there?	Dwell
Under what conditions?	Adamantine chains and penal fire

There are many other things to watch for if you wish to learn something of the power of Milton's verse. One of the most important is suggested by the opening of Satan's speech to Beelzebub:

> If thou beest he—but O how fallen! how changed
> From him, who in the happy realms of light
> Clothed with transcendent brightness didst outshine
> Myriads though bright—
>
> (lines 84–87)

Note the force of the interjection, "but O how fallen," introduced *before* the description of the terrible change the angel has undergone. Note also the weight and compression of "Myriads though bright," which calls up an impression of thousands of shining angels whom Beelzebub had outshone. No one save John Keats has ever exploited the possibilities of English so successfully.

Ceiling of the Ducal Palace (fresco) by Andrea Mantegna, Mantua, Italy,
showing the Blessed and the Angels looking down from Heaven.
Scala

John Bunyan
1628–1688

We know about Bunyan's life primarily from his autobiography, *Grace Abounding to the Chief of Sinners* (1666). His father was a poor village tinker (a maker and repairer of metal utensils), and Bunyan received only the simplest education before taking up his father's trade. He eventually married and fought with the Parliamentary army during the Civil War. But as the title of his autobiography suggests, the important thing in Bunyan's life was an intense religious struggle, through which he became convinced of his own sinful unworthiness, and eventually of the gift of grace and salvation. He joined one of the many Baptist sects flourishing in England during the Commonwealth and became a dedicated preacher. When Charles II reinstated the monarchy and the Church of England, he promised leniency to Protestant Dissenters such as Bunyan. But the Anglican hierarchy was less forgiving. Many from the Dissenting sects, including Bunyan, were imprisoned. Although he remained in jail for twelve years, Bunyan continued to preach to his fellow prisoners and to write religious books. He was released and allowed to become the pastor of a Nonconformist church in Bedford, but in 1675 he was imprisoned again. It was during this second imprisonment that he wrote his most inspired work, *The Pilgrim's Progress from This World to That Which Is To Come* (1678). Over the centuries it has been the most widely read work produced during the Puritan Age, and one of the most popular pieces of Christian writing ever to appear in English.

The Pilgrim's Progress is an allegory—a narrative in which general concepts such as sin, despair, and faith are represented as people or as aspects of the natural world. In *The Pilgrim's Progress*, the basis of the allegorical narrative is the idea of life as a journey. The traveler's name is Christian, and he

John Bunyan (detail) by T. Sadler.
National Portrait Gallery, London

represents every Christian. The figures and places Christian encounters on his journey stand for the various experiences every Christian must go through in the quest for salvation. The liveliness and power of Bunyan's allegory derive from his ability as a storyteller and from his skill at maintaining a convincing relationship between elements of the fiction and their spiritual significance. General Christian ideas are given vivid, immediate life. Bunyan's prose, modeled on that of the King James Bible, is clear enough to be followed by any reader, and it is always full of specific and plausible detail.

from The Pilgrim's Progress

The Vanity Fair episode from *The Pilgrim's Progress* is probably the best-known section of the book. Christian, the hero, and his companion, Faithful, are passing through a town called Vanity during the season of the local fair. Fairs were an ancient tradition in England, and even in Bunyan's day merchants from all over Europe would bring their wares for sale. Of course the serious business of fairs was accompanied by eating, drinking, and all forms of entertainment. In this episode Bunyan makes us feel the real atmosphere and excitement of such a fair, even as he uses the fair to represent the worldly corruption that stands between Christian and his salvation at the Celestial City. Bunyan as narrator tells his allegory as if he were recounting a dream.

Vanity Fair (engraving)
from *The Pilgrim's
Progress.*
The Mansell Collection

Vanity Fair

Then I saw in my dream, that when they were got out of the wilderness, they presently saw a town before them, and the name of that town is Vanity; and at the town there is a fair kept, called Vanity Fair. It is kept all the year long; it beareth the name of Vanity Fair, because the town where it is kept is lighter than vanity; and also because all that is there sold or that cometh thither is vanity. As is the saying of the wise, "All that cometh is Vanity."

This fair is no new-erected business, but a thing of ancient standing; I will show you the original of it.

Almost five thousand years agone, there were pilgrims walking to the Celestial City, as these two honest persons are: and Beelzebub, Apollyon, and Legion,[1] with their companions, perceiving by the path that the pilgrims made, that their way to the City lay through this town of Vanity, they contrived here to set up a fair; a fair wherein should be sold all sorts of vanity, and that it should last all the year long: therefore at this fair are all such merchandise sold, as houses, lands, trades, places, honors, preferments,[2] titles, countries, kingdoms, lusts, pleasures, and delights of all sorts, as wives, husbands, children, masters, servants, lives, blood, bodies, souls, silver, gold, pearls, precious stones, and whatnot.

And, moreover, at this fair there is at all times to be seen juggling, cheats, games, plays, fools, apes, knaves, and rogues, and that of every kind.

Here are to be seen, too, and that for nothing, thefts, murders, adulteries, and false swearers.

And as in other fairs of less moment, there are the several rows and streets, under their proper names, where such wares are vended; so here likewise you have the proper places, rows, streets (viz.[3] countries and kingdoms), where the wares of this fair are soonest to be found. Here is the Britain Row, the French Row, the Italian Row, the Spanish Row, the German Row, where several sorts of vanities are to be sold. But, as in other fairs, some one commodity is as the chief of all the fair, so the ware of Rome and her merchandise is greatly promoted in this fair; only our English nation, with some others, have taken a dislike thereat.

Now, as I said, the way to the Celestial City lies just through this town where this lusty[4] fair is kept; and he that will go to the City, and yet not go through this town, must needs go out of the world. The Prince of Princes himself, when here, went through this town[5] to his own country, and that upon a fair day too; yea, and as I think, it was Beelzebub, the chief lord of this fair, that invited him to buy of his vanities; yea, would have made him lord of the fair, would he but have done him reverence as he went through the town. Yea, because he was such a person of honor, Beelzebub had him from street to street, and showed him all the kingdoms of the world in a little time, that he might, if possible, allure the Blessed One to cheapen[6] and buy some of his vanities; but he had no mind to the merchandise, and therefore left the town without laying out so much as one farthing upon these vanities. This fair, therefore, is an ancient thing, of long standing, and a very great fair.

Now these pilgrims, as I said, must needs go through this fair. Well, so they did: but, behold, even as they entered into the fair, all the people in the fair were moved, and the

---

1. **Beelzebub** (bē-ĕl′zə-bŭb): Satan; **Apollyon** (ă-pŏl′yən): the angel of the bottomless pit; **Legion:** unclean spirits or devils.
2. **preferments:** appointments to political or ecclesiastical positions.

3. **viz.:** namely.
4. **lusty:** joyous.
5. **The Prince of Princes . . . town:** a reference to the temptation of Christ in the wilderness (Matthew 4:1–11).
6. **cheapen:** ask the price of.

town itself as it were in a hubbub about them; and that for several reasons: for—

First, the pilgrims were clothed with such kind of raiment as was diverse from the raiment of any that traded in that fair. The people therefore of the fair, made a great gazing upon them: some said they were fools, some they were bedlams,[7] and some, they are outlandish men.[8]

Secondly, and as they wondered at their apparel, so they did likewise at their speech; for few could understand what they said. They naturally spoke the language of Canaan,[9] but they that kept the fair were the men of this world; so that, from one end of the fair to the other, they seemed barbarians each to the other.

Thirdly, but that which did not a little amuse the merchandisers, was that these pilgrims set very light by all their wares; they cared not so much as to look upon them; and if they called upon them to buy, they would put their fingers in their ears, and cry, "Turn away mine eyes from beholding vanity," and look upwards, signifying that their trade and traffic was in heaven.

One chanced mockingly, beholding the carriages of the men, to say unto them, "What will ye buy?" But they, looking gravely upon him, answered, "We buy the truth." At that there was an occasion taken to despise the men the more; some mocking, some taunting, some speaking reproachfully, and some calling upon others to smite them. At last things came to a hubbub and great stir in the fair, insomuch that all order was confounded. Now was word presently brought to the great one of the fair, who quickly came down, and deputed some of his most trusty friends to take these men into examination, about whom the fair was almost overturned. . . .

---

7. **bedlams:** lunatics from Bethlehem Hospital, the insane asylum in London.
8. **outlandish men:** foreigners.
9. **Canaan** (kā'nən): the Promised Land. The "language of Canaan" is therefore the language of the Bible and of true religion.

A trial is held, in which Faithful is accused by three witnesses, Envy, Superstition, and Pickthank, a favor-seeker.

Then went the jury out, whose names were Mr. Blind-man, Mr. No-good, Mr. Malice, Mr. Love-lust, Mr. Live-loose, Mr. Heady, Mr. High-mind, Mr. Enmity, Mr. Liar, Mr. Cruelty, Mr. Hate-light, and Mr. Implacable; who every one gave in his private verdict against him among themselves, and afterwards unanimously concluded to bring him in guilty before the Judge. And first, among themselves, Mr. Blind-man, the foreman, said, "I see clearly that this man is a heretic." Then said Mr. No-good, "Away with such a fellow from the earth." "Aye," said Mr. Malice, "for I hate the very looks of him." Then said Mr. Love-lust, "I could never endure him." "Nor I," said Mr. Live-Loose, "for he would always be condemning my way." "Hang him, hang him," said Mr. Heady. "A sorry scrub," said Mr. High-mind. "My heart riseth against him," said Mr. Enmity. "He is a rogue," said Mr. Liar. "Hanging is too good for him," said Mr. Cruelty. "Let's dispatch him out of the way," said Mr. Hate-light. Then said Mr. Implacable, "Might I have all the world given me, I could not be reconciled to him; therefore, let us forthwith bring him in guilty of death." And so they did; therefore he was presently condemned to be had from the place where he was, to the place from whence he came, and there to be put to the most cruel death that could be invented.

They therefore brought him out to do with him according to their law; and, first, they scourged him, then they buffeted him, then they lanced his flesh with knives; after that, they stoned him with stones, then pricked him with their swords; and, last of all, they burned him to ashes at the stake. Thus came Faithful to his end.

Now I saw that there stood behind the multitude a chariot and a couple of horses, waiting for Faithful, who (so soon as his adversaries had dispatched him) was taken up into it, and straightway was carried up through the clouds, with sound of trumpet, the nearest way to the celestial gate.

But as for Christian, he had some respite, and was remanded back to prison. So he there remained for a space; but He that overrules all things, having the power of their rage in his own hand, so wrought it about, that Christian for that time escaped them, and went his way. . . .

Faithful is replaced by the convert, Hopeful.

FOR STUDY AND DISCUSSION

1. At the beginning of this episode, Bunyan establishes very clearly the moral and religious significance of Vanity Fair. How does he do this? What is the meaning of the Biblical quotation "All that cometh is Vanity"?
2. Why do Christian and Faithful arouse the ire of the people at Vanity Fair? What is probably the main reason for their arrest?
3. Point out how the persons on the jury are appropriate for Bunyan's purpose. Show how their words are in accordance with their names.
4. What do you think Bunyan meant to teach through the events at Vanity Fair?

The Celestial City

. . . I saw in my dream that these two men went in at the gate: and lo, as they entered, they were transfigured, and they had raiment put on that shone like gold. There were also that met them with harps and crowns and gave them to them—the harps to praise withal, and the crowns in token of honor. Then I heard in my dream that all the bells in the city rang again for joy, and that it was said unto them, "Enter ye into the joy of your Lord." I also heard the men themselves, that they sang with a loud voice, saying, "Blessing and honor, and glory, and power, be unto Him that sitteth upon the throne, and unto the Lamb, for ever and ever."

Now, just as the gates were opened to let in the men, I looked in after them, and, behold, the City shone like the sun; the streets also were paved with gold, and in them walked many men with crowns on their heads, palms in their hands, and golden harps to sing praises withal.

There were also of them that had wings, and they answered one another without intermission, saying, "Holy, holy, holy is the Lord." And after that they shut up the gates; which, when I had seen, I wished myself among them. . . .

The Seventeenth Century

One of the most remarkable things that happened to the English language in the course of the seventeenth century was that it reached a fairly stable form — at least so far as the written language is concerned. Writers of the previous century had often felt, with some reason, that they were completely reshaping their native tongue. They had borrowed words wholesale from foreign languages; they had developed elaborate prose styles (frequently in imitation of Latin prose); and they had delighted in rhetorical outpourings that overwhelmed readers with strange terms and fantastic figures of speech.

In the seventeenth century, however, this exuberant Elizabethan attitude gradually gave way to a concern for polishing and refining the language. Milton was one of the last writers to make a deliberate practice of borrowing words from Latin. He was also one of the last to pattern his style after classical models, using long, weighty sentences and Latinate constructions. Writers who were born later than Milton were no longer so interested in making English ornate, elaborate, or extravagant; they were more interested in trying to make it clear and accurate.

One thing that contributed to this new attitude toward language was the rapid rise of interest in scientific subjects. The modern "Age of Science" was beginning, and the educated public was fascinated by the experiments and discoveries that were taking place in medicine, astronomy, physics, and related fields. Writers on these subjects realized, of course, that clarity and accuracy were essential for their purposes. But they sometimes complained that English — although it had admittedly proved to be an excellent language for poetry and drama — was not suited for expressing exact ideas. For this reason, a few of the leading thinkers of the time continued the old practice of writing in Latin, feeling that it was easier to present ideas accurately in that language. Isaac Newton, for instance, used Latin to write *Principia Mathematica*, his famous work on mathematics.

However, many important philosophical works were being written in English. Thomas Hobbes's great political work, *Leviathan* (1651), was written in English, as was Bacon's *Advancement of Learning* (1605); and Harvey's extremely influential medical treatise, *Essay on the Motion of the Heart and the Blood*, appeared in an English translation in 1653.

The Reformation both on the Continent and in England dealt a blow to the prestige of Latin. As country after country withdrew from the universal church, worship began to be conducted in the local vernacular. English liturgies were published and revised under Edward VI and Elizabeth I. The Bible was also translated into vernacular tongues. This, along with growing national feelings, added enormously to the prestige of the local languages and tended to downgrade the preeminence of Latin. The Catholic church attempted to counteract this trend by initiating vernacular translations of its own: in 1609–1610 an English translation of the Bible called the Douay Version was published on the Continent and smuggled into England.

Knowledge of English outside of the British Isles was not widespread at the beginning of the seventeenth century, but with England's expansion in the New World and her widely expanding foreign trade, the English language began to spread to other lands and works written in English could expect to find an international readership and to exert an international influence.

The years 1607–1620 saw profound effects on the future of the English language. The English colonized Virginia and New England; these colonies were the first of a series that ultimately included English-speaking colonies around the world. Beginning with the seventeenth century, a distinct standard dialect of English began to grow up in America; new words were introduced to deal with new surroundings, and many of these words and new idioms were later introduced into the mother tongue in England. What England had exported, she began to import.

A date of special importance is 1611, the date of the publication of the Authorized or King James Version of the Bible. It has been said that during the seventeenth and eighteenth centuries, England was a nation of one book and that book was the Bible. It is impossible to overestimate the influence of this book on the poetry, prose, and daily speech of the English people everywhere. It became a standard of good English and its cadences sank deep into the hearts and minds of English people, many of whom could quote extensively from it by heart.

Nevertheless, words like *telleth, giveth, sayeth,* and *doth,* used in the 1611 Bible, had almost entirely dropped out by the end of the period in favor of the more modern *tells, gives, says,* and *does.* The system of articles was still not entirely set, so that one finds "creeping like snail," for example, instead of "creeping like *a* snail" and "at *the* last" instead of the more familiar "at last." The new neuter possessive *its* replaced the older *his* form that Queen Elizabeth had preferred.

Other changes in usage were of three basic sorts: in range of meaning, in degree of formality, and in frequency of use. The word *silly,* for example, meant "poor" or "mere"; its meaning by the end of the century had clearly narrowed. *Benignity* became much too formal and was replaced by *kindness* in most contexts. Except in prayers, there were very few contexts in which one would "beseech" rather than "ask."

FOR STUDY AND DISCUSSION

1. In Bacon's essay "Of Studies" there are a few words that are used in senses no longer common today. Using a college or an unabridged dictionary, look up *stond, stone,* and *rein.* Does the dictionary give definitions that fit the sense in which these words are used by Bacon?

2. Some dictionaries arrange definitions in chronological order, giving the earliest meaning first. Other dictionaries arrange definitions in order of frequency, giving the most common meanings first. If your dictionary has a definition for *silly* as "poor" or "mere," is this one of the first definitions given or does it come later in the list? Judging from this clue, what kind of arrangement does your dictionary follow?

The Restoration and Eighteenth Century

1660–1798

Scene from John Gay's *The Beggar's Opera* (detail)
by William Hogarth.
The Tate Gallery, London

It is customary to date the beginning of a new literary period with the Restoration in 1660, when the Stuarts returned from exile to the British throne. This historical convention has more to recommend it than most. It was a time when people sought to establish society and the arts on a firm basis, and a time when dislike of change became a guiding principle, so that there was a deliberate attempt to keep things the way they were. But change is inevitable, and order cannot survive except by evolving into new kinds of order. Literary tendencies after the middle of the eighteenth century, like the social scene they reflect, are filled with hints that the old order was breaking down and that new ways of understanding the world were bound to follow. In literary history a significant turning point is the publication in 1798 of *Lyrical Ballads,* a deliberately innovative collection of poems by William Wordsworth (1770–1850) and Samuel Taylor Coleridge (1773–1834). Here, then, is the end of our period.

THE POLITICAL BACKGROUND

Political history, the backbone on which we organize our knowledge of the past, is often more a reflection than a cause of human affairs. As Samuel Johnson (1709–1784) wisely wrote:

> How small, of all that human hearts endure,
> That part which laws or kings can cause or cure.

Nonetheless it is useful to know the reigns of the British monarchs in this period. The crucial date is 1660, when a country weary of civil war and Puritan dictatorship brought back the Stuart heir, King Charles II (1660–1685), from his exile in France. The Civil War had been fought to win religious freedom, but the Puritans were a minority group and could not have succeeded without the powerful

Coronation procession of Charles II (detail).

landowners who resented royal interference and supported the Puritan cause. By the time of the Restoration, the people who controlled power were convinced that the king's return would be a lesser evil than continued Puritan rule, and Charles was brought back without the shedding of a drop of blood.

From this time forward political life was dominated by the desire to assure stability. The British Civil War had been a traumatic experience that the nation was determined never to repeat. But before long a new threat emerged: Charles's brother, who came to the throne as James II in 1685, was openly committed to favoring Roman Catholicism and forming dangerous alliances with the Catholic powers of Europe. After three years James was expelled from the throne, in an upheaval long remembered as the "Glorious Revolution" because it, too, occurred without bloodshed. It was, in fact, no revolution at all, but an assertion of the status quo against a monarch who threatened to upset it.

The next heir to the throne was James's daughter Mary, a Protestant who ruled jointly with her Dutch husband, William of Orange (1689-1702). Mary's sister Queen Anne (1702-1714), who followed, died childless. Ordinarily the crown then would have passed to James Stuart, later called the "Old Pretender," son of the exiled (and dead) James II. But James, like his father, was a Catholic, and Parliament had passed an act that the British sovereign must be Protestant. A crucial decision was made: rather than continue the Stuart succession, Britain would be ruled by a more distant relative, the German Elector of Hanover, who assumed the throne in 1714 as George I (1714-1727). The powerful Louis XIV of France continued to harbor James Stuart and to back his claim to the British throne, and in Britain—particularly in Scotland and Ireland—there were many Stuart supporters, called "Jacobites" (from the Latin *Jacobus*, James). George I was succeeded by his son, George II (1727-1760), who like his father did not learn English well and showed greater interest in little Hanover than in Great Britain. These Georges therefore allowed control of the British government to fall almost completely into the hands of Parliament, where it remains to this day. The third King George (1760-1820), whose reign spanned sixty years, attempted to be what neither of the first two Georges had been—a strong English king. His attempt at ruling had some unfortunate results, notably the loss to Britain of thirteen of its American colonies. The Hanovers were not exactly admirable men, but two attempts—in 1715 and 1745—to restore the Stuarts were failures. (In 1745, however, the Scottish followers of "Bonnie Prince Charlie," the Old Pretender's son, reached the English Midlands before they were defeated. It is around this rebellion that so many romantic stories have been written.)

Coronation medal,
Queen Anne.
Radio Times Hulton

Coronation medal,
George I.
The Mansell Collection

Charles II (detail)

John Dryden (detail)

James II (detail)

1660   1660   **Charles II 1660–1685**

Restoration 1660   Royal Society incorporated   Great Fire 1666
                                             1662

Watt's steam engine 1765   Johnson's *Dictionary* 1755   Second Jacobite Rebellion
                                                         1745

                             1760   **George II 1727–1760**   **1740**

"Preface to Shakespeare"   Gray's *Elegy* 1751
       1765

Boston Tea Party 1773   War with the Colonies   French Revolution
                       1776–1783   Burns's *Poems* 1786   1789–1799

George III 1760–1820   **1780**

Alexander Pope (detail)

King of Brobdingnag and Gulliver from *Gulliver's Travels*

William III (detail)

Coronation of William and Mary (detail)

Queen Anne (detail), Edmond Lilley

Great Hall Blenheim Palace,
Woodstock, England

1680　　　　**James II 1685–1688**　　　　**William**

and Mary 1688–1702

An Essay of Dramatic Poesy 1668　　Newton's Theory 1687　　"A Song for St. Cecilia's Day" 1687　　Glorious Revolution 1688

First Jacobite Rebellion 1715　　Union of England and Scotland 1707

1720　　**George I 1714–1727**　　**Anne 1702–1714**　　**1700**

Gulliver's Travels 1726　　*The Rape of the Lock* 1712–1717　　Death of Dryden 1700

Songs of Innocence 1789　　*Life of Johnson* 1791　　*Lyrical Ballads* 1798

1790　　　　　　　　　　　　**1798**

Stoke Poges Churchyard

Samuel Johnson (detail)

Robert Burns (detail)

The Houghton Library,
Harvard University

A POISON TREE

Blake Illustration

The Department of Printing and Graphic Arts

The expulsion of James II in 1688 showed that whatever the excesses of the Puritans might have been, the principle of parliamentary supremacy was becoming firmly established in England. The king remained highly influential, but real power increasingly moved to the political parties of Parliament. In Parliament at this time the two-party political system came into being. The Whigs represented chiefly the financial and mercantile interests, the cities and towns, the progressive element, and were strongly opposed to any interference in politics by the monarchy. The Tories, many of them Jacobites in these earlier years, represented the country squires and their folk, all the people who favored old traditions. Though there were general elections then as now, only a comparatively small number of people were entitled to vote. Some quite large towns had no Member of Parliament at all, while some decaying little places known as "rotten boroughs" were still able to elect two members. There was no real political democracy as we know it today, but the ordinary people of the eighteenth century were public-spirited and often expressed their dissatisfaction by violent rioting that could be quelled only by military force.

For most of the eighteenth century, the Whig party was supreme, especially after Sir Robert Walpole consolidated its power during his long rule as prime minister from 1721 to 1742. Many of the greatest writers feared Walpole's power and sided with the Tory minority against him; he was brilliantly satirized by Alexander Pope, Jonathan Swift, John Gay, Samuel Johnson, and Henry Fielding. But Walpole was no dictator, only an able politician who knew how to use patronage as well as policies to win the broadest possible support. In later years Samuel Johnson admitted that Walpole had given Britain badly needed tranquillity at home and peace abroad.

Political power was centered in England, but the nation was Great Britain, a fourfold entity made up of England, Wales, Ireland, and (after the Act of Union in 1707) Scotland. Scotland achieved something like equal partnership; Ireland was always the least fortunate, treated by England as a colony for economic gain, and nursing hostilities that finally brought about its independence in the twentieth century.

RESTORATION ENGLAND

During the reign of Charles II, the greatest European power was France, where the despotic if magnificent Louis XIV ruled from his new palace at Versailles. What was fashionable in Paris soon became fashionable in London, with the result that the French classical style and manner were soon imitated.

Not long after the Restoration, London suffered two major disasters — the Plague in 1665 and the Great Fire in 1666. The fire devastated the old city, which was then rebuilt under the direction of the famous architect Christopher Wren (1632–1723). We know a great deal about the intimate life of London in these times because Samuel Pepys (1633–1703), Secretary of the Admiralty, kept a diary (in code).

In the London of Charles II, the new scientific and rational age was coming into existence. In 1662, the Royal Society, composed of distinguished scientists, philosophers, and scholars, was founded under the direct patronage of the king. London was the city of the great Isaac Newton (1642–1727), the mathematician and astronomer; of William Harvey (1578–1657), who discovered the circulation of the blood; of John Locke (1632–1704), whose *Essay Concerning Human Understanding* described our mental processes and whose influence on the eighteenth century was enormous.

ENGLAND IN THE EIGHTEENTH CENTURY

England at the start of the eighteenth century was a small and very traditional country. Its population numbered about five and a half million (half that of modern Ohio or Texas). London, by far the biggest city, had in excess of half a million people. No other town had more than thirty thousand, although industrial development at the end of the century brought about rapid growth in the cities of the north. It is not surprising that London dominates the literature of the period and that nearly every famous writer went there to make his name.

Many people were alarmed by the symptoms of urban sprawl. As Daniel Defoe (1660?–1731) complained, London was spreading out "in a most straggling, confused manner, out of all shape, uncompact and unequal, neither long nor broad, round or square." But he was also deeply impressed by the spectacle of its wealth and beauty: "gilded with noble palaces, strong fortifications, large hospitals and public buildings; with the greatest bridge, and the greatest City [that is, financial district] in the world, made famous by the opulence of its merchants, the increase and extensiveness of its commerce; by its invincible navies and by the innumerable fleets of ships, sailing to and from all parts of the world."

St. Paul's Cathedral, London, designed by Sir Christopher Wren after Old St. Paul's was destroyed in the Great Fire. Shostal Associates

The social order was based on a stratified class system, which most people regarded as inevitable and indeed as divinely ordained. Defoe summarized the hierarchy in 1709 in this way:

There are seven groups in English society:
1. The Great, who live profusely.
2. The Rich, who live very plentifully.
3. The Middle Sort, who live well.
4. The Working Trades, who labor hard, but feel no want.
5. The Country People, Farmers, etc., who fare indifferently.
6. The Poor, that fare hard.
7. The Miserable, that really pinch and suffer want.

At the top of the hierarchy were the hereditary nobility, whose ranks the wealthiest merchants sought to join by marriage or by purchasing titles. The country scene was dominated by the gentry, landowning squires who administered local justice as well as controlling the management of agriculture. Some were petty tyrants, some deeply loved. Joseph Addison's Sir Roger de Coverley is a portrait of a beloved squire. They tended to be suspicious of the rich wielders of power in far-off London (it took four days to get by stagecoach from York to London, a distance of 200 miles) and saw themselves as defenders of the older, established social order.

Then there were the professions: the church, the law, teachers, doctors and the military (where commissions were sold rather than assigned on merit). To a surprising degree these men were regarded as parasites. As Henry Fielding (1707–1754) wrote bitterly:

> Religion, law, and physic, were designed
> By Heaven the greatest blessing on mankind;
> But priests, and lawyers, and physicians made
> These general goods to each a private trade.
> With each they rob, with each they fill their purses.
> And turn our benefits into our curses.

Of these the law was the most constantly criticized. Unable to make adequate provision for the poor, eighteenth-century England was terrified of the crime caused by poverty and punished it ferociously. Many of the first English who came to America were convicts "transported" to the colonies for relatively minor offenses. There was a growing number of earnestly pious and intensely respectable people belonging to the middle and artisan classes, and finally the poor— sharply drawn not only by the writers of the time but also by the artist William Hogarth (1697–1764).

Universal education was far in the future, and was opposed by many on the ground that it would elevate humble people above their station. Oxford and Cambridge were the only two universities in the whole of England (Scotland had four). The majority of people were illiterate, though the growing middle class promoted a rapid rise in literacy. Women, even when wealthy, tended to receive a haphazard education, could not enter a university, and were barred from all professions. Only well-to-do males could vote (a system that did not begin to break down until 1832).

Marriage was commonly regarded as an economic arrangement uniting families and estates, though of course there were many happy marriages as well as unwelcome ones. The two most popular novels of the century, Henry Fielding's *The History of Tom Jones*

"The Marriage Contract" from *Marriage à la Mode,* a novellike set of paintings by William Hogarth.
Radio Times Hulton

and Samuel Richardson's *Clarissa,* both describe repulsive matches that parents try to force upon their daughters. And early in the next century, Jane Austen began *Pride and Prejudice* with the ironic remark, "It is a truth universally acknowledged, that a single man in possession of a good fortune, must be in want of a wife."

Religious life was dominated by the Anglican Church, with its hierarchy of bishops and its parish priest in every village (though not in the growing industrial towns). The minority who remained outside the state church, and were subject to various civil disabilities, were known as Dissenters. The old passions of the Puritans soon died down, especially after the death of the generation that had lived through the Civil War. John Milton died in 1674 and John Bunyan in 1688—the year of the Glorious Revolution and the year of Alexander Pope's birth. Some of the greatest writers of the period were Dissenters: Alexander Pope (1688–1744) was a Catholic and John Dryden (1631–1700) became one; Defoe was a Presbyterian; and William Blake (1757–1827) was a radical Protestant of some kind (possibly a Baptist, though he soon left organized religion). The most powerful religious movement of the century began within the Church of England. This was the evangelical revival led by John and Charles Wesley, who reluctantly broke away to form the Methodist denomination. Calling for spiritual rebirth, the Wesleys ministered especially to the laboring poor, whom the official church tended to neglect.

Chiswick House, London, designed by Lord Burlington and William Kent.
© 1973, Crown Copyright, Dept. of the Environment, London.

AN AGE OF ELEGANCE

During this period the upper classes lived on a superb scale. Never in European history do we see men and women so elaborately artificial, so far removed from natural appearance, as the men and women of the eighteenth century. The men wore wigs, which often had to be curled every day, and with them gaily colored and lace-trimmed satin coats and waistcoats, silk stockings, and buckled shoes. The women often had immense coiffures of powdered hair and enormous hooped skirts, and were carried to their parties in sedan chairs. An evening party in high society, taking place in a room lit with hundreds of candles, must have been an impressive spectacle.

These people lived better in some ways than similar people have done since. We know from pictures of the age and from the eighteenth-century houses, furniture, and domestic utensils still in existence that the outward trappings of their lives were truly magnificent. Only a small minority, however, lived on this superb scale. The mass of people dressed plainly, wore their own hair unpowdered, and drank out of clumsy mugs and cups.

The Etruscan Room at Osterley Park House, designed by Robert Adam.
J. Bethell, The National Trust, London

THE ARTS

The most striking characteristic of the arts during this period is their practical quality. It was not a great age of painting or sculpture: Sir Joshua Reynolds (1723–1792), aspired to an idea of grand allegorical scenes, but his best works were portraits of real people. Thomas Gainsborough (1727–1788), Reynolds' chief rival, likewise excelled in portraits and familiar landscapes. William Hogarth excelled as a cartoonist and caricaturist. Music was much cultivated, but at a level of competence rather than genius: the finest musicians in England during the eighteenth century were visiting foreigners like George Frederick Handel (1685–1759) and Franz Joseph Haydn (1732–1809). The drama was active, but after the Restoration there were more great actors than great playwrights. David Garrick's most brilliant performances were in the works of Shakespeare and other classics.

It was in everyday life that English arts excelled. This was a time of much building and "improvement" of towns and estates. Handsome streets and squares were put up, in a style known today as "Georgian," after the reigning monarchs. Country houses were designed in the fashionable classical mode. Furniture and interior decoration received the attention of skilled designers (the names of

Chippendale, Hepplewhite, Adam, and Sheraton are still well known today). In the far-off colonies it was quite natural for Thomas Jefferson to study architecture and to design for himself a classical mansion, Monticello, which has been described as "a portico in the wilderness."

The English made a favorite art form out of garden and landscape design, replacing the formal symmetry of the French-inspired garden with a more natural style. Meanwhile, landscapes began to be admired for their qualities of the "picturesque"—that is, for looking like pictures. After so many centuries of cultivation, the English countryside had become, as a historian has said, a handmade landscape. Thus the new gardens formed a harmonious part of the larger scene, which was itself, as a group of foreigners told Defoe, "all a planted garden." Borrowing the technical terms of the new art form, Defoe writes: "The enclosed cornfields made one grand parterre [decorative pattern], the thick-planted hedgerows, like a wilderness or labyrinth, divided in espaliers [plants trained to grow in a pattern]; the villages interspersed looked like so many several noble seats of gentlemen at a distance. In a word, it was all nature, and yet looked all like art." There precisely lies the eighteenth-century ideal: to make use of art in every aspect of life, but to do it in such a way that it becomes natural. For as Edmund Burke (1729–1797), the great orator, observed, "Art is man's nature."

Italian gardens at Compton Acres, Poole, England.
P. J. Sharpe, Shostal

THE COFFEEHOUSES

The middle class found its ideal social center in the coffeehouses, which came to occupy the area between the town houses of the aristocrats and the rough and roaring taverns of the Elizabethans and Jacobeans. The coffeehouses offered the same services to professional middle-class Londoners that clubs did later, and still do. So City men—financiers, merchants, shipowners—met at Lloyd's coffeehouse, where Lloyd's, the most famous insurance firm in the world, was established. Writers generally met at Will's. Other coffeehouse patrons, who might be City men, politicians, lawyers, writers, and the more free-and-easy aristocrats, foregathered at White's (now a rather exclusive club), St. James's, the Grecian, Buttons, and the Turk's Head. At such places, news could be gathered and exchanged, some business conducted, political secrets whispered. There also might be serious discussion of religion, philosophy, literature, domestic and foreign affairs, as well as a good deal of pleasant or malicious gossip. The result of this coffeehouse habit was a knitting together of the middle and upper sections of English society, which was a considerable benefit to the writer, among others, and to literature. It helped, too, to create a feeling that this closely knit and highly articulate society represented a new but enduring civilization, not unlike but superior to the ancient civilizations of Greece and Rome. This civilization belonged only to persons of some position, wealth, and influence; the common people

A London coffeehouse, 1668.
Radio Times Hulton

were still a long way outside it. If you were reasonably fortunate in your status, however, you could settle down to enjoy "the best of all possible worlds."

THE AGE OF REASON

During the eighteenth century the upper classes and the middle classes in Britain felt more complacent than they had ever felt before or since. Britain was free from the revolutionary, heated atmosphere of the seventeenth century and the growing doubts and dark divisions of the nineteenth century. Most people were strongly patriotic and welcomed the many signs of their country's greatness. Britain had always been a commercial nation, blessed with geographical advantages rather than with natural resources. Joseph Addison (1672–1719) spoke for nearly everyone when he wrote of a visit to London's financial center, "There is no place in the town which I so much love to frequent as the Royal Exchange. It gives me a secret satisfaction, and in some measure gratifies my vanity, as I am an Englishman, to see so rich an assembly of countrymen and foreigners consulting together upon the private business of mankind, and making this metropolis a kind of emporium for the whole earth." In the same vein, Pope celebrated the Peace of Utrecht, ending a war with France in 1713, with a poem proclaiming the moral advantages of an expansion of British trade:

> The time shall come, when free as seas or wind
> Unbounded Thames shall flow for all mankind,
> Whole nations enter with each swelling tide,
> And seas but join the regions they divide . . . .
> Oh stretch thy reign, fair Peace, from shore to shore,
> Till conquest cease, and slavery be no more.

Many people felt that they were living in the "best of all possible worlds" — a smug notion that was attacked by the great French satirist Voltaire (1694–1778) in *Candide*.

The complacency of the eighteenth century was due partly to the work of seventeenth-century scientists and philosophers. The age idolized the mathematician-philosopher Sir Isaac Newton, whose *Mathematical Principles of Natural Philosophy* (1687) provided the framework of a system that seemed capable of explaining everything in the universe. So great was Newton's influence that Alexander Pope was prompted to write, "God said, 'Let Newton be!' and all was light." It was the work of Newton and others that led to the philosophy of the universe as a smoothly running machine first set in motion by a benevolent deity. So long as people understood the working of this machine, they could be said to be the masters of it. This rational religion was known as Deism. Indeed, it is because human reason and the watchword "common sense" played so large and significant a role in this period that it is often referred to as "the Age of Reason."

LITERARY DEVELOPMENTS

One of the first things Charles II did was to reopen the theaters, which had been closed by the Puritans. The Restoration theater was very different from the Elizabethan theater. It was a theater for the court, the nobility, the men and women of fashion. Women's roles were now played by actresses, like the famous Nell Gwynn. The most characteristic dramas of the period were comedies of manners, particularly those of William Congreve (1670–1729), William Wycherley (1640–1716), and George Farquhar (1678–1707). These comedies have never been surpassed for their brilliant dialogue. Not until Oscar Wilde (1854–1900) produced *The Importance of Being Earnest* was the English stage to hear such sparkling and engaging prose.

Throughout much of this period there was a preference for public and general themes rather than private and individual ones. After the great lyric poems of the seventeenth century, the lyric suddenly fell into disuse except for playful purposes. Poets like Thomas Gray (1716–1771), William Collins (1721–1759), and William Cowper (1731–1800) struggled to revive it with only partial success. Not until Robert Burns (1759–1796) and William Blake, who foreshadow the Romantic poets, was the lyric again a major form. One reason for this development is that lyric poetry traditionally expresses personal feeling, which few poets of the age wanted (or in some cases dared) to write about. For the most part writers addressed themselves to universal human experience, to the problems of society, and to the recurring constants in human behavior. Henry Fielding, describing a typical lawyer in his novel *Joseph Andrews,* declared, "I describe not men, but manners; not an individual, but a species . . . . The lawyer is not only alive, but hath been so these four thousand years." When the French philosopher Jean Jacques Rousseau (1712–1778) wrote at the beginning of his *Confessions* that after making him Nature broke the mold, he wrote as a precursor to the Romantics: few writers of his age would have published "confessions."

At the opening of the eighteenth century, writers were largely dependent upon patronage. Writers were either rewarded directly by the wealthy patrons to whom they dedicated their work or given easy, well-paid government jobs, called "sinecures," that would enable them to keep on writing in comfortable circumstances. This system had its disadvantages—as we know from a famous bitter letter addressed by Samuel Johnson to his former patron Lord Chesterfield (see page 367)—but it had some advantages too. It meant that a writer could confidently address his work to cultivated, intelligent readers and could maintain a certain level in his writing.

Very soon, however, the complete dependence of authors upon patronage gave way to a system not unlike our own, except that publishers of books in those days were still themselves booksellers. Readers were no longer confined to a small class. The new middle class, especially its women members, took to buying and reading books. If they could not afford to buy them, they borrowed them from lending libraries, not free public libraries such as we now have in our cities, but libraries run by shopkeepers or various institutions demanding fees. An amusing scene in *The Rivals*, a comedy set in Bath, by Richard Sheridan (1751–1816), proves that young women visiting Bath borrowed fiction in large quantities from the lending libraries. By the 1770's the novel, though a comparatively new literary form, had won great popularity. Outstanding novelists of the day, such as Samuel Richardson (1689–1761), Henry Fielding, Laurence Sterne (1713–1768), and Tobias Smollett (1721–1771),

The trial of Macheath, a scene from John Gay's *The Beggar's Opera* by William Hogarth.
The Tate Gallery, London

were almost entirely dependent upon this new and growing reading public. Authors of more weighty works, however—Samuel Johnson, for instance, or Edward Gibbon (1737–1794), the great historian of the Roman Empire—usually brought out their works accompanied by a list of wealthy subscribers, whose support guaranteed that the books would at least pay for themselves.

Nevertheless, professional writers who had to earn their living and who had no government pension often led desperate lives scribbling away day and night to keep themselves from starvation. They would often undertake, for miserable payment, to write long books on subjects they knew little about, just because these were what the "booksellers" demanded from them. For years a man of genius like Oliver Goldsmith (1728–1774)—capable of writing comedy, fiction, and verse that would enchant future generations—wasted precious time and energy on this sort of hack work. If the rewards of good original work had been greater and more immediate than they were, the literature of this century might have been even richer.

LITERATURE: FROM THE RESTORATION TO THE ROMANTIC AGE

Our period may be conveniently divided into three parts. The first, the Restoration, is characterized by a cliquish culture centering on the court and deeply influenced by French classical taste. It sustains traditional values and admires "wit"—a brilliance and quickness of perception combined with a cleverness of expression. During the second era, known as the Age of Pope, satire increasingly becomes the dominant form, and there is great concern for moral analysis. The third era may be called the Age of Johnson, after its most conspicuous writer. This was the time of the rise of the novel, and of increasing demand for descriptions of actual life rather than of imaginary worlds. Much of the best writing was done in such forms as history, biography, philosophy, and political debate.

Just as the English garden sought to combine artifice with nature, so did English writing. The poems of Alexander Pope and Jonathan Swift used a mixture of ornate "poetic diction" and everyday colloquial language, carefully shaped into balanced couplets. Many people may find this poetry artificial, but we should recognize that its artificiality is skillfully controlled and is essential to its effect.

Similarly, the prose of the period, though based on conversational forms and striving for perfect clarity, was subtly structured to give pleasure as well as to communicate ideas. The first task of writers in this period was to replace the ornate prose of their forebears with a

"The Temple of Saturn" (etching, 1774) from *Views of Rome* by
G. B. Piranesi.
The Metropolitan Museum of Art

lucid "plain style" that reflected the vigor and ease of actual speech. Once this ideal was established—for instance, in the prose of Dryden, Swift, and Addison—it was possible to attempt variations that could organize complex materials while preserving clarity. Matthew Arnold (1822–1888), the nineteenth-century critic and poet, called the eighteenth century an age of prose, and he meant it in part as a compliment. Good prose is impossible without clear thinking and careful writing. And our best source of insight into the minds of people of that time, now so long ago, lies in the style with which they expressed themselves.

About the middle of the eighteenth century, a new mood made itself felt in literature, in which the inner world of wonder and strange feeling—what is essentially private rather than public—was given expression. This breakthrough is referred to as the beginning of Romanticism, and it showed itself in various ways. It showed itself in the curious hothouse sentimentality of Richardson's novels, and in the strongly personal mixture of humor and sentiment in Laurence Sterne's work. It showed itself in the publication of Bishop Percy's *Reliques of Ancient English Poetry* (1765), a collection of ballads that had a tremendous influence on the whole Romantic movement of the early nineteenth century. It showed itself in the new taste for ruins and Gothic castles and tales of mystery. It showed itself in the fashion during the latter half of the century for founding strange, secret societies interested in magic and in mysterious rites.

But this breakthrough was most obvious in poetry. Though they are all in many ways typical eighteenth-century men, Thomas Gray, Oliver Goldsmith, and William Cowper in their best verse began to show Romantic tendencies. Robert Burns, the national poet of Scotland, alternated between verse in the acceptable eighteenth-century style and impassioned lyrics or comic-pathetic narrative poems about the peasantry that are undoubtedly Romantic in feeling. And then there was William Blake, an astonishing character and one of the world's great originals, who in his earliest poems seems like another Elizabethan but then flashes out, completely disregarding the taste of the time, in work that blazes with his own highly original genius. By this time the Romantic Age had almost arrived.

THE END OF AN AGE

The last years of the eighteenth century were altogether different from its first years. The Industrial Revolution, which greatly increased the use of machinery and steam power in manufacturing, had transformed much of England into a blackened, ruined countryside of mine shafts, slag heaps, tall chimneys pouring out smoke, and horrible industrial towns in which people lived and worked in appalling conditions. The French Revolution (1789–1799), with its destructive fury, left nothing certain. Britain was sharply divided between those who feared and denounced the French Revolution and those who welcomed it. Old values and standards seemed to vanish in the smoke of burning buildings and the roar of Napoleon's cannons, which were heard everywhere in Europe from Spain to Moscow. Anything could happen now: it was that kind of world, that kind of universe. The social order was no longer as stable as it once had been. The old aristocracy was giving way to a rising middle class, and there was increasing sympathy for the underprivileged classes. Ideas of political freedom, of independence, of human brotherhood and "natural rights" had become more and more widespread, as revolutions on both sides of the Atlantic Ocean had attested. A new spirit was abroad. Gone were the philosophic calm, the complacency, the exultation of good taste, the curled wigs and lacy satin coats, the coffeehouse wits and critics: the whole age was dead.

The Restoration

The term *Restoration* refers to a specific event, Charles's recovery of his throne, rather than to a definable historical period. When the term is used in literary history, it is variously extended to include the years until the expulsion of James II in 1688 or until the death of John Dryden in 1700.

Coronation of Charles II (detail, etching) by Wenceslaus Hollar.
The Mansell Collection

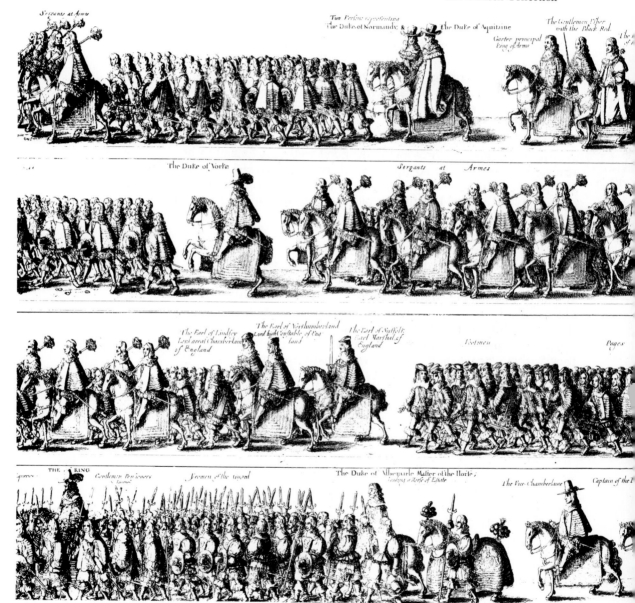

This was a time of vigorous activity in all areas of British life, but literature during this period, apart from the writings of steadfast Puritans like Milton and Bunyan, was dominated by the narrow interests of Charles's highly sophisticated court. Charles and his court had brought back from their exile on the Continent the new fashions in French wit, elegance, and literary taste. English writers began to imitate the strict order and regularity of French classicism. Dryden wrote in the prologue to one of his first plays:

> He who writ this, not without pains and thought,
> From French and English theaters has brought
> The exactest rules by which a play is wrought.

In fact, Dryden's writings were not really limited by strict "rules," but he understood that his fashionable audience expected him to claim that they were.

Those who wanted to get ahead took care to study Charles II closely. Charles loved his pleasures and understood well that England was ready for a monarch who preferred pleasure to bloodshed. The Marquess of Halifax wrote, "If he loved too much to lie upon his own down bed of ease, his subjects had the pleasure during his reign of lolling and stretching upon theirs."

In such a world, the range of literary experiment was not wide. Apart from some of Dryden's poems and his masterful prose, the greatest Restoration works are the worldly, witty comedies of William Congreve, William Wycherley, and others, many of which are still acted today. But on the whole, the writing of the age reflects the general mood of forced cleverness and anxious currying of favor at court. In a poem marking the end of the century, Dryden looked back without nostalgia on a time whose values seemed shaped by courtly recreations and intrigues:

> All, all of a piece throughout;
> Thy chase had a beast in view;
> Thy wars brought nothing about;
> Thy lovers were all untrue.
> 'Tis well an old age is out,
> And time to begin a new.

John Dryden
1631–1700

Born into a strongly Puritan family, Dryden lived as a young man through the dour decade of Commonwealth rule. He went to London where his early work was more striking for its political self-contradiction than for its literary quality: within two years he wrote *Heroic Stanzas* praising Oliver Cromwell and *Astrea Redux,* celebrating the Restoration of Charles II. In London Dryden married the daughter of an earl; and he joined the Royal Society, believing that "a man should be learned in several sciences . . . to be a complete and excellent poet." His best years were spent in court circles which reacted strongly against Cromwellian austerity. If he changed his opinions with the times, he was far from alone in doing so.

Dryden's long poetic career spanned the four decades from the Restoration in 1660 to the end of the seventeenth century. He wrote in most of the literary forms that were popular during that time. To make a living he wrote nearly thirty plays (a few are still performed today) and a series of distinguished translations of Virgil and other classical authors. His finest works were his long poems in rhymed couplets on political, religious, and literary themes. Dryden's best poetry was often inspired by some particular occasion like the great fire of London in 1666 or a plot against King Charles II in 1681. For almost twenty years Dryden was England's poet laureate, but had to resign in 1688 when James II was expelled and Catholics were deprived of public office.

Our selections show a number of facets of Dryden's many-sided talent. "A Song for St. Cecilia's Day" is an inventive testimony to the powers of music, intended to be sung as well as read (and given its noblest musical expression in Handel's setting, written some fifty years later than the poem). The excerpt from *Mac Flecknoe,* a witty attack on Thomas Shadwell, a minor poet and playwright, shows Dryden's superb gifts in verse satire. As he himself wrote, the great art of the satirist is to do his job elegantly rather than crudely: "There is a vast difference betwixt the slovenly butchering of a man, and the fineness of a stroke that separates the head from the body, and leaves it standing in its place." In poetry Dryden set an enduring style with his neat "heroic couplets"—paired lines of

John Dryden by Sir Godfrey Kneller.
National Portrait Gallery, London

rhymed iambic pentameter. In prose Dryden established the neoclassical standards of order, balance, and harmony; his greatest work of literary criticism is *An Essay of Dramatic Poesy,* in which appears his famous appreciation of Shakespeare.

Dryden's significance in the history of English literature is greater than that of any one of his works considered in itself. His influence was so great that the last quarter of the seventeenth century is, by common consent, the "Age of Dryden." His achievement was to unite a classical conception of order and clarity with traditional English energy and inventiveness. Both in his lucid prose and in his balanced, harmonious poetic couplets, he fashioned techniques that would dominate English writing for a century. For those whose minds were formed in that tradition, Dryden was a kind of founding father. As Samuel Johnson wrote in 1779, "What was said of Rome, adorned by Augustus, may be applied by an easy metaphor to English poetry embellished by Dryden: he found it brick, and he left it marble."

from An Essay of Dramatic Poesy

Before Dryden's time there was little of what we call "literary criticism"
—analysis of the merits and interesting aspects of pieces of literature. In
works like *An Essay of Dramatic Poesy,* which is an excellent example of
Dryden's prose and one of the first important works in English literary criticism, he launched the modern reputations of Chaucer and Shakespeare. In
the excerpt from the *Essay* given here, Dryden contrasts the "naturally
learned" Shakespeare with "the more correct poet," Ben Jonson.

To begin, then, with Shakespeare. He was the
man who of all modern, and perhaps ancient
poets, had the largest and most comprehensive soul. All the images of Nature were still
present in him, and he drew them, not laboriously, but luckily; when he describes anything, you more than see it, you feel it too.
Those who accuse him to have wanted[1] learning give him the greater commendation: he
was naturally learned. He needed not the
spectacles of books to read Nature; he looked
inwards, and found her there. I cannot say he
is everywhere alike; were he so, I should do
him injury to compare him with the greatest
of mankind. He is many times flat, insipid;
his comic wit degenerating into clenches,[2] his
serious swelling into bombast. But he is
always great when some great occasion is
presented to him; no man can say he ever had
a fit subject for his wit[3] and did not raise himself as high above the rest of poets.

*Quantum lenta solent inter viburna cu-
pressi.*[4]

The consideration of this made Mr. Hales of
Eton say that there is no subject of which any
poet ever wrote but he would produce it much
better done in Shakespeare; and, however
others are now more generally preferred before him, yet the age wherein he lived, which

had contemporaries with him Fletcher[5] and
Jonson, never equaled them to him in their esteem: and in the last King's court, when Ben's
reputation was at highest, Sir John Suckling,
and with him the greater part of the courtiers,
set our Shakespeare far above him.

Beaumont and Fletcher, of whom I am next
to speak, had, with the advantage of Shakespeare's wit, which was their precedent, great
natural gifts, improved by study. . . . The first
play that brought Fletcher and him in esteem
was their *Philaster:* for, before that, they had
written two or three very unsuccessfully, as
the like is reported of Ben Jonson, before he
writ *Every Man in His Humor.* Their plots
were generally more regular than Shakespeare's, especially those that were made before Beaumont's death; and they understood
and imitated the conversation of gentlemen
much better; whose wild debaucheries, and
quickness of wit in repartees, no poet before
them could paint as they have done. Humor,
which Ben Jonson derived from particular persons, they made it their business not to describe: they represented all the passions very
lively, but above all, love. I am apt to believe
the English language in them arrived to its
highest perfection: what words have since
been taken in are rather superfluous than or-

1. **wanted:** lacked.
2. **clenches:** puns (now obsolete).
3. **wit:** intelligence, imaginative mind. Throughout in
referring to "wit," Dryden means inventiveness and
imagination rather than humor.
4. *Quantum . . . cupressi:* as cypresses rise above shrubs.

5. **Fletcher:** John Fletcher (1579–1625), joint author
with Francis Beaumont (1584–1616), mentioned below,
of many plays popular in the Jacobean period.

namental. Their plays are now the most pleasant and frequent entertainments of the stage; two of theirs being acted through the year for one of Shakespeare's or Jonson's: the reason is because there is a certain gaiety in their comedies and pathos in their more serious plays, which suit generally with all men's humors. Shakespeare's language is likewise a little obsolete, and Ben Jonson's wit comes short of theirs.

As for Jonson, to whose character I am now arrived, if we look upon him while he was himself (for his last plays were but his dotage), I think him the most learned and judicious writer which any theater ever had. He was a most severe judge of himself, as well as others. One cannot say he wanted wit, but rather that he was frugal of it. In his works you find little to retrench or alter. Wit, and language, and humor also in some measure we had before him; but something of art was wanting to the drama till he came. He managed his strength to more advantage than any who preceded him. You seldom find him making love in any of his scenes, or endeavoring to move the passions; his genius was too sullen and saturnine to do it gracefully, especially when he knew he came after those who had performed both to such a height. Humor was his proper sphere; and in that he delighted most to represent mechanic people.[6] He was deeply conversant in the ancients, both Greek and Latin, and he borrowed boldly from them: there is scarcely a poet or historian among the Roman authors of those times whom he has not translated in *Sejanus* and *Catiline*.[7] But he has done his robberies so openly, that one may see he fears not to be taxed by any law. He invades authors like a monarch; and what would be theft in other poets is only victory in him. With the spoils of these writers he so represents old Rome to us, in its rites, ceremonies, and customs, that if one of their poets had written either of his

tragedies, we had seen less of it than in him. If there was any fault in his language, 'twas that he weaved it too closely and laboriously, in his comedies especially: perhaps, too, he did a little too much to Romanize our tongue, leaving the words which he translated almost as much Latin as when he found them: wherein, though he learnedly followed their language, he did not enough comply with the idiom of ours. If I would compare him with Shakespeare, I must acknowledge him the more correct poet, but Shakespeare the greater wit. Shakespeare was the Homer,[8] or father of our dramatic poets; Jonson was the Virgil,[9] the pattern of elaborate writing; I admire him, but I love Shakespeare. To conclude of him; as he has given us the most correct plays, so in the precepts which he has laid down in his *Discoveries*, we have as many and profitable rules for perfecting the stage, as any wherewith the French can furnish us. . . .

---

6. **mechanic people:** artisans.
7. *Sejanus* **and** *Catiline:* plays by Ben Jonson.

8. **Homer:** traditional author of the Greek epics, the *Iliad* and the *Odyssey*.
9. **Virgil:** author of the Roman epic, the *Aeneid*.

FOR STUDY AND DISCUSSION

1. According to Dryden, what are Jonson's strong points? His weak ones? Does Dryden condemn Jonson for borrowing from the ancient Greeks and Romans? Cite evidence to support your answer.

2. According to Dryden, what are Shakespeare's faults and merits? Do you agree? Cite examples of these faults and merits from *Macbeth*. In what sense does Dryden consider Shakespeare not a "correct" poet?

3. What difference, if any, is there between Dryden's evaluation of Shakespeare in this essay and Ben Jonson's in "To the Memory of My Beloved Master"? Which evaluation is more objective? Does that necessarily make it the superior judgment? Why?

4. Compare Dryden's prose style with that of Francis Bacon. Which is the simpler style? Justify your opinion.

from **Mac Flecknoe**

Thomas Shadwell, a rival playwright whom Dryden disliked, considered himself heir to the great Elizabethan poet Ben Jonson. In this superbly witty attack, written about 1678 but not published until 1682, Dryden suggests that Shadwell's true spiritual father was a grossly inept Irish poet named Richard Flecknoe, who had died in 1678. "Mac Flecknoe" would be an Irish expression for "Son of Flecknoe." Ironically, Shadwell later succeeded Dryden as poet laureate.

All human things are subject to decay,
And when fate summons, monarchs must obey.
This Flecknoe found, who, like Augustus,° young
Was called to empire, and had governed long;
In prose and verse was owned, without dispute,   5
Through all the realms of *Nonsense,* absolute.
This aged prince, now flourishing in peace,
And blessed with issue° of a large increase;
Worn out with business, did at length debate
To settle the succession of the state;   10
And, pondering which of all his sons was fit
To reign, and wage immortal war with wit,
Cried: " 'Tis resolved; for nature pleads that he
Should only rule, who most resembles me.
Sh— alone my perfect image bears,   15
Mature in dullness from his tender years:
Sh— alone of all my sons is he
Who stands confirmed in full stupidity.
The rest to some faint meaning make pretense,
But Sh— never deviates into sense.   20
Some beams of wit on other souls may fall,
Strike through, and make a lucid interval;
But Sh—'s genuine night admits no ray,
His rising fogs prevail upon the day.
Besides, his goodly fabric° fills the eye,   25
And seems designed for thoughtless° majesty;
Thoughtless as monarch oaks that shade the plain,
And, spread in solemn state, supinely reign."

---

3. **Augustus:** He became Roman Emperor at the age of thirty-two, and ruled for
forty-five years.   8. **issue:** children.   25. **fabric:** body. Shadwell was very fat.
26. **thoughtless:** carefree; but also mindless.

A Song for St. Cecilia's Day

An annual concert was given on November 22 in honor of Saint Cecilia, a Roman woman and early Christian martyr who was the patron saint of music and purported inventor of the organ. Dryden's song was performed in public in 1687.

I

From harmony, from heavenly harmony
    This universal frame° began:
    When Nature underneath a heap
      Of jarring atoms° lay,
    And could not heave her head,   5
The tuneful voice was heard from high:
    "Arise, ye more than dead."
Then cold, and hot, and moist, and dry,°
In order to their stations leap,
    And Music's power obey.°   10
From harmony, from heavenly harmony
    This universal frame began:
    From harmony to harmony
Through all the compass of the notes it ran,
The diapason° closing full in Man.   15

II

What passion cannot Music raise and quell!
    When Jubal° struck the corded shell,
    His listening brethren stood around,
    And, wondering, on their faces fell
    To worship that celestial sound.   20
Less than a god they thought there could not dwell
    Within the hollow of that shell
    That spoke so sweetly and so well.
What passion cannot Music raise and quell!

---

2. **universal frame:** the structure of the universe, the cosmos. 4. **jarring atoms:** the chaos before Creation. 8. **cold . . . dry:** the four elements of which all matter was said to be composed, according to the ancient Greeks. 10. **Music's power obey:** The forces organizing the universe were thought to be related to the mathematical proportions of musical harmony. 15. **diapason** (dī′ə-pā′sən): the organ stop that produces harmony across the whole range of octaves; by analogy, human beings are the fullest expression of the harmony of nature. 17. **Jubal:** legendary inventor of music (see Genesis 4:21) who made a harp from a tortoise shell (the "corded shell").

III

The trumpet's loud clangor 25
   Excites us to arms,
With shrill notes of anger
   And mortal alarms.
The double double double beat
   Of the thundering drum 30
Cries: "Hark! the foes come;
Charge, charge, 'tis too late to retreat."

IV

The soft complaining flute
In dying notes discovers
The woes of hopeless lovers, 35
Whose dirge is whispered by the warbling lute.

V

Sharp violins° proclaim
Their jealous pangs, and desperation,
Fury, frantic indignation,
Depth of pains, and height of passion, 40
   For the fair, disdainful dame.

VI

But O! what art can teach,
   What human voice can reach,
The sacred organ's praise?
   Notes inspiring holy love, 45
Notes that wing their heavenly ways
   To mend the choirs above.

VII

Orpheus° could lead the savage race;
And trees unrooted left their place,
   Sequacious of° the lyre; 50
But bright Cecilia raised the wonder higher:
When to her organ vocal breath was given,
   An angel heard, and straight appeared,
   Mistaking earth for heaven.

. 37. **Sharp violins:** The then recently invented violin had a much brighter tone than the softer Elizabethan viol. 48. **Orpheus:** the legendary singer in Greek myth whose playing of the lyre could charm rocks, trees, and wild beasts. 50. **Sequacious of:** following.

Grand Chorus

As from the power of sacred lays 55
The spheres began to move,°
And sung the great Creator's praise
To all the blest above;
So, when the last and dreadful hour°
This crumbling pageant° shall devour, 60
The trumpet shall be heard on high,
The dead shall live, the living die,
And Music shall untune the sky.°

---

56. *spheres . . . move:* It was believed that the planets or celestial bodies ("spheres") were put into motion by angelic song ("sacred lays"), producing the harmonious music of the spheres, i.e., a hymn to praise the Creator, sung by the created. 59. *last . . . hour:* the Last Judgment, the end of the universe. 60. *pageant:* the universe; also the stage performance itself, coming to an end. 63. *Music . . . sky:* The sound of the last trumpet (from I Corinthians 15:52) announces the end of the universe, and thus "untunes" the music of the spheres.

FOR STUDY AND DISCUSSION

Mac Flecknoe

Much of the humor in this poem lies in the contrast between the serious poetic style and the subject—poetic mediocrity. What examples of humorous contrast can you find in the poem? What does Flecknoe most admire in his chosen successor?

A Song for St. Cecilia's Day

1. In what sense is the word "harmony" in line 1 used? Why are the final two lines of the first stanza appropriate?
2. How does Dryden use the sounds of words to suggest musical effects? Why is it especially appropriate that a saint should be associated here with music?
3. According to Dryden, what passions are raised and quelled by music? With what instruments are the various passions associated? What instrument does Dryden praise most highly?
4. In line 40 Dryden uses *antithesis*, the balancing against each other of two contrasting words, thoughts, or phrases. Point out other examples of antithesis in the poem.
5. Explain the meaning of the "Grand Chorus."
6. In the first stanza of the poem, Dryden speaks of music as having organized the created world. This being so, do you think the last line of the poem is a paradox? Explain.

THE ODE

Its name based on a Greek word meaning "song," the ode, a form of long lyric poem, was originated by the Greeks to honor gods and heroes. The Greek odes of Pindar were sung and danced by a chorus, the various movements of the dance corresponding to the different sections of the poem. The characteristics of the original ode were modified by the Romans, and still later by the English. The English form, imitations of the classic Greek and Roman odes, was established by John Dryden. Early English odes were written in praise of a person, of music or poetry, or of abstract ideas, such as liberty. The elaborate address, irregular rhythm, and lofty feeling of the ode also appealed to the Romantic poets who wrote the most famous examples of this form in English. See, for example, Shelley's "To a Skylark" and Keats's "Ode on a Grecian Urn."

FOR COMPOSITION

Choose a subject for praise—a person, a place, or an idea. List the qualities you would want an ode on that subject to mention and comment on. List the images, metaphors, and similes you might use to convey those qualities to someone else.

Samuel Pepys
1633–1703

Samuel Pepys by Sir Godfrey Kneller.
National Portrait Gallery, London

On May 26, 1703, Samuel Pepys's friend John Evelyn wrote in his diary, "This day died Mr. Pepys, a very worthy, industrious and curious person, none in England exceeding him in knowledge of the navy. . . . He was universally beloved, hospitable, generous, learned in many things, skilled in music, a very great cherisher of learned men of whom he had conversation." What Evelyn did not know was that Pepys too had kept a diary, from which, long afterward, he would win a second and unexpected kind of reputation.

Pepys (pronounced "Peeps"), son of a prosperous tailor, was helped by an influential relative to attend Cambridge and to achieve public office. He worked hard and was able to pile up a small fortune, and rose to the rank of Secretary of the Admiralty, in which capacity he ran the British navy and made it a model of economy and efficiency. His career had its setbacks, including imprisonment on false charges of political intrigue, but he rose above them triumphantly. At the fall of King James II in 1688, however, Pepys's public life was over, and he retired to a comfortable leisure, writing letters and arranging an impressive library, which he bequeathed to one of the colleges at Cambridge.

Included in this library were six mysterious volumes of manuscript written in what appeared to be a secret code (Pepys had used the new and little-known shorthand). It was not until 1818 that someone took the trouble to break the code, and in 1825, after years of labor, Pepys's diary was fully deciphered and published. The world was delighted to discover the many-sided private man hidden behind the man of affairs, and also the fascinating narrative of life in the exciting 1660's (the diary stopped in 1669 when Pepys's eyesight began to fail). Along with remarkably candid pictures of his personal life, Pepys presents great public scenes: the splendid coronation of Charles II, a gruesome execution, the Plague of 1665, and the Great Fire of 1666.

Clearly Pepys concealed his diary from living eyes, but his bequest of the volumes to Cambridge University suggests that he may have hoped posterity would read it. Most people's diaries are of small interest to anyone but themselves. Pepys's achievement is the vivid re-creation of daily life, conveyed in clear and vigorous prose. He was a man of wide interests—he loved music and books and plays; he followed the progress of science and corresponded with Isaac Newton. Although he gives a lively sense of his own cheerful and practical personality, his attention is usually directed beyond himself to the teeming variety of his world. By reading Pepys we can imagine ourselves living as his contemporaries.

from **The Diary of Samuel Pepys**

Personal Affairs

August 19, 1660. (Lord's Day.) This morning Sir W. Batten, Pen,[1] and myself went to church to the churchwardens to demand a pew, which at present could not be given us, but we are resolved to have one built. So we stayed and heard Mr. Mills, a very good minister. Home to dinner, where my wife had on her new petticoat that she bought yesterday, which indeed is a very fine cloth, and a fine lace, but that being of a light color, and the lace all silver, it makes no great show. Mr. Creed and my brother Tom dined with me. After they were gone I went up to put my papers in order and finding my wife's clothes lie carelessly laid up, I was angry with her, which I was troubled for. After that my wife and I went and walked in the garden, and so home to bed.

November 21, 1660. This morning my wife and I went to Paternoster Row, and there we bought some green watered moire for a morning waistcoat. And after that we went to Mr. Cade's to choose some pictures for our house. After that my wife went home, and I to Pope's Head and bought me an agate-hafted knife, which cost me 5s.[2] So home to dinner, and so to the office all the afternoon, and at night to my violin (the first time that I have played on it since I came to this house) in my dining room, and afterward to my lute there, and I took much pleasure to have the neighbors come forth into the yard to hear me. So up to bed.

January 3, 1661. To the Theater: and here the first time that I ever saw women come upon the stage.[3]

March 27, 1661. To the Dolphin to a dinner of Mr. Harris' where Sir Williams both and my Lady Batten and her two daughters, and other company, where a great deal of mirth, and there stayed until 11 o'clock at night, and in our mirth I sang and sometimes fiddled. At last we fell to dancing, the first time that ever I did in my life, which I did wonder to see myself do.

May 31, 1661. I went to my father's, but to my great grief I found my father and mother in a great deal of discontent one with another, and indeed my mother is now grown so pettish that I know not how my father is able to bear with it. I did talk to her so as did not indeed become me, but I could not help it, she being so insufferably foolish and simple, so that my father, poor man, is become a very unhappy man.

December 31, 1661. My wife and I this morning to the painter's, and there she sat[4] the last time. After supper, and my barber had trimmed me, I sat down to end my journal for this year, and my condition at this time, by God's blessing, is thus: my health is very good, and so my wife's in all respects: my servants, W. Hewer, Sarah, Nell, and Wayneman: my house at the Navy Office. I suppose myself to be worth about £500 clear in the world, and my goods of my house my own,

---

1. **Sir W. Batten, Pen:** Sir William Batten and Sir William Pen (referred to later as "Sir Williams both") were members of the Navy Board of which Pepys was Clerk of the Acts.
2. **5s:** five shillings.

3. **women . . . stage:** In Elizabethan times boys played the roles of women on the stage, and this custom continued until almost the end of the seventeenth century.
4. **she sat:** She had been having her portrait painted.

and what is coming to me from Brampton when my father dies, which God defer. My chiefest thought is now to get a good wife for Tom, there being one offered by the Joyces, a cousin of theirs, worth £200 in ready money. But my greatest trouble is that I have for this last half year been a very great spendthrift in all manner of respects, that I am afeared to cast up my accounts, though I hope I am worth what I say above. But I will cast them up very shortly. I have newly taken a solemn oath about abstaining from plays and wine, which I am resolved to keep according to the letter of the oath which I keep by me.

June 8, 1662. (Lord's Day.) To my Lady's, and there supped with her; and merry among other things, with the parrot which my Lord hath brought from the sea, which speaks very well, and cries Poll so pleasantly that made my Lord give it to Lady Paulina; but my Lady her mother do not like it. Home and observe my man Will to walk with his cloak flung over his shoulder like a ruffian, which, whether it was that he might not be seen to walk along with the footboy I know not, but I was vexed at it; and coming home and after prayers, I did ask him where he learned that immodest garb, and he answered me that it was not immodest, or some such slight answer, at which I did give him two boxes on the ears, which I never did before, and so was after a little troubled at it.

The Execution of a Regicide

October 13, 1660. I went out to Charing Cross, to see Major General Harrison[5] hanged, drawn, and quartered; which was done there, he looking as cheerful as any man could do in that condition. He was presently cut down, and his head and heart shown to the people, at which there was great shouts of joy. It is said that he said that he was sure to come shortly at the right hand of Christ to judge them that now had judged him; and that his wife do expect his coming again. Thus it was my chance to see the King beheaded at Whitehall,[6] and to see the first blood shed in revenge for the blood of the King at Charing Cross. From thence to my Lord's, and took Captain Cuttance and Mr. Sheply to the Sun Tavern, and did give them some oysters. After that I went by water home, where I was angry with my wife for her things lying about, and in my passion kicked the little fine basket which I bought her in Holland, and broke it, which troubled me after I had done it. Within all the afternoon setting up shelves in my study. At night to bed.

The Coronation of Charles II

April 23, 1661. Coronation Day. About four I rose and got to the Abbey, where I followed Sir J. Denham,[7] the Surveyor, with some company that he was leading in. And with much ado, by the favor of Mr. Cooper, his man, did get up into a great scaffold across the north end of the Abbey, where with a great deal of patience I sat from past four till eleven before the King came in. And a great pleasure it was to see the Abbey raised in the middle, all covered with red, and a throne (that is a chair) and footstool on the top of it; and all the officers of all kinds, so much as the very fiddlers, in red vests.

At last comes in the Dean and Prebends[8] of Westminster, with the Bishops (many of them in cloth-of-gold copes), and after them the Nobility, all in their Parliament robes, which was a most magnificent sight. Then the Duke, and the King with a scepter (carried by

---

5. **Major General Harrison:** one of the signers of the death warrant of Charles I.

6. King Charles I was beheaded in 1649 when Pepys was sixteen.
7. **Sir J. Denham:** a popular poet who was also in charge of government buildings.
8. **Prebends** (prĕb'əndz): high officials in the church.

my Lord Sandwich) and sword and mond[9] before him, and the crown too. The King in his robes, bare-headed, which was very fine. And after all had placed themselves, there was a sermon and the service; and then in the Choir at the high altar, the King passed through all the ceremonies of the Coronation, which to my great grief I and most in the Abbey could not see. The crown being put upon his head, a great shout began, and he came forth to the throne; and there passed more ceremonies: as taking the oath, and having things read to him by the Bishop; and his Lords (who put on their caps as soon as the King put on his crown) and bishops came and kneeled before him. And three times the King at Arms[10] went to the three open places on the scaffold and proclaimed that if anyone could show any reason why Charles Stuart should not be King of England, that now he should come and speak. And a General Pardon also was read by the Lord Chancellor, and medals flung up and down by my Lord Cornwallis, of silver, but I could not come by any. But so great a noise that I could make but little of the music; and indeed, it was lost to everybody.

I went out a little while before the King had done all his ceremonies, and went round the Abbey to Westminster Hall, all the way within rails, and ten thousand people, with the ground covered with blue cloth; and scaffolds all the way. Into the Hall I got, where it was very fine with hangings and scaffolds one upon another full of brave ladies; and my wife in one little one, on the right hand. Here I stayed walking up and down, and at last, upon one of the side stalls, I stood and saw the King come in with all the persons (but the soldiers) that were yesterday in the cavalcade; and a most pleasant sight it was to see them in their several robes. And the King came in with his crown on, and his scepter in his hand, under a canopy borne up by six silver staves, carried by Barons of the Cinque Ports,[11] and little bells at every end.

And after a long time, he got up to the farther end, and all set themselves down at their several tables; and that was also a brave sight; and the King's first course carried up by the Knights of the Bath. And many fine ceremonies there was of the herald's leading up people before him, and bowing; and my Lord of Albemarle's going to the kitchen and eat a bit of the first dish that was to go to the King's table. But, above all, was these three Lords, Northumberland, and Suffolk, and the Duke of Ormond, coming before the courses on horseback, and staying so all dinnertime, and at last to bring up[12] [Dymock] the King's champion, all in armor on horseback, with his spear and target carried before him. And a herald proclaims, "That if any dare deny Charles Stuart to be lawful King of England, here was a champion that would fight with him"; and with these words, the champion flings down his gauntlet, and all this he do three times in his going up toward the King's table. At last when he is come, the King drinks to him and then sends him the cup, which is of gold, and he drinks it off and then rides back again with the cup in his hand. I went from table to table to see the bishops and all others at their dinner, and was infinitely pleased with it. And at the Lords' table, I met with William Howe, and he spoke to my Lord for me, and he did give me four rabbits and a pullet, and so I got it and Mr. Creed and I got Mr. Michell to give us some bread, and so we at a stall eat[13] it, as everybody else did what they could get. I took a great deal of

---

9. **mond:** an orb of gold, with a cross set with precious stones.
10. **King at Arms:** chief of the heralds.

11. **Cinque** (sĭngk) **Ports:** five ports on the English Channel: Hastings, Sandwich, Dover, Romney, and Hythe.
12. The ceremony here described is no longer observed as part of the coronation. It was a holdover from the days of chivalry.
13. **eat** (ĕt): meaning ate.

pleasure to go up and down, and look upon the ladies, and to hear the music of all sorts, but above all, the twenty-four violins.

The London Fire

September 2, 1666. (Lord's Day.) Some of our maids sitting up late last night to get things ready against our feast today, Jane called us up about three in the morning, to tell us of a great fire they saw in the city. So I rose and slipped on my nightgown, and went to her window, and thought it to be on the back side of Mark Lane at the farthest; but, being un-used to such fires as followed, I thought it far enough off; and so went to bed again and to sleep. About seven rose again to dress myself, and there looked out at the window, and saw the fire not so much as it was and farther off. So to my closet to set things to rights after yesterday's cleaning.

By and by Jane comes and tells me that she hears that above 300 houses have been burned down tonight by the fire we saw, and that it is now burning down all Fish Street, by London Bridge. So I made myself ready presently, and walked to the Tower,[14] and there got up upon one of the high places, Sir J. Robinson's little son going up with me; and there I did see the houses at the end of the bridge all on fire, and an infinite great fire on this and the other side the end of the bridge; which, among other people, did trouble me for poor little Michell and our Sarah on the bridge.[15] So down, with my heart full of trouble, to the Lieutenant of the Tower, who tells me that it begun this morning in the King's baker's house in Pudding Lane, and that it hath burned St. Magnus Church and most part of Fish Street already. So I down to the waterside, and there got a boat and through bridge, and there saw a lamentable fire. Poor Michell's house, as far as the Old Swan, already burned that way, and the fire running farther, that in a very little time it got as far as the Steel Yard, while I was there. Everybody endeavoring to remove their goods, and flinging into the river or bringing them into lighters that lay off; poor people staying in their houses as long as till the very fire touched them, and then running into boats, or clambering from one pair of stairs by the waterside to another. And among other things, the poor pigeons, I perceive, were loath to leave their houses, but hovered about the windows and balconies till they were, some of them burned, their wings, and fell down. Having stayed, and in an hour's time seen the fire rage every way, and nobody, to my sight, endeavoring to quench it, but to remove their goods, and leave all to the fire, and having seen it get as far as the Steel Yard, and the wind mighty high and driving it into the City; and everything, after so long a drought, proving combustible, even the very stones of churches. I to Whitehall, and there up to the King's closet in the Chapel, where people come about me, and I did give them an account dismayed them all, and word was carried in to the King. So I was called for and did tell the King and Duke of York what I saw, and that unless his Majesty did command houses to be pulled down nothing could stop the fire. They seemed much troubled, and the King commanded me to go to my Lord Mayor from him and command him to spare no houses, but to pull down before the fire every way. The Duke of York bid me tell him that if he would have any more soldiers he shall; and so did my Lord Arlington afterward, as a great secret. Here meeting with Captain Cocke, I in his coach, which he lent me, and Creed with me to Paul's[16] and there walked along Watling Street, as well as I could, every creature coming away laden with goods to save, and here and there sick people carried

---

14. **Tower:** the Tower of London.
15. **on the bridge:** Old London Bridge was like a street with houses built on either side of it.

16. **Paul's:** St. Paul's Cathedral.

The Great Fire of London (colored engraving, 1666).
The Mansell Collection

away in beds. Extraordinary good goods carried in carts and on backs. At last met my Lord Mayor in Canning Street, like a man spent, with a handkerchief about his neck. To the King's message he cried, like a fainting woman, "Lord! what can I do? I am spent: people will not obey me. I have been pulling down houses; but the fire overtakes us faster than we can do it." That he needed no more soldiers and that, for himself, he must go and refresh himself, having been up all night.

So he left me, and I him, and walked home, seeing people all almost distracted, and no manner of means used to quench the fire. The houses, too, so very thick thereabouts and full of matter for burning, as pitch and tar, in Thames Street; and warehouses of oil, and wines, and brandy, and other things. Here I saw Mr. Issake Houblon, the handsome man, prettily dressed and dirty, at his door at Dowgate, receiving some of his brothers' things, whose houses were on fire; and, as he says, have been removed twice already; and he doubts (as it soon proved) that they must be in a little time removed from his house also which was a sad consideration. And to see the churches all filling with goods by people who themselves should have been quietly there at this time.

By this time it was about twelve o'clock; and so home. Soon as dined, away, and walked through the city, the streets full of nothing but people and horses and carts laden with goods, ready to run over one another, and removing goods from one burned house to another. They now removing out of Canning Street (which received goods in the morning) into Lombard Street, and farther; and among others I now saw my little goldsmith, Stokes, receiving some friend's goods, whose house itself was burned the day after. We parted at Paul's; he home, and I to Paul's Wharf, where I had appointed a boat to attend me, and took in Mr. Carcasse and his brother, whom I met in the street, and carried them below and above bridge, to and again to see the fire, which was now got farther, both below and above, and no likelihood of stopping it. Met with the King and Duke of York in their barge, and with them to Queenhithe, and there called Sir Richard Browne to them. Their order was only to pull down houses apace, and so below bridge at the waterside; but little was or could be done, the fire coming upon them so fast. Good hopes there was of stopping it at the Three Cranes above, and at Buttolph's Wharf below bridge, if care be used; but the wind carries it into the City, so as we know not by the waterside what it do there. River full of lighters and boats taking in goods, and good goods swimming in the water, and only I observed that hardly one lighter or boat in three that had the goods of a house in, but there was a pair of virginals[17] in it.

Having seen as much as I could now, I away to Whitehall by appointment and there walked to St. James's Park, and there met my wife and Creed and walked to my boat; and there upon the water again, and to the fire up

and down, it still increasing, and the wind great. So near the fire as we could for smoke; and all over the Thames, with one's face in the wind, you were almost burned with a shower of firedrops. This is very true; so as houses were burned by these drops and flakes of fire, three or four, nay, five or six houses, one from another. When we could endure no more upon the water, we to a little alehouse on the Bankside, over against the Three Cranes, and there stayed till it was dark almost, and saw the fire grow; and, as it grew darker, appeared more and more, and in corners and upon steeples, and between churches and houses, as far as we could see up the hill of the City, in a most horrid malicious bloody flame not like the fine flame of an ordinary fire. Barbary and her husband away before us. We stayed till, it being darkish, we saw the fire as only one entire arch of fire from this to the other side of the bridge and in a bow up the hill for an arch of above a mile long: it made me weep to see it. The churches, houses, and all on fire and flaming at once; and a horrid noise the flames made, and the crackling of houses at their ruin.

So home with a sad heart, and there find everybody discoursing and lamenting the fire; and poor Tom Hater come with some few of his goods saved out of his house, which is burned upon Fish Street Hill. I invited him to lie at my house, and did receive his goods, but was deceived in his lying there, the news coming every moment of the growth of the fire; so as we were forced to begin to pack up our own goods and prepare for their removal; and did by moonshine (it being brave dry, and moonshine, and warm weather) carry much of my goods into the garden, and Mr. Hater and I did remove my money and iron chests into my cellar, as thinking that the safest place. And got my bags of gold into my office, ready to carry away, and my chief papers of accounts also there, and my tallies into a box by themselves. So great was our fear, as Sir W. Batten hath carts come out of the country to fetch away his goods this night. We did put

---

17. **pair of virginals:** a small, legless harpsichord popular in the sixteenth and seventeenth centuries.

Queen's Palace, St. James's Park (aquatint, 1809) by Thomas Rowlandson.
The Mansell Collection

Mr. Hater, poor man, to bed a little; but he got but very little rest, so much noise being in my house, taking down of goods.

3rd. About four o'clock in the morning, my Lady Batten sent me a cart to carry away all my money, and plate, and best things, to Sir W. Rider's at Bednall Green. Which I did, riding myself in my nightgown in the cart; and, Lord! to see how the streets and the highways are crowded with people running and riding, and getting of carts at any rate to fetch away things. I find Sir W. Rider tired with being called up all night, and receiving things from several friends. His house full of goods, and much of Sir W. Batten's and Sir W. Pen's. I am eased at my heart to have my treasure so well secured. Then home, with much ado to find a way, nor any sleep all this night to me nor my poor wife.

FOR STUDY AND DISCUSSION

1. What evidence can you find in the *Diary* to suggest that Pepys was businesslike, efficient, and civic-minded? That he was conscious of money and possessions and his own image? That he was given to comforts such as food, music, and entertainment? How would you describe Pepys's attitude toward his wife?

2. Do you think Pepys's *Diary* would be famous today if it contained descriptions only of great events and none of personal affairs? Explain your answer.

FOR COMPOSITION

The ability to observe closely, as Samuel Pepys did, is a rare and valuable skill. Imagining that you are a diarist, write a description of some school, local, or even national event that you have witnessed.

Samuel Pepys 325

The Age of Pope

In literary history, the first half of the eighteenth century is often called the Age of Pope. More than most literary periods, this one deserves to be named after a single writer. Even while criticizing his society Alexander Pope managed to express its deepest ideals. His work, as a result, is a true image of the spirit of the age. Above all, his poetry is public. Rather than expressing private feelings, it deals with general themes in social, political, and moral life. And in this it is supported by the work of the other major writers of the time: the satires of Jonathan Swift, the essays of Joseph Addison and Richard Steele, the novels of Henry Fielding. Only the Puritan tradition, no longer in the mainstream as it had been in the preceding century, continued to emphasize the inner qualities of human experience. The novels of Daniel Defoe and Samuel Richardson, superb expressions of the Puritan imagination, stand as an exception to the system of values embodied in the writings of Pope and the rest.

The period is also referred to as the Augustan Age or the Neoclassical Age, terms that usefully suggest both its hopes and its disappointments. Horace and Virgil, who lived during the reign of the first Roman emperor, Augustus, represented a classical ideal for many eighteenth-century people, both in their call for humane wisdom and self-control, and in their praise of the good life enjoyed in a setting of retired tranquillity among selected friends. Pope sought to create just such a life for himself in his villa and gardens at Twickenham. In a number of clever "imitations" of Horace, he applied the Roman poet's insights to contemporary parallels. But to a large extent England seemed to Pope and Swift a sad contrast to classical Roman civilization. Increasingly they came to feel that their world was collapsing in moral emptiness, political corruption, and gross abuse of the enormous wealth generated by a growing British Empire. Thus their writings took on an ironic tone, on the one hand confidently proclaiming traditional values, on the other bitterly accusing their contemporaries of failing to live up to them.

At the heart of these writers' thoughts was the belief that even the most unpleasant aspects of human nature are capable of control. Joseph Addison wrote in the *Spectator* that he intended "to enliven morality with wit, and to temper wit with morality." By *wit* he meant a quickness and brilliance of imagination that combined ideas in an unexpected and clever way. Confronted with much that they despised, Pope and Swift turned to satire, the form of writing in which moral indignation is supported by wit. But they never felt wholly isolated from their age, as some of the bleakest satirists have. Their works always assume the existence of readers of good sense and good will who can help to stem the tide of folly and vice. This is indeed a public conception of art: poet and reader are understood to share a set of values and to speak a common language. In the end, the Age of Pope is far from gloomy, and its literature celebrates traditional virtues and traditional social order.

Daniel Defoe

1660–1731

Born Daniel Foe, a merchant's son in London, Defoe adopted the aristocratic-sounding "De" in later life. After schooling that was intended to prepare him for the Presbyterian ministry, he embarked instead on as varied a career as any great English writer has ever had. He suffered two disastrous bankruptcies while trading in everything from diving bells to civet cats. Increasingly he supported himself as a writer, turning out immense numbers of essays and pamphlets on economic and religious themes.

No life demonstrates more dramatically than Defoe's both the peril and the power of the pen, especially the pen dipped in irony. Defoe's *The Shortest Way with Dissenters* reduced to absurdity the rabid intolerance prevalent in his time. Although an ardent Dissenter himself, he pretended to advocate an off-with-their-heads policy toward all those who dared to dissent from the tenets of the Church of England. The authorities at first took him literally and many unwary church officials endorsed his position, but, when they discovered that they had been deceived by his tone, they were not amused. Defoe was arrested, tried, and sentenced to prison and three successive appearances in the pillory. The pillory sentence, which was meant to degrade him publicly, turned to triumph when, instead of the expected jeering, a group of his friends sang a satiric song Defoe had composed for the occasion and pelted him with flowers rather than rocks and rotten eggs.

Much of Defoe's life remains mysterious, since he served the government for many years as a secret agent, operating under a series of assumed names. In his publications Defoe similarly made use of assumed names, preferring to give weight to his arguments by putting them in the mouth of some wise and trustworthy speaker. In the end he found himself writing pure fiction instead of fictionalized fact. In 1719, when he was nearly sixty, he published *The Life and Strange Surprising Adventures of Robinson Crusoe,* and discovered that almost by accident he had invented the English novel. In the next five years he brought out a series of further novels, each presented as autobiography and claiming to teach moral lessons about human life. Defoe's favorite form was the life story of a reformed criminal; *Moll Flanders* is his most famous novel of this sort.

Our selection is taken from his remarkably imaginative re-creation of the past, *A Journal of the Plague Year,* published in 1722. During 1721 there was much worry in England about a new outbreak on the Continent of bubonic plague, a disease that had ravaged England in 1665. In addition to several nonfiction works discussing how best to deal with the plague if it should come (which it did not), Defoe had the inspiration of writing a first-person account (ascribed to a tradesman called "H.F.") of the 1665 disaster. He hoped thereby to alert his readers to the dangers of plague and possible means of controlling it, but he also enjoyed the chance to create a convincing picture of human behavior in a time of great stress. In preparation for the work, Defoe interviewed survivors and made a close study of historical records. He himself had been a child of five at the time of the plague and could not have remembered many details, but undoubtedly the terror of that time remained vivid in his memory.

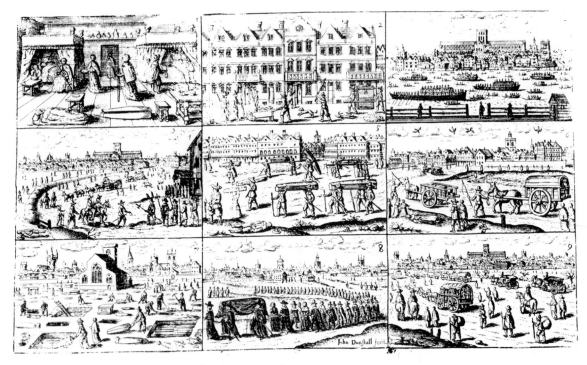

Scenes of the Great Plague of London (engraving from a contemporary broadsheet, 1665) by John Dunstall.
John Freeman, The Museum of London

from A Journal of the Plague Year

1665. It pleased God that I was still spared, and very hearty and sound in health, but very impatient of being pent up within doors without air, as I had been for fourteen days, or thereabouts; and I could not restrain myself, but I would go to carry a letter for my brother to the Posthouse. Then it was, indeed, that I observed a profound silence in the streets. When I came to the Posthouse, as I went to put in my letter, I saw a man stand in one corner of the yard, and talking to another at a window, and a third had opened a door belonging to the office. In the middle of the yard lay a small leather purse, with two keys hanging at it, and money in it, but nobody would meddle with it. I asked how long it had lain there; the man at the window said it had lain almost an hour, but they had not meddled with it, because they did not know but the person who dropped it might come back to look for it. I had no such need of money, nor was the sum so big that I had any inclination to meddle with it to get the money at the hazard it might be attended with; so I seemed to go away, when the man who had opened the door said he would take it up; but so that if the right owner came for it, he should be sure to have it. So he went in and fetched a pail of water, and set it down hard by the purse, then went again and fetched some gunpowder and cast a good deal of powder upon the purse, and then made a train from that which he had thrown loose upon the purse; the train reached about two yards. After this he goes in a third time, and fetches out a pair of tongs red hot, and which he had prepared, I suppose, on purpose; and first setting fire to the train of powder, that singed the purse, and also smoked the air sufficiently. But he was not content with that; but he then takes up the purse with the tongs, holding it so long till the tongs burnt through the purse, and then he shook the money out into the pail of water, so he carried it in. The money, as I remember, was about thirteen shillings, and some smooth groats, and brass farthings.

There might, perhaps, have been several poor people, as I have observed above, that would have been hardy enough to have ventured for the sake of the money; but you may easily see, by what I have observed, that the few people who were spared were very careful of themselves at that time when the distress was so exceeding great. . . .

It would pierce the hearts of all that came by to hear the piteous cries of those infected people, who being thus out of their understandings by the violence of their pain, or the heat of their blood, were either shut in, or perhaps tied in their beds and chairs, to prevent their doing themselves hurt, and who would make a dreadful outcry at their being confined, and at their not being permitted to "die at large," as they called it, and as they would have done before.

This running of distempered people about the streets was very dismal, and the Magistrates did their utmost to prevent it; but as it was generally in the night and always sudden, when such attempts were made, the officers could not be at hand to prevent it, and even when they got out in the day, the officers appointed did not care to meddle with them, because, as they were all grievously infected, to be sure, when they were come to that height, so they were more than ordinarily infectious, and it was one of the most dangerous things that could be to touch them. On the other hand, they generally ran on, not knowing what they did, till they dropped down stark dead, or till they had exhausted their spirits so as that they would fall, and then die in perhaps half an hour or an hour; and what was most piteous to hear, they were sure to come to themselves entirely in that half-hour or hour, and then to make most grievous and piercing cries and lamentations in the deep afflicting sense of the condition they were in. This was much of it before the order for shutting up of houses was strictly put in execution, for at first the watchmen were not so rigorous and severe, as they were afterward, in the keeping the people in; that is to say, before they were, I mean some of them, severely punished for their neglect, failing in their duty, and letting people who were under their care slip away, or conniving at their going abroad, whether sick or well. But after they saw the officers appointed to examine into their conduct were resolved to have them do their duty, or be punished for the omission, they were more exact, and the people were strictly restrained; which was a thing they took so ill, and bore so impatiently, that their discontents can hardly be described; but there was an absolute necessity for it, that must be confessed, unless some other measures had been timely entered upon, and it was too late for that.

Had not this particular of the sick being restrained as above, been our case at that time,[1] London would have been the most dreadful place that ever was in the world; there would, for aught I know, have as many people died in the streets as died in their houses; for when the Distemper was at its height, it generally made them raving and delirious, and when they were so, they would never be persuaded to keep in their beds but by force; and many, who were not tied, threw themselves out of windows, when they found they could not get leave to go out of their doors.

It was for want of people conversing one with another, in this time of calamity, that it

---

1. **Had not . . . time:** if we had not restrained the sick people in the manner described above.

was impossible any particular person could come at the knowledge of all the extraordinary cases that occurred in different families; and particularly I believe it was never known to this day how many people in their deliriums drowned themselves in the Thames, and in the river which runs from the marshes by Hackney, which we generally called Ware River, or Hackney River. As to those which were set down in the weekly bill,[2] they were indeed few; nor could it be known of any of those, whether they drowned themselves by accident or not. But I believe, I might reckon up more, who, within the compass of my knowledge or observation really drowned themselves in that year than are put down in the bill of all put together, for many of the bodies were never found, who yet were known to be so lost: and the like, in other methods of self-destruction. There was also one man, in or about Whitecross Street, who burnt himself to death in his bed; some said it was done by himself, others that it was by the treachery of the nurse that attended him; but that he had the Plague upon him was agreed by all. . . .

We that were Examiners[3] were often not able to come at the knowledge of the infection being entered into a house till it was too late to shut it up; and sometimes not till the people that were left were all dead. In Petticoat Lane two houses together were infected, and several people sick; but the Distemper was so well concealed that the Examiner, who was my neighbor, got no knowledge of it, till notice was sent him that the people were all dead, and that the carts[4] should call there to fetch them away. The two heads of the families concerted their measures, and so ordered their matters, as that when the Examiner was in the neighborhood, they appeared generally at a time, and answered, that is, lied for one another; or got some of the neighborhood to say they were all in health, and, perhaps, knew no better, till death making it impossible to keep it any longer as a secret, the Dead carts were called in the night to both houses, and so it became public; but when the Examiner ordered the constable to shut up the houses, there was nobody left in them but three people, two in one house, and one in the other, just dying, and a nurse in each house, who acknowledged that they had buried five before, that the houses had been infected nine or ten days, and that for all the rest of the two families, which were many, they were gone, some sick, some well, or whether sick or well, could not be known.

In like manner, at another house in the same lane, a man, having his family infected, but very unwilling to be shut up, when he could conceal it no longer, shut up himself; that is to say, he set the great Red Cross upon his door, with the words—"Lord have Mercy upon Us"; and so deluded the Examiner, who supposed it had been done by the constable by order of the other Examiner, for there were two Examiners to every district or precinct; by this means he had free egress and regress[5] into his house again, and out of it, as he pleased, notwithstanding it was infected; till at length his stratagem was found out, and then he, with the sound part of his servants and family, made off, and escaped; so they were not shut up at all. . . .

It is here, however, to be observed, that after the funerals became so many that people could not toll the bell, mourn, or weep, or wear black for one another, as they did before; no, nor so much as make coffins for those that died; so after a while the fury of the Infection

---

2. **bill:** a list of the dead from each parish with the cause of death.
3. **Examiners:** men whose job it was to determine which houses had been infected by the plague.
4. **carts:** Dead bodies were collected at night in carts and taken to a common burial ground, since the churchyards could not hold them all.

5. **egress and regress:** exit and entrance.

appeared to be so increased, that in short, they shut up no houses at all. It seemed enough that all the remedies of that kind had been used till they were found fruitless, and that the Plague spread itself with an irresistible fury; so that as the Fire, the succeeding year, spread itself, and burnt with such violence, that the citizens, in despair, gave over[6] their endeavors to extinguish it, so in the Plague, it came at last to such violence that the people sat still, looking at one another, and seemed quite abandoned to despair. Whole streets seemed to be desolated, and not to be shut up only, but to be emptied of their inhabitants; doors were left open, and windows stood shattering with the wind in empty houses for want of people to shut them. In a word, people began to give up themselves to their fears, and to think that all regulations and methods were in vain, and that there was nothing to be hoped for, but an universal Desolation; and it was even in the height of this general despair that it pleased God to stay his hand, and to slacken the fury of the Contagion, in such a manner as was even surprising (like its beginning), and demonstrated it to be his own particular Hand, and that above, if not without, the Agency of Means, as I shall take notice of in its proper place.

---

6. **over:** up.

FOR STUDY AND DISCUSSION

1. What kind of man is Defoe's imaginary reporter? What does the manner in which he describes the horrifying events he witnessed tell you about the narrator? Why do you think Defoe chose this kind of person as the narrator of an "eyewitness" account? Does he pass judgment on what he observes? How does this relate to the practice of a good reporter?

2. Defoe is a master at making a fictional account sound real by piling detail upon detail to create an atmosphere of complete authenticity. Show how he uses details to persuade the reader that his is an eyewitness account. Why do you think Defoe has his narrator use a calm, objective, matter-of-fact tone in describing events?

3. Compare Defoe's account of the plague with Pepys's account of the Great Fire. Which do you consider more graphic, more realistic in impression?

FOR COMPOSITION

By reading and by talking with people who remember it well, find out all you can about some event (an earthquake, fire, or other natural disaster) that occurred before you were old enough to be aware of it. Then, giving yourself a carefully chosen identity and clearly established viewpoint, bear in mind the devices by which Defoe achieves an impression of reality and write a first-person account of the event as though you had been there.

Jonathan Swift
1667–1745

Jonathan Swift (detail).
The Bodleian Library

Britain's greatest satirist, Jonathan Swift was a brilliant, troubled man who achieved literary fame and high standing in the church, but never felt that he had gained what he wanted and deserved. He was born in Dublin of English parents (his father died before he was born) and entered life as a member of the Protestant ruling class disliked by the Catholic majority. After studying at Trinity College, Dublin, Swift went to England to serve as private secretary to Sir William Temple, a retired diplomat and writer of essays who wanted help setting his papers in order. Swift found in Temple the father he never had, but frustration as well, for he expected Temple to help him begin a political career in England, and this never occurred. Abandoning his dream, Swift returned to Ireland and took orders in the church, but after an unhappy year in a rural parish he was back in Temple's household, where he remained until 1699.

The fifteen years that followed were in many ways his happiest. He made friends with Alexander Pope and other leading writers, and published anonymously in 1704 a brilliant satire called *A Tale of a Tub* that exposed abuses in religion and learning. In *The Battle of the Books* he involved himself in a literary controversy. The Tory administration found his talent for argument useful, and he produced a great deal of political writing for the government, feeling at last that he was near the center of power. He looked forward to being named an English bishop because of his well-placed friends. But when Queen Anne died in 1714 and the Tories fell from office, Swift's hopes vanished. He had to content himself with the position of Dean of St. Patrick's Cathedral in Dublin, where he remained for the next thirty years.

Swift's life in Ireland was far from miserable, particularly when he became a national hero for opposing a system of debased coinage which the government in London tried to introduce. He had a wide circle of friends, and his letters to Esther Johnson, the close confidante whom he called Stella, reveal his gift for affectionate humor. Yet he remained a deeply private man; he would never marry Stella, despite her wishes, and took care that

their meetings were always conducted with strict propriety. Ireland itself he regarded as a place of exile. *A Modest Proposal,* which suggests ironically that the English might as well eat Irish babies since they are already devouring the country economically, betrays a good deal of disgust for the people he was defending. He wrote, "What I do is owing to perfect rage and resentment, and the mortifying sight of slavery, folly, and baseness about me, among which I am forced to live."

In 1726 Swift published his immortal masterpiece, *Gulliver's Travels.* On the level of fantasy it is full of charming inventiveness and has always been loved by children. On the level of satire it rises, by the time of the final "Voyage," to deep moral indignation against what Swift elsewhere referred to as "that animal called man." In a letter to Pope, he objected to the standard definition of man as the rational animal, holding that man is capable of reason but seldom uses it.

Swift's favorite weapon was irony, the device of saying something outrageous with a straight face, while dropping enough clues to let the reader know what is really meant. The narrator of the *Travels* is Lemuel Gulliver, a well-meaning but not very bright Englishman who describes whatever he sees with simple innocence. (A "gull" was a term for someone easily duped or "gullible"; it is up to the reader to see the truths that Gulliver misses.)

Swift is one of the greatest masters of clear and simple writing. He once said that the secret of good prose is "proper words in proper places," and nothing is more difficult than that.

from **Gulliver's Travels**

Gulliver's Travels is Swift's final word on human beings as individuals and as social animals. All his contempt and hatred for the pettiness, cruelty, injustice, and stupidity that he saw in people was poured into this greatest of all prose satires. Though he claimed that "His satire points at no defect,/ But what all mortals may correct," the book nevertheless failed as a vehicle of social reform. Swift, through Gulliver, complained in a letter written after the initial reception of the book: "Yahoos [people reduced to a bestial state] were a species of animals utterly incapable of amendment by precepts or examples."

In the gullible Lemuel Gulliver, "first a surgeon, and then a captain of several ships," Swift found his ideal spokesman. Through Gulliver he exposes the corruption in every revered English institution, leaving no doubt as to the targets of his satire. Britain's political system is the recipient of his scorn in "The Voyage to Lilliput," a place where Gulliver discovers that members of political parties are distinguished by the height of their heels. In "A Voyage to Brobdingnag" Swift mocks the immorality and cruelty of English society. During Gulliver's trip to Laputa, false pedantry and learning are ridiculed when the scientists and scholars of this country conduct an eight-year experiment to extract sunbeams from cucumbers. But Swift deals his cruelest blow in Gulliver's journey to the land of the Houyhnhnms, where intelligent and noble horses govern the Yahoos, a breed of filthy, brutish humans. As a result of his travels, the honest, well-meaning Gulliver gradually comes to realize that there is often a discrepancy between appearance and reality, that people are not always what they seem to be, and that evil is present wherever people exist.

Astronomy (hand-colored engraving after a mezzotint) by Richard Houston. Swift and his contemporaries frequently satirized the pretensions of science. Museum of the History of Science, Oxford

A Voyage to Lilliput

Gulliver, shipwrecked somewhere in the South Pacific, struggles to an unknown shore and falls asleep. The Lilliputians (lĭl′ə-pyoo′shənz), who are only six inches tall, discover and tie down the sleeping "giant." After he awakens, they transport him with great difficulty to their capital and house him in an unused temple. He gradually begins to learn their language and to win their favor, although his sword and pistols are not returned to him and he remains a prisoner. The similarity between Gulliver's situation and English politics and court life, ridiculed by reduction to such tiny scale, reaches its peak in Chapter 3, which follows.

My gentleness and good behavior had gained so far on the emperor and his court, and indeed upon the army and people in general, that I began to conceive hopes of getting my liberty in a short time. I took all possible methods to cultivate this favorable disposition. The natives came by degrees to be less apprehensive of any danger from me. I would sometimes lie down and let five or six of them dance on my hand; and at last the boys and girls would venture to come and play at hide-and-seek in my hair. I had now made a good progress in understanding and speaking their language.

The emperor had a mind, one day, to entertain me with several of the country shows, wherein they exceed all nations I have known, both for dexterity and magnificence. I was diverted with none so much as that of the rope dancers, performed upon a slender white thread, extended about two feet and twelve inches from the ground. Upon which I shall desire liberty, with the reader's patience, to enlarge a little.

This diversion is only practiced by those persons who are candidates for great employments and high favor at court. They are trained in this art from their youth, and are not always of noble birth or liberal education. When a great office is vacant, either by death or disgrace (which often happens), five or six of those candidates petition the emperor to entertain his majesty and the court with a dance on the rope; and whoever jumps the highest, without falling, succeeds in the office. Very often the chief ministers themselves are commanded to show their skill, and to convince the emperor that they have not lost their faculty. Flimnap,[1] the treasurer, is allowed[2] to cut a caper on the strait rope at least an inch higher than any other lord in the whole empire. I have seen him do the somersault several times together upon a trencher,[3] fixed on a rope, which is no thicker than a common packthread in England. My friend Reldresal, principal secretary for private affairs, is, in my opinion, if I am not partial, the second after the treasurer; the rest of the great officers are much upon a par.

These diversions are often attended by fatal accidents, whereof great numbers are on record. I myself have seen two or three candidates break a limb. But the danger is much greater when the ministers themselves are commanded to show their dexterity! for, by contending to excel themselves and their fellows, they strain so far that there is hardly one of them who hath not received a fall,[4] and some of them two or three. I was assured that a year or two before my arrival, Flimnap

---

1. **Flimnap:** a caricature of Sir Robert Walpole, the Whig prime minister whom Swift and his friends often satirized.
2. **allowed:** admitted, considered.
3. **trencher:** wooden platter.
4. **fall:** While the Whigs held firmly to power when Swift was writing, many individual politicians had very uneven careers.

would have infallibly broke his neck if one of the king's cushions,[5] that accidentally lay on the ground, had not weakened the force of his fall.

There is likewise another diversion, which is only shown before the emperor and empress and first minister, upon particular occasions. The emperor lays on the table three fine silken threads,[6] of six inches long; one is blue, the other red, and the third green. These threads are proposed as prizes for those persons whom the emperor hath a mind to distinguish by a peculiar mark of his favor. The ceremony is performed in his majesty's great chamber of state, where the candidates are to undergo a trial of dexterity very different from the former, and such as I have not observed the least resemblance of in any other country of the old or the new world.

The emperor holds a stick in his hands, both ends parallel to the horizon, while the candidates, advancing one by one, sometimes leap over the stick, sometimes creep under it backward and forward several times, according as the stick is advanced or depressed. Sometimes the emperor holds one end of the stick, and his first minister the other; sometimes the minister has it entirely to himself. Whoever performs his part with most agility, and holds out the longest in leaping and creeping, is rewarded with the blue colored silk; the red is given to the next, and the green to the third, which they all wear girt twice round about the middle; and you see few great persons about this court who are not adorned with one of these girdles.

The horses of the army, and those of the royal stables, having been daily led before me, were no longer shy, but would come up to my very feet without starting. The riders would leap them over my hand as I held it on the ground; and one of the emperor's huntsmen, upon a larger courser, took[7] my foot, shoe and all, which was indeed a prodigious leap.

I had the good fortune to divert the emperor one day after a very extraordinary manner. I desired he would order several sticks of two feet high, and the thickness of an ordinary cane, to be brought me; whereupon his majesty commanded the master of his woods to give directions accordingly; and the next morning six woodmen arrived with as many carriages, drawn by eight horses to each.

I took nine of these sticks, and fixing them firmly in the ground in a quadrangular figure, two feet and a half square. I took four other sticks and tied them parallel at each corner, about two feet from the ground; then I fastened my handkerchief to the nine sticks that stood erect, and extended it on all sides, till it was as tight as the top of a drum; and the four parallel sticks, rising about five inches higher than the handkerchief, served as ledges on each side.

When I had finished my work, I desired the emperor to let a troop of his best horse, twenty-four in number, come and exercise upon this plain. His majesty approved of the proposal, and I took them up one by one in my hands, ready mounted and armed, with the proper officers to exercise them. As soon as they got into order, they divided into two parties, performed mock skirmishes, discharged blunt arrows, drew their swords, fled and pursued, attacked and retired, and, in short, discovered the best military discipline I ever beheld. The parallel sticks secured them and their horses from falling over the stage; and the emperor was so much delighted that he ordered this entertainment to be repeated several days, and once was pleased to be lifted up and give the word of command; and, with

---

5. **cushions:** an allusion to Walpole's receiving help from a favorite of the king.
6. **threads:** an allusion to the colors of the ribbons of three honorary titles much sought after by politicians — the Orders of the Garter, the Bath, and the Thistle.

7. **took:** cleared.

great difficulty, persuaded even the empress herself to let me hold her in her close chair within two yards of the stage, from whence she was able to take a full view of the whole performance.

It was my good fortune that no ill accident happened in these entertainments; only once a fiery horse, that belonged to one of the captains, pawing with his hoof, struck a hole in my handkerchief, and his foot slipping, he overthrew his rider and himself; but I immediately relieved them both, and covering the hole with one hand, I set down the troop with the other, in the same manner as I took them up. The horse that fell was strained in the left shoulder, but the rider got no hurt, and I repaired my handkerchief as well as I could; however, I would not trust to the strength of it any more in such dangerous enterprises.

About two or three days before I was set at liberty, as I was entertaining the court with these kinds of feats, there arrived an express to inform his majesty that some of his subjects riding near the place where I was first taken up had seen a great black substance lying on the ground, very oddly shaped, extending its edges round as wide as his majesty's bedchamber, and rising up in the middle as high as a man; that it was no living creature, as they at first apprehended, for it lay on the grass without motion; and some of them had walked round it several times; that, by mounting upon each other's shoulders, they had got to the top, which was flat and even, and, stamping upon it, they found it was hollow within; that they humbly conceived it might be something belonging to the man-mountain; and if his majesty pleased, they would undertake to bring it with only five horses.

I presently knew what they meant, and was glad at heart to receive this intelligence.[8] It seems, upon my first reaching the shore after our shipwreck, I was in such confusion that, before I came to the place where I went to sleep, my hat, which I had fastened with a string to my head while I was rowing, and had stuck on all the time I was swimming, fell off after I came to land; the string, as I conjecture, breaking by some accident which I never observed, but thought my hat had been lost at sea. I entreated his imperial majesty to give orders it might be brought to me as soon as possible, describing to him the use and nature of it; and the next day the wagoners arrived with it, but not in a very good condition; they had bored two holes in the brim, within an inch and a half of the edge, and fastened two hooks in the holes; these hooks were tied by a long cord to the harness, and thus my hat was dragged along for above half an English mile; but the ground in that country being extremely smooth and level, it received less damage than I expected.

Two days after this adventure, the emperor, having ordered that part of the army which quarters in and about his metropolis to be in readiness, took a fancy of diverting himself in a very singular manner. He desired I would stand like a colossus,[9] with my legs as far asunder as I conveniently could. He then commanded his general (who was an old, experienced leader and a great patron of mine) to draw up the troops in close order and march them under me; the foot by twenty-four in a breast and the horse by sixteen, with drums beating, colors flying, and pikes advanced. This body consisted of three thousand foot and a thousand horse. . . .

---

9. **colossus:** an enormous statue.

Gulliver's greatest service to Lilliput is his capture of the fleet of Blefuscu, an enemy country. By cutting the anchor ropes with his knife and attaching fifty ships to a central cable, he is able to drag them across the channel between the two countries. Warned by a friend that certain Lilliputians are planning to impeach him for high treason, Gulliver flees. Soon after, he discovers a derelict lifeboat which he uses to launch himself on his journey home.

---

8. **intelligence:** information, news.

"My little friend Grildrig you have made a most admirable
"panegyric upon yourself and Country but from what I can
"gather from your own relation & the answers I have with
"much pains wrung & extorted from you, I cannot but con
"clude you to be one of the most pernicious little odious
"reptiles that nature ever suffered to crawl upon the surface
of the Earth —

George III as the King of Brobdingnag inspects Napoleon as Gulliver.
Culver Pictures

A Voyage to Brobdingnag[10]

On his second voyage Gulliver finds himself in Brobdingnag, a country
Swift locates in then little-known Alaska. Here the natives are twelve times
as tall as Gulliver, instead of one-twelfth his height. As in Lilliput, Gulliver
learns the language and observes the ways of the people. Taken in by a
farmer, he is exhibited as a curiosity and finally sold to the Queen. His
diminutive size causes many misadventures: he is nearly trampled to death,
dropped from the palace roof by a court monkey, eaten alive by a baby, torn
to pieces by rats, drowned in a cream pitcher, and killed by a linnet. In trying to explain how admirable the English are, Gulliver succeeds only in horrifying the King of Brobdingnag. Their best-known discussion follows.

---

10. **Brobdingnag** (brŏb′dĭng-năg). The inhabitants of this land were called Brobdingnagians (brŏb′dĭng-năg′ē-ənz).

It is the custom that every Wednesday (which as I have before observed, was their Sabbath), the King and Queen, with the royal issue of both sexes, dine together in the apartment of his Majesty, to whom I was now become a great favorite; and at these times my little chair and table were placed at his left hand before one of the saltcellars. This Prince took a pleasure in conversing with me, inquiring into the manners, religion, laws, government, and learning of Europe, wherein I gave him the best account I was able. His apprehension was so clear, and his judgment so exact, that he made very wise reflections and observations upon all I said. But, I confess, that after I had been a little too copious in talking of my own beloved country, of our trade, and wars by sea and land, of our schisms in religion, and parties in the state, the prejudices of his education prevailed so far, that he could not forbear taking me up in his right hand, and stroking me gently with the other, after an hearty fit of laughing, asked me whether I were a Whig or a Tory. Then turning to his first Minister, who waited behind him with a white staff, near as tall as the mainmast of the *Royal Sovereign*,[11] he observed how contemptible a thing was human grandeur, which could be mimicked by such diminutive insects as I. And yet, said he, I dare engage, these creatures have their titles and distinctions of honor; they contrive little nests and burrows, that they call houses and cities; they make a figure in dress and equipage; they love, they fight, they dispute, they cheat, they betray. And thus he continued on, while my color came and went several times, with indignation to hear our noble country,[12] the Mistress of Arts and Arms, the Scourge of France, the Arbitress of Europe, the Seat of Virtue, Piety, Honor and Truth, the Pride and Envy of the World, so contemptuously treated. . . .

He was perfectly astonished with the historical account I gave him of our affairs during the last century, protesting it was only an heap of conspiracies, rebellions, murders, massacres, revolutions, banishments; the very worst effects that avarice, faction, hypocrisy, perfidiousness, cruelty, rage, madness, hatred, envy, lust, malice, and ambition could produce.

His Majesty, in another audience, was at the pains to recapitulate the sum of all I had spoken; compared the questions he made with the answers I had given; then taking me into his hands, and stroking me gently, delivered himself in these words, which I shall never forget, nor the manner he spoke them in. "My little friend Grildrig, you have made a most admirable panegyric upon your country. You have clearly proved that ignorance, idleness, and vice are the proper ingredients for qualifying a legislator: that laws are best explained, interpreted, and applied by those whose interest and abilities lie in perverting, confounding, and eluding them. I observe among you some lines of an institution, which in its original might have been tolerable, but these half erased, and the rest wholly blurred and blotted by corruptions. It doth not appear from all you have said how any one perfection is required towards the procurement of any one station among you; much less that men are ennobled on account of their virtue, that priests are advanced for their piety or learning, soldiers for their conduct or valor, judges for their integrity, senators for the love of their country, or counselors for their wisdom. As for yourself (continued the King), who have spent the greatest part of your life in traveling, I am well disposed to hope you may hitherto have escaped many vices of your country. But by what I have gathered from your own relation, and the answers I have with much pains wringed and extorted from you, I cannot but conclude the bulk of your natives to be the most pernicious race of little odious vermin that nature ever suffered to crawl upon the surface of the earth."

---

11. *Royal Sovereign:* one of the biggest ships in the Royal Navy.
12. **our noble country:** that is, England.

Nothing but an extreme love of truth could have hindered me from concealing this part of my story. It was in vain to discover my resentments, which were always turned into ridicule; and I was forced to rest with patience while my noble and most beloved country was so injuriously treated. I am heartily sorry as any of my readers can possibly be that such an occasion was given: but this prince happened to be so curious and inquisitive upon every particular that it could not consist either with gratitude or good manners to refuse giving him what satisfaction I was able. Yet thus much I may be allowed to say in my own vindication, that I artfully eluded many of his questions, and gave to every point a more favorable turn by many degrees than the strictness of truth would allow. For I have always borne that laudable partiality to my own country, which Dionysius Halicarnassensis[13] with so much justice recommends to an historian: I would hide the frailties and deformities of my political mother, and place her virtues and beauties in the most advantageous light. This was my sincere endeavor in those many discourses I had with that mighty monarch, although it unfortunately failed of success.

But great allowances should be given to a King who lives wholly secluded from the rest of the world, and must therefore be altogether unacquainted with the manners and customs that most prevail in other nations: the want of which knowledge will ever produce many prejudices, and a certain narrowness of thinking, from which we and the politer countries of Europe are wholly exempted. And it would be hard indeed, if so remote a prince's notions of virtue and vice were to be offered as a standard for all mankind.

To confirm what I have now said, and further to show the miserable effects of a confined education, I shall here insert a passage

which will hardly obtain belief. In hopes to ingratiate myself farther into his Majesty's favor, I told him of an invention discovered between three and four hundred years ago, to make a certain powder, into an heap of which the smallest spark of fire falling, would kindle the whole in a moment, although it were as big as a mountain, and make it all fly up in the air together, with a noise and agitation greater than thunder. That, a proper quantity of this powder rammed into an hollow tube of brass or iron, according to its bigness, would drive a ball of iron or lead with such violence and speed as nothing was able to sustain its force. That the largest balls thus discharged, would not only destroy whole ranks of an army at once, but batter the strongest walls to the ground, sink down ships with a thousand men in each, to the bottom of the sea; and when linked together by a chain, would cut through masts and rigging, divide hundreds of bodies in the middle, and lay all waste before them. That we often put this powder into large hollow balls of iron, and discharged them by an engine into some city we were besieging, which would rip up the pavements, tear the houses to pieces, burst and throw splinters on every side, dashing out the brains of all who came near. That I knew the ingredients very well, which were cheap, and common; I understood the manner of compounding them, and could direct his workmen how to make those tubes of a size proportionable to all other things in his Majesty's kingdom, and the largest need not be above two hundred foot long; twenty or thirty of which tubes, charged with the proper quantity of powder and balls, would batter down the walls of the strongest town in his dominions in a few hours, or destroy the whole metropolis, if ever it should pretend to dispute his absolute commands. This I humbly offered to his Majesty as a small tribute of acknowledgment in return of so many marks that I had received of his royal favor and protection.

The King was struck with horror at the description I had given of those terrible

---

13. **Dionysius Halicarnassensis:** a Greek writer living in Rome in the time of Augustus whose work praised the virtues of the Romans.

engines, and the proposal I had made. He was amazed how so impotent and groveling an insect as I (these were his expressions) could entertain such inhuman ideas, and in so familiar a manner as to appear wholly unmoved at all the scenes of blood and desolation, which I had painted as the common effects of those destructive machines, whereof he said, some evil genius, enemy to mankind, must have been the first contriver. As for himself, he protested, that although few things delighted him so much as new discoveries in art or in nature, yet he would rather lose half his kingdom than be privy to such a secret, which he commanded me, as I valued my life, never to mention any more.

FOR STUDY AND DISCUSSION

1. In "A Voyage to Lilliput," the Whig Prime Minister Robert Walpole and his ally Lord Townshend are satirized as Flimnap and Reldresal. Do you think that such attacks on individuals contradict Swift's statement, "I have ever hated all nations, professions, and communities, and all my love is toward individuals"? Explain your answer.
2. Which device do you think creates a more effective situation for satire: a hero who is a giant among Lilliputians or one who is a pygmy among Brobdingnagians? Or do you think these devices equally effective? Give examples from the text to support your viewpoint.
3. How does the tone of Swift's satire on human beings change as he moves from the Lilliputians to the Brobdingnagians? To what do you attribute this change of tone? What change of tone occurs at the very beginning of Gulliver's discourse to the King of Brobdingnag on "his own dear native country"?
4. What devices does Swift use to induce the reader to accept Gulliver's adventures as actual happenings—at least to the extent of willingly suspending disbelief? Compare Swift's method with Defoe's in the excerpt from A Journal of the Plague Year.

SATIRE

"Satire," wrote Jonathan Swift, "is a sort of glass wherein beholders do generally discover everybody's face but their own." Swift's wry comment on human nature was occasioned—in part, at least—by the failure of Gulliver's Travels to reform the English nation. Speaking through Gulliver, Swift wrote in the preface to the second edition: "Behold, after above six months' warning, I cannot learn that my book hath produced one single effect according to my intentions." The satirist is, above all, a reformer. The writer heaps ridicule on human heads, believing that satire is a form of therapy. "Those who are ashamed of nothing else," wrote Pope, "are so of being ridiculous."

The aims of satire vary, as does the tone of the critic. The satirist may desire to reform social conduct, ridicule a personal enemy, or denounce everything in human nature that he or she finds distasteful. The tone of the satirist's attack can range from that of light humor to scathing sarcasm, depending upon the degree of indignation.

Although, as author of Gulliver's Travels, Swift wrote what is probably the most famous satire in the English language, he was not the first to make use of this literary art. The good-natured and tolerant Chaucer satirized the worst follies of churchmen in his Pardoner. Shakespeare, in the play within a play in Hamlet, turns satire on his fellow actors. In the eighteenth century, a golden age of satire, Pope, Addison and Steele, and others used satire as a most effective weapon against their adversaries in intramural literary quarrels.

Compare Swift's satire with that of Chaucer. Discuss the aims, tone, and methods of both writers, using references to specific passages of their work.

LANGUAGE AND VOCABULARY

In describing the skills of the Lilliputians, Swift says that the "candidates for great employment" must undergo a trial of dexterity. The highest honors go to the one who exhibits the greatest agility. How are these two words related in meaning? How do they differ? List synonyms for these words and explain their exact use.

FOR COMPOSITION

Write an imaginary scene in which a modern Gulliver tries to initiate the King of Brobdingnag into some mysteries of modern society. Include the King's reactions.

Joseph Addison
1672–1719
Richard Steele
1672–1729

One of the most famous literary partnerships in English literature is that of Addison and Steele, who together created a new form and style of writing—that of the familiar essay. Though markedly different in temperament, Addison and Steele collaborated superbly, first in *The Tatler* and later in *The Spectator*, two early and popular periodicals (the forerunners of our present-day magazines) for which Addison and Steele between them wrote most of the essays.

Except for an unfortunate political quarrel a year before Addison's death, Addison and Steele were lifelong friends as well as collaborators. The two first met at the Charterhouse School in London and went on together to Oxford University. But Steele, witty, warmhearted, impulsive, and somewhat reckless in practical matters, left school to join the army, where he rose to the rank of captain. He also served as manager of a theater, for which he wrote several comedies, and as editor of the Whig party newspaper, an appointment he obtained through Addison, a fellow Whig. Later he turned to still other ventures as magazine publisher, poet, reformer, and Member of Parliament, and was generally known as a dashing man-about-town. Meanwhile, his more scholarly, withdrawn, and dignified friend, Addison, had taken his degree and embarked upon a literary career. A poem celebrating the victory of the Duke of Marlborough at Blenheim brought him to public attention when he was still fairly young. Though he is remembered chiefly as an essayist and stylist of English prose, he served his country in various political capacities as well. In 1717, shortly after he married the

Joseph Addison by Sir Godfrey Kneller.
National Portrait Gallery, London

Sir Richard Steele by Sir Godfrey Kneller.
National Portrait Gallery, London

Countess of Warwick, he was appointed Secretary of State, a position he enjoyed until his death two years later.

Steele started *The Tatler* in 1709. It was an immediate success. A modest one-page paper, it contained news, coffeehouse gossip, and comments on current events. In later issues Steele adopted the more serious purpose of serving as a moral influence and speaking out against the negligence and improprieties of his contemporaries. Addison began his collaboration with Steele by contributing articles to this paper.

When *The Tatler* was discontinued because of political difficulties, Addison and Steele decided to found together *The Spectator*, a new periodical which would take literature, manners, and morals as its subject matter. With good-natured satire, tolerance, and common sense, Addison and Steele sought to reform social tastes and behavior.

Although Steele may have been the more inventive and original member of this partnership, Addison was the more polished writer. Samuel Johnson in his conclusion to the *Life of Addison*, wrote, "His prose is the model of the middle style; on grave subjects not formal, on light occasions not groveling . . . always equable, and always easy." It was Steele who conceived the idea of the familiar essay, but it was Addison who perfected it.

THE

SPECTATOR.

VOLUME the FIRST.

LONDON:

Printed for J. and R. TONSON and S. DRAPER.

MDCCLIII.

Frontispiece to an edition of *The Spectator* (1753). The gentlemen on the left are Sir Roger de Coverley and members of the Spectator Club.
The Bettmann Archive

The Tatler

The Tatler (1709–1711) owed its inception partly to Steele's fear of bankruptcy and partly to his interest in the reform of morals and the betterment of his fellow creatures. His use of Isaac Bickerstaff as a pen name assured the paper public attention. Jonathan Swift had used the Bickerstaff name the year before when he played a practical joke on a quack astrologer named Partridge. Swift, writing under the imaginary name of Isaac Bickerstaff, predicted that according to the stars, Partridge was to die of a fever on March 28. On March 28, Swift printed a solemn announcement of Partridge's death and the newspapers carried detailed accounts of the funeral. Highly incensed, Partridge insisted that he was alive. Bickerstaff retorted that according to the stars, he could not be and that to pretend otherwise was an affront to stellar omniscience.

The audience that *The Tatler* addresses is mainly the growing middle class; the paper's tone is the casual, conversational one of the coffeehouse, the middle class's new-found fraternity house and practical university. In the Prospectus of *The Tatler*, in which Steele sets forth the general plan of his paper, we see the importance of the coffeehouse as a gathering place for the social, political, and literary life of the day. Steele prefaced many of his essays with an appropriate Greek or Latin motto, a practice that was continued in *The Spectator*. The motto accompanying the Prospectus was taken from the Roman poet Juvenal and, in Pope's translation, reads:

> Whate'er men do, or say, or think or dream,
> Our motley paper seizes for its theme.

Dueling

The Tatler, No. 25,
Tuesday, June 7, 1709

Quidquid agunt homines —
— nostri est farrago libelli.
— Juvenal, *Satire* I.85–86

White's Chocolate House, June 6
A letter from a young lady, written in the most passionate terms, wherein she laments the misfortune of a gentleman, her lover, who was lately wounded in a duel, has turned my thoughts to that subject, and inclined me to examine into the causes which precipitate men into so fatal a folly. And as it has been proposed to treat of subjects of gallantry in the article from hence, and no one point in nature is more proper to be considered by the company who frequent this place than that of duels, it is worth our consideration to examine into this chimerical groundless humor, and to lay every other thought aside, until we have stripped it of all its false pretenses to credit and reputation amongst men.

But I must confess, when I consider what I am going about, and run over in my imagination all the endless crowd of men of honor who will be offended at such a discourse, I am undertaking, methinks, a work worthy an invulnerable hero in romance, rather than a private gentleman with a single rapier; but as

I am pretty well acquainted by great opportunities with the nature of man, and know of a truth that all men fight against their will, the danger vanishes, and resolution rises upon this subject. For this reason, I shall talk very freely on a custom which all men wish exploded, though no man has courage enough to resist it.

But there is one unintelligible word, which I fear will extremely perplex my dissertation, and I confess to you I find very hard to explain, which is the term "satisfaction." An honest country gentleman had the misfortune to fall into company with two or three modern men of honor, where he happened to be very ill treated, and one of the company, being conscious of his offense, sends a note to him in the morning, and tells him he was ready to give him satisfaction. "This is fine doing," says the plain fellow; "last night he sent me away cursedly out of humor, and this morning he fancies it would be a satisfaction to be run through the body."

As the matter at present stands, it is not to do handsome actions denominates a man of honor; it is enough if he dares to defend ill ones. Thus you often see a common sharper[1] in competition with a gentleman of the first rank; though all mankind is convinced that a fighting gamester is only a pickpocket with the courage of an highwayman. One cannot with any patience reflect on the unaccountable jumble of persons and things in this town and nation, which occasions very frequently that a brave man falls by a hand below that of a common hangman, and yet his executioner escapes the clutches of the hangman for doing it. I shall therefore hereafter consider how the bravest men in other ages and nations have behaved themselves upon such incidents as we decide by combat; and show, from their practice, that this resentment neither has its foundation from true reason or solid fame: but is an imposture, made of cowardice, falsehood, and want of understanding. For this work, a good history of quarrels would be very edifying to the public, and I apply myself to the town for particulars and circumstances within their knowledge, which may serve to embellish the dissertation with proper cuts.[2] Most of the quarrels I have ever known have proceeded from some valiant coxcomb's[3] persisting in the wrong, to defend some prevailing folly, and preserve himself from the ingenuity of owning a mistake.

By this means it is called "giving a man satisfaction" to urge your offense against him with your sword; which puts me in mind of Peter's order to the keeper, in *The Tale of a Tub.*[4] "If you neglect to do all this, damn you and your generation forever: and so we bid you heartily farewell." If the contradiction in the very terms of one of our challenges were as well explained and turned into downright English, would it not run after this manner?

"SIR,
"Your extraordinary behavior last night, and the liberty you were pleased to take with me, makes me this morning give you this, to tell you, because you are an ill-bred puppy, I will meet you in Hyde Park an hour hence; and because you want both breeding and humanity, I desire you would come with a pistol in your hand, on horseback, and endeavor to shoot me through the head to teach you more manners. If you fail of doing me this pleasure, I shall say you are a rascal, on every post in town: and so, sir, if you will not injure me more, I shall never forgive what you have done already. Pray, sir, do not fail of getting everything ready; and you will infinitely oblige, sir, your most obedient humble servant, etc." . . .

---

1. **sharper:** a gambler who cheats.

2. **proper cuts:** woodcuts, or copper engravings.
3. **coxcomb:** a pretentious, conceited dandy.
4. **Peter's . . . Tub:** Peter is a character in Jonathan Swift's satire on religious controversy.

FOR STUDY AND DISCUSSION

1. What motives or reasons for the continuing popularity of dueling among gentlemen does Steele give in his essay? How does the anecdote Steele tells in his third paragraph support the points he has been making?

2. Steele says that "a man of honor" is not measured by the good acts he performs but by his willingness to defend "ill ones." What does he mean?

3. Challenges in Steele's day were often flowery and evasive, as the phrase "giving a man satisfaction" shows. How does Steele make fun of this phrase by recasting a challenge in "downright" English? How does Steele use humor to attack the practice of dueling?

LANGUAGE AND VOCABULARY

Steele's sentences are close to the spoken idiom of his time and ours. He writes in fairly loose sentences, joining his phrases and clauses with the common connectives *and, but, for,* and like words. And he uses semicolons and colons to mark strong pauses:

> I shall therefore hereafter consider how the bravest men in other ages and nations have behaved themselves upon such incidents as we decide by combat; *and* show, from their practice, that this resentment neither has its foundation from true reason or solid fame: *but* is an imposture, made of cowardice, falsehood, and want of understanding.

Steele's vocabulary is, by contrast, often formal—departing from the informal words of people in their daily conversations. Use your dictionary to decide the meaning of the following italicized words. Then rewrite each phrase in ordinary language:

"the causes which *precipitate* men into so fatal a *folly*"
"*chimerical* groundless humor"
"*resolution* rises upon this subject"
"will extremely *perplex* my *dissertation*"
"*denominates* a man of honor"
"an *imposture,* made of cowardice, falsehood, and want of understanding"
"*edifying* to the public"
"*embellish* the dissertation"
"the *ingenuity* of *owning* a mistake"

FOR COMPOSITION

1. Steele suggests that people pick fights—and accept challenges—because they think they must. Write an essay in which you agree or disagree with Steele.

2. Attack a custom you disapprove of—perhaps a custom observed by teen-agers or adults. Discuss the motives of those who adhere to the custom, as Steele discusses the motives of duelists.

The Spectator

The first issue of *The Spectator* (1711–1712) appeared two months after *The Tatler* was discontinued. *The Spectator* was not another *Tatler* under a new name. Its authors realized that in trying to be too many things to too many people, *The Tatler* had become a hodgepodge. Therefore they limited *The Spectator* to discussions of literature, manners, and morals, and confined each issue of the paper to a single theme. The purpose of the new paper was "to enliven morality with wit, and to temper wit with morality." The subject matter was both serious and amusing, ranging from discussions of ladies' fashions to discussions of religion. In a far more polished literary style than we are accustomed to in our own newspapers, *The Spectator* gently but pointedly satirized the extravagances of fashionable life. The paper, which became very popular, appeared daily and carried classified advertisements.

In *The Spectator*, as in *The Tatler*, Addison and Steele delivered their opinions through an imaginary spokesman, The Spectator, a quiet, sensible, and good-natured man whose signature appeared on every essay. Maintaining a position of detachment, he objectively observed and exposed social follies and pretensions and provided subtle advice in hopes of correcting them. Like the fashionable men of his time, The Spectator belonged to a club and regularly frequented the best coffeehouses. The members of his club, The Spectator Club, were carefully selected to represent the various classes and opinions of eighteenth-century society, thus creating a broad scope for satire. The club member who had the greatest popular appeal was Sir Roger de Coverley, a country gentleman to whom Addison devoted many of his most famous essays.

Sir Roger and the Witches

The Spectator, July 14, 1711

There are some opinions in which a man should stand neuter,[1] without engaging his assent to one side or the other. Such a hovering faith as this, which refuses to settle upon any determination, is absolutely necessary in a mind that is careful to avoid errors and prepossessions. When the arguments press equally on both sides in matters that are indifferent to us, the safest method is to give up ourselves to neither.

It is with this temper of mind that I consider the subject of witchcraft. When I hear the relations that are made from all parts of the world, not only from Norway and Lapland, from the East and West Indies, but from every particular nation in Europe, I cannot forbear thinking that there is such an intercourse and commerce with evil spirits as that which we express by the name of witchcraft. But when I consider that the ignorant and credulous parts of the world abound most in these relations, and that the persons among us who are supposed to engage in such an infernal commerce,[2] are people of a weak understanding and crazed imagination, and at the same time reflect upon the many impostures

---

1. **neuter:** neutral.

2. **infernal commerce:** dealing with the devil or other evil spirits.

and delusions of this nature that have been detected in all ages, I endeavor to suspend my belief till I hear more certain accounts than any which have yet come to my knowledge. In short, when I consider the question, whether there are such persons in the world as those we call witches, my mind is divided between two opposite opinions; or rather (to speak my thoughts freely) I believe in general that there is, and has been, such a thing as witchcraft; but at the same time can give no credit to any particular instance of it.

I am engaged in this speculation, by some occurrences that I met with yesterday, which I shall give my reader an account of at large. As I was walking with my friend Sir Roger[3] by the side of one of his woods, an old woman applied herself to me for my charity. Her dress and figure put me in mind of the following description in Otway:[4]

In a close lane, as I pursued my journey,
I spied a wrinkled hag, with age grown
   double,
Picking dry sticks, and mumbling to her-
   self;
Her eyes with scalding rheum were galled
   and red;
Cold palsy shook her head; her hands
   seemed withered,
And on her crooked shoulders had she
   wrapped
The tattered remnants of an old striped
   hanging,
Which served to keep her carcass from the
   cold;
So there was nothing of a piece about her:
Her lower weeds were all o'er coarsely
   patched
With different colored rags, black, red,
   white, yellow,
And seemed to speak variety of wretchedness.

As I was musing on this description and comparing it with the object before me, the knight told me that this very old woman had the reputation of a witch all over the country, that her lips were observed to be always in motion, and that there was not a switch[5] about her house which her neighbors did not believe had carried her several hundreds of miles. If she chanced to stumble, they always found sticks or straws that lay in the figure of a cross before her. If she made any mistake at church, and cried "Amen" in a wrong place, they never failed to conclude that she was saying her prayers backward. There was not a maid in the parish that would take a pin of her, though she should offer a bag of money with it. She goes by the name of Moll White and has made the country ring with several imaginary exploits which are palmed upon her. If the dairymaid does not make her butter to come so soon as she would have it, Moll White is at the bottom of the churn. If a horse sweats in the stable, Moll White has been upon his back. If a hare makes an unexpected escape from the hounds, the huntsman curses Moll White. Nay (says Sir Roger), I have known the master of the pack, upon such an occasion, send one of his servants to see if Moll White had been out that morning.

This account raised my curiosity so far, that I begged my friend Sir Roger to go with me into her hovel, which stood in a solitary corner under the side of the wood. Upon our first entering, Sir Roger winked to me and pointed to something that stood behind the door, which, upon looking that way, I found to be an old broom staff. At the same time he whispered me in the ear to take notice of a tabby cat[6] that sat in the chimney corner, which, as the knight told me, lay under as bad a report as Moll White herself; for besides that Moll is said often to accompany her in the same shape, the cat is reported to have spoken

---

3. **Sir Roger:** Sir Roger de Coverley.
4. **Otway:** Thomas Otway (1652–1685). This passage is a description of a beggar woman in Act Two of Otway's *The Orphan*, a very popular tragedy.

5. **switch:** a broom.
6. **tabby cat:** Witches were often supposed to use cats to assist them in their "spells."

twice or thrice in her life and to have played several pranks above the capacity of an ordinary cat.

I was secretly concerned to see human nature in so much wretchedness and disgrace, but at the same time could not forbear smiling to hear Sir Roger, who is a little puzzled about the old woman, advising her, as a justice of peace, to avoid all communication with the devil and never to hurt any of her neighbors' cattle. We concluded our visit with a bounty,[7] which was very acceptable.

On our return home, Sir Roger told me that old Moll had been often brought before him for making children spit pins, and giving maids the nightmare; and that the country people would be tossing her into a pond and trying experiments with her every day, if it was not for him and his chaplain.

I have since found, upon inquiry, that Sir Roger was several times staggered with the reports that had been brought him concerning this old woman and would frequently have bound her over to the county sessions, had not his chaplain with much ado persuaded him to the contrary.

I have been the more particular in this account, because I hear there is scarce a village in England that has not a Moll White in it. When an old woman begins to dote[8] and grow chargeable to a parish, she is generally turned into a witch and fills the whole country with extravagant fancies, imaginary distempers, and terrifying dreams. In the meantime the poor wretch that is the innocent occasion of so many evils begins to be frightened at herself, and sometimes confesses secret commerces and familiarities that her imagination forms in a delirious old age. This frequently cuts off charity from the greatest objects of compassion and inspires people with a malevolence toward those poor decrepit parts of our species, in whom human nature is defaced by infirmity and dotage.

---

7. **bounty:** a present of money.
8. **dote:** to grow old and feebleminded.

FOR STUDY AND DISCUSSION

1. Is this essay really about witchcraft? If not, what is Addison's main point in the essay? What examples does he use to develop this point? How does the conclusion emphasize his purpose?
2. What impression do you form of the speaker?
3. The avowed purpose of *The Spectator* was "to enliven morality with wit, and to temper wit with morality." How well do you think this essay illustrates that purpose?

THE ESSAY

Although Greek and Latin writers such as Cicero, Seneca, and Plutarch had written short prose pieces somewhat similar to the essay, the literary form known as the *essay* originated with a French writer, Michel de Montaigne, who in 1580 published two volumes of short prose pieces entitled *Essais*. Montaigne drew the title for his work from the French word meaning "attempt," or "endeavor." In his essays Montaigne expressed himself in a conversational style on a variety of subjects—on anything, in fact, that interested him. Then, in the late sixteenth century, Francis Bacon borrowed Montaigne's term and introduced the essay into English literature. With the creation in the eighteenth century of the periodical essay of Addison and Steele, the essay form gained great popularity.

In studying the essay form, it is useful to distinguish between the formal and the informal essay. In the *formal* essay, of which the essays of Bacon are a good example, the writer's purpose is to instruct or persuade, and the tone is usually dignified and impersonal. Ideas are developed through a logical arrangement of pertinent details. The *informal* essay is characterized by its personal and relaxed approach to its subject and by its conversational tone. Many informal essays are significant not so much for *what* the author says as for *how* he or she says it. That the informal essay spans a wide range of subject matter and approach is seen in such different works as Addison's gently satirical piece "Sir Roger and the Witches," Charles Lamb's whimsical "Dream Children," and George Orwell's thoughtful essay "Shooting an Elephant."

Compare Steele and Addison's informal essays with the formal essay "On Studies" by Bacon. Consider differences in subject matter and style.

Alexander Pope
1688–1744

Bust of Alexander Pope (c. 1741) by
L. F. Rubiliac.
Leeds City Art Galleries, Leeds, England

By his early twenties, Pope was established as the foremost poet of his generation, but if success came easily to him, tranquillity did not. He was deeply conscious of physical deformity, having suffered in childhood from tuberculosis of the spine, which left him hunchbacked and dwarfish. Moreover, his Roman Catholic faith excluded him from the university education and public positions that he might otherwise have expected. Pope's tireless literary labors were in some sense a compensation for the frustrations of what he called "this long disease, my life." But he strove with all his might to be more than just a clever poet. He formed friendships with many of the leading figures of the day, among them John Gay (author of *The Beggar's Opera*), Jonathan Swift, and Lord Bolingbroke, who for a time was Secretary of State and who suggested to Pope the composition of the *Essay on Man*. Pope devoted many hours to creating a harmonious world of his own in his house and gardens at Twickenham, just outside London.

In his youth, when Pope revealed himself to be a literary prodigy, he mapped out a career along classical lines, and began by publishing pastorals as Virgil, Spenser, and Milton had done. The obvious goal would have been a great epic poem, but for various reasons Pope came to believe that heroic ideals were no longer viable in the society of his time. He translated all of Homer into English verse, and in *The Rape of the Lock* (1712) wrote an affectionately humorous mock epic, but the bitter anti-epic of *The Dunciad* (1728) was his final assessment of the debased values (as he saw them) of eighteenth-century culture. While Pope is the great poet of civilization, he is far from complacent; the civilization he praises is under constant attack from corrupt politicians and the mindless hack writers whom he satirized as "dunces." Pope saw himself as drawn irresistibly to satire by an age that deserved rebuke. And it was for this reason, he declared, that he had to give up the more lyrical effects of his early works.

Pope wrote a number of "Essays" in verse. The first of these, *An Essay on Criticism*, appeared in 1711, when Pope was only twenty-three. In this long poem, Pope summed up neoclassical doctrine about literature and literary criticism. *The Essay on Man*, published in 1733–1734, was Pope's ambitious attempt to summarize the human condition, what he called a "general map of Man." It marked the beginning of his work as a philosophical poet. The *Moral Essays* appeared between 1731 and 1735. Pope considered these poems to be his best work. In them he set out to construct a system of ethics in imitation of Horace.

Pope's mastery of the heroic couplet seemed the perfect expression of the moral and intellectual values of an age that admired clarity and order. Part of Pope's skill was in reducing his meaning to unforgettable aphorisms, so that many of his lines have become proverbial: "Fools rush in where angels fear to tread"; "To err is human, to forgive, divine"; "Hope springs eternal in the human breast"; "The proper study of mankind is man." But above all he succeeded in giving infinite variety to the potentially rigid couplet, by subtle alterations of rhythm and vowel sounds. As Samuel Johnson remarked later in the century, "A thousand years may elapse before there shall appear another man with a power of versification equal to that of Pope."

from **The Rape of the Lock**

Although Pope was often quarrelsome, he had many friends to whom he showed the kindly side of his nature. On one notable occasion he attempted unsuccessfully to act as peacemaker. Because a foppish young baron named Lord Petre had snipped a curl from the head of a Miss Arabella Fermor and refused to give it up, there arose between the two families a quarrel which threatened to become a feud. Pope's friend, John Caryll, suggested that he write a poem about this trivial incident to show the absurdity of all the excitement. The result was "The Rape of the Lock," a mock-heroic, or mock-epic poem. The poem pokes fun at the combatants by describing them in exaggeratedly heroic language, but also has some very sensible things to say about social role playing and human behavior in general.

Pope himself described a mock epic as "using a vast force to lift a feather." Thus he wrote his poem in the grand epic style of the *Iliad,* the

The Mall in St. James's Park by Thomas Gainsborough. Copyright, The Frick Collection, New York

Odyssey, the *Aeneid,* and *Paradise Lost,* and filled it with amusing parallels to Homer, Virgil, and Milton. By recalling parallel situations of tragic or heroic importance in famous epic poems, he emphasized the triviality of his own subject. A card game, for example, is treated as if it were a battle outside the walls of Troy, though Pope's setting is "the level green" of the card table. Instead of being mortally wounded from the spears of Homeric warfare, the beaux fall dead before the angry glances of the ladies. Just before the lock is cut, sylphs gather to defend it just as the angels gather to defend Adam and Eve from Satan in *Paradise Lost.* Because Pope always maintains just the right degree of sympathy with the human characters in his poem, none of these parallels to the classical epic overload the poem or seem too weighty for Pope's delicate joke to bear.

The poem is written in five cantos, but because of its great length only a portion of it is given here. Canto I opens with a formal statement of the theme—"what mighty contests rise from trivial things"—and invokes the Muse to inspire the poet. Belinda, heroine of the poem, is visited by the sylph Ariel, who warns her that some dread fate hangs over her head. In Canto II, Belinda, on a pleasure boat on the Thames, is being conducted with other young fashionables to the palace of Hampton Court. An adventurous baron, admiring two of Belinda's curls, determines to obtain them. Belinda's protecting sylph Ariel exhorts a host of other airy beings to come to Belinda's defense. Canto III follows.

Canto III

Close by those meads, forever crowned with flowers,
Where Thames with pride surveys his rising towers,
There stands a structure of majestic frame,°
Which from the neighboring Hampton takes its name.
Here Britain's statesmen oft the fall foredoom   5
Of foreign tyrants and of nymphs at home;
Here thou, great Anna! whom three realms obey,°
Dost sometimes counsel take—and sometimes tea.°
    Hither the heroes and the nymphs resort,
To taste awhile the pleasures of a court;   10
In various talk th' instructive hours they passed,
Who gave the ball, or paid the visit last;
One speaks the glory of the British Queen,
And one describes a charming Indian screen;
A third interprets motions, looks, and eyes;   15
At every word a reputation dies.
Snuff, or the fan,° supply each pause of chat,
With singing, laughing, ogling, and all that.

A gay party of young gentlemen and ladies go up the Thames to Hampton Court.

---

3. **structure . . . frame:** Hampton Court, a handsome royal residence near London.   7. **Anna! . . . obey:** Queen Anne was ruler of England, Scotland, and Ireland.   8. **tea:** pronounced *tā.*   17. **Snuff . . . fan:** Taking snuff in the eighteenth century was almost as widespread among gentlemen as cigarette smoking is today. A lady was seldom without her fan to occupy her hands and often to help her flirtations.

Meanwhile, declining from the noon of day,
The sun obliquely shoots his burning ray;
The hungry judges soon the sentence sign,   20
And wretches hang that jurymen may dine;
The merchant from th' Exchange° returns in peace,
And the long labors° of the toilet cease.

In the afternoon Belinda and two lords engage in a three-handed game of cards.

Belinda now, whom thirst of fame invites,   25
Burns to encounter two adventurous knights,
At omber° singly to decide their doom;
And swells her breast with conquests yet to come.
Straight the three bands prepare in arms to join,
Each band the number of the sacred nine.°   30
Soon as she spreads her hand, th' aerial guard
Descend, and sit on each important card:
First, Ariel perched upon a Matador,°
Then each, according to the rank they bore;
For sylphs, yet mindful of their ancient race,   35
Are, as when women, wondrous fond of place.

Behold, four kings in majesty revered,
With hoary whiskers and a forky beard;
And four fair queens whose hands sustain a flower,

The game is compared to a great battle among kings.

The expressive emblem of their softer power;   40
Four knaves in garbs succinct,° a trusty band,
Caps on their heads, and halberts° in their hand;
And particolored troops, a shining train,
Draw forth to combat on the velvet plain.

The skillful nymph reviews her force with care: 45
Let spades be trumps! she said, and trumps they were.

Now move to war her sable Matadors,
In show like leaders of the swarthy Moors.
Spadillio° first, unconquerable lord!
Led off two captive trumps and swept the board.   50
As many more Manillio° forced to yield
And marched a victor from the verdant field.°
Him Basto° followed, but his fate more hard
Gained but one trump and one plebeian card.
With his broad saber next, a chief in years,   55

---

23. **Exchange:** a place where merchants, brokers, and bankers met to transact business.   24. **long labors:** Because of the elaborate, towering headdresses of that time, ladies often spent most of the day at their dressing tables preparing for a ball in the evening.   27. **omber:** a fashionable card game.   30. **the sacred nine:** The nine cards in each player's hand are compared to the nine Muses of the Greeks. 33. **Matador:** a card that had power to take a trick, derived from the Spanish word for bullfighter.   41. **succinct** (sək-sĭngkt'): belted.   42. **halberts** (hăl'bərts): long-handled weapons with metal heads.   49. **Spadillio:** the ace of spades.   51. **Manillio:** another trump card.   52. **verdant field:** The omber table was covered with green cloth.   53. **Basto:** the ace of clubs.

The hoary majesty of spades appears,
Puts forth one manly leg, to sight revealed,
The rest his many-colored robe concealed.
The rebel knave, who dares his prince engage,
Proves the just victim of his royal rage.   60
E'en mighty Pam,° that kings and queens o'erthrew,
And mowed down armies in the fights of Loo,
Sad chance of war! now destitute of aid,
Falls undistinguished by the victor spade!

    Thus far both armies to Belinda yield;   65
Now to the baron fate inclines the field.
His warlike Amazon her host invades,
The imperial consort of the crown of spades;
The club's black tyrant first her victim died,
Spite of his haughty mien, and barbarous pride.   70
What boots° the regal circle on his head,
His giant limbs, in state unwieldy spread;
That long behind he trails his pompous robe,
And, of all monarchs, only grasps the globe?

    The baron now his diamonds pours apace;   75
Th' embroidered king who shows but half his face,
And his refulgent° queen, with powers combined,
Of broken troops an easy conquest find.
Clubs, diamonds, hearts, in wild disorder seen,
With throngs promiscuous° strew the level green.   80
Thus when dispersed a routed army runs,
Of Asia's troops, and Afric's sable sons,
With like confusion different nations fly,
Of various habit, and of various dye,
The pierced battalions disunited fall,   85
In heaps on heaps; one fate o'erwhelms them all.

    The knave of diamonds tries his wily arts,
And wins (oh, shameful chance!) the queen of hearts.
At this the blood the virgin's cheek forsook,
A livid paleness spreads o'er all her look;   90
She sees, and trembles at the approaching ill,
Just in the jaws of ruin, and codille.°
And now (as oft in some distempered state)
On one nice trick depends the general fate.
An ace of hearts steps forth; the king unseen   95
Lurked in her hand, and mourned his captive queen:

Belinda's luck changes. The baron's queen of spades takes her king of clubs; his run of diamonds takes several tricks.

---

61. **Pam:** In a card game called "Loo," the knave of clubs, Pam, was the highest card and therefore "kings and queens o'erthrew" and "mowed down armies." In ombre, the game now being played, the knave was less powerful.   71. **What boots:** of what benefit is.   77. **refulgent** (rĭ-fŭl′jənt): radiant, resplendent.   80. **promiscuous:** mixed.   92. **codille:** a term meaning the defeat of the lone hand.

He springs to vengeance with an eager pace,

He springs to vengeance with an eager pace,
And falls like thunder on the prostrate ace.
The nymph exulting fills with shouts the sky;
The walls, the woods, and long canals reply.   100
    O thoughtless mortals; ever blind to fate,
Too soon dejected, and too soon elate.
Sudden, these honors shall be snatched away,
And cursed forever this victorious day.
    For lo! the board with cups and spoons is crowned,   105
The berries crackle, and the mill turns round;°
On shining altars of Japan° they raise
The silver lamp; the fiery spirits blaze;
From silver spouts the grateful liquors glide,
While China's earth° receives the smoking tide.   110
At once they gratify their scent and taste,
And frequent cups prolong the rich repast.
Straight hover round the fair her airy band;
Some, as she sipped, the fuming liquor fanned,
Some o'er her lap their careful plumes displayed,   115
Trembling, and conscious of the rich brocade.
Coffee (which makes the politician wise,
And see through all things with his half-shut eyes)
Sent up in vapors to the baron's brain
New stratagems the radiant locks to gain.   120
Ah, cease, rash youth! desist ere 'tis too late,
Fear the just gods, and think of Scylla's fate!°
Changed to a bird, and sent to flit in air,
She dearly pays for Nisus' injured hair!
    But when to mischief mortals bend their will,   125
How soon they find fit instruments of ill!
Just then Clarissa drew with tempting grace
A two-edged weapon from her shining case:
So ladies in romance assist their knight,
Present the spear, and arm him for the fight.   130
He takes the gift with reverence, and extends
The little engine on his fingers' ends;
This just behind Belinda's neck he spread,
As o'er the fragrant steams she bends her head.
Swift to the lock a thousand sprites repair,   135
A thousand wings, by turns, blow back the hair;

Belinda wins when her king of hearts takes the baron's ace of hearts.

The card game ended, coffee is served in a "rich repast."

Clarissa, one of the ladies, helps the baron's plan by handing him her scissors. The sprites scurry to protect Belinda.

---

106. **The berries . . . round:** Prepared coffee could not be bought in those days, but the coffee berries were ground in a small hand mill at the table.   107. **altars of Japan:** Imported lacquered tables were popular at this time. Pope suggests that the social custom has a ritualized quality.   110. **China's earth:** The cups were earthenware imported from China.   122. **Scylla's** (sīl'əz) **fate:** Scylla betrayed her father, King Nisus, by sending the enemy a lock of his hair.

And thrice they twitched the diamond in her ear;
Thrice she looked back and thrice the foe drew near.
Just in that instant, anxious Ariel sought
The close recesses of the virgin's thought;   140
As on the nosegay in her breast reclined,
He watched th' ideas rising in her mind,
Sudden he viewed, in spite of all her art,
An earthly lover lurking at her heart.°
Amazed, confused, he found his power expired,   145
Resigned to fate, and with a sigh retired.
    The peer now spreads the glittering *forfex*° wide,
T' inclose the lock; now joins it, to divide.
E'en then, before the fatal engine° closed,

Belinda's curl is severed — the rape of the lock!

A wretched sylph too fondly interposed: 150
Fate urged the shears, and cut the sylph in twain,
(But airy substance soon unites again).
The meeting points the sacred hair dissever
From the fair head, forever, and forever!
    Then flashed the living lightning from her eyes,   155
And screams of horror rend th' affrighted skies.
Not louder shrieks to pitying Heaven are cast,
When husbands, or when lap dogs breathe their last;
Or when rich China vessels, fallen from high,
In glittering dust and painted fragments lie!   160
"Let wreaths of triumph now my temples twine,"
The victor cried; "the glorious prize is mine!
While fish in streams, or birds delight in air,
Or in a coach and six the British fair,
As long as *Atalantis*° shall be read,   165
Or the small pillow grace a lady's bed,
While visits shall be paid on solemn days,

The baron exults over the permanent fame he has won by his conquest.

When numerous wax lights in bright order blaze,
While nymphs take treats, or assignations give,
So long my honor, name, and praise shall live!   170
What Time would spare, from steel receives its date,°
And monuments, like men, submit to fate!
Steel could the labor of the gods destroy,
And strike to dust th' imperial towers of Troy;
Steel could the works of mortal pride confound,   175
And hew triumphal arches to the ground.
What wonder then, fair nymph! thy hairs should feel,
The conquering force of unresisted steel?"

---

144. **earthly lover . . . heart:** The sylphs cannot protect Belinda if in her heart she
wants the Baron to succeed.   147. *forfex* (fôr′fəks): Latin for *shears.*   149. **engine:**
instrument; i.e., the shears.   165. *Atalantis:* a popular book of scandalous gossip.
171. **receives its date:** is destroyed.

Canto V

In Canto IV, Umbriel, a melancholy sprite, brings a bag (similar to the bag of winds once held by Ulysses) in which are contained "the force of female lungs, sighs, sobs, and passions, and the war of tongues." These he empties over the head of Belinda, who immediately bursts into loud lamentations on the loss of her lock. She then calls upon Sir Plume to aid her in regaining her lock. This ineffectual fop swears the favorite oaths of the time — "Zounds! Plague on 't! Prithee, pox!" — but fails to move the baron.

Then, in the beginning of Canto V, Clarissa urges good sense and good humor, but in vain. The story concludes with a mighty battle between the belles and the beaux.

The Drawing Room, St. James's Palace (aquatint, 1809) by
Thomas Rowlandson.
The Mansell Collection

"To arms, to arms!" the fierce virago cries,
And swift as lightning to the combat flies.
All side in parties, and begin th' attack;
Fans clap, silks rustle, and tough whalebones crack;
Heroes' and heroines' shouts confus'dly rise,   5
And bass and treble voices strike the skies.
No common weapons in their hands are found,
Like gods they fight, nor dread a mortal wound.°
    So when bold Homer makes the gods engage,
And heavenly breasts with human passions rage;   10
'Gainst Pallas, Mars, Latona, Hermes° arms;
And all Olympus° rings with loud alarms:
Jove's thunder roars, Heaven trembles all around,
Blue Neptune storms, the bellowing deeps resound;
Earth shakes her nodding towers, the ground gives way,   15
And the pale ghosts start at the flash of day!
    Triumphant Umbriel on a sconce's° height
Clapped his glad wings, and sat to view the fight;
Propped on their bodkin spears,° the sprites survey
The growing combat, or assist the fray.   20
    While through the press enraged Thalestris° flies,
And scatters death around from both her eyes,
A beau and witling° perished in the throng,
One died in metaphor, and one in song.
"O cruel nymph! a living death I bear,"   25
Cried Dapperwit, and sunk beside his chair.
A mournful glance Sir Fopling° upward cast,
"Those eyes are made so killing"—was his last.
Thus on Mæander's° flowery margin lies
Th' expiring swan, and as he sings he dies.   30
    When bold Sir Plume had drawn Clarissa down,
Chloe° stepped in and killed him with a frown;
She smiled to see the doughty hero slain,
But, at her smile, the beau revived again.
    Now Jove suspends his golden scales in air,   35
Weighs the men's wits against the lady's hair;
The doubtful beam long nods from side to side;

The lords and ladies engage in a battle—of words and looks—equal to those described by Homer in The Iliad.

The lock of hair is found to be heavier than the intelligence of the young lords.

---

8. **Like . . . wound:** The gods, being immortal, did not have to fear death in battle.   11. **Pallas, Mars, Latona, Hermes:** gods who directed the Trojan War. The first and fourth were on the side of the Greeks, the second and third on the Trojan side.   12. **Olympus:** the mountain in northern Greece on which the gods supposedly lived.   17. **sconce:** a candleholder attached to the wall.   19. **bodkin spears:** large needles.   21. **Thalestris** (thə-lĕs′trĭs): an Amazon who figured in medieval tales of Alexander the Great.   23. **witling:** a gentleman with empty pretensions to high intelligence.   26–27. **Dapperwit, Sir Fopling:** names of humorous characters in sophisticated comedies of the time.   29. **Mæander's:** The Mæander was a winding river in Asia.   32. **Chloe** (klō′ē): a shepherdess loved by Daphnis in a Greek pastoral romance.

At length the wits mount up, the hairs subside.
   See, fierce Belinda on the Baron flies,
With more than usual lightning in her eyes;   40
Nor feared the chief th' unequal fight to try,
Who sought no more than on his foe to die.
But this bold lord with manly strength endued,
She with one finger and a thumb subdued:
Just where the breath of life his nostrils drew,   45
A charge of snuff the wily virgin threw;
The gnomes direct, to every atom just,
The pungent grains of titillating dust.
Sudden, with starting tears each eye o'erflows,
And the high dome re-echoes to his nose.   50
   "Now meet thy fate," incensed Belinda cried,
And drew a deadly bodkin from her side. . . .
   "Boast not my fall," he cried, "insulting foe!
Thou by some other shalt be laid as low;
Nor think to die dejects my lofty mind;   55
All that I dread is leaving you behind!
Rather than so, ah, let me still survive,
And burn in Cupid's flames—but burn alive."
   "Restore the lock!" she cries; and all around
"Restore the lock!" the vaulted roofs rebound.   60
Not fierce Othello in so loud a strain
Roared for the handkerchief that caused his pain.°
But see how oft ambitious aims are crossed,
And chiefs contend till all the prize is lost!
The lock, obtained with guilt, and kept with pain,   65
In every place is sought, but sought in vain.
With such a prize no mortal must be blessed,
So Heav'n decrees! with Heav'n who can contest?
Some thought it mounted to the lunar sphere,
Since all things lost on earth are treasured there.   70
There heroes' wits are kept in ponderous vases,
And beaux' in snuffboxes and tweezer cases;
There broken vows and deathbed alms are found,
And lovers' hearts with ends of riband bound. . . .
   But trust the Muse—she saw it upward rise,   75
Though marked by none but quick, poetic eyes. . . .
A sudden star, it shot through liquid° air,
And drew behind a radiant trail of hair.° . . .

*Belinda's lost lock becomes
a star in the sky; and the
poet calls on Belinda to
cease mourning, for the
Muse of poetry will make
the lock immortal.*

61–62. **Not . . . pain:** In Shakespeare's tragedy *Othello,* the hero is convinced of
his wife's faithlessness when she cannot find a handkerchief he had given her. The
handkerchief had actually been stolen by an enemy to be used as evidence against
her. 77. **liquid:** clear. 78. **trail of hair:** The word *comet* comes from a Greek
word meaning "long-haired" (hence the expression, "the trail of a comet").

Then cease, bright nymph! to mourn thy ravished hair,
Which adds new glory to the shining sphere!   80
Not all the tresses that fair head can boast,
Shall draw such envy as the lock you lost.
For, after all the murders of your eye,°
When, after millions slain, yourself shall die;
When those fair suns shall set, as set they must,   85
And all those tresses shall be laid in dust:
This lock, the Muse shall consecrate to fame,
And 'midst the stars inscribe Belinda's name.

---

83. **murders . . . eye:** that is, lovers struck down by her beauty.

COMMENTARY

Pope's special gift, as Swift ruefully conceded, was the ability to use the balanced structure of the rhymed couplet to convey a rich complexity of meaning: "He can in one couplet fix / More sense than I can do in six." Consider just a few of the effects in *The Rape of the Lock*, for instance, the irreverent parallelism in these lines:

One speaks the glory of the British Queen,
And one describes a charming Indian screen . . .
(III, 13–14)

By joining the important with the trivial, Pope suggests that statecraft and interior decoration are of equal importance to these somewhat frivolous people.

Or again, Pope will make a single verb govern two widely different objects:

Here thou, great Anna! whom three realms obey,
Dost sometimes counsel take—and sometimes tea.

(III, 7–8)

("Tea" was pronounced "tay" in Pope's time.) Pope admired Queen Anne and had no wish to make fun of her, but he is signifying here that his subject is social behavior rather than larger issues. Sometimes she takes political advice at Hampton Court, but this poem will confine itself to the occasions when she takes tea. Another couplet a few lines later emphasizes this deliberate limitation:

The hungry judges soon the sentence sign,
And wretches hang that jurymen may dine.
(III, 21–22)

Pope is imitating Homer's poetic way of stating the time of day, in this instance by mentioning the time when judges rise from their work. But by hinting at "justice" that metes out hasty punishment so that both judge and jury can get on with their dinner, Pope tells the reader that his elegant, playful poem must exclude much of what goes on in the real world.

Finally, notice the range of diction that Pope commands. At one extreme, he can make the most casual idiom fall naturally into his verse: "With singing, laughing, ogling, and all that" (III, 18). And at the other, he can write lines of whose beauty a Romantic poet would be proud: "Waft on the breeze, or sink in clouds of gold" (II, 60); "And bask and whiten in the blaze of day" (II, 78). Pope's contemporaries admired him, above all else, because he knew how to capture the entire range of experience in the formal structure of the heroic couplet. In so doing, he set himself a specific challenge, like an athlete dedicating his life to a particular set of skills, and showed triumphantly that he was equal to it.

Pope's Epigrams

No authors except Shakespeare and Milton have given to our language so many quotable lines and phrases as Pope. His neat couplets are easy to remember, and his comments on life and learning are usually brief, clever, and exact.

Hope springs eternal in the human breast:
Man never is, but always to be blest.
An Essay on Man, Epistle I, lines 95–96.

All nature is but art, unknown to thee;
All chance, direction, which thou canst not see;
All discord, harmony not understood;
All partial evil, universal good;
And spite of pride, in erring reason's spite,
One truth is clear, Whatever is, is right.
Ibid., lines 289–294.

A wit's a feather, and a chief a rod;
An honest man's the noblest work of God.
Ibid., Epistle IV, lines 247–248.

'Tis education forms the common mind:
Just as the twig is bent the tree's inclined.
Moral Essays, Epistle I, lines 149–150.

A little learning is a dangerous thing;
Drink deep, or taste not the Pierian[1] spring:
There shallow drafts intoxicate the brain,
And drinking largely[2] sobers us again.
An Essay on Criticism, Part II, lines 15–18.

True ease in writing comes from art, not chance,
As those move easiest who have learned to dance.
'Tis not enough no harshness gives offense —
The sound must seem an echo to the sense.
Ibid., lines 162–165.

To err is human, to forgive divine.
Ibid., line 325.

For fools rush in where angels fear to tread.
Ibid., Part III, line 66.

---

1. **Pierian** (pī-îr'ē-ən): Pieria was the region where the Muses were first worshiped; hence, the spring represents the understanding of the arts and sciences.
2. **largely:** deeply.

"Breakfast Scene" from *Marriage à la Mode* by William Hogarth. The neglected household and unpaid bills indicate that the marriage is not going well.
Courtesy, Trustees of The National Gallery, London

FOR STUDY AND DISCUSSION

The Rape of the Lock

1. From what you know of the conventions of epic poetry, point out two or three incidents in *The Rape of the Lock* that parallel the action in *Beowulf* or *Paradise Lost* (or in the epics of Homer), and explain what each of these allusions contributes to the poem as a whole.

2. What purpose does the card game serve in the poem? How does Pope bring his card game to life?

3. Is there a victor and a victory at the close of *The Rape of the Lock*? If so, who is the victor and what is the nature of the victory?

Epigrams

Do you agree with Pope's ideas in all of these sayings? From your experience, can you support or attack these ideas?

LANGUAGE AND VOCABULARY

The description of the card game gives Pope an opportunity to introduce some color words. Begin-

ning with line 38 of Canto III, we see the four kings each with *hoary* (silvery white) whiskers. *Hoary* (from the Old English word for *frost*) suggests both color and age and is usually applied to hair, not to skin or to garments. In contrast to the white beards there are the *sable Matadors* and *swarthy Moors*. Look up the derivations of these words.

The card table is referred to as a *verdant* field. What does *verdant* mean? What word is it derived from? What physical quality of the card table makes it verdant?

FOR COMPOSITION

1. Pope, in *The Rape of the Lock*, and Swift, in *Gulliver's Travels*, make use of two related techniques of ridicule: inflating triviality by elevating it to grandeur, and deflating grandeur by reducing it to triviality. Referring to their works, explain each writer's use of both of these techniques.

2. How does Pope's satire compare with that of Addison and Steele? Explain, with references to specific selections.

3. Consider several subjects for a modern mock epic, and develop one of them in a brief essay.

Wit and Nature

The following lines from *An Essay on Criticism* are often cited for what they reveal about eighteenth-century literary doctrine:

> True wit is nature to advantage dressed,
> What oft was thought, but ne'er so well expressed . . .

Here we find two key terms, *wit* and *nature*. The following passage, also from *An Essay on Criticism*, casts light on the term *nature* and its relation to "the rules":

> When first young Maro in his boundless mind
> A work to outlast immortal Rome designed,
> Perhaps he seemed above the critic's law,
> And but from nature's fountains scorned to draw:
> But when to examine every part he came,
> Nature and Homer were, he found, the same.
> Convinced, amazed, he checks the bold design,
> And rules as strict his labored work confine
> As if the Stagirite o'erlooked each line.
> Learn hence for ancient rules a just esteem;
> To copy nature is to copy them.

Here, first of all, we are concerned with the relation of *nature* to Homer (the artist) and the "rules" (of art and of civilization). In these lines, Virgil, Homer's great successor as an epic poet (whom Pope refers to above as Maro), is said to have discovered that no better pattern—that is, nothing closer to nature—could be found than the one Homer had employed. *Nature* here does not mean beautiful scenery or the observed behavior of other people: it refers to the way in which the world reflects God's purposes. Pope maintains that a general view of the scheme of things enables us to discover what these purposes are. Our minds can take in the Creator's scheme because our minds, imperfect though they are, are nonetheless made in accord with the pattern or image of the divine mind. We can see that it is God's world because God has given us minds equipped to see just that. Of course, this sounds tidier than it was in practice because even in Pope's day there was disagreement about which aspects of the natural world supplied evidence of God's design. But Pope is making as much sense as he can, and he does not pretend to do more than follow the teachings of the philosophers.

In the passage just quoted, Pope says that Homer wrote an almost perfect poem because he followed nature almost perfectly. For this reason, he was the very best example to follow. Such rules as Aristotle (whom Pope calls "the Stagirite" because he was born at Stagira) drew from Homer were, therefore, almost perfect rules. These "rules" formulated by Aristotle were in turn applied by the critics of later days.

But where does *wit* come in? It is proper to call Pope a satirist. He certainly wrote satire—that is, amusing and ironic verse in which he denounced the follies and vices of his time—but what makes him a great satirist is his *wit*. The uses of this word are various, and more than one is important here. For example, Pope himself is *a* wit and moved in a great company of wits. The word also refers to cleverness and clever sayings, to literary figures of speech known as *conceits,* such as those in the line, "While China's earth receives the smoking tide" (page 354, line 110), which, as a literal description of an action, means "while coffee is poured into cups." But the root meaning of *wit* is the power some writers have to be the executives of nature, to make brilliant sense of a world that dull people cannot grasp. There is something happy or fortunate in wit. It is something more than following the rules: it is akin to *genius,* and this too is a favorite term for Pope and his fellows.

So *wit* is a word of great potency. By wit we may be reminded of certain contradictions as well as assertions. A wit both employs the rules and leaps beyond them. We may look back to a metaphysical poet such as John Donne and recall that the yoking together of things we ordinarily think of as far removed from one another is one of the properties of metaphysical poetry. With a far greater emphasis on the attempt to make rules for poetry and human behavior, Pope is also able to bring unlike things together. We see Pope's power and skill in his wonderfully modulated use of the heroic couplet: it stitches the world together and creates a sense of order. Thus it is really wit in the form of Pope's own genius that makes Pope's world —his view of nature and the rules—acceptable.

The Age of Johnson

The period coming after Pope and Swift (both of whom died in the mid-1740's) and preceding the Romantic poets in the 1790's is often called the Age of Johnson, since Johnson was a versatile writer and dominant personality whose career spanned most of those years. But it would be truer to say that no single writer epitomizes the age, which is more easily described as a highly varied transition between the Augustan and Romantic periods than as a unified whole.

The 1740's were the time of greatest experiment and change. Even while Pope's last poems were appearing, a number of younger writers rebelled against his standards and methods. They published odes and other lyric forms that represented a direct challenge to the epigrammatic couplets and moralized sentiments of Pope and his contemporaries. Pope had regarded his art as a craft that could be learned by disciplined labor. Poets like William Collins, in his *Ode on the Poetical Character*, and Thomas Gray, in *The Bard*, proclaimed poetry to be an inspiration that resembled divine creation. Some years later, in 1759, Edward Young summed up the new ideals in *Conjectures on Original Composition*, in which he called for originality rather than Augustan versification of "what oft was thought." Young denied that poetry could be rationally interpreted: "There is something in poetry beyond prose reason; there are mysteries in it not to be explained, but admired." The actual results of these poets, however, were often slender and disappointing. As the young William Blake would sarcastically observe, they called on the Muses for inspiration but seldom got it: "The languid strings do scarcely move! / The sound is forced, the notes are few!" And in fact the best poems of the period, before the great lyrics of Burns and Blake in the 1790's, were the most old-fashioned and conservative: Thomas Gray's *Elegy*, Oliver Goldsmith's *Deserted Village*, and Samuel Johnson's *Vanity of Human Wishes* and shorter pieces.

A more successful experiment took place in prose fiction, which made rapid advances in the 1740's and produced two masterpieces, Samuel Richardson's tragic *Clarissa* and Henry Fielding's comic *Tom Jones*. Thereafter, however, the novel too lost momentum, despite Tobias Smollett's lively narratives and Laurence Sterne's witty *Tristram Shandy*, which made fun of the usual conventions of novel writing. So in spite of its early promise, this form of literature too fell into decline, until it was revived in the early nineteenth century by Jane Austen and Walter Scott.

Much of the best writing in the second half of the eighteenth century was done outside the usual boundaries of "literature." If the

Samuel Johnson (1756) by
Sir Joshua Reynolds.
The Masters and Fellows of
Pembroke College, Oxford

years between 1740 and 1790 witnessed the appearance of no really
great poet or playwright, they saw the works of the greatest British
philosopher, David Hume; the greatest political writer and orator,
Edmund Burke; the greatest biographer, James Boswell; the greatest
historian, Edward Gibbon; and (some would argue) the greatest literary critic, Samuel Johnson. The work of each of these writers testifies to a special concern with real life. Many people looked down
on imaginary fictions, regarding them as trivial and escapist, and
preferred to read what modern scholars have called "the literature of
experience." But they enjoyed this kind of writing precisely because
it was imaginative as well as factually accurate. When Burke studied
the details of British administration in India or America, he made
them live through the power of his moral indignation. When Gibbon
pored over ancient coins and documents to reconstruct the history
of Rome, he did so with the passion of a man who had dedicated his
life to explaining why a great empire should decline and fall.
England too had gained a great empire and hoped to rule it wisely.
Burke and Gibbon, like Hume who served as a diplomat and Johnson
who wrote nobly against ill-considered war, were deeply committed
to making their learning and powers of expression useful to the life
of their country.

Samuel Johnson
1709–1784

Samuel Johnson was born in Lichfield, a country town where his father was a struggling bookseller. His parents soon recognized his genius and hoped to see him achieve great things, but his prospects at first appeared gloomy. Johnson was clumsy and physically unattractive, given to odd mannerisms, and socially inept. He studied briefly at Oxford University but was forced to leave for lack of money. Yet by the time of his death, near the end of the century, he was so famous a literary figure that the period between Pope and Wordsworth is often called the Age of Johnson.

Johnson won success by means of a vigorous, wide-ranging mind and a powerful will that overcame his laziness and fear of insanity. For many years he earned a scanty living in London by miscellaneous jobs of writing, translating, editing a monthly magazine, and ghost-writing parliamentary speeches. He first gained fame as a poet, but published little poetry; his major works were the *Dictionary of the English Language,* the periodical essays collected in *The Rambler* and *The Idler,* the philosophical novel *Rasselas,* and an important edition of Shakespeare's plays. Some of his other productions included biographies, political pamphlets, book reviews, legal arguments, sermons (for use by friends), a travel book, and a tragedy. Near the end of his life, he published *The Lives of the English Poets,* in which he combined his special gifts as biographer, literary critic, and essayist on human life. When he was sixty-six, Oxford finally recognized him with an honorary degree, and he is therefore often referred to as Dr. Johnson, but he never cared to use the title.

Johnson was a deeply loyal husband and friend. After his wife died in 1752, he spent much of his time with his wide circle of friends, among whom were some of the greatest men of the time: the painter Joshua Reynolds, the political thinker Edmund Burke, the poet and playwright Oliver Goldsmith. Fiercely competitive, Johnson loved argument, as can be seen in the conversations brilliantly reported in James Boswell's *Life of Johnson,* and he was capable of cutting sarcasm. But his temper was humorous rather than malicious, and as his friend Hester Thrale remarked, "No man loved laughing better."

Samuel Johnson (without a wig) by
Sir Joshua Reynolds.
National Portrait Gallery, London

Johnson's values were deeply conservative. He was committed to the established church and political order, and disliked much of the new literature of his time, such as the poems of Gray and the novels of Fielding and Sterne. But he always opposed the unreflecting acceptance of authority, and never hesitated to criticize those of all persuasions when he thought them mistaken. His main aim was to teach readers to think for themselves.

Johnson's prose style is elaborate and balanced, with a tendency to big words and lengthy constructions. Goldsmith told him, "If you were to make little fishes talk, they would talk like whales." But anyone who reads Johnson with care will find that his writing reflects a subtle and deep intelligence. He was the most learned man of his time—the economist Adam Smith said that he "knew more books than any man alive"—but he always insisted that knowledge was useless unless it helped its possessors to live in the real world.

Walter Jackson Bate has written of him: "In his ability to arouse—and sustain—an immediate and permanent trust, no other moralist in history excels or even begins to rival him."

Letter to Lord Chesterfield

Lord Chesterfield ignored Johnson's appeal for financial help with the *Dictionary*, but later hinted that he might like it dedicated to himself. Johnson's letter exposes the unfairness of the patronage system.

To the Right Honorable the Earl of Chesterfield

February 7, 1755.

My Lord: I have lately been informed by the proprietor of *The World*,[1] that two papers, in which my *Dictionary* is recommended to the public, were written by your Lordship. To be so distinguished is an honor which, being very little accustomed to favors from the great, I know not well how to receive, or in what terms to acknowledge.

When, upon some slight encouragement, I first visited your Lordship, I was overpowered, like the rest of mankind, by the enchantment of your address; and I could not forbear to wish that I might boast myself *"Le vainqueur du vainqueur de la terre"*;[2] that I might obtain that regard for which I saw the world contending; but I found my attendance so little encouraged, that neither pride nor modesty would suffer me to continue it. When I had once addressed your Lordship in public, I had exhausted all the art of pleasing which a retired and uncourtly scholar can possess. I had done all that I could; and no man is well pleased to have his all neglected, be it ever so little.

Seven years, my Lord, have now passed, since I waited in your outward rooms, or was repulsed from your door; during which time I have been pushing on my work through difficulties, of which it is useless to complain, and have brought it at last to the verge of publication, without one act of assistance, one word of encouragement, or one smile of favor. Such treatment I did not expect, for I never had a patron before.

The shepherd in Virgil grew at last acquainted with Love, and found him a native of the rocks.[3]

Is not a patron, my Lord, one who looks with unconcern on a man struggling for life in the water, and, when he has reached ground, encumbers him with help? The notice which you have been pleased to take of my labors, had it been early, had been kind; but it has been delayed till I am indifferent, and cannot enjoy it; till I am solitary,[4] and cannot impart it; till I am known, and do not want[5] it. I hope it is no very cynical asperity not to confess obligations where no benefit has been received, or to be unwilling that the public should consider me as owing that to a patron, which Providence has enabled me to do for myself.

Having carried on my work thus far with so little obligation to any favorer of learning, I shall not be disappointed though I should conclude it, if less be possible, with less; for I have been long wakened from that dream of hope, in which I once boasted myself with so much exaltation,

My Lord,

Your Lordship's most humble,

Most obedient servant,

Samuel Johnson.

---

1. **The World:** periodical in which Chesterfield had recently praised Johnson.
2. **Le . . . terre:** the conqueror of the conqueror of the world.
3. **The shepherd . . . rocks:** A shepherd in Virgil's eighth *Eclogue* laments bitterly that love must have been born among flinty rocks.
4. **till . . . solitary:** Johnson's wife died before she could see the results of his labors.
5. **want:** need.

Definitions from Johnson's *Dictionary*

In 1755 Johnson published his great *Dictionary of the English Language,* an extraordinary one-man undertaking, considering that a modern reprint of the entire work would fill ten large volumes. He hired assistants to copy out illustrative quotations. These illustrative quotations, or citations as they are called, provided a context for the word and showed how it had actually been used by the best writers. They enlivened as well as refined the definition. No other English dictionary had provided this service. Johnson took some of his technical definitions from other dictionaries, but the bulk of the labor was his own. Boswell says, "The world contemplated with wonder so stupendous a work achieved by one man, while other countries had thought such undertakings fit only for whole academies." The vast majority of the definitions are perfectly straightforward, and have been praised for the skill with which they present English as a living language rather than as a set of arbitrary rules. Occasionally Johnson indulged in wry or satiric definitions, like some of those printed here.

astro'logy. The practice of foretelling things by the knowledge of the stars; an art now generally exploded, as without reason.

> I know it hath been the opinion of the learned, who think of the art of *astrology,* that the stars do not force the actions or wills of men. Swift.

athle'tic. Strong of body; vigorous; lusty; robust.

> Science distinguishes a man of honor from one of those *athletic* brutes, whom undeservedly we call heroes. Dryden.

to ba'rbecue. A term used in the West Indies for dressing a hog whole; which, being split to the backbone, is laid flat upon a large gridiron, raised about two foot above a charcoal fire, with which it is surrounded.

> Oldfield, with more than harpy throat endu'd,
> Cries, send me, gods, a whole hog *barbecu'd.* Pope.

bo'okful. Full of notions gleaned from books; crowded with undigested knowledge.

> The *bookful* blockhead, ignorantly read,
> With loads of learned lumber in his head,

> With his own tongue still edifies his ears,
> And always listening to himself appears.
> Pope's *Essay on Criticism.*

chi'cken. A term for a young girl.

> Then, Chloe, still go on to prate
> Of thirty-six and thirty-eight;
> Pursue your trade of scandal-picking,
> Your hints, that Stella is no *chicken.*
> Swift.

cli'max. Gradation; ascent: a figure in rhetoric, by which the sentence rises gradually; as Cicero says to Catiline, Thou doest nothing, movest nothing, thinkest nothing; but I hear it, I see it, and perfectly understand it.

gru'bstreet. Originally the name of a street in Moorfields in London, much inhabited by writers of small histories, dictionaries, and temporary poems; whence any mean production is called grubstreet.

ina'ne. Empty; void.

> We sometimes speak of place in the great *inane,* beyond the confines of the world. Locke.

le'gend. A chronicle or register of the lives of saints.

There are in Rome two sets of antiquities, the christian and the heathen; the former, though of a fresher date, are so embroiled with fable and *legend,* that one receives but little satisfaction. Addison's *Remarks on Italy.*

mo′dern. In Shakespeare, vulgar; mean; common.

> We have our philosophical persons to make *modern* and familiar things supernatural and causeless. Shakespeare.

mo′dernism. Deviation from the ancient and classical manner. A word invented by Swift.

> Scribblers send us over their trash in prose and verse, with abominable curtailings and quaint *modernisms.* Swift.

oats. A grain, which in England is generally given to horses, but in Scotland supports the people.

pra′ctic.[1] (1) Relating to action; not merely theoretical.

> When he speaks,
> The air, a chartered libertine, is still;
> And the mute wonder lurketh in men's
>   ears,
> To steal his sweet and honied sentences;
> So that the act and *practic* part of life
> Must be the mistress to this theoric.
> Shakespeare.

(2) In Spenser it seems to signify, sly; artful.

> Thereto his subtile engines he doth bend,
> His *practic* wit, and his fair filed tongue,
> With thousand other slights. *Fairy Queen.*

pride. Insolence; rude treatment of others; insolent exultation.

> That witch
> Hath wrought this hellish mischief un
>   awares;
> That hardly we escaped the *pride* of
>   France. Shakespeare.

roma′nce. (1) a military fable of the middle ages; a tale of wild adventures in war and love. (2) a lie; a fiction. In common speech.

roma′ntic. Resembling the tales of romances; wild.

> Philosophers have maintained opinions, more absurd than any of the most fabulous poets or *romantic* writers. Keill.

shill-I-shall-I.[2] A corrupt reduplication of *shall I?* The question of a man hesitating. To stand *shill-I-shall-I,* is to continue hesitating and procrastinating.

> I am somewhat dainty in making a resolution, because when I make it, I keep it: I don't stand *shill-I-shall-I* then; if I say't, I'll do't. Congreve's *Way of the World.*

so′nnet. A short poem consisting of fourteen lines, of which the rhymes are adjusted by a particular rule. It is not very suitable to the English language, and has not been used by any man of eminence since Milton.

sto′ryteller. One who relates tales; an historian. In contempt.

> In such a satire all would seek a share,
> And every fool will fancy he is there;
> Old *storytellers* too must pine and die,
> To see their antiquated wit laid by;
> Like her, who missed her name in a lam
>   poon,
> And grieved to find herself decayed so
>   soon. Dryden.

to′ry. One who adheres to the ancient constitution of the State and the apostolical hierarchy of the Church of England; opposed to a whig.

whig. The name of a faction.

youth. The part of life succeeding to childhood and adolescence; the time from fourteen to twenty-eight.

ze′phyr. (*zephyrus,* Latin.) The west wind; and poetically any calm soft wind.

> They are as gentle
> As *zephyrs* blowing below the violet.
> Shakespeare's *Cymbeline.*
> *Zephyr,* you shall see a youth with a merry countenance, holding in his hand a swan with wings displayed, as about to sing. Peacham, *On Drawing.*

---

1. **practic:** in modern usage, practical.

2. **shill-I-shall-I:** pronounced *shilly-shally.*

from **Preface to Shakespeare**

Johnson's edition of Shakespeare is remembered today chiefly for two things: its clear interpretation of obscure passages and the sound judgments of its thoughtful Preface. As a neoclassical critic, Johnson wrote in a time strongly prejudiced in favor of tradition, authority, and, as regards drama, the classical rules, most important of which was the observation of the unities of time and place. Johnson, describing himself in his Preface as "almost frighted at my own temerity . . . when I estimate the fame and the strength of those that maintain the contrary opinion," proceeded to assess Shakespeare (who violated the rules more than he obeyed them) by his own standards of logic and common sense rather than by the generally accepted aesthetic standards of his day. Venerated though they were, Johnson argued, the unities "have given more trouble to the poet than pleasure to the auditor." Though he himself observed the rules in many ways, Johnson did not parrot prevailing beliefs. To the twentieth-century reader the Preface to Shakespeare may not seem particularly novel, but in Johnson's day, when Shakespeare's alleged irregularities as a dramatist required defense, Johnson defended them with daring and skill.

In the following passage from his Preface, Johnson suggests what to him are some of Shakespeare's admirable qualities as a dramatist.

Shakespeare is, above all writers, at least above all modern writers, the poet of nature; the poet that holds up to his readers a faithful mirror of manners and of life. His characters are not modified by the customs of particular places, unpracticed by the rest of the world; by the peculiarities of studies or professions, which can operate but upon small numbers; or by the accidents of transient fashions or temporary opinions; they are the genuine progeny of common humanity, such as the world will always supply and observation will always find. His persons act and speak by the influence of those general passions and principles by which all minds are agitated and the whole system of life is continued in motion. In the writings of other poets a character is too often an individual; in those of Shakespeare it is commonly a species.

It is from this wide extension of design that so much instruction is derived. It is this which fills the plays of Shakespeare with practical axioms and domestic wisdom. It was

said of Euripides[1] that every verse was a precept; and it may be said of Shakespeare that from his works may be collected a system of civil and economical prudence. Yet his real power is not shown in the splendor of particular passages, but by the progress of his fable and the tenor of his dialogue; and he that tries to recommend him by select quotations will succeed like the pedant in Hierocles,[2] who, when he offered his house to sale, carried a brick in his pocket as a specimen.

It will not easily be imagined how much Shakespeare excels in accommodating his sentiments to real life, but by comparing him with other authors. It was observed of the ancient schools of declamation that the more diligently they were frequented, the more was the student disqualified for the world, because he found nothing there which he should

---

1. **Euripides** (yŏo-rĭp′ə-dēz): Greek dramatist of the fifth century B.C.
2. **Hierocles** (hī′ər-ə-klēz′): fifth-century scholar and critic.

ever meet in any other place. The same remark may be applied to every stage but that of Shakespeare. The theater, when it is under any other direction, is peopled by such characters as were never seen, conversing in a language which was never heard, upon topics which will never arise in the commerce of mankind. But the dialogue of this author is often so evidently determined by the incident which produces it, and is pursued with so much ease and simplicity, that it seems scarcely to claim the merit of fiction, but to have been gleaned by diligent selection out of common conversation and common occurrences.

Upon every other stage the universal agent is love, by whose power all good and evil is distributed, and every action quickened or retarded. To bring a lover, a lady, and a rival into the fable; to entangle them in contradictory obligations, perplex them with oppositions of interest, and harass them with violence of desires inconsistent with each other; to make them meet in rapture and part in agony; to fill their mouths with hyperbolical joy and outrageous sorrow; to distress them as nothing human ever was distressed; to deliver them as nothing human ever was delivered — is the business of a modern dramatist. For this probability is violated, life is misrepresented, and language is depraved. But love is only one of many passions, and, as it has no great influence upon the sum of life, it has little operation in the dramas of a poet, who caught his ideas from the living world, and exhibited only what he saw before him. He knew that any other passion, as it was regular or exorbitant, was a cause of happiness or calamity.

Characters thus ample and general were not easily discriminated and preserved, yet perhaps no poet ever kept his personages more distinct from each other. I will not say with Pope that every speech may be assigned to the proper speaker, because many speeches there are which have nothing characteristical; but, perhaps, though some may be equally adapted to every person, it will be difficult to find any that can be properly transferred from the present possessor to another claimant. The choice is right when there is reason for choice.

Other dramatists can only gain attention by hyperbolical or aggravated characters, by fabulous and unexampled excellence or depravity, as the writers of barbarous romances invigorated the reader by a giant and a dwarf; and he that should form his expectations of human affairs from the play, or from the tale, would be equally deceived. Shakespeare has no heroes; his scenes are occupied only by men who act and speak as the reader thinks that he should himself have spoken or acted on the same occasion. Even where the agency is supernatural, the dialogue is level with life. Other writers disguise the most natural passions and most frequent incidents, so that he who contemplates them in the book will not know them in the world. Shakespeare approximates the remote, and familiarizes the wonderful; the event which he represents will not happen, but if it were possible, its effects would be probably such as he has assigned; and it may be said that he has not only shown human nature as it acts in real exigences, but as it would be found in trials to which it cannot be exposed.

This therefore is the praise of Shakespeare, that his drama is the mirror of life; that he who has mazed his imagination in following the phantoms which other writers raise up before him may here be cured of his delirious ecstasies by reading human sentiments in human language, by scenes from which a hermit may estimate the transactions of the world, and a confessor predict the progress of the passions.

FOR STUDY AND DISCUSSION

1. What light is cast upon Johnson's character by his conduct toward Lord Chesterfield?
2. How do Johnson's comments on Shakespeare compare with Dryden's in "An Essay of Dramatic Poesy"?
3. What does Johnson mean when he refers to Shakespeare as "the poet of nature"?
4. "Shakespeare," Johnson writes, "has no heroes; his scenes are occupied only by men who act and speak as the reader thinks that he should himself have spoken or acted on the same occasion." What do you think Johnson meant by "heroes"? Considering *Macbeth* (or any other Shakespeare play), do you agree that Shakespeare has no heroes?
5. How do Johnson's illustrative quotations help to define the words in his dictionary? Look at the quotation for *legend.* What meaning does it add to the definition?

FOR COMPOSITION

In imitation of the letter to Lord Chesterfield and with elaborate courtesy, write a letter to someone who has injured you.

James Boswell
1740–1795

James Boswell secured his position in English literature by assuring the immortality of Samuel Johnson, but had Johnson never lived Boswell would still deserve a high place as one of the best of diarists.

Only lately, through a series of unexpected discoveries as dramatic as any detective story, have we come to know Boswell not simply as author of *The Life of Samuel Johnson,* the world's greatest biography, but as a man of wide experience and many interests. Since 1840, thousands of pages of papers, letters, and diaries formerly thought to have been destroyed by his literary executors have been appearing in all sorts of unlikely places. One of the most spectacular finds was uncovered in the 1920's in an old Irish castle. In 1950 general publication of this great collection began with *Boswell's London Journal, 1762-1763.* For the first time the world came to know Boswell as he had been: a kaleidoscopic, moody, irrepressible man, by turns rakish and remorseful, taking his color from his company, vain, snobbish, aggressive, and at the same time able to win over almost anybody by his charm of manner.

Boswell's early life differed in nearly every way from Johnson's. He was born into a Scottish family of wealth, power, and position. To please his father, the Laird of Auchinleck, Boswell studied law. At one time he tried to get a commission in the peacetime army. His real career of celebrity chasing and writing began about the time he first met Johnson when visiting London in 1763. Recording this event along with other adventures during his stay, he then left on a tour of the Continent. Upon his return to London, he was admitted, under Johnson's sponsorship, to membership in the select Literary Club.

It was with Johnson that Boswell was at his best. Spurred by respect and near idolatry of his subject, willing to sustain Johnson's occasional exasperation at his continual questioning, Boswell noted his friend's every conversation, habit, and peculiarity with conscientious fidelity. One can only regard with awe the dedication and discipline required to devote thirty years to a single endeavor. While known to be a man of great vanity, Boswell more than fulfilled his prophecy in the opening

The young James Boswell by George Willison. Tom Scott, The Scottish National Portrait Gallery

pages of *The Life of Samuel Johnson:* "I will venture to say that he [Johnson] will be seen in this work more completely than any man who has ever yet lived."

Boswell's writings also include personal journals. *Journal of a Tour to Corsica* records his meeting with the Corsican patriot Paoli. *Journal of a Tour to the Hebrides* recounts his trip to the Scottish Highlands with Johnson. These journals go beyond the memorializing of a great man; Boswell dared to examine his own character and actions with open eyes. These works and his biography of Johnson serve to confirm Thomas Carlyle's remark that "Boswell wrote a good book because he had a heart and an eye to discern wisdom and an utterance to render it forth; because of his free insight, his lively talent, and, above all, of his love and childlike open-mindedness."

from The Life of Samuel Johnson

When *The Life of Samuel Johnson* was published in 1791, Boswell was at first criticized by many for so frankly revealing all of Johnson's weaknesses and idiosyncrasies as well as his strengths and virtues. Boswell insisted, however, that he would not make his "tiger a cat to please anybody." Time has proved Boswell correct in his belief that the greatness of his subject would enable him to withstand such truthful and candid exposure. The biography has resulted in lasting fame for both subject and author.

For many years Boswell's image has suffered from Thomas Macaulay's picture of him as a clownish puppy who followed Johnson about, fawning on him and waiting for the great man to throw him a bone of wit. This distorted view is based partly on Boswell's own unabashed record of his humiliation by Johnson at their first meeting. But a close reading of *The Life of Samuel Johnson* or of the *London Journal* will prove otherwise. Although a celebrity chaser, Boswell did not force himself on Johnson. Within a month after their initial meeting, it was Johnson who asked Boswell why he didn't call oftener, and toward the end of his life Johnson remembered a long trip to the Hebrides with Boswell so pleasantly that he wrote him asking whether they might ever enjoy such a trip again.

The following excerpt, which deals with the *Dictionary,* covers the period before Boswell's first meeting with Johnson.

How long this immense undertaking had been the object of his contemplation, I do not know. I once asked him by what means he had attained to that astonishing knowledge of our language by which he was enabled to realize a design of such extent and accumulated difficulty. He told me that "it was not the effect of particular study; but that it had grown up in his mind insensibly." . . .

That he was fully aware of the arduous nature of the undertaking, he acknowledges; and shows himself perfectly sensible of it in the conclusion of his "Plan"; but he had a noble consciousness of his own abilities, which enabled him to go on with undaunted spirit.

Dr. Adams found him one day busy at his Dictionary, when the following dialogue ensued:

Adams: "This is a great work, Sir. How are you to get all the etymologies?"[1]

Johnson: "Why, Sir, here is a shelf with Junius, and Skinner,[2] and others; and there is a Welsh gentleman who has published a collection of Welsh proverbs, who will help me with the Welsh."

Adams: "But, Sir, how can you do this in three years?"

Johnson: "Sir, I have no doubt that I can do it in three years."

Adams: "But the French Academy, which consists of forty members, took forty years to compile their Dictionary."

Johnson: "Sir, thus it is. This is the proportion. Let me see: forty times forty is sixteen hundred. As three to sixteen hundred so is the proportion of an Englishman to a Frenchman."

With so much ease and pleasantry could he talk of that prodigious labor which he had undertaken to execute.

---

1. **etymologies** (ĕt'ə-mŏl'ə-jēz): origins and derivations of words.

2. **Junius, and Skinner:** seventeenth-century English scholars, both of whom wrote books on etymology. Skinner was also a physician.

While the Dictionary was going forward, Johnson lived part of the time in Holborn, part in Gough Square, Fleet Street; and he had an upper room fitted up like a countinghouse for the purpose, in which he gave to the copyists their several tasks. The words, partly taken from other Dictionaries, and partly supplied by himself, having been first written down with spaces left between them, he delivered in writing their etymologies, definitions, and various significations. The authorities were copied from the books themselves, in which he had marked the passages with a black-lead pencil, the traces of which could be easily effaced. I have seen several of them in which that trouble had not been taken; so that they were just as when used by the copyists. It is remarkable that he was so attentive in the choice of the passages in which words were authorized that one may read page after page of his Dictionary with improvement and pleasure; and it should not pass unobserved that he has quoted no author whose writings had a tendency to hurt sound religion and morality.

The necessary expense of preparing a work of such magnitude for the press must have been a considerable deduction from the price stipulated to be paid for the copyright.[3] I understand that nothing was allowed by the booksellers on that account; and I remember his telling me that a large portion of it having, by mistake, been written upon both sides of the paper, so as to be inconvenient for the compositor, it cost him twenty pounds to have it transcribed upon one side only.

1763: The Meeting with Boswell

. . . Mr. Davies[4] recollected several of Johnson's remarkable sayings, and was one of the best of the many imitators of his voice and manner,

while relating them. He increased my impatience more and more to see the extraordinary man whose works I highly valued, and whose conversation was reported to be so peculiarly excellent.

At last, on Monday the 16th of May, when I was sitting in Mr. Davies' back parlor, after having drunk tea with him and Mrs. Davies, Johnson unexpectedly came into the shop; and Mr. Davies having perceived him through the glass door in the room in which we were sitting, advancing towards us — he announced his awful approach to me, somewhat in the manner of an actor in the part of Horatio, when he addresses Hamlet on the appearance of his father's ghost, "Look, my Lord, it comes." I found that I had a very perfect idea of Johnson's figure from the portrait of him painted by Sir Joshua Reynolds soon after he had published his Dictionary, in the attitude of sitting in his easy chair in deep meditation. . . . Mr. Davies mentioned my name, and respectfully introduced me to him. I was much agitated; and recollecting his prejudice against the Scotch, of which I had heard much, I said to Davies, "Don't tell where I come from."

"From Scotland," cried Davies roguishly.

"Mr. Johnson, (said I) I do indeed come from Scotland, but I cannot help it."

I am willing to flatter myself that I meant this as light pleasantry to soothe and conciliate him, and not as an humiliating abasement at the expense of my country. But however that might be, this speech was somewhat unlucky; for with that quickness of wit for which he was so remarkable, he seized the expression "come from Scotland," which I used in the sense of being of that country, and, as if I had said that I had come away from it or left it, retorted, "That, Sir, I find, is what a very great many of your countrymen cannot help."

This stroke stunned me a good deal; and when we had sat down, I felt myself not a little embarrassed, and apprehensive of what might come next.

---

3. **price . . . copyright:** The price was £1,575.
4. **Davies:** Thomas Davies, an actor and bookseller, in whose shop Boswell first met Johnson.

Samuel Johnson and James Boswell in a London fog (caricature)
by Thomas Rowlandson.
Culver Pictures

He then addressed himself to Davies: "What do you think of Garrick?[5] He has refused me an order for the play for Miss Williams,[6] because he knows the house will be full, and that an order would be worth three shillings."

Eager to take any opening to get into conversation with him, I ventured to say, "O, Sir, I cannot think Mr. Garrick would grudge such a trifle to you."

"Sir (said he, with a stern look), I have known David Garrick longer than you have done: and I know no right you have to talk to me on the subject."

Perhaps I deserved this check; for it was rather presumptuous in me, an entire stranger, to express any doubt of the justice of his animadversion[7] upon his old acquaintance and pupil. I now felt myself much mortified, and began to think that the hope which I had long indulged of obtaining his acquaintance was blasted. And, in truth, had not my ardor been uncommonly strong, and my resolution uncommonly persevering, so rough a reception might have deterred me forever from making any further attempts. Fortunately, however, I remained upon the field not wholly discomfited; and was soon rewarded

5. **Garrick:** David Garrick, the greatest actor of the eighteenth century, who had once been Johnson's pupil in a country school and had produced Johnson's tragedy *Irene.*
6. **Miss Williams:** Anna Williams, an impoverished friend for whom Garrick gave a benefit performance.

7. **animadversion:** criticism, hostile remarks.

by hearing some of his conversation, of which I preserved the following short minute, without marking the questions and observations by which it was produced.

"People (he remarked) may be taken in once, who imagine that an author is greater in private life than other men. Uncommon parts[8] require uncommon opportunities for their exertion."

"In barbarous society, superiority of parts is of real consequence. Great strength or great wisdom is of much value to an individual. But in more polished times there are people to do everything for money; and then there are a number of other superiorities, such as those of birth and fortune, and rank, that dissipate men's attention, and leave no extraordinary share of respect for personal and intellectual superiority. This is wisely ordered by Providence, to preserve some equality among mankind."

"Sir, this book (*The Elements of Criticism*,[9] which he had taken up), is a pretty essay, and deserves to be held in some estimation, though much of it is chimerical."

Speaking of one[10] who with more than ordinary boldness attacked public measures and the royal family, he said,

"I think he is safe from the law, but he is an abusive scoundrel; and instead of applying to my Lord Chief Justice to punish him, I would send half a dozen footmen and have him well ducked."

"The notion of liberty amuses the people of England, and helps to keep off the *tædium vitae*.[11] When a butcher tells you that *his heart bleeds for his country*, he has, in fact, no uneasy feeling."

"Sheridan[12] will not succeed at Bath with his oratory. Ridicule has gone down before him, and, I doubt, Derrick[13] is his enemy."

"Derrick may do very well, as long as he can outrun his character; but the moment his character gets up with him, it is all over."

It is, however, but just to record, that some years afterwards, when I reminded him of this sarcasm, he said, "Well, but Derrick has now got a character that he need not run away from."

I was highly pleased with the extraordinary vigor of his conversation, and regretted that I was drawn away from it by an engagement at another place. I had, for a part of the evening, been left alone with him, and had ventured to make an observation now and then, which he received very civilly; so that I was satisfied that though there was a roughness in his manner, there was no ill-nature in his disposition. Davies followed me to the door, and when I complained to him a little of the hard blows which the great man had given me, he kindly took upon him to console me by saying, "Don't be uneasy. I can see he likes you very well."

The Character of Samuel Johnson

The character of Samuel Johnson has, I trust, been so developed in the course of this work, that they who have honored it with a perusal, may be considered as well acquainted with him. As, however, it may be expected that I should collect into one view the capital and distinguishing features of this extraordinary

---

8. **parts:** abilities.

9. ***The Elements of Criticism:*** a theoretical work on literature, published two years previously by Henry Home, Lord Kames.

10. **one:** John Wilkes, a political radical who had attacked the government and called for "liberty," much to the disgust of Johnson, who was a Tory. Several American cities are named after him.

11. ***tædium vitae:*** boredom with life.

12. **Sheridan:** Thomas Sheridan, father of the playwright Richard Brinsley Sheridan, who was lecturing on oratory at the fashionable resort of Bath. Two years earlier, in Edinburgh, he had helped Boswell to rid himself of his Scottish accent.

13. **Derrick:** Samuel Derrick, master of ceremonies at Bath.

man, I shall endeavor to acquit myself of that part of my biographical undertaking, however difficult it may be to do that which many of my readers will do better for themselves.

His figure was large and well formed, and his countenance of the cast of an ancient statue; yet his appearance was rendered strange and somewhat uncouth by convulsive cramps, by the scars of that distemper[14] which it was once imagined the royal touch could cure,[15] and by a slovenly mode of dress. He had the use only of one eye; yet so much does mind govern and even supply the deficiency of organs that his visual perceptions, as far as they extended, were uncommonly quick and accurate. So morbid was his temperament that he never knew the natural joy of a free and vigorous use of his limbs: when he walked, it was like the struggling gait of one in fetters; when he rode, he had no command or direction of his horse, but was carried as if in a balloon. That with his constitution and habits of life he should have lived seventy-five years, is a proof that an inherent *vivida vis*[16] is a powerful preservative of the human frame.

He was prone to superstition, but not to credulity. Though his imagination might incline him to a belief of the marvelous and the mysterious, his vigorous reason examined the evidence with jealousy.[17] He was a sincere and zealous Christian, of high Church of England and monarchical principles, which he would not tamely suffer to be questioned; and had, perhaps, at an early period, narrowed his mind somewhat too much, both as to religion and politics. His being impressed with the danger of extreme latitude in either, though he was of a very independent spirit, occasioned his appearing somewhat unfavorable to the prevalence of that noble freedom of sentiment which is the best possession of man. Nor can it be denied that he had many prejudices; which, however, frequently suggested many of his pointed sayings, that rather show a playfulness of fancy than any settled malignity. He was steady and inflexible in maintaining the obligations of religion and morality; both from a regard for the order of society, and from a veneration for the Great Source of all order; correct, nay stern in his taste; hard to please, and easily offended; impetuous and irritable in his temper, but of a most humane and benevolent heart, which showed itself not only in a most liberal charity, as far as his circumstances would allow, but in a thousand instances of active benevolence.

He was afflicted with a bodily disease which made him often restless and fretful; and with a constitutional melancholy, the clouds of which darkened the brightness of his fancy and gave a gloomy cast to his whole course of thinking: we, therefore, ought not to wonder at his sallies of impatience and passion[18] at any time; especially when provoked by obtrusive ignorance or presuming petulance; and allowance must be made for his uttering hasty and satirical sallies, even against his best friends. And, surely, when it is considered, that, "amidst sickness and sorrow," he exerted his faculties in so many works for the benefit of mankind, and particularly that he achieved the great and admirable Dictionary of our language, we must be astonished at his resolution. The solemn text, "of him to whom much is given, much will be required,"[19] seems to have been ever present to his mind, in a rigorous sense, and to have

---

14. **distemper:** scrofula, a tubercular disease that caused facial disfigurement and impairment of sight; also known as the King's Evil.
15. **royal touch . . . cure:** As a small child Johnson was taken to London to be touched by Queen Anne, the last monarch to carry on the tradition.
16. *vivida vis:* lively force.
17. **jealousy:** suspicion.

18. **passion:** strong emotion.
19. **"of . . . required":** See Luke 12:48.

made him dissatisfied with his labors and acts of goodness, however comparatively great; so that the unavoidable consciousness of his superiority was, in that respect, a cause of disquiet. He suffered so much from this, and from the gloom which perpetually haunted him and made solitude frightful, that it may be said of him, "If in this life only he had hope, he was of all men most miserable."[20]

He loved praise, when it was brought to him; but was too proud to seek for it. He was somewhat susceptible of flattery. As he was general and unconfined in his studies, he cannot be considered as master of any one particular science; but he had accumulated a vast and various collection of learning and knowledge, which was so arranged in his mind, as to be ever in readiness to be brought forth. But his superiority over other learned men consisted chiefly in what may be called the art of thinking, the art of using his mind; a certain continual power of seizing the useful substance of all that he knew and exhibiting it in a clear and forcible manner; so that knowledge, which we often see to be no better than lumber[21] in men of dull understanding, was, in him, true, evident, and actual wisdom.

His moral precepts are practical; for they are drawn from an intimate acquaintance with human nature. His maxims carry conviction; for they are founded on the basis of common sense, and a very attentive and minute survey of real life. His mind was so full of imagery that he might have been perpetually a poet; yet it is remarkable that, however rich his prose is in this respect, his poetical pieces, in general, have not much of that splendor, but are rather distinguished by strong sentiment and acute observation, conveyed in harmonious and energetic verse, particularly in heroic couplets. Though usually grave, and even awful, in his deportment, he possessed uncommon and peculiar powers of wit and humor; he frequently indulged himself in colloquial pleasantry; and the heartiest merriment was often enjoyed in his company; with this great advantage, that as it was entirely free from any poisonous tincture of vice or impiety, it was salutary to those who shared in it. He had accustomed himself to such accuracy in his common conversation, that he at all times expressed his thoughts with great force, and an elegant choice of language, the effect of which was aided by his having a loud voice and a slow deliberate utterance.

In him were united a most logical head with a most fertile imagination, which gave him an extraordinary advantage in arguing: for he could reason close or wide, as he saw best for the moment. Exulting in his intellectual strength and dexterity, he could, when he pleased, be the greatest sophist[22] that ever contended in the lists of declamation; and, from a spirit of contradiction and a delight in showing his powers, he would often maintain the wrong side with equal warmth and ingenuity; so that when there was an audience, his real opinions could seldom be gathered from his talk; though when he was in company with a single friend, he would discuss a subject with genuine fairness: but he was too conscientious to make error permanent and pernicious by deliberately writing it; and, in all his numerous works, he earnestly inculcated what appeared to him to be the truth; his piety being constant, and the ruling principle of all his conduct.

Such was Samuel Johnson, a man whose talents, acquirements, and virtues were so extraordinary that the more his character is considered, the more he will be regarded by the present age, and by posterity, with admiration and reverence.

22. **sophist:** one who is adept at deviously misleading arguments.

20. **"If . . . miserable":** See I Corinthians 15:19.
21. **lumber:** clutter, rubbish.

FOR STUDY AND DISCUSSION

1. What qualities in Johnson does Boswell discover in their first meeting? What qualities in Boswell are revealed in his description of the meeting?

2. Even though Boswell was very much a personality in his own right, he submerged his personality in that of Dr. Johnson, a man thirty years his senior. Does he seem to you to be partial or impartial as a biographer? Explain your answer.

3. Johnson seems to have had a habit of speaking in *maxims*—concise statements expressing principles or rules of conduct. Select any two maxims and tell whether or not you agree with Johnson's generalizations. Be sure to explain your reasoning.

BIOGRAPHY AND AUTOBIOGRAPHY

In English the word *biography,* as a literary term, first came into use with John Dryden, who defined it as "the history of particular men's lives." Today we have an expanded definition: a biography is now denoted as a work that accurately presents the entire life of an individual, with the facts of the person's life and times interpreted in such a way as to give a complete and unified impression of character, personality, and mind.

People have always been fascinated by the lives of others, and the desire to satisfy this curiosity has been a prime reason for the reading of biographies. Self-education is another reason. Plutarch, the first-century Greek biographer, wrote that the lives he studied provided "a sort of looking glass in which I may see how to adjust and adorn my own

life." We also often read biographies to learn more about history; there is even a theory that history can be learned entirely through reading the lives of the great. The wish to relive periods of similar experience in our own lives or to share in the struggles and emotional experiences of outstanding people of the past also leads us to read biographies.

The advantage of autobiography, journals, and diaries is that in them the subjects speak for themselves. It is in diaries and journals, which are usually not intended for publication, that we are permitted the most revealing glimpses into an individual's personal life. The principal advantage of biography over autobiography is objectivity. A good biographer can stand apart and present a relatively unbiased picture of a person's life and times. But whether biography or autobiography, the value of the work can best be measured by how honestly and perceptively it defines the subject.

Compare the selections from Boswell's *Life of Johnson* with another biography you have read. Which do you think more clearly and candidly portrays its subject? Support your answer by referring to both texts.

FOR COMPOSITION

As readers, we get Boswell's picture of the events he describes in his *Life of Johnson*. How do you suppose Johnson himself would have described the same events? How might he have described young Mr. Boswell from Scotland? Pretending you are Johnson, write a journal entry describing an event or a conversation from this period of his life.

Thomas Gray
1716–1771

Although in his day Thomas Gray was considered England's foremost poet, he turned down the position of poet laureate. He is remembered today chiefly as the author of "Elegy Written in a Country Churchyard."

Gray was the only surviving child in a family of eight. By keeping shop, his mother earned the money to send him through Eton and Cambridge. After a three-year Continental tour with his former classmate and fellow writer, Horace Walpole, Gray settled in cloistered bachelor retirement at Cambridge, where he was a scholar of classical literature, a well-liked don, and a poet in residence. He enjoyed the quiet life of a Cambridge professor. On one occasion, however, a practical joke so shattered his nerves and disrupted the "noiseless tenor" of his ways that he moved to another of Cambridge's several colleges—a change which for him was a cataclysmic upheaval.

Although Gray's life was placid, his poetry was venturesome. Without discarding what he believed was good in the old, neoclassic tradition, he explored new and unfamiliar areas in poetry. His use of personification, high-flown allusions, and conventional poetic diction are representative of his ties to the earlier style. But while Pope reflected fashionable city tastes, Gray, like Wordsworth and other Romantic poets, turned to country life and humble people for inspiration. He dealt in honest and homely emotion and brought back into poetry the use of the first-person singular, considered a barbarism by eighteenth-century norms, which dictated suppression of the ego and concealment of emotion. Not only Gray's treatment of nature, but his interest in the past, in Celtic and Norse folklore and simple, primitive cultures, has been seen as a foreshadowing of themes that would find their fullest expression in the Romantic movement of the nineteenth century. But Gray can be appreciated on his own terms, free from theories about his preparing the way for the Romantic period.

A painstaking writer, Gray produced few poems. It took him nine years to complete "Elegy Written in a Country Churchyard." Samuel Johnson may have thought Gray dull, but most readers agreed with General Wolfe, who before the battle of Que-

Thomas Gray
National Portrait Gallery, London

bec in 1759, said of the "Elegy": "I would rather be the author of those lines than take Quebec."

The term *elegy*, first used to describe any serious meditative poem, is now used to refer to a poem that laments the death of a particular person. Gray's poem laments the passing of all people, but ends with an epitaph for a particular person, and is thus an elegy in both senses.

Elegy Written in a Country Churchyard

The curfew tolls the knell of parting day,
The lowing herd wind slowly o'er the lea,°
The plowman homeward plods his weary way,
And leaves the world to darkness and to me.

Now fades the glimmering landscape on the sight,   5
And all the air a solemn stillness holds,
Save where the beetle wheels his droning flight,
And drowsy tinklings lull the distant folds;

Save that from yonder ivy-mantled tower
The moping owl does to the moon complain   10
Of such as, wandering near her secret bower,
Molest her ancient solitary reign.

Beneath those rugged elms, that yew tree's shade,
Where heaves the turf in many a moldering heap,
Each in his narrow cell forever laid,   15
The rude° forefathers of the hamlet sleep.

The breezy call of incense-breathing morn,
The swallow twittering from the straw-built shed,
The cock's shrill clarion or the echoing horn,
No more shall rouse them from their lowly bed.   20

For them no more the blazing hearth shall burn,
Or busy housewife ply her evening care:
No children run to lisp their sire's return,
Or climb his knees the envied kiss to share.

Oft did the harvest to their sickle yield,   25
Their furrow oft the stubborn glebe° has broke;
How jocund did they drive their team afield!
How bowed the woods beneath their sturdy stroke!

Let not Ambition mock their useful toil,
Their homely joys and destiny obscure;   30
Nor Grandeur hear, with a disdainful smile,
The short and simple annals of the poor.

---

2. **lea:** meadow.   16. **rude:** humble, uneducated.   26. **glebe:** soil.

The boast of heraldry,° the pomp of power,
And all that beauty, all that wealth e'er gave,
Awaits alike the inevitable hour.   35
The paths of glory lead but to the grave.

Nor you, ye Proud, impute to these the fault,
If Memory o'er their tomb no trophies° raise,
Where through the long-drawn aisle and fretted vault°
The pealing anthem swells the note of praise.   40

Can storied urn° or animated° bust
Back to its mansion call the fleeting breath?
Can Honor's voice provoke° the silent dust,
Or Flattery soothe the dull cold ear of Death?

Perhaps in this neglected spot is laid   45
Some heart once pregnant with celestial fire;
Hands that the rod of empire might have swayed,
Or waked to ecstasy the living lyre.

But Knowledge to their eyes her ample page
Rich with the spoils of time did ne'er unroll;   50
Chill Penury repressed their noble rage,°
And froze the genial current° of the soul.

Full many a gem of purest ray serene
The dark unfathomed caves of ocean bear:
Full many a flower is born to blush unseen,   55
And waste its sweetness on the desert air.

Some village Hampden° that with dauntless breast
The little tyrant of his fields withstood;
Some mute inglorious Milton here may rest,
Some Cromwell° guiltless of his country's blood.   60

The applause of listening senates to command,
The threats of pain and ruin to despise,
To scatter plenty o'er a smiling land,
And read their history in a nation's eyes,°

The churchyard at
Stoke Poges, England,
the scene of Gray's
"Elegy Written in a
Country Churchyard."
Ace Williams, Shostal

33. **The boast of heraldry:** Heraldry is the study of family coats of arms; thus, the
pride of noble descent.   38. **trophies:** memorial sculptures.   39. **fretted vault:**
church roof ornamented by elaborate design.   41. **storied urn:** an urn with pictures that tell the story of the deceased.   **animated:** lifelike.   43. **provoke:**
arouse.   51. **rage:** ardor, vitality.   52. **genial current:** warm energies.   57. **Hampden:** John Hampden, a popular hero who defied the king over unjust taxation in
1636, shortly before the English Civil War.   60. **Cromwell:** Puritan leader during
the 1650's who became Lord Protector.   61–64: This whole stanza is the direct object of *forbade* in line 65.

Their lot forbade: nor circumscribed alone   65
Their growing virtues, but their crimes confined;
Forbade to wade through slaughter to a throne,
And shut the gates of mercy on mankind,

The struggling pangs of conscious° truth to hide,
To quench the blushes of ingenuous shame,°   70
Or heap the shrine of Luxury and Pride
With incense kindled at the Muse's flame.°

Far from the madding° crowd's ignoble strife
Their sober wishes never learned to stray;
Along the cool sequestered vale of life   75
They kept the noiseless tenor° of their way.

Yet even these bones from insult to protect
Some frail memorial° still erected nigh,
With uncouth rhymes and shapeless sculpture decked,
Implores the passing tribute of a sigh.   80

Their name, their years, spelt by the unlettered muse,°
The place of fame and elegy supply:
And many a holy text around she strews,
That teach the rustic moralist to die.

For who to dumb Forgetfulness a prey,   85
This pleasing anxious being e'er resigned,
Left the warm precincts of the cheerful day,
Nor cast one longing lingering look behind?

On some fond breast the parting soul relies,
Some pious drops° the closing eye requires;   90
Even from the tomb the voice of Nature cries,
Even in our ashes live their wonted fires.

For thee° who, mindful of the unhonored dead,
Dost in these lines their artless tale relate;
If chance, by lonely Contemplation led,   95
Some kindred spirit shall inquire thy fate,

---

69. **conscious**: guiltily aware (compare "conscience"). 70. **ingenuous shame**: a
naively innocent sense of virtue. 72. **incense . . . flame**: poetic praise. 73. **mad-
ding**: wild, irrational. 76. **tenor**: even course. 78. **frail memorial**: the humble
gravestones, contrasted with the elaborate tombs inside the church. 81. **the unlettered muse**: the uneducated gravestone carver. 90. **drops**: tears. 93. **thee**:
Gray himself.

Haply some hoary-headed swain° may say,
"Oft have we seen him at the peep of dawn
Brushing with hasty steps the dews away
To meet the sun upon the upland lawn.   100

"There at the foot of yonder nodding beech
That wreathes its old fantastic roots so high,
His listless length at noontide would he stretch,
And pore upon the brook that babbles by.

"Hard by yon wood, now smiling as in scorn,   105
Muttering his wayward fancies he would rove,
Now drooping, woeful wan, like one forlorn,
Or crazed with care, or crossed in hopeless love.

"One morn I missed him on the customed hill,
Along the heath and near his favorite tree;   110
Another came; nor yet beside the rill,°
Nor up the lawn, nor at the wood was he;

"The next with dirges due in sad array
Slow through the church-way path we saw him borne.
Approach and read (for thou canst read)° the lay,   115
Graved on the stone beneath yon aged thorn."°

The Epitaph

Here rests his head upon the lap of earth
A youth to Fortune and to Fame unknown.
Fair Science frowned not on his humble birth,°
And Melancholy marked him for her own.   120

Large was his bounty and his soul sincere,
Heaven did a recompense as largely send:
He gave to Misery all he had, a tear,
He gained from Heaven ('twas all he wished) a friend.

No farther seek his merits to disclose,   125
Or draw his frailties from their dread abode,
(There they alike in trembling hope repose)
The bosom of his Father and his God.

---

97. **hoary-headed swain:** white-haired rustic.   111. **rill:** brook.   115. **thou canst read:** Public education was not widespread until the nineteenth century, and many people were unable to read.   116. **thorn:** hawthorn bush.   119. **Fair . . . birth:** His humble birth did not prevent him from having a good education ("science" meant learning in general).

FOR STUDY AND DISCUSSION

1. The "Elegy" falls into clear-cut divisions of thought. What stanzas would you include in each of these first three divisions: (a) the setting; (b) the imagined life of the villagers; (c) death, the common end of all, rich and poor? Into what four divisions would you divide the rest of the poem? How would you describe each division? How do all of the divisions form a logical sequence that progresses from the general ("rude forefathers") to the particular ("A youth")?

2. Note how Gray uses vivid details to establish the mood of his poem. How does his use of imagery contribute to his restrained expression of sorrow? What effect does he achieve with the verb *tolls, wind, plods, fades,* and *lull* (lines 1–8)? What is the effect of "peep of dawn" and "hasty steps" in lines 98–100? What do they contrast with in lines 113–116? How does this contrast relate to the elegiac tone and subject matter?

3. Would the poem have been weaker or stronger if it had ended before the epitaph? Explain your answer.

4. To what extent does this poem echo Donne's "Meditation 17"?

INVERSION

The technique of inversion consists of reversing the normal English word order (subject, verb, object) of a sentence. As with other poetic devices, inversion should not be used for its own sake, but should have a definite relation to the thought and feeling of the poem, reinforcing a significant idea or emphasizing the dominant mood. If this relationship is not clear, inversion will result in artificiality and distortion. Inversion is effectively employed in Gray's "Elegy." Note for example, lines 5–6:

> Now fades the glimmering landscape on the
>   sight,
> And all the air a solemn stillness holds . . .

Cite other examples of inversion in this poem.

FOR COMPOSITION

Write your own epitaph. Will you want it to be short, witty, and general, or long, solemn, and meditative? How will you describe yourself?

Robert Burns

1759–1796

Tired and hungry, a traveler arrived one night at an inn in the heart of the Burns country. The place was alive with lights and laughter. When the traveler knocked, he got no answer. He tried shouting and banging, and finally resorted to the colorful rhetoric of an outraged Scotsman. Finally a window opened and a servant peered out and explained, "Oh, sir, Bobbie Burns is ben." When the celebrated Bobbie Burns was "ben" (within), it was understood that no one else should expect attention.

Even to this day "Bobbie Burns" is a magic name, one which kindles the loyalty and pride of his compatriots. Burns, the oldest of seven children, was born near Ayr, in southwestern Scotland, in a two-room cottage his father had built with his own hands. Although the family's poverty made possible only a meager education, Burns, according to Thomas Carlyle, "was fortunate in his father—a man of thoughtful, intense character . . . valuing knowledge, possessing some, and open-minded for more." It was from his father that Burns received most of his learning and his avid love for books. He supplemented his formal schooling by reading the Bible, *The Spectator*, and Pope's poems. His mother taught him old Scottish songs and stories, which he later turned into his best poems. He pored over small volumes of ballads when driving his cart or walking to the fields. His early life as a plowboy, he wrote, combined "the cheerless gloom of a hermit with the unceasing moil of a galley slave"; but his recollections of this life in his poetry, and particularly his love songs, reveal that his youth was not all toil and moil.

Burns developed into a handsome young man, but his wild ways and his verse satirizing local dignitaries made many enemies. At twenty-six—his father dead, the farm a failure, and his romance with Jean Armour blocked by her angry father—Burns was ready to flee to Jamaica to start a new life. To raise money for his passage, friends helped him to publish his first volume of poetry, called *Poems: Chiefly in Scottish Dialect* (1786). It was an immediate success. One contemporary claimed that "the country murmured of him from sea to sea . . . old and young, grave and gay, learned and igno-

Robert Burns
National Portrait Gallery, London

rant, were all alike transported." Canceling his trip to the West Indies, Burns went instead to Edinburgh where he was lionized, but where his peasant roughness soon jarred the refined sensibilities of polite society. When his novelty wore off, he took the £400 received from the publication of an enlarged edition of his book and toured Scotland and northern England collecting ballads. He then returned to his farm, married Jean Armour, and wrote some of his finest poetry. To supplement his meager income, he served as tax collector, a job he nearly lost because of his bold and outspoken advocacy of the principles of the French Revolution. His last years were clouded by ill health brought on by the chronic rheumatic heart condition that eventually killed him at the early age of thirty-seven. Upon his death, the whole country united to honor him and to contribute to the support of his destitute family. The recognition that had been only fleeting during his brief, unhappy lifetime flowered into lasting fame, and Burns was hailed as the national poet of Scotland. He was beloved by the Scottish people because, in their own idiom, he exalted and gave new dignity to the simple aspects of their lives.

Sweet Afton°

Flow gently, sweet Afton! among thy green braes,°
Flow gently, I'll sing thee a song in thy praise;
My Mary's asleep by thy murmuring stream,
Flow gently, sweet Afton, disturb not her dream.

Thou stock dove whose echo resounds through the glen,   5
Ye wild whistling blackbirds in yon thorny den,
Thou green-crested lapwing, thy screaming forbear,
I charge you, disturb not my slumbering Fair.

How lofty, sweet Afton, thy neighboring hills,
Far marked with the courses of clear, winding rills;   10
There daily I wander as noon rises high,
My flocks and my Mary's sweet cot° in my eye.

How pleasant thy banks and green valleys below,
Where, wild in the woodlands, the primroses blow;
There oft, as mild ev'ning weeps over the lea,°   15
The sweet-scented birk° shades my Mary and me.

Thy crystal stream, Afton, how lovely it glides,
And winds by the cot where my Mary resides;
How wanton thy waters her snowy feet lave,
As, gathering sweet flowerets, she stems thy clear wave.   20

Flow gently, sweet Afton, among thy green braes,
Flow gently, sweet river, the theme of my lays;
My Mary's asleep by thy murmuring stream,
Flow gently, sweet Afton, disturb not her dream.

° **Afton:** The Afton is a river in Burns's native Ayrshire.   1. **braes** (brāz):
slopes.   12. **cot:** cottage.   15. **lea:** meadow.   16. **birk:** birch.

The Banks o' Doon°

Ye Banks and braes o' bonie Doon,
  How can ye bloom sae° fresh and fair;
How can ye chant, ye little birds,
  And I sae weary fu'° o' care!
Thou'll break my heart thou warbling bird,   5
  That wantons thro' the flowering thorn:
Thou minds me o' departed joys,
  Departed never to return.

Oft hae° I rov'd by bonie Doon,
  To see the rose and woodbine twine;   10
And ilka° bird sang o' its luve,
  And fondly sae did I o' mine.
Wi' lightsome heart I pu'd° a rose,
  Fu' sweet upon its thorny tree;
And my fause luver staw° my rose,   15
  But, ah! he left the thorn wi' me.

°**Doon:** Another river in Ayrshire. 2. **sae:** so. 4. **fu':** full. 9. **hae:** have.
11. **ilka:** every. 13. **pu'd:** pulled. 15. **fause luver staw:** false lover stole.

To a Mouse

On Turning Her up in Her Nest with the Plough, November
  1785

Wee, sleekit,° cowrin', tim'rous beastie,
O, what a panic's in thy breastie!
Thou need na start awa sae hasty
    Wi' bickering brattle!°
I wad be laith° to rin an' chase thee   5
    Wi' murd'ring pattle!°

I'm truly sorry man's dominion
Has broken nature's social union,
And justifies that ill opinion
    Which makes thee startle   10
At me, thy poor, earthborn companion,
    An' fellow mortal!

---

1. **sleekit:** sleek. 4. **bickering brattle:** hasty scamper. 5. **laith** (lāth): loath, reluctant. 6. **pattle:** plowstaff.

I doubt na, whyles,° but thou may thieve;
What then? poor beastie, thou maun° live!
A daimen icker in a thrave°   15
    'S a sma' request;
I'll get a blessin' wi' the lave,°
    An' never miss 't!

Thy wee bit housie, too, in ruin!
It's silly wa's° the win's are strewin'!   20
An' naething, now, to big° a new ane,
    O' foggage° green!
An' bleak December's winds ensuin',
    Baith snell° an' keen!

Thou saw the fields laid bare and waste,   25
An' weary winter comin' fast,
An' cozie here, beneath the blast,
    Thou thought to dwell,
Till crash! the cruel coulter° passed
    Out through thy cell.   30

That wee bit heap o' leaves an' stibble
Has cost thee mony a weary nibble!
Now thou's turned out, for a' thy trouble,
    But house or hald,°
To thole° the winter's sleety dribble   35
    An' cranreuch° cauld!

But, Mousie, thou art no thy lane°
In proving foresight may be vain;
The best laid schemes o' mice an' men
    Gang aft agley,°   40
An' lea'e° us nought but grief an' pain,
    For promised joy.

Still thou art blest, compared wi' me,
The present only toucheth thee;
But och! I backward cast my e'e   45
    On prospects drear!
An' forward, though I canna see,
    I guess an' fear!

---

13. **whyles:** at times. 14. **maun:** must. 15. **A . . . thrave:** an occasional ear of grain in a bundle. 17. **lave:** rest. 20. **silly wa's:** feeble walls. 21. **big:** build. 22. **foggage:** coarse grass. 24. **baith:** both. **snell:** sharp, biting. 29. **coulter** (kōl′tər): plow blade. 34. **But . . . hald:** without house or holding (i.e., land). 35. **thole:** endure. 36. **cranreuch** (krən′rəkh): hoarfrost. 37. **no thy lane:** not alone. 40. **Gang aft agley** (ə-glē′): often go awry. 41. **lea'e:** leave.

To a Louse

On Seeing One on a Lady's Bonnet at Church

Ha! wh' are ye gaun, ye crowlin' ferlie!°
Your impudence protects you sairly;°
I canna say but ye strunt° rarely,
    Owre gauze and lace;
Though faith! I fear ye dine but sparely   5
    On sic a place.

Ye ugly, creepin', blastit wonner,°
Detested, shunned by saunt an' sinner!
How dare ye set your fit° upon her,
    Sae fine a lady?   10
Gae somewhere else, and seek your dinner
    On some poor body.

Swith, in some beggar's haffet squattle;°
There ye may creep, and sprawl, and sprattle°
Wi' ither kindred jumping cattle,   15
    In shoals and nations;
Where horn nor bane° ne'er dare unsettle
    Your thick plantations.

Now haud ye there,° ye're out o' sight,
Below the fatt'rels,° snug an' tight;   20
Na, faith ye yet! ye'll no be right
    Till ye've got on it,
The very tapmost tow'ring height
    O' Miss's bonnet.

My sooth! right bauld ye set your nose out,   25
As plump and gray as onie grozet;°
O for some rank mercurial rozet,°
    Or fell red smeddum!°
I'd gie you sic a hearty dose o't,
    Wad dress your droddum!°   30

---

1. **crowlin' ferlie** (fĕr′lī): crawling wonder. 2. **sairly:** greatly. 3. **strunt:** strut.
7. **blastit wonner:** blasted wonder. 9. **fit:** foot. 13. **Swith . . . squattle:** Be
off with you! Sprawl in some beggar's temple. 14. **sprattle:** struggle. 17. **horn
nor bane:** comb nor poison. 19. **haud ye there:** stay where you are. 20. **fatt'rels:**
ribbon ends. 26. **onie grozet** (grŏz′ĭt): any gooseberry. 27. **rozet:** rosin.
28. **smeddum:** powder. 30. **Wad . . . droddum:** would put an end to you.

I wad na been surprised to spy
You on an auld wife's flannen toy;°
Or aiblins some bit duddie boy,°
    On's wyliecoat;°
But Miss's fine Lunardi!° fie,   35
    How daur ye do 't?

O Jenny, dinna toss your head,
An' set your beauties a' abread!°
Ye little ken what cursèd speed
    The blastie's makin'!   40
Thae winks and finger ends,° I dread,
    Are notice takin'!

O wad some Pow'r the giftie gie us
To see oursels as ithers see us!
It wad frae mony a blunder free us,   45
    And foolish notion:
What airs in dress an' gait wad lea'e us,
    And e'en devotion!

---

32. **flannen toy:** flannel headdress. 33. **Or . . . boy:** or perhaps on some little
ragged boy. 34. **wyliecoat** (wī′lē-kōt′): flannel vest. 35. **Lunardi:** a bonnet named
for a balloonist of that day, probably with winglike ribbons. 38. **abread:** abroad.
41. **Thae . . . ends:** Those people winking and pointing.

FOR STUDY AND DISCUSSION

Songs
Apostrophe is a figure of speech in which an absent or dead person or something nonhuman is addressed directly. Find several examples of apostrophe in the songs. In "Sweet Afton," what mood or attitude toward nature does the speaker create through the use of apostrophe? In "Banks o' Doon," what mood of the speaker is contrasted with the lush beauty of nature? Does the contrast make the speaker's plight seem more touching or immediate?

Satires
"To a Mouse" and "To a Louse" are companion poems in several respects, but most strikingly in the author's use of homely subjects in homely situations to frame universal truths. In each case the truth is double-edged. Does Burns think that the plans of mice and human beings are, in general, comparable? Does he really think we would be happier if we could see ourselves as others see us? Explain.

FOR COMPOSITION

Burns's use of dialect in his poetry was a great departure from the elegant and artificial diction of eighteenth-century poetry. How does Burns's use of dialect, which is personal and emotional, reflect and illustrate the rural landscape of his native Scotland?

William Blake
1757–1827

One of William Blake's earlier biographers called him the "most spiritual of artists." The description still stands. Matter-of-fact objectors have called Blake mad; in recent years critics, while admitting his eccentricity, have elevated him as a major prophet—not only of the Romantic movement, but of the revolt against the mechanical tyranny of the modern world. It is said that Blake is only negatively related to the eighteenth century. Yet both as a revolutionary and a mystic, Blake was in his lonely way a child of his time. His revolt was against the intellectual patternmaking of the eighteenth century. His achievement—unrecognized in his own time—was a breakthrough into the Romantic movement.

Blake received little formal education, but his father, a poor tradesman, kept him well supplied with books and prints of great paintings. At the age of ten, Blake expressed a desire to be a painter and was sent to drawing school and then apprenticed to an engraver. It was during this period that he first began experimenting with verse, thus embarking upon the two separate careers that he would eventually make one. As a child, Blake had strangely intense religious experiences. He once reported seeing a tree filled with angels and, on another occasion, he saw the prophet Ezekiel under a tree in a field. To Blake the next world was as real as this one. Seeing God at his window was not, for him, unusual. Solitary by ordinary standards, Blake was surrounded from within by his own visitors. His devoted wife once said, "I have very little of Mr. Blake's company. He is always in Paradise."

Blake's trade as an engraver was an important means of livelihood, for his pictures and his poetry were not widely accepted during his lifetime. His talent for sketching is seen in his illustrations not only of his own poems but of specially decorated editions of Milton's *Paradise Lost*, Dante's *Divine Comedy*, and the Book of Job. All his life Blake devoted himself to expressing his mystical faith and his visions of a heavenly world. His concern, in both art and poetry, was to represent eternal things in terms of earthly symbols.

"Without contraries," wrote Blake, "there is no progression." His life and work are a confusion of

William Blake by Thomas Phillips.
National Portrait Gallery, London

contraries: infinite patience and painstaking workmanship in the dawn of the Industrial Age; the damning of "mind-forged manacles" in an age of rules; emotion in an age of reason; other-worldly presences involved in this world's work; genius called madness. His *Songs of Innocence* and *Songs of Experience,* two fanciful works which appealed so much to later Romantic poets, are also studies in contrast. In these two works, this great poet of contraries pointed out the need for both childhood's innocence and the wisdom—however painful and disillusioning—gained by experience. *Songs of Innocence* and *Songs of Experience,* though not appreciated until some fifty years after his death, contain some of the most beautiful lyrics in the English language.

The greatness of Blake lies less, perhaps, in his apocalyptic outlook than in his mastery, in art and verse, of an extreme and moving simplicity. William Wordsworth commented perceptively on this extraordinary artist and writer when he noted: "There is something in the madness of this man which interests me more than the sanity of Lord Byron or Walter Scott."

The *Songs of Innocence* were first published, with hand-colored illustrations, in 1789. In 1794 Blake added the *Songs of Experience* with the subtitle "Showing the Two Contrary States of the Human Soul." By setting one poem against another on a related theme (for instance, "The Lamb" and "The Tiger"), Blake forces the reader to think about "contrary" truths, the innocent faith of childhood and the facts of suffering and cruelty that an adult must learn to face.

from Songs of Innocence

Introduction

Piping down the valleys wild,
Piping songs of pleasant glee
On a cloud I saw a child,
And he laughing said to me:

"Pipe a song about a Lamb!"   5
So I piped with merry cheer.
"Piper pipe that song again—"
So I piped, he wept to hear.

"Drop thy pipe thy happy pipe
Sing thy songs of happy cheer."   10
So I sung the same again
While he wept with joy to hear.

"Piper sit thee down and write
In a book that all may read—"
So he vanished from my sight,   15
And I plucked a hollow reed,

And I made a rural pen,
And I stained the water clear,
And I wrote my happy songs,
Every child may joy to hear.   20

The Lamb

Little Lamb who made thee
    Dost thou know who made thee?
Gave thee life and bid thee feed,
By the stream and o'er the mead;
Gave thee clothing of delight,   5
Softest clothing, woolly bright;
Gave thee such a tender voice,
Making all the vales rejoice:
    Little Lamb who made thee
    Dost thou know who made thee?   10

    Little Lamb I'll tell thee,
    Little Lamb I'll tell thee;
He is callèd by thy name,
For he calls himself a Lamb:
He is meek and he is mild,   15
He became a little child:
I a child and thou a lamb,
We are callèd by his name.
    Little Lamb God bless thee.
    Little Lamb God bless thee.   20

An illustrated page
from *Songs of Inno-
cence*
(colored engraving) by
William Blake.
The Houghton Library,
Harvard University, The
Department of Printing
and Graphic Arts

The Chimney Sweeper

When my mother died I was very young,
And my father sold me while yet my tongue
Could scarcely cry " 'weep° 'weep 'weep 'weep."
So your chimneys I sweep and in soot I sleep.

There's little Tom Dacre, who cried when his head   5
That curled like a lamb's back, was shaved, so I said,
"Hush Tom never mind it, for when your head's bare,
You know that the soot cannot spoil your white hair."

And so he was quiet, and that very night
As Tom was a-sleeping he had such a sight,   10
That thousands of sweepers, Dick, Joe, Ned and Jack
Were all of them locked up in coffins of black.

And by came an Angel who had a bright key,
And he opened the coffins and set them all free.
Then down a green plain leaping laughing they run   15
And wash in a river and shine in the Sun.

Then naked and white, all their bags left behind,
They rise upon clouds, and sport in the wind.
And the Angel told Tom, if he'd be a good boy,
He'd have God for his father, and never want joy.   20

And so Tom awoke and we rose in the dark
And got with our bags and our brushes to work.
Tho' the morning was cold, Tom was happy and warm.
So if all do their duty, they need not fear harm.

---

3. **'weep:** "sweep," the cry of the chimney sweeper through the street.

from **Songs of Experience**

Introduction

Hear the voice of the Bard!
Who Present, Past, and Future sees
Whose ears have heard
The Holy Word,
That walked among the ancient trees.   5

Calling the lapsed Soul
And weeping in the evening dew:
That might control
The starry pole:
And fallen fallen light renew!   10

"O Earth O Earth return!
Arise from out the dewy grass:
Night is worn,
And the morn
Rises from the slumberous mass.   15

"Turn away no more:
Why wilt thou turn away
The starry floor
The watery shore
Is given thee till the break of day."   20

The Clod and the Pebble

"Love seeketh not itself to please,
Nor for itself hath any care;
But for another gives its ease,
And builds a Heaven in Hell's despair."

So sung a little Clod of Clay,   5
Trodden with the cattle's feet;
But a Pebble of the brook,
Warbled out these meters meet.

"Love seeketh only Self to please,
To bind another to its delight: 10
Joys in another's loss of ease,
And builds a Hell in Heaven's despite."

The Tiger

Tiger Tiger, burning bright,
In the forests of the night;
What immortal hand or eye,
Could frame thy fearful symmetry?

In what distant deeps or skies,   5
Burnt the fire of thine eyes?
On what wings dare he aspire?
What the hand, dare seize the fire?

And what shoulder, and what art,
Could twist the sinews of thy heart?   10
And when thy heart began to beat,
What dread hand? and what dread feet?

What the hammer? what the chain,
In what furnace was thy brain?
What the anvil? what dread grasp,   15
Dare its deadly terrors clasp?

When the stars threw down their spears
And watered heaven with their tears:°
Did he smile his work to see?
Did he who made the Lamb make thee?   20

Tiger Tiger burning bright,
In the forests of the night:
What immortal hand or eye,
Dare frame thy fearful symmetry?

17–18. **When . . . tears:** These lines refer to the angels who fell with Satan, weeping and throwing down their spears after defeat in the war in heaven.

A Poison Tree

I was angry with my friend:
I told my wrath, my wrath did end.
I was angry with my foe:
I told it not, my wrath did grow.

And I watered it in fears,   5
Night and morning with my tears:
And I sunned it with smiles,
And with soft deceitful wiles.

And it grew both day and night,
Till it bore an apple bright.   10
And my foe beheld it shine,
And he knew that it was mine.

And into my garden stole,
When the night had veiled the pole;
In the morning glad I see,   15
My foe outstretched beneath the tree.

An illustrated page from *Songs of Experience*
(colored engraving) by William Blake.
The Houghton Library, Harvard University,
The Department of Printing and Graphic Arts

Ah! Sunflower

Ah Sunflower! weary of time,
Who countest the steps of the Sun:°
Seeking after that sweet golden clime,°
Where the traveler's journey is done.

Where the Youth pined away with desire,
And the pale Virgin shrouded in snow:
Arise from their graves and aspire,°
Where my Sunflower wishes to go.

---

2. **Who countest . . . Sun:** The sunflower, which is
heliotropic, follows the sun across the sky.   3. **clime:**
climate.   7. **aspire:** to soar upward.

COMMENTARY

Though they were conceived independently, the *Songs of Innocence* (1789) should be read in conjunction with the *Songs of Experience* written a few years later. The two groups of lyrics depict, as Blake said in 1794, "the Two Contrary States of the Human Soul," and in many instances they develop opposite points of view toward the same subject matter. The speakers in the *Songs of Innocence* are children or childlike, and the songs express their emotions and their vision. To them the cosmos is one of "Mercy, Pity, Peace, and Love" received and bestowed by all creatures and by their Creator, who himself became a child and is called a Lamb. But if the speakers are innocent in their apprehension, the poems often are not. . . . In "The Chimney Sweeper" the child has been "sold" by his father to be a sweep and he is treated harshly. But with a child's terrible readiness to accept the only world he knows, he does not realize he is wronged, and he is happy. To adult readers, however, this abuse of a child's trust is a searing indictment. . . . The point is not that adults with their longer experience of the world have a truer vision. . . . "The Chimney Sweeper" may also be read as a celebration of the child's imaginative freedom to create the world in which he truly lives. But it may be noted that, as the pastoral imagery of shepherd and flock especially indicates, the imaginative world of the child is one in which he imagines himself to be dependent. While he is actually exercising his creative freedom he does not know it, and he may thus be contrasted with the artist who works in conscious liberty. For this among other reasons, the state of innocence does not represent Blake's final conception of man's highest joy. To attain this, man must go through experience.

— David Perkins
English Romantic Writers

FOR STUDY AND DISCUSSION

1. How would you describe the contrast in tone or mood between the two introductions?
2. Do you agree with this statement: " 'The Lamb' and 'The Tiger' may certainly be contrasted, but the animals should be regarded not as opposite but as different works of the same creation"? What do you think the animals represent? (For example, can you find evidence that the Lamb represents joy and innocence? That the Tiger represents a powerful force defying complete understanding?)
3. What is the central metaphor in "A Poison Tree"? Blake alludes to the Fall of Man in the third stanza, but how does his use of forbidden fruit differ from the Biblical account? Explain the last stanza of the poem. Does the speaker's foe literally die, or is the death figurative and symbolic?
4. Contrast the points of view of the Clod and the Pebble. In what way does this contrast illustrate innocence and experience?
5. In what way is the Sunflower compared and contrasted with the Youth and the Virgin? The Sunflower may symbolize the unending cycle of nature. What aspects of human nature do you think the Youth and the Virgin might represent?

SYMBOLISM

Because a symbol implies a meaning beyond its surface meaning, it can serve both to clarify the idea of a poem and to give it added dimensions. Like a metaphor, a symbol suggests a relationship between two objects. Symbols are often derived from conventional relationships familiar to and readily identifiable by most readers. Night, for example, often symbolizes death or evil; white stands for purity; the owl, for wisdom; the lion, for courage.

Although Blake's lamb and tiger can be thought of as real animals, their function as symbols should be emphasized. The lamb is used as a symbol of the innocence of childhood, the tiger mainly as a symbol of the fearful power of worldly experience. Point out lines in both poems in which the lamb and the tiger are pictured as animals and as symbols.

FOR COMPOSITION

1. Basing your answer on your comprehension of the poems "The Lamb" and "The Tiger," define fully the terms *innocence* and *experience* as you think Blake must have meant his readers to understand them.
2. Briefly discuss Blake's contrary states with specific references to selections in this unit.

The English Novel in
The Eighteenth Century

The novel was a comparatively late arrival in English literature; Italy, Spain, and France produced what we are entitled to call novels long before England did. But once English literature really got hold of the novel, in the 1700's, it became famous for its fiction and influenced writers in many countries.

Daniel Defoe, whose best-known book, *Robinson Crusoe*, appeared in 1719, was an important originator of realism in English fiction. He had to be realistic because while actually creating fiction—though usually with some basis of fact—he was pretending to offer his readers memoirs and autobiographies. In Defoe we have a journalist who was secretly a storyteller of quite remarkable talent. And because his stories had to seem solidly real, he did some valuable pioneer work for English fiction. His best characters, after his famous shipwrecked sailor, are raffish types like Moll Flanders and Captain Singleton.

Four English novelists came to prominence during the thirty-year period from 1740 to 1770: Samuel Richardson, Henry Fielding, Laurence Sterne, and Tobias Smollett. After Richardson, a retired printer, was commissioned to do a book of letters that readers could use as samples, he contrived a novel in the form of letters about a virtuous serving girl, Pamela Andrews, who repulsed her master until he consented to marry her. Though *Pamela, or Virtue Rewarded* (1740) is often referred to as the first English novel, it was Richardson's second and much longer novel, *Clarissa*, also written in letter form, that became the rage not only in England but all over the Continent. This narrative-in-letters method is entirely unreal, at least as Richardson used it (for his chief characters would be spending twelve hours a day writing letters). However, it has the great advantage, which Richardson made use of very artfully, of giving in turn everybody's points of view, thoughts, feelings, hopes, and fears.

Henry Fielding came from an old landed family, lived riotously, and then took to writing to earn a living, finally becoming a city magistrate—a very good one too. Fielding detested Richardson, whose work he burlesqued in *Shamela* (1741) and then in *The Adventures of Joseph Andrews* (1742). Fielding's masterpiece is *The History of Tom Jones* (1749), which is both a magnificent panorama of eighteenth-century life and the expression, unusual in the novel, of a powerful intellect, quick to observe all the ironies, absurdities, and hypocrisies of social life.

Laurence Sterne was enormously popular in his own time. His highly original method, ruthlessly cutting out everything that is not essential to our understanding of a character and a situation, is very "modern," like his extremely artful, intimate, and conversational style. His humor is "modern" too. *Tristram Shandy* (1760), his masterpiece, is a wonderful study of a family in which nobody understands anybody else.

Tobias Smollett, a Scot who had been a surgeon's mate in the navy, wrote long novels crammed with rough humor and knockabout incidents. His masterpiece, *The Expedition of Humphry Clinker* (1771), appeared shortly before his death. He had a very solid reputation for some fifty years after his death and had considerable influence upon Dickens in Dickens' earlier years.

One other figure needs to be included in this period. Oliver Goldsmith wrote only one novel, *The Vicar of Wakefield* (1766), which has been much admired for its humor and sentiment. After Goldsmith, there are no memorable novelists until the appearance of Jane Austen and Sir Walter Scott, whose major work falls in the nineteenth century.

The Restoration and Eighteenth Century

When we come to the prose of the late seventeenth century, we find the kind of sentence structure and paragraph organization that we are accustomed to in modern writing. The English had developed a sparse and sinuous style, easy and natural, closely resembling speech. T. S. Eliot attributed this development largely to Dryden's influence: "It's hardly too much to say that Dryden found the English speechless and he gave them speech." Except for a few words and idioms that are no longer current, the selection from Dryden's *Essay of Dramatic Poesy* (page 312) might almost have been written in the twentieth century.

The Royal Society was in part responsible for these changes in style. The Society, which began as a scientific and philosophical discussion group, came to interest itself in the English language. As the existence of the Society encouraged a great deal of scientific writing in English, it also provided an opportunity for members to discuss one another's scientific prose.

That the members of the Royal Society saw room for improvement in their prose is clear from the fact that in 1664, two years after the chartering of the Society, they set up a committee "to improve the English tongue, particularly for philosophic [that is, scientific] purposes." Dryden and several other eminent writers were among those who were appointed to the committee. The idea of forming such a committee had undoubtedly been suggested by the example of the French Academy, a group of French writers and critics that had been organized earlier in the seventeenth century for the purpose of improving the French language. The Academy was working on a French dictionary and also planned to compile treatises on French grammar, rhetoric, and poetics. The Royal Society's committee considered similar projects—a dictionary (there were no English dictionaries at that time, except for a few books that gave definitions of unusual words and technical terms), a grammar, a set of reformed spelling rules, a collection of translations from classical literature that could serve as models of elegant style for aspiring writers, and so forth.

For better or for worse, however, the committee made no headway on any of these projects and soon dissolved. Many people feel that this was just as well: the subsequent history of English literature might have been quite different if the committee had become a permanent body that insisted on dictating rules of style and usage to the country's writers.

The reform in English prose style that the committee had hoped to accomplish did come about, but it did so through the effort and example of individual writers. In striving to make their own writing clear, Dryden and other writers of his generation arrived at a kind of prose that was admired and imitated by succeeding generations.

During most of the eighteenth century, the English were strongly concerned with rules, form, and "correctness" in the use of language. The century began with a revival of interest in the idea of establishing an English Academy. Several leading writers of the time—including Defoe, Addison, and Swift—were interested in seeing such an Academy founded, and they wrote articles giving urgent reasons why it was needed.

Swift's ideas on the subject were especially influential. He wanted to see the language improved—but he wanted even more to see it protected from further change. "What I have most at heart," he wrote, "is, that some method be thought on for ascertaining and fixing our language forever . . . For I am of opinion, it is better a language should not be wholly perfect, than that it should be perpetually changing."

This attitude was notably different from the attitude that had been expressed in the Royal Society's resolution in 1664. The members of the Royal Society had taken it for granted that language changed, but they had not wanted to halt this process—on the contrary, they had wanted to encourage further development. What accounted for the change in opinion that had taken place by the beginning of the eighteenth century? For one thing, the English no longer felt that their own language was inferior to others (particularly Latin) for purposes of serious writing. But there was an even more important reason why Swift and his contemporaries feared further changes in the language. They were keenly aware that a great national literature had been produced in England during the past century and a half, and they were afraid that if the language kept on changing, soon all of this literature would be dead and lost. Alexander Pope expressed this conviction in *An Essay on Criticism*, where he said:

Short is the date, alas! of modern rhymes . . .
Our sons their fathers' failing language see,
And such as Chaucer is shall Dryden be.

Of course, we know that Pope's gloomy prediction about the future of the language has not come true. Approximately three centuries have now passed since the time that Dryden wrote, and Dryden's language—except for an occasional word or two—is still as clear to twentieth-century readers as it was to readers of Dryden's own day.

But why is it that Pope and Swift turned out to be wrong about the path of development that the language was following? One answer is that these men had no way of estimating the powerful influence that the written form of the language was coming to exert. Until the end of the Middle Ages, the written language had never had much effect on the kind of English that was used by the population as a whole—simply because most people had not been able to read or write. The introduction of the printing press in 1485 changed this situation by making inexpensive reading matter widely available. By Shakespeare's time, a century after the introduction of printing, probably about half the population of London could read and write. By the time of Pope and Swift, the literacy rate for the middle and upper classes in England was close to 100 percent.

Instead of being exposed only to the English spoken by their own circle of acquaintances, people were now being exposed continually to English that had been written by professional writers. Since the standard written form of the language was regarded as the "best" form or the "correct" form, educated people tended to give up local usages which differed from standard usage. Thus the influence of the written language acted to curb changes that might otherwise have taken wide hold in the spoken language.

The fact that the basic grammatical system and the basic vocabulary of English have not changed essentially since 1700 does not mean, however, that no changes at all have taken place. While the influence of the written language tends to keep old words and expressions from dropping out of the language, it also speeds the acceptance of new words and expressions. A new term that appears in a few newspaper and magazine articles can become part of the vocabulary of millions of people within a matter of days. Thus today's English vocabulary is indeed different from the vocabulary of Swift's time, but the difference is due almost entirely to the addition of new words and new meanings —not, as Swift had feared, to decay and loss of the old words.

FOR STUDY AND DISCUSSION

1. In Dryden's *Essay of Dramatic Poesy* there are a few words that are used in senses no longer common today. Using a college dictionary or an unabridged dictionary, look up the first three words that are footnoted on page 312 *want(ed)*, *clench(es)*, and *wit*. Does the dictionary give definitions that fit the senses in which these words were used by Dryden?

2. Some dictionaries arrange definitions in chronological order, giving the earliest meaning first. Other dictionaries arrange definitions in order of frequency, giving the most common meaning first. If your dictionary has a definition for *want* that fits Dryden's use of the word, is this one of the first definitions given for the word, or does it come later in the list? Judging from this clue, what kind of arrangement does your dictionary follow — chronological order or order of frequency?

3. Although Defoe's *Journal of the Plague Year* pretended to be an eyewitness account written by a Londoner of the 1660's, an observant reader could probably tell that the language of the *Journal* resembled the language of the 1720's much more than it did the language of the 1660's. Following are two short excerpts from Samuel Pepys's diary, which really was written in the 1660's, and two matching excerpts from Defoe's *Journal*. By looking at the italicized expressions, you should be able to tell which excerpt in each pair is by Pepys and which is by Defoe. Remember that Defoe's language is likely to be closer to modern speech.

a. (1) "I *did ask* him where he learned that immodest garb . . ."
   (2) "I *asked* how long it had lain there . . ."
b. (1) "they *did not know*"
   (2) "so as we *know not* . . ."

4. Another kind of language change that was not very much affected by the influence of the written language was change in pronunciation. Evidence that many changes in pronunciation have taken place during the past two hundred and fifty years can be found by examining the rhymes in an early eighteenth-century poem such as Pope's *Rape of the Lock* (page 350). Since "half-rhymes" were frowned on, we can assume that the following two couplets both ended with full rhymes according to Pope's pronunciation:

Here Britain's statesmen oft the fall foredoom
Of foreign tyrants and of nymphs at home . . .

At omber singly to decide their doom:
And swells her breast with conquests yet to come . . .

What can you conclude about the pronunciation of *doom, home,* and *come* in the early eighteenth century? Can you find other couplets in this poem containing rhyme words that no longer rhyme today?

What word in Blake's "The Tiger" would have to be pronounced differently to rhyme exactly in its couplet?

The Romantic Age
1798–1832

The Bard (detail, 1817) by John Martin.
Laing Art Gallery

"ROMANTICISM" AS A PERIOD AND A CONCEPT

The beginning of the Romantic Age in English literature is usually set in 1798, the year in which William Wordsworth and Samuel Taylor Coleridge published a book of their poems called *Lyrical Ballads*. The Romantic Age traditionally ends in 1832, with the death of Sir Walter Scott and the passage of the First Reform Bill in Parliament. Of course, these beginning and ending dates are not absolute. The literary concerns characteristic of Romanticism began to emerge early in the eighteenth century, and in altered form they extend through the Victorian era and into the twentieth century. We must also remember that Romanticism is a European, not just an English, development. In Germany, Romanticism established itself during the 1790's even more strongly than in England. In France, the

Jean Jacques Rousseau, father of Romanticism, by Allan Ramsay.
Lauros, Giraudon

great developments of Romantic literature and art were delayed for a time by the French Revolution and the Napoleonic Wars. Yet the French Revolution itself was the most significant historical event of the Romantic period, and a Swiss-born writer and philosopher who spent most of his life in France, Jean Jacques Rousseau (1712–1778), was the most important eighteenth-century influence on later European Romanticism.

More will be said later about these various determinants of the Romantic Age. But before looking at the main features of this period, we had better think for a moment about the words *Romantic* and *Romanticism*. The names we apply to broad periods of literary and cultural history can often be misleading, and this is especially true of the "Romantic" Age and "Romanticism." The word *romance* originally referred to highly imaginative medieval tales of knightly adventure written in the French derivative of the original *Roman* (or *romance*) language, Latin. (That these tales often involved amorous encounters between a knight and his lady is partly responsible for the modern meanings of *romance* and *romantic*.) When we speak of the "Romantic Age," we are using the word *romantic* in this older sense. We are referring indirectly to an interest in the charming, magical world of medieval "romance," and more generally to the rich imaginative activity displayed in that world, which is deeply characteristic of late eighteenth- and early nineteenth-century writers. To avoid confusion, we should remember that "romance" as "freely imaginative idealizing fiction," and not "romance" as "love between men and women," is the true basis for the terms "Romantic Age" and "Romanticism."

The chief characteristics of the Romantic Age are usually defined by contrast with those of the eighteenth century—the Age of Swift, Pope, and Johnson. Eighteenth-century writers stressed reason and judgment; Romantic writers emphasized imagination and emotion. Eighteenth-century writers were characteristically concerned with the general or universal in experience; Romantic writers were concerned with the particular. Eighteenth-century writers asserted the values of society as a whole; Romantic writers championed the value of the individual human being. Eighteenth-century writers sought to follow and to substantiate authority and the rules derived from authority; Romantic writers strove for freedom. Eighteenth-century writers took their primary inspiration from classical Greek and Roman authors; Romantic writers took a revitalized interest, as we have already seen, in medieval subjects and settings. These contrasts provide a useful way of approaching the Romantic Age, in part because most Romantic writers saw themselves as reacting against the thought and literary practice of the preceding century. Such contrasts can help put us in touch with what William Hazlitt and other

George III (detail)

Battle of Trafalgar

The Slave Ship (detail), J. M. W. Turner

1798 1800 **George III 1760–1820**

Lyrical Ballads 1798

Battle of Trafalgar 1805

Eve of St. Agnes 1820

Frankenstein 1818

1820

Essays of Elia 1820–1823

Shelley's
Defence of Poetry 1821

George IV 1820–1830

Samuel T. Coleridge

Mary Shelley (detail)

John Keats (detail)

The Royal Pavilion at Brighton

Lord Byron (detail)

Jane Austen

1810   **Regency Period 1811–1820**

Wordsworth's *Poems
in Two Volumes* 1807

Abolition of slave trade
1807

Childe Harold's Pilgrimage 1812

Biographia Literaria 1817

Pride and Prejudice 1813

Battle of Waterloo 1815

First Reform Bill 1832

Reform of the Poor Law 1834

1830   **William IV 1830–1837**   **1837**

Charles Lamb (detail)

Percy B. Shelley (detail)

George IV (detail)

William IV (detail)

Romantic writers called "the Spirit of the Age"—a shared sense of liberated energy and fresh departure similar in some respects to what we find in the Renaissance. Hazlitt spoke of "a time of promise, a renewal of the world—and of letters." Percy Bysshe Shelley claimed in his *Defence of Poetry* that the literature of the age "has arisen as it were from a new birth."

We must be careful, of course, not to exaggerate the generalized contrasts between the Romantic Age and the eighteenth century, or to take too literally the more exuberant and sweeping claims of Hazlitt and Shelley at their most confident. The early nineteenth century was indeed a period of enormous literary energy in England. The size of the reading public had increased rapidly during the eighteenth century. By the beginning of the nineteenth century, the number of readers who would buy Lord Byron's most recent book of poems, or Sir Walter Scott's latest novel, was much larger than ever before. Writers like Hazlitt and Coleridge gave public lectures that were attended by large audiences. Despite this trend, most Romantic writers felt that they were not understood or appreciated by their readers, that their values were not those accepted by English society as a whole. The Romantic Age is diverse and complex. To appreciate fully the achievements of this period, we need to examine the main political and social realities of these years, and to look more closely at the specific ideas and practices of writers who were far too individualistic ever to subordinate themselves to anything like a Romantic "school" or "movement."

THE HISTORICAL BACKGROUND: REVOLUTION AND REACTION

The eighteenth century was a time of great prosperity and confidence for England—at least for the upper and middle classes. Toward the end of the century, however, two major political revolutions disturbed the English sense of security and well-being. Although both revolutions occurred outside England and left the basic values and structures of English society unchanged for the moment, they nevertheless had a powerful effect on late eighteenth- and early nineteenth-century thinking in England. First, there was the revolt by the English colonies in America against the economic and political control of the mother country. The victory of the American movement for independence was certainly a blow to English confidence, but practically and philosophically it was less threatening than the second revolution, which took place in France in 1789. In practical political terms, the English could see in the French Revolution not merely a rejection of authority and control by a distant and as yet disorganized group of colonies, but a complete overthrow of the government of a great European power *from within*. Philosophically, the French Revolution seemed to signal the victory of even more radical democratic principles than those enunciated in the American Declaration of Independence.

In England the Crown and the ruling classes feared the effects of the French Revolution from the beginning. But English liberals and radicals, who themselves had been calling for the democratization of English society, saw in the early stages of the French Revolution – in the Declaration of the Rights of Man and in the storming of the Bastille on July 14, 1789, to release imprisoned political prisoners – a triumph of popular democracy. Among the enthusiastic supporters of the Revolution in its early stages were writers who would play a central role in English Romanticism. Wordsworth visited France during the summer of 1790 and was filled with hope and excitement as the country celebrated the first anniversary of the fall of the Bastille. William Godwin (1756–1836), a philosopher and novelist who exerted considerable influence on Wordsworth, Shelley, and other Romantic poets, predicted in *An Enquiry Concerning Political Justice* (1793) a peaceful version in England of what appeared to be happening in France. In *The Spirit of the Age,* Hazlitt said that the French Revolution seemed at first to announce that "a new impulse had been given to men's minds."

But the promise and expectation aroused by the early years of the Revolution in France soon gave way to bitter disappointment as events took an increasingly violent and repressive course. When revolutionary extremists gained control of the government in 1792, they executed hundreds of the imprisoned nobility in what came to be known as the "September Massacres." The year 1793 saw the execution of King Louis XVI and the establishment under Robespierre of the Reign of Terror, during which thousands of those associated with the old regime were guillotined. Most disturbing of all, perhaps, was the invasion of the Rhineland and the Netherlands by the army of the French Republic, and the French offer of armed assistance to all countries desiring to overthrow their present governments. Then, after savage reprisals against those who had held power during the Reign of Terror, Napoleon emerged as dictator, and eventually as emperor of France. Once a champion of the Revolution, Napoleon became a tyrannical despot who strove to conquer Europe and establish a new dynasty.

The reaction in England to these events in France was predictable. Even the most ardent supporters of the Revolution were left in disillusionment and despair. As Wordsworth expressed it in his greatest poem, *The Prelude:*

Frenchmen had changed a war of self-defense
For one of conquest, losing sight of all
Which they had struggled for . . . .

As for the government and the ruling classes, their fear of the Revolution was hardened into severe repressive measures at home against all those who sympathized with democratic ideals or reform, and into determined military opposition abroad against Napoleon's imperial army. (His navy had been destroyed by Lord Nelson at the Battle of Trafalgar in 1805.) Although emperor, with unlimited powers, Napoleon was in some respects still a man of the French Revolution, inheriting some of its liberating ideas, which were already triumphant in America. The Whigs in Britain recognized this fact and were in favor of trying to come to terms with Napoleon. But the Tories, who saw in him a threat to their political and social system, carried the country. The final defeat of Napoleon in 1815 at the Battle of Waterloo was cause for triumphant celebration by the conservative forces that ruled England during these years. But for some of the disillusioned English, such as Shelley and Byron, who had sympathized with the ideals of the French Revolution, Waterloo marked the defeat of one despotic power by another. Far from showing the way to democratic progress and reform, the French Revolution seemed to them to have consolidated the power of the wealthy and reactionary ruling classes.

General Bonaparte (sketch) by Jacques Louis David.
Clichés Musées Nationaux, Paris

THE INDUSTRIAL REVOLUTION

During these years of violent political revolution and reaction, another revolution was taking place throughout European society. This was the Industrial Revolution — the shift during the eighteenth and nineteenth centuries from hand labor to new methods of manufacturing made possible by power-driven machines. Though less sudden and obvious in its consequences than the political revolutions in America and France, the Industrial Revolution was ultimately more important in transforming European society, and in its own way more violent in its impact on human life. It was in England that the Industrial Revolution had its earliest and most substantial foundation. James Watt, an Englishman, perfected the steam engine in 1765. Soon many industries that had previously depended on traditional hand labor were converted to mills and factories where machines did the work, and where workers came to serve the machines.

The Industrial Revolution in England marks the beginning of our modern era, and it produced profound economic and social changes with which the existing principles and structures of government were totally unable to deal. Important cities in central and northern England that had previously been stable and orderly centers of skilled labor developed into sprawling, dirty industrial cities. Working and living conditions in these cities were terrible: women and children as well as men labored for long hours under intolerable conditions, for wages that were barely enough to keep them alive. Reports were not uncommon of young children being harnessed to coal-sledges and made to crawl on their hands and knees in the mines. Workers had no vote and were prevented by law from forming labor unions. When they turned in despair to petitions and meetings of protest, they were ruthlessly suppressed. One such occasion, in St. Peter's Fields, Manchester, in the summer of 1819, came to be known as the ''Peterloo Massacre,'' and it provoked a poem of satirical and visionary protest by Shelley called *The Mask of Anarchy*. To

Rain, Steam and Speed, The Great Western Railway by J. M. W. Turner. For many, the railroad was a romantic vision of the future.

feed the growing and increasingly urbanized populations, new systems of agriculture developed that required the enclosure and private ownership of lands formerly left open for communal cultivation and grazing. As a result, even more people were forced off the land and into the already crowded cities. More than ever before, England was sharply divided into two classes: a wealthy class of property owners who held economic and political power, and a poor class of wage earners deprived of virtually all rights and possessions.

The government's response to the changes brought about by the Industrial Revolution was guided by a policy of noninterference known as *laissez faire*—"allow to do." According to this belief, only the unhampered operation of economic laws (such as "supply and demand") would result in wealth and prosperity sufficient to secure the welfare of the country. Thus, very little was done by government to control and to organize the economic forces and social changes unleashed by the coming of the industrial age. The most decisive acts were those taken against the workers' demands for better conditions, and against those liberal or radical reformers who, the government thought, went too far in urging social change.

England suffered during these years from a serious lack of effective leadership. King George III, who had held the throne since 1760, was declared incurably insane in 1811. England was then ruled until 1820 by his son, the Prince of Wales, who acted as Regent. The years of the Regency were a time of lavish social display and indulgence by the upper classes in London and by the aristocratic families living in their great country houses in the provinces. Most of those who held power paid little attention to the alterations in English life or to the hardships of the working class.

Basically, then, the Romantic Age was a time of vast and largely unguided political and economic change. Most of the writers of this period were deeply affected by the promise and subsequent disappointment of the French Revolution, and by the contorting effects of the Industrial Revolution. In many ways, both direct and indirect, we can see the historical issues we have just been surveying reflected in the main literary concerns of Romantic writers. Much as the French Revolution signaled an attempt to break with the old order and to establish a new and revitalized social system, Romanticism sought to free itself from the rules and standards of eighteenth-century literature and to open up new areas of vision and expression. The democratic idealism and insistence on the rights and dignity of the individual, which characterized the early stages of the French Revolution, have their parallel in the Romantic writers'

The Royal Pavilion at Brighton (engraving) designed by John Nash for the Prince Regent.
Culver Pictures

interest in the language and experience of the common people, and in the belief that writers or artists must be free to explore their own imaginative worlds. The main consequences of the Industrial Revolution—the urbanization of English life and landscape, and the exploitation of the working class—underlie the Romantic writers' love of the unspoiled natural world or remote settings devoid of urban complexity, and their passionate concern for the downtrodden and the oppressed.

The main historical changes of the Romantic Age in England were not met with any serious political action until 1832. In this year Parliament passed the First Reform Bill, which extended the vote to more (but by no means to all) citizens, curtailed the political privileges of the aristocracy, and redistributed parliamentary representation. But 1832, as we have seen, is the year that traditionally marks the end of the Romantic Age. Historically, therefore, this is a time of soaring aspiration and bitter disappointment, rather than of progress and achievement. Yet in Romantic literature it is often the very expression of aspiration and disappointment that constitutes literary achievement.

William Wordsworth
(pencil drawing, 1805) by
Henry Edridge.
The Granger Collection

WORDSWORTH, COLERIDGE, AND THE FOUNDATIONS OF ENGLISH ROMANTIC POETRY

The Romantic Age in England began with perhaps the greatest act of collaboration in all of English literature. William Wordsworth (1770–1850) was a young man from the Lake District in the extreme northwest of England. He had been educated at Cambridge and had lived for a time in France, where he experienced both the bright hopes and the dark disillusionment of the French Revolution. Samuel Taylor Coleridge (1772–1834) came from a somewhat different background. Although born in Devonshire in southwest England, he attended school in London from the age of ten. He too had gone to Cambridge, but he left twice without taking a degree because he found the university atmosphere confining and uninteresting. Wordsworth and Coleridge were both leading disillusioned and somewhat aimless lives when they met in 1795. Their companionship gave both of them a new sense of purpose. Coleridge had already found signs of genius in Wordsworth's early poetry, which he read while still an undergraduate at Cambridge. Once he got to know Wordsworth personally and to read more of his work, he proclaimed him "the best poet of the age." The two men met almost daily, talking about poetry and working together on poems that would reflect their new ideas about what poetry should be. The result of this mutually inspiring collaboration was the first edition of *Lyrical Ballads,* published in 1798. A second edition was published in 1800, to which was added an extensive preface, written by Wordsworth but planned in close consultation with Coleridge.

There is no better introduction to English Romanticism than a careful study of the poetic practice and principles of *Lyrical Ballads.* In the various editions of this collection, Wordsworth and Coleridge announce and demonstrate fundamental changes in both the form and the subject matter of English poetry. It is important not to oversimplify the basic literary aims of *Lyrical Ballads,* or of English Romantic poetry in general. These aims are best understood, in fact, not as single, unvarying literary rules or standards, but as ideals that often embrace opposing or contrasting values. As Coleridge himself would later argue in his volume of literary musings, *Biographia Literaria* (1817), the power of the poetic imagination "reveals itself in the balance or reconciliation of opposite or discordant qualities."

As for the verbal form or style of poetry, Wordsworth makes it clear in the Preface to *Lyrical Ballads* that he and Coleridge were trying to leave behind the specialized, formal language of eighteenth-century poetry—what Wordsworth calls "poetic diction." Instead, Wordsworth says, his poems in *Lyrical Ballads* are experimental attempts to fit "to metrical arrangement a selection of the real language of men in a state of vivid sensation." The most memorable phrase here is "the real language of men." Wordsworth and other Romantic writers wanted to draw upon the expressive power of ordinary speech, instead of relying automatically upon an artificial, uniquely "poetic" way of using language. But Wordsworth did not naively believe that the language of poetry could ever be a direct imitation of the language of the man in the street or the worker in the field. He says, you will notice, that "the real language of men" must be *selected* by the poet, that it must be fitted "to metrical arrangement," and that it must be taken from "men in a state of vivid sensation." Thus we have the contrasting elements in Wordsworth's stylistic ideal: "real language" on the one hand, and its selection and transformation by the poet's mind and craft on the other.

Wordsworth and Coleridge also announce and demonstrate significant changes in the subject matter of poetry in *Lyrical Ballads.* Here, to begin with, we need to consider a certain division of labor in the composition of the poems in this collection. Wordsworth's main aim, he tells us in the Preface, was "to choose incidents and situations from common life." "Humble and rustic life was generally chosen," he goes on to explain, "because in that condition the essential passions of the heart find a better soil in which they can attain their maturity, are less under restraint, and speak a plainer and more emphatic language." This preference for the experiences and situations of the common people, particularly of those living close to nature in the country, away from the complexity and contamination of sophisticated urban existence, is one of the chief characteristics of Romanticism.

But the first poem in *Lyrical Ballads* is Coleridge's "The Rime of the Ancient Mariner," a work hardly corresponding to the sort of poetry Wordsworth describes in the Preface. Once again we may turn to Coleridge's *Biographia Literaria* for an account of how his role in *Lyrical Ballads* was mainly to explore another and quite different type of Romantic subject matter. "My endeavors," he says, were "directed to persons and characters supernatural, or at least romantic; yet so as to transfer from our inward nature a human interest and a semblance of truth sufficient to procure for these shadows of imagination that willing suspension of disbelief . . . which constitutes poetic faith." In other words, the reader willingly cooperates with the poet by giving up the need for literal truth.

We have in the plan of *Lyrical Ballads,* then, two favorite kinds of Romantic subjects: the natural or commonplace, and the supernatural or "romantic" (notice how Coleridge uses the word here). These kinds of subjects at first appear to be the very opposites of each other. But what Wordsworth and Coleridge are striving for is similar: to reveal what Wordsworth calls "the essential passions of the heart," and what Coleridge calls "our inward nature." Natural and commonplace, supernatural and romantic—both kinds of subjects are treated so as to make us aware of the basic operations of the human mind and human emotions.

Another important characteristic of the subject matter of Romantic literature proclaimed in *Lyrical Ballads* is the intense love of nature. Wordsworth, we are often told, is the greatest of all the Romantic "nature poets," and it is true that in both theory and practice the physical universe takes on a new significance in his writing. He speaks in the Preface of his interest in "the beautiful and permanent forms of nature," and the greatest of his poems in *Lyrical Ballads,* "Lines Composed a Few Miles Above Tintern Abbey," is one of the finest expressions in English poetry of the power and value of the natural world. But what really interests Wordsworth and other Romantic writers is not nature for its own sake, but nature as it affects the human mind and personality. He directs his attention toward rustic life because "in that condition *the passions of men are incorporated with* the beautiful and permanent forms of nature." Again and again in Wordsworth's poetry, and in that of his fellow Romantics, it is this relationship between the mind and the natural

The Bard by John Martin. The Romantic painters sought out the spectacular aspects of nature. The bard stood for vision and imagination.

Laing Art Gallery, Tyne and Wear County Museums

world that is the central focus. It is the mind of the poet, or of the figure in the poem through whom the poet expresses himself, that constitutes the ultimate subject for the Romantic writer, whether that mind is understood in relation to the actual physical universe or in relation to a mysterious, supernatural fiction.

Another aspect of Romantic subject matter is the concern with the poet's own life, emotions, and subjective experience. Wordsworth's very definition of poetry in the Preface to *Lyrical Ballads* confirms this emphasis on subjective emotion and personal experience. "All good poetry," he says, "is the spontaneous overflow of powerful feelings." For the Romantic writer, poetry must be based ultimately on the poet's own feelings and responses. It cannot be based on values or subjects derived primarily from books, or from society, or from abstract scientific reasoning. Wordsworth goes on to elaborate his definition in a famous passage: "I have said that poetry is the spontaneous overflow of powerful feelings: it takes its origin from emotion recollected in tranquillity. . . ." It is clear from what Wordsworth says here that sheer immediate emotion or "powerful feelings" is not enough for the poet. Emotion, once experienced, must be "recollected in tranquillity" or "contemplated," as Wordsworth goes on to say. Romantic poetry has its origin in strong and spontaneous personal feeling; but only when this feeling is given shape and organization by the reflective mind and adapted to the structures of language can it enter into poetry.

One final point that Wordsworth considers in the Preface to *Lyrical Ballads* is of major importance for Romanticism as a whole. This concerns the status of the poet in relation to the rest of humanity. Wordsworth has said that the poet uses "the real language of men," not a specialized poetic diction, and that he draws his subjects from "common life." This ideal may be appealingly democratic, but if it is true, what distinguishes a poet from anyone else? In trying to answer this question, Wordsworth preserves the democratic belief so important to Romanticism, while at the same time acknowledging an equally important Romantic belief in the uncommon sensitivity of the individual poet. A poet does not differ "in kind from other men," he says, "but only in degree." The poet "is chiefly distinguished from other men by a greater promptness to think and feel without immediate external excitement, and a greater power in expressing such thoughts and feelings as are produced in him in that manner." Once again we see that the Romantic attitude involves a "balance or reconciliation" of apparent opposites—in this case, democratic idealism on the one hand (the poet is just one person speaking to others in their own language), and heroic individualism on the other (each poet is gifted with unique powers of feeling and expression).

THE SECOND GENERATION OF ENGLISH ROMANTICS: BYRON, SHELLEY, AND KEATS

The poetic ideals announced by Wordsworth and Coleridge, and even more their actual poetic practice, provided a major inspiration for the brilliant young writers who make up the second generation of English Romantic poets. These poets were all precocious and intense, and had tragically short lives. In fact Wordsworth and Coleridge, although fifteen to twenty years older than Byron, Shelley, and Keats, long outlived them. The difference in age between the two generations is significant. Wordsworth and Coleridge both became more conservative politically after the democratic idealism and revolutionary fervor of their early years. The younger Romantics, particularly Byron and Shelley, felt the founders of English Romanticism had given in to the values of an unjust and reactionary society. Artistic admiration toward Wordsworth and Coleridge on the part of the second generation was mixed, therefore, with moral and political disillusionment. In a sense, however, this disillusionment may have left the younger Romantics free to develop their own artistic interests in a way that a more complete allegiance to Wordsworth and Coleridge would not have.

Although extremely different in personality and artistic temperament, George Gordon, Lord Byron (1788–1824) and Percy Bysshe Shelley (1792–1822) exhibit several striking similarities. Both were born into aristocratic families and attended prestigious private schools and universities; both eventually left England because of savage social pressures against their unconventional personal lives; both died prematurely in distant Mediterranean countries. Byron and Shelley came to be seen by their contemporaries—and to see themselves—as types of the outcast, alienated Romantic artist, whose refusal to compromise and live by the accepted norms of society results in isolation and suffering. Their poetic careers, however, were quite different. Before leaving England in 1815, Byron had become the most celebrated poet not only in England, but in all Europe. His long, romantic travel poem, *Childe Harold's Pilgrimage*, and his sensational, exotic verse narratives captured an enormous audience. Even *Don Juan*, his great satirical epic, written entirely after he had left England, was a popular success. Shelley's poetry, on the other hand, was never popular and was often misunderstood. Shelley himself realized that the philosophical difficulty and stylistic experimentation of some of his most ambitious work lay outside the interest and ability of many readers. Even when he attempted to make a direct impact on English opinion with his revolutionary and utopian political ideals, Shelley's intellectualism and imaginative daring sometimes got in the way of successful communication. Then, as now, the most widely appreciated of his poems were the shorter, intensely subjective lyrics.

John Keats (1795–1821) was the youngest of the second generation of English Romantic poets, and the first to die. His poetic career was perhaps the most richly promising in all English literature. Almost all his greatest poems—"The Eve of St. Agnes," the six magnificent odes, "Lamia," some of his finest sonnets—were written between January and September of 1819, when he was twenty-four years old, and when his remarkable poetic genius had just begun to realize itself. But he was stricken with tuberculosis in February of 1820 and died, in Rome, a year later. Although he left behind some of the most fully achieved poems ever written in English, Keats's early death deprived the Romantic Age of a talent that might have gone on to attain Shakespearean stature.

ROMANTIC PROSE: THE ESSAY AND THE NOVEL

Poetry was the major form of literary expression in England during the Romantic Age. The drama did not thrive in this period. Byron, Shelley, and other Romantic writers wrote "closet dramas"—poems in dramatic form that were never intended to be staged—but of the plays actually written for the theater, only Coleridge's *Remorse* and Shelley's *The Cenci* could be called successful. Romantic prose, on the other hand, contains many works of lasting importance. Two forms in particular, the familiar essay and the novel, underwent significant developments during this period.

The eighteenth century had been a time of great liveliness for the essay in English writing. The favorite type had been established early in the century by Joseph Addison and Richard Steele in the *Tatler* and the *Spectator:* brief, witty, instructive, filled with caricatures drawn from London life, and addressed to sophisticated readers from the leisure class. At the beginning of the nineteenth century, however, new types of journals and magazines began to appear, encouraging longer, more varied, and more personal essays from talented writers who were very well paid for their efforts. Perhaps the most interesting of all the new periodicals was the *London Magazine,* which began publication in 1820. Although its career was relatively short (publication ceased in 1829), the *London Magazine* included among its contributors the three greatest essayists of the Romantic Age: Charles Lamb (1775–1834), William Hazlitt (1778–

1830), and Thomas De Quincey (1785–1859). Brilliantly entertaining and moving in their own right, the essays of these three writers also offer us the best access we have to the quality of daily life and to the dominant personalities and cultural forces of the period.

Gothic novels, which had appeared on the scene during the late eighteenth century, became a popular form of fiction during the Romantic period. These novels were characteristically set in dark, mysterious castles amid an atmosphere of terror and gloom. A few well-known examples of this literary type are Horace Walpole's *The Castle of Otranto* (1764) and Ann Radcliffe's *The Mysteries of Udolpho* (1794) and *The Italian* (1797). In this tradition is Mary Shelley's famous *Frankenstein* (1818).

Mary Wollstonecraft Shelley, Percy Bysshe Shelley's second wife, was a novelist and travel writer whose mother, Mary Godwin, wrote *A Vindication of the Rights of Woman* (1792). National Portrait Gallery, London

The Romantic Age produced two novelists of the highest order: Jane Austen (1775–1817) and Sir Walter Scott (1771–1832). No two novelists could be more different. With her precisely controlled sense of order and her witty observation of a small segment of contemporary society, Jane Austen's novels seem to belong more to the eighteenth than to the nineteenth century. The concerns we normally think of as characteristic of Romantic writers enter her novels only with a subtle and often ironic indirectness. Scott, on the other hand, has been for many readers the very epitome of the Romantic novelist. A keen student of the remote past, particularly of his native Scotland, Scott gave his long, panoramic novels carefully detailed historical settings and atmosphere. Character and plot are rooted in history to a degree that is genuinely innovative. Yet Scott wrote in a mode that he himself called "romance," "the interest of which turns upon marvelous and uncommon incidents." This blend of the historically detailed and the marvelous made Scott, along with Byron, the most internationally famous of all the English Romantics.

The year in which Scott died, 1832, is commonly taken to mark the end of the Romantic period; certainly with Queen Victoria's accession to the throne in 1837, England entered a new phase in its cultural and literary history. But the importance for the Victorians of the great Romantic writers—of Scott and Byron, of Coleridge and Wordsworth (the latter lived on until 1850)—cannot be overestimated. The Romantic concern with the dignity, freedom, and creative potential of the human mind in a world that was becoming increasingly complicated and alien continued to be a major concern of Victorian writers. And it remains, of course, a major concern for us today.

William Wordsworth
1770–1850

William Wordsworth was born and grew up in the Lake District, the beautiful area of mountains, lakes, and streams near the Scottish border in northwest England. The natural beauty and grandeur of this area was a major source of inspiration for Wordsworth throughout his life. His family lived in the small town of Cockermouth in West Cumberland. His mother died when he was eight, and Wordsworth was sent to school at Hawkshead, a town further south in the Lake District. A lively though sometimes moody boy, he loved to spend his free time roaming about the countryside and getting to know the country people who lived there. Wordsworth's adult memories of these years are transformed into magnificent verse in the early books of *The Prelude,* his autobiographical poem.

Wordsworth was thirteen when his father died. The considerable sum of money left to the children was withheld for some years for legal reasons, but William was nevertheless able to attend Cambridge University in 1787. He found little in the formal university curriculum to interest him, however, and he longed restlessly for his summer vacations. During the vacation of his third year at Cambridge, Wordsworth went on a walking tour of France and the Alps with a close friend, Robert Jones. The year was 1790, and France was celebrating the first anniversary of the Revolution. Already sympathetic to the democratic ideals that inspired the French Revolution, Wordsworth was filled with enthusiastic hope that France might lead the way to a new and more just social order. He returned to France in 1791 after completing his degree at Cambridge. On this visit he became an even more fervent supporter of the Revolution, and he fell passionately in love with Annette Vallon, the daughter of a French surgeon. But lack of money forced Wordsworth to return to England, and by this time events in France had begun to take a grim and terribly destructive direction. The declaration of war between England and France in 1793 made it impossible for Wordsworth and Annette to be reunited. The unhappiness, guilt, and disillusionment of these years brought Wordsworth very near to mental collapse and despair.

In 1795, a friend and admirer of Wordsworth's died and left him enough money to live on while

William Wordsworth by Benjamin Robert Haydon. The Granger Collection

devoting himself entirely to writing poetry. With his sister Dorothy, to whom he was very close, Wordsworth settled in a small cottage at Racedown, Dorsetshire, in southwest England. Shortly afterward he was introduced to Samuel Taylor Coleridge, and thus began one of the most important and fruitful friendships in English literature. In 1797 Wordsworth and Dorothy moved to Alfoxden House in Somerset, to be near Coleridge, who lived only a few miles away at Nether Stowey. Already an admirer of Wordsworth's early poetry, Coleridge convinced Wordsworth that he had far more to offer the world than he had ever dreamed. By talking and working with Coleridge, Wordsworth moved beyond his period of sadness and despair and into the greatest creative phase of his life.

The concrete result of Wordsworth's friendship and collaboration with Coleridge was the first edition of *Lyrical Ballads,* published in 1798. This collection, as we have already seen in the general introduction to the Romantic Age, signaled a revolution in English poetic theory and practice and established the foundation of English Romanticism. In 1799, almost as a kind of living confirmation of the deepest source of his poetic vision, Wordsworth returned with Dorothy to their native Lake District and settled at Grasmere, in a small house later known as Dove Cottage. They would continue to live in this area for the rest of their lives. Coleridge followed them and rented a house at Keswick, thirteen miles away. In 1800 they published a second edition of *Lyrical Ballads,* which contains Wordsworth's Preface and a new volume of poems, including the famous "Lucy poems," many of which were written during a long and somber visit to Germany in the winter of 1798–1799.

In 1802 Wordsworth finally inherited the money left him by his father and married a childhood friend from the Lake District, Mary Hutchinson. But the years that followed, although they saw the full maturation of Wordsworth's powers as a poet, were filled with personal disaster. In 1805 his favorite brother, John, a ship captain, was drowned at sea. The event is reflected in the "Elegiac Stanzas Suggested by a Picture of Peele Castle," one of the finest poems to appear in *Poems in Two Volumes,* published in 1807. In 1810 the friendship between Wordsworth and Coleridge, which for various reasons had gradually become more cool and distant, was broken by an open quarrel. It was many years before the two men were reconciled. Two years later tragedy struck again—two of the Wordsworth children died. Offsetting the sadness of these middle years, however, was the steady growth of Wordsworth's reputation as a poet. In 1805 he accepted a government job as revenue collector for the county of Westmoreland, a sign not only of the national esteem he had won, but also of the growing conservatism of his political views. In 1843, at age seventy-three, he was made poet laureate.

Many of Wordsworth's admirers, both contemporary and modern, have seen a lamentable decline in Wordsworth's poetic powers after the decade of 1797–1807. And it is true that most of Wordsworth's finest poems were already included in *Lyrical Ballads* and in *Poems in Two Volumes.* But we must remember that when the great decade came to an end, Wordsworth was thirty-seven, an age that none of the younger Romantics who so often complained about Wordsworth's conservatism and declining powers ever reached. Is it reasonable to expect that the remarkable creative energy of that great decade could be sustained through such a long life? In any case, Wordsworth continued to write poems, some of which give evidence of his work at its best, until his death in 1850 at the age of eighty.

Only after his death was Wordsworth's masterpiece, *The Prelude,* published. In 1798 he had begun work on this monumental autobiographical poem, subtitled "Growth of a Poet's Mind," and in 1805 he completed a first version of it. But Wordsworth continued to revise *The Prelude* for the rest of his life. In it, the two forces or processes that underlie all Wordsworth's best poetry are most fully realized. The first of these, announced in the poem's subtitle, is *growth.* The growth of the poet's mind and moral character from earliest childhood to adult maturity is seen not simply in a strictly autobiographical perspective, but also in a more general perspective that takes in the universal patterns and processes common to all human minds. The second major force or process in Wordsworth's poetry is *memory.* All genuine poetry "takes its origin," Wordsworth says in the Preface to *Lyrical Ballads,* "from emotion recollected in tranquillity." It is memory that allows Wordsworth to retrace the growth of his own moral and artistic self, and it is both the content and the process of memory that give his poetry its life, beauty, and power. The characteristic moment in Wordsworth's poetry comes when some aspect of the poet's present experience triggers his recollection of a deeply meaningful experience in the past. What we see in the poem is the active, vital relationship of present to past experience.

The process of memory in Wordsworth's poetry is very often set in motion by his response to the natural world, and it is the natural world to which Wordsworth returns, again and again, as the great source of human happiness and fulfillment. Yet it is misleading to call Wordsworth a "nature poet," if we mean by that a poet whose main concern lies in recording the details of nature for their own sake. Wordsworth is interested in nature as it affects, guides, and nourishes the human mind. For Wordsworth, to think of nature apart from what it means, or can mean, to humanity is a virtual contradiction.

Lines Composed a Few Miles Above Tintern Abbey

The full title given to this poem by Wordsworth is "Lines Composed a Few Miles Above Tintern Abbey on Revisiting the Banks of the Wye During a Tour. July 13, 1798." Tintern Abbey was once a great medieval church with associated living quarters for monks of the Cistercian order. It was located in Monmouthshire, Wales, in the valley of the River Wye. The Abbey was broken up during the time of Henry VIII, however, and its buildings left in ruins. Wordsworth first visited these ruins on a walking tour of the Wye valley during August 1793, when he was twenty-three. He returned to the spot, as the poem tells us, almost exactly five years later. Wordsworth commented that "no poem of mine was composed under circumstances more pleasant for me to remember than this. I began it upon leaving Tintern, after crossing the Wye, and concluded it just as I was entering Bristol in the evening, after a ramble of four or five days, with my sister. Not a line of it was altered, and not any part of it written down till I reached Bristol."

After five years, the poet returns to the fertile river valley and from a cliff over the valley once again views the scene.

Five years have passed; five summers, with the length
Of five long winters! and again I hear
These waters, rolling from their mountain springs
With a soft inland murmur. — Once again
Do I behold these steep and lofty cliffs,   5
That on a wild secluded scene impress
Thoughts of more deep seclusion; and connect
The landscape with the quiet of the sky.
The day is come when I again repose
Here, under this dark sycamore, and view   10
These plots of cottage ground, these orchard tufts,
Which at this season, with their unripe fruits,
Are clad in one green hue, and lose themselves
'Mid groves and copses. Once again I see
These hedgerows, hardly hedgerows, little lines   15
Of sportive wood run wild: these pastoral farms,
Green to the very door; and wreaths of smoke
Sent up, in silence, from among the trees!
With some uncertain notice, as might seem
Of vagrant dwellers in the houseless woods,   20
Or of some hermit's cave, where by his fire
The hermit sits alone.
                These beauteous forms,
Through a long absence, have not been to me
As is a landscape to a blind man's eye;

The beauty of this scene had remained with the poet during his absence; its memory has influenced him to acts of kindness and love and given to him the serene mood that brings the deepest understanding of life.

But oft, in lonely rooms, and 'mid the din 25
Of towns and cities, I have owed to them
In hours of weariness, sensations sweet,
Felt in the blood, and felt along the heart;
And passing even into my purer mind,
With tranquil restoration:—feelings, too, 30
Of unremembered pleasure: such, perhaps,
As have no slight or trivial influence
On that best portion of a good man's life,
His little, nameless, unremembered acts
Of kindness and of love. Nor less, I trust, 35
To them I may have owed another gift,
Of aspect more sublime; that blessed mood
In which the burthen of the mystery,
In which the heavy and the weary weight
Of all this unintelligible world, 40
Is lightened—that serene and blessed mood,
In which the affections gently lead us on,
Until, the breath of this corporeal frame°
And even the motion of our human blood
Almost suspended, we are laid asleep 45
In body, and become a living soul;
While with an eye made quiet by the power
Of harmony, and the deep power of joy,
We see into the life of things.
                                    If this
Be but a vain belief, yet, oh! how oft— 50
In darkness and amid the many shapes
Of joyless daylight; when the fretful stir
Unprofitable, and the fever of the world,
Have hung upon the beatings of my heart—

In the past he had often returned in spirit to the Wye, and he now rejoices that this moment will give him pleasure in future years.

How oft, in spirit, have I turned to thee, 55
O sylvan° Wye! thou wanderer through the woods,
How often has my spirit turned to thee!
    And now, with gleams of half-extinguished thought,
With many recognitions dim and faint,
And somewhat of a sad perplexity, 60
The picture of the mind revives again;
While here I stand, not only with the sense
Of present pleasure, but with pleasing thoughts
That in this moment there is life and food
For future years. And so I dare to hope, 65
Though changed, no doubt, from what I was when first
I came among these hills; when like a roe
I bounded o'er the mountains, by the sides

---

43. **corporeal** (kôr-pôr'ē-əl) **frame:** the body.   56. **sylvan:** wooded.

Tintern Abbey
(watercolor, 1834) by
J. M. W. Turner.
Victoria and Albert Museum,
Crown Copyright

*When first he came here
as a young man,
whatever appealed to
his senses enraptured
him without stirring
him to meditation.*

Of the deep rivers, and the lonely streams,
Wherever nature led—more like a man   70
Flying from something that he dreads, than one
Who sought the thing he loved. For nature then
(The coarser pleasures of my boyish days,
And their glad animal movements all gone by)
To me was all in all.—I cannot paint   75
What then I was. The sounding cataract
Haunted me like a passion; the tall rock,

The mountain, and the deep and gloomy wood,
Their colors and their forms, were then to me
An appetite; a feeling and a love,   80
That had no need of a remoter charm,°
By thought supplied, nor any interest
Unborrowed from the eye. That time is past,
And all its aching joys are now no more,
And all its dizzy raptures. Not for this   85
Faint° I, nor mourn nor murmur; other gifts
Have followed; for such loss, I would believe,
Abundant recompense. For I have learned
To look on nature, not as in the hour
Of thoughtless youth; but hearing oftentimes   90
The still, sad music of humanity,
Nor harsh nor grating, though of ample power
To chasten and subdue. And I have felt
A presence that disturbs me with the joy
Of elevated thoughts; a sense sublime   95
Of something far more deeply interfused,
Whose dwelling is the light of setting suns,
And the round ocean and the living air,
And the blue sky, and in the mind of man;
A motion and a spirit, that impels   100
All thinking things, all objects of all thought,
And rolls through all things. Therefore am I still
A lover of the meadows and the woods
And mountains; and of all that we behold
From this green earth; of all the mighty world   105
Of eye, and ear—both what they half create,
And what perceive; well pleased to recognize
In nature and the language of the sense,
The anchor of my purest thoughts, the nurse,
The guide, the guardian of my heart, and soul   110
Of all my moral being.
                              Nor perchance,
If I were not thus taught, should I the more
Suffer my genial° spirits to decay;
For thou art with me here upon the banks
Of this fair river; thou my dearest Friend,°   115
My dear, dear Friend, and in thy voice I catch
The language of my former heart, and read
My former pleasures in the shooting lights
Of thy wild eyes. Oh! yet a little while
May I behold in thee what I was once,   120

Now the poet has found a divine spirit in nature, a spirit that he recognizes as a part of his own soul.

---

81. **remoter charm:** an attraction apart from the scene itself.   86. **Faint:** lose heart.
113. **genial:** cheerful, enlivening.   115. **Friend:** his sister Dorothy.

In his sister, Dorothy Wordsworth, his "dearest Friend," he sees his own former joy in nature for its outward beauty.

My dear, dear Sister! and this prayer I make,
Knowing that Nature never did betray
The heart that loved her; 'tis her privilege,
Through all the years of this our life, to lead
From joy to joy; for she can so inform   125
The mind that is within us, so impress
With quietness and beauty, and so feed
With lofty thoughts, that neither evil tongues,
Rash judgments, nor the sneers of selfish men,
Nor greetings where no kindness is, nor all   130
The dreary intercourse of daily life,
Shall e'er prevail against us, or disturb
Our cheerful faith, that all which we behold
Is full of blessings. Therefore let the moon
Shine on thee in thy solitary walk;   135
And let the misty mountain winds be free
To blow against thee: and, in after years,
When these wild ecstasies shall be matured
Into a sober pleasure; when thy mind
Shall be a mansion for all lovely forms,   140
Thy memory be as a dwelling place
For all sweet sounds and harmonies; oh! then,
If solitude, or fear, or pain, or grief,
Should be thy portion, with what healing thoughts
Of tender joy wilt thou remember me,   145
And these my exhortations! Nor, perchance—
If I should be where I no more can hear
Thy voice, nor catch from thy wild eyes these gleams
Of past existence—wilt thou then forget
That on the banks of this delightful stream   150
We stood together; and that I, so long
A worshiper of Nature, hither came
Unwearied in that service: rather say
With warmer love—oh! with far deeper zeal
Of holier love. Nor wilt thou then forget,   155
That after many wanderings, many years
Of absence, these steep woods and lofty cliffs,
And this green pastoral landscape, were to me
More dear, both for themselves and for thy sake!

COMMENTARY

"Tintern Abbey" is a magnificent example of Wordsworth's idea that poetry "takes its origin from emotion recollected in tranquillity. In this poem two emotional experiences of the same scene are recollected. The first experience is Wordsworth's original visit to Tintern Abbey in 1793. The second experience is his return to the same spot five years later. Wordsworth's meditation on the significance for his life of both experiences and of the relationship between them provides the structure as well as the subject matter of "Tintern Abbey."

Wordsworth looks back in "Tintern Abbey" — but he also looks forward to what the second or "present" visit will mean both for his own life and for his sister Dorothy's. Wordsworth's second visit is Dorothy's first, and he concludes the poem by hearing in her voice "The language of my former heart" (line 117), and by praying that in the future her memory will also be "a dwelling place / For all sweet sounds and harmonies" (lines 141–142).

THE STRUCTURE OF THE POEM

The divisions suggested here are not Wordsworth's; they simply offer a convenient way of approaching the study of the poem.

Lines 1–22. In this section the poet tells us that he is revisiting a secluded scene, the wild beauty of which suggests "Thoughts of more deep seclusion." The direction of his reflection is *away from* humanity and back into the past.

Lines 22–49. His visit to this place five years earlier had had two kinds of influence upon the poet. The first of these is moral. Remembering the banks of the Wye, their beauty and their grandeur, he has been saved from pettiness and has been made more loving and generous. But the second kind of influence had no reference to his fellow human beings; it was a mood of quietness and joy in which the incessant demands of the self were suspended, and the poet felt at one with the world.

Lines 49–57. Perhaps this exalted reverie is based on illusion; whether it is or not, the poet recalls instances when, oppressed by everyday concerns, he has returned in spirit to the wooded banks of the Wye. His reverie passes, and he is once more aware of the scene before his eyes.

Lines 58–111. No wonder the poet is perplexed; he is recognizing that his memories are those of a very different person: the person he was five years ago. He is reassured, not only by the pleasure he is now experiencing, but by the thought that memories of this present occasion will serve him in future years as well (lines 64–65). At the same time, he recalls how different he was upon his first visit to this scene. Then he was a youth rather than a man. The youth had passed the stage of boyhood's "glad animal movements" and had reached adolescence, when nature "To me was all in all." It is clear that Wordsworth is not scolding his adolescent self for being enthusiastic in his love for nature. He could not experience hearing the "still, sad music of humanity" if he had not first experienced being boy, then youth, then man. In his youth, Wordsworth says, the experience of nature was his master ("The sounding cataract / Haunted me like a passion"). Now the poet is aware that he cannot be at the mercy of his experience. As a man he must direct his own experience. He must move *toward* humanity. This is the key to the difference between lines 22–49 and lines 93–111. The latter passage is once more an account of a sense of union with the whole, but this union now has a different basis; the "presence" Wordsworth feels gives order to the world is felt not simply in nature but "in the mind of man" as well.

Lines 111–159. The fourth section of the poem moves quite logically from an account of Wordsworth's own growth to thoughts and hopes about his sister Dorothy. Does he expect her to pass through the same stages he himself experienced? What is Wordsworth's hope for his sister as she grows older (lines 137–159)?

FOR COMPOSITION

Think of a scene, either in the country or in the city, that is very familiar to you because you have seen it many times and because you often remember and perhaps daydream about it. Describe the scene as carefully as you can. Try to indicate how the scene appeared to you when you first experienced it, how it appeared to you in subsequent experiences, and how it makes you feel when you remember it. Finally, try to determine what it is about this scene that makes it memorable and important to you.

The Lucy Poems

The following three poems and three others not reprinted here are known as the "Lucy poems." Wordsworth wrote them while spending the winter of 1798–1799 in Germany with his sister Dorothy. There is no evidence that Wordsworth had an actual person in mind. Nevertheless, there has been widespread speculation about the identity of "Lucy." In speaking of "A Slumber Did My Spirit Seal," Coleridge commented: "Whether it had any reality I cannot say. Most probably, in some gloomier moment he had fancied the moment in which his sister might die."

She Dwelt Among the Untrodden Ways

She dwelt among the untrodden ways
   Beside the springs of Dove,°
A maid whom there were none to praise
   And very few to love:

A violet by a mossy stone   5
   Half hidden from the eye!
—Fair as a star, when only one
   Is shining in the sky.

She lived unknown, and few could know
   When Lucy ceased to be;   10
But she is in her grave, and, oh,
   The difference to me!

---

2. **Dove:** a river in the English Midlands.

FOR STUDY AND DISCUSSION

1. What do the comparisons in the second stanza suggest about Lucy?
2. The final line ends with "me." How does this sudden introduction of the speaker intensify the loss of Lucy?

Strange Fits of Passion
Have I Known

Strange fits of passion have I known:
And I will dare to tell,
But in the lover's ear alone,
What once to me befell.

When she I loved looked every day   5
Fresh as a rose in June,
I to her cottage bent my way,
Beneath an evening moon.

Upon the moon I fixed my eye,
All over the wide lea;   10
With quickening pace my horse drew nigh
Those paths so dear to me.

And now we reached the orchard plot;
And, as we climbed the hill,
The sinking moon to Lucy's cot   15
Came near, and nearer still.

In one of those sweet dreams I slept,
Kind Nature's gentle boon!
And all the while my eyes I kept
On the descending moon.   20

My horse moved on; hoof after hoof
He raised, and never stopped:
When down behind the cottage roof,
At once, the bright moon dropped.

What fond and wayward thoughts will slide   25
Into a lover's head!
"O mercy!" to myself I cried,
"If Lucy should be dead!"

Dove Cottage, Grasmere. Home of William Wordsworth from 1799 to 1808.
Syndication International, Photo Trends

COMMENTARY

These twenty-eight lines appear very simple when you first read them. Yet their effect is the result of a very deliberate artistry which plays the idea of motion, activity, life, against the idea of stillness, stoppage, arrest, death. In the third quatrain, there are two kinds of motion, and the innocent reader is quite unaware of their fateful meaning. There is the evening moon, and there is the horse, whose pace quickens as he approaches a familiar resting place. How does the very sound and pace of the fourth quatrain suggest something ominous?

In the fifth quatrain, we are made aware that the lover is enjoying a pleasant fantasy or dream, which involves no consciousness of time or motion. Meanwhile, his eye is on the sinking moon. This double consciousness of his fantasy and the movement of the moon becomes single and terrified in the sixth quatrain. Again the effect is secured by the movement of the verse. Compare the second quatrain with the sixth in this respect. How does the beat of the horse's hoofs enter in? Notice that in the last two quatrains there is a parallelism between the disappearance of the moon behind the cottage (lines 23–24) and the thought that "slides" into the lover's head. How is death suggested by movement in the poem?

A Slumber Did
My Spirit Seal

A slumber did my spirit seal;
  I had no human fears:
She seemed a thing that could not feel
  The touch of earthly years.

No motion has she now, no force;
  She neither hears nor sees;
Rolled round in earth's diurnal° course,
  With rocks, and stones, and trees.

---

7. **diurnal** (dī-ûr′nəl): daily.

My Heart Leaps Up
When I Behold

My heart leaps up when I behold
  A rainbow in the sky:
So was it when my life began;
So is it now I am a man;
So be it when I shall grow old,
  Or let me die!
The Child is father of the Man;
And I could wish my days to be
Bound each to each by natural piety.°

---

9. **natural piety:** reverent regard for nature.

COMMENTARY

This poem is probably the last of the so-called "Lucy poems." The question about the relation of motion and death in the poem may be answered in various ways, but one might first compare the fantasy of stanza 5 in "Strange Fits of Passion Have I Known" with the whole of the first stanza in this poem. Here are two instances describing the lover's view of his beloved and the tie that unites them as timeless ("I had no human fears"). And in both instances death is associated, by contrast, with motion and with activity that terminates: mortality. The fact that the conventional association of death is with stillness, not movement, accounts for the extraordinary effect of the last two lines of "A Slumber Did My Spirit Seal."

FOR COMPOSITION

Readers differ widely in their interpretation of the last two lines of "A Slumber Did My Spirit Seal." Is the speaker consoled by the fact that his beloved has become part of the apparently nonhuman natural world, or is he bitterly aware, by her death, of the mortality of human life? Try to support your view by referring to the poem as a whole. Consider, for instance, how the reference to "rocks, and stones, and trees" in the second stanza relates to the idea of "a *thing* that could not feel / The touch of earthly years" in the first stanza.

FOR STUDY AND DISCUSSION

1. In this poem, as in "Tintern Abbey," Wordsworth thinks of his life as existing in three phases, although here the phases are somewhat different. What are the three phases in this poem? How does his response to the rainbow connect the three phases?
2. The exact meaning of Wordsworth's poems often depends on a very simple, yet very important, choice of words or phrases. What is the significance of the shift in lines 3–5 from "So was it" to "So is it" to "So be it"? What is the meaning of line 8: "And I could wish my days to be" (as opposed to "And *I am sure* my days *will be*")?
3. A statement such as line 7, "The Child is father of the Man," is called a *paradox*, because at first it seems self-contradictory and therefore untrue, but on further thought it is seen to contain an element of truth. In what sense is a child the "father" of the man he eventually becomes? What does Wordsworth imply about the ways in which people's early experiences influence their later lives?

Sonnets

Although Wordsworth wrote sonnets throughout his poetic career, many of his finest achievements in the form were written between the summer of 1802, when he returned to France for the first time in ten years, and 1807, when his collected *Poems in Two Volumes* was published. The "Westminster Bridge" sonnet, Wordsworth said, was "composed on the roof of a coach on my way to France." "It Is a Beauteous Evening" was written later during this French journey, "on the beach near Calais in the autumn of 1802." And "London, 1802" was "written immediately after my return from France to London, when I could not but be struck . . . with the vanity and parade of our own country . . . as contrasted with the quiet, and I may say the desolation, that the revolution had produced in France."

Composed upon Westminster Bridge, September 3, 1802

Earth has not anything to show more fair:
Dull would he be of soul who could pass by
A sight so touching in its majesty:
This City now doth, like a garment, wear
The beauty of the morning; silent, bare,   5
Ships, towers, domes, theaters, and temples lie
Open unto the fields, and to the sky;
All bright and glittering in the smokeless air.
Never did sun more beautifully steep
In his first splendor, valley, rock, or hill;   10
Ne'er saw I, never felt, a calm so deep!
The river glideth at his own sweet will:
Dear God! the very houses seem asleep;
And all that mighty heart is lying still!

Westminster Bridge, London (engraving) by Charles Heath and P. Dewint.
Radio Times Hulton

It Is a Beauteous Evening, Calm and Free

It is a beauteous evening, calm and free,
The holy time is quiet as a Nun
Breathless with adoration; the broad sun
Is sinking down in its tranquillity;
The gentleness of heaven broods o'er the Sea: 5
Listen! the mighty Being is awake,
And doth with his eternal motion make
A sound like thunder—everlastingly.
Dear Child! dear Girl! that walkest with me here,
If thou appear untouched by solemn thought,   10
Thy nature is not therefore less divine:
Thou liest in Abraham's bosom° all the year;
And worship'st at the Temple's inner shrine,
God being with thee when we know it not.

---

12. **Abraham's bosom:** a metaphor for heaven (Luke 16:22). In other words, her spirit is at peace.

London, 1802

Milton! thou shouldst be living at this hour:
England hath need of thee: she is a fen°
Of stagnant waters: altar, sword, and pen,
Fireside, the heroic wealth of hall and bower,°
Have forfeited their ancient English dower   5
Of inward happiness. We are selfish men;
Oh! raise us up, return to us again;
And give us manners, virtue, freedom, power.
Thy soul was like a Star, and dwelt apart;
Thou hadst a voice whose sound was like the sea: 10
Pure as the naked heavens, majestic, free,
So didst thou travel on life's common way,
In cheerful godliness; and yet thy heart
The lowliest duties on herself did lay.

---

2. **fen:** a bog.   4. **hall and bower:** a reference to Anglo-Saxon times when the hall and bower were the main rooms in the large houses of various tribes.

The World Is Too Much with Us

The world is too much with us; late and soon,
Getting and spending, we lay waste our powers:
Little we see in Nature that is ours;
We have given our hearts away, a sordid boon!°
This sea that bares her bosom to the moon;   5
The winds that will be howling at all hours,
And are upgathered now like sleeping flowers;
For this, for everything, we are out of tune;
It moves us not.—Great God! I'd rather be
A Pagan suckled in a creed outworn;   10
So might I, standing on this pleasant lea,
Have glimpses that would make me less forlorn;
Have sight of Proteus rising from the sea;
Or hear old Triton blow his wreathèd horn.°

---

4. **boon:** a favor asked or granted.   13–14. **Proteus** (prō′tē-əs) and **Triton** (trīt′n): sea gods in Greek mythology.

COMMENTARY

In "London, 1802" Wordsworth calls upon the spirit of Milton, the great seventeenth-century poet, to return and stir nineteenth-century England from its moral and political stagnation. The appeal is doubly appropriate, for it was also Milton who provided Wordsworth with his most instructive example in the handling of sonnet form. The sonnet had fallen out of favor during the eighteenth century, but the Romantic poets revived it. Like Milton, Wordsworth uses the sonnet for moral and political reflection, and also for poetic statements of a more public kind. Also like Milton, Wordsworth may violate the strict rhyming divisions of octave and sestet to create dramatic emphasis. The magnificent turn and exclamation in "The World Is Too Much with Us" come not, as we might expect, just after the octave is completed, but in the middle of the ninth line, which opens with a prolongation of disappointment and defeat:

It moves us not.—Great God! I'd rather be
A Pagan suckled in a creed outworn . . .

Milton would have admired both the impulse and the placement of Wordsworth's outrage here. The early Romantic poet, like the late Renaissance poet, recognized the human value of breaking through the confinements of tradition and of a deadened imagination.

FOR STUDY AND DISCUSSION

Composed upon Westminster Bridge, September 3, 1802
1. Pick out the passages in which the city of London is presented as a living being. What is the effect of this personification?
2. Can you defend the statement that the key to the emotional power of this sonnet lies in the line, "A sight so touching in its majesty"? You might begin by referring to the kind of sight usually thought of as touching (puppies tumbling in the grass, a child taking its first steps, and so on) as compared to the majesty of the metropolis. Wordsworth's success may then be said to lie in coupling these apparent incompatibles.

It Is a Beauteous Evening, Calm and Free

1. How is the speaker's response to nature's power contrasted with that of the small girl who accompanies him on his walk? What does the speaker conclude about her experience?

2. One of the ways in which nature takes on a spiritual significance in this sonnet is through Wordsworth's use of religious references. Pick out as many such references as you can. What pattern of development can you see in these references as you move through the poem?

London, 1802

1. Wordsworth's vision of the city in "London, 1802" is very different from the one given in "Composed upon Westminster Bridge." How would you describe that difference?

2. We usually think of a hero as one who acts with splendid courage in some public emergency, such as a fire or a battle. In this sonnet Wordsworth is concerned not with such public acts, but with the social and moral conditions that nourish such men. What are they? Begin by considering the emphasis on "inward happiness" in line 6 and the comparison of Milton's powers to sea and sky in lines 10-11.

The World Is Too Much with Us

1. What does Wordsworth mean in this sonnet by "the world"? What does he mean by "Nature"? With which aspects of Nature has "getting and spending" made us "out of tune"?

2. In the second part of this sonnet (lines 9-14), Wordsworth expresses the need for a feeling of identity with the natural world that he thinks modern people lack. How do the concluding lines, which refer to the ancient pagan gods Proteus and Triton, express the more imaginative relation to nature that Wordsworth desires?

FOR COMPOSITION

Try your hand at composing a sonnet commemorating an event of historical importance with which you are familiar. If you need to review the specific requirements of sonnet form, consult the Guide to Literary Terms and Techniques. One of the main things you will need to do is to relate your own personal response to your sense of the event's more general public significance. Try to use the structure of the sonnet to bring out the most important features of your subject.

Samuel Taylor Coleridge
1772–1834

Samuel Taylor Coleridge had one of the most fertile and versatile minds in English literature. His poetic output is relatively small, although it contains such masterpieces as *The Rime of the Ancient Mariner*, "Kubla Khan," and "Frost at Midnight." His work as a literary critic and theorist, however, is massive; and his judgments and ideas are still enormously influential today. The fact that many of Coleridge's most ambitious literary projects were never completed should not obscure the awesome value and scope of what he actually accomplished.

Born in rural Devonshire, Coleridge was the son of a clergyman and the youngest of fourteen children. He was ten years old when his father died, and he was sent to live and attend school in London. Coleridge recalls his early years in London with a sense of dreamy sadness in "Frost at Midnight":

> For I was reared
> In the great city, pent 'mid cloisters dim,
> And saw nought lovely but the sky and stars.
> (lines 51–53)

Coleridge did more than gaze at the stars during these formative years. He was an enthusiastic and extraordinarily brilliant student. When he went on to attend Cambridge University in 1791, he was already a proficient scholar. Yet Coleridge found even less at Cambridge that really interested him than Wordsworth did. He fell into idleness, carelessness, and debt, and in 1793 he left Cambridge to join the army under the wonderful pseudonym of Silas Tomkyn Comberbacke. But Coleridge was miserable as a soldier, and with the help of his brothers he was sent back to Cambridge for a second chance. He left again in 1794, however, without taking a degree.

As a young man Coleridge held radical views on politics and religion. During the summer of 1794 he met the poet Robert Southey, who had similar views, and the two friends set about planning a small Utopian community in America to which Coleridge gave the name "Pantisocracy" ("equal rule by all"). In London, Coleridge met a real-estate agent who persuaded him that their com-

Samuel Taylor Coleridge (1795) by P. Vandyke.
The Granger Collection

munity ought to settle on the banks of the Susquehanna, in Pennsylvania. To further the cause of the community, Coleridge became engaged to Sara Fricker, the sister of Southey's own fiancée. Their hopelessly unrealistic scheme never materialized. Coleridge felt obligated, nevertheless, to go through with his marriage to Sara Fricker, although he characterized his attitude at the time as being "resolved, but wretched."

Coleridge and his wife Sara lived at Nether Stowey, in Somerset. In 1795 he met Wordsworth, who soon moved with his sister Dorothy to Alfoxden House only a few miles away. Thus began the great collaboration that would culminate in the publication of *Lyrical Ballads* in 1798, and the happiest and most productive time of Coleridge's life. Coleridge's specific role in *Lyrical Ballads*, as he later described it in his *Biographia Literaria*, was "directed to persons and characters supernatural." "With this view," he goes on to explain, "I wrote the *Ancient Mariner*," which was the opening poem of the collection. But in fact the collaboration between Coleridge and Wordsworth was more extensive than this division of labor suggests. Not only did they discuss their poems with each other, but one poet would actually contribute ideas, lines, and even entire stanzas to poems chiefly written by the other. Thus Wordsworth suggested the shooting of the albatross and contributed lines 13–16 and 222–227 of *The Rime of the Ancient Mariner*, and Coleridge contributed the first stanza of "We Are Seven" and suggested numerous other details in Wordsworth's poems. His most significant contribution came in the manner and structure of "Frost at Midnight," where the complex relation between meditation and natural description provided the basis for Wordsworth's technique in "Tintern Abbey."

Coleridge went with Wordsworth and Dorothy to Germany in the winter of 1798–1799. There, at the University of Göttingen, he began his lifelong study of Kant and other German philosophers. Coleridge was to become very important in introducing the advances of German philosophy to English poets and thinkers. Upon their return to England, both the Wordsworths and the Coleridges moved north to the Lake District, Coleridge and Sara settling at Greta Hall, Keswick, in 1800. This year marks the beginning of an agonizing period in Coleridge's life. He had become increasingly distant from his wife and had fallen in love with Sara Hutchinson, whose sister, Mary, Wordsworth was to marry in 1802. Sara Hutchinson did not return Coleridge's affections, however, and he suffered bitterly from her rejection. It was also about this time that Coleridge began taking large amounts of opium, the standard medical remedy in that day for the painful attacks of rheumatism from which he was suffering. But the effects of the drug, Coleridge soon realized, were more harmful than the disease: he became emotionally and psychologically distraught and unable to sustain his creative work. He expressed his despair in one of his major poems, "Dejection: An Ode," published in 1802:

> My genial spirits fail;
> And what can these avail
> To lift the smothering weight from off my
> breast?
>
> (lines 39–41)

By 1806, when he returned to London from an unsuccessful visit to the Mediterranean to restore his health, Coleridge's unhappiness and his addiction to opium had brought him to the verge of total collapse. A quarrel with Wordsworth in 1810 seemed to be the final blow. Yet the very fact that Coleridge was able to express his sense of physical and mental failure in such a powerful and accomplished poem as the "Dejection Ode" points up the extraordinary feat of his continuing literary efforts during these years. Those efforts may have been inconsistent and far inferior to what Coleridge was ideally capable of, but they are still remarkable.

In 1808 he began his career as a public lecturer in London. Coleridge was the most eloquent speaker and conversationalist of the Romantic Age. His lectures on Shakespeare and other writers have become classics of literary criticism. During the next few years he also wrote for newspapers and magazines, began a periodical called *The Friend*, and wrote a successful tragedy called *Remorse*.

In 1816 Coleridge moved to Highgate, a northern suburb of London, and placed himself in the care of Dr. James Gillman, a wise and kind physician who was able to control Coleridge's use of opium. Coleridge's recovery, though never complete and always dependent on the care of Dr. Gillman and his wife, was more successful than he had ever hoped. In 1817 he finished and published the *Biographia Literaria*, which he had begun and worked on intermittently since 1815. Coleridge himself saw the *Biographia* as an account of his "literary life and opinions," and it contains some of the central formulations of Romantic literary theory. The *Biographia* also contains some of Coleridge's best applied criticism of the poetry of previous periods and of his own time. It includes a searching discussion of Wordsworth's poetic ideals as they were expressed in the Preface to *Lyrical Ballads*. Through the *Biographia* and his public lectures, Coleridge joins Sir Philip Sidney, John Dryden, and Samuel Johnson in the select circle of great "poet-critics" in English literature.

The last years of Coleridge's life were relatively quiet and satisfying. He finally made up his quarrel with Wordsworth, and in 1828 they toured the Rhineland area of Germany together. In Highgate, Coleridge received a steady stream of admirers from both England and abroad. (One of his American visitors was Ralph Waldo Emerson.) They came to see the great man, and to hear his fascinating, eloquent, endlessly fluent conversation. When Coleridge died in 1834, the Romantic Age lost one of its greatest minds and personalities.

The Rime of the Ancient Mariner

The Rime of the Ancient Mariner opened the 1798 edition of *Lyrical Ballads.* The story was originally based on a dream of Coleridge's friend, John Cruikshank, and at first Coleridge and Wordsworth worked on the poem together. Eventually Wordsworth left the writing to Coleridge, but not before contributing a number of important elements, including the shooting of the albatross and the navigation of the ship by the dead sailors in Part V.

The comments in the margins of *The Rime of the Ancient Mariner* were added by Coleridge himself to later editions of the poem, as an aid to readers who wanted a clear indication of its simplest meanings. Coleridge did not intend these comments as a substitute for the verse itself, however. He would have expected us to realize that the marginal comments only begin to convey the poem's power and richness of suggestion.

Part I

An ancient Mariner meeteth three Gallants bidden to a wedding feast and detaineth one.

It is an ancient Mariner,
And he stoppeth one of three.
"By thy long gray beard and glittering eye,
Now wherefore stopp'st thou me?

"The Bridegroom's doors are opened wide,   5
And I am next of kin;
The guests are met, the feast is set;
May'st hear the merry din."

He holds him with his skinny hand;
"There was a ship," quoth he.   10
"Hold off! unhand me, graybeard loon!"
Eftsoons° his hand dropped he.

The Wedding Guest is spellbound by the eye of the old seafaring man and constrained to hear his tale.

He holds him with his glittering eye—
The Wedding Guest stood still,
And listens like a three years' child;   15
The Mariner hath his will.

The Wedding Guest sat on a stone;
He cannot choose but hear;
And thus spake on that ancient man,
The bright-eyed Mariner.   20

---

12. **Eftsoons:** immediately.

"The ship was cheered, the harbor cleared,
Merrily did we drop
Below the kirk,° below the hill,
Below the lighthouse top.

*The Mariner tells
how the ship sailed
southward with
a good wind and
fair weather till
it reached the
Line.°*

"The Sun came up upon the left,   25
Out of the sea came he—
And he shone bright, and on the right
Went down into the sea.

"Higher and higher every day,
Till over the mast at noon°—"   30
The Wedding Guest here beat his breast,
For he heard the loud bassoon.

*The Wedding Guest
heareth the
bridal music;
but the Mariner
continueth his tale.*

The bride hath paced into the hall,
Red as a rose is she;
Nodding their heads before her goes   35
The merry minstrelsy.

The Wedding Guest he beat his breast,
Yet he cannot choose but hear;
And thus spake on that ancient man,
The bright-eyed Mariner.   40

*The ship driven by a
storm toward
the South Pole.*

"And now the Storm blast came, and he
Was tyrannous and strong.
He struck with his o'ertaking wings,
And chased us south along.

"With sloping masts and dipping prow,   45
As who pursued with yell and blow
Still treads the shadow of his foe,
And forward bends his head,
The ship drove fast, loud roared the blast,
And southward aye we fled.   50

And now there came both mist and snow,
And it grew wondrous cold;
And ice, mast-high, came floating by,
As green as emerald.

---

23. **kirk**: church.   °**Line**: equator.   30. **over . . . noon**: The ship reaches the equator.

The land of ice, and of fearful sounds, where no living thing was to be seen.

K "And through the drifts° the snowy clifts°
    Did send a dismal sheen;
    Nor shapes of men nor beasts we ken—
    The ice was all between.
                                 55

J "The ice was here, the ice was there,
    The ice was all around;
    It cracked and growled, and roared and howled
    Like noises in a swound!°
                                 60

Till a great sea bird, called the Albatross, came through the snow-fog, and was received with great joy and hospitality.

M "At length did cross an Albatross,
    Thorough° the fog it came;
    As if it had been a Christian soul,
    We hailed it in God's name.
                                 65

K "It ate the food it n'er had eat,°
    And round and round it flew.
    The ice did split with a thunder fit;
    The helmsman steered us through!
                                 70

And lo! the Albatross proveth a bird of good omen, and followeth the ship as it returned northward through fog and floating ice.

J "And a good south wind sprung up behind;
    The Albatross did follow,
    And every day, for food or play,
    Came to the mariners' hollo!

M "In mist or cloud, on mast or shroud,°
    It perched for vespers° nine;
    Whiles all the night, through fog-smoke white,
    Glimmered the white moonshine."
                                 75

The ancient Mariner inhospitably killeth the pious bird of good omen.

K "God save thee, ancient Mariner!
    From the fiends, that plague thee thus!—
    Why look'st thou so?"°—"With my crossbow
    I shot the Albatross!
                                 80

Part II

J "The Sun now rose upon the right,°
    Out of the sea came he,
    Still hid in mist, and on the left
    Went down into the sea.
                                 85

---

55. **drifts:** mists. **clifts:** icebergs. 62. **swound:** swoon. 64. **Thorough:** through.
67. **eat:** pronounced *et*, old form of *eaten*. 75. **shroud:** rope of the rigging.
76. **vespers:** evenings. 79–81. **God . . . so:** spoken by the wedding guest.
83. **upon the right:** The ship has rounded the southern tip of South America and is heading north into the Pacific.

Samuel Taylor Coleridge 445

M "And the good south wind still blew behind,
But no sweet bird did follow,
Nor any day for food or play
Came to the mariners' hollo!   90

His shipmates cry out
against the
ancient Mariner
for killing the
bird of good
luck.

K "And I had done a hellish thing,
And it would work 'em woe;
For all averred, I had killed the bird
That made the breeze to blow.
Ah wretch! said they, the bird to slay,   95
That made the breeze to blow!

But when the fog
cleared off, they
justify the same,
and thus make
themselves
accomplices in
the crime.

J "Nor dim nor red, like God's own head,
The glorious Sun uprist;°
Then all averred, I had killed the bird
That brought the fog and mist.   100
'Twas right, said they, such birds to slay,
That bring the fog and mist.

The fair breeze continues;
the ship enters the
Pacific Ocean,
and sails northward, even
till it reaches the Line.

M "The fair breeze blew, the white foam flew,
The furrow° followed free;
We were the first that ever burst   105
Into that silent sea.

The ship hath been
suddenly
becalmed.

K "Down dropped the breeze, the sails dropped down,
'Twas sad as sad could be;
And we did speak only to break
The silence of the sea!   110

J "All in a hot and copper sky,
The bloody Sun, at noon,
Right up above the mast did stand,
No bigger than the Moon.

M "Day after day, day after day,   115
We stuck, nor breath nor motion;
As idle as a painted ship
Upon a painted ocean.

And the Albatross
begins to be
avenged.

K "Water, water, everywhere,
And all the boards did shrink;   120
Water, water, everywhere,
Nor any drop to drink.

---

98. **uprist:** arose. 104. **furrow:** wake of a ship.

J "The very deep did rot; O Christ!
That ever this should be!
Yea, slimy things did crawl with legs   125
Upon the slimy sea.

A Spirit had followed them: one of the invisible inhabitants of this planet, neither departed souls nor angels. They are very numerous, and there is no climate or element without one or more.

M "About, about, in reel and rout°
The death fires° danced at night;
The water, like a witch's oils,
Burnt green and blue and white.   130

K "And some in dreams assurèd were
Of the Spirit that plagued us so;
Nine fathom deep he had followed us
From the land of mist and snow.

The shipmates, in their sore distress, would fain throw the whole guilt on the ancient Mariner, in sign whereof they hang the dead sea bird round his neck.

J "And every tongue, through utter drought,   135
Was withered at the root;
We could not speak, no more than if
We had been choked with soot.

M "Ah, welladay! what evil looks
Had I from old and young!   140
Instead of the cross, the Albatross
About my neck was hung.

Part III

K "There passed a weary time. Each throat
Was parched, and glazed each eye.
A weary time! a weary time!   145
How glazed each weary eye,
When looking westward, I beheld
A something in the sky.

The ancient Mariner beholdeth a sign in the element afar off.

J "At first it seemed a little speck,
And then it seemed a mist;
It moved and moved, and took at last   150
A certain shape, I wist.°

M "A speck, a mist, a shape, I wist!
And still it neared and neared;
As if it dodged a water sprite,
It plunged and tacked and veered.   155

---

127. **rout:** tumultuous crowd. 128. **death fires:** St. Elmo's fires. A brush of electricity frequently appears on a ship's rigging. Sailors believed it was an omen of disaster. 152. **wist:** knew.

At its nearer
approach it
seemeth him to
be a ship, and at
a dear ransom
he freeth his
speech from the
bonds of thirst.

K "With throats unslaked, with black lips baked,
We could nor laugh nor wail;
Through utter drought all dumb we stood!
I bit my arm, I sucked the blood,   160
And cried, A sail! A sail!

J "With throats unslaked, with black lips baked,
Agape they heard me call;
Gramercy!° they for joy did grin,
And all at once their breath drew in,   165

A flash of joy.
As they were drinking all.

And horror follows.
For can it be a
ship that comes
onward without
wind or tide?
M "See! see! (I cried) she tacks no more!
Hither to work us weal;°
Without a breeze, without a tide,
She steadies with upright keel!   170

K "The western wave was all aflame.
The day was well-nigh done!
Almost upon the western wave
Rested the broad bright Sun;
When that strange shape drove suddenly   175
Betwixt us and the Sun.

It seemeth him but
the skeleton of a
ship.
J "And straight the Sun was flecked with bars,
(Heaven's Mother send us grace!)
As if through a dungeon grate he peered
With broad and burning face.   180

M "Alas! (thought I, and my heart beat loud)
How fast she nears and nears!
Are those her sails that glance in the Sun,
Like restless gossameres?°

And its ribs are seen
as bars on the
face of the
setting Sun. The
Specter-Woman
and her Death
mate, and no
other on board
the skeleton
ship.
K "Are those her ribs through which the Sun   185
Did peer, as through a grate?
And is that Woman all her crew?
Is that a Death? and are there two?
Is Death that woman's mate?

J "Her lips were red, her looks were free,°   190
Her locks were yellow as gold.
Her skin was as white as leprosy,

---

164. **Gramercy** (grə-mûr′sē): great thanks.   168. **work us weal:** help us.
184. **gossameres:** floating webs. The spelling has been changed from *gossamers* to
rhyme with *nears.*   190. **free:** wild.

Like vessel, like crew! The Nightmare Life-in-Death was she,
Who thicks man's blood with cold.

*Death and Life-in-
Death have
diced for the
ship's crew, and
she (the latter)
winneth the
ancient Mariner.*
"The naked hulk alongside came,
And the twain were casting dice;
'The game is done! I've won! I've won!'
Quoth she, and whistles thrice.   195

*No twilight within
the courts of the
Sun.*
"The Sun's rim dips; the stars rush out;
At one stride comes the dark;
With far-heard whisper, o'er the sea,   200
Off shot the specter bark.

"We listened and looked sideways up!
Fear at my heart, as at a cup,
*At the rising of the
Moon,*
My lifeblood seemed to sip!   205
The stars were dim, and thick the night,
The steersman's face by his lamp gleamed white;
From the sails the dew did drip—
Till clomb° above the eastern bar
The hornèd° Moon, with one bright star   210
Within the nether tip.

One after another,
"One after one, by the star-dogged Moon,°
Too quick for groan or sigh,
Each turned his face with a ghastly pang,
And cursed me with his eye,   215

*His shipmates drop
down dead.*
"Four times fifty living men,
(And I heard nor sigh nor groan)
With heavy thump, a lifeless lump,
They dropped down one by one.

*But Life-in-Death
begins her work
on the ancient
Mariner.*
"The souls did from their bodies fly—   220
They fled to bliss or woe!
And every soul, it passed me by,
Like the whizz of my crossbow!"

Part IV

*The Wedding Guest
feareth that a
Spirit is talking
to him.*
"I fear thee, ancient Mariner!
I fear thy skinny hand!   225
And thou art long, and lank, and brown,
As is the ribbed sea sand.

---

209. **clomb:** climbed.   210. **hornèd:** crescent.   212. **star-dogged Moon:** When a
star dogged the moon, it was a sign of evil to sailors.

"I fear thee and thy glittering eye,
    And thy skinny hand, so brown."—
"Fear not, fear not, thou Wedding Guest!   230
    This body dropped not down.

"Alone, alone, all, all alone,
    Alone on a wide, wide sea!
And never a saint took pity on
    My soul in agony.   235

"The many men, so beautiful!
    And they all dead did lie;
And a thousand thousand slimy things
    Lived on! and so did I.

"I looked upon the rotting sea,   240
    And drew my eyes away;
I looked upon the rotting deck,
    And there the dead men lay.

"I looked to heaven, and tried to pray;
    But or° ever a prayer had gushed,   245
A wicked whisper came, and made
    My heart as dry as dust.

"I closed my lids, and kept them close,
    And the balls like pulses beat;
For the sky and the sea, and the sea and the sky   250
Lay like a load on my weary eye,
    And the dead were at my feet.

"The cold sweat melted from their limbs,
    Nor rot nor reek did they;
The look with which they looked on me   255
    Had never passed away.

"An orphan's curse would drag to hell
    A spirit from on high;
But oh! more horrible than that
    Is a curse in a dead man's eye!   260
Seven days, seven nights, I saw that curse,
    And yet I could not die.

"The moving Moon went up the sky,
    And nowhere did abide;

But the ancient
Mariner
assureth him of
his bodily life,
and proceedeth
to relate his
horrible
penance.

He despiseth the
creatures of the
calm.

And envieth that they
should live, and
so many lie
dead.

But the curse liveth
for him in the
eye of the dead
men.

In his loneliness and
fixedness he yearneth
towards the journeying
Moon, and the stars that
still sojourn, yet still move
onward: and everywhere
the blue sky belongs to them,
and is their appointed rest,
and their native country and
their own natural homes—
which they enter

---

245. **or:** before.

unannounced, as lords that
are certainly expected; and
yet there is a silent joy at
their arrival.

Softly she was going up,   265
And a star or two beside—

"Her beams bemocked the sultry main,°
Like April hoarfrost spread;
But where the ship's huge shadow lay,
The charmèd water burnt alway   270
A still and awful red.

By the light of the Moon
he beholdeth God's creatures
of the great calm.

"Beyond the shadow of the ship,
I watched the water snakes.
They moved in tracks of shining white,
And when they reared, the elfish light   275
Fell off in hoary flakes.

"Within the shadow of the ship
I watched their rich attire;
Blue, glossy green, and velvet black,
They coiled and swam, and every track   280
Was a flash of golden fire.

Their beauty and
their happiness.

"Oh happy living things! no tongue
Their beauty might declare.
A spring of love gushed from my heart,

He blesseth them in
his heart.

And I blessed them unaware;   285
Sure my kind saint took pity on me,
And I blessed them unaware.

The spell begins to
break.

"The selfsame moment I could pray;
And from my neck so free
The Albatross fell off, and sank   290
Like lead into the sea.

Part V

"O sleep! it is a gentle thing,
Beloved from pole to pole!
To Mary Queen the praise be given!
She sent the gentle sleep from Heaven,   295
That slid into my soul.

By grace of the holy Mother
the ancient Mariner
is refreshed with rain.

"The silly° buckets on the deck,
That had so long remained,
I dreamt that they were filled with dew;
And when I awoke, it rained.   300

---

267. **main:** sea.   297. **silly:** empty, useless.

"My lips were wet, my throat was cold,
My garments all were dank;
Sure I had drunken in my dreams,
And still my body drank.

"I moved, and could not feel my limbs;   305
I was so light—almost
I thought that I had died in sleep,
And was a blessèd ghost.

*He heareth sounds
and seeth strange sights
and commotions
in the sky and
the element.*
"And soon I heard a roaring wind.
It did not come anear;   310
But with its sound it shook the sails,
That were so thin and sere.°

"The upper air burst into life!
And a hundred fire flags sheen,°
To and fro they were hurried about!   315
And to and fro, and in and out,
The wan stars danced between.°

"And the coming wind did roar more loud,
And the sails did sigh like sedge;°
And the rain poured down from one black cloud;   320
The Moon was at its edge.

"The thick black cloud was cleft, and still
The Moon was at its side;
Like waters shot from some high crag,
The lightning fell with never a jag,   325
A river steep and wide.

*The bodies of the ship's crew
are inspired, and the
ship moves on.*
"The loud wind never reached the ship,
Yet now the ship moved on!
Beneath the lightning and the Moon
The dead men gave a groan.   330

"They groaned, they stirred, they all uprose,
Nor spake, nor moved their eyes;
It had been strange, even in a dream,
To have seen those dead men rise.

---

312. **sere:** dried up.   314. **fire flags sheen:** bright lightning flashes.   313–317. **The upper . . . between.** The Mariner is witnessing the southern lights.   319. **sedge:** tall, coarse rushes that border lakes and streams.

"The helmsman steered, the ship moved on;   335
Yet never a breeze upblew;
The mariners all 'gan work the ropes,
Where they were wont° to do;
They raised their limbs like lifeless tools—
We were a ghastly crew.   340

"The body of my brother's son
Stood by me, knee to knee:
The body and I pulled at one rope,
But he said nought to me."

"I fear thee, ancient Mariner!"   345
"Be calm, thou Wedding Guest!
'Twas not those souls that fled in pain,
Which to their corses° came again,
But a troop of spirits blest;

"For when it dawned—they dropped their arms,   350
And clustered round the mast;
Sweet sounds rose slowly through their mouths,
And from their bodies passed.

"Around, around, flew each sweet sound,
Then darted to the Sun;   355
Slowly the sounds came back again,
Now mixed, now one by one.

"Sometimes a-dropping from the sky
I heard the skylark sing;
Sometimes all little birds that are,   360
How they seemed to fill the sea and air
With their sweet jargoning!°

"And now 'twas like all instruments,
Now like a lonely flute;
And now it is an angel's song,   365
That makes the heavens be mute.

"It ceased; yet still the sails made on
A pleasant noise till noon,
A noise like of a hidden brook
In the leafy month of June,   370
That to the sleeping woods all night
Singeth a quiet tune.

---

338. **wont:** accustomed.   348. **corses:** corpses.   362. **jargoning:** singing.

"Till noon we quietly sailed on,
Yet never a breeze did breathe;
Slowly and smoothly went the ship,   375
Moved onward from beneath.

"Under the keel nine fathom° deep,
From the land of mist and snow,
That Spirit slid; and it was he
That made the ship to go.   380
The sails at noon left off their tune,
And the ship stood still also.

"The Sun, right up above the mast,
Had fixed her to the ocean;
But in a minute she 'gan stir,   385
With a short uneasy motion—
Backwards and forwards half her length
With a short uneasy motion.

"Then like a pawing horse let go,
She made a sudden bound;   390
It flung the blood into my head,
And I fell down in a swound.

"How long in that same fit I lay,
I have not to declare;
But ere my living life returned,   395
I heard, and in my soul discerned,
Two voices in the air.

" 'Is it he?' quoth one, 'Is this the man?
By him who died on cross,
With his cruel bow he laid full low   400
The harmless Albatross.

" 'The Spirit who bideth by himself
In the land of mist and snow,
He loved the bird that loved the man
Who shot him with his bow.'   405

"The other was a softer voice,
As soft as honeydew;
Quoth he, 'The man hath penance done,
And penance more will do.'

---

377. **nine fathom:** fifty-four feet.

Part VI

First Voice

" 'But tell me, tell me! speak again,   410
Thy soft response renewing—
What makes that ship drive on so fast?
What is the ocean doing?'

Second Voice

" 'Still as a slave before his lord,
The ocean hath no blast;   415
His great bright eye most silently
Up to the Moon is cast—

" 'If he may know which way to go;
For she guides him smooth or grim.
See, brother, see! how graciously   420
She looketh down on him.'

First Voice

" 'But why drives on that ship so fast,
Without or wave or wind?'

Second Voice

" 'The air is cut away before,
And closes from behind.   425

" 'Fly, brother, fly! more high, more high!
Or we shall be belated;
For slow and slow that ship will go,
When the Mariner's trance is abated.'

"I woke, and we were sailing on   430
As in a gentle weather;
'Twas night, calm night, the Moon was high;
The dead men stood together.

"All stood together on the deck,
For a charnel dungeon° fitter;   435
All fixed on me their stony eyes,
That in the Moon did glitter.

"The pang, the curse, with which they died,
Had never passed away;
I could not draw my eyes from theirs,   440
Nor turn them up to pray.

The Mariner hath been cast into a trance, for the angelic power causeth the vessel to drive northward faster than human life could endure.

The supernatural motion is retarded; the Mariner awakes, and his penance begins anew.

---

435. **charnel dungeon:** burial vault.

Samuel Taylor Coleridge 455

The curse is finally
expiated.

"And now this spell was snapped; once more
I viewed the ocean green,
And looked far forth, yet little saw
Of what had else been seen—   445

"Like one, that on a lonesome road
Doth walk in fear and dread,
And having once turned round walks on,
And turns no more his head;
Because he knows a frightful fiend   450
Doth close behind him tread.

"But soon there breathed a wind on me,
Nor sound nor motion made;
Its path was not upon the sea,
In ripple or in shade.   455

"It raised my hair, it fanned my cheek
Like a meadow-gale of spring—
It mingled strangely with my fears,
Yet it felt like a welcoming.

"Swiftly, swiftly flew the ship,   460
Yet she sailed softly too;
Sweetly, sweetly blew the breeze—
On me alone it blew.

And the ancient Mariner
beholdeth his
native country.

"Oh! dream of joy! is this indeed
The lighthouse top I see?   465
Is this the hill? Is this the kirk?
Is this mine own countree?

"We drifted o'er the harbor bar,
And I with sobs did pray—
O let me be awake, my God!   470
Or let me sleep alway.

"The harbor bay was clear as glass,
So smoothly it was strewn!°
And on the bay the moonlight lay,
And the shadow of the Moon.   475

"The rock shone bright, the kirk no less,
That stands above the rock;

---

473. **strewn:** spread.

The moonlight steeped in silentness
The steady weathercock.

"And the bay was white with silent light   480
Till, rising from the same,
Full many shapes, that shadows were,
In crimson colors came.

*The angelic spirits
leave the dead bodies*

"A little distance from the prow
Those crimson shadows were;   485
I turned my eyes upon the deck—
Oh, Christ, what saw I there!

"Each corse lay flat, lifeless and flat,
And, by the holy rood!°
A man all light, a seraph°-man   490
On every corse there stood.

*And appear in their
own forms of light.*

"This seraph band, each waved his hand;
It was a heavenly sight!
They stood as signals to the land,
Each one a lovely light;   495

"This seraph band, each waved his hand;
No voice did they impart—
No voice; but oh! the silence sank
Like music on my heart.

"But soon I heard the dash of oars,   500
I heard the Pilot's cheer;
My heard was turned perforce away,
And I saw a boat appear.

"The Pilot and the Pilot's boy,
I heard them coming fast;   505
Dear Lord in Heaven! it was a joy
The dead men could not blast.

"I saw a third—I heard his voice;
It is the Hermit good!
He singeth loud his godly hymns   510
That he makes in the wood.
He'll shrieve° my soul, he'll wash away
The Albatross's blood.

---

489. **rood:** cross.   490. **seraph:** angel.   512. **shrieve** (shrēve): absolve from sin.

Part VII

The Hermit of the wood

"This Hermit good lives in that wood
Which slopes down to the sea.   515
How loudly his sweet voice he rears!
He loves to talk with mariners
That come from a far countree.

"He kneels at morn, and noon, and eve —
He hath a cushion plump;   520
It is the moss that wholly hides
The rotted old oak stump.

"The skiff boat neared; I heard them talk,
'Why, this is strange, I trow!°
Where are those lights so many and fair,   525
That signal made but now?'

Approacheth the ship with wonder.

" 'Strange, by my faith!' the Hermit said —
'And they answered not our cheer!°
The planks looked warped! and see those sails,
How thin they are and sere!   530
I never saw aught like to them,
Unless perchance it were

" 'Brown skeletons of leaves that lag
My forest brook along,
When the ivy tod° is heavy with snow,   535
And the owlet whoops to the wolf below,
That eats the she-wolf's young.'

" 'Dear Lord! it hath a fiendish look' —
(The Pilot made reply)
'I am afeared' — 'Push on, push on!'   540
Said the Hermit cheerily.

"The boat came closer to the ship,
But I nor spake nor stirred;
The boat came close beneath the ship,
And straight° a sound was heard.   545

---

524. **trow:** believe.   528. **cheer:** call, hail.   535. **ivy tod:** ivy bush.   545. **straight:** immediately.

The ship suddenly sinketh.
"Under the water it rumbled on,
Still louder and more dread;
It reached the ship, it split the bay;
The ship went down like lead.

*The ancient Mariner is
saved in the Pilot's boat.*
"Stunned by that loud and dreadful sound,   550
Which sky and ocean smote,
Like one that hath been seven days drowned
My body lay afloat;
But swift as dreams, myself I found
Within the Pilot's boat.   555

"Upon the whirl, where sank the ship,
The boat spun round and round;
And all was still, save that the hill
Was telling of the sound.

"I moved my lips—the Pilot shrieked   560
And fell down in a fit;
The holy Hermit raised his eyes,
And prayed where he did sit.

"I took the oars; the Pilot's boy,
Who now doth crazy go,   565
Laughed loud and long, and all the while
His eyes went to and fro.
'Ha! ha!' quoth he, 'full plain I see,
The Devil knows how to row.'

"And now, all in my own countree,   570
I stood on the firm land!
The Hermit stepped forth from the boat,
And scarcely he could stand.

*The ancient Mariner
earnestly entreateth
the Hermit to shrieve him,
and the penance of life
falls on him.*
" 'O shrieve me, shrieve me, holy man!'
The Hermit crossed his brow.°   575
'Say quick,' quoth he, 'I bid thee say—
What manner of man art thou?'

"Forthwith this frame of mine was wrenched
With a woeful agony,
Which forced me to begin my tale;   580
And then it left me free.

---

575. **crossed his brow:** made the sign of the cross on his forehead.

And ever and anon throughout his future life an agony constraineth him to travel from land to land

"Since then, at an uncertain hour,
That agony returns;
And till my ghastly tale is told,
This heart within me burns.

585

"I pass, like night, from land to land;
I have strange power of speech;
That moment that his face I see
I know the man that must hear me;
To him my tale I teach.

590

"What loud uproar bursts from that door!
The wedding guests are there;
But in the garden bower the bride
And bridemaids singing are;
And hark the little vesper bell,
Which biddeth me to prayer!

595

"O Wedding Guest! this soul hath been
Alone on a wide, wide sea;
So lonely 'twas, that God himself
Scarce seemèd there to be.

600

"O sweeter than the marriage feast,
'Tis sweeter far to me,
To walk together to the kirk
With a goodly company!—

"To walk together to the kirk,
And all together pray,
While each to his great Father bends,
Old men, and babes, and loving friends,
And youths and maidens gay!

605

And to teach by his own example love and reverence to all things that God made and loveth.

"Farewell, farewell; but this I tell
To thee, thou Wedding Guest!
He prayeth well, who loveth well
Both man and bird and beast.

610

"He prayeth best, who loveth best
All things both great and small;
For the dear God who loveth us,
He made and loveth all."

615

The Mariner, whose eye is bright,
Whose beard with age is hoar,
Is gone; and now the Wedding Guest   620
Turned from the bridegroom's door.

He went like one that hath been stunned,
And is of sense forlorn;
A sadder and a wiser man,
He rose the morrow morn.   625

FOR STUDY AND DISCUSSION

1. The accounts of the Wedding Guest's reactions in Parts I and VII serve as a kind of frame for the Mariner's tale by giving it a beginning and an end. To what extent does the presence of the Wedding Guest influence your own reactions to the poem?

2. What evidence can you find in the poem to show that the Albatross takes on a religious significance that would make the killing of it evil or "hellish"?

3. Contrast the two figures that cast dice for the Mariner in Part III. What does their presence suggest about the significance of the Mariner's offense?

4. The Mariner is punished for his contempt of living things. Which lines in Part IV show that he continues to despise or hate living creatures? At which point in the poem does his salvation or rebirth begin? How might the word *unaware* in line 285 suggest that the Mariner's salvation comes from heaven?

5. How does the conversation between the two spirits in Parts V and VI deepen your understanding of the Mariner's salvation?

6. Read aloud the lines in Part VII that sum up the theme of the poem. Coleridge once admitted that such a pat, explicit statement was a weakness in the poem. Do you agree? Explain. Find at least five other lines in the poem that point to this theme and make it more than simply a moral tag at the end of the poem.

7. Describe the atmosphere of the poem. Cite words, phrases, and vivid images that contribute to the atmosphere.

LANGUAGE AND VOCABULARY

To evoke the medieval folk ballads, Coleridge made deliberate use of archaic words in *The Rime of the Ancient Mariner*. For example, *wist* (line 152) is the past tense of the verb *wit*, meaning "to know." (*Wit* survives today only as a noun.) Consult an unabridged dictionary to explain the meaning and origin of the following old words: *eftsoons* (line 12); *ken* (line 57); *swound* (line 62); *rood* (line 489); *trow* (524). What does the use of such words add to the poem?

FOR COMPOSITION

Write a composition in which you describe the means Coleridge employs in *The Rime of the Ancient Mariner* to induce what he calls a "willing suspension of disbelief." Do you think Coleridge is successful in inducing such a suspension? Explain, using specific examples from the poem.

Kubla Khan

Kubla Khan (koō'blə kän') is a figure from ancient oriental history. He founded the Mongol dynasty in China in the thirteenth century ("Khan" means "King"). Coleridge had read about him in a seventeenth-century book by Samuel Purchas, entitled *Purchas His Pilgrimage* (1613): "In Xamdu did Cublai Can build a stately Palace; encompassing sixteene miles of plaine ground with a wall, wherein are fertile Meddowes, pleasant springs, delightful Streames, and all sorts of beasts of chase and game, and in the middest thereof a sumptuous house of pleasure, which may be removed from place to place." This description provides a basis for the elaborate imaginative vision of Kubla Khan's "pleasure dome" in Coleridge's poem, which was written in 1797–1798 but not published until 1816.

For an account of the circumstances under which Coleridge wrote "Kubla Khan," see the Commentary (page 464).

In Xanadu° did Kubla Khan
A stately pleasure dome decree,
Where Alph,° the sacred river, ran
Through caverns measureless to man
  Down to a sunless sea.   5
So twice five miles of fertile ground
With walls and towers were girdled round;
And here were gardens bright with sinuous rills,
Where blossomed many an incense-bearing tree;
And here were forests ancient as the hills,   10
Enfolding sunny spots of greenery.

But oh! that deep romantic chasm which slanted
Down the green hill athwart a cedarn cover!°
A savage place! as holy and enchanted
As e'er beneath a waning moon was haunted   15
By woman wailing for her demon lover!
And from this chasm, with ceaseless turmoil seething,
As if this earth in fast thick pants were breathing,
A mighty fountain momently was forced,
Amid whose swift half-intermitted burst   20
Huge fragments vaulted like rebounding hail,
Or chaffy grain beneath the thresher's flail;
And mid these dancing rocks at once and ever
It flung up momently the sacred river.
Five miles meandering with a mazy motion   25

---

1. **Xanadu** (zăn'ə-dōō): a region of Tartary, a vast, indefinite area in Asia and Europe. 3. **Alph:** Perhaps this name is taken from Alpheus, in classical mythology a river god who loved and pursued Arethusa until Diana changed her into a stream. Their waters united in a fountain in Sicily. 13. **athwart . . . cover:** across a thick covering of cedar trees.

Chingiz (Genghis) Khan (Persian miniature, 1397),
ancestor of Kubla Khan. British colonialism
helped to revive an interest in the Orient.
Courtesy, British Library

Through wood and dale the sacred river ran,
Then reached the caverns measureless to man,
And sank in tumult to a lifeless ocean;
And mid this tumult Kubla heard from far
Ancestral voices prophesying war! 30
   The shadow of the dome of pleasure
   Floated midway on the waves;
   Where was heard the mingled measure
   From the fountain and the caves.
It was a miracle of rare device, 35
A sunny pleasure dome with caves of ice!

   A damsel with a dulcimer°
   In a vision once I saw;
   It was an Abyssinian maid,
   And on her dulcimer she played, 40
   Singing of Mount Abora.°
   Could I revive within me
   Her symphony and song,
   To such a deep delight 'twould win me,
That with music loud and long, 45
I would build that dome in air,
That sunny dome! those caves of ice!
And all who heard should see them there,
And all should cry, Beware! Beware!
His flashing eyes, his floating hair! 50
Weave a circle round him thrice,
And close your eyes with holy dread,
For he on honeydew hath fed,
And drunk the milk of Paradise.

37. **dulcimer** (dŭl′sə-mər): a musical instrument having metallic wires played with
light hammers. The word means "sweet song," a phrase that well describes its
light, delicate tone. 41. **Mount Abora:** not positively identified; probably Amara,
a mountain in Abyssinia. On it, according to tradition, was an earthly paradise
like Kubla Khan's.

COMMENTARY

It was apparently Byron who insisted that Coleridge publish "Kubla Khan," and when the poem appeared in 1816, it was prefaced by Coleridge's account of the extraordinary circumstances under which it was composed. During the summer of 1797, Coleridge explains, he had retired in poor health to a lonely farmhouse. To relieve some of the discomfort of his illness, he had taken an "anodyne" prescribed by the doctor. (Coleridge later explained in a letter that this "anodyne" contained two grains of opium.) Coleridge was reading about Kubla Khan in *Purchas His Pilgrimage* at the time, but the effects of the "anodyne" caused him to fall asleep while he was reading the following sentence: "Here the Khan Kubla commanded a palace to be built, and a stately garden thereunto. And thus ten miles of fertile ground were inclosed with a wall."

Coleridge's account goes on: "The author continued for about three hours in a profound sleep, . . . during which time he has the most vivid confidence, that he could not have composed less than from two to three hundred lines . . . ." When he awoke, says Coleridge, he immediately began to write down the poem composed in his dream. But when he had written all that exists of the present version of "Kubla Khan," he was called away for an hour on business. When he returned to his room to write the rest of the dream-poem, he found that "with the exception of some eight or ten scattered lines and images, all the rest had passed away like the images on the surface of a stream into which a stone has been cast . . . ." Coleridge concludes by saying that he intends someday to complete the poem "from the still surviving recollections in his mind."

Coleridge's account of the composition of "Kubla Khan" has become a classic statement of the Romantic interest in unusual conditions of the mind, and of the Romantic belief that poetry should flow from the mind's deepest and most spontaneous impulses. It has also been taken to typify Coleridge's own poetic character—his inability to sustain or complete some of his finest initial inspirations. In any case, it is important to remember what Coleridge says he dreamed. His dream was not a vision of Xanadu itself, but the composition of a poem about that vision, part of which he was able to recall while awake. "Kubla Khan" is, therefore, partly a poem about writing a poem. This is particularly true of lines 37–54, where the speaker longs to recall a former "vision" which would enable him to build for himself "that dome in air." It is as if Coleridge's dream-poem anticipates the dreamer's own dilemma once he wakes up.

FOR STUDY AND DISCUSSION

1. Why has Kubla Khan enclosed the lush romantic landscape in a dome? What is the relation of the world inside the dome to the world outside it?

2. There is a sharp break at line 37 when the speaker introduces his past vision of "an Abyssinian maid." What does this past vision seem to mean to the speaker?

DEVICES OF SOUND

Coleridge's poems are notable for their use of sound to heighten emotion or deepen meaning, thus influencing the reader's reaction. Among other devices of sound, the following three devices are used in *The Rime of the Ancient Mariner* and "Kubla Khan":

Internal rhyme. Rhyme occurring within a poetic line, as in "The guests are *met,* the feast is *set.*"

Alliteration. The repetition of initial consonant sounds, as in "*D*own *d*ropped the breeze, the breeze *d*ropped *d*own."

Assonance. The repetition of vowel sounds, as in "So tw*i*ce f*i*ve m*i*les of f*e*rt*i*le ground."

Find three examples of the use of each device of sound in the two poems. What does the use of these devices add to the poem in each case?

FOR COMPOSITION

Coleridge's dream about writing "Kubla Khan" may remind you that we often hear of people dreaming about experiences that would be impossible in "real life." Think of such a dream you have had. Describe the dream, or as much of it as you can remember. Do you have the feeling that there were important aspects of the dream that you cannot recall? Then describe how you felt when you woke up from the dream.

Charles Lamb
1775–1834

Charles Lamb
National Portrait Gallery, London

Charles Lamb is one of the great essayists of the Romantic Age. What distinguishes his essays especially is the whimsical delicacy of his prose and the personal charm of his observations. A Londoner all his life, Lamb confessed in a letter to Wordsworth that he felt more at home in the city than in the wild nature so beloved by his fellow Romantics: "I have passed all my days in London, until I have formed as many and intense local attachments as any of you mountaineers can have done with dead nature." The subjects of Lamb's essays are often drawn from the richness of London life. He shows how a Romantic imagination can find its stimulus in society and people, as well as in what Wordsworth called "the beautiful and permanent forms of nature."

Lamb's life was characterized by an astounding combination of quiet normalcy and shocking tragedy. The son of a legal clerk, Lamb attended the famous Christ's Hospital School, where Coleridge was also a student. He left school at age fifteen, however, and took a position as clerk in an enormous commercial firm called the East India House. Lamb was to hold this job for thirty-three years.

Tragedy struck when he was twenty-two: his older sister, Mary, to whom he was very close all of his life, broke under the stress of caring for their invalid parents and, in a fit of insanity, stabbed her mother to death. Lamb was crushed, but he took on the full responsibility of seeing Mary confined to an asylum and, after her release, of taking care of her for the rest of his life.

Although subject to recurrent attacks of insanity, Mary was able most of the time to live a normal life with her brother. Together they enjoyed their London world of social events, books, theater, and art. Their home was the scene of weekly Wednesday- or Thursday-night gatherings of friends and literary acquaintances. Lamb himself was a superb host, delighting his guests with conversation which, as the wine flowed, became more and more whimsical and outrageously witty. When he finally retired from the East India House in 1824, he moved with Mary to a country house near London, where he spent the rest of his life.

Lamb began writing in a variety of forms early in life as a way of supplementing his salary at the East India House. His collected *Works,* published in 1818, contains poems, plays, a novel, and excellent literary criticism. In collaboration with his sister Mary, he had written a wonderful book for children called *Tales from Shakespeare.* But Lamb's real fame came two years later in 1820, when he began to contribute his *Essays of Elia* to the *London Magazine.* Under the pseudonym of an Italian clerk named Elia, whom he had actually known at the East India House, Lamb wrote about his own responses to a wide variety of subjects with that distinctive combination of nostalgia, humor, and refined observation that makes him one of the most enjoyable of all personal essayists.

With his love of the city, his charming sociability, and his unheroic perception of the world, Lamb has sometimes been said to lack the characteristics we usually associate with Romanticism. But memory—memory as a means of access to the writer's own growth and personality—is as important to Lamb as it is to Wordsworth. Many of his essays, including "Dream Children: A Reverie," are splendid examples in prose of what Wordsworth meant by "emotion recollected in tranquillity."

Dream Children: A Reverie

Children love to listen to stories about their elders, when *they* were children; to stretch their imagination to the conception of a traditionary great-uncle, or grandame, whom they never saw. It was in this spirit that my little ones crept about me the other evening to hear about their great-grandmother Field,[1] who lived in a great house in Norfolk (a hundred times bigger than that in which they and papa lived) which had been the scene (so at least it was generally believed in that part of the country) of the tragic incidents which they had lately become familiar with from the ballad of the "Children in the Wood." Certain it is that the whole story of the children and their cruel uncle was to be seen fairly carved out in wood upon the chimney piece of the great hall, the whole story down to the Robin Redbreasts;[2] till a foolish rich person pulled it down to set up a marble one of modern invention in its stead, with no story upon it. Here Alice put out one of her dear mother's looks, too tender to be called upbraiding.

Then I went on to say how religious and how good their great-grandmother Field was, how beloved and respected by everybody, though she was not indeed the mistress of this great house, but had only the charge of it (and yet in some respects she might be said to be the mistress of it too) committed to her by the owner, who preferred living in a newer and more fashionable mansion which he had purchased somewhere in the adjoining county; but still she lived in it in a manner as if it had been her own and kept up the dignity of the great house in a sort while she lived, which afterward came to decay and was nearly pulled down, and all its old ornaments stripped and carried away to the owner's other house, where they were set up and looked as awkward as if someone were to carry away the old tombs they had seen lately at the Abbey, and stick them up in Lady C.'s tawdry gilt drawing room. Here John smiled, as much as to say, "that would be foolish indeed."

And then I told how, when she came to die, her funeral was attended by a concourse of all the poor, and some of the gentry too, of the neighborhood for many miles round, to show their respect for her memory, because she had been such a good and religious woman; so good indeed that she knew all the Psaltery[3] by heart, aye, and a great part of the Testament besides. Here little Alice spread her hands.[4]

Then I told what a tall, upright, graceful person their great-grandmother Field once was; and how in her youth she was esteemed the best dancer—here Alice's little right foot played an involuntary movement, till, upon my looking grave, it desisted—the best dancer, I was saying, in the country, till a cruel disease, called a cancer, came, and bowed her down with pain; but it could never bend her good spirits, or make them stoop, but they were still upright, because she was so good and religious.

Then I told how she was used to sleep by herself in a lone chamber of the great lone house; and how she believed that an apparition of two infants was to be seen at midnight gliding up and down the great staircase near where she slept, but she said, "those innocents would do her no harm"; and how frightened I used to be, though in those days I had my maid to sleep with me, because I was never half so good or religious as she; and yet I

---

1. **great-grandmother Field:** a reference to Mary Field, Lamb's grandmother.
2. **Robin Redbreasts:** At the end of the ballad, the robin covers the bodies of the children with leaves.
3. **Psaltery** (sôl′tə-rē): Psalms of David, as they appear in the Book of Common Prayer.
4. **spread her hands:** a gesture of surprise.

never saw the infants. Here John expanded all his eyebrows and tried to look courageous.

Then I told how good she was to all her grandchildren, having us to the great house in the holidays, where I in particular used to spend many hours by myself in gazing upon the old busts of the Twelve Caesars that had been Emperors of Rome, till the old marble heads would seem to live again, or I to be turned into marble with them; how I never could be tired with roaming about that huge mansion, with its vast empty rooms, with their worn-out hangings, fluttering tapestry, and carved oaken panels, with the gilding almost rubbed out—sometimes in the spacious old-fashioned gardens, which I had almost to myself, unless when now and then a solitary gardening man would cross me—and how the nectarines and peaches hung upon the walls without my ever offering to pluck them because they were forbidden fruit, unless now and then—and because I had more pleasure in strolling about among the old melancholy-looking yew trees, or the firs, and picking up the red berries, and the fir apples,[5] which were good for nothing but to look at—or in lying about upon the fresh grass with all the fine garden smells around me—or basking in the orangery,[6] till I could almost fancy myself ripening too along with the oranges and the limes in that grateful warmth—or in watching the dace that darted to and fro in the fish-pond, at the bottom of the garden, with here and there a great sulky pike hanging midway down the water in silent state, as if it mocked at their impertinent friskings—I had more pleasure in these busy-idle diversions than in all the sweet flavors of peaches, nectarines, oranges, and suchlike common baits for children. Here John slyly deposited back upon the plate a bunch of grapes, which, not unobserved by Alice, he had meditated dividing with her, and both seemed willing to relinquish them for the present as irrelevant.

Then, in somewhat a more heightened tone, I told how, though their great-grandmother Field loved all her grandchildren, yet in an especial manner she might be said to love their uncle, John L——,[7] because he was so handsome and spirited a youth, and a king to the rest of us; and, instead of moping about in solitary corners, like some of us, he would mount the most mettlesome horse he could get, when but an imp no bigger than themselves, and make it carry him half over the county in a morning, and join the hunters when there were any out—and yet he loved the old great house and gardens too, but had too much spirit to be always pent up within their boundaries—and how their uncle grew up to man's estate as brave as he was handsome, to the admiration of everybody, but of their great-grandmother Field most especially; and how he used to carry me upon his back when I was a lame-footed boy—for he was a good bit older than me—many a mile when I could not walk for pain; and how in after life he became lame-footed too, and I did not always (I fear) make allowances enough for him when he was impatient and in pain, nor remember sufficiently how considerate he had been to me when I was lamefooted; and how when he died, though he had not been dead an hour, it seemed as if he had died a great while ago, such a distance there is betwixt life and death; and how I bore his death as I thought pretty well at first, but afterward it haunted and haunted me; and though I did not cry or take it to heart as some do, and as I think he would have done if I had died, yet I missed him all day long, and knew not till then how much I had loved him. I missed his kindness, and I missed his crossness, and wished him to be alive again to be quarreling

---

5. **fir apples:** fir cones.
6. **orangery:** a building or other protected place used for growing oranges in a mild climate.

7. **John L——:** John Lamb, Charles Lamb's eldest brother, who died shortly before this essay was written. His lameness, mentioned later in the essay, was due to an injury.

with him (for we quarreled sometimes) rather than not have him again, and was as uneasy without him as he, their poor uncle, must have been when the doctor took off his limb.[8] Here the children fell a-crying, and asked if their little mourning which they had on was not for uncle John, and they looked up and prayed me not to go on about their uncle, but to tell them some stories about their pretty dead mother.

Then I told how for seven long years, in hope sometimes, sometimes in despair, yet persisting ever, I courted the fair Alice W——n,[9] and, as much as children could understand, I explained to them what coyness, and difficulty, and denial, meant in maidens—when suddenly, turning to Alice, the soul of the first Alice looked out at her eyes with such a reality or representment[10] that I became in doubt which of them stood there before me, or whose that bright hair was; and while I stood gazing, both the children gradually grew fainter to my view, receding, and still receding, till nothing at last but two mournful features were seen in the uttermost distance, which, without speech, strangely impressed upon me the effects of speech: "We are not of Alice, nor of thee, nor are we children at all. The children of Alice call Bartrum father. We are nothing; less than nothing, and dreams. We are only what might have been, and must wait upon the tedious shores of Lethe[11] millions of ages before we have existence and a name"—and immediately awaking, I found myself quietly seated in my bachelor armchair, where I had fallen asleep with the faithful Bridget[12] unchanged by my side—but John L. (or James Elia) was gone forever.

8. **doctor . . . limb:** an imaginary detail.
9. **Alice W——n:** Alice Winterton, probably Ann Simmons, whom Lamb loved when he was young.
10. **representment:** portrayal, picturing.
11. **Lethe** (lē′thē): in Greek mythology, the river of forgetfulness. They wait on the shore of the river to return to mortal life.
12. **Bridget:** name given to Lamb's sister in the Elia essays.

FOR STUDY AND DISCUSSION

1. This essay is a blend of fact and fiction. Aside from the use of fact, how does this essay differ from a short story?
2. What details does Lamb use in this essay to make John and Alice seem like real children? Does the revelation that they are "only what might have been" make the ending seem sad and touching or does the ending seem merely clever?
3. What does this essay reveal about Lamb's attitude toward the world of reality and the world of imagination?

THE FAMILIAR ESSAY

The familiar, or informal, essay is characterized by its relaxed style, its conversational tone, and its wide range of subject matter. You have already encountered the informal essays of Addison and Steele (pages 343–348). The French essayist Montaigne said that in writing an essay, "It is myself that I portray." This is true not only of Montaigne but of most familiar essayists. No form of writing reveals more about the personality of a writer than the familiar essay.

Charles Lamb is generally considered the finest familiar essayist in English. What impression of Lamb's personality do you get from this essay? How do Lamb's choice of details and his style help to convey this impression? After reading this essay, do you think you would like to have known Lamb personally? Why or why not?

LANGUAGE AND VOCABULARY

At one point in the essay, Lamb uses adjectives in a unique way. In the phrase "busy-idle diversions," he has combined two adjectives with exactly opposite meanings by hyphenating them. Explain the meaning of this phrase. Why do you think Lamb wrote "busy-idle diversions" instead of "diversions that keep idle people busy"? What kind of situations can you think of that might account for the use of the following phrases: *sad-happy occasion, harsh-kind remark*? Invent a similar phrase and show how it might be used in a sentence.

Jane Austen
1775–1817

Although Jane Austen's career belongs chronologically to the Romantic period (she was a contemporary of Wordsworth and Coleridge), the spirit and the ideas embodied in her fiction hark back to the eighteenth century—to the brilliant satire of Alexander Pope and to the rational, commonsensical moral authority of Samuel Johnson. She was born at Steventon in Hampshire, a small town in southwest England where her father was rector of the church. "A life of usefulness, literature, and religion, was not by any means a life of event," reflected Jane's brother Henry Austen in an 1818 "Biographical Notice" of his sister. Jane Austen's life does seem remarkably quiet and uneventful to us today. Yet in her private reading and writing and in her observation of social behavior, she developed powers of subtle discrimination and shrewd perceptiveness. She referred to her own fiction as "the little bit (two inches wide) of ivory on which I work with so fine a brush, as produces little effect after much labor." In her modest way she became one of the two greatest English novelists of the period, Sir Walter Scott being the other.

Scott's own assessment of Jane Austen's achievement is telling: "The young lady had a talent for describing the involvements and feelings and characters of ordinary life which is to me the most wonderful I ever met with." Her earliest fictional ventures, written for her close friends and family before she was twenty, are full of charming and delicate comedy. In 1795 she began a first version of *Sense and Sensibility;* in 1796 of *Pride and Prejudice;* in 1797, or possibly earlier, of *Northanger Abbey.* In the revised versions of these early novels, we can see her perfecting her skill at social comedy while moving in the direction of the pointed social satire and refined moral understanding characteristic of her later work: *Mansfield Park* (begun in 1811), *Emma* (begun in 1814), and *Persuasion* (begun in 1815).

Jane Austen published most of her mature work while living at Chawton, a small village only a few miles away from her birthplace. She knew and wrote about fashionable resorts like Bath and

Jane Austen (contemporary drawing, artist unknown).
Brown Brothers

Southampton but preferred to keep her distance from them. The modest redbrick house at Chawton preserves very convincingly for present-day admirers the contrast between the appearance of her life and its inner character. Visitors to this house, like readers of her biography, sense the vitality and imagination that flourished within the well-bred serenity and restraint of her world. She died in Winchester, the ancient cathedral town of her native Hampshire. She is buried in the cathedral.

Jane Austen was popular all through the nineteenth century and in the twentieth century has become almost a cult figure to many well-known authors. E. M. Forster in a famous essay describes himself as a "Jane Austenite" and says that she is his favorite author.

from **Pride and Prejudice**

In the opinion of many readers, Jane Austen's novel *Pride and Prejudice* is her best work. The opening sentence of the book announces its theme and its tone: "It is a truth universally acknowledged that a single man in possession of a good fortune must be in want of a wife." Marriage—with all its social conventions and economic concerns—is Austen's subject, and she treats it with genial satire.

The central character of the novel is Elizabeth Bennet, one of five sisters, none of whom can inherit the Bennet estate of Longbourn for it has been entailed upon the nearest male heir, William Collins. Collins intends to marry and decides to choose one of the Bennet daughters as a way of making amends for inheriting their father's estate. Collins is a preposterous suitor, and his proposal to Elizabeth is one of the best comic scenes in the book. Collins' "declaration" not only reveals his pomposity and conceit but also tells us a great deal about attitudes toward marriage in Austen's time.

The next day opened a new scene at Longbourn. Mr. Collins made his declaration in form. Having resolved to do it without loss of time, as his leave of absence extended only to the following Saturday, and having no feelings of diffidence to make it distressing to himself even at the moment, he set about it in a very orderly manner, with all the observances which he supposed a regular part of the business. On finding Mrs. Bennet, Elizabeth and one of the younger girls together soon after breakfast, he addressed the mother in these words,

"May I hope, madam, for your interest with your fair daughter Elizabeth, when I solicit for the honor of a private audience with her in the course of this morning?"

Before Elizabeth had time for anything but a blush of surprise, Mrs. Bennet instantly answered,

"Oh dear!—Yes—certainly.—I am sure Lizzy will be very happy—I am sure she can have no objection.—Come Kitty, I want you upstairs." And gathering her work together, she was hastening away, when Elizabeth called out,

"Dear Ma'am, do not go.—I beg you will not go.—Mr. Collins must excuse me.—He can have nothing to say to me that anybody need not hear. I am going away myself."

"No, no, nonsense, Lizzy. I desire you will stay where you are."—And upon Elizabeth's seeming really, with vexed and embarrassed looks, about to escape, she added, "Lizzy, I *insist* upon your staying and hearing Mr. Collins."

Elizabeth would not oppose such an injunction—and a moment's consideration making her also sensible that it would be wisest to get it over as soon and as quietly as possible, she sat down again, and tried to conceal by incessant employment the feelings which were divided between distress and diversion. Mrs. Bennet and Kitty walked off, and as soon as they were gone Mr. Collins began.

"Believe me, my dear Miss Elizabeth, that your modesty, so far from doing you any disservice, rather adds to your other perfections. You would have been less amiable in my eyes had there *not* been this little unwillingness; but allow me to assure you that I have your respected mother's permission for this address. You can hardly doubt the purport of my discourse, however your natural delicacy may lead you to dissemble; my attentions have been too marked to be mistaken. Almost as soon as I entered the house I singled you out as the companion of my future life. But before I am run away with by my feelings on this subject, perhaps it will be advisable for me to state my reasons for marrying—and moreover for coming into Hertfordshire with the design of selecting a wife, as I certainly did.''

The idea of Mr. Collins, with all his solemn composure, being run away with by his feelings, made Elizabeth so near laughing that she could not use the short pause he allowed in any attempt to stop him farther, and he continued:

"My reasons for marrying are, first, that I think it a right thing for every clergyman in easy circumstances (like myself) to set the example of matrimony in his parish. Secondly, that I am convinced it will add very greatly to my happiness; and thirdly, which perhaps I ought to have mentioned earlier, that it is the particular advice and recommendation of the very noble lady whom I have the honor of calling patroness. Twice has she condescended to give me her opinion (unasked too!) on this subject; and it was but the very Saturday night before I left Hunsford—between our pools at quadrille,[1] while Mrs. Jenkinson was arranging Miss De Bourgh's footstool, that she said, 'Mr Collins, you must marry. A clergyman like you must marry. Choose properly, choose a gentlewoman for *my* sake; and for your *own*, let her be an active, useful sort of person, not brought up high, but able to make a small income go a good way. This is my advice. Find such a woman as soon as you can, bring her to Hunsford, and I will visit her.' Allow me, by the way, to observe, my fair cousin, that I do not reckon the notice and kindness of Lady Catherine de Bourgh as

---

1. **quadrille** (kwŏ-drĭl'): a popular card game in the eighteenth century.

among the least of the advantages in my power to offer. You will find her manners beyond anything I can describe; and your wit and vivacity I think must be acceptable to her, especially when tempered with the silence and respect which her rank will inevitably excite. Thus much for my general intention in favor of matrimony; it remains to be told why my views were directed to Longbourn instead of my own neighborhood, where I assure you there are many amiable young women. But the fact is that being, as I am, to inherit this estate after the death of your honored father (who, however, may live many years longer), I could not satisfy myself without resolving to choose a wife from among his daughters, that the loss to them might be as little as possible, when the melancholy event takes place—which, however, as I have already said, may not be for several years. This has been my motive, my fair cousin, and I flatter myself it will not sink me in your esteem. And now nothing remains for me but to assure you in the most animated language of the violence of my affection. To fortune I am perfectly indifferent, and shall make no demand of that nature on your father, since I am well aware that it could not be complied with; and that one thousand pounds in the 4 percents, which will not be yours till after your mother's decease, is all that you may ever be entitled to. On that head, therefore, I shall be uniformly silent; and you may assure yourself that no ungenerous reproach shall ever pass my lips when we are married.''

It was absolutely necessary to interrupt him now.

"You are too hasty, sir," she cried. "You forget that I have made no answer. Let me do it without farther loss of time. Accept my thanks for the compliment you are paying me. I am very sensible of the honor of your proposals, but it is impossible for me to do otherwise than decline them.''

"I am not now to learn," replied Mr. Collins, with a formal wave of the hand, "that it is usual with young ladies to reject the addresses of the man whom they secretly mean to accept, when he first applies for their favor; and that sometimes the refusal is repeated a second or even a third time. I am therefore by no means discouraged by what you have just said, and shall hope to lead you to the altar ere long."

"Upon my word, sir," cried Elizabeth, "your hope is rather an extraordinary one after my declaration. I do assure you that I am not one of those young ladies (if such young ladies there are) who are so daring as to risk their happiness on the chance of being asked a second time. I am perfectly serious in my refusal. — You could not make *me* happy, and I am convinced that I am the last woman in the world who would make *you* so. — Nay, were your friend Lady Catherine to know me, I am persuaded she would find me in every respect ill qualified for the situation."

"Were it certain that Lady Catherine would think so," said Mr. Collins very gravely — "but I cannot imagine that her ladyship would at all disapprove of you. And you may be certain that when I have the honor of seeing her again I shall speak in the highest terms of your modesty, economy, and other amiable qualifications."

"Indeed, Mr. Collins, all praise of me will be unnecessary. You must give me leave to judge for myself, and pay me the compliment of believing what I say. I wish you very happy and very rich, and by refusing your hand, do all in my power to prevent your being otherwise. In making me the offer, you must have satisfied the delicacy of your feelings with regard to my family, and may take possession of Longbourn estate whenever it falls, without any self-reproach. This matter may be considered, therefore, as finally settled." And rising as she thus spoke, she would have quitted the room had not Mr. Collins thus addressed her,

"When I do myself the honor of speaking to you next on this subject I shall hope to receive a more favorable answer than you have now given me; though I am far from accusing you of cruelty at present, because I know it to be the established custom of your sex to reject a man on the first application, and perhaps you have even now said as much to encourage my suit as would be consistent with the true delicacy of the female character."

"Really, Mr. Collins," cried Elizabeth with some warmth, "you puzzle me exceedingly. If what I have hitherto said can appear to you in the form of encouragement, I know not how to express my refusal in such a way as may convince you of its being one."

"You must give me leave to flatter myself, my dear cousin, that your refusal of my addresses is merely words of course. My reasons for believing it are briefly these: it does not appear to me that my hand is unworthy your acceptance, or that the establishment I can offer would be any other than highly desirable. My situation in life, my connections with the family of De Bourgh, and my relationship to your own, are circumstances highly in my favor; and you should take it into farther consideration that in spite of your manifold attractions, it is by no means certain that another offer of marriage may ever be made you. Your portion is unhappily so small that it will in all likelihood undo the effects of your loveliness and amiable qualifications. As I must therefore conclude that you are not serious in your rejection of me, I shall choose to attribute it to your wish of increasing my love by suspense, according to the usual practice of elegant females."

"I do assure you, sir, that I have no pretension whatever to that kind of elegance which consists in tormenting a respectable man. I would rather be paid the compliment of being believed sincere. I thank you again and again for the honor you have done me in your proposals, but to accept them is absolutely impossible. My feelings in every respect forbid it. Can I speak plainer? Do not consider me now as an elegant female intending to plague you, but as a rational creature speaking the truth from her heart."

Tenderly Flirting (drawing for an early edition of *Pride and Prejudice*) by Hugh Thomson. One of Elizabeth's less judicious sisters flirts with a group of soldiers.
Culver Pictures

"You are uniformly charming!" cried he, with an air of awkward gallantry; "and I am persuaded that when sanctioned by the express authority of both your excellent parents, my proposals will not fail of being acceptable."

To such perseverance in willful self-deception Elizabeth would make no reply, and immediately and in silence withdrew; determined, that if he persisted in considering her repeated refusals as flattering encouragement, to apply to her father, whose negative might be uttered in such a manner as must be decisive, and whose behavior at least could not be mistaken for the affectation and coquetry of an elegant female.

FOR STUDY AND DISCUSSION

1. Collins feels that it is proper to give his reasons for marrying. Which of the three reasons he offers seems to be most important to him? What does this tell you about Collins?

2. Collins refuses to take Elizabeth's rejection of his proposal seriously. Why does he consider his offer "highly desirable"? Why does he assume Elizabeth will have few offers of marriage?

3. Jane Austen's characters frequently reveal themselves through their modes of speech. Compare the speeches of Collins and Elizabeth. What do the differences in their manner of speaking to one another tell you about them as individuals? What is the contrast between Collins' elaborate flattery and the real message of his proposal?

George Gordon, Lord Byron
1788–1824

For many of his contemporaries in England, Europe, and America, Byron was the embodiment of the Romantic spirit, both in his poetry and in his personal life. Proud, passionate, rebellious, deeply marked by painful and often mysterious experiences in the past, yet fiercely and defiantly committed to following his own individual destiny— this was the image that Byron created for his contemporaries and passed on to subsequent ages.

Byron was descended from two aristocratic but violent and undisciplined families. His father, a reckless English sea captain and fortune hunter, was called "Mad Jack" Byron; his mother, Catharine Gordon of Gight, came from a line of fiery-tempered, lawless Scottish nobles. Byron was born in London, but at the age of three, shortly after his father died, he was taken by his mother to Aberdeen, where he was brought up in the strict religious environment of Scottish Presbyterianism. Byron's mother was loving but very ill-tempered, and she often quarreled with her impetuous, high-spirited son. Although an extremely handsome boy, Byron had been born with a clubfoot. The pain and self-consciousness caused by this deformity was aggravated by a corrective shoe, which Byron's mother, on the advice of an inept physician, forced him to wear. Byron struggled all his life with the physical and psychological effects of his deformity. He was especially proud of his athletic prowess at swimming, riding, boxing, and cricket, and of his good looks, which he was always fearful of losing.

When Byron was ten years old, his great uncle, known as the "Wicked Lord," died, and Byron inherited his title to become the sixth Lord Byron. Byron was also heir to the ancestral estate, Newstead Abbey. He was sent to Harrow, one of England's most prestigious private schools, and then to Cambridge University. It was at Cambridge that Byron began to write poetry, and to assume a flamboyant, outrageous style of life that would become his trademark. He spent much of the money he inherited on expensive clothes and decorations for his college rooms; he entertained lavishly; he kept horses and a pet bear; and he loved to shock his friends by drinking out of a cup made from a human skull. In 1807 Byron published his lyric poems in a small volume called *Hours of Idleness*.

George Gordon, Lord Byron by Thomas Phillips.
The Bettmann Archive

The volume was sharply attacked in the influential *Edinburgh Review,* and Byron responded with his first important poem, a biting satire in the eighteenth-century manner, called *English Bards and Scotch Reviewers.*

In 1809, after graduating from Cambridge, Byron set out with a close friend on an extended tour of countries not immediately involved in the Napoleonic Wars: Spain, Portugal, Albania, Greece, Asia Minor. He used the experiences of this journey as the basis for the first two cantos of a marvelous poetic travelogue entitled *Childe Harold's Pilgrimage,* which he published soon after his return to England in 1812. The work was enormously successful. As Byron himself recalled, "I awoke one morning and found myself famous." He became the greatest literary and social celebrity of Regency London. His reputation grew still further with the publication of a series of Romantic verse narratives with exotic, Near-Eastern settings: *The Giaour, The Corsair,* and *Lara.*

The appeal of these poems lay only partly in their descriptions of foreign scenes and customs. In them, and in the verse dramas a few years later, Byron created the figure subsequently known as the "Byronic hero": a passionate, moody, restless character who has exhausted most of the world's excitements, and who lives under the weight of some mysterious sin committed in the past. His proud, defiant individualism refuses to be limited by the normal institutional and moral strictures of society. He is an "outsider" whose daring life both isolates him and makes him attractive. Most of Byron's readers identified him personally with his heroes. And despite his protests that such connections should never be taken seriously, it seems clear that Byron partly enjoyed the identity, at least at the beginning of his career, and sometimes tried to project it in his own behavior.

In 1815, at the height of his popularity, Byron married Annabella Milbanke, who sought to make him into a conventional and respectable husband. But Byron was soon involved in bitter quarrels with his wife over his unconventional behavior and his continuing love affairs. When she left him after only a year of marriage, Byron found himself surrounded by scandal and ostracized by the very society that had made him its favorite. Bitter but defiant as always, Byron left England on April 25, 1816, and was never to return.

Byron resumed his travels in Europe, living first at Geneva in Switzerland, where he became close friends with Shelley and where he produced a magnificent third canto of *Childe Harold.* Then he moved to Venice, where he perpetuated his reputation for fast living and began his greatest work, the satirical epic *Don Juan.* Byron's hero is not, as we would expect, the adult Don Juan, the notorious lover who would seem to lie closest to Byron's own personality and to that of his earlier "Byronic heroes." He is rather an original version of the boyish and youthful Don Juan, a fresh, energetic, impressionable young man whose curiosity and attractiveness to women enable Byron to expose both the foolishness and cruelty of life and the wonderful richness of earthly experience. Byron himself makes his presence felt in *Don Juan* primarily through the voice of the narrator, who appears to be making up his poem as he goes along

and who recounts the adventures of Don Juan (a younger version of himself) with a splendid balance of satire and sympathy.

Byron eventually moved to Pisa where he again joined Shelley, who was living there among a small circle of friends. After Shelley's death and the breakup of the "Pisan Circle," Byron again grew restless. Always an ardent spokesman for political freedom, he saw Greece, the ancient home of democracy, struggling to win its independence from Turkey. He invested a great deal of money and energy in organizing an expedition, which he himself led, to help the Greek cause. While training troops in the squalid, marshy town of Missolonghi, he was stricken with a severe fever. Byron died on April 19, 1824, shortly after his thirty-sixth birthday. Although his practical contribution to the Greek army was insignificant, his presence and tragic death produced a vital spark of inspiration for the eventual liberation of the country. He is still regarded in Greece as a national hero.

Despite his status as the archetypal Romantic, Byron had stronger ties to the eighteenth century than any of his contemporaries. He was a great admirer of Dryden and Pope, and he was sharply critical of all his fellow Romantics, except Shelley, for having devoted themselves to "a wrong revolutionary poetical system." His affinities with the eighteenth century are apparent not only in *English Bards and Scotch Reviewers, Don Juan,* and his other satires, but also in many of his shorter lyrics and songs. Some of these extend the Cavalier tradition of elegant, graceful compliment to a lady. Others belong to the gentlemanly eighteenth-century tradition of witty, extemporaneous reflection on a passing occasion. As a man Byron was capable of many moods and many roles, and we can see this reflected in the variety of his poetry. But behind all the different roles and postures we sense that powerful, self-conscious personality that holds as much fascination for us today as it did for Byron's own era.

Written After Swimming from Sestos to Abydos

According to legend, Leander of Abydos swam nightly across the Hellespont (the modern Dardanelles) to visit his lover, Hero, a priestess of Aphrodite at Sestos. Leander drowned when the light by which Hero guided him was put out by a storm, and she then threw herself into the sea after him. Attracted by the legend, Byron and a friend decided to attempt the swimming feat themselves. The distance across the strait is only one mile but the strong and hazardous current made the actual swim four miles, taking them just over an hour.

I

If, in the month of dark December,
   Leander, who was nightly wont
(What maid will not the tale remember?)
   To cross thy stream, broad Hellespont!

II

If, when the wintry tempest roared,   5
   He sped to Hero, nothing loath,
And thus of old thy current poured,
   Fair Venus! how I pity both!

III

For *me*, degenerate modern wretch,
   Though in the genial month of May   10
My dripping limbs I faintly stretch,
   And think I've done a feat today.

IV

But since he crossed the rapid tide,
   According to the doubtful story,
To woo—and—Lord knows what beside,   15
   And swam for Love, as I for Glory;

V

'Twere hard to say who fared the best:
   Sad mortals! thus the Gods still plague you!
He lost his labor, I my jest:
   For he was drowned, and I've the ague.°   20

---

20. **ague** (ā′gyo͞o): an attack of fever, often with chills.

She Walks in Beauty

This lyric, which has been set to music, was inspired by the poet's first meeting with his cousin by marriage, Lady Wilmot Horton. The occasion of their meeting was an evening party at which she appeared in a black dress with spangles.

She walks in beauty, like the night
  Of cloudless climes and starry skies;
And all that's best of dark and bright
  Meet in her aspect° and her eyes:
Thus mellowed to that tender light   5
  Which heaven to gaudy day denies.

One shade the more, one ray the less,
  Had half impaired the nameless grace
Which waves in every raven tress,
  Or softly lightens o'er her face;   10
Where thoughts serenely sweet express
  How pure, how dear their dwelling place.

And on that cheek, and o'er that brow,
  So soft, so calm, yet eloquent,
The smiles that win, the tints that glow,   15
  But tell of days in goodness spent,
A mind at peace with all below,
  A heart whose love is innocent!

---

4. **aspect:** facial expression.

Stanzas Written on the Road Between Florence and Pisa°

In this poem one can almost hear the hoofbeats of the horse Byron was riding. This meter was one of Byron's favorites, for it conveyed the vigor and exuberance that contributed to his great popularity as a poet.

Oh, talk not to me of a name great in story—
The days of our youth are the days of our glory;
And the myrtle and ivy° of sweet two-and-twenty
Are worth all your laurels,° though ever so plenty.

What are garlands and crowns to the brow that is wrinkled?   5
'Tis but a dead flower with May dew besprinkled:
Then away with all such from a head that is hoary!
What care I for the wreaths that can *only* give glory?

Oh Fame!—if I e'er took delight in thy praises,
'Twas less for the sake of thy high-sounding phrases   10
Than to see the bright eyes of the dear one discover
She thought that I was not unworthy to love her.

There chiefly I sought thee, *there* only I found thee;
Her glance was the best of the rays that surround thee;
When it sparkled o'er aught that was bright in my story,   15
I knew it was love, and I felt it was glory.

° **Pisa** (pē'zä).   3. **myrtle . . . ivy:** Myrtle, an evergreen plant, was sacred to Venus, goddess of love. Ivy, an evergreen vine, was sacred to Bacchus, god of revelry.
4. **laurels:** Laurel leaves were used by the ancient Greeks for crowns (wreaths) to honor the winners of athletic games and other contests.

from Childe Harold's Pilgrimage

These stanzas (178–184 of Canto IV of *Childe Harold's Pilgrimage*), considered among Byron's most sublime lines, are a worthy tribute not only to the time-defying ocean but to its effects on the empires that border it. Byron observes that great empires of the past, once centers of art, religion, and law, are now ruins washed by the ever-changing, yet changeless, sea.

Characteristically, Byron delighted in the grand aspects of nature, such as mountain ranges and the turbulent ocean. His enduring love of the sea can be paralleled with that of both earlier and later English writers.

Apostrophe to the Ocean

There is a pleasure in the pathless woods,
There is a rapture on the lonely shore,
There is society, where none intrudes,
By the deep sea, and music in its roar;
I love not man the less, but nature more,   5
From these our interviews, in which I steal
From all I may be, or have been before,
To mingle with the universe, and feel
What I can ne'er express, yet cannot all conceal.

Roll on, thou deep and dark blue Ocean—roll!   10
Ten thousand fleets sweep over thee in vain;
Man marks the earth with ruin—his control
Stops with the shore—upon the watery plain
The wrecks are all thy deed, nor doth remain
A shadow of man's ravage, save his own,°   15
When, for a moment, like a drop of rain,
He sinks into thy depths with bubbling groan—
Without a grave, unknelled, uncoffined, and unknown.

His steps are not upon thy paths—thy fields
Are not a spoil for him—thou dost arise   20
And shake him from thee; the vile strength he wields
For earth's destruction thou dost all despise,
Spurning him from thy bosom to the skies,
And send'st him, shivering in thy playful spray
And howling, to his gods, where haply° lies   25
His petty hope in some near port or bay,
And dashest him again to earth; there let him lay.°

---

15. **save his own:** except his own destruction (*ravage*).   25. **haply:** perhaps.
27. **lay:** Byron's note on his galley proof suggests that he made this grammatical error purposely for the sake of the rhyme.

The armaments which thunderstrike the walls
Of rock-built cities, bidding nations quake
And monarchs tremble in their capitals,   30
The oak leviathans,° whose huge ribs make
Their clay creator° the vain title take
Of lord of thee, and arbiter of war—
These are thy toys, and as the snowy flake,
They melt into thy yeast of waves, which mar   35
Alike the Armada's° pride, or spoils of Trafalgar.°

Thy shores are empires, changed in all save thee—
Assyria, Greece, Rome, Carthage, what are they?
Thy waters washed them power while they were free,
And many a tyrant since;° their shores obey   40
The stranger, slave, or savage; their decay
Has dried up realms to deserts—not so thou,
Unchangeable save to thy wild waves' play.
Time writes no wrinkle on thine azure brow;
Such as creation's dawn beheld, thou rollest now.   45

Thou glorious mirror, where the Almighty's form
Glasses itself in tempest; in all time,
Calm or convulsed—in breeze, or gale, or storm,
Icing the pole, or in the torrid clime
Dark-heaving—boundless, endless, and sublime;   50
The image of eternity, the throne
Of the Invisible; even from out thy slime
The monsters of the deep are made; each zone
Obeys thee; thou goest forth, dread, fathomless, alone.

And I have loved thee, Ocean! and my joy   55
Of youthful sports was on thy breast to be
Borne, like thy bubbles, onward; from a boy
I wantoned with thy breakers°—they to me
Were a delight; and if the freshening sea
Made them a terror—'twas a pleasing fear,   60
For I was as it were a child of thee,
And trusted to thy billows far and near,
And laid my hand upon thy mane—as I do here.

---

31. **leviathans** (lə-vī′ə-thənz): monstrous sea animals, described several times in
the Old Testament. Here the word means huge ships. 32. **clay creator:** human
beings. 36. **Armada** (är-mä′də): refers to the defeat of the Spanish Armada in
1588. **Trafalgar** (trə-făl′gər, but here must be accented on the first syllable for the
meter): Nelson's memorable victory over the French and Spanish fleets in
1805. 39-40. **Thy . . . since:** The ocean brought power to these empires, and,
when they had fallen, it brought tyrants to rule them. 58. **I . . . breakers:** Byron
was a famous swimmer (see "Written After Swimming from Sestos to Abydos,"
page 476).

from **Don Juan**

Don Juan (dŏn jōō′ŭn), Byron's comic masterpiece, is considered one of the great long poems in English. The main character is a legendary figure whose only occupation is to woo beautiful women. In various stories and plays and in *Don Giovanni,* a famous opera by Mozart, Don Juan is depicted as a thoroughly immoral person who will do anything to win a woman's love. In Byron's poem, Juan is an innocent young man who, because of his extreme handsomeness, finds himself involved, usually against his will, in many embarrassing situations.

Don Juan does not move in a straight line but meanders in many directions. Again and again Byron departs from his story to comment on politics, relations between men and women, other poets, and the social vices, follies, and absurdities of his time. In the third canto of *Don Juan,* Byron apologizes for his digressions from the main thread of his story: "I must own / If I have any fault, it is digression, / Leaving my people to proceed alone, / While I soliloquize beyond expression. . . ." Most admirers of *Don Juan* agree that without the digressions, it would be a far inferior poem. Byron completed sixteen cantos before his death.

One of Byron's most frequent targets in *Don Juan* and in other poems is a trio of Romantic poets of an older generation—Wordsworth, Coleridge, and Robert Southey. Byron disliked these men not only because he thought they were bad poets but also because he considered them political renegades, men who had turned away from the republicanism of their youth to support the conservative cause. The stanzas that follow are the last twenty-three stanzas of the first canto.

Here Byron defends his mock-heroic epic by playfully comparing it to the tradition of classical epics and by harking back to the English epics of Milton, Dryden, and Pope. While making fun of others, he also makes fun of himself.

from **Canto I**

My poem's epic, and is meant to be
   Divided in twelve books; each book containing,
With love, and war, a heavy gale at sea,
   A list of ships, and captains, and kings reigning,
New characters; the episodes are three: 5
   A panoramic view of hell's in training,
After the style of Virgil and of Homer,
So that my name of Epic's no misnomer.°

---

8. **my . . . misnomer:** Traditionally, an epic poem, such as Homer's *Odyssey,* was supposed to contain all the elements Byron names.

All these things will be specified in time,
    With strict regard to Aristotle's rules,°   10
The *Vade Mecum*° of the true sublime,
Which makes so many poets, and some fools:
Prose poets like blank verse, I'm fond of rhyme,
    Good workmen never quarrel with their tools;
I've got new mythological machinery,   15
And very handsome supernatural scenery.

There's only one slight difference between
    Me and my epic brethren gone before,
And here the advantage is my own, I ween°
    (Not that I have not several merits more,   20
But this will more peculiarly be seen);
    They so embellish, that 'tis quite a bore
Their labyrinth of fables to thread through,
Whereas this story's actually true.

If any person doubt it, I appeal   25
    To history, tradition, and to facts,
To newspapers, whose truth all know and feel,
    To plays in five, and operas in three acts;
All these confirm my statement a good deal,
    But that which more completely faith exacts   30
Is, that myself, and several now in Seville,
Saw Juan's last elopement with the devil.°

If ever I should condescend to prose,
    I'll write poetical commandments, which
Shall supersede beyond all doubt all those   35
    That went before; in these I shall enrich
My text with many things that no one knows,
    And carry precept to the highest pitch:
I'll call the work "Longinus o'er a Bottle,
Or, Every Poet his *own* Aristotle."°   40

---

10. **Aristotle's rules:** The rule holding that a tragedy should observe the unities of
time, place, and action is popularly attributed to Aristotle, although Aristotle discusses only unity of action in his critical work, the *Poetics*.   11. *Vade Mecum:*
handbook.   19. **ween** (archaic): think.   32. **devil:** In several plays about Don Juan,
he meets his end by being dragged off to Hell by the devil.   39–40. **"Longinus . . .
Aristotle":** Longinus' *On the Sublime* and Aristotle's *Poetics* were regarded as two
basic critical works in ancient Greece and Rome.

Thou shalt believe in Milton, Dryden, Pope;°
   Thou shalt not set up Wordsworth, Coleridge, Southey;
Because the first is crazed beyond all hope,
   The second drunk, the third so quaint and mouthy:
With Crabbe° it may be difficult to cope,   45
   And Campbell's Hippocrene° is somewhat drouthy:
Thou shalt not steal from Samuel Rogers,° nor
Commit—flirtation with the muse of Moore.°

Thou shalt not covet Mr. Sotheby's° Muse,
   His Pegasus,° nor anything that's his;   50
Thou shalt not bear false witness like "the Blues"°—
   (There's one, at least, is very fond of this);
Thou shalt not write, in short, but what I choose:
   This is true criticism, and you may kiss—
Exactly as you please, or not,—the rod;   55
But if you don't, I'll lay it on, by G—d!

If any person should presume to assert
   This story is not moral, first, I pray,
That they will not cry out before they're hurt,
   Then that they'll read it o'er again, and say   60
(But, doubtless, nobody will be so pert),
   That this is not a moral tale, though gay;
Besides, in Canto Twelfth, I mean to show
The very place where wicked people go.

If, after all, there should be some so blind   65
   To their own good this warning to despise,
Let by some tortuosity of mind,
   Not to believe my verse and their own eyes,
And cry that they "the moral cannot find,"
   I tell him, if a clergyman, he lies;   70
Should captains the remark, or critics, make,
They also lie too—under a mistake.

---

41. **Thou . . . Pope:** Byron often defended Dryden and Pope against his Romantic
contemporaries. 45. **Crabbe:** George Crabbe (1754–1832), author of the poem *The
Village.* 46. **Campbell's Hippocrene** (hip'ə-krēn'): that is, Campbell's fountain of
inspiration. Thomas Campbell (1777–1844) was a minor Romantic poet.
47. **Samuel Rogers:** Rogers (1763–1855), like Crabbe and Campbell, was a minor
poet of the Romantic period and a friend of Byron. 48. **Moore:** Thomas Moore
(1779–1852), a poet and friend of Byron. 49. **Sotheby:** William Sotheby
(1757–1833), the translator of Homer and Virgil. 50. **Pegasus:** the winged horse of
classical mythology, a symbol of poetic inspiration. 51. **"the Blues":** that is,
bluestockings; a term applied to pedantic intellectuals, among whom Byron
included his wife.

The public approbation I expect,
    And beg they'll take my word about the moral,
Which I with their amusement will connect   75
    (So children cutting teeth receive a coral);
Meantime they'll doubtless please to recollect
    My epical pretensions to the laurel:
For fear some prudish readers should grow skittish,
I've bribed my grandmother's review—the British.   80

I sent it in a letter to the Editor,
    Who thanked me duly by return of post—
I'm for a handsome article his creditor;
    Yet, if my gentle Muse he please to roast,
And break a promise after having made it her,   85
    Denying the receipt of what it cost,
And smear his page with gall instead of honey,
All I can say is—that he had the money.

I think that with this holy new alliance
    I may ensure the public, and defy   90
All other magazines of art or science,
    Daily, or monthly or three monthly; I
Have not essayed to multiply their clients,
    Because they tell me 'twere in vain to try,
And that the Edinburgh Review and Quarterly°   95
Treat a dissenting author very martyrly.

"Non ego hoc ferrem calida juventâ
    Consule Planco,"° Horace said, and so
Say I; by which quotation there is meant a
    Hint that some six or seven good years ago   100
(Long ere I dreamt of dating from the Brenta)°
    I was most ready to return a blow,
And would not brook at all this sort of thing
In my hot youth—when George the Third was King.

But now at thirty years my hair is gray—   105
    (I wonder what it will be like at forty?
I thought of a peruke° the other day—)
    My heart is not much greener; and, in short, I

---

95. **Edinburgh Review and Quarterly:** Whig and Tory periodicals, respectively; both journals were hostile to Byron. 97–98. **"Non . . . Planco":** I should not have tolerated this in the heat of my youth when Plancus was consul" (Horace, *Odes*). 101. **Brenta:** that is, long before I started dating my letters as written from near Brenta, a river near Venice. 107. **peruke:** wig.

Have squandered my whole summer while 'twas May,
   And feel no more the spirit to retort; I   110
Have spent my life, both interest and principal,
And deem not, what I deemed, my soul invincible.

No more—no more—Oh! never more on me
   The freshness of the heart can fall like dew,
Which out of all the lovely things we see   115
   Extracts emotions beautiful and new;
Hived in our bosoms like the bag o' the bee.
   Think'st thou the honey with those objects grew?
Alas! 'twas not in them, but in thy power
To double even the sweetness of a flower.   120

No more—no more—Oh! never more, my heart,
   Canst thou be my sole world, my universe!
Once all in all, but now a thing apart,
   Thou canst not be my blessing or my curse:
The illusion's gone for ever, and thou art   125
   Insensible, I trust, but none the worse,
And in thy stead I've got a deal of judgment,
Though heaven knows how it ever found a lodgment.

My days of love are over; me no more
   The charms of maid, wife, and still less of widow,   130
Can make the fool of which they made before—
   In short, I must not lead the life I did do;
The credulous hope of mutual minds is o'er,
   The copious use of claret is forbid too,
So for a good old-gentlemanly vice,   135
I think I must take up with avarice.

Ambition was my idol, which was broken
   Before the shrines of Sorrow, and of Pleasure;
And the two last have left me many a token
   O'er which reflection may be made at leisure;   140
Now, like Friar Bacon's brazen head, I've spoken,
   "Time is, Time was, Time's past:"°—a chymic° treasure
Is glittering youth, which I have spent betimes—
My heart in passion, and my head on rhymes.

141–142. **Friar Bacon's . . . Time's past:** a legendary speaking head of brass, made
by Friar Bacon, says these words in Robert Greene's play *Friar Bacon and Friar
Bungay* (1594). 142. **chymic** (kĭm'ĭk): counterfeit; archaic for *chemic* and suggestive of alchemy or magic.

What is the end of fame? 'tis but to fill   145
    A certain portion of uncertain paper:
Some liken it to climbing up a hill,
    Whose summit, like all hills, is lost in vapor;
For this men write, speak, preach, and heroes kill,
    And bards burn what they call their "midnight taper,"   150
To have, when the original is dust,
A name, a wretched picture, and worst bust.

What are the hopes of man? Old Egypt's King
    Cheops° erected the first pyramid
And largest, thinking it was just the thing   155
    To keep his memory whole, and mummy hid:
But somebody or other rummaging,
    Burglariously broke his coffin's lid.
Let not a monument give you or me hopes,
Since not a pinch of dust remains of Cheops.   160

But I, being fond of true philosophy,
    Say very often to myself, "Alas!
All things that have been born were born to die,
    And flesh (which Death mows down to hay) is grass;
You've passed your youth not so unpleasantly.   165
    And if you had it o'er again—'twould pass—
So thank your stars that matters are no worse,
And read your Bible, sir, and mind your purse."

But for the present, gentle reader! and
    Still gentler purchaser! the bard—that's I—   170
Must, with permission, shake you by the hand,
    And so your humble servant, and goodbye!
We meet again, if we should understand
    Each other; and if not, I shall not try
Your patience further than by this short sample—   175
'Twere well if others followed my example.

"Go, little book, from this my solitude!
    I cast thee on the waters—go thy ways!
And if, as I believe, thy vein be good,
    The world will find thee after many days."°   180
When Southey's read, and Wordsworth understood,
    I can't help putting in my claim to praise—
The four first rhymes are Southey's, every line:
For God's sake, reader! take them not for mine!

---

154. **Cheops** (kē′ŏps). 177–180. **"Go . . . days"**: The lines are from Southey's
"Epilogue to the Lay of the Laureate."

On This Day I Complete My Thirty–Sixth Year°

'Tis time this heart should be unmoved,
   Since others it hath ceased to move:
Yet, though I cannot be beloved,
      Still let me love!

My days are in the yellow leaf;°   5
   The flowers and fruits of love are gone;
The worm, the canker, and the grief
      Are mine alone!

The fire that on my bosom preys
   Is lone as some volcanic isle;   10
No torch is kindled at its blaze—
      A funeral pile.

The hope, the fear, the jealous care,
   The exalted portion of the pain
And power of love, I cannot share,   15
      But wear the chain.

But 'tis not *thus*—and 'tis not *here*—
   Such thoughts should shake my soul, nor *now*,
Where glory decks the hero's bier,
      Or binds his brow.   20

The sword, the banner, and the field,
   Glory and Greece, around me see!
The Spartan, borne upon his shield,
      Was not more free.

Awake! (not Greece—she *is* awake!)   25
   Awake, my spirit! Think through *whom*
Thy lifeblood tracks its parent lake,
      And then strike home!

Tread those reviving passions down,
   Unworthy manhood!—unto thee   30
Indifferent should the smile or frown
      Of beauty be.

°Dated "Missolonghi, January 22, 1824." Byron died on April 19 of that year.
5. **My days are in the yellow leaf:** an echo of Macbeth's "My way of life / Is fall'n into the sear, the yellow leaf" (V, 3, 22–23).

If thou regret'st thy youth, *why live?*
   The land of honorable death
Is here:—up to the field, and give 35
     Away thy breath!

Seek out—less often sought than found—
   A soldier's grave, for thee the best;
Then look around, and choose thy ground,
     And take thy rest. 40

FOR STUDY AND DISCUSSION

Written After Swimming from Sestos to Abydos

1. The first two stanzas of the poem begin with "If." What does this word suggest about the speaker's attitude toward the classical legend?
2. What words and images does the speaker use to create an ironic tone?

She Walks in Beauty

1. The lady being praised is compared to the night. What particular aspects of the night are singled out in the comparison? Why does the speaker use the word *gaudy* to describe day?
2. How do we know that the lady's beauty depends on a balance of opposites? How does her appearance express her thoughts and past experience?

Stanzas Written on the Road Between Florence and Pisa

What is the meaning of line 5? Explain the different uses of the words *love* and *glory* in the poem.

Apostrophe to the Ocean

1. What aspect of the ocean is emphasized throughout the poem? In what way is the ocean superior to human beings and their works?
2. Byron uses a figure of speech when he says, "Roll on, thou deep and dark blue Ocean—roll!" This figure of speech, called an *apostrophe*, can be direct address: to the dead as if living; to the absent as if present; and to animals, objects, or ideas as if they were persons. Find other lines in which the poet speaks directly to the ocean. Why is the apostrophe effective as used here?

Don Juan

1. *Don Juan* pokes fun at subjects regarded as time-honored and firmly established. What subjects are satirized in this selection from Canto I?
2. *Don Juan* is known for its sudden changes of subject and of mood. Cite two examples of each kind of change.
3. Examine carefully one of the stanzas in the selection from Canto I. Describe the rhyme scheme. How does the rhyming in the last two lines give force to the stanza? Cite examples of strange or unexpected rhymes. How do they add to the comic effect of the poem?
4. Unlike most Romantic poets, Byron was an admirer of Pope. What comparisons can you make between this poem and *The Rape of the Lock?*

On This Day I Complete My Thirty-Sixth Year

1. What attitude does the speaker take toward himself in the first four stanzas of this poem? What has happened to the powerful emotions that moved him in younger days? What does he mean when he says, in lines 15–16: "And power of love, I cannot share, / But wear the chain"?
2. Describe the shift in attitude that begins to take place in the fifth stanza. What wish is expressed at the end of the poem?

FOR COMPOSITION

Write an essay in which you compare Byron's view of nature with Wordsworth's. Cite evidence from their poems to support your conclusions.

Percy Bysshe Shelley
1792–1822

Percy Bysshe Shelley
The Bodleian Library

Shelley is a contradictory and challenging figure. His writing is at once the most passionate and intense of all the Romantic poets, and yet the most intellectual, the fullest of philosophical speculation and technical experiment. And although he was the most committed of the Romantic poets to social action, to improving the lot of all people, his political writing is harder to grasp and less accessible than that of the others. He made brilliant innovations and experiments in poetic language, and he wrote a magnificent essay on the meaning and importance of poetry (*The Defence of Poetry*, 1821). Yet it is precisely Shelley's stylistic experiments and his fervent ambition to push language into the realm of the inexpressible that make him at times forbiddingly difficult. In his personal life Shelley was uncommonly generous, responsive, and sympathetic to the sufferings of others—yet his fierce devotion to ideals about what human life could attain sometimes put him out of touch with the immediate feelings and needs of those around

him. One thing is certain: the only way for any reader to come to terms with Shelley as a man and a writer is with an open mind and a willingness to envision new possibilities for human experience and expression.

Like Byron, Shelley was born into an upper-class family. His father, Timothy Shelley, was a rather conservative member of Parliament from Sussex, a county just south of London. Shelley was sent to Eton, the famous private school, where he was mercilessly taunted by the other boys because of his slight, unathletic build and his imaginative, eccentric manner. They called him "mad Shelley." It was at Eton that Shelley first became determined to fight against the forces of injustice and oppression in life. In 1810 he went to Oxford University, where he and a close friend wrote a pamphlet called "The Necessity of Atheism." Shelley refused to deny that he had written the pamphlet when called before the authorities, and he was expelled after only six months at Oxford.

Shelley then went to London, where he fell in love and eloped with Harriet Westbrook, an attractive, warmhearted girl who Shelley thought was being oppressed by her father. Harriet was sixteen when they were married, Shelley eighteen. Both families were, of course, unhappy about the marriage, and Harriet and Shelley had to live on their own with little money. They went to Ireland for a time to work for Catholic emancipation and improved living conditions for the poor. Returning to London, Shelley joined the circle of the radical social philosopher William Godwin, whose wife, Mary Wollstonecraft, had been one of the earliest and most effective advocates for the rights of women. In 1814 Shelley fell in love with Mary, the brilliant daughter of Godwin and Mary Wollstonecraft. Committed to the idea that human relationships should not be restricted by law or social convention, Shelley went to live with Mary in France for a time.

When Shelley returned with Mary to England, he found himself branded a revolutionary and a social outcast. He was happiest living abroad, and he spent the summer of 1816 on the shores of Lake Geneva, in Switzerland, where he was visited by and became friends with Byron. But a crisis arose later that year—Harriet drowned herself in a fit of despair. Shelley was stricken with grief and remorse, and to make matters worse, the courts denied Shelley custody of the two children born to him and Harriet. Like Byron, Shelley felt himself an alien and an outcast in his own country. In 1818, soon after he and Mary were married, they left England for Italy, where Shelley would live for the rest of his life.

Shelley's four years in Italy, from 1818 until his death in 1822, were a time of poor health, of financial difficulty, of restless moving about from place to place, and of further personal tragedy. In 1818–1819 two of his children by Mary, Clara and William, died. Yet Shelley was able during these years to produce an astonishing amount and range of magnificent poetry. In 1818 he began the philosophical drama that many readers consider his masterpiece, *Prometheus Unbound*. In 1819 he completed *Prometheus Unbound* and wrote his great "Ode to the West Wind." In 1820 he produced a visionary satire called *The Mask of Anarchy* and a delicate philosophical nature-fable called *The Sensitive Plant*. The year 1821 saw the publication of *Epipsychidion*, a difficult and experimental poem about the transcendent possibilities of human love, and of *Adonais*, Shelley's great elegy on the death of John Keats. In 1822 he completed *Hellas*, a lyrical drama about the Greek war of liberation against the Turks. At his death he was at work on *The Triumph of Life*, which some readers think would have been his finest work had he lived to complete it. In addition to these major works, Shelley wrote in each of these years many of the intense, beautifully crafted shorter lyrics for which he is so well known.

The last two years of Shelley's "Italian Period" were happier than the first two. He and Mary finally settled at Pisa, where they were joined by a group of close friends who came to be known as the "Pisan Circle." Byron left Venice to live with them for a time. Shelley's accidental death came suddenly and in a manner almost miraculously predicted in the famous concluding stanza of *Adonais*:

> . . . my spirit's bark is driven,
> Far from the shore, far from the trembling throng
> Whose sails were never to the tempest given;
> The massy earth and sphered skies are riven!

Shelley loved boats and frequently used them as images or symbols in his poetry. On July 8, 1822, he and his friend Edward Williams set out in Shelley's small boat, the *Don Juan*, to sail across the Gulf of Spezzia. A violent storm arose and both Williams and Shelley, who could not swim, were swept overboard. Their bodies were found on the beach several days later, where they were cremated by a group of friends, including Byron. Shelley's ashes were buried in the Protestant cemetery at Rome, near the grave of Keats.

Byron said of Shelley that he "was, without exception, the *best* and least selfish man I ever knew. I never knew one who was not a beast in comparison." Matthew Arnold thought that Shelley's character was too sensitive for a really great writer and called him a "beautiful and ineffectual angel, beating in the void his luminous wings in vain." But Shelley was not ineffectual, and he was not so cut off from the realities of life as Arnold suggests. Although dedicated to the idea that by perfecting their own natures people could liberate themselves from the pain and injustice of present existence, Shelley had a shrewd and informed comprehension of the complexities of earthly life. And his generous, unselfish personality also contained elements of sophisticated playfulness and good humor—he was not beyond laughing at himself. Intellectually, he was an immensely learned and well-read man capable of more refined and original philosophical thinking than any other English Romantic, including Coleridge. And as a poet, as Wordsworth said, "Shelley is one of the best *artists* of us all: I mean in workmanship of style."

Ozymandias°

I met a traveler from an antique land
Who said: Two vast and trunkless legs of stone
Stand in the desert . . . Near them on the sand,
Half sunk, a shattered visage lies, whose frown,
And wrinkled lip, and sneer of cold command,   5
Tell that its sculptor well those passions read
Which yet survive, stamped on these lifeless things,
The hand that mocked them, and the heart that fed:
And on the pedestal these words appear:
"My name is Ozymandias, king of kings: 10
Look on my works, ye Mighty, and despair!"
Nothing beside remains. Round the decay
Of that colossal wreck, boundless and bare
The lone and level sands stretch far away.

° **Ozymandias** (ŏz′ĭ-măn′dē-əs): another version of the Egyptian name Rameses.
The king referred to in the poem is Rameses II, a great builder of palaces and
temples who ruled Egypt during the thirteenth century B.C., and who left a number of statues of himself.

*The Artist Moved by the Magnitude of
Antique Fragments* by Henry Fuseli. Like
the poet Shelley, the Swiss painter
Fuseli mourns the passing of a great
civilization and meditates on the vanity
of human monuments.
Kunsthaus, Zurich

Percy Bysshe Shelley 491

Sonnet: England in 1819

An old, mad, blind, despised, and dying king°—
Princes, the dregs of their dull race, who flow
Through public scorn—mud from a muddy spring,—
Rulers who neither see, nor feel, nor know,
But leechlike to their fainting country cling,   5
Till they drop, blind in blood, without a blow—
A people starved and stabbed in the untilled field—
An army, which liberticide° and prey
Makes as a two-edged sword to all who wield—
Golden and sanguine laws° which tempt and slay;   10
Religion Christless, Godless—a book sealed;
A Senate—Time's worst statute unrepealed°—
Are graves, from which a glorious Phantom° may
Burst, to illumine our tempestuous day.

---

1. **An old, mad . . . king:** King George III, who had ruled since 1760 and was declared incurably insane in 1811. He died in 1820. 8. **liberticide:** the death or killing of freedom. 10. **Golden and sanguine laws:** corrupt and unjust laws, passed through financial bribery and resulting in bloodshed. 12. **statute unrepealed:** the law forbidding Catholics to hold office. 13. **Phantom:** spirit, vision.

FOR STUDY AND DISCUSSION

Ozymandias
The inscription on the pedestal of the statue proclaims Ozymandias' great pride and confidence. How does this inscription appear ironic, considering the condition of the statue and landscape as the traveler describes them? How would you state the theme of the poem?

Sonnet: England in 1819
1. How does Shelley characterize the leaders of England in this sonnet? How does he characterize the people?

2. Shelley gives his sonnet something of a surprise ending by saying that all the present evils he has enumerated are "graves." What does he mean by this? Where earlier in the sonnet can you find suggestions that the forces of evil controlling England in 1819 are self-defeating?

3. Shelley organizes the clauses and lines in this sonnet very effectively in order to build up a sense of the tension of intolerable evil. What happens to this accumulated tension at the beginning of line 13? What additional twist in the movement of the sonnet occurs with the rhyme-word "may" at the end of line 13?

Ode to the West Wind

Shelley wrote of this poem that it "was conceived and chiefly written in a wood that skirts the Arno, near Florence [Italy], and on a day when that tempestuous wind, whose temperature is at once mild and animating, was collecting the vapors which pour down the autumnal rains. They began, as I foresaw, at sunset with a violent tempest of hail and rain, attended by that magnificent thunder and lightning peculiar to the Cisalpine regions."

I

O wild West Wind, thou breath of Autumn's being,
Thou, from whose unseen presence the leaves dead
Are driven, like ghosts from an enchanter fleeing,

Yellow, and black, and pale, and hectic red,
Pestilence-stricken multitudes: O thou,   5
Who chariotest° to their dark wintry bed

The wingèd seeds, where they lie cold and low,
Each like a corpse within its grave, until
Thine azure sister of the Spring° shall blow

Her clarion° o'er the dreaming earth, and fill   10
(Driving sweet buds like flocks to feed in air)
With living hues and odors plain and hill:

Wild Spirit, which art moving everywhere;
Destroyer and preserver; hear, oh, hear!

II

Thou on whose stream, 'mid the steep sky's commotion,   15
Loose clouds like earth's decaying leaves are shed,
Shook from the tangled boughs of Heaven and Ocean,

Angels° of rain and lightning: there are spread
On the blue surface of thine aëry surge,
Like the bright hair uplifted from the head   20

---

6. **chariotest:** In Shelley's poetry the chariot is an image of irresistible power.
9. **sister . . . Spring:** south wind.   10. **clarion:** a trumpet with a pure, clear tone.
18. **Angels:** messengers (from the Greek *angelos*).

Of some fierce Maenad,° even from the dim verge
Of the horizon to the zenith's° height,
The locks of the approaching storm. Thou dirge

Of the dying year, to which this closing night
Will be the dome of a vast sepulcher,   25
Vaulted with all thy congregated might

Of vapors, from whose solid atmosphere
Black rain, and fire, and hail will burst: oh, hear!

III

Thou who didst waken from his summer dreams
The blue Mediterranean, where he lay,   30
Lulled by the coil of his crystàlline streams,

Beside a pumice° isle in Baiae's bay,°
And saw in sleep old palaces and towers
Quivering within the wave's intenser day,

All overgrown with azure moss and flowers   35
So sweet, the sense faints picturing them! Thou
For whose path the Atlantic's level powers°

Cleave themselves into chasms, while far below
The sea-blooms and the oozy woods which wear
The sapless foliage of the ocean, know   40

Thy voice, and suddenly grow gray with fear,
And tremble and despoil themselves: oh, hear!

IV

If I were a dead leaf thou mightest bear;
If I were a swift cloud to fly with thee;
A wave to pant beneath thy power, and share   45

The impulse of thy strength, only less free
Than thou, O uncontrollable! If even
I were as in my boyhood, and could be

---

21. **Maenad** (mē'năd): a priestess of Bacchus, "fierce" because she engaged in wild
and frenzied ceremonies in honor of the god.   22. **zenith**: the point in the heavens
directly overhead.   32. **pumice** (pŭm'ĭs): formed from lava.   **Baiae's** (bā'yəz) **bay**,
near Naples, is close to nearly extinct volcanoes that still rumble and erupt occasionally. The area was famous as a resort of the ancient Romans.   37. **level
powers**: surfaces.

The comrade of thy wanderings over Heaven,
As then, when to outstrip thy skyey speed   50
Scarce seemed a vision;° I would ne'er have striven

As thus with thee in prayer in my sore need.
Oh, lift me as a wave, a leaf, a cloud!
I fall upon the thorns of life! I bleed!

A heavy weight of hours has chained and bowed   55
One too like thee: tameless, and swift, and proud.

V

Make me thy lyre,° even as the forest is:
What if my leaves are falling like its own!
The tumult of thy mighty harmonies

Will take from both a deep, autumnal tone,   60
Sweet though in sadness. Be thou, Spirit fierce,
My spirit! Be thou me, impetuous one!

Drive my dead thoughts over the universe
Like withered leaves to quicken a new birth!
And, by the incantation of this verse,   65

Scatter, as from an unextinguished hearth
Ashes and sparks, my words among mankind!
Be through my lips to unawakened earth

The trumpet of a prophecy! O Wind,
If Winter comes, can Spring be far behind?   70

---

51. **vision:** that is, something impossible to attain.   57. **lyre:** Aeolian lute, or
wind harp, which makes musical sounds when the wind blows through it. Also, a
reference to Pindar, who wrote odes to be accompanied by a lyre.

COMMENTARY

In the five magnificent stanzas of the "Ode," Shelley addresses the west wind directly as a force that is both destructive and creative. He longs to establish a vital contact between his own poetic powers and the wind, and he begins by focusing on three natural objects of the wind's power: the autumn leaves in stanza 1, the clouds in stanza 2, and the waves in stanza 3. Stanza 4 marks a crisis in the poem, as Shelley longs to identify himself with these objects of the wind's power; but he fails to recover the spontaneous, imaginative confidence of his boyhood, which would link him positively with the wind itself.

In stanza 5, Shelley discovers his true relationship to the west wind. Instead of being a passive object of the wind's power, he will be its active, cooperative instrument: he will be its "lyre," receiving its "mighty harmonies" like a wind harp, or like the forest itself, and converting them into words of poetry. These words, like the leaves of stanza 1, will be scattered everywhere to prophesy and to awaken a rebirth of human imagination. The "Ode" itself succeeds in expressing just that relationship between imagination and the power of nature which Shelley longs for.

The stanza Shelley invents for this ode is a highly complicated fusion of the *sonnet* and of *terza rima*. Like a sonnet, each stanza is fourteen lines long, "turns" or shifts its argument near the middle, and ends in a couplet. However, the rhyme scheme of the opening twelve lines of each stanza is in *terza rima*. This form, derived from Italian poetry, is composed of interlocking sequences of three-line groups (hence *terza*, the Italian word for "third"). Shelley's rhyme scheme for his stanzas may be represented as *aba bcb cdc ded ee*. Notice especially the *interlocking rhyme scheme* of the four three-line groups: the middle rhyme of each triplet becomes the first and third rhyme of the next triplet: *aba, bcb,* and so on.

It has been suggested that the tumbling effect of this scheme creates a sense of the turbulent, swirling activity of the wind as it drives and tosses the leaves, clouds, and waves. Certainly the way in which the stanzas unite an impression of wild irregularity with an amazing degree of artistic control is beautifully appropriate to expressing a relationship between imagination and the power of nature.

FOR STUDY AND DISCUSSION

1. What are the three dominant images in the first three parts of the poem? How does the effect of the wind on each of these elements in nature bear out Shelley's characterization of the wind as "destroyer and preserver"?

2. The speaker's relation to the wind develops in a dramatic way during the course of the poem, particularly in stanzas 4 and 5. What is the speaker's attitude toward himself and his relation to the wind at the end of stanza 4? How does this change in stanza 5?

3. Line 54 has often been criticized by modern critics as showing too much self-pity. Do you agree with this criticism, or do you think that the feeling of the line is justified by the violent descriptions that precede it? Explain.

THE ODE AS A POETIC FORM

Ode comes from a Greek word meaning "song," and originally an ode was simply a poem meant to be sung to instrumental accompaniment. But eventually Greek poets, especially Pindar, developed the ode into a special poetic form divided into three main parts: *strophe, antistrophe,* and *epode.* In style and tone Pindar's odes were very grand and heroic, and still today the term *Pindaric Ode* denotes a poem of this type. The ode was a favorite form of the Romantic poets because it allowed for intense and expansive personal expression.

Although some English poets have followed the Greek practice of arranging the ode into unequal strophes or stanzas with lines of varying length, many English odes use equal stanzas and lines of regular length. The one thing common to almost all odes is that they are poems of address: the poet speaks directly in the first person to some other person, being, or power, the "thou" or "thee" of the poem.

FOR COMPOSITION

"Ode to the West Wind" depends heavily on figures of speech for effectiveness. Find examples of the use of *simile, metaphor,* and *personification* in the poem. Explain how each example enriches the poem's meaning or contributes to its mood.

To a Skylark

Shelley wrote "To a Skylark" in 1820, when he and Mary were staying at the house of some friends near the Mediterranean coast of Italy. Mary later said of the origins of this poem: "It was on a beautiful summer evening, while wandering among the lanes whose myrtle hedges were the bowers of fireflies, that we heard the caroling of the skylark which inspired one of the most beautiful of his poems."

The skylark is notable for its sustained, high-pitched musical song, which it utters during its spectacular ascending and descending flights. Shelley addresses the skylark, which has soared high above the earth and beyond the reach of all senses except hearing, as a kind of natural poet. The skylark's song, unlike that of the human poet, is "unpremeditated art" (line 5). Also, unlike the human poet's song, the skylark's "clear keen joyance" (line 76) is free from all consciousness of pain or sadness. Shelley longs for the skylark's completely natural happiness and music, but he realizes that the human poet is bound to earthly cares and to a more complicated mental and emotional life.

Hail to thee, blithe Spirit!
  Bird thou never wert,
That from Heaven, or near it,
  Pourest thy full heart
In profuse strains of unpremeditated art.   5

Higher still and higher
  From the earth thou springest
Like a cloud of fire;
  The blue deep thou wingest,
And singing still dost soar, and soaring ever singest.   10

In the golden lightning
  Of the sunken sun,
O'er which clouds are bright'ning,
  Thou dost float and run;
Like an unbodied joy whose race is just begun.   15

The pale purple even°
  Melts around thy flight;
Like a star of Heaven
  In the broad daylight
Thou art unseen, but yet I hear thy shrill delight,   20

---

16. **even:** evening.

Keen as are the arrows
    Of that silver sphere,°
Whose intense lamp narrows
    In the white dawn clear,
Until we hardly see—we feel that it is there.   25

All the earth and air
    With thy voice is loud,
As, when night is bare,
    From one lonely cloud
The moon rains out her beams, and Heaven is overflowed.   30

What thou art we know not;
    What is most like thee?
From rainbow clouds there flow not
    Drops so bright to see,
As from thy presence showers a rain of melody.   35

Like a Poet hidden
    In the light of thought,
Singing hymns unbidden,
    Till the world is wrought
To sympathy with hopes and fears it heeded not: 40

Like a highborn maiden
    In a palace tower,
Soothing her love-laden
    Soul in secret hour
With music sweet as love, which overflows her bower: 45

Like a glowworm golden
    In a dell of dew,
Scattering unbeholden
    Its aerial hue
Among the flowers and grass, which screen it from the view!   50

Like a rose embowered
    In its own green leaves,
By warm winds deflowered,°
    Till the scent it gives
Makes faint with too much sweet those heavy-wingèd
    thieves°:   55

---

22. **silver sphere:** the morning star.   53. **deflowered:** fully opened.   55. **thieves:**
the "warm winds" of line 53.

Sound of vernal showers
   On the twinkling grass,
Rain-awakened flowers,
   All that ever was
Joyous, and clear, and fresh, thy music doth surpass: 60

Teach us, Sprite or Bird,
   What sweet thoughts are thine;
I have never heard
   Praise of love or wine
That panted forth a flood of rapture so divine.   65

Chorus Hymeneal,°
   Or triumphal chant,
Matched with thine, would be all
   But an empty vaunt,°
A thing wherein we feel there is some hidden want.   70

What objects are the fountains°
   Of thy happy strain?
What fields, or waves, or mountains?
   What shapes of sky or plain?
What love of thine own kind? what ignorance of pain?   75

With thy clear keen joyance
   Languor cannot be;
Shadow of annoyance
   Never came near thee;
Thou lovest—but ne'er knew love's sad satiety.   80

Waking or asleep,
   Thou of death must deem°
Things more true and deep
   Than we mortals dream,
Or how could thy notes flow in such a crystal stream?   85

We look before and after,
   And pine for what is not;
Our sincerest laughter
   With some pain is fraught;
Our sweetest songs are those that tell of saddest thought.   90

---

66. **Chorus Hymeneal** (hī′mə-nē′əl): marriage chant. Hymen was the Greek god of
marriage. 69. **vaunt:** ostentatious display. 71. **fountains:** sources, inspiration.
82. **deem:** know.

Yet if° we could scorn
    Hate, and pride, and fear;
If we were things born
    Not to shed a tear,
I know not how thy joy we ever should come near. 95

Better than all measures
    Of delightful sound
Better than all treasures
    That in books are found,
Thy skill to poet were,° thou scorner of the ground! 100

Teach me half the gladness
    That thy brain must know,
Such harmonious madness
    From my lips would flow,
The world should listen then—as I am listening now. 105

---

91. **if:** even if.   100. **were:** would be.

FOR STUDY AND DISCUSSION

1. Why is it important that the bird is "unseen"? Which words in the poem suggest that the bird does not seem to be a physical being?
2. To what different things does Shelley compare the skylark? What qualities do all these things have in common with the bird? Why are they less lovely to the poet than the bird is?
3. Line 90 says "Our sweetest songs are those that tell of saddest thought." What difference is there between the skylark's song and the song of the human poet? Why in the final stanza does the poet ask the skylark, "Teach me half the gladness / That thy brain must know" (lines 101–102)?

READING LYRIC POETRY

Most Romantic poets believed with Wordsworth that all good poetry was based on "the spontaneous overflow of powerful feelings." For this reason lyric poetry is especially important in the Romantic period. Even when the "I" of a Romantic lyric addresses some outside force or being, it is the speaker's perception of and relation to that apparently external force or being that really matters. The speaking "I" in a Romantic lyric often tries to identify and unite with some powerful or beautiful external presence. The poem then becomes an account of the speaker's attempt to achieve such a union, and sometimes of the inability to achieve or sustain that relationship completely. This is the pattern of Shelley's "Ode to the West Wind" and "To a Skylark," and of Keats's "Ode to a Nightingale" (page 518) and "Ode on a Grecian Urn" (page 521).

A lyric poem may create the impression of spontaneous, unpremeditated emotional experience. But we must not assume from this that lyric poems lack structure and organization, or that they are written without a great deal of careful thought and skill. A lyric poem is an artistic presentation of subjective experience. As Wordsworth, Shelley, and Keats show very clearly, the lyric poet begins with spontaneous feelings, but the effective presentation of those feelings requires revision and hard work.

To ——

Music, when soft voices die,
Vibrates in the memory—
Odors, when sweet violets sicken,
Live within the sense they quicken.

Rose leaves, when the rose is dead,
Are heaped for the beloved's bed;
And so thy thoughts,° when thou art gone,
Love itself shall slumber on.

---

7. **thy thoughts:** thoughts of, or about, thee.

FOR STUDY AND DISCUSSION

1. In this poem Shelley emphasizes that our experience of certain lovely things may last even when the original source of the experience disappears or fades. What examples of this process does he offer?
2. In lines 5–6 Shelley uses the image of a rose, whose fallen petals are still lovely even when the rose itself has died. To what does he compare the fallen rose petal? In what sense may love "slumber" upon thoughts or recollections of a departed loved one?

A Dirge

Rough wind, that moanest loud
    Grief too sad for song;
Wild wind, when sullen cloud
    Knells all the night long;
Sad storm, whose tears are vain,
Bare woods, whose branches strain,
Deep caves and dreary main—
    Wail, for the world's wrong!

FOR STUDY AND DISCUSSION

Shelley personifies a stormy natural scene in order to express his sense of the world's moral or spiritual decline. How does Shelley use *hyperbole* (exaggeration) to express his idea?

John Keats
1795–1821

John Keats died when he was only twenty-five, an age at which Wordsworth had still not begun to write the poems for which he is known today. The brevity and intensity of Keats's career are unmatched in English poetry. He achieved so much at such a young age that readers have always speculated about his potential had he lived to reach artistic maturity.

Keats came from very humble origins. His father, the keeper of a livery stable, was killed in a fall from a horse when Keats was eight; his mother died of tuberculosis when he was fourteen. Keats had been fortunate enough as a boy to attend an excellent private school near London, where his teacher introduced him to poetry, music, and the theater. But soon after his mother died, his guardian, a hard-headed businessman, took Keats out of school and made him an apprentice to a surgeon and apothecary. In 1815 Keats continued his study of medicine more formally at Guy's Hospital in London. He qualified the next year to practice as an apothecary, but it was at this time that he decided, much to his guardian's displeasure, to devote his life to poetry.

Keats had become friends in London with Leigh Hunt, a well-known literary critic and political radical, who encouraged Keats to take himself seriously as a writer. Hunt also introduced him to other leading literary figures of the day, among whom were Hazlitt, Lamb, and Shelley. Hunt and his circle provided Keats with a friendly and encouraging audience. But Keats had his difficulties at first. Some of his early poems lack the control and originality of expression that characterize his best verse. A long mythological poem entitled *Endymion,* published in 1818, was severely attacked by the reviewers, and at least some of their criticisms were justified. Keats himself realized that *Endymion* had its faults, that in writing it he was learning and experimenting—"fitting myself for verses fit to live," as he says in the preface. He was already at work on an even more ambitious project, an epic inspired by Milton's *Paradise Lost,* which he was to call *Hyperion.* Keats was driven by an increasingly independent sense of his own artistic

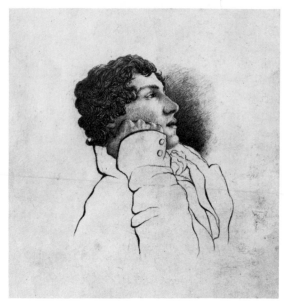

John Keats (drawing, study of the head).
National Portrait Gallery, London

potential, and by a burning ambition to measure himself against the greatest English poets: Spenser, Shakespeare, Milton, and Wordsworth.

The year 1818 was a difficult one for Keats. He was able to take the negative reviews of *Endymion* in his stride, but personal problems began to weigh heavily on him. As the eldest of four children, Keats felt a special responsibility and closeness to his two brothers and his sister. When his brother George, who had emigrated to America, ran into financial difficulties, Keats worked hard to earn extra money to help him. His younger brother Tom contracted tuberculosis, and Keats cared for him constantly, running the risk, as he well knew, of contracting the disease himself. In the autumn of 1818, Keats fell desperately in love with Fanny Brawne, a pretty, vivacious girl to whom he soon became engaged. But by this time Keats's own poor health, poverty, and relentless devotion to poetry made an immediate marriage impossible. The year came to a dismal end with Tom's death in December.

In January 1819 Keats took a much-needed vacation from London and spent a few days with some very good friends near the southern coast of England. As a relief from his taxing work on *Hyperion,* Keats set about writing a less ambitious, more romantic poem based on the legend of Saint Agnes' Eve (which falls on January 20). The result was one of Keats's greatest poems, *The Eve of St. Agnes,* and it marks the beginning of one of the most extraordinarily productive periods in all of English literature. In less than nine months, from January to September, Keats produced an astonishing sequence of masterpieces: "La Belle Dame Sans Merci," six great odes, "Lamia," and a group of magnificent sonnets. During the last few months of 1819 Keats went back to *Hyperion,* this time with a new vision of what his most ambitious undertaking could become.

But Keats's career was to be cut tragically short just as he was beginning to realize his full potential. The first clear signs of the tuberculosis he had always feared became apparent in February 1820. He weakened rapidly during the spring and summer. His close friend, the painter Joseph Severn, persuaded him to spend the fall and winter in Italy. But Keats had given up all hope of recovery. He died in Rome on February 23, 1821.

Keats's power as a poet comes from his remarkable ability to embody the complexity and concreteness of experience, and from the force and integrity of his character. He has always been known as a sensuous poet, and certainly his ability to appeal to the senses through language is virtually unrivaled. But there is much more to Keats than sensuousness. He is also a poet of ideas, of complicated and contradictory states of mind, and above all of deeply serious artistic enterprise—of what Matthew Arnold called "high and severe work." In contrast to most of his fellow Romantics, Keats sought to subordinate his own personality in his poetry and to focus attention on the complex individuality of his subject. "A poet," he wrote, "is the most unpoetical of any thing in existence.... The sun, the moon, the sea and men and women who are creatures of impulse are poetical and have about them an unchangeable attribute—the poet has none; no identity . . . ." He characterized the ideal poetic attitude as the capacity for forgetting oneself in a concentration on, or identification with, the subject of the poem. He called this attitude "*Negative Capability,* that is when a man is capable of being in uncertainties, mysteries, doubts, without any irritable reaching after fact and reason." Yet despite his deemphasizing the direct expression of the artist's conscious needs and values, Keats's own personality emerges very clearly in his poems, and especially in his letters, which are perhaps the most interesting of any English poet. In them we can see the deep connection between Keats's greatness as a poet and his greatness as a human being.

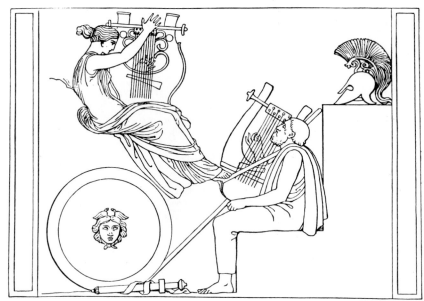

Homer Invoking the Muse by John Flaxman, from an early edition of Chapman's *Homer.* New York Public Library Picture Collection

On First Looking into Chapman's Homer

When Keats was about twenty-one he borrowed a translation of Homer by George Chapman, an Elizabethan poet. With an old friend, he sat up all night reading it. The next morning his friend found this sonnet on his breakfast table.

Much have I traveled in the realms of gold,
   And many goodly states and kingdoms seen;
   Round many western islands have I been
Which bards in fealty to Apollo° hold.
Oft of one wide expanse had I been told   5
   That deep-browed Homer ruled as his demesne;°
   Yet did I never breathe its pure serene°
Till I heard Chapman speak out loud and bold.
Then felt I like some watcher of the skies
   When a new planet swims into his ken;   10
Or like stout Cortez° when with eagle eyes
   He stared at the Pacific—and all his men
Looked at each other with a wild surmise—
   Silent, upon a peak in Darien.°

---

4. **Apollo:** Greek god of poetry and music. 6. **demesne** (dĭ-mān′): domain, here the *Iliad* and the *Odyssey.* 7. **serene:** clear air. 11. **Cortez:** Balboa discovered the Pacific Ocean in 1513, not Cortez; a celebrated mistake. 14. **Darien:** (dä-ryĕn′): the eastern part of the Isthmus of Panama.

Bright Star!
Would I Were Steadfast As Thou Art

Bright star! would I were steadfast as thou art—
   Not in lone splendor hung aloft the night
And watching, with eternal lids apart,
   Like nature's patient, sleepless Eremite,°
The moving waters at their priestlike task
   Of pure ablution round earth's human shores,
Or gazing on the new soft-fallen mask
   Of snow upon the mountains and the moors—
No—yet still steadfast, still unchangeable,
   Pillowed upon my fair love's ripening breast,
To feel forever its soft fall and swell,
   Awake forever in a sweet unrest,
Still, still to hear her tender-taken breath,
And so live ever—or else swoon to death.

Deathbed portrait of John Keats by Joseph Severn. London Borough of Camden, Keats House, Hampstead

---

4. **Eremite** (ĕr′ə-mīt′): hermit.

When I Have Fears That I May Cease to Be

When I have fears that I may cease to be
  Before my pen has gleaned my teeming brain,
Before high-pilèd books, in charactery,°
  Hold like rich garners the full-ripened grain;
When I behold, upon the night's starred face,   5
  Huge cloudy symbols of a high romance,
And think that I may never live to trace
  Their shadows, with the magic hand of chance;°
And when I feel, fair creature of an hour,
  That I shall never look upon thee more,   10
Never have relish in the fairy power
  Of unreflecting love—then on the shore
Of the wide world I stand alone, and think
Till love and fame to nothingness do sink.

---

3. **charactery:** handwriting.   8. **chance:** inspiration.

COMMENTARY

This sonnet has a high proportion of lines that oblige the reader to pause at the end. Only a few lines vary this effect of regularity, most notably lines 12 and 13, which, with their long open vowels (in *shore, wide world, alone*), provide a change of pace and underline the emotional climax of these lines.

FOR STUDY AND DISCUSSION

On First Looking into Chapman's Homer
The basic metaphor in this poem is one of travel: physical travel to various areas of the earth is Keats's way of expressing mental or imaginative voyages into the world of literature. How is Keats using this metaphor when he says that the "western islands" visited in the first part of the poem are held by "bards in fealty to Apollo" (lines 3–4)? How does the metaphor of travel change when the speaker says he felt "like some watcher of the skies" (line 9)? How does the image of Cortez at the end of the sonnet further alter the original idea of the speaker as one who has often "traveled in the realms of gold" (line 1)?

Bright Star! Would I Were Steadfast As Thou Art
1. How is the atmosphere of warmth and peacefulness in the final six lines (sestet) contrasted with the atmosphere of remoteness, coldness, and lack of involvement in the first eight lines (octave)?
2. What is the significance of the mention of death in the last line? The star is watchful: it can see. What does the lover have that the star does not?

When I Have Fears That I May Cease to Be
Describe the progress in thought in the three quatrains. Is there a progression of emotion also? Explain. How does the variation from the Shakespearean sonnet (see lines 12–13) call attention to the meaning of the poem?

FOR COMPOSITION

Compare Keats's sonnet "When I Have Fears That I May Cease to Be" with Milton's sonnet "On His Blindness." How does Keats's fear that his poetic talent will be cut short and never fully ripen differ from Milton's fear of the same thing? For Milton, what force or knowledge greater than poetic talent offers him consolation?

Keats and the Sonnet Form

Keats was highly conscious of the rich tradition of sonnet writing in English poetry. His first great sonnet, "On First Looking into Chapman's Homer," is written in the regular Italian or Petrarchan form and makes powerful use of the dramatic shift from octave to sestet. Most of his sonnets, however, follow the Shakespearean pattern of three quatrains and a couplet. This is true of "When I Have Fears That I May Cease to Be" and "Bright Star." But Keats eventually came to feel that both these traditional forms, despite the beauty and control made possible by their internal organization, were too artificial and constricting. In April 1819 he wrote "On the Sonnet," in which he simultaneously called for and demonstrated a more organically interwoven sonnet form:

> If by dull rhymes our English must be chained,
> And, like Andromeda,° the Sonnet sweet
> Fettered, in spite of painèd loveliness,
> Let us find out, if we must be constrained,
> Sandals more interwoven and complete   5
> To fit the naked foot of Poesy:
> Let us inspect the Lyre, and weigh the stress
> Of every chord, and see what may be gained
> By ear industrious, and attention meet;
> Misers of sound and syllable, no less   10
> Than Midas° of his coinage, let us be
> Jealous of dead leaves in the bay wreath crown;
> So, if we may not let the Muse° be free,
> She will be bound with garlands of her own.

---

2. **Andromeda** (ăn-drŏm′ə-də): a character in Greek mythology who was chained to a rock. She was rescued from a sea monster by Perseus.   11. **Midas:** a legendary king who was given the power to turn everything he touched to gold.   13. **Muse:** in Greek mythology the nine Muses presided over the arts.

The rhyme scheme of this sonnet is *abc abd cabc dede,* an intricate departure from the Petrarchan and Shakespearean forms.

Keats's attitude toward the sonnet is characteristic of his poetic career as a whole. Deeply committed to the great traditions of the past and fully capable of excelling within them, he nevertheless felt the need to bring those traditions into line with his own ideals about the relationship of art to life.

The Eve of St. Agnes

In this metrical romance the poet uses as his setting a castle in medieval Italy. The chapel with its stone images of lords and ladies, the great hall, and the chamber of Madeline with its triple-arched casement are pictured in vivid detail. The medieval characters of beadsman (an old man supported by a family in return for his regular prayers), nurse, warrior guests, and romantic lovers combine with archaic language to weave a spell of rare, unearthly beauty. The theme, like that of *Romeo and Juliet*, is the flowering of young love against a background of age, death, and human intolerance.

Saint Agnes was an early Christian martyr who, after her death, appeared to her parents in a vision with a lamb. Thereafter the white lamb, symbol of purity, was sacred to her. The legend on which this story is based is that a maiden, by observing certain rites on Saint Agnes' Eve, which occurs on January 20, may have a glimpse of her future husband.

St. Agnes' Eve—Ah, bitter chill it was!
The owl, for all his feathers, was a-cold;
The hare limped trembling through the frozen grass,
And silent was the flock in woolly fold;
Numb were the Beadsman's fingers, while he told   5
His rosary, and while his frosted breath,
Like pious incense from a censer old,
Seemed taking flight for heaven, without a death,
Past the sweet Virgin's picture, while his prayer he saith.

His prayer he saith, this patient, holy man;   10
Then takes his lamp, and riseth from his knees,
And back returneth, meager, barefoot, wan,
Along the chapel aisle by slow degrees;
The sculptured dead, on each side, seem to freeze,
Imprisoned in black, purgatorial rails;°   15
Knights, ladies, praying in dumb orat'ries,°
He passeth by; and his weak spirit fails
To think how they may ache in icy hoods and mails.°

Northward he turneth through a little door,
And scarce three steps, ere Music's golden tongue   20
Flattered to tears this aged man and poor;
But no—already had his deathbell rung;
The joys of all his life were said and sung;
His was harsh penance on St. Agnes' Eve;

---

15. **purgatorial rails:** burial robes.   16. **orat'ries:** oratories, small chapels for private prayers.   18. **mails:** coats of armor.

Another way he went, and soon among   25
Rough ashes sat he for his soul's reprieve,
And all night kept awake, for sinners' sake to grieve.

That ancient Beadsman heard the prelude soft;
And so it chanced, for many a door was wide,
From hurry to and fro. Soon, up aloft,   30
The silver, snarling trumpets 'gan to chide;
The level chambers, ready with their pride,
Were glowing to receive a thousand guests;
The carvèd angels, ever eager-eyed,
Stared, where upon their heads the cornice rests,   35
With hair blown back, and wings put crosswise on their
    breasts.

At length burst in the argent revelry,°
With plume, tiara, and all rich array,
Numerous as shadows, haunting fairily
The brain, new stuffed, in youth, with triumphs gay   40
Of old romance. These let us wish away,
And turn, sole-thoughted, to one Lady there,
Whose heart had brooded, all that wintry day,
On love, and winged St. Agnes' saintly care,
As she had heard old dames full many times declare.   45

They told her how, upon St. Agnes' Eve,
Young virgins might have visions of delight,
And soft adorings from their loves receive
Upon the honeyed middle of the night,
If ceremonies due they did aright;   50
As, supperless to bed they must retire,
And couch supine° their beauties, lily white;
Nor look behind, nor sideways, but require
Of Heaven with upward eyes for all that they desire.

Full of this whim was thoughtful Madeline;   55
The music, yearning like a god in pain,
She scarcely heard; her maiden eyes divine,
Fixed on the floor, saw many a sweeping train
Pass by—she heeded not at all; in vain
Came many a tiptoe, amorous cavalier,   60
And back retired; not cooled by high disdain,
But she saw not; her heart was otherwhere;
She sighed for Agnes' dreams, the sweetest of the year.

---

37. **argent revelry:** shining group of revelers.   52. **couch supine** (sōō-pīn′): lay flat.

She danced along with vague, regardless eyes,
Anxious her lips, her breathing quick and short;   65
The hallowed hour was near at hand; she sighs
Amid the timbrels, and the thronged resort
Of whisperers in anger, or in sport;
'Mid looks of love, defiance, hate, and scorn,
Hoodwinked with fairy fancy; all amort,°   70
Save to St. Agnes and her lambs unshorn,°
And all the bliss to be before tomorrow morn.

So, purposing each moment to retire,
She lingered still. Meantime, across the moors,
Had come young Porphyro,° with heart on fire   75
For Madeline. Beside the portal doors,
Buttressed from moonlight,° stands he, and implores
All saints to give him sight of Madeline,
But for one moment in the tedious hours,
That he might gaze and worship all unseen;   80
Perchance speak, kneel, touch, kiss — in sooth such things have
    been.

He ventures in; let no buzzed whisper tell;
All eyes be muffled, or a hundred swords
Will storm his heart, Love's fev'rous citadel;
For him, those chambers held barbarian hordes,   85
Hyena foemen, and hot-blooded lords,
Whose very dogs would execrations howl
Against his lineage; not one breast affords
Him any mercy, in that mansion foul,
Save one old beldame,° weak in body and in soul.   90

Ah, happy chance! the aged creature came,
Shuffling along with ivory-headed wand,
To where he stood, hid from the torch's flame,
Behind a broad hall pillar, far beyond
The sound of merriment and chorus bland.   95
He startled her; but soon she knew his face,
And grasped his fingers in her palsied hand,
Saying, "Mercy, Porphyro! hie thee from this place;
They are all here tonight, the whole bloodthirsty race!

---

70. **amort:** as if dead.   71. **lambs unshorn:** In honor of St. Agnes, the symbol
of youth and innocence, two lambs were sacrificed annually in the church on her
eve. The wool was later spun and woven by the nuns into garments for the poor.
75. **Porphyro** (pôr′fĭ-rō).   77. **Buttressed from moonlight:** He is standing in the
shadow of one of the buttresses that supported the walls of the castle.   90. **beldame** (bĕl′dăm): an old woman.

"Get hence; get hence! there's dwarfish Hildebrand;   100
He had a fever late, and in the fit
He cursèd thee and thine, both house and land;
Then there's that old Lord Maurice, not a whit
More tame for his gray hairs—Alas me! flit!
Flit like a ghost away."—"Ah, Gossip° dear,   105
We're safe enough; here in this armchair sit
And tell me how"—"Good Saints! not here, not here;
Follow me, child, or else these stones will be thy bier."

He followed through a lowly archèd way,
Brushing the cobwebs with his lofty plume;   110
And as she muttered, "Wella—welladay!"
He found him in a little moonlight room,
Pale, latticed, chill, and silent as a tomb.
"Now tell me where is Madeline," said he,
"O tell me, Angela, by the holy loom   115
Which none but secret sisterhood may see,
When they St. Agnes' wool are weaving piously."

"St. Agnes! Ah! it is St. Agnes' Eve—
Yet men will murder upon holy days.
Thou must hold water in a witch's sieve,°   120
And be liege lord of all the Elves and Fays,
To venture so: it fills me with amaze
To see thee, Porphyro!—St. Agnes' Eve!
God's help! my lady fair the conjurer plays
This very night; good angels her deceive!   125
But let me laugh awhile, I've mickle° time to grieve."

Feebly she laugheth in the languid moon,
While Porphyro upon her face doth look,
Like puzzled urchin on an aged crone
Who keepeth closed a wondrous riddle book,   130
As spectacled she sits in chimney nook.
But soon his eyes grew brilliant, when she told
His lady's purpose; and he scarce could brook
Tears, at the thought of those enchantments cold,
And Madeline asleep in lap of legends old.   135

Sudden a thought came like a fullblown rose,
Flushing his brow, and in his painèd heart
Made purple riot; then doth he propose
A stratagem, that makes the beldame start.

---

105. **Gossip:** godmother. 120. **hold . . . sieve:** have supernatural powers.
126. **mickle:** much (a Scottish expression).

"A cruel man and impious thou art.   140
Sweet lady, let her pray, and sleep, and dream
Alone with her good angels, far apart
From wicked men like thee. Go, go!—I deem
Thou canst not surely be the same that thou didst seem."°

"I will not harm her, by all saints I swear,"   145
Quoth Porphyro: "O may I ne'er find grace
When my weak voice shall whisper its last prayer,
If one of her soft ringlets I displace,
Or look with ruffian passion in her face.
Good Angela, believe me by these tears;   150
Or, I will, even in a moment's space,
Awake, with horrid shout, my foemen's ears,
And beard them, though they be more fanged than wolves and
    bears."

"Ah! why wilt thou affright a feeble soul?
A poor, weak, palsy-stricken churchyard thing,   155
Whose passing bell may ere the midnight toll;
Whose prayers for thee, each morn and evening,
Were never missed." Thus plaining,° doth she bring
A gentler speech from burning Porphyro;
So woeful, and of such deep sorrowing,   160
That Angela gives promise she will do
Whatever he shall wish, betide her weal or woe.°

Which was, to lead him, in close secrecy,
Even to Madeline's chamber, and there hide
Him in a closet, of such privacy   165
That he might see her beauty unespied,
And win perhaps that night a peerless bride,
While legioned fairies paced the coverlet,
And pale enchantment held her sleepy-eyed.
Never on such a night have lovers met,   170
Since Merlin° paid his Demon all the monstrous debt.

"It shall be as thou wishest," said the Dame;
"All cates° and dainties shall be storèd there
Quickly on this feast night; by the tambour frame°
Her own lute thou wilt see; no time to spare,   175

---

144. **Thou . . . seem:** You cannot be as honorable as I thought you were.
158. **plaining:** complaining.   162. **betide . . . woe:** whether good or evil come of
it.   171. **Merlin:** a magician, the offspring of demons, who was at last overpowered by means of one of his own spells reversed.   173. **cates:** dainty, choice
food.   174. **tambour frame:** embroidery hoops, shaped like a tambour or drum.

For I am slow and feeble, and scarce dare
On such a catering trust my dizzy head.
Wait here, my child, with patience; kneel in prayer
The while. Ah! thou must needs the lady wed,
Or may I never leave my grave among the dead." 180

So saying, she hobbled off with busy fear.
The lover's endless minutes slowly passed;
The dame returned, and whispered in his ear
To follow her; with aged eyes aghast
From fright of dim espial. Safe at last, 185
Through many a dusky gallery, they gain
The maiden's chamber, silken, hushed, and chaste;
Where Porphyro took covert, pleased amain.°
His poor guide hurried back with agues° in her brain.

Her falt'ring hand upon the balustrade, 190
Old Angela was feeling for the stair,
When Madeline, St. Agnes' charmèd maid,
Rose, like a missioned spirit, unaware:
With silver taper's light, and pious care,
She turned, and down the aged gossip led 195
To a safe level matting. Now prepare,
Young Porphyro, for gazing on that bed;
She comes, she comes again, like ringdove frayed° and fled.

Out went the taper as she hurried in;
Its little smoke, in pallid moonshine, died; 200
She closed the door, she panted, all akin
To spirits of the air, and visions wide;
No uttered syllable or woe betide!
But to her heart, her heart was voluble,
Paining with eloquence her balmy side; 205
As though a tongueless nightingale should swell
Her throat in vain, and die, heart-stifled, in her dell.

A casement high and triple-arched there was,
All garlanded with carven imageries
Of fruits, and flowers, and bunches of knotgrass, 210
And diamonded with panes of quaint device,
Innumerable of stains and splendid dyes,
As are the tiger moth's deep-damasked° wings;
And in the midst, 'mong thousand heraldries,

---

188. **amain:** greatly.   189. **agues** (ā'gyōoz): An ague causes one to shake from either fever or cold; in other words, she was frightened.   198. **frayed:** frightened.
213. **deep-damasked:** patterned.

And twilight saints, and dim emblazonings,   215
A shielded scutcheon blushed with blood of queens and kings.°

Full on this casement shone the wintry moon,
And threw warm gules° on Madeline's fair breast,
As down she knelt for heaven's grace and boon;
Rose bloom fell on her hands, together pressed,   220
And on her silver cross soft amethyst,
And on her hair a glory, like a saint:
She seemed a splendid angel, newly dressed,
Save wings, for heaven:—Porphyro grew faint;
She knelt, so pure a thing, so free from mortal taint.   225

Anon his heart revives; her vespers done,
Of all its wreathèd pearls her hair she frees;
Unclasped her warmèd jewels one by one;
Loosens her fragrant bodice; by degrees
Her rich attire creeps rustling to her knees;   230
Half-hidden, like a mermaid in seaweed,
Pensive awhile she dreams awake, and sees,
In fancy, fair St. Agnes in her bed,
But dares not look behind, or all the charm is fled.

Soon, trembling in her soft and chilly nest,   235
In sort of wakeful swoon, perplexed she lay,
Until the poppied° warmth of sleep oppressed
Her soothèd limbs, and soul fatigued away;
Flown, like a thought, until the morrow day;
Blissfully havened both from joy and pain;   240
Clasped like a missal° where swart Paynims° pray;
Blinded alike from sunshine and from rain,
As though a rose should shut, and be a bud again.

Stol'n to this paradise, and so entranced,
Porphyro gazed upon her empty dress,   245
And listened to her breathing, if it chanced
To wake into a slumberous tenderness;
Which when he heard, that minute did he bless,
And breathed himself; then from the closet crept,
Noiseless as fear in a wide wilderness,   250
And over the hushed carpet, silent, stepped,
And 'tween the curtains peeped, where, lo! how fast she slept.

---

216. **A shielded . . . kings:** A coat of arms shaped like a shield was colored red to
indicate a royal family.   218. **gules** (gyo͞olz): red, represented in heraldry by parallel
lines.   237. **poppied:** druglike.   241. **missal:** Mass book. **Paynims:** pagans. Her
eyes were as tightly closed in sleep as a prayer book would be in pagan lands.

Then by the bedside, where the faded moon
Made a dim, silver twilight, soft he set
A table, and half-anguished, threw thereon   255
A cloth of woven crimson, gold, and jet—
O for some drowsy Morphean amulet!°
The boisterous, midnight, festive clarion,
The kettledrum, and far-heard clarinet,
Affray° his ears, though but in dying tone—   260
The hall door shuts again, and all the noise is gone.

And still she slept an azure-lidded sleep,
In blanchèd linen, smooth, and lavendered,°
While he from forth the closet brought a heap
Of candied apple, quince, and plum, and gourd;   265
With jellies soother° than the creamy curd,
And lucent° syrups, tinct° with cinnamon;
Manna and dates, in argosy transferred
From Fez;° and spicèd dainties, every one,
From silken Samarkand° to cedared Lebanon.°   270

These delicates he heaped with glowing hand
On golden dishes and in baskets bright
Of wreathèd silver; sumptuous they stand
In the retirèd quiet of the night,
Filling the chilly room with perfume light.—   275
"And now, my love, my seraph fair, awake!
Thou art my heaven, and I thine eremite;
Open thine eyes, for meek St. Agnes' sake,
Or I shall drowse beside thee, so my soul doth ache."

Thus whispering, his warm, unnervèd arm   280
Sank in her pillow. Shaded was her dream
By the dusk curtains—'twas a midnight charm
Impossible to melt as icèd stream;
The lustrous salvers in the moonlight gleam;
Broad golden fringe upon the carpet lies;   285
It seemed he never, never could redeem
From such a steadfast spell his lady's eyes;
So mused awhile, entoiled in woofèd° phantasies.

---

257. **Morphean amulet:** a charm pertaining to the god of dreams; that is, one to keep her asleep.   260. **Affray:** frighten.   263. **lavendered:** perfumed with lavender.   266. **soother:** smoother.   267. **lucent** (lōō′sĕnt): clear.   **tinct:** delicately flavored.   269. **Fez:** a city in Morocco.   270. **Samarkand:** a city of Turkestan, famous for its manufacture of silk.   **Lebanon:** a country at the eastern end of the Mediterranean. From it came the timbers of cedar that were used in Solomon's temple.   288. **woofèd:** intertwined, as the threads are in weaving.

Awakening up, he took her hollow lute—
Tumultuous—and, in chords that tenderest be,   290
He played an ancient ditty, long since mute,
In Provence called "La belle dame sans merci";°
Close to her ear touching the melody;
Wherewith disturbed, she uttered a soft moan;
He ceased—she panted quick—and suddenly   295
Her blue affrayèd eyes wide open shone;
Upon his knees he sank, pale as smooth-sculptured stone.

Her eyes were open, but she still beheld,
Now wide awake, the vision of her sleep;
There was a painful change, that night expelled   300
The blisses of her dreams so pure and deep,
At which fair Madeline began to weep,
And moan forth witless words with many a sigh;
While still her gaze on Porphyro would keep;
Who knelt, with joinèd hands and piteous eyes,   305
Fearing to move or speak, she looked so dreamingly.

"Ah, Porphyro!" said she, "but even now
Thy voice was at sweet tremble in mine ear,
Made tunable with every sweetest vow;
And those sad eyes were spiritual and clear;   310
How changed thou art! how pallid, chill, and drear!
Give me that voice again, my Porphyro,
Those looks immortal, those complainings dear!
Oh, leave me not in this eternal woe,
For if thou diest, my Love, I know not where to go."   315

Beyond a mortal man impassioned far
At those voluptuous accents, he arose,
Ethereal, flushed, and like a throbbing star
Seen mid the sapphire heaven's deep repose;
Into her dream he melted, as the rose   320
Blendeth its odor with the violet—
Solution sweet; meantime the frost wind blows
Like Love's alarum pattering the sharp sleet
Against the windowpanes; St. Agnes' moon hath set.

'Tis dark; quick pattereth the flaw-blown° sleet;   325
"This is no dream, my bride, my Madeline!"
'Tis dark; the icèd gusts still rave and beat.

---

292. **"La belle dame sans merci"**: the beautiful lady without mercy. 325. **flaw-blown**: squall-blown.

"No dream, alas! alas! and woe is mine!
Porphyro will leave me here to fade and pine. —
Cruel! what traitor could thee hither bring?   330
I curse not, for my heart is lost in thine,
Though thou forsakest a deceivèd thing —
A dove forlorn and lost with sick unprunèd wing."

"My Madeline! sweet dreamer! lovely bride!
Say, may I be for aye thy vassal° blest?   335
Thy beauty's shield, heart-shaped and vermeil-dyed?°
Ah, silver shrine, here will I take my rest
After so many hours of toil and quest,
A famished pilgrim — saved by miracle.
Though I have found, I will not rob thy nest   340
Saving of thy sweet self; if thou think'st well
To trust, fair Madeline, to no rude infidel.

"Hark! 'tis an elfin storm from fairyland,
Of haggard seeming,° but a boon indeed.
Arise — arise! the morning is at hand —   345
The bloated wassailers will never heed —
Let us away, my love, with happy speed;
There are no ears to hear, or eyes to see —
Drowned all in Rhenish° and the sleepy mead.°
Awake! arise! my love, and fearless be,   350
For o'er the southern moors I have a home for thee."

She hurried at his words, beset with fears,
For there were sleeping dragons all around,
At glaring watch, perhaps, with ready spears —
Down the wide stairs a darkling way they found —   355
In all the house was heard no human sound.
A chain-drooped lamp° was flickering by each door;
The arras,° rich with horseman, hawk, and hound,
Fluttered in the besieging wind's uproar;
And the long carpets rose along the gusty floor.   360

They glide, like phantoms, into the wide hall;
Like phantoms, to the iron porch, they glide;
Where lay the Porter, in uneasy sprawl,
With a huge empty flagon by his side.

---

335. **vassal:** in feudal times, a knight who pledged allegiance to his overlord.
336. **vermeil-dyed** (vûr'mĭl): vermilion, bright red.   344. **haggard seeming:** wild in aspect.   349. **Rhenish** (rĕn'ĭsh): wine made near the Rhine River.   **mead:** a drink made of fermented honey.   357. **chain-drooped lamp:** lamp hanging on a chain.
358. **arras** (ăr'ăs): tapestry hanging on the wall to keep out drafts.

The wakeful bloodhound rose, and shook his hide,   365
But his sagacious eye an inmate owns;
By one and one, the bolts full easy slide—
The chains lie silent on the footworn stones—
The key turns, and the door upon its hinges groans.

And they are gone; aye, ages long ago   370
These lovers fled away into the storm.
That night the Baron dreamt of many a woe,
And all his warrior guests, with shade and form
Of witch, and demon, and large coffin worm,
Were long benightmared. Angela the old   375
Died palsy-twitched, with meager face deform;
The Beadsman, after thousand aves told,
For aye unsought-for slept among his ashes cold.

FOR STUDY AND DISCUSSION

1. What details does Keats use to give a medieval flavor to the story?
2. At the end of the story, what becomes of the lovers, the beadsman, the nurse, the baron, and the guests? How is a veil of mystery thrown over the conclusion? Does this add to the romantic appeal of the poem, in your opinion?
3. What stanza form does Keats use in this poem? What other poems that you have read are written in this form?

KEATS'S IMAGERY

Keats is a master of language; his magical phrasing and his harmoniously flowing lines are comparable to those of Shakespeare. What sets Keats apart from most poets, however, is his sensuous imagery. He is able to stimulate our senses as they would be if the objects depicted were physically present.

Keats's masterful appeal to the senses is illustrated by two pairs of contrasting stanzas from "The Eve of St. Agnes." In the opening stanza of the poem the reader cannot escape the dominant note of cold. Many lines have at least one word to add to the sensation: *bitter chill, a-cold, limped trembling, frozen, silent, numb, frosted.* The crowning simile suggests a striking image by likening the beadsman's frosted breath to the cloud of incense from an old censer rising toward heaven.

The cold of the outside world is contrasted with the richness and beauty of the scene in Madeline's chamber. The two stanzas from lines 253–270 appeal to every one of the five senses:

sight: a dim silver twilight; a cloth of woven crimson, gold, and jet; azure-lidded sleep; blanchèd linen, smooth; all the foods in lines 265–269; silken Samarkand and cedared Lebanon.

sound: the musical instruments "affray his ears," then are silent.

smell and taste: the fruits, jellies, and syrups mentioned appeal to *three* senses, smell, taste, and sight; lavendered linen; spicèd dainties.

touch: smooth linen (to the hands); jellies soother than the creamy curd (to the tongue).

Make a list of the images appealing to the senses that the poet uses in the next three stanzas (lines 271–297).

Ode to a Nightingale

Keats wrote this poem in May of 1819 while living with his friend Charles Brown in Hampstead, in northwest London. Brown commented as follows on its composition: "In the spring of 1819 a nightingale had built her nest near my house. Keats felt a tranquil and continual joy in her song; and one morning he took his chair from the breakfast table to the grass plot under a plum tree, where he sat for two or three hours. When he came into the house, I perceived he had some scraps of paper in his hand, and these he was quietly thrusting behind the books. On inquiry, I found those scraps, four or five in number, contained his poetic feeling on the song of our nightingale."

Keats's imagination in this poem, like Shelley's in "To a Skylark," focuses on a natural creature whose joyful state of being he both identifies with and yet ultimately feels separated from. The song of the nightingale puts Keats in a kind of imaginative trance, which he desires to sustain forever. But near the end of the poem, Keats realizes that his intense experience of beauty cannot be sustained. As the song of the nightingale fades away into the distance, he is left to wonder whether his experience was real or only a dream.

My heart aches, and a drowsy numbness pains
   My sense, as though of hemlock° I had drunk,
Or emptied some dull opiate to the drains
   One minute past, and Lethe-wards° had sunk;
Tis not through envy of thy happy lot,   5
   But being too happy in thine happiness—
      That thou, light-wingèd Dryad° of the trees,
         In some melodious plot
Of beechen green, and shadows numberless,
      Singest of summer in full-throated ease.   10

O for a draught of vintage! that hath been
   Cooled a long age in the deep-delvèd earth.
Tasting of Flora° and the country green,
   Dance, and Provençal° song, and sunburnt mirth!
O for a beaker full of the warm South,   15
   Full of the true, the blushful Hippocrene,°
      With beaded bubbles winking at the brim,
         And purple-stainèd mouth;
That I might drink, and leave the world unseen,
      And with thee fade away into the forest dim;   20

---

2. **hemlock:** a poison.   4. **Lethe-wards:** toward the Greek mythological river of forgetfulness, whose waters prepared the good to enter the bliss of the Elysian fields.   7. **Dryad:** a wood nymph.   13. **Flora:** goddess of flowers.   14. **Provençal** (prō'vən-säl'): pertaining to Provence, a region in southern France, home of the medieval troubadours.   16. **Hippocrene** (hĭp'ə-krēn'): a fountain on Mount Helicon, sacred to the Muses.

Fade far away, dissolve, and quite forget
    What thou among the leaves hast never known,
The weariness, the fever, and the fret
    Here, where men sit and hear each other groan;
Where palsy shakes a few, sad, last gray hairs;   25
    Where youth grows pale and specter-thin, and dies;°
        Where but to think is to be full of sorrow
            And leaden-eyed despairs;
    Where Beauty cannot keep her lustrous eyes
        Or new Love pine at them beyond tomorrow.   30

Away! away! for I will fly to thee,
    Not charioted by Bacchus and his pards,°
But on the viewless° wings of Poesy,
    Though the dull brain perplexes and retards:
Already with thee! tender is the night,   35
    And haply the Queen Moon is on her throne,
        Clustered around by all her starry Fays;°
            But here there is no light,
    Save what from heaven is with the breezes blown
        Through verdurous glooms and winding mossy ways.   40

I cannot see what flowers are at my feet,
    Nor what soft incense hangs upon the boughs,
But, in embalmèd° darkness, guess each sweet
    Wherewith the seasonable month endows
The grass, the thicket, and the fruit tree wild;   45
    White hawthorn, and the pastoral eglantine;
        Fast fading violets covered up in leaves;
            And mid-May's eldest child,
    The coming musk rose, full of dewy wine,
        The murmurous haunt of flies on summer eves.   50

Darkling° I listen; and, for many a time
    I have been half in love with easeful Death,
Called him soft names in many a musèd rhyme,
    To take into the air my quiet breath;
Now more than ever seems it rich to die,   55
    To cease upon the midnight with no pain,
        While thou art pouring forth thy soul abroad
            In such an ecstasy!
    Still wouldst thou sing, and I have ears in vain—
        To thy high requiem become a sod.   60

---

26. **youth . . . dies:** Keats recalls the death of his young brother Tom a few months
before this poem was written.   32. **Bacchus** (băk′əs) . . . **pards:** The Roman god of
wine rode in a chariot drawn by leopards.   33. **viewless:** invisible.   37. **Fays:**
fairies.   43. **embalmed:** balmy.   51. **Darkling:** in the dark.

Thou wast not born for death, immortal Bird!
    No hungry generations tread thee down;
The voice I hear this passing night was heard
    In ancient days by emperor and clown;
Perhaps the selfsame song that found a path   65
    Through the sad heart of Ruth,° when, sick for home,
      She stood in tears amid the alien corn;
        The same that ofttimes hath
    Charmed magic casements, opening on the foam
      Of perilous seas, in fairylands forlorn.   70

Forlorn! the very word is like a bell
    To toll me back from thee to my sole self!
Adieu! the fancy cannot cheat so well
    As she is famed° to do, deceiving elf.
Adieu! adieu! thy plaintive anthem fades   75
    Past the near meadows, over the still stream,
      Up the hillside; and now 'tis buried deep
        In the next valley glades.
    Was it a vision, or a waking dream?
    Fled is that music—Do I wake or sleep?   80

---

66. **Ruth:** According to the Bible (Ruth 2:1–23), the widow Ruth left her home and
went to Judah, where she worked in the corn (wheat) fields. 74. **famed:** reported.

COMMENTARY

Keats's central symbol is the song of the nightin-gale. In the first stanza the poet is overcome by the song and almost loses himself, so powerful is its ef-fect. In the second stanza he imagines a drink that might take him out of himself completely and carry him off into the nightingale's retreat. The third stanza turns back to the sadness of the world, in which youth dies (as had Keats's brother Tom a few months before the poem was written). The poet's attempted flight from that world takes an-other form in the fourth stanza—not a liquor, an external thing, but "poesy," is to free him. At this point the poem takes an unexpected turn, almost a somersault, for after proclaiming that the poet is "Already with thee!"—as if he could at a leap join mortal hopes to an eternal being, "a Queen Moon" —he falls back into a world of time and change, a world in which "there is no light" (line 38).

    The wood in which the poet finds himself in the fifth stanza is one in which flowers bloom and die and seasons come and go. There he is conscious of his mortality and is drawn by the fantasy of dying to the nightingale's music. In the sixth stanza Keats imagines a death which is an ecstatic conclu-sion, but then acknowledges that if he were dead the song would go unheard.

FOR STUDY AND DISCUSSION

1. What is the speaker's mental and emotional state at the opening of the poem? Why is he in this state? What emotions are aroused in him by the song of the nightingale?
2. At the end of stanza 7, the "fairylands" are described as "forlorn." How does the word *forlorn* in line 71 bring the speaker back to reality?
3. How may this ode be read as a poem in which the self has an adventure of the imagination?
4. In the final stanza the speaker says that "fancy cannot cheat so well / As she is famed to do" (lines 73–74). How do these lines relate to the speaker's earlier confidence that he will fly to the nightingale "on the viewless wings of Poesy" (lines 31–33)? In what way does the speaker feel betrayed by fancy or imagination at the end of the poem?

Ode on a Grecian Urn

The Francois Vase (Attic black figure,
c. 575 B.C.).
Museo Archaelogico, Florence, The Mansell Collection

Thou still unravished bride of quietness,
    Thou foster child of silence and slow time,
Sylvan historian, who canst thus express
    A flowery tale more sweetly than our rhyme:
What leaf-fringed legend haunts about thy shape   5
    Of deities or mortals, or of both,
        In Tempe° or the dales of Arcady?°
What men or gods are these? What maidens loath?
    What mad pursuit? What struggle to escape?
        What pipes and timbrels?° What wild ecstasy?   10

Heard melodies are sweet, but those unheard
    Are sweeter; therefore, ye soft pipes, play on;
Not to the sensual° ear, but, more endeared,
    Pipe to the spirit ditties of no tone.
Fair youth, beneath the trees, thou canst not leave   15
    Thy song, nor ever can those trees be bare;
        Bold Lover, never, never canst thou kiss,
Though winning near the goal—yet, do not grieve;
    She cannot fade, though thou hast not thy bliss,
        Forever wilt thou love, and she be fair!   20

---

7. **Tempe** (tĕm′pē): a lovely valley in Thessaly, Greece. **Arcady** (är′kə-dē): a pastoral region in Greece. 10. **timbrels:** hand drums or tambourines. 13. **sensual:** appealing to the sense (of hearing).

Ah, happy, happy boughs! that cannot shed
   Your leaves, nor ever bid the Spring adieu;
And, happy melodist, unwearièd,
   Forever piping songs forever new;
More happy love! more happy, happy love!   25
   Forever warm and still to be enjoyed,
      Forever panting, and forever young;
All breathing human passion far above,
   That leaves a heart high-sorrowful and cloyed,
      A burning forehead, and a parching tongue.   30

Who are these coming to the sacrifice?
   To what green altar, O mysterious priest,
Lead'st thou that heifer lowing at the skies,
   And all her silken flanks with garlands dressed?
What little town by river or seashore,   35
   Or mountain-built with peaceful citadel,
      Is emptied of this folk, this pious morn?
And, little town, thy streets for evermore
   Will silent be; and not a soul to tell
      Why thou art desolate, can e'er return.   40

O Attic° shape! Fair attitude! with brede°
   Of marble men and maidens overwrought,
With forest branches and the trodden weed;
   Thou, silent form, dost tease us out of thought
As doth eternity. Cold° Pastoral.   45
   When old age shall this generation waste,
      Thou shalt remain, in midst of other woe
Than ours, a friend to man, to whom thou say'st,
   "Beauty is truth, truth beauty—that is all
      Ye know on earth, and all ye need to know."   50

---

41. **Attic:** that is, Athenian, a style marked by grace and simplicity.   **brede:** embroidery.   45. **Cold:** unchanging, immortal.

COMMENTARY

Many readers of this poem have wondered about the actual Grecian urn that inspired it, and various attempts have been made to identify this or that urn as Keats's. Although scenes like those described in the "Ode" can be found on examples of Greek pottery surviving in museums, the many details taken together seem to have existed only in Keats's imagination. This fact bears an important relation to Keats's theme. The poem celebrates the urn as a perfect work of art in which the contrary energies of human experience are suspended in ideal perfection; but it also makes us aware of certain aspects of life that the art of the urn does not express. The urn is "far above" "All breathing human passion" (line 28), in the sense that it transcends the changes and uncertainties of such passion, and is remote from, even oblivious to, such passion. The art of the urn is very great, but the "Ode" points indirectly to another kind of art embodying a fuller relationship to "breathing human passion." This other kind of art is Keats's own poetry, which is able to imagine the urn in its ideal perfection and, at the same time, to take in aspects of experience that the urn leaves out. The urn may be able to "express/A flowery tale more sweetly than our rhyme" (lines 3–4), but in the end Keats's rhyme succeeds in expressing more than a flowery tale, and its range of tone and mood includes, but is not confined to, happiness and sweetness.

FOR STUDY AND DISCUSSION

1. In the first stanza of "Ode on a Grecian Urn," Keats addresses the urn as an "historian" who describes a scene of "mad pursuit" and "ecstasy." Why does the speaker say that the lover on the urn can never kiss the maiden he pursues (line 17)? Why can the "happy boughs" in lines 21–22 never shed their leaves?

2. "Heard melodies" are those of the senses (hearing) while "unheard" melodies are those created by the imagination. How is the entire "Ode on a Grecian Urn" an expression of "unheard" melodies?

3. In stanza 4 Keats shifts our attention to another scene on the urn. What does this scene seem to show? Is the "little town" referred to in line 35 actually depicted on the urn? How does the speaker imagine this little town?

4. In the course of praising the eternal beauty and happiness of the figures in the scenes on the urn, Keats refers again and again to qualities these figures do *not* possess, to experiences they *cannot* undergo. The "Fair youth" playing his pipe beneath the trees in line 15, for example, can never stop his song. What other examples can you find where Keats emphasizes experiences not embodied in the scenes on the urn? What is the effect of praising the urn in this way?

FOR COMPOSITION

Readers of "Ode on a Grecian Urn" have long debated the significance of the final two lines. Some readers believe that the urn says "Beauty is truth, truth beauty," and that Keats adds his support to this message in the last line and a half. Other readers think that what the urn says includes all of the final two lines, and that Keats expects us to realize that the message of the urn is not necessarily the message of the poem as a whole. (These readers point out that in some versions of the poem printed while Keats was alive there are no quotation marks separating "Beauty is truth, truth beauty" from what follows.) Which view do you support? Give reasons based upon your reading of the entire poem to support your position. Your answer may depend upon whether or not you think the statement is true.

To Autumn

Season of mists and mellow fruitfulness,
  Close bosom-friend of the maturing sun;
Conspiring with him how to load and bless
  With fruit the vines that round the thatch-eaves run;
To bend with apples the mossed cottage-trees,   5
  And fill all fruit with ripeness to the core;
    To swell the gourd, and plump the hazel shells
With a sweet kernel; to set budding more,
  And still more, later flowers for the bees,
  Until they think warm days will never cease,   10
    For Summer has o'er-brimmed their clammy cells.

Who hath not seen thee oft amid thy store?
  Sometimes whoever seeks abroad may find
Thee sitting careless on a granary floor,
  Thy hair soft-lifted by the winnowing wind;   15
Or on a half-reaped furrow sound asleep,
  Drowsed with the fume of poppies, while thy hook
    Spares the next swath and all its twinèd flowers:
And sometimes like a gleaner thou dost keep
  Steady thy laden head across a brook;   20
  Or by a cider-press, with patient look,
    Thou watchest the last oozings hours by hours.

Where are the songs of Spring? Aye, where are they?
  Think not of them, thou hast thy music too—
While barred clouds bloom the soft-dying day,   25
  And touch the stubble-plains with rosy hue;
Then in a wailful choir the small gnats mourn
  Among the river sallows,° borne aloft
    Or sinking as the light wind lives or dies;
And full-grown lambs loud bleat from hilly bourn;°   30
  Hedge crickets sing; and now with treble soft
  The redbreast whistles from a garden croft;°
    And gathering swallows twitter in the skies.

---

28. **sallows:** willow trees.   30. **bourn:** region.   32. **croft:** a fenced plot.

COMMENTARY

This was the last of Keats's odes, and some readers consider it the finest of all. Two days after it was composed (on September 19, 1819), Keats wrote to a friend: "I never liked stubble fields so much as now—Aye, better than the chilly green of the spring. Somehow a stubble plain looks warm—in the same way that some pictures look warm—this struck me so much in my Sunday's walk that I composed upon it."

Keats addresses autumn as a time of rich fullness and fruition. The decay and decline that will follow and lead into winter are only implied. The consciousness of the speaker is almost totally absorbed in the scene he describes—there is a perfect "greeting," as Keats called it, between his spirit or mood and the natural presence he contemplates. Autumn itself is addressed in the poem as a personified or mythical being, but this being emerges from and flows back into the specific aspects of the natural scene with an artistry that itself seems entirely natural.

FOR STUDY AND DISCUSSION

1. What particular aspects of autumn does Keats focus on in stanza 1? What overall feeling do these images create? How do the important images in stanza 1 compare with those in stanza 3? How is your feeling about autumn affected by the last seven lines of the poem, which describe the music of autumn?

2. In stanza 2 Keats describes the personified figure of autumn. In what particular situations or experiences may this figure be seen? Why does Keats single out these situations and experiences?

3. Keats has an amazing ability to evoke an almost physical sense of autumn's presence—a reality which is at once natural and imaginary. He does this in the first stanza by repeating the sounds of the letters *s* and *m* and *l*; he does it in the second stanza by describing Autumn's hair as "soft-lifted by the winnowing wind" (line 15). Find other examples in the poem where the sound and imagery give you a very strong sense of autumn's presence. Try to describe the relation between language and poetic effect as carefully as you can.

STANZA FORM

We have already seen how Keats experimented with sonnet form. This experimentation carries over into the great series of odes that he wrote during the spring of 1819. The ode provided Keats with a freer and more expansive range of poetic possibilities for expressing his perceptions about art, nature, and the human mind. All Keats's odes are poems of address: the poet speaks directly to a Grecian Urn, or to a Nightingale, or to Autumn.

Like Shelley, Keats created his own stanza form for his odes. In both "Ode on a Grecian Urn" and "Ode to a Nightingale" he uses a ten-line stanza. In "Grecian Urn" all lines are of equal length, but the rhyme scheme varies subtly. Each of the five stanzas begins with a regular *abab* pattern, but the first stanza ends *cdedce*, the second stanza *cdeced*, the third stanza *cdecde*, and so forth. In "Ode to a Nightingale," the rhyme scheme is regular throughout (*ababcdecde*). Although the line length varies slightly, the variation itself is regular. The eighth line of each stanza is short, containing just six syllables instead of the usual ten. (The only real irregularity comes in the final line of stanza 2, which contains two extra syllables.) "To Autumn" contains the most delicately varied rhyme scheme of all. Here Keats expands the length of the stanza to eleven lines and varies the pattern of stanzas 2 and 3 ever so slightly from that of stanza 1: *ababcdedcce* becomes *ababcdecdde*.

In reading Keats's odes, we should be alert to ways in which his experimentation with stanza form relates to the feelings and ideas peculiar to each individual poem. Expanding the stanza length from ten to eleven lines in "To Autumn," for example, helps create just the sensation of ripeness or overripeness that is part of the poem's subject. For an attentive reader, the odes reveal with astonishing complexity how a great poet expresses himself.

A Famous American Novelist on Keats

Poetry is either something that lives like fire inside of you . . . or else it is nothing, an empty, formalized bore around which pedants can endlessly drone their notes and explanations. "The Grecian Urn" is unbearably beautiful with every syllable as inevitable as the notes in Beethoven's *Ninth Symphony*, or it's just something you don't understand. It is what it is because an extraordinary genius passed at that point in history and touched it. I suppose I've read it a hundred times. About the tenth time I began to know what it is about, and caught the chime in it and the exquisite inner mechanics. Likewise with the "Nightingale" which I can never read through without tears in my eyes; likewise the "Pot of Basil" with its great stanzas about the two brothers; and "The Eve of Saint Agnes" which has the richest, most sensuous imagery in English, not excepting Shakespeare. And finally his three or four great sonnets, "Bright Star" and the others.

Knowing those things young and granted an ear, one can scarcely ever afterwards be unable to distinguish between gold and dross in what one reads. In themselves those eight poems are a scale of workmanship for anybody who wants to know truly about words, their most utter value for evocation, persuasion, or charm. For a while after you quit Keats all other poetry seems to be only whistling or humming.

F. Scott Fitzgerald

—*From a letter quoted in the*
Princeton Alumni Weekly, *March 9, 1956.*

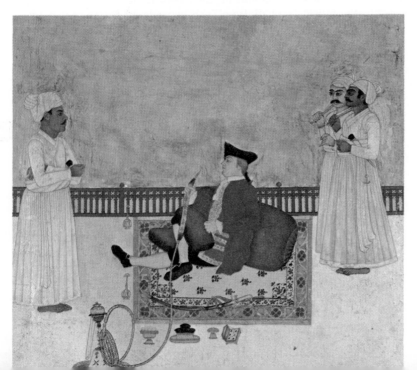

Bengal miniature (1760).
A British East India
Company employee adapts
to his Indian environment.
Victoria and Albert Museum,
Crown Copyright

The Romantic Age

By the beginning of the nineteenth century the English language had spread around the globe. The East India House had established settlements in Madras, Bombay, and Calcutta. Captain Cook's voyages had opened New Zealand and Australia to English settlers. During the Napoleonic Wars, the English annexed the Dutch settlement at Cape Town in Africa. The British fleet's success during the Napoleonic War, culminating in Admiral Nelson's triumph at the Battle of Trafalgar in 1805, left England the undisputed master of the seas and in control of most of the world's commerce.

From the new settlements and from the United States came a flood of new words for the English language. From the North American Indians came *hickory, caribou, hominy, moose, moccasin, opposum, raccoon, skunk, squaw, toboggan, totem, wampum, wigwam*, and many others. From Spanish and Portuguese territories came *chili, chocolate, coyote, tomato, barbeque, cannibal, canoe, hammock, hurricane, maize, potato, tobacco, jerky, buccaneer, petunia, poncho*, and *tapioca*, to name a few. India gave us *bandanna, bungalow, calico, cashmere, china, chintz, coolie, cot, curry, jungle, punch, tom-tom, veranda*, and scores of others. Australia has provided fewer words to common use, though we could mention *kangaroo* and *boomerang*.

Some anxiety about "correctness" in language carried over into the nineteenth century. This anxiety centered mainly on the use of slang. The word *slang* does not appear in Johnson's dictionary. By the time Byron published *Don Juan*, the conservative critics of his day took him to task for his racy conversational style and his use of fashionable slang. In this he was following the practice of Dryden, Swift, and Pope (who were not criticized in their day). For example, De Quincey con-

demned as slang the phrase *what on earth*, used as an intensive, and expressed horror at hearing it used by an educated public official. No one, of course, would remark on it today. The term *row* used to describe a noisy quarrel or brawl would be quite standard usage today. In 1818, H. J. Todd called it "a very low expression."

On our side of the Atlantic, in 1828, Noah Webster described slang as "low, vulgar, unmeaning language." Webster was concerned about "correctness" but he also had the reformer's zeal. He wanted to make sense out of American English. "We have . . . the fairest opportunity of establishing a national language . . . in North America that ever presented itself to mankind." He set about reforming American spelling by eliminating the British *u* from such words as *colour, favour, flavour, harbour, labour*, and *neighbour* and the final *k* from such words as *energetick, musick, physick, publick*, and *traffick*. Webster also reversed the British *re*, giving us *caliber, center, sepulcher*, and *theater* rather than the British *calibre, centre, sepulchre*, and *theatre*.

The one grammatical change that can be noted in the late eighteenth and early nineteenth century is the development of progressive verb forms. These forms allowed the speaker to designate ongoing action. At first the grammatical construction was a participle used as a noun, governed by the preposition *on*: "The house was on building." This weakened to "The house was a-building" or "He was a-laughing." While one can still hear in some local dialects "The barn is a-building," at about this time the standard form for expressing continuous or progressive action became "The house is being built."

As far as the literary language was concerned, the poets and novelists of the Romantic period reacted against what they regarded as the "high-flown" style of the eighteenth century. Whereas the eighteenth-century writers wanted to express general truths and tended to use abstract words, the Romantics were interested in particular states of being and personal experience. They tended to use concrete words, to describe nature in minute detail rather than in broad generalized landscapes. It seemed to them that eighteenth-century literary English, careful and elegant though it might be, had often proved limited and artificial. Deliberately rejecting the literary style of the immediate past, they looked for inspiration to sources that eighteenth-century purists had scorned—the literature of the Elizabethan period, the language of folk ballads, the speech of everyday life. Coleridge employed the techniques and some of the archaic language of the old ballads in *The Rime of the Ancient Mariner.* Wordsworth tried to capture the simplicity and directness of rural speech in his poetry. Sir Walter Scott put archaic English into the mouth of his hero in *Ivanhoe* and Scottish dialect into the mouth of his heroine in *The Heart of Midlothian.*

The appearance of "nonliterary" English in so many literary works marked a turning point in the history of the written language. The earlier ideal of creating a lofty literary English, different in style from spoken English, was overthrown. Since the beginning of the nineteenth century, written English has become progressively less formal and closer to the spoken language. This change has affected not just the work of professional writers, but all the writing that each of us does—even our letterwriting.

FOR STUDY AND DISCUSSION

1. One feature of eighteenth-century literary language to which writers of the Romantic period particularly objected was the use of elaborate and roundabout ways of expressing simple ideas. Following are two pairs of excerpts from poetry. The excerpts in each pair express approximately the same idea: one is from mid-eighteenth-century poetry and the other from poetry of the Romantic period. You should be able to tell which is which, and to point out the specific expressions in each excerpt that helped you to form your judgment.

    a. (1) The birds are singing in the distant woods . . .

       (2) . . . Every Copse
Deep-tangled, Tree irregular, and Bush
Bending with dewy Moisture, o'er the Heads
Of the coy Quiristers[1] that lodge within,
Are prodigal of Harmony.

    b. (1) And redning Phoebus lifts his golden Fire . . .

       (2) But now the sun is rising calm and bright. . .

---

1. **Quiristers:** choristers, choir singers.

2. The excerpts immediately above are printed with the original spelling and capitalization. What specific differences from modern spelling and capitalization can you point out? Do these differences tend to occur chiefly in the excerpts you identified as being from eighteenth-century poetry? Would you say that English habits of spelling and capitalization probably changed between the middle of the eighteenth century and the beginning of the nineteenth century? Explain.

3. To help create a sense of distant past in "The Eve of St. Agnes," Keats uses such archaic words as *saith* and *amain.* Find other examples of archaic language in the poem.

The Victorian Age
1832–1900

Omnibus Life in London (detail) by William Maw Egely.
The Tate Gallery, London

VICTORIAN ENGLAND: PROMISES AND PROBLEMS OF AN INDUSTRIAL SOCIETY

The Victorian Age began in the strict sense in 1837, when the eighteen-year-old Victoria succeeded her uncle, William IV, and became Queen of England. Victoria's life and reign were prodigiously long. When she died in 1901, she was eighty-two; her Diamond Jubilee in 1897 had celebrated her sixtieth year on the throne. During this period England became the world's wealthiest nation and, through the creation and expansion of the British Empire, its most influential colonial power. The Victorians also made the first serious and large-scale attempts to solve the problems of the industrial and democratic revolutions that had taken place during the Romantic Age. Standing as it does between the Romantic era and our own twentieth century, the Victorian Age has a special relevance for us today.

We are much closer to the Victorian era than we often realize. Many people alive today were born during the reign of Queen Victoria; many of us have parents or grandparents who were raised by Victorian mothers and fathers. Because of this historical proximity, and because of the natural tendency of one generation to rebel against the style and values of its parents' generation, it is sometimes hard to be objective about the Victorians. People still use the word *Victorian* as a synonym for "prude" and think of the Victorian era as a time of extreme repression, when even furniture legs had to be concealed under heavy brocade cloth so as not to be too suggestive.

This view of the Victorians is very limited and misleading. In no other period of English culture before or since were new ideas discussed and debated so vigorously by such a large segment of society. The Victorians were voracious readers: they thrived not only on the massive novels of Charles Dickens, William Thackeray, and George Eliot, but also on lengthy political and religious tracts. The intellectual seriousness and vitality of the age were part of the larger process of growth, change, and adjustment. If the Victorians were not always capable of fully understanding and solving the problems confronting them, we must nevertheless acknowledge that many of those problems remain unsolved today. It is not at all clear, moreover, that our willingness to confront the difficulties of modern industrial society is equal — much less superior — to that of the Victorians. We have much to learn from Victorian literature. The writers of this period offer a fascinating variety of artistic responses to a rapidly changing world that is not far removed from our own.

Queen Victoria in Her Coronation Robes by John Hayton. National Portrait Gallery, London

THE HISTORICAL AND POLITICAL BACKGROUND

The Victorian Age was a time of extensive social and political development. In order to clarify the main events and issues of this complicated period, it is convenient to divide the Victorian Age into three phases—early, middle, and late.

The Early Period (1832–1848). Although Queen Victoria did not come to the throne until 1837, we may think of the early Victorian period as beginning in 1832, when Parliament passed the First Reform Bill. From the time of the American and French revolutions, England had been increasingly distressed by the need for democratic reform. The first real step in this direction, however, came with the Reform Bill of 1832, which gave greater power to the middle class by extending the vote to all men owning property worth ten pounds or more in annual rent. The Reform Bill also reduced the power of upper-class landowners by redistributing parliamentary representation. In addition, it abolished the system of "rotten boroughs," which had allotted seats to the squires controlling underpopulated rural areas while more populous urban areas went unrepresented. The First Reform Bill demonstrated that social change could take place peacefully, without violent revolution, and it marked the emergence of the middle class as the dominant force in English politics.

Moorish arch as seen from a tunnel of the Liverpool and Manchester Railway (colored engraving, 1841).
Radio Times Hulton

Dickens, First Edition
Newman of the Oxford Movement (detail)
Queen Victoria in Coronation Robes (detail)

1837 **Early Victorian Period 1837–1848** **1840**

Dickens'
Pickwick Papers 1837

The People's Charter 1839

Oxford Movement
late 1830's

Mill's *On the Subjection
of Women* 1869

Second Reform Bill 1867

Period 1870–1901 **1870**

Late Victorian

Eliot's *Middlemarch*
1872

Empress of India 1876

Das Kapital 1867
"Dover Beach" 1867

H.M.S. Pinafore 1878

Treasure Island 1883

Death of Hopkins 1889

1880 **1890**

Darwin Pursuing an Elephant Tortoise

Benjamin Disraeli (detail)

The Lady of Shalott (detail), Holman Hunt

Alfred Tennyson (detail)

Crystal Palace Interior

Middle Victorian Period 1848–1870   1850

Repeal of the
Corn Law 1846

Pre-Raphaelite
Brotherhood 1848

Tennyson made
Poet Laureate 1850

Browning's
Men and Women 1855

Great Exhibition 1851

1860

The Origin of Species 1859

Crimean War 1854–1856

*The Importance
of Being Earnest* 1894

Diamond Jubilee 1897

Hardy's *Wessex Poems*
1898

1900   **1901**

Queen Victoria as Empress of India

George Eliot (Mary Ann Evans)

Victoria near the Diamond Jubilee (detail)

Despite improvements made possible by the Reform Bill, however, the early years of Victoria's reign continued to be a time of considerable hardship, injustice, and unrest. Living and working conditions in the industrial cities of northern England were as terrible as they ever had been. The working class and lower middle class still did not have the right to vote, and the hardships they suffered in nineteenth-century industrial society were still waiting for redress. In the early 1840's severe economic depression and widespread unemployment led to working-class protest and rioting. The "Chartists" drew up a "People's Charter" demanding further extension of the right to vote, the use of the secret ballot, and additional democratic reforms. The lower classes also suffered from the potato blight in Ireland in 1845, and from the Corn Laws, which used import tariffs to protect the price of grain for English farmers and landowners while making the price of bread and other foods intolerably high. Only with the repeal of the Corn Laws in 1846 and the introduction of a policy of Free Trade did England begin to move toward the greater prosperity and improved living conditions that characterize the later phases of the Victorian Age.

The Middle Period (1848–1870). During these two decades England reached the height of its wealth and productivity as an industrial nation. Under the system of Free Trade, the world markets were dominated by Lancashire cotton goods, Yorkshire woolens, and metal products from the cities of Sheffield and Birmingham. The city of

The Crystal Palace at the Great Exhibition (colored lithograph, 1851).
The Mansell Collection

Interior of the Crystal Palace (colored lithograph, 1851).
The Mansell Collection

London, which had a population of two million when Victoria became queen and was growing more rapidly than ever, had become the world center for banking, insurance, and shipping. A new system of railways covered the country and played a vital role in England's prosperity. Technological and scientific inventions, such as Michael Faraday's development of electromagnetic machinery, amazed the world and promised even greater prosperity for the future. Presiding over the entire panorama of mid-Victorian achievement were Queen Victoria and her husband Albert, the Prince Consort, whom she had married in 1840. It was Prince Albert who officially opened the Great Exhibition of 1851, which was held in an enormous structure of glass and steel known as the Crystal Palace. This was the first World's Fair, and it was designed to show, through the wonders of modern science and industry, England's confidence in her present and future accomplishments.

The Albert Memorial designed by
Sir George Gilbert Scott (colored
engraving, 1872).
The Mansell Collection

The most eloquent spokesman for Victorian progress and optimism
was Thomas Babington Macaulay (1800–1859). Replying to an attack on the forces of industry and mechanization by Robert
Southey (1774–1843), a supporter of the older Romantic ideal of a
feudal and agrarian culture, Macaulay based his optimism on the
conviction that history, technology, free enterprise, and God were
all working in harmony toward the betterment of human beings:

> [Southey] thinks, that to all outward appearance, the country is
> hastening to destruction; but . . . we rely on the natural tend-
> ency of the human intellect to truth, and on the natural tend-
> ency of society to improvement. . . . History is full of the signs
> of this natural progress of society. . . . If any person had told the

Parliament which met in perplexity and terror after the crash in 1720 that in 1830 the wealth of England would surpass all their wildest dreams, that the annual revenue would equal the principal of that debt which they considered as an intolerable burden, that for one man of ten thousand pounds then living there would be five men of fifty thousand pounds, that London would be twice as large and twice as populous . . . , that men would be in the habit of sailing without wind, and would be beginning to ride without horses, our ancestors would have given as much credit to the prediction as they gave to *Gulliver's Travels*. Yet the prediction would have been true . . . .

For Macaulay, the very nature of human society would lead it toward improvement and progress as long as the "general laws" established by God in the "moral and physical world" were left free to operate. Evil and poverty were the result not of neglecting social control, but of imposing such control in the form of governmental "prohibitions" or "protections." According to Macaulay, democratic reform was desirable, as long as it did not limit economic freedom and progress. Macaulay was the voice of what in political terms was known as liberal Whiggism, and it was a voice that became increasingly prominent during the mid-Victorian period.

English political life during this middle period was dominated by complicated infighting between the Whigs and the Tories, or the Liberals and the Conservatives as they were coming to be called. The Whigs, once the party of the landed aristocracy, had come increasingly to represent the interests of the newly wealthy middle class, and were in favor of gradual democratic reform as long as it did not conflict with economic growth and expansion. The Tories, originally the party of traditional English values and institutions as represented in the monarchy, the Church of England, and the ideal of a strict but benevolent class system, had moved past the reactionary phase of the early decades of the century into a more modern and enlightened position. Both major parties sought the support of the enlarged voting public. They feared the demands of the radical representatives of the working class and realized that despite widespread prosperity, further social reforms were necessary.

During the 1840's and early 1850's leaders from both parties had joined in persuading Parliament to pass a series of Factory Acts, which restricted child labor and limited hours of employment. As early as 1845, Benjamin Disraeli, later to become a brilliant Conservative leader and Prime Minister, had seen that England was being divided into "two nations," the rich and the poor. In 1867 Disraeli and the Conservatives daringly seized the initiative for reform from William Gladstone and the progressive element in the Liberal party and passed the Second Reform Bill, which extended the vote to all members of the working class except agricultural laborers. Although passed largely for reasons of political expediency, the Second Reform Bill had a profound effect on the subsequent development of English political life.

Omnibus Life in London (1859) by
William Maw Egely.
The Tate Gallery, London

The Late Period (1870–1901). The last thirty years of Victoria's reign appear on the surface to be a continuation of mid-Victorian prosperity, gradual reform, and expansion. During these years the British Empire reached the height of its power and influence. Disraeli himself became the great spokesman for English imperialism—not as a system of economic expansion and exploitation but as the realization of an ideal of the Anglo-Saxon race spreading its supposedly superior civilization throughout the world. The English boast that the sun "never sets on the British Empire" was literally true: English rule extended to Canada, Australia, New Zealand, India, South Africa, and many other parts of the world. Queen Victoria was made Empress of India in 1876 as part of Disraeli's romantic imperialism. Rudyard Kipling (1865–1936), who was already famous when he was in his twenties, introduced readers to this larger world through his tales and ballads of British India. He was essentially the poet and storyteller of the spirit of the new imperialism, the pride in controlling and managing a vast empire, which flourished between 1880 and 1914.

Mr. Rudyard Kipling Takes a Bloomin' Day aht on the Blasted 'eath, along with Britannia, 'is Gurl (caricature) by Max Beerbohm. Kipling, here satirized as an arch-imperialist, frequently wrote in the local dialects of various parts of England.
New York Public Library, Print Room

At home, more Victorians than ever were enjoying the comfort and serenity of middle-class prosperity. London was a gay and fashionable city; new rows of fanciful late-Victorian houses were built in the suburbs to suit the taste of those whose prosperity allowed them to "move up in the world." The two great Jubilee celebrations of 1887 and 1897 (marking the fiftieth and sixtieth years of the Queen's reign) displayed the nation's confidence with triumphant pomp and ceremony.

Beneath this surface of progress, comfort, and satisfaction, however, there were signs of new tensions in Victorian life. In foreign affairs, the rapid emergence of Chancellor Otto von Bismarck's Germany as a great military and industrial power began to pose a threat to England's preeminence. At home, the extension of the vote to the working class and the development of labor unions meant that the Liberals and the Conservatives found it increasingly difficult to stave off the demands of workers with gradual reforms that posed no real threat to their own economic and political interests. During the 1880's and 1890's the Labor Party arose to argue for an entirely new

A Summer's Day in Hyde Park by John Ritchie (1858).
The Museum of London

conception of the relationship between the owners of industry and the workers. Socialism promised to become a major force in British politics because it responded to the needs of those whose lives had still not been improved significantly by the old Victorian politics of compromise and gradual, self-protective reform.

VICTORIAN ATTITUDES: EARNESTNESS, SELF–SATISFACTION, AND ANXIETY

The attitudes we regard as typically Victorian are primarily those of the middle class—the new industrialists, merchants, professional men, and property owners who benefited most directly from Victorian prosperity and progress. Middle-class Victorians believed in hard work, moral seriousness, and social respectability. They were progressive in that they favored the new discoveries of science and the gradual attempts to make England a more democratic society. They were conservative and often repressive in their attitudes toward worldly pleasures, private emotions, and personal relationships. The twentieth century has often found it easy to caricature the typical Victorian as prudish, hypocritical, and smugly complacent. But this caricature, more than most, is biased and oversimplified. Although proud of their country's wealth and power, and confident of England's ability to solve the problems of the modern world, the Victorians felt that happiness and success could be achieved only through strenuous effort and constant devotion to duty.

The basis for many Victorian attitudes lay in the religious movement known as *Evangelicalism*. This movement began in the late eighteenth century among members of the established Church of England who were inspired by the teachings of John Wesley (1703–1791), the founder of Methodism. Wesley emphasized individual religious experience and spiritual zeal, and the Evangelicals sought to bring his enthusiasm and sense of commitment into the established Church. The Evangelicals were vigorously dedicated to humane causes and social reform: their influence was instrumental in the passage of the First Reform Bill in 1832, and in 1833 they were responsible for the emancipation of all slaves in the British Empire. On the other hand, the Evangelicals believed in a strict, puritanical code of morality. They were behind a severe new Sunday Observance Bill introduced into Parliament in 1837, and in general they opposed many forms of popular public entertainment. Together with the various groups of Nonconformists whose views were virtually identical with their own—Baptists, Methodists, Congregationalists, and other Protestant sects outside the Church of England—the Evangelicals became a significant force in English life.

The Houses of Parliament (1836–1867).
Kurt Scholz, Shostal Associates

As the century wore on, the Evangelical spirit came to permeate Victorian life in ways no longer directly tied to religious doctrine. Many members of the rising or newly wealthy middle class came from Evangelical and Nonconformist backgrounds. The widespread interest in social reform, the habitual sober Sunday of churchgoing and Bible reading, the puritanical moral code—all these aspects of Victorian life were outgrowths of Evangelical influence. The Evangelical spirit could be made to support even the material and commercial aspirations of the Victorian middle class, since hard work, individualism, sobriety, and avoidance of worldly pleasures led not only to spiritual worthiness but to success in business as well. But as Dickens and other writers of the age indignantly pointed out, selfishly prosperous Victorians would sometimes twist Evangelical principles to justify their own success, a success that in fact depended upon their blindness to the real meaning of Evangelical morality.

542   *The Victorian Age*

Another movement exerting an important, if less pervasive, influence on Victorian attitudes was *Utilitarianism*. The philosophy of Utilitarianism was first developed by Jeremy Bentham (1748–1832), and it sought to subject all human practices and institutions to the scrutiny of scientific reasoning in order to determine their fundamental usefulness, or utility. The Utilitarians' basic standard for judging utility was whether a law, practice, or institution contributed to the greatest happiness of the greatest number of people. Utilitarianism appealed to and helped shape those aspects of Victorian thinking that were modern, progressive, and rooted in an enlightened self-interest. It contributed to the Victorian belief that through reason and the free interplay of individual points of view, no problem was too great to overcome. Politically the strict Utilitarians tended to be classed as radicals, but their influence on both major parties, particularly on the Whigs, or Liberals, was significant. Although basically antireligious in their emphasis on reason and science, the Utilitarians joined the Evangelicals in urging many of the most important democratic reforms in the early and middle phases of the Victorian Age.

From both the Evangelicals and the Utilitarians the Victorian middle class learned concern for conditions among the working-class poor. Much of this concern was genuine and led to sincere attempts at reform. But the Evangelical spirit sometimes encouraged a condescending and sentimental attitude toward the poor among prosperous Victorians proud of the material comforts and social status they

Backyards of a London slum near the railway aqueduct (engraving, 1871) from *London: A Pilgrimage* by Gustave Doré and B. Jerrold. New York Public Library, Print Room

had worked so hard to attain. And while the Utilitarians argued for improved conditions among the working class, their scientific and rather mechanical view of life could on occasion make them brutally indifferent to ordinary human needs. In 1834, for example, they supported a Poor Law which forced impoverished people to accept an employer's conditions of work or be sent to a workhouse, where the standard of life was usually abominable. Throughout the Victorian Age, then, there was much talk about conditions among the poor, and some concrete reform, but the deepest interests of the working class were still not fully represented. Even after the passage of the Second Reform Bill in 1867 and the development of labor unions and the Labor Party, middle-class interests came first.

During the latter decades of Victoria's reign, anxiety gradually began to make itself felt within the prevailing mood of confidence and security. The very forces that had led to Victorian progress and prosperity had also created a rapidly changing and unstable world. Society had become much more fluid, and many people lived in circumstances to which they were not entirely accustomed. Some of those recently arrived in the middle class began to feel defensive and wary of the increasing power of the workers; others settled into a complacent and often vulgar enjoyment of their new position. The workers themselves, though reform had given them greater political power, often felt frustrated and disoriented as they were cut off from their traditional sources of identity and purpose in life. And members of the aristocracy tended to retreat into their own world of heedless high living. Beneath the high public spirits of the Jubilee celebrations there was a vague feeling that the positive energies of Victorian progress were being exhausted, and that the future of the modern world might not be so predictably rosy after all.

NEW IDEAS AND INTELLECTUAL CONTROVERSY

Even during the middle phase of the Victorian Age, the confidence of those who read widely and kept in touch with the main intellectual trends of the century was disturbed by new sources of uncertainty. Among the great scientific advances of the age, those in geology and particularly biology carried far-reaching implications that seemed to contradict traditional assumptions about the origin and place of human beings in the world. In 1830 Sir Charles Lyell's *Principles of Geology* attempted to show that the earth in its present form had not been created by God virtually overnight, but had developed slowly over vast stretches of time. And in 1859 Charles Darwin, in his *Origin of Species*, theorized that the various forms of life on earth, including human beings, had evolved over millions of years through the process of natural selection, which in turn

Darwin testing the speed
of an elephant tortoise
in the Galapagos Islands
(engraving).
The Bettmann Archive

operated on the principle of the survival of the fittest in an endless
struggle for existence. These and numerous other scientific works
proposing similar views posed a great threat to the traditional concept of Biblical creation and of human beings' preeminent role in the
world. This threat to religious belief was most powerfully expressed
by the poet Alfred, Lord Tennyson, who wondered whether man
could retain his faith when "Nature, red in tooth and claw / With
ravine, shrieked against his creed." Although some Victorians
thought that these new theories could be reconciled with Christian
values and other accepted ideas (Darwin's theory of evolution, for
example, was interpreted by a few readers as the ultimate confirmation of the ideal of progress), many people were deeply disturbed.
Religion had been attacked by the Utilitarians with their belief in
scientific rationalism; now it was being more directly challenged by
science itself.

What was the Church to do in the face of such serious challenges?
One answer was to reinvigorate itself, not by emphasizing individual spiritual zeal, as the Evangelicals had done, nor by making its
beliefs more liberal and flexible, but by returning to the ancient doc-
trines, rituals, and sacraments of the Church when its authority was
strongest. This kind of reform was advocated at Oxford University,
where a group of intellectuals and clergymen, led by the brilliant
John Henry Newman (1801–1890), published a series of persuasively
written pamphlets, or tracts, thus beginning what was called the Oxford Movement or Tractarianism. The Oxford Movement lost its
impetus after 1845 when Newman, having tried to elevate the

John Henry, Cardinal Newman by W. W.
Oueless. An influential English ecclesiastic,
Newman and a group of Oxford clerics at-
tempted a renewal of the Church early in the
nineteenth century and established the Anglo-
Catholic movement.
Masters and Fellows of Oriel College, Oxford

Church of England and give it a new idealism and authority, joined
the Roman Catholic Church. But the Oxford Movement raised the
intellectual level of religious controversy in England and had a lasting influence on many Victorian writers.

The Victorian Age saw the development of radical new ideas in economic and political theory as well as in the physical sciences. Although the writings of Karl Marx had little immediate influence on
the minds of English workers, it is significant that his theories were
based upon research done in England, the most advanced European
industrial nation. Marx lived in England for many years and worked
out his ideas in the Reading Room of the British Museum. In 1867
he published the first volume of his immensely important treatise,
Capital (Das Kapital). Of the English writers and political leaders
who read Marx and responded positively to some of his ideas, the
most important was the poet and artist William Morris (1834–1896).
Although he rejected some of the more extreme assertions of Marx-
ist theory and advocated instead a social ideal based upon the simplicity and beauty of the Middle Ages, Morris shared Marx's conviction that the deep-rooted problems of industrial society could be
solved only by a massive movement among the workers themselves.
As we have already noted, the time for British socialism had not yet
arrived. But the development of radical socialist ideas is a crucial
part of the intellectual ferment of the Victorian Age.

VICTORIAN LITERATURE: NONFICTION PROSE AND DRAMA

Perhaps the most important idea to grasp in approaching literature of the Victorian Age is that the major writers of this period simultaneously embodied and rebelled against the attitudes we have been surveying. This is especially true of the writers of nonfiction prose. If the Romantic Age distinguishes itself as a great period of English poetry, the Victorian Age is an equally great age of English prose. Seldom before had the problems of English society been addressed so directly and with so much creative energy by writers of essays, pamphlets, and longer works of historical, philosophical, and artistic analysis. Victorian prose writers reflected critically and prophetically on the main issues of the day in ways that both embraced and transcended the dominant characteristics of Victorian culture as a whole. These writers often seem to be anti-Victorian in their opposition to the superficial conception of Victorian progress celebrated by journalists, self-congratulatory businessmen, and speechmaking politicians. But in the fundamental sources of their beliefs and in their tireless commitment to transforming English society according to those beliefs, they are very much of their age.

The dominant figure in early Victorian literature was Thomas Carlyle (1795–1881). In speaking out against the materialism and the lack of spiritual courage and direction of his era, Carlyle combined the fervor and belief in hard work of the Evangelical tradition with the Romantic ideal of the preeminence of the imagination. Carlyle opposed the Utilitarians' rational and often mechanical conception of human nature. In his partly fictionalized autobiography, *Sartor Resartus* (1833), he recounts a quest to replace belief in traditional religion with a new "natural supernaturalism," a commitment to all that is vital in oneself and in the world.

Through his own fiercely energetic and eccentric prose, Carlyle exerted a strong influence on all the major Victorian writers. His influence was particularly important for John Ruskin (1819–1900), the most wide-ranging and eloquent genius of the entire Victorian era. Ruskin began his career as the greatest art critic of his age. But during the 1860's, inspired by Carlyle's attack on Victorian materialism and by his own outrage at the injustice and spiritual emptiness of industrial society, Ruskin turned his attention to economics and social reform. Having taught his contemporaries to appreciate the human and spiritual value of art, Ruskin now sought to persuade them to make their society more humane, less ugly and alienating. "Life without industry is guilt," he agreed with those who extolled hard work, but "industry without art is brutality." Although sometimes dismissed as farfetched and unrealistic, Ruskin's later writings were a major inspiration for British socialism and the labor movement, as well as for such important and diverse modern figures as Frank Lloyd Wright and Mahatma Gandhi.

Among the prose writers of the mid-Victorian period, one of the most influential and forward-looking was John Stuart Mill (1806–1873). Mill's father, James, had been an important follower of the Utilitarianism of Jeremy Bentham, and in his *Principles of Political Economy* (1848), John Stuart Mill extended and refined the Utilitarian emphasis on rational analysis. But Mill's views are much less narrow and mechanical than those of his Utilitarian predecessors. He admired Wordsworth and Coleridge as much as Carlyle did, and he recognized that human intelligence expresses itself through imagination as well as through reason. Most important, Mill was a great Victorian spokesman for individual liberty, and it is in this capacity that Americans have tended to find him the most sympathetic of the major prose writers of the era. In his essay *On Liberty* (1859), he argued that in society's pursuit of "the greatest good for the greatest number," the individual must be free not only from political and religious tyranny, but from the tyranny of the opinion of others. In a later work, *On The Subjection of Women* (1869), Mill specifically extended his ideal of individual freedom and self-reliance to include women, who were both oppressed and falsely idealized under the middle-class Victorian code of moral respectability.

One of the most representative writers of the Victorian Age, and also one of its most intelligent critics, was Matthew Arnold (1822–1888). Arnold began his career as a poet, but in the 1860's he began to devote himself to literary and social criticism. He exposed the ignorance, narrow-mindedness, and intellectual dullness of the Victorian middle class—the "Philistines," as he called them—and argued for the civilizing power of liberal education and of literature. For Arnold, great literature was itself a "criticism of life," which could provide individuals with the standards of excellence, truth, and self-improvement that they had traditionally sought in philosophy and religion.

In their different ways both Arnold and Ruskin elevated literature and art to positions of supreme significance in human culture by insisting on their moral and spiritual value. This elevation of the status of art came to have a new and in some respects quite different significance for certain late Victorian writers. In the essays of Walter Pater (1839–1894), the intense experience of beauty becomes the only source of certain value in a modern world in which rapid and

The Day Dream by Dante Gabriel Rossetti. Rossetti was a poet and a painter, and with some fellow painters and designers founded the Pre-Raphaelite Brotherhood, one of the most important artistic movements of the Victorian period.
Victoria and Albert Museum, Crown Copyright

unexpected change makes all other standards of truth seem relative. In a series of essays entitled *Studies in the History of the Renaissance* (1873), Pater interpreted Arnold's claim that the basis for a true understanding of art is "to see the object as in itself it really is" in an extremely subjective and impressionistic way. For Pater the key question was, What is this song or picture, this engaging personality presented in life or in a book, to *me*? Pater shares with Carlyle an insistence on the importance of personal vitality and energy, but otherwise his creed of artistic supremacy could hardly differ more from Carlyle's call to hard work, duty, and social responsibility.

Toward the end of the century, Pater's ideas were extended with dazzling wit and paradoxical irony by Oscar Wilde (1854–1900), who laughed at the old forms of Victorian moral seriousness. Wilde even made a joke about that most characteristic of all Victorian virtues, earnestness, the basis of a brilliant comedy, *The Importance of Being Earnest* (1894). But it is important to see that while he represents a reaction against Victorian attitudes, Wilde's views are an extreme extension, as well as a satirical criticism, of the attempts of Ruskin and Arnold to discover in art those human values missing from a society obsessed with material progress and financial profit. Moreover, the movement involving Pater, Wilde, and many other European writers, which came to be identified by the slogan "Art for Art's sake," was in part a response to the chaotic uncertainty of modern life which we, in the latter part of the twentieth century, have not yet fully learned to cope with.

VICTORIAN LITERATURE: POETRY

Following the magnificent achievements of Romantic poetry, it is not surprising that the poetry of the Victorian Age should in many respects represent a further development of themes and attitudes first explored by the Romantics. The two greatest Victorian poets, Alfred, Lord Tennyson (1809–1892), and Robert Browning (1812–1889), both began writing poetry in emulation of the major Romantic poets. Tennyson's early poetry was strongly influenced by Byron, Scott, and Keats, while Browning's chief model was Shelley. But the Victorian poet was confronted with new problems of meaning and expression. The rapid changes in England's industrial society and the new theories of science and philosophy made it even more difficult than it had been in the early years of the century for human beings to feel at home in the world. There is a deep impulse in Victorian poetry to express doubt and a sense of alienation at finding oneself, in the words of Matthew Arnold, "wandering between two worlds, one dead, / The other powerless to be born." But as Arnold himself saw, it was not enough for the poet simply to express the pain of being born after the age of secure religious belief, and before an age that would find another form of conviction. Nor was it enough, as the Romantics had done, to retreat into the poet's private imagination. Victorian poets saw the need for a more objective and socially engaged poetic vision. This sense of public obligation was heightened by the demands of Victorian readers for poetry that would celebrate the progress of the age and provide them with the reassurance they needed to confront the problems accompanying that progress.

Much Victorian poetry does give expression to the optimism and progressive vitality of the age. As poet laureate, for instance, Tennyson often celebrated the great occasions and achievements of his era; Browning, less frequently and more indirectly, did the same. But

Victorian poetry is best when it does not turn aside from doubt, uncertainty, and loss, or from the poet's personal response to the difficulty of life. Tennyson is at his finest when he uses his amazing technical resources to evoke a sense of wistful, melancholy longing for an experience in the remote past or remote distance, or to record his own struggle for faith and understanding in a world full of hostility and contradiction. Arnold's most famous poem, "Dover Beach," concludes with the speaker's finding himself "on a darkling plain/ Swept with confused alarms of struggle and flight,/Where ignorant armies clash by night." And Browning, in spite of the optimism and vitality often attributed to his poetry, uses the indirection of the dramatic monologue to explore the motives and attitudes of fictional speakers who are often obsessed with the darker aspects of life— failure, self-doubt, greed, evil, and ugliness. The best Victorian poetry builds upon the Romantic concern with the complexities of human consciousness, and it adapts that concern to the problems of a new era.

Taken as a whole, Victorian poetry is remarkably varied and diverse. There was no clearly defined "school" or "movement" to which a Victorian poet could become attached. Even the Pre-Raphaelite Brotherhood, formed in 1848 by Dante Gabriel Rossetti along with other young artists and writers, was of greater significance for painting than for poetry, and lasted for only a few years. This lack of cohesion in Victorian poetry might be taken as a sign of confusion and uncertainty, but in fact it left individual poets free to develop their own voice and style. There is a strain of vigorous experimentalism in Victorian poetry that has proved extremely important

The Browning Society (caricature) by Max Beerbohm. Browning's great popularity as a poet and as a public figure attracted admirers of every sort.
The Mansell Collection

for poets in the twentieth century. The sometimes radical and unsettling stylistic exploration of Browning and of Gerard Manley Hopkins (1844–1889) pointed the way to the verbal dislocations and dissonances characteristic of modern poetry. Even the rugged, eccentric plainness of the poetry of Thomas Hardy (1840–1928) has been freshly appreciated by readers in our own era.

VICTORIAN LITERATURE: THE NOVEL

For many readers the novel is the literary form best adapted to the expression of the Victorian sensibility. Like the nonfiction prose of this era, most Victorian novels are directly concerned with the

A wallpaper design by William Morris. Morris, prolific as a writer of both prose and verse, was also a designer and a member of the influential English arts and crafts movement.
Kenneth Karp,
courtesy of Sylvia Sleigh

issues and problems of contemporary society. Unlike the novels of the Romantic era, which were often set in remote historical periods and encouraged a taste for the exotic and the fantastic, Victorian novels usually create a richly detailed and "realistic" sense of nineteenth-century life. And most of them are, of course, very long. This length is owing partly to the fact that Victorian novels were often published in serial form: single chapters or installments appeared monthly or at even longer intervals. Such serial publication is also partly responsible for the dramatically episodic plots of Victorian novels. The novelist needed to gratify readers' interest with each individual installment while at the same time stimulating and sustaining interest in the novel as a whole. Novelists inevitably found themselves responding to the public's response to earlier portions of a book while working on later installments. This is another sense in which the Victorian novel is generally more closely in touch with the actual life it describes than are the novels of any earlier period.

Charles Dickens (1812–1870) was the master of serial publication and the leading Victorian novelist from 1837 until his death. Dickens was loved by contemporary readers because he gave them what they thought of as a completely realistic, and often hilariously funny, portrayal of London life in home, tavern, office, and factory. Dickens was in fact an immensely inventive writer with a special fondness for the theater. The appeal of his novels is due largely to his brilliant dramatic heightening of ordinary Victorian life. Dickens was also deeply concerned with the political problems and the social injustice of his age, and his novels were increasingly filled with bitter satirical attacks on the ugliness, greed, hypocrisy, and social pretension that went along with Victorian prosperity. More successfully than any other contemporary novelist, Dickens demonstrates the paradox that just those writers who seem most typically Victorian are often the most anti-Victorian in their criticisms.

Some contemporary Victorian novelists admired Dickens' comic and dramatic inventiveness, but felt that his novels were too theatrical and even melodramatic to represent reality accurately, or to concentrate sufficiently on characters' inner lives. William Makepeace Thackeray (1811–1863) and Anthony Trollope (1815–1882) were more restrained and traditional than Dickens, more concerned with precise shades of Victorian manners and behavior. And the great Victorian novelist of the inner moral life is George Eliot (1819–1880), whose real name was Mary Ann Evans. The political and social worlds of her novels are as vast and detailed as anything in Dickens or Thackeray, yet their primary concern is always with the free will and moral intelligence of her characters as they try to establish their true identity and role in life. With their astonishing depth of perception and compassion, George Eliot's novels are not

George Eliot (drawing) by
F. W. Burton. The novelist Mary
Ann Evans wrote under the pen name
George Eliot.
Radio Times Hulton

only among the greatest of the age; they are among the greatest novels ever written in English. Thomas Hardy was another, slightly later Victorian novelist who focused on the inner lives of his characters and on the question of free will and self-determination, although his emphasis was very different from George Eliot's. For Hardy, the fate of human beings is shaped by forces outside their control—by passions, coincidences, and historical forces beyond their moral will and understanding. Like his poems, Hardy's novels are set in Wessex, a predominantly rural area in southwest England, far removed from Dickens' London.

Considered in all their variety, Victorian novels represent almost every aspect of nineteenth-century life. Like so much of Victorian literature, they simultaneously describe and reflect upon, include and criticize, the values and attitudes of this energetic, rapidly changing, contradictory period in English history.

Alfred, Lord Tennyson
1809–1892

For more than fifty years, Tennyson was recognized among his contemporaries as the greatest poet of Victorian England. He was made poet laureate in 1850 when Wordsworth died, and as decade followed decade, Victorian readers looked to him for poetic pronouncements on the major issues affecting their lives. Yet Tennyson's status as a public poet is only part of his identity. As a man he was intensely private and introspective, and some of his greatest work as an artist depends upon the creation of very personal and subjective moods or states of mind. In the largest sense it is this division in Tennyson between his public and private selves, between social and purely artistic commitments, that makes him such a central figure for the Victorian Age.

Tennyson was born in the village of Somersby, in Lincolnshire, and was the fourth of twelve children. His father, the Reverend George Tennyson, was an intelligent and cultivated but very unhappy man given to periods of severe depression. He educated his children himself in classical and modern languages, but he also disturbed and terrified them with his emotional instability. Thus Tennyson grew up as a sensitive and well-read but often melancholy boy. He enjoyed the companionship of his brothers and sisters, but he also spent long periods of time by himself, roaming the Lincolnshire countryside both day and night. He began writing poetry before he was ten, and in 1827, when he was eighteen, he and his brother Charles published anonymously *Poems by Two Brothers*. More than half of the poems in this volume are by Tennyson himself, and they are strongly influenced by Byron and by Scott.

Also in 1827 Tennyson went to study at Cambridge University, and the poems he had published drew him to the attention of a small group of brilliant undergraduates who called themselves the "Apostles." These friends encouraged Tennyson to devote his life to poetry, and their intellectual and artistic interests played a significant role in shaping his early career. Tennyson found his closest friend among this group — Arthur Henry Hallam, a highly gifted and charismatic young writer who Tennyson later said was "as near perfection as a mortal man could be." Hallam's urbanity and charm offset Tennyson's own shyness

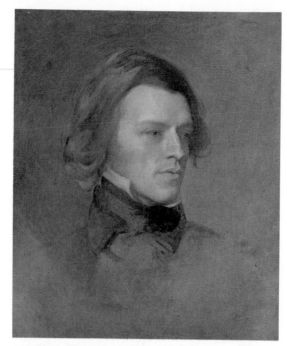

Alfred, Lord Tennyson by Samuel Lawrence. National Portrait Gallery, London

and awkwardness. In 1830 the two friends traveled together in Europe, and Hallam became engaged to Tennyson's sister Emily. In the same year Tennyson published *Poems, Chiefly Lyrical*, the first volume of verse to appear under his own name. Though not a critical success, it was a clear reflection of his development as a poet during the years at Cambridge.

In 1831 Tennyson had to leave Cambridge without a degree because of financial difficulties and family dissension. He published another volume of poems in 1832, but this collection, like that of 1830, was not well received by the reviewers. Already discouraged and uncertain of his future, Tennyson was absolutely shattered in 1833 by the news that his friend Hallam had died suddenly in Vienna. The immediate effect of his grief and of the other setbacks he had suffered was a period in Tennyson's life sometimes referred to as the "ten years' silence." Tennyson published nothing during this time, and most of his friends thought he would never write again. But Tennyson spent these years privately revising his published poems and working on new and more ambitious projects. It was during these years, as he later told his son, that "in silence, obscurity, and solitude he perfected his art."

Tennyson returned to public notice in 1842 with the publication of *Poems,* in two volumes. This collection firmly established his reputation and initiated the fifty-year period in which he was the major figure in Victorian poetry. In 1850 he published *In Memoriam,* a sequence of elegiac and meditative poems recalling the experience of Hallam's death. In that same year he was made poet laureate, and he married Emily Sellwood, with whom he had first fallen in love in 1836. In 1883 he was made a peer of the realm and was thus accorded the title of Lord. He died in 1892, with a reputation among all classes of readers that grew until it eventually exceeded Byron's in the early years of the twentieth century.

In his appearance and behavior as well as in his writing, Tennyson fulfilled the Victorian idea of what a poet should be. He was a huge man with a great mane and shaggy beard, he often dressed in a picturesque fashion, and he read his poems in public with a resounding voice and with the rough manners of a man from the country. He earned considerable money from his poetry—as much as £10,000 a year—and was able to buy a house on the Isle of Wight, where he lived quietly, as he preferred. He also became the personal friend of Queen Victoria and often read to her privately at Buckingham Palace. His most ambitious project, *Idylls of the King,* is a series of poetic narratives based on the legend of King Arthur and the Round Table (an "idyll" is a poetic picture or description). Addressed to Prince Albert, *Idylls of the King* uses a medieval context to assess the values and achievements of Victorian England.

Tennyson's poetic output was vast and extremely varied: he wrote lyrics, dramatic monologues, plays, long poetic narratives, elegies, and poems commemorating specific occasions. But three characteristics distinguish all his best verse, from the beginning to the end of his long career. First, there is Tennyson's total mastery of the sounds and rhythms of the English language. The twentieth-century poet W. H. Auden said that Tennyson had "the finest ear, perhaps, of any English poet." Tennyson was so skillful at controlling the imitative and musical sounds of language that individual lines from his poems have become famous as isolated examples of this dimension of poetry:

The shallop flitteth silken-sailed.
("The Lady of Shalott")

The mild-eyed melancholy Lotos-eaters came.
("The Lotos-Eaters")

The moan of doves in immemorial elms
And murmuring of innumerable bees.
(*The Princess*)

Second, Tennyson has a genius for evoking moods and states of mind in his poems. Particularly characteristic is his ability to create a sense of nostalgia, a wistful longing for the past or for remote experiences. And no English poet surpasses Tennyson at linking descriptions of nature or setting to a state of mind. The opening of "Mariana," for example, takes us inside the mental world of the title figure without saying a word directly about what she thinks or feels:

With blackest moss the flower-plots
  Were thickly crusted, one and all;
The rusted nails fell from the knots
  That held the pear to the gable wall.
The broken sheds looked sad and strange:
  Unlifted was the clinking latch;
  Weeded and worn the ancient thatch
Upon the lonely moated grange.

Third, and in partial contrast to the mainly artistic skills we have just been considering, there is Tennyson's engagement with the main political, religious, and scientific issues of his day. Tennyson is not a philosophical or intellectual poet, but his mind brooded honestly and responsively on the problems of Victorian industrialism and material progress, on war and colonial expansion, and on the threats to Christian belief posed by Darwinian theory and other biological and geological discoveries:

Are God and Nature then at strife,
  That Nature lends such evil dreams?
So careful of the type she seems
So careless of the single life . . .
(*In Memoriam* 55, lines 5–8)

Tennyson's willingness to extend his attention to such large public questions in a poem based initially on his own grief shows the importance of his work for Victorian readers and for us today.

The Lady of Shalott

In his boyhood Tennyson was fascinated by the stories of King Arthur's knights, and it was natural for him to turn to them later as subjects for poetry. The twelve metrical tales included in *Idylls of the King* were composed over a period of twenty-six years (1859–1885). But long before that time, in 1832, the poet had written this legend of the Lady of Shalott.

Part I

On either side the river lie
Long fields of barley and of rye,
That clothe the wold° and meet the
    sky;
And through the field the road runs by
       To many-towered Camelot;°   5
And up and down the people go,
Gazing where the lilies blow
Round an island there below,
       The island of Shalott.

Willows whiten,° aspens quiver,   10
Little breezes dusk and shiver
Through the wave that runs forever
By the island in the river
       Flowing down to Camelot.
Four gray walls, and four gray towers,   15
Overlook a space of flowers,
And the silent isle embowers
       The Lady of Shalott.

By the margin, willow-veiled,
Slide the heavy barges° trailed   20
By slow horses; and unhailed
The shallop° flitteth silken-sailed
       Skimming down to Camelot:
But who hath seen her wave her hand?
Or at the casement seen her stand?   25
Or is she known in all the land,
       The Lady of Shalott?

Only reapers, reaping early
In among the bearded barley,
Hear a song that echoes cheerly   30
From the river winding clearly
       Down to towered Camelot;
And by the moon the reaper weary,
Piling sheaves in uplands airy,
Listening, whispers, " 'Tis the fairy   35
       Lady of Shalott."

Part II

There she weaves by night and day
A magic web with colors gay.
She has heard a whisper say,
A curse is on her if she stay   40
       To look down to Camelot.
She knows not what the curse may be,
And so she weaveth steadily,
And little other care hath she,
       The Lady of Shalott.   45

And moving through a mirror clear
That hangs before her all the year,
Shadows of the world appear.
There she sees the highway near
       Winding down to Camelot;   50
There the river eddy whirls,
And there the surly village churls,°
And the red cloaks of market girls,
       Pass onward from Shalott.

---

3. **wold:** an open stretch of rising ground. 5. **Camelot:** a mysterious city where King Arthur and his knights held court in medieval romances. 10. **whiten:** Leaves turned by the breeze show their white undersides. 20. **barges:** roomy, flat-bottomed freight boats; here drawn by horses along the river banks. 22. **shallop:** a light pleasure boat.

52. **churls:** country folk.

Sometimes a troop of damsels glad,   55
An abbot on an ambling pad,°
Sometimes a curly shepherd lad,
Or long-haired page in crimson clad,
        Goes by to towered Camelot;
And sometimes through the mirror
        blue   60
The knights come riding two and two:

---

56. **pad:** an easy-paced riding horse.

The Lady of Shalott by William Holman Hunt. A
Pre-Raphaelite, Hunt painted this illustration
of Tennyson's poem.
City Art Gallery, Manchester

She hath no loyal knight and true,
        The Lady of Shalott.

But in her web she still delights
To weave the mirror's magic sights,   65
For often through the silent nights
A funeral, with plumes and lights
        And music, went to Camelot;
Or when the moon was overhead,
Came two young lovers lately wed: 70
"I am half sick of shadows," said
        The Lady of Shalott.

Part III
A bowshot from her bower eaves,
He rode between the barley sheaves,
The sun came dazzling through the
        leaves,   75
And flamed upon the brazen greaves°
        Of bold Sir Lancelot.
A red-cross knight° forever kneeled
To a lady in his shield,
That sparkled on the yellow field,   80
        Beside remote Shalott.

The gemmy° bridle glittered free,
Like to some branch of stars we see
Hung in the golden Galaxy.°
The bridle bells rang merrily   85
        As he rode down to Camelot;
And from his blazoned baldric° slung,
A mighty silver bugle hung,
And as he rode his armor rung,
        Beside remote Shalott.   90

All in the blue unclouded weather
Thick-jeweled shone the saddle
        leather,
The helmet and the helmet feather

---

76. **greaves:** armor for the legs below the knees.
78. **red-cross knight:** a symbol of Saint George, patron
saint of England. He slew the dragon and thus saved a
maiden from sacrifice. 82. **gemmy:** studded with
jewels. 84. **Galaxy:** the Milky Way, a pathway of
myriad stars stretching across the middle heavens.
87. **blazoned baldric:** a decorated belt worn diagonally
across the chest.

Burned like one burning flame together
    As he rode down to Camelot;
As often through the purple night,   95
Below the starry clusters bright,
Some bearded meteor, trailing light,
    Moves over still Shalott.

His broad clear brow in sunlight
    glowed;   100
On burnished hoofs his war horse
    trode;
From underneath his helmet flowed
His coal-black curls as on he rode,
    As he rode down to Camelot.
From the bank and from the river   105
He flashed into the crystal mirror,
"Tirra lirra," by the river
    Sang Sir Lancelot.

She left the web, she left the loom,
She made three paces through the
    room,   110
She saw the water lily bloom,
She saw the helmet and the plume,
    She looked down to Camelot.
Out flew the web and floated wide;
The mirror cracked from side to side;   115
"The curse is come upon me," cried
    The Lady of Shalott.

Part IV
In the stormy east wind straining,
The pale yellow woods were waning,
The broad stream in his banks com-
    plaining,
Heavily the low sky raining   120
    Over towered Camelot;
Down she came and found a boat
Beneath a willow left afloat,
And round about the prow she wrote   125
    The Lady of Shalott.

And down the river's dim expanse—
Like some bold seër in a trance,
Seeing all his own mischance—
With a glassy countenance   130
    Did she look to Camelot.

And at the closing of the day
She loosed the chain, and down she lay,
The broad stream bore her far away,
    The Lady of Shalott.   135

Lying, robed in snowy white
That loosely flew to left and right—
The leaves upon her falling light—
Through the noises of the night
    She floated down to Camelot;   140
And as the boathead wound along
The willowy hills and fields among,
They heard her singing her last song,
    The Lady of Shalott.

Heard a carol, mournful, holy,   145
Chanted loudly, chanted lowly,
Till her blood was frozen slowly,
And her eyes were darkened wholly,
    Turned to towered Camelot.
For ere she reached upon the tide   150
The first house by the waterside,
Singing in her song she died,
    The Lady of Shalott.

Under tower and balcony,
By garden wall and gallery,   155
A gleaming shape she floated by,
Dead-pale between the houses high,
    Silent into Camelot.
Out upon the wharves they came
Knight and burgher,° lord and dame,   160
And round the prow they read her
    name,
    The Lady of Shalott.

Who is this? and what is here?
And in the lighted palace near
Died the sound of royal cheer;   165
And they crossed themselves for fear,
    All the knights at Camelot:
But Lancelot mused a little space;
He said, "She has a lovely face;
God in his mercy lend her grace,   170
    The Lady of Shalott."

---

160. **burgher:** citizen.

COMMENTARY

Although "The Lady of Shalott" is a narrative poem of some length, it has qualities suggesting a lyric that could be set to music. The fifth and ninth lines of every stanza serve as refrains, with some variations in wording. The rhythm is heavy and regular. The rhymes are very audible, even insistent, partly because the first four lines of each stanza all rhyme on the same sound (e.g., *lie, rye, sky, by* in the first stanza). The sixth, seventh, and eighth lines also rhyme on a single sound (in the first stanza, *go, blow,* and *below*), while the short refrain lines use "Camelot" and "Shalott" as rhyme words in all the stanzas except two.

The musical quality of this poem has sometimes been criticized for being intrusive and calling too much attention to itself, but it is surely appropriate to the romantic legend that the poem recounts. In "The Lady of Shalott" Tennyson's lifelong interest in "the haunted region of Celtic romance" combines with his interest in what a modern critic calls "the predicament of a mind trying to free itself from a web of fantasy." The medieval tale is used to present a distinctively modern problem: the plight of the dedicated artist who must, because of temperament and the nature of artistic work, experience life and emotion secondhand. Thus the Lady sits endlessly weaving her magic web and sees the world only in the reflections cast in the mirror before her.

Tennyson himself said that the key to the poem's meaning lay in the closing lines of Part II: " 'I am half sick of shadows,' said/The Lady of Shalott." And he said of the poem as a whole: "The newborn love for something, for someone in the wide world from which she has been so long excluded, takes her out of the region of shadows into that of realities." When the Lady sees the image of two young lovers in her mirror, she becomes "half sick of shadows." After seeing the dazzling vision of Sir Lancelot, she turns from the web and the mirror, and for the first time looks down to Camelot. As Tennyson says, she turns from shadows to realities. But the awakening is a fatal one. The curse of the web and the mirror may have imprisoned the Lady in isolation, but when she leaves them she goes to her death.

FOR STUDY AND DISCUSSION

1. What is the main subject of each part of "The Lady of Shalott"? Why do you think Tennyson constructed this poem in four parts?

2. How is the entrance of Lancelot in Part III prepared for in Part II? Explain the pathos of Lancelot's words in the last stanza of the poem.

3. Sir Lancelot appears in bright sunlight, and everything about him is dazzling, glittering, burnished, flamelike—from his "gemmy bridle" to his "blazoned baldric." Cite examples to show how the imagery of flaming and shining things that dominates Part III contrasts with the imagery of the other three parts of the poem.

Ulysses

Ulysses (yōō-lǐs′ēz) is the hero of Homer's ancient Greek epic poem, the *Odyssey*. Homer tells of Ulysses' adventures on his way home to Ithaca from the Trojan Wars. Tennyson's poem picks up the story long after Ulysses has returned. The aging hero has grown restless and is preparing to set out with a band of his followers on his legendary last voyage.

It little profits that an idle king,
By this still hearth, among these barren crags,
Matched with an aged wife, I mete and dole°
Unequal laws° unto a savage race,
That hoard, and sleep, and feed, and know not me.   5
I cannot rest from travel; I will drink
Life to the lees. All times I have enjoyed
Greatly, have suffered greatly, both with those
That loved me, and alone; on shore, and when
Through scudding drifts the rainy Hyades°   10
Vexed the dim sea. I am become a name;
For always roaming with a hungry heart
Much have I seen and known—cities of men
And manners, climates, councils, governments,
Myself not least, but honored of them all—   15
And drunk delight of battle with my peers,
Far on the ringing plains of windy Troy.
I am a part of all that I have met;
Yet all experience is an arch wherethrough
Gleams that untraveled world whose margin fades   20
Forever and forever when I move.
How dull it is to pause, to make an end,
To rust unburnished, not to shine in use!
As though to breathe were life! Life piled on life
Were all too little, and of one to me   25
Little remains; but every hour is saved
From that eternal silence, something more,
A bringer of new things; and vile it were
For some three suns to store and hoard myself,
And this gray spirit yearning in desire   30
To follow knowledge like a sinking star,
Beyond the utmost bound of human thought.

Head of a Greek
(marble, 5th century B.C.).
The Metropolitan Museum of Art, New York

---

3. **mete and dole:** measure and give out.   4. **Unequal laws:** unfair laws. The people were not civilized enough to be governed by the kinds of laws Ulysses approved.   10. **Hyades** (hī′ə-dēz): stars in the constellation Taurus, supposed to bring rain.

This is my son, mine own Telemachus,
To whom I leave the scepter and the isle°—
Well-loved of me, discerning to fulfill   35
This labor, by slow prudence to make mild
A rugged people, and through soft degrees
Subdue them to the useful and the good.
Most blameless is he, centered in the sphere
Of common duties, decent not to fail   40
In offices of tenderness, and pay
Meet adoration to my household gods,
When I am gone. He works his work, I mine.
    There lies the port; the vessel puffs her sail;
There gloom the dark, broad seas. My mariners,   45
Souls that have toiled, and wrought, and thought with me—
That ever with a frolic welcome took
The thunder and the sunshine, and opposed
Free hearts, free foreheads—you and I are old;
Old age hath yet his honor and his toil.   50
Death closes all; but something ere the end,
Some work of noble note, may yet be done,
Not unbecoming men that strove with Gods.
The lights begin to twinkle from the rocks;
The long day wanes; the slow moon climbs; the deep   55
Moans round with many voices. Come, my friends,
'Tis not too late to seek a newer world.
Push off, and sitting well in order smite
The sounding furrows; for my purpose holds
To sail beyond the sunset, and the baths   60
Of all the western stars, until I die.
It may be that the gulfs will wash us down;
It may be we shall touch the Happy Isles,°
And see the great Achilles,° whom we knew.
Though much is taken, much abides; and though   65
We are not now that strength which in old days
Moved earth and heaven, that which we are, we are—
One equal temper of heroic hearts,
Made weak by time and fate, but strong in will
To strive, to seek, to find, and not to yield.   70

34. **isle:** Ithaca, an island off the west coast of Greece. Telemachus (tə-lĕm′ə-kəs),
a youth in the *Odyssey,* is now a mature man, well suited to rule the kingdom.
63. **Happy Isles:** Elysium, the place where heroes went after death.   64. **Achilles**
(ə-kĭl′ēz): the Greek hero of the Trojan War, in which Ulysses had taken part
before his long series of adventures on the return journey.

COMMENTARY

The dramatic monologue is related to the soliloquy used in Shakespeare's plays. In each of Macbeth's soliloquies, for example, the character addresses himself and the audience, usually in a moment of self-exploration. In the dramatic monologue, the speaker addresses one or more characters who are present but who remain silent.

Although the most famous Victorian author of dramatic monologues was Robert Browning, Tennyson also excelled in this poetic form. "Ulysses" is Tennyson's best-known dramatic monologue.

The speaker of the monologue is Ulysses himself, the hero of Homer's *Odyssey*. According to a later extension of the story recounted in Dante's *Divine Comedy*, Ulysses grew restless after returning to his island kingdom of Ithaca and desired to set out on a new voyage of exploration. As an old man, he persuaded some of his followers to accompany him on the voyage.

Like *In Memoriam*, "Ulysses" reflects Tennyson's response to the death of his closest friend, Arthur Hallam. According to Tennyson himself, the poem expresses "the need of going forward and braving the struggle of life perhaps more simply than anything in *In Memoriam*." Ulysses' vigorous speech conveys this grave, forward-looking energy. But many readers have noticed that the movement of the blank verse in the poem is often slow and retarded, as if to present a countermovement of melancholy yearning for the peacefulness of death, or of a sad recognition of diminished power, which Tennyson wishes to set against the more obvious impulse toward adventure. We must remember that Ulysses is an old man, and that what he proposes is a voyage into the unknown. Yet his age and the impracticality of his motives make his energetic questing all the more extraordinary, particularly when set against the "slow prudence" (line 36) of his son Telemachus, who is to become the young king of Ithaca after Ulysses departs.

FOR STUDY AND DISCUSSION

1. How does Ulysses describe his present life on the island of Ithaca? What was his life like in the past, before he returned home from the Trojan War? What phrases or lines show Ulysses' spirit and attitude toward life?

2. In lines 33–43 Ulysses speaks of his son Telemachus. What attitude does he take toward him? What does Ulysses mean when he says, "He works his work, I mine"?

3. Much of the imagery of "Ulysses" is designed to recall the epic world of adventure in Homer's *Iliad* and *Odyssey*, a world Ulysses himself does not want to leave behind. One example of such imagery is the reference to "the ringing plains of windy Troy" (line 17). What other examples of such imagery can you find in the poem?

4. How would you state the theme of this poem?

FOR COMPOSITION

Write a monologue in your own words expressing the thoughts and feelings of some heroic figure from literature who looks back on his or her adventures. You might wish to imagine what King Arthur would say, looking back on his life from Avalon. Or you might imagine a monologue by Adam or Eve, looking back at their experiences in Paradise after being driven from the Garden of Eden. You might even think of a speech for the ghost of Macbeth, as he recalls his rise to power and eventual defeat. Try to express the feelings of the figure you choose in close relation to the main facts of his or her former life as we know them from literature.

Break, Break, Break

Break, break, break,
   On thy cold gray stones, O Sea!
And I would that my tongue could utter
   The thoughts that arise in me.

O well for the fisherman's boy,   5
   That he shouts with his sister at play!
O well for the sailor lad,
   That he sings in his boat on the bay!

And the stately ships go on
   To their haven under the hill;   10
But O for the touch of a vanished hand,
   And the sound of a voice that is still!

Break, break, break,
   At the foot of thy crags, O Sea!
But the tender grace of a day that is dead   15
   Will never come back to me.

The Eagle

He clasps the crag with crooked hands;
Close to the sun in lonely lands,
Ringed with the azure world, he stands.

The wrinkled sea beneath him crawls;
He watches from his mountain walls,
And like a thunderbolt he falls.

FOR STUDY AND DISCUSSION

Break, Break, Break
What feelings of loss arise in the speaker as he looks out at the sea breaking endlessly against the shore? How does his mental state compare to that of "the fisherman's boy" (line 5) and "the sailor lad" (line 7)? How does the setting intensify the speaker's mood?

The Eagle
1. What qualities of natural power and grandeur does the eagle possess in Tennyson's poem? What is the importance of the eagle's situation and of the speaker's perspective on him?
2. What element of contrast or tension can you find between the two stanzas of the poem? (Notice that line 3 ends with the words "he stands"; line 6 with the words "he falls.")

from **The Princess**

The Princess is a long narrative poem that deals with the role of women in modern society. Although the poem as a whole is not considered one of Tennyson's best works, the songs occasionally interspersed throughout the narrative are among the finest of Tennyson's lyrics.

Tears, Idle Tears

Tears, idle tears, I know not what they mean,
Tears from the depth of some divine despair
Rise in the heart, and gather to the eyes,
In looking on the happy autumn fields,
And thinking of the days that are no more.   5

Fresh as the first beam glittering on a sail,
That brings our friends up from the underworld,
Sad as the last which reddens over one
That sinks with all we love below the verge;
So sad, so fresh, the days that are no more.   10

Ah, sad and strange as in dark summer dawns
The earliest pipe of half-awakened birds
To dying ears, when unto dying eyes
The casement slowly grows a glimmering square;
So sad, so strange, the days that are no more.   15

Dear as remembered kisses after death,
And sweet as those by hopeless fancy feigned
On lips that are for others; deep as love,
Deep as first love, and wild with all regret;
O Death in Life, the days that are no more.   20

Now Sleeps the Crimson Petal

Now sleeps the crimson petal, now the white;
Nor waves the cypress in the palace walk;
Nor winks the gold fin in the porphyry° font.°
The firefly wakens: waken thou with me.

Now droops the milk-white peacock like a ghost,　　　　　5
And like a ghost she glimmers on to me.

Now lies the Earth all Danaë° to the stars,
And all thy heart lies open unto me.

Now slides the silent meteor on, and leaves
A shining furrow, as thy thoughts in me.　　　　　10

Now folds the lily all her sweetness up,
And slips into the bosom of the lake.
So fold thyself, my dearest, thou, and slip
Into my bosom and be lost in me.

---

3. **porphyry** (pôr′fə-rē): a purplish-red stone. **font:** a fountain.　7. **Danaë** (dăn′ə-ē′): a character in Greek mythology. Zeus visited her in the form of a shower of gold.

FOR STUDY AND DISCUSSION

Tears, Idle Tears
1. What is the main source of the speaker's sadness in this poem? How is this source emphasized in the final line of each stanza?
2. One of the ways in which Tennyson expresses melancholy here is through images of nature. Find as many references to the natural world as you can in the poem. In which of these images does the sadness come from the freshness and beauty of the natural world, rather than from its decaying or fading away? What, for example, is "sad and strange" about the "earliest pipe of half-awakened birds" (lines 11–12)?

Now Sleeps the Crimson Petal
1. The contrasting movements of closing and opening are very important in this poem. Find as many instances of these two processes as you can. How do these contrasting movements help define the time of day and the atmosphere in the poem? How do they express the speaker's desires and emotion in terms of the activity of the natural world?
2. This song is a good example of Tennyson's skill in using words to produce a desired emotional effect. Note these verbs: *sleeps, droops, glimmers, lies, slides, folds,* and *slips.* What effect do they have on the mood of the song? How does the word *Nor* (lines 2 and 3) assist the effect?

from **In Memoriam**

Tennyson's *In Memoriam* is one of the finest elegiac poems in English literature. Like *Lycidas*, Milton's elegy on the death of his Cambridge friend Edward King, and *Adonais*, Shelley's elegy on the death of Keats, Tennyson's work laments the death of a young man of great talent, cut off before he could fulfill the promise of his early years. Also like them, it relates the significance of this death to larger questions about the meaning of life and art. But unlike its two great predecessors, *In Memoriam* is made up of poetic units which may be read and appreciated on their own.

   The sudden death in 1833 of Arthur Henry Hallam, at the age of twenty-two, was a tremendous blow to Tennyson. Hallam's death deprived Tennyson of his most intimate relationship and left him overwhelmed with doubts about the purpose of life. He began writing a kind of poetic diary to record his feelings and reflections during the years following Hallam's death. Eventually the individual poetic meditations were grouped into one long sequence and published anonymously, in 1850.

7

Dark house, by which once more I
    stand
  Here in the long unlovely street,
  Doors, where my heart was used to
    beat
So quickly, waiting for a hand,

A hand that can be clasped no more—   5
  Behold me, for I cannot sleep,
  And like a guilty thing I creep
At earliest morning to the door.

He is not here; but far away
  The noise of life begins again,   10
  And ghastly through the drizzling
    rain
On the bald street breaks the blank
    day.

54

O, yet we trust that somehow good
  Will be the final goal of ill,
  To pangs of nature, sins of will,
Defects of doubt, and taints of blood;°

That nothing walks with aimless feet;   5
  That not one life shall be destroyed,
  Or cast as rubbish to the void,
When God hath made the pile com-
    plete;

That not a worm is cloven in vain;
  That not a moth with vain desire   10
  Is shriveled in a fruitless fire,
Or but subserves another's gain.

Behold, we know not anything;
  I can but trust that good shall fall
  At last—far off—at last, to all,   15
And every winter change to spring.

So runs my dream; but what am I?
  An infant crying in the night;
  An infant crying for the light,
And with no language but a cry.   20

3-4. **To . . . blood:** Four kinds of ills are specified: physical, moral, spiritual, and inherited.

130

Thy voice is on the rolling air;
　I hear thee where the waters run;
　Thou standest in the rising sun,
And in the setting thou art fair.

What art thou then? I cannot guess;　　　　5
　But though I seem in star and flower
　To feel thee some diffusive power,
I do not therefore love thee less.

My love involves the love before;
　My love is vaster passion now;　　　　10
　Though mixed with God and Nature
　　thou,
I seem to love thee more and more.

Far off thou art, but ever nigh;
　I have thee still, and I rejoice;
　I prosper, circled with thy voice;　　　　15
I shall not lose thee though I die.

FOR STUDY AND DISCUSSION

In Memoriam 7

1. Where does the speaker find himself in this poem? How do his memories of visiting this place in the past contrast with his present experience? What seems to be the speaker's attitude at the end of the poem as he describes the breaking of day?
2. The poem makes no direct mention of death—it might very well be a poem about paying a social call to a friend's house and finding that the friend is not at home ("He is not here," line 9). Why does Tennyson deal with Hallam's death here in this indirect manner?

In Memoriam 54

1. What common assumption about the presence of evil, death, and loss in the world does Tennyson present in the first three stanzas of this poem? What examples does he offer of this assumption? How does the thought of the poem turn against this assumption in the last two stanzas?
2. It has often been remarked that the rhyme scheme of *In Memoriam*, in which a closely rhymed couplet is surrounded by more distantly rhymed first and fourth lines, is perfectly suited to

the movement between faith and doubt in the poem. What examples of such matching of form and content can you find in this poem? Why, for instance, is it appropriate that we should have to wait for three lines, past the thought expressed in lines 14–15, before the rhyme word of line 13 ("Behold, we know not *anything*") is answered by the rhyme word of line 16 ("And every winter change to *spring*")?

In Memoriam 130

1. In this poem, which comes near the end of *In Memoriam*, Tennyson triumphs over his despair at the loss of his friend by rediscovering him as a spiritual presence in the world. In what aspects of the natural world does he find his friend's presence? Why does he say, "My love is vaster passion now" (line 10)?
2. Examine carefully lines 5–8, the most difficult stanza in this poem. Why does Tennyson respond to the question "What art thou then?" by saying "I cannot guess" (line 5)? What does he mean when he says that he feels Hallam as "some diffusive power" (line 7)? Why does he protest, at the end of the stanza, "I do not therefore love thee less"?
3. Explain the paradox in the last line.

Crossing the Bar

Tennyson wrote this poem in October 1889, three years before his death in October of 1892. It was written while he was crossing the Solent, a channel separating the Isle of Wight from the southern coast of England. Tennyson requested that the poem be printed at the end of all editions of his poems.

Sunset and evening star,
   And one clear call for me!
And may there be no moaning of the bar,
   When I put out to sea,

But such a tide as moving seems asleep,   5
   Too full for sound and foam,
When that° which drew from out the boundless deep
   Turns again home.

Twilight and evening bell,
   And after that the dark!   10
And may there be no sadness of farewell,
   When I embark;

For though from out our bourne° of Time and Place
   The flood may bear me far,
I hope to see my Pilot face to face   15
   When I have crossed the bar.

---

7. **that:** the soul.   13. **bourne:** boundary.

FOR STUDY AND DISCUSSION

1. What overall mood and attitude does Tennyson create in this poem? How do the images of the tide and the sea contribute to this mood and attitude?
2. Tennyson uses the experience of a sailor embarking at evening on a long voyage across the sea as a metaphor for another experience. What is that experience? What particular details help define the real subject of the poem? Why is "Pilot" in line 15 capitalized?

Robert Browning
1812–1889

Robert Browning is thought of today as the most important Victorian poet after Tennyson. During much of his own career, however, he was better appreciated by readers of a younger generation than by his immediate contemporaries. Browning was an adventurous and experimental poet, and his verse seemed to open new possibilities to younger Victorians who felt that Tennyson had done all that could be done with traditional subjects and forms. Toward the end of his career, Browning came to be revered by a wide range of readers, many of whom insisted on making him the voice of wise and reassuring optimism. Browning Societies sprang up in England and America to study the "message" of his writing. But as Browning himself seems to have realized, the meaning of his best poetry was more evasive and complicated than these organized admirers were prepared to allow.

Browning was born in Camberwell, then a comfortable, attractive suburb only three miles from central London. His father, an official of the Bank of England, was a well-read and cultivated man, and although Browning attended a boarding school, he was also tutored at home in ancient and modern languages, in music, and in horsemanship. He read constantly in his father's excellent library, and he spent hours looking at the Italian Renaissance paintings in the Dulwich Art Gallery, only half an hour's walk from his house. Browning's mother, to whom he was particularly close, was a gentle, loving woman with strong religious convictions. Browning spent most of his early life in this comfortable, cultivated family environment. It was not until he was married, at age thirty-four, that he established his own life independent of his parents.

Browning began writing poetry at a very early age: according to his own recollection, he was barely five years old when he wrote his first poem and hid it under a sofa cushion. His first book of poetry, a highly personal and confessional work entitled *Pauline*, appeared when he was twenty-one, and shows the influence of Byron and especially of Shelley, his idol among the Romantic poets. *Pauline* was sharply and accurately criticized by the philosopher John Stuart Mill for its "intense and morbid self-consciousness." In his next two volumes of verse Browning moved away

Robert Browning
National Portrait Gallery, London

from the subjective immaturity of *Pauline* toward a more objective and analytical approach to experience. For ten years, between 1837 and 1847, Browning devoted himself to writing for the theater. Although he was not successful as a playwright, he discovered during these years that his real ability as a writer lay in adapting the techniques of dramatic writing to poetry. His development is reflected in a remarkable series of poetic pamphlets called *Bells and Pomegranates*, written between 1841 and 1846. Included in these pamphlets is *Pippa Passes*, the most interesting of his early poetic dramas.

Browning met Elizabeth Barrett in 1845. She was six years older and much better known as a poet than he was. She was in poor health and living a life of unhappy seclusion because of her tyrannical and overprotective father. The story of the love and courtship of Browning and Elizabeth Barrett is well known through the letters they exchanged and through Elizabeth's own love sonnets. After sixteen months of frustrated courtship, Browning finally decided that Elizabeth's father would never allow her to marry and that she had to be "rescued" for the sake of her own health and happiness. They were secretly married in the autumn of

1846, and eloped to Italy, where they lived until her death in 1861.

The Brownings seem to have been almost ideally happy in Italy. Browning himself had always been interested in Italian art and history. He delighted in studying the great paintings in Florence, where they lived for most of the time, and in championing the cause of Italian independence. His literary imagination flourished as never before. It was while living in Italy that he published his finest volume of poems, *Men and Women* (1855). This collection reflects Browning's intense interest in the Italian Renaissance, and it displays his complete mastery of the poetic form through which he was to achieve his greatest success, the *dramatic monologue*. Browning himself described his "poetry always dramatic in principle" as "so many utterances of so many imaginary persons, not mine." This formulation is central to Browning's dramatic monologues, in which imagined speakers other than Browning himself—often based upon famous figures from history or art but sometimes entirely Browning's own invention—utter their thoughts to implied listeners. In the process these speakers reveal to us, as readers, aspects of themselves and their feelings of which they are unaware. Browning's models in writing this kind of poem were the soliloquies in Shakespeare's plays and the poems of John Donne. Previous writers of the nineteenth century, Byron and Tennyson for example, had written in this form, but it was Browning who explored its possibilities to the full.

When Elizabeth Barrett Browning died in 1861, Browning returned to London and began working on *Dramatis Personae* (1864), another collection of dramatic monologues. He also wrote *The Ring and the Book* (1868–1869), his longest and most ambitious work, in which the principle of the dramatic monologue is extended to project a single murder story from ten different points of view. Browning's fame as a poet gradually spread beyond the small group of young intellectuals who had admired his earlier work. He enjoyed the life of a literary celebrity, dining out so often at the homes and clubs of friends and admirers that Tennyson sarcastically predicted that Browning would die in his dinner jacket. He spoke out vigorously on most of the main issues of the day, and this contributed to his image as a Victorian sage. But Browning remained curiously reluctant to comment on the meaning of his own poems, preferring to express himself indirectly through the personages he created in them. Some people have felt that the image of the socially confident literary celebrity Browning adopted in his later years was itself a kind of mask, behind which Browning's true character remains mysterious. In any case, Browning had the satisfaction of enormous public fame during the last part of his career, even if this fame was not always based on an open and accurate understanding of his work. He died at the age of seventy-two, and was buried in Westminster Abbey.

Two aspects of Browning's poetry are particularly significant for understanding his influence on twentieth-century poetry and his appeal to readers today. First, there is Browning's interest in what we may loosely call psychology, in the conscious and unconscious workings of the human mind. In his concern with the devious thinking and complex motives of the characters in his dramatic monologues, Browning is closer to later Victorian novelists such as George Eliot and George Meredith than to the poets of his own generation. But Browning goes beyond these novelists in his extraordinary openness to evil, obsessive, and abnormal states of mind. He once commented that "all morbidness of the soul is worth the soul's study." Browning also differs from his contemporaries in the degree of objectivity with which he presents the personalities of the speakers in his dramatic monologues. Browning does not pass judgment on these speakers for us. Instead, he involves us fully in the desires and energies, both good and bad, of his speakers, and then leaves us to get our own moral bearings and to pass judgment on what we have experienced.

Second, Browning's importance derives from his stylistic experimentation. Following the example of Donne and his own desire to break with the traditional decorum of most English poetry, Browning makes deliberate use of rough colloquial diction and word order, of surprising and even grotesque rhymes, and of harsh rhythms and metrical patterns. Browning's general purpose in exploring these uses of language was to bring his poetry more closely in touch with the irregular, unpredictable, and often distorted movements of the minds of his speakers. More conservative readers have sometimes found Browning's style unpleasing in its deliberate awkwardnesses and lack of musicality. But for writers and readers interested in expanding the expressive resources of English poetry, Browning opened up new possibilities and helped prepare the way for some of the best poetry of our own era.

My Last Duchess

This poem is perhaps the most popular of Browning's dramatic monologues. The scene is the castle of the Duke of Ferrara, the speaker in the poem, who is a powerful Italian nobleman of the Renaissance period. The Duke is showing a painting of his first wife to an envoy who has been sent to arrange the details of a second marriage.

That's my last Duchess painted on the wall,
Looking as if she were alive. I call
That piece a wonder, now: Frà Pandolf's° hands
Worked busily a day, and there she stands.
Will 't please you sit and look at her? I said   5
"Frà Pandolf" by design, for never read
Strangers like you that pictured countenance,
The depth and passion of its earnest glance,
But to myself they turned (since none puts by
The curtain I have drawn for you, but I)   10
And seemed as they would ask me, if they durst,
How such a glance came there; so, not the first
Are you to turn and ask thus. Sir, 'twas not
Her husband's presence only, called that spot
Of joy into the Duchess' cheek; perhaps   15
Frà Pandolf chanced to say, "Her mantle laps
Over my lady's wrist too much," or "Paint
Must never hope to reproduce the faint
Half flush that dies along her throat." Such stuff
Was courtesy, she thought, and cause enough   20
For calling up that spot of joy. She had
A heart—how shall I say?—too soon made glad,
Too easily impressed; she liked whate'er
She looked on, and her looks went everywhere.
Sir, 'twas all one! My favor at her breast,   25
The dropping of the daylight in the West,
The bough of cherries some officious fool
Broke in the orchard for her, the white mule
She rode with round the terrace—all and each
Would draw from her alike the approving speech,   30
Or blush, at least. She thanked men—good! but thanked
Somehow—I know not how—as if she ranked
My gift of a nine-hundred-years-old name

---

3. **Frà Pandolf:** an imaginary monk and painter of the Italian Renaissance period. "Frà" means "Brother."

Giovanna Tornabuoni (1488) by Domenico Ghirlandaio. Stylized portraits of Italian Renaissance women in elegant costumes and jewelry were common during the period Browning evokes in "My Last Duchess."
Stichting Collectie Thyssen-Bornemisza, Lugano

With anybody's gift. Who'd stoop to blame
This sort of trifling? Even had you skill
In speech—which I have not—to make your will
Quite clear to such an one, and say, "Just this
Or that in you disgusts me; here you miss,
Or there exceed the mark"—and if she let
Herself be lessoned so, nor plainly set
Her wits to yours, forsooth, and made excuse
—E'en then would be some stooping; and I choose
Never to stoop. Oh, sir, she smiled, no doubt,
Whene'er I passed her; but who passed without
Much the same smile? This grew; I gave commands;   45
Then all smiles stopped together. There she stands
As if alive. Will 't please you rise? We'll meet
The company below, then. I repeat,
The Count your master's known munificence
Is ample warrant that no just pretense   50
Of mine for dowry will be disallowed;
Though his fair daughter's self, as I avowed
At starting, is my object. Nay, we'll go
Together down, sir.° Notice Neptune,° though,
Taming a sea horse, thought a rarity,   55
Which Claus of Innsbruck° cast in bronze for me!

53–54. **we'll . . . down:** The envoy, out of respect, has dropped behind the duke, who calls him forward to a position of equality.   54. **Neptune:** the Roman god of the sea.   56. **Claus of Innsbruck:** an imaginary sculptor.

COMMENTARY

As has already been suggested in the general introduction to Browning, dramatic monologues such as "My Last Duchess" are closely related to the longer speeches in Shakespeare's plays. They are like speeches in a play without any surrounding dramatic context. In a dramatic monologue, an imaginary context of situation, action, and character development is implied by what the speaker of the monologue says, and by the way in which he or she says it. The speaker in Browning's dramatic monologues is always a fictional figure—never the poet himself. And this speaker is imagined as addressing a fictional listener, whose presence and identity we infer from the speaker's language. The speaker does not address us, as readers, directly. Rather, it is as if we are overhearing the speaker talking to someone else. It is partly because we are overhearing the speaker from a privileged vantage point that we gain insight into aspects of the speaker's life and personality that he or she is unaware of disclosing.

In Browning's "My Last Duchess," for example, the Duke wants to present himself as powerful and sophisticated, and in part he succeeds in creating this impression. But when he says, in explaining to the envoy that he has shown the portrait of his former wife to other visitors, "But to myself they turned (since none puts by / The curtain I have drawn for you, but I)," we may also find him arrogant and possessive. We have to infer these aspects of the Duke's character from the way he speaks, just as we must infer details of setting and situation. The reader is also invited to make other inferences: about the personality of the Duke's former wife (although we hear about her, of course, only from the Duke), about the cause of her death, about the Duke's motives for telling the envoy about his former wife in the first place, and so forth. Although we stand outside the situation implied in "My Last Duchess," we are also encouraged by the language to participate very actively in creating the full dramatic reality suggested in the poem. Part of

Browning's genius lies in his ability to provoke the right kind of imaginative participation and contribution from his readers.

Browning was fascinated all his life by the Italian Renaissance, and "My Last Duchess," like several other of his dramatic monologues, reflects his interest in this period of energetic and often violent self-assertion, worldly confidence, and artistic sophistication. The Duke is not, then, just an individualized study of power, cleverness, and refinement combined with ruthless ambition, greed, and cruelty. He is also a representative figure who embodies attitudes Browning thought of as characteristic of the Renaissance as a whole.

FOR STUDY AND DISCUSSION

1. What passages in the Duke's monologue suggest that he is an intelligent, cultivated Renaissance nobleman? What passages suggest that he is egotistical, tyrannical, and ruthless?

2. According to the Duke, what was his last duchess like? What does he mean when he says, "She had / A heart . . . too soon made glad" (lines 21–22)?

3. The critical point in the Duke's monologue comes in lines 45–46: "This grew; I gave commands; / Then all smiles stopped together." What seems to have been the duchess' fate? Why do you think Browning suggests this fate so indirectly and ambiguously?

4. Although "My Last Duchess" is written in iambic pentameter couplets, we hardly notice this regularity of form because the language of the Duke's monologue is so colloquial and natural. What examples can you find in the poem where Browning's writing gives the impression of actual speech?

5. At the end of "My Last Duchess," the Duke asks the envoy to notice another work of art, a bronze sculpture showing "Neptune . . . / Taming a sea horse . . ." (lines 54–55). What does this work of art suggest about the theme of the poem as a whole?

Home Thoughts, from Abroad

Although Browning was not actually abroad in 1845 when this poem was written, it is presented from the point of view of an Englishman thinking about his country from a distant land. The "brushwood sheaf" (line 5), "elm tree" (line 6—a "bole" is a tree trunk), "chaffinch" (line 7), and "whitethroat" (line 10) are plants or birds characteristic of the English countryside, while the "melon flower" (line 20) is typical of a warmer, more southerly environment.

Oh, to be in England
Now that April's there,
And whoever wakes in England
Sees, some morning, unaware,
That the lowest boughs and the brushwood sheaf 5
Round the elm tree bole are in tiny leaf,
While the chaffinch sings on the orchard bough
In England—now!

And after April, when May follows,
And the whitethroat builds, and all the swallows! 10
Hark, where my blossomed pear tree in the hedge
Leans to the field and scatters on the clover
Blossoms and dewdrops—at the bent spray's edge—
That's the wise thrush; he sings each song twice over,
Lest you should think he never could recapture 15
The first fine careless rapture!
And though the fields look rough with hoary dew,
All will be gay when noontide wakes anew
The buttercups, the little children's dower
—Far brighter than this gaudy melon flower! 20

FOR STUDY AND DISCUSSION

1. It is often the case that we do not appreciate the beauty of places with which we are very familiar until we are removed from them. Does this seem to be true of the speaker in "Home Thoughts, from Abroad"? What is the significance of the word *unaware* in line 4?

2. What is the meaning of the final contrast in the poem between the bright "buttercups" and "this gaudy melon flower" (lines 19–20)?

Love Among the Ruins

The scene of this monologue may be the Campagna di Roma (käm-pä′nyä dē rô′mä), the open country surrounding the capital city. The speaker is a shepherd who eagerly anticipates his return to his young wife. Their home is a ruined turret, on the spot where, in ancient days, stood a tower from which the monarch and his court watched chariot races. The poem contrasts the quiet countryside with the tumult of the ancient city, the temporary nature of all earthly things with the realization that "love is best."

Where the quiet-colored end of evening smiles
    Miles and miles
On the solitary pastures where our sheep
    Half-asleep
Tinkle homeward through the twilight, stray or stop   5
    As they crop—
Was the site once of a city great and gay
    (So they say),°
Of our country's very capital, its prince
    Ages since   10
Held his court in, gathered councils, wielding far
    Peace or war.

Now—the country does not even boast a tree,
    As you see,
To distinguish slopes of verdure, certain rills   15
    From the hills
Intersect and give a name to (else they run
    Into one),
Where the domed and daring palace shot its spires
    Up like fires   20
O'er the hundred-gated circuit of a wall
    Bounding all,
Made of marble, men might march on nor be pressed,
    Twelve abreast.

And such plenty and perfection, see, of grass   25
    Never was!
Such a carpet as, this summertime, o'erspreads
    And embeds
Every vestige of the city, guessed alone,°
    Stock or stone—   30

---

8. **they say:** The archaeologists alone can determine this fact; so the shepherd takes his data from them.   29. **guessed alone:** Now one can only guess where the city was because the site is covered by grass.

Where a multitude of men breathed joy and woe
    Long ago;
Lust of glory pricked their hearts up, dread of shame
    Struck them tame;
And that glory and that shame alike, the gold   35
    Bought and sold.

Now—the single little turret that remains
    On the plains,
By the caper° overrooted, by the gourd
    Overscored,°   40
While the patching houseleek's° head of blossom winks
    Through the chinks—
Marks the basement whence a tower in ancient time
    Sprang sublime,
And a burning ring, all round, the chariots traced   45
    As they raced,
And the monarch and his minions° and his dames
    Viewed the games.

And I know—while thus the quiet-colored eve
    Smiles to leave   50
To their folding, all our many tinkling fleece
    In such peace,
And the slopes and rills in undistinguished gray
    Melt away—
That a girl with eager eyes and yellow hair   55
    Waits me there
In the turret whence the charioteers caught soul
    For the goal,
When the king looked, where she looks now, breathless, dumb
    Till I come.   60

But he looked upon the city, every side,
    Far and wide,
All the mountains topped with temples, all the glades'
    Colonnades,°
All the causeys,° bridges, aqueducts—and then,   65
    All the men!

---

39. **caper:** a Mediterranean shrub, abundant on old walls and rocks. Its flower buds are often used as a seasoning. 39–40. **gourd/Overscored:** The climbing vine, overrunning the turret, has marked or scored it as if with lines. 41. **houseleek:** a common plant with thick, fleshy leaves and yellow or purple flowers, frequently found on old walls and roofs. 47. **minions:** attendants; more strictly, favorites. 63–64. **glades'/Colonnades:** The open spaces in the woods are enclosed by trees, just as a large building is often enclosed by a series of columns. 65. **causeys:** Ruins of old causeways, or raised sidewalks, and aqueducts may still be seen in the Roman Campagna.

When I do come, she will speak not, she will stand,
    Either hand
On my shoulder, give her eyes the first embrace
    Of my face,   70
Ere we rush, ere we extinguish sight and speech
    Each on each.

In one year they sent a million fighters forth
    South and North,
And they built their gods a brazen pillar high   75
    As the sky,
Yet reserved a thousand chariots in full force—
    Gold, of course.
O heart! O blood that freezes, blood that burns!
    Earth's returns°   80
For whole centuries of folly, noise and sin!
    Shut them in,
With their triumphs and their glories and the rest!
    Love is best.

---

80. **Earth's returns:** the rewards of temporal or earthly efforts.

FOR STUDY AND DISCUSSION

How is the contrast between the past grandeur and
the present bareness emphasized? How do the motives behind the sports, buildings, and wars of the
vanished civilization compare with the emotions
of the two young people?

Prospice

Prospice (prō-spĭk′ē) means "look forward." As an expression of Browning's attitude toward death, it should be compared with Tennyson's "Crossing the Bar." Browning probably wrote the poem soon after Elizabeth Barrett Browning's death in 1861. She is the "soul of my soul" referred to in the last three lines.

Fear death?—to feel the fog in my throat,
    The mist in my face,
When the snows begin, and the blasts denote
    I am nearing the place,
The power of the night, the press of the storm,   5
    The post of the foe;
Where he stands, the Arch Fear in a visible form,
    Yet the strong man must go.
For the journey is done and the summit attained,
    And the barriers fall,   10
Though a battle's to fight ere the guerdon be gained,
    The reward of it all.
I was ever a fighter, so—one fight more,
    The best and the last!
I would hate that death bandaged my eyes, and forbore,   15
    And bade me creep past.
No! let me taste the whole of it, fare like my peers,
    The heroes of old,
Bear the brunt, in a minute pay glad life's arrears
    Of pain, darkness, and cold.   20
For sudden the worst turns the best to the brave,
    The black minute's at end,
And the elements' rage, the fiend-voices° that rave,
    Shall dwindle, shall blend,
Shall change, shall become first a peace out of pain,   25
    Then a light, then thy breast,
O thou soul of my soul! I shall clasp thee again,
    And with God be the rest!

---

23. **fiend-voices:** This term refers to a legend that, as the soul leaves the body, fiends try to snatch it away from the powers of light.

COMMENTARY

Although more directly personal and grave in subject than many of Browning's other poems, "Prospice" opens with a colloquial abruptness that is very characteristic of the dramatic quality of his verse. The poem is a meditation on death, but it takes the form of a pilgrimage or journey which includes a heroic battle and a sudden bursting through cold and darkness into peace and light. Death is seen not as a slow, passive ebbing away of life and a gradual loss of consciousness, but as a heroic climax in which all the speaker's courage and power of resistance are brought into play. The speaker approaches death as a warrior laying siege to the "post of the foe" (line 6), confronting with all his might the terrifying "Arch Fear" (line 7).

At the end of the poem, the speaker is rewarded for his bravery in the ultimate battle of death by being reunited with the person he loves most. Browning once translated Dante's words on his beloved Beatrice: "Thus I believe, thus I affirm, thus I am certain it is, that from this life I shall pass to another, there, where the lady lives of whom my soul was enamored."

FOR STUDY AND DISCUSSION

1. What feelings of danger and fearfulness does the speaker of "Prospice" experience at the approach of death in the opening lines of the poem? With what attitude and self-image will the speaker confront these feelings? What happens to the powers of darkness and fear when "The black minute's at end" (line 22)?

2. Compare the attitude toward death expressed in Browning's "Prospice" with that expressed by Tennyson in "Crossing the Bar." How do these two poems differ in the images they use to suggest the experience of death? How do the poems differ in the vision they suggest of life after death?

FOR COMPOSITION

Like Browning's "My Last Duchess," Tennyson's "Ulysses" (page 561) is a famous dramatic monologue of the Victorian period. Compare the two poems in a brief composition in which you consider the following points: Which poem presents a more interesting character? Which poem is the more musical? Which poem depends more on direct statement? Which on implication? Does either poem give you the impression that the poet was more concerned with creating a symbol than a convincing character? Explain.

Matthew Arnold
1822–1888

Matthew Arnold by G. F. Watts.
National Portrait Gallery, London

Readers have long debated whether Matthew Arnold is more important as a poet or as a critic. Certainly his achievement in both literary forms is impressive. In his poetry, Arnold confronts more directly than either Tennyson or Browning the central Victorian problem of remaining human in the dehumanizing atmosphere of a modern industrial society. In his critical essays, Arnold tries to provide answers to the questions about modern life that he poses but leaves for the most part unanswered in his poems.

Arnold's father, Dr. Thomas Arnold, was an important religious and educational reformer who became headmaster of the Rugby School, one of the most prestigious private schools in England. Arnold was deeply influenced by his father's ideas, as we might expect, but he also showed a certain rebellious defiance of his father's rigorous principles. When Arnold left Rugby to attend Oxford University in 1841, he assumed the style of an aristocratic wit and dandy, famous for his elegant, colorful clothes and flippant manner. He did not work particularly hard at Oxford, and only by desperate last-minute cramming did he manage a respectable performance on his final examinations. But underneath the casual manner that Arnold cultivated as a young man was a wide-ranging intellect and a sensitive, brooding imagination. Even before he abandoned his youthful dandyism, Arnold was beginning to write poems that would surprise his closest friends and family with their meditative intensity and their power of symbolic suggestion.

In 1851 Arnold became a government inspector of schools, a position he held for over thirty years. The job was a demanding one and left him with less free time for his own writing than was enjoyed by other major Victorian writers. Yet Arnold wrote continually throughout these years.

Arnold's career as a writer may be divided roughly into four phases. Most of his poems appeared during the 1850's: a volume entitled *The Strayed Reveller and Other Poems,* published in 1849, was followed by additional volumes in 1852 and 1853. During the 1860's the focus of his writing shifted from poetry to literary and social criticism. In 1865 the first series of his *Essays in Criticism* was published, and in 1869, *Culture and Anarchy,* a fierce attack on middle-class materialism and narrow-mindedness, considered by many to be his finest work. In the 1870's Arnold devoted himself mainly to writing about education and religion. Finally, in the 1880's, he returned to literary criticism and wrote the second series of his *Essays in Criticism,* published soon after his death in 1888.

One of the most fascinating questions presented by Arnold's career is why he virtually gave up writing poetry after 1860. Some have suggested that he was discouraged by the cool public reception to his poems; others have thought that he felt he had exhausted his sources of poetic inspiration. The main reason, however, seems to have been that Arnold was uneasy about the kind of poetry he was producing. Many of his best poems convey a melancholy, pessimistic sense of the dilemmas of modern life, without offering any secure source of hope, joy, and permanent value. Arnold described the limitations of this kind of poetry in criticizing one of his own major poems in the preface to his collection of 1853: ". . . the suffering finds no vent in action; . . . a continuous state of mental distress is prolonged, unrelieved by incident, hope, or resistance; . . . there is everything to be endured, nothing to be done." It was not enough, Arnold felt, for poetry to express the pain and difficulty of life—it must also "inspirit and rejoice the reader." But if, in being true to his own poetic instincts, Arnold could not provide readers with sufficient spirit and joy, he could still help them find permanent values in other writers—in the Greeks, in Dante, in Shakespeare, and in the best writers of his own century. Arnold's literary criticism became in part a quest for those qualities that he found lacking or imperfectly realized in his own poems.

Whatever Arnold's sense of his own poetic shortcomings may have been, today his poetry seems distinctively expressive of mid-Victorian anxiety precisely because it avoids offering optimistic answers to the doubtful questions it raises. From the more balanced and objective perspective of his later years, Arnold himself came to feel confident that he had after all spoken responsibly to and for his era. Writing to his mother in 1869, Arnold observed: "My poems represent, on the whole, the main movement of mind of the last quarter of a century, and thus they will probably have their day as people become conscious to themselves of what that movement of mind is, and interested in the literary productions which reflect it. It might be fairly urged that I have less poetic sentiment than Tennyson, and less intellectual vigor and abundance than Browning; yet, because I have perhaps more of a fusion of the two than either of them, and have more regularly applied that fusion to the main line of modern development, I am likely enough to have my turn, as they have had theirs." Arnold has indeed had his turn in our own century, as readers have responded to the haunting sense of loneliness and isolation in his poems, and to the beauty of his verse.

In Harmony with Nature

To a Preacher

"In harmony with Nature?" Restless fool,
Who with such heat dost preach what were to thee,
When true, the last impossibility—
To be like Nature strong, like Nature cool!

Know, man hath all which Nature hath, but more,   5
And in that *more* lie all his hopes of good.
Nature is cruel, man is sick of blood;
Nature is stubborn, man would fain adore;

Nature is fickle, man hath need of rest;
Nature forgives no debt, and fears no grave;   10
Man would be mild, and with safe conscience blest.

Man must begin, know this, where Nature ends;
Nature and man can never be fast friends.
Fool, if thou canst not pass her, rest her slave!

To Marguerite—Continued

In the 1840's Arnold wrote several poems to a young woman called Marguerite. Arnold always insisted during his lifetime that Marguerite was only an imaginary figure, but recent scholarship has shown that the "Marguerite" of these poems was Mary Claude, a young Frenchwoman, with whom Arnold fell in love.

Yes! in the sea of life enisled,
With echoing straits between us thrown,
Dotting the shoreless watery wild,
We mortal millions live *alone.*
The islands feel the enclasping flow,   5
And then their endless bounds they know.

But when the moon their hollows lights,
And they are swept by balms of spring,
And in their glens, on starry nights,
The nightingales divinely sing;   10
And lovely notes, from shore to shore,
Across the sounds and channels pour—

Oh! then a longing like despair
Is to their farthest caverns sent;
For surely once, they feel, we were   15
Parts of a single continent!
Now round us spreads the watery plain—
Oh, might our marges meet again!

Who ordered, that their longing's fire
Should be, as soon as kindled, cooled?   20
Who renders vain their deep desire?—
A god, a god their severance ruled!
And bade betwixt their shores to be
The unplumbed, salt, estranging sea.

FOR STUDY AND DISCUSSION

In Harmony with Nature

1. Why does Arnold consider the preacher's message, that human beings should be in harmony with nature, foolish and superficial? Has the preacher himself acted in accord with the doctrine he preaches?

2. Why, according to Arnold, must people "begin . . . where Nature ends" (line 12)?

To Marguerite—Continued

1. How does Arnold use the image of islands surrounded by a vast ocean to convey the idea of the isolated individual? Who, according to Arnold, is responsible for this isolation?

2. What images does Arnold use in lines 7–16 to suggest those moments when the individual longs most deeply for connection with someone else? Why is the despair of the isolated individual particularly keen at such moments?

Dover Beach

The sea is calm tonight.
The tide is full, the moon lies fair
Upon the straits;°— on the French coast the light
Gleams and is gone; the cliffs of England stand,
Glimmering and vast, out in the tranquil bay.   5
Come to the window, sweet is the night air!
Only, from the long line of spray
Where the sea meets the moon-blanched land,
Listen! you hear the grating roar
Of pebbles which the waves draw back, and fling,   10
At their return, up the high strand,
Begin, and cease, and then again begin,
With tremulous cadence slow, and bring
The eternal note of sadness in.

Sophocles° long ago   15
Heard it on the Aegean,° and it brought
Into his mind the turbid ebb and flow
Of human misery; we
Find also in the sound a thought,
Hearing it by this distant northern sea.   20

The Sea of Faith
Was once, too, at the full, and round earth's shore
Lay like the folds of a bright girdle furled.
But now I only hear
Its melancholy, long, withdrawing roar,   25
Retreating, to the breath
Of the night wind, down the vast edges drear
And naked shingles° of the world.

Ah, love, let us be true
To one another! for the world, which seems   30
To lie before us like a land of dreams,
So various, so beautiful, so new,
Hath really neither joy, nor love, nor light,
Nor certitude, nor peace, nor help for pain;
And we are here as on a darkling plain   35
Swept with confused alarms of struggle and flight,
Where ignorant armies clash by night.

---

3. **straits:** Strait of Dover, a crossing between England and France.   15. **Sophocles**
(sŏf′ə-klēz′): an Athenian writer (496?–406 B.C.), one of the three greatest trage-
dians in the golden age of Greek drama.   16. **Aegean** (ĭ-jē′ən): an arm of the Mediterranean Sea.   28. **shingles:** shores of large coarse gravel.

COMMENTARY

The main theme of "Dover Beach" is one that appears throughout Arnold's poetry: the anxiety experienced by an isolated individual as he confronts the turbulent historical forces and the loss of religious faith in the modern world. But in no other poem does Arnold embody this theme so effectively in the movement of the speaker's mind, and in the natural setting to which the speaker responds.

As the poem opens, the speaker looks out on the moonlit water of the Strait of Dover with a sense of peaceful, fulfilled beauty. The only disturbing hint in the opening lines is the light from the French coast across the water: it "Gleams and is gone" (line 4), in contrast to the full, steady moonlight. The speaker invites the person he is with to "Come to the window" (line 6) and share the lovely scene with him. But as soon as he makes this gesture, he begins to listen to the sea, as well as to look at it. The "grating roar" (line 9) of the waves breaking against the shore alters his mood entirely, and he begins to hear in the sea the "eternal note of sadness" (line 14).

In the second section, the speaker makes the sadness he hears in the sea timeless and universal by extending the idea beyond his own immediate response. He remembers that Sophocles, the great Greek tragedian, had a similar response to the sound of the sea, even though he lived more than two thousand years ago in an entirely different part of the world.

In the third section of "Dover Beach," we move from actual seas—the speaker looking at and listening to the Strait of Dover, Sophocles listening to the Aegean—to a metaphorical sea, the "Sea of Faith" (line 21). In a difficult image, Arnold imagines that in the past the tide of religious faith was at its height, and the world was completely encircled by its bright and reassuring presence. "But now," the speaker says, "I only hear/Its melancholy, long, withdrawing roar" (lines 24–25). In contrast to the full tide of the sea before him (line 2), but with a disturbing force similar to that which the speaker senses in the waves crashing against and flowing away from the coast of England, the Sea of Faith has withdrawn its protective presence, leaving the world "naked" (line 28) and vulnerable.

In the last section the speaker again addresses his companion directly, but in a different mood and tone of voice from his earlier invitation to "Come to the window." He now asks that they be faithful to each other, since the personal faith of human love is all he believes remains in a world that only "seems" beautiful and full of promise (lines 30–32). What the world is really like is conveyed in the concluding lines of the poem, where the equivalent of the dark, agitated, withdrawing sea appears as "a darkling plain, / Swept with confused alarms of struggle and flight, / Where ignorant armies clash by night."

FOR STUDY AND DISCUSSION

1. What mood or feeling is created by the description of the moonlit sea in the opening lines of "Dover Beach"? How does this mood begin to change with the word *Only* at the beginning of line 7?

2. In lines 15–18 Arnold refers to Sophocles, the great Greek tragedian. What, in Arnold's imagination, did Sophocles hear in the ebb and flow of the Aegean Sea? How does Arnold broaden the meaning of his poem by relating his experience of the sea to that of Sophocles?

3. In the third section of "Dover Beach," Arnold presents faith as a sea that once, at high tide, encircled the entire world. What has happened to this sea?

4. To whom is the speaker of "Dover Beach" addressing his meditations? How does the speaker's attitude toward "the world" affect his need for love and for private trust and fidelity?

5. Study carefully the image that Arnold places at the end of "Dover Beach" (lines 35–37). Why does Arnold think of himself and the person he loves as being situated "on a darkling plain"? What double sense of error and confusion is suggested by the idea of "*ignorant* armies" clashing "by *night*"?

FOR COMPOSITION

In "To Marguerite—Continued" and "Dover Beach," Arnold uses similar seaside settings to express the speaker's feeling of isolation and his desire for personal relationship. How are the two settings alike? How are they different? What importance does this difference have for the overall meaning and attitude in each poem? Write a short paper that addresses these questions.

Thomas Hardy
1840–1928

W. STRANG.
1893

Thomas Hardy
National Portrait Gallery, London

Today Thomas Hardy is better known as a novelist than as a poet. Yet he began his literary career writing poems, and after the hostile public response to his last novel, *Jude the Obscure* (1896), he devoted the final thirty years of his life almost exclusively to poetry. The appeal of Hardy's poetry is not as obvious as that of the other major Victorian poets, but his reputation, having declined somewhat after the first quarter of the twentieth century, has grown steadily in recent years. The main concerns of his poetry are essentially those of his fiction—the forces both inside and outside human life that lead, almost inevitably, to sorrow, regret, frustration, and loss.

Hardy was born near Dorchester, in the center of the area of southwest England which he referred to in his fiction by the ancient name of Wessex. He was trained as an architect, and in 1861 he went to London for further study and to practice his profession. He also began writing poems and short stories. In 1868 he submitted his first novel to a publisher. It was rejected, but Hardy was encouraged to try again, and in 1871 a second novel, *Desperate Remedies,* was published. Another novel appeared the following year, and Hardy gave up his profession as an architect to devote full time to his writing. His career as a novelist extended from 1871 to 1896. After that, as we have noted, he returned to poetry. His first collection, *Wessex Poems,* was published in 1898. Between 1903 and 1908 appeared *The Dynasts,* a vast epic-drama based upon the Napoleonic Wars. At his death in 1928, he was widely admired. His ashes were buried in Westminster Abbey, but in accordance with his wishes, his heart was removed and buried in the parish churchyard of his native village in Dorsetshire.

Hardy's best poems usually present situations that illustrate his concern with circumstances or forces beyond human control. Hardy is often described as a gloomy pessimist who believed in the impersonal and generally negative power of fate. But it is important to recognize that while the sadness in Hardy's writing is sometimes attributed to causes remote from human will and consciousness, more often it springs from within, from our own insatiable desires, emotions, and illusions. And while the prevailing mood in Hardy's poetry is somber, there is also a very rich and positive feeling for the ancient landscape and cultural roots of rural England, for patterns of life so old that they come to seem archetypal.

In style Hardy's poems create an impression of plainness or ruggedness, in keeping with his rural background and his lack of extensive formal education. But the colloquial directness of his language is very much a matter of conscious selection and craft. Even Hardy's frequent use of archaic words or of homely diction is part of a deliberate reaction against the ornate, elaborate language of some late-Victorian verse. Hardy's poetry may appear to lack sophisticated complexity and glamour, but its surface simplicity is deceptive. Its deep integrity will consistently reward a reader who is free of presumptions about what fine poetry should be.

The Darkling Thrush

I leant upon a coppice gate
    When Frost was specter-gray,
And Winter's dregs made desolate
   . The weakening eye of day.
The tangled bine-stems scored the sky   5
    Like strings of broken lyres,
And all mankind that haunted nigh
    Had sought their household fires.

The land's sharp features seemed to be
    The Century's corpse° outleant,   10
His crypt the cloudy canopy,
    The wind his death lament.
The ancient pulse of germ° and birth
    Was shrunken hard and dry,
And every spirit upon earth   15
    Seemed fervorless as I.

At once a voice arose among
    The bleak twigs overhead
In a full-hearted evensong
    Of joy illimited;   20
An aged thrush, frail, gaunt, and small,
    In blast-beruffled plume,
Had chosen thus to fling his soul
    Upon the growing gloom.

So little cause for carolings   25
    Of such ecstatic sound
Was written on terrestrial things
    Afar or nigh around,
That I could think there trembled through
    His happy good-night air   30
Some blessèd Hope, whereof he knew
    And I was unaware.

---

10. **Century's corpse:** This poem was written on December 31, 1900, the last day of the nineteenth century. 13. **germ:** seed or bud.

The Man He Killed

"Had he and I but met
    By some old ancient inn,
We should have sat us down to wet
    Right many a nipperkin!°

"But ranged as infantry,   5
    And staring face to face,
I shot at him as he at me,
    And killed him in his place.

"I shot him dead because—
    Because he was my foe,   10
Just so: my foe of course he was;
    That's clear enough; although

"He thought he'd 'list,° perhaps,
    Offhand like—just as I—
Was out of work—had sold his traps—   15
    No other reason why.

"Yes; quaint and curious war is!
    You shoot a fellow down
You'd treat if met where any bar is,
    Or help to half-a-crown."°   20

---

4. **nipperkin:** a small cup or glass for drinking beer and wine. 13. **'list:** enlist. 20. **help to half-a-crown:** lend a coin worth two and a half shillings.

Ah, Are You Digging on My Grave?

This poem, written in the form of a dialogue, is a good illustration of Hardy's often grim sense of humor, and of his tendency to expose romantic or sentimental illusions about love, life, and death.

"Ah, are you digging on my grave
    My loved one?—planting rue?"
—"No; yesterday he went to wed
One of the brightest wealth has bred.
'It cannot hurt her now,' he said,   5
    'That I should not be true.'"

"Then who is digging on my grave?
    My nearest dearest kin?"
—"Ah, no; they sit and think, 'What use!
What good will planting flowers produce?   10
No tendance of her mound can loose
    Her spirit from Death's gin.'"

"But someone digs upon my grave?
    My enemy?—prodding sly?"
—"Nay; when she heard you had passed the Gate   15
That shuts on all flesh soon or late,
She thought you no more worth her hate,
    And cares not where you lie."

"Then, who is digging on my grave?
    Say—since I have not guessed!"   20
—"O it is I, my mistress dear,
Your little dog, who still lives near,
And much I hope my movements here
    Have not disturbed your rest?"

"Ah, yes! *You* dig upon my grave . . .   25
    Why flashed it not on me
That one true heart was left behind!
What feeling do we ever find
To equal among humankind
    A dog's fidelity!"   30

"Mistress, I dug upon your grave
    To bury a bone, in case
I should be hungry near this spot
When passing on my daily trot.
I am sorry, but I quite forgot   35
    It was your resting place."

In Time of "The Breaking of Nations"

This poem was written during World War I. The title is derived from a passage in the Bible: "Thou art my battle ax and weapons of war: for with thee will I break in pieces the nations" (Jeremiah 51:20).

Only a man harrowing clods
    In a slow silent walk
With an old horse that stumbles and nods
    Half asleep as they stalk.

Only thin smoke without flame   5
    From the heaps of couch-grass;°
Yet this will go onward the same
    Though Dynasties pass.

Yonder a maid and her wight°
    Come whispering by: 10
War's annals will fade into night
    Ere their story die.

---

6. **couch-grass:** a type of grass with long creeping root-stalks. 9. **wight:** young man, fellow.

FOR STUDY AND DISCUSSION

The Darkling Thrush
The vocabulary and imagery of the poem are directed mainly toward creating a sense of the bleakness and sadness of the winter landscape. In line 2, for example, the "Frost" is described as "specter-gray." How else does Hardy's language give to the wintry scene a dreariness that is more than just visual or physical?

The Man He Killed
1. Who is the speaker in this poem? What experience has he just gone through?
2. How does Hardy create the sense in this poem that human life is subject to circumstances and forces beyond our control? Why does the speaker pause and then repeat the word *because?*

Ah, Are You Digging on My Grave?
1. The rather grim irony in this poem is created through the interplay of two different voices. To whom does the first voice belong? What various guesses does this speaker make about the identity of the second speaker? Where in the poem is the identity of the second speaker finally revealed?
2. Hardy's poem may be seen as a satire on conventional romantic attitudes toward the death of young lovers. What sentimental or romantic attitudes are revealed in the questions of the first speaker? To what extent is the reader drawn into sharing these attitudes? How does the second speaker begin to undermine these attitudes even before revealing his own identity?

In Time of "The Breaking of Nations"
1. The three short stanzas of this poem present three examples of peaceful rural life. Describe these examples in your own words. What attitude does Hardy's speaker take toward these simple scenes or moments? What is the relation between these kinds of experiences and the "Dynasties" in line 8, or "War's annals" in line 11?
2. Hardy makes effective use in this poem of simple, "unpoetic" words like *clods* (line 1), and of old-fashioned words like *wight* (line 9). Find other examples of such language. Why are these words appropriate to Hardy's theme?

Gerard Manley Hopkins
1844–1889

Gerard Manley Hopkins
Oxford University Press

Although not widely read or appreciated until the twentieth century—his poems were not published until 1918—Hopkins is in many respects a deeply characteristic Victorian writer. He is, to be sure, a remarkable experimenter and innovator in the rhythm, vocabulary, and formal arrangements of English verse. As much as any other Victorian poet, including Browning, Hopkins has influenced the direction of modern English and American poetry. Yet in his expressions of intense spiritual anxiety and in his passionate devotion to the unique, particularized beauty of the natural world, he is very much a nineteenth-century poet. To read Hopkins well, we must learn to value the Victorian dimension of his writing as well as its advanced, forward-looking modernity.

Hopkins was born into a large and very religious English family. He was often unhappy while attending the Highgate School in northwest London, but in 1863 he went to study classics at Oxford University, and there his brilliant intellect and imagination began to flower. He was a student of Walter Pater, the eloquent late-Victorian spokesman for artistic experience as the only stable source of value in the modern world. And he was influenced by the Oxford Movement, which sought to revive the ritualistic and dogmatic traditions of the Church of England. The original leader of the Oxford Movement, John Henry Newman, had left the Church of England in 1845 to become a Roman Catholic. After a period of deep religious turmoil, Hopkins himself, under Newman's sponsorship, joined the Catholic Church in 1866. In 1868 he entered the Society of Jesus, one of the most intellectually demanding and disciplined orders of the Church. Before becoming a Jesuit, Hopkins burned all the poems he had written up to that time, feeling that his artistic interests were incompatible with strict devotion to his religious obligations. He did not begin writing poetry again until 1875 or 1876, and even then he resisted his friends' suggestion that he publish at least some of his work. In 1877 he became an ordained priest and served in a number of parishes, including one in a depressing working-class district of Liverpool. In 1884 he was appointed Professor of Classics at University College, Dublin. Hopkins died in Dublin of typhoid fever in 1889, when he was only forty-four. His poems were finally published in 1918 by his close friend, the poet Robert Bridges.

God's Grandeur

The world is charged with the grandeur of God.
    It will flame out, like shining from shook foil;°
    It gathers to a greatness, like the ooze of oil
Crushed. Why do men then now not reck his rod?°
Generations have trod, have trod, have trod;   5
    And all is seared with trade; bleared, smeared with toil;
    And wears man's smudge and shares man's smell: the soil
Is bare now, nor can foot feel, being shod.

And for all this, nature is never spent;
    There lives the dearest freshness deep down things;   10
And though the last lights off the black West went
    Oh, morning, at the brown brink eastward, springs—
Because the Holy Ghost over the bent
    World broods with warm breast and with ah! bright wings.

---

2. **foil:** tinfoil, or tinsel.   4. **reck his rod:** heed God's authority.

FOR STUDY AND DISCUSSION

1. According to the poet, how is the grandeur of God revealed through the physical world? What effect have human beings had on this grandeur?

2. Hopkins ends the poem with contrasting images of darkness and light. What is the source of light? In what way does the final image of the "bright wings" of the Holy Ghost look back to the beginning of the poem?

3. The image in the last two lines recalls a famous passage from the beginning of Milton's *Paradise Lost:* ". . . thou from the first / Wast present, and with mighty wings outspread / Dovelike sat'st brooding on the vast abyss / And mad'st it pregnant: what in me is dark / Illumine . . ." (Book I, lines 19-23). Which words and phrases from Milton's poem does Hopkins take over? In what way is the overall meaning of Milton's passage relevant to Hopkins' sonnet?

The Windhover

"Windhover" is another name for the kestrel, a type of falcon very similar to
the American sparrow hawk. It is a bird capable of extremely rapid flight
and also of hovering in the air in an almost stationary position.

To Christ Our Lord

I caught this morning morning's minion,° king-
    dom of daylight's dauphin, dapple-dawn-drawn Falcon, in
      his riding
    Of the rolling level underneath him steady air, and striding
High there, how he rung upon the rein of a wimpling° wing
In his ecstasy! then off, off forth on swing,   5
    As a skate's heel sweeps smooth on a bow-bend: the hurl
      and gliding
    Rebuffed the big wind. My heart in hiding
Stirred for a bird—the achieve of, the mastery of the thing!

Brute beauty and valor and act, oh, air, pride, plume, here
    Buckle! AND the fire that breaks from thee then, a billion   10
Times told lovelier, more dangerous, O my chevalier!°

    No wonder of it: shéer plód makes plough down sillion°
Shine, and blue-bleak embers, ah, my dear,
    Fall, gall themselves, and gash gold-vermilion.

---

1. **minion** (mĭn′-yən): favorite. 4. **wimpling:** rippling. 11. **chevalier** (shĕv-ə-lîr′):
knight. 12. **sillion:** ridge between two plow rows.

COMMENTARY

The poem is about and addresses the windhover (a
falcon) and Christ. It states that true greatness of
character shines out in the self-mastery that
ensues under stress and conflict with outward
forces. The greater a man is, the more is his true
glory revealed under the greatest odds. Thus, the
innate beauty of the windhover is revealed in its
meeting with and mastering of the *big wind*, just
as the true glory of Christ is revealed in His Passion and Crucifixion when He suffered and died for
the salvation of mankind. The heart of the poet, his
entire capacity and love, watches *in hiding*—that
is, watches in secret, abashed, and even from the
holy and withdrawn "retreat" of the Jesuit priest.
The bird is the favorite (*minion*) of the morning,
the prince of the kingdom of delight, and it rides
the rolling yet steady air beneath it like a horse,
sometimes striding on high, sometimes making a
swinging circle like the heel of a skater rounding a
bend. The poet's heart is stirred with admiration
for the achievement and mastery of the bird, and
he cries out that here, in this bird and in the world,
outward things like plumes and action, and inward
things like valor and pride, *buckle*—that is, under
stress and strain they gather together, are enclosed
and enclose (as in "buckle in"), are crumpled,
broken, and sacrificed ("buckle under"), and grapple and engage in battle ("buckle to"). The beauty
of the bird's mastery of the wind in joy, and the
beauty of Christ's mastery of the world and flesh in
sacrifice and death are one and the same thing. The
poet (continuing the metaphor of the horse) ad-

dresses both the bird and Christ as his knight (*chevalier*), from whose gallant and dangerous action a glorious radiance shines. There is nothing to wonder in this, says the poet, for the opposition which the plough meets as it cuts through the furrow (*sillion*) is what makes it shine, just as an ember, which seems blue and bleak with ash on the outside, as it falls through and meets the resistance of the air, is "wounded" and breaks open, revealing in its gashes the fiery, golden and vermilion inward flame. The use of such words as *fall*, *gall* and *gash* in the last line suggests the wounds and suffering of Christ and His Glory, the fire and glory that shine in His sacrifice.

—Kimon Friar and John Brinnin
Modern Poetry: American and British

FOR STUDY AND DISCUSSION

1. In the first eight lines of "The Windhover," how is the speaker affected by his sight of the bird as it hovers and wheels in flight? What does he mean by "My heart in hiding/Stirred for a bird"?
2. Hopkins first introduces the idea that the falcon makes him aware of qualities in Christ's power and glory that seem to contradict His meekness and humility (lines 9–11); then he concludes the poem with two images that, by way of further example, help us comprehend this mysterious contradiction. Describe these two images in your own words. How do the details of these images suggest both the paradoxical qualities of Christ and the physical appearance of the bird?

Pied Beauty

Glory be to God for dappled things—
    For skies of couple-color as a brinded° cow;
        For rose-moles all in stipple° upon trout that swim;
Fresh-firecoal chestnut-falls; finches' wings;
    Landscape plotted and pieced—fold, fallow, and plow;   5
        And áll trádes, their gear and tackle and trim.

All things counter, original, spare, strange;
    Whatever is fickle, freckled (who knows how?)
        With swift, slow; sweet, sour; adazzle, dim;
He fathers-forth° whose beauty is past change: 10
        Praise him.

---

2. **brinded:** streaked with dark hairs.   3. **stipple:** dots or spots.   10. **fathers-forth:** creates.

FOR STUDY AND DISCUSSION

1. What kind of beauty in the natural world is Hopkins celebrating in this poem? What specific examples of this kind of beauty does he give?
2. Hopkins begins and ends this poem by directing our attention to the source of the "pied beauty" in the world. Who is that source? In what way is His own beauty unlike that of the natural world "He fathers-forth" (line 10)?

3. The look and sound of individual words in "Pied Beauty" are important aspects of the poem's meaning. What do *dappled* (line 1), *couple-color* (line 2), and *stipple* (line 3) have in common? What other words in the poem can you relate to these through their look and sound? (Notice *plotted* in line 5, for example.) In what sense is Hopkins imitating in language the "pied beauty" he celebrates in nature? What does Hopkins mean by "All things counter"? How are they part of the "pied beauty"?

Spring and Fall: To a Young Child

In this poem an adult speaker addresses himself to the sadness a young girl feels about the autumnal decline and decay of nature's beauty. Homer says (in Pope's translation of the *Iliad*), "Like leaves on trees the race of man is found,/Now green in youth, now withering on the ground." The central theme of this poem might be said to be the same identification between the fall of the year and the young girl's intuitive sense that everything human must die.

Márgarét, are you gríeving
Over Goldengrove unleaving?
Leáves, líke the things of man, you
With your fresh thoughts care for, can you?
Ah! ás the heart grows older   5
It will come to such sights colder
By and by, nor spare a sigh
Though worlds of wanwood° leafmeal° lie;
And yet you wíll° weep and know why.
Now no matter, child, the name: 10
Sórrow's spríngs áre the same.
Nor° mouth had, no nor mind, expressed
What heart heard of, ghost guessed:
It ís the blight man was born for,
It is Margaret you mourn for.   15

---

8. **wanwood:** literally, pale wood.   **leafmeal:** dried and ground-up leaves. The adverbial use here suggests piecemeal or scattered.   9. **wíll:** Because line 9 is ambiguous, Hopkins puts an accent on the verb *will*. This accent distinguishes between a simple future action and a continuous, persistent one.   12. **Nor:** neither.

COMMENTARY

The beauty of this poem arises from the way in which Hopkins fuses two perspectives: the child's sorrow over the loss of nature's beauty, and the speaker's sorrow over the loss of innocence and the awareness of death. In the first half of the poem, the speaker seems to feel that Margaret's grief is naively misdirected, that as she grows older she will become more detached from and suspicious of natural beauty and "the things of man." But the second half of the poem turns upon his recognition that Margaret's sadness over autumnal decay is not misdirected, since it is both an anticipation of and a metaphor for the greater sadness of mortality that she will eventually come to feel: "Sórrow's springs áre the same." At the end of the poem, the speaker emphasizes the similarity, rather than the difference, between the death of a leaf and the death of a human being. The speaker also realizes that in grieving over the autumnal blighting of "Goldengrove," Margaret is grieving, appropriately and unconsciously, over the inevitable loss of her own childhood innocence.

The structural organization of the poem provides superb reinforcement for its meaning. The scheme of rhyme in the poem is six couplets, or pairs of consecutively rhymed lines—except for the middle, where the speaker's thoughts about Margaret shift (lines 7–9). Here the "sigh"/"lie" pair is extended into a third rhyme word, "and know *why*." Elsewhere in the poem, individual pairs of rhymes carry great thematic meaning: "grieving" and "unleaving," for instance, or "born for" and "mourn for." Hopkins' mastery of traditional poetic resources as well as of his own personal experiments with word combinations and word order is nowhere more delicately effective.

FOR STUDY AND DISCUSSION

1. What attitude does the speaker take toward Margaret at the beginning of the poem? In what way does the speaker's attitude shift?

2. *Fall* and *leaves* are both used as nouns in this poem. Because of the theme of the poem, these two words could also have been used as verbs. What things "fall" in this poem? What things "leave"? Remembering the Eden story in Genesis, and its

relation to death, what other "fall" is Hopkins suggesting here?

3. What exactly does the speaker mean when he says in line 11, "Sórrow's springs áre the same"? What does the plural "springs" refer to? Remember that the title of the poem is "Spring and Fall."

SPRUNG RHYTHM

Hopkins was passionately interested in rejuvenating the language of poetry and in opening up new sources of verbal expression. He discovered fresh power and vitality in the English language by using familiar words in unusual, often startling, contexts, by reviving ancient words, and by creating entirely new words based upon already existing words. His approach to the rhythm and meter of poetry was daringly original.

Hopkins' fascination with rhythm led to his popularization of a metrical system resembling natural speech and called *sprung rhythm*. As Hopkins himself explained his technique, "It consists in scanning by accents alone or stresses alone, so that a foot may be one strong syllable or it may be many light and one strong." Conventional poetic rhythm consists of a number of metrical feet each having a fixed number of stressed and unstressed syllables. Sprung rhythm differs from conventional rhythm in that it is not concerned with the number of syllables in a foot. The flexibility of sprung rhythm allows any kind of foot to follow any other. However, Hopkins most frequently used a foot consisting of a single stressed syllable or dactyls and trochees—that is, a stressed syllable followed by one or two unstressed syllables:

And fór all/this/na túre is/ név er/ spent.

It is not unusual in one of Hopkins' poems to find the startling combination of a number of stressed syllables followed by a succession of unstressed syllables.

Scan the first stanza of the poem "Pied Beauty," placing the stresses where you think they should fall. Is there an equal number of stresses in each line? What else besides verse stress contributes to the rhythm of this poem? Is the rhythm in keeping with the main thought and feeling of the poem? Explain.

A. E. Housman
1859–1936

A. E. Housman's poetic output was small and concentrated, both in the number of poems he published and in the succinctness of his individual lyrics. Yet he was regarded by many of his contemporaries as the finest lyric poet since Tennyson. By profession he was an eminent classical scholar, and as a poet his chief aim was to follow the lyric poets of classical antiquity in conveying emotional intensity and profundity by the simplest and most efficient poetic means possible.

Alfred Edward Housman was born in Worcestershire, a county in western England, near the Shropshire border. He studied classical literature and philosophy at Oxford University, but in 1881 he amazed his teachers and fellow students by failing his honors examination. He had to take a civil service job, but he continued to pursue classical studies independently, and he gradually built up an excellent reputation through his meticulous scholarly contributions to learned periodicals. His classical scholarship is characterized by an impersonal striving for accuracy that shows almost no trace of the poignant feelings often expressed in his poetry. He was a brilliant and bitter controversialist, capable of delivering the most savage attacks on other scholars with whom he disagreed. In 1892 Housman was made professor of Latin at University College, London, and from 1911 until his death in 1936 he held a similar professorship at Cambridge University.

Housman published only two small volumes of poems during his lifetime—*A Shropshire Lad* (1896) and *Last Poems* (1922). Most of the poems have a rural or pastoral setting, and many of them focus on the experiences of the "Shropshire lad," whom Housman himself described as "an imaginary figure, with something of my own temper and view of life." Housman's favorite subject is the ill-fated "lad" enacting his tragic and brief

Alfred Edward Housman
National Portrait Gallery, London

life against a background of the passing beauties and eternal patterns of the natural world. Housman is as aware as Hardy of the grimness and pain of life, but his awareness takes the form of a more subdued irony and a more poignant melancholy. In contrast to the often harsh, rugged qualities of Hardy's verse, Housman's writing has a smooth, carefully wrought cadence. In 1933 Housman gave a lecture entitled "The Name and Nature of Poetry," in which he argued that poetry had an almost physical effect on the reader, so intimate that it was impossible to analyze and explain it. For many readers Housman's finest poems create just this sort of direct intimacy.

To an Athlete Dying Young

The time you won your town the race
We chaired you through the market-
    place;
Man and boy stood cheering by,
And home we brought you shoulder-
    high.

Today, the road all runners come,   5
Shoulder-high we bring you home,
And set you at your threshold down,
Townsman of a stiller town.

Smart lad, to slip betimes away
From fields where glory does not stay   10
And early though the laurel grows
It withers quicker than the rose.

Eyes the shady night has shut
Cannot see the record cut,
And silence sounds no worse than
    cheers   15
After earth has stopped the ears:

Now you will not swell the rout
Of lads that wore their honors out,
Runners whom renown outran
And the name died before the man.   20

So set, before its echoes fade,
The fleet foot on the sill of shade,
And hold to the low lintel up
The still-defended challenge cup.

And round that early-laureled head   25
Will flock to gaze the strengthless
    dead,
And find unwithered on its curls
The garland briefer than a girl's.

Is My Team Ploughing

"Is my team ploughing,
    That I was used to drive
And hear the harness jingle
    When I was man alive?"

Aye, the horses trample,   5
    The harness jingles now;
No change though you lie under
    The land you used to plough.

"Is football playing
    Along the river shore,   10
With lads to chase the leather,
    Now I stand up no more?"

Aye, the ball is flying,
    The lads play heart and soul;
The goal stands up, the keeper   15
    Stands up to keep the goal.

"Is my girl happy,
    That I thought hard to leave,
And has she tired of weeping
    As she lies down at eve?"   20

Aye, she lies down lightly,
    She lies not down to weep:
Your girl is well contented.
    Be still, my lad, and sleep.

"Is my friend hearty,   25
    Now I am thin and pine,
And has he found to sleep in
    A better bed than mine?"

Yes, lad, I lie easy,
    I lie as lads would choose;   30
I cheer a dead man's sweetheart,
    Never ask me whose.

When I Was
One-and-Twenty

When I was one-and-twenty
  I heard a wise man say,
"Give crowns and pounds and guineas,
  But not your heart away;
Give pearls away and rubies   5
  But keep your fancy free."
But I was one-and-twenty,
  No use to talk to me.

When I was one-and-twenty
  I heard him say again,   10
"The heart out of the bosom
  Was never given in vain;
'Tis paid with sighs a plenty
  And sold for endless rue."
And I am two-and-twenty,   15
  And oh, 'tis true, 'tis true.

With Rue My
Heart Is Laden

With rue my heart is laden
  For golden friends I had,
For many a rose-lipt maiden
  And many a lightfoot lad.

By brooks too broad for leaping
  The lightfoot boys are laid;
The rose-lipt girls are sleeping
  In fields where roses fade.

FOR STUDY AND DISCUSSION

To an Athlete Dying Young
1. What two processions are contrasted in the opening stanzas of the poem? How does this contrast create a sense of the transience of life and the passing of earthly success and value?
2. In lines 9–20 of this poem, the speaker seems to praise the young athlete who has died. Why does he say that the young man was fortunate to have died so young? Does he really think him fortunate? How would you characterize the speaker's attitude toward death?
3. Several of the images in the poem are drawn from classical Greek and Roman traditions of athletic competition and triumph. The victorious procession described in the first stanza is one such classical image. What other classical details can you find in the poem? How do these details contribute to Housman's attitude and perspective?

Is My Team Ploughing
This poem is written in the form of a dialogue. Who is the first speaker? What aspects of the life he once knew does he ask about? Who does the second speaker turn out to be?

When I Was One-and-Twenty
1. What was the speaker's first reaction to the advice he was given? How does he feel about the advice now that he is a year older? What must have happened to him to make him change his mind?
2. Housman is often praised for the succinctness with which he expresses emotion in his poems. What evidence can you find in "When I Was One-and-Twenty" to support this view? Look particularly at the last two lines of each stanza.

With Rue My Heart Is Laden
What does Housman convey about the speaker's sadness through the two contrasting images of nature in the last stanza—the "brooks too broad for leaping" and the "fields where roses fade"? How do these natural images relate to the repeated epithets applied to the speaker's friends, "lightfoot" (lines 4 and 6) and "rose-lipt" (lines 3 and 7)?

FOR COMPOSITION

Housman's poetry has been said to reveal "a bitter but fearless philosophy." Write a composition in which you agree or disagree with this statement, citing evidence from Housman's poems.

Other Victorian Poets

Although Victorian poetry had its major figures—Tennyson, Browning, Arnold—it was by no means totally dominated by these writers or confined to their particular styles. It has been said, in fact, that extreme variety of style and theme is the most striking characteristic of the poetry of this period. The other Victorian poets represented in this section reveal a fascinating array of subjects and attitudes.

Some of these Victorian poets have become, like Hardy, better known for their novels than for their poems. George Meredith (1828–1909) is remembered today mainly as the author of such novels as *The Ordeal of Richard Feverel* (1859) and *The Egoist* (1879). But he also produced some extremely powerful and subtle poetry, including a sequence of sixteen-line sonnets called *Modern Love* (1862). A novelist-poet of a very different sort is Robert Louis Stevenson (1850–1894). Today we know him best through his romantic adventure novels and short stories: *Treasure Island* (1883), *The Strange Case of Dr. Jekyll and Mr. Hyde* (1886), *Kidnapped* (1886), and numerous others. But he also wrote several collections of well-crafted and memorable poems. These include the popular *Child's Garden of Verses* (1885), and a volume published in 1887 entitled *Underwoods*, from which the poem "Requiem" is taken.

Two interesting mid-Victorian poets were famous—or perhaps one should say notorious—for exploring states of mind and emotion that many Victorian readers considered shockingly offensive. Dante Gabriel Rossetti (1828–1882), the son of an Italian patriot who had been forced to emigrate to England, was a painter and poet who, when he was just twenty years old, helped found the Pre-Raphaelite Brotherhood. The painters and writers who joined Rossetti in this group wished to revitalize English art by returning to the simple designs and pure colors that prevailed in Italian painting before the time of Raphael, the great Renaissance master. Rossetti himself was particularly obsessed with an imaginary ideal of feminine beauty, an ideal inspired both by Dante and other early Italian poets and by Keats. In 1850 Rossetti found what he thought was a living embodiment of that ideal in Elizabeth Siddall, the favorite model of the Pre-Raphaelite painters. Much of Rossetti's poetry was inspired by his love for her. But their relationship was a troubled one, and in 1862, two years after they were married, Elizabeth committed suicide. Rossetti was stricken with grief and guilt, and in a romantic gesture he buried the manuscripts of his poems with her. Several years later he had second thoughts. The manuscripts were dug up, and in 1870 Rossetti published them as a series of sonnets called *The House of Life*. Rossetti's poetic exploration of the relation of the spirit to the body in human love was violently attacked as immoral in a pamphlet entitled "The Fleshly School of Poetry." The attack contributed to the mental instability that plagued Rossetti for the rest of his life.

The poetry of Algernon Charles Swinburne (1837–1909) threatened the Victorian sense of decency even more than Rossetti's. Swinburne came from a conservative upper-class English background and had attended Eton and Oxford University. But he rebelled against established codes of behavior and sought out the bohemian artistic worlds of Paris and London. For a time he was closely associated with Rossetti and the Pre-Raphaelites. His collection of *Poems and Ballads* (1866) often treats human love in ways mid-Victorian readers found scandalous, but Swinburne's poems have undeniably stunning rhythmical and musical effects. Although sometimes criticized for subordinating the meaning of his verse to beautiful, seductive sounds, Swinburne's best poems, such as "When the Hounds of Spring" from *Atalanta in Calydon*, fuse sound, image, atmosphere, and idea in a way that enhances each of these elements, as the following stanza shows:

> The full streams feed on flower of rushes,
> Ripe grasses trammel a traveling foot,
> The faint fresh flame of the young year flushes
> From leaf to flower and flower to fruit,
> And fruit and leaf are as gold and fire,
> And the oat is heard above the lyre,
> And the hoofèd heel of a satyr crushes
> The chestnut-husk at the chestnut-root . . .
> (lines 33–40)

The Victorian Age produced a number of fine women poets. Before she met Robert Browning and married him in 1846, Elizabeth Barrett (1806–1861) was a better-known poet than he was. During their courtship she wrote a series of forty-four sonnets celebrating their love. When she showed the poems to Browning after their marriage, he immediately insisted that they be published. Because of their private nature, they were given the deliberately misleading title of *Sonnets from the Portuguese,* as if Elizabeth had translated the poems from that language. Browning thought them "the finest sonnets in any language since Shakespeare." The judgment is understandably exaggerated, but the best of the *Sonnets* do possess a fervent and arresting eloquence that may remind us of the Elizabethans.

In many people's view the finest woman poet of the Victorian era was Christina Rossetti (1830–1894), the sister of Dante Gabriel Rossetti. In character and poetic temperament Christina and Dante Gabriel were completely different. Christina was a devout adherent of the more formal tradition within the Church of England, and twice in her life, with feelings of great frustration and loss, she rejected proposals of marriage because she thought they conflicted with her Christian duty. Although her volume of 1862, *Goblin Market and Other Poems,* reflects the Pre-Raphaelite interest in stylistic simplicity, her poems display a unique lyric intensity. They are the finely wrought products of a sensibility shaped by painful and difficult self-sacrifice.

One of the most amazing writers of the nineteenth century was Emily Brontë (1818–1848). Raised in a small, isolated village in northern England and with almost no contact with other children or families, Emily joined her sisters Anne and Charlotte, who also became writers, and her brother Branwell, who became an artist, in creating their own world of exotic childhood fiction. Emily's poems were originally part of this early fiction, and they often contain personages and motifs that belong to the imaginary kingdom she called Gondal. The major work of Emily Brontë's mature imagination is *Wuthering Heights,* one of the greatest novels in English literature. It was published in 1847, a year before she died of tuberculosis. Like this remarkable novel, her poems, published with her sisters' in 1846, are full of a fierce, haunting passion, and an uncanny sensitivity to the wild grandeur of the countryside where she spent her short life.

Elizabeth Barrett Browning
National Portrait Gallery, London

from **Sonnets from the Portuguese**
Elizabeth Barrett Browning

14

If thou must love me, let it be for nought
Except for love's sake only. Do not say
"I love her for her smile—her look—her way
Of speaking gently—for a trick of thought
That falls in well with mine, and certes° brought   5
A sense of pleasant ease on such a day"—
For these things in themselves, Belovèd, may
Be changed, or change for thee,—and love, so wrought,
May be unwrought so. Neither love me for
Thine own dear pity's wiping my cheeks dry—   10
A creature might forget to weep, who bore
Thy comfort long, and lose thy love thereby!
But love me for <u>love's</u> sake, that evermore
Thou may'st love on, through love's eternity.

---

5. **certes:** certainly.

43

How do I love thee? Let me count the ways.
I love thee to the depth and breadth and height
My soul can reach, when feeling out of sight
For the ends of Being and ideal Grace.
I love thee to the level of every day's   5
Most quiet need, by sun and candlelight.
I love thee freely, as men strive for Right;
I love thee purely, as they turn from Praise.
I love thee with the passion put to use
In my old griefs, and with my childhood's faith.   10
I love thee with a love I seemed to lose
With my lost saints,—I love thee with the breath,
Smiles, tears, of all my life!—and, if God choose,
I shall but love thee better after death.

The Woodspurge   *Dante Gabriel Rossetti*

The wind flapped loose, the wind was still,
Shaken out dead from tree and hill;
I had walked on at the wind's will—
I sat now, for the wind was still.

Between my knees my forehead was—   5
My lips, drawn in, said not Alas!
My hair was over in the grass,
My naked ears heard the day pass.

My eyes, wide open, had the run
Of some ten weeds to fix upon;   10
Among those few, out of the sun,
The woodspurge flowered, three cups in one.

From perfect grief there need not be
Wisdom or even memory;
One thing then learned remains to me—   15
The woodspurge has a cup of three.

Silent Noon   *Dante Gabriel Rossetti*

Your hands lie open in the long fresh grass,—
The finger-points look through like rosy blooms:
Your eyes smile peace. The pasture gleams and glooms
'Neath billowing skies that scatter and amass.
All round our nest, far as the eye can pass,   5
Are golden kingcup-fields with silver edge
Where the cow parsley skirts the hawthorn hedge.
'Tis visible silence, still as the hourglass.
Deep in the sun-searched growths the dragonfly
Hangs like a blue thread loosened from the sky—   10
So this winged hour is dropped to us from above.
Oh! clasp we to our hearts, for deathless dower,
This close-companioned inarticulate hour
When twofold silence was the song of love.

Song   *Emily Brontë*

The linnet in the rocky dells,
  The moor lark in the air,
The bee among the heather bells
  That hide my lady fair:

The wild deer browse above her breast;   5
  The wild birds raise their brood;
And they, her smiles of love caressed,
  Have left her solitude.

I ween that, when the grave's dark wall
  Did first her form retain,   10
They thought their hearts could ne'er recall
  The light of joy again.

They thought the tide of grief would flow
  Unchecked through future years;
But where is all their anguish now,   15
  And where are all their tears?

Well, let them fight for honor's breath,
  Or pleasures shade pursue—
The dweller in the land of death
  Is changed and careless too.   20

And, if their eyes should watch and weep
  Till sorrow's source were dry,
She would not, in her tranquil sleep,
  Return a single sigh.

Blow, west wind, by the lonely mound,   25
  And murmur, summer streams!
There is no need of other sound
  To soothe my lady's dreams.

Lucifer in Starlight   *George Meredith*

On a starred night Prince Lucifer uprose.
Tired of his dark dominion swung the fiend
Above the rolling ball in cloud part screened,
Where sinners hugged their specter of repose.
Poor prey to his hot fit of pride were those.   5
And now upon his western wing he leaned,
Now his huge bulk o'er Afric's sands careened,
Now the black planet shadowed Arctic snows.
Soaring through wider zones that pricked his scars
With memory of the old revolt from Awe,   10
He reached the middle height, and at the stars,
Which are the brain of heaven, he looked, and sank.
Around the ancient track marched, rank on rank,
The army of unalterable law.

Sleeping at Last   *Christina Rossetti*

Sleeping at last, the trouble and tumult over,
   Sleeping at last, the struggle and horror past,
Cold and white, out of sight of friend and of lover,
        Sleeping at last.

   No more a tired heart downcast or overcast,   5
No more pangs that wring or shifting fears that hover,
   Sleeping at last in a dreamless sleep locked fast.

Fast asleep. Singing birds in their leafy cover
   Cannot wake her, nor shake her the gusty blast.
Under the purple thyme and the purple clover   10
        Sleeping at last.

Requiem   *Robert Louis Stevenson*

Under the wide and starry sky,
Dig the grave and let me lie.
Glad did I live and gladly die,
   And I laid me down with a will.

This be the verse you grave for me:
Here he lies where he longed to be;
Home is the sailor, home from sea,
   And the hunter home from the hill.

FOR STUDY AND DISCUSSION

Sonnets from the Portuguese
1. In Sonnet 14, what does the speaker mean when she asks to be loved "for love's sake only" (line 2)? Why does she not wish to be loved for more particular qualities in herself, or for more particular emotions in the person to whom she is speaking?
2. How does the speaker in Sonnet 43 define the scope and the all-consuming intensity of her love? What images does she use to convey the sense that she loves with her entire being? What does the definition of her love suggest about the character of the person to whom she is speaking?
3. Study the poet's handling of traditional sonnet form. Does she follow the Petrarchan or the Shakespearean pattern? Find specific ways in which she uses the rhyming patterns of the sonnet to organize and emphasize her meaning.
4. The sonnets of Elizabeth Barrett Browning are considered by many to be the most genuine and the most skilled expressions of love in English literature. These critics point to the emotional unity of her poems, to her sensitivity in choosing the exact words and details necessary to convey her feelings. Others think that the feelings in these sonnets are overexpressed, that her poems attempt to communicate more emotion than is appropriate to the means, or that the poet has not set forth sufficient concrete details to support her feelings. Form your own opinion on these questions with special attention to Sonnet 43.

The Woodspurge
1. Although the speaker does not reveal his grief directly until the last four lines, his grief is hinted at in various details earlier in the poem. What, for example, is the relationship between the speaker and the wind in lines 1–4? What does this relationship suggest? What other details anticipate the "perfect grief" in line 13?
2. The speaker's precise observation of an aspect of nature grows out of his sense of almost total exhaustion and passivity. Why do you think his attention has been caught by the woodspurge, with its "three cups in one," flowering "out of the sun" (lines 11–12)? Why has his observation of this fact remained with him? Compare the psychological significance of precise observation of nature in this poem with that in "Silent Noon."

Silent Noon
1. The primary goal of the poet is to convey a sense of deep silence. Do you think that the clarity of detail and the specifically named objects contribute to the mood of the poem? Give reasons for your opinion.
2. The rhyme scheme of this sonnet is *abba, acca, dd, effe*. What is the effect of having a couplet between two quatrains? Where is the turning point in the sonnet?

Song

1. Who is the speaker in the poem? Where is the "lady fair" whom he addresses in the poem? To whom is the speaker referring when he says, in lines 7–8: "And they, her smiles of love caressed,/ Have left her solitude"?

2. What attitude does the speaker take toward the wild creatures and forces of nature? What does the separation of his "lady fair" from all human contact and emotion except his own ("The dweller in the land of death / Is changed and careless too," lines 19–20) have to do with his attitude toward nature?

Lucifer in Starlight

1. George Meredith's sonnet dramatizes Satan's attempt to escape from Hell ("his dark dominion," line 2) where God had confined him after his revolt in Heaven ("the old revolt from Awe," line 10). Why does looking up cause Satan to "sink"? Who make up the "army" that "marched, rank on rank" (line 13) around the "ancient track"?

2. Compare Meredith's account of Satan's rebellion against God and confinement in Hell with Milton's in *Paradise Lost* (Book I, lines 27–49). Which details from Milton's account does Meredith's sonnet make us remember? What does Meredith add with his emphasis on stars? (You may find it helpful to know that Lucifer, in addition to being another name for Satan, is also another name for the morning star. See the Biblical references to this in Revelation 9:1 and 12:7–10, and in Luke 10:18.)

Sleeping at Last

1. The attitude toward death expressed in the poem is closely tied to the speaker's attitude toward life. What has life been like for the speaker? How do the references to nature in the final stanza alter the feeling about life conveyed in lines 1–7?

2. Study Christina Rossetti's use of verbal repetition. What effect is produced by the repeated phrase "Sleeping at last"? How is the word *last* related in meaning to the other words in the poem with which it rhymes: *past* (line 2), *downcast* or *overcast* (line 5), *fast* (line 7), *blast* (line 9)?

Requiem

1. Where does the speaker wish to be buried? Why is the location appropriate, given the references to "the sailor" and "the hunter" in the last two lines of the poem?

2. Robert Louis Stevenson's "Requiem" is an interesting version of an *epitaph*, a poem conceived as an inscription on a gravestone or monument. Which part of this poem is the actual epitaph? In what sense is this a poem within a poem?

Victorian Prose

Charles Dickens
1812–1870

In the early years of the nineteenth century, the great majority of public institutions in England — schools, courts, prisons, hospitals, and poorhouses — were in a deplorable condition. The spirit of reform aroused by these abuses found its most able and effective champion in Charles Dickens.

The son of a government clerk who became bankrupt and was thrown into prison, Dickens received little education and was forced to work in a factory at an early age. Many of the unhappy experiences of his youth are related in the semiau-tobiographical *David Copperfield.* While working as a newspaper reporter in London at the age of twenty-two, Dickens began his *Sketches by Boz.* Soon afterward he achieved fame and fortune through the publication of *Pickwick Papers,* another series of rambling adventures, which appeared in a monthly magazine. Acclaimed as the most popular fiction writer of his day, he succeeded Sir Walter Scott in the affection of the reading public in both Great Britain and the United States and soon became well known for platform readings from his works throughout Europe and the United States. Dickens was a strange, divided man, but for the art of fiction he had a blazing genius. It has been said that he had the power to create scores of characters who talk themselves alive.

Dickens' Dream (pen and watercolor) by R. W. Buss.
The Dickens House

from **Hard Times**

Hard Times, Charles Dickens' tenth major novel, was published in 1854. It originally appeared in weekly installments in Dickens' own periodicals, *Household Words* and *All the Year Round.* Written shortly after Dickens had visited the grimy, depressing industrial cities of northern England, *Hard Times* expresses more directly than any of his previous novels Dickens' sense of the brutal living conditions in such areas and of the attitudes responsible for their existence. *Hard Times* remains one of the most powerful attacks ever made on the inhumanity of an industrial, materialistic society.

The novel takes place in Coketown, a fictional version of a city like those Dickens had actually visited. In the opening chapters we are introduced to Thomas Gradgrind, a prominent citizen and educator ruthlessly committed to a narrow version of the Utilitarian theory of education. We see Gradgrind's theory put into practice in the second chapter of the novel, printed below, when, on a visit to his school, he bullies one of the students, Sissy Jupe, with his doctrine of "Fact, fact, fact."

from **Chapter 2**

Murdering the Innocents

Thomas Gradgrind, Sir. A man of realities. A man of facts and calculations. A man who proceeds upon the principle that two and two are four, and nothing over, and who is not to be talked into allowing for anything over. Thomas Gradgrind, Sir—peremptorily Thomas—Thomas Gradgrind. With a rule and a pair of scales, and the multiplication table always in his pocket, Sir, ready to weigh and measure any parcel of human nature, and tell you exactly what it comes to. It is a mere question of figures, a case of simple arithmetic. You might hope to get some other nonsensical belief into the head of George Gradgrind, or Augustus Gradgrind, or John Gradgrind, or Joseph Gradgrind (all supposititious,[1] nonexistent persons), but into the head of Thomas Gradgrind—no, Sir!

In such terms Mr. Gradgrind always mentally introduced himself, whether to his private circle of acquaintance, or to the public in general. In such terms, no doubt, substituting the words "boys and girls," for "Sir," Thomas Gradgrind now presented Thomas Gradgrind to the little pitchers before him, who were to be filled so full of facts.

Indeed, as he eagerly sparkled at them from the cellarage before mentioned, he seemed a kind of cannon loaded to the muzzle with facts, and prepared to blow them clean out of the regions of childhood at one discharge. He seemed a galvanizing apparatus, too, charged with a grim mechanical substitute for the tender young imaginations that were to be stormed away.

"Girl number twenty," said Mr. Gradgrind, squarely pointing with his square forefinger, "I don't know that girl. Who is that girl?"

"Sissy Jupe, Sir," explained number twenty, blushing, standing up, and curtseying.

"Sissy is not a name," said Mr. Gradgrind. "Don't call yourself Sissy. Call yourself Cecilia."

---

1. **supposititious** (sə-pŏz'ə-tĭsh'əs): supposed, conjectural, imaginary.

A Victorian schoolroom.
The Reverend Thomas
Guthrie in his school in
Edinburgh (c. 1857).
Radio Times Hulton

"It's father as calls me Sissy, Sir," returned the young girl in a trembling voice, and with another curtsey.

"Then he has no business to do it," said Mr. Gradgrind. "Tell him he mustn't. Cecilia Jupe. Let me see. What is your father?"

"He belongs to the horse-riding, if you please, Sir."

Mr. Gradgrind frowned, and waved off the objectionable calling with his hand.

"We don't want to know anything about that, here. You mustn't tell us about that, here. Your father breaks horses, don't he?"

"If you please, Sir, when they can get any to break, they do break horses in the ring, Sir."

"You mustn't tell us about the ring, here. Very well, then. Describe your father as a horsebreaker. He doctors sick horses, I dare say?"

"Oh yes, Sir."

"Very well, then. He is a veterinary surgeon, a farrier, and horsebreaker. Give me your definition of a horse."

(Sissy Jupe thrown into the greatest alarm by this demand.)

"Girl number twenty unable to define a horse!" said Mr. Gradgrind, for the general behoof of all the little pitchers. "Girl number twenty possessed of no facts, in reference to one of the commonest of animals! Some boy's definition of a horse. Bitzer, yours."

The square finger, moving here and there, lighted suddenly on Bitzer, perhaps because he chanced to sit in the same ray of sunlight which, darting in at one of the bare windows of the intensely whitewashed room, irradiated Sissy. For, the boys and girls sat on the face of the inclined plane in two compact bodies, divided up the center by a narrow interval; and Sissy, being at the corner of a row on the sunny side, came in for the beginning of a sunbeam, of which Bitzer, being at the corner of a row on the other side, a few rows in advance, caught the end. But, whereas the girl was so dark-eyed and dark-haired that she seemed to receive a deeper and more lustrous color from the sun, when it shone upon her, the boy was so light-eyed and light-haired that the selfsame rays appeared to draw out of him what little color he ever possessed. His cold eyes would hardly have been eyes, but for the short ends of lashes which, by bringing them into immediate contrast with something paler than themselves, expressed their form. His short-cropped hair might have been a mere continuation of the sandy freckles on his forehead and face. His skin was so unwholesomely deficient in the natural tinge that he looked as though, if he were cut, he would bleed white.

"Bitzer," said Thomas Gradgrind. "Your definition of a horse."

"Quadruped. Graminivorous.[2] Forty teeth, namely, twenty-four grinders, four eye-teeth, and twelve incisive. Sheds coat in the spring; in marshy countries, sheds hoofs, too. Hoofs hard, but requiring to be shod with iron. Age known by marks in mouth." Thus (and much more) Bitzer.

"Now girl number twenty," said Mr. Gradgrind. "You know what a horse is."

She curtseyed again, and would have blushed deeper, if she could have blushed deeper than she had blushed all this time. Bitzer, after rapidly blinking at Thomas Gradgrind with both eyes at once, and so catching the light upon his quivering ends of lashes that they looked like the antennae of busy insects, put his knuckles to his freckled forehead, and sat down again.

The third gentleman now stepped forth. A mighty man at cutting and drying, he was; a government officer; in his way (and in most other people's too), a professed pugilist; always in training, always with a system to force down the general throat like a bolus,[3] always to be heard of at the bar of his little Public-office, ready to fight all England. To continue in fistic phraseology, he had a genius for coming up to the scratch, wherever and whatever it was, and proving himself an ugly customer. He would go in and damage any subject whatever with his right, follow up with his left, stop, exchange, counter, bore his opponent (he always fought All England) to the ropes, and fall upon him neatly. He was certain to knock the wind out of common sense, and render that unlucky adversary deaf to the call of time. And he had it in charge from high authority to bring about the great public-office Millennium,[4] when Commissioners should reign upon earth.

"Very well," said this gentleman, briskly smiling, and folding his arms. "That's a horse. Now, let me ask you girls and boys, Would you paper a room with representations of horses?"

After a pause, one half of the children cried in chorus, "Yes, Sir!" Upon which the other half, seeing in the gentleman's face that Yes was wrong, cried out in chorus, "No, Sir!"—as the custom is, in these examinations.

"Of course, No. Why wouldn't you?"

A pause. One corpulent slow boy, with a wheezy manner of breathing, ventured the answer, Because he wouldn't paper a room at all, but would paint it.

"You *must* paper it," said the gentleman, rather warmly.

"You must paper it," said Thomas Gradgrind, "whether you like it or not. Don't tell *us* you wouldn't paper it. What do you mean, boy?"

"I'll explain to you, then," said the gentleman, after another and a dismal pause, "why you wouldn't paper a room with representations of horses. Do you ever see horses walking up and down the sides of rooms in reality—in fact? Do you?"

"Yes, Sir!" from one half. "No, Sir!" from the other.

"Of course, No," said the gentleman, with an indignant look at the wrong half. "Why, then, you are not to see anywhere, what you

---

2. **graminivorous** (grăm′ə-nĭv′ər-əs): feeding on grass.
3. **bolus** (bō′ləs): a large pill.

4. **Millennium** (mə-lĕn′ē-əm): a hoped-for golden age; a period of great happiness, peace, and prosperity.

don't see in fact; you are not to have anywhere, what you don't have in fact. What is called Taste, is only another name for Fact."

Thomas Gradgrind nodded his approbation.

"This is a new principle, a discovery, a great discovery," said the gentleman. "Now, I'll try you again. Suppose you were going to carpet a room. Would you use a carpet having a representation of flowers upon it?"

There being a general conviction by this time that "No, Sir!" was always the right answer to this gentleman, the chorus of No was very strong. Only a few feeble stragglers said Yes: among them Sissy Jupe.

"Girl number twenty," said the gentleman, smiling in the calm strength of knowledge.

Sissy blushed, and stood up.

"So you would carpet your room—or your husband's room, if you were a grown woman, and had a husband—with representations of flowers, would you?" said the gentleman. "Why would you?"

"If you please, Sir, I am very fond of flowers," returned the girl.

"And is that why you would put tables and chairs upon them, and have people walking over them with heavy boots?"

"It wouldn't hurt them, Sir. They wouldn't crush, and wither, if you please, Sir. They would be the pictures of what was very pretty and pleasant, and I would fancy—"

"Aye, aye, aye! But you mustn't fancy," cried the gentleman, quite elated by coming so happily to his point. "That's it! You are never to fancy."

"You are not, Cecilia Jupe," Thomas Gradgrind solemnly repeated, "to do anything of that kind."

"Fact, fact, fact!" said the gentleman. And "Fact, fact, fact!" repeated Thomas Gradgrind.

"You are to be in all things regulated and governed," said the gentleman, "by fact. We hope to have, before long, a board of fact, composed of commissioners of fact, who will force the people to be a people of fact, and of nothing but fact. You must discard the word Fancy altogether. You have nothing to do with it. You are not to have, in any object of use or ornament, what would be a contradiction in fact. You don't walk upon flowers in fact; you cannot be allowed to walk upon flowers in carpets. You don't find that foreign birds and butterflies come and perch upon your crockery; you cannot be permitted to paint foreign birds and butterflies upon your crockery. You never meet with quadrupeds going up and down walls; you must not have quadrupeds represented upon walls. You must use," said the gentleman, "for all these purposes, combinations and modifications (in primary colors) of mathematical figures which are susceptible of proof and demonstration. This is the new discovery. This is fact. This is taste."

The girl curtseyed, and sat down. She was very young, and she looked as if she were frightened by the matter-of-fact prospect the world afforded. . . .

FOR STUDY AND DISCUSSION

1. What is Thomas Gradgrind's basic attitude toward human experience? Why is he described with "a rule and a pair of scales, and the multiplication table always in his pocket"? What attitude does Dickens want the reader to take toward Gradgrind? **2.** According to the government officer, why should one never carpet a room with representations of flowers? How does Sissy Jupe respond to the teacher's argument? How does Dickens use this exchange to dramatize the stupidity of denying the value of "fancy" or the imagination?

FOR COMPOSITION

One of the main techniques of satire in Dickens' novels is *caricature*—the use of exaggeration or distortion to make a figure appear comic or ridiculous. Write an essay about Bitzer, the student whose definition of a horse Mr. Gradgrind finds so satisfactory. Point out what elements of caricature Dickens uses and what aspects of Gradgrind's theory of education he satirizes.

The Three Strangers   *Thomas Hardy*

That Thomas Hardy was equally concerned in his short stories as in his novels and poems with the part that chance, or fate, plays in people's lives is evident in "The Three Strangers." The setting of this story is the remote and wind-swept downs of "Wessex," a name Hardy used for the six southwest counties of England, including his native Dorset. The sense of specific place is always strong in Hardy's fiction and poetry. Here his rich use of local color acquaints us with a rural celebration—with the mead-drinking, the singing and dancing, the Wessex dialect, and the homely philosophy of the people. For a detailed account of the author's life, see page 586.

Among the few features of agricultural England which retain an appearance but little modified by the lapse of centuries may be reckoned the high, grassy and furzy downs, coombs,[1] or ewe-leases, as they are indifferently called, that fill a large area of certain counties in the south and southwest. If any mark of human occupation is met with hereon, it usually takes the form of the solitary cottage of some shepherd.

Fifty years ago such a lonely cottage stood on such a down, and may possibly be standing there now. In spite of its loneliness, however, the spot, by actual measurement, was not more than five miles from a county town. Yet that affected it little. Five miles of irregular upland, during the long inimical seasons, with their sleets, snows, rains, and mists, afford withdrawing space enough to isolate a Timon[2] or a Nebuchadnezzar;[3] much less, in fair weather, to please that less repellent tribe, the poets, philosophers, artists, and others who "conceive and meditate of pleasant things."

Some old earthen camp or barrow,[4] some clump of trees, at least some starved fragment of ancient hedge is usually taken advantage of in the erection of these forlorn dwellings. But, in the present case, such a kind of shelter had been disregarded. Higher Crowstairs, as the house was called, stood quite detached and undefended. The only reason for its precise situation seemed to be the crossing of two footpaths at right angles hard by, which may have crossed there and thus for a good five hundred years. Hence the house was exposed to the elements on all sides. But, though the wind up here blew unmistakably when it did blow, and the rain hit hard whenever it fell, the various weathers of the winter season were not quite so formidable on the coomb as they were imagined to be by dwellers on low ground. The raw rimes[5] were not so pernicious as in the hollows, and the frosts were scarcely so severe. When the shepherd and his family who tenanted the house were pitied for their sufferings from the exposure, they said that upon the whole they were less incon-

---

1. **coombs** (kōōms): open uplands.
2. **Timon** (tī'mən): a Greek of the fifth century who hated people and preferred to live in a cave.
3. **Nebuchadnezzar** (nĕb'ə-kəd-nĕz'ər): a Babylonian king who went to live alone in the fields when he became insane.

4. **barrow:** a hill or mound, often an ancient burial ground.
5. **rimes** (rīms): white frost.

venienced by "wuzzes and flames" (hoarses and phlegms) than when they had lived by the stream of a snug neighboring valley.

The night of March 28, 182— was precisely one of the nights that were wont to call forth these expressions of commiseration. The level rainstorm smote walls, slopes, and hedges like the clothyard shafts of Senlac[6] and Crécy.[7] Such sheep and outdoor animals as had no shelter stood with their buttocks to the winds; while the tails of little birds trying to roost on some scraggy thorn were blown inside out like umbrellas. The gable-end of the cottage was stained with wet, and the eaves-droppings flapped against the wall. Yet never was commiseration for the shepherd more misplaced. For that cheerful rustic was entertaining a large party in glorification of the christening of his second girl.

The guests had arrived before the rain began to fall, and they were all now assembled in the chief or living room of the dwelling. A glance into the apartment at eight o'clock on this eventful evening would have resulted in the opinion that it was as cozy and comfortable a nook as could be wished for in boisterous weather. The calling of its inhabitant was proclaimed by a number of highly polished sheep crooks without stems that were hung ornamentally over the fireplace, the curl of each shining crook varying from the antiquated type engraved in the patriarchal pictures of old family Bibles to the most approved fashion of the last local sheep fair. The room was lighted by half a dozen candles having wicks only a trifle smaller than the grease which enveloped them, in candlesticks that were never used but at high days, holy days, and family feasts. The lights were scattered about the room, two of them standing on the

chimney piece. This position of candles was in itself significant. Candles on the chimney piece always meant a party.

On the hearth, in front of a backbrand to give substance, blazed a fire of thorns, that crackled "like the laughter of the fool."

Nineteen persons were gathered here. Of these, five women, wearing gowns of various bright hues, sat in chairs along the wall; girls shy and not shy filled the window bench; four men, including Charley Jake, the hedge carpenter, Elijah New, the parish clerk, and John Pitcher, a neighboring dairyman, the shepherd's father-in-law, lolled in the settle; a young man and maid, who were blushing over tentative *pourparlers*[8] on a life companionship, sat beneath the corner cupboard; and an elderly engaged man of fifty or upward moved restlessly about from spots where his betrothed was not to the spot where she was. Enjoyment was pretty general, and so much the more prevailed in being unhampered by conventional restrictions. Absolute confidence in each other's good opinion begat perfect ease, while the finishing stroke of manner, amounting to a truly princely serenity, was lent to the majority by the absence of any expression or trait denoting that they wished to get on in the world, enlarge their minds, or do any eclipsing thing whatever— which nowadays so generally nips the bloom and bonhomie[9] of all except the two extremes of the social scale.

Shepherd Fennel had married well, his wife being a dairyman's daughter from a vale at a distance, who brought fifty guineas in her pocket—and kept them there, till they should be required for ministering to the needs of a coming family. This frugal woman had been somewhat exercised as to the character that

---

6. **Senlac:** hill near Hastings in southeastern England, where the Normans defeated the Saxons in 1066.
7. **Crécy** (krā-sē'): town in northern France where English archers defeated the French in 1346 during the Hundred Years War between France and England. The *clothyard shafts* referred to are the yard-long arrows of the English archers.

8. *pourparlers* (pŏŏr'pär-lāz'): informal discussions (French).
9. **bonhomie** (bŏn'ə-mē'): good nature (French).

should be given to the gathering. A sit-still party had its advantages; but an undisturbed position of ease in chairs and settles was apt to lead on the men to such an unconscious deal of toping[10] that they would sometimes fairly drink the house dry. A dancing party was the alternative; but this, while avoiding the foregoing objection on the score of good drink, had a counterbalancing disadvantage in the matter of good victuals, the ravenous appetites engendered by the exercise causing immense havoc in the buttery. Shepherdess Fennel fell back upon the intermediate plan of mingling short dances with short periods of talk and singing, so as to hinder any ungovernable rage in either. But this scheme was entirely confined to her own gentle mind: the shepherd himself was in the mood to exhibit the most reckless phases of hospitality.

The fiddler was a boy of those parts, about twelve years of age, who had a wonderful dexterity in jigs and reels, though his fingers were so small and short as to necessitate a constant shifting for the high notes, from which he scrambled back to the first position with sounds not of unmixed purity of tone. At seven the shrill tweedle-dee of this youngster had begun, accompanied by a booming ground bass from Elijah New, the parish clerk, who had thoughtfully brought with him his favorite musical instrument, the serpent.[11] Dancing was instantaneous, Mrs. Fennel privately enjoining the players on no account to let the dance exceed the length of a quarter of an hour.

But Elijah and the boy, in the excitement of their position, quite forgot the injunction. Moreover, Oliver Giles, a man of seventeen, one of the dancers, who was enamored of his partner, a fair girl of thirty-three rolling years, had recklessly handed a new crown-piece to the musicians, as a bribe to keep going as long as they had muscle and wind. Mrs. Fennel, seeing the steam begin to generate on the countenances of her guests, crossed over and touched the fiddler's elbow and put her hand on the serpent's mouth. But they took no notice, and fearing she might lose her character of genial hostess if she were to interfere too markedly, she retired and sat down helpless. And so the dance whizzed on with cumulative fury, the performers moving in their planetlike courses, direct and retrograde, from apogee to perigee,[12] till the hand of the well-kicked clock at the bottom of the room had traveled over the circumference of an hour.

While these cheerful events were in course of enactment within Fennel's pastoral dwelling, an incident having considerable bearing on the party had occurred in the gloomy night without. Mrs. Fennel's concern about the growing fierceness of the dance corresponded in point of time with the ascent of a human figure to the solitary hill of Higher Crowstairs from the direction of the distant town. This personage strode on through the rain without a pause, following the little-worn path which, further on in its course, skirted the shepherd's cottage.

It was nearly the time of full moon, and on this account, though the sky was lined with a uniform sheet of dripping cloud, ordinary objects out of doors were readily visible. The sad, wan light revealed the lonely pedestrian to be a man of supple frame; his gait suggested that he had somewhat passed the period of perfect and instinctive agility, though not so far as to be otherwise than rapid of motion when occasion required. At a rough guess, he might have been about forty years of age. He appeared tall, but a recruiting sergeant, or other person accustomed to the judging of men's heights by the eye, would have discerned that this was chiefly owing to his gauntness, and that he was not more than five-feet-eight or -nine.

---

10. **toping:** drinking.
11. **serpent:** an obsolete bass wind instrument of the trumpet type.

12. **apogee . . . perigee:** the points at which the orbit of a planet is, respectively, farthest from and nearest to the earth.

Notwithstanding the regularity of his tread, there was caution in it, as in that of one who mentally feels his way; and despite the fact that it was not a black coat nor a dark garment of any sort that he wore, there was something about him which suggested that he naturally belonged to the black-coated tribes[13] of men. His clothes were of fustian,[14] and his boots hobnailed, yet in his progress he showed not the mud-accustomed bearing of hobnailed and fustianed peasantry.

By the time that he had arrived abreast of the shepherd's premises the rain came down, or rather came along, with yet more determined violence. The outskirts of the little settlement partially broke the force of wind and rain, and this induced him to stand still. The most salient of the shepherd's domestic erections was an empty sty at the forward corner of his hedgeless garden, for in these latitudes the principle of masking the homelier features of your establishment by a conventional frontage was unknown. The traveler's eye was attracted to this small building by the pallid shine of the wet slates that covered it. He turned aside, and, finding it empty, stood under the pent roof for shelter.

While he stood, the boom of the serpent within the adjacent house, and the lesser strains of the fiddler, reached the spot as an accompaniment to the surging hiss of the flying rain on the sod, its louder beating on the cabbage leaves of the garden, on the eight or ten beehives just discernible by the path, and its dripping from the eaves into a row of buckets and pans that had been placed under the walls of the cottage. For at Higher Crowstairs, as at all such elevated domiciles, the grand difficulty of housekeeping was an insufficiency of water; and a casual rainfall was utilized by turning out, as catchers, every utensil that the house contained. Some queer stories might be told of the contrivances for economy in suds and dishwaters that are ab-

solutely necessitated in upland habitations during the droughts of summer. But at this season there were no such exigencies; a mere acceptance of what the skies bestowed was sufficient for an abundant store.

At last the notes of the serpent ceased and the house was silent. This cessation of activity aroused the solitary pedestrian from the reverie into which he had elapsed, and, emerging from the shed, with an apparently new intention, he walked up the path to the house door. Arrived here, his first act was to kneel down on a large stone beside the row of vessels, and to drink a copious draft from one of them. Having quenched his thirst, he rose and lifted his hand to knock, but paused with his eye upon the panel. Since the dark surface of the wood revealed absolutely nothing, it was evident that he must be mentally looking through the door, as if he wished to measure thereby all the possibilities that a house of this sort might include, and how they might bear upon the question of his entry.

In his indecision he turned and surveyed the scene around. Not a soul was anywhere visible. The garden path stretched downward from his feet, gleaming like the track of a snail; the roof of the little well (mostly dry), the well cover, the top rail of the garden gate, were varnished with the same dull liquid glaze; while, far away in the vale, a faint whiteness of more than usual extent showed that the rivers were high in the meads. Beyond all this winked a few bleared lamplights through the beating drops — lights that denoted the situation of the county town from which he had appeared to come. The absence of all notes of life in that direction seemed to clinch his intentions, and he knocked at the door.

Within, a desultory chat had taken the place of movement and musical sound. The hedge carpenter was suggesting a song to the company, which nobody just then was inclined to undertake, so that the knock afforded a not unwelcome diversion.

"Walk in!" said the shepherd, promptly.

The latch clicked upward, and out of the

---

13. **black-coated tribes:** middle class.
14. **fustian** (fŭs′chən): a type of coarse cotton.

night our pedestrian appeared upon the door-mat. The shepherd arose, snuffed two of the nearest candles, and turned to look at him.

Their light disclosed that the stranger was dark in complexion and not unprepossessing as to feature. His hat, which for a moment he did not remove, hung low over his eyes, without concealing that they were large, open, and determined, moving with a flash rather than a glance round the room. He seemed pleased with his survey, and, baring his shaggy head, said, in a rich, deep voice: "The rain is so heavy, friends, that I ask leave to come in and rest awhile."

"To be sure, Stranger," said the shepherd. "And faith, you've been lucky in choosing your time, for we are having a bit of a fling for a glad cause — though, to be sure, a man could hardly wish that glad cause to happen more than once a year."

"Nor less," spoke up a woman. "For 'tis best to get your family over and done with, as soon as you can, so as to be all the earlier out of the fag o't."[15]

"And what may be this glad cause?" asked the stranger.

"A birth and christening," said the shepherd.

The stranger hoped his host might not be made unhappy either by too many or too few of such episodes and, being invited by a gesture to a pull at the mug, he readily acquiesced. His manner, which, before entering, had been so dubious, was now altogether that of a careless and candid man.

"Late to be traipsing athwart this coomb — hey?" said the engaged man of fifty.

"Late it is, Master, as you say — I'll take a seat in the chimney corner, if you have nothing to urge against it, Ma'am; for I am a little moist on the side that was next the rain."

Mrs. Shepherd Fennel assented, and made room for the self-invited comer, who, having got completely inside the chimney corner, stretched out his legs and arms with the expansiveness of a person quite at home.

"Yes, I am rather cracked in the vamp,"[16] he said freely, seeing that the eyes of the shepherd's wife fell upon his boots, "and I am not well fitted either. I have had some rough times lately, and have been forced to pick up what I can get in the way of wearing, but I must find a suit better fit for working days when I reach home."

"One of hereabouts?" she inquired.

"Not quite that — further up the country."

"I thought so. And so be I; and by your tongue you come from my neighborhood."

"But you would hardly have heard of me," he said quickly. "My time would be long before yours, Ma'am, you see."

This testimony to the youthfulness of his hostess had the effect of stopping her cross-examination.

"There is only one thing more wanted to make me happy," continued the newcomer, "and that is a little baccy, which I am sorry to say I am out of."

"I'll fill your pipe," said the shepherd.

"I must ask you to lend me a pipe likewise."

"A smoker, and no pipe about 'ee?"

"I have dropped it somewhere on the road."

The shepherd filled and handed him a new clay pipe, saying, as he did so, "Hand me your baccy-box — I'll fill that too, now I am about it."

The man went through the movement of searching his pockets.

"Lost that too?" said his entertainer, with some surprise.

"I am afraid so," said the man with some confusion. "Give it to me in a screw of paper." Lighting his pipe at the candle with a suction that drew the whole flame into the bowl, he resettled himself in the corner and bent his looks upon the faint steam from his damp legs, as if he wished to say no more.

---

15. **fag o't:** the fatigue of it.

16. **vamp:** the part of a shoe above the sole and in front of the ankle seam.

Meanwhile the general body of guests had been taking little notice of this visitor by reason of an absorbing discussion in which they were engaged with the band about a tune for the next dance. The matter being settled, they were about to stand up when an interruption came in the shape of another knock at the door.

At sound of the same the man in the chimney corner took up the poker and began stirring the brands as if doing it thoroughly were the one aim of his existence; and a second time the shepherd said, "Walk in!" In a moment another man stood upon the straw-woven doormat. He too was a stranger.

This individual was one of a type radically different from the first. There was more of the commonplace in his manner, and a certain jovial cosmopolitanism sat upon his features. He was several years older than the first arrival, his hair being slightly frosted, his eyebrows bristly, and his whiskers cut back from his cheeks. His face was rather full and flabby, and yet it was not altogether a face without power. A few grog-blossoms marked the neighborhood of his nose. He flung back his long drab greatcoat, revealing that beneath it he wore a suit of cinder-gray shade throughout, large heavy seals, of some metal or other that would take a polish, dangling from his fob as his only personal ornament. Shaking the water drops from his low-crowned glazed hat, he said, "I must ask for a few minutes' shelter, comrades, or I shall be wetted to my skin before I get to Casterbridge."

"Make yourself at home, Master," said the shepherd, perhaps a trifle less heartily than on the first occasion. Not that Fennel had the least tinge of niggardliness in his composition; but the room was far from large, spare chairs were not numerous, and damp companions were not altogether desirable at close quarters for the women and girls in their bright-colored gowns.

However, the second comer, after taking off his greatcoat, and hanging his hat on a nail in one of the ceiling beams as if he had been specially invited to put it there, advanced and sat down at the table. This had been pushed so closely into the chimney corner, to give all available room to the dancers, that its inner edge grazed the elbow of the man who had ensconced himself by the fire; and thus the two strangers were brought into close companionship. They nodded to each other by way of breaking the ice of unacquaintance, and the first stranger handed his neighbor the family mug—a huge vessel of brown ware, having its upper edge worn away like a threshold by the rub of whole generations of thirsty lips that had gone the way of all flesh, and bearing the following inscription burnt upon its rotund side in yellow letters:

THERE IS NO FUN
UNTiL i CUM.

The other man, nothing loth,[17] raised the mug to his lips, and drank on, and on, and on—till a curious blueness overspread the countenance of the shepherd's wife, who had regarded with no little surprise the first stranger's free offer to the second of what did not belong to him to dispense.

"I knew it!" said the toper to the shepherd with much satisfaction. "When I walked up your garden before coming in, and saw the hives all of a row, I said to myself, 'Where there's bees there's honey, and where there's honey there's mead.' But mead of such a truly comfortable sort as this I really didn't expect to meet in my older days." He took yet another pull at the mug, till it assumed an ominous elevation.

"Glad you enjoy it!" said the shepherd warmly.

"It is goodish mead," assented Mrs. Fennel, with an absence of enthusiasm which seemed to say that it was possible to buy praise for one's cellar at too heavy a price. "It is trouble enough to make—and really I hardly think we

---

17. **nothing loth:** not reluctant.

shall make any more. For honey sells well, and we ourselves can make shift with a drop o' small mead and metheglin[18] for common use from the comb-washings."

"Oh, but you'll never have the heart!" reproachfully cried the stranger in cinder gray, after taking up the mug a third time and setting it down empty. "I love mead, when 'tis old like this, as I love to go to church o' Sundays, or to relieve the needy any day of the week."

"Ha, ha, ha!" said the man in the chimney corner, who, in spite of the taciturnity induced by the pipe of tobacco, could not or would not refrain from this slight testimony to his comrade's humor.

Now the old mead of those days, brewed of the purest first-year or maiden honey, four pounds to the gallon—with its due complement of white of eggs, cinnamon, ginger, cloves, mace, rosemary, yeast, and processes of working, bottling, and cellaring—tasted remarkably strong; but it did not taste so strong as it actually was. Hence presently, the stranger in cinder gray at the table, moved by its creeping influence, unbuttoned his waistcoat, threw himself back in his chair, spread his legs, and made his presence felt in various ways.

"Well, well, as I say," he resumed, "I am going to Casterbridge, and to Casterbridge I must go. I should have been almost there by this time; but the rain drove me into your dwelling, and I'm not sorry for it."

"You don't live in Casterbridge?" said the shepherd.

"Not as yet; though I shortly mean to move there."

"Going to set up in trade, perhaps?"

"No, no," said the shepherd's wife. "It is easy to see that the gentleman is rich, and don't want to work at anything."

The cinder-gray stranger paused, as if to consider whether he would accept that definition of himself. He presently rejected it by answering. "Rich is not quite the word for me, Dame. I do work, and I must work. And even if I only get to Casterbridge by midnight I must begin work there at eight tomorrow morning. Yes, het or wet, blow or snow, famine or sword, my day's work tomorrow must be done."

"Poor man! Then, in spite o'seeming, you be worse off than we," replied the shepherd's wife.

" 'Tis the nature of my trade, men and maidens. 'Tis the nature of my trade more than my poverty. . . . But really and truly I must up and off, or I shan't get a lodging in the town." However, the speaker did not move, and directly added, "There's time for one more draft of friendship before I go; and I'd perform it at once if the mug were not dry."

"Here's a mug o' small," said Mrs. Fennel. "Small, we call it, though to be sure 'tis only the first wash o' the combs."

"No," said the stranger, disdainfully. "I won't spoil your first kindness by partaking o' your second."

"Certainly not," broke in Fennel. "We don't increase and multiply every day, and I'll fill the mug again." He went away to the dark place under the stairs where the barrel stood. The shepherdess followed him.

"Why should you do this?" she said, reproachfully, as soon as they were alone. "He's emptied it once, though it held enough for ten people; and now he's not contented wi' the small, but must needs call for more o' the strong! And a stranger unbeknown to any of us. For my part, I don't like the look o' the man at all."

"But he's in the house, my honey; and 'tis a wet night, and a christening. Daze it, what's a cup of mead more or less? There'll be plenty more next bee-burning."

"Very well—this time, then," she answered, looking wistfully at the barrel. "But what is the man's calling, and where is he one of, that he should come in and join us like this?"

18. **small mead and metheglin:** weaker forms of mead.

"I don't know. I'll ask him again."

The catastrophe of having the mug drained dry at one pull by the stranger in cinder gray was effectively guarded against this time by Mrs. Fennel. She poured out his allowance in a small cup, keeping the large one at a discreet distance from him. When he had tossed off his portion the shepherd renewed his inquiry about the stranger's occupation.

The latter did not immediately reply, and the man in the chimney corner, with sudden demonstrativeness, said, "Anybody may know my trade—I'm a wheelwright."

"A very good trade for these parts," said the shepherd.

"And anybody may know mine—if they've the sense to find it out," said the stranger in cinder gray.

"You may generally tell what a man is by his claws," observed the hedge carpenter, looking at his own hands. "My fingers be as full of thorns as an old pincushion is of pins."

The hands of the man in the chimney corner instinctively sought the shade, and he gazed into the fire as he resumed his pipe. The man at the table took up the hedge carpenter's remark, and added smartly, "True; but the oddity of my trade is that, instead of setting a mark upon me, it sets a mark upon my customers."

No observation being offered by anybody in elucidation of this enigma, the shepherd's wife once more called for a song. The same obstacles presented themselves as at the former time—one had no voice, another had forgotten the first verse. The stranger at the table, whose soul had now risen to a good working temperature, relieved the difficulty by exclaiming that, to start the company, he would sing himself. Thrusting one thumb into the armhole of his waistcoat, he waved the other hand in the air, and, with an extemporizing gaze at the shining sheep crooks above the mantelpiece, began:

O my trade it is the rarest one,
　　　　Simple shepherds all—

My trade is a sight to see:
For my customers I tie, and take them up
　　on high,
And waft 'em to a far countree!

The room was silent when he had finished the verse—with one exception, that of the man in the chimney corner, who at the singer's word, "Chorus!" joined him in a deep bass voice of musical relish:

And waft 'em to a far countree!

Oliver Giles, John Pitcher the dairyman, the parish clerk, the engaged man of fifty, the row of young women against the wall, seemed lost in thought not of the gayest kind. The shepherd looked meditatively on the ground, the shepherdess gazed keenly at the singer, and with some suspicion; she was doubting whether this stranger were merely singing an old song from recollection, or was composing one there and then for the occasion. All were as perplexed at the obscure revelation as the guests at Belshazzar's Feast,[19] except the man in the chimney corner, who quietly said, "Second verse, stranger," and smoked on.

The singer thoroughly moistened himself from his lips inward, and went on with the next stanza as requested:

My tools are but common ones,
　　　　Simple shepherds all—
My tools are no sight to see:
A little hempen string, and a post where-
　　on to swing,
Are implements enough for me!

Shepherd Fennel glanced round. There was no longer any doubt that the stranger was answering his question rhythmically. The guests one and all started back with suppressed exclamations. The young woman

---

19. **All . . . Belshazzar's** (bĕl-shăz′ərz) **Feast:** According to the Old Testament, writing appeared on the wall prophesying the destruction of Babylonia.

engaged to the man of fifty fainted halfway, and would have proceeded, but finding him wanting in alacrity for catching her she sat down trembling.

"Oh, he's the—!" whispered the people in the background, mentioning the name of an ominous public officer. "He's come to do it! 'Tis to be at Casterbridge jail tomorrow—the man for sheep-stealing—the poor clockmaker we heard of, who used to live away at Shottsford and had no work to do—Timothy Summers, whose family were astarving, and so he went out of Shottsford by the highroad, and took a sheep in open daylight, defying the farmer and the farmer's wife and the farmer's lad, and every man jack among 'em. He" (and they nodded toward the stranger of the deadly trade) "is come from up the country to do it because there's not enough to do in his own county town, and he's got the place here now our own countryman's dead; he's going to live in the same cottage under the prison wall."

The stranger in cinder gray took no notice of this whispered string of observations, but again wetted his lips. Seeing that his friend in the chimney corner was the only one who reciprocated his joviality in any way, he held out his cup toward that appreciative comrade, who also held out his own. They clinked together, the eyes of the rest of the room hanging upon the singer's actions. He parted his lips for the third verse; but at that moment another knock was audible upon the door. This time the knock was faint and hesitating.

The company seemed scared; the shepherd looked with consternation toward the entrance, and it was with some effort that he resisted his alarmed wife's deprecatory glance, and uttered for the third time the welcoming words, "Walk in!"

The door was gently opened, and another man stood upon the mat. He, like those who had preceded him, was a stranger. This time it was a short, small personage, of fair complexion, and dressed in a decent suit of dark clothes.

"Can you tell me the way to—?" he began:

when, gazing round the room to observe the nature of the company among whom he had fallen, his eyes lighted on the stranger in cinder gray. It was just at the instant when the latter, who had thrown his mind into his song with such a will that he scarcely heeded the interruption, silenced all whispers and inquiries by bursting into his third verse:

Tomorrow is my working day,
          Simple shepherds all—
Tomorrow is a working day for me:
For the farmer's sheep is slain, and lad who
    did it ta'en.
And on his soul may God ha' merc-y!

The stranger in the chimney corner, waving cups with the singer so heartily that his mead splashed over the hearth, repeated in his bass voice as before:

And on his soul may God ha' merc-y!

All this time the third stranger had been standing in the doorway. Finding now that he did not come forward or go on speaking, the guests particularly regarded him. They noticed to their surprise that he stood before them the picture of abject terror—his knees trembling, his hand shaking so violently that the door latch by which he supported himself rattled audibly; his white lips were parted, and his eyes fixed on the merry officer of justice in the middle of the room. A moment more and he had turned, closed the door, and fled.

"What a man can it be?" said the shepherd.

The rest, between the awfulness of their late discovery and the odd conduct of this third visitor, looked as if they knew not what to think, and said nothing. Instinctively they withdrew further and further from the grim gentleman in their midst, whom some of them seemed to take for the Prince of Darkness himself, till they formed a remote circle, an empty space of floor being left between them and him— . . . *circulus, cujus centrum diabolus.*[20] The room was so silent — though there were more than twenty people in it — that nothing could be heard but the patter of the rain against the window shutters, accompanied by the occasional hiss of a stray drop that fell down the chimney into the fire, and the steady puffing of the man in the corner, who had now resumed his pipe of long clay.

The stillness was unexpectedly broken. The distant sound of a gun reverberated through the air — apparently from the direction of the county town.

"Be jiggered!" cried the stranger who had sung the song, jumping up.

"What does that mean?" asked several.

"A prisoner escaped from the jail — that's what it means."

All listened. The sound was repeated, and none of them spoke but the man in the chimney corner, who said quietly, "I've often been told that in this county they fire a gun at such times; but I never heard it till now."

"I wonder if it is *my* man?" murmured the personage in cinder gray.

"Surely it is!" said the shepherd involuntarily. "And surely we've zeed him! That little man who looked in at the door by now, and quivered like a leaf when he zeed ye and heard your song!"

"His teeth chattered, and the breath went out of his body," said the dairyman.

"And his heart seemed to sink within him like a stone," said Oliver Giles.

"And he bolted as if he'd been shot at," said the hedge carpenter.

"True — his teeth chattered, and his heart seemed to sink; and he bolted as if he'd been shot at," slowly summed up the man in the chimney corner.

"I didn't notice it," remarked the hangman.

"We were all awondering what made him run off in such a fright," faltered one of the women against the wall, "and now 'tis explained!"

---

20. *circulus . . . diabolus:* a circle with the devil at its center.

The firing of the alarm gun went on at intervals, low and sullenly, and their suspicions became a certainty. The sinister gentleman in cinder gray roused himself. "Is there a constable here?" he asked, in thick tones. "If so, let him step forward."

The engaged man of fifty stepped quavering out from the wall, his betrothed beginning to sob on the back of the chair.

"You are a sworn constable?"

"I be. Sir."

"Then pursue the criminal at once, with assistance, and bring him back here. He can't have gone far."

"I will, Sir, I will — when I've got my staff. I'll go home and get it, and come sharp here, and start in a body."

"Staff! — never mind your staff; the man'll be gone!"

"But I can't do nothing without my staff — can I, William, and John, and Charles Jake? No; for there's the king's royal crown apainted on en in yaller and gold, and the lion and the unicorn, so as when I raise en up and hit my prisoner, 'tis made a lawful blow thereby. I wouldn't 'tempt to take up a man without my staff — no, not I. If I hadn't the law to gie me courage, why, instead o' my taking up him he might take up me!"

"Now, I'm a king's man myself, and can give you authority enough for this," said the formidable officer in gray. "Now then, all of ye, be ready. Have ye any lanterns?"

"Yes — have ye any lanterns? I demand it!" said the constable.

"And the rest of you able-bodied — "

"Able-bodied men — yes — the rest of ye!" said the constable.

"Have you some good stout staves and pitchforks — "

"Staves and pitchforks — in the name o' the law! And take 'em in yer hands and go in quest, and do as we in authority tell ye!"

Thus aroused, the men prepared to give chase. The evidence was, indeed, though circumstantial, so convincing that but little argument was needed to show the shepherd's guests that after what they had seen it would look very much like connivance if they did not instantly pursue the unhappy third stranger, who could not as yet have gone more than a few hundred yards over such uneven country.

A shepherd is always well provided with lanterns; and, lighting these hastily, and with hurdle staves in their hands, they poured out of the door, taking a direction along the crest of the hill, away from the town, the rain having fortunately a little abated.

Disturbed by the noise, or possibly by unpleasant dreams of her baptism, the child who had been christened began to cry heartbrokenly in the room overhead. These notes of grief came down through the chinks of the floor to the ears of the women below, who jumped up one by one and seemed glad of the excuse to ascend and comfort the baby, for the incidents of the last half-hour greatly oppressed them. Thus in the space of two or three minutes the room on the ground floor was deserted quite.

But it was not for long. Hardly had the sound of footsteps died away when a man returned round the corner of the house from the direction the pursuers had taken. Peeping in at the door, and seeing nobody there, he entered leisurely. It was the stranger of the chimney corner, who had gone out with the rest. The motive of his return was shown by his helping himself to a cut piece of skimmer cake that lay on a ledge beside where he had sat, and which he had apparently forgotten to take with him. He also poured out half a cup more mead from the quantity that remained, ravenously eating and drinking these as he stood. He had not finished when another figure came in just as quietly—his friend in cinder gray.

"Oh—you here?" said the latter, smiling. "I thought you had gone to help in the capture." And this speaker also revealed the object of his return by looking solicitously round for the fascinating mug of old mead.

"And I thought you had gone," said the other, continuing his skimmer cake with some effort.

"Well, on second thoughts, I felt there were enough without me," said the first confidentially, "and such a night as it is, too. Besides, 'tis the business o' the government to take care of its criminals—not mine."

"True; so it is. And I felt as you did, that there were enough without me."

"I don't want to break my limbs running over the humps and hollows of this wild country."

"Nor I neither, between you and me."

"These shepherd people are used to it—simple-minded souls, you know, stirred up to anything in a moment. They'll have him ready for me before the morning, and no trouble to me at all."

"They'll have him, and we shall have saved ourselves all labor in the matter."

"True, true. Well, my way is to Casterbridge; and 'tis as much as my legs will do to take me that far. Going the same way?"

"No, I am sorry to say! I have to get home over there" (he nodded indefinitely to the right), "and I feel as you do, that it is quite enough for my legs to do before bedtime."

The other had by this time finished the mead in the mug, after which, shaking hands heartily at the door, and wishing each other well, they went their several ways.

In the meantime the company of pursuers had reached the end of the hog's-back elevation which dominated this part of the down. They had decided on no particular plan of action; and, finding that the man of the baleful trade was no longer in their company, they seemed quite unable to form any such plan now. They descended in all directions down the hill, and straightway several of the party fell into the snare set by Nature for all misguided midnight ramblers over this part of the cretaceous[21] formation. The "lanchets," or flint slopes, which belted the escarpment

---

21. **cretaceous**: (krĭ-tā'shəs): chalky.

at intervals of a dozen yards, took the less cautious ones unawares, and losing their footing on the rubbly steep they slid sharply downward, the lanterns rolling from their hands to the bottom, and there lying on their sides till the horn[22] was scorched through.

When they had again gathered themselves together, the shepherd, as the man who knew the country best, took the lead, and guided them round these treacherous inclines. The lanterns, which seemed rather to dazzle their eyes and warn the fugitive than to assist them in the exploration, were extinguished, due silence was observed; and in this more rational order they plunged into the vale. It was a grassy, briery, moist defile, affording some shelter to any person who had sought it; but the party perambulated it in vain, and ascended on the other side. Here they wandered apart, and after an interval closed together again to report progress. At the second time of closing in they found themselves near a lonely ash, the single tree on this part of the coomb, probably sown there by a passing bird some fifty years before. And here, standing a little to one side of the trunk, as motionless as the trunk itself appeared the man they were in quest of, his outline being well defined against the sky beyond. The band noiselessly drew up and faced him.

"Your money or your life!" said the constable sternly to the still figure.

"No, no," whispered John Pitcher. " 'Tisn't our side ought to say that. That's the doctrine of vagabonds like him, and we be on the side of the law."

"Well, well," replied the constable, impatiently; "I must say something, mustn't I? and if you had all the weight o' this undertaking upon your mind, perhaps you'd say the wrong thing, too! Prisoner at the bar, surrender in the name of the Father—the Crown, I mane!"

The man under the tree seemed now to notice them for the first time, and, giving them

no opportunity whatever for exhibiting their courage, he strolled slowly toward them. He was, indeed, the little man, the third stranger; but his trepidation had in a great measure gone.

"Well, travelers," he said, "did I hear you speak to me?"

"You did; you've got to come and be our prisoner at once!" said the constable. "We arrest 'ee on the charge of not biding in Casterbridge jail in a decent proper manner to be hung tomorrow morning. Neighbors, do your duty, and seize the culpet!"

On hearing the charge, the man seemed enlightened and, saying not another word, resigned himself with preternatural civility to the search party, who, with their staves in their hands, surrounded him on all sides and marched him back toward the shepherd's cottage.

It was eleven o'clock by the time they arrived. The light shining from the open door, a sound of men's voices within, proclaimed to them as they approached the house that some new events had arisen in their absence. On entering they discovered the shepherd's living room to be invaded by two officers from Casterbridge jail, and a well-known magistrate who lived at the nearest county seat, intelligence of the escape having become generally circulated.

"Gentlemen," said the constable, "I have brought back your man—not without risk and danger; but everyone must do his duty! He is inside this circle of able-bodied persons, who have lent me useful aid, considering their ignorance of Crown work.—Men, bring forward your prisoner!" And the third stranger was led to the light.

"Who is this?" said one of the officials.

"The man," said the constable.

"Certainly not," said the turnkey; and the first corroborated his statement.

"But how can it be otherwise?" asked the constable. "Or why was he so terrified at sight o' the singing instrument of the law who sat there?" Here he related the strange behavior

---

22. **horn:** Scraped horn was sometimes used instead of glass in lanterns.

of the third stranger on entering the house during the hangman's song.

"Can't understand it," said the officer coolly. "All I know is that it is not the condemned man. He's quite a different character from this one; a gauntish fellow, with dark hair and eyes, rather good-looking, and with a musical bass voice that if you heard it once you'd never mistake as long as you lived."

"Why, souls—'twas the man in the chimney corner!"

"Hey—what?" said the magistrate, coming forward after inquiring particulars from the shepherd in the background. "Haven't you got the man after all?"

"Well, Sir," said the constable, "he's the man we were in search of, that's true; and yet he's not the man we were in search of. For the man we were in search of was not the man we wanted, Sir, if you understand my everyday way; for 'twas the man in the chimney corner!"

"A pretty kettle of fish altogether!" said the magistrate. "You had better start for the other man at once."

The prisoner now spoke for the first time. The mention of the man in the chimney corner seemed to have moved him as nothing else could do. "Sir," he said, stepping forward to the magistrate, "take no more trouble about me. The time is come when I may as well speak. I have done nothing, my crime is that the condemned man is my brother. Early this afternoon I left home at Shottsford to tramp it all the way to Casterbridge jail to bid him farewell. I was benighted, and called here to rest and ask the way. When I opened the door I saw before me the very man, my brother, that I thought to see in the condemned cell at Casterbridge. He was in this chimney corner; and jammed close to him, so that he could not have got out if he had tried, was the executioner who'd come to take his life, singing a song about it and not knowing that it was his victim who was close by, joining in to save appearances. My brother looked a glance of agony at me, and I know he

meant, 'Don't reveal what you see; my life depends on it.' I was so terror-struck that I could hardly stand, and, not knowing what I did, I turned and hurried away."

The narrator's manner and tone had the stamp of truth, and his story made a great impression on all around. "And do you know where your brother is at the present time?" asked the magistrate.

"I do not. I have never seen him since I closed this door."

"I can testify to that, for we've been between ye ever since," said the constable.

"Where does he think to fly to?—what is his occupation?"

"He's a watch-and-clock-maker, Sir."

"'A said 'a was a wheelwright—a wicked rogue," said the constable.

"The wheels of clocks and watches he meant, no doubt," said Shepherd Fennel. "I thought his hands were palish for's trade."

"Well, it appears to me that nothing can be gained by retaining this poor man in custody," said the magistrate; "your business lies with the other, unquestionably."

And so the little man was released offhand; but he looked nothing the less sad on that account, it being beyond the power of magistrate or constable to raze out the written troubles in his brain, for they concerned another whom he regarded with more solicitude than himself. When this was done, and the man had gone his way, the night was found to be so far advanced that it was deemed useless to renew the search before the next morning.

Next day, accordingly, the quest for the clever sheep stealer became general and keen, to all appearance at least. But the intended punishment was cruelly disproportioned to the transgression, and the sympathy of a great many country-folk in that district was strongly on the side of the fugitive. Moreover, his marvelous coolness and daring in hob-and-nobbing with the hangman, under the unprecedented circumstances of the shepherd's party, won their admiration. So that it may be questioned if all those who ostensibly made themselves so busy in exploring woods and fields and lanes were quite so thorough when it came to the private examination of their own lofts and outhouses. Stories were afloat of a mysterious figure being occasionally seen in some old overgrown trackway or other, remote from turnpike roads, but when a search was instituted in any of these suspected quarters nobody was found. Thus the days and weeks passed without tidings.

In brief, the bass-voiced man of the chimney corner was never recaptured. Some said that he went across the sea, others that he did not, but buried himself in the depths of a populous city. At any rate, the gentleman in cinder gray never did his morning's work at Casterbridge, nor met anywhere at all, for business purposes, the genial comrade with whom he had passed an hour of relaxation in the lonely house on the coomb.

The grass has long been green on the graves of Shepherd Fennel and his frugal wife; the guests who made up the christening party have mainly followed their entertainers to the tomb; the baby in whose honor they all had met is a matron in the sere and yellow leaf. But the arrival of the three strangers at the shepherd's that night, and the details connected therewith, is a story as well known as ever in the country about Higher Crowstairs.

FOR STUDY AND DISCUSSION

1. How does Hardy create interest in the first stranger as he begins to ascend the solitary hill of Higher Crowstairs? What impression does he make on the guests?
2. The second stranger was "one of a type radically different from the first." Compare the two. Why does Mrs. Fennel dislike him? How does he arouse the curiosity of the guests? Hardy reveals this stranger's identity in an oblique manner. Does this device enrich the story, or would a straight exposition have been more effective? Give reasons for your opinion.
3. The guests are quick to conclude that the third stranger is the escaped prisoner. At this point in the story, do you have any reason to suspect either of the other two strangers? What effect does Hardy achieve by introducing the long silence after the stranger leaves?

4. At what point in the story did you first recognize the hangman and the prisoner? Does the revelation of their identities come at the same time? Point out phrases and sentences in which Hardy prepares you to rejoice at the escape of the condemned man.
5. Hardy's work is frequently marked by subtle touches of humor. Give some examples of the use of humor in this story. Do you think Hardy introduced these lighter moments simply for amusement, or might he have had another purpose? Explain.

FOR COMPOSITION

Write a short essay on Hardy's view of human beings as subject to the indifferent forces of chance and circumstance, using the adventure of the escaped prisoner as your example.

Rudyard Kipling
1865–1936

Like Hardy, Kipling belongs to both the Victorian and the modern age. His life was at midpoint at the turn of the century, and while his reputation was definitely established during the eighties and nineties, he was probably the most widely read British author in the first decades of the twentieth century. In both verse and fiction Kipling has been a favorite storyteller of millions. Children treasure the animal stories of India told in *The Jungle Book*, and later they thrill to the excitement of *Kim*, his best-known novel. Readers of all ages enjoy the quick sketching of his army ballads such as "Danny Deever" and "Gunga Din." But Kipling's fame rests most securely on his numerous volumes of short stories, filled with the hilarious antics and sometimes strange fates of the British soldier.

Rudyard Kipling was born in Bombay, and he is always associated with India, though he was educated and lived in England most of his life. At seventeen he became editor of a newspaper in Lahore, and for the next nine years he gathered material for many of his later books—exotic Indian backgrounds of dusty villages and colonial military posts, of lush jungles and remote mountain passes. In 1892 Kipling married an American girl from Vermont and spent five years there. One of his novels, *Captains Courageous*, has a New England setting. Travel was one of Kipling's delights; there are few places "east and west" he did not visit and write about.

It is often noted that while other writers of the period sought romance in idyllic surroundings, Kipling found it in the everyday world of engineers, soldiers, and bridge builders. Somerset Maugham has said of him: "Rudyard Kipling was the first to blaze the trail through new-found country, and no one has invested it with more glamour, no one has made it more exciting, and no one has presented it so vividly and with such a wealth of color."

Kipling was out of favor with officialdom in his own day and with critics of later days. Though he was the most eligible of poets, Queen Victoria kept him from becoming poet laureate because of his satiric descriptions (he called her the "Widow of Windsor" in *Barrack-Room Ballads*). However, Kipling won the Nobel Prize in literature in 1907.

Rudyard Kipling by Philip Burne-Jones.
National Portrait Gallery, London

Afterward, he was criticized as a defender of British imperialism. But that issue, at least since India has been granted independence, has passed, and readers continue to enjoy Kipling as a master storyteller.

Miss Youghal's *Sais*°

This story from *Plain Tales from the Hills* illustrates in small space several points about Kipling's stories. It deals with British official and army life in India, and suggests that Kipling himself must have been, like Strickland, capable of "going native" so completely that he was lost in the crowd. At the end of this story of the *sais* we find a typical mannerism of the author. Because his brain was overflowing with so many stories, he seldom concluded one tale without hinting that he had another good story up his sleeve. He often ends—"But that is another story."

When Man and Woman are agreed, what can the Kazi° do? —MOHAMMEDAN PROVERB

Some people say that there is no romance in India. Those people are wrong. Our lives hold quite as much romance as is good for us. Sometimes more.

Strickland was in the police, and people did not understand him; so they said he was a doubtful sort of man and passed by on the other side. Strickland had himself to thank for this. He held the extraordinary theory that a policeman in India should try to know as much about the natives as the natives themselves. Now, in the whole of upper India, there is only *one* man who can pass for Hindu or Mohammedan, *chamar*[1] or *faquir*,[2] as he pleases. He is feared and respected by the natives from the Ghor Kathri to the Jamma Musjid; and he is supposed to have the gift of invisibility and executive control over many devils. But what good has this done him with the government? None in the world. He has never got Simla[3] for his charge; and his name is almost unknown to Englishmen.

Strickland was foolish enough to take that man for his model; and, following out his absurd theory, dabbled in unsavory places no respectable man would think of exploring—all among the native riffraff. He educated himself in this peculiar way for seven years, and people could not appreciate it. He was perpetually "going Fantee" among natives, which, of course, no man with any sense believes in. He was initiated into the *Sat Bhai* at Allahabad[4] once, when he was on leave; he knew the Lizard Song of the Sansis, and the *Hálli-Hukk* dance, which is a religious cancan of a startling kind. When a man knows who dances the *Hálli-Hukk*, and how, and when, and where, he knows something to be proud of. He has gone deeper than the skin. But Strickland was not proud, though he had helped once, at Jagadhri, at the Painting of the Death Bull, which no Englishman must even look upon; had mastered the thieves' patter of the *chángars*; had taken a Eusufzai horse

---

° **Youghal** (youl): *Sais* (sīs): A sais is a servant in charge of horses.
° *Kazi:* military judge of the Ottoman Empire.
1. *chamar* (shă-mär′): skin dresser.
2. *faquir* (fə-kîr′): priest.
3. **Simla:** the summer capital of India; situated in the Himalayas.

4. **Allahabad** (ăl′ə-hă-băd′): an important city on the Ganges at the foot of the Himalayas.

thief alone near Attock; and had stood under the *mimbar* board[5] of a Border mosque and conducted service in the manner of a Sunni Mollah.

His crowning achievement was spending eleven days as a *faquir* in the gardens of Baba Atal at Amritsar,[6] and there picking up the threads of the great Nasiban murder case. But people said, justly enough, "Why on earth can't Strickland sit in his office and write up his diary, and recruit, and keep quiet, instead of showing up the incapacity of his seniors?" So the Nasiban murder case did him no good departmentally; but, after his first feeling of wrath, he returned to his outlandish custom of prying into native life. By the way, when a man once acquires a taste for this particular amusement, it abides with him all his days. It is the most fascinating thing in the world; Love not excepted. Where other men took ten days to the Hills, Strickland took leave for what he called *shikar*,[7] put on the disguise that appealed to him at the time, stepped down into the brown crowd, and was swallowed up for a while. He was a quiet, dark young fellow—spare; black eyes—and, when he was not thinking of something else, a very interesting companion. Strickland on Native Progress as he had seen it was worth hearing. Natives hated Strickland; but they were afraid of him. He knew too much.

When the Youghals came into the station, Strickland—very gravely, as he did everything—fell in love with Miss Youghal; and she, after a while, fell in love with him because she could not understand him. Then Strickland told the parents; but Mrs. Youghal said she was not going to throw her daughter into the worst-paid department in the Empire, and old Youghal said, in so many words, that he mistrusted Strickland's ways and works,

and would thank him not to speak or write to his daughter anymore. "Very well," said Strickland, for he did not wish to make his ladylove's life a burden. After one long talk with Miss Youghal he dropped the business entirely.

The Youghals went up to Simla in April.

In July Strickland secured three months' leave on "urgent private affairs." He locked up his house—though not a native in the province would wittingly have touched "Estreek-in Sahib's" gear for the world—and went down to see a friend of his, an old dyer, at Tarn Taran.

Here all trace of him was lost, until a *sais* met me on the Simla Mall with this extraordinary note:

Dear Old Man,

Please give bearer a box of cheroots— Supers, No. 1, for preference. They are freshest at the Club. I'll repay when I reappear; but at present I'm out of society.

Yours,
E. Strickland.

I ordered two boxes, and handed them over to the *sais* with my love. That *sais* was Strickland, and he was in old Youghal's employ, attached to Miss Youghal's Arab. The poor fellow was suffering for an English smoke, and knew that, whatever happened, I should hold my tongue till the business was over.

Later on, Mrs. Youghal, who was wrapped up in her servants, began talking at houses where she called of her paragon among *saises* —the man who was never too busy to get up in the morning and pick flowers for the breakfast table, and who blacked—actually *blacked* —the hoofs of his horse like a London coachman! The turnout of Miss Youghal's Arab was a wonder and a delight. Strickland—Dulloo, I mean—found his reward in the pretty things that Miss Youghal said to him when she went out riding. Her parents were pleased to find she had forgotten all her foolishness for young Strickland and said she was a good girl.

---

5. *mimbar* **board:** sounding board, a structure over a pulpit.
6. **Amritsar** (ŭm-rĭt′sər): a city in the Punjab, the northwest province of India.
7. *shikar* (shə-kär′): hunting.

Strickland vows that the two months of his service were the most rigid mental discipline he has ever gone through. Quite apart from the little fact that the wife of one of his fellow *saises* fell in love with him and then tried to poison him with arsenic because he would have nothing to do with her, he had to school himself into keeping quiet when Miss Youghal went out riding with some man who tried to flirt with her, and he was forced to trot behind, carrying the blanket and hearing every word! Also, he had to keep his temper when he was slanged in Benmore porch[8] by a policeman—especially once when he was abused by a Naik he had himself recruited from Isser Jang village—or, worse still, when a young subaltern called him a pig for not making way quickly enough.

But the life had its compensations. He obtained great insight into the ways and thefts of *saises*—enough, he says, to have summarily convicted half the *chamar* population of the Punjab if he had been on business. He became one of the leading players at knucklebones, which all *jampanis*[9] and many *saises* play while they are waiting outside the Government House or the Gaiety Theater of nights; he learned to smoke tobacco that was three-fourths cow-dung; and he heard the wisdom of the grizzled *Jemadar*[10] of the Government Houses *saises*, whose words are valuable. He saw many things which amused him; and he states, on honor, that no man can appreciate Simla properly till he has seen it from the *sais's* point of view. He also says that if he chose to write all he saw, his head would be broken in several places.

Strickland's account of the agony he endured on wet nights, hearing the music and seeing the lights in "Benmore," with his toes tingling for a waltz and his head in a horse blanket, is rather amusing. One of these days,

Strickland is going to write a little book on his experiences. That book will be worth buying; and even more worth suppressing.

Thus, he served faithfully as Jacob served for Rachel;[11] and his leave was nearly at an end when the explosion came. He had really done his best to keep his temper in the hearing of the flirtations I have mentioned; but he broke down at last. An old and very distinguished general took Miss Youghal for a ride, and began that specially offensive "you're-only-a-little-girl" sort of flirtation—most difficult for a woman to turn aside deftly, and most maddening to listen to. Miss Youghal was shaking with fear at the things he said in the hearing of her *sais*. Dulloo—Strickland—stood it as long as he could. Then he caught hold of the general's bridle, and, in most fluent English, invited him to step off and be heaved over the cliff. Next minute Miss Youghal began crying; and Strickland saw that he had hopelessly given himself away, and everything was over.

The general nearly had a fit, while Miss Youghal was sobbing out the story of the disguise and the engagement that was not recognized by the parents. Strickland was furiously angry with himself, and more angry with the general for forcing his hand; so he said nothing, but held the horse's head and prepared to thrash the general as some sort of satisfaction. But when the general had thoroughly grasped the story, and knew who Strickland was, he began to puff and blow in the saddle, and nearly rolled off with laughing. He said Strickland deserved a V. C.,[12] if it were only for putting on a *sais's* blanket. Then he called himself names, and vowed that he deserved a thrashing, but he was too old to take it from Strickland. Then he complimented Miss Youghal on her lover. The scandal of the business never struck him; for

---

8. **Benmore porch:** entrance to the reception center.
9. *jampanis* (jăm-pə-nēz´): bearers of a jampan—like a sedan chair.
10. *Jemadar* (jĕm-ə-där´): a native sergeant.

11. **Jacob . . . Rachel:** The story of Jacob and Rachel is in Genesis 29:15–30.
12. **V. C.:** Victoria Cross, the highest Crown award for military valor.

he was a nice old man, with a weakness for flirtations. Then he laughed again, and said that old Youghal was a fool. Strickland let go of the cob's head, and suggested that the general had better help them, if that was his opinion. Strickland knew Youghal's weakness for men with titles and letters after their names and high official position. "It's rather like a forty-minute farce," said the general, "but, begad, I *will* help, if it's only to escape that tremendous thrashing I deserve. Go along to your home, my *sais*-policeman, and change into decent kit, and I'll attack Mr. Youghal. Miss Youghal, may I ask you to canter home and wait?"

About seven minutes later, there was a wild hurroosh at the club. A *sais*, with blanket and headrobe, was asking all the men he knew: "For Heaven's sake lend me decent clothes!" As the men did not recognize him, there were some peculiar scenes before Strickland could get a hot bath, with soda in it, in one room, a shirt here, a collar there, a pair of trousers elsewhere, and so on. He galloped off, with half the club wardrobe on his back, and an utter stranger's pony under him, to the house of old Youghal. The general, arrayed in purple and fine linen, was before him. What the general had said Strickland never knew, but Youghal received Strickland with moderate civility; and Mrs. Youghal, touched by the devotion of the transformed Dulloo, was almost kind. The general beamed and chuckled, and Miss Youghal came in, and almost before old Youghal knew where he was, the parental consent had been wrenched out, and Strickland had departed with Miss Youghal to the telegraph office to wire for his kit. The final embarrassment was when a stranger attacked him on the Mall and asked for the stolen pony.

So, in the end, Strickland and Miss Youghal were married, on the strict understanding that Strickland should drop his old ways, and stick to departmental routine, which pays best and leads to Simla. Strickland was far too fond of his wife, just then, to break his word, but it was a sore trial to him; for the streets and the bazaars, and the sounds in them, were full of meaning to Strickland, and these called to him to come back and take up his wanderings and his discoveries. Someday I will tell you how he broke his promise to help a friend. That was long since, and he has, by this time, been nearly spoiled for what he would call *shikar*. He is forgetting the slang, and the beggar's cant, and the marks, and the signs, and the drift of the undercurrents, which, if a man would master, he must always continue to learn.

But he fills in his departmental returns beautifully.

FOR STUDY AND DISCUSSION

1. In what kind of predicament did Strickland find himself? What personal qualities and past experience enabled him to carry out his plan? Did his conduct in any way differ from that of a native *sais*?

2. What do you learn of Indian life and customs from this story? Does the life of the English colony sound pleasant or unpleasant as described? What traits of the English in India during the time of the Empire do you observe?

Oscar Wilde
1854–1900

Oscar Wilde (1891).
The Mansell Collection

Oscar Wilde was born in Dublin. His father was a distinguished physician; his mother wrote poetry and was a prominent figure in Dublin literary society. Wilde excelled as a student of classical literature at Trinity College, Dublin, and eventually won a scholarship to Magdalen College, Oxford. He soon became famous for his brilliant conversation and his flamboyant manner of dress and behavior. At a time when most Victorian men wore sober wool suits and stiff white shirts, Wilde often appeared in a velvet coat edged with braid, knee-breeches, silk stockings, a soft loose shirt with a wide collar, and a large, flowing, richly colored tie. He was a student of Walter Pater, the writer who began what is usually known as the "aesthetic movement" by rejecting the older Victorian insistence on the moral purpose of art and celebrating instead the value of "art for art's sake."

Upon leaving Oxford, Wilde settled in London. Through his stories, poems, and essays, he became himself the most famous champion of the "art-for-art's-sake" creed. With his dazzling and often paradoxical wit he delighted in mocking Victorian notions about the moral seriousness of great art. Yet underlying the brilliant and deliberately outrageous playfulness of Wilde's manner is a commitment to the power of art that has genuine intellectual integrity.

Wilde's career as a successful dramatist began in 1892 with *Lady Windermere's Fan.* In the years that followed he wrote several successful comedies. His best and most brilliant is *The Importance of Being Earnest,* which was produced in 1895. The plot turns upon the fortunes and misfortunes of two young upper-class Englishmen, John Worthing and Algernon Moncrieff. Each of them is living a kind of double life, having created for himself another personality to provide an escape from tedious social or family obligations. In London, John (known as Jack) assumes the role of a nonexistent brother, Ernest, while Algernon pretends to have a close friend, an invalid, called Bunbury, whom he visits in the country when he needs an excuse to leave London. Jack is in love with Gwendolen Fairfax, Algernon's cousin, but he is at first thwarted in his attempt to marry her by the scruples of Gwendolen's mother, Lady Bracknell. Algernon is interested in Jack's ward, Cecily Cardew, who is always watched by her governess, Miss Prism.

The plot becomes hilariously complicated when Algernon decides to pass himself off as Ernest in order to spend time with Cecily; at the same time John, for reasons having to do with his own courtship of Gwendolen, announces that his poor brother Ernest has died of a chill in Paris.

The plot of *The Importance of Being Earnest* is brilliantly constructed, but it is composed of events of the most improbable and trivial significance. The real substance of the play is Wilde's dazzlingly witty, perfectly polished dialogue. Even the title of the play is based upon a satirical double meaning: "Ernest" is the name of a fictitious character, but it also designates the moral virtue of sincere aspiration which had been so important in the earlier Victorian Period. In making the earnestness of his Ernest the key to an outrageous social comedy, Wilde pokes fun at conventional Victorian seriousness by fitting solemn moral language to frivolous and ridiculous action. The speeches of Lady Bracknell, Miss Prism, and Reverend Chasuble consistently depend upon this comic technique. In the speeches of Algernon and John, Wilde exploits more directly the fun and charm of language as it might ideally be used by sophisticated young men who avoid boredom by treating it as a challenge for their own verbal cleverness.

The Importance of Being Earnest

Characters

John Worthing, alias Ernest Worthing
Algernon Moncrieff, friend of John
Lady Bracknell, Algernon's aunt
Honorable Gwendolen Fairfax, daughter of
 Lady Bracknell
Cecily Cardew, ward of John Worthing
Miss Prism, governess to Cecily
The Reverend Canon Chasuble, rector
Lane, Algernon's butler
Merriman, butler at Manor House

Act One

Morning room[1] in Algernon's flat in Half-Moon Street. The room is luxuriously and artistically furnished. The sound of a piano is heard in the adjoining room. Lane *is arranging afternoon tea on the table, and after the music has ceased,* Algernon *enters.*

Algernon. Did you hear what I was playing, Lane?

Lane. I didn't think it polite to listen, sir.

Algernon. I'm sorry for that, for your sake. I don't play accurately—anyone can play accurately—but I play with wonderful expression. As far as the piano is concerned, sentiment is my forte. I keep science for life.

Lane. Yes, sir.

Algernon. And, speaking of the science of life, have you got the cucumber sandwiches cut for Lady Bracknell?

Lane. Yes, sir. (*Hands them on a salver[2]*)

Algernon (*inspects them, takes two, and sits down on the sofa*). Oh! . . . By the way, Lane, I see from your book that on Thursday night,

when Lord Shoreman and Mr. Worthing were dining with me, eight bottles of champagne are entered as having been consumed.

Lane. Yes, sir; eight bottles and a pint.

Algernon. Why is it that at a bachelor's establishment the servants invariably drink the champagne? I ask merely for information.

Lane. I attribute it to the superior quality of the wine, sir. I have often observed that in married households the champagne is rarely of a first-rate brand.

Algernon. Good heavens! Is marriage so demoralizing as that?

Lane. I believe it *is* a very pleasant state, sir. I have had very little experience of it myself up to the present. I have only been married once. That was in consequence of a misunderstanding between myself and a young person.

Algernon (*languidly*). I don't know that I am much interested in your family life, Lane.

Lane. No, sir; it is not a very interesting subject. I never think of it myself.

Algernon. Very natural, I am sure. That will do, Lane, thank you.

Lane. Thank you, sir. (Lane *goes out.*)

Algernon. Lane's views on marriage seem somewhat lax. Really, if the lower orders don't set us a good example, what on earth is the use of them? They seem, as a class, to have absolutely no sense of moral responsibility.

[*Enter* Lane.]

Lane. Mr. Ernest Worthing.

[*Enter* Jack. Lane *goes out.*]

Algernon. How are you, my dear Ernest? What brings you up to town?

Jack. Oh, pleasure, pleasure! What else should bring one anywhere? Eating as usual, I see, Algy!

---

1. **Morning room:** an informal sitting room, different from the more formal drawing room.
2. **salver:** a tray.

Algernon (*stiffly*). I believe it is customary in good society to take some slight refreshment at five o'clock. Where have you been since last Thursday?

Jack (*sitting down on the sofa*). In the country.

Algernon. What on earth do you do there?

Jack (*pulling off his gloves*). When one is in town, one amuses oneself. When one is in the country, one amuses other people. It is excessively boring.

Algernon. And who are the people you amuse?

Jack (*airily*). Oh, neighbors, neighbors.

Algernon. Got nice neighbors in your part of Shropshire?

Jack. Perfectly horrid! Never speak to one of them.

Algernon. How immensely you must amuse them! (*Goes over and takes sandwich*) By the way, Shropshire is your county, is it not?

Jack. Eh? Shropshire? Yes, of course. Hallo! Why all these cups? Why cucumber sandwiches? Why such reckless extravagance in one so young? Who is coming to tea?

Algernon. Oh! Merely Aunt Augusta and Gwendolen.

Jack. How perfectly delightful!

Algernon. Yes, that is all very well; but I am afraid Aunt Augusta won't quite approve of your being here.

Jack. May I ask why?

Algernon. My dear fellow, the way you flirt with Gwendolen is perfectly disgraceful. It is almost as bad as the way Gwendolen flirts with you.

Jack. I am in love with Gwendolen. I have come up to town expressly to propose to her.

Algernon. I thought you had come up for pleasure? . . . I call that business.

Jack. How utterly unromantic you are!

Algernon. I really don't see anything romantic in proposing. It is very romantic to be in love. But there is nothing romantic about a definite proposal. Why, one may be accepted. One usually is, I believe. Then the excitement is all over. The very essence of romance is un-certainty. If ever I get married, I'll certainly try to forget the fact.

Jack. I have no doubt about that, dear Algy. The Divorce Court was specially invented for people whose memories are so curiously constituted.

Algernon. Oh! There is no use speculating on that subject. Divorces are made in heaven— (Jack *puts out his hand to take a sandwich.* Algernon *at once interferes.*) Please don't touch the cucumber sandwiches. They are ordered specially for Aunt Augusta. (*Takes one and eats it*)

Jack. Well, you have been eating them all the time.

Algernon. That is quite a different matter. She is my aunt. (*Takes plate from below*) Have some bread and butter. The bread and butter is for Gwendolen. Gwendolen is devoted to bread and butter.

Jack (*advancing to table and helping himself*). And very good bread and butter it is too.

Algernon. Well, my dear fellow, you need not eat as if you were going to eat it all. You behave as if you were married to her already. You are not married to her already, and I don't think you ever will be.

Jack. Why on earth do you say that?

Algernon. Well, in the first place, girls never marry the men they flirt with. Girls don't think it right.

Jack. Oh, that is nonsense!

Algernon. It isn't. It is a great truth. It accounts for the extraordinary number of bachelors that one sees all over the place. In the second place, I don't give my consent.

Jack. Your consent!

Algernon. My dear fellow, Gwendolen is my first cousin. And before I allow you to marry her, you will have to clear up the whole question of Cecily. (*Rings bell*)

Jack. Cecily! What on earth do you mean? What do you mean, Algy, by Cecily! I don't know anyone of the name of Cecily.

[*Enter* Lane.]

Algernon. Bring me that cigarette case Mr. Worthing left in the smoking room the last time he dined here.

Lane. Yes, sir. (Lane *goes out.*)

Jack. Do you mean to say you have had my cigarette case all this time? I wish to goodness you had let me know. I have been writing frantic letters to Scotland Yard about it. I was very nearly offering a large reward.

Algernon. Well, I wish you would offer one. I happen to be more than usually hard up.

Jack. There is no good offering a large reward now that the thing is found.

[*Enter* Lane *with the cigarette case on a salver.* Algernon *takes it at once.* Lane *goes out.*]

Algernon. I think that is rather mean of you, Ernest, I must say. (*Opens case and examines it*) However, it makes no matter, for, now that I look at the inscription inside, I find that the thing isn't yours after all.

Jack. Of course it's mine. (*Moving to him*) You have seen me with it a hundred times, and you have no right whatsoever to read what is written inside. It is a very ungentlemanly thing to read a private cigarette case.

Algernon. Oh! It is absurd to have a hard and fast rule about what one should read and what one shouldn't. More than half of modern culture depends on what one shouldn't read.

Jack. I am quite aware of the fact, and I don't propose to discuss modern culture. It isn't the sort of thing one should talk of in private. I simply want my cigarette case back.

Algernon. Yes; but this isn't your cigarette case. This cigarette case is a present from someone of the name of Cecily, and you said you didn't know anyone of that name.

Jack. Well, if you want to know, Cecily happens to be my aunt.

Algernon. Your aunt!

Jack. Yes. Charming old lady she is, too. Lives at Tunbridge Wells. Just give it back to me, Algy.

Algernon (*retreating to back of sofa*). But why does she call herself little Cecily if she is your aunt and lives at Tunbridge Wells? (*Reading*) "From little Cecily with her fondest love."

Jack (*moving to sofa and kneeling upon it*). My dear fellow, what on earth is there in that? Some aunts are tall, some aunts are not tall. That is a matter that surely an aunt may be allowed to decide for herself. You seem to think that every aunt should be exactly like your aunt! That is absurd. For heaven's sake, give me back my cigarette case. (*Follows* Algernon *round the room*)

Algernon. Yes. But why does your aunt call you her uncle? "From little Cecily, with her fondest love to her dear Uncle Jack." There is no objection, I admit, to an aunt being a small aunt, but why an aunt, no matter what her size may be, should call her own nephew her uncle, I can't quite make out. Besides, your name isn't Jack at all; it is Ernest.

Jack. It isn't Ernest; it's Jack.

Algernon. You have always told me it was Ernest. I have introduced you to everyone as Ernest. You answer to the name of Ernest. You look as if your name was Ernest. You are the most earnest-looking person I ever saw in my life. It is perfectly absurd your saying that your name isn't Ernest. It's on your cards. Here is one of them: (*taking it from case*) "Mr. Ernest Worthing, B.4, The Albany, W." I'll keep this as a proof that your name is Ernest if ever you attempt to deny it to me, or to Gwendolen, or to anyone else. (*Puts the card in his pocket*)

Jack. Well, my name is Ernest in town and Jack in the country, and the cigarette case was given to me in the country.

Algernon. Yes, but that does not account for the fact that your small Aunt Cecily, who lives at Tunbridge Wells, calls you her dear uncle. Come, old boy, you had much better have the thing out at once.

Jack. My dear Algy, you talk exactly as if you were a dentist. It is very vulgar to talk like a dentist when one isn't a dentist. It produces a false impression.

Algernon. Well, that is exactly what dentists always do. Now, go on! Tell me the whole thing. I may mention that I have always suspected you of being a confirmed and secret Bunburyist; and I am quite sure of it now.

Jack. Bunburyist? What on earth do you mean by a Bunburyist?

Algernon. I'll reveal to you the meaning of that incomparable expression as soon as you are kind enough to inform me why you are Ernest in town and Jack in the country.

Jack. Well, produce my cigarette case first.

Algernon. Here it is. (*Hands cigarette case*) Now produce your explanation, and pray make it improbable. (*Sits on sofa*)

Jack. My dear fellow, there is nothing improbable about my explanation at all. In fact it's perfectly ordinary. Old Mr. Thomas Cardew, who adopted me when I was a little boy, made me in his will guardian to his granddaughter, Miss Cecily Cardew. Cecily, who addresses me as her uncle from motives of respect that you could not possibly appreciate, lives at my place in the country under the charge of her admirable governess, Miss Prism.

Algernon. Where is that place in the country, by the way?

Jack. That is nothing to you, dear boy. You are not going to be invited. . . . I may tell you candidly that the place is not in Shropshire.

Algernon. I suspected that, my dear fellow! I have Bunburyed all over Shropshire on two separate occasions. Now, go on. Why are you Ernest in town and Jack in the country?

Jack. My dear Algy, I don't know whether you will be able to understand my real motives. You are hardly serious enough. When one is placed in the position of guardian, one has to adopt a very high moral tone on all subjects. It's one's duty to do so. And as a high moral tone can hardly be said to conduce very much to either one's health or one's happiness, in order to get up to town I have always pretended to have a younger brother of the name of Ernest, who lives in the Albany, and gets into the most dreadful scrapes. That, my

dear Algy, is the whole truth pure and simple.

Algernon. The truth is rarely pure and never simple. Modern life would be very tedious if it were either, and modern literature a complete impossibility!

Jack. That wouldn't be at all a bad thing.

Algernon. Literary criticism is not your forte, my dear fellow. Don't try it. You should leave that to people who haven't been at a University. They do it so well in the daily papers. What you really are is a Bunburyist. I was quite right in saying you were a Bunburyist. You are one of the most advanced Bunburyists I know.

Jack. What on earth do you mean?

Algernon. You have invented a very useful younger brother called Ernest, in order that you may be able to come up to town as often as you like. I have invented an invaluable permanent invalid called Bunbury, in order that I may be able to go down into the country whenever I choose. Bunbury is perfectly invaluable. If it wasn't for Bunbury's extraordinary bad health, for instance, I wouldn't be able to dine with you at Willis' tonight, for I have been really engaged to Aunt Augusta for more than a week.

Jack. I haven't asked you to dine with me anywhere tonight.

Algernon. I know. You are absurdly careless about sending out invitations. It is very foolish of you. Nothing annoys people so much as not receiving invitations.

Jack. You had much better dine with your Aunt Augusta.

Algernon. I haven't the smallest intention of doing anything of the kind. To begin with, I dined there on Monday, and once a week is quite enough to dine with one's own relations. In the second place, whenever I do dine there I am always treated as a member of the family, and sent down with either no woman at all, or two. In the third place, I know perfectly well whom she will place me next to, tonight. She will place me next Mary Farquhar, who always flirts with her own husband across the dinner table. That is not very pleasant. Indeed, it is not even decent . . . and that sort of thing is enormously on the increase. The amount of women in London who flirt with their own husbands is perfectly scandalous. It looks so bad. It is simply washing one's clean linen in public. Besides, now that I know you to be a confirmed Bunburyist I naturally want to talk to you about Bunburying. I want to tell you the rules.

Jack. I'm not a Bunburyist at all. If Gwendolen accepts me, I am going to kill my brother, indeed I think I'll kill him in any case. Cecily is a little too much interested in him. It is rather a bore. So I am going to get rid of Ernest. And I strongly advise you to do the same with Mr. . . . with your invalid friend who has the absurd name.

Algernon. Nothing will induce me to part with Bunbury, and if you ever get married, which seems to me extremely problematic, you will be very glad to know Bunbury. A man who marries without knowing Bunbury has a very tedious time of it.

Jack. That is nonsense. If I marry a charming girl like Gwendolen, and she is the only girl I ever saw in my life that I would marry, I certainly won't want to know Bunbury.

Algernon. Then your wife will. You don't seem to realize that in married life three is company and two is none.

Jack (*sententiously*). That, my dear young friend, is the theory that the corrupt French drama has been propounding for the last fifty years.[3]

Algernon. Yes; and that the happy English home has proved in half the time.

Jack. For heaven's sake, don't try to be cynical. It's perfectly easy to be cynical.

Algernon. My dear fellow, it isn't easy to be anything nowadays. There's such a lot of beastly competition about. (*The sound of an electric bell is heard.*) Ah! That must be Aunt Augusta. Only relatives, or creditors, ever ring in that Wagnerian[4] manner. Now, if I get her out of the way for ten minutes, so that you can have an opportunity for proposing to Gwendolen, may I dine with you tonight at Willis'?

Jack. I suppose so, if you want to.

Algernon. Yes, but you must be serious about it. I hate people who are not serious about meals. It is so shallow of them.

[*Enter* Lane.]

Lane. Lady Bracknell and Miss Fairfax.

[Algernon *goes forward to meet them. Enter* Lady Bracknell *and* Gwendolen.]

Lady Bracknell. Good afternoon, dear Algernon, I hope you are behaving very well.

Algernon. I'm feeling very well, Aunt Augusta.

Lady Bracknell. That's not quite the same thing. In fact the two things rarely go together. (*Sees* Jack *and bows to him with icy coldness*)

Algernon (*to* Gwendolen). Dear me, you are smart!

Gwendolen. I am always smart! Am I not, Mr. Worthing?

Jack. You're quite perfect, Miss Fairfax.

Gwendolen. Oh! I hope I am not that. It would leave no room for developments, and I intend to develop in many directions. (Gwendolen *and* Jack *sit down together in the corner.*)

Lady Bracknell. I'm sorry if we are a little late, Algernon, but I was obliged to call on dear Lady Harbury. I hadn't been there since her poor husband's death. I never saw a woman so altered; she looks quite twenty years younger. And now I'll have a cup of tea

---

3. **corrupt . . . years:** The "love triangle" was a popular plot in French novels and plays of the late nineteenth century.

4. **Wagnerian** (väg'nîr'ē-ən): operatic. Richard Wagner (1813–1883), a German composer, had startled the music world by his stirring and dramatic music.

Scene from a 1953 film version of *The Importance of Being Earnest.*
Museum of Modern Art, New York

and one of those nice cucumber sandwiches you promised me.

Algernon. Certainly, Aunt Augusta. (*Goes over to tea table*)

Lady Bracknell. Won't you come and sit here, Gwendolen?

Gwendolen. Thanks, Mama, I'm quite comfortable where I am.

Algernon (*picking up empty plate in horror*). Good heavens! Lane! Why are there no cucumber sandwiches? I ordered them specially.

Lane (*gravely*). There were no cucumbers in the market this morning, sir. I went down twice.

Algernon. No cucumbers!

Lane. No, sir. Not even for ready money.

Algernon. That will do, Lane, thank you.

Lane. Thank you, sir. (*Goes out*)

Algernon. I am greatly distressed, Aunt Augusta, about there being no cucumbers, not even for ready money.

Lady Bracknell. It really makes no matter,

Algernon. I had some crumpets with Lady Harbury, who seems to me to be living entirely for pleasure now.

Algernon. I hear her hair has turned quite gold from grief.

Lady Bracknell. It certainly has changed its color. From what cause I, of course, cannot say. (Algernon *crosses and hands tea*) Thank you, I've quite a treat for you tonight, Algernon. I am going to send you down with Mary Farquhar. She is such a nice woman, and so attentive to her husband. It's delightful to watch them.

Algernon. I am afraid, Aunt Augusta, I shall have to give up the pleasure of dining with you tonight after all.

Lady Bracknell (*frowning*). I hope not, Algernon. It would put my table completely out. Your uncle would have to dine upstairs. Fortunately he is accustomed to that.

Algernon. It is a great bore, and, I need hardly say, a terrible disappointment to me, but the fact is I have just had a telegram to say that my poor friend Bunbury is very ill again. (*Exchanges glances with* Jack) They seem to think I should be with him.

Lady Bracknell. It is very strange. This Mr. Bunbury seems to suffer from curiously bad health.

Algernon. Yes; poor Bunbury is a dreadful invalid.

Lady Bracknell. Well, I must say, Algernon, that I think it is high time that Mr. Bunbury made up his mind whether he was going to live or to die. This shilly-shallying with the question is absurd. Nor do I in any way approve of the modern sympathy with invalids. I consider it morbid. Illness of any kind is hardly a thing to be encouraged in others. Health is the primary duty of life. I am always telling that to your poor uncle, but he never seems to take much notice . . . as far as any improvement in his ailments goes. I should be much obliged if you would ask Mr. Bunbury, from me, to be kind enough not to have a relapse on Saturday, for I rely on you to arrange my music for me. It is my last reception, and one wants something that will encourage conversation, particularly at the end of the season when everyone has practically said whatever they had to say, which, in most cases, was probably not much.

Algernon. I'll speak to Bunbury, Aunt Augusta, if he is still conscious, and I think I can promise you he'll be all right by Saturday. Of course the music is a great difficulty. You see, if one plays good music, people don't listen, and if one plays bad music, people don't talk. But I'll run over the program I've drawn out, if you will kindly come into the next room for a moment.

Lady Bracknell. Thank you, Algernon. It is very thoughtful of you. (*Rising, and following* Algernon) I'm sure the program will be delightful, after a few expurgations. French songs I cannot possibly allow. People always seem to think that they are improper, and either look shocked, which is vulgar, or laugh, which is worse. But German sounds a thoroughly respectable language, and indeed I

believe is so. Gwendolen, you will accompany me.

Gwendolen. Certainly, Mama.

[Lady Bracknell *and* Algernon *go into the music room;* Gwendolen *remains behind.*]

Jack. Charming day it has been, Miss Fairfax.

Gwendolen. Pray don't talk to me about the weather, Mr. Worthing. Whenever people talk to me about the weather, I always feel quite certain that they mean something else. And that makes me so nervous.

Jack. I do mean something else.

Gwendolen. I thought so. In fact, I am never wrong.

Jack. And I would like to be allowed to take advantage of Lady Bracknell's temporary absence . . .

Gwendolen. I would certainly advise you to do so. Mama has a way of coming back suddenly into a room that I have often had to speak to her about.

Jack (*nervously*). Miss Fairfax, ever since I met you I have admired you more than any girl . . . I have ever met since . . . I met you.

Gwendolen. Yes, I am quite aware of the fact. And I often wish that in public, at any rate, you had been more demonstrative. For me you have always had an irresistible fascination. Even before I met you I was far from indifferent to you. (Jack *looks at her in amazement.*) We live, as I hope you know, Mr. Worthing, in an age of ideals. The fact is constantly mentioned in the more expensive monthly magazines, and has reached the provincial pulpits, I am told; and my ideal has always been to love someone of the name of Ernest. There is something in that name that inspires absolute confidence. The moment Algernon first mentioned to me that he had a friend called Ernest, I knew I was destined to love you.

Jack. You really love me, Gwendolen?

Gwendolen. Passionately!

Jack. Darling! You don't know how happy you've made me.

Gwendolen. My own Ernest!

Jack. But you don't really mean to say that you couldn't love me if my name wasn't Ernest?

Gwendolen. But your name is Ernest.

Jack. Yes, I know it is. But supposing it was something else? Do you mean to say you couldn't love me then?

Gwendolen (*glibly*). Ah! That is clearly a metaphysical speculation,[5] and like most metaphysical speculations has very little reference at all to the actual facts of real life, as we know them.

Jack. Personally, darling, to speak quite candidly, I don't much care about the name of Ernest. . . . I don't think the name suits me at all.

Gwendolen. It suits you perfectly. It is a divine name. It has a music of its own. It produces vibrations.

Jack. Well, really, Gwendolen, I must say that I think there are lots of other much nicer names. I think Jack, for instance, a charming name.

Gwendolen. Jack? . . . No, there is very little music in the name Jack, if any at all, indeed. It does not thrill. It produces absolutely no vibrations. . . . I have known several Jacks, and they all, without exception, were more than usually plain. Besides, Jack is a notorious domesticity for John! And I pity any woman who is married to a man called John. She would probably never be allowed to know the entrancing pleasure of a single moment's solitude. The only really safe name is Ernest.

Jack. Gwendolen, I must get christened at once—I mean we must get married at once. There is no time to be lost.

Gwendolen. Married, Mr. Worthing?

Jack (*astounded*). Well . . . surely. You know that I love you, and you led me to believe, Miss Fairfax, that you were not absolutely indifferent to me.

Gwendolen. I adore you. But you haven't proposed to me yet. Nothing has been said at all about marriage. The subject has not even been touched on.

Jack. Well . . . may I propose to you now?

Gwendolen. I think it would be an admirable opportunity. And to spare you any possible disappointment, Mr. Worthing, I think it only fair to tell you quite frankly beforehand that I am fully determined to accept you.

Jack. Gwendolen!

Gwendolen. Yes, Mr. Worthing, what have you got to say to me?

Jack. You know what I have got to say to you.

Gwendolen. Yes, but you don't say it.

Jack (*goes on his knees*). Gwendolen, will you marry me?

Gwendolen. Of course I will, darling. How long you have been about it! I am afraid you have had very little experience in how to propose.

Jack. My own one, I have never loved anyone in the world but you.

Gwendolen. Yes, but men often propose for practice. I know my brother Gerald does. All my girlfriends tell me so. What wonderfully blue eyes you have, Ernest! They are quite, quite blue. I hope you will always look at me just like that, especially when there are other people present.

[*Enter* Lady Bracknell.]

Lady Bracknell. Mr. Worthing! Rise, sir, from this semirecumbent posture. It is most indecorous.

Gwendolen. Mama! (*He tries to rise; she restrains him.*) I must beg you to retire. This is no place for you. Besides, Mr. Worthing has not quite finished yet.

Lady Bracknell. Finished what, may I ask?

Gwendolen. I am engaged to Mr. Worthing, Mama. (*They rise together.*)

Lady Bracknell. Pardon me, you are not engaged to anyone. When you do become engaged to someone, I, or your father, should his health permit him, will inform you of the

---

5. **metaphysical speculation:** abstract philosophical inquiry.

fact. An engagement should come on a young girl as a surprise, pleasant or unpleasant, as the case may be. It is hardly a matter that she could be allowed to arrange for herself. . . . And now I have a few questions to put to you, Mr. Worthing. While I am making these inquiries, you, Gwendolen, will wait for me below in the carriage.

Gwendolen (*reproachfully*). Mama!

Lady Bracknell. In the carriage, Gwendolen! (Gwendolen *goes to the door. She and* Jack *blow kisses to each other behind* Lady Bracknell*'s back.* Lady Bracknell *looks vaguely about as if she could not understand what the noise was. Finally turns round.*) Gwendolen, the carriage!

Gwendolen. Yes, Mama. (*Goes out, looking back at* Jack)

Lady Bracknell (*sitting down*). You can take a seat, Mr. Worthing. (*Looks in her pocket for notebook and pencil*)

Jack. Thank you, Lady Bracknell, I prefer standing.

Lady Bracknell (*pencil and notebook in hand*). I feel bound to tell you that you are not down on my list of eligible young men, although I have the same list as the dear Duchess of Bolton has. We work together, in fact. However, I am quite ready to enter your name, should your answers be what a really affectionate mother requires. Do you smoke?

Jack. Well, yes, I must admit I smoke.

Lady Bracknell. I am glad to hear it. A man should always have an occupation of some kind. There are far too many idle men in London as it is. How old are you?

Jack. Twenty-nine.

Lady Bracknell. A very good age to be married at. I have always been of opinion that a man who desires to get married should know either everything or nothing. Which do you know?

Jack (*after some hesitation*). I know nothing, Lady Bracknell.

Lady Bracknell. I am pleased to hear it. I do not approve of anything that tampers with natural ignorance. Ignorance is like a delicate exotic fruit; touch it and the bloom is gone. The whole theory of modern education is radically unsound. Fortunately in England, at any rate, education produces no effect whatsoever. If it did, it would prove a serious danger to the upper classes, and probably lead to acts of violence in Grosvenor Square.[6] What is your income?

Jack. Between seven and eight thousand a year.

Lady Bracknell (*makes a note in her book*). In land or in investments?

Jack. In investments, chiefly.

Lady Bracknell. That is satisfactory. What between the duties expected of one during one's lifetime, and the duties exacted from one after one's death, land has ceased to be either a profit or a pleasure. It gives one position and prevents one from keeping it up. That's all that can be said about land.

Jack. I have a country house with some land, of course, attached to it, about fifteen hundred acres, I believe; but I don't depend on that for my real income. In fact, as far as I can make out, the poachers are the only people who make anything out of it.

Lady Bracknell. A country house! How many bedrooms? Well, that point can be cleared up afterward. You have a town house, I hope? A girl with a simple, unspoiled nature, like Gwendolen, could hardly be expected to reside in the country.

Jack. Well, I own a house in Belgrave Square, but it is let by the year to Lady Bloxham. Of course, I can get it back whenever I like, at six months' notice.

Lady Bracknell. Lady Bloxham? I don't know her.

Jack. Oh, she goes about very little. She is a lady considerably advanced in years.

Lady Bracknell. Ah, nowadays that is no guarantee of respectability of character. What number in Belgrave Square?

---

6. **Grosvenor** (grōv′nər) **Square:** a fashionable square in Mayfair, east of Hyde Park.

Jack. One hundred and forty-nine.

Lady Bracknell (*shaking her head*). The un-fashionable side. I thought there was something. However, that could easily be altered.

Jack. Do you mean the fashion, or the side?

Lady Bracknell (*sternly*). Both, if necessary, I presume. What are your politics?

Jack. Well, I am afraid I really have none. I am a Liberal Unionist.[7]

Lady Bracknell. Oh, they count as Tories. They dine with us. Or come in the evening, at any rate. Now to minor matters. Are your parents living?

Jack. I have lost both my parents.

Lady Bracknell. To lose one parent, Mr. Worthing, may be regarded as a misfortune; to lose both looks like carelessness. Who was your father? He was evidently a man of some wealth. Was he born in what the Radical papers call the purple of commerce, or did he rise from the ranks of the aristocracy?

Jack. I am afraid I really don't know. The fact is, Lady Bracknell, I said I had lost my parents. It would be nearer the truth to say that my parents seem to have lost me. . . . I don't actually know who I am by birth. I was . . . well, I was found.

Lady Bracknell. Found!

Jack. The late Mr. Thomas Cardew, an old gentleman of a very charitable and kindly disposition, found me and gave me the name of Worthing, because he happened to have a first-class ticket for Worthing in his pocket at the time. Worthing is a place in Sussex. It is a seaside resort.

Lady Bracknell. Where did the charitable gentleman who had a first-class ticket for this seaside resort find you?

Jack (*gravely*). In a handbag.

Lady Bracknell. A handbag?

Jack (*very seriously*). Yes, Lady Bracknell. I was in a handbag—a somewhat large, black leather handbag, with handles to it—an ordinary handbag in fact.

Lady Bracknell. In what locality did this Mr. James, or Thomas, Cardew come across this ordinary handbag?

Jack. In the cloakroom at Victoria Station. It was given to him in mistake for his own.

Lady Bracknell. The cloakroom at Victoria Station?

Jack. Yes. The Brighton line.

Lady Bracknell. The line is immaterial. Mr. Worthing, I confess I feel somewhat bewildered by what you have just told me. To be born, or at any rate bred, in a handbag, whether it had handles or not, seems to me to display a contempt for the ordinary decencies of family life that reminds one of the worst excesses of the French Revolution. And I presume you know what that unfortunate movement led to? As for the particular locality in which the handbag was found, a cloakroom at a railway station might serve to conceal a social indiscretion—has probably, indeed, been used for that purpose before now—but it could hardly be regarded as an assured basis for a recognized position in good society.

Jack. May I ask you then what you would advise me to do? I need hardly say I would do anything in the world to ensure Gwendolen's happiness.

Lady Bracknell. I would strongly advise you, Mr. Worthing, to try and acquire some relations as soon as possible, and to make a definite effort to produce at any rate one parent, of either sex, before the season is quite over.

Jack. Well, I don't see how I could possibly manage to do that. I can produce the handbag at any moment. It is in my dressing room at home. I really think that should satisfy you, Lady Bracknell.

Lady Bracknell. Me, sir! What has it to do with me? You can hardly imagine that I and Lord Bracknell would dream of allowing our only daughter—a girl brought up with the utmost care—to marry into a cloakroom, and form an alliance with a parcel. Good morning, Mr. Worthing!

---

7. **Liberal Unionist:** Liberal Unionists were members of the Liberal party who opposed home rule for Ireland in 1886, and, therefore, would be more acceptable to Lord and Lady Bracknell than strict Liberals.

[Lady Bracknell *sweeps out in majestic indignation.*]

Jack. Good morning! (Algernon, *from the other room, strikes up the Wedding March. Jack looks perfectly furious, and goes to the door.*) For goodness' sake, don't play that ghastly tune, Algy! How idiotic you are!

[*The music stops, and* Algernon *enters cheerily.*]

Algernon. Didn't it go off all right, old boy? You don't mean to say Gwendolen refused you? I know it is a way she has. She is always refusing people. I think it is most ill-natured of her.

Jack. Oh, Gwendolen is as right as a trivet.[8] As far as she is concerned, we are engaged. Her mother is perfectly unbearable. Never met such a Gorgon.[9] . . . I don't really know what a Gorgon is like, but I am quite sure that Lady Bracknell is one. In any case, she is a monster, without being a myth, which is rather unfair. . . . I beg your pardon, Algy, I suppose I shouldn't talk about your own aunt in that way before you.

Algernon. My dear boy, I love hearing my relations abused. It is the only thing that makes me put up with them at all. Relations are simply a tedious pack of people, who haven't got the remotest knowledge of how to live, nor the smallest instinct about when to die.

Jack. Oh, that is nonsense!

Algernon. It isn't!

Jack. Well, I won't argue about the matter. You always want to argue about things.

Algernon. That is exactly what things were originally made for.

Jack. Upon my word, if I thought that, I'd shoot myself. . . . (*A pause*) You don't think there is any chance of Gwendolen becoming like her mother in about a hundred and fifty years, do you, Algy?

Algernon. All women become like their mothers. That is their tragedy. No man does. That's his.

Jack. Is that clever?

Algernon. It is perfectly phrased! And quite as true as any observation in civilized life should be.

Jack. I am sick to death of cleverness. Everybody is clever nowadays. You can't go anywhere without meeting clever people. The thing has become an absolute public nuisance. I wish to goodness we had a few fools left.

Algernon. We have.

Jack. I should extremely like to meet them. What do they talk about?

Algernon. The fools? Oh! About the clever people, of course.

Jack. What fools.

Algernon. By the way, did you tell Gwendolen the truth about your being Ernest in town and Jack in the country?

Jack (*in a very patronizing manner*). My dear fellow, the truth isn't quite the sort of thing one tells to a nice, sweet, refined girl. What extraordinary ideas you have about the way to behave to a woman!

Algernon. The only way to behave to a woman is to make love to her, if she is pretty, and to someone else, if she is plain.

Jack. Oh, that is nonsense.

Algernon. What about your brother? What about the profligate Ernest?

Jack. Oh, before the end of the week I shall have got rid of him. I'll say he died in Paris of apoplexy.[10] Lots of people die of apoplexy, quite suddenly, don't they?

---

8. **right as a trivet:** A trivet is a stool or stand perfectly balanced on three legs; therefore, Gwendolen is standing firm.

9. **Gorgon:** In Greek mythology the Gorgons were three sisters who had snakes for hair. The sight of any one of them would turn the beholder to stone.

10. **apoplexy:** a stroke.

Algernon. Yes, but it's hereditary, my dear fellow. It's a sort of thing that runs in families. You had much better say a severe chill.

Jack. You are sure a severe chill isn't hereditary, or anything of that kind?

Algernon. Of course it isn't!

Jack. Very well, then. My poor brother Ernest is carried off suddenly, in Paris, by a severe chill. That gets rid of him.

Algernon. But I thought you said that . . . Miss Cardew was a little too much interested in your poor brother Ernest? Won't she feel his loss a good deal?

Jack. Oh, that is all right. Cecily is not a silly romantic girl, I am glad to say. She has got a capital appetite, goes for long walks, and pays no attention at all to her lessons.

Algernon. I would rather like to see Cecily.

Jack. I will take very good care you never do. She is excessively pretty, and she is only just eighteen.

Algernon. Have you told Gwendolen yet that you have an excessively pretty ward who is only just eighteen?

Jack. Oh! One doesn't blurt these things out to people. Cecily and Gwendolen are perfectly certain to be extremely great friends. I'll bet you anything you like that half an hour after they have met, they will be calling each other sister.

Algernon. Women only do that when they have called each other a lot of other things first. Now, my dear boy, if we want to get a good table at Willis', we really must go and dress. Do you know it is nearly seven?

Jack (*irritably*). Oh! It always is nearly seven.

Algernon. Well, I'm hungry.

Jack. I never knew you when you weren't. . . .

Algernon. What shall we do after dinner? Go to a theater?

Jack. Oh, no! I loathe listening.

Algernon. Well, let us go to the club?

Jack. Oh, no! I hate talking.

Algernon. Well, we might trot round to the Empire[11] at ten?

---

11. **the Empire:** a popular amusement hall of the time.

Jack. Oh, no! I can't bear looking at things. It is so silly.

Algernon. Well, what shall we do?

Jack. Nothing!

Algernon. It is awfully hard work doing nothing. However, I don't mind hard work where there is no definite object of any kind.

[*Enter* Lane.]

Lane. Miss Fairfax.

[*Enter* Gwendolen. Lane *goes out.*]

Algernon. Gwendolen, upon my word!

Gwendolen. Algy, kindly turn your back. I have something very particular to say to Mr. Worthing.

Algernon. Really, Gwendolen, I don't think I can allow this at all.

Gwendolen. Algy, you always adopt a strictly immoral attitude toward life. You are not quite old enough to do that. (Algernon *retires to the fireplace.*)

Jack. My own darling!

Gwendolen. Ernest, we may never be married. From the expression on Mama's face I fear we never shall. Few parents nowadays pay any regard to what their children say to them. The old-fashioned respect for the young is fast dying out. Whatever influence I ever had over Mama, I lost at the age of three. But although she may prevent us from becoming man and wife, and I may marry someone else, and marry often, nothing that she can possibly do can alter my eternal devotion to you.

Jack. Dear Gwendolen!

Gwendolen. The story of your romantic origin, as related to me by Mama, with unpleasing comments, has naturally stirred the deeper fibers of my nature. Your Christian name has an irresistible fascination. The simplicity of your character makes you exquisitely incomprehensible to me. Your town address at the Albany I have. What is your address in the country?

Jack. The Manor House, Woolton, Hertfordshire.

[Algernon, *who has been carefully listening, smiles to himself, and writes the address on his shirt cuff. Then picks up the* Railway Guide.]

Gwendolen. There is a good postal service, I suppose? It may be necessary to do something desperate. That, of course, will require serious consideration. I will communicate with you daily.
Jack. My own one!
Gwendolen. How long do you remain in town?
Jack. Till Monday.
Gwendolen. Good! Algy, you may turn round now.
Algernon. Thanks, I've turned round already.
Gwendolen. You may also ring the bell.
Jack. You will let me see you to your carriage, my own darling?
Gwendolen. Certainly.
Jack (*to* Lane, *who now enters*). I will see Miss Fairfax out.
Lane. Yes, sir. (Jack *and* Gwendolen *go off.*)

[Lane *presents several letters on a salver to* Algernon. *It is to be surmised that they are bills, as* Algernon, *after looking at the envelopes, tears them up.*]

Algernon. A glass of sherry, Lane.
Lane. Yes, sir.
Algernon. Tomorrow, Lane, I'm going Bunburying.
Lane. Yes, sir.
Algernon. I shall probably not be back till Monday. You can put up my dress clothes, my smoking jacket, and all the Bunbury suits. . . .
Lane. Yes, sir. (*Handing sherry*)
Algernon. I hope tomorrow will be a fine day, Lane.
Lane. It never is, sir.
Algernon. Lane, you're a perfect pessimist.
Lane. I do my best to give satisfaction, sir.

[*Enter* Jack. Lane *goes off.*]

Jack. There's a sensible, intellectual girl! The only girl I ever cared for in my life. (Algernon *is laughing immoderately.*) What on earth are you so amused at?
Algernon. Oh, I'm a little anxious about poor Bunbury, that is all.
Jack. If you don't take care, your friend Bunbury will get you into a serious scrape some day.
Algernon. I love scrapes. They are the only things that are never serious.
Jack. Oh, that's nonsense, Algy. You never talk anything but nonsense.
Algernon. Nobody ever does.

[Jack *looks indignantly at him, and leaves the room.* Algernon *lights a cigarette, reads his shirt cuff, and smiles.*]

FOR STUDY AND DISCUSSION

1. Explain the double lives led by Jack and Algernon. Where and to whom is Jack known as "Ernest"? What does Algernon mean when he says to Jack: "I have always suspected you of being a confirmed and secret Bunburyist"?
2. Why does Algernon say to Jack just before the arrival of Lady Bracknell: "I am afraid Aunt Augusta won't quite approve of your being here"? What evidence do we have that Lady Bracknell does not approve of Jack's presence? What are Lady Bracknell's requirements for a proper suitor for Gwendolen?
3. One conventional feature of most social comedy is the presence of what is often called the *blocking figure,* a character in the play, often an old and ill-tempered person, whose opposition to the romantic impulses of the other main characters provides the basis for much of the comic action. In what sense could Lady Bracknell be described as the blocking figure in *The Importance of Being Earnest?*
4. The comic wit of Wilde's writing often depends upon a character's directly contradicting what we normally assume to be logical or true. We can see an example of this in Algernon's comment that "the amount of women in London who flirt with their own husbands is perfectly scandalous." Find other examples in Act One of this kind of wit.

Act Two

Garden at the Manor House. A flight of gray stone steps leads up to the house. The garden, an old-fashioned one, full of roses. Time of year, July. Basket chairs, and a table covered with books, are set under a large yew tree.

Miss Prism *discovered seated at the table. Cecily is at the back, watering flowers.*

Miss Prism (*calling*). Cecily, Cecily! Surely such a utilitarian occupation as the watering of flowers is rather Moulton's duty than yours? Especially at a moment when intellectual pleasures await you. Your German grammar is on the table. Pray open it at page fifteen. We will repeat yesterday's lesson.

Cecily (*coming over very slowly*). But I don't like German. It isn't at all a becoming language. I know perfectly well that I look quite plain after my German lesson.

Miss Prism. Child, you know how anxious your guardian is that you should improve yourself in every way. He laid particular stress on your German, as he was leaving for town yesterday. Indeed, he always lays stress on your German when he is leaving for town.

Cecily. Dear Uncle Jack is so very serious! Sometimes he is so serious that I think he cannot be quite well.

Miss Prism (*drawing herself up*). Your guardian enjoys the best of health, and his gravity of demeanor is especially to be commended in one so comparatively young as he is. I know no one who has a higher sense of duty and responsibility.

Cecily. I suppose that is why he often looks a little bored when we three are together.

Miss Prism. Cecily! I am surprised at you. Mr. Worthing has many troubles in his life. Idle merriment and triviality would be out of place in his conversation. You must remember his constant anxiety about that unfortunate young man, his brother.

Cecily. I wish Uncle Jack would allow that unfortunate young man, his brother, to come down here sometimes. We might have a good influence over him, Miss Prism. I am sure you certainly would. You know German and geology, and things of that kind influence a man very much. (Cecily *begins to write in her diary.*)

Miss Prism (*shaking her head*). I do not think that even I could produce any effect on a character that according to his own brother's admission is irretrievably weak and vacillating. Indeed I am not sure that I would desire to reclaim him. I am not in favor of this modern mania for turning bad people into good people at a moment's notice. As a man sows, so let him reap. You must put away your diary, Cecily. I really don't see why you should keep a diary at all.

Cecily. I keep a diary in order to enter the wonderful secrets of my life. If I didn't write them down, I should probably forget all about them.

Miss Prism. Memory, my dear Cecily, is the diary that we all carry about with us.

Cecily. Yes, but it usually chronicles the things that have never happened, and couldn't possibly have happened. I believe that memory is responsible for nearly all the three-volume novels that Mudie[1] sends us.

Miss Prism. Do not speak slightingly of the three-volume novel, Cecily. I wrote one myself in earlier days.

Cecily. Did you really, Miss Prism? How wonderfully clever you are! I hope it did not end happily? I don't like novels that end happily. They depress me so much.

Miss Prism. The good ended happily, and the bad unhappily. That is what fiction means.

Cecily. I suppose so. But it seems very unfair. And was your novel ever published?

Miss Prism. Alas! No. The manuscript unfortunately was abandoned. (Cecily *starts.*) I used the word in the sense of lost or mislaid. To your work, child, these speculations are profitless.

---

1. **Mudie:** a London book shop. Victorian novels were frequently published in two or three volumes.

Cecily (*smiling*). But I see dear Dr. Chasuble coming up through the garden.

Miss Prism (*rising and advancing*). Dr. Chasuble! This is indeed a pleasure.

[*Enter* Canon Chasuble.]

Chasuble. And how are we this morning? Miss Prism, you are, I trust, well?

Cecily. Miss Prism has just been complaining of a slight headache. I think it would do her so much good to have a short stroll with you in the park, Dr. Chasuble.

Miss Prism. Cecily, I have not mentioned anything about a headache.

Cecily. No, dear Miss Prism, I know that, but I felt instinctively that you had a headache. Indeed I was thinking about that, and not about my German lesson, when the Rector came in.

Chasuble. I hope, Cecily, you are not inattentive.

Cecily. Oh, I am afraid I am.

Chasuble. That is strange. Were I fortunate enough to be Miss Prism's pupil, I would hang upon her lips. (Miss Prism *glares.*) I spoke metaphorically. My metaphor was drawn from bees. Ahem! Mr. Worthing, I suppose, has not returned from town yet?

Miss Prism. We do not expect him till Monday afternoon.

Chasuble. Ah, yes, he usually likes to spend his Sunday in London. He is not one of those whose sole aim is enjoyment, as, by all accounts, that unfortunate young man his brother seems to be. But I must not disturb Egeria[2] and her pupil any longer.

Miss Prism. Egeria? My name is Laetitia, Doctor.

Chasuble (*bowing*). A classical allusion merely, drawn from the pagan authors. I shall see you both no doubt at Evensong?[3]

Miss Prism. I think, dear Doctor, I will have a stroll with you. I find I have a headache after all, and a walk might do it good.

Chasuble. With pleasure, Miss Prism, with pleasure. We might go as far as the schools and back.

Miss Prism. That would be delightful. Cecily, you will read your political economy in my absence. The chapter on the fall of the rupee you may omit. It is somewhat too sensational. Even these metallic problems have their melodramatic side. (*Goes down the garden with* Dr. Chasuble)

Cecily (*picks up books and throws them back on table*). Horrid political economy! Horrid geography! Horrid, horrid German!

[*Enter* Merriman *with a card on a salver.*]

Merriman. Mr. Ernest Worthing has just driven over from the station. He has brought his luggage with him.

Cecily (*takes the card and reads it*). "Mr. Ernest Worthing, B.4, The Albany, W." Uncle Jack's brother! Did you tell him Mr. Worthing was in town?

Merriman. Yes, miss. He seemed very much disappointed. I mentioned that you and Miss Prism were in the garden. He said he was anxious to speak to you privately for a moment.

Cecily. Ask Mr. Ernest Worthing to come here. I suppose you had better talk to the housekeeper about a room for him.

Merriman. Yes, miss. (Merriman *goes off.*)

Cecily. I have never met any really wicked person before. I feel rather frightened. I am so afraid he will look just like everyone else. (*Enter* Algernon, *very gay and debonair.*) He does!

Algernon (*raising his hat*). You are my little cousin Cecily, I'm sure.

Cecily. You are under some strange mistake. I am not little. In fact, I believe I am more than usually tall for my age. (Algernon *is rather taken aback.*) But I am your cousin Cecily. You, I see from your card, are Uncle Jack's brother, my cousin Ernest, my wicked cousin Ernest.

---

2. **Egeria** (Latin *aegeria*): a female adviser.
3. **Evensong:** Evening Prayer service, which is sung.

Algernon. Oh! I am not really wicked at all, Cousin Cecily. You mustn't think that I am wicked.

Cecily. If you are not, then you have certainly been deceiving us all in a very inexcusable manner. I hope you have not been leading a double life, pretending to be wicked and being really good all the time. That would be hypocrisy.

Algernon (*looks at her in amazement*). Oh! Of course I have been rather reckless.

Cecily. I am glad to hear it.

Algernon. In fact, now you mention the subject, I have been very bad in my own small way.

Cecily. I don't think you should be so proud of that, though I am sure it must have been very pleasant.

Algernon. It is much pleasanter being here with you.

Cecily. I can't understand how you are here at all. Uncle Jack won't be back till Monday afternoon.

Algernon. That is a great disappointment. I am obliged to go up by the first train on Monday morning. I have a business appointment that I am anxious . . . to miss!

Cecily. Couldn't you miss it anywhere but in London?

Algernon. No, the appointment is in London.

Cecily. Well, I know, of course, how important it is not to keep a business engagement, if one wants to retain any sense of the beauty of life, but still I think you had better wait till Uncle Jack arrives. I know he wants to speak to you about your emigrating.

Algernon. About my what?

Cecily. Your emigrating. He has gone up to buy your outfit.

Algernon. I certainly wouldn't let Jack buy my outfit. He has no taste in neckties at all.

Cecily. I don't think you will require neckties. Uncle Jack is sending you to Australia.

Algernon. Australia! I'd sooner die.

Cecily. Well, he said at dinner on Wednesday night that you would have to choose between this world, the next world, and Australia.

Algernon. Oh, well! The accounts I have received of Australia and the next world are not particularly encouraging. This world is good enough for me, Cousin Cecily.

Cecily. Yes, but are you good enough for it?

Algernon. I'm afraid I'm not that. That is why I want you to reform me. You might make that your mission, if you don't mind, Cousin Cecily.

Cecily. I'm afraid I've no time, this afternoon.

Algernon. Well, would you mind my reforming myself this afternoon?

Cecily. It is rather Quixotic[4] of you. But I think you should try.

Algernon. I will. I feel better already.

Cecily. You are looking a little worse.

Algernon. That is because I am hungry.

Cecily. How thoughtless of me. I should have remembered that when one is going to lead an entirely new life, one requires regular and wholesome meals. Won't you come in?

Algernon. Thank you. Might I have a buttonhole first? I never have any appetite unless I have a buttonhole first.

Cecily. A Maréchal Niel?[5] (*Picks up scissors*)

Algernon. No, I'd sooner have a pink rose.

Cecily. Why? (*Cuts a flower*)

Algernon. Because you are like a pink rose, Cousin Cecily.

Cecily. I don't think it can be right for you to talk to me like that. Miss Prism never says such things to me.

Algernon. Then Miss Prism is a shortsighted old lady. (Cecily *puts the rose in his buttonhole.*) You are the prettiest girl I ever saw.

Cecily. Miss Prism says that all good looks are a snare.

Algernon. They are a snare that every sensible man would like to be caught in.

---

4. **Quixotic** (kwĭk-sŏt′ĭk): rash, idealistic; from the name *Don Quixote*, a character in a seventeenth-century epic who displayed these characteristics.
5. **Maréchal Niel:** a climbing yellow rose. Many roses are named for people; Adolphe Niel (1801–1869) was a marshal of France.

Cecily. Oh, I don't think I would care to catch a sensible man. I shouldn't know what to talk to him about.

[*They pass into the house.* Miss Prism *and* Dr. Chasuble *return.*]

Miss Prism. You are too much alone, dear Dr. Chasuble. You should get married. A misanthrope I can understand—a womanthrope, never!

Chasuble (*with a scholar's shudder*). Believe me, I do not deserve so neologistic[6] a phrase. The precept as well as the practice of the Primitive Church[7] was distinctly against matrimony.

Miss Prism (*sententiously*). That is obviously the reason why the Primitive Church has not lasted up to the present day. And you do not seem to realize, dear Doctor, that by persistently remaining single, a man converts himself into a permanent public temptation. Men should be more careful; this very celibacy leads weaker vessels astray.

Chasuble. But is a man not equally attractive when married?

Miss Prism. No married man is ever attractive except to his wife.

Chasuble. And often, I've been told, not even to her.

Miss Prism. That depends on the intellectual sympathies of the woman. Maturity can always be depended on. Ripeness can be trusted. Young women are green. (Dr. Chasuble *starts.*) I spoke horticulturally. My metaphor was drawn from fruits. But where is Cecily?

Chasuble. Perhaps she followed us to the schools.

---

6. **neologistic:** coining new words, from *neo-* ("new") and the Greek word *logos,* which means "word."
7. **Primitive Church:** the early church during the first three centuries after Christ. Marriage was discouraged because many people expected the end of the world to occur momentarily.

[*Enter* Jack *slowly from the back of the garden. He is dressed in the deepest mourning, with crepe hatband and black gloves.*]

Miss Prism. Mr. Worthing!
Chasuble. Mr. Worthing?
Miss Prism. This is indeed a surprise. We did not look for you till Monday afternoon.
Jack (*shakes* Miss Prism's *hand in a tragic manner*). I have returned sooner than I expected. Dr. Chasuble, I hope you are well?
Chasuble. Dear Mr. Worthing, I trust this garb of woe does not betoken some terrible calamity?
Jack. My brother.
Miss Prism. More shameful debts and extravagance?
Chasuble. Still leading his life of pleasure?
Jack (*shaking his head*). Dead!
Chasuble. Your brother Ernest dead?
Jack. Quite dead.
Miss Prism. What a lesson for him! I trust he will profit by it.
Chasuble. Mr. Worthing, I offer you my sincere condolence. You have at least the consolation of knowing that you were always the most generous and forgiving of brothers.
Jack. Poor Ernest! He had many faults, but it is a sad, sad blow.
Chasuble. Very sad indeed. Were you with him at the end?
Jack. No. He died abroad; in Paris, in fact. I had a telegram last night from the manager of the Grand Hotel.
Chasuble. Was the cause of death mentioned?
Jack. A severe chill, it seems.
Miss Prism. As a man sows, so shall he reap.
Chasuble (*raising his hand*). Charity, dear Miss Prism, charity! None of us are perfect. I myself am peculiarly susceptible to drafts. Will the interment take place here?
Jack. No. He seems to have expressed a desire to be buried in Paris.
Chasuble. In Paris. (*Shakes his head*) I fear that hardly points to any very serious state of mind at the last. You would no doubt wish

me to make some slight allusion to this tragic domestic affliction next Sunday. (Jack *presses his hand convulsively.*) My sermon on the meaning of the manna in the wilderness can be adapted to almost any occasion, joyful, or, as in the present case, distressing. (*All sigh.*) I have preached it at harvest celebrations, christenings, confirmations, on days of humiliation and festal days. The last time I delivered it was in the Cathedral, as a charity sermon on behalf of the Society for the Prevention of Discontent among the Upper Orders. The Bishop, who was present, was much struck by some of the analogies I drew.

Jack. Ah! That reminds me, you mentioned christenings, I think, Dr. Chasuble? I suppose you know how to christen all right? (Dr. Chasuble *looks astounded.*) I mean, of course, you are continually christening, aren't you?

Miss Prism. It is, I regret to say, one of the Rector's most constant duties in this parish. I have often spoken to the poorer classes on the subject. But they don't seem to know what thrift is.

Chasuble. But is there any particular infant in whom you are interested, Mr. Worthing? Your brother was, I believe, unmarried, was he not?

Jack. Oh, yes.

Miss Prism (*bitterly*). People who live entirely for pleasure usually are.

Jack. But it is not for any child, dear Doctor. I am very fond of children. No! The fact is, I would like to be christened myself, this afternoon, if you have nothing better to do.

Chasuble. But surely, Mr. Worthing, you have been christened already?

Jack. I don't remember anything about it.

Chasuble. But have you any grave doubts on the subject?

Jack. I certainly intend to have. Of course, I don't know if the thing would bother you in any way, or if you think I am a little too old now.

Chasuble. Not at all. The sprinkling and, indeed, the immersion of adults is a perfectly canonical practice.

Jack. Immersion!

Chasuble. You need have no apprehensions. Sprinkling is all that is necessary, or indeed I think advisable. Our weather is so changeable. At what hour would you wish the ceremony performed?

Jack. Oh, I might trot round about five if that would suit you.

Chasuble. Perfectly, perfectly! In fact I have two similar ceremonies to perform at that time. A case of twins that occurred recently in one of the outlying cottages on your own estate. Poor Jenkins the carter, a most hard-working man.

Jack. Oh! I don't see much fun in being christened along with other babies. It would be childish. Would half-past five do?

Chasuble. Admirably! Admirably! (*Takes out watch*) And now, dear Mr. Worthing, I will not intrude any longer into a house of sorrow. I would merely beg you not to be too much bowed down by grief. What seems to us bitter trials are often blessings in disguise.

Miss Prism. This seems to me a blessing of an extremely obvious kind.

[*Enter* Cecily *from the house.*]

Cecily. Uncle Jack! Oh, I am pleased to see you back. But what horrid clothes you have got on. Do go and change them.

Miss Prism. Cecily!

Chasuble. My child! My child! (Cecily *goes toward* Jack; *he kisses her brow in a melancholy manner.*)

Cecily. What is the matter, Uncle Jack? Do look happy! You look as if you had a toothache, and I have got such a surprise for you. Who do you think is in the dining room? Your brother!

Jack. Who?

Cecily. Your brother Ernest. He arrived about half an hour ago.

Jack. What nonsense! I haven't got a brother.

Cecily. Oh, don't say that. However badly he may have behaved to you in the past he is still your brother. You couldn't be so heartless as to disown him. I'll tell him to come out. And you will shake hands with him, won't you, Uncle Jack? (*Runs back into the house*)

Chasuble. These are very joyful tidings.

Miss Prism. After we had all been resigned to his loss, his sudden return seems to me peculiarly distressing.

Jack. My brother is in the dining room? I don't know what it all means. I think it is perfectly absurd.

[*Enter* Algernon *and* Cecily *hand in hand. They come slowly up to* Jack.]

Jack. Good heavens! (*Motions* Algernon *away*)

Algernon. Brother John, I have come down from town to tell you that I am very sorry for all the trouble I have given you, and that I intend to lead a better life in the future. (Jack *glares at him and does not take his hand.*)

Cecily. Uncle Jack, you are not going to refuse your own brother's hand?

Jack. Nothing will induce me to take his hand. I think his coming down here disgraceful. He knows perfectly well why.

Cecily. Uncle Jack, do be nice. There is some good in everyone. Ernest has just been telling me about his poor invalid friend, Mr. Bunbury, whom he goes to visit so often. And surely there must be much good in one who is kind to an invalid, and leaves the pleasures of London to sit by a bed of pain.

Jack. Oh! He has been talking about Bunbury, has he?

Cecily. Yes, he has told me all about poor Mr. Bunbury, and his terrible state of health.

Jack. Bunbury! Well, I won't have him talk to you about Bunbury or about anything else. It is enough to drive one perfectly frantic.

Algernon. Of course I admit that the faults were all on my side. But I must say that I think that Brother John's coldness to me is peculiarly painful. I expected a more enthusiastic welcome, especially considering it is the first time I have come here.

Algernon meets Jack in the country. Jack is in mourning for his brother Ernest.
Museum of Modern Art, New York

Cecily. Uncle Jack, if you don't shake hands with Ernest, I will never forgive you.

Jack. Never forgive me?

Cecily. Never, never, never!

Jack. Well, this is the last time I shall ever do it. (*Shakes hands with* Algernon *and glares*)

Chasuble. It's pleasant, is it not, to see so perfect a reconciliation? I think we might leave the two brothers together.

Miss Prism. Cecily, you will come with us.

Cecily. Certainly, Miss Prism. My little task of reconciliation is over.

Chasuble. You have done a beautiful action today, dear child.

Miss Prism. We must not be premature in our judgments.

Cecily. I feel very happy. (*They all go off except* Jack *and* Algernon.)

Jack. You young scoundrel, Algy, you must get out of this place as soon as possible. I don't allow any Bunburying here.

[*Enter* Merriman.]

Merriman. I have put Mr. Ernest's things in the room next to yours, sir. I suppose that is all right?

Jack. What?

Merriman. Mr. Ernest's luggage, sir. I have unpacked it and put it in the room next to your own.

Jack. His luggage?

Merriman. Yes, sir. Three portmanteaus,[8] a dressing case, two hat-boxes, and a large luncheon basket.

Algernon. I am afraid I can't stay more than a week this time.

Jack. Merriman, order the dogcart[9] at once. Mr. Ernest has been suddenly called back to town.

Merriman. Yes, sir. (*Goes back into the house*)

Algernon. What a fearful liar you are, Jack. I have not been called back to town at all.

---

8. **portmanteaus** (pôrt-măn′tōz): large suitcases.
9. **dogcart**: an open horse-drawn cart.

Jack. Yes, you have.

Algernon. I haven't heard anyone call me.

Jack. Your duty as a gentleman calls you back.

Algernon. My duty as a gentleman has never interfered with my pleasures in the smallest degree.

Jack. I can quite understand that.

Algernon. Well, Cecily is a darling.

Jack. You are not to talk of Miss Cardew like that. I don't like it.

Algernon. Well, I don't like your clothes. You look perfectly ridiculous in them. Why on earth don't you go up and change? It is perfectly childish to be in deep mourning for a man who is actually staying for a whole week with you in your house as a guest. I call it grotesque.

Jack. You are certainly not staying with me for a whole week as a guest or anything else. You have got to leave . . . by the four-five train.

Algernon. I certainly won't leave you so long as you are in mourning. It would be most unfriendly. If I were in mourning, you would stay with me, I suppose. I should think it very unkind if you didn't.

Jack. Well, will you go if I change my clothes?

Algernon. Yes, if you are not too long. I never saw anybody take so long to dress, and with such little result.

Jack. Well, at any rate, that is better than being always overdressed as you are.

Algernon. If I am occasionally a little overdressed, I make up for it by being always immensely overeducated.

Jack. Your vanity is ridiculous, your conduct an outrage, and your presence in my garden utterly absurd. However, you have got to catch the four-five, and I hope you will have a pleasant journey back to town. This Bunburying, as you call it, has not been a great success for you. (*Goes into the house*)

Algernon. I think it has been a great success. I'm in love with Cecily, and that is everything. (*Enter* Cecily *at the back of the garden.*

She picks up the can and begins to water the flowers.) But I must see her before I go, and make arrangements for another Bunbury. Ah, there she is.

Cecily. Oh, I merely came back to water the roses. I thought you were with Uncle Jack.

Algernon. He's gone to order the dogcart for me.

Cecily. Oh, is he going to take you for a nice drive?

Algernon. He's going to send me away.

Cecily. Then have we got to part?

Algernon. I am afraid so. It's a very painful parting.

Cecily. It is always painful to part from people whom one has known for a very brief space of time. The absence of old friends one can endure with equanimity. But even a momentary separation from anyone to whom one has just been introduced is almost unbearable.

Algernon. Thank you.

[*Enter* Merriman.]

Merriman. The dogcart is at the door, sir.

[Algernon *looks at* Cecily *appealingly.*]

Cecily. It can wait, Merriman . . . for . . . five minutes.

Merriman. Yes, miss. (*Exit.*)

Algernon. I hope, Cecily, I shall not offend you if I state quite frankly and openly that you seem to me to be in every way the visible personification of absolute perfection.

Cecily. I think your frankness does you great credit, Ernest. If you will allow me, I will copy your remarks into my diary. (*Goes over to table and begins writing in diary*)

Algernon. Do you really keep a diary? I'd give anything to look at it. May I?

Cecily. Oh, no. (*Puts her hand over it*) You see, it is simply a very young girl's record of her own thoughts and impressions, and consequently meant for publication. When it appears in volume form, I hope you will order a copy. But pray, Ernest, don't stop. I delight in taking down from dictation. I have reached "absolute perfection." You can go on, I am quite ready for more.

Algernon (*somewhat taken aback*). Ahem! Ahem!

Cecily. Oh, don't cough, Ernest. When one is dictating one should speak fluently and not cough. Besides, I don't know how to spell a cough. (*Writes as* Algernon *speaks*)

Algernon (*speaking very rapidly*). Cecily, ever since I first looked upon your wonderful and incomparable beauty, I have dared to love you wildly, passionately, devotedly, hopelessly.

Cecily. I don't think that you should tell me that you love me wildly, passionately, devotedly, hopelessly. Hopelessly doesn't seem to make much sense, does it?

Algernon. Cecily.

[*Enter* Merriman.]

Merriman. The dogcart is waiting, sir.

Algernon. Tell it to come round next week, at the same hour.

Merriman (*looks at* Cecily, *who makes no sign*). Yes, sir. (Merriman *retires.*)

Cecily. Uncle Jack would be very much annoyed if he knew you were staying on till next week, at the same hour.

Algernon. Oh, I don't care about Jack. I don't care for anybody in the whole world but you. I love you, Cecily. You will marry me, won't you?

Cecily. You silly boy! Of course. Why, we have been engaged for the last three months.

Algernon. For the last three months?

Cecily. Yes, it will be exactly three months on Thursday.

Algernon. But how did we become engaged?

Cecily. Well, ever since dear Uncle Jack first confessed to us that he had a younger brother who was very wicked and bad, you, of course, have formed the chief topic of conversation between myself and Miss Prism. And of course a man who is much talked about is always very attractive. One feels there must be something in him, after all. I daresay it was foolish of me; but I fell in love with you, Ernest.

Algernon. Darling. And when was the engagement actually settled?

Cecily. On the fourteenth of February last. Worn out by your entire ignorance of my existence, I determined to end the matter one way or the other, and after a long struggle with myself, I accepted you under this dear old tree here. The next day I bought this little ring in your name, and this is the little bangle with the true lovers' knot I promised you always to wear.

Algernon. Did I give you this? It's very pretty, isn't it?

Cecily. Yes, you've wonderfully good taste, Ernest. It's the excuse I've always given for your leading such a bad life. And this is the box in which I keep all your dear letters. (*Kneels at table, opens box, and produces letters tied up with blue ribbon*)

Algernon. My letters! But, my own sweet Cecily, I have never written you any letters.

Cecily. You need hardly remind me of that, Ernest. I remember only too well that I was forced to write your letters for you. I wrote always three times a week, and sometimes oftener.

Algernon. Oh, do let me read them, Cecily?

Cecily. Oh, I couldn't possibly. They would make you far too conceited. (*Replaces box*) The three you wrote me after I had broken off the engagement are so beautiful, and so badly spelled, that even now I can hardly read them without crying a little.

Algernon. But was our engagement ever broken off?

Cecily. Of course it was. On the twenty-second of last March. You can see the entry if you like. (*Shows diary*) "Today I broke off my engagement with Ernest. I feel it is better to do so. The weather still continues charming."

Algernon. But why on earth did you break it off? What had I done? I had done nothing at all. Cecily, I am very much hurt indeed to hear you broke it off. Particularly when the weather was so charming.

Cecily. It would hardly have been a really serious engagement if it hadn't been broken off at least once. But I forgave you before the week was out.

Algernon (*crossing to her, and kneeling*). What a perfect angel you are, Cecily.

Cecily. You dear romantic boy. (*He kisses her, she puts her fingers through his hair.*) I hope your hair curls naturally, does it?

Algernon. Yes, darling, with a little help from others.

Cecily. I am so glad.

Algernon. You'll never break off our engagement again, Cecily?

Cecily. I don't think I could break it off now that I have actually met you. Besides, of course, there is the question of your name.

Algernon (*nervously*). Yes, of course.

Cecily. You must not laugh at me, darling, but it had always been a girlish dream of mine to love someone whose name was Ernest. (Algernon *rises,* Cecily *also.*) There is something in that name that seems to inspire absolute confidence. I pity any poor married woman whose husband is not called Ernest.

Algernon. But, my dear child, do you mean to say you could not love me if I had some other name?

Cecily. But what name?

Algernon. Oh, any name you like—Algernon—for instance . . .

Cecily. But I don't like the name of Algernon.

Algernon. Well, my own dear, sweet, loving little darling, I really can't see why you should object to the name of Algernon. It is not at all a bad name. In fact, it is rather an aristocratic name. Half of the chaps who get into the Bankruptcy Court are called Algernon. But seriously, Cecily (*moving to her*), if my name was Algy, couldn't you love me?

Cecily (*rising*). I might respect you, Ernest, I might admire your character, but I fear that I should not be able to give you my undivided attention.

Algernon. Ahem! Cecily! (*Picking up hat*)

Your Rector here is, I suppose, thoroughly experienced in the practice of all the rites and ceremonials of the church?

Cecily. Oh, yes. Dr. Chasuble is a most learned man. He has never written a single book, so you can imagine how much he knows.

Algernon. I must see him at once on a most important christening—I mean on most important business.

Cecily. Oh!

Algernon. I shan't be away more than half an hour.

Cecily. Considering that we have been engaged since February the fourteenth, and that I only met you today for the first time, I think it is rather hard that you should leave me for so long a period as half an hour. Couldn't you make it twenty minutes?

Algernon. I'll be back in no time. (*Kisses her and rushes down the garden*)

Cecily. What an impetuous boy he is! I like his hair so much. I must enter his proposal in my diary.

[*Enter* Merriman.]

Merriman. A Miss Fairfax just called to see Mr. Worthing. On very important business, Miss Fairfax states.

Cecily. Isn't Mr. Worthing in his library?

Merriman. Mr. Worthing went over in the direction of the Rectory some time ago.

Cecily. Pray ask the lady to come out here; Mr. Worthing is sure to be back soon. And you can bring tea.

Merriman. Yes, miss. (*Goes out*)

Cecily. Miss Fairfax! I suppose one of the many good elderly women who are associated with Uncle Jack in some of his philanthropic work in London. I don't quite like women who are interested in philanthropic work. I think it is so forward of them.

[*Enter* Merriman.]

Merriman. Miss Fairfax.

[*Enter* Gwendolen. *Exit* Merriman.]

Cecily (*advancing to meet her*). Pray let me introduce myself to you. My name is Cecily Cardew.

Gwendolen. Cecily Cardew? (*Moving to her and shaking hands*) What a very sweet name! Something tells me that we are going to be great friends. I like you already more than I can say. My first impressions of people are never wrong.

Cecily. How nice of you to like me so much after we have known each other such a comparatively short time. Pray sit down.

Gwendolen (*still standing up*). I may call you Cecily, may I not?

Cecily. With pleasure!

Gwendolen. And you will always call me Gwendolen, won't you?

Cecily. If you wish.

Gwendolen. Then that is all quite settled, is it not?

Cecily. I hope so. (*A pause. They both sit down together.*)

Gwendolen. Perhaps this might be a favorable opportunity for my mentioning who I am. My father is Lord Bracknell. You have never heard of Papa, I suppose?

Cecily. I don't think so.

Gwendolen. Outside the family circle, Papa, I am glad to say, is entirely unknown. I think that is quite as it should be. The home seems to me to be the proper sphere for the man. And certainly once a man begins to neglect his domestic duties he becomes painfully effeminate, does he not? And I don't like that. It makes men so very attractive. Cecily, Mama, whose views on education are remarkably strict, has brought me up to be extremely shortsighted; it is part of her system; so do you mind my looking at you through my glasses?

Cecily. Oh! Not at all, Gwendolen. I am very fond of being looked at.

Gwendolen (*after examining* Cecily *carefully through a lorgnette[10]*). You are here on a short visit, I suppose.

---

10. **lorgnette** (lôrn-yĕt′): eyeglasses attached to a handle.

Cecily. Oh, no! I live here.

Gwendolen (*severely*). Really? Your mother, no doubt, or some female relative of advanced years resides here also?

Cecily. Oh, no! I have no mother, nor, in fact, any relations.

Gwendolen. Indeed?

Cecily. My dear guardian, with the assistance of Miss Prism, has the arduous task of looking after me.

Gwendolen. Your guardian?

Cecily. Yes, I am Mr. Worthing's ward.

Gwendolen. Oh! It is strange he never mentioned to me that he had a ward. How secretive of him! He grows more interesting hourly. I am not sure, however, that the news inspires me with feelings of unmixed delight. (*Rising and going to her*) I am very fond of you, Cecily; I have liked you ever since I met you! But I am bound to state that now that I know that you are Mr. Worthing's ward, I cannot help expressing a wish you were—well, just a little older than you seem to be—and not quite so very alluring in appearance. In fact, if I may speak candidly—

Cecily. Pray do! I think that whenever one has anything unpleasant to say, one should always be quite candid.

Gwendolen. Well, to speak with perfect candor, Cecily, I wish that you were fully forty-two, and more than usually plain for your age. Ernest has a strong upright nature. He is the very soul of truth and honor. Disloyalty would be as impossible to him as deception. But even men of the noblest possible moral character are extremely susceptible to the influence of the physical charms of others. Modern, no less than ancient history, supplies us with many most painful examples of what I refer to. If it were not so, indeed, history would be quite unreadable.

Cecily. I beg your pardon, Gwendolen, did you say Ernest?

Gwendolen. Yes.

Cecily. Oh, but it is not Mr. Ernest Worthing who is my guardian. It is his brother—his elder brother.

Gwendolen (*sitting down again*). Ernest never mentioned to me that he had a brother.

Cecily. I am sorry to say they have not been on good terms for a long time.

Gwendolen. Ah! That accounts for it. And now that I think of it, I have never heard any man mention his brother. The subject seems distasteful to most men. Cecily, you have lifted a load from my mind. I was growing almost anxious. It would have been terrible if any cloud had come across a friendship like ours, would it not? Of course you are quite, quite sure that it is not Mr. Ernest Worthing who is your guardian?

Cecily. Quite sure. (*A pause*) In fact, I am going to be his.

Gwendolen (*inquiringly*). I beg your pardon?

Cecily (*rather shy and confidingly*). Dearest Gwendolen, there is no reason why I should make a secret of it to you. Our little country newspaper is sure to chronicle the fact next week. Mr. Ernest Worthing and I are engaged to be married.

Gwendolen (*quite politely, rising*). My darling Cecily, I think there must be some slight error. Mr. Ernest Worthing is engaged to me. The announcement will appear in the *Morning Post* on Saturday at the latest.

Cecily (*very politely, rising*). I am afraid you must be under some misconception. Ernest proposed to me exactly ten minutes ago. (*Shows diary*)

Gwendolen (*examines diary through her lorgnette carefully*). It is very curious, for he asked me to be his wife yesterday afternoon at five-thirty. If you would care to verify the incident, pray do so. (*Produces diary of her own*) I never travel without my diary. One should always have something sensational to read in the train. I am so sorry, dear Cecily, if it is any disappointment to you, but I am afraid I have the prior claim.

Cecily. It would distress me more than I can tell you, dear Gwendolen, if it caused you any mental or physical anguish, but I feel bound to point out that since Ernest proposed to you he clearly has changed his mind.

Gwendolen (*meditatively*). If the poor fellow has been entrapped into any foolish promise, I shall consider it my duty to rescue him at once, and with a firm hand.

Cecily (*thoughtfully and sadly*). Whatever unfortunate entanglement my dear boy may have got into, I will never reproach him with it after we are married.

Gwendolen. Do you allude to me, Miss Cardew, as an entanglement? You are presumptuous. On an occasion of this kind it becomes more than a moral duty to speak one's mind. It becomes a pleasure.

Cecily. Do you suggest, Miss Fairfax, that I entrapped Ernest into an engagement? How dare you? This is no time for wearing the shallow mask of manners. When I see a spade, I call it a spade.

Gwendolen (*satirically*). I am glad to say that I have never seen a spade. It is obvious that our social spheres have been widely different.

[*Enter Merriman, followed by the footman. He carries a salver, tablecloth, and plate stand. Cecily is about to retort. The presence of the servants exercises a restraining influence, under which both girls chafe.*]

Merriman. Shall I lay tea here as usual, miss?

Cecily (*sternly, in a calm voice*). Yes, as usual. (Merriman *begins to clear table and lay cloth. A long pause. Cecily and Gwendolen glare at each other.*)

Gwendolen. Are there many interesting walks in the vicinity, Miss Cardew?

Cecily. Oh, yes! A great many. From the top of one of the hills quite close one can see five counties.

Gwendolen. Five counties! I don't think I should like that; I hate crowds.

Cecily (*sweetly*). I suppose that is why you live in town? (Gwendolen *bites her lip, and beats her foot nervously with her parasol.*)

Gwendolen (*looking round*). Quite a well-kept garden this is, Miss Cardew.

Cecily. So glad you like it, Miss Fairfax.

Gwendolen. I had no idea there were any flowers in the country.

Cecily. Oh, flowers are as common here, Miss Fairfax, as people are in London.

Gwendolen. Personally I cannot understand how anybody manages to exist in the country, if anybody who is anybody does. The country always bores me to death.

Cecily. Ah! This is what the newspapers call agricultural depression, is it not? I believe the aristocracy are suffering very much from it just at present. It is almost an epidemic amongst them, I have been told. May I offer you some tea, Miss Fairfax?

Gwendolen (*with elaborate politeness*). Thank you. (*Aside*) Detestable girl! But I require tea!

Cecily (*sweetly*). Sugar?

Gwendolen (*superciliously*). No, thank you. Sugar is not fashionable anymore. (Cecily *looks angrily at her, takes up the tongs and puts four lumps of sugar into the cup.*)

Cecily (*severely*). Cake or bread and butter?

Gwendolen (*in a bored manner*). Bread and butter, please. Cake is rarely seen at the best houses nowadays.

Cecily (*cuts a very large slice of cake and puts it on the tray*). Hand that to Miss Fairfax.

[Merriman *does so, and goes out with footman. Gwendolen drinks the tea and makes a grimace. Puts down cup at once, reaches out her hand to the bread and butter, looks at it, and finds it is cake. Rises in indignation.*]

Gwendolen. You have filled my tea with lumps of sugar, and though I asked most distinctly for bread and butter, you have given me cake. I am known for the gentleness of my disposition, and the extraordinary sweetness of my nature, but I warn you, Miss Cardew, you may go too far.

Cecily (*rising*). To save my poor, innocent, trusting boy from the machinations of any other girl, there are no lengths to which I would not go.

Gwendolen. From the moment I saw you I distrusted you. I felt that you were false and deceitful. I am never deceived in such matters. My first impressions of people are invariably right.

Cecily. It seems to me, Miss Fairfax, that I am trespassing on your valuable time. No doubt you have many other calls of a similar character to make in the neighborhood.

[*Enter* Jack.]

Gwendolen (*catches sight of him*). Ernest! My own Ernest!

Jack. Gwendolen! Darling! (*Offers to kiss her*)

Gwendolen (*drawing back*). A moment! May I ask if you are engaged to be married to this young lady? (*Points to* Cecily)

Jack (*laughing*). To dear little Cecily! Of course not! What could have put such an idea into your pretty little head?

Gwendolen. Thank you. You may! (*Offers her cheek*)

Cecily (*very sweetly*). I knew there must be some misunderstanding, Miss Fairfax. The gentleman whose arm is at present round your waist is my dear guardian, Mr. John Worthing.

Gwendolen. I beg your pardon?

Cecily. This is Uncle Jack.

Gwendolen (*receding*). Jack! Oh!

[*Enter* Algernon.]

Cecily. Here is Ernest.

Algernon (*goes straight over to* Cecily *without noticing anyone else*). My own love! (*Offers to kiss her*)

Cecily (*drawing back*). A moment, Ernest! May I ask you—are you engaged to be married to this young lady?

Algernon (*looking round*). To what young lady? Good heavens! Gwendolen!

Cecily. Yes, to good heavens, Gwendolen. I mean to Gwendolen.

Algernon (*laughing*). Of course not. What could have put such an idea into your pretty little head?

Cecily. Thank you. (*Presenting her cheek to be kissed*) You may. (Algernon *kisses her.*)

Gwendolen. I felt there was some slight error, Miss Cardew. The gentleman who is now embracing you is my cousin, Mr. Algernon Moncrieff.

Cecily (*breaking away from* Algernon). Algernon Moncrieff! Oh!

[*The two girls move toward each other and put their arms round each other's waists as if for protection.*]

Cecily. Are you called Algernon?

Algernon. I cannot deny it.

Cecily. Oh!

Gwendolen. Is your name really John?

Jack (*standing rather proudly*). I could deny it if I liked. I could deny anything if I liked. But my name certainly is John. It has been John for years.

Cecily (*to* Gwendolen). A gross deception has been practiced on both of us.

Gwendolen. My poor, wounded Cecily!

Cecily. My sweet, wronged Gwendolen!

Gwendolen (*slowly and seriously*). You will call me sister, will you not?

[*They embrace,* Jack *and* Algernon *groan and walk up and down.*]

Cecily (*rather brightly*). There is just one question I would like to be allowed to ask my guardian.

Gwendolen. An admirable idea! Mr. Worthing, there is just one question I would like to be permitted to put to you. Where is your brother Ernest? We are both engaged to be married to your brother Ernest, so it is a matter of some importance to us to know where your brother Ernest is at present.

Jack (*slowly and hesitatingly*). Gwendolen—Cecily—it is very painful for me to be forced to speak the truth. It is the first time in my life that I have ever been reduced to such a painful position, and I am really quite inexperienced in doing anything of the kind. However, I will tell you quite frankly that I have no brother Ernest. I have no brother at all. I never had a brother in my life, and I certainly have not the smallest intention of ever having one in the future.

Cecily (*surprised*). No brother at all?

Jack (*cheerily*). None!

Gwendolen (*severely*). Had you never a brother of any kind?

Jack (*pleasantly*). Never. Not even of any kind.

Gwendolen. I am afraid it is quite clear, Cecily, that neither of us is engaged to be married to anyone.

Cecily. It is not a very pleasant position for a young girl suddenly to find herself in. Is it?

Gwendolen. Let us go into the house. They will hardly venture to come after us there.

Cecily. No, men are so cowardly, aren't they?

[*They retire into the house with scornful looks.*]

Jack. This ghastly state of things is what you call Bunburying, I suppose?

Algernon. Yes, and a perfectly wonderful Bunbury it is. The most wonderful Bunbury I have ever had in my life.

Jack. Well, you've no right whatsoever to Bunbury here.

Algernon. That is absurd. One has a right to Bunbury anywhere one chooses. Every serious Bunburyist knows that.

Jack. Serious Bunburyist? Good heavens!

Algernon. Well, one must be serious about something, if one wants to have any amusement in life. I happen to be serious about Bunburying. What on earth you are serious about I haven't got the remotest idea. About everything, I should fancy. You have such an absolutely trivial nature.

Jack. Well, the only small satisfaction I have in the whole of this wretched business is that your friend Bunbury is quite exploded. You won't be able to run down to the country quite so often as you used to do, dear Algy. And a very good thing too.

Algernon. Your brother is a little off color,

isn't he, dear Jack? You won't be able to disappear to London quite so frequently as your wicked custom was. And not a bad thing either.

Jack. As for your conduct toward Miss Cardew, I must say that your taking in a sweet, simple, innocent girl like that is quite inexcusable. To say nothing of the fact that she is my ward.

Algernon. I can see no possible defense at all for your deceiving a brilliant, clever, thoroughly experienced young lady like Miss Fairfax. To say nothing of the fact that she is my cousin.

Jack. I wanted to be engaged to Gwendolen, that is all. I love her.

Algernon. Well, I simply wanted to be engaged to Cecily. I adore her.

Jack. There is certainly no chance of your marrying Miss Cardew.

Algernon. I don't think there is much likelihood, Jack, of you and Miss Fairfax being united.

Jack. Well, that is no business of yours.

Algernon. If it was my business, I wouldn't talk about it. (*Begins to eat muffins*) It is very vulgar to talk about one's business. Only people like stockbrokers do that, and then merely at dinner parties.

Jack. How you can sit there, calmly eating muffins when we are in this horrible trouble, I can't make out. You seem to me to be perfectly heartless.

Algernon. Well, I can't eat muffins in an agitated manner. The butter would probably get on my cuffs. One should always eat muffins quite calmly. It is the only way to eat them.

Jack. I say it's perfectly heartless your eating muffins at all, under the circumstances.

Algernon. When I am in trouble, eating is the only thing that consoles me. Indeed, when I am in really great trouble, as anyone who knows me intimately will tell you, I refuse everything except food and drink. At the present moment I am eating muffins because I am unhappy. Besides, I am particularly fond of muffins. (*Rising*)

Jack (*rising*). Well, there is no reason why you should eat them all in that greedy way. (*Takes muffins from* Algernon)

Algernon (*offering teacake*). I wish you would have teacake instead. I don't like teacake.

Jack. Good heavens! I suppose a man may eat his own muffins in his own garden.

Algernon. But you have just said it was perfectly heartless to eat muffins.

Jack. I said it was perfectly heartless of you, under the circumstances. That is a very different thing.

Algernon. That may be. But the muffins are the same. (*He seizes the muffin dish from* Jack.)

Jack. Algy, I wish to goodness you would go.

Algernon. You can't possibly ask me to go without having some dinner. It's absurd. I never go without my dinner. No one ever does, except vegetarians and people like that. Besides I have just made arrangements with Dr. Chasuble to be christened at a quarter to six under the name of Ernest.

Jack. My dear fellow, the sooner you give up that nonsense the better. I made arrangements this morning with Dr. Chasuble to be christened at five-thirty, and I naturally will take the name of Ernest. Gwendolen would wish it. We can't both be christened Ernest. It's absurd. Besides, I have a perfect right to be christened if I like. There is no evidence at all that I have ever been christened by anybody. I should think it extremely probable I never was, and so does Dr. Chasuble. It is entirely different in your case. You have been christened already.

Algernon. Yes, but I have not been christened for years.

Jack. Yes, but you have been christened. That is the important thing.

Algernon. Quite so. So I know my constitution can stand it. If you are not quite sure about your ever having been christened, I must say I think it rather dangerous your venturing on it now. It might make you very unwell. You can hardly have forgotten that someone very closely connected with you was very nearly carried off this week in Paris by a severe chill.

Jack. Yes, but you said yourself that a severe chill was not hereditary.

Algernon. It usen't to be, I know — but I daresay it is now. Science is always making wonderful improvements in things.

Jack (*picking up the muffin dish*). Oh, that is nonsense; you are always talking nonsense.

Algernon. Jack, you are at the muffins again! I wish you wouldn't. There are only two left. (*Takes them*) I told you I was particularly fond of muffins.

Jack. But I hate teacake.

Algernon. Why on earth then do you allow teacake to be served up for your guests? What ideas you have of hospitality!

Jack. Algernon! I have already told you to go. I don't want you here. Why don't you go!

Algernon. I haven't quite finished my tea yet! And there is still one muffin left.

[Jack *groans, and sinks into a chair.* Algernon *still continues eating.*]

FOR STUDY AND DISCUSSION

1. How do Gwendolen and Cecily respond to each other when they first meet in this act? How do their feelings about each other change as the act progresses? What finally unites the two girls as they go into the house together "with scornful looks"?

2. The comedy of mistaken identity is a very old dramatic form — as old, in fact, as comedy itself — which Wilde manages to revitalize in *The Importance of Being Earnest*. The key mistaken identity in this play, of course, is that of "Ernest" himself. What comic consequences result from Algernon's assuming the role of Ernest Worthing? How are these consequences made more complicated when Gwendolen arrives on the scene from London?

Act Three

Morning room at the Manor House. Gwendolen *and* Cecily *are at the window, looking into the garden.*

Gwendolen. The fact that they did not follow us at once into the house, as anyone else would have done, seems to me to show that they have some sense of shame left.

Cecily. They have been eating muffins. That looks like repentance.

Gwendolen (*after a pause*). They don't seem to notice us at all. Couldn't you cough?

Cecily. But I haven't got a cough.

Gwendolen. They're looking at us. What effrontery!

Cecily. They're approaching. That's very forward of them.

Gwendolen. Let us preserve a dignified silence.

Cecily. Certainly. It's the only thing to do now.

[*Enter* Jack *followed by* Algernon. *They whistle some dreadful popular air from a British opera.*]

Gwendolen. This dignified silence seems to produce an unpleasant effect.

Cecily. A most distasteful one.

Gwendolen. But we will not be the first to speak.

Cecily. Certainly not.

Gwendolen. Mr. Worthing, I have something very particular to ask you. Much depends on your reply.

Cecily. Gwendolen, your common sense is invaluable. Mr. Moncrieff, kindly answer me the following question. Why did you pretend to be my guardian's brother?

Algernon. In order that I might have an opportunity of meeting you.

Cecily (*to* Gwendolen). That certainly seems a satisfactory explanation, does it not?

Gwendolen. Yes, dear, if you can believe him.

Cecily. I don't. But that does not affect the wonderful beauty of his answer.

Gwendolen. True. In matters of grave importance, style, not sincerity, is the vital thing. Mr. Worthing, what explanation can you offer to me for pretending to have a brother? Was it in order that you might have an opportunity of coming up to town to see me as often as possible?

Jack. Can you doubt it, Miss Fairfax?

Gwendolen. I have the gravest doubts upon the subject. But I intend to crush them. This is not the moment for German skepticism.[1] (*Moving to* Cecily) Their explanations appear to be quite satisfactory, especially Mr. Worthing's. That seems to me to have the stamp of truth upon it.

Cecily. I am more than content with what Mr. Moncrieff said. His voice alone inspires one with absolute credulity.

Gwendolen. Then you think we should forgive them?

Cecily. Yes. I mean no.

Gwendolen. True! I had forgotten. There are principles at stake that one cannot surrender. Which of us should tell them? The task is not a pleasant one.

Cecily. Could we not both speak at the same time?

Gwendolen. An excellent idea! I nearly always speak at the same time as other people. Will you take the time from me?

Cecily. Certainly. (Gwendolen *beats time with uplifted finger.*)

Gwendolen and Cecily (*speaking together*). Your Christian names are still an insuperable barrier. That is all!

Jack and Algernon (*speaking together*). Our Christian names! Is that all? But we are going to be christened this afternoon.

Gwendolen (*to* Jack). For my sake you are prepared to do this terrible thing?

Jack. I am.

---

1. **German skepticism:** a school of philosophy which taught that the truth of all knowledge must be questioned.

Cecily (*to* Algernon). To please me you are ready to face this fearful ordeal?

Algernon. I am!

Gwendolen. How absurd to talk of the equality of the sexes! Where questions of self-sacrifice are concerned, men are infinitely beyond us.

Jack. We are. (*Clasps hands with* Algernon)

Cecily. They have moments of physical courage of which we women know absolutely nothing.

Gwendolen (*to* Jack). Darling!

Algernon (*to* Cecily). Darling! (*They fall into each other's arms.*)

[*Enter* Merriman. *When he enters, he coughs loudly, seeing the situation.*]

Merriman. Ahem! Ahem! Lady Bracknell.

Jack. Good heavens!

[*Enter* Lady Bracknell. *The couples separate in alarm. Exit* Merriman.]

Lady Bracknell. Gwendolen! What does this mean?

Gwendolen. Merely that I am engaged to be married to Mr. Worthing, Mama.

Lady Bracknell. Come here. Sit down. Sit down immediately. Hesitation of any kind is a sign of mental decay in the young, of physical weakness in the old. (*Turns to* Jack) Apprised, sir, of my daughter's sudden flight by her trusty maid, whose confidence I purchased by means of a small coin, I followed her at once by a luggage train. Her unhappy father is, I am glad to say, under the impression that she is attending a more than usually lengthy lecture by the University Extension Scheme on the Influence of a Permanent Income on Thought. I do not propose to undeceive him. Indeed I have never undeceived him on any question. I would consider it wrong. But of course, you will clearly understand that all communication between yourself and my daughter must cease immediately from this moment. On this point, as indeed on all points, I am firm.

Jack. I am engaged to be married to Gwendolen, Lady Bracknell!

Lady Bracknell. You are nothing of the kind, sir. And now as regards Algernon! . . . Algernon!

Algernon. Yes, Aunt Augusta.

Lady Bracknell. May I ask if it is in this house that your invalid friend Mr. Bunbury resides?

Algernon (*stammering*). Oh! No! Bunbury doesn't live here. Bunbury is somewhere else at present. In fact, Bunbury is dead.

Lady Bracknell. Dead! When did Mr. Bunbury die? His death must have been extremely sudden.

Algernon (*airily*). Oh! I killed Bunbury this afternoon. I mean poor Bunbury died this afternoon.

Lady Bracknell. What did he die of?

Algernon. Bunbury? Oh, he was quite exploded.

Lady Bracknell. Exploded! Was he the victim of a revolutionary outrage? I was not aware that Mr. Bunbury was interested in social legislation. If so, he is well punished for his morbidity.

Algernon. My dear Aunt Augusta, I mean he was found out! The doctors found out that Bunbury could not live, that is what I mean—so Bunbury died.

Lady Bracknell. He seems to have had great confidence in the opinion of his physicians. I am glad, however, that he made up his mind at the last to some definite course of action, and acted under proper medical advice. And now that we have finally got rid of this Mr. Bunbury, may I ask, Mr. Worthing, who is that young person whose hand my nephew Algernon is now holding in what seems to me a peculiarly unnecessary manner?

Jack. That lady is Miss Cecily Cardew, my ward. (Lady Bracknell *bows coldly to* Cecily.)

Algernon. I am engaged to be married to Cecily, Aunt Augusta.

Lady Bracknell. I beg your pardon?

Cecily. Mr. Moncrieff and I are engaged to be married, Lady Bracknell.

Lady Bracknell (*with a shiver, crossing to the sofa and sitting down*). I do not know whether there is anything peculiarly exciting in the air of this particular part of Hertfordshire, but the number of engagements that go on seems to me considerably above the proper average that statistics have laid down for our guidance. I think some preliminary inquiry on my part would not be out of place. Mr. Worthing, is Miss Cardew at all connected with any of the larger railway stations in London? I merely desire information. Until yesterday I had no idea that there were any families or persons whose origin was a Terminus.[2] (Jack *looks perfectly furious, but restrains himself.*)

Jack (*in a cold, clear voice*). Miss Cardew is the granddaughter of the late Mr. Thomas Cardew of 149 Belgrave Square, S.W.; Gervase Park, Dorking, Surrey; and the Sporran, Fifeshire, N.B.

Lady Bracknell. That sounds not unsatisfactory. Three addresses always inspire confidence, even in tradesmen. But what proof have I of their authenticity?

Jack. I have carefully preserved the Court Guides[3] of the period. They are open to your inspection, Lady Bracknell.

Lady Bracknell (*grimly*). I have known strange errors in that publication.

Jack. Miss Cardew's family solicitors are Messrs. Markby, Markby, and Markby.

Lady Bracknell. Markby, Markby, and Markby? A firm of the very highest position in the profession. Indeed I am told that one of the Mr. Markbys is occasionally to be seen at dinner parties. So far I am satisfied.

Jack (*very irritably*). How extremely kind of you, Lady Bracknell! I have also in my possession, you will be pleased to hear, certificates of Miss Cardew's birth, baptism, whooping cough, registration, vaccination, confirma-

tion, and the measles; both the German and the English variety.

Lady Bracknell. Ah! A life crowded with incident, I see; though perhaps somewhat too exciting for a young girl. I am not myself in favor of premature experiences. (*Rises, looks at her watch*) Gwendolen! The time approaches for our departure. We have not a moment to lose. As a matter of form, Mr. Worthing, I had better ask you if Miss Cardew has any little fortune?

Jack. Oh! About a hundred and thirty thousand pounds in the Funds.[4] That is all. Good-bye, Lady Bracknell. So pleased to have seen you.

Lady Bracknell (*sitting down again*). A moment, Mr. Worthing. A hundred and thirty thousand pounds! And in the Funds! Miss Cardew seems to me a most attractive young lady, now that I look at her. Few girls of the present day have any really solid qualities, any of the qualities that last, and improve with time. We live, I regret to say, in an age of surfaces. (*To Cecily*) Come over here, dear. (Cecily *goes across.*) Pretty child! Your dress is sadly simple, and your hair seems almost as nature might have left it. But we can soon alter all that. A thoroughly experienced French maid produces a really marvelous result in a very brief space of time. I remember recommending one to young Lady Lancing, and after three months her own husband did not know her.

Jack. And after six months nobody knew her.

Lady Bracknell (*glares at* Jack *for a few moments. Then bends, with a practiced smile, to* Cecily). Kindly turn round, sweet child. (Cecily *turns completely round.*) No, the side view is what I want. (Cicely *presents her profile.*) Yes, quite as I expected. There are distinct social possibilities in your profile. The two weak points in our age are its want of

---

2. **Terminus:** a railway terminal. In Latin, *terminus* means "end." It is used as a play on words with *origin.*
3. **Court Guides:** a book containing the names and addresses of titled and prominent people.

4. **Funds:** government bonds.

principle and its want of profile. The chin a little higher, dear. Style largely depends on the way the chin is worn. They are worn very high, just at present. Algernon!

Algernon. Yes, Aunt Augusta!

Lady Bracknell. There are distinct social possibilities in Miss Cardew's profile.

Algernon. Cecily is the sweetest, dearest, prettiest girl in the whole world. And I don't care twopence about social possibilities.

Lady Bracknell. Never speak disrespectfully of Society, Algernon. Only people who can't get into it do that. (*To* Cecily) Dear child, of course you know that Algernon has nothing but his debts to depend upon. But I do not approve of mercenary marriages. When I married Lord Bracknell, I had no fortune of any kind. But I never dreamed for a moment of allowing that to stand in my way. Well, I suppose I must give my consent.

Algernon. Thank you, Aunt Augusta.

Lady Bracknell. Cecily, you may kiss me!

Cecily (*kisses her*). Thank you, Lady Bracknell.

Lady Bracknell. You may also address me as Aunt Augusta for the future.

Cecily. Thank you, Aunt Augusta.

Lady Bracknell. The marriage, I think, had better take place quite soon.

Algernon. Thank you, Aunt Augusta.

Cecily. Thank you, Aunt Augusta.

Lady Bracknell. To speak frankly, I am not in favor of long engagements. They give people the opportunity of finding out each other's character before marriage, which I think is never advisable.

Jack. I beg your pardon for interrupting you, Lady Bracknell, but this engagement is quite out of the question. I am Miss Cardew's guardian, and she cannot marry without my consent until she comes of age. That consent I absolutely decline to give.

Lady Bracknell. Upon what grounds, may I ask? Algernon is an extremely, I may almost say an ostentatiously, eligible young man. He has nothing, but he looks everything. What more can one desire?

Jack. It pains me very much to have to speak frankly to you, Lady Bracknell, about your nephew, but the fact is that I do not approve at all of his moral character. I suspect him of being untruthful.

[Algernon *and* Cecily *look at him in indignant amazement.*]

Lady Bracknell. Untruthful! My nephew Algernon? Impossible! He is an Oxonian.[5]

Jack. I fear there can be no possible doubt about the matter. This afternoon during my temporary absence in London on an important question of romance, he obtained admission to my house by means of the false pretense of being my brother. Under an assumed name he drank, I've just been informed by my butler, an entire pint bottle of my Perrier-Jouet, Brut, '89; wine I was specially reserving for myself. Continuing his disgraceful deception, he succeeded in the course of the afternoon in alienating the affections of my only ward. He subsequently stayed to tea, and devoured every single muffin. And what makes his conduct all the more heartless is that he was perfectly well aware from the first that I have no brother, that I never had a brother, and that I don't intend to have a brother, not even of any kind. I distinctly told him so myself yesterday afternoon.

Lady Bracknell. Ahem! Mr. Worthing, after careful consideration I have decided entirely to overlook my nephew's conduct to you.

Jack. That is very generous of you, Lady Bracknell. My own decision, however, is unalterable. I decline to give my consent.

Lady Bracknell (*to* Cecily). Come here, sweet child. (Cecily *goes over.*) How old are you, dear?

Cecily. Well, I am really only eighteen, but I always admit to twenty when I go to evening parties.

Lady Bracknell. You are perfectly right in making some slight alteration. Indeed, no

---

5. **Oxonian:** student at or graduate of Oxford University.

woman should ever be quite accurate about her age. It looks so calculating. . . . (*In a meditative manner*) Eighteen, but admitting to twenty at evening parties. Well, it will not be very long before you are of age and free from the restraints of tutelage. So I don't think your guardian's consent is, after all, a matter of any importance.

Jack. Pray excuse me, Lady Bracknell, for interrupting you again, but it is only fair to tell you that according to the terms of her grandfather's will Miss Cardew does not come legally of age till she is thirty-five.

Lady Bracknell. That does not seem to me to be a grave objection. Thirty-five is a very attractive age. London society is full of women of the very highest birth who have, of their own free choice, remained thirty-five for years. Lady Dumbleton is an instance in point. To my own knowledge she has been thirty-five ever since she arrived at the age of forty, which was many years ago now. I see no reason why our dear Cecily should not be even still more attractive at the age you mention than she is at present. There will be a large accumulation of property.

Cecily. Algy, could you wait for me till I was thirty-five?

Algernon. Of course I could, Cecily. You know I could.

Cecily. Yes, I felt it instinctively, but I couldn't wait all that time. I hate waiting even five minutes for anybody. It always makes me rather cross. I am not punctual myself, I know, but I do like punctuality in others, and waiting, even to be married, is quite out of the question.

Algernon. Then what is to be done, Cecily?

Cecily. I don't know, Mr. Moncrieff.

Lady Bracknell. My dear Mr. Worthing, as Miss Cardew states positively that she cannot wait till she is thirty-five—a remark which I am bound to say seems to me to show a somewhat impatient nature—I would beg of you to reconsider your decision.

Jack. But my dear Lady Bracknell, the matter is entirely in your own hands. The moment you consent to my marriage with Gwendolen, I will most gladly allow your nephew to form an alliance with my ward.

Lady Bracknell (*rising and drawing herself up*). You must be quite aware that what you propose is out of the question.

Jack. Then a passionate celibacy is all that any of us can look forward to.

Lady Bracknell. That is not the destiny I propose for Gwendolen. Algernon, of course, can choose for himself. (*Pulls out her watch*) Come, dear (Gwendolen *rises*), we have already missed five, if not six, trains. To miss any more might expose us to comment on the platform.

[*Enter* Dr. Chasuble.]

Chasuble. Everything is quite ready for the christenings.

Lady Bracknell. The christenings, sir! Is not that somewhat premature?

Chasuble (*looking rather puzzled, and pointing to* Jack *and* Algernon). Both these gentlemen have expressed a desire for immediate baptism.

Lady Bracknell. At their age? The idea is grotesque and irreligious! Algernon, I forbid you to be baptized. I will not hear of such excesses. Lord Bracknell would be highly displeased if he learned that that was the way in which you wasted your time and money.

Chasuble. Am I to understand then that there are to be no christenings at all this afternoon?

Jack. I don't think that, as things are now, it would be of much practical value to either of us, Dr. Chasuble.

Chasuble. I am grieved to hear such sentiments from you, Mr. Worthing. They savor of the heretical views of the Anabaptists,[6] views that I have completely refuted in four of my unpublished sermons. However, as your present mood seems to be one peculiarly sec-

---

6. **Anabaptists:** a religious sect founded in Switzerland in the sixteenth century which did not believe in infant baptism.

Jack discovers who his real parents are in Act Three.
Radio Times Hulton

ular, I will return to the church at once. Indeed, I have just been informed by the pew-
opener that for the last hour and a half Miss
Prism has been waiting for me in the vestry.

Lady Bracknell (*starting*). Miss Prism! Did I
hear you mention a Miss Prism?

Chasuble. Yes, Lady Bracknell. I am on my
way to join her.

Lady Bracknell. Pray allow me to detain you
for a moment. This matter may prove to be
one of vital importance to Lord Bracknell and
myself. Is this Miss Prism a female of repellent aspect, remotely connected with education?

Chasuble (*somewhat indignantly*). She is the
most cultivated of ladies, and the very picture
of respectability.

Lady Bracknell. It is obviously the same person. May I ask what position she holds in
your household?

Chasuble (*severely*). I am a celibate, madam.

Jack (*interposing*). Miss Prism, Lady Bracknell, has been for the last three years Miss

Cardew's esteemed governess and valued
companion.

Lady Bracknell. In spite of what I hear of her,
I must see her at once. Let her be sent for.

Chasuble (*looking off*). She approaches; she is
nigh.

[*Enter* Miss Prism *hurriedly.*]

Miss Prism. I was told you expected me in
the vestry, dear Canon. I have been waiting
for you there for an hour and three-quarters.
(*Catches sight of* Lady Bracknell, *who has
fixed her with a stony glare.* Miss Prism
grows pale and quails. She looks anxiously
round as if desirous to escape.*)

Lady Bracknell (*in a severe, judicial
voice*). Prism! (Miss Prism *bows her head in
shame.*) Come here, Prism! (Miss Prism
approaches in a humble manner.*) Prism!
Where is that baby? (*General consternation.
The* Canon *starts back in horror.* Algernon
and Jack *pretend to be anxious to shield*

The Importance of Being Earnest Act Three 665

Cecily *and* Gwendolen *from hearing the details of a terrible public scandal.*) Twenty-eight years ago, Prism, you left Lord Bracknell's house, Number 104, Upper Grosvenor Square, in charge of a perambulator[7] that contained a baby of the male sex. You never returned. A few weeks later, through the elaborate investigations of the Metropolitan police, the perambulator was discovered at midnight standing by itself in a remote corner of Bayswater. It contained the manuscript of a three-volume novel of more than usually revolting sentimentality. (Miss Prism *starts in involuntary indignation.*) But the baby was not there. (*Everyone looks at* Miss Prism.) Prism! Where is that baby? (*A pause*)

Miss Prism. Lady Bracknell, I admit with shame that I do not know. I only wish I did. The plain facts of the case are these. On the morning of the day you mention, a day that is forever branded on my memory, I prepared as usual to take the baby out in its perambulator. I had also with me a somewhat old, but capacious, handbag in which I had intended to place the manuscript of a work of fiction that I had written during my few unoccupied hours. In a moment of mental abstraction, for which I can never forgive myself, I deposited the manuscript in the bassinette and placed the baby in the handbag.

Jack (*who has been listening attentively*). But where did you deposit the handbag?

Miss Prism. Do not ask me, Mr. Worthing.

Jack. Miss Prism, this is a matter of no small importance to me. I insist on knowing where you deposited the handbag that contained that infant.

Miss Prism. I left it in the cloakroom of one of the larger railway stations in London.

Jack. What railway station?

Miss Prism (*quite crushed*). Victoria. The Brighton line. (*Sinks into a chair*)

Jack. I must retire to my room for a moment. Gwendolen, wait here for me.

---

7. **perambulator:** baby carriage.

Gwendolen. If you are not too long, I will wait here for you all my life. (*Exit* Jack *in great excitement.*)

Chasuble. What do you think this means, Lady Bracknell?

Lady Bracknell. I dare not even suspect, Dr. Chasuble. I need hardly tell you that in families of high position strange coincidences are not supposed to occur. They are hardly considered the thing.

[*Noises heard overhead as if someone was throwing trunks about. Everyone looks up.*]

Cecily. Uncle Jack seems strangely agitated.

Chasuble. Your guardian has a very emotional nature.

Lady Bracknell. This noise is extremely unpleasant. It sounds as if he was having an argument. I dislike arguments of any kind. They are always vulgar, and often convincing.

Chasuble (*looking up*). It has stopped now.

[*The noise is redoubled.*]

Lady Bracknell. I wish he would arrive at some conclusion.

Gwendolen. This suspense is terrible. I hope it will last.

[*Enter* Jack *with a handbag of black leather in his hand.*]

Jack (*rushing over to* Miss Prism). Is this the handbag, Miss Prism? Examine it carefully before you speak. The happiness of more than one life depends on your answer.

Miss Prism (*calmly*). It seems to be mine. Yes, here is the injury it received through the upsetting of a Gower Street omnibus in younger and happier days. Here is the stain on the lining caused by the explosion of a temperance beverage, an incident that occurred at Leamington. And here, on the lock, are my initials. I had forgotten that in an extravagant mood I had had them placed there. The bag is undoubtedly mine. I am delighted to have it so unexpectedly restored to me. It has been a great inconvenience being without it all these years.

Jack (*in a pathetic voice*). Miss Prism, more is restored to you than this handbag. I was the baby you placed in it.

Miss Prism (*amazed*). You?

Jack (*embracing her*). Yes . . . Mother!

Miss Prism (*recoiling in indignant astonishment*). Mr. Worthing. I am unmarried!

Jack. Unmarried! I do not deny that is a serious blow. But after all, who has the right to cast a stone against one who has suffered? Cannot repentance wipe out an act of folly? Why should there be one law for men and another for women? Mother, I forgive you. (*Tries to embrace her again*)

Miss Prism (*still more indignant*). Mr. Worthing, there is some error. (*Pointing to Lady Bracknell.*) There is the lady who can tell you who you really are.

Jack (*after a pause*). Lady Bracknell, I hate to seem inquisitive, but would you kindly inform me who I am?

Lady Bracknell. I am afraid that the news I have to give you will not altogether please you. You are the son of my poor sister, Mrs. Moncrieff, and consequently Algernon's elder brother.

Jack. Algy's elder brother! Then I have a brother after all. I knew I had a brother! I always said I had a brother! Cecily—how could you have ever doubted that I had a brother? (*Seizes hold of* Algernon) Dr. Chasuble, my unfortunate brother. Miss Prism, my unfortunate brother. Gwendolen, my unfortunate brother. Algy, you young scoundrel, you will have to treat me with more respect in the future. You have never behaved to me like a brother in all your life.

Algernon. Well, not till today, old boy, I admit. I did my best, however, though I was out of practice. (*Shakes hands*)

Gwendolen (*to* Jack). My own! But what own are you? What is your Christian name, now that you have become someone else?

Jack. Good heavens! . . . I had quite forgotten that point. Your decision on the subject of my name is irrevocable, I suppose?

Gwendolen. I never change, except in my affections.

Cecily. What a noble nature you have, Gwendolen!

Jack. Then the question had better be cleared up at once. Aunt Augusta, a moment. At the time when Miss Prism left me in the handbag, had I been christened already?

Lady Bracknell. Every luxury that money could buy, including christening, had been lavished on you by your fond and doting parents.

Jack. Then I was christened! That is settled. Now, what name was I given? Let me know the worst.

Lady Bracknell. Being the eldest son you were naturally christened after your father.

Jack (*irritably*). Yes, but what was my father's Christian name?

Lady Bracknell (*meditatively*). I cannot at the present moment recall what the General's Christian name was. But I have no doubt he had one. He was eccentric, I admit. But only in later years. And that was the result of the Indian climate, and marriage, and indigestion, and other things of that kind.

Jack. Algy! Can't you recollect what our father's Christian name was?

Algernon. My dear boy, we were never even on speaking terms. He died before I was a year old.

Jack. His name would appear in the Army Lists of the period, I suppose, Aunt Augusta?

Lady Bracknell. The General was essentially a man of peace, except in his domestic life. But I have no doubt his name would appear in any military directory.

Jack. The Army Lists of the last forty years are here. These delightful records should have been my constant study. (*Rushes to bookcase and tears the books out*) M. Generals . . . Mallam, Maxbohm, Magley—what ghastly names they have—Markby, Migsby, Mobbs, Moncrieff! Lieutenant 1840, Captain, Lieutenant-Colonel, Colonel, General 1869,

Christian names, Ernest John. (*Puts book very quietly down and speaks quite calmly*) I always told you, Gwendolen, my name was Ernest, didn't I? Well, it is Ernest after all. I mean it naturally is Ernest.

Lady Bracknell. Yes, I remember now that the General was called Ernest. I knew I had some particular reason for disliking the name.

Gwendolen. Ernest! My own Ernest! I felt from the first that you could have no other name!

Jack. Gwendolen, it is a terrible thing for a man to find out suddenly that all his life he has been speaking nothing but the truth. Can you forgive me?

Gwendolen. I can. For I feel that you are sure to change.

Jack. My own one!

Chasuble (*to* Miss Prism). Laetitia! (*Embraces her*)

Miss Prism (*enthusiastically*). Frederick! At last!

Algernon. Cecily! (*Embraces her*) At last!

Jack. Gwendolen! (*Embraces her*) At last!

Lady Bracknell. My nephew, you seem to be displaying signs of triviality.

Jack. On the contrary, Aunt Augusta. I've now realized for the first time in my life the vital Importance of Being Earnest.

FOR STUDY AND DISCUSSION

1. Describe in your own words the story Miss Prism tells when she is recognized and questioned by Lady Bracknell. Looking back now at Miss Prism's speeches early in the play, what is amusing about her having told Cecily near the beginning of Act Two: "Do not speak slightingly of the three-volume novel, Cecily. I wrote one myself in earlier days"?

2. A *recognition scene* is a scene near the end of a play when characters who have previously had mistaken roles finally discover or reveal their true identities. Describe the recognition scene in *The Importance of Being Earnest*. In how many senses is John Worthing's discovery of his real identity ironic?

3. Another traditional feature of comedy is the all-inclusive nature of the final resolution, when minor as well as major characters are brought into harmonious relationship. How is this tradition of inclusiveness comically emphasized at the end of *The Importance of Being Earnest*? Why is it significant that Reverend Chasuble and Miss Prism join the two young couples in openly expressing their love for each other? What role does Lady Bracknell play in the final resolution?

FOR COMPOSITION

Many people have resorted to Bunburying. Relate an experience of yours or a friend's in which an attempt to avoid an unpleasant situation resulted in being found out. If this experience has never happened to you, try writing a comic sketch in which it happens to a fictional character.

The English Novel in

The Nineteenth Century

Two important novelists whose work comes at the beginning of this period are Jane Austen (1775–1817) and Sir Walter Scott (1771–1832). Jane Austen, with her very acute and exquisite sense of character and scene, has probably never been equaled within her deliberately limited range. Her novels are classics of the art of fiction, and once enjoyed they are our friends for life. Scott is a curious case, for in his own time, when he had stupendous success and very wide influence as author of medieval romances such as *Ivanhoe* (1819), he was thought to be not so much a novelist as a historical romancer. In point of fact, however, he has many weaknesses as a historical romancer and much enduring strength and appeal as a novelist. His finest stories are those with an eighteenth-century background.

The years 1840 to 1890 represent a peak in English novel writing. The 1840–1890 group begins with Charles Dickens (1812–1870), one of the acknowledged world masters of fiction. Dickens began to write in a slapdash, improvising way, mixing glorious fun with unreal melodrama; then he gradually planned his work more and more and, while keeping his inimitable humor, filled his writings with a searching criticism of mid-Victorian society. William Makepeace Thackeray (1811–1863) had no such genius, but he had great qualities of his own: a wide knowledge of social life, a wonderful eye and ear for character and scene, and an easy narrative style that could rise to passages of great force and beauty. These qualities are perhaps found at their best in *Vanity Fair*, although many critics consider his historical novel, *Henry Esmond*, his masterpiece. Anthony Trollope (1815–1882), who was one of Thackeray's most enthusiastic admirers, is less distinguished in style and lacks Thackeray's flashes of insight, but his solid novels about mid-Vic-

torian churchmen and politicians, after being almost forgotten, are once more being widely read and appreciated.

The chief women in this group are Charlotte Brontë (1816–1855), who brought an intense realism into fiction; her sister, Emily (1818–1848), whose *Wuthering Heights* (1847) is hardly a novel at all in the ordinary sense but rather an impassioned and symbolic prose poem; and Mary Ann Evans (1819–1880), who wrote under the name of George Eliot. The latter was a deeply serious woman with a good intellect as well as a sound knowledge of English provincial life; her very solid virtues are found at their best in *Middlemarch* (1871), which thoroughly analyzes a certain type of English society.

George Meredith (1828–1909) and Thomas Hardy (1840–1928) both preferred their poetry to their fiction, although they wrote many long novels. They are both philosophical novelists, making their fiction express certain ideas about life. But whereas Meredith is a high-spirited if rather affected comic-romantic, Hardy is broodingly pessimistic, at his best when his characters are rustic types surrounded by the heaths and vales of the author's native "Wessex." With them may be mentioned Robert Louis Stevenson (1850–1894), who died too young—at forty-four—to fulfill completely all his promise, but who has retained his hold on successive generations of readers by the romantic zest of his narrative and a curious charm of style.

From 1890 onward, English prose fiction suddenly began to travel to very distant places. Before this time, from Richardson to Hardy, every major novel, except for a few chapters here and there, had been concerned with the British scene. Now came a much wider sweep. Stevenson began it with his tales of the South Seas. Then Rudyard Kipling

(1865–1936) arrived from India, W. H. Hudson (1841–1922) from South America, and Joseph Conrad (1857–1924) from worldwide travels. The last, a Pole by birth who became a captain in the British merchant marine, is the most important of these three as a novelist. Conrad is often thought to be simply a romantic storyteller just because he shows us so many sailors and ships in far-off places. However, he is really a novelist who happens to be indifferent to the usual social themes but who is deeply concerned with character, with behavior of individuals in moments of great stress, and with the fundamental nature of human life and destiny. These themes he often treats in a symbolical way, as poets are apt to do, so that in reading Conrad we must always try to be aware of depths of meaning below the surface of the narrative.

In the years before World War I, three writers came to prominence who might be described as "sociological" novelists. By this we mean that their chief concern is with society itself—its organization, outlook, values, and tone. H. G. Wells (1866–1946), Arnold Bennett (1867–1931), and John Galsworthy (1867–1933), the three writers in question, are far from being alike either as men or as writers, but in their fiction they all have a sociological foundation in common.

Wells, the most brilliant, never thought of himself as a literary artist (though he was), and made no secret of the fact that he made use of the novel as a critic of society. But his genius in the creation of character and scene often triumphs over his sociology, as in *Mr. Polly* (1910) and *Tono-Bungay* (1909). Arnold Bennett's fiction is varied and uneven, but the best of it is a solidly realistic record of the society he knew as a boy in that provincial region known, because it was the center of the pottery industry, as "The Potteries." There is, however, in Bennett an easy, unforced charm as well as a solid realism, which he learned from French novelists during the years he lived in France. Bennett's masterpiece is *The Old Wives' Tale* (1908).

John Galsworthy made his reputation in Britain before World War I, not only through his novels, which were sharply critical studies of the property-owning class to which he himself belonged, but also through his realistic and well-constructed plays. It was, however, with the publication of *The Forsyte Saga* (1906–1921) that he achieved during the 1920's a worldwide body of admiring readers who felt that his wide social range, his honest criticism of his own class, his deep compassion, his essential Englishness, made him the representative English novelist of his time. He was awarded the Nobel Prize in 1932, the first English writer of fiction after Kipling to be so honored.

During most of the nineteenth century, novels of any importance were originally published in three volumes and at prices that only wealthier readers and libraries could afford to pay. Dickens and Thackeray, however, brought out most of their novels first in what were called "parts," that is, in separate installments published every month. Cheap one-volume editions began to be published chiefly for the benefit of railroad travelers. Then, in the 1890's, enterprising publishers brought out one-volume editions of new novels, at a quarter of the price of the old three-volume editions. Libraries could now afford to buy more copies; ordinary readers became novel-buyers; and the trade in fiction increased enormously. All manner of tastes were catered to by enterprising publishers and popular authors.

The Victorian Age

When Victoria ascended the throne in 1837, her country was already in the midst of a period of great social and economic upheaval. Great Britain, which only two centuries earlier had been a tiny island country on the fringes of European civilization, had now become the most powerful nation in the world and the governing center of a vast colonial empire. Many English people who might formerly have spent their lives quietly in the towns where they had been born now found themselves assigned to the far corners of the earth as government officials or as soldiers. Even for those who did stay at home, life was no longer the same. The Industrial Revolution had begun; factories were springing up everywhere, cities were growing rapidly, railways were extending over the countryside. The English way of life was changing rapidly, and these changes were reflected in the language and literature.

The English who saw service in outlying parts of the British Empire returned home with a new vocabulary of exotic terms, some of which quickly made their way into the standard vocabulary of the language. Names of African animals became familiar words— *aardvark, bushbuck, eland, gnu.* Australia and New Zealand also contributed exotic animal names— *cassowary, wombat, kookaburra, wallaby.*

Meanwhile, in England itself, the vocabulary of modern science and technology was taking shape. An "engine" to the eighteenth-century English had been any kind of tool or device; to the nineteenth-century English it began to assume its present-day meaning of a machine that converts energy into mechanical force. The arrival of the steam engine was marked by the appearance of new terms such as *piston valve, drive shaft, steamship,* and *steamroller.* During the last half of the cen-

tury, many words associated with electrical power put in their first appearance: *dynamo, ampere, ohm, volt, watt.*

At the same time that the scientific and technological vocabulary was expanding rapidly, other specialized vocabularies were beginning to shrink and fall into disuse. When the stagecoach gave way to the railroad, for instance, terms like *postilion, splinter bar,* and *swingle* began to disappear from common speech. But the railroad brought its own terms: *locomotive, timetable,* and *turntable.* A little later, with the coming of the automobile, almost all horse-drawn vehicles vanished from the scene; and with them went an enormous group of specialized terms. Everyone today knows the difference between a *sports car,* a *taxi,* a *trailer truck,* and a *bus.* But how many people could distinguish between a *victoria,* a *hackney,* a *dray,* and a *tallyho?*

The writers of the Victorian period were keenly aware that they were living in a time of change. On the whole, they found the changes disturbing and unsettling. They had good reason for looking on modern developments with a gloomy eye: among the most visible signs of "progress" were ugly factory districts, growing urban slums, and an ever-increasing stream of cheap, shoddy manufactured items. Some writers, such as Carlyle, spoke out directly against the ugliness and the suffering they saw in contemporary life. But many others, especially the poets, reacted by turning away from modern civilization and concentrating on pleasant rural scenes or on a romantically idealized past. It was left for twentieth-century writers to adopt urban life as their theme; few nineteenth-century English writers felt quite at home in the city streets. To some extent, therefore, the language of Victorian literature is the language of a vanishing country life or of a vanished past. Many modern readers owe to Tennyson their familiarity with medieval terms such as *greaves* and *baldric* (see "The Lady of Shalott," page 557), and they owe to Hardy their familiarity with certain rural English dialects (see the dialogue in "The Three Strangers," page 612).

The love of the past that was so strong an element in Victorian thought was often combined, however, with an equally strong passion for scientific accuracy. One of the aspects of the past that particularly fascinated Victorian thinkers was the history of language. During the seventeenth and eighteenth centuries, the little research that had been done into Old English and Middle English had been based mainly on guesswork. Nineteenth-century researchers, however, began to go systematically through collections of old manuscripts, classifying and comparing them in minute detail. Scholarly societies devoted to the study of language history were formed: the Philological Society was founded in 1842, the Early English Text Society in 1864, the Chaucer Society in 1868.

Perhaps the greatest single product of nineteenth-century language scholarship was the *Oxford English Dictionary*, a dictionary that traces the origin of hundreds of thousands of English words, giving the date when each word was first found in English writing and showing the development of new meanings by giving definitions and carefully dated quotations. The preparation of this dictionary was an immense task. Work on it was begun in 1857, and by the time the first volume appeared in 1884, approximately one thousand readers and editors had given their time to the project. The complete twelve-volume dictionary took more than seventy years to finish. The dictionary has now grown to fifteen volumes and is still being revised.

FOR STUDY AND DISCUSSION

1. Using a dictionary that gives etymologies (word origins), look up the following words and find out from which language each of them entered the English language. All are terms that were acquired from far-reaching parts of the British Empire. From which specific part of the world did each of them come?

bangle	gingham	pariah
cooey	loot	polo
dinghy	nirvana	thug

2. Find out whether there is a set of the *Oxford English Dictionary* available in a local library. (You might find an older edition under the title *A New English Dictionary;* this will serve your purpose just as well.) If you find a set, read the Historical Introduction near the beginning of the first volume, and prepare a brief report, answering one of the following questions:

  a. What led up to the Philological Society's decision to prepare a dictionary based on historical principles?
  b. Who were the chief editors involved with work on the dictionary over the years? What did each of these editors accomplish?
  c. Exactly how were the entry slips prepared?

3. Using either the *Oxford English Dictionary (New English Dictionary)* or the *Shorter Oxford English Dictionary,* look up the following words and find the date given for the first recorded appearance of the word in English writing. The *Shorter Oxford English Dictionary* is an abridged version available in many libraries that may not have the unabridged multivolume set. What does the date given for the word's first appearance tell you about the historical development of science or technology?

aeronaut	gasoline	pasteurize
automobile	hydroelectric	radium
bacterium	ion	X-rays

The Twentieth Century

Elizabeth II riding in the Gold State Coach during her Silver Jubilee
(1977) celebrating the twenty-fifth year of her reign.
Sipa, Black Star

Many achievements of this century have raised expectations for improving the quality of life throughout the world. Advances in medical science have prolonged life and reduced the threat of epidemics. New sources of energy and improved agriculture offer hope of solution to the world population crisis. Mass communication is raising the level of education in many parts of the world, and has increased the pressure for human rights in totalitarian regimes. Knowledge of the environment and the universe has advanced at an astonishing rate.

Despite the achievements of our culture and its growing technology, few of its accomplishments have been prevailing themes in modern literature. Twentieth-century literature has been more concerned with tragic and fragmented experience than with positive achievement. These overriding concerns are understandable, given the cataclysmic events of our time: two devastating world wars, the destruction of millions in the Nazi Holocaust, the confinement and immense suffering of millions in the prisons and labor camps that stretched across the Soviet Union in the Stalin years, the mass starvation of millions in Asia and Africa even in recent years, and nuclear armament that poses a constant threat to world peace. Perhaps at no other time in history has there been such widespread awareness of the gap between ideals and reality—between the high expectations for happiness and the frustration of those hopes.

For Britain, the twentieth century has been generally a time of declining national fortune. The country has had to face two ruinous wars that have cost many lives and the destruction of much property. In order to pay for the wars, Britain has had to give up many of its investments abroad that during the nineteenth century had made London the financial capital of the world. Britain has lost the dominant position in world politics that it had during the nineteenth century. And while there have been many gains in social and economic legislation and in the standard of living, Britain has had difficulty modernizing and expanding its industry. Yet, during these years, Britain has continued to produce an outstanding literature.

EARLY TWENTIETH-CENTURY LITERATURE

The early years of the twentieth century in Britain saw momentous changes in social and political life. The struggle for women's rights was reaching a climax, the movement for Irish independence gained momentum with the Easter uprising of 1916 and ended with the creation of the Irish Free State in 1921, and the laboring class made important gains in political power and living standards.

Air raid damage in
London, 1941.
Radio Times Hulton

Early twentieth-century literature reflected these changes, turning increasingly to lower middle-class and working-class life, as in the Dublin stories of James Joyce (1882–1941) and the novels of Arnold Bennett (1867–1931) and H. G. Wells (1866–1946). In *Sons and Lovers*, D. H. Lawrence (1885–1930) wrote about the life of a miner's family in the industrial North of England. Irish drama, reborn in the founding of the Abbey Theater and the distinguished plays of William Butler Yeats (1865–1939), John Millington Synge (1871–1909), and Lady Gregory (1852–1932), often dealt realistically with the daily life of Irish country people. Political and social themes continued to occupy writers. The plays of Bernard Shaw (1856–1950) written at the beginning of the century explore a range of social themes, including middle-class British society, militarism, education, and the situation of women.

Joseph Conrad

A scene from the film *Pygmalion*

Battle of Langermarch (1917)

1900   **Edward VII 1901–1910**   **1910**   **World War I 1914–1918**

Conrad's
Nostromo 1904

Yeats's
The Green Hamlet 1910

Shaw's *Pygmalion*
1912

Battle of the Somme
1916

Orwell's *1984* 1948

Commonwealth
of Nations 1947

Yalta Conference 1945

After the War 1945–   **World War II 1939–1945**

Larkin's
The North Ship 1945

Thomas'
Collected Poems 1952

Beckett's *Waiting for Godot*
1954

Hughes's
Hawk in the Rain 1957

Coventry Cathedral
rebuilt 1962

1950   **Elizabeth II (1953–**   **1960**

Guernica, Pablo Picasso. On extended loan to the Museum of Modern Art, New York

Edward, Prince of Wales (1926)

T. S. Eliot (detail), Wyndham Lewis

The General Strike (1926)

1920   George V 1910–1936

Women's Suffrage
1918

Eliot's *The Waste Land*
and Joyce's *Ulysses* 1922

Forster's *A Passage to India*
1924

General Strike
1926

Bombing of Guernica
1937

Woolf's
To the Lighthouse 1927

1940   George VI 1936–1953   **1930**

Eliot's
Four Quartets 1942

Abdication
of Edward VIII 1936

Graves's
Collected Poems 1965

North Sea
oil discovered 1970

The Common Market
1973

Silver Jubilee 1977

1970   **1980   1990**

Dylan Thomas (detail)

Coventry Cathedral

Elizabeth II (detail), P. Annigoni

Fewer poets wrote in the large forms favored earlier by the Victorians—the extended elegy and dramatic monologue, the epic narrative of Tennyson's *Idylls of the King.* The short lyric flourished in the poetry of A. E. Housman, Thomas Hardy, and Yeats. Impressionism in literature—focusing on individual moments of experience, and not seeking to interpret life or moralize experience as Victorian literature had—became increasingly important in poetry and fiction. Impressionism ushered in the Imagist movement. "Direct treatment of the 'thing' whether subjective or objective"—that was the aim of Imagist poetry, Ezra Pound wrote in 1913.

Closer to Romantic and Victorian ideals was literary symbolism, of which Yeats was the leading exponent at the turn of the century. The essential idea of Symbolism was that certain mysterious feelings and ideas could be experienced only through a symbol that represented and evoked these meanings.

Maud Gonne by Sarah Purser. Gonne was active in the Irish struggle for independence and was for Yeats a symbol of Ireland: beautiful, proud, heroic.
National Gallery of Ireland, Dublin

WORLD WAR I

In Europe, World War I began in August 1914 and continued to November 1918. The older heroic ideal of Tennyson's "Charge of the Light Brigade"—"When can their glory fade?/O the wild charge they made!"—is voiced by Rupert Brooke (1887–1915), who had fought briefly in Belgium and died en route to the Dardanelles:

> Now God be thanked who has matched us with His Hour,
> And caught our youth, and wakened us from sleeping.

The war itself soon silenced those who thought they would find heroism and beauty in it. The realities of trench warfare were soon impressed on civilians and poets fighting in the war. The slaughter was immense, particularly at the Battle of the Somme in 1916, in which virtually all the young men of some small towns in England perished. Poison gas, explosive bullets, the filth and vermin of the trenches, the machine gun and barbed wire: these were the new realities of war, a sharp contrast to the mounted glory of the Light Brigade. On the Allied side, more than seven million men died, five million in direct action or from wounds. Wilfred Owen, who died shortly before the Armistice, captured the physical horror in poems like "Arms and the Boy":

> Let the boy try along this bayonet-blade
> How cold steel is, and keen with hunger of blood . . .
> Lend him to stroke these blind, blunt bullet-heads
> Which long to nuzzle in the hearts of lads,
> Or give him cartridges of fine zinc teeth,
> Sharp with the sharpness of grief and death.

The effect of these ghastly casualties was powerful and lasting, both on surviving soldiers themselves—poets like Siegfried Sassoon (1886–1967) and Robert Graves (1895–   )—and on the civilians at home. From 1919 onward, many of the younger writers turned in disgust from public affairs. Whatever was associated with the world before the war was condemned or ignored because it was that world that had produced the war.

Battle of Langermarch, 1917.
Radio Times Hulton

THE NEW WRITING

The war poetry strongly influenced a new literary movement sometimes called Modernist. Poets and novelists with diverse subjects and points of view joined in their rejection of prewar literary tradition. Modernist trends were influenced by Impressionist and Symbolist ideas, by the poems of Gerard Manley Hopkins, and by the ideas of the British Idealists, who were opposed to the materialism that had dominated the nineteenth century. The Bloomsbury group of artists and writers, which included Virginia Woolf (1882–1941), E. M. Forster (1879–1970), and Lytton Strachey (1880–1932), disseminated Modernist ideas even though their practice as writers varied. Virginia Woolf wrote in 1924:

> We are sharply cut off from our predecessors. A shift in the scale — the war, the sudden slip of masses held in position for ages — has shaken the fabric from top to bottom, alienated us from the past and made us perhaps too vividly conscious of the present. Every day we find ourselves doing, saying, or thinking things that would have been impossible to our fathers.

Virginia Woolf
Man Ray, courtesy *Harper's Bazaar*

T. S. Eliot by Wyndham Lewis.
Fogg Art Museum, Harvard University

A major influence during the 1920's was T. S. Eliot (1888–1965), who sought in his poems and critical essays to create a new literary tradition out of what he considered most vital in the past. Eliot revived interest in the seventeenth-century writers, chiefly John Donne and the so-called metaphysical poets. In them he found the basis of a new classicism. The publication of his long poem *The Waste Land* in 1922, the same year that James Joyce's long and complex novel *Ulysses* was published, brought to public attention a new kind of literature. It was highly allusive and "crossed" many traditions of thought and literary expression in an immense variety of forms and voices. In these works no single voice could be identified with the author: that was perhaps the most significant idea of the Modernist movement.

Virginia Woolf was to achieve the same effect in her magnificent novel of 1931, *The Waves*. Yeats, in the remarkable poems he wrote in the 1920's and 1930's, shows what Eliot had in mind. Yeats established many voices and many images of himself. No single poem speaks for the "real" Yeats. Indeed, the central theme of his poetry is the continuing discovery of many selves, moods, and modes of thinking and feeling.

A number of younger poets, including W. H. Auden (1907–1973), Stephen Spender (1909–   ), and C. Day Lewis (1904–1972) were enormously influenced not only by Eliot's Modernist verse but also by his examination of social and religious questions. Increasingly, their poetry and that of others became directly concerned with ideas, and they were willing to speak in their own voice.

There were, of course, other writers whose work was less affected by the war and the disillusionment that it bred. Joseph Conrad (1857–1924) and Katherine Mansfield (1888–1923), whose careers as writers of fiction began well before the war and ended shortly after it, exercised much influence on later writers. Among poets, A. E. Housman wrote a small number of exquisitely polished lyrics. An important novelist, contemporary with Joyce and Woolf but markedly different in his approach, was D. H. Lawrence.

THE RISE OF FASCISM

The rise of fascism — with its ideal of the great leader and exaltation of physical force — was the central political event in the years between the two world wars. The immediate causes of its appearance were nationalism and economic hardship. Germany had been humiliated by the Versailles Treaty, which exacted heavy war reparations; the inflation of 1923 severely weakened the government and ruined thousands of the lower middle class who lost homes and savings. During these years of hardship, Adolf Hitler was building the Nazi movement in Germany; Benito Mussolini established a fascist dictatorship in Italy in 1922; the Bolshevists, who had seized power in Russia in 1917, established a Communist dictatorship.

Great Britain was not exempt from economic crisis. The British seizure of the German merchant marine as part of the war reparations ironically created unemployment in the British shipbuilding industry. Beginning with the nine-day general strike in 1926, a series of governments failed to solve growing economic problems.

The Great Depression, beginning in the United States in 1929 and intensifying the severe economic crisis throughout Europe, created even greater political turmoil. The abolition of German war reparations at a conference of the Allied powers in 1932 did not prevent Hitler's coming to power in 1933. The League of Nations failed to deal effectively with Mussolini's conquest of Ethiopia in 1935. The British and French governments failed to respond decisively to Hitler's revival of military power, his occupation of the Rhineland in 1936, and other treaty violations. Hitler's annexation of Austria and occupation of western Czechoslovakia, in 1938, were the prelude to the outbreak of World War II on September 1, 1939, with the German invasion of Poland.

A decisive experience for many writers was the Spanish Civil War, which began in 1936. The Loyalist government of Spain was supported by the Soviet Union and socialists in other countries, as well as by the Western democracies, though not wholeheartedly. The Franco forces were supported by Germany and Italy. Some British writers

Patrol wagon escorted by police in Southwark during the general strike of 1926.
Radio Times Hulton

like W. H. Auden, Stephen Spender, and George Orwell (1903–1950),
who had been attracted to Marxism or one of the several contemporary socialist movements, were soon disillusioned by Soviet
opportunism or confirmed in growing disbelief of communistic doc-
trines. Many, realizing that no simple political solution existed for
long-standing evils, sought new answers. Like Eliot, who had entered the Church of England in 1927, Auden turned to Christianity
for an answer to the impasse of the "low dishonest decade" he char-
acterizes in his poem "September 1, 1939." George Orwell, who
fought for several months on the Loyalist side, returned to England,
and wrote about his experiences in *Homage to Catalonia*. The
England he returned to, he wrote, was "sleeping the deep, deep sleep
of England, from which I sometimes fear that we shall never wake
till we are jerked out of it by the roar of bombs."

WORLD WAR II

In Europe, World War II lasted from 1939 to 1945. Though civilian
populations have always been subject to attack in war, and have frequently suffered greater torments and casualties than men in the
field, the effect of World War II on civilian populations throughout
Europe was catastrophic. The German bombing of the Basque town

Guernica by Pablo Picasso (oil, 1937).
On loan to the Museum of Modern Art, New York, from
the artist's estate

of Guernica in northern Spain, on April 26, 1937, virtually destroying the town, and killing or wounding more than a third of its five thousand inhabitants, demonstrated the new, immensely destructive power of "blitz" bombing, and pointed to the fate of towns and cities in the coming war. Ahead were the German death camps, in which millions were to be tortured and slaughtered, an event slower to seize the imagination of people in America and Europe than the German "blitzkrieg" that swept east into the Balkans and the Soviet Union and west into Norway, Holland, Belgium, Denmark, and France.

The German "blitz" of London in the first years of the war, and other acts like the destruction of the English town of Coventry, strengthened British resolve to win a war fought under enormous handicaps. The more than a quarter million civilian casualties brought home a grisly horror of modern warfare: whole populations were now hostage to war. Eliot wrote in his wartime poem, "Little Gidding," that the solution for human beings lay in a "fire" as fierce as the holocaust of the bombing:

> The only hope, or else despair
> Lies in the choice of pyre or pyre—
> To be redeemed from fire by fire.

The overriding question for many postwar writers was whether Western civilization could be reconstructed—indeed whether humane values had long been taken for granted by complacent people.

THE AFTERMATH OF WORLD WAR II

After World War II a movement that had been long under way reached its climax—namely, the transformation of the British Empire into the Commonwealth of Nations. Lands once governed by Britain became independent, self-governing nations, tied to Britain by bonds of tradition and language. This status had been achieved in 1867 by Canada, in the early twentieth century by Australia, New Zealand, and South Africa, and in 1921 by the Irish Free State. The two decades immediately following World War II saw the triumph of movements for national independence in almost all British colonies—the most important being the division of India in 1947 into the two independent states of India and Pakistan.

At the same time that the Empire was being transformed into the Commonwealth, far-reaching changes were taking place at home. Most notable was the continuing demand for extensive social legislation. The government took over a large share of the responsibility for the health, employment, housing, education, and pensions of the great mass of the population. Despite many gains in domestic policy, Britain was plagued by economic problems. British industry was not growing at the same rate achieved by industry in other countries. British exports encountered competition from other nations—a far more serious problem for Britain than for most other countries, for Britain must export industrial goods in order to pay for the large quantities of food imported to feed its population. In addition, several financial crises contributed to the lowering of national morale.

A continuing theme of much postwar literature was how people were to live in the modern state. Postwar writers looked for concrete solutions and renewal of what seemed best in the British character. Writing in 1941, Orwell spoke for many British postwar writers:

> It needs some very great disaster, such as prolonged subjection by a foreign enemy, to destroy a national culture. The Stock Exchange will be pulled down, the horse plow will give way to the tractor, the country houses will be turned into children's holiday camps, the Eton and Harrow match will be forgotten, but England will still be England, an everlasting animal stretching into the future and the past, and like all living things, having the power to change out of recognition and yet remain the same.

CONTEMPORARY BRITISH WRITING

Several prominent writers of contemporary fiction made their first appearance in the twenties. This group includes Aldous Huxley (1894–1963), Elizabeth Bowen (1899–1973), Evelyn Waugh (1903–1966), and Graham Greene (1904–   ). Other novelists of this older generation include Joyce Cary (1888–1957), Liam O'Flaherty (1896–   ), and C. P. Snow (1905–   ).

Since World War II a new group of English novelists has appeared: William Golding (1911–   ), Pamela Hansford Johnson (1912–   ), Angus Wilson (1913–   ), Anthony Burgess (1917–   ), Iris Murdoch (1919–   ), Alan Sillitoe (1928–   ) and Margaret Drabble (1939–   ). In addition there is the work of writers in the Commonwealth: Alan Paton (1903–   ), Doris Lessing (1919–   ), and Nadine Gordimer (1923–   ), for example, have written about Africa; Patrick White (1912–   ) and Colleen McCullough (1937–   ), about Australia; Morley Callaghan (1903–   ) and Margaret Atwood (1939–   ), about Canada.

Psychological and social problems continue to be the major concerns of contemporary writing. Fiction in the 1960's and 1970's has dealt increasingly with both psychological introspection—what Doris Lessing calls "inner space"—and with social questions.

Among those dramatists who established reputations in the 1950's is John Osborne, one of the "Angry Young Men," who in his play *Look Back in Anger* attacked the British class system for denying the highly educated working-class person an opportunity to rise in the world. Harold Pinter, among the most innovative writers of modern British drama, also has explored the dilemmas of human existence, revealing disturbing overtones in seemingly ordinary situations.

Coventry Cathedral. Remains of the old cathedral are at the left.
Larry Mulvehill, Photo Researchers

English poets today seem to share this preference for looking realistically at modern experience, regardless of how disquieting their realizations may be. A group of poets writing since the mid-1950's and known as "Movement" poets have avoided flamboyant, emotional statements. They have found it important to use controlled simple language. The poetry of Philip Larkin and Thom Gunn is representative of this group. To a century of disorder and conflict, to a modern world growing in complexity, the Movement poets have responded with order and clarity. Other poets, Ted Hughes among them, have broken away from the direction of the Movement and have revealed more urgent feeling as well as a wide range of popular and sophisticated poetic forms. Modern English poetry, like twentieth-century writing as a whole, derives its undeniable power from its great diversity.

A view of Piccadilly Circus, center of London theatrical life. The word *Circus* refers to an open, circular area where several streets meet.
Ray Manley, Shostal Associates

Prose

Joseph Conrad
1857–1924

Two facts have long obscured the full meaning of Conrad's work: first, that he did not learn to speak and write English until he was twenty-one; and second, that his early work centered on the sea and exotic regions of the Far East. While these aspects of his life are important, the attempts of Conrad's early critics to use one or both of them to define his achievement were misleading. That the young Polish man learned English is less interesting than his use of that language to achieve a new kind of fiction; that he excelled at describing the sights, sounds, and smells of Malaysia, or the absorbing craft of the sea and the lonely trials of command, is less important than his discovery of our common humanity in these unfamiliar settings.

In one of his prefaces Conrad describes the writer's calling in this way: "He [the writer] speaks to our capacity for delight and wonder, to the sense of mystery surrounding our lives; to our sense of pity, and beauty, and pain; to the latent feeling of fellowship with all creation. . . ." Conrad insists on a community based on aspiration, illusion, and dream. A number of important writers at the end of the nineteenth century tried to find some basis outside the state and outside organized religion for defining our common humanity and for creating a bond that might hold people together. For Conrad the ideal of the nation-state lay in the past. He found a kind of bond, a partial order, in the code of the sea, which bound officers and men in a network of defined responsibilities to each other, to their passengers, and to the vessel.

Conrad did more than discover a usable code of conduct, a bond between people. In his novels he measured this code against the pressures of Western civilization in his time. In some of his works he may, in fact, to a superficial reader, seem more concerned with the pressures of civilization than with the code. In *Heart of Darkness*, he deals with the merciless exploitation of Africans in the Belgian Congo. In *Nostromo*, he exposes the weakness of commercial interests. But underlying these

Joseph Conrad by W. Rothenstein.
National Portrait Gallery, London

works as well as such masterpieces as *Victory, The Secret Agent,* and *Lord Jim,* there is always Conrad's greatest theme: the way in which our dreams of ourselves work either to join us with, or to cut us off from, the rest of humanity. In the process of exploring this theme, he is to an extent one of the finest modern psychological novelists. He penetrates the obscure places of the human heart and shows how our lives are wrecked or sustained by our dreams and illusions. In Conrad, however, the psychological as well as the social is subordinated to a basic concern with "the truth, manifold and one" about us and the world we inhabit and shape. Conrad has no very happy view of this adventure of dream and reality. Almost always he remains the stern shipmaster of souls: act on your dream you must, he says, but take good care that it reaches out to include your fellows, otherwise you will lose your humanity.

Josef Teodor Conrad Nalecz Korzeniowski was

born in Russian Poland in December 1857. His father was a nobleman, a Polish patriot, whose efforts to liberate his country from Russia led in 1862 to his exile with his wife and son. Conrad's mother died in 1865, and her young son was then sent to live with his maternal uncle, Tadeusz Bobrowski, with whom he remained for two years. He then rejoined his father, who had been permitted to move closer to home. In 1869 his father died, and Conrad's uncle Tadeusz again became responsible for the slight, emotional youngster. For some years thereafter, Conrad was educated by a tutor, with whom he made a European tour in 1873.

In 1874 Tadeusz gave in to an extraordinary request. His ward wished to become a seaman. The firm, practical, and affectionate guardian apprenticed him to a banking and shipping company in Marseilles. There Conrad learned seamanship in voyages to the West Indies. In 1877 and 1878, on a small vessel of which he was part owner, he was involved in smuggling arms to the forces of a pretender to the Spanish throne. In the latter year, having lost all his money and perhaps (no one knows) having had an unhappy love affair, he shot himself in the chest. (He later made up a tale about a duel to account for this episode.) Under the care of his attentive uncle Tadeusz, he recovered, and that same year shipped out on a British vessel for the first time. In 1886 he became a British subject, as well as a licensed ship's captain, and until 1894 he was to serve as seaman and officer on British ships, sailing to Asia, South America, and South Africa, with only occasional intervals ashore.

From 1889 until the publication of *Almayer's Folly* in 1895, Conrad spent all his leisure moments working on the manuscript of this first novel. In the year following its publication, he married an Englishwoman and became a householder and the head of a family. But even with marriage he did not achieve tranquillity. He was a nervous, irritable, passionate man, who labored long, agonized hours at his desk, was in constant need of money, and never received full public recognition during the years when he did his best work. When recognition finally came in the form of an offer of knighthood, Conrad refused it.

The Lagoon

The white man, leaning with both arms over the roof of the little house in the stern of the boat, said to the steersman:

"We will pass the night in Arsat's clearing. It is late."

The Malay only grunted, and went on looking fixedly at the river. The white man rested his chin on his crossed arms and gazed at the wake of the boat. At the end of the straight avenue of forests cut by the intense glitter of the river, the sun appeared unclouded and dazzling, poised low over the water that shone smoothly like a band of metal. The forests, somber and dull, stood motionless and silent on each side of the broad stream. At the foot of big, towering trees, trunkless nipa palms rose from the mud of the bank, in bunches of leaves enormous and heavy, that hung unstirring over the brown swirl of eddies. In the stillness of the air every tree, every leaf, every bough, every tendril of creeper and every petal of minute blossoms seemed to have been bewitched into an immobility perfect and final. Nothing moved on the river but the eight paddles that rose flashing regularly, dipped together with a single splash, while the steersman swept right and left with a periodic and sudden flourish of his blade describing a glinting semicircle above his head. The churned-up water frothed alongside with a confused murmur. And the white man's canoe, advancing upstream in the short-lived disturbance of its own making, seemed to enter the portals of a land from which the very memory of motion had forever departed.

The white man, turning his back upon the setting sun, looked along the empty and broad expanse of the sea reach. For the last three

Sunset over lagoon and rice paddy in Indonesia.
Paul Fusco, Magnum

miles of its course the wandering, hesitating river, as if enticed irresistibly by the freedom of an open horizon, flows straight into the sea, flows straight to the east—to the east that harbors both light and darkness. Astern of the boat the repeated call of some bird, a cry discordant and feeble, skipped along over the smooth water and lost itself before it could reach the other shore in the breathless silence of the world.

The steersman dug his paddle into the stream, and held hard with stiffened arms, his body thrown forward. The water gurgled aloud; and suddenly the long straight reach seemed to pivot on its center, the forests swung in a semicircle, and the slanting beams of sunset touched the broadside of the canoe with a fiery glow, throwing the slender and distorted shadows of its crew upon the streaked glitter of the river. The white man turned to look ahead. The course of the boat had been altered at right angles to the stream, and the carved dragonhead on its prow was pointing now at a gap in the fringing bushes of the bank. It glided through, brushing the overhanging twigs, and disappeared from the river like some slim and amphibious creature leaving the water for its lair in the forests.

The narrow creek was like a ditch: tortuous, fabulously deep; filled with gloom under the thin strip of pure and shining blue of the heaven. Immense trees soared up, invisible behind the festooned draperies of creepers. Here and there, near the glistening blackness of the water, a twisted root of some tall tree showed among the tracery of small ferns, black and dull, writhing and motionless, like an arrested snake. The short words of the paddlers reverberated loudly between the thick and somber walls of vegetation. Darkness oozed out from between the trees, through the tangled maze of the creepers, from behind the great fantastic and unstirring leaves; the darkness, mysterious and invincible; the darkness scented and poisonous of impenetrable forests.

Joseph Conrad 691

The men poled in the shoaling water. The creek broadened, opening out into a wide sweep of a stagnant lagoon. The forests receded from the marshy bank, leaving a level strip of bright green, reedy grass to frame the reflected blueness of the sky. A fleecy pink cloud drifted high above, trailing the delicate coloring of its image under the floating leaves and the silver blossoms of the lotus. A little house, perched on high piles, appeared black in the distance. Near it, two tall nibong palms that seemed to have come out of the forests in the background leaned slightly over the ragged roof, with a suggestion of sad tenderness and care in the droop of their leafy and soaring heads.

The steersman, pointing with his paddle, said, "Arsat is there. I see his canoe fast between the piles."

The polers ran along the sides of the boat glancing over their shoulders at the end of the day's journey. They would have preferred to spend the night somewhere else than on this lagoon of weird aspect and ghostly reputation. Moreover, they disliked Arsat, first as a stranger, and also because he who repairs a ruined house, and dwells in it, proclaims that he is not afraid to live amongst the spirits that haunt the places abandoned by mankind. Such a man can disturb the course of fate by glances or words; while his familiar ghosts are not easy to propitiate[1] by casual wayfarers upon whom they long to wreak the malice of their human master. White men care not for such things, being unbelievers and in league with the Father of Evil, who leads them unharmed through the invisible dangers of this world. To the warnings of the righteous they oppose an offensive pretense of disbelief. What is there to be done?

So they thought, throwing their weight on the end of their long poles. The big canoe glided on swiftly, noiselessly, and smoothly, toward Arsat's clearing, till, in a great rattling of poles thrown down, and the loud murmurs of "Allah be praised!" it came with a gentle knock against the crooked piles below the house.

The boatmen with uplifted faces shouted discordantly, "Arsat! O Arsat!" Nobody came. The white man began to climb the rude ladder giving access to the bamboo platform before the house. The juragan[2] of the boat said sulkily, "We will cook in the sampan,[3] and sleep on the water."

"Pass my blankets and the basket," said the white man curtly.

He knelt on the edge of the platform to receive the bundle. Then the boat shoved off, and the white man, standing up, confronted Arsat, who had come out through the low door of his hut. He was a man young, powerful, with broad chest and muscular arms. He had nothing on but his sarong.[4] His head was bare. His big, soft eyes stared eagerly at the white man, but his voice and demeanor were composed as he asked, without any words of greeting:

"Have you medicine, Tuan?"[5]

"No," said the visitor in a startled tone. "No. Why? Is there sickness in the house?"

"Enter and see," replied Arsat, in the same calm manner, and turning short round, passed again through the small doorway. The white man, dropping his bundles, followed.

In the dim light of the dwelling he made out on a couch of bamboos a woman stretched on her back under a broad sheet of red cotton cloth. She lay still, as if dead; but her big eyes, wide open, glittered in the gloom, staring upward at the slender rafters, motionless and unseeing. She was in a high fever, and evi-

---

1. **familiar . . . propitiate:** attendant spirits are difficult to appease.

2. **juragan:** native leader or captain.
3. **sampan:** flat-bottomed boat used in river and harbor traffic.
4. **sarong:** skirt or kilt worn by both sexes in the Malay Peninsula.
5. **Tuan:** term of respect, like *Sir*.

dently unconscious. Her cheeks were sunk slightly, her lips were partly open, and on the young face there was the ominous and fixed expression—the absorbed, contemplating expression of the unconscious who are going to die. The two men stood looking down at her in silence.

"Has she been long ill?" asked the traveler.

"I have not slept for five nights," answered the Malay in a deliberate tone. "At first she heard voices calling her from the water and struggled against me who held her. But since the sun of today rose she hears nothing—she hears not me. She sees nothing. She sees not me—me!"

He remained silent for a minute, then asked softly:

"Tuan, will she die?"

"I fear so," said the white man, sorrowfully. He had known Arsat years ago, in a far country in times of trouble and danger, when no friendship is to be despised. And since his Malay friend had come unexpectedly to dwell in the hut on the lagoon with a strange woman, he had slept many times there, in his journeys up and down the river. He liked the man who knew how to keep faith in council and how to fight without fear by the side of his white friend. He liked him—not so much perhaps as a man likes his favorite dog—but still he liked him well enough to help and ask no questions, to think sometimes vaguely and hazily in the midst of his own pursuits about the lonely man and the long-haired woman with audacious face and triumphant eyes, who lived together hidden by the forests —alone and feared.

The white man came out of the hut in time to see the enormous conflagration of sunset put out by the swift and stealthy shadows that, rising like a black and impalpable vapor above the treetops, spread over the heaven, extinguishing the crimson glow of floating clouds and the red brilliance of departing daylight. In a few moments all the stars came out above the intense blackness of the earth, and the great lagoon gleaming suddenly with reflected lights resembled an oval patch of night sky flung down into the hopeless and abysmal night of the wilderness. The white man had some supper out of the basket, then collecting a few sticks that lay about the platform, made up a small fire, not for warmth, but for the sake of the smoke, which would keep off the mosquitoes. He wrapped himself in the blankets and sat with his back against the reed wall of the house, smoking thoughtfully.

Arsat came through the doorway with noiseless steps and squatted down by the fire. The white man moved his outstretched legs a little.

"She breathes," said Arsat in a low voice, anticipating the expected question. "She breathes and burns as if with a great fire. She speaks not; she hears not—and burns!"

He paused for a moment, then asked in a quiet, incurious tone:

"Tuan . . . will she die?"

The white man moved his shoulders uneasily and uttered in a hesitating manner:

"If such is her fate."

"No, Tuan," said Arsat, calmly. "If such is my fate. I hear, I see, I wait. I remember . . . Tuan, do you remember the old days? Do you remember my brother?"

"Yes," said the white man. The Malay rose suddenly and went in. The other, sitting still outside, could hear the voice in the hut. Arsat said: "Hear me! Speak!" His words were succeeded by a complete silence. "O Diamelen!" he cried suddenly. After that cry there was a deep sigh. Arsat came out and sank down again in his old place.

They sat in silence before the fire. There was no sound within the house, there was no sound near them; but far away on the lagoon they could hear the voices of the boatmen ringing fitful and distinct on the calm water. The fire in the bow of the sampan shone faintly in the distance with a hazy red glow. Then it died out. The voices ceased. The land and the water slept invisible, unstirring, and mute. It was as though there had been nothing left in the world but the glitter of stars streaming, ceaseless and vain, through the black stillness of the night.

The white man gazed straight before him into the darkness with wide-open eyes. The fear and fascination, the inspiration and the wonder of death—of death near, unavoidable, and unseen, soothed the unrest of his race and stirred the most indistinct, the most intimate of his thoughts. The ever-ready suspicion of evil, the gnawing suspicion that lurks in our hearts, flowed out into the stillness round him—into the stillness profound and dumb, and made it appear untrustworthy and infamous, like the placid and impenetrable mask of an unjustifiable violence. In that fleeting and powerful disturbance of his being, the earth, enfolded in the starlight peace, became a shadowy country of inhuman strife, a battlefield of phantoms terrible and charming, august or ignoble, struggling ardently for the possession of our helpless hearts. An unquiet and mysterious country of inextinguishable desires and fears.

A plaintive murmur rose in the night; a murmur saddening and startling, as if the great solitudes of surrounding woods had tried to whisper into his ear the wisdom of their immense and lofty indifference. Sounds hesitating and vague floated in the air round him, shaped themselves slowly into words; and at last flowed on gently in a murmuring stream of soft and monotonous sentences. He stirred like a man waking up and changed his position slightly. Arsat, motionless and shadowy, sitting with bowed head under the stars, was speaking in a low and dreamy tone:

". . . for where can we lay down the heaviness of our trouble but in a friend's heart? A man must speak of war and of love. You, Tuan, know what war is, and you have seen me in time of danger seek death as other men seek life! A writing may be lost; a lie may be written; but what the eye has seen is truth and remains in the mind!"

"I remember," said the white man, quietly. Arsat went on with mournful composure:

"Therefore I shall speak to you of love. Speak in the night. Speak before both night and love are gone—and the eye of day looks upon my sorrow and my shame; upon my blackened face; upon my burnt-up heart."

A sigh, short and faint, marked an almost imperceptible pause, and then his words flowed on, without a stir, without a gesture.

"After the time of trouble and war was over and you went away from my country in the pursuit of your desires, which we, men of the islands, cannot understand, I and my brother became again, as we had been before, the swordbearers of the Ruler. You know we were men of family, belonging to a ruling race, and more fit than any to carry on our right shoulder the emblem of power. And in the time of prosperity Si Dendring showed us favor, as we, in time of sorrow, had showed to him the faithfulness of our courage. It was a time of peace. A time of deer hunts and cockfights; of idle talks and foolish squabbles between men whose bellies are full and weapons are rusty. But the sower watched the young rice shoots grow up without fear, and the traders came and went, departed lean and returned fat into the river of peace. They brought news, too. Brought lies and truth mixed together, so that no man knew when to rejoice and when to be sorry. We heard from them about you also. They had seen you here and had seen you there. And I was glad to hear, for I remembered the stirring times, and I always remembered you, Tuan, till the time came when my eyes could see nothing in the past, because they had looked upon the one who is dying there—in the house."

He stopped to exclaim in an intense whisper, "O Mara bahia! O Calamity!" then went on speaking a little louder:

"There's no worse enemy and no better friend than a brother, Tuan, for one brother knows another, and in perfect knowledge is strength for good or evil. I loved my brother. I went to him and told him that I could see nothing but one face, hear nothing but one voice. He told me: 'Open your heart so that she can see what is in it—and wait. Patience is wisdom. Inchi Midah may die or our Ruler may throw off his fear of a woman!' . . . I waited. . . . You remember the lady with the veiled face, Tuan, and the fear of our Ruler before her cunning and temper. And if she wanted her servant, what could I do? But I fed the hunger of my heart on short glances and stealthy words. I loitered on the path to the bathhouses in the daytime, and when the sun had fallen behind the forest I crept along the jasmine hedges of the women's courtyard. Unseeing, we spoke to one another through the scent of flowers, through the veil of leaves, through the blades of long grass that stood still before our lips; so great was our prudence, so faint was the murmur of our great longing. The time passed swiftly . . . and there were whispers among women—and our enemies watched—my brother was gloomy, and I began to think of killing and of a fierce death. . . . We are of a people who take what they want—like you whites. There is a time when a man should forget loyalty and respect. Might and authority are given to rulers, but to all men is given love and strength and courage. My brother said, 'You shall take her from their midst. We are two who are like one.' And I answered, 'Let it be soon, for I find no warmth in sunlight that does not shine upon her.' Our time came when the Ruler and all the great people went to the mouth of the river to fish by torchlight. There were hundreds of boats, and on the white sand, between the water and the forests, dwellings of leaves were built for the households of the Rajahs.[6] The smoke of cooking fires was like a blue mist of the evening, and many voices rang in it joyfully. While they were making the boats ready to beat up the fish, my brother came to me and said, 'Tonight!' I looked to my weapons, and when the time came our canoe took its place in the circle of boats carrying the torches. The lights blazed on the water, but behind the boats there was dark-

ness. When the shouting began and the excitement made them like mad we dropped out. The water swallowed our fire, and we floated back to the shore that was dark with only here and there the glimmer of embers. We could hear the talk of slave girls among the sheds. Then we found a place deserted and silent. We waited there. She came. She came running along the shore, rapid and leaving no trace, like a leaf driven by the wind into the sea. My brother said gloomily, 'Go and take her; carry her into our boat.' I lifted her in my arms. She panted. Her heart was beating against my breast. I said, 'I take you from those people. You came to the cry of my heart, but my arms take you into my boat against the will of the great!' 'It is right,' said my brother. 'We are men who take what we want and can hold it against many. We should have taken her in daylight.' I said, 'Let us be off'; for since she was in my boat I began to think of our Ruler's many men. 'Yes. Let us be off,' said my brother. 'We are cast out and this boat is our country now—and the sea is our refuge.' He lingered with his foot on the shore, and I entreated him to hasten, for I remembered the strokes of her heart against my breast and thought that two men cannot withstand a hundred. We left, paddling downstream close to the bank; and as we passed by the creek where they were fishing, the great shouting had ceased, but the murmur of voices was loud like the humming of insects flying at noonday. The boats floated, clustered together, in the red light of torches, under a black roof of smoke; and men talked of their sport. Men that boasted, and praised, and jeered—men that would have been our friends in the morning, but on that night were already our enemies. We paddled swiftly past. We had not more friends in the country of our birth. She sat in the middle of the canoe with covered face; silent as she is now; unseeing as she is now—and I had no regret at what I was leaving because I could hear her breathing close to me—as I can hear her now."

He paused, listened with his ear turned to

6. **Rajah:** a Malay prince or chief.

the doorway, then shook his head and went on:

"My brother wanted to shout the cry of challenge—one cry only—to let the people know we were freeborn robbers who trusted our arms and the great sea. And again I begged him in the name of our love to be silent. Could I not hear her breathing close to me? I knew the pursuit would come quick enough. My brother loved me. He dipped his paddle without a splash. He only said, 'There is half a man in you now—the other half is in that woman. I can wait. When you are a whole man again, you will come back with me here to shout defiance. We are sons of the same mother.' I made no answer. All my strength and all my spirit were in my hands that held the paddle—for I longed to be with her in a safe place beyond the reach of men's anger and of women's spite. My love was so great that I thought it could guide me to a country where death was unknown, if I could only escape from Inchi Midah's fury and from our Ruler's sword. We paddled with haste, breathing through our teeth. The blades bit deep into the smooth water. We passed out of the river; we flew in clear channels among the shallows. We skirted the black coast; we skirted the sand beaches where the sea speaks in whispers to the land; and the gleam of white sand flashed back past our boat, so swiftly she ran upon the water. We spoke not. Only once I said, 'Sleep, Diamelen, for soon you may want all your strength.' I heard the sweetness of her voice, but I never turned my head. The sun rose and still we went on. Water fell from my face like rain from a cloud. We flew in the light and heat. I never looked back, but I knew that my brother's eyes, behind me, were looking steadily ahead, for the boat went as straight as a bushman's dart when it leaves the end of the sumpitan.[7] There was no better paddler, no better steersman than my brother. Many times, together,

we had won races in that canoe. But we never had put out our strength as we did then—then, when for the last time we paddled together! There was no braver or stronger man in our country than my brother. I could not spare the strength to turn my head and look at him, but every moment I heard the hiss of his breath getting louder behind me. Still he did not speak. The sun was high. The heat clung to my back like a flame of fire. My ribs were ready to burst, but I could no longer get enough air into my chest. And then I felt I must cry out with my last breath, 'Let us rest!' . . . 'Good!' he answered; and his voice was firm. He was strong. He was brave. He knew not fear and no fatigue. . . . My brother!"

A murmur powerful and gentle, a murmur vast and faint; the murmur of trembling leaves, of stirring boughs, ran through the tangled depths of the forests, ran over the starry smoothness of the lagoon, and the water between the piles lapped the slimy timber once with a sudden splash. A breath of warm air touched the two men's faces and passed on with a mournful sound—a breath loud and short like an uneasy sigh of the dreaming earth.

Arsat went on in an even, low voice.

"We ran our canoe on the white beach of a little bay close to a long tongue of land that seemed to bar our road; a long wooded cape going far into the sea. My brother knew that place. Beyond the cape a river has its entrance, and through the jungle of that land there is a narrow path. We made a fire and cooked rice. Then we lay down to sleep on the soft sand in the shade of our canoe, while she watched. No sooner had I closed my eyes than I heard her cry of alarm. We leaped up. The sun was halfway down the sky already, and coming in sight in the opening of the bay we saw a prau[8] manned by many paddlers. We knew it at once; it was one of our Rajah's praus. They were watching the shore, and saw

---

7. **sumpitan:** a kind of blowgun for discharging a dart, used by inhabitants of Borneo and adjacent islands.

8. **prau:** swift Malayan vessel with sharp prow and stern, which can sail equally well prow or stern first.

us. They beat the gong, and turned the head of the prau into the bay. I felt my heart become weak within my breast. Diamelen sat on the sand and covered her face. There was no escape by sea. My brother laughed. He had the gun you had given him, Tuan, before you went away, but there was only a handful of powder. He spoke to me quickly: 'Run with her along the path. I shall keep them back, for they have no firearms, and landing in the face of a man with a gun is certain death for some. Run with her. On the other side of that wood there is a fisherman's house—and a canoe. When I have fired all the shots I will follow. I am a great runner, and before they can come up we shall be gone. I will hold out as long as I can, for she is but a woman—that can neither run nor fight, but she has your heart in her weak hands.' He dropped behind the canoe. The prau was coming. She and I ran, and as we rushed along the path I heard shots. My brother fired—once—twice—and the booming of the gong ceased. There was silence behind us. That neck of land is narrow. Before I heard my brother fire the third shot I saw the shelving shore, and I saw the water again; the mouth of a broad river. We crossed a grassy glade. We ran down to the water. I saw a low hut above the black mud, and a small canoe hauled up. I heard another shot behind me. I thought, 'That is his last charge.' We rushed down to the canoe; a man came running from the hut, but I leaped on him, and we rolled together in the mud. Then I got up, and he lay still at my feet. I don't know whether I had killed him or not. I and Diamelen pushed the canoe afloat. I heard yells behind me, and I saw my brother run across the glade. Many men were bounding after him. I took her in my arms and threw her into the boat, then leaped in myself. When I looked back I saw that my brother had fallen. He fell and was up again, but the men were closing round him. He shouted, 'I am coming!' The men were close to him. I looked. Many men. Then I looked at her. Tuan, I pushed the canoe! I pushed it into deep water. She was kneeling forward looking at me, and I said, 'Take your paddle,' while I struck the water with mine. Tuan, I heard him cry. I heard him cry my name twice; and I heard voices shouting, 'Kill! Strike!' I never turned back. I heard him calling my name again with a great shriek, as when life is going out together with the voice—and I never turned my head. My own name! . . . My brother! Three times he called—but I was not afraid of life. Was she not there in that canoe? And could I not with her find a country where death is forgotten—where death is unknown!"

The white man sat up. Arsat rose and stood, an indistinct and silent figure above the dying embers of the fire. Over the lagoon a mist drifting and low had crept, erasing slowly the glittering images of the stars. And now a great expanse of white vapor covered the land: it flowed cold and gray in the darkness, eddied in noiseless whirls round the tree trunks and about the platform of the house, which seemed to float upon a restless and impalpable illusion of a sea. Only far away the tops of the trees stood outlined on the twinkle of heaven, like a somber and forbidding shore—a coast deceptive, pitiless and black.

Arsat's voice vibrated loudly in the profound peace.

"I had her there! I had her! To get her I would have faced all mankind. But I had her—and——"

His words went out ringing into the empty distances. He paused and seemed to listen to them dying away very far—beyond help and beyond recall. Then he said quietly:

"Tuan, I loved my brother."

A breath of wind made him shiver. High above his head, high above the silent sea of mist the drooping leaves of the palms rattled together with a mournful and expiring sound. The white man stretched his legs. His chin rested on his chest, and he murmured sadly without lifting his head:

"We all love our brothers."

Arsat burst out with an intense whispering violence:

"What did I care who died? I wanted peace in my own heart."

He seemed to hear a stir in the house—listened—then stepped in noiselessly. The white man stood up. A breeze was coming in fitful puffs. The stars shone paler as if they had retreated into the frozen depths of immense space. After a chill gust of wind there were a few seconds of perfect calm and absolute silence. Then from behind the black and wavy line of the forests a column of golden light shot up into the heavens and spread over the semicircle of the eastern horizon. The sun had risen. The mist lifted, broke into drifting patches, vanished into thin flying wreaths; and the unveiled lagoon lay, polished and black, in the heavy shadows at the foot of the wall of trees. A white eagle rose over it with a slanting and ponderous flight, reached the clear sunshine and appeared dazzlingly brilliant for a moment, then, soaring higher, became a dark and motionless speck before it vanished into the blue as if it had left the earth forever. The white man, standing gazing upward before the doorway, heard in the hut a confused and broken murmur of distracted words ending with a loud groan. Suddenly Arsat stumbled out with outstretched hands, shivered, and stood still for some time with fixed eyes. Then he said:

"She burns no more."

Before his face the sun showed its edge above the treetops, rising steadily. The breeze freshened; a great brilliance burst upon the lagoon, sparkled on the rippling water. The forests came out of the clear shadows of the morning, became distinct, as if they had rushed nearer—to stop short in a great stir of leaves, of nodding boughs, of swaying branches. In the merciless sunshine the whisper of unconscious life grew louder, speaking in an incomprehensible voice round the dumb darkness of that human sorrow. Arsat's eyes wandered slowly, then stared at the rising sun.

"I can see nothing," he said half aloud to himself.

"There is nothing," said the white man, moving to the edge of the platform and waving his hand to the boat. A shout came faintly over the lagoon and the sampan began to glide toward the abode of the friend of ghosts.

"If you want to come with me, I will wait all the morning," said the white man, looking away upon the water.

"No, Tuan," said Arsat softly. "I shall not eat or sleep in this house, but I must first see my road. Now I can see nothing—see nothing! There is no light and no peace in the world; but there is death—death for many. We are sons of the same mother—and I left him in the midst of enemies; but I am going back now."

He drew a long breath and went on in a dreamy tone:

"In a little while I shall see clear enough to strike—to strike. But she has died, and . . . now . . . darkness."

He flung his arms wide open, let them fall along his body, then stood still with unmoved face and stony eyes, staring at the sun. The white man got down into his canoe. The polers ran smartly along the sides of the boat, looking over their shoulders at the beginning of a weary journey. High in the stern, his head muffled up in white rags, the juragan sat moody, letting his paddle trail in the water. The white man, leaning with both arms over the grass roof of the little cabin, looked at the shining ripple of the boat's wake. Before the sampan passed out of the lagoon into the creek he lifted his eyes. Arsat had not moved. He stood lonely in the searching sunshine; and he looked beyond the great light of a cloudless day into the darkness of a world of illusions.

COMMENTARY

How simply we can summarize the action of this story! Arsat's brother has been killed in helping him to escape their homeland with Diamelen. When she dies Arsat realizes that while she lived his tie to her had bound him to live, no matter how or where. Now that she is dead a profounder tie obliges him to die in order to avenge his brother. If you like the story you may well exclaim: "There is much more to it than that!" This "more," which eludes a simple summary, is the additional burden of feeling that results from actually reading the story. This comes from what we may call "frames," the different perspectives from which the reader is led to look at the story's simple sequence of events.

The first and most obvious frame is the consciousness of the white man, a witness from another culture moving in a world not his own. In the consciousness of the white man, all the things that are familiar to his paddlers add up to total strangeness for him. In this foreigner's mind, the world he is moving through is a *whole*. We seldom see anything this way unless we are far from our own home. Descriptive passages in the first part of the story add to the effect of strangeness: "The narrow creek was like a ditch: tortuous, fabulously deep; filled with gloom under the thin strip of pure and shining blue of the heaven. Immense trees soared up, invisible behind the festooned draperies of creepers. Here and there, near the glistening blackness of the water, a twisted root of some tall tree showed among the tracery of small ferns, black and dull, writhing and motionless, like an arrested snake."

The second frame is the disconnection (what critics call the "alienation") of Arsat himself, living as he does in a world in which he is an impious intruder. He disregards the spirts of those now dead who have lived in the house on the lagoon. The paddlers think of him as cut off from them altogether. His isolation intensifies the terrible plight he is in: the woman for whom he had sacrificed his brother's life is dying, and she is his whole world.

A third, more general, frame is the cosmic view behind the story—the sense of human beings as strangers moving through a mysterious country toward an unknown end. The white man has this sense as he looks into the darkness while Diamelen is dying: "In that fleeting and powerful disturbance of his being, the earth, enfolded in the starlight peace, became a shadowy country of inhuman strife, a battlefield of phantoms terrible and charming, august or ignoble, struggling ardently for the possession of our helpless hearts." Placed against such a view, simple virtues such as loyalty become supremely important—as our only surety, our defense against our own weaknesses and against the fear that the world is only an illusion.

FOR STUDY AND DISCUSSION

1. "There is half a man in you now—the other half is in that woman. I can wait. When you are a whole man again, you will come back with me here to shout defiance. We are sons of the same mother." Use this passage to analyze Arsat's moral obligations.

2. Cite the crucial passage that shows Arsat failing his obligations. How does the white man's comment "We all love our brothers" frame this episode?

3. What use does Conrad make of the great stillness at the opening of the story?

4. Both the white man and Arsat are alienated from their countries and their people. Does the white man's alienation seem self-imposed? What is the relationship of the two men? Does the white man's attitude toward Arsat seem somewhat detached? If so, how does this attitude further illustrate the cosmic, or universal, theme of Conrad's story?

5. Divide the story into episodes, describing briefly what happens in each. What effect on the reader is each episode meant to produce?

6. Choose a single episode and study Conrad's use of adjectives in that episode to discover how often he tells you what to feel, and how often he creates a situation or picture that inspires your feeling.

7. Explain why, in your opinion, Conrad chose to call his story "The Lagoon."

Saki (Hector Hugh Munro)

1870–1916

"Saki" was the pseudonym of one of England's finest satirists and short-story writers. He was born in Burma, where his father was an officer in the Burmese police, and following his mother's death, he was sent to England to be educated. In his early twenties, after a year's service with the Burmese police, he left for London, where he began his literary career as a political satirist with the *Westminster Gazette*. It was at this time that he chose the pseudonym Saki—the name of the cup-bearer in the *Rubáiyát of Omar Khayyám*. After serving as foreign correspondent for a London newspaper, he gave up journalism to devote full time to writing short stories. He also wrote novels and plays, but he is best known for his stories. They are distinctive in their satire of pretentious upper-class English life, their humorous treatment of childhood and adult fantasies, and their considerable wit. His only serious work, a book on Russian history, was published in his own name. At the beginning of World War I, he enlisted as a private, was sent to France, and was killed in action.

The Schartz-Metterklume Method

Lady Carlotta stepped out onto the platform of the small wayside station and took a turn or two up and down its uninteresting length, to kill time till the train should be pleased to proceed on its way. Then, in the roadway beyond, she saw a horse struggling with a more than ample load, and a carter of the sort that seems to bear a sullen hatred against the animal that helps him to earn a living. Lady Carlotta promptly betook her to the roadway, and put rather a different complexion on the struggle. Certain of her acquaintances were wont to give her plentiful admonition as to the undesirability of interfering on behalf of a distressed animal, such interference being "none of her business." Only once had she put the doctrine of noninterference into practice, when one of its most eloquent exponents had been besieged for nearly three hours in a small and extremely uncomfortable may tree by an angry boar-pig, while Lady Carlotta, on the other side of the fence, had proceeded with the water-color sketch she was engaged on, and refused to interfere between the boar and his prisoner. It is to be feared that she lost the friendship of the ultimately rescued lady. On this occasion she merely lost the train, which gave way to the first sign of impatience it had shown throughout the journey, and steamed off without her. She bore the desertion with philosophical indifference; her friends and relations were thoroughly well used to the fact of her luggage arriving without her. She wired a vague noncommittal message to her destination to say that she was coming on "by another train." Before she had time to think what her next move might be, she was confronted by an imposingly attired lady, who seemed to be taking a prolonged mental inventory of her clothes and looks.

"You must be Miss Hope, the governess I've come to meet," said the apparition, in a tone that admitted of very little argument.

"Very well, if I must I must," said Lady Carlotta to herself with dangerous meekness.

"I am Mrs. Quabarl," continued the lady; "and where, pray, is your luggage?"

"It's gone astray," said the alleged governess, falling in with the excellent rule of life that the absent are always to blame; the

Nineteenth-century railway station.
Culver Pictures

luggage had, in point of fact, behaved with perfect correctitude. "I've just telegraphed about it," she added, with a nearer approach to truth.

"How provoking," said Mrs. Quabarl; "these railway companies are so careless. However, my maid can lend you things for the night," and she led the way to her car.

During the drive to the Quabarl mansion Lady Carlotta was impressively introduced to the nature of the charge that had been thrust upon her; she learned that Claude and Wilfrid were delicate, sensitive young people, that Irene had the artistic temperament highly developed, and that Viola was something or other else of a mold equally commonplace among children of that class and type in the twentieth century.

"I wish them not only to be *taught*," said Mrs. Quabarl, "but *interested* in what they learn. In their history lessons, for instance, you must try to make them feel that they are being introduced to the life stories of men and women who really lived, not merely committing a mass of names and dates to memory. French, of course, I shall expect you to talk at mealtimes several days in the week."

"I shall talk French four days of the week and Russian in the remaining three."

"Russian? My dear Miss Hope, no one in the house speaks or understands Russian."

"That will not embarrass me in the least," said Lady Carlotta coldly.

Mrs. Quabarl, to use a colloquial expression, was knocked off her perch. She was one of those imperfectly self-assured individuals who are magnificent and autocratic as long as they are not seriously opposed. The least show of unexpected resistance goes a long way towards rendering them cowed and apologetic. When the new governess failed to express wondering admiration of the large newly purchased and expensive car, and lightly alluded to the superior advantages of one or two makes which had just been put on the market, the discomfiture of her patroness became almost abject. Her feelings were those which might have animated a general of ancient warfaring days, on beholding his heaviest battle-elephant ignominiously driven off the field by slingers and javelin throwers.

At dinner that evening, although reinforced by her husband, who usually duplicated her opinions and lent her moral support generally, Mrs. Quabarl regained none of her lost ground. The governess not only helped herself well and truly to wine, but held forth with considerable show of critical knowledge on various vintage matters, concerning which the Quabarls were in no wise able to pose as authorities. Previous governesses had limited their conversation on the wine topic to a respectful and doubtless sincere expression of a preference for water. When this one went as far as to recommend a wine firm in whose hands you could not go very far wrong Mrs. Quabarl thought it time to turn the conversation into more usual channels.

"We got very satisfactory references about you from Canon Teep," she observed; "a very estimable man, I should think."

"Drinks like a fish and beats his wife, otherwise a very lovable character," said the governess imperturbably.

"My *dear* Miss Hope! I trust you are exaggerating," exclaimed the Quabarls in unison.

"One must in justice admit that there is some provocation," continued the romancer. "Mrs. Teep is quite the most irritating bridge player that I have ever sat down with; her leads and declarations would condone a certain amount of brutality in her partner, but to souse her with the contents of the only soda-water siphon in the house on a Sunday afternoon, when one couldn't get another, argues

an indifference to the comfort of others which I cannot altogether overlook. You may think me hasty in my judgments, but it was practically on account of the siphon incident that I left."

"We will talk of this some other time," said Mrs. Quabarl hastily.

"I shall never allude to it again," said the governess with decision.

Mr. Quabarl made a welcome diversion by asking what studies the new instructress proposed to inaugurate on the morrow.

"History to begin with," she informed him.

"Ah, history," he observed sagely; "now in teaching them history you must take care to interest them in what they learn. You must make them feel that they are being introduced to the life stories of men and women who really lived——"

"I've told her all that," interposed Mrs. Quabarl.

"I teach history on the Schartz-Metterklume method," said the governess loftily. .

"Ah, yes," said her listeners, thinking it expedient to assume an acquaintance at least with the name.

"What are you children doing out here?" demanded Mrs. Quabarl the next morning, on finding Irene sitting rather glumly at the head of the stairs, while her sister was perched in an attitude of depressed discomfort on the window seat behind her, with a wolfskin rug almost covering her.

"We are having a history lesson," came the unexpected reply. "I am supposed to be Rome, and Viola up there is the she-wolf; not a real wolf, but the figure of one that the Romans used to set store by—I forget why. Claude and Wilfrid have gone to fetch the shabby women."

"The shabby women?"

"Yes, they've got to carry them off. They didn't want to, but Miss Hope got one of father's fives bats[1] and said she'd give them a

---

1. **fives bats:** wooden bats used in a variation of *fives*, a handball-like game.

number nine spanking if they didn't, so they've gone to do it."

A loud, angry screaming from the direction of the lawn drew Mrs. Quabarl thither in hot haste, fearful lest the threatened castigation might even now be in process of infliction. The outcry, however, came principally from the two small daughters of the lodge-keeper, who were being hauled and pushed towards the house by the panting and disheveled Claude and Wilfrid, whose task was rendered even more arduous by the incessant, if not very effectual, attacks of the captured maidens' small brother. The governess, fives bat in hand, sat negligently on the stone balustrade, presiding over the scene with the cold impartiality of a goddess of battles. A furious and repeated chorus of "I'll tell muvver" rose from the lodge children, but the lodge mother, who was hard of hearing, was for the moment immersed in the preoccupation of her wash-tub. After an apprehensive glance in the direction of the lodge (the good woman was gifted with the highly militant temper which is sometimes the privilege of deafness) Mrs. Quabarl flew indignantly to the rescue of the struggling captives.

"Wilfrid! Claude! Let those children go at once. Miss Hope, what on earth is the meaning of this scene?"

"Early Roman history; the Sabine women, don't you know? It's the Schartz-Metterklume method to make children understand history by acting it themselves; fixes it in their memory, you know. Of course, if, thanks to your interference, your boys go through life thinking that the Sabine women ultimately escaped, I really cannot be held responsible."

"You may be very clever and modern, Miss Hope," said Mrs. Quabarl firmly, "but I should like you to leave here by the next train. Your luggage will be sent after you as soon as it arrives."

"I'm not certain exactly where I shall be for the next few days," said the dismissed instructress of youth; "you might keep my luggage till I wire my address. There are only a couple of trunks and some golf clubs and a leopard cub."

"A leopard cub!" gasped Mrs. Quabarl. Even in her departure this extraordinary person seemed destined to leave a trail of embarrassment behind her.

"Well, it's rather left off being a cub; it's more than half grown, you know. A fowl every day and a rabbit on Sundays is what it usually gets. Raw beef makes it too excitable. Don't trouble about getting the car for me, I'm rather inclined for a walk."

And Lady Carlotta strode out of the Quabarl horizon.

The advent of the genuine Miss Hope, who had made a mistake as to the day on which she was due to arrive, caused a turmoil which that good lady was quite unused to inspiring. Obviously the Quabarl family had been woefully befooled, but a certain amount of relief came with the knowledge.

"How tiresome for you, dear Carlotta," said her hostess, when the overdue guest ultimately arrived; "how very tiresome losing your train and having to stop overnight in a strange place."

"Oh, dear, no," said Lady Carlotta; "not at all tiresome — for me."

FOR STUDY AND DISCUSSION

1. The ironic flavor of the story arises from Lady Carlotta's tendency to take people at their word: this is not what we expect in life. What kind of education does Mrs. Quabarl request for her children? How does Lady Carlotta take Mrs. Quabarl at her word?

2. What is the "Schartz-Metterklume" method of teaching? What modern notions or methods of education is it used to satirize?

3. Through Lady Carlotta, Saki lightly ridicules the pretensions and hypocrisies of upper-class people like the Quabarls. What social etiquette or manners does Saki satirize during the interview in the car? At dinner?

E. M. Forster

1879–1970

E. M. Forster
Radio Times Hulton

Edward Morgan Forster's reputation as one of the great novelists of this century is based on six fine novels written between 1905 and 1924. The most distinguished of these are *Howards End* (1910) and *A Passage to India* (1924). Most of his writing after 1924 was in the form of essays. Like his novels, Forster's highly regarded essays, of which "Notes on the English Character" is one, display a complex moral awareness and a graceful, sensitive style that is one of the finest in modern literature.

In 1939, in his essay "What I Believe," Forster drew away from the moral absolutes that were typically English and expressed his concern with the new values needed to live in the twentieth century. He wrote "Tolerance, good temper, and sympathy—they are what matter really, and if the human race is not to collapse, they must come to the front before long." He offered no overwhelming faith that could sustain human beings through a long struggle. Instead he noted, "I believe in an aristocracy. . . . Not an aristocracy of power, based upon rank and influence, but an aristocracy of the sensitive, the considerate, and the plucky. Its members are to be found in all nations and classes. . . . They represent the true human tradition, the one permanent victory of our race over cruelty and chaos."

Forster was born in the town of Tonbridge in Kent. Growing to manhood, he was horrified by the narrow-mindedness and indifference of middle-class England to art and culture. As he grew older and began to travel, his attitudes toward the English were confirmed. Under all his work lies a hatred of hypocrisy and convention, an aspiration toward a free, honest life. Forster was in the lucky position of having just enough money to make him independent. A man of few and simple tastes, he devoted himself to his friends, most of whom were associated with Cambridge University and had studied under the philosopher G. E. Moore, a man whose teachings had a great influence on Forster and others. Later Forster and his friends—among them Virginia Woolf, the novelist; Lytton Strachey, the biographer; and Roger Fry, the art critic—became known as the Bloomsbury Group, after a section of London where some of them lived. The men and women of the circle were known for their interest in literary and artistic experiments, their creativity, and their rejection of Victorian values.

For a while Forster was a secretary to an Indian prince, an experience he put to fine use in *A Passage to India*. A stay in Egypt during World War I led to two delightful short books about the city of Alexandria. Having lost his home in Abinger, England, during World War II, he moved to King's College, Cambridge. There he established himself as a wise counselor and a philosophic companion to people of all ages, beliefs, and racial backgrounds. His own interests were wide. He was an excellent musician and a charming talker.

Notes on the English Character

First Note. I had better let the cat out of the bag at once and record my opinion that the character of the English is essentially middle-class. There is a sound historical reason for this, for, since the end of the eighteenth century, the middle classes have been the dominant force in our community. They gained wealth by the Industrial Revolution, political power by the Reform Bill of 1832; they are connected with the rise and organization of the British Empire; they are responsible for the literature of the nineteenth century. Solidity, caution, integrity, efficiency. Lack of imagination, hypocrisy. These qualities characterize the middle classes in every country, but in England they are national characteristics also, because only in England have the middle classes been in power for one hundred and fifty years. Napoleon, in his rude way, called us "a nation of shopkeepers." We prefer to call ourselves "a great commercial nation"—it sounds more dignified—but the two phrases amount to the same. Of course there are other classes: there is an aristocracy, there are the poor. But it is on the middle classes that the eye of the critic rests—just as it rests on the poor in Russia and on the aristocracy in Japan. Russia is symbolized by the peasant or by the factory worker; Japan by the samurai;[1] the national figure of England is Mr. Bull with his top hat, his comfortable clothes, his substantial stomach, and his substantial balance at the bank. Saint George may caper on banners and in the speeches of politicians, but it is John Bull who delivers the goods. And even Saint George—if Gibbon[2] is correct—wore a top hat once; he was an army contractor and supplied indifferent bacon. It all amounts to the same in the end.

---

1. **samurai** (săm′oo-rī′): In feudal Japan, the samurai were a special class of warriors.
2. **Gibbon** (gĭb′ən): Edward Gibbon (1737–1794), an English historian.

Mr. Bull: "Now mind—money is no object—but we'll have money's worth." Cartoon from *Punch,* 1859.
Radio Times Hulton

Second Note. Just as the heart of England is the middle classes, so the heart of the middle classes is the public-school[3] system. This extraordinary institution is local. It does not even exist all over the British Isles. It is unknown in Ireland, almost unknown in Scotland (countries excluded from my survey), and though it may inspire other great institutions—Aligarh,[4] for example, and some of the schools in the United States—it remains unique, because it was created by the Anglo-Saxon middle classes, and can flourish only where they flourish. How perfectly it expresses their character—far better, for instance, than does the university, into which social and spiritual complexities have already entered. With its boardinghouses, its compulsory games, its system of prefects and fagging,[5] its insistence on good form and on *esprit de corps,*[6] it produces a type whose weight is out of all proportion to its numbers.

On leaving his school, the boy either sets to work at once—goes into the army or into business, or emigrates—or else proceeds to the university, and after three or four years there enters some other profession—becomes a barrister, doctor, civil servant, schoolmaster, or journalist. (If through some mishap he does not become a manual worker or an artist.) In all these careers his education, or the absence of it, influences him. Its memories influence him also. Many men look back on their school days as the happiest of their lives. They remember with regret that golden time when life, though hard, was not yet complex; when they all worked together and played together and thought together, so far as they thought at all; when they were taught that school is the world in miniature, and believed that no one can love his country who does not love his school. And they prolong that time as best they can by joining their Old Boys' society;[7] indeed, some of them remain Old Boys and nothing else for the rest of their lives. They attribute all good to the school. They worship it. They quote the remark that "the battle of Waterloo[8] was won on the playing fields of Eton." It is nothing to them that the remark is inapplicable historically and was never made by the Duke of Wellington, and that the Duke of Wellington was an Irishman. They go on quoting it because it expresses their sentiments; they feel that if the Duke of Wellington didn't make it he ought to have, and if he wasn't an Englishman he ought to have been. And they go forth into a world that is not entirely composed of public-school men or even of Anglo-Saxons, but of men who are as various as the sands of the sea; into a world of whose richness and subtlety they have no conception. They go forth into it with well-developed bodies, fairly developed minds, and undeveloped hearts. And it is this undeveloped heart that is largely responsible for the difficulties of Englishmen abroad. An undeveloped heart—not a cold one. The difference is important, and on it my next note will be based.

For it is not that the Englishman can't feel —it is that he is afraid to feel. He has been taught at this public school that feeling is bad form. He must not express great joy or sorrow, or even open his mouth too wide when he talks—his pipe might fall out if he did. He must bottle up his emotions, or let them out only on a very special occasion.

---

3. **public school:** corresponds to the American private school. English grammar schools correspond to our public schools.
4. **Aligarh** (ăl´ĭ-gûr´): a school in the city of Aligarh, India.
5. **fagging:** a system wherein underclassmen run errands and do chores for upperclassmen.
6. *esprit de corps* (ĕ-sprē´ də kôr´): group spirit, such as "school spirit."

7. **Old Boys' society:** alumni organization.
8. **battle of Waterloo:** a decisive battle in English history in which the Duke of Wellington defeated the forces of Napoleon.

Fourth of June celebrations at Eton (1911).
Radio Times Hulton

Once upon a time (this is an anecdote) I went for a week's holiday on the Continent with an Indian friend. We both enjoyed ourselves and were sorry when the week was over, but on parting our behavior was absolutely different. He was plunged in despair. He felt that because the holiday was over, all happiness was over until the world ended. He could not express his sorrow too much. But in me the Englishman came out strong. I reflected that we should meet again in a month or two, and could write in the interval if we had anything to say; and under these circumstances I could not see what there was to make a fuss about. It wasn't as if we were parting forever or dying. "Buck up," I said, "do buck up." He refused to buck up, and I left him plunged in gloom.

The conclusion of the anecdote is even more instructive. For when we met the next month our conversation threw a good deal of light on the English character. I began by scolding my friend. I told him that he had been wrong to feel and display so much emotion upon so slight an occasion; that it was inappropriate. The word *inappropriate* roused him to fury. "What?" he cried. "Do you measure out your emotions as if they were potatoes?" I did not like the simile of the potatoes, but after a moment's reflection I said, "Yes, I do; and what's more, I think I ought to. A small occasion demands a little emotion, just as a large occasion demands a great one. I would like my emotions to be appropriate. This may be measuring them like potatoes, but it is better than slopping them about like water from a pail, which is what you did." He did not like the simile of the pail. "If those are your opinions, they part us forever," he cried, and left the room. Returning immediately, he added: "No—but your whole attitude toward emotion is wrong. Emotion has nothing to do with appropriateness. It matters only that it shall be sincere. I happened to feel deeply. I showed it. It doesn't matter whether I ought to have felt deeply or not."

This remark impressed me very much. Yet I could not agree with it, and said that I valued emotion as much as he did, but used it differently; if I poured it out on small occasions I was afraid of having none left for the great ones, and of being bankrupt at the crises of life. Note the word *bankrupt*. I spoke as a member of a prudent middle-class nation, always anxious to meet my liabilities. But my friend spoke as an Oriental, and the Oriental has behind him a tradition, not of middle-class prudence, but of kingly munificence and splendor. He feels his resources are endless, just as John Bull feels his are finite. As regards material resources, the Oriental is clearly unwise. Money isn't endless. If we spend or give away all the money we have, we haven't any more, and must take the consequences, which are frequently unpleasant. But, as regards the resources of the spirit, he may be right. The emotions may be endless. The more we express them, the more we may have to express.

True love in this differs from gold and clay,
That to divide is not to take away,

says Shelley. Shelley, at all events, believes that the wealth of the spirit is endless; that we may express it copiously, passionately, and always; and that we can never feel sorrow or joy too acutely.

In the above anecdote, I have figured as a typical Englishman. I will now descend from that dizzy and somewhat unfamiliar height, and return to my business of note-taking. A note on the *slowness* of the English character. The Englishman appears to be cold and unemotional because he is really slow. When an event happens, he may understand it quickly enough with his mind, but he takes quite a while to feel it. Once upon a time a coach, containing some Englishmen and some Frenchmen, was driving over the Alps. The horses ran away, and as they were dashing across a bridge the coach caught on the stonework, tottered, and nearly fell into the ravine below. The Frenchmen were frantic with terror: they screamed and gesticulated and flung themselves about, as Frenchmen would. The Englishmen sat quite calm. An hour later the coach drew up at an inn to change horses, and by that time the situations were exactly reversed. The Frenchmen had forgotten all about the danger, and were chattering gaily; the Englishmen had just begun to feel it, and one had a nervous breakdown and was obliged to go to bed. We have here a clear physical difference between the two races—a difference that goes deep into character. The Frenchmen responded at once; the Englishmen responded in time. They were slow and they were also practical. Their instinct forbade them to throw themselves about in the coach, because it was more likely to tip over if they did. They had this extraordinary appreciation of *fact* that we shall notice again and again. When a disaster comes, the English instinct is to do what can be done first, and to postpone the feeling as long as possible. Hence they are splendid at emergencies. No doubt they are brave—no one will deny that—but bravery is partly an affair of the nerves, and the English nervous system is well equipped for meeting a physical emergency. It acts promptly and feels slowly. Such a combination is fruitful, and anyone who possesses it has gone a long way toward being brave. And when the action is over, then the Englishman can feel.

There is one more consideration—a most important one. If the English nature is cold, how is it that it has produced a great literature and a literature that is particularly great in poetry? Judged by its prose, English literature would not stand in the first rank. It is its poetry that raises it to the level of Greek, Persian, or French. And yet the English are supposed to be so unpoetical. How is this? The nation that produced the Elizabethan drama and the Lake Poets[9] cannot be a cold, unpo-

---

9. **Lake Poets:** Coleridge, Wordsworth, and Southey, who lived for a while in the Lake District in northwestern England.

etical nation. We can't get fire out of ice. Since literature always rests upon national character, there must be in the English nature hidden springs of fire to produce the fire we see. The warm sympathy, the romance, the imagination, that we look for in Englishmen whom we meet, and too often vainly look for, must exist in the nation as a whole, or we could not have this outburst of national song. An undeveloped heart—not a cold one.

The trouble is that the English nature is not at all easy to understand. It has a great air of simplicity, it advertises itself as simple, but the more we consider it, the greater the problems we shall encounter. People talk of the mysterious East, but the West also is mysterious. It has depths that do not reveal themselves at the first gaze. We know what the sea looks like from a distance: it is of one color, and level, and obviously cannot contain such creatures as fish. But if we look into the sea over the edge of a boat, we see a dozen colors, and depth below depth, and fish swimming in them. That sea is the English character—apparently imperturbable and even. The depths and the colors are the English romanticism and the English sensitiveness—we do not expect to find such things, but they exist. And—to continue my metaphor—the fish are the English emotions, which are always trying to get up to the surface, but don't quite know how. For the most part we see them moving far below, distorted and obscure. Now and then they succeed and we exclaim, "Why, the Englishman has emotions! He actually can feel!" And occasionally we see that beautiful creature the flying fish, which rises out of the water altogether into the air and the sunlight. English literature is a flying fish. It is a sample of the life that goes on day after day beneath the surface; it is a proof that beauty and emotion exist in the salt, inhospitable sea.

And now let's get back to terra firma.[10] The Englishman's attitude toward criticism will give us another starting point. He is not annoyed by criticism. He listens or not as the case may be, smiles and passes on, saying, "Oh, the fellow's jealous"; "Oh, I'm used to Bernard Shaw, monkey tricks don't hurt me." It never occurs to him that the fellow may be accurate as well as jealous, and that he might do well to take the criticism to heart and profit by it. It never strikes him—except as a form of words—that he is capable of improvement; his self-complacency is abysmal. Other nations, both Oriental and European, have an uneasy feeling that they are not quite perfect. In consequence they resent criticism. It hurts them; and their snappy answers often mask a determination to improve themselves. Not so the Englishman. He has no uneasy feeling. Let the critics bark. And the "tolerant, humorous attitude" with which he confronts them is not really tolerant, because it is insensitive, and not really humorous, because it is bounded by the titter and the guffaw.

Turn over the pages of *Punch*.[11] There is neither wit, laughter, nor satire in our national jester—only the snigger of a suburban householder who can understand nothing that does not resemble himself. Week after week, under Mr. Punch's supervision, a man falls off his horse, or a colonel misses a golf ball, or a little girl makes a mistake in her prayers. Week after week ladies show not too much of their legs, foreigners are deprecated, originality condemned. Week after week a bricklayer does not do as much work as he ought and a futurist does more than he need. It is all supposed to be so good-tempered and clean; it is also supposed to be funny. It is actually an outstanding example of our attitude toward criticism: the middle-class Englishman, with a smile on his clean-shaven lips, is engaged in admiring himself and ignoring the rest of mankind. If, in those colorless pages, he came across anything that really was

---

10. **terra firma:** solid ground.

11. ***Punch:*** a well-known humorous and satirical weekly.

funny—a drawing by Max Beerbohm,[12] for instance—his smile would disappear, and he would say to himself, "The fellow's a bit of a crank," and pass on.

This particular attitude reveals such insensitiveness as to suggest a more serious charge: Is the Englishman altogether indifferent to the things of the spirit? Let us glance for a moment at his religion—not, indeed, at his theology, which would not merit inspection, but at the action on his daily life of his belief in the unseen. Here again his attitude is practical. But an innate decency comes out: he is thinking of others rather than of himself. Right conduct is his aim. He asks of his religion that it shall make him a better man in daily life; that he shall be more kind, more just, more merciful, more desirous to fight what is evil and to protect what is good. No one could call this a low conception. It is, as far as it goes, a spiritual one. Yet—and this seems to me typical of the race—it is only half the religious idea. Religion is more than an ethical code with a divine sanction. It is also a means through which man may get into direct connection with the divine, and, judging by history, few Englishmen have succeeded in doing this. We have produced no series of prophets, as has Judaism or Islam.[13] We have not even produced a Joan of Arc, or a Savonarola.[14] We have produced few saints. In Germany the Reformation was due to the passionate conviction of Luther. In England it was due to a palace intrigue.[15] We can show a steady level of piety, a fixed determination to live decently according to our lights—little more.

Well, it is something. It clears us of the charge of being an unspiritual nation. That facile contrast between the spiritual East and the materialistic West can be pushed too far. The West also is spiritual. Only it expresses its belief, not in fasting and visions, not in prophetic rapture, but in the daily round, the common task. An incomplete expression, if you like. I agree. But the argument underlying these scattered notes is that the Englishman is an incomplete person. Not a cold or an unspiritual one. But undeveloped, incomplete.

I have suggested earlier that the English are sometimes hypocrites, and it is now my duty to develop this rather painful subject. Hypocrisy is the prime charge that is always brought against us. The Germans are called brutal, the Spanish cruel, the Americans superficial, and so on; but we are *perfide Albion*,[16] the island of hypocrites, the people who have built up an Empire with a Bible in one hand, a pistol in the other, and financial concessions in both pockets. Is the charge true? I think it is; but while making it we must be quite clear as to what we mean by hypocrisy. Do we mean *conscious* deceit? Well, the English are comparatively guiltless of this; they have little of the Renaissance villain about them. Do we mean *unconscious* deceit? Muddle-headedness? Of this I believe them to be guilty. When an Englishman has been led into a course of wrong action, he has nearly always begun by muddling himself. A public-school education does not make for mental clearness, and he possesses to a very high degree the power of confusing his own mind. We

---

12. **Max Beerbohm:** an English essayist and caricaturist (1872–1956).
13. **Islam:** the Moslem religion.
14. **Savonarola** (săv'ə-nə-rō'lə): an Italian monk (1452–1498), a political and religious reformer, who was burned as a heretic.
15. **due . . . intrigue:** Henry VIII (1509–1547) initiated the break between England and the Church of Rome when the Pope refused to grant him a divorce from Catherine of Aragon.

16. *perfide Albion:* false England; Albion (ăl'bē-ən) is an ancient name for England still retained in poetry.

Woodcut for Jane Austen's *Sense and Sensibility*.
New York Public Library Picture Collection

have seen this tendency at work in the domain of theology; how does it work in the domain of conduct?

Jane Austen[17] may seem an odd authority to cite, but Jane Austen has, within her limits, a marvelous insight into the English mind. Her range is limited, her characters never attempt any of the more scarlet sins. But she has a merciless eye for questions of conduct, and the classical example of two English people muddling themselves before they embark upon a wrong course of action is to be found in the opening chapters of *Sense and Sensibility*. Old Mr. Dashwood has just died. He has been twice married. By his first marriage he has a son, John; by his second marriage, three daughters. The son is well off; the young ladies and their mother—for Mr. Dashwood's second wife survives him—are badly off. He has called his son to his deathbed and has solemnly adjured him to provide for the second family. Much moved, the young man

promises, and mentally decides to give each of his sisters a thousand pounds; and then the comedy begins. For he announces his generous intention to his wife, and Mrs. John Dashwood by no means approves of depriving their own little boy of so large a sum. The thousand pounds are accordingly reduced to five hundred. But even this seems rather much. Might not an annuity to the stepmother be less of a wrench? Yes—but though less of a wrench it might be more of a drain, for "she is very stout and healthy, and scarcely forty." An occasional present of fifty pounds will be better, "and will, I think, be amply discharging my promise to my father." Or, better still, an occasional present of fish. And in the end nothing is done, nothing; the four impecunious ladies are not even helped in the moving of their furniture.

Well, are the John Dashwoods hypocrites? It depends upon our definition of hypocrisy. The young man could not see his evil impulses as they gathered force and gained on him. And even his wife, though a worse character, is also self-deceived. She reflects that

---

17. **Jane Austen:** English novelist (1775–1817).

old Mr. Dashwood may have been out of his mind at his death. She thinks of her own little boy—and surely a mother ought to think of her own child. She has muddled herself so completely that in one sentence she can refuse the ladies the income that would enable them to keep a carriage and in the next can say that they will not be keeping a carriage and so will have no expenses. No doubt men and women in other lands can muddle themselves, too, yet the state of mind of Mr. and Mrs. John Dashwood seems to me typical of England. They are slow—they take time even to do wrong; whereas people in other lands do wrong quickly.

There are national faults as there are national diseases, and perhaps one can draw a parallel between them. It has always impressed me that the national diseases of England should be cancer and consumption—slow, insidious, pretending to be something else; while the diseases proper to the South should be cholera and plague, which strike at a man when he is perfectly well and may leave him a corpse by evening. Mr. and Mrs. John Dashwood are moral consumptives. They collapse gradually without realizing what the disease is. There is nothing dramatic or violent about their sin. You cannot call them villains.

Here is the place to glance at some of the other charges that have been brought against the English as a nation. They have, for instance, been accused of treachery, cruelty, and fanaticism. In these charges I have never been able to see the least point, because treachery and cruelty are conscious sins. The man knows he is doing wrong, and does it deliberately, like Tartuffe[18] or Iago.[19] He betrays his friend because he wishes to. He tortures his prisoners because he enjoys seeing the blood flow. He worships the Devil because he prefers evil to good. From villainies such as these the average Englishman is free. His character, which prevents his rising to certain heights, also prevents him from sinking to these depths. Because he doesn't produce mystics he doesn't produce villains either; he gives the world no prophets, but no anarchists, no fanatics—religious or political.

Of course there are cruel and treacherous people in England—one has only to look at the police courts—and examples of public infamy can be found, such as the Amritsar massacre.[20] But one does not look at the police courts or the military mind to find the soul of any nation; and the more English people one meets, the more convinced one becomes that the charges as a whole are untrue. Yet foreign critics often make them. Why? Partly because they fix their eyes on the criminal classes, partly because they are annoyed with certain genuine defects in the English character, and in their irritation throw in cruelty in order to make the problem simpler. Moral indignation is always agreeable, but nearly always misplaced. It is indulged in both by the English and by the critics of the English. They all find it great fun. The drawback is that while they are amusing themselves the world becomes neither wiser nor better.

The main point of these notes is that the English character is incomplete. No national character is complete. We have to look for some qualities in one part of the world and others in another. But the English character is incomplete in a way that is particularly annoying to the foreign observer. It has a bad surface—self-complacent, unsympathetic, and reserved. There is plenty of emotion further down, but it never gets used. There is plenty of brainpower, but it is more often

---

18. **Tartuffe** (tär-tōof′): a hypocrite in Molière's comedy *Tartuffe* who swindles his benefactor.
19. **Iago** (ē-ä′gō): the villain in Shakespeare's *Othello*, who deceives Othello and makes him think that his wife has been unfaithful.

20. **Amritsar massacre:** During a riot in 1919 in Amritsar (ŭm-rĭt′sər), India, British soldiers fired into a crowd and killed nearly four hundred people.

used to confirm prejudices than to dispel them. With such an equipment the Englishman cannot be popular. Only I would repeat: There is little vice in him and no real coldness. It is the machinery that is wrong.

I hope and believe myself that in the next twenty years we shall see a great change, and that the national character will alter into something that is less unique but more lovable. The supremacy of the middle classes is probably ending. What new element the working classes will introduce one cannot say, but at all events they will not have been educated at public schools. And whether these notes praise or blame the English character—that is only incidental. They are the notes of a student who is trying to get at the truth and would value the assistance of others. I believe myself that the truth is great and that it shall prevail. I have no faith in official caution and reticence. The cats are all out of their bags, and diplomacy cannot recall them. The nations *must* understand one another, and quickly; and without the interposition of their governments, for the shrinkage of the globe is throwing them into one another's arms. To that understanding these notes are a feeble contribution—notes on the English character as it has struck a novelist.

FOR STUDY AND DISCUSSION

1. According to Forster, the qualities of "solidity, caution, integrity, efficiency, lack of imagination," and "hypocrisy," which characterize the English middle class, are promoted by the English public school system. Why does Forster feel this system leaves the English unprepared for adult life? What are the qualities of "an undeveloped heart"?
2. What point about English character is illustrated in the account of the Englishmen and the Frenchmen driving together over the Alps?
3. Forster develops an analogy between the sea and the English character. What paradox is he trying to account for by using this metaphor?
4. With what qualities of character do the English protect themselves from criticism? Why does Forster criticize these qualities?
5. Near the conclusion of the essay, Forster blames the "machinery" for the shortcomings of the English. What does he mean by "machinery"?

FOR COMPOSITION

Write several paragraphs in the manner of Forster on the characteristics of Americans. You might answer these questions: What qualities are distinctively American? How has education influenced the national character? What is American humor like?

Virginia Woolf
1882–1941

Virginia Woolf
Radio Times Hulton

To the outside observer, Virginia Woolf was an exceptionally lucky person. She was the daughter of Sir Leslie Stephen, an eminent Victorian scholar, critic, and writer. Throughout her life, she moved in the company of highly intelligent and articulate writers, artists, critics, and philosophers. Her father's first wife was the daughter of the novelist William Makepeace Thackeray, and Virginia herself married a keenly intelligent writer, Leonard Woolf. Her elder sister, Vanessa, was an excellent painter who married the eminent art critic Clive Bell. Roger Fry, whose biography she wrote, and whose insights as a critic of painting did much to revolutionize British taste by introducing the work of the Post-Impressionists, was a close friend. So were John Maynard Keynes, the economist; Lytton Strachey, the biographer; Bertrand Russell, the philosopher; and E. M. Forster, the novelist. Bound together by a common outlook, working and living in the Bloomsbury section of London, the Woolfs and some of their friends formed an intellectual circle known as the "Bloomsbury Group."

Beneath this surface, however, she had constantly to fight a mental instability that led to several severe breakdowns and eventual suicide at the age of fifty-nine. A penetrating critic herself, she was painfully sensitive to the criticism of others.

Latent genius she undoubtedly possessed. *The Waves*, a poetic statement rather than a novel, stands out as a truly remarkable, highly stylized creation. More conventional in form, the novels *To the Lighthouse* and *Mrs. Dalloway*, the better essays in the two volumes of *The Common Reader*, and *A Room of One's Own*, a short defense of women's rights, have lost none of their freshness.

What made her fiction distinctive was its attempt to go beyond what she regarded as the tyranny of plot, to get close to life as it is actually experienced. "Examine for a moment an ordinary mind on an ordinary day. The mind receives myriad impressions — trivial, fantastic, evanescent, or engraved with the sharpness of steel . . . Is it not the task of the novelist to convey this varying, this unknown and uncircumscribed spirit . . . ?" To approach the experience of life, she often employed the "stream-of-consciousness" technique in her novels. Although she did not invent this technique, she refined and brightened by her own wit and observation the procedure by which the characters of a novel reveal themselves through their unspoken thoughts. Her method was to assemble in language of great poetic force tiny fragments of perception. She tried, as far as possible, to catch each moment as it passed rather than to thrust her characters into the contrivances of a plot.

Inevitably, Woolf's writing grew less and less concerned with ordinary life and concentrated more and more on moments of great subtlety and sensitivity. Her friend E. M. Forster characterized her as "a poet who wants to write something as near to a novel as possible." She recorded her own anxieties and frustrations in a diary, part of which was posthumously published as *A Writer's Diary*. *The Death of the Moth and Other Essays* was also published after her death. A complete edition of the *Diaries* in five volumes is in preparation. Volume One appeared in 1977.

The New Dress

Mabel had her first serious suspicion that something was wrong as she took her cloak off and Mrs. Barnet, while handing her the mirror and touching the brushes and thus drawing her attention, perhaps rather markedly, to all the appliances for tidying and improving hair, complexion, clothes, which existed on the dressing table, confirmed the suspicion—that it was not right, not quite right, which growing stronger as she went upstairs and springing at her with conviction as she greeted Clarissa Dalloway, she went straight to the far end of the room, to a shaded corner where a looking glass hung and looked. No! It was not *right*. And at once the misery which she always tried to hide, the profound dissatisfaction—the sense she had had, ever since she was a child, of being inferior to other people—set upon her, relentlessly, remorselessly, with an intensity which she could not beat off, as she would when she woke at night at home, by reading Borrow[1] or Scott;[2] for oh these men, oh these women, all were thinking—"What's Mabel wearing? What a fright she looks! What a hideous new dress!"—their eyelids flickering as they came up and then their lids shutting rather tight. It was her own appalling inadequacy; her cowardice; her mean, water-sprinkled blood that depressed her. And at once the whole of the room where, for ever so many hours, she had planned with the little dressmaker how it was to go, seemed sordid, repulsive; and her own drawing room so shabby, and herself, going out, puffed up with vanity as she touched the letters on the hall table and said, "How dull!" to show off—all this now seemed unutterably silly, paltry, and provincial. All this had been

absolutely destroyed, shown up, exploded, the moment she came into Mrs. Dalloway's drawing room.

What she had thought that evening when, sitting over the teacups, Mrs. Dalloway's invitation came, was that, of course, she could not be fashionable. It was absurd to pretend it even—fashion meant cut, meant style, meant thirty guineas at least—but why not be original? Why not be herself, anyhow? And, getting up, she had taken that old fashion book of her mother's, a Paris fashion book of the time of the Empire, and had thought how much prettier, more dignified, and more womanly they were then, and so set herself—oh, it was foolish—trying to be like them, pluming herself in fact, upon being modest and old-fashioned and very charming, giving herself up, no doubt about it, to an orgy of self-love, which deserved to be chastised, and so rigged herself out like this.

But she dared not look in the glass. She could not face the whole horror—the pale yellow, idiotically old-fashioned silk dress with its long skirt and its high sleeves and its waist and all the things that looked so charming in the fashion book, but not on her, not among all these ordinary people. She felt like a dressmaker's dummy standing there, for young people to stick pins into.

"But, my dear, it's perfectly charming!" Rose Shaw said, looking her up and down with that little satirical pucker of the lips which she expected—Rose herself being dressed in the height of the fashion, precisely like everybody else, always.

We are all like flies trying to crawl over the edge of the saucer, Mabel thought, and repeated the phrase as if she were crossing herself, as if she were trying to find some spell to annul this pain, to make this agony endurable. Tags of Shakespeare, lines from books she had read ages ago, suddenly came to her

---

1. **Borrow:** George Henry Borrow (1803–1881), English writer.
2. **Scott:** Sir Walter Scott (1771–1832), Scottish novelist and poet.

when she was in agony, and she repeated them over and over again. "Flies trying to crawl," she repeated. If she could say that over often enough and make herself see the flies, she would become numb, chill, frozen, dumb. Now she could see flies crawling slowly out of a saucer of milk with their wings stuck together; and she strained and strained (standing in front of the looking glass, listening to Rose Shaw) to make herself see Rose Shaw and all the other people there as flies, trying to hoist themselves out of something, or into something, meager, insignificant, toiling flies. But she could not see them like that, not other people. She saw herself like that—she was a fly, but the others were dragonflies, butterflies, beautiful insects, dancing, fluttering, skimming, while she alone dragged herself up out of the saucer. (Envy and spite, the most detestable of the vices, were her chief faults.)

"I feel like some dowdy, decrepit, horribly dingy old fly," she said, making Robert Haydon stop just to hear her say that, just to reassure herself by furbishing up a poor weak-kneed phrase and so showing how detached she was, how witty, that she did not feel in the least out of anything. And, of course, Robert Haydon answered something quite polite, quite insincere, which she saw through instantly, and said to herself, directly he went (again from some book), "Lies, lies, lies!" For a party makes things either much more real, or much less real, she thought; she saw in a flash to the bottom of Robert Haydon's heart; she saw through everything. She saw the truth. *This* was true, this drawing room, this self, and the other false. Miss Milan's little workroom was really terribly hot, stuffy, sordid. It smelled of clothes and cabbage cooking; and yet, when Miss Milan put the glass in her hand, and she looked at herself with the dress on, finished, an extraordinary bliss shot through her heart. Suffused with light, she sprang into existence. Rid of cares and wrinkles, what she had dreamed of herself was there —a beautiful woman. Just for a second (she

had not dared look longer, Miss Milan wanted to know about the length of the skirt), there looked at her, framed in the scrolloping mahogany, a gray-white, mysteriously smiling, charming girl, the core of herself, the soul of herself; and it was not vanity only, not only self-love that made her think it good, tender, and true. Miss Milan said that the skirt could not well be longer; if anything the skirt, said Miss Milan, puckering her forehead, considering with all her wits about her, must be shorter; and she felt, suddenly, honestly, full of love for Miss Milan, much, much fonder of Miss Milan than of anyone in the whole world, and could have cried for pity that she should be crawling on the floor with her mouth full of pins, and her face red and her eyes bulging—that one human being should be doing this for another, and she saw them all as human beings merely, and herself going off to her party, and Miss Milan pulling the cover over the canary's cage, or letting him pick a hempseed from between her lips, and the thought of it, of this side of human nature and its patience and its endurance and its being content with such miserable, scanty, sordid little pleasures filled her eyes with tears.

And now the whole thing had vanished. The dress, the room, the love, the pity, the scrolloping looking glass, and the canary's cage—all had vanished, and here she was in a corner of Mrs. Dalloway's drawing room, suffering tortures, woken wide awake to reality.

But it was all so paltry, weak-blooded, and petty-minded to care so much at her age with two children, to be still so utterly dependent on people's opinions and not have principles or convictions, not to be able to say as other people did, "There's Shakespeare! There's death! We're all weevils in a captain's biscuit" —or whatever it was that people did say.

She faced herself straight in the glass; she pecked at her left shoulder; she issued out into the room, as if spears were thrown at her yellow dress from all sides. But instead of looking fierce or tragic, as Rose Shaw would have done—Rose would have looked like Boadicea[3]—she looked foolish and self-conscious, and simpered like a schoolgirl and slouched across the room, positively slinking, as if she were a beaten mongrel, and looked at a picture, an engraving. As if one went to a party to look at a picture! Everybody knew why she did it—it was from shame, from humiliation.

"Now the fly's in the saucer," she said to herself, "right in the middle, and can't get out, and the milk," she thought, rigidly staring at the picture, "is sticking its wings together."

"It's so old-fashioned," she said to Charles Burt, making him stop (which by itself he hated) on his way to talk to someone else.

She meant, or she tried to make herself think that she meant, that it was the picture and not her dress that was old-fashioned. And one word of praise, one word of affection from Charles would have made all the difference to her at the moment. If he had only said, "Mabel, you're looking charming tonight!" it would have changed her life. But then she ought to have been truthful and direct. Charles said nothing of the kind, of course. He was malice itself. He always saw through one, especially if one were feeling particularly mean, paltry, or feeble-minded.

"Mabel's got a new dress!" he said, and the poor fly was absolutely shoved into the middle of the saucer. Really, he would like her to drown, she believed. He had no heart, no fundamental kindness, only a veneer of friendliness. Miss Milan was much more real, much kinder. If only one could feel that and stick to it always. "Why," she asked herself—replying to Charles much too pertly, letting him see that she was out of temper, or "ruffled" as he called it ("Rather ruffled?" he said and went on to laugh at her with some woman over there)—"Why," she asked herself, "can't I feel one thing always, feel quite sure that Miss Milan is right, and Charles wrong and stick to it, feel sure about the canary and pity and love and not be whipped all round in a second by coming into a room full of people?" It was her odious, weak, vacillating character again, always giving at the critical moment and not being seriously interested in conchology, etymology, botany, archeology, cutting up potatoes and watching them fructify like Mary Dennis, like Violet Searle.

Then Mrs. Holman, seeing her standing there, bore down upon her. Of course a thing like a dress was beneath Mrs. Holman's notice, with her family always tumbling downstairs or having the scarlet fever. Could Mabel tell her if Elmthorpe was ever let for August and September? Oh, it was a conversation that bored her unutterably!—it made her furious to be treated like a house agent or a messenger boy, to be made use of. Not to have value, that was it, she thought, trying to grasp something hard, something real, while she tried to answer sensibly about the bathroom and the south aspect and the hot water to the top of the house; and all the time she could see little bits of her yellow dress in the round looking glass which made them all the size of boot-buttons or tadpoles; and it was amazing to think how much humiliation and agony and self-loathing and effort and passionate ups and downs of feeling were contained in a thing the size of a threepenny bit. And what was still odder, this thing, this Mabel Waring, was separate, quite disconnected; and though Mrs. Holman (the black button) was leaning forward and telling her how her eldest boy had strained his heart running, she could see her, too, quite detached in the looking glass, and it was impossible that the black dot, leaning forward, gesticulating, should make the yellow dot, sitting solitary, self-centered, feel what the black dot was feeling, yet they pretended.

"So impossible to keep boys quiet"—that was the kind of thing one said.

And Mrs. Holman, who could never get

3. **Boadicea** (bō´ăd-ə-sē´ə): a British queen who in A.D. 62 poisoned herself after suffering defeat by the Romans.

enough sympathy and snatched what little there was greedily, as if it were her right (but she deserved much more for there was her little girl who had come down this morning with a swollen kneejoint), took this miserable offering and looked at it suspiciously, grudgingly, as if it were a half-penny when it ought to have been a pound and put it away in her purse, must put up with it, mean and miserly though it was, times being hard, so very hard; and on she went, creaking, injured Mrs. Holman, about the girl with the swollen joints. Ah, it was tragic, this greed, this clamor of human beings, like a row of cormorants,[4] barking and flapping their wings for sympathy — it was tragic, could one have felt it and not merely pretended to feel it!

But in her yellow dress tonight she could not wring out one drop more; she wanted it all, all for herself. She knew (she kept on looking into the glass, dipping into that dreadfully showing up blue pool) that she was condemned, despised, left like this in a backwater, because of her being like this a feeble, vacillating creature; and it seemed to her that the yellow dress was a penance which she had deserved, and if she had been dressed like Rose Shaw, in lovely, clinging green with a ruffle of swansdown, she would have deserved that; and she thought that there was no escape for her—none whatever. But it was not her fault altogether, after all. It was being one of a family of ten; never having money enough, always skimping and paring; and her mother carrying great cans, and the linoleum worn on the stair edges, and one sordid little domestic tragedy after another—nothing catastrophic, the sheep farm failing, but not utterly; her eldest brother marrying beneath him but not very much—there was no romance, nothing extreme about them all. They petered out respectably in seaside resorts; every watering place had one of her aunts even now asleep in some lodging with the

Girl Before a Mirror by Pablo Picasso (1932). Museum of Modern Art, New York

front windows not quite facing the sea. That was so like them—they had to squint at things always. And she had done the same— she was just like her aunts. For all her dreams of living in India, married to some hero like Sir Henry Lawrence, some empire builder (still the sight of a native in a turban filled her with romance), she had failed utterly. She had married Hubert, with his safe, permanent underling's job in the Law Courts, and they managed tolerably in a smallish house without proper maids and hash when she was alone or just bread and butter, but now and then—Mrs. Holman was off, thinking her the most dried up, unsympathetic twig she had

---

4. **cormorants:** large, web-footed aquatic birds.

ever met, absurdly dressed, too, and would tell everyone about Mabel's fantastic appearance—now and then, thought Mabel Waring, left alone on the blue sofa, punching the cushion in order to look occupied, for she would not join Charles Burt and Rose Shaw, chattering like magpies and perhaps laughing at her by the fireplace—now and then, there did come to her delicious moments, reading the other night in bed, for instance, or down by the sea on the sand in the sun at Easter—let her recall it—a great tuft of pale sand grass standing all twisted like a shock of spears against the sky, which was blue like a smooth china egg, so firm, so hard, and then the melody of the waves—"Hush, hush," they said, and the children's shouts paddling—yes, it was a divine moment, and there she lay, she felt, in the hand of the Goddess who was the world; rather a hard-hearted, but very beautiful Goddess, a little lamb laid on the altar (one did think these silly things, and it didn't matter so long as one never said them). And also with Hubert sometimes she had quite unexpectedly—carving the mutton for Sunday lunch, for no reason, opening a letter, coming into a room—divine moments, when she said to herself (for she would never say this to anybody else), "This is it. This has happened. This is it!" And the other way about it was equally surprising—that is, when everything was arranged—music, weather, holidays, every reason for happiness was there—then nothing happened at all. One wasn't happy. It was flat, just flat, that was all.

Her wretched self again, no doubt! She had always been a fretful, weak, unsatisfactory mother, a wobbly wife, lolling about in a kind of twilight existence with nothing very clear or very bold, or more one thing than another, like all her brothers and sisters, except perhaps Herbert—they were all the same poor water-veined creatures who did nothing. Then in the midst of this creeping, crawling life, suddenly she was on the crest of a wave. That wretched fly—where had she read the story that kept coming into her mind about the fly and the saucer?—struggled out. Yes, she had those moments. But now that she was forty, they might come more and more seldom. By degrees she would cease to struggle any more. But that was deplorable! That was not to be endured! That made her feel ashamed of herself!

She would go to the London Library tomorrow. She would find some wonderful, helpful, astonishing book, quite by chance, a book by a clergyman, by an American no one had ever heard of; or she would walk down the Strand and drop, accidentally, into a hall where a miner was telling about the life in the pit, and suddenly she would become a new person. She would be absolutely transformed. She would wear a uniform; she would be called Sister Somebody; she would never give a thought to clothes again. And for ever after she would be perfectly clear about Charles Burt and Miss Milan and this room and that room; and it would be always, day after day, as if she were lying in the sun or carving the mutton. It would be it!

So she got up from the blue sofa, and the yellow button in the looking glass got up too, and she waved her hand to Charles and Rose to show them she did not depend on them one scrap, and the yellow button moved out of the looking glass, and all the spears were gathered into her breast as she walked towards Mrs. Dalloway and said, "Good night."

"But it's too early to go," said Mrs. Dalloway, who was always so charming.

"I'm afraid I must," said Mabel Waring. "But," she added in her weak, wobbly voice which only sounded ridiculous when she tried to strengthen it, "I have enjoyed myself enormously."

"I have enjoyed myself," she said to Mr. Dalloway, whom she met on the stairs.

"Lies, lies, lies!" she said to herself, going downstairs, and "Right in the saucer!" she said to herself as she thanked Mrs. Barnet for helping her and wrapped herself round and round and round in the Chinese cloak she had worn these twenty years.

FOR STUDY AND DISCUSSION

1. How would you describe Mabel's relationship to the other people at the party? Does she "belong"? Why or why not?

2. How does what you learn of Mabel's past explain her behavior at the party? Why do you think this information is given so late in the story?

3. There are repeated references to Mabel's enjoyment of reading. Why does she turn to books? What satisfaction does she find in them?

4. What do you learn of Mrs. Dalloway, Rose Shaw, Robert Haydon, Miss Milan, and the other people at the party? Do they emerge as distinct individuals? Why or why not?

5. A simile involving a "fly trying to crawl over the edge of the saucer" occurs with variations several times in the story. Describe the variations. What is the significance of this simile in the story?

6. Cite at least three references to mirrors in "The New Dress." Why do mirrors play such an important role in this story?

7. In Shakespeare's *Hamlet*, the hero says, "There's nothing good or bad but thinking makes it so." How may this statement be applied to Mabel Waring?

THE STREAM-OF-CONSCIOUSNESS TECHNIQUE

Twentieth-century writers such as Virginia Woolf and James Joyce (page 721) have tried not merely to describe how a character might think; they have also attempted to present a record of the character's consciousness—that is, the stream of the character's thoughts as he or she is thinking them. For example, in her novel *Mrs. Dalloway,* Woolf records the consciousness of Clarissa Dalloway as she thinks about a party she is giving:

> But to go deeper, beneath what people said (and these judgments, how superficial, how fragmentary they are!) in her own mind now, what did it mean to her, this thing she called life? Oh, it was very queer. Here was So-and-so in South Kensington; someone up in Bayswater; and someone else, say, in Mayfair [districts of London]. And she felt continuously a sense of their existence; and she felt a waste; and she felt what a pity; and she felt if only they could be brought together; so she did it. And it was an offering; to combine, to create, but to whom?

Notice that the author does not try to be especially clear. Instead, she follows the mind wherever it goes, seeking to give an impression of spontaneity rather than order.

1. Find passages in "The New Dress" that employ the stream-of-consciousness technique. Do the sentences follow one another logically? If not, what relationship do they have to one another?

2. In terms of sentence order and the kinds of sentences used, compare a passage in "The New Dress" with a passage in "The Lagoon" (page 690) that describes the white man's thoughts as he looks at the sky.

James Joyce
1882–1941

During the nineteenth century England gave a somewhat grudging and uncertain approval to the abilities of contemporary foreign writers. But today when modern literature is spoken of, the term is naturally understood to refer to literary works in several languages and implies that great works in any one of these languages have been built, in part, upon an awareness and appreciation of literature in other tongues.

James Joyce, whose work is at once intensely local and universal, is a striking instance of this interdependence. He attributed his most famous innovation in fictional method to a Frenchman, Edouard Dujardin, and he ransacked the world's languages and literatures for his own purposes, yet he never wrote anything of consequence that did not deal with his native Dublin and his life there. He is known for six works: a book of poems, a play, and four works of fiction—*Dubliners* (1914), *A Portrait of the Artist as a Young Man* (1916), *Ulysses* (1922), and *Finnegans Wake* (1939).

Joyce came to manhood in an Ireland full of the stirrings of the Irish Renaissance, whose most notable figures were W. B. Yeats, George Moore, Lady Gregory, and J. M. Synge. Ireland was at this time trying rather self-consciously to achieve a sense of national identity, and, as part of this endeavor, an attempt was made to revive Gaelic as a national language. Believing this movement would separate Ireland further from the mainstream of European culture, Joyce was resolutely against it. He thought it superficial and sentimental and preferred to tell the bitter truth about Dublin; and since for him this involved telling the truth about growing up there, he planned *Dubliners* very carefully to reflect the grim reality of Irish life. However, the stories in *Dubliners* reveal a certain lyricism as well: the wild cry of youth is in the book, muted but always seeking an escape from ugliness. Joyce said of this collection of short stories that it was written "for the most part in a style of scrupulous meanness." This does not apply to certain passages in "Araby," but it is a good way to note the historical position of *Dubliners*, for this book marks a sharp break with the techniques of nineteenth-century fiction. Each word and phrase has a precise function; incident and plot are minimized; the au-

James Joyce
Radio Times Hulton

thor does not seem to be manipulating characters and emotions; form and theme are intimately connected. Lyricism springs not only out of the promise that youth offers us all, but out of a strong sense of the power of art to shape a world no matter how wretched and shabby it may be. This power enables Joyce ultimately to triumph over the meanness that betrays itself in the impoverished emotions and the cadences of speech which are so faithfully recorded in *Dubliners*.

A Portrait of the Artist is much more directly autobiographical, although its hero, Stephen Dedalus, is a "young man" on whom the writer looks back with sometimes ironical detachment. This young man renounces his family and country and sets out to "encounter the reality of experience and to forge in the smithy of my soul the uncreated conscience of my race." In French, *conscience* means "consciousness," and, if we combine this with the English meaning, we arrive at a notion of Joyce's ambition. He named his hero after Daedalus, the legendary Greek inventor who designed the labyrinth of Crete, was imprisoned to protect its secret, and then made wings to escape. Stephen similarly escapes from Ireland and takes flight, only to penetrate the labyrinth of Irish consciousness from afar and to judge all he has known.

Dubliners and *A Portrait of the Artist* do not present the difficulties of *Ulysses*, a work that reflects the consciousness of its characters in a literal sense: that is, the book is composed of the characters' internal monologues. This device, often referred to as "stream of consciousness" (see page 720), is the innovation Joyce said he had found in Dujardin. Although the use of stream of consciousness was a radical shift in fictional technique, the aim of *Ulysses* was newer still. *Ulysses* is told chiefly through the consciousness of its principal figure, Leopold Bloom. Bloom's consciousness is made to embrace not only the multitudinous details of the life of the city of Dublin on just one day—June 16, 1904—but the whole journey of human beings from birth to grave. In this novel Joyce attempts to embody the significance of all human history, the meaning of the family, of manhood and womanhood, war, politics, and human achievement of every sort, but preeminently the achievements of those artists who have found in words the means of binding people together. Words are Joyce's obsession, his delight, the source of his power. So wonderfully are words used by this great artificer that the whole world of Dublin springs up out of their sounds, colors, reverberations, and linkages with each other. Almost nothing is *seen* in this book. We hear, rather, torrents of words that flow out into rivers of meaning.

The content of *Dubliners, A Portrait of the Artist,* and *Ulysses* is in a sense all the same: Joyce's childhood and youth in Dublin. It is no surprise, therefore, to learn that his final achievement, *Finnegans Wake,* is also based on Dublin. In this book, however, the artificer is no longer content with existing words; he takes apart, combines, and rebuilds words into a pattern of meanings that no single language alone (but all languages taken together) affords. Joyce was a linguist who for many years earned his living by teaching English to foreigners. He knew Latin, Italian, French, German, and numerous other tongues, and in this final work drew upon all his knowledge.

As *Ulysses* is an account of a day, *Finnegans Wake* is the account of a night, or rather a night dreamed by a man in whose consciousness all recorded history finds a meaning and a home. It is interesting that *wake* is not only the Irish term for funeral, but a part of the verb *to awaken.* Thus the novel is concerned with the death and rebirth of Finnegan, builder of cities and a Dublin bricklayer, a compound of all the heroes of myth. Full of riddles, allusions, and ambiguities, it is a tremendous performance, a book about everything.

Joyce spent most of his adult life trying to make sense of an environment that must have been hard for a youngster to endure or understand. His father, John Joyce, who had inherited some property, frittered it away. The family kept moving to meaner quarters, and the father, who was jovial, savage, extravagantly affectionate, and brutal by turns, was more likely to come home drunk than with food for his family. John Joyce had been devoted to Charles Stewart Parnell, the advocate of Irish freedom, and his betrayal and death affected both the elder Joyce and his son James deeply.

Joyce's mother tried to hold the large family together. After her death, Joyce finally fled Dublin for good, in the company of Nora Barnacle, the beautiful and maternal woman who was to become his wife. The mileposts in the years that followed are the names of the cities in which Joyce successively lived, the publication of the books over which he labored for years, the gradual deterioration of his always poor eyesight, and the names of the patrons who gave him the financial freedom which he needed in order to write. Joyce acquired his first patron himself by getting his steady, responsible brother, Stanislaus, to share (and help support) his household in Trieste, where he had settled as a teacher of English at the Berlitz School. On the surface his life seemed to be one of improvidence very much like his father's, but in fact it was centered wholly on his writing. World War I forced him to Switzerland, where he remained until he was able to move to Paris in 1920. There he lived through the triumphant period of the publication of *Ulysses.* Driven again to Switzerland by the Nazi occupation of France, he died in 1941, nearly blind and almost worn out by a combination of hard work and hard living. Joyce lived in an atmosphere of conspiracy at times. He was quick to feel insulted and equally quick to return defiance to the world. At other times he was full of gaiety and a delightful companion. But, in reviewing his troubled life, the most vivid picture is that of a man fiercely guarding his talent and doing the work that he knew he alone could do.

Araby°

North Richmond Street, being blind,[1] was a quiet street except at the hour when the Christian Brothers' School set the boys free. An uninhabited house of two stories stood at the blind end, detached from its neighbors in a square ground. The other houses of the street, conscious of decent lives within them, gazed at one another with brown imperturbable faces.

The former tenant of our house, a priest, had died in the back drawing room. Air, musty from having been long enclosed, hung in all the rooms, and the waste room behind the kitchen was littered with old useless papers. Among these I found a few paper-covered books, the pages of which were curled and damp: *The Abbot,* by Walter Scott, *The Devout Communicant* and *The Memoirs of Vidocq.*[2] I liked the last best because its leaves were yellow. The wild garden behind the house contained a central apple tree and a few straggling bushes under one of which I found the late tenant's rusty bicycle pump. He had been a very charitable priest; in his will he had left all his money to institutions and the furniture of his house to his sister.

When the short days of winter came dusk fell before we had well eaten our dinners. When we met in the street the houses had grown somber. The space of sky above us was the color of ever-changing violet and towards it the lamps of the street lifted their feeble lanterns. The cold air stung us and we played till our bodies glowed. Our shouts echoed in the silent street. The career of our play brought us through the dark muddy lanes behind the houses where we ran the gantlet of the rough tribes from the cottages, to the back doors of the dark dripping gardens where odors arose from the ashpits, to the dark odorous stables where a coachman smoothed and combed the horse or shook music from the buckled harness. When we returned to the street, light from the kitchen windows had filled the areas. If my uncle was seen turning the corner we hid in the shadow until we had seen him safely housed. Or if Mangan's sister came out on the doorstep to call her brother in to his tea we watched her from our shadow peer up and down the street. We waited to see whether she would remain or go in and, if she remained, we left our shadow and walked up to Mangan's steps resignedly. She was waiting for us, her figure defined by the light from the half-opened door. Her brother always teased her before he obeyed and I stood by the railings looking at her. Her dress swung as she moved her body and the soft rope of her hair tossed from side to side.

Every morning I lay on the floor in the front parlor watching her door. The blind was pulled down to within an inch of the sash so that I could not be seen. When she came out on the doorstep my heart leaped. I ran to the hall, seized my books and followed her. I kept her brown figure always in my eye and, when we came near the point at which our ways diverged, I quickened my pace and passed her. This happened morning after morning. I had never spoken to her, except for a few casual words, and yet her name was like a summons to all my foolish blood.

Her image accompanied me even in places the most hostile to romance. On Saturday evenings when my aunt went marketing I had to go to carry some of the parcels. We walked through the flaring streets, jostled by drunken men and bargaining women, amid the curses

---

° **Araby:** ancient name for Arabia; in this story, an Oriental bazaar in Dublin.
1. **blind:** dead end.
2. *The Abbot . . . Vidocq:* a historical romance, a religious manual, and the reminiscences of a French adventurer, respectively.

of laborers, the shrill litanies of shopboys who stood on guard by the barrels of pigs' cheeks, the nasal chanting of street singers, who sang a *come-all-you* about O'Donovan Rossa,[3] or a ballad about the troubles in our native land. These noises converged in a single sensation of life for me: I imagined that I bore my chalice safely through a throng of foes. Her name sprang to my lips at moments in strange prayers and praises which I myself did not understand. My eyes were often full of tears (I could not tell why) and at times a flood from my heart seemed to pour itself out into my bosom. I thought little of the future. I did not know whether I would ever speak to her or not or, if I spoke to her, how I could tell her of my confused adoration. But my body was like a harp and her words and gestures were like fingers running upon the wires.

One evening I went into the back drawing room in which the priest had died. It was a dark rainy evening and there was no sound in the house. Through one of the broken panes I heard the rain impinge upon the earth, the fine incessant needles of water playing in the sodden beds. Some distant lamp or lighted window gleamed below me. I was thankful that I could see so little. All my senses seemed to desire to veil themselves and, feeling that I was about to slip from them, I pressed the palms of my hands together until they trembled, murmuring: *"O love! O love!"* many times.

At last she spoke to me. When she addressed the first words to me I was so confused that I did not know what to answer. She asked me was I going to *Araby.* I forget whether I answered yes or no. It would be a splendid bazaar, she said; she would love to go.

"And why can't you?" I asked.

While she spoke she turned a silver bracelet round and round her wrist. She could not go, she said, because there would be a retreat[4] that week in her convent. Her brother and two other boys were fighting for their caps and I was alone at the railings. She held one of the spikes, bowing her head towards me. The light from the lamp opposite our door caught the white curve of her neck, lit up her hair that rested there and, falling, lit up the hand upon the railing. It fell over one side of her dress and caught the white border of a petticoat, just visible as she stood at ease.

"It's well for you," she said.

"If I go," I said, "I will bring you something."

What innumerable follies laid waste my waking and sleeping thoughts after that evening! I wished to annihilate the tedious intervening days. I chafed against the work of school. At night in my bedroom and by day in the classroom her image came between me and the page I strove to read. The syllables of the word *Araby* were called to me through the silence in which my soul luxuriated and cast an Eastern enchantment over me. I asked for leave to go to the bazaar on Saturday night. My aunt was surprised and hoped it was not some Freemason[5] affair. I answered few questions in class. I watched my master's face pass from amiability to sternness; he hoped I was not beginning to idle. I could not call my wandering thoughts together. I had hardly any patience with the serious work of life which, now that it stood between me and my desire, seemed to me child's play, ugly monotonous child's play.

On Saturday morning I reminded my uncle that I wished to go to the bazaar in the evening. He was fussing at the hallstand, looking for the hat brush, and answered me curtly:

"Yes, boy, I know."

As he was in the hall I could not go into the

---

3. *come-all-you* . . . **Rossa:** opening of a street ballad about an Irish hero.

4. **retreat:** a group withdrawal and seclusion for prayer, religious study, and meditation.
5. **Freemason:** a fraternal society called the Free and Accepted Masons, which has some secret rituals.

front parlor and lie at the window. I left the house in bad humor and walked slowly towards the school. The air was pitilessly raw and already my heart misgave me.

When I came home to dinner my uncle had not yet been home. Still it was early. I sat staring at the clock for some time and, when its ticking began to irritate me, I left the room. I mounted the staircase and gained the upper part of the house. The high cold empty gloomy rooms liberated me and I went from room to room singing. From the front window I saw my companions playing below in the street. Their cries reached me weakened and indistinct and, leaning my forehead against the cool glass, I looked over at the dark house where she lived. I may have stood there for an hour, seeing nothing but the brown-clad figure cast by my imagination, touched discreetly by the lamplight at the curved neck, at the hand upon the railings and at the border below the dress.

When I came downstairs again I found Mrs. Mercer sitting at the fire. She was an old garrulous woman, a pawnbroker's widow, who collected used stamps for some pious purpose. I had to endure the gossip of the tea table. The meal was prolonged beyond an hour and still my uncle did not come. Mrs. Mercer stood up to go: she was sorry she couldn't wait any longer, but it was after eight o'clock and she did not like to be out late, as the night air was bad for her. When she had gone I began to walk up and down the room, clenching my fists. My aunt said:

"I'm afraid you may put off your bazaar for this night of Our Lord."

At nine o'clock I heard my uncle's latchkey in the hall door. I heard him talking to himself and heard the hallstand rocking when it had received the weight of his overcoat. I could interpret these signs. When he was midway through his dinner I asked him to give me the money to go to the bazaar. He had forgotten.

"The people are in bed and after their first sleep now," he said.

I did not smile. My aunt said to him energetically:

"Can't you give him the money and let him go? You've kept him late enough as it is."

My uncle said he was very sorry he had forgotten. He said he believed in the old saying: *All work and no play makes Jack a dull boy.* He asked me where I was going and, when I had told him a second time he asked me did I know *The Arab's Farewell to His Steed.*[6] When I left the kitchen he was about to recite the opening lines of the piece to my aunt.

I held a florin[7] tightly in my hand as I strode down Buckingham Street towards the station. The sight of the streets thronged with buyers and glaring with gas recalled to me the purpose of my journey. I took my seat in a third-class carriage of a deserted train. After an intolerable delay the train moved out of the station slowly. It crept onward among ruinous houses and over the twinkling river. At Westland Row Station a crowd of people pressed to the carriage doors; but the porters moved them back, saying that it was a special train for the bazaar. I remained alone in the bare carriage. In a few minutes the train drew up beside an improvised wooden platform. I passed out onto the road and saw by the lighted dial of a clock that it was ten minutes to ten. In front of me was a large building which displayed the magical name.

I could not find any sixpenny entrance and, fearing that the bazaar would be closed, I passed in quickly through a turnstile, handing a shilling to a weary-looking man. I found myself in a big hall girdled at half its height by a gallery. Nearly all the stalls were closed and the greater part of the hall was in darkness. I recognized a silence like that which pervades a church after a service. I walked into the

---

6. *The Arab's . . . Steed:* a popular sentimental nineteenth-century poem.
7. **florin:** a two-shilling coin, no longer used, that at the time was worth approximately forty-nine American cents.

center of the bazaar timidly. A few people were gathered about the stalls which were still open. Before a curtain, over which the words *Café Chantant*[8] were written in colored lamps, two men were counting money on a salver. I listened to the fall of the coins.

Remembering with difficulty why I had come I went over to one of the stalls and examined porcelain vases and flowered tea sets. At the door of the stall a young lady was talking and laughing with two young gentlemen. I remarked their English accents and listened vaguely to their conversation.

"O, I never said such a thing!"

"O, but you did!"

"O, but I didn't!"

"Didn't she say that?"

"Yes. I heard her."

"O, there's a . . . fib!"

Observing me the young lady came over and asked me did I wish to buy anything. The tone of her voice was not encouraging; she seemed to have spoken to me out of a sense of duty. I looked humbly at the great jars that stood like Eastern guards at either side of the dark entrance to the stall and murmured:

"No, thank you."

The young lady changed the position of one of the vases and went back to the two young men. They began to talk of the same subject. Once or twice the young lady glanced at me over her shoulder.

I lingered before her stall, though I knew my stay was useless, to make my interest in her wares seem the more real. Then I turned away slowly and walked down the middle of the bazaar. I allowed the two pennies to fall against the sixpence in my pocket. I heard a voice call from one end of the gallery that the light was out. The upper part of the hall was now completely dark.

Gazing up into the darkness I saw myself as a creature driven and derided by vanity; and my eyes burned with anguish and anger.

---

8. *Café Chantant:* café providing musical entertainment.

COMMENTARY

"Araby" puts clearly before us the disproportion between our passionate dreams as children and the world that denies those dreams. It may be pointed out that the dream of this story was in one way realized. The child who bore his chalice "safely through a throng of foes" is also the young artist conscious of the vessel of his powers which he must guard. But the movement of the story is not to such a symbolic conclusion. The little boy makes a brave offer of a present to the girl, and he succeeds in his effort to visit the bazaar with the mysterious and wonderful name. But all ends in dull and meaningless talk as the hall is darkened; no trace of the exotic lingers. The splendid bazaar is simply a place that is closing, a place where small boys aren't welcome. "Araby" vanishes, and the child is beset by "anguish and anger."

The uncle in this story is a version of Joyce's own father; there actually was such an oriental bazaar in Dublin; one of the houses in which Joyce lived was on North Richmond Street; and there was in fact such a girl, the sister of Joyce's friend— but it is astonishing how little all this matters. What does matter is the power to order and choose out of the welter of the past. Only that power turns the past to rich account.

FOR STUDY AND DISCUSSION

1. Important details of setting and personality are given in the first two paragraphs of the story. How does the description of North Richmond Street and its houses convey the emotional life of the inhabitants? What do the priest's books reveal about him? Was the priest really "charitable"?

2. How does the narrator's trip to the market with his aunt contribute to his feeling of separation from real life? Which words in this paragraph reinforce the contrast between Dublin life and the boy's desire for romance?

3. Explain how Joyce reveals the restrictions in the lives of the narrator, the uncle, Mangan's sister, and the dead priest.

4. What exotic associations does the bazaar have for the narrator? Contrast these associations with what he finds at the bazaar. What do you think is the purpose of the dialogue between the woman and the two men?

5. What does the narrator come to realize about himself at the end of the story? Do you think he is being too harsh in his judgment?

FOR COMPOSITION

1. Notice that "Araby" begins and ends in darkness. Trace the various images of light and shadow through the story and show how they define the boy's feelings at each point.

2. The musty books found in the back room include a romantic novel by Sir Walter Scott, a religious tract written by a friar, and a memoir attributed to a French detective of the early nineteenth century—three very different kinds of literature. The boy's overall impression of these books, however, is a romantic one; his preference for *The Memoirs of Vidocq* has nothing to do with its contents. "I liked the last because its leaves were yellow." Find several other examples in the story of the contrast between an actual object and the boy's perception of it. Then discuss how these differences help develop the theme of the story.

D. H. Lawrence
1885–1930

D. H. Lawrence
British Information Service

David Herbert Lawrence was born in a village in the industrial midlands of England. His father was a coal miner and his mother a schoolteacher. By birth and education he was therefore a man apart from the typical writer of the early twentieth century, who was very unlikely to be of working-class stock. By the time Lawrence's first book, *The White Peacock,* was published in 1911, he had begun to glory in his apartness, an attitude reinforced by his elopement the following year with Frieda von Richthofen, the German-born wife of a Nottingham professor.

From 1912 until his death from tuberculosis in 1930, the Lawrences spent most of their time abroad: in Italy, Australia, and New Mexico. Their relationship was a stormy one. Lawrence always felt uneasy in conventional surroundings. Before World War I he had been accepted by the English social and literary world as a budding genius, but friendship with him required a degree of patience that not all his would-be helpers were able to sustain. His difficult temperament went hand in hand with a powerful imagination and a prose style which, if humorless, beautifully matched the blunt and challenging situations into which he liked to plunge his fictional characters.

All his life Lawrence sought a Utopia, an ideally civilized community in which he could live with a few chosen followers. His dislike of British puritanism and snobbery, as he saw it, made him bitterly dislike his own country. He thought for a time that he had found what he sought in Queensland, Australia, and in Taos, New Mexico. But as time passed, his deteriorating health made him always harder to satisfy.

Those of Lawrence's contemporaries who knew him well never accepted his view of himself as a tiger; they considered him a sick man living on his nerves. But they, like posterity, were forced to acknowledge the fineness of his best short stories, such as "The Prussian Officer," and his best novels, among which *Sons and Lovers, The Rainbow,* and *Women in Love* are outstanding. Lawrence was also a more than ordinarily skillful writer of free verse, with an acute understanding of animals and a warmly sensuous view of nature. Artifice was as abhorrent to him as convention. He liked to think himself a child of the Mediterranean dawn—as a child of the Italy of the Etruscans, who preceded the coming of the Romans. In more primitive human beings Lawrence attempted to find the wholeness and balance he felt had been lost by civilization.

In addition to his strikingly original fiction and poetry, Lawrence wrote some remarkable travel books, such as *Sea and Sardinia* and *Twilight in Italy.* When he chose, he also could be a refreshingly original critic. His *Studies in Classical American Literature* remains one of the best unprofessional pieces of critical writing to be published in this century.

The Rocking-Horse Winner

There was a woman who was beautiful, who started with all the advantages, yet she had no luck. She married for love, and the love turned to dust. She had bonny children, yet she felt they had been thrust upon her, and she could not love them. They looked at her coldly, as if they were finding fault with her. And hurriedly she felt she must cover up some fault in herself. Yet what it was that she must cover up she never knew. Nevertheless, when her children were present, she always felt the center of her heart go hard. This troubled her, and in her manner she was all the more gentle and anxious for her children, as if she loved them very much. Only she herself knew that at the center of her heart was a hard little place that could not feel love, no, not for anybody. Everybody else said of her: "She is such a good mother. She adores her children." Only she herself, and her children themselves, knew it was not so. They read it in each other's eyes.

There were a boy and two little girls. They lived in a pleasant house, with a garden, and they had discreet servants, and felt themselves superior to anyone in the neighborhood.

Although they lived in style, they felt always an anxiety in the house. There was never enough money. The mother had a small income, and the father had a small income, but not nearly enough for the social position which they had to keep up. The father went in to town to some office. But though he had good prospects, these prospects never materialized. There was always the grinding sense of the shortage of money, though the style was always kept up.

At last the mother said: "I will see if *I* can't make something." But she did not know where to begin. She racked her brains, and tried this thing and the other, but could not find anything successful. The failure made deep lines come into her face. Her children were growing up, they would have to go to school. There must be more money, there must be more money. The father, who was always very handsome and expensive in his tastes, seemed as if he never *would* be able to do anything worth doing. And the mother, who had a great belief in herself, did not succeed any better, and her tastes were just as expensive.

And so the house came to be haunted by the unspoken phrase: *There must be more money! There must be more money!* The children could hear it all the time, though nobody said it aloud. They heard it at Christmas, when the expensive and splendid toys filled the nursery. Behind the shining modern rocking horse, behind the smart doll's house, a voice would start whispering: "There *must* be more money! There *must* be more money!" And the children would stop playing, to listen for a moment. They would look into each other's eyes, to see if they had all heard. And each one saw in the eyes of the other two that they too had heard. "There *must* be more money! There *must* be more money!"

It came whispering from the springs of the still-swaying rocking horse, and even the horse, bending his wooden, champing head, heard it. The big doll, sitting so pink and smirking in her new pram, could hear it quite plainly, and seemed to be smirking all the more self-consciously because of it. The foolish puppy, too, that took the place of the teddy bear, he was looking so extraordinarily foolish for no other reason but that he heard the secret whisper all over the house: "There *must* be more money!"

Yet nobody ever said it aloud. The whisper was everywhere, and therefore no one spoke it. Just as no one ever says: "We are breathing!'' in spite of the fact that breath is coming and going all the time.

"Mother," said the boy Paul one day, "why don't we keep a car of our own? Why do we always use Uncle's, or else a taxi?"

"Because we're the poor members of the family," said the mother.

"But why *are* we, Mother?"

"Well—I suppose," she said slowly and bitterly, "it's because your father has no luck."

The boy was silent for some time.

"Is luck money, Mother?" he asked rather timidly.

"No, Paul. Not quite. It's what causes you to have money."

"Oh!" said Paul vaguely. "I thought when Uncle Oscar said *filthy lucker*, it meant money."

"*Filthy lucre* does mean money," said the mother. "But it's lucre, not luck."

"Oh!" said the boy. "Then what *is* luck, Mother?"

"It's what causes you to have money. If you're lucky you have money. That's why it's better to be born lucky than rich. If you're rich, you may lose your money. But if you're lucky, you will always get more money."

"Oh! Will you? And is Father not lucky?"

"Very unlucky, I should say," she said bitterly.

The boy watched her with unsure eyes.

"Why?" he asked.

"I don't know. Nobody ever knows why one person is lucky and another unlucky."

"Don't they? Nobody at all? Does *nobody* know?"

"Perhaps God. But He never tells."

"He ought to, then. And aren't you lucky either, Mother?"

"I can't be, if I married an unlucky husband."

"But by yourself, aren't you?"

"I used to think I was, before I married. Now I think I am very unlucky indeed."

"Why?"

"Well—never mind! Perhaps I'm not really," she said.

The child looked at her, to see if she meant it. But he saw, by the lines of her mouth, that she was only trying to hide something from him.

"Well, anyhow," he said stoutly, "I'm a lucky person."

"Why?" said his mother, with a sudden laugh.

He stared at her. He didn't even know why he had said it.

"God told me," he asserted, brazening it out.

"I hope He did, dear!" she said, again with a laugh, but rather bitter.

"He did, Mother!"

"Excellent!" said the mother, using one of her husband's exclamations.

The boy saw she did not believe him; or, rather, that she paid no attention to his assertion. This angered him somewhat, and made him want to compel her attention.

He went off by himself, vaguely, in a childish way, seeking for the clue to "luck." Absorbed, taking no heed of other people, he went about with a sort of stealth, seeking inwardly for luck. He wanted luck, he wanted it, he wanted it. When the two girls were playing dolls in the nursery, he would sit on his big rocking horse, charging madly into space, with a frenzy that made the little girls peer at him uneasily. Wildly the horse careered, the waving dark hair of the boy tossed, his eyes had a strange glare in them. The little girls dared not speak to him.

When he had ridden to the end of his mad little journey, he climbed down and stood in front of his rocking horse, staring fixedly into its lowered face. Its red mouth was slightly open, its big eye was wide and glassy-bright.

"Now!" he would silently command the snorting steed. "Now, take me to where there is luck! Now take me!"

And he would slash the horse on the neck with the little whip he had asked Uncle Oscar for. He *knew* the horse could take him to where there was luck, if only he forced it. So he would mount again, and start on his furious ride, hoping at last to get there. He knew he could get there.

"You'll break your horse, Paul!" said the nurse.

"He's always riding like that! I wish he'd leave off!" said his elder sister Joan.

But he only glared down on them in silence. Nurse gave him up. She could make nothing of him. Anyhow he was growing beyond her.

One day his mother and his Uncle Oscar came in when he was on one of his furious rides. He did not speak to them.

"Hallo, you young jockey! Riding a winner?" said his uncle.

"Aren't you growing too big for a rocking horse? You're not a very little boy any longer, you know," said his mother.

But Paul only gave a blue glare from his big, rather close-set eyes. He would speak to nobody when he was in full tilt. His mother watched him with an anxious expression on her face.

At last he suddenly stopped forcing his horse into the mechanical gallop, and slid down.

"Well, I got there!" he announced fiercely, his blue eyes still flaring, and his sturdy long legs straddling apart.

"Where did you get to?" asked his mother.

"Where I wanted to go," he flared back at her.

"That's right, son!" said Uncle Oscar. "Don't you stop till you get there. What's the horse's name?"

"He doesn't have a name," said the boy.

"Gets on without all right?" asked the uncle.

"Well, he has different names. He was called Sansovino last week."

"Sansovino, eh? Won the Ascot.[1] How did you know his name?"

"He always talks about horse races with Bassett," said Joan.

The uncle was delighted to find that his small nephew was posted with all the racing news. Bassett, the young gardener, who had been wounded in the left foot in the war and had got his present job through Oscar Cresswell, whose batman[2] he had been, was a perfect blade of the "turf."[3] He lived in the racing events, and the small boy lived with him.

Oscar Cresswell got it all from Bassett.

"Master Paul comes and asks me, so I can't do more than tell him, sir," said Bassett, his face terribly serious, as if he were speaking of religious matters.

"And does he ever put anything on a horse he fancies?"

"Well—I don't want to give him away— he's a young sport, a fine sport, sir. Would you mind asking him yourself? He sort of takes a pleasure in it, and perhaps he'd feel I was giving him away, sir, if you don't mind.

Bassett was serious as a church.

The uncle went back to his nephew and took him off for a ride in the car.

"Say, Paul, old man, do you ever put anything on a horse?" the uncle asked.

The boy watched the handsome man closely.

"Why, do you think I oughtn't to?" he parried.

"Not a bit of it! I thought perhaps you might give me a tip for the Lincoln."

The car sped on into the country, going down to Uncle Oscar's place in Hampshire.

"Honor bright?" said the nephew.

"Honor bright, son!" said the uncle.

"Well, then, Daffodil."

"Daffodil! I doubt it, sonny. What about Mirza?"

"I only know the winner," said the boy. "That's Daffodil."

"Daffodil, eh?"

There was a pause. Daffodil was an obscure horse comparatively.

"Uncle!"

"Yes, son?"

---

1. **Ascot:** a prestigious thoroughbred horse race.

2. **batman:** a military officer's orderly.
3. **turf:** the racing world.

"You won't let it go any further, will you? I promised Bassett."

"Bassett be damned, old man! What's he got to do with it?"

"We're partners. We've been partners from the first. Uncle, he lent me my first five shillings, which I lost. I promised him, honor bright, it was only between me and him; only you gave me that ten-shilling note I started winning with, so I thought you were lucky. You won't let it go any further, will you?"

The boy gazed at his uncle from those big, hot, blue eyes, set rather close together. The uncle stirred and laughed uneasily.

"Right you are, son! I'll keep your tip private. Daffodil, eh? How much are you putting on him?"

"All except twenty pounds," said the boy. "I keep that in reserve."

The uncle thought it a good joke.

"You keep twenty pounds in reserve, do you, you young romancer? What are you betting, then?"

"I'm betting three hundred," said the boy, gravely. "But it's between you and me, Uncle Oscar! Honor bright?"

The uncle burst into a roar of laughter.

"It's between you and me all right, you young Nat Gould,"[4] he said, laughing. "But where's your three hundred?"

"Bassett keeps it for me. We're partners."

"You are, are you! And what is Bassett putting on Daffodil?"

"He won't go quite as high as I do, I expect. Perhaps he'll go a hundred and fifty."

"What, pennies?" laughed the uncle.

"Pounds," said the child, with a surprised look at his uncle. "Bassett keeps a bigger reserve than I do."

Between wonder and amusement Uncle Oscar was silent. He pursued the matter no further, but he determined to take his nephew with him to the Lincoln races.

"Now, son," he said, "I'm putting twenty

on Mirza, and I'll put five for you on any horse you fancy. What's your pick?"

"Daffodil, Uncle."

"No, not the fiver on Daffodil!"

"I should if it was my own fiver," said the child.

"Good! Good! Right you are! A fiver for me and a fiver for you on Daffodil."

The child had never been to a race meeting before, and his eyes were blue fire. He pursed his mouth tight, and watched. A Frenchman just in front had put his money on Lancelot. Wild with excitement, he flayed his arms up and down, yelling *Lancelot! Lancelot!* in his French accent.

Daffodil came in first, Lancelot second, Mirza third. The child, flushed and with eyes blazing, was curiously serene. His uncle brought him four five-pound notes, four to one.

"What am I to do with these?" he cried, waving them before the boy's eyes.

"I suppose we'll talk to Bassett," said the boy. "I expect I have fifteen hundred now; and twenty in reserve; and this twenty."

His uncle studied him for some moments.

"Look here, son!" he said. "You're not serious about Bassett and that fifteen hundred, are you?"

"Yes, I am. But it's between you and me, Uncle. Honor bright!"

"Honor bright all right, son! But I must talk to Bassett."

"If you'd like to be a partner, Uncle, with Bassett and me, we could all be partners. Only, you'd have to promise, honor bright, Uncle, not to let it go beyond us three. Bassett and I are lucky, and you must be lucky, because it was your ten shillings I started winning with. . . ."

Uncle Oscar took both Bassett and Paul into Richmond Park for an afternoon, and there they talked.

"It's like this, you see, sir," Bassett said. "Master Paul would get me talking about racing events, spinning yarns, you know, sir. And he was always keen on knowing if I'd

---

4. **Nat Gould:** a famous authority on racing.

made or if I'd lost. It's about a year since, now, that I put five shillings on Blush of Dawn for him—and we lost. Then the luck turned, with that ten shillings he had from you, that we put on Singhalese. And since that time, it's been pretty steady, all things considering. What do you say, Master Paul?"

"We're all right when we're sure," said Paul. "It's when we're not quite sure that we go down."

"Oh, but we're careful then," said Bassett.

"But when are you *sure?*" smiled Uncle Oscar.

"It's Master Paul, sir," said Bassett, in a secret, religious voice. "It's as if he had it from heaven. Like Daffodil, now, for the Lincoln. That was as sure as eggs."

"Did you put anything on Daffodil?" asked Oscar Cresswell.

"Yes, sir. I made my bit."

"And my nephew?"

Bassett was obstinately silent, looking at Paul.

"I made twelve hundred, didn't I, Bassett? I told Uncle I was putting three hundred on Daffodil."

"That's right," said Bassett, nodding.

"But where's the money?" asked the uncle.

"I keep it safe locked up, sir. Master Paul he can have it any minute he likes to ask for it."

"What, fifteen hundred pounds?"

"And twenty! And *forty,* that is, with the twenty he made on the course."

"It's amazing!" said the uncle.

"If Master Paul offers you to be partners, sir, I would, if I were you; if you'll excuse me," said Bassett.

Oscar Cresswell thought about it.

"I'll see the money," he said.

They drove home again, and sure enough, Bassett came round to the garden house with fifteen hundred pounds in notes. The twenty pounds reserve was left with Joe Glee, in the Turf Commission deposit.

"You see, it's all right, Uncle, when I'm *sure!* Then we go strong, for all we're worth. Don't we, Bassett?"

"We do that, Master Paul."

"And when are you sure?" said the uncle, laughing.

"Oh, well, sometimes I'm *absolutely* sure, like about Daffodil," said the boy; "and sometimes I have an idea; and sometimes I haven't even an idea, have I, Bassett? Then we're careful, because we mostly go down."

"You do, do you! And when you're sure, like about Daffodil, what makes you sure, sonny?"

"Oh, well, I don't know," said the boy uneasily. "I'm sure, you know, Uncle; that's all."

"It's as if he had it from heaven, sir," Bassett reiterated.

"I should say so!" said the uncle.

But he became a partner. And when the Leger was coming on, Paul was "sure" about Lively Spark, which was a quite inconsiderable horse. The boy insisted on putting a thousand on the horse, Bassett went for five hundred, and Oscar Cresswell two hundred. Lively Spark came in first, and the betting had been ten to one against him. Paul had made ten thousand.

"You see," he said, "I was absolutely sure of him."

Even Oscar Cresswell had cleared two thousand.

"Look here, son," he said, "this sort of thing makes me nervous."

"It needn't, Uncle! Perhaps I shan't be sure again for a long time."

"But what are you going to do with your money?" asked the uncle.

"Of course," said the boy, "I started it for Mother. She said she had no luck, because Father is unlucky, so I thought if *I* was lucky, it might stop whispering."

"What might stop whispering?"

"Our house. I *hate* our house for whispering."

"What does it whisper?"

"Why—why"—the boy fidgeted—"why, I don't know. But it's always short of money, you know, Uncle."

"I know it, son, I know it."

"You know people send mother writs, don't you, Uncle?"

"I'm afraid I do," said the uncle.

"And then the house whispers, like people laughing at you behind your back. It's awful, that is! I thought if I was lucky . . ."

"You might stop it," added the uncle.

The boy watched him with big blue eyes, that had an uncanny cold fire in them, and he said never a word.

"Well, then!" said the uncle. "What are we doing?"

"I shouldn't like Mother to know I was lucky," said the boy.

"Why not, son?"

"She'd stop me."

"I don't think she would."

"Oh!"—and the boy writhed in an odd way—"I *don't* want her to know, Uncle."

"All right, son! We'll manage it without her knowing."

They managed it very easily. Paul, at the other's suggestion, handed over five thousand pounds to his uncle, who deposited it with the family lawyer, who was then to inform Paul's mother that a relative had put five thousand pounds into his hands, which sum was to be paid out a thousand pounds at a time, on the mother's birthday, for the next five years.

"So she'll have a birthday present of a thousand pounds for five successive years," said Uncle Oscar. "I hope it won't make it all the harder for her later."

Paul's mother had her birthday in November. The house had been "whispering" worse than ever lately, and, even in spite of his luck, Paul could not bear up against it. He was very anxious to see the effect of the birthday letter, telling his mother about the thousand pounds.

When there were no visitors, Paul now took his meals with his parents, as he was beyond the nursery control. His mother went into town nearly every day. She had discovered that she had an odd knack of sketching furs and dress materials, so she worked secretly in the studio of a friend who was the chief "artist" for the leading drapers. She drew the figures of ladies in furs and ladies in silk and sequins for the newspaper advertisements. This young woman artist earned several thousand pounds a year, but Paul's mother only made several hundreds, and she was again dissatisfied. She so wanted to be first in something, and she did not succeed, even in making sketches for drapery advertisements.

She was down to breakfast on the morning of her birthday. Paul watched her face as she read her letters. He knew the lawyer's letter. As his mother read it, her face hardened and became more expressionless. Then a cold, determined look came on her mouth. She hid the letter under the pile of others, and said not a word about it.

"Didn't you have anything nice in the post for your birthday, Mother?" said Paul.

"Quite moderately nice," she said, her voice cold and absent.

She went away to town without saying more.

But in the afternoon Uncle Oscar appeared. He said Paul's mother had had a long interview with the lawyer, asking if the whole five thousand could not be advanced at once, as she was in debt.

"What do you think, Uncle?" said the boy.

"I leave it to you, son."

"Oh, let her have it, then! We can get some more with the other," said the boy.

"A bird in the hand is worth two in the bush, laddie!" said Uncle Oscar.

"But I'm sure to *know* for the Grand National; or the Lincolnshire; or else the Derby. I'm sure to know for *one* of them," said Paul.

So Uncle Oscar signed the agreement, and Paul's mother touched the whole five thousand. Then something very curious happened. The voices in the house suddenly went mad, like a chorus of frogs on a spring evening. There were certain new furnishings, and Paul had a tutor. He was *really* going to Eton, his father's school, in the following autumn.

There were flowers in the winter, and a blossoming of the luxury Paul's mother had been used to. And yet the voices in the house, behind the sprays of mimosa and almond blossom, and from under the piles of iridescent cushions, simply trilled and screamed in a sort of ecstasy: "There *must* be more money! Oh-h-h; there *must* be more money. Oh, now, now-w! Now-w-w—there *must* be more money!—more than ever! More than ever!"

It frightened Paul terribly. He studied away at his Latin and Greek with his tutors. But his intense hours were spent with Bassett. The Grand National had gone by: he had not "known," and had lost a hundred pounds. Summer was at hand. He was in agony for the Lincoln. But even for the Lincoln he didn't "know," and he lost fifty pounds. He became wild-eyed and strange, as if something were going to explode in him.

"Let it alone, son! Don't you bother about it!" urged Uncle Oscar. But it was as if the boy couldn't really hear what his uncle was saying.

"I've got to know for the Derby! I've got to know for the Derby!" the child reiterated, his big blue eyes blazing with a sort of madness.

His mother noticed how overwrought he was.

"You'd better go to the seaside. Wouldn't you like to go now to the seaside, instead of waiting? I think you'd better," she said, looking down at him anxiously, her heart curiously heavy because of him.

But the child lifted his uncanny blue eyes.

"I couldn't possibly go before the Derby, Mother!" he said. "I couldn't possibly!"

"Why not?" she said, her voice becoming heavy when she was opposed. "Why not? You can still go from the seaside to see the Derby with your Uncle Oscar, if that's what you wish. No need for you to wait here. Besides, I think you care too much about these races. It's a bad sign. My family has been a gambling family, and you won't know till you grow up how much damage it has done. But it has done damage. I shall have to send Bassett away, and ask Uncle Oscar not to talk racing to you, unless you promise to be reasonable about it; go away to the seaside and forget it. You're all nerves!"

"I'll do what you like, Mother, so long as you don't send me away till after the Derby," the boy said.

"Send you away from where? Just from this house?"

"Yes," he said, gazing at her.

"Why, you curious child, what makes you care about this house so much, suddenly? I never knew you loved it."

He gazed at her without speaking. He had a secret within a secret, something he had not divulged, even to Bassett or to his Uncle Oscar.

But his mother, after standing undecided and a little bit sullen for some moments, said:

"Very well, then! Don't go to the seaside till after the Derby, if you don't wish it. But promise me you won't let your nerves go to pieces. Promise you won't think so much about horse racing and *events*, as you call them!"

"Oh, no," said the boy casually. "I won't think much about them, Mother. You needn't worry. I wouldn't worry, Mother, if I were you."

"If you were me and I were you," said his mother, "I wonder what we *should* do!"

"But you know you needn't worry, Mother, don't you?" the boy repeated.

"I should be awfully glad to know it," she said wearily.

"Oh, well, you *can*, you know. I mean, you *ought* to know you needn't worry," he insisted.

"Ought I? Then I'll see about it," she said.

Paul's secret of secrets was his wooden horse, that which had no name. Since he was emancipated from a nurse and a nursery governess, he had had his rocking horse removed to his own bedroom at the top of the house.

"Surely, you're too big for a rocking horse!" his mother had remonstrated.

"Well, you see, Mother, till I can have a *real*

horse, I like to have *some* sort of animal about," had been his quaint answer.

"Do you feel he keeps you company?" she laughed.

"Oh, yes! He's very good, he always keeps me company, when I'm there," said Paul.

So the horse, rather shabby, stood in an arrested prance in the boy's bedroom.

The Derby was drawing near, and the boy grew more and more tense. He hardly heard what was spoken to him, he was very frail, and his eyes were really uncanny. His mother had sudden strange seizures of uneasiness about him. Sometimes, for half an hour, she would feel a sudden anxiety about him that was almost anguish. She wanted to rush to him at once, and know he was safe.

Two nights before the Derby, she was at a big party in town, when one of her rushes of anxiety about her boy, her firstborn, gripped her heart till she could hardly speak. She fought with the feeling, might and main, for she believed in common sense. But it was too strong. She had to leave the dance and go downstairs to telephone to the country. The children's nursery governess was terribly surprised and startled at being rung up in the night.

"Are the children all right, Miss Wilmot?"

"Oh, yes, they are quite all right."

"Master Paul? Is he all right?"

"He went to bed as right as a trivet. Shall I run up and look at him?"

"No," said Paul's mother reluctantly. "No! Don't trouble. It's all right. Don't sit up. We shall be home fairly soon." She did not want her son's privacy intruded upon.

"Very good," said the governess.

It was about one o'clock when Paul's mother and father drove up to their house. All was still. Paul's mother went to her room and slipped off her white fur cloak. She had told her maid not to wait up for her. She heard her husband downstairs, mixing a whiskey-and-soda.

And then, because of the strange anxiety at her heart, she stole upstairs to her son's room.

Noiselessly she went along the upper corridor. Was there a faint noise? What was it?

She stood, with arrested muscles, outside his door, listening. There was a strange, heavy, and yet not loud noise. Her heart stood still. It was a soundless noise, yet rushing and powerful. Something huge, in violent, hushed motion. What was it? What in God's name was it? She ought to know. She felt that she knew the noise. She knew what it was.

Yet she could not place it. She couldn't say what it was. And on and on it went, like a madness.

Softly, frozen with anxiety and fear, she turned the door handle.

The room was dark. Yet in the space near the window, she heard and saw something plunging to and fro. She gazed in fear and amazement.

Then suddenly she switched on the light, and saw her son, in his green pajamas, madly surging on the rocking horse. The blaze of light suddenly lit him up, as he urged the wooden horse, and lit her up, as she stood, blond, in her dress of pale green and crystal, in the doorway.

"Paul!" she cried. "Whatever are you doing?"

"It's Malabar!" he screamed, in a powerful, strange voice. "It's Malabar!"

His eyes blazed at her for one strange and senseless second, as he ceased urging his wooden horse. Then he fell with a crash to the ground, and she, all her tormented motherhood flooding upon her, rushed to gather him up.

But he was unconscious, and unconscious he remained, with some brain fever. He talked and tossed, and his mother sat stonily by his side.

"Malabar! It's Malabar! Bassett, Bassett, I *know*! It's Malabar!"

So the child cried, trying to get up and urge the rocking horse that gave him his inspiration.

"What does he mean by Malabar?" asked the heartbroken mother.

"I don't know," said the father stonily.

"What does he mean by Malabar?" she asked her brother Oscar.

"It's one of the horses running for the Derby," was the answer.

And, in spite of himself, Oscar Cresswell spoke to Bassett, and himself put a thousand on Malabar: at fourteen to one.

The third day of the illness was critical: they were waiting for a change. The boy, with his rather long, curly hair, was tossing ceaselessly on the pillow. He neither slept nor regained consciousness, and his eyes were like blue stones. His mother sat, feeling her heart had gone, turned actually into a stone.

In the evening, Oscar Cresswell did not come, but Bassett sent a message, saying could he come up for one moment, just one moment? Paul's mother was very angry at the intrusion, but on second thought she agreed. The boy was the same. Perhaps Bassett might bring him to consciousness.

The gardener, a shortish fellow with a little brown mustache, and sharp little brown eyes, tiptoed into the room, touched his imaginary cap to Paul's mother, and stole to the bedside, staring with glittering, smallish eyes, at the tossing, dying child.

"Master Paul!" he whispered. "Master Paul!

Malabar came in first all right, a clean win. I did as you told me. You've made over seventy thousand pounds, you have; you've got over eighty thousand. Malabar came in all right, Master Paul."

"Malabar! Malabar! Did I say Malabar, Mother? Did I say Malabar? Do you think I'm lucky, Mother? I knew Malabar, didn't I? Over eighty thousand pounds! I call that lucky, don't you, Mother? Over eighty thousand pounds! I knew, didn't I know I knew! Malabar came in all right. If I ride my horse till I'm sure, then I tell you, Bassett, you can go as high as you like. Did you go for all you were worth, Bassett?"

"I went a thousand on it, Master Paul."

"I never told you, Mother, that if I can ride my horse, and *get there*, then I'm absolutely sure—oh, absolutely! Mother, did I ever tell you? I *am* lucky!"

"No, you never did," said the mother.

But the boy died in the night.

And even as he lay dead, his mother heard her brother's voice saying to her: "My God, Hester, you're eighty-odd thousand to the good, and a poor devil of a son to the bad. But, poor devil, poor devil, he's best gone out of a life where he rides his rocking horse to find a winner."

D. H. Lawrence 737

COMMENTARY

At first glance "The Rocking-Horse Winner" seems a simple, almost fairy-tale-like story. The son of a disappointed and greedy woman comes to share her obsession about money—to such an extent that he begins to hear voices insisting, "There must be more money!" Believing that the magic of his rocking horse has made it possible for him to predict winners of horse races, the boy, through sheer "luck," amasses a small fortune. His obsession produces a brain fever from which he dies.

The fairy-tale quality of the story seems to support a simple interpretation. However, Paul's "knowing" about the horses and the whisperings throughout the house represent more than an active imagination. When Paul is inspired by his rocking horse, when he is "sure," emotions and visions are unleashed, and he is invariably right, not held back by a shallow society or frustrated mother. Ironically, even Paul's mother, out of her own childhood and lost innocence, half remembers these feelings of what Lawrence calls "blood" and intuition:

It was a soundless noise, yet rushing and powerful. Something huge, in violent, hushed motion. What was it? What in God's name was it? She ought to know. She felt that she knew the noise. She knew what it was.

Yet she could not place it.

The voices Paul has heard are his mother's. It is her *will* that exerts magic in the house, that impels him to make money in a way that his mother, his uncle, indeed the whole of the mercenary society represented in the story, would approve. For Lawrence, the story's voices are ever present in life. They are what he calls "the voices of my education," the forces that completely submerge the world of feeling.

The fairy-tale mode through which Lawrence tells the story is not merely a "frame," or a way of representing the child's view of reality. The world of the story is as demonic—ridden with dark mysterious forces that control the lives of human beings—as is the world of Sleeping Beauty or Rapunzel. The *will* is for Lawrence a demonic force, originating in powerful, unconscious drives that have no name and can only be symbolized. The destructive will acts in secrecy, as Paul rides his horse in a magical tower, away from the eyes of his mother. The discovery of his act seems to break the spell: the source of magic has been exposed. For a moment the proud, cold woman is tormented into "motherhood" and rushes to pick up her unconscious child. But the harm caused is irreparable. There is no fairy-tale ending to this tragedy.

FOR STUDY AND DISCUSSION

1. Do you think the mother is to blame for her obsession with money, or do you think the fault lies with what society has led her to value?

2. The critic Robert Gorham Davis has observed that at the heart of the story "is an incapacity for love" and a search for "satisfaction instead in social status, in material display, in spending for the sake of spending." What evidence do you find to support this comment?

3. What evidence do you find to show that Paul's mother's need for money can never be satisfied? How does Lawrence use her greed to increase the tension and horror of the story?

4. Do you think Lawrence succeeds in making believable Paul's odd gift of "knowing"? What explanation is offered for Paul's "luck"?

FOR COMPOSITION

Luck and *lucky* are key terms in the story. Study the different occasions in which these words are used, and show how their meaning develops throughout the story until Paul's last words, "I *am* lucky." What significance does the repeated use of these words add to the story? Does Lawrence use the words ironically? What does the boy really need?

Katherine Mansfield

1888–1923

Katherine Mansfield
Courtesy, Alfred Knopf, Inc.

Katherine Mansfield performed for the English short story what the great Russian writer Anton Chekhov performed for the European story. In 1911, when she began to write the stories that made her famous, readers expected short stories to be "well made" with cleverly devised plots that had a beginning, a middle, and an end; with characters about whom readers could feel that they knew almost everything; often with tricky but logically constructed endings, as in the short stories of O. Henry. Mansfield took the opposite course. As far as possible, she directed herself to the untidiness of real life. She became a mistress of small gestures, tiny fragments of significance, intuitive moments. She hardly ever told a story from A to Z, but took its inner core as her theme. The truth of a situation was immensely important to her. She was very conscious of the lies that human beings tell to protect themselves, and attempted in her stories to carry the reader past these lies. Giving an intense sense of participation in life, she showed a concern with essentials only, a deep appreciation of situations that seem ordinary only on the surface. Her style, with its quick strokes, and its shifting evocative quality, is an instrument that conveys almost perfectly her special sense of life.

Katherine Mansfield's real name was Kathleen Beauchamp. Born of a wealthy family in Wellington, New Zealand, she studied in London as a young girl and later settled there. An attack of tuberculosis forced her to go to Germany to recuperate, and there she began to write. In England once again, she married the editor and critic J. Middleton Murry and became known as a literary reviewer and story writer. But appreciation of her work came too late for her to enjoy. Constantly ill, she spent most of her last years trying to regain her health in the warmer climates of Italy and France, where she died at an early age.

Katherine Mansfield wrote three volumes that are particularly notable: *The Garden Party* and *The Dove's Nest,* which contain some of her best short stories; and her *Journal,* which reveals her aims and methods as a writer and is a legacy to all short-story writers who followed her. Almost all her writing, whether fiction or nonfiction, reveals her special personality. In a memoir, her husband described her as "spontaneous as no other human being I have ever met. She seemed to adjust herself to life as a flower adjusts itself to the earth and to the sun. She suffered greatly, she delighted greatly; but her suffering and her delight were never partial, they filled the whole of her."

A Dill Pickle

And then, after six years, she saw him again. He was seated at one of those little bamboo tables decorated with a Japanese vase of paper daffodils. There was a tall plate of fruit in front of him, and very carefully, in a way she recognized immediately as his "special" way, he was peeling an orange.

He must have felt that shock of recognition in her for he looked up and met her eyes. Incredible! He didn't know her! She smiled; he frowned. She came towards him. He closed his eyes an instant, but opening them his face lit up as though he had struck a match in a dark room. He laid down the orange and pushed back his chair, and she took her little warm hand out of her muff and gave it to him.

"Vera!" he exclaimed. "How strange. Really, for a moment I didn't know you. Won't you sit down? You've had lunch? Won't you have some coffee?"

She hesitated, but of course she meant to.

"Yes, I'd like some coffee." And she sat down opposite him.

"You've changed. You've changed very much," he said, staring at her with that eager, lighted look. "You look so well. I've never seen you look so well before."

"Really?" She raised her veil and unbuttoned her high fur collar. "I don't feel very well. I can't bear this weather, you know."

"Ah, no. You hate the cold. . . ."

"Loathe it." She shuddered. "And the worst of it is that the older one grows . . ."

He interrupted her. "Excuse me," and tapped on the table for the waitress. "Please bring some coffee and cream." To her: "You are sure you won't eat anything? Some fruit, perhaps. The fruit here is very good."

"No, thanks. Nothing."

"Then that's settled." And smiling just a hint too broadly he took up the orange again. "You were saying—the older one grows—"

"The colder," she laughed. But she was thinking how well she remembered that trick of his—the trick of interrupting her—and of how it used to exasperate her six years ago. She used to feel then as though he, quite suddenly, in the middle of what she was saying, put his hand over her lips, turned from her, attended to something different, and then took his hand away, and with just the same slightly too broad smile, gave her his attention again. . . . Now we are ready. That is settled.

"The colder!" He echoed her words, laughing too. "Ah, ah. You still say the same things. And there is another thing about you that is not changed at all—your beautiful voice—your beautiful way of speaking." Now he was very grave; he leaned towards her, and she smelled the warm, stinging scent of the orange peel. "You have only to say one word and I would know your voice among all other voices. I don't know what it is—I've often wondered—that makes your voice such a—haunting memory. . . . Do you remember that first afternoon we spent together at Kew Gardens? You were so surprised because I did not know the names of any flowers. I am still just as ignorant for all your telling me. But whenever it is very fine and warm, and I see some bright colors—it's awfully strange—I hear your voice saying: 'Geranium, marigold and verbena.' And I feel those three words are all I recall of some forgotten, heavenly language. . . . You remember that afternoon?"

"Oh, yes, very well." She drew a long, soft breath, as though the paper daffodils between them were almost too sweet to bear. Yet, what had remained in her mind of that particular afternoon was an absurd scene over the tea table. A great many people taking tea in a Chinese pagoda, and he behaving like a maniac about the wasps—waving them away, flapping at them with his straw hat, serious and infuriated out of all proportion to the occasion. How delighted the sniggering tea drinkers had been. And how she had suffered.

But now, as he spoke, that memory faded. His was the truer. Yes, it had been a wonderful afternoon, full of geranium and marigold and verbena, and—warm sunshine. Her thoughts lingered over the last two words as though she sang them.

In the warmth, as it were, another memory unfolded. She saw herself sitting on a lawn. He lay beside her, and suddenly, after a long silence, he rolled over and put his head in her lap.

"I wish," he said, in a low, troubled voice, "I wish that I had taken poison and were about to die—here now!"

At that moment a little girl in a white dress, holding a long, dripping water lily, dodged from behind a bush, stared at them, and dodged back again. But he did not see. She leaned over him.

"Ah, why do you say that? I could not say that."

But he gave a kind of soft moan, and taking her hand he held it to his cheek.

"Because I know I am going to love you too much—far too much. And I shall suffer so terribly, Vera, because you never, never will love me."

He was certainly far better-looking now than he had been then. He had lost all that dreamy vagueness and indecision. Now he had the air of a man who has found his place in life, and fills it with a confidence and an assurance which was, to say the least, impressive. He must have made money, too. His clothes were admirable, and at that moment he pulled a Russian cigarette case out of his pocket.

"Won't you smoke?"

"Yes, I will." She hovered over them. "They look very good."

"I think they are. I get them made for me by a little man in St. James's Street. I don't smoke very much. I'm not like you—but when I do, they must be delicious, very fresh cigarettes. Smoking isn't a habit with me; it's

a luxury—like perfume. Are you still so fond of perfumes? Ah, when I was in Russia . . ."

She broke in: "You've really been to Russia?"

"Oh, yes. I was there for over a year. Have you forgotten how we used to talk of going there?"

"No, I've not forgotten."

He gave a strange half laugh and leaned back in his chair. "Isn't it curious. I have really carried out all those journeys that we planned. Yes, I have been to all those places that we talked of, and stayed in them long enough to—as you used to say, 'air oneself' in them. In fact, I have spent the last three years of my life traveling all the time. Spain, Corsica, Siberia, Russia, Egypt. The only country left is China, and I mean to go there, too, when the war is over."

As he spoke, so lightly, tapping the end of his cigarette against the ashtry, she felt the strange beast that had slumbered so long within her bosom stir, stretch itself, yawn, prick up its ears, and suddenly bound to its feet, and fix its longing, hungry stare upon those faraway places. But all she said was, smiling gently: "How I envy you."

He accepted that. "It has been," he said, "very wonderful—especially Russia. Russia was all that we had imagined, and far, far more. I even spent some days on a riverboat on the Volga. Do you remember that boatman's song that you used to play?"

"Yes." It began to play in her mind as she spoke.

"Do you ever play it now?"

"No, I've no piano."

He was amazed at that. "But what has become of your beautiful piano?"

She made a little grimace. "Sold. Ages ago."

"But you were so fond of music," he wondered.

"I've no time for it now," said she.

He let it go at that. "That river life," he went on, "is something quite special. After a day or two you cannot realize that you have ever known another. And it is not necessary to know the language—the life of the boat creates a bond between you and the people that's more than sufficient. You eat with them, pass the day with them, and in the evening there is that endless singing."

She shivered, hearing the boatman's song break out again loud and tragic, and seeing the boat floating on the darkening river with melancholy trees on either side. . . . "Yes, I should like that," said she, stroking her muff.

"You'd like almost everything about Russian life," he said warmly. "It's so informal, so impulsive, so free without question. And then the peasants are so splendid. They are such human beings—yes, that is it. Even the man who drives your carriage has—has some real part in what is happening. I remember the evening a party of us, two friends of mine and the wife of one of them, went for a picnic by the Black Sea. We took supper and champagne and ate and drank on the grass. And while we were eating the coachman came up. 'Have a dill pickle,' he said. He wanted to share with us. That seemed to me so right, so—you know what I mean?"

And she seemed at that moment to be sitting on the grass beside the mysteriously Black Sea, black as velvet, and rippling against the banks in silent, velvet waves. She saw the carriage drawn up to one side of the road, and the little group on the grass, their faces and hands white in the moonlight. She saw the pale dress of the woman outspread and her folded parasol, lying on the grass like a huge pearl crochet hook. Apart from them, with his supper in a cloth on his knees, sat the coachman. "Have a dill pickle," said he, and although she was not certain what a dill pickle was, she saw the greenish glass jar with a red chili like a parrot's beak glimmering through. She sucked in her cheeks; the dill pickle was terribly sour. . . .

"Yes, I know perfectly what you mean," she said.

In the pause that followed they looked at each other. In the past when they had looked at each other like that they had felt such a boundless understanding between them that their souls had, as it were, put their arms round each other and dropped into the same sea, content to be drowned, like mournful lovers. But now, the surprising thing was that it was he who held back. He who said:

"What a marvelous listener you are. When you look at me with those wild eyes I feel that I could tell you things that I would never breathe to another human being."

Was there just a hint of mockery in his voice or was it her fancy? She could not be sure.

"Before I met you," he said, "I had never spoken of myself to anybody. How well I remember one night, the night that I brought you the little Christmas tree, telling you all about my childhood. And of how I was so miserable that I ran away and lived under a cart in our yard for two days without being discovered. And you listened, and your eyes shone, and I felt that you had even made the little Christmas tree listen too, as in a fairy story."

But of that evening she had remembered a little pot of caviar. It had cost seven and sixpence. He could not get over it. Think of it—a tiny jar like that costing seven and sixpence. While she ate it he watched her, delighted and shocked.

"No, really, that is eating money. You could not get seven shillings into a little pot that size. Only think of the profit they must make. . . ." And he had begun some immensely complicated calculations. . . . But now goodbye to the caviar. The Christmas tree was on the table, and the little boy lay under the cart with his head pillowed on the yard dog.

"The dog was called Bosun," she cried delightedly.

But he did not follow. "Which dog? Had you a dog? I don't remember a dog at all."

"No, no. I mean the yard dog when you were a little boy." He laughed and snapped the cigarette case to.

"Was he? Do you know I had forgotten that. It seems such ages ago. I cannot believe that it is only six years. After I had recognized you today—I had to take such a leap—I had to take a leap over my whole life to get back to that time. I was such a kid then." He drummed on the table. "I've often thought how I must have bored you. And now I understand so perfectly why you wrote to me as you did—although at the time that letter nearly finished my life. I found it again the other day, and I couldn't help laughing as I read it. It was so clever—such a true picture of me." He glanced up. "You're not going?"

She had buttoned her collar again and drawn down her veil.

"Yes, I am afraid I must," she said, and managed a smile. Now she knew that he had been mocking.

"Ah, no, please," he pleaded. "Don't go just for a moment," and he caught up one of her gloves from the table and clutched at it as if that would hold her. "I see so few people to talk to nowadays, that I have turned into a sort of barbarian," he said. "Have I said something to hurt you?"

"Not a bit," she lied. But as she watched him draw her glove through his fingers, gently, gently, her anger really did die down, and besides, at the moment he looked more like himself of six years ago. . . .

"What I really wanted then," he said softly, "was to be a sort of carpet—to make myself into a sort of carpet for you to walk on so that you need not be hurt by the sharp stones and the mud that you hated so. It was nothing more positive than that—nothing more selfish. Only I did desire, eventually, to turn into a magic carpet and carry you away to all those lands you longed to see."

As he spoke she lifted her head as though she drank something; the strange beast in her bosom began to purr. . . .

"I felt that you were more lonely than anybody else in the world," he went on, "and yet, perhaps, that you were the only person in the world who was really, truly alive. Born out of your time," he murmured, stroking the glove, "fated."

What had she done! How had she dared to throw away her happiness like this. This was the only man who had ever understood her. Was it too late? Could it be too late? *She* was that glove that he held in his fingers. . . .

"And then the fact that you had no friends and never had made friends with people. How I understood that, for neither had I. Is it just the same now?"

"Yes," she breathed. "Just the same. I am as alone as ever."

"So am I," he laughed gently, "just the same."

Suddenly with a quick gesture he handed her back the glove and scraped his chair on the floor. "But what seemed to me so mysterious then is perfectly plain to me now. And to you, too, of course. . . . It simply was that we were such egoists, so self-engrossed, so wrapped up in ourselves that we hadn't a corner in our hearts for anybody else. Do you know," he cried, naive and hearty, and dreadfully like another side of that old self again, "I began studying a Mind System when I was in Russia, and I found that we were not peculiar at all. It's quite a well-known form of . . ."

She had gone. He sat there, thunderstruck, astounded beyond words. . . . And then he asked the waitress for his bill.

"But the cream has not been touched," he said. "Please do not charge me for it."

FOR STUDY AND DISCUSSION

1. What does the title "A Dill Pickle" suggest about the relationship between Vera and the man?
2. How would you describe the personalities of both characters? Are they both self-centered? Stingy? What does the man's habit of interrupting the conversation tell you?

FOR COMPOSITION

Katherine Mansfield uses symbols to define feelings and situations. Show how she does this with the dill pickle.

Liam O'Flaherty
1897–1984

Liam O'Flaherty (ō-flä'hĕr-tē) was born in the Aran Islands, in County Galway, off the west coast of Ireland, about which he wrote his most distinguished fiction. Gaelic was his original language, and in later years he began to write stories in this native Irish tongue. O'Flaherty enlisted in the Irish Guards following his education at University College, Dublin, and served in France. Suffering from shell shock, he was given a medical discharge in 1917. After traveling widely, he returned to Ireland and involved himself in the civil war that had broken out. Eventually, discouraged with political life, he left for England where his career as a writer began in 1923.

Many of his stories and novels are drawn from involvement in the Irish Civil War of the early 1920's. His most famous novel, *The Informer*, deals with this period in modern Irish history. His most commonly treated theme involves the conflict or struggle for survival that underlies all life, the struggle between beasts, between people, between people and nature. "The Wild Goat's Kid," a particularly fine example of his nature writing, was a favorite work of the author.

Liam O'Flaherty
UPI

The Wild Goat's Kid

Her nimble hoofs made music on the crags all winter, as she roamed along the clifftops over the sea.

During the previous autumn, when goats were mating, she had wandered away, one of a small herd that trotted gaily after a handsome fellow, with a splendid gray-black hide and winding horns. It was her first mating. Then, with the end of autumn, peasant boys came looking for their goats. The herd was broken up. The gallant buck was captured and slain by two hungry dogs from the village of Drumranny. The white goat alone remained. She had wandered too far away from her master's village. He couldn't find her. She was given up as lost.

So that she became a wild one of the cliffs, where the sea gulls and the cormorants were lords, and the great eagle of Mohur soared high over the thundering sea. Her big, soft, yellow eyes became wild from looking down often at the sea, with her long chin whiskers swaying gracefully in the wind. She was a long, slender thing, with short, straight horns and ringlets of matted hair trailing far down on either haunch.

With her tail in the air, snorting, tossing her horns, she fled when anybody approached. Her hoofs would patter over the crags until she was far away. Then she would stand on some eminence and turn about to survey the person who had disturbed her, calmly, confident in the power of her slender legs to carry her beyond pursuit.

She roamed at will. No stone fence, however high, could resist her long leap, as she sprang on muscular thighs that bent like silk. She was so supple that she could trot on the top of a thin fence, carelessly, without a sound except the gentle tapping of her delicate hoofs. She hardly ever left the clifftops. There was plenty of food there, for the winter was mild, and the leaves and grasses that grew between the crevices of the crags were flavored by the strong, salt taste of the brine carried up on the wind. She grew sleek and comely.

Towards the end of winter a subtle change came over her. Her hearing became more acute. She took fright at the least sound. She began to shun the sea except on very calm days, when it did not roar. She ate less. She grew very particular about what she ate. She hunted around a long time before she chose a morsel. She often went on her knees, reaching down into the bottom of a crevice to nibble at a brier that was inferior to the more accessible ones. She became corpulent. Her udder increased.

Winter passed. Green leaves began to sprout. Larks sang in the morning. There was sweetness in the air and a great urge of life. The white goat, one morning a little after dawn, gave birth to a gray-black kid.

The kid was born in a tiny, green glen under an overhanging ledge of low rock that sheltered it from the wind. It was a male kid, an exquisite, fragile thing, tinted delicately with many colors. His slender belly was milky-white. The insides of his thighs were of the same color. He had deep rings of gray, like bracelets, above his hoofs. He had black knee-caps on his forelegs, like pads, to protect him when he knelt to take his mother's teats into his silky, black mouth. His back and sides were gray-black. His ears were black, long, and drooping with the weakness of infancy.

The white goat bleated over him, with soft eyes and shivering flanks, gloating over the exquisite thing that had been created within her by the miraculous power of life. And she had this delicate creature all to herself, in the wild solitude of the beautiful little glen, within earshot of the murmuring sea, with little birds whistling their spring songs around about her, and the winds coming with their slow murmurs over the crags. The first tender hours of her first motherhood were undisturbed by any restraint, not even by the restraint of a mate's presence. In absolute freedom and quiet, she watched with her young.

How she maneuvered to make him stand! She breathed on him to warm him. She raised him gently with her forehead, uttering strange, soft sounds to encourage him. Then he stood up, trembling, staggering, swaying on his curiously long legs. She became very excited, rushing around him, bleating nervously, afraid that he should fall again. He fell. She was in agony. Bitter wails came from her distended jaws and she crunched her teeth. But she renewed her efforts, urging the kid to rise, to rise and live . . . to live, live, live.

He rose again. Now he was steadier. He shook his head. He wagged his long ears as his mother breathed into them. He took a few staggering steps, came to his padded knees, and rose again immediately. Slowly, gently, gradually, she pushed him towards her udder with her horns. At last he took the teat within his mouth, he pushed joyously, sank to his knees and began to drink.

She stayed with him all day in the tiny glen, just nibbling a few mouthfuls of the short grass that grew around. Most of the time she spent exercising her kid. With a great show of anxiety and importance, she brought him on little expeditions across the glen to the opposite rock, three yards away and back again. At first he staggered clumsily against her sides, and his tiny hoofs often lost their balance on tufts of grass, such was his weakness. But he gained strength with amazing speed, and the goat's joy and pride increased. She suckled and caressed him after each tiny journey.

When the sun had set he was able to walk steadily, to take little short runs, to toss his head. They lay all night beneath the shelter of the ledge, with the kid between his mother's legs, against her warm udder.

Next morning she hid him securely in a crevice of the neighboring crag, in a small groove between two flags that were covered with a withered growth of wild grass and ferns. The kid crawled instinctively into the warm hole without any resistance to the gentle push of his mother's horns. He lay down with his head towards his doubled hind legs, and closed his eyes. Then the goat scraped the grass and fern stalks over the entrance hole with her forefeet, and she hurried away to graze, as carelessly as if she had no kid hidden.

All the morning, as she grazed hurriedly and fiercely around the crag, she took great pains to pretend that she was not aware of her kid's nearness. Even when she grazed almost beside the hiding place, she never noticed him, by look or by cry. But still, she pricked her little ears at every distant sound.

At noon she took him out and gave him suck. She played with him on a grassy knoll and watched him prance about. She taught him how to rear on his hind legs and fight the air with his forehead. Then she put him back into his hiding place and returned to graze. She continued to graze until nightfall.

Just when she was about to fetch him from his hole and take him to the overhanging ledge to rest for the night, a startling sound reached her ears. It came from afar, from the south, from beyond a low fence that ran across the crag on the skyline. It was indistinct, barely audible, a deep, purring sound. But to the ears of the mother goat, it was loud and ominous as a thunderclap. It was the heavy breathing of a dog sniffing the wind.

She listened stock-still, with her head in the air and her short tail lying stiff along her back, twitching one ear. The sound came again. It was nearer. Then there was a patter of feet. Then a clumsy, black figure hurtled over the fence and dropped on to the crag, with awkward secrecy. The goat saw a black dog, a large, curly fellow, standing by the fence in the dim twilight, with his forepaw raised and his long, red tongue hanging. Then he shut his mouth suddenly, and raising his snout upwards sniffed several times, contracting his nostrils as he did so, as if in pain. Then he whined savagely, and trotted towards the goat sideways.

She snorted. It was a sharp, dull thud, like a blow from a rubber sledge. Then she rapped the crag three times with her left forefoot, loudly and sharply. The dog stood still and raised his forepaw again. He bent down his head and looked at her with narrowed eyes. Then he licked his breast and began to run swiftly to the left. He was running towards the kid's hiding place, with his tail stretched out straight and his snout to the wind.

With another fierce snort the goat charged him at full speed, in order to cut him off from his advance on the kid's hiding place. He stopped immediately when she charged. The goat halted too, five yards from the hiding place, facing the dog.

The dog stood still. His eyes wandered around in all directions, with the bashfulness of a sly brute, caught suddenly in an awkward position. Then slowly he raised his bloodshot eyes to the goat. He bared his fangs. His mane rose like a fan. His tail shot out. Picking his steps like a lazy cat, he approached her without a sound. The goat shivered along her left flank, and she snorted twice in rapid succession.

When he was within six yards of her he uttered a ferocious roar—a deep, rumbling sound in his throat. He raced towards her, and leaped clean into the air, as if she were a fence that he was trying to vault. She parried him subtly with her horns, like a sword thrust, without moving her forefeet. Her sharp horns just grazed his belly as he whizzed past her head. But the slight blow deflected his course. Instead of falling on his feet, as he had intended cunningly to do, between the goat and the kid, he was thrown to the left and fell on his side, with a thud. The goat whirled about and charged him.

But he had arisen immediately and jerked himself away, with his haunches low down, making a devilish scraping and yelping and growling noise. He wanted to terrify the kid out of his hiding place. Then it would be easy to overpower the goat, hampered by the task of hiding the kid between her legs.

The kid uttered a faint, querulous cry, but the goat immediately replied with a sharp, low cry. The kid mumbled something indistinct, and then remained silent. There was a brushing sound among the ferns that covered him. He was settling himself down farther. The goat trotted rigidly to the opposite side of the hiding place to face the dog again.

The dog had run away some distance, and lay on his belly, licking his paws. Now he meant to settle himself down properly to the prolonged attack, after the failure of his first onslaught. He yawned lazily and made peculiar mournful noises, thrusting his head into the air and twitching his snout. The goat watched every single movement and sound, with her ears thrust forward past her horns. Her great, soft eyes were very wild and timorous in spite of the valiant posture of her body, and the terrific force of the blows she delivered occasionally on the hard crag with her little hoofs.

The dog remained lying for half an hour or so, continuing his weird pantomime. The night fell completely. Everything became unreal and ghostly under the light of the distant myriads of stars. An infant moon had arisen. The sharp rushing wind and the thunder of the sea only made the silent loneliness of the night more menacing to the white goat, as she stood bravely on the limestone crag defending her newborn young. On all sides the horizon was a tumultuous line of barren crag, dented with shallow glens and seamed with low, stone fences that hung like tattered curtains against the rim of the sky.

Then the dog attacked again. Rising suddenly, he set off at a long, swinging gallop, with his head turned sideways towards the goat, whining as he ran. He ran around the goat in a wide circle, gradually increasing his speed. A white spot on his breast flashed and vanished as he rose and fell in the undulating stretches of his flight. The goat watched him, fiercely rigid from tail to snout. She pawed the crag methodically, turning around on her own ground slowly to face him.

When he passed his starting point, he was flying at full speed, a black ball shooting along the gloomy surface of the crag, with a sharp rattle of claws. The rattle of his claws, his whining and the sharp tapping of the goat's forefeet as she turned about, were the only sounds that rose into the night from this sinister engagement.

He sped round and round the goat, approaching her imperceptibly each round, until he was so close that she could see his glittering eyes and the white lather of rage on his half-open jaws. She became slightly dizzy and confused, turning about so methodically in a confined space, confused and amazed by the subtle strategy of the horrid beast. His whining grew louder and more savage. The rattle of his claws was like the clamor of hailstones driven by a wind. He was upon her.

He came in a whirl on her flank. He came with a savage roar that deafened her. She shivered and then stiffened in rigid silence to receive him. The kid uttered a shrill cry. Then the black bulk hurtled through the air, close up, with hot breathing, snarling, with reddened fangs and . . . smash.

He had dived for her left flank. But as he went past her head she turned like lightning and met him again with her horns. This time she grazed his side, to the rear of the shoulder. He yelped and tumbled sideways, rolling over twice. With a savage snort she was upon him. He was on his haunches, rising, when her horns thudded into his head. He went down again with another yelp. He rolled over and then suddenly, with amazing speed, swept to his feet, whirled about on swinging tail and dived for her flank once more. The goat uttered a shriek of terror. He had passed her horns. His fangs had embedded themselves in the matted ringlet that trailed along her right flank. The dog's flying weight, swinging onto the ringlet as he fell, brought her to her haunches.

But she was ferocious now. As she wriggled to her feet beside the rolling dog that gripped her flank, she wrenched herself around and gored him savagely in the belly. He yelled and loosed his hold. She rose on her hind legs in a flash, and with a snort she gored him again. Her sharp, pointed horns penetrated his side between the ribs. He gasped and shook his four feet in the air. Then she pounded on him with her forefeet, beating his prostrate body furiously. Her little hoofs pattered with tremendous speed for almost a minute. She beat him blindly, without looking at him.

Then she suddenly stopped. She snorted. The dog was still. She shivered and looked down at him curiously. He was dead. Her terror was passed. She lifted her right forefoot and shook it with a curious movement. Then she uttered a wild, joyous cry and ran towards her kid's hiding place.

Night passed into a glorious dawn that came over a rippling sea from the east. A wild, sweet dawn, scented with dew and the many perfumes of the germinating earth. The sleepy sun rose brooding from the sea, golden and soft, searching far horizons with its concave shafts of light. The dawn was still. Still and soft and pure.

The white goat and her kid were traveling eastwards along the clifftops over the sea. They had traveled all night, flying from the horrid carcass of the beast that lay stretched on the crag beside the little glen. Now they were far away, on the summit of the giant white Precipice of Cahir. The white goat rested to give suck to her kid, and to look out over the clifftop at the rising sun.

Then she continued her flight eastwards, pushing her tired kid gently before her with her horns.

FOR STUDY AND DISCUSSION

1. Do the actions of the animals suggest human qualities? Does the author wish us to think of the goat, the kid, and the dog as human types? Or is the story simply about the world of nature divorced from human considerations?

2. Does the conflict provide a clear distinction between good and evil? What point do you think the author is making in the story?

FOR COMPOSITION

Discuss the details used by O'Flaherty to create mood and atmosphere and to give the reader a picture of the western Irish countryside. Compare his techniques with those of Joseph Conrad in the opening paragraphs of "The Lagoon" (page 690).

Elizabeth Bowen
1898–1973

Elizabeth Bowen was born in Dublin, Ireland, of Anglo-Irish parents, who had an estate in County Cork. At the age of seven, she moved to England, and for most of her life she lived near Oxford with her husband. She began her writing career when she was twenty. The deepest influences on her writing were Henry James and Virginia Woolf, particularly the impressionism of the latter.

Elizabeth Bowen's fiction is concerned with the qualities of ordinary experience, the mysterious process of growing up and coming to understand the world as it is and not as it seems in childhood and adolescence—"the death of the heart," as she refers to it in the title of her greatest novel. Whereas the novel is reserved for the exploration of character, the short story is for Bowen "linked with poetry," bearing the qualities of the lyric, which need not be "weighed down . . . by facts, explanation, or analysis." The short story is by its nature concerned with the episode rather than the extended plot; it is "framed for simplification," centering on a single crisis to which everything in the story immediately relates. About her work Bowen said, "When I reread a story, I relive the moment from which it sprang. A scene burned itself into me, a building magnetized me, a mood or season of Nature's penetrated me, history suddenly appeared to me in some tiny act, or a face had begun to haunt me before I glanced at it." Unlike Joyce, Bowen does not make any greater claim than this for the reality or truth of her fiction. Hers is more a world of possibilities and appearances, of qualified truths and judgments. Concerned with the surface of experience, she touches the depths of character without seeking ultimate philosophical truths.

Tears, Idle Tears

Frederick burst into tears in the middle of Regent's Park. His mother, seeing what was about to happen, had cried: "Frederick, you *can't*—in the middle of Regent's Park!" Really, this was a corner, one of those lively corners just inside a big gate, where two walks meet and a bridge starts across the pretty winding lake. People were passing quickly; the bridge rang with feet. Poplars stood up like delicate green brooms; diaphanous willows whose weeping was not shocking quivered over the lake. May sun spattered gold through the breezy trees; the tulips though falling open were still gay; three girls in a long boat shot under the bridge. Frederick, knees trembling, butted towards his mother a crimson convulsed face, as though he had the idea of burying himself in her. She whipped out a handkerchief and dabbed at him with it under his gray felt hat, exclaiming meanwhile in fearful mortification: "You really haven't got to be such a *baby!*" Her tone attracted the notice of several people, who might otherwise have thought he was having something taken out of his eye.

He was too big to cry: the whole scene was disgraceful. He wore a gray flannel knickerbocker suit and looked like a schoolboy; though in fact he was seven, still doing lessons at home. His mother said to him almost every week: "I don't know what they will think when you go to school!" His tears were a shame of which she could speak to no one; no offensive weakness of body could have upset her more. Once she had got so far as taking her pen up to write to the Mother's Advice Column of a helpful woman's weekly about them. She began: "I am a widow; young, good-tempered, and my friends all tell me that I have great control. But my little boy——" She intended to sign herself "Mrs. D., Surrey." But

then she had stopped and thought no, no: after all, he is Toppy's son. . . . She was a gallant-looking, correct woman, wearing today in London a coat and skirt, a silver fox, white gloves and a dark-blue toque put on exactly right—not the sort of woman you ought to see in a park with a great blubbering boy belonging to her. She looked a mother of sons, but not of a son of this kind, and should more properly, really, have been walking a dog. "Come on!" she said, as though the bridge, the poplars, the people staring were to be borne no longer. She began to walk on quickly, along the edge of the lake, parallel with the park's girdle of trees and the dark, haughty windows of Cornwall Terrace looking at her over the red may. They had meant to go to the Zoo, but now she had changed her mind: Frederick did not deserve the Zoo.

Frederick stumbled along beside her, too miserable to notice. His mother seldom openly punished him, but often revenged herself on him in small ways. He could feel how just this was. His own incontinence in the matter of tears was as shocking to him, as bowing-down, as annulling, as it could be to her. He never knew what happened—a cold black pit with no bottom opened inside himself; a red-hot bell wire jagged up through him from the pit of his frozen belly to the caves of his eyes. Then the hot gummy rush of tears, the convulsion of his features, the terrible square grin he felt his mouth take all made him his own shameful and squalid enemy. Despair howled round his inside like a wind, and through his streaming eyes he saw everything quake. Anyone's being there—and most of all his mother—drove this catastrophe on him. He never cried like this when he was alone.

Crying made him so abject, so outcast from other people that he went on crying out of despair. His crying was not just reflex, like a baby's; it dragged up all unseemliness into view. No wonder everyone was repelled. There is something about an abject person that rouses cruelty in the kindest breast. The plate-glass windows of the lordly houses looked at him through the may trees with judges' eyes. Girls with their knees crossed, reading on the park benches, looked up with unkind smiles. His apathetic stumbling, his not seeing or caring that they had given up their trip to the Zoo, became more than Mrs. Dickinson, his mother, could bear. She pointed out, in a voice tense with dislike: "I'm not taking you to the Zoo."

"Mmmph-mmph-mmph," sobbed Frederick.

"You know, I so often wonder what your father would think."

"Mmmph-mmph-mmph."

"He used to be so proud of you. He and I used to look forward to what you'd be like when you were a big boy. One of the last things he ever said was: 'Frederick will take care of you.' You almost make me glad he's not here now."

"Oough-oough."

"What do you say?"

"I'm t-t-trying to stop."

"Everybody's looking at you, you know."

She was one of those women who have an unfailing sense of what not to say, and say it: despair, perversity or stubborn virtue must actuate them. She had a horror, also, of the abnormal and had to hit out at it before it could hit at her. Her husband, an RAF pilot who had died two days after a ghastly crash, after two or three harrowing spaces of consciousness, had never made her ashamed or puzzled her. Their intimacies, then even his death, had had a bold naturalness.

"Listen, I shall walk on ahead," said Frederick's mother, lifting her chin with that noble, decided movement so many people liked. "You stay here and look at that duck till you've stopped that noise. Don't catch me up till you have. No, I'm really ashamed of you."

She walked on. He had *not* been making, really, so very much noise. Drawing choppy breaths, he stood still and looked at the duck that sat folded into a sleek white cipher on the green grassy margin of the lake. When it rolled one eye open over a curve, something unseeing in its expression calmed him. His mother walked away under the gay tree-shadows; her step quickened lightly, the tip of her fox fur swung. She thought of the lunch she had had with Major and Mrs. Williams, the party she would be going to at five. First, she must leave Frederick at Aunt Mary's, and what would Aunt Mary say to his bloated face? She walked fast; the gap between her and Frederick widened: she was a charming woman walking by herself.

Everybody had noticed how much courage she had; they said: "How plucky Mrs. Dickinson is." It was five years since her tragedy and she had not remarried, so that her gallantness kept on coming into play. She helped a friend with a little hat shop called *Isobel* near where they lived in Surrey, bred puppies for sale and gave the rest of her time to making a man of Frederick. She smiled nicely and carried her head high. Those two days while Toppy had lain dying she had hardly turned a hair, for his sake: no one knew when he might come conscious again. When she was not by his bed she was waiting about the hospital. The chaplain hanging about her and the doctor had given thanks that there were women like this; another officer's wife who had been her friend had said she was braver than could be good for anyone. When Toppy finally died the other woman had put the unflinching widow into a taxi and driven back with her to the Dickinsons' bungalow. She kept saying: "Cry, dear, cry: you'd feel better." She made tea and clattered about, repeating: "Don't mind me, darling: just have a big cry." The strain became so great that tears streamed down her own face. Mrs. Dickinson looked past her palely, with a polite smile. The empty-feeling bungalow with its rustling curtains still smelt of Toppy's pipe; his slippers were under a chair. Then Mrs. Dickinson's friend, almost tittering with despair, thought of a poem of Tennyson's she had learnt as a child. She said:

"Where's Frederick? He's quiet. Do you think he's asleep?" The widow, rising, perfectly automatic, led her into the room where Frederick lay in his cot. A nursemaid rose from beside him, gave them one morbid look and scurried away. The two-year-old baby, flushed, and drawing up his upper lip in his sleep as his father used to do, lay curved under his blue blanket, clenching one fist on nothing. Something suddenly seemed to strike his mother, who, slumping down by the cot, ground her face and forehead into the fluffy blanket, then began winding the blanket round her two fists. Her convulsions, though proper, were fearful: the cot shook. The friend crept away into the kitchen, where she stayed an half-hour, muttering to the maid. They made more tea and waited for Mrs. Dickinson to give full birth to her grief. Then extreme silence drew them back to the cot. Mrs. Dickinson knelt asleep, her profile pressed to the blanket, one arm crooked over the baby's form. Under his mother's arm, as still as an image, Frederick lay wide awake, not making a sound. In conjunction with a certain look in his eyes, the baby's silence gave the two women the horrors. The servant said to the friend: "You would think he knew."

Mrs. Dickinson's making so few demands on pity soon rather alienated her women friends, but men liked her better for it: several of them found in her straight look an involuntary appeal to themselves alone, more exciting than coquetry, deeply, nobly exciting: several wanted to marry her. But courage had given her a new intractable kind of virgin pride: she loved it too much; she could never surrender it. "No, don't ask me that," she would say, lifting her chin and with that calm, gallant smile. "Don't spoil things. You've been splendid to me: such a support. But you see, there's Frederick. He's the man in my life now. I'm bound to put him first. That wouldn't be fair, would it?" After that, she would simply go on shaking her head. She became the perfect friend for men who wished to wish to marry but were just as glad not to, and for married men who liked just a little pathos without being upset.

Frederick had stopped crying. This left him perfectly blank, so that he stared at the duck with abstract intensity, perceiving its molded feathers and porcelain-smooth neck. The burning, swirling film had cleared away from his eyes, and his diaphragm felt relief, as when retching has stopped. He forgot his focus of grief and forgot his mother, but saw with joy a quivering bough of willow that, drooping into his gaze under his swollen eyelids, looked as pure and strong as something after the Flood. His thought clutched at the willow, weak and wrecked but happy. He knew he was now qualified to walk after his mother, but without feeling either guilty or recalcitrant did not wish to do so. He stepped over the rail—no park keeper being at hand to stop him—and, tenderly and respectfully, attempted to touch the white duck's tail. Without a blink, with automatic uncoyness, the duck slid away from Frederick into the lake. Its lovely white china body balanced on the green glass water as it propelled itself gently round the curve of the bank. Frederick saw with a passion of observation its shadowy webbed feet lazily striking out.

"The keeper'll eat you," said a voice behind him.

Frederick looked cautiously round with his bunged-up eyes. The *individual* who had spoken sat on a park bench; it was a girl with a dispatch case beside her. Her big bony knee joints stuck out through her thin crepe de Chine dress; she was hatless and her hair made a frizzy, pretty outline, but she wore spectacles, her skin had burnt dull red: her smile and the cock of her head had about them something pungent and energetic, not like a girl's at all. "Whatcher mean, eat me?"

"You're on his grass. And putting salt on his duck's tail."

Frederick stepped back carefully over the low rail. "I haven't got any salt." He looked up and down the walk: his mother was out of sight but from the direction of the bridge a keeper was approaching, still distant but with an awesome gait. "My goodness," the girl said, "what's been biting *you?*" Frederick was at a loss. "Here," she said, "have an apple." She opened her case, which was full of folded grease paper that must have held sandwiches, and rummaged out an apple with a waxy, bright skin. Frederick came up, tentative as a pony, and finally took the apple. His breath was still hitching and catching; he did not wish to speak.

"Go on," she said, "swallow: it'll settle your chest. Where's your mother gone off to? What's all the noise about?" Frederick only opened his jaws as wide as they would go, then bit slowly, deeply into the apple. The girl recrossed her legs and tucked her thin crepe de Chine skirt round the other knee. "What had you done—cheeked her?"

Frederick swept the mouthful of apple into one cheek. "No," he said shortly. "Cried."

"I should say you did. Bellowed. I watched you all down the path." There was something ruminative in the girl's tone that made her remark really not at all offensive; in fact, she looked at Frederick as though she were meeting an artist who had just done a turn. He had been standing about, licking and biting the apple, but now he came and sat down at the other end of the bench. "How do you do it?" she said.

Frederick only turned away: his ears began burning again.

"What gets at you?" she said.

"Don't know."

"Someone coming it over you? I know another boy who cries like you, but he's older. He knots himself up and bellows."

"What's his name?"

"George."

"Does he go to school?"

"Oh, no; he's a boy at the place where I used to work." She raised one arm, leaned back, and watched four celluloid bangles, each of a different color, slide down it to her elbow joint, where they stuck. "He doesn't know why he does it," she said, "but he's got to. It's

as though he saw something. You can't ask him. Some people take him that way: girls do. I never did. It's as if he knew about something he'd better not. I said once, well, what just *is* it, and he said if he *could* tell me he wouldn't do it. I said, well, what's the *reason,* and he said, well, what's the reason not to? I knew him well at one time."

Frederick spat out two pips, looked round cautiously for the keeper, then dropped the apple core down the back of the seat. "Where's George live?"

"I don't know now," she said, "I often wonder. I got sacked from that place where I used to work, and he went right off and I never saw him again. You snap out of that, if you can, before you are George's age. It does you no good. It's all in the way you see things. Look, there's your mother back. Better move, or there'll be *more* trouble." She held out her hand to Frederick, and when he put his in it shook hands so cheerfully, with such tough decision, that the four celluloid bangles danced on her wrist. "You and George," she said. "Funny to meet two of you. Well, goodbye, Henry: cheer up."

"I'm Frederick."

"Well, cheer up, Freddie."

As Frederick walked away, she smoothed down the sandwich papers inside her dispatch case and snapped the case shut again. Then she put a finger under her hair at each side, to tuck her spectacles firmly down on her ears. Her mouth, an unreddened line across her harshly burnt face, still wore the same truculent, homely smile. She crossed her arms under the flat chest, across her stomach, and sat there holding her elbows idly, wagging one foot in its fawn sandal, looking fixedly at the lake through her spectacles, wondering about George. She had the afternoon, as she had no work. She saw George's face lifted abjectly from his arms on a table, blotchy over his clerk's collar. The eyes of George and Frederick seemed to her to be wounds in the world's surface, through which its inner, terrible, unassuageable, necessary sorrow constantly bled away and as constantly welled up.

Mrs. Dickinson came down the walk under the band of trees, carefully unanxious, looking lightly at objects to see if Frederick were near them; he had been a long time. Then she saw Frederick shaking hands with a sort of girl on a bench and starting to come her way. So she quickly turned her frank, friendly glance on the lake, down which, as though to greet her, a swan came swimming. She touched her fox fur lightly, sliding it up her shoulder. What a lovely mother to have. "Well, Frederick," she said, as he came into earshot, "coming?" Wind sent a puff of red mayflowers through the air. She stood still and waited for Frederick to come up. She could not think what to do now: they had an hour to put in before they were due at Aunt Mary's. But this only made her manner calmer and more decisive.

Frederick gave a great skip, opened his mouth wide, shouted: "Oo, I say, Mother, I nearly caught a duck!"

"Frederick, dear, how silly you are: you couldn't."

"Oo, yes, I could, I could. If I'd had salt for its tail!" Years later, Frederick could still remember, with ease, pleasure and with a sense of lonely shame being gone, that calm white duck swimming off round the bank. But George's friend with the bangles, and George's trouble, fell through a cleft in his memory and were forgotten soon.

FOR STUDY AND DISCUSSION

1. How would you describe the character and personality of Frederick's mother? What qualities of character keep her from crying over her husband's death?
2. Does Frederick recognize the cause of his sudden fits of crying? What is the point of the scene in which his mother seems to repress her grief as she falls asleep beside the two-year-old Frederick?
3. In what ways does Mrs. Dickinson's reaction to Frederick's crying contrast with the reaction of the girl on the bench?
4. Laurence Perrine has suggested that the theme of the story might be expressed this way:

A boy whose irrational behavior is only aggravated by attempts to make him feel guilty and ashamed may be cured when his behavior is accepted calmly and he learns that it is not unique.

Explain why you agree or disagree with this interpretation.
5. What might the duck represent for Frederick? Why do you suppose Frederick forgets about the girl with the bangles?
6. The title of the story alludes to Tennyson's poem of the same name. How might this allusion be relevant to the meaning of the story?

FOR COMPOSITION

After the death of Frederick's father, Mrs. Dickinson's friend is reminded of "a poem of Tennyson's," apparently "Home They Brought Her Warrior Dead":

Home they brought her warrior dead,
She nor swooned nor uttered cry.
All her maidens, watching, said,
"She must weep or she will die."

Then they praised him, soft and low,   5
Called him worthy to be loved,
Truest friend and noblest foe;
Yet she neither spoke nor moved.

Stole a maiden from her place,
Lightly to the warrior stepped,   10
Took the face cloth from the face;
Yet she neither moved nor wept.

Rose a nurse of ninety years,
Set his child upon her knee—
Like summer tempest came her tears—   15
"Sweet my child, I live for thee."

In an essay explain the relation of the poem to events in the story.

Frank O'Connor
1903–1966

Frank O'Connor is generally regarded as one of the best short-story writers of the twentieth century. His stories have an outstanding honesty and craftsmanship about them and reveal a deep knowledge of modern Ireland. O'Connor was a born storyteller, and he wrote with a refreshing directness and lack of pretension. As a short-story writer, he declared himself a follower of the great Russian writer Anton Chekhov, who, more than anyone else, turned writers away from the neatly plotted, "well-made" story and created the modern short story. O'Connor once wrote that the short story "is the nearest thing one can get to the quality of a pure lyric poem. It doesn't deal with problems; it doesn't have any solutions to offer; it just states the human condition."

Frank O'Connor was the pseudonym adopted by Michael O'Donovan, who was born and grew up in Cork, Ireland. His childhood was the classic childhood of the underprivileged Irish at the turn of the century: the father a laborer, the mother going out to work as a cleaning woman, the child's future darkened by the difficulty of getting an education and by the narrowness of a life in which money is a perpetual problem. Michael O'Donovan did, however, receive an elementary education from the Christian Brothers and contrived by voracious reading to extend that education. Between odd jobs, he managed to make a start as a writer. After spending a year in jail for his political support of the Irish Republican cause, he became a librarian in Cork and in Dublin. For a time he was a director of the Abbey Theater, where he worked with William Butler Yeats. Although he collaborated on a number of plays, his main interest was in the short story.

Frank O'Connor
Department of Foreign Affairs, Ireland

During the last twenty years of his life, O'Connor lived largely in the United States, although he returned periodically to Ireland. He taught at Northwestern University and at Harvard. Most American readers came to know him from his many stories that appeared in *The New Yorker* magazine. Even while he lived in the United States, he continued to write about Ireland. "I prefer to write about Ireland and the Irish people," he said, "merely because I know to a syllable how everything in Ireland can be said." In addition to his plays and poetry, he published critical studies of the short story and the novel and several collections of verse.

Masculine Protest

For months things had been getting worse between Mother and me. At the time I was twelve, and we were living in Boharna, a small town twenty miles from the city—Father, Mother, Martha, and I. Father worked in the County Council and we didn't see much of him. I suppose that threw me more on Mother, but I could be perfectly happy sitting with her all day if only she let me. She didn't, though. She was always inventing excuses to get rid of me, even giving me money to go to the pictures, which she knew Father didn't like because I wasn't very bright at school and he thought the pictures were bad for me.

I blamed a lot of it on Martha at first. Martha was sly, and she was always trying to get inside me with Mother. She was always saving, whereas I always found money burned a hole in my pocket, and it was only to spite her that I kept a savings bank at all. As well as that, she told Mother about all the scrapes I got into. They weren't what you'd really call scrapes. It was just that we had a gang in our neighborhood, which was the classy one of the town, and we were always having battles with the slummy kids from the other side of town who wanted to play in our neighborhood. I was the Chief Gang Leader, and it was my job to keep them from expanding beyond their own frontiers.

Martha let on not to understand why I should be Chief Gang Leader. She let on not to know why we didn't want the slum kids overrunning our locality. Though she knew better than to tell Mother when I made Viking raids on the housekeeping money, she was always at me in a low, bloodcurdling voice, following me round like a witch. "You'll be caught yet, Denis Halligan. You'll be caught. The police will be after you. You took three shillings out of Mummy's purse. God sees

you!" Sometimes she drove me so wild that I went mad and twisted her arm or pulled her hair, and she went off screeching, and I got a licking.

I had managed to kid myself into the belief that one day Mother would understand; one day she would wake up and see that the affection of Dad and Martha was insincere; that the two of them had long ago ganged up against her, and that I, the black sheep, was the one who really loved her.

This revelation was due to take place in rather unusual circumstances. We were all to be stranded in some dangerous desert, and Mother, with her ankle broken, would tell us to leave her to her fate, the way they did in storybooks. Dad and Martha, of course, would leave her, with only a pretense of concern, but I, in my casual way, would simply fold my arms about my knees and ask listlessly: "What use is life to me without you?" Nothing more; I was against any false drama, any raising of the voice. I had never been one for high-flown expressions like Martha: just the lift of the shoulder, the way I pulled a grass blade to chew (it needn't be a desert), and Mother would realize at last that though I wasn't demonstrative—just a plain, rough, willing chap—I really had a heart of gold.

The trouble about Mother was that she had a genius for subjecting hearts of gold to intolerable strain. It wasn't that she was actively unkind, for she thought far too much of the impression she wanted to make to be anything like that. It was just that she didn't care. She was always away from home. She visited friends in Galway, Dublin, Birr, and Athlone, and all we ever got to see of her was the flurry between one foray and the next, while she was packing and unpacking.

Things came to a head when she told me she wouldn't be at home for my birthday. At the same time, always conscientious, she had arranged a very nice treat for Martha and me. But the treat wasn't the same thing that I had been planning, when I proposed to bring a couple of fellows along and show Mother off to them, and I began to bawl. The trouble was that the moment I did, I seemed to have no reasons on my side. It was always like that with Mother; she invariably had all the reasons on her side, and made you feel contrary and a pig, but that was worse instead of better. You felt then that she was taking advantage of you. I sobbed and stamped and asked why she hadn't done that to Martha and why she was doing it to me. She looked at me coldly and said I was a pretty picture and that I had no manliness. Of course, I saw she was in the right about that too, and that there was no excuse for a fellow of my age complaining against not being treated like his younger sister, and that only made me madder still.

"Go on!" I screamed. "Who's trying to stop you? All you want is people to admire you."

I knew when I had said it that it was awful, and expected her to give me a clout, but she only drew herself up, looking twice as dignified and beautiful.

"That is a contemptible remark, Denis," she said in a biting tone. "It's one I wouldn't have expected even from you."

The way she said it made me feel like the scum of the earth. And then she went off for the evening in a car with the Clarkes, leaving Martha and me alone. Martha looked at me, half in pity, half in amusement. She was never really disappointed in Mother, because she expected less of her. Martha was born sly.

"What did I tell you?" she said, though she hadn't told me anything.

"Go on!" I said in a thick voice. "You sucker!" Then I went upstairs and bawled and used all the dirty words I knew. I knew now it was all over between Mother and me; that no circumstances would ever occur which would show how much I loved her, because after what had happened I could not live in the same house with her again. For quite a while I

thought about suicide, but I put that on one side, because the only way I could contemplate committing suicide was by shooting, and my air pistol was not strong enough for that. I took out my post-office book. I had four pounds fifteen in the bank. As I've said, it was purely out of spite against Martha, but that made no difference now. It was enough to keep me for a month or so till I found some corner where people wanted me; a plain rough-spoken chap who only needed a little affection. I was afraid of nothing in the way of work. I was strong and energetic. At the worst, I could always make for Dublin, where my grandfather and Auntie May lived. I knew they would be glad to help me, because they thought that Dad had married the wrong woman and never pretended to like Mother. When Mother had told me this I was furious, but now I saw that they were probably cleverer than I was. It would give me great satisfaction to reach their door and tell Auntie May in my plain straightforward way: "You were right and I was wrong." For the last time I looked round my bedroom and burst into fresh tears. There is something heart-rending about leaving for the last time a place where you have spent so much of your life. Then, trying to steady myself, I grabbed a little holy picture from the mantlepiece and a favorite storybook from the bookshelf and ran downstairs. Martha heard me taking out my bike and came to see. It had a dynamo lamp and a three-speed gear; a smashing bike!

"Where are you off to?" she asked.

"Never mind!" I said as I cycled off.

I had no particular feelings about seeing Martha for the last time.

Then I had my first shock, because as I cycled into Main Street I saw that all the shops were shuttered for the weekly half-holiday and I knew the post office would be shut too and I could not draw out my savings. It was the first time I felt what people so often feel in after life, that Fate has made a plaything of you. Why should I have had my final quarrel with Mother on the one day in the week when I could not get away from her? If that wasn't Fate, what was? And I knew my own weakness of character better than anyone. I knew that if I put it off until the next day, the sight of Mother would be sufficient to set me servilely seeking for pardon. Even setting off across Ireland without a penny would be better than that.

Then I had what I thought was an inspiration. The city was only twenty miles away, and the General Post Office was bound to be open. I had calculated my time to and from school at twelve miles an hour; even allowing for the distance, it wouldn't take me more than two hours. As well as that, I had been to the city for the Christmas shopping, so I knew the look of it. I could get my money and stay in a hotel or have tea and then set off for Dublin. I liked that idea. Cycling all the way up through Ireland in the dark, through sleeping towns and villages; seeing the dawn break over Dublin as I cycled down the slopes of the Dublin mountains; arriving at Auntie May's door in the Shelbourne Road when she was lighting the fire—that would be smashing. I could imagine how she would greet me—"Child of grace, where did you come from?" "Ah, just cycled." My natural modesty always came out in those daydreams of mind, for I never, under any circumstances, made a fuss. Absolutely smashing!

All the same, it was no joke, a trip like that. I cycled slowly and undecidedly out the familiar main road where we walked on Sunday, past the little suburban houses. It was queer how hard it was to break away from places and people and things you knew. I thought of letting it go and of doing the best I could to patch it up with Mother. I thought of the gang and at that a real lump rose in my throat. Tomorrow night, when my absence was noticed, there would be a new Chief Gang Leader; somebody like Eddie Humphreys who would be so prim and cautious that he would be afraid to engage the enemy which threatened us on every side. In that moment of weakness I nearly turned back. At the same moment it brought me renewed decision, for I knew that I had not been chosen Chief Gang Leader because I was a little sissy like Eddie Humphreys but because I was afraid of nothing.

At one moment my feet had nearly stopped pedaling; at the next I was pedaling for all I was worth. It was as sudden as that, like the moment when you find yourself out of your depth and two inclinations struggle in you—to swim back to the shallows or strike out boldly for the other side. Up to that I had thought mainly of what was behind me; now I thought only of what was ahead of me, and it was frightening enough. I was aware of great distances, of big cloud masses on the horizon, of the fragility of my tires compared with the rough surface of the road, and I thought only of the two-hour journey ahead of me. The romantic picture of myself cycling across Ireland in the dark disappeared. I should be quite content to get the first stage over me.

For the last ten miles I wasn't even tempted to look at the scenery. I was doubled over the handlebars. Things just happened; the road bent away under me; wide green rivers rose up and slipped away again under me; castles soared from the roadside with great arches blocked out in masses of shadow.

Then at last the little rocky fields closed behind me like a book, and the blessed electric-light poles escorted me up the last hill, and I floated proudly down between comfortable villas with long gardens till I reached the bridge. The city was stretched out on the other side of the river, shining in the evening light, and my heart rose at the thought that I had at least shown Mother whether or not I had manliness. I dismounted from my bicycle and pushed it along the Main Street, looking at the shops. They were far more interesting than the shops at home, and the people looked better too.

I found the post office in a side street and went up to the counter with my savings-bank book.

"I want to draw out my money," I said.

Macroon, Ireland.
L. Robert Tschirky, Annan Photos/Photo Trends

The clerk looked at the clock.

"You can't do that, sonny," he said. "The savings-bank counter is shut."

"When will it open again?" I asked.

"Not till tomorrow. Any time after nine."

"But can't I get it now?"

"No. The clerk is gone home now."

I slouched out of the post office with despair in my heart. I took my bicycle and pushed it wearily back to the Main Street. The crowds were still going by, but now it looked long and wide and lonesome, for I had no money and I didn't know a soul. Without a meal and a rest, I could not even set out for Dublin, if I had the heart, which I knew I hadn't. Nor could I even return home, for it was already late and I was dropping with weariness. One side of the Main Street was in shadow; the shadow seemed to spread with extraordinary rapidity, and you felt that the city was being quenched as with snuffers.

It was only then that I thought of Father. It was funny that I had not thought of him before, even when thinking of Grandfather and Auntie May. I had thought of these as allies against Mother, but I hadn't even considered him as an ally. Now as I thought of him, everything about him seemed different. It wasn't only the hunger and panic. It was

something new for me. It was almost love. With fresh energy I pushed my bicycle back to the post office, left it outside the door where I could see it, and went up to the clerk I had already spoken to.

"Could I make a telephone call?" I asked.

"You could to be sure," he said. "Have you the money?"

"No, sir."

"Well, you can't make a call without the money. Where is it to?"

"Boharna," I said.

At once his face took on a severe expression.

"That's one and threepence," he said.

"And I can't ring unless I have the money?"

"Begor, you can't. I couldn't ring myself without that."

I went out and took my bicycle again. This time I could see no way out. I dawdled along the street, leaving my bicycle by the curb and gazing in shop windows. In one I found a mirror in which I could see myself full-length. I looked old and heartbroken. It was just like a picture of a child without a home, and I blinked away my tears.

Then, as I approached a public house, I saw a barman in shirt sleeves standing by the door. I remembered that I had seen him already on my way down and that he had looked at me. He nodded and smiled and I stopped. I was glad of anyone making a friendly gesture in that strange place.

"Are you waiting for someone?" he asked.

"No," I said. "I wanted to make a phone call."

"You're not from these parts?"

"No," I said. "I'm from Boharna."

"Are you, begor?" he said. "Was it on the bus you came?"

"No," I replied modestly. "I biked it."

"Biked it?"

"Yes."

"That's a devil of a distance," he said.

"It is long," I agreed.

"What did you come all that way for?" he asked in surprise.

"Ah, I was running away from home," I said despondently.

"You were what?" he asked in astonishment. "You're not serious."

"But I am," I said, very close to tears. "I did my best, but then I couldn't stick it any longer and I cleared out." I turned my head away because this time I was really crying.

"Oh, begor, I know what 'tis like," he said in a friendlier tone. "I did it myself."

"Did you?" I asked eagerly, forgetting my grief. This, I felt, was the very man I wanted to meet.

"Ah, indeed I did. I did it three times, what's more. By that time they were getting fed up with me. Anyway, they say practice makes perfect. Tell me, is it your old fellow?"

"No," I said with a sigh. "My mother."

"Ah, do you tell me so? That's worse again. 'Tis bad enough to have the old man at you, but 'tis the devil entirely when the mother is against you. What are you going to do now?"

"I don't know," I said. "I wanted to get to Dublin, but the savings bank is shut, and all my money is in it."

"That's tough luck. Sure, you can't get anywhere without money. I'm afraid you'll have to go back and put up with it for another while."

"But I can't," I said. "'Tis twenty miles."

"'Tis all of that, begor. You couldn't go on the bus?"

"I can't. I haven't the money. That's what I asked them in the post office, to let me ring up Daddy, but they wouldn't."

"Where's your daddy?" he asked, and when I told him: "Ah, we'll try and get him for you anyway. Come on in."

There was a phone in the corner, and he rang up and asked for Daddy. Then he gave me a big smile and handed me the receiver. I heard Daddy's voice and I nearly wept with delight.

"Hullo, Son," he said in astonishment. "Where on earth are you?"

"In the city, Daddy," I said modestly—even then I couldn't bring myself to make a lot of it, the way another fellow would.

"The city?" he repeated incredulously. "What took you there?"

"I ran away from home, Dad," I said, trying to make it sound as casual as possible.

"Oh!" he exclaimed and there was a moment's pause. I was afraid he was going to get angry, but his tone remained the same. "Had a row?"

"Yes, Dad."

"And how did you get there?"

"On the bike."

"All the way? But you must be dead."

"Just a bit tired," I said modestly.

"Tell me, did you even get a meal?"

"No, Dad. The savings bank was shut."

"Ah, blazes!" he said softly. "Of course, it's the half-day. And what are you going to do now?"

"I don't know, Dad. I thought you might tell me."

"Well, what about coming home?" he said, beginning to laugh.

"I don't mind, Dad. Whatever you say."

"Hold on now till I see what the buses are like. . . . Hullo! You can get one in forty minutes' time—seven ten. Tell the conductor I'll be meeting you and I'll pay your fare. Will that be all right?"

"That's grand, Dad," I said, feeling that the world was almost right again.

When I finished, the barman was waiting for me with his coat on. He had got another man to look after the bar for him.

"Now, you'd better come and have a cup of tea with me before your bus goes," he said. "The old bike will be safe outside."

He took me to a café, and I ate cake after cake and drank tea and he told me about how he'd run away himself. You could see he was a real hard case, worse even than I was. The first time, he'd pinched a bicycle and cycled all the way to Dublin, sleeping in barns and deserted cottages. The police had brought him home and his father had belted him. They caught him again the second time, but the third time he'd joined the army and not returned home for years.

He put me and my bicycle on the bus and paid my fare. He made me promise to tell Dad that he'd done it and that Dad owed me the money. He said in this world you had to stand up for your rights. He was a rough chap, but you could see he had a good heart. It struck me that maybe only rough chaps had hearts as good as that.

Dad was waiting for me at the bus stop, and he looked at me and laughed.

"Well, the gouger!" he said. "Who ever would think that the son of a good-living, upright man like me would turn into a common tramp."

All the same I could see he was pleased, and as he pushed my bike down the street he made me tell him all about my experiences. He laughed over the barman and promised to give me the fare. Then, seeing him so friendly, I asked the question that had been on my mind the whole way back on the bus.

"Mummy back yet, Dad?"

"No, Son," he said. "Not yet. She probably won't be in till late."

What I was really asking him, of course, was "Does she know?" and now I was torn by the desire to ask him not to tell her, but it choked me. It would have seemed too much like trying to gang up against her. But he seemed to know what I was thinking, for he added with a sort of careful casualness that he had sent Martha to the pictures. I guessed that that was to get her out of the way so that she couldn't bring the story to Mother, and when we had supper together and washed up afterwards, I knew I was right.

Mother came in before we went to bed, and Father talked to her just as though nothing had happened. He was a little bit more forthcoming than usual, but that was the only indication he gave, and I was fascinated, watching him create an understanding between us. It was an understanding in more ways than one, because it dawned on me gradually that, like myself and the barman, Dad too had once run away from home, and for some reason—perhaps because the bank was shut or because he was hungry, tired, and lonely—he had come back. People mostly came back, but their protest remained to distinguish them from all the others who had never run away. It was the real sign of their manhood.

I never ran away after that. I never felt I needed to.

FOR STUDY AND DISCUSSION

1. Denis describes himself as possessing a "weakness of character," but in his daydreams, he sees himself as "a plain rough-spoken chap," who is "strong and energetic." In what ways has Denis' mother contributed to his feeling that, in reality, he has "no manliness"?

2. Denis' running away from home, his "masculine protest," creates a bond between Denis and his father. What evidence do you find toward the end of the story to indicate their improved relationship?

FOR COMPOSITION

Explain how the story might have been different if the narrator had been Martha instead of Denis. What reasons might Martha have had for running away from home?

Frank O'Connor 761

George Orwell
1903–1950

George Orwell was a writer who disliked frills, both in life and in art. Pursuing his own brand of integrity, he liked ugly rather than beautiful rooms, worn clothes rather than new ones, and abrupt rather than ingratiating personalities. As a writer he cultivated a beautifully clear prose style and strove to cut out "all stale or mixed images, all prefabricated phrases, needless repetitions, and humbug and vagueness generally." He believed that a muddled style could lead to vague thinking and that precision in both thought and writing was one of the chief defenses against political tyranny. As a writer his chief concern was to warn against such tyranny. His two most famous books, *Animal Farm* and *Nineteen Eighty-Four*, are both reminders that no country's liberty is ever completely secure. *Animal Farm*, a brilliant fable, traces the downward path of a revolution of animals from the initial decree that "All animals are equal" to the revised version, "All animals are equal, but some are more equal than others." *Nineteen Eighty-Four* is a stern warning, a nightmarish tale of a future in which freedom has lost its meaning. Orwell was a liberal in the British sense, a firm believer in freedom and a hater of tyranny from both right and left. His main preoccupation was to save modern civilization from the results of its own follies.

"George Orwell" was the pseudonym adopted by Eric Blair. Born in India, he was sent to boarding school in England at an early age and completed his formal education at Eton. His service with the Imperial Police in Burma led not only to his essay "Shooting an Elephant" but also to a novel, *Burmese Days*. Orwell was born into "the lower upper-middle-class," the term he used to characterize people with upper-middle-class pretensions who lacked the money to live up to these pretensions. As Orwell wrote, "Theoretically you knew how to wear your clothes and how to order a good dinner, although in practice you could never afford to go to a decent tailor or a decent restaurant." Very early and in part because of his Burmese experiences, he turned against the attitudes of mind

George Orwell
British Information Service

that might have been expected of him. He chose poverty, a working-class background, and anonymity in preference to the conventional career a young man of his gifts might have followed.

In 1936, Orwell was wounded after fighting on the Loyalist side in the Spanish Civil War. He described his war experiences in one of his books, *Homage to Catalonia*. From the middle 1930's on, Orwell wrote novels and essays until ill health undermined him. He became famous only in the 1940's after *Animal Farm* and *Nineteen Eighty-Four*, his greatest success, were published. At the very end of his life he married. Through the kindness of friends he was given a home in the western islands of Scotland to fight the lung illness that finally killed him at the age of forty-six.

Shooting an Elephant

In Moulmein,[1] in Lower Burma, I was hated by large numbers of people—the only time in my life that I have been important enough for this to happen to me. I was subdivisional police officer of the town, and in an aimless, petty kind of way anti-European feeling was very bitter. No one had the guts to raise a riot, but if a European woman went through the bazaars alone somebody would probably spit betel juice over her dress. As a police officer I was an obvious target and was baited whenever it seemed safe to do so. When a nimble Burman tripped me up on the football field and the referee (another Burman) looked the other way, the crowd yelled with hideous laughter. This happened more than once. In the end the sneering yellow faces of young men that met me everywhere, the insults hooted after me when I was at a safe distance, got badly on my nerves. The young Buddhist priests were the worst of all. There were several thousands of them in the town and none of them seemed to have anything to do except stand on street corners and jeer at Europeans.

All this was perplexing and upsetting. For at that time I had already made up my mind that imperialism was an evil thing and the sooner I chucked up my job and got out of it the better. Theoretically—and secretly, of course—I was all for the Burmese and all against their oppressors, the British. As for the job I was doing, I hated it more bitterly than I can perhaps make clear. In a job like that you see the dirty work of Empire at close quarters. The wretched prisoners huddling in the stinking cages of the lockups, the gray, cowed faces of the long-term convicts, the scarred buttocks of the men who had been flogged with bamboos—all these oppressed me with an intolerable sense of guilt. But I could get nothing into perspective. I was young and ill-educated and I had had to think out my problems in the utter silence that is imposed on every Englishman in the East. I did not even know that the British Empire is dying, still less did I know that it is a great deal better than the younger empires that are going to supplant it. All I knew was that I was stuck between my hatred of the empire I served and my rage against the evil-spirited little beasts who tried to make my job impossible. With one part of my mind I thought of the British Raj[2] as an unbreakable tyranny, as something clamped down, *in saecula saeculorum,*[3] upon the will of prostrate peoples; with another part I thought that the greatest joy in the world would be to drive a bayonet into a Buddhist priest's guts. Feelings like these are the normal byproducts of imperialism; ask any Anglo-Indian official, if you can catch him off duty.

One day something happened which in a roundabout way was enlightening. It was a tiny incident in itself, but it gave me a better glimpse than I had had before of the real nature of imperialism—the real motives for which despotic governments act. Early one morning the subinspector at a police station the other end of the town rang me up on the phone and said that an elephant was ravaging the bazaar. Would I please come and do something about it? I did not know what I could do, but I wanted to see what was happening and I got onto a pony and started out. I took my rifle, an old .44 Winchester and much too small to kill an elephant, but I thought the

---

1. **Moulmein** (mo͞ol-mān′).

2. **Raj** (räj): government or rule.
3. *in saecula saeculorum* (sē′ko͞o-lə sē′ko͞o-lôr′əm): forever and ever (Latin).

noise might be useful *in terrorem*.[4] Various Burmans stopped me on the way and told me about the elephant's doings. It was not, of course, a wild elephant, but a tame one which had gone "must."[5] It had been chained up as tame elephants always are when their attack of "must" is due, but on the previous night it had broken its chain and escaped. Its mahout,[6] the only person who could manage it when it was in that state, had set out in pursuit, but he had taken the wrong direction and was now twelve hours' journey away, and in the morning the elephant had suddenly reappeared in the town. The Burmese population had no weapons and were quite helpless against it. It had already destroyed somebody's bamboo hut, killed a cow and raided some fruit stalls and devoured the stock; also it had met the municipal rubbish van, and, when the driver jumped out and took to his heels, had turned the van over and inflicted violence upon it.

The Burmese subinspector and some Indian constables were waiting for me in the quarter where the elephant had been seen. It was a very poor quarter, a labyrinth of squalid bamboo huts, thatched with palm leaf, winding all over a steep hillside. I remember that it was a cloudy stuffy morning at the beginning of the rains. We began questioning the people as to where the elephant had gone, and, as usual, failed to get any definite information. That is invariably the case in the East; a story always sounds clear enough at a distance, but the nearer you get to the scene of events the vaguer it becomes. Some of the people said that the elephant had gone in one direction, some said that he had gone in another, some professed not even to have heard of any elephant. I had almost made up my mind that the whole story was a pack of lies, when we heard yells a little distance away. There was a loud, scandalized cry of "Go away, child! Go away this instant!" and an old woman with a switch in her hand came round the corner of a hut, violently shooing away a crowd of naked children. Some more women followed, clicking their tongues and exclaiming; evidently there was something there that the children ought not to have seen. I rounded the hut and saw a man's dead body sprawling in the mud. He was an Indian, a black Dravidian[7] coolie, almost naked, and he could not have been dead many minutes. The people said that the elephant had come suddenly upon him round the corner of the hut, caught him with its trunk, put its foot on his back and ground him into the earth. This was the rainy season and the ground was soft, and his face had scored a trench a foot deep and a couple of yards long. He was lying on his belly with arms crucified and head sharply twisted to one side. His face was coated with mud, the eyes wide open, the teeth bared and grinning with an expression of unendurable agony. (Never tell me, by the way, that the dead look peaceful. Most of the corpses I have seen looked devilish.) The friction of the great beast's foot had stripped the skin from his back as neatly as one skins a rabbit. As soon as I saw the dead man I sent an orderly to a friend's house nearby to borrow an elephant rifle. I had already sent back the pony, not wanting it to go mad with fright and throw me if it smelled the elephant.

The orderly came back in a few minutes with a rifle and five cartridges, and meanwhile some Burmans had arrived and told us that the elephant was in the paddy fields below, only a few hundred yards away. As I started forward practically the whole population of the quarter flocked out of their houses and followed me. They had seen the rifle and were all shouting excitedly that I was going to shoot the elephant. They had not shown much interest in the elephant when he was merely ravaging their homes, but it was dif-

---

4. *in terrorem:* for terror.
5. **"must":** a state of dangerous frenzy in animals.
6. **mahout** (mə-hoōt′): elephant's keeper and driver.

7. **Dravidian:** a race of people that comprise the majority of the population of southern India.

ferent now that he was going to be shot. It was a bit of fun to them, as it would be to an English crowd; besides, they wanted the meat. It made me vaguely uneasy. I had no intention of shooting the elephant—I had merely sent for the rifle to defend myself if necessary—and it is always unnerving to have a crowd following you. I marched down the hill, looking and feeling a fool, with the rifle over my shoulder and an ever-growing army of people jostling at my heels. At the bottom, when you got away from the huts, there was a metaled[8] road and beyond that a miry waste of paddy fields a thousand yards across, not yet plowed but soggy from the first rains and dotted with coarse grass. The elephant was standing eighty yards from the road, his left side towards us. He took not the slightest notice of the crowd's approach. He was tearing up bunches of grass, beating them against his knees to clean them and stuffing them into his mouth.

I had halted on the road. As soon as I saw the elephant I knew with perfect certainty that I ought not to shoot him. It is a serious matter to shoot a working elephant—it is comparable to destroying a huge and costly piece of machinery—and obviously one ought not to do it if it can possibly be avoided. And at that distance, peacefully eating, the elephant looked no more dangerous than a cow. I thought then and I think now that his attack of "must" was already passing off; in which case he would merely wander harmlessly about until the mahout came back and caught him. Moreover, I did not in the least want to shoot him. I decided that I would watch him for a little while to make sure that he did not turn savage again, and then go home.

But at that moment I glanced round at the crowd that had followed me. It was an immense crowd, two thousand at the least and growing every minute. It blocked the road for a long distance on either side. I looked at the sea of yellow faces above the garish clothes—faces all happy and excited over this bit of fun, all certain that the elephant was going to be shot. They were watching me as they would watch a conjurer about to perform a trick. They did not like me, but with the magical rifle in my hands I was momentarily worth watching. And suddenly I realized that I should have to shoot the elephant after all. The people expected it of me and I had got to do it; I could feel their two thousand wills pressing me forward, irresistibly. And it was at this moment, as I stood there with the rifle in my hands, that I first grasped the hollowness, the futility of the white man's dominion in the East. Here was I, the white man with his gun, standing in front of the unarmed native crowd —seemingly the leading actor of the piece; but in reality I was only an absurd puppet pushed to and fro by the will of those yellow faces behind. I perceived in this moment that when the white man turns tyrant it is his own freedom that he destroys. He becomes a sort of hollow, posing dummy, the conventionalized figure of a sahib.[9] For it is the condition of his rule that he shall spend his life in trying to impress the "natives" and so in every crisis he has got to do what the "natives" expect of him. He wears a mask, and his face grows to fit it. I had got to shoot the elephant. I had committed myself to doing it when I sent for the rifle. A sahib has got to act like a sahib; he has got to appear resolute, to know his own mind and do definite things. To come all that way, rifle in hand, with two thousand people marching at my heels, and then to trail feebly away, having done nothing —no, that was impossible. The crowd would laugh at me. And my whole life, every white man's life in the East, was one long struggle not to be laughed at.

But I did not want to shoot the elephant. I watched him beating his bunch of grass against his knees, with that preoccupied

---

8. **metaled:** paved.

9. **sahib** (sä′ĭb): during the colonial period, a title used by Indians for a European gentleman.

grandmotherly air that elephants have. It seemed to me that it would be murder to shoot him. At that age I was not squeamish about killing animals, but I had never shot an elephant and never wanted to. (Somehow it always seems worse to kill a *large* animal.) Besides, there was the beast's owner to be considered. Alive, the elephant was worth at least a hundred pounds; dead, he would only be worth the value of his tusks—five pounds, possibly. But I had got to act quickly. I turned to some experienced-looking Burmans who had been there when we arrived, and asked them how the elephant had been behaving. They all said the same thing: he took no notice of you if you left him alone, but he might charge if you went too close to him.

It was perfectly clear to me what I ought to do. I ought to walk up to within, say, twenty-five yards of the elephant and test his behavior. If he charged I could shoot; if he took no notice of me it would be safe to leave him until the mahout came back. But also I knew that I was going to do no such thing. I was a poor shot with a rifle and the ground was soft mud into which one would sink at every step. If the elephant charged and I missed him, I should have about as much chance as a toad under a steamroller. But even then I was not thinking particularly of my own skin, only the watchful yellow faces behind. For at that moment, with the crowd watching me, I was not afraid in the ordinary sense, as I would have been if I had been alone. A white man mustn't be frightened in front of "natives"; and so, in general, he isn't frightened. The sole thought in my mind was that if anything went wrong those two thousand Burmans would see me pursued, caught, trampled on and reduced to a grinning corpse like that Indian up the hill. And if that happened it was quite probable that some of them would laugh. That would never do. There was only one alternative. I shoved the cartridges into the magazine and lay down on the road to get a better aim.

The crowd grew very still, and a deep, low,

happy sigh, as of people who see the theater curtain go up at last, breathed from innumerable throats. They were going to have their bit of fun after all. The rifle was a beautiful German thing with cross-hair sights. I did not then know that in shooting an elephant one should shoot to cut an imaginary bar running from earhole to earhole. I ought therefore, as the elephant was sideways on, to have aimed straight at his earhole; actually I aimed several inches in front of this, thinking the brain would be further forward.

When I pulled the trigger I did not hear the bang or feel the kick—one never does when a shot goes home—but I heard the devilish roar of glee that went up from the crowd. In that instant, in too short a time, one would have thought, even for the bullet to get there, a mysterious, terrible change had come over the elephant. He neither stirred nor fell, but every line of his body had altered. He looked suddenly stricken, shrunken, immensely old, as though the frightful impact of the bullet had paralyzed him without knocking him down. At last, after what seemed a long time —it might have been five seconds, I dare say—he sagged flabbily to his knees. His mouth slobbered. An enormous senility seemed to have settled upon him. One could have imagined him thousands of years old. I fired again into the same spot. At the second shot he did not collapse but climbed with desperate slowness to his feet and stood weakly upright, with legs sagging and head drooping. I fired a third time. That was the shot that did for him. You could see the agony of it jolt his whole body and knock the last remnant of strength from his legs. But in falling he seemed for a moment to rise, for as his hind legs collapsed beneath him he seemed to tower upwards like a huge rock toppling, his trunk reaching skyward like a tree. He trumpeted, for the first and only time. And then down he came, his belly towards me, with a crash that seemed to shake the ground even where I lay.

I got up. The Burmans were already racing

past me across the mud. It was obvious that the elephant would never rise again, but he was not dead. He was breathing very rhythmically with long rattling gasps, his great mound of a side painfully rising and falling. His mouth was wide open—I could see far down into caverns of pale pink throat. I waited a long time for him to die, but his breathing did not weaken. Finally I fired my two remaining shots into the spot where I thought his heart must be. The thick blood welled out of him like red velvet, but still he did not die. His body did not even jerk when the shots hit him, the tortured breathing continued without a pause. He was dying, very slowly and in great agony, but in some world remote from me where not even a bullet could damage him further. I felt that I had got to put an end to that dreadful noise. It seemed dreadful to see the great beast lying there, powerless to move and yet powerless to die, and not even to be able to finish him. I sent back for my small rifle and poured shot after shot into his heart and down his throat. They seemed to make no impression. The tortured gasps continued as steadily as the ticking of a clock.

In the end I could not stand it any longer and went away. I heard later that it took him half an hour to die. Burmans were arriving with dahs[10] and baskets even before I left, and I was told they had stripped his body almost to the bones by the afternoon.

Afterwards, of course, there were endless discussions about the shooting of the elephant. The owner was furious, but he was only an Indian and could do nothing. Besides, legally I had done the right thing, for a mad elephant has to be killed, like a mad dog, if its owner fails to control it. Among the Europeans opinion was divided. The older men said I was right, the younger men said it was a damn shame to shoot an elephant for killing a coolie, because an elephant was worth more than any damn Coringhee[11] coolie. And afterwards I was very glad that the coolie had been killed; it put me legally in the right and it gave me a sufficient pretext for shooting the elephant. I often wondered whether any of the others grasped that I had done it solely to avoid looking a fool.

---

11. **Coringhee** (kôr-ĭng′ē).

FOR STUDY AND DISCUSSION

1. Orwell says that the incident concerning the elephant "gave me a better glimpse than I had had before of the real nature of imperialism." What does the incident illustrate about imperialism?

2. Ironically, the elephant has turned peaceful when Orwell is forced to destroy it. How does this situation (of doing what is expected of you merely to impress others) illustrate Orwell's concern with the loss of individual freedom? What other examples of irony do you find in the essay?

3. What do you think is the older Orwell's attitude toward his younger self? In what ways have his ideas and attitudes changed? Cite passages from the essay to support your answer.

4. What is the tone of the opening and concluding paragraphs?

FOR COMPOSITION

Select one sentence from this essay which you think expresses Orwell's basic point better than any other. Write a composition defending your choice.

---

10. **dahs** (däz): large knives.

Graham Greene

1904–

Graham Greene
Karsh of Ottawa, Camera Press/Photo Trends

Graham Greene is probably the most gifted British storyteller of his generation. Nobody can plan taut, exciting action better than he; nobody possesses a sharper insight into the kinks and fissures of human personality. Adverse critics may accuse him of a morbid interest in the run-down, the second-rate, the pathological, but nobody is likely to question his skill in catching and holding his reader's attention.

Greene was born in Berkhamstead, England, and graduated from Oxford. From early youth on, he developed an individual pattern of living. He has told in an autobiographical essay how, as an adolescent, in order to stimulate a jaded zest for life, he used to play the dangerous game of Russian roulette. By the time he was twenty-three, he had been very briefly a member of the Communist Party; then he became a convert to Roman Catholicism. As a writer he has explored a wide range of experience and unusual mental states. He has little use for the ordinary or the safe. His special bent as a writer has been to wrest out of unpromising material an unexpected affirmation, a stinging paradox, or an unsuspected nobility.

His first entirely successful novel, *Brighton Rock*, is a case in point. Its central character, Pinkie, is a minor gangster. It is typical of Greene not only to prefer him to those few in the book who represent conventional standards of conduct, but to give him moral superiority over the upholders of law and order. A verse tag quoted in this book may be taken as a motto for all Greene's work. It signifies that even at the eleventh hour a destiny can be reversed: "Between the stirrup and the ground/He mercy sought and mercy found." Much of Greene's work has been a prolonged brooding over the eleventh hour: the moment at which a rider, in falling, has time not only to face the reality of his dilemma, but to take a last desperate action.

There is, for example, the priest in Greene's finest novel, *The Power and the Glory*, who, by sacrificing himself to his duty at the last possible moment, buys back a lifetime of personal failure. There is Scobie in *The Heart of the Matter*, struggling to overcome the wreck of a marriage, and Sarah in *The End of the Affair*, attaining a degree of sainthood after renouncing the man who loves her. These are the kinds of men and women who appeal to Greene, and again and again he returns to the struggle they engage in to transcend some crippling weakness.

Greene's novels still appear at regular intervals, often as the result of a journey to some trouble-center currently in the news. *The Quiet American* sprang out of a trip to Indochina; *Our Man in Havana* was inspired by a stay in Cuba; *A Burnt-Out Case* followed a journey into the Congo. *The Comedians* was the result of a trip to Haiti. Greene classifies his fiction as "novels" and "entertainments," the latter consisting of superior thrillers. His autobiography, *A Kind of Life*, is one of the most distinguished works in this genre in recent years.

Across the Bridge

"They say he's worth a million," Lucia said. He sat there in the little hot damp Mexican square, a dog at his feet, with an air of immense and forlorn patience. The dog attracted your attention at once; for it was very nearly an English setter, only something had gone wrong with the tail and the feathering. Palms wilted over his head, it was all shade and stuffiness round the bandstand, radios talked loudly in Spanish from the little wooden sheds where they changed your pesos into dollars at a loss. I could tell he didn't understand a word from the way he read his newspaper—as I did myself, picking out the words which were like English ones. "He's been here a month," Lucia said. "They turned him out of Guatemala and Honduras."

You couldn't keep any secrets for five hours in this border town. Lucia had only been twenty-four hours in the place, but she knew all about Mr. Joseph Calloway. The only reason I didn't know about him (and I'd been in the place two weeks) was because I couldn't talk the language any more than Mr. Calloway could. There wasn't another soul in the place who didn't know the story—the whole story of the Halling Investment Trust and the proceedings of extradition. Any man doing dusty business in any of the wooden booths in the town is better fitted by long observation to tell Mr. Calloway's tale than I am, except that I was in—literally—at the finish. They all watched the drama proceed with immense interest, sympathy and respect. For, after all, he had a million.

Every once in a while through the long steamy day, a boy came and cleaned Mr. Calloway's shoes: he hadn't the right words to resist them—they pretended not to know his English. He must have had his shoes cleaned the day Lucia and I watched him at least half a dozen times. At midday he took a stroll across the square to the Antonio Bar and had a bottle of beer, the setter sticking to heel as if they were out for a country walk in England (he had, you may remember, one of the biggest estates in Norfolk). After his bottle of beer, he would walk down between the money-changers' huts to the Rio Grande and look across the bridge into the United States: people came and went constantly in cars. Then back to the square till lunchtime. He was staying in the best hotel, but you don't get good hotels in this border town: nobody stays in them more than a night. The good hotels were on the other side of the bridge: you could see their electric signs twenty stories high from the little square at night, like lighthouses marking the United States.

You may ask what I'd been doing in so drab a spot for a fortnight. There was no interest in the place for anyone; it was just damp and dust and poverty, a kind of shabby replica of the town across the river: both had squares in the same spots; both had the same number of cinemas. One was cleaner than the other, that was all, and more expensive, much more expensive. I'd stayed across there a couple of nights waiting for a man a tourist bureau said was driving down from Detroit to Yucatan and would sell a place in his car for some fantastically small figure—twenty dollars, I think it was. I don't know if he existed or was invented by the optimistic half-caste in the agency; anyway, he never turned up and so I waited, not much caring, on the cheap side of the river. It didn't much matter; I was living. One day I meant to give up the man from Detroit and go home or go south, but it was easier not to decide anything in a hurry. Lucia was just waiting for a car going the other way, but she didn't have to wait so long. We waited together and watched Mr. Calloway waiting —for God knows what.

I don't know how to treat this story—it was a tragedy for Mr. Calloway, it was poetic retribution, I suppose, in the eyes of the shareholders he'd ruined with his bogus transactions, and to Lucia and me, at this stage, it was pure comedy—except when he kicked the dog. I'm not a sentimentalist about dogs, I prefer people to be cruel to animals rather than to human beings, but I couldn't help being revolted at the way he'd kick that animal—with a hint of cold-blooded venom, not in anger but as if he were getting even for some trick it had played him a long while ago. That generally happened when he returned from the bridge: it was the only sign of anything resembling emotion he showed. Otherwise he looked a small, set, gentle creature with silver hair and a silver mustache, and gold-rimmed glasses, and one gold tooth like a flaw in character.

Lucia hadn't been accurate when she said he'd been turned out of Guatemala and Honduras; he'd left voluntarily when the extradition proceedings seemed likely to go through and moved north. Mexico is still not a very centralized state, and it is possible to get round governors as you can't get round cabinet ministers or judges. And so he waited there on the border for the next move. That earlier part of the story is, I suppose, dramatic, but I didn't watch it and I can't invent what I haven't seen—the long waiting in anterooms, the bribes taken and refused, the growing fear of arrest, and then the flight—in gold-rimmed glasses—covering his tracks as well as he could, but this wasn't finance and he was an amateur at escape. And so he'd washed up here, under my eyes and Lucia's eyes, sitting all day under the bandstand, nothing to read but a Mexican paper, nothing to do but look across the river at the United States, quite unaware, I suppose, that everyone knew everything about him, once a day kicking his dog. Perhaps in its semi-setter way it reminded him too much of the Norfolk estate—though that too, I suppose, was the reason he kept it.

And the next act again was pure comedy. I hesitate to think what this man worth a million was costing his country as they edged him out from this land and that. Perhaps somebody was getting tired of the business, careless; anyway, they sent across two detectives, with an old photograph. He'd grown his silvery mustache since that had been taken, and he'd aged a lot, and they couldn't catch sight of him. They hadn't been across the bridge two hours when everybody knew that there were two foreign detectives in town looking for Mr. Calloway—everybody knew, that is to say, except Mr. Calloway, who couldn't talk Spanish. There were plenty of people who could have told him in English, but they didn't. It wasn't cruelty, it was a sort of awe and respect: like a bull, he was on show, sitting there mournfully in the plaza with his dog, a magnificent spectacle for which we all had ringside seats.

I ran into one of the policemen in the Bar Antonio. He was disgusted; he had had some idea that when he crossed the bridge life was going to be different, so much more color and sun, and—I suspect—love, and all he found were wide mud streets where the nocturnal rain lay in pools, and mangy dogs, smells and cockroaches in his bedroom, and the nearest to love, the open door of the Academia Comercial, where pretty mestizo[1] girls sat all the morning learning to typewrite. Tip-tap-tip-tap-tip—perhaps they had a dream, too—jobs on the other side of the bridge, where life was going to be so much more luxurious, refined and amusing.

We got into conversation; he seemed surprised that I knew who they both were and what they wanted. He said, "We've got information this man Calloway's in town."

"He's knocking around somewhere," I said.

"Could you point him out?"

"Oh, I don't know him by sight," I said.

He drank his beer and thought awhile. "I'll go out and sit in the plaza. He's sure to pass sometime."

I finished my beer and went quickly off and

---

1. **mestizo** (mĕs-tē′zō): a person of Spanish and Indian blood.

found Lucia. I said, "Hurry, we're going to see an arrest." We didn't care a thing about Mr. Calloway, he was just an elderly man who kicked his dog and swindled the poor, and who deserved anything he got. So we made for the plaza; we knew Calloway would be there, but it had never occurred to either of us that the detectives wouldn't recognize him. There was quite a surge of people round the place; all the fruit-sellers and bootblacks in town seemed to have arrived together; we had to force our way through, and there in the little green stuffy center of the place, sitting on adjoining seats, were the two plainclothesmen and Mr. Calloway. I've never known the place so silent; everybody was on tiptoe, and the plainclothesmen were staring at the crowd looking for Mr. Calloway, and Mr. Calloway sat on his usual seat staring out over the money-changing booths at the United States.

"It can't go on. It just can't," Lucia said. But it did. It got more fantastic still. Somebody ought to write a play about it. We sat as close as we dared. We were afraid all the time we were going to laugh. The semi-setter scratched for fleas and Mr. Calloway watched the USA. The two detectives watched the crowd, and the crowd watched the show with solemn satisfaction. Then one of the detectives got up and went over to Mr. Calloway. That's the end, I thought. But it wasn't, it was the beginning. For some reason they had eliminated him from their list of suspects. I shall never know why.

The man said, "You speak English?"

"I *am* English," Mr. Calloway said.

Even that didn't tear it, and the strangest thing of all was the way Mr. Calloway came alive. I don't think anybody had spoken to him like that for weeks. The Mexicans were too respectful—he was a man with a million—and it had never occurred to Lucia and me to treat him casually like a human being; even in our eyes he had been magnified by the colossal theft and the worldwide pursuit.

He said, "This is rather a dreadful place, don't you think?"

"It is," the policeman said.

"I can't think what brings anybody across the bridge."

"Duty," the policeman said gloomily. "I suppose you are passing through."

"Yes," Mr. Calloway said.

"I'd have expected over here there'd have been—you know what I mean—life. You read things about Mexico."

"Oh, life," Mr. Calloway said. He spoke firmly and precisely, as if to a committee of shareholders. "That begins on the other side."

"You don't appreciate your own country until you leave it."

"That's very true," Mr. Calloway said. "Very true."

At first it was difficult not to laugh, and then after a while there didn't seem to be much to laugh at; an old man imagining all the fine things going on beyond the international bridge. I think he thought of the town opposite as a combination of London and Norfolk—theaters and cocktail bars, a little shooting and a walk round the field at evening with the dog—that miserable imitation of a setter—poking the ditches. He'd never been across, he couldn't know that it was just the same thing over again—even the same layout; only the streets were paved and the hotels had ten more stories, and life was more expensive, and everything was a little bit cleaner. There wasn't anything Mr. Calloway would have called living—no galleries, no bookshops, just *Film Fun* and the local paper, and *Click* and *Focus* and the tabloids.

"Well," said Mr. Calloway, "I think I'll take a stroll before lunch. You need an appetite to swallow the food here. I generally go down and look at the bridge about now. Care to come too?"

The detective shook his head. "No," he said, "I'm on duty. I'm looking for a fellow." And that, of course, gave *him* away. As far as Mr. Calloway could understand, there was only one "fellow" in the world anyone was looking for—his brain had eliminated friends who were seeking their friends, husbands who might be waiting for their wives, all objectives of any search but just the one. The power of elimination was what had made him a financier—he could forget the people behind the shares.

That was the last we saw of him for a while. We didn't see him going into the Botica Paris to get his aspirin, or walking back from the bridge with his dog. He simply disappeared, and when he disappeared, people began to talk, and the detectives heard the talk. They looked silly enough, and they got busy after the very man they'd been sitting next to in the garden. Then they too disappeared. They, as well as Mr. Calloway, had gone to the state capital to see the Governor and the Chief of Police, and it must have been an amusing sight there too, as they bumped into Mr. Calloway and sat with him in the waiting rooms. I suspect Mr. Calloway was generally shown in first, for everyone knew he was worth a million. Only in Europe is it possible for a man to be a criminal as well as a rich man.

Anyway, after about a week the whole pack of them returned by the same train. Mr. Calloway traveled Pullman, and the two policemen traveled in the day coach. It was evident that they hadn't got their extradition order.

Lucia had left by that time. The car came and went across the bridge. I stood in Mexico and watched her get out at the United States Customs. She wasn't anything in particular but she looked beautiful at a distance as she gave me a wave out of the United States and got back into the car. And I suddenly felt sympathy for Mr. Calloway, as if there were something over there which you couldn't find here, and turning round I saw him back on his old beat, with the dog at his heels.

I said, "Good afternoon," as if it had been all along our habit to greet each other. He looked tired and ill and dusty, and I felt sorry for him—to think of the kind of victory he'd been winning, with so much expenditure of cash and care—the prize this dirty and dreary town, the booths of the money-changers, the awful little beauty parlors with their wicker chairs and sofas looking like the reception rooms of brothels, that hot and stuffy garden by the bandstand.

He replied gloomily, "Good morning," and the dog started to sniff at some ordure and he turned and kicked it with fury, with depression, with despair.

And at that moment a taxi with the two policemen in it passed us on its way to the bridge. They must have seen that kick; perhaps they were cleverer than I had given them credit for, perhaps they were just sentimental about animals, and thought they'd do a good deed, and the rest happened by accident. But the fact remains—those two pillars of the law set about the stealing of Mr. Calloway's dog.

He watched them go by. Then he said, "Why don't you go across?"

"It's cheaper here," I said.

"I mean just for an evening. Have a meal at that place we can see at night in the sky. Go to the theater."

"There isn't a chance."

He said angrily, sucking his gold tooth, "Well, anyway, get away from here." He stared down the hill and up the other side. He couldn't see that that street climbing up from the bridge contained only the same money-changers' booths as this one.

I said, "Why don't *you* go?"

He said evasively. "Oh—business."

I said, "It's only a question of money. You don't *have* to pass by the bridge."

He said with faint interest, "I don't talk Spanish."

"There isn't a soul here," I said, "who doesn't talk English."

He looked at me with surprise. "Is that so?" he said. "Is that so?"

It's as I have said; he'd never tried to talk to anyone, and they respected him too much to talk to him—he was worth a million. I don't know whether I'm glad or sorry that I told him that. If I hadn't, he might be there now, sitting by the bandstand having his shoes cleaned—alive and suffering.

Three days later his dog disappeared. I found him looking for it, calling it softly and shamefacedly between the palms of the garden. He looked embarrassed. He said in a low angry voice, "I *hate* that dog. The beastly mongrel," and called "Rover, Rover," in a voice which didn't carry five yards. He said, "I bred setters once. I'd have shot a dog like that." It reminded him, I *was* right, of Norfolk, and he lived in the memory, and he hated it for its imperfection. He was a man without a family and without friends, and his only enemy was that dog. You couldn't call the law an enemy; you have to be intimate with an enemy.

Late that afternoon someone told him they'd seen the dog walking across the bridge. It wasn't true, of course, but we didn't know that then—they'd paid a Mexican five pesos to smuggle it across. So all that afternoon and the next Mr. Calloway sat in the garden having his shoes cleaned over and over again, and thinking how a dog could just walk across like that, and a human being, an immortal soul, was bound here in the awful routine of the little walk and the unspeakable meals and the aspirin at the *botica*. That dog was seeing things he couldn't see—that hateful dog. It made him mad—I think literally mad. You must remember the man had been going on for months. He had a million and he was living on two pounds a week, with nothing to spend his money on. He sat there and brooded on the hideous injustice of it. I think he'd have crossed over one day in any case, but the dog was the last straw.

Next day when he wasn't to be seen I guessed he'd gone across, and I went too. The American town is as small as the Mexican. I knew I couldn't miss him if he was there, and I was still curious. A little sorry for him, but not much.

I caught sight of him first in the only drugstore, having a Coca-Cola, and then once outside a cinema looking at the posters; he had dressed with extreme neatness, as if for a party, but there was no party. On my third time round, I came on the detectives—they were having Coca-Colas in the drugstore, and they must have missed Mr. Calloway by inches. I went in and sat down at the bar.

"Hello," I said, "you still about?" I suddenly felt anxious for Mr. Calloway, I didn't want them to meet.

One of them said, "Where's Calloway?"

"Oh," I said, "he's hanging on."

"But not his dog," he said, and laughed. The other looked a little shocked, he didn't like anyone to *talk* cynically about a dog. Then they got up—they had a car outside.

"Have another?" I said.

"No, thanks. We've got to keep moving."

The man bent close and confided to me, "Calloway's on this side."

"No!" I said.

"And his dog."

"He's looking for it," the other said.

"I'm damned if he is," I said, and again one of them looked a little shocked, as if I'd insulted the dog.

I don't think Mr. Calloway was looking for his dog, but his dog certainly found him. There was a sudden hilarious yapping from the car and out plunged the semi-setter and gamboled furiously down the street. One of the detectives—the sentimental one—was into the car before we got to the door and was off after the dog. Near the bottom of the long road to the bridge was Mr. Calloway—I do believe he'd come down to look at the Mexican side when he found there was nothing but the drugstore and the cinemas and the paper shops on the American. He saw the dog coming and yelled at it to go home—"home, home, home," as if they were in Norfolk—it took no notice at all, pelting toward him. Then he saw the police car coming and ran. After that, everything happened too quickly, but I think the order of events was this—the dog started across the road right in front of the car, and Mr. Calloway yelled, at the dog or the car, I don't know which. Anyway, the detective swerved—he said later, weakly, at the inquiry, that he couldn't run over a dog, and down went Mr. Calloway, in a mess of broken glass and gold rims and silver hair, and blood. The dog was onto him before any of us could reach him, licking and whimpering and licking. I saw Mr. Calloway put up his hand, and down it went across the dog's neck and the whimper rose to a stupid bark of triumph, but Mr. Calloway was dead—shock and a weak heart.

"Poor old geezer," the detective said, "I bet he really loved that dog," and it's true that the attitude in which he lay looked more like a caress than a blow. I thought it was meant to be a blow, but the detective may have been right. It all seemed to me a little too touching to be true as the old crook lay there with his arm over the dog's neck, dead with his million between the money-changers' huts, but it's as well to be humble in the face of human nature. He had come across the river for something, and it may, after all, have been the dog he was looking for. It sat there, baying its stupid and mongrel triumph across his body, like a piece of sentimental statuary. The nearest he could get to the fields, ditches, the horizon of his home. It was comic and it was pitiable; but it wasn't less comic because the man was dead. Death doesn't change comedy to tragedy, and if that last gesture was one of affection, I suppose it was only one more indication of a human being's capacity for self-deception, our baseless optimism that is so much more appalling than our despair.

COMMENTARY

The reader's experience of "Across the Bridge" is the experience of the narrator, of *his* sense of Calloway's character and the meaning of his final gesture. Is the kicking of the dog a true revelation of Calloway's character? The narrator suggests that it is—Calloway is capable of acting in "cold-blooded venom"; perhaps that is how he was able to swindle so many people. But what about Calloway's final gesture in death? Is it a caress or a blow? The narrator believes it was a blow, but is

not sure, and can only speculate about the appearances and probabilities of character: "It all seemed to me a little too touching to be true as the old crook lay there with his arm over the dog's neck, dead with his million between the money-changers' huts, but it's as well to be humble in the face of human nature." That is the mysterious entity of the story: human nature. Out of what feelings Calloway has acted we cannot know with certainty. The narrator finds comedy in "a human being's capacity for self-deception," but to other observers the death would have been pure tragedy. If the narrator is right in interpreting Calloway's attitude toward the dog, then the scene is saturated with a grim comic irony. But to know what was in Calloway's heart is to know human nature. And that, we are warned by the narrator, is what we cannot know.

Greene uses this special point of view to remind us of the mystery of character. This is a major theme of his longer works. Only God knows "the heart of the matter," he suggests in the great novel of that title. No human being can judge the life or know what is in the heart of another. Our experience of "Across the Bridge" is our experience of the narrator, one mere hole "in a dead wall."

FOR STUDY AND DISCUSSION

1. How do Calloway's actions, and those of other characters throughout the story, suggest a "capacity for self-deception" and "baseless optimism" to which the narrator alludes in the closing lines?
2. What significance does the title have?
3. The narrator sees the story's events as comic instead of tragic. What reasons can you offer to support or refute his view?
4. Irony pervades the story: Calloway "is worth a million" but can't use his money to escape the border town; he thinks he can begin life all over again across the bridge, but he dies there. What other examples of irony do you find in the story?

FOR COMPOSITION

Discuss the narrator's role in making clear the theme of this story. Consider how the story might be different if another narrator—for example, a brash, aggressive salesperson—had told it.

Doris Lessing
1919–

Doris Lessing
Mark Gerson, Camera Press/Photo Trends

Doris Lessing is one of a number of African authors writing in English who have settled in Europe. A characteristic most of these writers have in common is a deep affection for their own continent coupled with a reluctance to live in it and a sharp eye for its defects. Lessing has written that writers brought up in Africa have the advantage of "being at the center of a modern battlefield, part of a society in rapid, dramatic change." But, she notes, being too close to this battlefield, too exposed to the brutalities that are a part of the battle, tends to limit the writer's point of view and dry up the imagination. Therefore, it becomes necessary for African writers to leave their countries and gain the perspective that travel and distance give. "I believe that the chief gift from Africa to writers, white and black, is the continent itself, its presence, which for some people is like an old fever, latent always in their blood; or like an old wound throbbing in the bones as the air changes."

The daughter of British parents, Lessing was born in Persia and grew up in Southern Rhodesia. In 1949 she settled in England. Since living there, she has written a number of novels, many short stories, and some poetry. In her book *In Pursuit of the English,* she gives an absorbing account of her early years in England. Her typical heroine is a frustrated, highly intellectual young woman who struggles, against the inadequacies of her environment, to realize herself. Her great novel *The Golden Notebook* marks the beginning of wide experimentation in psychological fiction. In two remarkable novels of the 1970's, *Briefing for a Descent into Hell* and *The Memoirs of a Survivor,* Lessing turns to what she calls the mysterious "inner space" of the mind. Her great theme is the growth in "how we see things," the real feelings of people and how they come to discover them.

Lessing is a very conscious, probing writer, greatly preoccupied with social questions. One critic has summed up her work as "enormously lucid sociological journalism." There is a strong didactic streak in her work: not only do her novels explore social questions but they take a very clear stand on them. The London *Times* has called her "not only the best woman novelist we have, but one of the most serious and intelligent and honest writers of the whole postwar generation."

A Sunrise on the Veld

Every night that winter he said aloud into the dark of the pillow: Half past four! Half past four! till he felt his brain had gripped the words and held them fast. Then he fell asleep at once, as if a shutter had fallen; and lay with his face turned to the clock so that he could see it first thing when he woke.

It was half past four to the minute, every morning. Triumphantly pressing down the alarm knob of the clock, which the dark half of his mind had outwitted, remaining vigilant all night and counting the hours as he lay relaxed in sleep, he huddled down for a last warm moment under the clothes, playing with the idea of lying abed for this once only. But he played with it for the fun of knowing that it was a weakness he could defeat without effort; just as he set the alarm each night for the delight of the moment when he woke and stretched his limbs, feeling the muscles tighten, and thought: Even my brain—even that! I can control every part of myself.

Luxury of warm rested body, with the arms and legs and fingers waiting like soldiers for a word of command! Joy of knowing that the precious hours were given to sleep voluntarily!—for he had once stayed awake three nights running, to prove that he could, and then worked all day, refusing even to admit that he was tired; and now sleep seemed to him a servant to be commanded and refused.

The boy stretched his frame full length, touching the wall at his head with his hands, and the bedfoot with his toes; then he sprung out, like a fish leaping from water. And it was cold, cold.

He always dressed rapidly, so as to try and conserve his night-warmth till the sun rose two hours later; but by the time he had on his clothes his hands were numbed and he could scarcely hold his shoes. These he could not put on for fear of waking his parents, who never came to know how early he rose.

As soon as he stepped over the lintel, the flesh of his soles contracted on the chilled earth, and his legs began to ache with cold. It was night: the stars were glittering, the trees standing black and still. He looked for signs of day, for the graying of the edge of a stone, or a lightening in the sky where the sun would rise, but there was nothing yet. Alert as an animal he crept past the dangerous window, standing poised with his hand on the sill for one proudly fastidious moment, looking in at the stuffy blackness of the room where his parents lay.

Feeling for the grass-edge of the path with his toes, he reached inside another window further along the wall, where his gun had been set in readiness the night before. The steel was icy, and numbed fingers slipped along it, so that he had to hold it in the crook of his arm for safety. Then he tiptoed to the room where the dogs slept, and was fearful that they might have been tempted to go before him; but they were waiting, their haunches crouched in reluctance at the cold, but ears and swinging tails greeting the gun ecstatically. His warning undertone kept them secret and silent till the house was a hundred yards back: then they bolted off into the bush, yelping excitedly. The boy imagined his parents turning in their beds and muttering: Those dogs again! before they were dragged back in sleep; and he smiled scornfully. He always looked back over his shoulder at the house before he passed a wall of trees that shut it from sight. It looked so low and small, crouching there under a tall and brilliant sky. Then he turned his back on it, and on the frowsting[1] sleepers, and forgot them.

He would have to hurry. Before the light grew strong he must be four miles away; and

---

1. **frowsting:** lounging, late-sleeping.

already a tint of green stood in the hollow of a leaf, and the air smelled of morning and the stars were dimming.

He slung the shoes over his shoulder, veld *skoen* that were crinkled and hard with the dews of a hundred mornings. They would be necessary when the ground became too hot to bear. Now he felt the chilled dust push up between his toes, and he let the muscles of his feet spread and settle into the shapes of the earth; and he thought: I could walk a hundred miles on feet like these! I could walk all day, and never tire!

He was walking swiftly through the dark tunnel of foliage that in daytime was a road. The dogs were invisibly ranging the lower travelways of the bush, and he heard them panting. Sometimes he felt a cold muzzle on his leg before they were off again, scouting for a trail to follow. They were not trained, but free-running companions of the hunt, who often tired of the long stalk before the final shots, and went off on their own pleasure. Soon he could see them, small and wild-looking in a wild strange light, now that the bush stood trembling on the verge of color, waiting for the sun to paint earth and grass afresh.

The grass stood to his shoulders; and the trees were showering a faint silvery rain. He was soaked; his whole body was clenched in a steady shiver.

Once he bent to the road that was newly scored with animal trails, and regretfully straightened, reminding himself that the pleasure of tracking must wait till another day.

He began to run along the edge of a field, noting jerkily how it was filmed over with fresh spider web, so that the long reaches of great black clods seemed netted in glistening gray. He was using the steady lope he had learned by watching the natives, the run that is a dropping of the weight of the body from one foot to the next in a slow balancing movement that never tires, nor shortens the breath; and he felt the blood pulsing down his legs and along his arms, and the exultation and pride of body mounted in him till he was

shutting his teeth hard against a violent desire to shout his triumph.

Soon he had left the cultivated part of the farm. Behind him the bush was low and black. In front was a long vlei,[2] acres of long pale grass that sent back a hollowing gleam of light to a satiny sky. Near him thick swaths of grass were bent with the weight of water, and diamond drops sparkled on each frond.

The first bird woke at his feet and at once a flock of them sprang into the air calling shrilly that day had come; and suddenly, behind him, the bush woke into song, and he could hear the guinea fowl calling far ahead of him. That meant they would now be sailing down from their trees into thick grass, and it was for them he had come: he was too late. But he did not mind. He forgot he had come to shoot. He set his legs wide, and balanced from foot to foot, and swung his gun up and down in both hands horizontally, in a kind of improvised exercise, and let his head sink back till it was pillowed in his neck muscles, and watched how above him small rosy clouds floated in a lake of gold.

Suddenly it all rose in him: it was unbearable. He leapt up into the air, shouting and yelling wild, unrecognizable noises. Then he began to run, not carefully, as he had before, but madly, like a wild thing. He was clean crazy, yelling mad with the joy of living and a superfluity of youth. He rushed down the vlei under a tumult of crimson and gold, while all the birds of the world sang about him. He ran in great leaping strides, and shouted as he ran, feeling his body rise into the crisp rushing air and fall back surely onto sure feet; and thought briefly, not believing that such a thing could happen to him, that he could break his ankle any moment, in this thick tangled grass. He cleared bushes like a duiker,[3] leapt over rocks; and finally came to a dead stop at a place where the ground fell abruptly away below him to the river. It had

---

2. **vlei** (flā): a meadow or valley.
3. **duiker** (dīk′ər): small African antelope.

been a two-mile-long dash through waist-high growth, and he was breathing hoarsely and could no longer sing. But he poised on a rock and looked down at stretches of water that gleamed through stooping trees, and thought suddenly, I am fifteen! Fifteen! The words came new to him; so that he kept repeating them wonderingly, with swelling excitement; and he felt the years of his life with his hands, as if he were counting marbles, each one hard and separate and compact, each one a wonderful shining thing. That was what he was: fifteen years of this rich soil, and this slow-moving water, and air that smelt like a challenge whether it was warm and sultry at noon, or as brisk as cold water, like it was now.

There was nothing he couldn't do, nothing! A vision came to him, as he stood there, like when a child hears the word *eternity* and tries to understand it, and time takes possession of the mind. He felt his life ahead of him as a great and wonderful thing, something that was his; and he said aloud, with the blood rising to his head: All the great men of the world have been as I am now, and there is nothing I can't become, nothing I can't do; there is no country in the world I cannot make part of myself, if I choose. I contain the world. I can make of it what I want. If I choose, I can change everything that is going to happen: it depends on me, and what I decide now.

The urgency and the truth and the courage of what his voice was saying exulted him so that he began to sing again, at the top of his voice, and the sound went echoing down the river gorge. He stopped for the echo, and sang again: stopped and shouted. That was what he was! — he sang, if he chose; and the world had to answer him.

And for minutes he stood there, shouting and singing and waiting for the lovely eddying sound of the echo; so that his own new strong thoughts came back and washed round his head, as if someone were answering him and encouraging him; till the gorge was full of soft voices clashing back and forth from rock to rock over the river. And then it seemed as if there was a new voice. He listened, puzzled, for it was not his own. Soon he was leaning forward, all his nerves alert, quite still: somewhere close to him there was a noise that was no joyful bird, nor tinkle of falling water, nor ponderous movement of cattle.

There it was again. In the deep morning hush that held his future and his past, was a sound of pain, and repeated over and over: it was a kind of shortened scream, as if someone, something, had no breath to scream. He came to himself, looked about him, and called for the dogs. They did not appear: they had gone off on their own business, and he was alone. Now he was clean sober, all the madness gone. His heart beating fast, because of that frightened screaming, he stepped carefully off the rock and went towards a belt of trees. He was moving cautiously, for not so long ago he had seen a leopard in just this spot.

At the edge of the trees he stopped and peered, holding his gun ready; he advanced, looking steadily about him, his eyes narrowed. Then, all at once, in the middle of a step, he faltered, and his face was puzzled. He shook his head impatiently, as if he doubted his own sight.

There, between two trees, against a background of gaunt black rocks, was a figure from a dream, a strange beast that was horned and drunken-legged, but like something he had never even imagined. It seemed to be ragged. It looked like a small buck that had black ragged tufts of fur standing up irregularly all over it, with patches of raw flesh beneath . . . but the patches of rawness were disappearing under moving black and came again elsewhere; and all the time the creature screamed, in small gasping screams, and leaped drunkenly from side to side, as if it were blind.

Then the boy understood: it *was* a buck. He ran closer, and again stood still, stopped by a new fear. Around him the grass was whispering and alive. He looked wildly about, and then down. The ground was black with ants, great energetic ants that took no notice of him, but hurried and scurried towards the fighting shape, like glistening black water flowing through the grass.

And, as he drew in his breath and pity and terror seized him, the beast fell and the screaming stopped. Now he could hear nothing but one bird singing, and the sound of the rustling, whispering ants.

He peered over at the writhing blackness that jerked convulsively with the jerking nerves. It grew quieter. There were small twitches from the mass that still looked vaguely like the shape of a small animal.

It came into his mind that he should shoot it and end its pain; and he raised the gun. Then he lowered it again. The buck could no longer feel; its fighting was a mechanical protest of the nerves. But it was not that which made him put down the gun. It was a swelling feeling of rage and misery and protest that expressed itself in the thought: If I had not come it would have died like this: so why should I interfere? All over the bush things like this happen; they happen all the time; this is how life goes on, by living things dying in anguish. He gripped the gun between his knees and felt in his own limbs the myriad swarming pain of the twitching animal that could no longer feel, and set his teeth, and said over and over again under his breath: I can't stop it. I can't stop it. There is nothing I can do.

He was glad that the buck was unconscious and had gone past suffering so that he did not have to make a decision to kill it even when he was feeling with his whole body: This is what happens, this is how things work.

It was right—that was what he was feeling. *It was right and nothing could alter it.*

The knowledge of fatality, of what has to be, had gripped him and for the first time in his life; and he was left unable to make any movement of brain or body, except to say: "Yes, yes. That is what living is." It had entered his flesh and his bones and grown in to the furthest corners of his brain and would

never leave him. And at that moment he could not have performed the smallest action of mercy, knowing as he did, having lived on it all his life, the vast unalterable, cruel veld, where at any moment one might stumble over a skull or crush the skeleton of some small creature.

Suffering, sick, and angry, but also grimly satisfied with his new stoicism, he stood there leaning on his rifle, and watched the seething black mound grow smaller. At his feet, now, were ants trickling back with pink fragments in their mouths, and there was a fresh acid smell in his nostrils. He sternly controlled the uselessly convulsing muscles of his empty stomach, and reminded himself: The ants must eat too! At the same time he found that the tears were streaming down his face, and his clothes were soaked with the sweat of that other creature's pain.

The shape had grown small. Now it looked like nothing recognizable. He did not know how long it was before he saw the blackness thin, and bits of white showed through, shining in the sun—yes, there was the sun, just up, glowing over the rocks. Why, the whole thing could not have taken longer than a few minutes.

He began to swear, as if the shortness of the time was in itself unbearable, using the words he had heard his father say. He strode forward, crushing ants with each step, and brushing them off his clothes, till he stood above the skeleton, which lay sprawled under a small bush. It was clean-picked. It might have been lying there years, save that on the white bone were pink fragments of gristle. About the bones ants were ebbing away, their pincers full of meat.

The boy looked at them, big black ugly insects. A few were standing and gazing up at him with small glittering eyes.

"Go away!" he said to the ants, very coldly. "I am not for you—not just yet, at any rate. Go away." And he fancied that the ants turned and went away.

He bent over the bones and touched the

sockets in the skull; that was where the eyes were, he thought incredulously, remembering the liquid dark eyes of a buck. And then he bent the slim foreleg bone, swinging it horizontally in his palm.

That morning, perhaps an hour ago, this small creature had been stepping proud and free through the bush, feeling the chill on its hide even as he himself had done, exhilarated by it. Proudly stepping the earth, tossing its horns, frisking a pretty white tail, it had sniffed the cold morning air. Walking like kings and conquerors it had moved through this free-held bush, where each blade of grass grew for it alone, and where the river ran pure sparkling water for its slaking.

And then—what had happened? Such a swift sure-footed thing could surely not be trapped by a swarm of ants?

The boy bent curiously to the skeleton. Then he saw that the back leg that lay uppermost and strained out in the tension of death, was snapped midway in the thigh, so that broken bones jutted over each other uselessly. So that was it! Limping into the ant-masses it could not escape, once it had sensed the danger. Yes, but how had the leg been broken? Had it fallen, perhaps? Impossible, a buck was too light and graceful. Had some jealous rival horned it?

What could possibly have happened? Perhaps some Africans had thrown stones at it, as they do, trying to kill it for meat, and had broken its leg. Yes, that must be it.

Even as he imagined the crowd of running, shouting natives, and the flying stones, and the leaping buck, another picture came into his mind. He saw himself, on any one of these bright ringing mornings, drunk with excitement, taking a snap shot at some half-seen buck. He saw himself with the gun lowered, wondering whether he had missed or not; and thinking at last that it was late, and he wanted his breakfast, and it was not worthwhile to track miles after an animal that would very likely get away from him in any case.

For a moment he would not face it. He was a small boy again, kicking sulkily at the skeleton, hanging his head, refusing to accept the responsibility.

Then he straightened up, and looked down at the bones with an odd expression of dismay, all the anger gone out of him. His mind went quite empty: all around him he could see trickles of ants disappearing into the grass. The whispering noise was faint and dry, like the rustling of a cast snakeskin.

At last he picked up his gun and walked homewards. He was telling himself half defiantly that he wanted his breakfast. He was telling himself that it was getting very hot, much too hot to be out roaming the bush.

Really, he was tired. He walked heavily, not looking where he put his feet. When he came within sight of his home he stopped, knitting his brows. There was something he had to think out. The death of that small animal was a thing that concerned him, and he was by no means finished with it. It lay at the back of his mind uncomfortably.

Soon, the very next morning, he would get clear of everybody and go to the bush and think about it.

FOR STUDY AND DISCUSSION

1. How do the boy's feelings on waking contrast with his feelings at the end of the story? What is the unexpected discovery he makes about himself and the world of nature?

2. What progression of thoughts and feelings about the dying buck and the skeleton in the bush does the boy have?

3. How important is the African setting to the boy's experience? To what extent does the setting help to define the boy's character?

FOR COMPOSITION

Compare the view of nature developed in "A Sunrise on the Veld" with the view developed in O'Flaherty's "The Wild Goat's Kid" (page 744). Contrast the ways in which these views emerge.

Nadine Gordimer

1923–

Nadine Gordimer was born in Springs, near Johannesburg, South Africa, and educated at the University of Witwatersrand. She possesses a skill for penetrating emotionally complex moments. In her stories and novels she deals with modern South Africa, the racial tensions in that country and the dilemma of the individual conscience in situations of political and racial stress. Though traditional in techniques of characterization and narrative, her writing bears the influence of experimental fiction in this century. This modern influence is particularly evident in "The Train from Rhodesia," where Gordimer subtly communicates the tensions of daily living. Her writing has been compared to that of Virginia Woolf — "crystalline and gentle" — yet she does not ignore the grim realities of much of South African life.

The Train from Rhodesia

The train came out of the red horizon and bore down toward them over the single straight track.

The stationmaster came out of his little brick station with its pointed chalet roof, feeling the creases in his serge uniform in his legs as well. A stir of preparedness rippled through the squatting native vendors waiting in the dust; the face of a carved wooden animal, eternally surprised, stuck out of a sack. The stationmaster's barefoot children wandered over. From the gray mud huts with the untidy heads that stood within a decorated mud wall, chickens, and dogs with their skin stretched like parchment over their bones, followed the piccanins[1] down to the track. The flushed and perspiring west cast a reflection, faint, without heat, upon the station, upon the tin shed marked "Goods," upon the walled kraal,[2] upon the gray tin house of the stationmaster and upon the sand, that lapped all around, from sky to sky, cast little rhythmical cups of shadow, so that the sand became the sea, and closed over the children's black feet softly and without imprint.

---

1. **piccanins:** native children.
2. **kraal** (kräl): an enclosure for livestock.

The stationmaster's wife sat behind the mesh of her veranda. Above her head the hunk of a sheep's carcass moved slightly, dangling in a current of air.

They waited.

The train called out, along the sky; but there was no answer; and the cry hung on: I'm coming . . . I'm coming . . .

The engine flared out now, big, whisking a dwindling body behind it; the track flared out to let it in.

Creaking, jerking, jostling, gasping, the train filled the station.

Here, let me see that one — the young woman curved her body further out of the corridor window. Missus? smiled the old boy, looking at the creatures he held in his hand. From a piece of string on his gray finger hung a tiny woven basket; he lifted it, questioning. No, no, she urged, leaning down toward him, across the height of the train, toward the man in the piece of old rug; that one, that one, her hand commanded. It was a lion, carved out of soft dry wood that looked like spongecake; heraldic, black and white, with impressionistic detail burnt in. The old man held it up to her still smiling, not from the heart, but at the customer. Between its Vandyke teeth, in the mouth opened in an endless roar too terrible to be heard, it had a black tongue. Look, said the young husband, if you don't mind! And round the neck of the thing, a piece of fur (rat? rabbit? meerkat?); a real mane, majestic, telling you somehow that the artist had delight in the lion.

All up and down the length of the train in the dust the artists sprang, walking bent, like performing animals, the better to exhibit the fantasy held toward the faces on the train. Buck, startled and stiff, staring with round black and white eyes. More lions, standing erect, grappling with strange, thin, elongated warriors who clutched spears and showed no fear in their slits of eyes. How much, they asked from the train, how much?

Give me penny, said the little ones with nothing to sell. The dogs went and sat, quite still, under the dining car, where the train breathed out the smell of meat cooking with onion.

A man passed beneath the arch of reaching arms meeting gray-black and white in the exchange of money for the staring wooden eyes, the stiff wooden legs sticking up in the air; went along under the voices and the bargaining, interrogating the wheels. Past the dogs; glancing up at the dining car where he could stare at the faces, behind glass, drinking beer, two by two, on either side of a uniform railway vase with its pale dead flower. Right to the end, to the guard's van, where the stationmaster's children had just collected their mother's two loaves of bread; to the engine itself, where the stationmaster and the driver stood talking against the steaming complaint of the resting beast.

The man called out to them, something loud and joking. They turned to laugh, in a twirl of steam. The two children careered over the sand, clutching the bread, and burst through the iron gate and up the path through the garden in which nothing grew.

Passengers drew themselves in at the corridor windows and turned into compartments to fetch money, to call someone to look. Those sitting inside looked up: suddenly different, caged faces, boxed in, cut off, after the contact of outside. There was an orange a piccanin would like. . . . What about that chocolate? It wasn't very nice. . . .

A young girl had collected a handful of the hard kind, that no one liked, out of the chocolate box, and was throwing them to the dogs, over at the dining car. But the hens darted in, and swallowed the chocolates, incredibly quick and accurate, before they had even dropped in the dust, and the dogs, a little bewildered, looked up with their brown eyes, not expecting anything.

— No, leave it, said the girl, don't take it. . . .

Too expensive, too much, she shook her head and raised her voice to the old boy, giving up the lion. He held it up where she had handed it to him. No, she said, shaking her head. Three-and-six?[3] insisted her husband, loudly. Yes baas! laughed the boy. *Three-and-six?* — the young man was incredulous. Oh leave it — she said. The young man stopped. Don't you want it? he said, keeping his face closed to the boy. No, never mind, she said, leave it. The old native kept his head on one side, looking at them sideways, holding the lion. Three-and-six, he murmured, as old people repeat things to themselves.

The young woman drew her head in. She went into the coupé and sat down. Out of the window, on the other side, there was nothing; sand and bush; a thorn tree. Back through the open doorway, past the figure of her husband in the corridor, there was the station, the voices, wooden animals waving, running feet. Her eye followed the funny little valance of scrolled wood that outlined the chalet roof of the station; she thought of the lion and smiled. That bit of fur round the neck. But the wooden buck, the hippos, the elephants, the baskets that already bulked out of their brown paper under the seat and on the luggage rack! How will they look at home? Where will you

---

3. **Three-and-six:** three shillings and sixpence; at the time of the story, approximately thirty-four American cents.

put them? What will they mean away from the places you found them? Away from the unreality of the last few weeks? The man outside. But he is not part of the unreality; he is for good now. Odd . . . somewhere there was an idea that he, that living with him, was part of the holiday, the strange places.

Outside, a bell rang. The stationmaster was leaning against the end of the train, green flag rolled in readiness. A few men who had got down to stretch their legs sprang on to the train, clinging to the observation platforms, or perhaps merely standing on the iron step, holding the rail; but on the train, safe from the one dusty platform, the one tin house, the empty sand.

There was a grunt. The train jerked. Through the glass the beer drinkers looked out, as if they could not see beyond it. Behind the flyscreen, the stationmaster's wife sat facing back at them beneath the darkening hunk of meat.

There was a shout. The flag drooped out. Joints not yet coordinated, the segmented body of the train heaved and bumped back against itself. It began to move; slowly the scrolled chalet moved past it, the yells of the natives, running alongside, jetted up into the air, fell back at different levels. Staring wooden faces waved drunkenly, there, then gone, questioning for the last time at the windows. Here, one-and-six baas!— As one automatically opens a hand to catch a thrown ball, a man fumbled wildly down his pocket, brought up the shilling and sixpence and threw them out; the old native, gasping, his skinny toes splaying the sand, flung the lion.

The piccanins were waving, the dogs stood, tails uncertain, watching the train go: past the mud huts, where a woman turned to look, up from the smoke of the fire, her hand pausing on her hip.

The stationmaster went slowly in under the chalet.

The old native stood, breath blowing out the skin between his ribs, feet tense, balanced in the sand, smiling and shaking his head. In his opened palm, held in the attitude of receiving, was the retrieved shilling and sixpence.

The blind end of the train was being pulled helplessly out of the station.

The young man swung in from the corridor, breathless. He was shaking his head with laughter and triumph. Here! he said. And waggled the lion at her. One-and-six!

What? she said.

He laughed. I was arguing with him for fun, bargaining—when the train had pulled out already, he came tearing after. . . . One-and-six baas! So there's your lion.

She was holding it away from her, the head with the open jaws, the pointed teeth, the black tongue, the wonderful ruff of fur facing her. She was looking at it with an expression of not seeing, of seeing something different. Her face was drawn up, wryly, like the face of a discomforted child. Her mouth lifted nervously at the corner. Very slowly, cautious, she lifted her finger and touched the mane, where it was joined to the wood.

But how could you, she said. He was shocked by the dismay of her face.

Good heavens, he said, what's the matter?

If you wanted the thing, she said, her voice rising and breaking with the shrill impotence of anger, why didn't you buy it in the first place? If you wanted it, why didn't you pay for it? Why didn't you take it decently, when he offered it? Why did you have to wait for him to run after the train with it, and give him one-and-six? One-and-six!

She was pushing it at him, trying to force him to take it. He stood astonished, his hands hanging at his sides.

But you wanted it! You liked it so much?

—It's a beautiful piece of work, she said fiercely, as if to protect it from him.

You liked it so much! You said yourself it was too expensive—

Oh *you*—she said, hopeless and furious. *You*. . . . She threw the lion onto the seat.

He stood looking at her.

She sat down again in the corner and, her face slumped in her hand, stared out of the window. Everything was turning round inside her. One-and-six. One-and-six. One-and-six for the wood and the carving and the sinews of the legs and the switch of the tail. The mouth open like that and the teeth. The black tongue, rolling, like a wave. The mane round the neck. To give one-and-six for that. The heat of shame mounted through her legs and body and sounded in her ears like the sound of sand pouring. Pouring, pouring. She sat there, sick. A weariness, a tastelessness, the discovery of a void made her hands slacken their grip, atrophy emptily, as if the hour was not worth their grasp. She was feeling like this again. She had thought it was something to do with singleness, with being alone and belonging too much to oneself.

She sat there not wanting to move or speak, or to look at anything, even; so that the mood should be associated with nothing, no object, word or sight that might recur and so recall the feeling again. . . . Smuts blew in grittily, settled on her hands. Her back remained at exactly the same angle, turned against the young man sitting with his hands drooping between his sprawled legs, and the lion, fallen on its side in the corner.

The train had cast the station like a skin. It called out to the sky, I'm coming, I'm coming; and again, there was no answer.

COMMENTARY

Nadine Gordimer chooses to characterize the people of the small-town station through the *setting* of the story. The single important event in the lives of these people—the stationmaster and his wife, their children, the natives who sit waiting to sell their wares, their children waiting to beg pennies—is the arrival of the train from Rhodesia. The physical inertness of this hot and dusty world reflects the emotional and moral sterility of a society in which connections are few, and those that exist are transitory and mercenary.

The young husband in "The Train from Rhodesia" believes that he has argued with the old man "for fun." To the end of the story he remains uncomprehending of his wife's sudden shift in attitude toward what he has done—sudden because he has bargained with natives before this episode, and she has not objected. The purchases made during their holiday in Rhodesia bulge under the train seat and on the rack above their heads. These details are part of the setting, too, and they tell us a great deal about the lives of this young couple, their acceptance of their world and its values. We do not know, however, what in the scene causes the young woman suddenly to feel an old feeling, to discover "a weariness, a tastelessness, . . . a void." We know only that although she once attached this emptiness to her being alone, the mood's return is beyond her control. Our final view of her is one of physical inertness. Our attention returns to the scene outside—the disappearing station, cast off by the train as if it has molted into a new life. The sky gives no answer to its cry, "I'm coming, I'm coming."

FOR STUDY AND DISCUSSION

1. How do the details of the story's setting suggest the dreary emptiness of the world of the station? In what ways are both life aboard the train and life at the station disconnected or cut off from the outside?
2. What does the young woman see from the window? How is her attitude toward her husband affected by his purchase of the lion? What does the lion represent to her? What does it represent to her husband?
3. What do you think accounts for the woman's shift in mood? What qualities of life described in the story might cause her to feel weary and unfulfilled?

FOR COMPOSITION

Compare the use of setting in "The Train from Rhodesia" with its use in "Across the Bridge" (page 769). To what extent does Greene also use setting to help define characters and their values?

Poetry

William Butler Yeats
1865–1939

Early in his life William Butler Yeats resolved to become a great literary artist, and by the end of his life he was judged by many to be among the greatest poets who had ever lived. The British poet Edwin Muir has defined the source of Yeats's poetry as "a magnificent temperament associated with a magnificent style."

Yeats was an Irishman of Anglo-Norman descent. He spent part of his childhood in Sligo, on the northwest coast of Ireland. There he became acquainted with traditional Irish legends and lore. His father, a painter, moved the family between Dublin and London, where Yeats attended school and spent much time reading, pursuing his interests in Irish legend and Romantic idealism and occult philosophies. Mixed into his thought were the mysticism of Blake, the Romantic idealism of Shelley, and the aesthetic ideas of the Pre-Raphaelites.

By the time he moved to London in 1887, his goals as an artist were fixed. He was particularly interested in making the Irish people conscious of their past and in resurrecting a heroic ideal by which they could live. His first book of poetry, published in 1889, and *The Celtic Twilight*, published in 1893, drew on ancient Irish legend. The beautiful Maud Gonne, whom Yeats met in 1889, drew him into the Irish National movement, about which Yeats had strong doubts. Lady Gregory, who shared his interest in Irish legend, joined with him in founding an Irish National Theater. After returning to Ireland in 1896, Yeats gave less attention to poetry and devoted himself largely to drama and forming the Abbey Theater.

Maud Gonne's marriage to John MacBride, in 1903, marked an important change in Yeats's life. Disappointed in love, he was resolved to make great poetry out of his experience, seeking perfec-

William Butler Yeats by John B. Yeats.
National Gallery of Ireland, Dublin

tion "of the work" instead of "perfection of the life," as he called it in a late poem. Yeats was working to toughen his poetry and to bring it more into touch with the language and preoccupations of the modern world. He was working to simplify his style, to rid it of Romantic vagueness, and to bring it close to the rhythms of everyday speech. His aim was to write poems "as cold and passionate as the dawn." In his aims and practice, and rejection of late Victorian poetic modes, Yeats gave impetus to the Modernist movement in poetry, which in Ezra Pound, T. S. Eliot, Edith Sitwell and others sought a fresh language, new rhythms, and an extension of poetic subjects.

Yeats's Tower
(Thor Ballylee). It was
used as a symbol in a
number of his poems.
Bettina Cirone,
Photo Researchers

Throughout his poetic career, Yeats sought to unify his experience of the world and gain for his poems a central illuminating vision comparable to that of Dante and Shelley, one that would pull together the thousand separate fragments of everyday life. He sought that vision in the mysticism of Blake and occult philosophies, drawing these various ideas together in his philosophical and historical book, *A Vision,* published in 1925. He saturated his poetry with these ideas, constructing in various volumes of poetry a composite portrait of a complex modern being. No single poem revealed Yeats's personality completely: each poem provided some insight into a moment of thought or feeling. At the same time, these poems took the pulse of current thought and feeling.

In 1917 Yeats married the Englishwoman Georgie Hyde-Lees, and his two children were born in 1919 and 1921. He became a senator in the Irish Free State, founded in 1921. In 1923, he was awarded the Nobel Prize for literature. By the time of his death in 1939, Yeats had become the leading poet of his age, who had taught "the free man how to praise," W. H. Auden wrote of him in his great elegiac poem, "In Memory of W. B. Yeats (D. Jan. 1939)."

When You Are Old

When you are old and gray and full of sleep,
And nodding by the fire, take down this book,
And slowly read, and dream of the soft look
Your eyes had once, and of their shadows deep;

How many loved your moments of glad grace,   5
And loved your beauty with love false or true;
But one man loved the pilgrim soul in you,
And loved the sorrows of your changing face.

And bending down beside the glowing bars,
Murmur, a little sadly, how Love fled   10
And paced upon the mountains overhead
And hid his face amid a crowd of stars.

The Song of Wandering Aengus

I went out to the hazel wood,
Because a fire was in my head,
And cut and peeled a hazel wand,
And hooked a berry to a thread;
And when white moths were on the wing,   5
And moth-like stars were flickering out,
I dropped the berry in a stream
And caught a little silver trout.

When I had laid it on the floor
I went to blow the fire aflame,   10
But something rustled on the floor,
And someone called me by my name:
It had become a glimmering girl
With apple blossom in her hair
Who called me by my name and ran   15
And faded through the brightening air.

Though I am old with wandering
Through hollow lands and hilly lands,
I will find out where she has gone,
And kiss her lips and take her hands;   20
And walk among long dappled grass,
And pluck till time and times are done
The silver apples of the moon,
The golden apples of the sun.

The Wild Swans at Coole°

The trees are in their autumn beauty,
The woodland paths are dry,
Under the October twilight the water
Mirrors a still sky;
Upon the brimming water among the stones   5
Are nine-and-fifty swans.

The nineteenth autumn has come upon me
Since I first made my count;
I saw, before I had well finished,
All suddenly mount   10
And scatter wheeling in great broken rings
Upon their clamorous wings.

I have looked upon those brilliant creatures,
And now my heart is sore.
All's changed since I, hearing at twilight,   15
The first time on this shore,
The bell-beat of their wings above my head,
Trod with a lighter tread.

Unwearied still, lover by lover,
They paddle in the cold   20
Companionable streams or climb the air;
Their hearts have not grown old;
Passion or conquest, wander where they will,
Attend upon them still.

But now they drift on the still water   25
Mysterious, beautiful;
Among what rushes will they build,
By what lake's edge or pool
Delight men's eyes when I awake some day
To find they have flown away?   30

° **Coole** (kōōl′): the estate of Yeats's friend and fellow dramatist, Lady Gregory,
whom Yeats often visited.

An Irish Airman Foresees His Death

This poem concerns Major Robert Gregory, an Irish volunteer in England's
Royal Flying Corps, which fought against Germany in World War I.

I know that I shall meet my fate
Somewhere among the clouds above;
Those that I fight I do not hate,
Those that I guard I do not love;°
My country is Kiltartan Cross,   5
My countrymen Kiltartan's poor,°
No likely end could bring them loss
Or leave them happier than before.
Nor law, nor duty bade me fight,
Nor public men, nor cheering crowds,   10
A lonely impulse of delight
Drove to this tumult in the clouds;
I balanced all, brought all to mind,
The years to come seemed waste of breath,
A waste of breath the years behind   15
In balance with this life, this death.

3–4. **Those . . . love:** Ireland was still under English rule in World War I. The
hatred of the Irish was directed at their rulers rather than against Germany.
6. **Kiltartan's poor:** the poor of Ireland.

FOR STUDY AND DISCUSSION

When You Are Old
1. What book do you think the speaker is asking
the woman to read?
2. What does the phrase "pilgrim soul" tell you
about the woman? How does the speaker contrast
his love for her with the love of others?
3. What evidence can you find to show that the
speaker's love was not reciprocated and was finally
withdrawn?

The Song of Wandering Aengus
Aengus, an ancient Celtic god in Irish mythology,
was for Yeats the god of youthful love, poetry, and
beauty. Some readers think the poem celebrates
the pursuit of elusive ideals by artists or poets.
What evidence do you find in the poem to support
this interpretation?

The Wild Swans at Coole
1. What aspects of setting reinforce the speaker's
mood?
2. How are the swans contrasted with the speaker?
What do they symbolize to him? Why do you think
they are called "mysterious" (line 26)?

An Irish Airman Foresees His Death
1. The airman says he is not fighting in any holy
war or even for any ideal. His death would not
change the lives of any of his countrymen. Why,
then, do you think he has volunteered to fly a
warplane?
2. In lines 13–16, the airman decides that concern
about the past or the future is pointless. What does
he conclude is important in the present?

The Second Coming

Turning and turning in the widening gyre
The falcon cannot hear the falconer;
Things fall apart; the center cannot hold;
Mere anarchy is loosed upon the world,
The blood-dimmed tide is loosed, and everywhere   5
The ceremony of innocence is drowned;
The best lack all conviction, while the worst
Are full of passionate intensity.

Surely some revelation is at hand;
Surely the Second Coming is at hand.   10
The Second Coming! Hardly are those words out
When a vast image out of *Spiritus Mundi*°
Troubles my sight: somewhere in sands of the desert
A shape with lion body and the head of a man,°
A gaze blank and pitiless as the sun,   15
Is moving its slow thighs, while all about it
Reel shadows of the indignant desert birds.
The darkness drops again; but now I know
That twenty centuries° of stony sleep
Were vexed to nightmare by a rocking cradle,°   20
And what rough beast, its hour come round at last,
Slouches towards Bethlehem to be born?

---

12. *Spiritus Mundi:* World Spirit or Soul, the Great Memory of Nature, "a general
storehouse of images" on which the imagination of the poet draws.   14. **shape** . . .
man: an image that had come to Yeats in an early occult experience, described
later as "a brazen winged beast that I associated with laughing destruction."
19. **twenty centuries:** the two-thousand-year period preceding the birth of Christ.
20. **rocking cradle:** the cradle of the Christ child.

Hawking scene, pendant, late sixteenth century.
Courtesy, British Museum

COMMENTARY

Written in 1919, "The Second Coming" reveals the impact of the World War, the Bolshevik Revolution in Russia, and the British effort to suppress the rebellion in Ireland. Further, the poem reflects Yeats's complex theory of history.

Yeats believed that history occurs in two-thousand-year periods or cycles, one cycle subjective and emotional, the other objective and rational. As each historical cycle comes to an end or unwinds, another cycle—its opposite—begins, inaugurating the new era with a momentous event. For example, the birth of Christ, which inaugurated the era of Christianity, marked the end of the classical era, which had lasted for two thousand years. The two cycles (symbolized by a gyre or vortex) also intertwine, one winding up as the other winds down, their energies sometimes in conflict, sometimes in momentary balance. Yeats uses this system in "The Second Coming" to explain the breakdown of society in the beginning of the twentieth century. Although the specific identity of the "rough beast" is not revealed to us here, Yeats suggested toward the end of his life that the poem predicted the rise of fascism in Europe—a reign of anarchy and terror in keeping with the historical cycle.

In the poem, the unwinding of an era or cycle is symbolized in the opening lines by the "widening gyre," or spiral, which like the falcon leaving the hand of the falconer rises in larger and larger circular orbits. As the orbit of flight widens, the falconer loses control of the bird—"Things fall apart; the center cannot hold;/"Mere anarchy is loosed upon the world."

FOR STUDY AND DISCUSSION

1. In falconry the bird flies in circles and eventually returns at the call of its master. What change does Yeats make in this pattern? How does Yeats use this change as a symbol?

2. In the second stanza, what does Yeats suggest will be characteristic of the new era symbolized by the "rough beast" that "Slouches towards Bethlehem to be born"?

3. According to a Biblical prophecy, Christ is to return and establish a new era of peace and prosperity. What ironic use does Yeats make of the phrase "Second Coming"?

Sailing to Byzantium°

I

That is no country for old men. The young
In one another's arms, birds in the trees
— Those dying generations — at their song,
The salmon-falls, the mackerel-crowded seas,
Fish, flesh, or fowl, commend all summer long   5
Whatever is begotten, born, and dies.
Caught in that sensual music all neglect
Monuments of unaging intellect.

° **Byzantium:** now Istanbul, Turkey; the ancient seat of the Eastern Roman Empire
and the Greek Christian Church. For Yeats, it symbolized a unification of artistic
and spiritual values.

Court of Justinian (mosaic), Church of San Vitale, Ravenna, Italy.
Scala/Editorial Photocolor Archives

II

An aged man is but a paltry thing,
A tattered coat upon a stick, unless   10
Soul clap its hands and sing, and louder sing
For every tatter in its mortal dress,
Nor is there singing school but studying
Monuments of its own magnificence;
And therefore I have sailed the seas and come 15
To the holy city of Byzantium.

III

O sages standing in God's holy fire
As in the gold mosaic of a wall,°
Come from the holy fire, perne in a gyre,°
And be the singing-masters of my soul.   20
Consume my heart away; sick with desire
And fastened to a dying animal
It knows not what it is; and gather me
Into the artifice of eternity.

IV

Once out of nature I shall never take   25
My bodily form from any natural thing,
But such a form as Grecian goldsmiths make
Of hammered gold and gold enameling°
To keep a drowsy Emperor awake;
Or set upon a golden bough to sing   30
To lords and ladies of Byzantium
Of what is past, or passing, or to come.

17–18. **sages . . . wall:** Wise men and saints are depicted in gold mosaic on the
walls of Byzantine churches in Ravenna, Italy, and Sicily, which Yeats visited in
1924.   19. **perne . . . gyre:** spin in a spiraling motion. *Pern* is a spool. For Yeats,
this is an image of historical cycles.   27–28. **such . . . enameling:** Yeats wrote, "I
have read somewhere that in the Emperor's palace at Byzantium was a tree made
of gold and silver, and artificial birds that sang."

FOR STUDY AND DISCUSSION

1. In the first stanza, the cycle of birth, life, and death of all living things is contrasted with seemingly eternal monuments of art. In the second stanza, what human element does the speaker suggest is an integral part of these great artistic monuments?

2. In the third stanza, what request does the speaker make of the sages?

3. In the last stanza, what "form" does the speaker choose as a reflection of his soul? What does his choice tell you of his feelings about old age and death?

4. What do you think Yeats might be saying about the purposes of art in general and the motives that impel the artist?

SYMBOLS AND THE SYMBOLIST MOVEMENT

A *symbol* is anything used to stand for an idea. By using symbols, writers can make general ideas vivid and specific. They can charge an otherwise neutral concept with emotion and, since a symbol tends to suggest other symbols, they can give an idea an evocative quality it would otherwise lack.

Much twentieth-century poetry relies heavily upon symbols. The two most influential modern British poets, William Butler Yeats and T. S. Eliot, were themselves deeply influenced by the French Symbolist movement. French Symbolist poets such as Baudelaire, Mallarmé, and Rimbaud wrote musically evocative poems that usually suggested ideas rather than stating them directly. Yeats used symbols in his poems as a path to an inner vision, a complex system which he described in his book *A Vision* and which he hoped would be a unifying core for his poetry. In an essay, "The Symbolism of Poetry," Yeats asserted that the power of poetry comes chiefly from symbols, both emotional symbols "that evoke emotions alone" and intellectual symbols "that evoke ideas alone or ideas mingled with emotions." Calling for a rejection from a direct discussion of intellectual and moral issues in poetry, Yeats wrote:

> If people were to accept the theory that poetry moves us because of its symbolism, what change should one look for in the manner of our poetry? A return to the way of our fathers, a casting out of descriptions of nature for the sake of nature, of the moral law for the sake of the moral law, a casting out of all anecdotes and of that brooding over scientific opinion that so often extinguished the central flame in Tennyson. . . . With this change of substance, this return to imagination, this understanding of the laws of art . . . would come a change of style . . . we would seek out those wavering, meditative, organic rhythms, which are the embodiment of the imagination, that neither desires nor hates, because it has done with time, and only wishes to gaze upon some reality, some beauty . . .

Cite examples of the use of symbols in "Sailing to Byzantium." To what extent, in your opinion, does the emotional power of this poem rely on use of symbols? How do symbols give this poem a visionary quality, a sense that Yeats was looking through an immediate situation to something deeper and eternal?

FOR COMPOSITION

1. Using several of Yeats's poems as examples, write a composition in which you discuss the use of symbols in poetry. You may also wish to use poems such as Shelley's "Ode to the West Wind" and Blake's "The Tiger."

2. Compare the themes of "Sailing to Byzantium" and Keats's "Ode on a Grecian Urn." Referring to specific passages, discuss what shows one poem to be the work of a young man and the other the work of a man growing old.

Walter de la Mare
1873–1956

Songs of Childhood was Walter de la Mare's first book of verse. After its publication in 1902, he came to be identified with the Georgian poets of the first two decades of the twentieth century— poets considered conservative and anti-Modernist in their verse. This group was influenced more by Milton than by Donne and the metaphysical poets, and less influenced by modern European poetry than were Ezra Pound, T. S. Eliot, and other Modernist poets of the 1920's.

De la Mare is a poet of wistful dream and the supernatural, often Romantic in his themes but also aware of the hidden terrors that the Romantic view of life often disguises. Of the Georgian poets, De la Mare was the most influenced by the Symbolists. The results are apparent in his fresh and unusual use of familiar words and his dependence on highly suggestive images to convey experiences and feelings that are only hinted at rather than named explicitly.

All That's Past

Very old are the woods;
   And the buds that break
Out of the brier's boughs,
   When March winds wake,
So old with their beauty are—   5
   Oh, no man knows
Through what wild centuries
   Roves back the rose.

Very old are the brooks;
   And the rills° that rise   10
Where snow sleeps cold beneath
   The azure skies
Sing such a history
   Of come and gone,
Their every drop is as wise   15
   As Solomon.

Very old are we men;
   Our dreams are tales
Told in dim Eden
   By Eve's nightingales;   20
We wake and whisper awhile,
   But, the day gone by,
Silence and sleep like fields
   Of amaranth° lie.

---

10. **rills:** little brooks or rivulets.   24. **amaranth:** an imaginary flower that does not fade or die.

Richard Perrine, Taurus Photo

FOR STUDY AND DISCUSSION

1. What do the first two stanzas reveal about the permanence of nature's beauty and wisdom?

2. In the final stanza, how are human beings depicted in contrast to nature? How does the Biblical allusion to Eden help intensify the contrast?

3. De la Mare uses various poetic techniques to create a dreamlike effect or sense of unreality in his poetry. *Alliteration*—the repetition of consonants in initial positions mainly—is one means to reinforce sounds so that we linger over and are able to recall the experience as in a dream. The technique is used, for example, in lines 2 and 3:

> And the *b*uds that *b*reak
> Out of the *b*rier's *b*oughs,

What other examples of alliteration do you find in the poem?

4. The repetition of the same *vowel* sound within a passage is called *assonance*. De la Mare uses assonance to join words that form a pattern of meaning:

> S*o* *o*ld with their beauty are—
>   *O*h, n*o* man kn*o*ws
> Through what wild centuries
>   R*o*ves back the r*o*se.

In these lines "roves" and "rose" reinforce each other through their similarity in sound. What pattern of meaning is created in the other words marked for assonance? How is this pattern developed in later lines of the poem?

D. H. Lawrence
1885–1930

D. H. Lawrence's major literary activity was the writing of stories and novels, but he was also an outstanding poet. Strongly influenced by Whitman, Lawrence favored free verse, for he wished to capture the feeling of the moment and to be as unpremeditated as possible. In breaking from the major movements of poetry, Lawrence used his poems to make direct statements about basic qualities of human beings and to express the "instant, whole man." He wanted to rediscover the fundamental sources of energy and vitality, and he looked to nature and the physical world: "My great religion is a belief in the blood, the flesh, as being wiser than the intellect. We can go wrong in our minds. But what our blood feels and believes and says is always true. . . ."

For a detailed account of the author's life, see page 728.

Snake

A snake came to my water-trough
On a hot, hot day, and I in pajamas for the heat,
To drink there.

In the deep, strange-scented shade of the great dark carob-tree
I came down the steps with my pitcher   5
And must wait, must stand and wait, for there he was at the
    trough before me.

He reached down from a fissure in the earth-wall in the gloom
And trailed his yellow-brown slackness soft-bellied down, over
    the edge of the stone trough
And rested his throat upon the stone bottom,
And where the water had dripped from the tap, in a small clear-
    ness,   10
He sipped with his straight mouth,
Softly drank through his straight gums, into his slack long
    body,
Silently.

Someone was before me at my water-trough,
And I, like a second comer, waiting.   15

He lifted his head from his drinking, as cattle do,
And looked at me vaguely, as drinking cattle do,
And flickered his two-forked tongue from his lips, and mused a
    moment,
And stooped and drank a little more,
Being earth-brown, earth-golden from the burning bowels of
    the earth   20
On the day of Sicilian July, with Etna° smoking.

---

21. **Etna:** Mount Etna, a volcano in Sicily.

The voice of my education said to me
He must be killed,
For in Sicily the black, black snakes are innocent, the gold are
    venomous.

And voices in me said, If you were a man   25
You would take a stick and break him now, and finish him off.

But must I confess how I liked him,
How glad I was he had come like a guest in quiet, to drink at
    my water-trough
And depart peaceful, pacified, and thankless,
Into the burning bowels of this earth?   30

Was it cowardice, that I dared not kill him?
Was it perversity, that I longed to talk to him?
Was it humility, to feel so honored?
I felt so honored.

And yet those voices: 35
If you were not afraid, you would kill him!

And truly I was afraid, I was most afraid,
But even so, honored still more
That he should seek my hospitality
From out the dark door of the secret earth.   40

He drank enough
And lifted his head, dreamily, as one who has drunken,
And flickered his tongue like a forked night on the air, so
    black;
Seeming to lick his lips,
And looked around like a god, unseeing, into the air,   45
And slowly turned his head,
And slowly, very slowly, as if thrice adream,
Proceeded to draw his slow length curving round
And climb again the broken bank of my wall-face.

And as he put his head into that dreadful hole,   50
And as he slowly drew up, snake-easing his shoulders, and en-
    tered farther,
A sort of horror, a sort of protest against his withdrawing into
    that horrid black hole,
Deliberately going into the blackness, and slowly drawing
    himself after,
Overcame me now his back was turned.

I looked round, I put down my pitcher, 55
I picked up a clumsy log
And threw it at the water-trough with a clatter.

I think it did not hit him,
But suddenly that part of him that was left behind convulsed in
    undignified haste,
Writhed like lightning, and was gone 60
Into the black hole, the earth-lipped fissure in the wall front,
At which, in the intense still noon, I stared with fascination.

And immediately I regretted it.
I thought how paltry, how vulgar, what a mean act!
I despised myself and the voices of my accursed human educa-
    tion. 65

And I thought of the albatross,°
And I wished he would come back, my snake.

For he seemed to me again like a king,
Like a king in exile, uncrowned in the underworld,
Now due to be crowned again. 70

And so, I missed my chance with one of the lords
Of life.
And I have something to expiate;
A pettiness.

---

66. **albatross:** the bird killed by the Mariner in Coleridge's "The Rime of the Ancient Mariner." Traditionally, the albatross symbolized good luck.

FOR STUDY AND DISCUSSION

1. What internal conflict does the speaker experience while watching the snake (lines 22–40)? How
does he resolve the conflict?
2. The snake is traditionally a symbol of evil.
What does the snake represent for the speaker?
Why do you think the speaker feels honored to
have the snake drink from his water trough?

3. One of Lawrence's themes in "Snake" contrasts
what we are taught to think about certain creatures with what we may instinctively feel about
them. Notice the line in the concluding stanza of
the poem, "And I have something to expiate."
What sin has the speaker committed? What does
the poem imply about the proper relationship of
human beings to the natural world? Why might the
poet regard the snake as a "lord of life"?

Siegfried Sassoon

1886–1967

Siegfried Sassoon was born into a wealthy London family. He was educated at Clare College, Cambridge University, and before World War I lived the life of leisure as an English country gentleman. His early romantic poetry appeared in the Georgian collections that began publication in 1912. He enlisted in the British army in 1914, but it was not until later in the war that he became disillusioned and began writing poems of angry protest against the war and the brutality he had witnessed. In contrast to his earlier poems of ordered loveliness, those written between 1916 and 1918 are undisguised in their bitterness and filled with shocking, realistic details whose intended purpose is to awaken the comfortable civilian to the horrors of trench warfare. He sought in his poetry the "full and living voice, seemingly natural, though often using the language of a personal poetic idiom. I mean the true vocal cadence of something urgently communicated . . ." The poetry Sassoon wrote after the war is usually quieter in mood than his war poems, though still drawing on these earlier painful experiences. In later years, Sassoon wrote about his life and new-found spiritualism in a series of memoirs.

Everyone Sang

Everyone suddenly burst out singing;
And I was filled with such delight
As prisoned birds must find in freedom
Winging wildly across the white
Orchards and dark green fields; on; on;   5
   and out of sight.

Everyone's voice was suddenly lifted,
And beauty came like the setting sun.
My heart was shaken with tears, and horror
Drifted away. . . . O, but everyone   10
Was a bird; and the song was wordless; the
   singing will never be done.

FOR STUDY AND DISCUSSION

1. What similes does Sassoon employ to suggest the joy of release from war? What do you think the speaker means by saying the song of everyone was "wordless"?

2. How does the poem illustrate Sassoon's belief that poetry must be written in "the true vocal cadence of something urgently communicated"?

Rupert Brooke
1887–1915

Though Rupert Brooke was early identified with the Georgian poets, much of his verse reflected his interest in John Donne and the early seventeenth-century dramatist John Webster, on whom he wrote a dissertation at Cambridge University. In the years before World War I, Brooke suffered an unhappy love affair that brought him close to nervous collapse. He broke with friends and turned back to traditional Victorian attitudes that he had repudiated in his college days. In 1913 he traveled in the United States, Canada, and the Pacific, spending several months in Tahiti, where he wrote some of his most famous poems. Following his enlistment in the navy and brief service in Belgium, he wrote his war sonnets, among them "The Soldier." Traditional not only in form, these poems were the last of that period to express idealistic patriotism in the face of war. Unlike Siegfried Sassoon and Wilfred Owen, Brooke did not live to witness the horrors of trench warfare, for he died of blood poisoning en route to the Dardanelles with the British Mediterranean Expeditionary Force.

The Soldier

If I should die, think only this of me;
   That there's some corner of a foreign field
That is forever England. There shall be
   In that rich earth a richer dust concealed;
A dust whom England bore, shaped, made aware,
   Gave, once, her flowers to love, her ways to roam,
A body of England's breathing English air,
   Washed by the rivers, blest by suns of home.

And think, this heart, all evil shed away,
   A pulse in the eternal mind, no less
     Gives somewhere back the thoughts by England given;
Her sights and sounds; dreams happy as her day;
   And laughter, learnt of friends; and gentleness,
     In hearts at peace, under an English heaven.

10   Rupert Brooke
Radio Times Hulton

FOR STUDY AND DISCUSSION

1. What are the poet's feelings toward England and the cause for which he may die? What traditional English qualities does he stress?

2. Brooke expresses an ideal of happiness, not the actual reality of his life. What statements in the poem show his awareness of the courage and hope needed to achieve that ideal?

3. T. S. Eliot characterized Georgian poetry in these words: ". . . the Georgian poets insist upon the English countryside, and are even positively patriotic. . . ." To what extent does "The Soldier" fit this characterization?

Edwin Muir

1887–1959

Edwin Muir was born in the Orkney Islands, northeast of Scotland, where his father had a farm. The simple folk culture of the islands, bound to ancient custom and belief, instilled in the boy a heroic view of life that strongly influenced his later writings. When Edwin was thirteen, his family moved to Glasgow, an uprooting that haunted him for the rest of his life. He left school the following year, educating himself and trying his hand at writing. His marriage to novelist and critic Willa Anderson in 1919 precipitated his departure for London, where he worked as a journalist and teacher, and with his wife translated the works of a number of European writers, including Franz Kafka.

Muir belonged to no modern school but found his own style in a combination of grace, wisdom, and a seemingly effortless mastery of the language. His poetry is saturated with Christian and Platonic ideas, with the belief that human existence is in touch always with an immortal world from which people descend into life. He is fascinated by time, by links between generations, by the modern meaning of ancient myths. "As I look back on the part of the mystery which is my own life, my own fable," Muir wrote in his autobiography, "what I am most aware of is that we receive more than we can ever give; we receive it from the past, on which we draw with every breath, but also—and this is a point of faith—from the Source of the mystery itself, by the means which religious people call Grace."

The critic John Holloway writes that for Muir the powers of good were greater than the powers of evil because "they were also humbler, more primeval, nearer to life in its archaic simplicity; which Muir was able to see not far below life's surface distractions."

Red Horses by Franz Marc.
Harbrace, courtesy Franz Hanfstaengl, Munich, Germany

The Horses

Barely a twelvemonth after
The seven days war that put the world to sleep,
Late in the evening the strange horses came.
By then we had made our covenant with silence,
But in the first few days it was so still   5
We listened to our breathing and were afraid.
On the second day
The radios failed; we turned the knobs; no answer.
On the third day a warship passed us, heading north,
Dead bodies piled on the deck. On the sixth day   10
A plane plunged over us into the sea. Thereafter
Nothing. The radios dumb;
And still they stand in corners of our kitchens,
And stand, perhaps, turned on, in a million rooms
All over the world. But now if they should speak,   15
If on a sudden they should speak again,
If on the stroke of noon a voice should speak,
We would not listen, we would not let it bring
That old bad world that swallowed its children quick°
At one great gulp. We would not have it again.   20
Sometimes we think of the nations lying asleep,
Curled blindly in impenetrable sorrow,
And then the thought confounds us with its strangeness.
The tractors lie about our fields; at evening
They look like dank sea-monsters crouched and waiting.   25
We leave them where they are and let them rust:
'They'll moulder away and be like other loam.'
We make our oxen drag our rusty ploughs,
Long laid aside. We have gone back
Far past our fathers' land.   30
                          And then, that evening
Late in the summer the strange horses came.
We heard a distant tapping on the road,
A deepening drumming; it stopped, went on again
And at the corner changed to hollow thunder.   35
We saw the heads
Like a wild wave charging and were afraid.
We had sold our horses in our fathers' time
To buy new tractors. Now they were strange to us
As fabulous steeds set on an ancient shield   40
Or illustrations in a book of knights.

---

19. **quick:** alive.

We did not dare go near them. Yet they waited,
Stubborn and shy, as if they had been sent
By an old command to find our whereabouts
And that long-lost archaic companionship.   45
In the first moment we had never a thought
That they were creatures to be owned and used.
Among them were some half-a-dozen colts
Dropped in some wilderness of the broken world,
Yet new as if they had come from their own Eden.   50
Since then they have pulled our ploughs and borne our loads,
But that free servitude still can pierce our hearts.
Our life is changed; their coming our beginning.

FOR STUDY AND DISCUSSION

1. T. S. Eliot, in his preface to the 1952 edition of Muir's poems, refers to "The Horses" as "that great, that terrifying poem of the 'atomic age.'" What details tell the reader that the war is modern and devastating?

2. Biblical allusions remind the speaker of another world long past. What are these allusions, and what do they reveal about that world?

3. Does the speaker know from where the horses have come? How does he explain their coming? What do they bring or provide for the survivors of the war?

4. What qualities of horses—not specifically named in the poem—are important to understanding the meaning they have for the speaker? Would mules or donkeys have been equally appropriate symbols?

FOR COMPOSITION

Compare and contrast "The Horses" with Brooke's "The Soldier," with attention to the following:

the attitude toward war and death in war
the images by which the poets express their attitudes
the dominant tone

Edith Sitwell

1887–1964

Reacting to what she regarded as "the dead and expected patterns" of Georgian poetry, Edith Sitwell brought into her poetry the new rhythms and images of modern art. A nonconformist always, outspoken and flamboyant, she tried to see the world through new eyes, and the vision she communicates in her verse is often startling and fantastic, joining words and images in surprising combinations. Behind the surfaces of life, she sought a spiritual reality. Increasingly she saw her poetry as a celebration of life, caught in its separate rhythms. She wrote in notes to her poems: "Rhythm is one of the principal translators between dream and reality. Rhythm might be described as, to the world of sound, what light is to the world of sight." She sought, she tells us, "to produce a poetry that is the light of the Great Morning, wherein all beings whom we see passing in the common street are transformed into the epitome of all beauty, or of all joy, or of all sorrow." Many of her poems are satiric in their comments on human pretensions and inhumanity. Despite her own birth to aristocratic parents, she was especially critical of London's fashionable, wealthy people who were oblivious to the suffering of the poor.

Edith Sitwell by Wyndham Lewis.
The Tate Gallery, London

Sir Beelzebub

WHEN
Sir
Beelzebub° called for his syllabub° in the hotel in Hell
    Where Proserpine first fell,
Blue as the gendarmerie° were the waves of the sea,   5

    (Rocking and shocking the bar-maid).

Nobody comes to give him his rum but the
Rim of the sky hippopotamus-glum
Enhances the chances to bless with a benison
Alfred Lord Tennyson crossing the bar laid   10
With cold vegetation from pale deputations
Of temperance workers (all signed in Memoriam)°
Hoping with glory to trip up the Laureate's° feet,

    (Moving in classical meters). . . .

Like Balaclava,° the lava came down from the   15
Roof, and the sea's blue wooden gendarmerie
Took them in charge while Beelzebub roared for his rum.

. . . None of them come!

---

3. **Beelzebub:** one of the chief devils. **syllabub:** sweet, alcoholic drink. 5. **gendarmerie:** headquarters of the French police, whose officers wear blue uniforms. 12. **in Memoriam:** *In Memoriam* is a long elegiac poem by Alfred, Lord Tennyson. 13. **Laureate:** Tennyson became poet laureate in 1850, the year of *In Memoriam.* 15. **Balaclava:** the site of the charge of the Light Brigade, the subject of Tennyson's poem of that name.

FOR STUDY AND DISCUSSION

1. In "Sir Beelzebub," Hell is a world of unchanging horizons, purposelessness, eternal waiting. One of the chief devils waits for drinks that never come; "deputations/Of temperance workers" wait to trip up a famous poet who never arrives. How does Sitwell characterize Sir Beelzebub? What significance do you find in his waiting for his drinks in a fashionable hotel?

2. What images are repeated to convey a sense of monotony? How do the internal rhymes heighten this effect? Are the meter and the line length regular enough to convey monotony?

3. What attitudes in modern life is Sitwell satirizing in the poem?

T. S. Eliot
1888–1965

T. S. Eliot
Rollie McKenna

If one figure had to be named as the pivotal leader among writers in English during the first half of the twentieth century, it would be Thomas Stearns Eliot. Not only was he a great poet, a great critic, a fine playwright, and a far-reaching influence on others, but he sought to become the conscience of his generation, deliberately fitting himself for this role, which he summed up in a celebrated phrase when he defined his beliefs as "classicist in literature, royalist in politics, and Anglo-Catholic in religion."

When Eliot began to publish verse at the age of twenty-six, his first few readers were generally shocked by what they took to be a dry, overclever, revolutionary use of language and syntax. Fifty years later, when his name was surrounded by an air of majesty unique in his time, that same verse still had a contemporary ring to it. Today he seems representative of an age in which many people, feeling themselves barren because of their doubt, searched for an experience of faith.

Eliot was born in St. Louis, Missouri, attended Harvard University, and subsequently the Sorbonne in Paris and Oxford University in England. World War I caught him in England, where he worked for a time in Lloyd's Bank, married, and finally settled for good. In the 1920's he joined the London publishing house that later became Faber and Faber, and in 1927 he became a British subject. In the years following, he avoided publicity and deliberately cultivated a shy aloofness, lightened by an almost youthful sense of humor.

What Eliot achieved was an exact expression for the spiritual disease of the twentieth century. After the unquenchable optimism of the Victorian Age had burned itself out in World War I, a period of intense questioning began. One by one, what had seemed established certainties were questioned; a society that had appeared both stable and progressive for over a century broke into fragments. Eliot's classic expression of the temper of his age is *The Waste Land,* a poem which, despite its extreme difficulty, brought him immediate fame. "The Hollow Men," published two years after *The Waste Land,* is almost as powerful an expression of an age of doubt that longs in despair for belief. In the early 1920's Eliot's attitude toward the world was negative. He watched it carefully and hated what he saw. He cultivated an ironic, detached, corrosive manner in his poetry, and when he wrote prose, it was with the didactic purpose of turning his readers away from what he considered the self-indulgence of the Romantics and toward the sterner splendors of Elizabethan drama and seventeenth-century metaphysical poetry. He wished to discourage the easy acceptance of popular favorites like Milton or Shelley in order to make room for neglected masters like John Donne.

Little by little Eliot's negative attitude toward society changed. Close study of Dante brought him to consider traditional Christianity as the one chance of finding a still center in the midst of chaos. His poem *Ash Wednesday*, written following his confirmation in 1927 in the Church of England, was a significant step in this direction. But the final expression of a long process of thought took place nine years later when he wrote the first of *Four Quartets*. These poems were published in 1943 and conclude his major work as a poet with a new serenity of outlook.

In the latter part of his life, Eliot turned more and more to playwriting and to the writing of essays and books discussing social and religious themes, notably *Notes Toward a Definition of Culture* and *The Aims of Education*. It was his aim to revitalize poetic drama, to write plays that would seem perfectly natural to audiences although the characters were speaking poetry. One of his modern plays, *The Cocktail Party*, had a long run in both London and New York, but his earlier play, *Murder in the Cathedral*, is closest to traditional poetic drama.

As a poet, Eliot is above all an intellectual, one who has put much hard thinking into his verse and who demands an equal amount of thought from the reader. He can encompass poignant feeling when he chooses, but his habitual choice is to establish an exact equation between feeling and thought. Some of his poems are difficult because the links between the ideas have been suppressed. Consequently, the reader must study these poems carefully to piece together into a logical sequence the seemingly isolated statements.

Eliot may be said to have changed the direction of modern writing more sharply than did any of his contemporaries. He changed it in the direction of precision and complexity, and of wide-ranging reference, so that all of history is brought into his poetry. And he moved it toward deep but highly controlled emotion—emotion, as some of his poems imply, that is much too serious to be stated in consciously "poetic" language. In 1948 he was awarded the Nobel Prize in literature.

Preludes

I

The winter evening settles down
With smell of steaks in passageways.°
Six o'clock.
The burnt-out ends of smoky days.
And now a gusty shower wraps   5
The grimy scraps
Of withered leaves about your feet
And newspapers from vacant lots;
The showers beat
On broken blinds and chimney-pots,   10
And at the corner of the street
A lonely cab-horse steams and stamps.

And then the lighting of the lamps.

II

The morning comes to consciousness
Of faint stale smells of beer   15
From the sawdust-trampled street
With all its muddy feet that press
To early coffee-stands.

With the other masquerades
That time resumes,   20
One thinks of all the hands
That are raising dingy shades
In a thousand furnished rooms.

---

2. **smell . . . passageways:** In 1910, the time of the poem's writing, steaks were inexpensive and associated with tenement living.

III

You tossed a blanket from the bed,
You lay upon your back, and waited;   25
You dozed, and watched the night re-
      vealing
The thousand sordid images
Of which your soul was constituted;
They flickered against the ceiling.
And when all the world came back   30
And the light crept up between the
      shutters
And you heard the sparrows in the gut-
      ters,
You had such a vision of the street
As the street hardly understands;
Sitting along the bed's edge, where   35
You curled the papers from your hair,
Or clasped the yellow soles of feet
In the palms of both soiled hands.

IV

His soul stretched tight across the
      skies
That fade behind a city block,   40
Or trampled by insistent feet
At four and five and six o'clock;
And short square fingers stuffing pipes,
And evening newspapers, and eyes
Assured of certain certainties.   45
The conscience of a blackened street
Impatient to assume the world.

I am moved by fancies that are curled
Around these images, and cling:
The notion of some infinitely gentle   50
Infinitely suffering thing.

Wipe your hand across your mouth,
      and laugh;
The worlds revolve like ancient
      women
Gathering fuel in vacant lots.

FOR STUDY AND DISCUSSION

1. A prelude is a short piece of music that prepares the listener for the spoken or musical drama that is to follow. The preludes of some composers stand by themselves and express a single mood. How would you describe the mood of this poem? How does the speaker feel about city life?

2. In the second prelude, how does Eliot use *synecdoche*—a part to stand for the whole—to suggest the dehumanizing elements of modern urban life?

3. How does the image in the last two lines sum up the speaker's feelings about the effects of city life on people?

The Hollow Men

Mistah Kurtz—he dead.°

A penny for the Old Guy°

I

We are the hollow men
We are the stuffed men
Leaning together
Headpiece filled with straw. Alas!
Our dried voices, when   5
We whisper together
Are quiet and meaningless
As wind in dry grass
Or rats' feet over broken glass
In our dry cellar   10

Shape without form, shade without color,
Paralyzed force, gesture without motion;

Those who have crossed
With direct eyes, to death's other Kingdom°
Remember us—if at all—not as lost   15
Violent souls, but only
As the hollow men
The stuffed men.

II

Eyes I dare not meet in dreams
In death's dream kingdom   20
These do not appear:
There, the eyes are
Sunlight on a broken column
There, is a tree swinging
And voices are   25
In the wind's singing
More distant and more solemn
Than a fading star.

° **Mistah Kurtz:** a character in Joseph Conrad's *Heart of Darkness* who goes to Africa with the idea of reforming the natives but, because of his own inner weakness, is instead corrupted by the primitive environment. All his base instincts are aroused, and he is eventually destroyed by the horror of what he has become. **A . . . Guy:** a cry used by children on Guy Fawkes Day when, in England, they carry stuffed effigies of Fawkes and beg for handouts to buy firecrackers. Fawkes was a traitor who in 1605 unsuccessfully attempted to blow up the Houses of Parliament. **13-14. Those . . . Kingdom:** Those with "direct eyes" are the blessed in Paradise. The allusion is to Dante's *Paradiso*.

Let me be no nearer
In death's dream kingdom   30
Let me also wear
Such deliberate disguises
Rat's coat, crowskin, crossed staves°
In a field
Behaving as the wind behaves   35
No nearer—

Not that final meeting
In the twilight kingdom

III
This is the dead land
This is the cactus land   40
Here the stone images
Are raised, here they receive
The supplication of a dead man's hand
Under the twinkle of a fading star.

Is it like this   45
In death's other kingdom
Waking alone
At the hour when we are
Trembling with tenderness
Lips that would kiss   50
Form prayers to broken stone.

IV
The eyes are not here
There are no eyes here
In this valley of dying stars
In this hollow valley   55
This broken jaw of our lost kingdoms

In this last of meeting places
We grope together
And avoid speech
Gathered on this beach of the tumid river°   60

Sightless, unless
The eyes reappear
As the perpetual star
Multifoliate rose°

---

33. **staves:** rods or staffs; "crossed staves/In a field" refers to scarecrows.   60. **tumid river:** the River Acheron in Hell in Dante's *Inferno,* over which the damned must cross into the land of the dead.   64. **Multifoliate rose:** Dante's description of Paradise as a rose of many leaves.

Of death's twilight kingdom   65
The hope only
Of empty men.

V

Here we go round the prickly pear°
Prickly pear prickly pear
Here we go round the prickly pear   70
At five o'clock in the morning.

Between the idea
And the reality
Between the motion
And the act°   75
Falls the Shadow
     For Thine is the Kingdom°

Between the conception
And the creation
Between the emotion   80
And the response
Falls the Shadow
     Life is very long

Between the desire
And the spasm   85
Between the potency
And the existence
Between the essence
And the descent
Falls the Shadow   90
     For Thine is the Kingdom

For Thine is
Life is
For Thine is the

This is the way the world ends   95
This is the way the world ends
This is the way the world ends
Not with a bang but a whimper.

---

68. *prickly pear:* cactus. 74–75. **Between . . . act:** a reference to *Julius Caesar,*
"Between the acting of a dreadful thing / And the first motion, all the interim is /
Like a phantasma or a hideous dream" (II, 1, 63–65). 77. *For . . . **Kingdom:*** closing
words of the Lord's Prayer, "For thine is the kingdom, and the power, and the
glory, forever and ever."

COMMENTARY

For Eliot, the hollow men are the straw-filled members of modern civilization who have reached a point of stagnation, who believe in nothing, and in whom all desire for change has been paralyzed. Their world is a twilight world between life and death, where all is a flat "cactus land." The hollow men are contrasted with the specters of Kurtz and Guy Fawkes, who have met death "With direct eyes" because they were strong men, if misguided. Even their self-destruction is better than that pointless wait on the "beach of the tumid river." But the hollow men will neither return to life nor cross the river of death to peace; and to attain a new life or salvation, they must receive a new sign, a new faith. In the face of such a decision, they are loath to take any responsibility but try to hide among the other scarecrow shapes, allowing the wind of fate to blow them where it will. Their chance for salvation is at best, however, ambiguous, for, although Eliot describes the way to salvation, it is not certain whether he is saying (line 66) *the only hope* or *only a hope*. Again and again the "shadow" comes between the idea and the act. It is this paralyzing inability to connect the two which proves terminal, and the hollow men seem to waste away with a disjointed and confused "whimper."

FOR STUDY AND DISCUSSION

1. What purpose do the two epigraphs have? How do Kurtz and Guy Fawkes differ from the "hollow men"?
2. In Part I, what images does Eliot use to suggest sterility or lack of will and purpose in modern life?
3. In Part II, why do you think the hollow men want to avoid meeting the "eyes" (those people who lived purposeful lives)?
4. In Part III and Part IV, Eliot uses images that suggest a spiritual wasteland inhabited by the hollow men. What is their hope?
5. In Part V, what do you think Eliot means by "the shadow" that prevents the hollow men from accomplishing anything?
6. How do the closing lines of the poem characterize modern people as ineffectual?

FOR COMPOSITION

Eliot wrote in *The Use of Poetry and the Use of Criticism*, "But the essential advantage for a poet is not to have a beautiful world with which to deal: it is to be able to see beneath both beauty and ugliness; to see the boredom, and the horror, and the glory." To what extent does "The Hollow Men" illustrate this statement?

Wilfred Owen

1893–1918

Of the poets who came to maturity in World War I, Owen exerted the greatest influence on twentieth-century poetry. Though not in good health, he enlisted in the service in 1915, experienced the horrors of trench warfare in France in 1916 and 1917, suffered a collapse, and was hospitalized in England. Returning to the front fourteen months later, he received the Military Cross for his heroism. He was killed in action seven days before the Armistice.

Like Sassoon, Owen was unsparing in his details of the carnage and waste of war, evoking what he called the "pity of war." It was, however, his experiments with slant rhyme and consonance that influenced poets in the 1920's. By diminishing the euphony of vowel patterns and using consonant clusters to create a harsh or dissonant sound, Owen was able to convey the brutal tragedy of the scenes described in his poems. Owen also used the caesura or rhetorical pause freely in his lines to convey the halting speech and colloquial tone appropriate to his subject. The following lines employ slant rhyme and consonance to underscore the confusion of feeling and the harsh sight:

> Gas! Gas! Quick, boys! — An ecstasy of fumbling,
> Fitting the clumsy helmets just in time . . .

The italicized consonants recur in stressed positions. Though assonance occurs in these lines (fumbling, clumsy), it is less prominent. The effect is one of dissonance.

A sentence in one of Owen's letters to his mother, written following the Battle of the Somme, reveals the experience that produced the remarkable poems of 1917 and 1918: "I have not seen any dead. I have done worse. In the dark air I have perceived it, and in the darkness, felt."

Cemetery in France.
Erich Hartmann, Magnum

Dulce et Decorum Est

Bent double, like old beggars under sacks,
Knock-kneed, coughing like hags, we cursed through sludge,
Till on the haunting flares we turned our backs
And towards our distant rest began to trudge.
Men marched asleep. Many had lost their boots   5
But limped on, blood-shod. All went lame; all blind;
Drunk with fatigue; deaf even to the hoots
Of tired, outstripped Five-Nines° that dropped behind.

Gas! GAS! Quick, boys!—An ecstasy of fumbling,
Fitting the clumsy helmets just in time;   10
But someone still was yelling out and stumbling
And flound'ring like a man in fire or lime . . .
Dim, through the misty panes and thick green light,
As under a green sea, I saw him drowning.

In all my dreams, before my helpless sight,   15
He plunges at me, guttering, choking, drowning.

If in some smothering dreams you too could pace
Behind the wagon that we flung him in,
And watch the white eyes writhing in his face,
His hanging face, like a devil's sick of sin;   20
If you could hear, at every jolt, the blood
Come gargling from the froth-corrupted lungs,
Obscene as cancer, bitter as the cud
Of vile, incurable sores on innocent tongues,—
My friend, you would not tell with such high zest   25
To children ardent for some desperate glory,
The old Lie: Dulce et decorum est
Pro patria mori.°

---

8. **Five-Nines:** gas shells.   27–28. **Dulce . . . mori:** It is sweet and proper to die for
one's country (Horace).

FOR STUDY AND DISCUSSION

1. Owen builds to the statement of his theme: the heroic view of war as glory is "The old Lie." How different would the effect of the poem be if he had begun with this statement?

2. What is the central contrast that Owen develops, and how does it illustrate his theme?

3. Owen is concerned also with the unexpected and sudden terror of war. How do his images and the central contrast of the poem help to convey this terror?

Robert Graves

1895–

Robert Graves enlisted in 1914 and served with Siegfried Sassoon in a regiment of the Royal Welsh Fusiliers. He was wounded and later suffered shell shock. Graves, like Sassoon, refused to glorify war.

In the years following the war, Graves became a prolific poet, experimenting with a wide variety of verse forms, including folksongs, ballads, and poems in the metaphysical vein—employing highly subtle and complex metaphors. In *A Survey of Modernist Poetry* in 1927, Graves, along with his co-author Laura Riding, defined what he felt poetry was now to be engaged in: "The ideal modernist poem is its own clearest, fullest, and most accurate meaning . . . the poem does not give a rendering of a poetical picture or idea existing outside the poem, but . . . the poem has the character of a creature by itself." "His poems," declared Richard Wilbur, ". . . have the air of being spontaneous answers to actual experience."

Graves has also written distinguished fiction, much of it retelling historical and mythological stories. His most controversial book, *The White Goddess,* is a study of the poetic imagination, which Graves claims has its origins in ancient fertility rites.

Robert Graves
Tom Blau, Camera Press/Photo Trends

The Troll's Nosegay

A simple nosegay!° was that much to ask?
(Winter still nagged, with scarce a bud yet showing.)
He loved her ill, if he resigned the task.
"Somewhere," she cried, "there *must* be blossom blowing."°
It seems my lady wept and the troll swore   5
By Heaven he hated tears: he'd cure her spleen°—
Where she had begged one flower he'd shower fourscore,
A bunch fit to amaze a China Queen.

Cold fog-drawn Lily, pale mist-magic Rose
He conjured, and in a glassy caldron set   10
With elvish unsubstantial Mignonette
And such vague bloom as wandering dreams enclose.
But she?
      Awed,
          Charmed to tears,
                Distracted,
                      Yet—
Even yet, perhaps, a trifle piqued—who knows?

---

1. **nosegay:** a bouquet of flowers. 4. **blowing:** blooming. 6. **spleen:** peevishness.

She Tells Her Love While Half Asleep

She tells her love while half asleep
  In the dark hours,
    With half-words whispered low:
As Earth stirs in her winter sleep
  And puts out grass and flowers
    Despite the snow,
    Despite the falling snow.

Mermaid, Dragon, Fiend

In my childhood rumors ran
   Of a world beyond our door—
Terrors to the life of man
   That the highroad held in store.

Of the mermaids' doleful game   5
   In deep water I heard tell,
Of lofty dragons belching flame,
   Of the hornèd fiend of Hell.

Tales like these were too absurd
   For my laughter-loving ear: 10
Soon I mocked at all I heard,
   Though with cause indeed for fear.

Now I know the mermaid kin
   I find them bound by natural laws:
They have neither tail nor fin,   15
   But are deadlier for that cause.

Dragons have no darting tongues,
   Teeth saw-edged, nor rattling scales;
No fire issues from their lungs,
   No black poison from their tails: 20

For they are creatures of dark air,
   Unsubstantial tossing forms,
Thunderclaps of man's despair
   In mid-whirl of mental storms.

And there's a true and only fiend   25
   Worse than prophets prophesy,
Whose full powers to hurt are screened
   Lest the race of man should die.

Ever in vain will courage plot
   The dragon's death, in coat of proof;   30
Or love abjure the mermaid grot;
   Or faith denounce the cloven hoof.

Mermaids will not be denied
   The last bubbles of our shame,
The dragon flaunts an unpierced hide,   35
   The true fiend governs in God's name.

FOR STUDY AND DISCUSSION

The Troll's Nosegay
1. Although the poem deals with fairy-tale characters (one of whom asks another to perform a near impossible task), they seem very human. Given the lady's response to the bouquet, what might the poet be suggesting about human nature?
2. What is the form of the poem? Do you think it is appropriate to the situation developed in the poem?

She Tells Her Love While Half Asleep
1. What is the central metaphor of this poem?
2. How is this a poem about new birth?

Mermaid, Dragon, Fiend
1. As a child, how did the speaker react to stories of dragons, mermaids, and fiends?
2. As an adult, how has the speaker encountered mermaid, dragon, and fiend? What do these creatures symbolize to him?

W. H. Auden
1907–1973

W. H. Auden
Rollie McKenna

Wystan Hugh Auden was born, raised, and educated in England. His first poems were published in 1928, and early in his career he became a friend of T. S. Eliot, whose ideas on poetry influenced his work. He was also a friend and colleague of Stephen Spender, Louis MacNeice, and C. Day Lewis, who shared with Auden an interest in politics and who saw themselves bringing new techniques and attitudes to English poetry. In 1939 Auden emigrated to the United States. He became an American citizen in 1946 and made his living teaching and writing poetry. In 1956, once again back in England, he was elected Professor of Poetry at Oxford University, a post he held until 1961.

Auden's early poems were concerned with revealing the ills of his native country and were intended to shock their readers. He often combined deliberate irreverence with verbal craftsmanship to awaken what he saw as the complacent middle class to the hollowness of their society and the need for reform. It was his impatience with the limits imposed by English society that prompted Auden to move to the United States. To some extent, Auden must have felt that Europe was slowly dying and that his residence in a young nation would bring with it new life. Like Eliot, Auden later in his life returned to the formal practice of Christianity, having grown disenchanted with the socialism he had professed in his youth. His later poetry, though often as satirical as the early poems had been, became increasingly concerned with religious themes.

Auden wrote three ambitious long poems: *For the Time Being,* a Christmas oratorio in which he explores the modern significance of the Nativity; *The Sea and the Mirror,* a discourse in poetic form on the relationship between life and art, which takes the form of a commentary on Shakespeare's *The Tempest;* and *The Age of Anxiety,* a work that presents four individuals attempting to find a way out of their spiritual dilemmas. Toward the end of his life, Auden's poetry tended to become mellower, reflecting a spirit that was less urgent in its denunciation of evil. His poetry never lost its moral quality, however, nor did it abandon its concern with the troubles of the modern world.

Auden's poetry has been praised for its vitality, variety, and originality. He imposes new and unexpected patterns on a wide range of forms — from archaic ballads to street-corner blues. Perhaps Auden's most important contribution to twentieth-century poetry is his experimentation in many verse forms and meters, combining an offhand informality with remarkable technical skill.

Ballad

O what is that sound which so thrills the ear
  Down in the valley drumming, drumming?
Only the scarlet soldiers, dear,
  The soldiers coming.

O what is that light I see flashing so clear   5
  Over the distance brightly, brightly?
Only the sun on their weapons, dear,
  As they step lightly.

O what are they doing with all that gear;
  What are they doing this morning, this morning?   10
Only the usual maneuvers, dear,
  Or perhaps a warning.

O why have they left the road down there;
  Why are they suddenly wheeling, wheeling?
Perhaps a change in the orders, dear;   15
  Why are you kneeling?

O haven't they stopped for the doctor's care;
  Haven't they reined their horses, their horses?
Why, they are none of them wounded, dear.
  None of these forces.   20

O is it the parson they want, with white hair;
  Is it the parson, is it, is it?
No, they are passing his gateway, dear,
  Without a visit.

O it must be the farmer who lives so near,   25
  It must be the farmer, so cunning, cunning;
They have passed the farm already, dear,
  And now they are running.

O where are you going? stay with me here.
  Were the vows you swore me deceiving, deceiving?   30
No, I promised to love you, my dear,
  But I must be leaving.

O it's broken the lock and splintered the door,
  O it's the gate where they're turning, turning;
Their feet are heavy on the floor   35
  And their eyes are burning.

That Night When Joy Began

That night when joy began
Our narrowest veins to flush,
We waited for the flash
Of morning's levelled gun.

But morning let us pass,   5
And day by day relief
Outgrew his nervous laugh,
Grows credulous of peace.

As mile by mile is seen
No trespasser's reproach,   10
And love's best glasses reach
No fields but are his own.

COMMENTARY

The metaphor in lines 3–4 beautifully combines the visual image of the sun's horizontal rays awakening [the travelers] from their dream and the metaphorical idea of the landowner's shooting them for trespassing — that is, destroying their temporary illusion of love. But as they hike for additional miles (days), they outgrow their nervousness and begin to believe in spiritual peace, for they are not reproached for trespassing and they can see in the future (through love's field glasses) nothing that is not genuine and lasting love.

The rhyme pattern:

Lines 1 and 4 (of each stanza): alliteration and consonance
Lines 2 and 3 (of each stanza): alliteration and consonance
Lines 1 and 3 (of each stanza): assonance
Lines 2 and 4 (of each stanza): assonance

In line 10 the last syllable must be thought of as beginning with *r* rather than with *p* to preserve the integrity of this pattern, and in line 12 the final syllable must be thought of as including the final *s* (really a *z*) of *his*. The whole is ingeniously worked out, along with the extended metaphor, and the poet's pleasure (and ours) lies partly in the working out of this design.

— *Laurence Perrine*

Musée des Beaux Arts°

About suffering they were never wrong,
The Old Masters: how well they understood
Its human position; how it takes place
While someone else is eating or opening a window or just
    walking dully along;
How, when the aged are reverently, passionately waiting   5
For the miraculous birth, there always must be
Children who did not specially want it to happen, skating
On a pond at the edge of the wood:
They never forgot
That even the dreadful martyrdom must run its course   10
Anyhow in a corner, some untidy spot
Where the dogs go on with their doggy life and the torturer's
    horse
Scratches its innocent behind on a tree.

In Brueghel's° *Icarus*, for instance: how everything turns away
Quite leisurely from the disaster; the plowman may   15
Have heard the splash, the forsaken cry,
But for him it was not an important failure; the sun shone
As it had to on the white legs disappearing into the green
Water; and the expensive delicate ship that must have seen
Something amazing, a boy falling out of the sky,   20
Had somewhere to get to and sailed calmly on.

° **Musée des Beaux Arts:** the Museum of Fine Arts in Brussels.   14. **Brueghel**
(brœ′gǝl): Pieter Brueghel the Elder (1522?–1569), Flemish artist who painted *The
Fall of Icarus.*

The Fall of Icarus by Pieter Brueghel the Elder.
Royal Museum of Fine Arts, Brussels, Belgium

FOR STUDY AND DISCUSSION

Ballad

1. Auden uses the traditional ballad form to describe the terror of the modern world. What narrative technique is used to increase gradually the poem's mood of terror?

2. Although the speakers are not identified, what can you infer about their relationship?

3. The word *dear* is repeated in every stanza but the last. In what way is the use of this word ironic? What evidence do you find in the poem to suggest that one of the speakers has betrayed the other? Cite specific lines.

That Night When Joy Began

What is the tone or attitude of the speaker in this poem?

Musée des Beaux Arts

1. Details in the first part of the poem seem to refer to two paintings by the Flemish master Pieter Brueghel: *The Massacre of the Innocents* and *The Numbering at Bethlehem (The Census).* In the second part of the poem, Auden describes Brueghel's painting *The Fall of Icarus.* How do these various details characterize the ordinary world?

2. What suggests that Auden is writing about the modern world as well as that of the past?

3. In Greek mythology, Icarus was given wings of wax and warned by his father Daedalus not to fly too close to the sun. Icarus, who was overbold, disobeyed and fell to his death in the sea. How is his death viewed by the other figures in the painting?

4. What do Auden and "The Old Masters" suggest about the significance and experience of human suffering?

W. H. Auden 823

Louis MacNeice

1907–1963

Louis MacNeice was born and raised in Belfast, Ireland, where his father was a Protestant clergyman. Following his graduation from Oxford University, he taught at various universities and wrote poetry; later he became a writer and producer for the British Broadcasting Company. Though associated early in his career with Auden, Spender, and other liberal-minded poets of protest of the early 1930's, MacNeice was less interested in politics and more doubtful about what poetry could accomplish. The poet is "a blend of the entertainer and the critic or informer," he wrote in 1938; "he is not a legislator, however, unacknowledged, nor yet essentially a prophet." And he added: "I would have a poet able-bodied, fond of talking, a reader of the newspapers, capable of pity and laughter, informed in economics, appreciative of women, involved in personal relationships, actively interested in politics, susceptible to physical impressions." He is at one with Auden in rejecting the Romantic conception of the poet exemplified in Yeats. MacNeice's poetry deals with the everyday world, the ordinary affairs of people; he does not attempt to make profound statements about life or provide final truths.

Louis MacNeice
Rollie McKenna

The Sunlight on the Garden

The sunlight on the garden
Hardens and grows cold,
We cannot cage the minute
Within its nets of gold;
When all is told   5
We cannot beg for pardon.

Our freedom as free lances
Advances towards its end;
The earth compels, upon it
Sonnets and birds descend;   10
And soon, my friend,
We shall have no time for dances.

The sky was good for flying
Defying the church bells
And every evil iron   15
Siren and what it tells:
The earth compels,
We are dying, Egypt, dying°

And not expecting pardon,
Hardened in heart anew,   20
But glad to have sat under
Thunder and rain with you,
And grateful too
For sunlight on the garden.

---

18. **We . . . dying:** an allusion to Antony's speech in
Shakespeare's play *Antony and Cleopatra*, "I am dying,
Egypt, dying," a famous example of acceptance of
death.

The Wiper

Through purblind° night the wiper
Reaps a swathe of water
On the screen;° we shudder on
   And hardly hold the road,
All we can see a segment   5
Of blackly shining asphalt
With the wiper moving across it
   Clearing, blurring, clearing.

But what to say of the road?
The monotony of its hardly   10
Visible camber, the mystery
   Of its far invisible margins,
Will these be always with us,
The night being broken only
By lights that pass or meet us   15
   From others in moving boxes?

---

1. **purblind:** nearly blind; here, without light.
3. **screen:** windshield.

Boxes of glass and water
Upholstered, equipped with dials
Professing to tell the distance
   We have gone, the speed we are
      going,   20
But never a gauge nor needle
To tell us where we are going
Or when day will come, supposing
   This road exists in daytime.

For now we cannot remember   25
Where we were when it was not
Night, when it was not raining,
   Before this car moved forward
And the wiper backward and forward
Lighting so little before us   30
Of a road that, crouching forward,
   We watch move always towards us,

Which through the tiny segment
Cleared and blurred by the wiper
Is sucked in under the axle   35
   To be spewed behind us and lost
While we, dazzled by darkness,
Haul the black future towards us
Peeling the skin from our hands;
   And yet we hold the road.   40

FOR STUDY AND DISCUSSION

The Sunlight on the Garden

1. The surprising rhyme scheme of each stanza throws unusual emphasis on certain words: the last words of the first and third lines rhyme in some way with the first words of the second and fourth lines. Some of these are slant rhymes. How various are these rhymes, and what special emphasis do they provide?

2. What is the speaker's attitude toward death? What in the poem suggests that MacNeice is writing about the death of an era—perhaps the death of the postwar era in England as a new war approached—and not merely the death of an individual?

3. In telling us how death should be faced, how does MacNeice imply life should be lived?

The Wiper

1. The car, the wiper, the road, and other details of the poem form a metaphor for life. What do the details of the car, the passing traffic, and the nature of the road reveal about the isolation of people from one another? What do they reveal about the quality of modern living?

2. Why does MacNeice describe the experience of driving at night instead of driving in daylight? How is the darkness, which limits vision, symbolic?

3. Does MacNeice refer to his own perception of the world or does he suggest that most people see what is missing in their lives?

Stephen Spender
1909–

Stephen Spender was one of a group of young poets of the 1930's who tried to incorporate the modern world into their poetry. Unlike those poets who railed at the modern world and saw it as a wasteland or a scene of bloody chaos, these younger poets tried to discover beauty and order in contemporary technological society. Thus, in one of his most famous poems, Spender celebrated the beauty of an express train. Like other members of his group, Spender did not strive for a perpetually optimistic note. He was as much concerned with protesting the evils of his time as with proclaiming its beauties.

As an adolescent, Spender believed in "pure poetry, an invocation which one understands imperfectly but which is yet expressed exactly . . ." At Oxford—falling under the influence of his friend W. H. Auden and reading writers such as T. S. Eliot, James Joyce, and Ernest Hemingway—Spender's views changed. "I began to realize that unpoetic-seeming things were material for poetry. . . . What excited me . . . was the inclusion within new forms of material which seemed ugly, antipoetic, and inhuman . . . [The modern poems and novels] showed me . . . that the poet, instead of having to set himself apart from his time, could create out of an acceptance of it."

In addition to poetry, Spender has written a novel, short stories, and a number of books on the situation of the writer in modern society. As a magazine editor, he helped found two important literary journals, *Horizon* and *Encounter.* In 1951, he published an unusually penetrating autobiography, *World Within World.* In recent years, he has taught at American and British universities and continues to comment on the intellectual and political life of his time.

Stephen Spender
Rollie McKenna

The Express

After the first powerful, plain manifesto
The black statement of pistons, without more fuss
But gliding like a queen, she leaves the station.
Without bowing and with restrained unconcern
She passes the houses which humbly crowd outside,   5
The gasworks, and at last the heavy page
Of death, printed by gravestones in the cemetery.
Beyond the town, there lies the open country
Where, gathering speed, she acquires mystery,
The luminous self-possession of ships on ocean.   10
It is now she begins to sing—at first quite low
Then loud, and at last with a jazzy madness—
The song of her whistle screaming at curves,
Of deafening tunnels, brakes, innumerable bolts.
And always light, aerial, underneath,   15
Retreats the elate° meter of her wheels.
Steaming through metal landscape on her lines,
She plunges new eras of wild happiness,
Where speed throws up strange shapes, broad curves
And parallels clean like trajectories from guns.   20
At last, further than Edinburgh or Rome,
Beyond the crest of the world, she reaches night
Where only a low streamline brightness
Of phosphorus on the tossing hills is light.
Ah, like a comet through flame, she moves entranced,   25
Wrapt in her music no bird song, no, nor bough
Breaking with honey buds, shall ever equal.

---

16. **elate:** joyful.

What I Expected

What I expected was
Thunder, fighting,
Long struggles with men
And climbing.
After continual straining   5
I should grow strong;
Then the rocks would shake
And I should rest long.

What I had not foreseen
Was the gradual day   10
Weakening the will
Leaking the brightness away,
The lack of good to touch
The fading of body and soul
Like smoke before wind   15
Corrupt, unsubstantial.

The wearing of Time,
And the watching of cripples pass
With limbs shaped like questions
In their odd twist,   20
The pulverous grief
Melting the bones with pity,
The sick falling from earth—
These, I could not foresee.

For I had expected always   25
Some brightness to hold in trust,
Some final innocence
To save from dust;
That, hanging solid,
Would dangle through all   30
Like the created poem
Or the dazzling crystal.

FOR STUDY AND DISCUSSION

The Express

1. What "personality" has been attributed to the express?
2. What does the speaker think of the moving express when it is compared to bird song and flowering boughs? What does the comparison imply about traditional symbols of beauty?

What I Expected

What, in your opinion, is the "brightness" (lines 12, 26) that the speaker values as highly as the "created poem" or the "dazzling crystal"?

Henry Reed

1914–

Henry Reed was born and educated in Birmingham, England, and later served in the British
Army and the Foreign Office. He has worked as a
journalist and written plays for radio, including a
version of *Moby Dick*. As a poet, Reed has experimented in many styles, including parody and bur-
lesque. "Naming of Parts" is a satirical section of a
longer poem entitled "Lessons of War."

Naming of Parts

Today we have naming of parts. Yesterday,
We had daily cleaning. And tomorrow morning,
We shall have what to do after firing. But today,
Today we have naming of parts. Japonica
Glistens like coral in all of the neighboring gardens,   5
   And today we have naming of parts.

This is the lower sling swivel. And this
Is the upper sling swivel, whose use you will see,
When you are given your slings. And this is the piling swivel,
Which in your case you have not got. The branches   10
Hold in the gardens their silent, eloquent gestures,
   Which in our case we have not got.

This is the safety-catch, which is always released
With an easy flick of the thumb. And please do not let me
See anyone using his finger. You can do it quite easy   15
If you have any strength in your thumb. The blossoms
Are fragile and motionless, never letting anyone see
   Any of them using their finger.

And this you can see is the bolt. The purpose of this
Is to open the breech, as you see. We can slide it   20
Rapidly backwards and forwards; we call this
Easing the spring. And rapidly backwards and forwards
The early bees are assaulting and fumbling the flowers:
   They call it easing the Spring.

They call it easing the Spring. It is perfectly easy   25
If you have any strength in your thumb: like the bolt,
And the breech, and the cocking-piece, and the point of bal-
    ance,
Which in our case we have not got; and the almond-blossom
Silent in all of the gardens and the bees going backwards and
    forwards,
    For today we have naming of parts.   30

Japonica tree
Bruce Coleman

FOR STUDY AND DISCUSSION

1. There are two voices in the poem: that of a rifle instructor and that of a recruit. Identify the lines spoken by each voice. Who speaks in the final stanza?

2. In what way is the setting of the gardens contrasted with the details of rifle instruction?

3. What meanings can you find in "easing the spring" (line 22) and in "point of balance" (line 27)?

4. What is the poet mocking? How would you state the theme of the poem?

Dylan Thomas
1914–1953

More than any other poet following W. H. Auden and Stephen Spender, it was Dylan Thomas who returned English poetry to a personal, lyrical romanticism. Auden and his friends wrote poems that were cool, mocking, and jazzy, and that reflected their divided attitude toward the modern world: their desire to belong to it and, at the same time, their distrust of it. Thomas' poems, with their rush of feeling, either ignored the world or took it by storm. His resonant language and evocative images are frequently compressed and personal, and several of his poems are among the most difficult in the English language. Yet many readers, even when they do not fully understand Thomas' poems, find themselves responding to his magnificent use of words and sense of driving emotion. Thomas' manuscripts reveal that he was a careful craftsman who revised his poems many times to get the effects he wanted. And intensive study of his best poems uncovers not an impulsive wildness but a coherent expression of Thomas' personal view of the world: his joy in love and physical beauty, his rage against death, his search for a means of overcoming mortality. Thomas himself said of his poetry, "My poems are written for the love of man and the praise of God—and I'd be a fool if they weren't."

Dylan Thomas was born in Swansea, a seacoast town in Southern Wales. As he records it in *Quite Early One Morning,* he spent a happy childhood in Swansea, a great industrial center surrounded by fine natural scenery. Although he later went to London, he settled once again in Wales in his later years, and the Welsh countryside obviously left its mark on his poetry. His first volume, *Eighteen Poems,* was published in 1934 when he was only twenty. Elder poets like Edith Sitwell at once recognized in Thomas' early work a distinctive

Dylan Thomas by Augustus John.
National Museum of Wales, Cardiff

voice and acclaimed him as an important new talent, perhaps even a genius. Later poetry was collected in *25 Poems* (1936), *The Map of Love* (1939), and *New Poems* (1943). Although as he grew older he wrote fewer and fewer poems—only six in the last six years of his life—his later work shows that he was moving toward a simpler, clearer, more direct poetic language. His *Collected Poems* was published the year before his death.

Thomas reached an increasingly large audience through his verse plays and recordings of his poetry. He toured the United States several times, giving readings and lectures. At the time of his death at thirty-nine, he was recognized as one of the major British poets of the twentieth century.

The Force That Through the Green Fuse Drives the Flower

The force that through the green fuse drives the flower
Drives my green age; that blasts the roots of trees
Is my destroyer.
And I am dumb to tell° the crooked rose
My youth is bent by the same wintry fever.   5

The force that drives the water through the rocks
Drives my red blood; that dries the mouthing streams
Turns mine to wax.
And I am dumb to mouth unto my veins
How at the mountain spring the same mouth sucks.   10

The hand that whirls the water in the pool
Stirs the quicksand; that ropes the blowing wind
Hauls my shroud° sail.
And I am dumb to tell the hanging man
How of my clay is made the hangman's lime.°   15

The lips of time leech to the fountain head;
Love drips and gathers, but the fallen blood
Shall calm her sores.
And I am dumb to tell a weather's wind
How time has ticked a heaven round the stars.   20

And I am dumb to tell the lover's tomb
How at my sheet goes the same crooked worm.

---

4. **dumb to tell:** unable to tell; inarticulate.   13. **shroud:** winding sheet used to
wrap a corpse.   15. **hangman's lime:** quicklime in which those hanged were
buried.

Fern Hill

Now as I was young and easy under the apple boughs
About the lilting house and happy as the grass was green,
 The night above the dingle° starry,
  Time let me hail and climb
  Golden in the heydays of his eyes,   5
And honored among wagons I was prince of the apple towns
And once below a time I lordly had the trees and leaves
  Trail with daisies and barley
 Down the rivers of the windfall light.

And as I was green and carefree, famous among the barns   10
About the happy yard and singing as the farm was home,
 In the sun that is young once only,
  Time let me play and be
 Golden in the mercy of his means,
And green and golden I was huntsman and herdsman, the calves   15
Sang to my horn, the foxes on the hills barked clear and cold,
  And the sabbath rang slowly
 In the pebbles of the holy streams.

All the sun long it was running, it was lovely, the hay
Fields high as the house, the tunes from the chimneys, it was air   20
 And playing, lovely and watery
  And fire green as grass.
 And nightly under the simple stars
As I rode to sleep the owls were bearing the farm away,
All the moon long I heard, blessed among stables, the nightjars°   25
 Flying with the ricks,° and the horses
  Flashing into the dark.

And then to awake, and the farm, like a wanderer white
With the dew, come back, the cock on his shoulder: it was all
 Shining, it was Adam and maiden,   30
  The sky gathered again
 And the sun grew round that very day.
So it must have been after the birth of the simple light
In the first, spinning place, the spellbound horses walking warm
 Out of the whinnying green stable   35
  On to the fields of praise.

---

3. **dingle:** small, deep valley. 25. **nightjars:** night hawks, whippoorwills, and other nocturnal birds. 26. **ricks:** haystacks.

Garden of Eden by Jan Brueghel, Provincial Museum, Seville, Spain.
Scala/Editorial Photocolor Archives

And honored among foxes and pheasants by the gay house
Under the new made clouds and happy as the heart was long,
   In the sun born over and over,
      I ran my heedless ways,   40
   My wishes raced through the house high hay
And nothing I cared, at my sky blue trades, that time allows
In all his tuneful turning so few and such morning songs
   Before the children green and golden
      Follow him out of grace.   45

Nothing I cared, in the lamb white days, that time would take me
Up to the swallow thronged loft by the shadow of my hand,
   In the moon that is always rising,
      Nor that riding to sleep
   I should hear him fly with the high fields
And wake to the farm forever fled from the childless land.   50
Oh as I was young and easy in the mercy of his means,
     Time held me green and dying
   Though I sang in my chains like the sea.

Do Not Go Gentle into That Good Night

Do not go gentle into that good night,
Old age should burn and rave at close of day;
Rage, rage against the dying of the light.

Though wise men at their end know dark is right,
Because their words had forked no lightning they   5
Do not go gentle into that good night.

Good men, the last wave by, crying how bright
Their frail deeds might have danced in a green bay,
Rage, rage against the dying of the light.

Wild men who caught and sang the sun in flight,   10
And learn, too late, they grieved it on its way,
Do not go gentle into that good night.

Grave men, near death, who see with blinding sight
Blind eyes could blaze like meteors and be gay,
Rage, rage against the dying of the light.   15

And you, my father, there on the sad height,
Curse, bless, me now with your fierce tears, I pray.
Do not go gentle into that good night.
Rage, rage against the dying of the light.

FOR STUDY AND DISCUSSION

The Force That Through the Green Fuse Drives the Flower

1. Explain the "force" that is the subject of the poem. Is this force identical with life or with death, is it both life and death, or does it link one with the other?
2. What "wintry fever" bends youth? Note that the phrase is an *oxymoron* joining heat and cold. What other contrast of this sort do you find in the poem? How does this contrast help to define the "force" of the poem?
3. How many images of death (or the means to death) do you find? How do these images join human life to nature? What is Thomas saying about the relation between human life and nature?
4. A graveside anthem claims that "In the midst of life we are in death." How does the nautical imagery of this poem relate that point?

Fern Hill

1. What specific scenes and childhood activities does Thomas mention in the poem?
2. What do the colors green and golden represent in the poem? What does the paradox "green and dying" (line 53) signify about Thomas' view of life and death?
3. How does the rapid movement of the lines help to create the dominant mood of the poem? What is that mood?
4. How does the mood of the poem change in the last stanza? What details in previous stanzas anticipate this change of mood?
5. What details have a religious implication? How do they call up a state of innocence—or of grace— that was the human state before the Fall? How does the poet see himself as a child and as a man?

Do Not Go Gentle into That Good Night

1. What knowledge have "wise men at their end" gained? What about good men? Wild men? Grave men?
2. What ideas do the various images of light (including meteors) symbolize? How do these images contrast with images of darkness?
3. How would you describe the poet's attitude toward death?
4. "Do Not Go Gentle" is a *villanelle*, an intricately patterned poem containing two rhymes. The first and third lines of the first *tercet*, or three-line stanza, alternate as refrains in the succeeding stanzas and combine to form the concluding couplet of the final quatrain. Because of this intricate design, the villanelle is often associated with light poems designed to display the poet's technical skill. How has Thomas used the repetitive rhymes and sentences of the villanelle to gain unusual emphasis in the poem? What ideas and feelings receive the most emphasis?

FOR COMPOSITION

1. Select a theme in one of Thomas' poems—the continuing process of life and death, the role of nature in this process, the force of time, the joy of experience—and discuss its treatment in two of the poems. Point out similarities and differences in what Thomas says and how he says it.
2. Write about a childhood experience as Thomas does, evoking its special qualities through images and concrete details. Develop a dominant mood as you write.
3. Analyze the use and effect of sound patterns in a stanza in "Fern Hill" with attention to alliteration, internal rhyme, consonance, and assonance.

Philip Larkin
1922–

World War II produced a series of poets like Dylan Thomas whose response to the catastrophe was emotionally intense and often highly rhetorical. This group of poets is sometimes referred to as the "New Apocalypse." In contrast to this group is "The Movement"—a group of poets educated at Oxford University and strongly influenced by W. H. Auden. They are concerned with creating a less intense and colloquial style of poetry, and with writing about ordinary experience and the changes in everyday English life. Philip Larkin has proved to be one of the best poets of this group. He began his career as a novelist and makes his living as a university librarian. In their quiet, reflective tone and ironic understatement, his best poems continue the tradition associated with Thomas Hardy, whose influence Larkin acknowledges: "When I came to Hardy it was with the sense of relief that I didn't have to try and jack myself up to a concept of poetry that lay outside my own life. . . . One could simply relapse back into one's own life and write from it." He has the rare gift of clarity and of casually suggesting the importance of the ordinary.

Philip Larkin
Rollie McKenna

Going

There is an evening coming in
Across the fields, one never seen before,
That lights no lamps.

Silken it seems at a distance, yet
When it is drawn up over the knees and breast   5
It brings no comfort.

Where has the tree gone, that locked
Earth to the sky? What is under my hands,
That I cannot feel?

What loads my hands down?   10

Days

What are days for?
Days are where we live.
They come, they wake us
Time and time over.
They are to be happy in: 5
Where can we live but days?
Ah, solving that question
Brings the priest and the doctor
In their long coats
Running over the fields.   10

Coming

On longer evenings,
Light, chill and yellow,
Bathes the serene
Foreheads of houses.
A thrush sings,   5
Laurel-surrounded
In the deep bare garden,
Its fresh-peeled voice
Astonishing the brickwork.
It will be spring soon,   10
It will be spring soon—
And I, whose childhood
Is a forgotten boredom,
Feel like a child
Who comes on a scene   15
Of adult reconciling,
And can understand nothing
But the unusual laughter,
And starts to be happy.

FOR STUDY AND DISCUSSION

Going
1. Evening is presented as a metaphor for oncoming death. What details develop the metaphor?
2. Why does death seem "silken" at a distance? Why does Larkin stress the experience of hands?

Days
1. Why should the answer to the question that opens the poem bring priest and doctor "running over the fields"?
2. How would you describe the tone of the poem? Is it sarcastic or ironic? Matter-of-fact or deeply serious?
3. What qualities of tone and diction does "Days" share with "Going"? What difference do you notice between these poems and those of Dylan Thomas?

Coming
1. How would you describe the dominant mood of this poem?
2. What is spring compared to?
3. What is the significance of the speaker feeling like a child again?

Thom Gunn

1929–

Thom (son William) Gunn is the youngest poet associated with "The Movement" of the 1950's. He lived for a time in the United States. He was educated at Cambridge and Stanford universities and from 1958 to 1966 taught at the University of California at Berkeley. His poetry is distinctive in its frequent unity of vivid physical detail and abstract statement, which, in Gunn's words, sometimes constitutes "the only possible full confrontation of one's subject matter." A major theme of his poetry is the importance of action in a world of uncertain values and certain death.

Thom Gunn
Rollie McKenna

On the Move

> *Man, you gotta Go.*

The blue jay scuffling in the bushes follows
Some hidden purpose, and the gust of birds
That spurts across the field, the wheeling swallows,
Have nested in the trees and undergrowth.
Seeking their instinct, or their poise, or both,   5
One moves with an uncertain violence
Under the dust thrown by a baffled sense
Or the dull thunder of approximate words.

On motorcycles, up the road, they come:
Small, black, as flies hanging in heat, the Boys,   10
Until the distance throws them forth, their hum
Bulges to thunder held by calf and thigh.
In goggles, donned impersonality,
In gleaming jackets trophied with the dust,
They strap in doubt—by hiding it, robust—   15
And almost hear a meaning in their noise.

Exact conclusion of their hardiness
Has no shape yet, but from known whereabouts
They ride, direction where the tires press.
They scare a flight of birds across the field: 20
Much that is natural, to the will must yield.
Men manufacture both machine and soul,
And use what they imperfectly control
To dare a future from the taken routes.

It is a part solution, after all.   25
One is not necessarily discord
On earth; or damned because, half animal,
One lacks direct instinct, because one wakes
Afloat on movement that divides and breaks.
One joins the movement in a valueless world,   30
Choosing it, till, both hurler and the hurled,
One moves as well, always toward, toward.

A minute holds them, who have come to go:
The self-defined, astride the created will
They burst away; the towns they travel through   35
Are home for neither bird nor holiness,
For birds and saints complete their purposes.
At worst, one is in motion; and at best,
Reaching no absolute, in which to rest,
One is always nearer by not keeping still.   40

FOR STUDY AND DISCUSSION

1. In the first stanza, what do the birds follow that
the motorcyclists can't find?
2. What do you think is the "doubt" that the Boys
strap in? Is it uncertainty about their masculine
"hardiness," or doubt about what to do with their
youthful strength? Why do they seek "impersonality" in goggles and leather jackets?
3. What significance does the speaker attach to
their imperfect control over the machines they
ride? What exactly can they not control?
4. Why does the speaker describe the cyclists' lives
as "a part solution"? What is the unstated problem
they are trying to solve?
5. What is the meaning of the final line? What is
one "always nearer by not keeping still"?

Ted Hughes
1930–

Ted Hughes stands apart from the poets who came to maturity in the 1950's. Looking at the dark aspects of nature, he has stressed the ferocious and demonic rather than the idyllic and beautiful. Within the cruelty and violence of nature, Hughes looks for an understanding of human life and its mysterious bonds with nature. He has been named a "survivor-poet" by the critic A. Alvarez because he parallels human beings with lower animals, creatures that will do anything to ensure survival.

Hughes was born in Yorkshire and educated at Cambridge University. He has made his living mainly as a teacher and writer. He was married to the American poet Sylvia Plath, who died in 1963.

Ted Hughes
Rollie McKenna

View of a Pig

The pig lay on a barrow dead.
It weighed, they said, as much as three men.
Its eyes closed, pink white eyelashes.
Its trotters° stuck straight out.

Such weight and thick pink bulk   5
Set in death seemed not just dead.
It was less than lifeless, further off.
It was like a sack of wheat.

I thumped it without feeling remorse.
One feels guilty insulting the dead,   10
Walking on graves. But this pig
Did not seem able to accuse.

It was too dead. Just so much
A poundage of lard and pork.
Its last dignity had entirely gone.   15
It was not a figure of fun.

Too dead now to pity.
To remember its life, din, stronghold
Of earthly pleasure as it had been,
Seemed a false effort, and off the point.   20

Too deadly factual. Its weight
Oppressed me—how could it be moved?
And the trouble of cutting it up!
The gash in its throat was shocking, but not pathetic.

Once I ran at a fair in the noise   25
To catch a greased piglet
That was faster and nimbler than a cat,
Its squeal was the rending of metal.

Pigs must have hot blood, they feel like ovens.
Their bite is worse than a horse's—   30
They chop a half-moon clean out.
They eat cinders, dead cats.

Distinctions and admirations such
As this one was long finished with.
I stared at it a long time. They were going to scald it,   35
Scald it and scour it like a doorstep.

---

4. **trotters:** legs.

Hawk Roosting

I sit in the top of the wood, my eyes closed.
Inaction, no falsifying dream
Between my hooked head and hooked feet:
Or in sleep rehearse perfect kills and eat.

The convenience of the high trees!   5
The air's buoyancy and the sun's ray
Are of advantage to me;
And.the earth's face upward for my inspection.

My feet are locked upon the rough bark.
It took the whole of Creation   10
To produce my foot, my each feather:
Now I hold Creation in my foot

Or fly up, and revolve it all slowly—
I kill where I please because it is all mine.
There is no sophistry° in my body: 15
My manners are tearing off heads—

The allotment of death.
For the one path of my flight is direct
Through the bones of the living.
No arguments assert my right: 20

The sun is behind me.
Nothing has changed since I began.
My eye has permitted no change.
I am going to keep things like this.

---

15. **sophistry** (sŏf'əs-trē): the use of clever but misleading arguments.

FOR STUDY AND DISCUSSION

View of a Pig

1. What details does the speaker emphasize in contrasting the dead pig with living pigs? How would you describe the speaker's feeling about the dead pig?

2. Is the dead pig the real subject of the poem, or is the poet making a statement about the loss of individuality and dignity through death? Give reasons for your answer.

3. Why is the use of short, clipped sentences effective in this poem?

Hawk Roosting

1. The "falsifying dream" that the hawk rejects is the romantic view that animals are not malicious or cruel. What does the hawk reveal about its own nature? What is the motive for its cruelty?

2. The hawk is roosting: the scene is a peaceful one. How does this detail point up the contrast between the appearance and reality of nature?

3. What view of nature emerges in the poem? What does the poet suggest should be our attitude toward the natural world?

4. By imparting human motives to the hawk, what might the poet be implying about human tyranny?

Drama

Bernard Shaw

1856–1950

Bernard Shaw was born in Dublin, Ireland, of Irish Protestant parents. His father was an improvident man, and Shaw's early years were not happy ones. He attended school sporadically, and felt that he had learned nothing. In 1876 he followed his mother to London, where she had gone with his two sisters to make a living giving singing lessons. Shaw lived with and was supported by his mother: "I did not throw myself into the struggle for life," he said later. "I threw my mother into it." Shaw spent his time reading, visiting museums, and writing unsuccessful novels. In 1881 he became a vegetarian, which he remained throughout his long life. "A man of my spiritual intensity does not eat corpses," he explained. In 1884 he joined the recently formed Fabian Society, which was later to be the nucleus of the British Labor Party, and he began to write and speak on political and economic topics and social reform.

In 1885 his friend William Archer secured him a position as an art critic. Shaw's only credentials for the job, he said, was that he was the only Irishman who had ever entered the National Gallery of Ireland, "except the officials." Three years later he began writing music criticism under the name Corno di Bassetto and continued to do so until 1894. Though an amateur in this field also, his writings on music are among the most distinguished in the nineteenth century.

Archer, an ardent supporter of the Norwegian dramatist Henrik Ibsen, whose plays he translated, heightened Shaw's interest in drama. In 1891 Shaw wrote his commentary on Ibsen's plays, *The Quintessence of Ibsenism*, in which he praises Ibsen for attacking middle-class conventionality and hypocrisy. In 1892 he began his own career as a dramatist, first collaborating with Archer in *Widowers' Houses*, and in the years immediately following writing some of his most famous plays, including *Mrs. Warren's Profession, Arms and the Man*, and *Candida*. In contrast to much of the drama then current on the London stage, these plays dealt with contemporary social problems, problems considered unmentionable in genteel society and hardly suited to stage presentation. Shaw portrayed his situations frankly and honestly, intending to shock his audiences with a new view of society. He presented many of his characters as fools. He believed, however, in the power of human reason— what he called the "Life Force"— to cut through all pretense in the end. In their realism and wit, his plays were largely comedies of ideas in the tradition of the French dramatist Molière, as Shaw himself claimed, and marked a turning to a realism and naturalism that was increasingly to dominate British drama.

Shaw's plays were slow to find a wide audience, and disappointed in not having them produced often or at all, he began to publish them as plays to be read rather than performed. Almost all of his plays were published with long prefaces that dealt in depth with the issues of the play. Shaw continued this practice in later years, after his plays had achieved wide popularity in performance. *Pygmalion* is distinctive in having a long afterword or "sequel," in which Shaw discusses the lives of his characters following the events of the play itself. The play is, however, complete as it stands.

In 1898 Shaw married, and from the turn of the century to his death in 1950 continued to write plays, engage in politics and social reform, and comment on a wide range of topics that included evolution, criminology, war, education, marriage, and religion. The preface to *Androcles and the Lion* is an extensive commentary on the synoptic Gospels; the preface to *Saint Joan* is an examination of the Medieval Church and sainthood. He was awarded the Nobel Prize for literature in 1925. By the time of his death, he had become the foremost English dramatist of his time.

Discussing his practice as a dramatist, Shaw explained that character was far more important to him than plot. It is this concentration on characters

Bernard Shaw by Bernard Partridge.
National Portrait Gallery, London

Sometimes I do not see what the play was driving at until a long time after I have finished it. . . ." Aware of the criticism that he created mouth-pieces for his ideas instead of characters existing in their own right, Shaw defended his accomplishment in these words:

I was always in the classic tradition, recognizing that stage characters must be endowed by the author with a conscious self-knowledge . . . , a freedom from inhibitions, which in real life would make them monsters of genius. It is the power to do this that differentiates me (or Shakespeare) from a gramophone and a camera.

Although Shaw was not alone in pioneering theatrical realism — his great Irish contemporary John Synge brought the language and everyday life of Irish country people to the stage — his influence on later English dramatists has been immense. The play of ideas and the comedy of manners continued to flourish in the work of John Galsworthy, J. B. Priestley, Noel Coward, and others. More recent dramatists have kept the theater alive to the portrayal and discussion of serious social problems. The intense social realism of Arnold Wesker, John Osborne, Shelagh Delaney, and Simon Gray — more outspoken and naturalistic than Shaw and his contemporaries could have imagined possible on the stage — is directly descended from Shaw's own social drama.

Pygmalion was written in 1912 and first performed in 1913. The name of the play is derived from a Greek myth. Pygmalion was a sculptor who fell in love with the statue he had carved. He implored Aphrodite, the goddess of love, to bring the statue to life, and the goddess did so. The Eliza of the play bears some resemblance to Galatea, the girl of the legend, and Professor Higgins is the modern Pygmalion.

Shaw believed in phonetic spelling, and he introduced into his work some of his own spelling simplifications. In 1902 he wrote in an article: "I have written aint, dont, havnt, shant, shouldnt and wont for twenty years with perfect impunity, using the apostrophe only where its omission would suggest another word: for example, hell for he'll . . . . I also write thats, whats, lets, for the colloquial forms of that is, what is, let us. . . ." Shaw's simplifications are retained here in the text of *Pygmalion*.

and on the ideas they represent that separates him from most English dramatists at the end of the nineteenth century and the beginning of the twentieth. "When I am writing a play I never invent a plot," Shaw said. "I let the play write itself and shape itself, which it always does even when up to the last moment I do not foresee the way out.

Preface to *Pygmalion*

A Professor of Phonetics

The English have no respect for their language, and will not teach their children to speak it. They cannot spell it because they have nothing to spell it with but an old foreign alphabet of which only the consonants — and not all of them — have any agreed speech value. Consequently no man can teach himself what it should sound like from reading it; and it is impossible for an Englishman to open his mouth without making some other Englishman despise him. Most European languages are now accessible in black and white to foreigners: English and French are not thus accessible even to Englishmen and Frenchmen. The reformer we need most today is an energetic phonetic enthusiast: that is why I have made such a one the hero of a popular play.

There have been heroes of that kind crying in the wilderness for many years past. When I became interested in the subject towards the end of the eighteen-seventies, the illustrious Alexander Melville Bell, the inventor of Visible Speech, had emigrated to Canada, where his son invented the telephone; but Alexander J. Ellis was still a London Patriarch, with an impressive head always covered by a velvet skull cap, for which he would apologize to public meetings in a very courtly manner. He and Tito Pagliardini, another phonetic veteran, were men whom it was impossible to dislike. Henry Sweet, then a young man, lacked their sweetness of character: he was about as conciliatory to conventional mortals as Ibsen or Samuel Butler. His great ability as a phonetician (he was, I think the best of them all at his job) would have entitled him to high official recognition, and perhaps enabled him to popularize his subject, but for his Satanic contempt for all academic dignitaries and persons in general who thought more of Greek than of phonetics. Once, in the days

when the Imperial Institute rose in South Kensington, and Joseph Chamberlain was booming the Empire, I induced the editor of a leading monthly review to commission an article from Sweet on the imperial importance of his subject. When it arrived, it contained nothing but a savagely derisive attack on a professor of language and literature whose chair Sweet regarded as proper to a phonetic expert only. The article, being libellous, had to be returned as impossible; and I had to renounce my dream of dragging its author into the limelight. When I met him afterwards, for the first time for many years, I found to my astonishment that he, who had been a quite tolerably presentable young man, had actually managed by sheer scorn to alter his personal appearance until he had become a sort of walking repudiation of Oxford and all its traditions. It must have been largely in his own despite that he was squeezed into something called a Readership of phonetics there. The future of phonetics rests probably with his pupils, who all swore by him; but nothing could bring the man himself into any sort of compliance with the university to which he nevertheless clung by divine right in an intensely Oxonian way. I daresay his papers, if he has left any, include some satires that may be published without too destructive results fifty years hence. He was, I believe, not in the least an ill-natured man: very much the opposite, I should say; but he would not suffer fools gladly; and to him all scholars who were not rabid phoneticians were fools.

Those who knew him will recognize in my third act the allusion to the Current Shorthand in which he used to write postcards. It may be acquired from a four and sixpenny manual published by the Clarendon Press. The postcards which Mrs Higgins describes are such as I have received from Sweet. I would decipher a sound which a cockney would represent by *zerr*, and a Frenchman by *seu*, and then write demanding with some heat what on earth it meant. Sweet, with boundless contempt for my stupidity, would reply that it not only meant but obviously was the word Result, as no other word containing that sound, and capable of making sense with the context, existed in any language spoken on earth. That less expert mortals should require fuller indications was beyond Sweet's patience. Therefore, though the whole point of his Current Shorthand is that it can express every sound in the language perfectly, vowels as well as consonants, and that your hand has to make no stroke except the easy and current ones with which you write m, n, and u, l, p, and q, scribbling them at whatever angle comes easiest to you, his unfortunate determination to make this remarkable and quite legible script serve also as a shorthand reduced it in his own practice to the most inscrutable of cryptograms. His true objective was the provision of a full, accurate, legible script for our language; but he was led past that by his contempt for the popular Pitman system of shorthand, which he called the Pitfall system. The triumph of Pitman was a triumph of business organization: there was a weekly paper to persuade you to learn Pitman: there were cheap textbooks and exercise books and transcripts of speeches for you to copy, and schools where experienced teachers coached you up to the necessary proficiency. Sweet could not organize his market in that fashion. He might as well have been the Sybil who tore up the leaves of prophecy that nobody would attend to. The four and sixpenny manual, mostly in his lithographed handwriting, that was never vulgarly advertized, may perhaps some day be taken up by a syndicate and pushed upon the public as The Times pushed the Encyclopædia Britannica; but until then it will certainly not prevail against Pitman. I have bought three copies of it during my lifetime; and I am informed by the publishers that its cloistered existence is still a steady and healthy one. I actually learned the system two several times; and yet the shorthand in which I am writing these lines is Pitman's. And the reason is, that my secretary cannot transcribe Sweet, having been perforce taught in the schools of Pitman. In America I could use the commercially organized Gregg shorthand, which has taken a hint from Sweet by making its letters writable (current, Sweet would have called them) instead of having to be geometrically drawn like Pitman's; but all these systems, including Sweet's, are spoilt by making them available for verbatim reporting, in which complete and exact spelling and word division are impossible. A complete and exact phonetic script is neither practicable nor necessary for ordinary use; but if we enlarge our alphabet to the Russian size, and make our spelling as phonetic as Spanish, the advance will be prodigious.

Pygmalion Higgins is not a portrait of Sweet, to whom the adventure of Eliza Doolittle would have been impossible; still, as will be seen, there are touches of Sweet in the play. With Higgins's physique and temperament Sweet might have set the Thames on fire. As it was, he impressed himself professionally on Europe to an extent that made his comparative personal obscurity, and the failure of Oxford to do justice to his eminence, a puzzle to foreign specialists in his subject. I do not blame Oxford, because I think Oxford is quite right in demanding a certain social amenity from its nurslings (heavens knows it is not exorbitant in its requirement!); for although I well know how hard it is for a man of genius with a seriously underrated subject to maintain serene and kindly relations with the men who underrate it, and who keep all the best places for less important subjects which they profess without originality and sometimes without much capacity for them, still, if he overwhelms them with wrath and disdain, he cannot expect them to heap honors on him.

Of the later generations of phoneticians I know little. Among them towered Robert Bridges, to whom perhaps Higgins may owe his Miltonic sympathies, though here again I must disclaim all portraiture. But if the play makes the public aware that there are such people as phoneticians, and that they are among the most important people in England at present, it will serve its turn.

I wish to boast that Pygmalion has been an extremely successful play, both on stage and screen, all over Europe and North America as well as at home. It is so intensely and deliberately didactic, and its subject is esteemed so dry, that I delight in throwing it at the heads of the wiseacres who repeat the parrot cry that art should never be didactic. It goes to prove my contention that great art can never be anything else.

Finally, and for the encouragement of people troubled with accents that cut them off from all high employment, I may add that the change wrought by Professor Higgings in the flower-girl is neither impossible nor uncommon. The modern concierge's daughter who fulfills her ambition by playing the Queen of Spain in Ruy Blas at the Théâtre Français is only one of many thousands of men and women who have sloughed off their native dialects and acquired a new tongue. Our West End shop assistants and domestic servants are bilingual. But the thing has to be done scientifically, or the last state of the aspirant may be worse than the first. An honest slum dialect is more tolerable than the attempts of phonetically untaught persons to imitate the plutocracy. Ambitious flower-girls who read this play must not imagine that they can pass themselves off as fine ladies by untutored imitation. They must learn their alphabet over again, and different, from a phonetic expert. Imitation will only make them ridiculous.

NOTE FOR TECHNICIANS. A complete representation of the play as printed in this edition is technically possible only on the cinema screen or on stages furnished with exceptionally elaborate machinery. For ordinary theatrical use the scenes separated by rows of asterisks are to be omitted.

In the dialogue an e upside down indicates the indefinite vowel, sometimes called obscure or neutral, for which, though it is one of the commonest sounds in English speech, our wretched alphabet has no letter.

Pygmalion

Characters

Henry Higgins	Mrs Higgins
Colonel Pickering	Mrs Pearce
Freddy Eynsford Hill	Parlormaid
Alfred Doolittle	Taximen
Bystanders	Count Nepommuck
Eliza Doolittle	Host
Mrs Eynsford Hill	Hostess
Miss Eynsford Hill	Footmen
Constables	

Act One

London at 11.15 P.M. Torrents of heavy summer rain. Cab whistles blowing frantically in all directions. Pedestrians running for shelter into the portico of St Paul's church (not Wren's cathedral but Inigo Jones's church in Covent Garden vegetable market), among them a lady and her daughter in evening dress. All are peering out gloomily at the rain, except one man with his back turned to the rest, wholly preoccupied with a notebook in which he is writing.

The church clock strikes the first quarter.

The Daughter (*in the space between the central pillars, close to the one on her left*) I'm getting chilled to the bone. What can Freddy be doing all this time? He's been gone twenty minutes.

The Mother (*on her daughter's right*) Not so long. But he ought to have got us a cab by this.

A Bystander (*on the lady's right*) He wont get no cab not until half-past eleven, missus, when they come back after dropping their theatre fares.

The Mother. But we must have a cab. We cant stand here until half-past eleven. It's too bad.

The Bystander. Well, it ain't my fault, missus.

The Daughter. If Freddy had a bit of gumption, he would have got one at the theatre door.

The Mother. What could he have done, poor boy?

The Daughter. Other people got cabs. Why couldnt he?

Freddy rushes in out of the rain from the Southampton Street side, and comes between them closing a dripping umbrella. He is a young man of twenty, in evening dress, very wet round the ankles.

The Daughter. Well, havnt you got a cab?

Freddy. Theres not one to be had for love or money.

The Mother. Oh, Freddy, there must be one. You cant have tried.

The Daughter. It's too tiresome. Do you expect us to go and get one ourselves?

Freddy. I tell you theyre all engaged. The rain was so sudden: nobody was prepared; and everybody had to take a cab. Ive been to Charing Cross one way and nearly to Ludgate Circus the other; and they were all engaged.

The Mother. Did you try Trafalgar Square?

Freddy. There wasn't one at Trafalgar Square.

The Daughter. Did you try?

Freddy. I tried as far as Charing Cross Station. Did you expect me to walk to Hammersmith?

The Daughter. You havnt tried at all.

The Mother. You really are very helpless, Freddy. Go again; and dont come back until you have found a cab.

Freddy. I shall simply get soaked for nothing.

The Daughter. And what about us? Are we to stay here all night in this draught,[1] with next to nothing on? You selfish pig——

Freddy. Oh, very well: I'll go, I'll go. (*He opens his umbrella and dashes off Strandwards, but comes into collision with a flower girl who is hurrying in for shelter, knocking her basket out of her hands. A blinding flash of lightning, followed instantly by a rattling peal of thunder, orchestrates the incident*).

The Flower Girl. Nah then, Freddy: look wh' y' gowin, deah.

Freddy. Sorry (*he rushes off*).

The Flower Girl (*picking up her scattered flowers and replacing them in the basket*) Theres menners f' yer! Tə-oo banches o voylets trod into the mad. (*She sits down on the plinth[2] of the column sorting her flowers, on the lady's right. She is not at all a romantic figure. She is perhaps eighteen, perhaps twenty, hardly older. She wears a little sailor hat of black straw that has long been exposed to the dust and soot of London and has seldom if ever been brushed. Her hair needs washing rather badly: its mousy color can hardly be natural. She wears a shoddy black coat that reaches nearly to her knees and is shaped to her waist. She has a brown skirt with a coarse apron. Her boots are much the worse for wear. She is no doubt as clean as she can afford to be; but compared to the ladies she is very dirty. Her features are no worse than theirs; but their condition leaves something to be desired; and she needs the services of a dentist*).

The Mother. How do you know that my son's name is Freddy, pray?

The Flower Girl. Ow, eez yə-ooa, san, is e? Wal, fewd dan y' də-ooty bawmz a mather should, eed now bettern to spawl a pore gel's flahrzn than ran awy athaht pyin. Will ye-oo py me f'them? (*Here, with apologies, this desperate attempt to represent her dialect without a phonetic alphabet must be abandoned as unintelligible outside London*).

The Daughter. Do nothing of the sort, mother. The idea!

The Mother. Please allow me, Clara. Have you any pennies?

The Daughter. No. Ive nothing smaller than sixpence.

The Flower Girl (*hopefully*) I can give you change for a tanner,[3] kind lady.

The Mother (*to Clara*) Give it to me. (*Clara parts reluctantly*). Now (*to the Girl*) This is for your flowers.

The Flower Girl. Thank you kindly, lady.

The Daughter. Make her give you the change. These things are only a penny a bunch.

The Mother. Do hold your tongue, Clara. (*To the Girl*) You can keep the change.

The Flower Girl. Oh, thank you, lady.

The Mother. Now tell me how you know that young gentleman's name.

The Flower Girl. I didnt.

The Mother. I heard you call him by it. Dont try to deceive me.

The Flower Girl (*protesting*) Who's trying to deceive you? I called him Freddy or Charlie same as you might yourself if you was talking to a stranger and wished to be pleasant.

The Daughter. Sixpence thrown away! Really, mamma, you might have spared Freddy that. (*She retreats in disgust behind the pillar*).

An elderly gentleman of the amiable military type rushes into the shelter, and closes a dripping umbrella. He is in the same plight as Freddy, very wet above the ankles. He is in evening dress, with a light overcoat. He takes the place left vacant by the Daughter.

The Gentleman. Phew!

The Mother (*to the* Gentleman) Oh, sir, is there any sign of its stopping?

The Gentleman. I'm afraid not. It started worse than ever about two minutes ago (*he*

---

1. **draught:** draft.
2. **plinth:** the square block at the base of a column.

3. **tanner:** English slang for a sixpence.

Liza selling flowers in Covent Garden.
Penguin Photos

goes to the plinth beside the Flower Girl; *puts up his foot on it; and stoops to turn down his trouser ends).*

The Mother. Oh dear! (*She retires sadly and joins her daughter).*

The Flower Girl (*taking advantage of the military gentleman's proximity to establish friendly relations with him*) If it's worse, it's a sign it's nearly over. So cheer up, Captain; and buy a flower off a poor girl.

The Gentleman. I'm sorry. I havnt any change.

The Flower Girl. I can give you change, Captain.

The Gentleman. For a sovereign? Ive nothing less.

The Flower Girl. Garn! Oh do buy a flower off me, Captain. I can change half-a-crown. Take this for tuppence.

The Gentleman. Now dont be troublesome: theres a good girl. (*Trying his pockets*) I really havnt any change — Stop: heres three hapence, if thats any use to you (*he retreats to the other pillar*).

The Flower Girl (*disappointed, but thinking three half-pence better than nothing*) Thank you, sir.

The Bystander (*to the* Girl) You be careful: give him a flower for it. Theres a bloke here behind taking down every blessed word youre saying. (*All turn to the man who is taking notes*).

The Flower Girl (*springing up terrified*) I aint done nothing wrong by speaking to the gentleman. Ive a right to sell flowers if I keep off the kerb. (*Hysterically*) I'm a respectable girl: so help me, I never spoke to him except to ask him to buy a flower off me.

General hubbub, mostly sympathetic to the Flower Girl, *but deprecating her excessive sensibility. Cries of* Dont start hollerin. Who's hurting you? Nobody's going to touch you. Whats the good of fussing? Steady on. Easy, easy, etc., *come from the elderly staid spectators, who pat her comfortingly. Less patient ones bid her shut her head, or ask her roughly what is wrong with her. A remoter* group, *not knowing what the matter is, crowd in and increase the noise with question and answer:* What's the row? What-she do? Where is he? A tec taking her down. What! him? Yes: him over there: Took money off the gentleman, etc.

The Flower Girl (*breaking through them to the* Gentleman, *crying wildly*) Oh, sir, dont let him charge me. You dunno what it means to me. Theyll take away my character and drive me on the streets for speaking to gentlemen. They——

The Note Taker (*coming forward on her right, the rest crowding after him*) There! there! there! there! who's hurting you, you silly girl? What do you take me for?

The Bystander. It's aw rawt: e's a genleman: look at his bə-oots. (*Explaining to the* Note Taker) She thought you was a copper's nark, sir.

The Note Taker (*with quick interest*) Whats a copper's nark?

The Bystander (*inapt at definition*) It's a—well, it's a copper's nark, as you might say. What else would you call it? A sort of informer.

The Flower Girl (*still hysterical*) I take my Bible oath I never said a word——

The Note Taker (*overbearing but good-humored*) Oh, shut up, shut up. Do I look like a policeman?

The Flower Girl (*far from reassured*) Then what did you take down my words for? How do I know whether you took me down right? You just shew[4] me what youve wrote about me. (*The* Note Taker *opens his book and holds it steadily under her nose, though the pressure of the mob trying to read it over his shoulders would upset a weaker man*). Whats that? That aint proper writing. I cant read that.

The Note Taker. I can. (*Reads, reproducing her pronunciation exactly*) "Cheer ap, Keptin; n' baw ya flahr orf a pore gel."

The Flower Girl (*much distressed*) It's because I called him Captain. I meant no harm. (*To the* Gentleman) Oh, sir, dont let him lay a charge agen me for a word like that. You—

The Gentleman. Charge! I make no charge. (*To the* Note Taker) Really, sir, if you are a detective, you need not begin protecting me against molestation by young women until I ask you. Anybody could see that the girl meant no harm.

The Bystanders Generally (*demonstrating against police espionage*) Course they could. What business is it of yours? You mind your own affairs. He wants promotion, he does. Taking down people's words! Girl never said a word to him. What harm if she did? Nice thing a girl cant shelter from the rain without being insulted, etc., etc., etc. (*She is conducted by the more sympathetic demonstrators back to her plinth, where she resumes her seat and struggles with her emotion*).

The Bystander. He aint a tec. He's a blooming busybody: thats what he is. I tell you, look at his bə-oots.

The Note Taker (*turning on him genially*) And how are all your people down at Selsey?

The Bystander (*suspiciously*) Who told you my people come from Selsey?

The Note Taker. Never you mind. They did. (*To the* Girl) How do you come to be up so far east? You were born in Lisson Grove.

The Flower Girl (*appalled*) Oh, what harm is there in my leaving Lisson Grove? It wasnt fit for a pig to live in; and I had to pay four-and-six a week. (*In tears*) Oh, boo—hoo—oo——

The Note Taker. Live where you like; but stop that noise.

The Gentleman (*to the* Girl) Come, come! he cant touch you: you have a right to live where you please.

A Sarcastic Bystander (*thrusting himself between the* Note Taker *and the* Gentleman) Park Lane, for instance. I'd like to go into the Housing Question with you, I would.

---

4. **shew:** show.

The Flower Girl (*subsiding into a brooding melancholy over her basket, and talking very low-spiritedly to herself*) I'm a good girl, I am.

The Sarcastic Bystander (*not attending to her*) Do you know where *I* come from?

The Note Taker (*promptly*) Hoxton.

Titterings. Popular interest in the Note Taker's *performance increases.*

The Sarcastic One (*amazed*) Well, who said I didnt? Bly me! you know everything, you do.

The Flower Girl (*still nursing her sense of injury*) Aint no call to meddle with me, he aint.

The Bystander (*to her*) Of course he aint. Dont you stand it from him. (*To the* Note Taker) See here: what call have you to know about people what never offered to meddle with you?

The Flower Girl. Let him say what he likes. I dont want to have no truck with him.

The Bystander. You take us for dirt under your feet, dont you? Catch you taking liberties with a gentleman!

The Sarcastic Bystander. Yes: tell him where he come from if you want to go fortune-telling.

The Note Taker. Cheltenham, Harrow, Cambridge, and India.

The Gentleman. Quite right.

Great laughter. Reaction in the Note Taker's *favor. Exclamations of* He knows all about it. Told him proper. Hear him tell the toff[5] where he come from? etc.

The Gentleman. May I ask, sir, do you do this for your living at a music hall?

The Note Taker. I've thought of that. Perhaps I shall some day.

The rain has stopped; and the persons on the outside of the crowd begin to drop off.

The Flower Girl (*resenting the reaction*) He's no gentleman, he aint, to interfere with a poor girl.

---

5. **toff:** English slang for a dandy.

The Daughter (*out of patience, pushing her way rudely to the front and displacing the* Gentleman, *who politely retires to the other side of the pillar*) What on earth is Freddy doing? I shall get pneumownia if I stay in this draught any longer.

The Note Taker (*to himself, hastily making a note of her pronunciation of "monia"*) Earls-court.

The Daughter (*violently*) Will you please keep your impertinent remarks to yourself.

The Note Taker. Did I say that out loud? I didn't mean to. I beg your pardon. Your mother's Epsom, unmistakeably.

The Mother (*advancing between the* Daughter *and the* Note Taker) How very curious! I was brought up in Largelady Park, near Epsom.

The Note Taker (*uproariously amused*) Ha! ha! What a devil of a name! Excuse me. (*To the* Daughter) You want a cab, do you?

The Daughter. Dont dare speak to me.

The Mother. Oh please, please, Clara. (*Her daughter repudiates her with an angry shrug and retires haughtily*) We should be so grateful to you, sir, if you found us a cab. (*The* Note Taker *produces a whistle*) Oh, thank you. (*She joins her daughter*).

The Note Taker *blows a piercing blast.*

The Sarcastic Bystander. There! I knowed he was a plainclothes copper.

The Bystander. That aint a police whistle: thats a sporting whistle.

The Flower Girl (*still preoccupied with her wounded feelings*) He's no right to take away my character. My character is the same to me as any lady's.

The Note Taker. I dont know whether youve noticed it; but the rain stopped about two minutes ago.

The Bystander. So it has. Why didn't you say so before? and us losing our time listening to your silliness! (*He walks off towards the Strand*).

The Sarcastic Bystander. I can tell where you come from. You come from Anwell. Go back there.

The Note Taker (*helpfully*) Hanwell.

The Sarcastic Bystander (*affecting great distinction of speech*) Thenk you, teacher. Haw haw! So long (*he touches his hat with mock respect and strolls off*).

The Flower Girl. Frightening people like that! How would he like it himself?

The Mother. It's quite fine now, Clara. We can walk to a motor bus. Come. (*She gathers her skirts above her ankles and hurries off towards the Strand*).

The Daughter. But the cab—(*her mother is out of hearing*). Oh, how tiresome! (*She follows angrily*).

All the rest have gone except the Note Taker, *the* Gentleman, *and the* Flower Girl, *who sits arranging her basket, and still pitying herself in murmurs.*

The Flower Girl. Poor girl! Hard enough for her to live without being worrited and chivied.[6]

The Gentleman (*returning to his former place on the* Note Taker's *left*) How do you do it, if I may ask?

The Note Taker. Simply phonetics. The science of speech. Thats my profession: also my hobby. Happy is the man who can make a living by his hobby! You can spot an Irishman or a Yorkshireman by his brogue. *I* can place any man within six miles. I can place him within two miles in London. Sometimes within two streets.

The Flower Girl. Ought to be ashamed of himself, unmanly coward.

The Gentleman. But is there a living in that?

The Note Taker. Oh yes. Quite a fat one. This is an age of upstarts. Men begin in Kentish Town with £80 a year, and end in Park Lane with a hundred thousand. They want to drop Kentish Town; but they give themselves away every time they open their mouths. Now I can teach them—

The Flower Girl. Let him mind his own business and leave a poor girl—

The Note Taker (*Explosively*) Woman: cease this detestable boohooing instantly; or else seek the shelter of some other place of worship.

The Flower Girl (*with feeble defiance*) Ive a right to be here if I like, same as you.

The Note Taker. A woman who utters such depressing and disgusting sounds has no right to be anywhere—no right to live. Remember that you are a human being with a soul and the divine gift of articulate speech: that your native language is the language of Shakespear and Milton and The Bible; and dont sit there crooning like a bilious pigeon.

The Flower Girl (*quite overwhelmed, looking up at him in mingled wonder and deprecation without daring to raise her head*) Ah-ah-ah-ow-ow-ow-oo!

The Note Taker (*whipping out his book*) Heavens! what a sound! (*He writes; then holds out the book and reads, reproducing her vowels exactly*) Ah-ah-ah-ow-ow-ow-oo!

The Flower Girl (*tickled by the performance, and laughing in spite of herself*) Garn!

The Note Taker. You see this creature with her kerbstone English: the English that will keep her in the gutter to the end of her days. Well, sir, in three months I could pass that girl off as a duchess at an ambassador's garden party. I could even get her a place as lady's maid or shop assistant, which requires better English.

The Flower Girl. What's that you say?

The Note Taker. Yes, you squashed cabbage leaf, you disgrace to the noble architecture of these columns, you incarnate insult to the English language: I could pass you off as the Queen of Sheba. (*To the* Gentleman) Can you believe that?

The Gentleman. Of course I can. I am myself a student of Indian dialects; and—

---

6. **worrited and chivied:** worried and tormented.

The Note Taker (*eagerly*) Are you? Do you know Colonel Pickering, the author of Spoken Sanscrit?

The Gentleman. I am Colonel Pickering. Who are you?

The Note Taker. Henry Higgins, author of Higgins's Universal Alphabet.

Pickering (*with enthusiasm*) I came from India to meet you.

Higgins. I was going to India to meet you.

Pickering. Where do you live?

Higgins. 27A Wimpole Street. Come and see me tomorrow.

Pickering. I'm at the Carlton. Come with me now and lets have a jaw over some supper.

Higgins. Right you are.

The Flower Girl (*to Pickering, as he passes her*) Buy a flower, kind gentleman. I'm short for my lodging.

Pickering. I really havnt any change. I'm sorry (*he goes away*).

Higgins (*shocked at the* Girl's *mendacity*) Liar. You said you could change half-a-crown.

The Flower Girl (*rising in desperation*) You ought to be stuffed with nails, you ought. (*Flinging the basket at his feet*) Take the whole blooming basket for sixpence.

The church clock strikes the second quarter.

Higgins (*hearing in it the voice of God, rebuking him for his Pharisaic[7] want of charity to the poor girl*) A reminder. (*He raises his hat solemnly; then throws a handful of money into the basket and follows* Pickering).

The Flower Girl (*picking up a half-crown*) Ahow-ooh! (*Picking up a couple of florins*) Aaahow-ooh! (*Picking up several coins*) Aaaaahow-ooh! (*Picking up a half-sovereign*) Aaaaaaaaaaaah-ow-ooh!!!

Freddy (*springing out of a taxicab*) Got one at last. Hallo! (*To the* Girl) Where are the two ladies that were here?

---

7. **Pharisaic** (făr′ə-sā′ĭk): The Pharisees were a group among the ancient Jews known for their formality and strictness.

The Flower Girl. They walked to the bus when the rain stopped.

Freddy. And left me with a cab on my hands! Damnation!

The Flower Girl (*with grandeur*) Never mind, young man. *I'm* going home in a taxi. (*She sails off to the cab. The driver puts his hand behind him and holds the door firmly shut against her. Quite understanding his mistrust, she shews him her handful of money*). A taxi fare aint no object to me, Charlie. (*He grins and opens the door*). Here. What about the basket?

The Taximan. Give it here. Tuppence extra.

Liza. No: I dont want nobody to see it. (*She crushes it into the cab and gets in, continuing the conversation through the window*) Goodbye, Freddy.

Freddy (*dazedly raising his hat*) Goodbye.

Taximan. Where to?

Liza. Bucknam Pellis [Buckingham Palace].

Taximan. What d'ye mean—Bucknam Pellis?

Liza. Dont you know where it is? In the Green Park, where the King lives. Goodbye, Freddy. Dont let me keep you standing there. Goodbye.

Freddy. Goodbye. (*He goes*).

Taximan. Here? Whats this about Bucknam Pellis? What business have you at Bucknam Pellis?

Liza. Of course I havnt none. But I wasn't going to let him know that. You drive me home.

Taximan. And wheres home?

Liza. Angel Court, Drury Lane, next Meiklejohn's oil shop.

Taximan. That sounds more like it, Judy. (*He drives off*).

*　　*　　*　　*　　*　　*

Let us follow the taxi to the entrance to Angel Court, a narrow little archway between two shops, one of them Meiklejohn's oil shop. When it stops there, Eliza gets out, dragging her basket with her.

Liza. How much?

Taximan (*indicating the taximeter*) Cant you read? A shilling.

Liza. A shilling for two minutes!!

Taximan. Two minutes or ten: it's all the same.

Liza. Well, I dont call it right.

Taximan. Ever been in a taxi before?

Liza (*with dignity*) Hundreds and thousands of times, young man.

Taximan (*laughing at her*) Good for you, Judy. Keep the shilling, darling, with best love from all at home. Good luck! (*He drives off*).

Liza (*humiliated*) Impidence!

She picks up the basket and trudges up the alley with it to her lodging: a small room with very old wall paper hanging loose in the damp places. A broken pane in the window is mended with paper. A portrait of a popular actor and a fashion plate of ladies' dresses, all wildly beyond poor Eliza's means, both torn from newspapers, are pinned up on the wall. A birdcage hangs in the window; but its tenant died long ago: it remains as a memorial only.

These are the only visible luxuries: the rest is the irreducible minimum of poverty's needs: a wretched bed heaped with all sorts of coverings that have any warmth in them, a draped packing case with a basin and jug on it and a little looking glass over it, a chair and table, the refuse of some suburban kitchen, and an American alarum clock on the shelf above the unused fireplace: the whole lighted with a gas lamp with a penny in the slot meter. Rent: four shillings a week.

Here Eliza, chronically weary, but too excited to go to bed, sits, counting her new riches and dreaming and planning what to do with them, until the gas goes out, when she enjoys for the first time the sensation of being able to put in another penny without grudging it. This prodigal mood does not extinguish her gnawing sense of the need for economy sufficiently to prevent her from calculating that she can dream and plan in bed more cheaply and warmly than sitting up without a fire. So she takes off her shawl and skirt and adds them to the miscellaneous bedclothes. Then she kicks off her shoes and gets into bed without any further change.

FOR STUDY AND DISCUSSION

1. In the opening scene, why do you think Shaw attaches labels rather than specific names to his characters? How would you describe the types of characters represented in Act One?

2. What actions and statements by the flower girl reveal that she has integrity and is also streetwise or shrewd? How would you define other aspects of her character?

3. What is the note taker's attitude toward people in general and women in particular—especially the flower girl? How is he affected by the sound of the church bells?

4. Does Higgins' boast, "in three months I could pass that girl off as a duchess," raise expectations about the nature of the flower girl's coming relationship with Higgins? Or do you feel their personal relationship is not of interest in Act One?

LANGUAGE AND VOCABULARY

The City of London, now a financial center of worldwide importance, is the oldest part of London. It is in that area of one square mile that Cockneys are born—if we adhere to the strictest definition of the term *Cockney*. Or they are defined, equally strictly, as those born within the sound of Bow-bells, which ring out from the old church of Saint Mary-le-Bow.

The Cockney dialect—the dialect spoken by the flower girl—has several characteristic features. Perhaps the most striking variation in the consonants is the sound of *f* or *v* used instead of the standard *th* sound ("fing" for *thing*). Dickens' Sam Weller and his friends, early in the nineteenth century, used *v* for *w* and vice versa, but this is no longer heard. As for vowel sounds, *about* is pronounced "abaht" and *today* becomes "to dye." Cockneys do not pronounce *h* (saying " 'orrible" for *horrible*), but this omission occurs in other varieties of English also. It might be noted, finally, that Cockneys do *not* add the *h* sound to words that begin with a vowel in standard English. Such curiosities as "hindignant" are uttered by actors playing British butlers in American films.

Etymology, the study of the derivation of words (from Greek *etymon* "true meaning" and *logos* "word" or "study"), offers two theories of the history of *Cockney*. Some dictionaries trace it back to a Middle English word meaning a cock's egg. (The *thing* never existed, but the word did.) But Eric Partridge, in his dictionary *Origins*, prefers to derive *Cockney* from French.

What shifts of meaning lie behind the word? According to the first derivation proposed, the Middle English *cokeney* or *cokenay* meant (1) a small or misshapen egg. Then (2) the word was used for a milksop, for example, the city dweller as he appeared to country folk. In the next stages it came to mean (3) a city dweller and (4), by restriction of meaning, a Londoner. According to the second derivation, French *acoquiné*, which meant, first, "rascally" and, later, "pampered," lost its initial vowel in English speech. The later shifts in meaning are those listed under (3) and (4).

Act Two

Next day at 11 A.M. Higgins's *laboratory in Wimpole Street. It is a room on the first floor, looking on the street, and was meant for the drawing room. The double doors are in the middle of the back wall; and persons entering find in the corner to their right two tall file cabinets at right angles to one another against the walls. In this corner stands a flat writing-table, on which are a phonograph, a laryngoscope, a row of tiny organ pipes with a bellows, a set of lamp chimneys for singing flames with burners attached to a gas plug in the wall by an indiarubber tube, several tuning-forks of different sizes, a life-size image of half a human head, shewing in section the vocal organs, and a box containing a supply of wax cylinders for the phonograph.*

Further down the room, on the same side, is a fireplace, with a comfortable leather-covered easy-chair at the side of the hearth nearest the door, and a coal-scuttle. There is a clock on the mantlepiece. Between the fireplace and the phonograph table is a stand for newspapers.

On the other side of the central door, to the left of the visitor, is a cabinet of shallow drawers. On it is a telephone and the telephone directory. The corner beyond, and most of the side wall, is occupied by a grand piano, with the keyboard at the end furthest from the door, and a bench for the players extending the full length of the keyboard. On the piano is a dessert dish heaped with fruit and sweets, mostly chocolates.

The middle of the room is clear. Besides the easy-chair, the piano bench, and two chairs at the phonograph table, there is one stray chair. It stands near the fireplace. On the walls, engravings: mostly Piranesis[1] and mezzotint[2] portraits. No paintings.

---

1. **Piranesis:** the engravings of Giambattista Piranesi (1720–1778), an Italian artist.
2. **mezzotint:** a copper or steel engraving.

Pickering *is seated at the table, putting down some cards and a tuning-fork which he has been using.* Higgins *is standing up near him, closing two or three file drawers which are hanging out. He appears in the morning light as a robust, vital, appetizing sort of man of forty or thereabouts, dressed in a professional-looking black frock-coat with a white linen collar and black silk tie. He is of energetic, scientific type, heartily, even violently interested in everything that can be studied as a scientific subject, and careless about himself and other people, including their feelings. He is, in fact, but for his years and size, rather like a very impetuous baby "taking notice" eagerly and loudly, and requiring almost as much watching to keep him out of unintended mischief. His manner varies from genial bullying when he is in a good humor to stormy petulance when anything goes wrong; but he is so entirely frank and void of malice that he remains likeable even in his least reasonable moments.*

Higgins (*as he shuts the last drawer*) Well, I think thats the whole show.

Pickering. It's really amazing. I havnt taken half of it in, you know.

Higgins. Would you like to go over any of it again?

Pickering (*rising and coming to the fireplace, where he plants himself with his back to the fire*) No, thank you: not now. I'm quite done up for this morning.

Higgins (*following him, and standing beside him on his left*) Tired of listening to sounds?

Pickering. Yes. It's a fearful strain. I rather fancied myself because I can pronounce twenty-four distinct vowel sounds; but your hundred and thirty beat me. I cant hear a bit of difference between most of them.

Higgins (*chuckling, and going over to the piano to eat sweets*) Oh, that comes with practice. You hear no difference at first; but you keep on listening, and presently you find theyre all as different as A from B. (Mrs Pearce

looks in: *she is* Higgins's *housekeeper*). Whats the matter?

Mrs Pearce (*hesitating, evidently perplexed*) A young woman asks to see you, sir.

Higgins. A young woman! What does she want?

Mrs Pearce. Well, sir, she says youll be glad to see her when you know what she's come about. She's quite a common girl, sir. Very common indeed. I should have sent her away, only I thought perhaps you wanted her to talk into your machines. I hope Ive not done wrong; but really you see such queer people sometimes—youll excuse me, I'm sure, sir—

Higgins. Oh, thats all right, Mrs Pearce. Has she an interesting accent?

Mrs Pearce. Oh, something dreadful, sir, really. I dont know how you can take an interest in it.

Higgins (*to* Pickering) Lets have her up. Shew her up, Mrs Pearce (*he rushes across to his working table and picks out a cylinder to use on the phonograph*).

Mrs Pearce (*only half resigned to it*) Very well, sir. It's for you to say. (*She goes downstairs*).

Higgins. This is rather a bit of luck. I'll shew you how I make records. We'll set her talking; and I'll take it down first in Bell's Visible Speech; then in broad Romic; and then we'll get her on the phonograph so that you can turn her on as often as you like with the written transcript before you.

Mrs Pearce (*returning*) This is the young woman, sir.

The Flower Girl *enters in state. She has a hat with three ostrich feathers, orange, sky-blue, and red. She has a nearly clean apron, and the shoddy coat has been tidied a little. The pathos of this deplorable figure, with its innocent vanity and consequential air, touches* Pickering, *who has already straightened himself in the presence of* Mrs Pearce. *But as to* Higgins, *the only distinction he makes between men and women is that when he is neither bullying nor exclaiming to the heav-*

ens *against some feather-weight cross,*[3] *he coaxes women as a child coaxes its nurse when it wants to get anything out of her.*

Higgins (*brusquely, recognizing her with unconcealed disappointment, and at once, babylike, making an intolerable grievance of it*) Why, this is the girl I jotted down last night. She's no use: I've got all the records I want of the Lisson Grove lingo; and I'm not going to waste another cylinder on it. (*To the* Girl) Be off with you: I dont want you.

The Flower Girl. Dont you be so saucy. You aint heard what I come for yet. (*To* Mrs Pearce, *who is waiting at the door for further instructions*) Did you tell him I come in a taxi?

Mrs Pearce. Nonsense, girl! What do you think a gentleman like Mr Higgins cares what you came in?

The Flower Girl. Oh, we are proud! He aint above giving lessons, not him: I heard him say so. Well, I aint come here to ask for any compliment; and if my money's not good enough I can go elsewhere.

Higgins. Good enough for what?

The Flower Girl. Good enough for yə-oo. Now you know, dont you? I've come to have lessons, I am. And to pay for em tə-oo: make no mistake.

Higgins (*stupent*[4]) Well!!! (*Recovering his breath with a gasp*) What do you expect me to say to you?

The Flower Girl. Well, if you was a gentleman, you might ask me to sit down, I think. Dont I tell you I'm bringing you business?

Higgins. Pickering: shall we ask this baggage to sit down, or shall we throw her out of the window?

The Flower Girl (*running away in terror to the piano, where she turns at bay*) Ah-ah-oh-ow-ow-ow-oo! (*Wounded and whimpering*) I wont be called a baggage when Ive offered to pay like any lady.

Motionless, the two men stare at her from the other side of the room, amazed.

Pickering (*gently*) But what is it you want?

The Flower Girl. I want to be a lady in a flower shop stead of sellin at the corner of Tottenham Court Road. But they wont take me unless I can talk more genteel. He said he could teach me. Well, here I am ready to pay him—not asking any favor—and he treats me zif I was dirt.

Mrs Pearce. How can you be such a foolish ignorant girl as to think you could afford to pay Mr Higgins?

The Flower Girl. Why shouldnt I? I know what lessons cost as well as you do; and I'm ready to pay.

Higgins. How much?

The Flower Girl (*coming back to him, triumphant*) Now youre talking! I thought youd come off it when you saw a chance of getting back a bit of what you chucked at me last night. (*Confidentially*) Youd had a drop in,[5] hadn't you?

Higgins (*peremptorily*) Sit down.

The Flower Girl. Oh, if youre going to make a compliment of it —

Higgins (*thundering at her*) Sit down.

Mrs Pearce (*severely*) Sit down, girl. Do as youre told.

The Flower Girl. Ah-ah-ah-ow-ow-oo! (*She stands, half rebellious, half bewildered*).

Pickering (*very courteous*) Wont you sit down? (*He places the stray chair near the hearthrug between himself and* Higgins.)

Liza (*coyly*) Dont mind if I do. (*She sits down.* Pickering *returns to the hearthrug*).

Higgins. Whats your name?

The Flower Girl. Liza Doolittle.

Higgins (*declaiming gravely*)
Eliza, Elizabeth, Betsy and Bess,
They went to the woods to get a bird's nes':

Pickering. They found a nest with four eggs in it:

---

3. **feather-weight cross:** a very small burden or inconvenience.
4. **stupent:** dumbfounded.

5. **had a drop in:** been drinking.

Higgins. They took one apiece, and left three in it.

They laugh heartily at their own fun.

Liza. Oh, dont be silly.

Mrs Pearce (*placing herself behind* Eliza's *chair*) You mustnt speak to the gentleman like that.

Liza. Well, why wont he speak sensible to me?

Higgins. Come back to business. How much do you propose to pay me for the lessons?

Liza. Oh, I know whats right. A lady friend of mine gets French lessons for eighteenpence an hour from a real French·gentleman. Well, you wouldnt have the face to ask me the same for teaching me my own language as you would for French; so I wont give more than a shilling. Take it or leave it.

Higgins (*walking up and down the room, rattling his keys and his cash in his pockets*) You know, Pickering, if you consider a shilling, not as a simple shilling, but as a percentage of this girl's income, it works out as fully equivalent to sixty or seventy guineas from a millionaire.

Pickering. How so?

Higgins. Figure it out. A millionaire has about £150 a day. She earns about half-a-crown.

Liza (*haughtily*) Who told you I only——

Higgins (*continuing*) She offers me two-fifths of her day's income for a lesson. Two-fifths of a millionaire's income for a day would be somewhere about £60. It's handsome. By George, it's enormous! it's the biggest offer I ever had.

Liza (*rising, terrified*) Sixty pounds! What are you talking? I never offered you sixty pounds. Where would I get——

Higgins. Hold your tongue.

Liza (*weeping*) But I aint got sixty pounds. Oh—

Mrs Pearce. Dont cry, you silly girl. Sit down. Nobody is going to touch your money.

Higgins. Somebody is going to touch you, with a broomstick, if you dont stop snivelling. Sit down.

Liza (*obeying slowly*) Ah-ah-ah-ow-oo-o! One would think you was my father.

Higgins. If I decide to teach you, I'll be worse than two fathers to you. Here (*he offers her his silk handkerchief*)!

Liza. Whats this for?

Higgins. To wipe your eyes. To wipe any part of your face that feels moist. Remember: thats your handkerchief; and thats your sleeve. Dont mistake the one for the other if you wish to become a lady in a shop.

Liza, utterly bewildered, stares helplessly at him.

Mrs Pearce. It's no use talking to her like that, Mr Higgins: she doesnt understand you. Besides, youre quite wrong: she doesnt do it that way at all (*she takes the handkerchief*).

Liza (*snatching it*) Here! You give me that handkerchief. He gev it to me, not to you.

Pickering (*laughing*) He did. I think it must be regarded as her property, Mrs Pearce.

Mrs Pearce (*resigning herself*) Serve you right, Mr Higgins.

Pickering. Higgins: I'm interested. What about the ambassador's garden party? I'll say youre the greatest teacher alive if you make that good. I'll bet you all the expenses of the experiment you cant do it. And I'll pay for the lessons.

Liza. Oh, you are real good. Thank you, Captain.

Higgins (*tempted, looking at her*) It's almost irresistible. She's so deliciously low—so horribly dirty——

Liza (*protesting extremely*) Ah-ah-ah-ah-ow-ow-oo-oo!!! I aint dirty: I washed my face and hands afore I come, I did.

Pickering. Youre certainly not going to turn her head with flattery, Higgins.

Mrs Pearce (*uneasy*) Oh, dont say that, sir: theres more ways than one of turning a girl's head; and nobody can do it better than Mr Higgins, though he may not always mean it. I do hope, sir, you wont encourage him to do anything foolish.

Higgins (*becoming excited as the idea grows on him*) What is life but a series of inspired follies? The difficulty is to find them to do. Never lose a chance: it doesnt come every day. I shall make a duchess of this draggle-tailed guttersnipe.

Liza (*strongly deprecating this view of her*) Ah-ah-ah-ow-ow-oo!

Higgins (*carried away*) Yes: in six months—in three if she has a good ear and a quick tongue—I'll take her anywhere and pass her off as anything. We'll start today: now! this moment! Take her away and clean her, Mrs Pearce. Monkey Brand, if it wont come off any other way. Is there a good fire in the kitchen?

Mrs Pearce (*protesting*) Yes; but——

Higgins (*storming on*) Take all her clothes off and burn them. Ring up Whitely or somebody for new ones. Wrap her up in brown paper til they come.

Liza. Youre no gentleman, youre not, to talk of such things. I'm a good girl, I am; and I know what the like of you are, I do.

Higgins. We want none of your Lisson Grove prudery here, young woman. Youve got to learn to behave like a duchess. Take her away, Mrs Pearce. If she gives you any trouble, wallop her.

Liza (*springing up and running between* Pickering *and* Mrs Pearce *for protection*) No! I'll call the police, I will.

Mrs Pearce. But Ive no place to put her.

Higgins. Put her in the dustbin.

Liza. Ah-ah-ah-ow-ow-oo!

Pickering. Oh come, Higgins! be reasonable.

Mrs Pearce (*resolutely*) You must be reasonable, Mr Higgins: really you must. You cant walk over everybody like this.

Higgins, *thus scolded, subsides. The hurricane is succeeded by a zephyr of amiable surprise.*

Higgins (*with professional exquisiteness of modulation*) I walk over everybody! My dear Mrs Pearce, my dear Pickering, I never had the slightest intention of walking over anyone. All I propose is that we should be kind to this poor girl. We must help her to prepare and fit herself for her new station in life. If I did not express myself clearly it was because I did not wish to hurt her delicacy, or yours.

Liza, *reassured, steals back to her chair.*

Mrs Pearce (*to* Pickering) Well, did you ever hear anything like that, sir?

Pickering (*laughing heartily*) Never, Mrs Pearce: never.

Higgins (*patiently*) Whats the matter?

Mrs Pearce. Well, the matter is, sir, that you cant take a girl up like that as if you were picking up a pebble on the beach.

Higgins. Why not?

Mrs Pearce. Why not! But you don't know anything about her. What about her parents? She may be married.

Liza. Garn!

Higgins. There! As the girl very properly says, Garn! Married indeed! Dont you know that a woman of that class looks a worn out drudge of fifty a year after she's married?

Liza. Whood marry me?

Higgins (*suddenly resorting to the most thrillingly beautiful low tones in his best elocutionary style*) By George, Eliza, the streets will be strewn with the bodies of men shooting themselves for your sake before Ive done with you.

Mrs Pearce. Nonsense, sir. You mustnt talk like that to her.

Liza (*rising and squaring herself determinedly*) I'm going away. He's off his chump, he is. I dont want no balmies teaching me.

Higgins (*wounded in his tenderest point by her insensibility to his elocution*) Oh, indeed! I'm mad, am I? Very well, Mrs Pearce: you neednt order the new clothes for her. Throw her out.

Liza (*whimpering*) Nah-ow. You got no right to touch me.

Mrs Pearce. You see now what comes of being

saucy. (*Indicating the door*) This way, please.
Liza (*almost in tears*) I didnt want no clothes. I wouldnt have taken them (*she throws away the handkerchief*). I can buy my own clothes.
Higgins (*deftly retrieving the handkerchief and intercepting her on her reluctant way to the door*) Youre an ungrateful wicked girl. This is my return for offering to take you out of the gutter and dress you beautifully and make a lady of you.
Mrs Pearce. Stop, Mr Higgins. I wont allow it. It's you that are wicked. Go home to your parents, girl; and tell them to take better care of you.
Liza. I aint got no parents. They told me I was big enough to earn my own living and turned me out.
Mrs Pearce. Wheres your mother?
Liza. I aint got no mother. Her that turned me out was my sixth stepmother. But I done without them. And I'm a good girl, I am.
Higgins. Very well, then, what on earth is all this fuss about? The girl doesnt belong to anybody—is no use to anybody but me. (*He goes to* Mrs Pearce *and begins coaxing*). You can adopt her, Mrs Pearce: I'm sure a daughter would be a great amusement to you. Now don't make any more fuss. Take her downstairs; and—
Mrs Pearce. But whats to become of her? Is she to be paid anything? Do be sensible, sir.
Higgins. Oh, pay her whatever is necessary: put it down in the housekeeping book. (*Impatiently*) What on earth will she want with money? She'll have her food and her clothes. She'll only drink if you give her money.
Liza (*turning on him*) Oh you are a brute. It's a lie: nobody ever saw the sign of liquor on me. (*To* Pickering) Oh, sir: youre a gentleman: dont let him speak to me like that.
Pickering (*in good-humored remonstrance*) Does it occur to you, Higgins, that the girl has some feelings?
Higgins (*looking critically at her*) Oh no, I dont think so. Not any feelings that we need bother about. (*Cheerily*) Have you, Eliza?
Liza. I got my feelings same as anyone else.

Higgins (*to* Pickering, *reflectively*) You see the difficulty?
Pickering. Eh? What difficulty?
Higgins. To get her to talk grammar. The mere pronunciation is easy enough.
Liza. I dont want to talk grammar. I want to talk like a lady in a flower-shop.
Mrs Pearce. Will you please keep to the point, Mr Higgins. I want to know on what terms the girl is to be here. Is she to have any wages? And what is to become of her when youve finished your teaching? You must look ahead a little.
Higgins (*impatiently*) Whats to become of her if I leave her in the gutter? Tell me that, Mrs Pearce.
Mrs Pearce. Thats her own business, not yours, Mr Higgins.
Higgins. Well, when Ive done with her, we can throw her back into the gutter; and then it will be her own business again; so thats all right.
Liza. Oh, youve no feeling heart in you: you dont care for nothing but yourself. (*She rises and takes the floor resolutely*). Here! Ive had enough of this. I'm going (*making for the door*). You ought to be ashamed of yourself, you ought.
Higgins (*snatching a chocolate cream from the piano, his eyes suddenly beginning to twinkle with mischief*) Have some chocolates, Eliza.
Liza (*halting, tempted*) How do I know what might be in them? Ive heard of girls being drugged by the like of you.

Higgins *whips out his penknife; cuts a chocolate in two; puts one half into his mouth and bolts it; and offers her the other half.*

Higgins. Pledge of good faith, Eliza. I eat one half: you eat the other. (Liza *opens her mouth to retort: he pops the half chocolate into it*). You shall have boxes of them, barrels of them, every day. You shall live on them. Eh?

Liza (*who has disposed of the chocolate after being nearly choked by it*) I wouldnt have ate it, only I'm too ladylike to take it out of my mouth.

Higgins. Listen, Eliza. I think you said you came in a taxi.

Liza. Well, what if I did? Ive as good a right to take a taxi as anyone else.

Higgins. You have, Eliza; and in future you shall have as many taxis as you want. You shall go up and down and round the town in a taxi every day. Think of that, Eliza.

Mrs Pearce. Mr Higgins: youre tempting the girl. It's not right. She should think of the future.

Higgins. At her age! Nonsense! Time enough to think of the future when you havnt any future to think of. No, Eliza: do as this lady does: think of other people's futures; but never think of your own. Think of chocolates, and taxis, and gold, and diamonds.

Liza. No: I dont want no gold and no diamonds. I'm a good girl, I am. (*She sits down again, with an attempt at dignity*).

Higgins. You shall remain so, Eliza, under the care of Mrs Pearce. And you shall marry an officer in the Guards, with a beautiful moustache: the son of a marquis, who will disinherit him for marrying you, but will relent when he sees your beauty and goodness——

Pickering. Excuse me, Higgins; but I really must interfere. Mrs Pearce is quite right. If this girl is to put herself in your hands for six months for an experiment in teaching, she must understand thoroughly what she's doing.

Higgins. How can she? She's incapable of understanding anything. Besides, do any of us understand what we are doing? If we did, would we ever do it?

Pickering. Very clever, Higgins; but not to the present point. (*To Eliza*) Miss Doolittle——

Liza (*overwhelmed*) Ah-ah-ow-oo!

Higgins. There! Thats all youll get out of Eliza. Ah-ah-ow-oo! No use explaining. As a military man you ought to know that. Give her her orders: thats enough for her. Eliza: you

are to live here for the next six months, learning how to speak beautifully, like a lady in a florist's shop. If youre good and do whatever youre told, you shall sleep in a proper bedroom, and have lots to eat, and money to buy chocolates and take rides in taxis. If youre naughty and idle you will sleep in the back kitchen among the black beetles, and be walloped by Mrs Pearce with a broomstick. At the end of six months you shall go to Buckingham Palace in a carriage, beautifully dressed. If the King finds out youre not a lady, you will be taken by the police to the Tower of London, where your head will be cut off as a warning to other presumptuous flower girls. If you are not found out, you shall have a present of seven-and-sixpence to start life with as a lady in a shop. If you refuse this offer you will be a most ungrateful wicked girl; and the angels will weep for you. (*To Pickering*) Now are you satisfied, Pickering? (*To Mrs Pearce*) Can I put it more plainly and fairly, Mrs Pearce?

Mrs Pearce (*patiently*) I think youd better let me speak to the girl properly in private. I dont know that I can take charge of her or consent to the arrangement at all. Of course I know you dont mean her any harm; but when you get what you call interested in people's accents, you never think or care what may happen to them or you. Come with me, Eliza.

Higgins. Thats all right. Thank you, Mrs Pearce. Bundle her off to the bath-room.

Liza (*rising reluctantly and suspiciously*) Youre a great bully, you are. I wont stay here if I dont like. I wont let nobody wallop me. I never asked to go to Bucknam Palace, I didnt. I was never in trouble with the police, not me. I'm a good girl——

Mrs Pearce. Dont answer back, girl. You dont understand the gentleman. Come with me. (*She leads the way to the door, and holds it open for* Eliza).

Liza (*as she goes out*) Well, what I say is right. I wont go near the King, not if I'm going to have my head cut off. If I'd known what I was letting myself in for, I wouldnt have come

here. I always been a good girl; and I never offered to say a word to him; and I dont owe him
nothing; and I dont care; and I wont be put
upon; and I have my feelings the same as anyone else——

Mrs Pearce *shuts the door; and* Eliza's *plaints
are no longer audible.*

      ★   ★   ★   ★   ★   ★

Eliza is taken upstairs to the third floor
greatly to her surprise; for she expected to be
taken down to the scullery. There Mrs Pearce
opens a door and takes her into a spare bedroom.

Mrs Pearce. I will have to put you here. This
will be your bedroom.
Liza. O-h, I couldnt sleep here, missus. It's too
good for the likes of me. I should be afraid to
touch anything. I aint a duchess yet, you
know.
Mrs Pearce. You have got to make yourself as
clean as the room: then you wont be afraid of
it. And you must call me Mrs Pearce, not
missus. (*She throws open the door of the dres-
singroom, now modernized as a bathroom*).
Liza. Gawd! whats this? Is this where you
wash clothes? Funny sort of copper[6] I call it.
Mrs Pearce. It is not a copper. This is where
we wash ourselves, Eliza, and where I am
going to wash you.
Liza. You expect me to get into that and wet
myself all over! Not me. I should catch my
death. I knew a woman did it every Saturday
night; and she died of it.
Mrs Pearce. Mr Higgins has the gentlemen's
bathroom downstairs; and he has a bath every
morning, in cold water.
Liza. Ugh! He's made of iron, that man.
Mrs Pearce. If you are to sit with him and the
Colonel and be taught you will have to do the
same. They wont like the smell of you if you
don't. But you can have the water as hot as you
like. There are two taps: hot and cold.

---

6. **copper:** a large boiler used for washing clothes.

Liza (*weeping*) I couldnt. I dursnt. Its not natural: it would kill me. I've never had a bath in
my life: not what youd call a proper one.
Mrs Pearce. Well, dont you want to be clean
and sweet and decent, like a lady? You know
you cant be a nice girl inside if youre a dirty
slut outside.
Liza. Boohoo!!!!
Mrs Pearce. Now stop crying and go back into
your room and take off all your clothes. Then
wrap yourself in this (*Taking down a gown
from its peg and handing it to her*) and come
back to me. I will get the bath ready.
Liza (*all tears*) I cant. I wont. I'm not used to
it. Ive never took off all my clothes before.
It's not right: it's not decent.
Mrs Pearce. Nonsense, child. Dont you take
off all your clothes every night when you go to
bed?
Liza (*amazed*) No. Why should I? I should
catch my death. Of course I take off my skirt.
Mrs Pearce. Do you mean that you sleep in
the underclothes you wear in the daytime?
Liza. What else have I to sleep in?
Mrs Pearce. You will never do that again as
long as you live here. I will get you a proper
nightdress.
Liza. Do you mean change into cold things
and lie awake shivering half the night? You
want to kill me, you do.
Mrs Pearce. I want to change you from a
frowzy slut to a clean respectable girl fit to sit
with the gentlemen in the study. Are you
going to trust me and do what I tell you or be
thrown out and sent back to your flower
basket?
Liza. But you dont know what the cold is to
me. You dont know how I dread it.
Mrs Pearce. Your bed won't be cold here: I will
put a hot water bottle in it. (*Pushing her into
the bedroom*) Off with you and undress.
Liza. Oh, if only I'd known what a dreadful
thing it is to be clean I'd never have come. I
didnt know when I was well off. I—— (Mrs
Pearce *pushes her through the door, but
leaves it partly open lest her prisoner should
take to flight*).

Mrs Pearce *puts on a pair of white rubber sleeves, and fills the bath, mixing hot and cold, and testing the result with the bath thermometer. She perfumes it with a handful of bath salts and adds a palmful of mustard. She then takes a formidable looking long handled scrubbing brush and soaps it profusely with a ball of scented soap.*

Eliza *comes back with nothing on but the bath gown huddled tightly round her, a piteous spectacle of abject terror.*

Mrs Pearce. Now come along. Take that thing off.

Liza. Oh I couldnt, Mrs Pearce: I reely couldnt. I never done such a thing.

Mrs Pearce. Nonsense. Here: step in and tell me whether its hot enough for you.

Liza. Ah-oo! Ah-oo! It's too hot.

Mrs Pearce (*deftly snatching the gown away and throwing* Eliza *down on her back*). It wont hurt you. (*She sets to work with the scrubbing brush*).

Eliza's *screams are heartrending.*

  ★ ★ ★ ★ ★ ★

Meanwhile the Colonel has been having it out with Higgins about Eliza. Pickering has come from the hearth to the chair and seated himself astride of it with his arms on the back to cross-examine him.

Pickering. Excuse the straight question, Higgins. Are you a man of good character where women are concerned?

Higgins (*moodily*) Have you ever met a man of good character where women are concerned?

Pickering. Yes: very frequently.

Higgins (*dogmatically, lifting himself on his hands to the level of the piano, and sitting on it with a bounce*) Well, I havnt. I find that the moment I let a woman make friends with me, she becomes jealous, exacting, suspicious, and a damned nuisance. I find that the moment I let myself make friends with a women, I become selfish and tyrannical. Women upset everything. When you let them

into your life, you find that the woman is driving at one thing and youre driving at another.

Pickering. At what, for example?

Higgins (*coming off the piano restlessly*) Oh, Lord knows! I suppose the woman wants to live her own life; and the man wants to live his; and each tries to drag the other on to the wrong track. One wants to go north and the other south; and the result is that both have to go east, though they both hate the east wind. (*He sits down on the bench at the keyboard*). So here I am, a confirmed old bachelor, and likely to remain so.

Pickering (*rising and standing over him gravely*) Come, Higgins! You know what I mean. If I'm to be in this business I shall feel responsible for that girl. I hope it's understood that no advantage is to be taken of her position.

Higgins. What! That thing! Sacred, I assure you. (*Rising to explain*) You see, she'll be a pupil; and teaching would be impossible unless pupils were sacred. Ive taught scores of American millionairesses how to speak English: the best looking women in the world. I'm seasoned. They might as well be blocks of wood. *I* might as well be a block of wood. It's——

Mrs Pearce *opens the door. She has* Eliza's *hat in her hand.* Pickering *retires to the easy-chair at the hearth and sits down.*

Higgins (*eagerly*) Well, Mrs Pearce: is it all right?

Mrs Pearce (*at the door*) I just wish to trouble you with a word, if I may, Mr. Higgins.

Higgins. Yes, certainly. Come in. (*She comes forward*). Dont burn that, Mrs Pearce. I'll keep it as a curiosity. (*He takes the hat*).

Mrs Pearce. Handle it carefully, sir, please. I had to promise her not to burn it; but I had better put it in the oven for a while.

Higgins (*putting it down hastily on the piano*) Oh! thank you. Well, what have you to say to me?

Pickering. Am I in the way?

Mrs Pearce. Not in the least, sir. Mr Higgins: will you please be very particular what you say before the girl?

Higgins (*sternly*) Of course. I'm always particular about what I say. Why do you say this to me?

Mrs Pearce (*unmoved*) No, sir: youre not at all particular when youve mislaid anything or when you get a little impatient. Now it doesnt matter before me: I'm used to it. But you really must not swear before the girl.

Higgins (*indignantly*) I swear! (*Most emphatically*) I never swear. I detest the habit. What the devil do you mean?

Mrs Pearce (*stolidly*) Thats what I mean, sir. You swear a great deal too much. I dont mind your damning and blasting, and what the devil and where the devil and who the devil—

Higgins. Mrs Pearce: this language from your lips! Really!

Mrs Pearce (*not to be put off*) — but there is a certain word I must ask you not to use. The girl used it herself when she began to enjoy the bath. It begins with the same letter as bath. She knows no better: she learnt it at her mother's knee. But she must not hear it from your lips.

Higgins (*loftily*) I cannot charge myself with having ever uttered it, Mrs Pearce. (*She looks at him steadfastly. He adds, hiding an uneasy conscience with a judicial air*) Except perhaps in a moment of extreme and justifiable excitement.

Mrs Pearce. Only this morning, sir, you applied it to your boots, to the butter, and to the brown bread.

Higgins. Oh, that! Mere alliteration, Mrs Pearce, natural to a poet.

Mrs Pearce. Well, sir, whatever you choose to call it, I beg you not to let the girl hear you repeat it.

Higgins. Oh, very well, very well. Is that all?

Mrs Pearce. No, sir. We shall have to be very particular with this girl as to personal cleanliness.

Higgins. Certainly. Quite right. Most important.

Mrs Pearce. I mean not to be slovenly about her dress or untidy in leaving things about.

Higgins (*going to her solemnly*) Just so. I intended to call your attention to that. (*He passes on to* Pickering, *who is enjoying the conversation immensely*). It is these little things that matter, Pickering. Take care of the pence and the pounds will take care of themselves is as true of personal habits as of money. (*He comes to anchor on the hearthrug, with the air of a man in an unassailable position*).

Mrs Pearce. Yes, sir. Then might I ask you not to come down to breakfast in your dressing-gown, or at any rate not to use it as a napkin to the extent you do, sir. And if you would be so good as not to eat everything off the same plate, and to remember not to put the porridge saucepan out of your hand on the clean table-cloth, it would be a better example to the girl. You know you nearly choked yourself with a fishbone in a jam only last week.

Higgins (*routed from the hearthrug and drifting back to the piano*) I may do these things sometimes in absence of mind; but surely I dont do them habitually. (*Angrily*) By the way: my dressing-gown smells most damnably of benzine.

Mrs Pearce. No doubt it does, Mr Higgins. But if you will wipe your fingers—

Higgins (*yelling*) Oh very well, very well: I'll wipe them in my hair in future.

Mrs Pearce. I hope youre not offended, Mr Higgins.

Higgins (*shocked at finding himself thought capable of an unamiable sentiment*) Not at all, not at all. Youre quite right, Mrs Pearce: I shall be particularly careful before the girl. Is that all?

Mrs Pearce. No, sir. Might she use some of those Japanese dresses you brought from abroad? I really cant put her back into her old things.

Higgins. Certainly. Anything you like. Is that all?

Higgins accuses Doolittle of blackmail.
Culver Pictures

Mrs Pearce. Thank you, sir. Thats all. (*She goes out*).

Higgins. You know, Pickering, that woman has the most extraordinary ideas about me. Here I am, a shy, diffident sort of man. I've never been able to feel really grown-up and tremendous, like other chaps. And yet she's firmly persuaded that I'm an arbitrary overbearing bossing kind of person. I cant account for it.

Mrs Pearce *returns.*

Mrs Pearce. If you please, sir, the trouble's beginning already. Theres a dustman[7] downstairs, Alfred Doolittle, wants to see you. He says you have his daughter here.

Pickering (*rising*) Phew! I say!

Higgins (*promptly*) Send the blackguard up.

Mrs Pearce. Oh, very well, sir. (*She goes out*).

Pickering. He may not be a blackguard, Higgins.

Higgins. Nonsense. Of course he's a blackguard.

Pickering. Whether he is or not, I'm afraid we shall have some trouble with him.

Higgins (*confidently*) Oh no: I think not. If theres any trouble he shall have it with me, not I with him. And we are sure to get something interesting out of him.

Pickering. About the girl?

Higgins. No. I mean his dialect.

Pickering. Oh!

Mrs Pearce (*at the door*) Doolittle, sir. (*She admits* Doolittle *and retires*).

Alfred *is an elderly but vigorous dustman, clad in the costume of his profession, including a hat with a back brim covering his neck and shoulders. He has well marked and rather interesting features, and seems equally free from fear and conscience. He has a remarkably expressive voice, the result of a habit of giving vent to his feelings without reserve. His present pose is that of wounded honor and stern resolution.*

7. **dustman:** a garbage collector.

Doolittle (*at the door, uncertain which of the two gentlemen is his man*) Professor Iggins?

Higgins. Here. Good morning. Sit down.

Doolittle. Morning, Governor. (*He sits down magisterially*). I come about a very serious matter, Governor.

Higgins (*to* Pickering) Brought up in Hounslow. Mother Welsh, I should think. (Doolittle *opens his mouth, amazed.* Higgins *continues*) What do you want, Doolittle?

Doolittle (*menacingly*) I want my daughter: thats what I want. See?

Higgins. Of course you do. Youre her father, arnt you? You dont suppose anyone else wants her, do you? I'm glad to see you have some spark of family feeling left. She's upstairs. Take her away at once.

Doolittle (*rising, fearfully taken aback*) What!

Higgins. Take her away. Do you suppose I'm going to keep your daughter for you?

Doolittle (*remonstrating*) Now, now, look here, Governor. Is this reasonable? Is it fairity to take advantage of a man like this? The girl belongs to me. You got her. Where do I come in? (*He sits down again*).

Higgins. Your daughter had the audacity to come to my house and ask me to teach her how to speak properly so that she could get a place in a flower-shop. This gentleman and my housekeeper have been here all the time. (*Bullying him*) How dare you come here and attempt to blackmail me? You sent her here on purpose.

Doolittle (*protesting*) No, Governor.

Higgins. You must have. How else could you possibly know that she is here?

Doolittle. Don't take a man up like that, Governor.

Higgins. The police shall take you up. This is a plant—a plot to extort money by threats. I shall telephone for the police (*he goes resolutely to the telephone and opens the directory*)

Doolittle. Have I asked you for a brass farthing? I leave it to the gentleman here: have I said a word about money?

Higgins (*throwing the book aside and marching down on* Doolittle *with a poser*) What else did you come for?

Doolittle (*sweetly*) Well, what would a man come for? Be human, Governor.

Higgins (*disarmed*) Alfred: did you put her up to it?

Doolittle. So help me, Governor. I never did. I take my Bible oath I aint seen the girl these two months past.

Higgins. Then how did you know she was here?

Doolittle (*"most musical, most melancholy"*) I'll tell you, Governor, if youll only let me get a word in. I'm willing to tell you. I'm wanting to tell you. I'm waiting to tell you.

Higgins. Pickering: this chap has a certain natural gift of rhetoric. Observe the rhythm of his native woodnotes wild. "I'm willing to tell you: I'm wanting to tell you: I'm waiting to tell you." Sentimental rhetoric! thats the Welsh strain in him. It also accounts for his mendacity and dishonesty.

Pickering. Oh, please, Higgins: I'm west country myself. (*To* Doolittle) How did you know the girl was here if you didnt send her?

Doolittle. It was like this, Governor. The girl took a boy in the taxi to give him a jaunt. Son of her landlady, he is. He hung about on the chance of her giving him another ride home. Well, she sent him back for her luggage when she heard you was willing for her to stop here. I met the boy at the corner of Long Acre and Endell Street.

Higgins. Public house. Yes?

Doolittle. The poor man's club, Governor: why shouldnt I?

Pickering. Do let him tell his story, Higgins.

Doolittle. He told me what was up. And I ask you, what was my feelings and my duty as a father? I says to the boy, "You bring me the luggage," I says—

Pickering. Why didnt you go for it yourself?

Doolittle. Landlady wouldnt have trusted me with it, Governor. She's that kind of woman: you know. I had to give the boy a penny afore he trusted me with it, the little swine. I brought it to her just to oblige you like, and make myself agreeable. Thats all.

Higgins. How much luggage?

Doolittle. Musical instrument, Governor. A few pictures, a trifle of jewelry, and a birdcage. She said she didn't want no clothes. What was I to think from that, Governor? I ask you as a parent what was I to think?

Higgins. So you came to rescue her from worse than death, eh?

Doolittle (*appreciatively: relieved at being so well understood*) Just so, Governor. That's right.

Pickering. But why did you bring her luggage if you intended to take her away?

Doolittle. Have I said a word about taking her away? Have I now?

Higgins (*determinedly*) Youre going to take her away, double quick. (*He crosses to the hearth and rings the bell*).

Doolittle (*rising*) No, Governor. Dont say that. I'm not the man to stand in my girl's light. Heres a career opening for her, as you might say; and——

Mrs Pearce *opens the door and awaits orders.*

Higgins. Mrs Pearce: this is Eliza's father. He has come to take her away. Give her to him. (*He goes back to the piano, with an air of washing his hands of the whole affair*).

Doolittle. No. This is a misunderstanding. Listen here——

Mrs Pearce. He cant take her away. Mr Higgins: how can he? You told me to burn her clothes.

Doolittle. Thats right. I cant carry the girl through the streets like a blooming monkey, can I? I put it to you.

Higgins. You have put it to me that you want your daughter. Take your daughter. If she has no clothes go out and buy her some.

Doolittle (*desperate*) Wheres the clothes she come in? Did I burn them or did your missus here?

Mrs Pearce. I am the housekeeper, if you please. I have sent for some clothes for your girl. When they come you can take her away. You can wait in the kitchen. This way, please.

Doolittle, *much troubled, accompanies her to the door; then hesitates; finally turns confidentially to* Higgins.

Doolittle. Listen here, Governor. You and me is men of the world, aint we?

Higgins. Oh! Men of the world, are we? Youd better go, Mrs Pearce.

Mrs Pearce. I think so, indeed, sir. (*She goes, with dignity*).

Pickering. The floor is yours, Mr Doolittle.

Doolittle (*to* Pickering) I thank you, Governor. (*To* Higgins, *who takes refuge on the piano bench, a little overwhelmed by the proximity of his visitor; for* Doolittle *has a professional flavour of dust about him*). Well, the truth is, I've taken a sort of fancy to you, Governor; and if you want the girl, I'm not so set on having her back home again but what I might be open to an arrangement. Regarded in the light of a young woman, she's a fine handsome girl. As a daughter she's not worth her keep; and so I tell you straight. All I ask is my rights as a father; and youre the last man alive to expect me to let her go for nothing; for I can see youre one of the straight sort, Governor. Well, whats a five-pound note to you? and whats Eliza to me? (*He turns to his chair and sits down judicially*).

Pickering. I think you ought to know, Doolittle, that Mr Higgins's intentions are entirely honorable.

Doolittle. Course they are, Governor. If I thought they wasnt, I'd ask fifty.

Higgins (*revolted*) Do you mean to say that you would sell your daughter for £50?

Doolittle. Not in a general way I would; but to oblige a gentleman like you I'd do a good deal, I do assure you.

Pickering. Have you no morals, man?

Doolittle (*unabashed*) Cant afford them, Governor. Neither could you if you was as poor as me. Not that I mean any harm, you know. But if Liza is going to have a bit out of this, why not me too?

Higgins (*troubled*) I dont know what to do, Pickering. There can be no question that as a matter of morals it's a positive crime to give this chap a farthing. And yet I feel a sort of rough justice in his claim.

Doolittle. Thats it, Governor. Thats all I say. A father's heart, as it were.

Pickering. Well, I know the feeling; but really it seems hardly right——

Doolittle. Dont say that, Governor. Dont look at it that way. What am I, Governors both? I ask you, what am I? I'm one of the undeserving poor: thats what I am. Think of what that means to a man. It means that he's up agen middle class morality all the time. If theres anything going, and I put in for a bit of it, it's always the same story: "Youre undeserving; so you cant have it." But my needs is as great as the most deserving widows' that ever got money out of six different charities in one week for the death of the same husband. I dont need less than a deserving man: I need more. I dont eat less hearty than him; and I drink a lot more. I want a bit of amusement, cause I'm a thinking man. I want cheerfulness and a song and a band when I feel low. Well, they charge me just the same for everything as they charge the deserving. What is middle class morality? Just an excuse for never giving me anything. Therefore, I ask you, as two gentlemen, not to play that game on me. I'm playing straight with you. I aint pretending to be deserving. I'm undeserving; and I mean to go on being undeserving. I like it; and thats the truth. Will you take advantage of a man's nature to do him out of the price of his own daughter what he's brought up and fed and clothed by the sweat of his brow until she's growed big enough to be interesting to you two gentlemen? Is five pounds unreasonable? I put it to you; and I leave it to you.

Higgins (*rising, and going over to* Pickering) Pickering: if we were to take this man in hand for three months, he could choose between a seat in the Cabinet and a popular pulpit in Wales.

Pickering. What do you say to that, Doolittle?

Doolittle. Not me, Governor, thank you kindly. Ive heard all the preachers and all the prime ministers—for I'm a thinking man and game for politics or religion or social reform same as all the other amusements—and I tell you it's a dog's life any way you look at it. Undeserving poverty is my line. Taking one station in society with another, it's—it's—well, it's the only one that has any ginger in it, to my taste.

Higgins. I suppose we must give him a fiver.

Pickering. He'll make a bad use of it, I'm afraid.

Doolittle. Not me, Governor, so help me I wont. Dont you be afraid that I'll save it and spare it and live idle on it. There wont be a penny of it left by Monday: I'll have to go to work same as if I'd never had it. It wont pauperize me, you bet. Just one good spree for myself and the missus, giving pleasure to ourselves and employment to others, and satisfaction to you to think it's not been throwed away. You couldnt spend it better.

Higgins (*taking out his pocket book and coming between* Doolittle *and the piano*) This is irresistible. Lets give him ten. (*He offers two notes to the* Dustman)

Doolittle. No, Governor. She wouldnt have the heart to spend ten; and perhaps I shouldnt neither. Ten pounds is a lot of money: it makes a man feel prudent like; and then goodbye to happiness. You give me what I ask you, Governor: not a penny more, and not a penny less.

Pickering. Why dont you marry that missus of yours? I rather draw the line at encouraging that sort of immorality.

Doolittle. Tell her so, Governor: tell her so. I'm willing. It's me that suffers by it. Ive no hold on her. I got to be agreeable to her. I got to give her presents. I got to buy her clothes something sinful. I'm a slave to that woman, Governor, just because I'm not her lawful husband. And she knows it too. Catch her marrying me! Take my advice, Governor: marry Eliza while she's young and dont know no better. If you dont youll be sorry for it after. If you do, she'll be sorry for it after; but better her than you, because youre a man, and she's only a woman and dont know how to be happy anyhow.

Higgins. Pickering: if we listen to this man another minute, we shall have no convictions left. (*To Doolittle*) Five pounds I think you said.

Doolittle. Thank you kindly, Governor.

Higgins. Youre sure you wont take ten?

Doolittle. Not now. Another time, Governor.

Higgins (*handing him a five-pound note*) Here you are.

Doolittle. Thank you, Governor. Good morning. (*He hurries to the door, anxious to get away with his booty. When he opens it he is confronted with a dainty and exquisitely clean young Japanese lady in a simple blue cotton kimono printed cunningly with small white jasmine blossoms. Mrs Pearce is with her. He gets out of her way deferentially and apologizes*). Beg pardon, miss.

The Japanese Lady. Garn! Dont you know your own daughter?

Doolittle ⌈ *exclaiming* ⌉ Bly me! it's Eliza!
Higgins ⟨ *simul-* ⟩ Whats that? This!
Pickering ⌊ *taneously* ⌋ By Jove!

Liza. Dont I look silly?

Higgins. Silly?

Mrs Pearce (*at the door*) Now, Mr Higgins, please dont say anything to make the girl conceited about herself.

Higgins (*conscientiously*) Oh! Quite right, Mrs Pearce. (*To Eliza*) Yes: damned silly.

Mrs Pearce. Please, sir.

Higgins (*correcting himself*) I mean extremely silly.

Liza. I should look all right with my hat on. (*She takes up her hat; puts it on; and walks across the room to the fireplace with a fashionable air*).

Higgins. A new fashion, by George! And it ought to look horrible!

Doolittle (*with fatherly pride*) Well, I never thought she'd clean up as good looking as that, Governor. She's a credit to me, aint she?

Liza. I tell you, it's easy to clean up here. Hot and cold water on tap, just as much as you like, there is. Woolly towels, there is; and a towel horse[8] so hot, it burns your fingers. Soft brushes to scrub yourself, and a wooden bowl of soap smelling like primroses. Now I know why ladies is so clean. Washing's a treat for them. Wish they could see what it is for the like of me!

Higgins. I'm glad the bathroom met with your approval.

Liza. It didnt: not all of it; and I dont care who hears me say it. Mrs Pearce knows.

Higgins. What was wrong, Mrs Pearce?

Mrs Pearce (*blandly*) Oh, nothing, sir. It doesnt matter.

Liza. I had a good mind to break it. I didnt know which way to look. But I hung a towel over it, I did.

Higgins. Over what?

Mrs Pearce. Over the looking-glass, sir.

Higgins. Doolittle: you have brought your daughter up too strictly.

Doolittle. Me! I never brought her up at all, except to give her a lick of a strap now and again. Dont put it on me, Governor. She aint accustomed to it, you see: thats all. But she'll soon pick up your free-and-easy ways.

Liza. I'm a good girl, I am; and I wont pick up no free-and-easy ways.

Higgins. Eliza: if you say again that youre a good girl, your father shall take you home.

Liza. Not him. You dont know my father. All he come here for was to touch you for some money to get drunk on.

Doolittle. Well, what else would I want money for? To put into the plate in church, I suppose. (*She puts out her tongue at him. He is so incensed by this that* Pickering *presently finds it necessary to step between them*). Dont you give me none of your lip; and dont let me hear you giving this gentleman any of it neither, or youll hear from me about it. See?

Higgins. Have you any further advice to give her before you go, Doolittle? Your blessing, for instance.

---

8. **towel horse:** towel rack, here with a heater for drying the towels.

Doolittle. No, Governor: I aint such a mug as to put up my children to all I know myself. Hard enough to hold them in without that. If you want Eliza's mind improved, Governor, you do it yourself with a strap. So long, gentlemen. (*He turns to go*).

Higgins (*impressively*) Stop. Youll come regularly to see your daughter. It's your duty, you know. My brother is a clergyman; and he could help you in your talks with her.

Doolittle (*evasively*) Certainly, I'll come, Governor. Not just this week, because I have a job at a distance. But later on you may depend on me. Afternoon, gentlemen. Afternoon, maam. (*He touches his hat to* Mrs Pearce, *who disdains the salutation and goes out. He winks at* Higgins, *thinking him probably a fellow-sufferer from* Mrs Pearce's *difficult disposition, and follows her*).

Liza. Don't you believe the old liar. He'd as soon you set a bulldog on him as a clergyman. You wont see him again in a hurry.

Higgins. I dont want to, Eliza. Do you?

Liza. Not me. I dont want never to see him again, I dont. He's a disgrace to me, he is, collecting dust, instead of working at his trade.

Pickering. What is his trade, Eliza?

Liza. Talking money out of other people's pockets into his own. His proper trade's a navvy;[9] and he works at it sometimes too—for exercise—and earns good money at it. Aint you going to call me Miss Doolittle any more?

Pickering. I beg your pardon, Miss Doolittle. It was a slip of the tongue.

Liza. Oh, I dont mind; only it sounded so genteel. I should just like to take a taxi to the corner of Tottenham Court Road and get out there and tell it to wait for me, just to put the girls in their place a bit. I wouldnt speak to them, you know.

Pickering. Better wait til we get you something really fashionable.

Higgins. Besides, you shouldnt cut your old friends now that you have risen in the world. Thats what we call snobbery.

Liza. You dont call the like of them my friends now, I should hope. Theyve took it out of me often enough with their ridicule when they had the chance; and now I mean to get a bit of my own back. But if I'm to have fashionable clothes, I'll wait. I should like to have some. Mrs Pearce says youre going to give me some to wear in bed at night different to what I wear in the daytime; but it do seem a waste of money when you could get something to shew. Besides, I never could fancy changing into cold things on a winter night.

Mrs Pearce (*coming back*) Now, Eliza. The new things have come for you to try on.

Liza. Ah-ow-oo-ooh! (*She rushes out*).

Mrs Pearce (*following her*) Oh, dont rush about like that, girl. (*She shuts the door behind her*).

Higgins. Pickering: we have taken on a stiff job.

Pickering (*with conviction*) Higgins: we have.

*   *   *   *   *   *

There seems to be some curiosity as to what Higgins's lessons to Eliza were like. Well, here is a sample: the first one.

Picture Eliza, in her new clothes, and feeling her inside put out of step by a lunch, dinner, and breakfast of a kind to which it is unaccustomed, seated with Higgins and the Colonel in the study, feeling like a hospital out-patient at a first encounter with the doctors.

Higgins, constitutionally unable to sit still, discomposes her still more by striding restlessly about. But for the reassuring presence and quietude of her friend the Colonel she would run for her life, even back to Drury Lane.

Higgins. Say your alphabet.

Liza. I know my alphabet. Do you think I know nothing? I dont need to be taught like a child.

Higgins (*thundering*) Say your alphabet.

---

9. **navvy** (năv′ē): an unskilled laborer.

Pickering. Say it, Miss Doolittle. You will understand presently. Do what he tells you; and let him teach you in his own way.

Liza. Oh well, if you put it like that—Ahyee, bəyee, cəyee, dəyee—

Higgins (*with the roar of a wounded lion*) Stop. Listen to this, Pickering. This is what we pay for as elementary education. This unfortunate animal has been locked up for nine years in school at our expense to teach her to speak and read the language of Shakespear and Milton. And the result is Ahyee, Bə-yee, Cə-yee, Dəyee. (*To Eliza*) Say A, B, C, D.

Liza (*almost in tears*) But I'm sayin it. Ahyee, Bəyee, Cəyee—

Higgins. Stop. Say a cup of tea.

Liza. A cappətə-ee.

Higgins. Put your tongue forward until it squeezes against the top of your lower teeth. Now say cup.

Liza. C-c-c—I cant. C-Cup.

Pickering. Good. Splendid, Miss Doolittle.

Higgins. By Jupiter, she's done it the first shot. Pickering: we shall make a duchess of her. (*To* Eliza) Now do you think you could possibly say tea? Not tə-yee, mind: if you ever say bə-yee cə-yee də-yee again you shall be dragged round the room three times by the hair of your head. (*Fortissimo*) T, T, T, T.

Liza (*weeping*) I cant hear no difference cep that it sounds more genteel-like when you say it.

Higgins. Well, if you can hear the difference, what the devil are you crying for? Pickering: give her a chocolate.

Pickering. No, no. Never mind crying a little, Miss Doolittle: you are doing very well; and the lessons wont hurt. I promise you I wont let him drag you round the room by your hair.

Higgins. Be off with you to Mrs Pearce and tell her about it. Think about it. Try to do it by yourself: and keep your tongue well forward in your mouth instead of trying to roll it up and swallow it. Another lesson at half-past four this afternoon. Away with you.

Eliza, *still sobbing, rushes from the room.*

And that is the sort of ordeal Eliza has to go through for months before we meet her again on her first appearance in London society of the professional class.

FOR STUDY AND DISCUSSION

1. What reason does Eliza give for wanting lessons in speaking? Why is Higgins willing to take her as a student?

2. Consider Colonel Pickering in his role as a foil to Higgins. How does he differ from him in character, drive, ability, and attitudes—especially in his attitude to Eliza? In what way does he stand up for her and represent her best interests?

3. How does Mrs. Pearce react to Eliza? On what points are Pickering and Mrs. Pearce in agreement?

4. Eliza reveals her self-esteem through her bargaining with Higgins and her snatching from Pickering the handkerchief that Higgins had "given" her. Find other examples of her feelings of self-worth.

5. Doolittle exposes the pretensions of what he calls "middle-class morality," an excuse for never giving to the poor. Why does Doolittle prefer his own "undeserving poverty"?

Act Three

It is Mrs Higgins's *at-home day. Nobody has yet arrived. Her drawing room, in a flat on Chelsea Embankment, has three windows looking on the river; and the ceiling is not so lofty as it would be in an older house of the same pretension. The windows are open, giving access to a balcony with flowers in pots. If you stand with your face to the windows, you have the fireplace on your left and the door in the right-hand wall close to the corner nearest the windows.*

Mrs Higgins *was brought up on Morris[1] and Burne Jones;[2] and her room, which is very unlike her son's room in Wimpole Street, is not crowded with furniture and little tables and nicknacks. In the middle of the room there is a big ottoman; and this, with the carpet, the Morris wall-papers, and the Morris chintz window curtains and brocade covers of the ottoman and its cushions, supply all the ornament, and are much too handsome to be hidden by odds and ends of useless things. A few good oil-paintings from the exhibitions in the Grosvenor Gallery thirty years ago (the Burne Jones, not the Whistler[3] side of them) are on the walls. The only landscape is a Cecil Lawson[4] on the scale of a Rubens.[5] There is a portrait of* Mrs Higgins *as she was when she defied the fashion in her youth in one of the beautiful Rossettian costumes which, when caricatured by people who did not understand, led to the absurdities of popular estheticism in the eighteen-seventies.*

In the corner diagonally opposite the door Mrs Higgins, *now over sixty and long past taking the trouble to dress out of the fashion, sits writing at an elegantly simple writing-table with a bell button within reach of her hand. There is a Chippendale chair further back in the room between her and the window nearest her side. At the other side of the room, further forward, is an Elizabethan chair roughly carved in the taste of Inigo Jones.[6] On the same side a piano in a decorated case. The corner between the fireplace and the window is occupied by a divan cushioned in Morris chintz.*

It is between four and five in the afternoon.

The door is opened violently; and Higgins *enters with his hat on.*

Mrs Higgins (*dismayed*) Henry! (*Scolding him*) What are you doing here today? It is my at-home day: you promised not to come. (*As he bends to kiss her, she takes his hat off, and presents it to him*).

Higgins. Oh bother! (*He throws the hat down on the table*).

Mrs Higgins. Go home at once.

Higgins (*kissing her*) I know, mother. I came on purpose.

Mrs Higgins. But you mustnt. I'm serious, Henry. You offend all my friends: they stop coming whenever they meet you.

Higgins. Nonsense! I know I have no small talk; but people dont mind. (*He sits on the settee*).

Mrs Higgins. Oh! dont they? Small talk indeed! What about your large talk? Really, dear, you mustnt stay.

---

1. **Morris:** William Morris (1834–1896), English poet and decorative designer.
2. **Burne Jones:** Sir Edward Coley Burne-Jones (1833–1898), an English Pre-Raphaelite painter.
3. **Whistler:** James Abbott McNeill Whistler (1834–1903), a fashionable American portrait painter who spent many years in England.
4. **Cecil Lawson:** Cecil Gordon Lawson (1851–1882), English landscape painter.
5. **Rubens:** Peter Paul Rubens (1577–1640), a Flemish painter known for his large paintings.

6. **Inigo Jones:** English architect and stage designer (1573–1652) who created elaborate sets for masques.

Higgins. I must. Ive a job for you. A phonetic job.

Mrs Higgins. No use, dear. I'm sorry; but I cant get round your vowels; and though I like to get pretty postcards in your patent shorthand, I always have to read the copies in ordinary writing you so thoughtfully send me.

Higgins. Well, this isnt a phonetic job.

Mrs Higgins. You said it was.

Higgins. Not your part of it. Ive picked up a girl.

Mrs Higgins. Does that mean that some girl has picked you up?

Higgins. Not at all. I dont mean a love affair.

Mrs Higgins. What a pity!

Higgins. Why?

Mrs Higgins. Well, you never fall in love with anyone under forty-five. When will you discover that there are some rather nice-looking young women about?

Higgins. Oh, I cant be bothered with young women. My idea of a lovable woman is somebody as like you as possible. I shall never get into the way of seriously liking young women: some habits lie too deep to be changed. (*Rising abruptly and walking about, jingling his money and his keys in his trouser pockets*) Besides, theyre all idiots.

Mrs Higgins. Do you know what you would do if you really loved me, Henry?

Higgins. Oh bother! What? Marry, I suppose.

Mrs Higgins. No. Stop fidgeting and take your hands out of your pockets. (*With a gesture of despair, he obeys and sits down again*). Thats a good boy. Now tell me about the girl.

Higgins. She's coming to see you.

Mrs Higgins. I dont remember asking her.

Higgins. You didnt. *I* asked her. If youd known her you wouldnt have asked her.

Mrs Higgins. Indeed! Why?

Higgins. Well, it's like this. She's a common flower girl. I picked her off the kerbstone.

Mrs Higgins. And invited her to my at-home!

Higgins (*rising and coming to her to coax her*) Oh, thatll be all right. Ive taught her to speak properly; and she has strict orders as to her behavior. She's to keep to two subjects: the weather and everybody's health — Fine day and How do you do, you know — and not to let herself go on things in general. That will be safe.

Mrs Higgins. Safe! To talk about our health! about our insides! perhaps about our outsides! How could you be so silly, Henry?

Higgins (*impatiently*) Well, she must talk about something. (*He controls himself and sits down again*). Oh, she'll be all right: dont you fuss. Pickering is in it with me. Ive a sort of bet on that I'll pass her off as a duchess in six months. I started on her some months ago; and she's getting on like a house on fire. I shall win my bet. She has a quick ear; and she's easier to teach than my middle-class pupils because she's had to learn a complete new language. She talks English almost as you talk French.

Mrs Higgins. Thats satisfactory, at all events.

Higgins. Well, it is and it isnt.

Mrs Higgins. What does that mean?

Higgins. You see, Ive got her pronunciation all right; but you have to consider not only how a girl pronounces, but what she pronounces; and that's where —

They are interrupted by the Parlormaid, *announcing guests.*

The Parlormaid. Mrs and Miss Eynsford Hill. (*She withdraws*).

Higgins. Oh Lord! (*He rises; snatches his hat from the table; and makes for the door; but before he reaches it his mother introduces him*).

Mrs and Miss Eynsford Hill are the mother and daughter who sheltered from the rain in Covent Garden. The mother is well bred, quiet, and has the habitual anxiety of straitened means. The daughter has acquired a gay air of being very much at home in society: the bravado of genteel poverty.

Mrs Eynsford Hill (*to Mrs Higgins*) How do you do? (*They shake hands*).

Miss Eynsford Hill. How d'you do? (*She shakes*).

Mrs Higgins (*introducing*) My son Henry.

Mrs Eynsford Hill. Your celebrated son! I have so longed to meet you, Professor Higgins.

Higgins (*glumly, making no movement in her direction*) Delighted. (*He backs against the piano and bows brusquely*).

Miss Eynsford Hill (*going to him with confident familiarity*) How do you do?

Higgins (*staring at her*) Ive seen you before somewhere. I havnt the ghost of a notion where; but Ive heard your voice. (*Drearily*) It doesnt matter. Youd better sit down.

Mrs Higgins. I'm sorry to say that my celebrated son has no manners. You mustnt mind him.

Miss Eynsford Hill (*gaily*) I dont. (*She sits in the Elizabethan chair*).

Mrs Eynsford Hill (*a little bewildered*) Not at all. (*She sits on the ottoman between her daughter and* Mrs Higgins, *who has turned her chair away from the writing-table*).

Higgins. Oh, have I been rude? I didnt mean to be.

He goes to the central window, through which, with his back to the company, he contemplates the river and the flowers in Battersea Park on the opposite bank as if they were a frozen desert.

The Parlormaid *returns, ushering in* Pickering.

The Parlormaid. Colonel Pickering. (*She withdraws*).

Pickering. How do you do, Mrs Higgins?

Mrs Higgins. So glad youve come. Do you know Mrs Eynsford Hill — Miss Eynsford Hill? (*Exchange of bows. The* Colonel *brings the Chippendale chair a little forward between* Mrs Hill *and* Mrs Higgins, *and sits down*).

Pickering. Has Henry told you what weve come for?

Higgins (*over his shoulder*) We were interrupted: damn it!

Mrs Higgins. Oh, Henry, Henry, really!

Mrs Eynsford Hill (*half rising*) Are we in the way?

Mrs Higgins (*rising and making her sit down again*) No, no. You couldnt have come more fortunately: we want you to meet a friend of ours.

Higgins (*turning hopefully*) Yes, by George! We want two or three people. You'll do as well as anybody else.

The Parlormaid *returns, ushering* Freddy.

The Parlormaid. Mr Eynsford Hill.

Higgins (*almost audibly, past endurance*) God of Heaven! another of them.

Freddy (*shaking hands with* Mrs Higgins) Ahdedo?

Mrs Higgins. Very good of you to come. (*Introducing*) Colonel Pickering.

Freddy (*bowing*) Ahdedo?

Mrs Higgins. I dont think you know my son, Professor Higgins.

Freddy (*going to* Higgins) Ahdedo?

Higgins (*looking at him much as if he were a pickpocket*) I'll take my oath Ive met you before somewhere. Where was it?

Freddy. I dont think so.

Higgins (*resignedly*) It dont matter, anyhow. Sit down.

He shakes Freddy's *hand, and almost slings him on to the ottoman with his face to the window; then comes round to the other side of it.*

Higgins. Well, here we are, anyhow! (*He sits down on the ottoman next* Mrs Eynsford Hill, *on her left*) And now, what the devil are we going to talk about until Eliza comes?

Mrs Higgins. Henry: you are the life and soul of the Royal Society's soirées; but really youre rather trying on more commonplace occasions.

Higgins. Am I? Very sorry. (*Beaming suddenly*) I suppose I am, you know. (*Uproariously*) Ha, ha!

Miss Eynsford Hill (*who considers* Higgins

quite eligible matrimonially) I sympathize. *I havnt any small talk. If people would only be frank and say what they really think!*

Higgins (*relapsing into gloom*) Lord forbid!

Mrs Eynsford Hill (*taking up her daughter's cue*) But why?

Higgins. What they think they ought to think is bad enough, Lord knows; but what they really think would break up the whole show. Do you suppose it would be really agreeable if I were to come out now with what *I* really think?

Miss Eynsford Hill (*gaily*) Is it so very cynical?

Higgins. Cynical! Who the dickens said it was cynical? I mean it wouldnt be decent.

Mrs Eynsford Hill (*seriously*) Oh! I'm sure you dont mean that, Mr Higgins.

Higgins. You see, we're all savages, more or less. We're supposed to be civilized and cultured—to know all about poetry and philosophy and art and science, and so on; but how many of us know even the meanings of these names? (*To* Miss Hill) What do you know of poetry? (*To* Mrs Hill) What do you know of science? (*Indicating* Freddy) What does he know of art or science or anything else? What the devil do you imagine I know of philosophy?

Mrs Higgins (*warningly*) Or of manners, Henry?

The Parlormaid (*opening the door*) Miss Doolittle. (*She withdraws*).

Higgins (*rising hastily and running to* Mrs Higgins) Here she is, mother. (*He stands on tiptoe and makes signs over his mother's head to* Eliza *to indicate to her which lady is her hostess*).

Eliza, *who is exquisitely dressed, produces an impression of such remarkable distinction and beauty as she enters that they all rise, quite fluttered. Guided by* Higgins's *signals, she comes to* Mrs Higgins *with studied grace.*

Liza (*speaking with pedantic correctness of pronunciation and great beauty of tone*) How do you do, Mrs Higgins? (*She gasps slightly in making sure of the H in Higgins, but is quite successful*). Mr Higgins told me I might come.

Mrs Higgins (*cordially*) Quite right: I'm very glad indeed to see you.

Pickering. How do you do, Miss Doolittle?

Liza (*shaking hands with him*) Colonel Pickering, is it not?

Mrs Eynsford Hill. I feel sure we have met before, Miss Doolittle. I remember your eyes.

Liza. How do you do? (*She sits down on the ottoman gracefully in the place just left vacant by* Higgins).

Mrs Eynsford Hill (*introducing*) My daughter Clara.

Liza. How do you do?

Clara (*impulsively*) How do you do? (*She sits down on the ottoman beside* Eliza, *devouring her with her eyes*).

Freddy (*coming to their side of the ottoman*) Ive certainly had the pleasure.

Mrs Eynsford Hill (*introducing*) My son Freddy.

Liza. How do you do?

Freddy *bows and sits down in the Elizabethan chair, infatuated.*

Higgins (*suddenly*) By George, yes: it all comes back to me! (*They stare at him*). Covent Garden! (*Lamentably*) What a damned thing!

Mrs Higgins. Henry, please! (*He is about to sit on the edge of the table*) Dont sit on my writing-table: youll break it.

Higgins (*sulkily*) Sorry.

He goes to the divan, stumbling into the fender and over the fire-irons on his way; extricating himself with muttered imprecations; and finishing his disastrous journey by throwing himself so impatiently on the divan that he almost breaks it. Mrs Higgins looks at him, but controls herself and says nothing.

A long and painful pause ensues.

The "new small talk" is introduced in Chelsea.
Culver Pictures

Mrs Higgins (*at last, conversationally*) Will it rain, do you think?

Liza. The shallow depression in the west of these islands is likely to move slowly in an easterly direction. There are no indications of any great change in the barometrical situation.

Freddy. Ha! ha! how awfully funny!

Liza. What is wrong with that, young man? I bet I got it right.

Freddy. Killing!

Mrs Eynsford Hill. I'm sure I hope it wont turn cold. Theres so much influenza about. It runs right through our whole family regularly every spring.

Liza (*darkly*) My aunt died of influenza: so they said.

Mrs Eynsford Hill (*clicks her tongue sympathetically*)!!!

Liza (*in the same tragic tone*) But it's my belief they done the old woman in.

Mrs Higgins (*puzzled*) Done her in?

Liza. Y-e-e-e-es, Lord love you! Why should she die of influenza? She come through diphtheria right enough the year before. I saw her with my own eyes. Fairly blue with it, she was. They all thought she was dead; but my father he kept ladling gin down her throat til she came to so sudden that she bit the bowl off the spoon.

Mrs Eynsford Hill (*startled*) Dear me!

Liza (*piling up the indictment*) What call would a woman with that strength in her have to die of influenza? What become of her new straw hat that should have come to me? Somebody pinched it; and what I say is, them as pinched it done her in.

Mrs Eynsford Hill. What does doing her in mean?

Higgins (*hastily*) Oh, thats the new small talk. To do a person in means to kill them.

Mrs Eynsford Hill (*to* Eliza, *horrified*) You surely dont believe that your aunt was killed?

Liza. Do I not! Them she lived with would have killed her for a hat-pin, let alone a hat.

Mrs Eynsford Hill. But it cant have been right for your father to pour spirits down her throat like that. It might have killed her.

Liza. Not her. Gin was mother's milk to her. Besides, he'd poured so much down his own throat that he knew the good of it.

Mrs. Eynsford Hill. Do you mean that he drank?

Liza. Drank! My word! Something chronic.

Mrs Eynsford Hill. How dreadful for you!

Liza. Not a bit. It never did him no harm what I could see. But then he did not keep it up regular. (*Cheerfully*) On the burst, as you might say, from time to time. And always more agreeable when he had a drop in. When he was out of work, my mother used to give him fourpence and tell him to go out and not come back until he'd drunk himself cheerful and loving-like. Theres lots of women has to make their husbands drunk to make them fit to live with. (*Now quite at her ease*) You see, it's like this. If a man has a bit of conscience, it always takes him when he's sober; and then it makes him low-spirited. A drop of booze just takes that off and makes him happy. (*To* Freddy, *who is in convulsions of suppressed laughter*) Here! what are you sniggering at?

Freddy. The new small talk. You do it so awfully well.

Liza. If I was doing it proper, what was you laughing at? (*To* Higgins) Have I said anything I oughtnt?

Mrs Higgins (*interposing*) Not at all, Miss Doolittle.

Liza. Well, thats a mercy, anyhow. (*Expansively*) What I always say is —

Higgins (*rising and looking at his watch*) Ahem!

Liza (*looking round at him; taking the hint; and rising*) Well: I must go. (*They all rise.* Freddy *goes to the door*). So pleased to have met you. Goodbye. (*She shakes hands with* Mrs Higgins).

Mrs Higgins. Goodbye.

Liza. Goodbye, Colonel Pickering.

Pickering. Goodbye, Miss Doolittle. (*They shake hands*).

Liza (*nodding to the others*) Goodbye, all.

Freddy (*opening the door for her*) Are you walking across the Park, Miss Doolittle? If so —

Liza (*with perfectly elegant diction*) Walk! Not bloody likely. (*Sensation*). I am going in a taxi. (*She goes out*).

Pickering *gasps and sits down.* Freddy *goes out on the balcony to catch another glimpse of* Eliza.

Mrs Eynsford Hill (*suffering from shock*) Well, I really cant get used to the new ways.

Clara (*throwing herself discontentedly into the Elizabethan chair*) Oh, it's all right, mamma, quite right. People will think we never go anywhere or see anybody if you are so old-fashioned.

Mrs Eynsford Hill. I daresay I am very old-fashioned; but I do hope you wont begin using that expression, Clara. I have got accustomed to hear you talking about men as rotters, and calling everything filthy and beastly; though I do think it horrible and unladylike. But this last is really too much. Dont you think so, Colonel Pickering?

Pickering. Dont ask me. Ive been away in India for several years; and manners have changed so much that I sometimes dont know whether I'm at a respectable dinnertable or in a ship's forecastle.

Clara. It's all a matter of habit. Theres no right or wrong in it. Nobody means anything by it. And it's so quaint, and gives such a smart emphasis to things that are not in themselves very witty. I find the new small talk delightful and quite innocent.

Mrs Eynsford Hill (*rising*) Well, after that, I think it's time for us to go.

Pickering *and* Higgins *rise.*

Clara (*rising*) Oh yes: we have three at-homes to go to still. Goodbye, Mrs Higgins. Goodbye, Colonel Pickering. Goodbye, Professor Higgins.

Higgins (*coming grimly at her from the divan, and accompanying her to the door*) Goodbye. Be sure you try on that small talk at the three at-homes. Dont be nervous about it. Pitch it in strong.

Clara (*all smiles*) I will. Goodbye. Such nonsense, all this early Victorian prudery!

Higgins (*tempting her*) Such damned nonsense!

Clara. Such bloody nonsense!

Mrs Eynsford Hill (*convulsively*) Clara!

Clara. Ha! ha! (*She goes out radiant, conscious of being thoroughly up to date, and is heard descending the stairs in a stream of silvery laughter*).

Freddy (*to the heavens at large*) Well, I ask you— (*He gives it up, and comes to* Mrs Higgins). Goodbye.

Mrs Higgins (*shaking hands*) Goodbye. Would you like to meet Miss Doolittle again?

Freddy (*eagerly*) Yes, I should, most awfully.

Mrs Higgins. Well, you know my days.

Freddy. Yes. Thanks awfully. Goodbye. (*He goes out*).

Mrs Eynsford Hill. Goodbye, Mr Higgins.

Higgins. Goodbye. Goodbye.

Mrs Eynsford Hill (*to* Pickering) It's no use. I shall never be able to bring myself to use that word.

Pickering. Dont. It's not compulsory, you know. Youll get on quite well without it.

Mrs Eynsford Hill. Only, Clara is so down on me if I am not positively reeking with the latest slang. Goodbye.

Pickering. Goodbye (*They shake hands*).

Mrs Eynsford Hill (*to* Mrs Higgins) You mustnt mind Clara. (Pickering, *catching from her lowered tone that this is not meant for him to hear, discreetly joins* Higgins *at the window*). We're so poor! and she gets so few parties, poor child! She doesnt quite know. (Mrs Higgins, *seeing that her eyes are moist, takes her hand sympathetically and goes with her to the door*). But the boy is nice. Dont you think so?

Mrs Higgins. Oh, quite nice. I shall always be delighted to see him.

Mrs Eynsford Hill. Thank you, dear. Goodbye. (*She goes out*).

Higgins (*eagerly*) Well? Is Eliza presentable (*he swoops on his mother and drags her to the ottoman, where she sits down in* Eliza's *place with her son on her left*)?

Pickering *returns to his chair on her right.*

Mrs Higgins. You silly boy, of course she's not presentable. She's a triumph of your art and of her dressmaker's; but if you suppose for a moment that she doesn't give herself away in every sentence she utters, you must be perfectly cracked about her.

Pickering. But dont you think something might be done? I mean something to eliminate the sanguinary[7] element from her conversation.

Mrs Higgins. Not as long as she is in Henry's hands.

Higgins (*aggrieved*) Do you mean that my language is improper?

Mrs Higgins. No, dearest: it would be quite proper—say on a canal barge; but it would not be proper for her at a garden party.

Higgins (*deeply injured*) Well I must say—

Pickering (*interrupting him*) Come, Higgins: you must learn to know yourself. I havnt heard such language as yours since we used to review the volunteers in Hyde Park twenty years ago.

Higgins (*sulkily*) Oh, well, if you say so, I suppose I dont always talk like a bishop.

Mrs Higgins (*quieting* Henry *with a touch*) Colonel Pickering: will you tell me what is the exact state of things in Wimpole Street?

Pickering (*cheerfully: as if this completely changed the subject*) Well, I have come to live

---

7. **sanguinary** (săng′gwə-nĕr′ē): bloody; a reference to Eliza's use of the slang term "bloody" in her conversation.

there with Henry. We work together at my Indian Dialects; and we think it more convenient——

Mrs Higgins. Quite so. I know all about that: it's an excellent arrangement. But where does this girl live?

Higgins. With us, of course. Where should she live?

Mrs Higgins. But on what terms? Is she a servant? If not, what is she?

Pickering (*slowly*) I think I know what you mean, Mrs Higgins.

Higgins. Well, dash me if *I* do! Ive had to work at the girl every day for months to get her to her present pitch. Besides, she's useful. She knows where my things are, and remembers my appointments and so forth.

Mrs Higgins. How does your housekeeper get on with her?

Higgins. Mrs Pearce? Oh, she's jolly glad to get so much taken off her hands; for before Eliza came, she used to have to find things and remind me of my appointments. But she's got some silly bee in her bonnet about Eliza. She keeps saying "You dont think, sir": doesnt she, Pick?

Pickering. Yes: thats the formula. "You dont think, sir." Thats the end of every conversation about Eliza.

Higgins. As if I ever stop thinking about the girl and her confounded vowels and consonants. I'm worn out, thinking about her, and watching her lips and her teeth and her tongue, not to mention her soul, which is the quaintest of the lot.

Mrs Higgins. You certainly are a pretty pair of babies, playing with your live doll.

Higgins. Playing! The hardest job I ever tackled: make no mistake about that, mother. But you have no idea how frightfully interesting it is to take a human being and change her into a quite different human being by creating a new speech for her. It's filling up the deepest gulf that separates class from class and soul from soul.

Pickering (*drawing his chair closer to* Mrs Higgins *and bending over to her eagerly*) Yes: it's enormously interesting. I assure you, Mrs Higgins, we take Eliza very seriously. Every week – every day almost – there is some new change. (*Closer again*) We keep records of every stage – dozens of gramophone disks and photographs——

Higgins (*assailing her at the other ear*) Yes, by George: it's the most absorbing experiment I ever tackled. She regularly fills our lives up: doesnt she, Pick?

Pickering. We're always talking Eliza.

Higgins. Teaching Eliza.

Pickering. Dressing Eliza.

Mrs Higgins. What!

Higgins. Inventing new Elizas.

Higgins.	(*speaking together*)	You know, she has the most extraordinary quickness of ear:
Pickering.		I assure you, my dear Mrs Higgins, that girl
Higgins.		just like a parrot. Ive tried her with every
Pickering.		is a genius. She can play the piano quite beautifully.
Higgins.		possible sort of sound that a human being can make——
Pickering.		We have taken her to classical concerts and to music
Higgins.		Continental dialects, African dialects, Hottentot
Pickering.		halls; and it's all the same to her: she plays everything
Higgins.		clicks, things it took me years to get hold of; and
Pickering.		she hears right off when she comes home, whether it's

Higgins. *(speaking together)* she picks them up like a shot, right away, as if she had Beethoven and Brahms or Lehar, and Lionel Monckton;

Pickering.

Higgins.
Pickering. been at it all her life. though six months ago, she'd never as much as touched a piano —

Mrs Higgins *(putting her fingers in her ears, as they are by this time shouting one another down with an intolerable noise)* Sh-sh-sh—sh! *(They stop)*.

Pickering. I beg your pardon. *(He draws his chair back apologetically)*.

Higgins. Sorry. When Pickering starts shouting nobody can get a word in edgeways.

Mrs Higgins. Be quiet, Henry. Colonel Pickering: dont you realize that when Eliza walked in Wimpole Street, something walked in with her?

Pickering. Her father did. But Henry soon got rid of him.

Mrs Higgins. It would have been more to the point if her mother had. But as her mother didnt something else did.

Pickering. But what?

Mrs Higgins *(unconsciously dating herself by the word)* A problem.

Pickering. Oh, I see. The problem of how to pass her off as a lady.

Higgins. I'll solve that problem. Ive half solved it already.

Mrs Higgins. No, you two infinitely stupid male creatures: the problem of what is to be done with her afterwards.

Higgins. I dont see anything in that. She can go her own way, with all the advantages I have given her.

Mrs Higgins. The advantages of that poor woman who was here just now! The manners and habits that disqualify a fine lady from earning her own living without giving her a fine lady's income! Is that what you mean?

Pickering *(indulgently, being rather bored)* Oh, that will be all right, Mrs Higgins. *(He rises to go)*.

Higgins *(rising also)* We'll find her some light employment.

Pickering. She's happy enough. Dont you worry about her. Goodbye. *(He shakes hands as if he were consoling a frightened child, and makes for the door)*.

Higgins. Anyhow, theres no good bothering now. The thing's done. Goodbye, mother. *(He kisses her, and follows* Pickering*)*.

Pickering *(turning for a final consolation)* There are plenty of openings. We'll do whats right. Goodbye.

Higgins *(to* Pickering *as they go out together)* Lets take her to the Shakespear exhibition at Earls Court.

Pickering. Yes: lets. Her remarks will be delicious.

Higgins. She'll mimic all the people for us when we get home.

Pickering. Ripping. *(Both are heard laughing as they go downstairs)*.

Mrs Higgins *(rises with an impatient bounce, and returns to her work at the writing-table. She sweeps a litter of disarranged papers out of the way; snatches a sheet of paper from her stationery case; and tries resolutely to write. At the third time she gives it up; flings down her pen; grips the table angrily and exclaims)* Oh, men! men!! men!!!

   *   *   *   *   *   *

Clearly Eliza will not pass as a duchess yet; and Higgins's bet remains unwon. But the six months are not yet exhausted and just in time Eliza does actually pass as a princess. For a glimpse of how she did it imagine an Embassy in London one summer evening after dark. The hall door has an awning and a carpet across the sidewalk to the kerb, because a grand reception is in progress. A small crowd is lined up to see the guests arrive.

A Rolls-Royce car drives up. Pickering in evening dress, with medals and orders, alights, and hands out Eliza, in opera cloak, evening dress, diamonds, fan, flowers and all accessories. Higgins follows. The car drives off; and the three go up the steps and into the house, the door opening for them as they approach.

Inside the house they find themselves in a spacious hall from which the grand staircase rises. On the left are the arrangements for the gentlemen's cloaks. The male guests are depositing their hats and wraps there.

On the right is a door leading to the ladies' cloakroom. Ladies are going in cloaked and coming out in splendor. Pickering whispers to Eliza and points out the ladies' room. She goes into it. Higgins and Pickering take off their overcoats and take tickets for them from the attendant.

One of the guests, occupied in the same way, has his back turned. Having taken his ticket, he turns round and reveals himself as an important looking young man with an astonishingly hairy face. He has an enormous moustache, flowing out into luxuriant whiskers. Waves of hair cluster on his brow. His hair is cropped closely at the back, and glows with oil. Otherwise he is very smart. He wears several worthless orders. He is evidently a foreigner, guessable as a whiskered Pandour[8] from Hungary; but in spite of the ferocity of his moustache he is amiable and genially voluble.

Recognizing Higgins, he flings his arms wide apart and approaches him enthusiastically.

Whiskers. Maestro, maestro (*he embraces Higgins and kisses him on both cheeks*). You remember me?
Higgins. No I dont. Who the devil are you?
Whiskers. I am your pupil: your first pupil, your best and greatest pupil. I am little Nepommuck, the marvellous boy. I have made your name famous throughout Europe. You teach me phonetic. You cannot forget ME.
Higgins. Why dont you shave?
Nepommuck. I have not your imposing appearance, your chin, your brow. Nobody notice me when I shave. Now I am famous: they call me Hairy Faced Dick.
Higgins. And what are you doing here among all these swells?
Nepommuck. I am interpreter. I speak 32 languages. I am indispensable at these international parties. You are great cockney specialist: you place a man anywhere in London the moment he open his mouth. I place any man in Europe.

A Footman *hurries down the grand staircase and comes to* Nepommuck.

Footman. You are wanted upstairs. Her Excellency cannot understand the Greek gentleman.
Nepommuck. Thank you, yes, immediately.

The Footman *goes and is lost in the crowd.*

Nepommuck (*to* Higgins) This Greek diplomatist pretends he cannot speak nor understand English. He cannot deceive me. He is the son of a Clerkenwell watchmaker. He speaks English so villainously that he dare not utter a word of it without betraying his origin. I help him to pretend; but I make him pay through the nose. I make them all pay. Ha ha! (*He hurries upstairs*).
Pickering. Is this fellow really an expert? Can he find out Eliza and blackmail her?
Higgins. We shall see. If he finds her out I lose my bet.

Eliza *comes from the cloakroom and joins them.*

Pickering. Well, Eliza, now for it. Are you ready?

---

8. **Pandour:** an armed servant or retainer of Hungarian nobles.

Liza. Are you nervous, Colonel?

Pickering. Frightfully. I feel exactly as I felt before my first battle. It's the first time that frightens.

Liza. It is not the first time for me, Colonel. I have done this fifty times—hundreds of times—in my little piggery in Angel Court in my day-dreams. I am in a dream now. Promise me not to let Professor Higgins wake me; for if he does I shall forget everything and talk as I used to in Drury Lane.

Pickering. Not a word, Higgins. (*To* Eliza) Now, ready?

Liza. Ready.

Pickering. Go.

They mount the stairs, Higgins *last.* Pickering *whispers to the* Footman *on the first landing.*

First Landing Footman. Miss Doolittle, Colonel Pickering, Professor Higgins.

Second Landing Footman. Miss Doolittle, Colonel Pickering, Professor Higgins.

At the top of the staircase the Ambassador *and his* Wife, *with* Nepommuck *at her elbow, are receiving.*

Hostess (*taking* Eliza's *hand*) How d'ye do?

Host (*same play*) How d'ye do? How d'ye do, Pickering?

Liza (*with a beautiful gravity that awes her hostess*) How do you do? (*She passes on to the drawingroom*).

Hostess. Is that your adopted daughter, Colonel Pickering? She will make a sensation.

Pickering. Most kind of you to invite her for me. (*He passes on*).

Hostess (*to* Nepommuck) Find out all about her.

Nepommuck (*bowing*) Excellency—(*he goes into the crowd*).

Host. How d'ye do, Higgins? You have a rival here tonight. He introduced himself as your pupil. Is he any good?

Higgins. He can learn a language in a fortnight —knows dozens of them. A sure mark of a fool. As a phonetician, no good whatever.

Hostess. How d'ye do, Professor?

Higgins. How do you do? Fearful bore for you this sort of thing. Forgive my part in it. (*He passes on*).

In the drawing room and its suite of salons the reception is in full swing. Eliza passes through. She is so intent on her ordeal that she walks like a somnambulist in a desert instead of a débutante in a fashionable crowd. They stop talking to look at her, admiring her dress, her jewels, and her strangely attractive self. Some of the younger ones at the back stand on their chairs to see.

The Host and Hostess come in from the staircase and mingle with their guests. Higgins, gloomy and contemptuous of the whole business, comes into the group where they are chatting.

Hostess. Ah, here is Professor Higgins: he will tell us. Tell us all about the wonderful young lady, Professor.

Higgins (*almost morosely*) What wonderful young lady?

Hostess. You know very well. They tell me there has been nothing like her in London since people stood on their chairs to look at Mrs Langtry.[9]

Nepommuck *joins the group, full of news.*

Hostess. Ah, here you are at last, Nepommuck. Have you found out all about the Doolittle lady?

Nepommuck. I have found out all about her. She is a fraud.

Hostess. A fraud! Oh no.

Nepommuck. YES, yes. She cannot deceive me. Her name cannot be Doolittle.

Higgins. Why?

Nepommuck. Because Doolittle is an English name. And she is not English.

---

9. **Mrs. Langtry:** Lily Langtry (1852–1929), an English actress of great beauty and style.

Hostess. Oh, nonsense! She speaks English perfectly.

Nepommuck. Too perfectly. Can you shew me any English woman who speaks English as it should be spoken? Only foreigners who have been taught to speak it speak it well.

Hostess. Certainly she terrified me by the way she said How d'ye do. I had a school-mistress who talked like that; and I was mortally afraid of her. But if she is not English what is she?

Nepommuck. Hungarian.

All the Rest. Hungarian!

Nepommuck. Hungarian. And of royal blood. I am Hungarian. My blood is royal.

Higgins. Did you speak to her in Hungarian?

Nepommuck. I did. She was very clever. She said "Please speak to me in English: I do not understand French." French! She pretend not to know the difference between Hungarian and French. Impossible: she knows both.

Higgins. And the blood royal? How did you find that out?

Nepommuck. Instinct, maestro, instinct. Only the Magyar races can produce that air of the divine right, those resolute eyes. She is a princess.

Host. What do you say, Professor?

Higgins. I say an ordinary London girl out of the gutter and taught to speak by an expert. I place her in Drury Lane.

Nepommuck. Ha ha ha! Oh, maestro, maestro, you are mad on the subject of cockney dialects. The London gutter is the whole world for you.

Higgins (*to the* Hostess) What does your Excellency say?

Hostess. Oh, of course I agree with Nepommuck. She must be a princess at least.

Host. Not necessarily legitimate, of course. Morganatic[10] perhaps. But that is undoubtedly her class.

Higgins. I stick to my opinion.

---

10. **Morganatic** (môr′gə-năt′ĭk): a marriage between a member of a royal family and someone of inferior rank. Though the marriage is valid, offspring of it do not inherit titles.

Hostess. Oh, you are incorrigible.

The group breaks up, leaving Higgins *isolated.* Pickering *joins him.*

Pickering. Where is Eliza? We must keep an eye on her.

Eliza *joins them.*

Liza. I dont think I can bear much more. The people all stare so at me. An old lady has just told me that I speak exactly like Queen Victoria. I am sorry if I have lost your bet. I have done my best; but nothing can make me the same as these people.

Pickering. You have not lost it, my dear. You have won it ten times over.

Higgins. Let us get out of this. I have had enough of chattering to these fools.

Pickering. Eliza is tired; and I am hungry. Let us clear out and have supper somewhere.

FOR STUDY AND DISCUSSION

1. In what ways is Mrs. Higgins a contrast in manners and attitudes to her son and to Mrs. Eynsford Hill and Clara?
2. What is Mrs. Higgins' reaction to Eliza? Find passages to show that she finds her son and Pickering selfish and irresponsible in their attitudes toward Eliza. How does her view of Eliza's future compare with the view of Mrs. Pearce in Act Two?
3. Despite Eliza's tragic tones in describing the death of her aunt, the scene retains its comedy. Why? How does Clara's believing Eliza's slang to be "the new small talk" provide an example of Shaw's satire of class pretensions? What does Freddy say that shows he is infatuated with Eliza?
4. How does the Eliza of Act Three compare with the Eliza of Acts One and Two?

Act Four

The Wimpole Street laboratory. Midnight. Nobody in the room. The clock on the mantelpiece strikes twelve. The fire is not alight: it is a summer night.

Presently Higgins *and* Pickering *are heard on the stairs.*

Higgins (*calling down to* Pickering) I say, Pick: lock up, will you? I shant be going out again.
Pickering. Right. Can Mrs Pearce go to bed? We dont want anything more, do we?
Higgins. Lord, no!

Eliza *opens the door and is seen on the lighted landing in all the finery in which she has just won* Higgins's *bet for him. She comes to the hearth, and switches on the electric lights there. She is tired: her pallor contrasts strongly with her dark eyes and hair; and her expression is almost tragic. She takes off her cloak; puts her fan and gloves on the piano; and sits down on the bench, brooding and silent.* Higgins, *in evening dress, with overcoat and hat, comes in, carrying a smoking jacket which he has picked up downstairs. He takes off the hat and overcoat; throws them carelessly on the newspaper stand; disposes of his coat in the same way; puts on the smoking jacket; and throws himself wearily into the easy-chair at the hearth.* Pickering, *similarly attired, comes in. He also takes off his hat and overcoat, and is about to throw them on* Higgins's *when he hesitates.*

Pickering. I say: Mrs Pearce will row if we leave these things lying about in the drawing room.
Higgins. Oh, chuck them over the bannisters into the hall. She'll find them there in the morning and put them away all right. She'll think we were drunk.
Pickering. We are, slightly. Are there any letters?

Higgins. I didnt look. (Pickering *takes the overcoats and hats and goes downstairs.* Higgins *begins half singing half yawning an air from* La Fanciulla del Golden West.[1] *Suddenly he stops and exclaims*) I wonder where the devil my slippers are!

Eliza *looks at him darkly; then rises suddenly and leaves the room.*

Higgins *yawns again, and resumes his song.*

Pickering *returns, with the contents of the letter-box in his hand.*

Pickering. Only circulars, and this coroneted billet-doux[2] for you. (*He throws the circulars into the fender, and posts himself on the hearthrug, with his back to the grate*).
Higgins (*glancing at the billet-doux*) Moneylender. (*He throws the letter after the circulars*).

Eliza *returns with a pair of large down-at-heel slippers. She places them on the carpet before* Higgins, *and sits as before without a word.*

Higgins (*yawning again*) Oh Lord! What an evening! What a crew! What a silly tomfoolery! (*He raises his shoe to unlace it, and catches sight of the slippers. He stops unlacing and looks at them as if they had appeared there of their own accord*). Oh! theyre there, are they?
Pickering (*stretching himself*). Well, I feel a bit tired. It's been a long day. The garden party, a dinner party, and the reception! Rather too much of a good thing. But youve won your bet, Higgins. Eliza did the trick, and something to spare, eh?
Higgins (*fervently*) Thank God it's over!

Eliza *flinches violently; but they take no notice of her; and she recovers herself and sits stonily as before.*

---

1. **La Fanciulla del Golden West:** *The Girl of the Golden West,* an opera by Giacomo Puccini (1858–1924).
2. **billet-doux** (bĭl′ā-dōō′): a love letter.

Pickering. Were you nervous at the garden party? *I* was. Eliza didnt seem a bit nervous.
Higgins. Oh, she wasnt nervous. I knew she'd be all right. No: it's the strain of putting the job through all these months that has told on me. It was interesting enough at first, while we were at the phonetics; but after that I got deadly sick of it. If I hadnt backed myself to do it I should have chucked the whole thing up two months ago. It was a silly notion: the whole thing has been a bore.
Pickering. Oh come! the garden party was frightfully exciting. My heart began beating like anything.
Higgins. Yes, for the first three minutes. But when I saw we were going to win hands down, I felt like a bear in a cage, hanging about doing nothing. The dinner was worse: sitting gorging there for over an hour, with nobody but a damned fool of a fashionable woman to talk to! I tell you, Pickering, never again for me. No more artificial duchesses. The whole thing has been simple purgatory.
Pickering. Youve never been broken in properly to the social routine. (*Strolling over to the piano*) I rather enjoy dipping into it occasionally myself: it makes me feel young again. Anyhow, it was a great success: an immense success. I was quite frightened once or twice because Eliza was doing it so well. You see, lots of the real people cant do it at all: theyre such fools that they think style comes by nature to people in their position; and so they never learn. Theres always something professional about doing a thing superlatively well.
Higgins. Yes: thats what drives me mad: the silly people dont know their own silly business. (*Rising*) However, it's over and done with; and now I can go to bed at last without dreading tomorrow.

Eliza's *beauty becomes murderous.*

Pickering. I think I shall turn in too. Still, it's been a great occasion: a triumph for you. Goodnight. (*He goes*).

Higgins (*following him*) Goodnight. (*Over his shoulder, at the door*) Put out the lights, Eliza; and tell Mrs Pearce not to make coffee for me in the morning: I'll take tea. (*He goes out*).

Eliza *tries to control herself and feel indifferent as she rises and walks across to the hearth to switch off the lights. By the time she gets there she is on the point of screaming. She sits down in* Higgins's *chair and holds on hard to the arms. Finally she gives way and flings herself furiously on the floor, raging.*

Higgins (*in despairing wrath outside*) What the devil have I done with my slippers? (*He appears at the door*).
Liza (*snatching up the slippers, and hurling them at him one after the other with all her force*) There are your slippers. And there. Take your slippers; and may you never have a day's luck with them!
Higgins (*astounded*) What on earth——! (*He comes to her*). Whats the matter? Get up. (*He pulls her up*) Anything wrong?
Liza (*breathless*) Nothing wrong—with you. Ive won your bet for you, havnt I? Thats enough for you. *I* dont matter, I suppose.
Higgins. You won my bet! You! Presumptuous insect! *I* won it. What did you throw those slippers at me for?
Liza. Because I wanted to smash your face. I'd like to kill you, you selfish brute. Why didnt you leave me where you picked me out of—in the gutter? You thank God it's all over, and that now you can throw me back again there, do you? (*She crisps her fingers[3] frantically*).
Higgins (*looking at her in cool wonder*) The creature is nervous, after all.
Liza (*gives a suffocated scream of fury, and instinctively darts her nails at his face*)!!
Higgins (*catching her wrists*) Ah! would you? Claws in, you cat. How dare you shew your

---

3. **crisps her fingers:** clenches and unclenches her fists.

temper to me? Sit down and be quiet. (*He throws her roughly into the easy-chair*).

Liza (*crushed by superior strength and weight*) Whats to become of me? Whats to become of me?

Higgins. How the devil do I know whats to become of you? What does it matter what becomes of you?

Liza. You dont care. I know you dont care. You wouldnt care if I was dead. I'm nothing to you—not so much as them slippers.

Higgins (*thundering*) Those slippers.

Liza (*with bitter submission*) Those slippers. I didnt think it made any difference now.

A pause. Eliza *hopeless and crushed.* Higgins *a little uneasy.*

Higgins (*in his loftiest manner*) Why have you begun going on like this? May I ask whether you complain of your treatment here?

Liza. No.

Higgins. Has anybody behaved badly to you? Colonel Pickering? Mrs Pearce? Any of the servants?

Liza. No.

Higgins. I presume you dont pretend that *I* have treated you badly?

Liza. No.

Higgins. I am glad to hear it. (*He moderates his tone*). Perhaps youre tired after the strain of the day. Will you have a glass of champagne? (*He moves towards the door*).

Liza. No. (*Recollecting her manners*) Thank you.

Higgins (*good-humored again*) This has been coming on you for some days. I suppose it was natural for you to be anxious about the garden party. But thats all over now. (*He pats her kindly on the shoulder. She writhes*). Theres nothing more to worry about.

Liza. No. Nothing more for you to worry about. (*She suddenly rises and gets away from him by going to the piano bench, where she sits and hides her face*). Oh God! I wish I was dead.

Higgins (*staring after her in sincere surprise*) Why? In heaven's name, why? (*Reasonably, going to her*) Listen to me, Eliza. All this irritation is purely subjective.

Liza. I dont understand. I'm too ignorant.

Higgins. It's only imagination. Low spirits and nothing else. Nobody's hurting you. Nothing's wrong. You go to bed like a good girl and sleep it off. Have a little cry and say your prayers: that will make you comfortable.

Liza. I heard your prayers. "Thank God it's all over!"

Higgins (*impatiently*) Well, dont you thank God it's all over? Now you are free and can do what you like.

Liza (*pulling herself together in desperation*) What am I fit for? What have you left me fit for? Where am I to go? What am I to do? Whats to become of me?

Higgins (*enlightened, but not at all impressed*) Oh, thats whats worrying you, is it? (*He thrusts his hands into his pockets, and walks about in his usual manner, rattling the contents of his pockets, as if condescending to a trivial subject out of pure kindness*). I shouldnt bother about it if I were you. I should imagine you wont have much difficulty in settling yourself somewhere or other, though I hadnt quite realized that you were going away. (*She looks quickly at him: he does not look at her, but examines the dessert stand on the piano and decides that he will eat an apple*). You might marry, you know. (*He bites a large piece out of the apple and munches it noisily*). You see, Eliza, all men are not confirmed old bachelors like me and the Colonel. Most men are the marrying sort (poor devils!); and youre not bad-looking: it's quite a pleasure to look at you sometimes—not now, of course, because youre crying and looking as ugly as the very devil; but when youre all right and quite yourself, youre what I should call attractive. That is, to the people in the marrying line, you understand. You go to bed and have a good nice rest; and then get up and look at yourself in the glass; and you wont feel so cheap.

Eliza *again looks at him, speechless, and does not stir.*

The look is quite lost on him: he eats his apple with a dreamy expression of happiness, as it is quite a good one.

Higgins (*a genial afterthought occurring to him*) I daresay my mother could find some chap or other who would do very well.

Liza. We were above that at the corner of Tottenham Court Road.

Higgins (*waking up*) What do you mean?

Liza. I sold flowers. I didnt sell myself. Now youve made a lady of me I'm not fit to sell anything else. I wish youd left me where you found me.

Higgins (*slinging the core of the apple decisively into the grate*) Tosh, Eliza. Dont you insult human relations by dragging all this cant about buying and selling into it. You neednt marry the fellow if you dont like him.

Liza. What else am I to do?

Higgins. Oh, lots of things. What about your old idea of a florist's shop? Pickering could set you up in one: he has lots of money. (*Chuckling*) He'll have to pay for all those togs you have been wearing today; and that, with the hire of the jewellery, will make a big hole in two hundred pounds. Why, six months ago you would have thought it the millennium to have a flower shop of your own. Come! youll be all right. I must clear off to bed: I'm devilish sleepy. By the way, I came down for something: I forgot what it was.

Liza. Your slippers.

Higgins. Oh yes, of course. You shied them at me. (*He picks them up, and is going out when she rises and speaks to him*).

Liza. Before you go, sir——

Higgins (*dropping the slippers in his surprise at her calling him Sir*) Eh?

Liza. Do my clothes belong to me or to Colonel Pickering?

Higgins (*coming back into the room as if her question were the very climax of unreason*) What the devil use would they be to Pickering?

Liza. He might want them for the next girl you pick up to experiment on.

Higgins (*shocked and hurt*) Is that the way you feel towards us?

Liza. I dont want to hear anything more about that. All I want to know is whether anything belongs to me. My own clothes were burnt.

Higgins. But what does it matter? Why need you start bothering about that in the middle of the night?

Liza. I want to know what I may take away with me. I dont want to be accused of stealing.

Higgins (*now deeply wounded*) Stealing! You shouldnt have said that, Eliza. That shews a want of feeling.

Liza. I'm sorry. I'm only a common ignorant girl; and in my station I have to be careful. There cant be any feelings between the like of you and the like of me. Please will you tell me what belongs to me and what doesnt?

Higgins (*very sulky*) You may take the whole damned houseful if you like. Except the jewels. Theyre hired. Will that satisfy you? (*He turns on his heel and is about to go in extreme dudgeon*).

Liza (*drinking in his emotion like nectar, and nagging him to provoke a further supply*) Stop, please. (*She takes off her jewels*). Will you take these to your room and keep them safe? I dont want to run the risk of their being missing.

Higgins (*furious*) Hand them over. (*She puts them into his hands*). If these belonged to me instead of to the jeweller, I'd ram them down your ungrateful throat. (*He perfunctorily thrusts them into his pockets, unconsciously decorating himself with the protruding ends of the chains*).

Liza (*taking a ring off*). This ring isnt the jeweller's: it's the one you bought me in Brighton. I dont want it now. (Higgins *dashes the ring violently into the fireplace, and turns on her so threateningly that she crouches over the piano with her hands over her face, and exclaims*) Dont you hit me.

Higgins. Hit you! You infamous creature, how

Higgins takes leave of "a heartless
guttersnipe."
Penguin Photos

dare you accuse me of such a thing? It is you
who have hit me. You have wounded me to
the heart.

Liza (*thrilling with hidden joy*) I'm glad. Ive
got a little of my own back, anyhow.

Higgins (*with dignity, in his finest professional style*) You have caused me to lose my
temper: a thing that has hardly ever happened
to me before. I prefer to say nothing more tonight. I am going to bed.

Liza (*pertly*) Youd better leave a note for Mrs
Pearce about the coffee; for she wont be told
by me.

Higgins (*formally*) Damn Mrs Pearce; and
damn the coffee; and damn you; and (*wildly*)
damn my own folly in having lavished my
hard-earned knowledge and the treasure of
my regard and intimacy on a heartless guttersnipe. (*He goes out with impressive decorum, and spoils it by slamming the door
savagely*).

Eliza *goes down on her knees on the
hearthrug to look for the ring. When she finds
it she considers for a moment what to do
with it. Finally she flings it down on the dessert stand and goes upstairs in a tearing rage.*

*   *   *   *   *   *

The furniture of Eliza's room has been increased by a big wardrobe and a sumptuous
dressing-table. She comes in and switches on
the electric light. She goes to the wardrobe;
opens it; and pulls out a walking dress, a hat,
and a pair of shoes, which she throws on the
bed. She takes off her evening dress and shoes;
then takes a padded hanger from the wardrobe; adjusts it carefully in the evening dress;
and hangs it in the wardrobe, which she shuts
with a slam. She puts on her walking shoes,
her walking dress, and hat. She takes her
wrist watch from the dressing-table and fas-
tens it on. She pulls on her gloves; takes her
vanity bag; and looks into it to see that her
purse is there before hanging it on her wrist.
She makes for the door. Every movement
expresses her furious resolution.

She takes a last look at herself in the glass.

She suddenly puts out her tongue at herself;
then leaves the room, switching off the electric light at the door.

Meanwhile, in the street outside, Freddy
Eynsford Hill, lovelorn, is gazing up at the
second floor, in which one of the windows is
still lighted.

The light goes out.

Freddy. Goodnight, darling, darling, darling.

Eliza *comes out, giving the door a considerable bang behind her.*

Liza. Whatever are you doing here?

Freddy. Nothing. I spend most of my nights here. It's the only place where I'm happy. Dont laugh at me, Miss Doolittle.

Liza. Dont you call me Miss Doolittle, do you hear? Liza's good enough for me. (*She breaks down and grabs him by the shoulders*) Freddy: you dont think I'm a heartless guttersnipe, do you?

Freddy. Oh no, no, darling: how can you imagine such a thing? You are the loveliest, dearest——

He loses all self-control and smothers her with kisses. She, hungry for comfort, responds. They stand there in one another's arms.
An elderly police constable arrives.

Constable (*scandalized*) Now then! Now then!! Now then!!!

They release one another hastily.

Freddy. Sorry, constable. Weve only just become engaged.

They run away.

The constable shakes his head, reflecting on his own courtship and on the vanity of human hopes. He moves off in the opposite direction with slow professional steps.

The flight of the lovers takes them to Cavendish Square. There they halt to consider their next move.

Liza (*out of breath*) He didnt half give me a fright, that copper. But you answered him proper.

Freddy. I hope I havnt taken you out of your way. Where were you going?

Liza. To the river.

Freddy. What for?

Liza. To make a hole in it.

Freddy (*horrified*) Eliza, darling. What do you mean? What's the matter?

Liza. Never mind. It doesnt matter now. There's nobody in the world now but you and me, is there?

Freddy. Not a soul.

They indulge in another embrace, and are again surprised by a much younger constable.

Second Constable. Now then, you two! What's this? Where do you think you are? Move along here, double quick.

Freddy. As you say, sir, double quick.

They run away again, and are in Hanover Square before they stop for another conference.

Freddy. I had no idea the police were so devilishly prudish.

Liza. It's their business to hunt girls off the streets.

Freddy. We must go somewhere. We cant wander about the streets all night.

Liza. Cant we? I think it'd be lovely to wander about for ever.

Freddy. Oh, darling.

They embrace again, oblivious of the arrival of a crawling taxi. It stops.

Taximan. Can I drive you and the lady anywhere, sir?

They start asunder.

Liza. Oh, Freddy, a taxi. The very thing.

Freddy. But, damn it, I've no money.

Liza. I have plenty. The Colonel thinks you should never go out without ten pounds in your pocket. Listen. We'll drive about all night; and in the morning I'll call on old Mrs

Higgins and ask her what I ought to do. I'll tell you all about it in the cab. And the police wont touch us there.

Freddy. Righto! Ripping. (*To the* Taximan) Wimbledon Common. (*They drive off*).

FOR STUDY AND DISCUSSION

1. The experiment is finished and Higgins has won his bet. How does he react to his victory? What gratefulness, if any, does he show for Eliza's hard work and achievement—and what regard for her feelings?
2. What fears has Eliza for the future? What do you think Eliza's feelings for Higgins are?
3. The fourth act, which presents the first major crisis to erupt in the unconventional Higgins household, is unusually short—hardly more than a scene. What advantages might Shaw see in introducing the crisis in the fourth of his five acts and in keeping this act very short?

Act Five

Mrs Higgins's *drawing room. She is at her writing-table as before. The* Parlormaid *comes in.*

The Parlormaid (*at the door*) Mr Henry, maam, is downstairs with Colonel Pickering.
Mrs Higgins. Well, shew them up.
The Parlormaid. Theyre using the telephone, maam. Telephoning to the police, I think.
Mrs Higgins. What!
The Parlormaid (*coming further in and lowering her voice*) Mr Henry is in a state, maam. I thought I'd better tell you.
Mrs Higgins. If you had told me that Mr Henry was not in a state it would have been more surprising. Tell them to come up when theyve finished with the police. I suppose he's lost something.
The Parlormaid. Yes, maam (*going*).
Mrs Higgins. Go upstairs and tell Miss Doolittle that Mr. Henry and the Colonel are here. Ask her not to come down til I send for her.
The Parlormaid. Yes, maam.

Higgins *bursts in. He is, as the* Parlormaid *has said, in a state.*

Higgins. Look here, mother: heres a confounded thing!
Mrs Higgins. Yes, dear. Good morning. (*He checks his impatience and kisses her, whilst the* Parlormaid *goes out*). What is it?
Higgins. Eliza's bolted.
Mrs Higgins (*calmly continuing her writing*) You must have frightened her.
Higgins. Frightened her! nonsense! She was left last night, as usual, to turn out the lights and all that; and instead of going to bed she changed her clothes and went right off: her bed wasnt slept in. She came in a cab for her things before seven this morning; and that fool Mrs Pearce let her have them without telling me a word about it. What am I to do?
Mrs Higgins. Do without, I'm afraid, Henry.

The girl has a perfect right to leave if she chooses.

Higgins (*wandering distractedly across the room*) But I cant find anything. I dont know what appointments Ive got. I'm—— (*Pickering comes in.* Mrs Higgins *puts down her pen and turns away from the writing-table*).

Pickering (*shaking hands*) Good morning, Mrs Higgins. Has Henry told you? (*He sits down on the ottoman*).

Higgins. What does that ass of an inspector say? Have you offered a reward?

Mrs Higgins (*rising in indignant amazement*) You dont mean to say you have set the police after Eliza.

Higgins. Of course. What are the police for? What else could we do? (*He sits in the Elizabethan chair*).

Pickering. The inspector made a lot of difficulties. I really think he suspected us of some improper purpose.

Mrs Higgins. Well, of course he did. What right have you to go to the police and give the girl's name as if she were a thief, or a lost umbrella, or something? Really! (*She sits down again, deeply vexed*).

Higgins. But we want to find her.

Pickering. We cant let her go like this, you know, Mrs Higgins. What were we to do?

Mrs Higgins. You have no more sense, either of you, than two children. Why——

The Parlormaid *comes in and breaks off the conversation.*

The Parlormaid. Mr Henry: a gentleman wants to see you very particular. He's been sent on from Wimpole Street.

Higgins. Oh, bother! I cant see anyone now. Who is it?

The Parlormaid. A Mr Doolittle, sir.

Pickering. Doolittle! Do you mean the dustman?

The Parlormaid. Dustman! Oh no, sir: a gentleman.

Higgins (*springing up excitedly*) By George, Pick, it's some relative of hers that she's gone

to. Somebody we know nothing about. (*To the Parlormaid*) Send him up, quick.

The Parlomaid. Yes, sir. (*She goes*).

Higgins (*eagerly, going to his mother*) Genteel relatives! now we shall hear something. (*He sits down in the Chippendale chair*).

Mrs Higgins. Do you know any of her people?

Pickering. Only her father: the fellow we told you about.

The Parlormaid (*announcing*) Mr Doolittle. (*She withdraws*).

Doolittle *enters. He is resplendently dressed as for a fashionable wedding, and might, in fact, be the bridegroom. A flower in his buttonhole, a dazzling silk hat, and patent leather shoes complete the effect. He is too concerned with the business he has come on to notice Mrs Higgins. He walks straight to* Higgins, *and accosts him with vehement reproach.*

Doolittle (*indicating his own person*) See here! Do you see this? You done this.

Higgins. Done what, man?

Doolittle. This, I tell you. Look at it. Look at this hat. Look at this coat.

Pickering. Has Eliza been buying you clothes?

Doolittle. Eliza! not she. Why would she buy me clothes?

Mrs Higgins. Good morning, Mr Doolittle. Wont you sit down?

Doolittle (*taken aback as he becomes conscious that he has forgotten his hostess*) Asking your pardon, maam. (*He approaches her and shakes her proffered hand*). Thank you. (*He sits down on the ottoman, on* Pickering's *right*). I am that full of what has happened to me that I cant think of anything else.

Higgins. What the dickens has happened to you?

Doolittle. I shouldnt mind if it had only happened to me: anything might happen to anybody and nobody to blame but Providence, as you might say. But this is something that you done to me: yes, you, Enry Iggins.

Higgins. Have you found Eliza?

Doolittle. Have you lost her?

Higgins. Yes.

Doolittle. You have all the luck, you have. I aint found her; but she'll find me quick enough now after what you done to me.

Mrs Higgins. But what has my son done to you, Mr Doolittle?

Doolittle. Done to me! Ruined me. Destroyed my happiness. Tied me up and delivered me into the hands of middle class morality.

Higgins (*rising intolerantly and standing over* Doolittle) Youre raving. Youre drunk. Youre mad. I gave you five pounds. After that I had two conversations with you, at half-a-crown an hour. Ive never seen you since.

Doolittle. Oh! Drunk am I? Mad am I? Tell me this. Did you or did you not write a letter to an old blighter in America that was giving five millions to found Moral Reform Societies all over the world, and that wanted you to invent a universal language for him?

Higgins. What! Ezra D. Wannafeller! He's dead. (*He sits down again carelessly*).

Doolittle. Yes: he's dead; and I'm done for. Now did you or did you not write a letter to him to say that the most original moralist at present in England, to the best of your knowledge, was Alfred Doolittle, a common dustman?

Higgins. Oh, after your first visit I remember making some silly joke of the kind.

Doolittle. Ah! You may well call it a silly joke. It put the lid on me right enough. Just give him the chance he wanted to shew that Americans is not like us: that they reckonize and respect merit in every class of life, however humble. Them words is in his blooming will, in which, Henry Higgins, thanks to your silly joking, he leaves me a share in his Predigested Cheese Trust worth [three] thousand a year on condition that I lecture for his Wannafeller Moral Reform World League as often as they ask me up to six times a year.

Higgins. The devil he does! Whew! (*Brightening suddenly*) What a lark!

Pickering. A safe thing for you, Doolittle. They wont ask you twice.

Doolittle. It aint the lecturing I mind. I'll lecture them blue in the face, I will, and not turn a hair. It's making a gentleman of me that I object to. Who asked him to make a gentleman of me? I was happy. I was free. I touched pretty nigh everybody for money when I wanted it, same as I touched you, Enry Iggins. Now I am worrited; tied neck and heels; and everybody touches me for money. It's a fine thing for you, says my solicitor. Is it? says I. You mean it's a good thing for you, I says. When I was a poor man and had a solicitor once when they found a pram in the dust cart, he got me off, and got shut of me and got me shut of him as quick as he could. Same with the doctors: used to shove me out of the hospital before I could hardly stand on my legs, and nothing to pay. Now they finds out that I'm not a healthy man and cant live unless they looks after me twice a day. In the house I'm not let do a hand's turn for myself: somebody else must do it and touch me for it. A year ago I hadnt a relative in the world except two or three that wouldnt speak to me. Now Ive fifty, and not a decent week's wages among the lot of them. I have to live for others and not for myself: thats middle class morality. You talk of losing Eliza. Dont you be anxious: I bet she's on my doorstep by this: she that could support herself easy by selling flowers if I wasnt respectable. And the next one to touch me will be you, Enry Iggins. I'll have to learn to speak middle class language from you, instead of speaking proper English. Thats where youll come in; and I daresay thats what you done it for.

Mrs Higgins. But, my dear Mr Doolittle, you need not suffer all this if you are really in earnest. Nobody can force you to accept this bequest. You can repudiate it. Isnt that so, Colonel Pickering?

Pickering. I believe so.

Doolittle (*softening his manner in deference to her sex*) Thats the tragedy of it, maam. It's easy to say chuck it; but I havnt the nerve. Which of us has? We're all intimidated. Intimidated, maam: thats what we are. What is there for me if I chuck it but the workhouse in my old age? I have to dye my hair already to keep my job as a dustman. If I was one of the deserving poor, and had put by a bit, I could chuck it; but then why should I, acause the deserving poor might as well be millionaires for all the happiness they ever has. They dont know what happiness is. But I, as one of the undeserving poor, have nothing between me and the pauper's uniform but this here blasted three thousand a year that shoves me into the middle class. (Excuse the expression, maam; youd use it yourself if you had my provocation.) Theyve got you every way you turn: it's a choice between the Skilly of the workhouse and the Char Bydis[1] of the middle class; and I havnt the nerve for the workhouse. Intimidated: thats what I am. Broke. Bought up. Happier men than me will call for my dust, and touch me for their tip; and I'll look on helpless, and envy them. And thats what your son has brought me to. (He is overcome by emotion).

Mrs Higgins. Well, I'm very glad youre not going to do anything foolish, Mr Doolittle. For this solves the problem of Eliza's future. You can provide for her now.

Doolittle (with melancholy resignation) Yes, maam: I'm expected to provide for everyone now, out of [three] thousand a year.

Higgins (jumping up) Nonsense! he cant provide for her. He shant provide for her. She doesnt belong to him. I paid him five pounds for her. Doolittle: either youre an honest man or a rogue.

Doolittle (tolerantly) A little of both, Henry, like the rest of us: a little of both.

Higgins. Well, you took that money for the girl; and you have no right to take her as well.

---

1. **Skilly . . . Char Bydis:** Doolittle's distortion of Scylla (sĭl′ə) and Charybdis (kə-rĭb′dĭs), a dangerous rock and whirlpool on either side of a narrow strait between Sicily and Italy. The ancient Greeks personified them as two monsters, and they have come to symbolize two dangers between which it is almost impossible to steer a safe course.

Mrs Higgins. Henry: dont be absurd. If you want to know where Eliza is, she is upstairs.

Higgins (amazed) Upstairs!!! Then I shall jolly soon fetch her downstairs. (He makes resolutely for the door).

Mrs Higgins (rising and following him) Be quiet, Henry. Sit down.

Higgins. I——

Mrs Higgins. Sit down, dear; and listen to me.

Higgins. Oh very well, very well, very well. (He throws himself ungraciously on the ottoman, with his face towards the windows). But I think you might have told us this half an hour ago.

Mrs Higgins. Eliza came to me this morning. She told me of the brutal way you two treated her.

Higgins (bounding up again) What!

Pickering (rising also) My dear Mrs Higgins, she's been telling you stories. We didnt treat her brutally. We hardly said a word to her; and we parted on particularly good terms. (Turning on Higgins) Higgins: did you bully her after I went to bed?

Higgins. Just the other way about. She threw my slippers in my face. She behaved in the most outrageous way. I never gave her the slightest provocation. The slippers came bang into my face the moment I entered the room — before I had uttered a word. And used perfectly awful language.

Pickering (astonished) But why? What did we do to her?

Mrs Higgins. I think I know pretty well what you did. The girl is naturally rather affectionate, I think. Isnt she, Mr Doolittle?

Doolittle. Very tender-hearted, maam. Takes after me.

Mrs Higgins. Just so. She had become attached to you both. She worked very hard for you, Henry. I dont think you quite realize what anything in the nature of brain work means to a girl of her class. Well, it seems that when the great day of trial came, and she did this wonderful thing for you without making a single mistake, you two sat there and never said a word to her, but talked together of how glad you were that it was all over and how you had been bored with the whole thing. And then you were surprised because she threw your slippers at you! *I* should have thrown the fire-irons at you.

Higgins. We said nothing except that we were tired and wanted to go to bed. Did we, Pick?

Pickering (*shrugging his shoulders*) That was all.

Mrs Higgins (*ironically*) Quite sure?

Pickering. Absolutely. Really, that was all.

Mrs Higgins. You didnt thank her, or pet her, or admire her, or tell her how splendid she'd been.

Higgins (*impatiently*) But she knew all about that. We didnt make speeches to her, if thats what you mean.

Pickering (*conscience stricken*) Perhaps we were a little inconsiderate. Is she very angry?

Mrs Higgins (*returning to her place at the writing-table*) Well, I'm afraid she wont go back to Wimpole Street, especially now that Mr Doolittle is able to keep up the position you have thrust on her; but she says she is quite willing to meet you on friendly terms and to let bygones be bygones.

Higgins (*furious*) Is she, by George? Ho!

Mrs Higgins. If you promise to behave yourself, Henry, I'll ask her to come down. If not, go home; for you have taken up quite enough of my time.

Higgins. Oh, all right. Very well. Pick: you behave yourself. Let us put on our best Sunday manners for this creature that we picked out of the mud. (*He flings himself sulkily into the Elizabethan chair*).

Doolittle (*remonstrating*) Now, now, Enry Iggins! Have some consideration for my feelings as a middle class man.

Mrs Higgins. Remember your promise, Henry. (*She presses the bell-button on the writing-table*). Mr Doolittle: will you be so good as to step out on the balcony for a moment. I dont want Eliza to have the shock of your news until she has made it up with these two gentlemen. Would you mind?

Doolittle. As you wish, lady. Anything to help Henry to keep her off my hands. (*He disappears through the window*).

The Parlormaid *answers the bell.* Pickering *sits down in* Doolittle's *place.*

Mrs Higgins. Ask Miss Doolittle to come down, please.

The Parlormaid. Yes, maam. (*She goes out*).

Mrs Higgins. Now, Henry: be good.

Higgins. I am behaving myself perfectly.

Pickering. He is doing his best, Mrs Higgins.

A pause. Higgins *throws back his head; stretches out his legs; and begins to whistle.*

Mrs Higgins. Henry, dearest, you dont look at all nice in that attitude.

Higgins (*pulling himself together*) I was not trying to look nice, mother.

Mrs Higgins. It doesnt matter, dear. I only wanted to make you speak.

Higgins. Why?

Mrs Higgins. Because you cant speak and whistle at the same time.

Higgins *groans. Another very trying pause.*

Higgins (*springing up, out of patience*) Where the devil is that girl? Are we to wait here all day?

Eliza *enters, sunny, self-possessed, and giving a staggeringly convincing exhibition of ease of manner. She carries a little workbasket, and is very much at home.* Pickering *is too much taken aback to rise.*

Liza. How do you do, Professor Higgins? Are you quite well?

Higgins (*choking*) Am I— (*He can say no more*).

Liza. But of course you are: you are never ill. So glad to see you again, Colonel Pickering. (*He rises hastily; and they shake hands*). Quite chilly this morning, isnt it? (*She sits down on his left. He sits beside her*).

Higgins. Dont you dare try this game on me. I taught it to you; and it doesnt take me in. Get up and come home; and dont be a fool.

Higgins proclaims victory.
Penguin Photos

Eliza *takes a piece of needlework from her basket, and begins to stitch at it, without taking the least notice of this outburst.*

Mrs Higgins. Very nicely put, indeed, Henry. No woman could resist such an invitation.
Higgins. You let her alone, mother. Let her speak for herself. You will jolly soon see whether she has an idea that I havnt put into her head or a word that I havnt put into her mouth. I tell you I have created this thing out of the squashed cabbage leaves of Covent Garden; and now she pretends to play the fine lady with me.
Mrs Higgins (*placidly*) Yes, dear; but youll sit down, wont you?

Higgins *sits down again, savagely.*

Liza (*to* Pickering, *taking no apparent notice of* Higgins, *and working away deftly*) Will you drop me altogether now that the experiment is over, Colonel Pickering?

Pickering. Oh dont. You mustnt think of it as an experiment. It shocks me, somehow.
Liza. Oh, I'm only a squashed cabbage leaf——
Pickering (*impulsively*) No.
Liza (*continuing · quietly*)——but I owe so much to you that I should be very unhappy if you forgot me.
Pickering. It's very kind of you to say so, Miss Doolittle.
Liza. It's not because you paid for my dresses. I know you are generous to everybody with money. But it was from you that I learnt really nice manners; and that is what makes one a lady, isnt it? You see it was so very difficult for me with the example of Professor Higgins always before me. I was brought up to be just like him, unable to control myself, and using bad language on the slightest provocation. And I should never have known that ladies and gentlemen didnt behave like that if you hadnt been there.
Higgins. Well!!

Pickering. Oh, thats only his way, you know. He doesnt mean it.

Liza. Oh, *I* didnt mean it either, when I was a flower girl. It was only my way. But you see I did it; and thats what makes the difference after all.

Pickering. No doubt. Still, he taught you to speak; and I couldnt have done that, you know.

Liza (*trivially*) Of course: that is his profession.

Higgins. Damnation!

Liza (*continuing*) It was just like learning to dance in the fashionable way: there was nothing more than that in it. But do you know what began my real education?

Pickering. What?

Liza (*stopping her work for a moment*) Your calling me Miss Doolittle that day when I first came to Wimpole Street. That was the beginning of self-respect for me. (*She resumes her stitching*) And there were a hundred little things you never noticed, because they came naturally to you. Things about standing up and taking off your hat and opening doors —

Pickering. Oh, that was nothing.

Liza. Yes: things that shewed you thought and felt about me as if I were something better than a scullery-maid; though of course I know you would have been just the same to a scullery-maid if she had been let into the drawing room. You never took off your boots in the dining room when I was there.

Pickering. You mustnt mind that. Higgins takes off his boots all over the place.

Liza. I know. I am not blaming him. It is his way, isnt it? But it made such a difference to me that you didnt do it. You see, really and truly, apart from the things anyone can pick up (the dressing and the proper way of speaking, and so on), the difference between a lady and a flower girl is not how she behaves, but how she's treated. I shall always be a flower girl to Professor Higgins, because he always treats me as a flower girl, and always will; but I know I can be a lady to you, because you always treat me as a lady, and always will.

Mrs Higgins. Please dont grind your teeth, Henry.

Pickering. Well, this is really very nice of you, Miss Doolittle.

Liza. I should like you to call me Eliza, now, if you would.

Pickering. Thank you. Eliza, of course.

Liza. And I should like Professor Higgins to call me Miss Doolittle.

Higgins. I'll see you damned first.

Mrs Higgins. Henry! Henry!

Pickering (*laughing*) Why dont you slang back at him? Dont stand it. It would do him a lot of good.

Liza. I cant. I could have done it once; but now I cant go back to it. You told me, you know, that when a child is brought to a foreign country, it picks up the language in a few weeks, and forgets its own. Well, I am a child in your country. I have forgotten my own language, and can speak nothing but yours. Thats the real break-off with the corner of Tottenham Court Road. Leaving Wimpole Street finishes it.

Pickering (*much alarmed*) Oh! but youre coming back to Wimpole Street, arnt you? Youll forgive Higgins?

Higgins (*rising*) Forgive! Will she, by George! Let her go. Let her find out how she can get on without us. She will relapse into the gutter in three weeks without me at her elbow.

Doolittle *appears at the centre window. With a look of dignified reproach at* Higgins, *he comes slowly and silently to his daughter, who, with her back to the window, is unconscious of his approach.*

Pickering. He's incorrigible, Eliza. You wont relapse, will you?

Liza. No: not now. Never again. I have learnt my lesson. I dont believe I could utter one of the old sounds if I tried. (Doolittle *touches her on the left shoulder. She drops her work, losing her self-possession utterly at the spectacle* *of her father's splendor*) A-a-a-a-ah-ow-ooh!

Higgins (*with a crow of triumph*) Aha! Just so. A-a-a-a-ahowooh! A-a-a-a-ahowooh! A-a-a-a-ahowooh! Victory! Victory! (*He throws himself on the divan, folding his arms, and spraddling arrogantly*).

Doolittle. Can you blame the girl? Dont look at me like that, Eliza. It aint my fault. Ive come into some money.

Liza. You must have touched a millionaire this time, dad.

Doolittle. I have. But I'm dressed something special today. I'm going to St George's, Hanover Square. Your stepmother is going to marry me.

Liza (*angrily*) Youre going to let yourself down to marry that low common woman!

Pickering (*quietly*) He ought to, Eliza. (*To* Doolittle) Why has she changed her mind?

Doolittle (*sadly*) Intimidated, Governor. Intimidated. Middle class morality claims its victim. Wont you put on your hat, Liza, and come and see me turned off?

Liza. If the Colonel says I must, I—I'll (*almost sobbing*) I'll demean myself. And get insulted for my pains, like enough.

Doolittle. Dont be afraid: she never comes to words with anyone now, poor woman! respectability has broke all the spirit out of her.

Pickering (*squeezing* Eliza's *elbow gently*) Be kind to them, Eliza. Make the best of it.

Liza (*forcing a little smile for him through her vexation*) Oh well, just to shew theres no ill feeling. I'll be back in a moment. (*She goes out*).

Doolittle (*sitting down beside* Pickering) I feel uncommon nervous about the ceremony, Colonel. I wish youd come and see me through it.

Pickering. But youve been through it before, man. You were married to Eliza's mother.

Doolittle. Who told you that, Colonel?

Pickering. Well, nobody told me. But I concluded—naturally—

Doolittle. No: that aint the natural way, Colonel: it's only the middle class way. My way was always the undeserving way. But

dont say nothing to Eliza. She dont know: I always had a delicacy about telling her.

Pickering. Quite right. We'll leave it so, if you dont mind.

Doolittle. And youll come to the church, Colonel, and put me through straight?

Pickering. With pleasure. As far as a bachelor can.

Mrs Higgins. May I come, Mr Doolittle? I should be very sorry to miss your wedding.

Doolittle. I should indeed be honored by your condescension, maam; and my poor old woman would take it as a tremenjous compliment. She's been very low, thinking of the happy days that are no more.

Mrs Higgins (*rising*) I'll order the carriage and get ready. (*The men rise, except* Higgins). I shant be more than fifteen minutes. (*As she goes to the door* Eliza *comes in, hatted and buttoning her gloves*). I'm going to the church to see your father married, Eliza. You had better come in the brougham[2] with me. Colonel Pickering can go on with the bridegroom.

Mrs Higgins *goes out.* Eliza *comes to the middle of the room between the centre window and the ottoman.* Pickering *joins her.*

Doolittle. Bridegroom. What a word! It makes a man realize his position, somehow. (*He takes up his hat and goes towards the door*).

Pickering. Before I go, Eliza, do forgive Higgins and come back to us.

Liza. I dont think dad would allow me. Would you, dad?

Doolittle (*sad but magnanimous*) They played you off very cunning, Eliza, them two sportsmen. If it had been only one of them, you could have nailed him. But you see, there was two; and one of them chaperoned the other, as you might say. (*To* Pickering) It was artful of you, Colonel; but I bear no malice: I should have done the same myself. I been the victim

---

2. **brougham** (broom): a four-wheeled carriage.

of one woman after another all my life, and I dont grudge you two getting the better of Liza. I shant interfere. It's time for us to go, Colonel. So long, Henry. See you in St George's, Eliza. (*He goes out*).

Pickering (*coaxing*) Do stay with us, Eliza. (*He follows Doolittle*).

Eliza *goes out on the balcony to avoid being alone with* Higgins. *He rises and joins her there. She immediately comes back into the room and makes for the door; but he goes along the balcony and gets his back to the door before she reaches it.*

Higgins. Well, Eliza, youve had a bit of your own back, as you call it. Have you had enough? and are you going to be reasonable? Or do you want any more?

Liza. You want me back only to pick up your slippers and put up with your tempers and fetch and carry for you.

Higgins. I havnt said I wanted you back at all.

Liza. Oh, indeed. Then what are we talking about?

Higgins. About you, not about me. If you come back I shall treat you just as I have always treated you. I cant change my nature; and I dont intend to change my manners. My manners are exactly the same as Colonel Pickering's.

Liza. Thats not true. He treats a flower girl as if she was a duchess.

Higgins. And I treat a duchess as if she was a flower girl.

Liza. I see (*She turns away composedly, and sits on the ottoman, facing the window*). The same to everybody.

Higgins. Just so.

Liza. Like father.

Higgins (*grinning, a little taken down*) Without accepting the comparison at all points, Eliza, it's quite true that your father is not a snob, and that he will be quite at home in any station of life to which his eccentric destiny may call him. (*Seriously*) The great secret, Eliza, is not having bad manners or good manners or any other particular sort of manners,

but having the same manner for all human souls: in short, behaving as if you were in Heaven, where there are no third-class carriages, and one soul is as good as another.

Liza. Amen. You are a born preacher.

Higgins (*irritated*) The question is not whether I treat you rudely, but whether you ever heard me treat anyone else better.

Liza (*with sudden sincerity*) I dont care how you treat me. I dont mind your swearing at me. I shouldnt mind a black eye: Ive had one before this. But (*standing up and facing him*) I wont be passed over.

Higgins. Then get out of my way; for I wont stop for you. You talk about me as if I were a motor bus.

Liza. So you are a motor bus: all bounce and go, and no consideration for anyone. But I can do without you: dont think I cant.

Higgins. I know you can. I told you you could.

Liza (*wounded, getting away from him to the other side of the ottoman with her face to the hearth*) I know you did, you brute. You wanted to get rid of me.

Higgins. Liar.

Liza. Thank you. (*She sits down with dignity*)

Higgins. You never asked yourself, I suppose, whether *I* could do without you.

Liza (*earnestly*) Dont you try to get round me. Youll have to do without me.

Higgins (*arrogant*) I can do without anybody. I have my own soul: my own spark of divine fire. But (*with sudden humility*) I shall miss you, Eliza. (*He sits down near her on the ottoman*) I have learnt something from your idiotic notions: I confess that humbly and gratefully. And I have grown accustomed to your voice and appearance. I like them, rather.

Liza. Well, you have both of them on your gramophone and in your book of photographs. When you feel lonely without me, you can turn the machine on. It's got no feelings to hurt.

Higgins. I cant turn your soul on. Leave me those feelings; and you can take away the voice and the face. They are not you.

Liza. Oh, you are a devil. You can twist the

heart in a girl as easy as some could twist her arms to hurt her. Mrs Pearce warned me. Time and again she has wanted to leave you; and you always got round her at the last minute. And you dont care a bit for her. And you dont care a bit for me.

Higgins. I care for life, for humanity; and you are a part of it that has come my way and been built into my house. What more can you or anyone ask?

Liza. I wont care for anybody that doesnt care for me.

Higgins. Commercial principles, Eliza. Like (*reproducing her Covent Garden pronunciation with professional exactness*) s'yollin voylets [selling violets], isnt it?

Liza. Dont sneer at me. It's mean to sneer at me.

Higgins. I have never sneered in my life. Sneering doesnt become either the human face or the human soul. I am expressing my righteous contempt for Commercialism. I dont and wont trade in affection. You call me a brute because you couldnt buy a claim on me by fetching my slippers and finding my spectacles. You were a fool: I think a woman fetching a man's slippers is a disgusting sight: did I ever fetch your slippers? I think a good deal more of you for throwing them in my face. No use slaving for me and then saying you want to be cared for: who cares for a slave? If you come back, come back for the sake of good fellowship; for youll get nothing else. Youve had a thousand times as much out of me as I have out of you; and if you dare to set up your little dog's tricks of fetching and carrying slippers against my creation of a Duchess Eliza, I'll slam the door in your silly face.

Liza. What did you do it for if you didnt care for me?

Higgins (*heartily*) Why, because it was my job.

Liza. You never thought of the trouble it would make for me.

Higgins. Would the world ever have been made if its maker had been afraid of making trouble? Making life means making trouble. Theres only one way of escaping trouble; and thats killing things. Cowards, you notice, are always shrieking to have troublesome people killed.

Liza. I'm no preacher: I dont notice things like that. I notice that you dont notice me.

Higgins (*jumping up and walking about intolerantly*) Eliza: youre an idiot. I waste the treasures of my Miltonic mind by spreading them before you. Once for all, understand that I go my way and do my work without caring twopence what happens to either of us. I am not intimidated, like your father and your stepmother. So you can come back or go to the devil: which you please.

Liza. What am I to come back for?

Higgins (*bouncing up on his knees on the ottoman and leaning over it to her*) For the fun of it. Thats why I took you on.

Liza (*with averted face*) And you may throw me out tomorrow if I dont do everything you want me to?

Higgins. Yes; and you may walk out tomorrow if I dont do everything you want me to.

Liza. And live with my stepmother?

Higgins. Yes, or sell flowers.

Liza. Oh, if I only could go back to my flower basket! I should be independent of both you and father and all the world! Why did you take my independence from me? Why did I give it up? I'm a slave now, for all my fine clothes.

Higgins. Not a bit. I'll adopt you as my daughter and settle money on you if you like. Or would you rather marry Pickering?

Liza (*looking fiercely round at him*) I wouldnt marry you if you asked me; and youre nearer my age than what he is.

Higgins (*gently*) Than he is: not "than what he is."

Liza (*losing her temper and rising*) I'll talk as I like. Youre not my teacher now.

Higgins (*reflectively*) I dont suppose Pickering would, though. He's as confirmed an old bachelor as I am.

Liza. Thats not what I want; and dont you think it. I've always had chaps enough wanting me that way. Freddy Hill writes to me twice and three times a day, sheets and sheets.

Higgins (*disagreeably surprised*) Damn his impudence! (*He recoils and finds himself sitting on his heels*).

Liza. He has a right to if he likes, poor lad. And he does love me.

Higgins (*getting off the ottoman*) You have no right to encourage him.

Liza. Every girl has a right to be loved.

Higgins. What! By fools like that?

Liza. Freddy's not a fool. And if he's weak and poor and wants me, may be he'd make me happier than my betters that bully me and dont want me.

Higgins. Can he make anything of you? Thats the point.

Liza. Perhaps I could make something of him. But I never thought of us making anything of one another; and you never think of anything else. I only want to be natural.

Higgins. In short, you want me to be as infatuated about you as Freddy? Is that it?

Liza. No I dont. Thats not the sort of feeling I want from you. And dont you be too sure of yourself or of me. I could have been a bad girl if I'd liked. Ive seen more of some things than you, for all your learning. Girls like me can drag gentlemen down to make love to them easy enough. And they wish each other dead the next minute.

Higgins. Of course they do. Then what in thunder are we quarrelling about?

Liza (*much troubled*) I want a little kindness. I know I'm a common ignorant girl, and you a book-learned gentleman; but I'm not dirt under your feet. What I done (*correcting herself*) what I did was not for the dresses and the taxis: I did it because we were pleasant together and I come—came—to care for you; not to want you to make love to me, and not forgetting the difference between us, but more friendly like.

Higgins. Well, of course. Thats just how I feel. And how Pickering feels. Eliza: youre a fool.

Liza. Thats not a proper answer to give me

(*she sinks on the chair at the writing-table in tears*).

Higgins. It's all youll get until you stop being a common idiot. If youre going to be a lady, youll have to give up feeling neglected if the men you know dont spend half their time snivelling over you and the other half giving you black eyes. If you cant stand the coldness of my sort of life, and the strain of it, go back to the gutter. Work til youre more a brute than a human being; and then cuddle and squabble and drink til you fall asleep. Oh, it's a fine life, the life of the gutter. It's real: it's warm: it's violent: you can feel it through the thickest skin: you can taste it and smell it without any training or any work. Not like Science and Literature and Classical Music and Philosophy and Art. You find me cold, unfeeling, selfish, dont you? Very well: be off with you to the sort of people you like. Marry some sentimental hog or other with lots of money, and a thick pair of lips to kiss you with and a thick pair of boots to kick you with. If you cant appreciate what youve got, youd better get what you can appreciate.

Liza (*desperate*) Oh, you are a cruel tyrant. I cant talk to you: you turn everything against me: I'm always in the wrong. But you know very well all the time that youre nothing but a bully. You know I cant go back to the gutter, as you call it, and that I have no real friends in the world but you and the Colonel. You know well I couldnt bear to live with a low common man after you two; and it's wicked and cruel of you to insult me by pretending I could. You think I must go back to Wimpole Street because I have nowhere else to go but father's. But dont you be too sure that you have me under your feet to be trampled on and talked down. I'll marry Freddy, I will, as soon as I'm able to support him.

Higgins (*thunderstruck*) Freddy!!! that young fool! That poor devil who couldnt get a job as an errand boy even if he had the guts to try for it! Woman: do you not understand that I have made you a consort for a king?

Liza. Freddy loves me: that makes him king

enough for me. I dont want him to work: he wasnt brought up to it as I was. I'll go and be a teacher.

Higgins. Whatll you teach, in heaven's name?

Liza. What you taught me. I'll teach phonetics.

Higgins. Ha! ha! ha!

Liza. I'll offer myself as an assistant to that hairyfaced Hungarian.

Higgins (*rising in a fury*) What! That imposter! that humbug! that toadying ignoramus! Teach him my methods! my discoveries! You take one step in his direction and I'll wring your neck. (*He lays hands on her*). Do you hear?

Liza (*defiantly non-resistant*) Wring away. What do I care? I knew youd strike me some day. (*He lets her go, stamping with rage at having forgotten himself, and recoils so hastily that he stumbles back into his seat on the ottoman*). Aha! Now I know how to deal with you. What a fool I was not to think of it before! You cant take away the knowledge you gave me. You said I had a finer ear than you. And I can be civil and kind to people, which is more than you can. Aha! (*Purposely dropping her aitches to annoy him*) Thats done you, Enry Iggins, it az. Now I dont care that (*snapping her fingers*) for your bullying and your big talk. I'll advertize it in the papers that your duchess is only a flower girl that you taught, and that she'll teach anybody to be a duchess just the same in six months for a thousand guineas. Oh, when I think of myself crawling under your feet and being trampled on and called names, when all the time I had only to lift up my finger to be as good as you, I could just kick myself.

Higgins (*wondering at her*) You damned impudent slut, you! But it's better than snivelling; better than fetching slippers and finding spectacles, isnt it? (*Rising*) By George, Eliza. I said I'd make a woman of you; and I have. I like you like this.

Liza. Yes: you turn round and make up to me now that I'm not afraid of you, and can do without you.

Higgins. Of course I do, you little fool. Five minutes ago you were like a millstone round my neck. Now youre a tower of strength: a consort battleship. You and I and Pickering will be three old bachelors instead of only two men and a silly girl.

Mrs Higgins *returns, dressed for the wedding.* Eliza *instantly becomes cool and elegant.*

Mrs Higgins. The carriage is waiting, Eliza. Are you ready?

Liza. Quite. Is the Professor coming?

Mrs Higgins. Certainly not. He cant behave himself in church. He makes remarks out loud all the time on the clergyman's pronunciation.

Liza. Then I shall not see you again, Professor. Goodbye. (*She goes to the door*).

Mrs Higgins (*coming to* Higgins) Goodbye, dear.

Higgins. Goodbye, mother. (*He is about to kiss her, when he recollects something*). Oh, by the way, Eliza, order a ham and a Stilton cheese, will you? And buy me a pair of reindeer gloves, number eights, and a tie to match that new suit of mine. You can choose the color. (*His cheerful, careless, vigorous voice shews that he is incorrigible*).

Liza (*disdainfully*) Number eights are too small for you if you want them lined with lamb's wool. You have three new ties that you have forgotten in the drawer of your washstand. Colonel Pickering prefers double Gloucester to Stilton; and you dont notice the difference. I telephoned Mrs Pearce this morning not to forget the ham. What you are to do without me I cannot imagine. (*She sweeps out*).

Mrs Higgins. I'm afraid youve spoilt that girl, Henry. I should be uneasy about you and her if she were less fond of Colonel Pickering.

Higgins. Pickering! Nonsense: she's going to marry Freddy. Ha ha! Freddy! Freddy!! Ha ha ha ha ha!!!!! (*He roars with laughter as the play ends*).

Epilogue

The rest of the story need not be shewn in action, and indeed, would hardly need telling if our imaginations were not so enfeebled by their lazy dependence on the ready-mades and reach-me-downs of the ragshop in which Romance keeps its stock of "happy endings" to misfit all stories. Now, the history of Eliza Doolittle, though called a romance because the transfiguration it records seems exceedingly improbable, is common enough. Such transfigurations have been achieved by hundreds of resolutely ambitious young women since Nell Gwynne[1] set them the example by playing queens and fascinating kings in the theatre in which she began by selling oranges. Nevertheless, people in all directions have assumed, for no other reason than that she became the heroine of a romance, that she must have married the hero of it. This is unbearable, not only because her little drama, if acted on such a thoughtless assumption, must be spoiled, but because the true sequel is patent to anyone with a sense of human nature in general, and of feminine instinct in particular.

Eliza, in telling Higgins she would not marry him if he asked her, was not coquetting: she was announcing a well-considered decision. When a bachelor interests, and dominates, and teaches, and becomes important to a spinster, as Higgins with Eliza, she always, if she has character enough to be capable of it, considers very seriously indeed whether she will play for becoming that bachelor's wife, especially if he is so little interested in marriage that a determined and devoted woman might capture him if she set herself resolutely to do it. Her decision will depend a good deal on whether she is really free to choose; and that, again, will depend on her age and income. If she is at the end of her youth, and has no security for her livelihood, she will marry him because she must marry anybody who will provide for her. But at Eliza's age a good-looking girl does not feel that pressure: she feels free to pick and choose. She is therefore guided by her instinct in the matter. Eliza's instinct tells her not to marry Higgins. It does not tell her to give him up. It is not in the slightest doubt as to his remaining one of the strongest personal interests in her life. It would be very sorely strained if there was another woman likely to supplant her with him. But as she feels sure of him on that last point, she has no doubt at all as to her course, and would not have any, even if the difference of twenty years in age, which seems so great to youth, did not exist between them.

As our own instincts are not appealed to by her conclusion, let us see whether we cannot discover some reason in it. When Higgins excused his indifference to young women on the ground that they had an irresistible rival in his mother, he gave the clue to his inveterate old-bachelordom. The case is uncommon only to the extent that remarkable mothers are uncommon. If an imaginative boy has a sufficiently rich mother who has intelligence, personal grace, dignity of character without harshness, and a cultivated sense of the best art of her time to enable her to make her house beautiful, she sets a standard for him against which very few women can struggle, besides effecting for him a disengagement of his affections, his sense of beauty, and his idealism from his specifically sexual impulses. This makes him a standing puzzle to the huge number of uncultivated people who have been brought up in tasteless homes by commonplace or disagreeable parents, and to whom, consequently, literature, painting, sculpture, music, and affectionate personal relations come as modes of sex if they come at all. The word passion means nothing else to them; and that Higgins could have a passion for phonetics and idealize his mother instead of Eliza, would seem to them absurd and unnatural. Nevertheless, when we look round and see that hardly anyone is too ugly or disagreeable to find a wife or a husband if he or she wants one, whilst many old maids and bachelors are above the average in quality and culture, we cannot help suspecting that the disentanglement of sex from the associations with which it is so commonly confused, a disentanglement which persons of genius achieve by sheer intellectual analysis, is sometimes produced or aided by parental fascination.

Now, though Eliza was incapable of thus explaining to herself Higgins's formidable powers of resistance to the charm that prostrated Freddy at the first glance, she was instinctively aware that she could never obtain a complete grip of him, or come between him and his mother (the first necessity of the married woman). To put it shortly, she

---

1. **Nell Gwynne:** Eleanor Gwynne or Gwyn (1650–1687), an English actress who became the favorite of Charles II.

knew that for some mysterious reason he had not the makings of a married man in him, according to her conception of a husband as one to whom she would be his nearest and fondest and warmest interest. Even had there been no mother-rival, she would still have refused to accept an interest in herself that was secondary to philosophic interests. Had Mrs Higgins died, there would still have been Milton and the Universal Alphabet. Landor's[2] remark that to those who have the greatest power of loving, love is a secondary affair, would not have recommended Landor to Eliza. Put that along with her resentment of Higgins's domineering superiority, and her mistrust of his coaxing cleverness in getting round her and evading her wrath when he had gone too far with his impetuous bullying, and you will see that Eliza's instinct had good grounds for warning her not to marry her Pygmalion.

And now, whom did Eliza marry? For if Higgins was a predestinate old bachelor, she was most certainly not a predestinate old maid. Well, that can be told very shortly to those who have not guessed it from the indications she has herself given them.

Almost immediately after Eliza is stung into proclaiming her considered determination not to marry Higgins, she mentions the fact that young Mr Frederick Eynsford Hill is pouring out his love for her daily through the post. Now Freddy is young, practically twenty years younger than Higgins: he is a gentleman (or, as Eliza would qualify him, a toff), and speaks like one. He is nicely dressed, is treated by the Colonel as an equal, loves her unaffectedly, and is not her master, nor ever likely to dominate her in spite of his advantage of social standing. Eliza has no use for the foolish romantic tradition that all women love to be mastered, if not actually bullied and beaten. "When you go to women" says Nietzsche[3] "take your whip with you." Sensible despots have never confined that precaution to women: they have taken their whips with them when they have dealt with men, and been slavishly idealized by the men over whom they have flourished the whip much more than by women. No doubt there are slavish women as well as slavish men; and women, like men, ad-

mire those that are stronger than themselves. But to admire a strong person and to live under that strong person's thumb are two different things. The weak may not be admired and hero-worshipped; but they are by no means disliked or shunned; and they never seem to have the least difficulty in marrying people who are too good for them. They may fail in emergencies; but life is not one long emergency: it is mostly a string of situations for which no exceptional strength is needed, and with which even rather weak people can cope if they have a stronger partner to help them out. Accordingly, it is a truth everywhere in evidence that strong people, masculine or feminine, not only do not marry stronger people, but do not shew any preference for them in selecting their friends. When a lion meets another with a louder roar "the first lion thinks the last a bore." The man or woman who feels strong enough for two, seeks for every other quality in a partner than strength.

The converse is also true. Weak people want to marry strong people who do not frighten them too much; and this often leads them to make the mistake we describe metaphorically as "biting off more than they can chew." They want too much for too little; and when the bargain is unreasonable beyond all bearing, the union becomes impossible: it ends in the weaker party being either discarded or borne as a cross, which is worse. People who are not only weak, but silly or obtuse as well, are often in these difficulties.

This being the state of human affairs, what is Eliza fairly sure to do when she is placed between Freddy and Higgins? Will she look forward to a lifetime of fetching Higgins's slippers or to a lifetime of Freddy fetching hers? There can be no doubt about the answer. Unless Freddy is biologically repulsive to her, and Higgins biologically attractive to a degree that overwhelms all her other instincts, she will, if she marries either of them, marry Freddy.

And that is just what Eliza did.

Complications ensued; but they were economic, not romantic. Freddy had no money and no occupation. His mother's jointure, a last relic of the opulence of Largelady Park, had enabled her to struggle along in Earlscourt with an air of gentility, but not to procure any serious secondary education for her children, much less give the boy a profession. A clerkship at thirty shillings a week was beneath Freddy's dignity, and extremely distasteful to him

---

2. **Landor:** Walter Savage Landor (1775–1864), an English writer.
3. **Nietzsche** (nē′chə, -chē): Friedrich Wilhelm Nietzsche (1844–1900), German philosopher.

besides. His prospects consisted of a hope that if he kept up appearances somebody would do something for him. The something appeared vaguely to his imagination as a private secretaryship or a sinecure of some sort. To his mother it perhaps appeared as a marriage to some lady of means who could not resist her boy's niceness. Fancy her feelings when he married a flower girl who had become disclassed under extraordinary circumstances which were now notorious!

It is true that Eliza's situation did not seem wholly ineligible. Her father, though formerly a dustman, and now fantastically disclassed, had become extremely popular in the smartest society by a social talent which triumphed over every prejudice and every disadvantage. Rejected by the middle class, which he loathed, he had shot up at once into the highest circles by his wit, his dustmanship (which he carried like a banner), and his Nietzschean transcendence of good and evil. At intimate ducal dinners he sat on the right hand of the Duchess; and in country houses he smoked in the pantry and was made much of by the butler when he was not feeding in the dining room and being consulted by cabinet ministers. But he found it almost as hard to do all this on [three] thousand a year as Mrs Eynsford Hill to live in Earlscourt on an income so pitiably smaller that I have not the heart to disclose its exact figure. He absolutely refused to add the last straw to his burden by contributing to Eliza's support.

Thus Freddy and Eliza, now Mr and Mrs Eynsford Hill, would have spent a penniless honeymoon but for a wedding present of £500 from the Colonel to Eliza. It lasted a long time because Freddy did not know how to spend money, never having had any to spend, and Eliza, socially trained by a pair of old bachelors, wore her clothes as long as they held together and looked pretty, without the least regard to their being many months out of fashion. Still, £500 will not last two young people for ever; and they both knew, and Eliza felt as well, that they must shift for themselves in the end. She could quarter herself on Wimpole Street because it had come to be her home; but she was quite aware that she ought not to quarter Freddy there, and that it would not be good for his character if she did.

Not that the Wimpole Street bachelors objected. When she consulted them, Higgins declined to be bothered about her housing problem when that solution was so simple. Eliza's desire to have Freddy in the house with her seemed of no more importance than if she had wanted an extra piece of bedroom furniture. Pleas as to Freddy's character, and the moral obligation on him to earn his own living, were lost on Higgins. He denied that Freddy had any character, and declared that if he tried to do any useful work some competent person would have the trouble of undoing it: a procedure involving a net loss to the community, and great unhappiness to Freddy himself, who was obviously intended by Nature for such light work as amusing Eliza, which, Higgins declared, was a much more useful and honorable occupation than working in the city. When Eliza referred again to her project of teaching phonetics, Higgins abated not a jot of his violent opposition to it. He said she was not within ten years of being qualified to meddle with his pet subject; and as it was evident that the Colonel agreed with him, she felt she could not go against them in this grave matter, and that she had no right, without Higgins's consent, to exploit the knowledge he had given her; for his knowledge seemed to her as much his private property as his watch: Eliza was no communist. Besides, she was superstitiously devoted to them, both, more entirely and frankly after her marriage than before it.

It was the Colonel who finally solved the problem, which had cost him much perplexed cogitation. He one day asked Eliza, rather shyly, whether she had quite given up her notion of keeping a flower shop. She replied that she had thought of it, but had put it out of her head, because the Colonel had said, that day at Mrs Higgins's, that it would never do. The Colonel confessed that when he said that, he had not quite recovered from the dazzling impression of the day before. They broke the matter to Higgins that evening. The sole comment vouchsafed by him very nearly led to a serious quarrel with Eliza. It was to the effect that she would have in Freddy an ideal errand boy.

Freddy himself was next sounded on the subject. He said he had been thinking of a shop himself; though it had presented itself to his pennilessness as a small place in which Eliza should sell tobacco at one counter whilst he sold newspapers at the opposite one. But he agreed that it would be extraordinarily jolly to go early every morning with Eliza, to Covent Garden and buy flowers on the scene of their first meeting: a sentiment which earned him many kisses from his wife. He added that he had always been afraid to propose anything of the sort, because Clara would make an awful row about a step that must damage her matrimonial chances, and his mother could not be expected to like it after clinging for so many years to that step of the social ladder on which retail trade is impossible.

This difficulty was removed by an event highly unexpected by Freddy's mother. Clara, in the course of her incursions into those artistic circles which were the highest within her reach, discovered that her conversational qualifications were expected to include a grounding in the novels of Mr H. G. Wells. She borrowed them in various directions so energetically that she swallowed them all within two months. The result was a conversion of a kind quite common today. A modern Acts of the Apostles would fill fifty whole Bibles if anyone were capable of writing it.

Poor Clara, who appeared to Higgins and his mother as a disagreeable and ridiculous person, and to her own mother as in some inexplicable way a social failure, had never seen herself in either light; for, though to some extent ridiculed and mimicked in West Kensington like everybody else there, she was accepted as a rational and normal—or shall we say inevitable?—sort of human being. At worst they called her The Pusher; but to them no more than to herself had it ever occurred that she was pushing the air, and pushing it in a wrong direction. Still, she was not happy. She was growing desperate. Her one asset, the fact that her mother was what the Epsom greengrocer called a carriage lady, had no exchange value, apparently. It had prevented her from getting educated, because the only education she could have afforded was education with the Earlscourt greengrocer's daughter. It had led her to seek the society of her mother's class; and that class simply would not have her, because she was much poorer than the greengrocer, and, far from being able to afford a maid, could not afford even a housemaid, and had to scrape along at home with an illiberally treated general servant. Under such circumstances nothing could give her an air of being a genuine product of Largelady Park. And yet its tradition made her regard a marriage with anyone within her reach as an unbearable humiliation. Commercial people and professional people in a small way were odious to her. She ran after painters and novelists; but she did not charm them; and her bold attempts to pick up and practise artistic and literary talk irritated them. She was, in short, an utter failure, an ignorant, incompetent, pretentious, unwelcome, penniless, useless little snob; and though she did not admit these disqualifications (for nobody ever faces unpleasant truths of this kind until the possibility of a way out dawns on them) she felt their effects too keenly to be satisfied with her position.

Clara had a startling eyeopener when, on being suddenly wakened to enthusiasm by a girl of her own age who dazzled her and produced in her a gushing desire to take her for a model, and gain her friendship, she discovered that this exquisite apparition had graduated from the gutter in a few months time. It shook her so violently, that when Mr H. G. Wells lifted her on the point of his puissant pen, and placed her at the angle of view from which the life she was leading and the society to which she clung appeared in its true relation to real human needs and worthy social structure, he effected a conversion and a conviction of sin comparable to the most sensational feats of General Booth[4] or Gypsy Smith. Clara's snobbery went bang. Life suddenly began to move with her. Without knowing how or why, she began to make friends and enemies. Some of the acquaintances to whom she had been a tedious or indifferent or ridiculous affliction, dropped her: others became cordial. To her amazement she found that some "quite nice" people were saturated with Wells, and that this accessibility to ideas was the secret of their niceness. People she had thought deeply religious, and had tried to conciliate on that tack with disastrous results, suddenly took an interest in her, and revealed a hostility to conventional religion which she had never conceived possible except among the most desperate characters. They made her read Galsworthy; and Galsworthy exposed the vanity of Largelady Park and finished her. It exasperated her to think that the dungeon in which she had languished for so many unhappy years had been unlocked all the time, and that the impulses she had so carefully struggled with and stifled for the sake of keeping well with society, were precisely those by which alone she could have come into any sort of sincere human contact. In the radiance of these discoveries, and the tumult of their reaction, she made a fool of herself as freely and conspicuously as when she so rashly adopted Eliza's expletive in Mrs Higgins's drawing room;

---

4. **General Booth:** the evangelist William Booth (1829–1912), who founded the Salvation Army.

for the new-born Wellsian had to find her bearings almost as ridiculously as a baby; but nobody hates a baby for its ineptitudes, or thinks the worse of it for trying to eat the matches; and Clara lost no friends by her follies. They laughed at her to her face this time; and she had to defend herself and fight it out as best she could.

When Freddy paid a visit to Earlscourt (which he never did when he could possibly help it) to make the desolating announcement that he and his Eliza were thinking of blackening the Largelady scutcheon by opening a shop, he found the little household already convulsed by a prior announcement from Clara that she also was going to work in an old furniture shop in Dover Street, which had been started by a fellow Wellsian. This appointment Clara owed, after all, to her old social accomplishment of Push. She had made up her mind that, cost what it might, she would see Mr Wells in the flesh; and she had achieved her end at a garden party. She had better luck than so rash an enterprise deserved. Mr Wells came up to her expectations. Age had not withered him, nor could custom stale his infinite variety in half an hour. His pleasant neatness and compactness, his small hands and feet, his teeming ready brain, his unaffected accessibility, and a certain fine apprehensiveness which stamped him as susceptible from his topmost hair to his tipmost toe, proved irresistible. Clara talked of nothing else for weeks and weeks afterwards. And as she happened to talk to the lady of the furniture shop, and that lady also desired above all things to know Mr Wells and sell pretty things to him, she offered Clara a job on the chance of achieving that end through her.

And so it came about that Eliza's luck held, and the expected opposition to the flower shop melted away. The shop is in the arcade of a railway station not very far from the Victoria and Albert Museum; and if you live in that neighbourhood you may go there any day and buy a buttonhole from Eliza.

Now here is a last opportunity for romance. Would you not like to be assured that the shop was an immense success, thanks to Eliza's charms and her early business experience in Covent Garden? Alas! the truth is the truth: the shop did not pay for a long time, simply because Eliza and her Freddy did not know how to keep it. True, Eliza had not to begin at the very beginning: she knew the names and prices of the cheaper flowers; and her elation was unbounded when she found that Freddy, like

all youths educated at cheap, pretentious, and thoroughly inefficient schools, knew a little Latin. It was very little, but enough to make him appear to her a Porson or Bentley, and to put him at his ease with botanical nomenclature. Unfortunately he knew nothing else; and Eliza, though she could count money up to eighteen shillings or so, and had acquired a certain familiarity with the language of Milton from her struggles to qualify herself for winning Higgins's bet, could not write out a bill without utterly disgracing the establishment. Freddy's power of stating in Latin and Balbus built a wall and that Gaul was divided into three parts did not carry with it the slightest knowledge of accounts or business: Colonel Pickering had to explain to him what a cheque book and a bank account meant. And the pair were by no means easily teachable. Freddy backed up Eliza in her obstinate refusal to believe that they could save money by engaging a bookkeeper with some knowledge of the business. How, they argued, could you possibly save money by going to extra expense when you already could not make both ends meet? But the Colonel, after making the ends meet over and over again, at last gently insisted; and Eliza, humbled to the dust by having to beg from him so often, and stung by the uproarious derision of Higgins, to whom the notion of Freddy succeeding at anything was a joke that never palled, grasped the fact that business, like phonetics, has to be learned.

On the piteous spectacle of the pair spending their evenings in shorthand schools and polytechnic classes, learning bookkeeping and typewriting with incipient junior clerks, male and female, from the elementary schools, let me not dwell. There were even classes at the London School of Economics, and a humble personal appeal to the director of that institution to recommend a course bearing on the flower business. He, being a humorist, explained to them the method of the celebrated Dickensian essay on Chinese Metaphysics by the gentleman who read an article on China and an article on Metaphysics and combined the information. He suggested that they should combine the London School with Kew Gardens. Eliza, to whom the procedure of the Dickensian gentleman seemed perfectly correct (as in fact it was) and not in the least funny (which was only her ignorance), took the advice with entire gravity. But the effort that cost her the deepest humiliation was a request to Higgins, whose pet artistic fancy, next to Milton's verse, was calligraphy, and who himself wrote a most beautiful Italian hand, that he would teach her to write. He declared that she was congenitally incapable of forming a single letter worthy of the least of Milton's words; but she persisted; and again he suddenly threw himself into the task of teaching her with a combination of stormy intensity, concentrated patience, and occasional bursts of interesting disquisition on the beauty and nobility, the august mission and destiny, of human handwriting. Eliza ended by acquiring an extremely uncommercial script which was a positive extension of her personal beauty, and spending three times as much on stationery as anyone else because certain qualities and shapes on paper became indispensable to her. She could not even address an envelope in the usual way because it made the margins all wrong.

Their commercial schooldays were a period of disgrace and despair for the young couple. They seemed to be learning nothing about flower shops. At last they gave it up as hopeless, and shook the dust of the shorthand schools, and the polytechnics, and the London School of Economics from their feet for ever. Besides, the business was in some mysterious way beginning to take care of itself. They had somehow forgotten their objections to employing other people. They came to the conclusion that their own way was the best, and that they had really a remarkable talent for business. The Colonel, who had been compelled for some years to keep a sufficient sum on current account at his bankers to make up their deficits, found that the provision was unnecessary: the young people were prospering. It is true that there was not quite fair play between them and their competitors in trade. Their week-ends in the country cost them nothing, and saved them the price of their Sunday dinners; for the motor car was the Colonel's; and he and Higgins paid the hotel bills. Mr F. Hill, florist and greengrocer (they soon discovered that there was money in asparagus; and asparagus led to other vegetables), had an air which stamped the business as classy; and in private life he was still Frederick Eynsford Hill, Esquire. Not that there was any swank about him: nobody but Eliza knew that he had been christened Frederick Chaloner. Eliza herself swanked like anything.

That is all. That is how it has turned out. It is astonishing how much Eliza still manages to meddle in the housekeeping at Wimpole Street in spite of the shop and her own family. And it is notable that though she never nags her husband, and frankly loves the Colonel as if she were his favorite daughter, she has never got out of the habit of nagging Higgins that was established on the fatal night when she won his bet for him. She snaps his head off on the faintest provocation, or on none. He no longer dares to tease her by assuming an abysmal inferiority of Freddy's mind to his own. He storms and bullies and derides; but she stands up to him so ruthlessly that the Colonel has to ask her from time to time to be kinder to Higgins; and it is the only request of his that brings a mulish expression into her face. Nothing but some emergency or calamity great enough to break down all likes and dislikes, and throw them both back on their common humanity—and may they be spared any such trial!—will ever alter this. She knows that Higgins does not need her, just as her father did not need her. The very scrupulousness with which he told her that day that he had become used to having her there, and dependent on her for all sorts of little services, and that he should miss her if she went away (it would never have occurred to Freddy or the Colonel to say anything of the sort) deepens her inner certainty that she is "no more to him than them slippers"; yet she has a sense, too, that his indifference is deeper than the infatuation of commoner souls. She is immensely interested in him. She has even secret mischievous moments in which she wishes she could get him alone, on a desert island, away from all ties and with nobody else in the world to consider, and just drag him off his pedestal and see him making love like any common man. We all have private imaginations of that sort. But when it comes to business, to the life that she really leads as distinguished from the life of dreams and fancies, she likes Freddy and she likes the Colonel; and she does not like Higgins and Mr Doolittle. Galatea never does quite like Pygmalion: his relation to her is too godlike to be altogether agreeable.

1. Why does Eliza, in her distress, turn to Mrs. Higgins? How has Eliza changed in the course of the play beyond adopting the appearance and behavior of a lady? What evidence do you find of new self-confidence and self-esteem?

2. How has Higgins' view of Eliza changed? Does his wanting her back "for the fun of it" indicate any real change in his own character by the end of the play?

3. In what ways does Alfred Doolittle's acceptance of affluence conflict with his earlier criticisms of middle-class morality? Through Doolittle, what might Shaw be saying about English society?

THE PLAY AS A WHOLE

1. Consider the plot of *Pygmalion.* How does it use suspense—about both the basic question "Will Higgins win his bet?" and minor instances? What is the question after he has won his bet? Is this a success story? Do you think it ends happily or unhappily? Give reasons.

2. Consider the truth of the play. What is revealed about human nature in general or about particular human beings? What is revealed about the society of the play and the classes that make up that society? Is the society static or evolving? If evolving, is it progressing or backsliding?

3. Shaw has a considerable, and deserved, reputation as a moralist. What moral picture do you find here of the relations between human beings? What vices or weaknesses appear to be condemned? What virtues are praised? What characters, if any, speak the author's views? Which characters does the author approve of? Disapprove of? For what purpose does he use each of his major characters?

4. Shaw was also a social reformer. Consider whether any call to improve society emerges from this play. If so, what is it and how does it affect the play?

COMMENTARY

Pygmalion exhibits a highly sophisticated and artificial world in the context of which romantic themes are explored. Shaw's Professor Higgins and Eliza Doolittle are not, however, the traditional romantic couple, nor does Shaw provide a conventional romantic ending, as he points out in the afterword or "sequel" to the play:

> The rest of the story need not be shewn in action, and indeed, would hardly need telling if our imaginations were not so enfeebled by their lazy dependence on the ready-mades and reach-me-downs of the rag shop in which Romance keeps its stock of "happy endings" to misfit all stories.

Shaw was determined to be true to the characters he had created. As he stated in the afterword, Higgins "had not the makings of a married man in him," at least as Eliza imagined a husband to be. He tells us that Eliza married Freddy instead. The reason that he gives is an interesting revelation of his view of marriage and the general relations of the sexes:

> . . . it is a truth everywhere in evidence that strong people, masculine or feminine, not only do not marry stronger people, but do not shew any preference for them in selecting their friends.

It is worth nothing that in *My Fair Lady,* the musical based on *Pygmalion,* Higgins declares a romantic interest in Eliza at the end, and the audience is left in no doubt about the outcome. Shaw, indeed, allowed the ending of the 1938 film of *Pygmalion* to suggest this possibility. But in 1913, the year in which the play was first performed, Shaw saw his characters in a different light: "Galatea never does quite like Pygmalion: his relation to her is too godlike to be altogether agreeable."

Shaw's primary interests lie not in the romantic possibilities of the play but in the social satire that the transformation of Eliza permits him to develop. Shaw is plain about his intentions in the short preface to the play:

> It is so intensely and deliberately didactic, and its subject is esteemed so dry, that I delight in throwing it at the heads of the wiseacres who

repeat the parrot cry that art should never be didactic. It goes to prove my contention that art should never be anything else.

In *Pygmalion* ideas are absorbed into character and action. Though Higgins and Alfred Doolittle ridicule the false values of a society that cherishes class and breeding and that engages in the hypocrisies of "middle-class morality," we would understand Shaw's satirical points even if Doolittle never appeared and Higgins remained silent about his intentions. Shaw was never closer to the spirit of the French satirist Molière than he was in *Pygmalion*. As in the best comedies of Molière, the comedy emerges from full-blooded characters, not one-dimensional types or "humor" characters such as we find in some comic writers. Shaw's characters have that unpredictable quality that all truly rounded characters in fiction and drama display. The experience of *Pygmalion* is the experience of discovering new possibilities and qualities in Higgins and Eliza as the play progresses, not in watching the same fixed qualities in action from scene to scene. Shaw wants us to *think* about his characters as we enjoy hearing them talk and seeing them in action throughout the play. In a preface written much earlier in his career, to *Three Plays for Puritans*, he stated the principle that governs the theatrical experience he created: "The pleasures of the senses I can sympathize with and share; but the substitution of sensuous ecstasy for intellectual activity is the very devil."

SHAW'S SATIRE

The humor of Bernard Shaw always has a touch of satire—a sharp social lash that he uses with superb skill. Satire, a device for exposing and discrediting vice or folly, was used by ancient Roman poets, and it has been developed into an effective and amusing literary art.

Satirists have moved from private animosity, or bitterness toward individuals, to elements in public life with which we all are concerned. All types of literature may be vehicles for satire. The spirit behind satirical writing, while it is always critical, ranges from lighthearted fun to angry denunciation.

1. *Pygmalion* is a satire on the false values of society. What classes is Shaw satirizing? What social standards does he criticize? According to Shaw, what is the most important thing each group or class does not have?
2. Make a list of the different aspects of society that Shaw satirizes in this play. How many of them do you think are justifiably ridiculed? In which instances do you disagree with Shaw's point of view?
3. Review the play, noticing what types of people are represented. For what purposes does Shaw use each of the following characters: Eliza, Higgins, Pickering, Mrs. Higgins, Mrs. Eynsford Hill, Clara, Freddy, Alfred Doolittle, Mrs. Pearce? To what extent are these characters individuals or representatives of types of people? What kind of people did Shaw admire? What kind did he dislike? Give definite evidence in support of your answers.

FOR COMPOSITION

1. *My Fair Lady*, the Broadway musical based on *Pygmalion*, ends on a note of romantic promise: Eliza will most probably return to Higgins. Given Higgins' attitudes toward women and Eliza's attitudes toward men, do you find an ending of romantic promise to be plausible? Explain your answer.
2. What major transformation would you be willing to experience in yourself? Imagine that you meet someone who claims to have the skills required, and that you accept this person as trainer or miracle worker. Relate the story of your transformation.

The English Novel in

The Twentieth Century

World War I removed the interest of the more literary critics of fiction from the sociological novels of Wells, Bennett, and Galsworthy, and fixed that interest on novels and novelists of a very different kind. Instead of looking outward toward society itself, these new novelists tended to look inward and describe what was happening in the minds of their characters. So Virginia Woolf (1882–1941), one of these new novelists and a very brilliant woman, could attack Bennett because he did not seem to her to bring any illusion of life into the novel. (But this was true only from her own point of view, and if a Bennett novel is weak in its inward life, a Virginia Woolf novel is weak in its outward life—in the relation of its characters to society.) Literary fashion in London, following a general European movement, now insisted that fiction, to be of any significance, should explore the depths and recesses of personality, revealing an unending stream of impressions, feelings, and thoughts, and showing us fewer people if necessary, but telling us everything about them.

A master of this method, which he finally carried to an extreme that lies outside the novel proper, was James Joyce (1882–1941). His genius, especially in *Ulysses* (1922), cannot be questioned, but his stature and influence as a novelist may have been overestimated. Joyce is best regarded as a kind of humorous prose-poet with an astonishing passion for and knowledge of language—a master of words.

E. M. Forster (1879–1970) published most of his novels well before World War I, but his finest novel, *A Passage to India* (1924), did not arrive until the twenties, and he stands quite apart from the older sociological novelists. His work is easier to enjoy than to describe. He cares nothing for a broad picture of people and society. His own point of view

shapes and colors all his novels, and he tries—as a rule very successfully—to give the reader certain supremely important, all-revealing moments in the lives of his characters. There is a kind of magic in Forster at his best, but he can also be oddly improbable and unconvincing.

Virginia Woolf, as we have seen, believed that the significant modern novel should reflect the inner life of its characters, and with this aim in mind, she made several difficult, subtle, and not always successful experiments. But in novels like *To the Lighthouse* (1927) and *Between the Acts* (1941), she succeeds triumphantly, creating fiction of deep human interest and strange beauty. Elsewhere, character and situation almost seem to vanish, and her work seems more like that of a prose poet than that of a real novelist.

There can be no doubt that D. H. Lawrence (1885–1930), especially in his earlier work, was a real novelist. He too looks inward, not to show us a stream of impressions as Virginia Woolf does, but to explore those mysterious areas of feeling of which we are hardly conscious but which can strongly influence our lives. Lawrence was certainly a man of genius, and his writing reveals a marvelously sensitive feeling for nature and a gift for description.

Younger novelists who made their first appearance in the twenties are Aldous Huxley (1894–1963), who succeeds in fiction by sheer intelligence but who is really more a philosophical essayist than a novelist proper; Evelyn Waugh (1903–1966), who in his first two stories, *Decline and Fall* (1928) and *Vile Bodies* (1930), achieved something very rare—namely a new kind of humor that quickly became fashionable and much imitated; and Graham Greene (1904–   ), whose best work is concerned with good and evil and who is haunted by a feeling of guilt that many of his readers cannot help sharing. Among the women novelists first published during this decade were Elizabeth Bowen (1899–1973), Rosamund Lehmann (1903–   ), and Ivy Compton-Burnett (1892–1969).

During the thirties, good novelists were bringing out excellent new work. But it is difficult not to feel that sometime not long after 1930 much of the earlier excitement about the English novel began to subside. Most of the experiments had already been made. The inner life had been explored and recorded up to a point beyond which fiction would become unreadable. Novels were being written and read, but the form itself seemed to lose its primary importance. Moreover, as the various dictators in Europe became ever more powerful and menacing, political events and books dealing with those events attracted more and more attention. Fiction has always been at its best during comparatively peaceful eras, and this period, which ended with World War II, was anything but peaceful.

Since the Second World War, much new fiction has been published. The craftsmanship, the writing, are on a high level. But this contemporary fiction lacks size and weight, profound originality, and the kind of urgency that makes the novel seem important. These shortcomings may be due to a change of attitude in the reading public itself, for it will be found that it is precisely at those times when people are passionately eager to read fiction — as they were, for example, during the middle years of the nineteenth century, not only in England but all over Europe and in America — that the novel reaches toward greatness.

The Twentieth Century

Sir James A. H. Murray, editor, with the staff of the *Oxford English Dictionary*.
Courtesy Yale University Press, London

One of the most interesting developments in the English language during the present century has been the swift rise in importance of the spoken language. During previous centuries, the only practical way of communicating with someone at a distance was by writing a letter, and the only practical way of reaching a large audience was through print. Today, however, the spoken word—on the telephone, over public-address systems, on television and radio—makes certain kinds of written communication unnecessary.

The spoken forms of the language have become a subject of increasing interest to language specialists. In the nineteenth century, language research had focused chiefly on the study of historical dialects and on the tracing of language history. Much of what we know about Old English and Middle English, for instance, was first discovered by nineteenth-century researchers. But research into living forms of speech had been largely ignored until the very end of the century. Although this field is therefore still relatively new, many important discoveries have already been made. For example, one of the tasks that researchers are undertaking is the mapping of regional and local dialect areas, both in the British Isles and in the United States. Although this work is far from finished, some interesting results have already come about — for instance, dialect mapping has shed a good deal of light on patterns of historical settlement and migration within the United States.

Twentieth-century writers have taken full advantage of the great range of possibilities offered by the spoken language. Although nineteenth-century writers had also been interested in this aspect of language, the feeling had lingered until the end of the century that informal spoken English was not entirely respectable. For instance, while Wordsworth admired the simplicity and directness of rural speech, he believed that for literary purposes it must be "purified" — by which he seems to have meant that all dialect expressions and any grammatical departures from standard English must be avoided. The language of Wordsworth's poetry may indeed be simple and direct, but it is also unquestionably standard written English, not a country dialect. Dickens also delicately refrained from assigning dialect-speech to his humblest heroes and heroines.

Today the prejudice against nonstandard English in literature has practically disappeared. This is partly due to the concern for realism and accurate detail that marks much of the writing of the present century, but it is due in even greater part to the increasing democratization of society and to the growing belief that an individual's worth does not depend on having been born into the "right" social class. Irish writers were among the first to employ their own spoken English in preference to standard literary English. The poets and playwrights who were associated with the Irish Nationalist movement deliberately tried to free themselves from literary dependence on England. At first, writers like Yeats and J. M. Synge frequently turned to Irish folklore and the Irish peasantry for their themes and their language. Writers of a later generation — James Joyce, Liam O'Flaherty, Frank O'Connor — tended to write directly out of their own experience, using contemporary Irish settings and current speech.

This tendency to write from experience and to develop a written style based on the spoken language has become a characteristic of twentieth-century English literature as a whole. Dylan Thomas' poetry reflects the speech of his native Wales. Hugh McDiarmid and other Scottish poets have revived the old tradition of writing in Scots dialect. Even writers whose own spoken dialect happens to be standard British English, such as Evelyn Waugh and E. M. Forster, have proved expert at capturing in writing the nuances of this spoken language.

During this century English has continued to adopt new words and to adapt old ones to new contexts, giving them new meanings. Scientific terms have proliferated, made necessary by inventions and discoveries. The terms needed for living in the space age, for example, would fill countless pages.

Also, our history continues to be reflected in the words we use. The two world wars this century has survived have contributed countless words to our vocabulary, some of which will probably continue to be used even in times of peace. World War I gave us *air raid, antiaircraft, tank, blimp, gas mask, liaison officer, camouflage* (adopted from the French), *sector, barrage,* and *dud.* World War I also popularized or gave new meanings to old words: *hand grenade* (first used in 1661), *dugout* (once a hollowed-out log for primitive navigation, now an underground hiding place). There is also *machine gun, periscope, no man's land, slacker, trench foot,* and *war bride.* World War II has given us words that were unknown to the 1933 supplement of the *Oxford English Dictionary: blackout, blockbuster, pinup, beachhead, parachutist, paratrooper, roadblock, jeep, foxhole, bulldozer, decontamination, task force, resistance movement,* and *radar.* World War II also gave us some new verbs: *to spearhead, to mop up,* and *to appease. Blitz* is new and can be used as either a noun or a verb.

Many new self-explaining compounds have also entered the language. Combining old words is one of the oldest methods we know of forming new words. Here are a few recent ones that we could hardly live without: *hitchhike, know-how, lipstick, road hog, steamroll, mudguard, manhole, bluegrass, madman, first-rate, trigger-happy, breakdown, setback, cookout, sit-in, overanxious, oncoming, uptight, overland, washed-up,* and *carryings-on.*

English has grown from small beginnings to become an international language, the second language for many nations, and a major subject of study and research. But English is also a personal matter. We all have our own personal history of English and our own characteristic vocabulary and turns of phrase by which others know us.

FOR STUDY AND DISCUSSION

1. Although most of the expressions in the following list are now familiar throughout the English-speaking world, each of them was originally a local term used by speakers in a particular part of the British Isles or of the British Empire. In a dictionary that gives etymologies, look up each expression and find out where it originated.

auld lang syne	trek
pundit	veld
smithereens	wallah
swagman	whiskey

2. The language is growing at such a rapid rate that no dictionary can keep up with the new words that enter our vocabulary each year. *Sit-in,* a term used in the late fifties and early sixties, was old enough to be included in *Webster's Third New International Dictionary,* 1961. *Uptight,* a compound from the late sixties, was too new to be included. Make a list of words or phrases used daily by you and your friends that are too new or perhaps too faddish to be included in your own dictionary.

Reading and Writing About Literature

INTRODUCTION

In English class students are often asked to write essays on literary topics in response to homework assignments, examination questions, or research projects. You may have been given assignments such as the following: discuss the theme of a short story; compare two characters in a play; analyze the symbolism in a poem; agree or disagree with an interpretation of some work. Such writing assignments are an important part of literary study, which aims at greater understanding and appreciation of the works you read.

Writing about a literary work is a way of getting to know it better, of becoming more fully involved with it. Before you can formulate your thoughts on paper, you must read and reread the selection carefully. You must sort out your ideas, weigh evidence, and reach conclusions.

Throughout your studies you have acquired a substantial body of information and skills that you can use in writing about literature. You have learned a special language of terms and techniques that is useful in examining literary works. You can safely assume that your readers will understand what you mean when you identify a poem as a *Shakespearean sonnet*, or when you refer to such terms as *epic* and *paradox*. These words are part of a common vocabulary used in writing about literature. (See the *Guide to Literary Terms and Techniques*, page 983.)

There are, as well, certain topics or approaches that are considered appropriate in writing about literature. It is quite acceptable, for example, to examine one part of a literary work in order to make clear its relationship to the whole. Thus, you might focus on a key episode in a story in order to explain its function. You might take a short passage in a long poem and *explicate* it (examine it line by line) in order to focus on its significance in the entire work. Or you might approach a work in broader terms, choosing to comment on its structure or its relationship to other works of the same period. (A fuller discussion of sample topics appears on page 945.) The object of all such literary inquiry is to discover the meaning of a work (or group of works) and to transmit your insights and conclusions to others who share your interest.

The material on the following pages offers help in planning and writing papers about literature. Here you will find suggestions for reading and analyzing literature, answering examination questions, choosing topics, gathering evidence, organizing essays, and writing and revising papers. Also included are model essays and several new selections for analysis along with suggested writing topics.

READING LITERATURE

To write effectively about literature, you must first know how to read literature skillfully. To read for explicit meaning alone is not sufficient. Often an author does not tell you everything directly, but leads you to make discoveries by drawing *inferences* about the events, the characters, or the meaning of a work. To read literature well, you have to be an active reader, aware of *what* the author is doing, *how* the author is doing it, and *why*. A good reader probes beneath the surface of a work, asking the right questions at the right time.

When you are asked to write about a literary work, be sure you read it carefully before you begin writing. Read actively, asking yourself questions as you work through the selection.

Close Reading of a Short Story

Here is a brief story that has been read carefully by an experienced reader. The notes and questions in the margin show how this reader thinks in working through a story. Read the story at least twice before proceeding to the commentary on page 923. You may wish to make notes of your own on a separate sheet of paper as you read.

The Japanese Quince   *John Galsworthy*

As Mr. Nilson, well known in the City,[1] opened the window of his dressing room on Campden Hill, he experienced a peculiar sweetish sensation in the back of his throat, and a feeling of emptiness just under his fifth rib. Hooking the window back, he noticed that a little tree in the Square Gardens had come out in blossom, and that the thermometer stood at sixty. "Perfect morning," he thought; "spring at last!"

Resuming some meditations on the price of Tintos,[2] he took up an ivory-backed handglass and scrutinized his face. His firm, well-colored cheeks, with their neat brown mustaches, and his round, well-opened, clear gray eyes, wore a reassuring appearance of good health. Putting on his black frock coat,[3] he went downstairs.

[margin notes]
a business man
private dressing room indicates a man of means
his heart

concern with business
handglass sign of affluence
no physical disorder apparent

---

1. **the City:** the financial and commercial district of London.
2. **Tintos:** red Madeira wines.
3. **frock coat:** a double-breasted dress overcoat with knee-length skirts, worn in the nineteenth century.

In the dining room his morning paper was laid out on the sideboard. Mr. Nilson had scarcely taken it in his hand when he again became aware of that queer feeling. Somewhat concerned, he went to the French window and descended the scrolled iron steps into the fresh air. A cuckoo clock struck eight.

"Half an hour to breakfast," he thought; "I'll take a turn in the Gardens."

He had them to himself, and proceeded to pace the circular path with his morning paper clasped behind him. He had scarcely made two revolutions, however, when it was borne in on him that, instead of going away in the fresh air, the feeling had increased. He drew several deep breaths, having heard deep breathing recommended by his wife's doctor; but they augmented rather than diminished the sensation—as of some sweetish liquor in course within him, together with a faint aching just above his heart. Running over what he had eaten the night before, he could recollect no unusual dish, and it occurred to him that it might possibly be some smell affecting him. But he could detect nothing except a faint sweet lemony scent, rather agreeable than otherwise, which evidently emanated from the bushes budding in the sunshine. He was on the point of resuming his promenade, when a blackbird close by burst into song, and, looking up, Mr. Nilson saw at a distance of perhaps five yards a little tree, in the heart of whose branches the bird was perched. He stood staring curiously at this tree, recognizing it for that which he had noticed from his window. It was covered with young blossoms, pink and white, and little bright green leaves both round and spiky; and on all this blossom and these leaves the sunlight glistened. Mr. Nilson smiled; the little tree was so alive and pretty! And instead of passing on, he stayed there smiling at the tree.

"Morning like this!" he thought; "and here I am the only person in the Square who has the—to come out and——!" But he had no sooner conceived this thought than he saw quite near him a man with his hands behind him, who was also staring up and smiling at the little tree. Rather taken aback, Mr. Nilson ceased to smile, and looked furtively at the stranger. It was his next-door neighbor, Mr. Tandram, well known in the City, who had occupied the adjoining house for some five years. Mr. Nilson perceived at once the awkwardness of his position, for, being married, they had not yet had occasion to speak to one another. Doubtful as to his proper conduct, he decided at last to murmur: "Fine morning!" and was passing on, when Mr. Tandram answered: "Beautiful, for the time of year!" Detecting a slight nervousness in his neighbor's voice, Mr. Nilson was emboldened to regard him openly. He was of about Mr. Nilson's own height, with firm, well-colored cheeks, neat brown mustaches, and round, well-opened, clear gray eyes; and he was wearing a black frock coat. Mr. Nilson noticed that he had his morning paper clasped behind him as he looked up at the little tree. And, visited somehow by the feeling that he had been caught out, he said abruptly:

"Er—can you give me the name of that tree?"

Mr. Tandram answered:

"I was about to ask you that," and stepped towards it. Mr. Nilson also approached the tree.

"Sure to have its name on, I should think," he said.

Mr. Tandram was the first to see the little label, close to where the blackbird had been sitting. He read it out.

"Japanese quince!"

"Ah!" said Mr. Nilson, "thought so. Early flowerers."

"Very," assented Mr. Tandram, and added: "Quite a feelin' in the air today."

Mr. Nilson nodded.

"It was a blackbird singin'," he said.

"Blackbirds," answered Mr. Tandram, "I prefer them to thrushes myself; more body in the note." And he looked at Mr. Nilson in an almost friendly way.

"Quite," murmured Mr. Nilson. "These exotics, they don't bear fruit. Pretty blossoms!" and he again glanced up at the blossom, thinking: "Nice fellow, this, I rather like him."

tree is without practical purpose
exists for its beauty alone

Mr. Tandram also gazed at the blossom. And the little tree, as if appreciating their attention, quivered and glowed. From a distance the blackbird gave a loud, clear call. Mr. Nilson dropped his eyes. It struck him suddenly that Mr. Tandram looked a little foolish; and, as if he had seen himself, he said: "I must be going in. Good morning!"

display of feeling causes embarrassment

A shade passed over Mr. Tandram's face, as if he, too, had suddenly noticed something about Mr. Nilson.

"Good morning," he replied, and clasping their journals to their backs they separated.

Mr. Nilson retraced his steps towards his garden window, walking slowly so as to avoid arriving at the same time as his neighbor. Having seen Mr. Tandram mount his scrolled iron steps, he ascended his own in turn. On the top step he paused.

With the slanting spring sunlight darting and quivering into it, the Japanese quince seemed more living than a tree. The blackbird had returned to it, and was chanting out his heart.

renewed emphasis on the life of the tree, suggesting what is missing from the lives of the characters

Mr. Nilson sighed; again he felt that queer sensation, that choky feeling in his throat.

The sound of a cough or sigh attracted his attention. There, in the shadow of his French window, stood Mr. Tandram, also looking forth across the Gardens at the little quince tree.

Unaccountably upset, Mr. Nilson turned abruptly into the house, and opened his morning paper.

Nilson distressed by these sensations turns back to his familiar existence

Commentary on "The Japanese Quince"

To an inexperienced reader, this may seem a rather slight story. Nothing much appears to be happening. On a certain morning in spring, the main character, Mr. Nilson, experiences odd physical sensations that he cannot explain. Finding that he has time before breakfast, he takes a walk in the gardens and is drawn to a little blossoming tree, in which a bird is perched and singing. As he stands looking at the tree, he becomes aware of another man who is also staring up and smiling at the tree. This man is similar to Mr. Nilson in appearance and bearing. Recognizing him as his neighbor, Mr. Tandram, to whom he has never spoken, Mr. Nilson hesitates to address him. After a somewhat awkward beginning, they begin to make small talk about the tree. As Mr. Nilson regards his neighbor's actions, he becomes embarrassed. Taking his leave abruptly, he returns to his garden window. He cannot overcome the peculiar sensation as he looks at the little tree. Seeing that Mr. Tandram is similarly affected, Mr. Nilson becomes upset, turns into his house, and opens his newspaper.

The reader who finds nothing more than this summary to the story has not grasped its essential meaning and artistry. That reader has failed to respond to the author's clues. All the clues needed to uncover meaning are contained in the story, but they are not given away without some effort on the reader's part. The skillful reader cooperates with the author by attending to every significant detail.

The opening paragraphs of the story are important in establishing the setting and social background of the characters. Mr. Nilson, "well known in the City," is representative of a prosperous middle class, accustomed to comfort, order, and conventions. The details of household life point to affluence—the private dressing room, the ivory-backed handglass, the scrolled iron steps—and regularity—the morning paper laid out on the sideboard and the serving of breakfast exactly at eight-thirty.

In this world there is a simple, organic explanation for "peculiar sensations." Mr. Nilson does not recognize that his sensations are a manifestation of spring fever. He seeks an explanation in his complexion and in his diet, and takes exercise to alleviate his symptoms.

Despite his pragmatic nature, he is drawn to the little blossoming tree in the garden which is so pretty and alive. The tree, which blossoms but does not bear fruit—a significant detail—clearly is a symbol of life, joy, and beauty, and its existence contrasts markedly with that of the two characters who admire it. The similarities in the description of Mr. Nilson and Mr. Tandram are intentional; these figures delineate an entire class which is ruled by rigid standards of dress and conduct, and by materialistic values.

Galsworthy's imagery emphasizes the aliveness of the tree: it "glistened," "quivered," "glowed," with "slanting spring sunlight darting and quivering into it." In the context of the story, such language does not merely contrast the beauty of nature with the stuffy formality of the characters: it also suggests what is lacking in the lives of these people—spontaneity, beauty, and joy. The conflict between Mr. Nilson's strange impulses and his desire for order may be seen as Galsworthy's comment on a certain way of life. That Mr. Nilson suppresses his urges and returns to the comfortable world indoors is a natural resolution of the conflict, and quite in keeping with the portrait of upper middle-class life Galsworthy presents in this remarkable story.

This reader has arrived at an interpretation of the story by actively considering the author's intent. The commentary accounts for the significant details of description and action; it focuses on the key passages in the narrative; it comes to grips with the "point" of the story—its overall meaning or theme.

With practice, you can develop skill in reading and analyzing a literary work. Here are some guidelines for reading fiction.

Guidelines for Reading Fiction

1. *Look up unfamiliar words and references.* In Galsworthy's story, the word *City* (which has been defined in a footnote) has a specific meaning that is important. A careful reader would be sure to check such words in a standard dictionary or other reference book.

2. *Learn to probe beneath the surface.* The author does not tell you directly that Mr. Nilson is a man of regular habits. However, there are several references to the orderliness of his household and his concern with routine that lead to this inference.

3. *Actively question the author's purpose and method.* Ask yourself what significance there might be to details the author gives you. In the opening paragraph of "The Japanese Quince," for example, Galsworthy alerts the reader to a connection between Mr. Nilson's strange sensation and the little tree in the Square Gardens.

4. *Be alert to the author's emphasis.* In "The Japanese Quince," Galsworthy refers to the life of the tree in several key passages. Such clues as repetition and prominence help to reveal meaning.

5. *Account for all significant elements of the work.* It is important, for example, to understand the role of the second character, Mr. Tandram, as a mirror image of Mr. Nilson.

6. *Probe for the central idea or point—the underlying meaning of the work.* Try to state this theme in one or two sentences in the following manner: *On one level, Galsworthy's story is about a curious case of spring fever, but on a deeper, more satisfying level, it is about a conflict in values.*

Practice in Close Reading

Each of the following passages is accompanied by a set of questions.
Read carefully before answering the questions. If you need to, look
up unfamiliar words or references.

I

There was no possibility of taking a walk that day. We had been wandering, indeed, in the leafless shrubbery an hour in the morning; but since dinner (Mrs. Reed, when there was no company, dined early) the cold winter wind had brought with it clouds so somber and a rain so penetrating, that further outdoor exercise was now out of the question.

I was glad of it: I never liked long walks, especially on chilly afternoons: dreadful to me was the coming home in the raw twilight, with nipped fingers and toes, and a heart saddened by the chidings of Bessie, the nurse, and humbled by the consciousness of my physical inferiority to Eliza, John, and Georgiana Reed.

The said Eliza, John, and Georgiana were now clustered round their mamma in the drawing room: she lay reclined on the sofa by the fireside, and with her darlings about her (for the time neither quarreling nor crying) looked perfectly happy. Me, she had dispensed from joining the group; saying, "She regretted to be under the necessity of keeping me at a distance; but that until she heard from Bessie and could discover by her own observation that I was endeavoring in good earnest to acquire a more sociable and childlike disposition, a more attractive and sprightly manner—something lighter, franker, more natural, as it were—she really must exclude me from privileges intended only for contented, happy, little children."

"What does Bessie say I have done?" I asked.

"Jane, I don't like cavilers[1] or questioners: besides, there is something truly forbidding in a child taking up her elders in that manner. Be seated somewhere; and until you can speak pleasantly, remain silent."

A small breakfast room adjoined the drawing room. I slipped in there. It contained a bookcase: I soon possessed myself of a volume, taking care that it should be one stored with pictures. I mounted into the window seat: gathering up my feet, I sat cross-legged like a Turk; and, having drawn the red moreen[2] curtain nearly close, I was shrined in double retirement.

Folds of scarlet drapery shut in my view to the right hand; to the left were the clear panes of glass, protecting, but not separating me from the drear November day. At intervals, while turning over the leaves of my book, I studied the aspect of that winter afternoon. Afar, it offered a pale blank of mist and cloud; near, a scene of wet lawn and storm-beat shrub, with ceaseless rain sweeping away wildly before a long and lamentable blast.

Charlotte Brontë
from *Jane Eyre*

---

1. **cavilers** (kăv′əl-ərz): people who find fault or criticize.
2. **moreen** (mə-rēn′, mô-): sturdy fabric, often embossed.

FOR STUDY AND DISCUSSION

1. What mood is set by this passage? How does it complement the state of mind of the narrator?

2. What difficulties are evident in Jane's relationship to Mrs. Reed and her children?

3. What indicates that although she is a child, Jane already has a marked independence of mind?

In the days when the spinning wheels hummed busily in the farmhouses—and even great ladies, clothed in silk and thread lace,[1] had their toy spinning wheels of polished oak—there might be seen in districts far away among the lanes, or deep in the bosom of the hills, certain pallid undersized men, who, by the side of the brawny countryfolk, looked like the remnants of a disinherited race. The shepherd's dog barked fiercely when one of these alien-looking men appeared on the upland, dark against the early winter sunset; for what dog likes a figure bent under a heavy bag?—and these pale men rarely stirred abroad without that mysterious burden. The shepherd himself, though he had good reason to believe that the bag held nothing but flaxen thread, or else the long rolls of strong linen spun from that thread, was not quite sure that this trade of weaving, indispensable though it was, could be carried on entirely without the help of the Evil One. In that far-off time superstition clung easily round every person or thing that was at all unwonted, or even intermittent and occasional merely, like the visits of the pedlar or the knife grinder. No one knew where wandering men had their homes or their origin; and how was a man to be explained unless you at least knew somebody who knew his father and mother? To the peasants of old times, the world outside their own direct experience was a region of vagueness and mystery: to their untraveled thought a state of wandering was a conception as dim as the winter life of the swallows that came back with the spring; and even a settler, if he came from distant parts, hardly ever ceased to be viewed with a remnant of distrust, which would have prevented any surprise if a long course of inoffensive conduct on his part had ended in the commission of a crime; especially if he had any reputation for knowledge, or showed any skill in handicraft. All cleverness, whether in the rapid use of that difficult instrument the tongue, or in some other art unfamiliar to villagers, was in itself suspicious: honest folk, born and bred in a visible manner, were mostly not overwise or clever—at least, not beyond such a matter as knowing the signs of the weather; and the process by which rapidity and dexterity of any kind were acquired was so wholly hidden, that they partook of the nature of conjuring. In this way it came to pass that those scattered linen weavers—emigrants from the town into the country—were to the last regarded as aliens by their rustic neighbors, and usually contracted the eccentric habits which belong to a state of loneliness.

In the early years of this century,[2] such a linen weaver, named Silas Marner, worked at his vocation in a stone cottage that stood among the nutty hedgerows near the village of Raveloe, and not far from the edge of a deserted stone pit. The questionable sound of Silas' loom, so unlike the natural cheerful trotting of the winnowing machine, or the simpler rhythm of the flail, had a half-fearful fascination for the Raveloe boys, who would often leave off their nutting or birds'-nesting to peep in at the window of the stone cottage, counterbalancing a certain awe at the mysterious action of the loom, by a pleasant sense of scornful superiority, drawn from the mockery of its alternating noises, along with the bent, treadmill attitude of the weaver. But sometimes it happened that Marner, pausing to adjust an irregularity in his thread, became aware of the small scoundrels, and, though chary of his time, he liked their intrusion so ill that he would descend from his loom, and, opening the door, would fix

---

1. **thread lace:** lace made of linen thread.

2. **this century:** the nineteenth century. The first edition of this book appeared in 1861.

on them a gaze that was always enough to make them take to their legs in terror. For how was it possible to believe that those large brown protuberant eyes in Silas Marner's pale face really saw nothing very distinctly that was not close to them, and not rather that their dreadful stare could dart cramp, or rickets, or a wry mouth at any boy who happened to be in the rear? They had, perhaps, heard their fathers and mothers hint that Silas Marner could cure folks' rheumatism if he had a mind, and add, still more darkly, that if you could only speak the devil fair enough, he might save you the cost of the doctor. Such strange lingering echoes of the old demon worship might perhaps even now be caught by the diligent listener among the gray-haired peasantry; for the rude mind with difficulty associates the ideas of power and benignity. A shadowy conception of power that by much persuasion can be induced to refrain from inflicting harm, is the shape most easily taken by the sense of the Invisible in the minds of men who have always been pressed close by primitive wants, and to whom a life of hard toil has never been illuminated by any enthusiastic religious faith. To them pain and mishap present a far wider range of possibilities than gladness and enjoyment: their imagination is almost barren of the images that feed desire and hope, but is all overgrown by recollections that are a perpetual pasture to fear. "Is there anything you can fancy that you would like to eat?" I once said to an old laboring man, who was in his last illness, and who had refused all the food his wife had offered him. "No," he answered, "I've never been used to nothing but common victual, and I can't eat that." Experience had bred no fancies in him that could raise the phantasm of appetite.

George Eliot
from *Silas Marner*

FOR STUDY AND DISCUSSION

1. At the opening of this novel, Eliot establishes the social and moral climate of an English village at the turn of the nineteenth century. Why are individuals like Silas Marner viewed with suspicion and hostility by this community?
2. The Industrial Revolution caused many changes in social and economic organization in England after 1760. One consequence was the replacement of hand tools by machine and power tools. How does Eliot suggest the dehumanizing effect of machine toil?
3. How does Eliot explain the superstitious nature of the peasantry?
4. What is the point of the anecdote about the laboring man who refused all food? What does it reveal about the limitations of village people?

Close Reading of a Poem

It is a good idea to read a selection more than once. A poem ought to be read several times, and aloud at least once. Often it is helpful to write a prose paraphrase of a poem, restating all its ideas in plain language. A paraphrase is no substitute for the "meaning" of a poem, but it helps you clarify and simplify the author's text.

The more information and experience you bring to a poem, the greater will be your understanding and appreciation of what you read.

The reader who understands the conventions of the Petrarchan sonneteers takes added pleasure in the anti-Petrarchan sentiments of Shakespeare's Sonnet 130 ("My mistress' eyes are nothing like the sun," page 131).

Here is a well-known poem from *A Shropshire Lad* by A. E. Housman. Read the poem several times, using the notes in the margin to guide you in interpreting the poem. When you are satisfied that you have understood the poem, read the explication that follows.

On Wenlock Edge° the Wood's in Trouble

A. E. Housman

On Wenlock Edge the wood's in trouble;
  His forest fleece the Wrekin° heaves;
The gale, it plies the saplings double,
  And thick on Severn snow the leaves.

> note personification of nature; human feelings of distress attributed to trees

'Twould blow like this through holt° and hanger°   5
  When Uricon° the city stood:

> unchanging character of nature

'Tis the old wind in the old anger,
  But then it threshed another wood.

> note personification; feeling and purpose attributed to wind

Then, 'twas before my time, the Roman
  At yonder heaving hill would stare: 10
The blood that warms an English yeoman,°
  The thoughts that hurt him, they were there.

> unchanging character of human beings
> *blood* represents passions human frustrations

There, like the wind through woods in riot,
  Through him the gale of life blew high;

> wind and trees key symbols wind symbol for life (14)

The tree of man was never quiet: 15
  Then 'twas the Roman, now 'tis I.

> trees symbol for human beings (15)

The gale, it plies the saplings double,
  It blows so hard, 'twill soon be gone:

> repetition in last stanza of key words unifies poem

Today the Roman and his trouble
  Are ashes under Uricon.   20

> resolution of life's anguish in death

° **Wenlock Edge:** Wenlock is a borough in the county of Shropshire, on the Severn River. Wenlock Edge is a ridge of hills.   2. **Wrekin** (rē′kən): a sugarloaf hill, an extinct volcano in Shropshire.   5. **holt:** a small wood (archaic). **hanger:** a steep wooded slope.   6. **Uricon:** the ancient Roman town Uriconium or Viroconium. Ruins of public baths, a town hall, and market have been excavated.   11. **yeoman** (yō′mən): small landowner.

Explication of "On Wenlock Edge the Wood's in Trouble"

The setting of the poem is established in the opening stanza. The speaker, who identifies himself in line 11 as "an English yeoman," is observing the effects of a strong wind on the landscape. He sees nature turning against itself. He views the physical disturbance of the natural world in human terms. The wood, personified in line 1, is "in trouble"; the Wrekin hurls off *his* "forest fleece," a metaphor for the soft natural covering of leaves. The powerful wind bends and twists ("plies") young trees ("saplings") to the point of snapping them. The leaves shower like snow on the river Severn. The words *trouble, heaves, plies,* and *double* connote effort, strenuous movement, pain. Thus Housman sets the tone for the human dilemma that is the subject of the poem.

In the second stanza the speaker reflects on the unchanging character of nature. He recalls that centuries ago a different civilization, that of the Romans, existed on this very site. The wind behaved similarly then. Animated by its "old anger," the wind thrashed ("threshed") other trees then just as it does now. This thought prompts the speaker to reflect also upon the unchanging nature of human beings. In the third stanza he imagines an unknown figure from the past, referred to as the Roman, observing a similar scene. This man was subject to the same passions ("blood") and the same heartache ("thoughts that hurt") as an English yeoman of the present.

In the fourth stanza the speaker establishes an analogy between the violent spirit in nature and the spirit of human life. The trees function as a symbol for human beings (line 15); the wind for life (line 14). Like the wind that blows through the wood "in riot," causing confusion and disorder, the spirit of life in the Roman caused tumult and anguish. In line 16 the speaker identifies with the Roman, concluding that all human beings share a common fate.

The only consolation the speaker finds is that finally there is an end to the suffering. The strong wind soon vanishes. Similarly, the breath of life soon passes from the body, and with it the pain of life:

> Today the Roman and his trouble
> Are ashes under Uricon.

Housman uses certain rhythmical and musical devices to reinforce the meaning of his poem. The predominant meter is iambic tetrameter. The regularity of the end-stopped lines contributes to the restrained tone of the poem. Housman uses pauses to gain variety, as in line 9, where the parenthetic phrase "'twas before my time" makes the speaker's presence felt; and in lines 12 and 16, where the pauses are necessary for emphasis. Rhyme gives added weight to the theme by stressing disturbance (*trouble/double*) and by linking the past with the present (*Roman/yeoman*).

The first four stanzas are linked to the final stanza by repetition. Note the repetition of key words: *trouble* (lines 1, 19); *gale* (lines 3, 14); *Uricon* (lines 6, 20); *Roman* (lines 9, 16, 19). The third line of the poem is repeated as line 17. The phrase "Roman and his trouble" in line 19 recalls "the wood's in trouble" in line 1. This association emphasizes the symbolic meaning of trees and underscores the unity of human beings and nature, integral to the meaning of this poem.

The language of the poem is appropriately stark, made up chiefly of nouns and verbs. Some lines are completely monosyllabic (lines 12, 14, 18); others are virtually monosyllabic (lines 4, 5, 7, 13). This unembellished quality suits well the melancholy theme of the poem.

This explication examines the poem line by line for its meaning. In analyzing the poem, the reader has attended to such important elements as the speaker, the tone, figurative language, symbols, meter, and rhyme.

Guidelines for Reading a Poem

1. *Read the poem aloud at least once, following the author's clues for phrasing.* Although Housman's poem uses strong regular end rhymes, he does not expect the reader to pause at the end of each line. Some lines run over (see lines 5, 9, 19). Others have more than one pause (see lines 3, 9, 12, 16, 17, 18).

2. *Identify the speaker and the occasion.* The speaker of a poem is not necessarily the author. In line 11, the speaker identifies himself as a small landowner ("an English yeoman"). He is observing the woods on Wenlock Edge during a gale.

3. *Be alert to key words and references.* In a poem the connotative meanings of words are often more important than their denotative meanings. Note how many words in the poem are associated with pain or sorrow: *trouble,*

threshed, heaving, hurt, riot, for example. Look up any unfamiliar words.

4. *Write a paraphrase of any lines that need clarification or simplification.* Paraphrase can help a reader understand the syntax of a poem. For example, the reader writing a paraphrase of line 2 would first have to invert word order: The trees on Wrekin hill are throwing off their leaves as if with effort.

5. *Look for the relationship of content and technique.* The use of metonymy in line 11, for instance, emphasizes the theme. The word *blood* refers to human desires.

6. *Arrive at the central idea or meaning of the poem.* Try to state this theme briefly. Housman's poem expresses a pessimistic view: *Life is filled with troubles. Our only solace is that our stay on earth is brief.*

Practice in Close Reading

The Pulley   *George Herbert*

When God at first made man,
Having a glass of blessings standing by—
"Let us," said he, "pour on him all we can;
Let the world's riches, which dispersèd lie,
   Contract into a span."°

So strength first made a way,
Then beauty flowed, then wisdom, honor, pleasure:
When almost all was out, God made a stay,
Perceiving that, alone of all his treasure,
   Rest in the bottom lay.

"For if I should," said he,
"Bestow this jewel also on my creature,
He would adore my gifts instead of me,
And rest in nature, not the God of nature:
   So both should losers be.

"Yet let him keep the rest,
But keep them with repining restlessness;
Let him be rich and weary, that at least
If goodness lead him not, yet weariness
   May toss him to my breast."

---

5. **span:** small or limited space.

FOR STUDY AND DISCUSSION

1. Why does God withhold the last blessing?

2. Give the different meanings of the word *rest* in the poem.

3. A *paradox* is a statement that seems to be contradictory, yet reveals a kind of truth. Explain the paradox in the last stanza.

4. Using the last three lines, explain the metaphor in the title of the poem.

Close Reading of a Play

While many of the elements studied in connection with short stories and poetry are relevant to the study of drama, there are several additional elements that need to be taken into account. Drama has its own conventions, or practices. Elizabethan drama, for example, makes use of soliloquies, monologues, and asides. In the poetic drama *Macbeth* (page 149), prose is reserved for the comic passages, such as the Porter's speech in Act Two, Scene 3, and for the sleepwalking scene, Act Five, Scene 2. Dramatists frequently make use of stage directions to create setting and to give players instructions for acting. Sound effects are often important in creating setting and mood. Generally, however, dialogue is the dramatist's most important device for presenting character and for moving the action along.

The following sketch, *Last to Go*, is by Harold Pinter, a contemporary English playwright, who has earned a reputation for the realistic quality and subtlety of his dialogue. As you read, be alert not only to the content of the speeches, but to Pinter's use of pauses and repetition. Read the sketch several times, and aloud at least once. Then turn to the commentary on page 933.

Last to Go   *Harold Pinter*

A coffee stall. A Barman *and an old* Newspaper Seller. *The* Barman *leans on his counter, the* Old Man *stands with tea. Silence.*

Man. You was a bit busier earlier.
Barman. Ah.
Man. Round about ten.
Barman. Ten, was it?
Man. About then.

Pause.

I passed by here about then.
Barman. Oh yes?
Man. I noticed you were doing a bit of trade.

Pause.

Barman. Yes, trade was very brisk here about ten.
Man. Yes, I noticed.

Pause.

I sold my last one about then. Yes. About nine forty-five.
Barman. Sold your last then, did you?

Man. Yes, my last *Evening News* it was. Went about twenty to ten.

Pause.

Barman. *Evening News*, was it?
Man. Yes.

Pause.

Sometimes it's the *Star* is the last to go.
Barman. Ah.
Man. Or the . . . whatsisname.
Barman. *Standard.*
Man. Yes.

Pause.

All I had left tonight was the *Evening News.*

Pause.

Barman. Then that went, did it?
Man. Yes.

Pause.

Like a shot.

Pause.

Barman. You didn't have any left, eh?

Man. No. Not after I sold that one.

Pause.

Barman. It was after that you must have come by here then, was it?

Man. Yes, I come by here after that, see, after I packed up.

Barman. You didn't stop here though, did you?

Man. When?

Barman. I mean, you didn't stop here and have a cup of tea then, did you?

Man. What, about ten?

Barman. Yes.

Man. No, I went up to Victoria.[1]

Barman. No, I thought I didn't see you.

Man. I had to go up to Victoria.

Pause.

Barman. Yes, trade was very brisk here about then.

Pause.

Man. I went to see if I could get hold of George.

Barman. Who?

Man. George.

Pause.

Barman. George who?

Man. George . . . whatsisname.

Barman. Oh.

Pause.

Did you get hold of him?

---

1. **Victoria:** one of the principal railway stations in London.

Man. No. No, I couldn't get hold of him. I couldn't locate him.

Barman. He's not about much now, is he?

Pause.

Man. When did you last see him then?

Barman. Oh, I haven't seen him for years.

Man. No, nor me.

Pause.

Barman. Used to suffer very bad from arthritis.

Man. Arthritis?

Barman. Yes.

Man. He never suffered from arthritis.

Barman. Suffered very bad.

Pause.

Man. Not when I knew him.

Pause.

Barman. I think he must have left the area.

Pause.

Man. Yes, it was the *Evening News* was the last to go tonight.

Barman. Not always the last though, is it, though?

Man. No. Oh no. I mean sometimes it's the *News*. Other times it's one of the others. No way of telling beforehand. Until you've got your last one left, of course. Then you can tell which one it's going to be.

Barman. Yes.

Pause.

Man. Oh yes.

Pause.

I think he must have left the area.

Commentary on *Last to Go*

If the essence of drama is conflict, what is the conflict in Pinter's *Last to Go?* There is no collision here of wills, no opposition of ideas, no incompatible interests. What we do experience is a failure of the characters to engage on any meaningful level. The conflict arises from their frustrated desire to communicate.

The dialogue in this short sketch takes place between two people whose relationship is incidental: a barman in a coffee stall and an old newspaper seller, who is his customer. We have almost no information about the characters. They are not identified by name; it is likely that they do not know each other's names, or need to. The content of their conversation is trivial. What is of significance is what the dialogue suggests about the quality of the characters' lives and the nature of their communication.

The setting conveys loneliness and isolation. It is late evening. The barman's trade is no longer "brisk"; his patrons have left. The old man has sold his last paper; he seems to be hanging about the stall aimlessly. The two men do not really have anything to say to each other. They have a desire to communicate, but are unable to. They repeat each other's phrases almost mindlessly. Their exchange is vague and confusing. We never find out why the old man wants to get hold of George after not having seen him for years, whether George has indeed left the area, and whether or not George suffers from arthritis. The dialogue ends without verifying whether both characters are even thinking of the same "George whatsisname."

The dialogue is punctuated by pauses, by repetition, by digressions, as if it were realistically transcribed from life. But language does not reveal self; rather than serving as a bridge to communication, it sets the characters apart. They do not succeed in conveying their ideas and feelings or clarifying their experiences. They talk at cross-purposes and evasively. Perhaps this is Pinter's way of saying that people can never really know each other and that words are ultimately of no help.

Guidelines for Reading a Play

1. *Note any information that establishes the setting and the situation.* In *Last to Go,* we listen to a conversation between two men in a coffee stall in London late at night. The characters are of the working class: a barman and a newspaper seller.

2. *Note clues that tell what the players are doing or how the lines are spoken.* In Pinter's sketch there are no stage directions that tell what the players are doing or how the lines are spoken. However, the emphasis on pauses, repetition, and non-sequiturs (statements that do not follow from what has just been said) indicates a style of delivery that is real-istic, like snatches of everyday conversation.

3. *Be alert to the mood of the play.* In *Last to Go,* we get a sense of futility and isolation. Talk is empty or evasive. Words are no comfort since the characters are unable to articulate their experiences.

4. *Examine the relationship between style and subject matter.* The effect of Pinter's sketch is to leave us with no sure sense of the action, the characters' relationships to one another, or the reliability of their speeches. The inane dialogue, with its digressions and repetitions, is a suitable vehicle for the drama's ambiguities.

Practice in Close Reading

The comedy of manners flourished during the Restoration and eighteenth century. This kind of comedy is generally satirical and deals with the manners and attitudes of elegant society. The characters tend to be types rather than individuals. A recurrent character in Restoration drama is the fop, who is a favorite target of satire. The most characteristic element of the comedy of manners is its brilliant and witty dialogue. The action often grows out of characters' attempts to outwit each other. A conventional scene is the battle of words. The following passage is the opening of *The School for Scandal* (1777), a highly celebrated play written when its author, Richard Brinsley Sheridan, was twenty-six.

[Lady Sneerwell *at her dressing table with* Lappet, *her maid*; Miss Verjuice *drinking chocolate*.]

Lady Sneerwell. The paragraphs you say were all inserted?

Verjuice. They were, madam — and as I copied them myself in a feigned hand, there can be no suspicion whence they came.

Lady Sneerwell. Did you circulate the report of Lady Brittle's intrigue with Captain Boastall?

Verjuice. Madam, by this time Lady Brittle is the talk of half the town — and I doubt not in a week the men will toast her as a demirep.[1]

Lady Sneerwell. What have you done as to the insinuation as to a certain baronet's lady and a certain cook?

Verjuice. That is in as fine a train as your Ladyship could wish. I told the story yesterday to my own maid with directions to communicate it directly to my hairdresser. He, I am informed, has a brother who courts a milliner's prentice in Pall Mall,[2] whose mistress has a first cousin whose sister is *femme de chambre*[3] to Mrs. Clackit — so that in the common course of things it must reach Mrs. Clackit's ears within four-and-twenty hours, and then you know the business is as good as done.

Lady Sneerwell. Why, truly, Mrs. Clackit has a very pretty talent — a great deal of industry — yet — yes — been tolerably successful in her way. To my knowledge she has been the cause of breaking off six matches, of three sons being disinherited and four daughters being turned out of doors; of three several elopements, as many close confinements, nine separate maintenances, and two divorces. — Nay, I have more than once traced her causing a *tête-a-tête*[4] in the Town and Country Magazine,[5] when the parties perhaps had never seen each other's faces before in the course of their lives.

Verjuice. She certainly has talents.

Lady Sneerwell. But her manner is gross.

---

1. **demirep:** an adventuress; a woman of bad reputation.

2. **Pall Mall** (pĕl'mĕl'): a London street where many clubs are located.
3. *femme de chambre* (fȧm'də shäm'brə): French for "chambermaid."
4. *tête-a-tête* (tāt'ə-tāt'): French for "head to head"; a private conversation between two people.
5. **Town and Country Magazine:** a publication known for its gossip.

Verjuice. 'Tis very true. She generally designs well, has a free tongue, and a bold invention; but her coloring is too dark and her outline often extravagant. She wants that delicacy of tint and mellowness of sneer which distinguish your ladyship's scandal.

Lady Sneerwell. Ah, you are partial, Verjuice.

Verjuice. Not in the least; everybody allows that Lady Sneerwell can do more with a word or a look than many can with the most labored detail, even when they happen to have a little truth on their side to support it.

Lady Sneerwell. Yes, my dear Verjuice, I am no hypocrite to deny the satisfaction I reap from the success of my efforts. Wounded myself in the early part of my life by the envenomed tongue of slander, I confess I have since known no pleasure equal to the reducing others to the level of my own injured reputation.

Verjuice. Nothing can be more natural. But, my dear Lady Sneerwell, there is one affair in which you have lately employed me, wherein, I confess, I am at a loss to guess your motives.

Lady Sneerwell. I conceive you mean with respect to my neighbor, Sir Peter Teazle, and his family—Lappet. *(Exit Maid)*—And has my conduct in this matter really appeared to you so mysterious?

Richard Brinsley Sheridan
from *The School for Scandal*

FOR STUDY AND DISCUSSION

1. This is the opening scene of one of the most brilliant comedies in English literature. What do you learn about the activities of Lady Sneerwell and Miss Verjuice?

2. What are Lady Sneerwell's motives for scandal-mongering? Why does she consider her qualifications superior to those of Mrs. Clackit?

3. The names in Sheridan's play are revealing of character. For example, *verjuice* (vûr'jōōs') is the juice of some sour or unripe fruit. How is this name appropriate for the character? What do the other names tell you about the characters?

4. What human failing is the object of Sheridan's satire in this scene?

5. How is an element of suspense introduced at the end of the scene?

WRITING ABOUT LITERATURE

The Writing Process

We often refer to writing an essay as a *process*, which consists of three key stages or phases: **prewriting, writing,** and **revising.** In this process, much of the critical work precedes the actual writing of the paper. In the prewriting stage, the writer makes decisions about what to say and how to say it. Prewriting activities include choosing and limiting a topic, gathering ideas, organizing ideas, and arriving at a *thesis*—the controlling idea for the paper. In the next stage, the writer uses the working plan to write a first draft of the essay. In the revising stage, the writer rewrites the draft, several times perhaps, adding or deleting ideas, rearranging order, rephrasing for clarity, and correcting errors in spelling, punctuation, and grammar. The steps in the process are interdependent. For example, as ideas are developed on paper, the writer may find that additional evidence is needed to support a point or that some parts of the paper need to be reorganized.

The amount of time devoted to each stage will vary with individual assignments. During a classroom examination, you will have limited time to plan your essay and to proofread your paper. For a term paper, you may have weeks or even months to prepare your essay.

On the following pages the steps in this process are illustrated through the development of several model papers.

Answering Examination Questions

From time to time you will be asked to demonstrate your understanding of a literary work or a topic by writing a short essay in class. Usually, your teacher will designate the subject of the essay. How well you respond will depend not only on how carefully you have prepared for the examination but on how carefully you read and interpret the question.

Before you begin to answer an examination question, be sure you understand what the question calls for. If you are asked to cite examples of the use of symbols in *three* poems by Yeats, be sure to include three. If you refer to *two* poems only, your answer will be unacceptable. If you are asked to demonstrate the conventions of Elizabethan sonnets, you may choose from the works of Spenser, Sidney, and Shakespeare in this anthology. You should not include the sonnets of John Milton. No matter how good your essay is, it will be unsatisfactory if you do not respond to the question accurately.

Remember that you are expected to demonstrate specific knowledge of the literature. Any general statement should be supported by evidence. If you wish to show that a character changes, for example, you should refer to specific actions, dialogue, thoughts and feelings, or direct comments by the author in order to illustrate your point. If you are allowed to use your textbook during the examination, you may occasionally quote short passages or refer to a specific page in order to provide supporting evidence.

At the start, it may be helpful to jot down some notes to guide you in writing the essay. If you have several points to make, decide what the most effective order of presentation will be. You might build up to your strongest point, or you might present your points to develop a striking contrast. Aim for a logical organization.

Also remember that length alone is not satisfactory. Your answer must be relevant, and presented in acceptable, correct English. Always take time to proofread your paper.

The key word in examination questions is the *verb*. Let us look briefly at some common instructions used in examinations.

Analysis. A question may ask you to *analyze* some aspect of a literary work or topic. When you analyze something, you take it apart to see how each part works. On an examination, you will generally be directed to focus on some limited but essential aspect of a work in order to demonstrate your knowledge and understanding. A common type of exercise is *character analysis*, in which you draw on the most significant details of characterization in order to reach conclusions about a specific figure. For example, you might be asked to analyze the character of one of the leading figures in *Macbeth* (page 149), pointing out how that character is revealed through action, dialogue, soliloquies, and other characters' reactions. You might be asked to analyze the use and effect of sound patterns in "To a Skylark" (page 497). You might be asked to analyze the major theme and variations in Donne's "Meditation 17" (page 243). Analysis may be applied to form, technique, or ideas.

Comparison/Contrast. A question may ask that you *compare* (or *contrast*) two things, such as techniques, ideas, characters, or works. When you *compare*, you point out likenesses; when you *contrast*, you point out differences. At times you may be asked to *compare and contrast*. In that event, you will be expected to deal with similarities and

differences. You might be asked to compare the Monk and the Parson in the *Prologue* to *The Canterbury Tales* (page 51). You might be asked to contrast the philosophies in two Cavalier poems: "Why So Pale and Wan" (page 262) and "To Lucasta, on Going to the Wars" (page 263). You might compare and contrast the seaside settings in two works by Arnold: "To Marguerite—Continued" (page 583) and "Dover Beach" (page 584). Sometimes the instruction to *compare* implies both comparison and contrast. Always check with your teacher to make sure how inclusive the term *compare* is intended to be.

Description. If a question asks you to *describe* a setting or a character, you are expected to give a picture in words. In describing a setting, include not only features that establish time and place, but those features that contribute to atmosphere or mood. In describing a character, deal with both direct and indirect methods of characterization (see page 985). You might be asked to describe the setting of the Green Knight's chapel in *Sir Gawain and the Green Knight* (page 87) and its effect on Gawain. You might be asked to describe the character of Dr. Johnson as it is revealed in Boswell's *The Life of Samuel Johnson* (page 374).

Discussion. The word *discuss* in a question is much more general than the other words we've looked at. When you are asked to discuss a subject, you are expected to examine the subject thoroughly and to treat it in all significant aspects. You might be asked to discuss the Anglo-Saxon ideals of conduct reflected in the epic poem *Beowulf* (page 9). You might be asked to discuss contrary states in Blake's *Songs of Innocence* and *Songs of Experience* (pages 394–399). You might be asked to discuss Wilde's attitude toward Victorian earnestness in *The Importance of Being Earnest* (page 632).

Explanation. A question may ask you to *explain* something. When you explain, you give reasons for something being the way it is. You make clear a character's actions, or you show how something has come about. You might, for example, be asked to explain the targets of Swift's political satire in "A Voyage to Lilliput" (page 334). You might be asked to explain the poetic principles of Romanticism outlined in the preface to the *Lyrical Ballads* (see pages 416–420). You might be asked to explain the stream-of-consciousness technique used in "The New Dress" (page 715).

Illustration. The word *illustrate, demonstrate,* or *show* asks that you provide examples to support a point. You might be asked to provide examples of pagan and Christian elements in *Beowulf* (page 9). You might be asked to illustrate Shakespeare's use of dramatic irony in *Macbeth* (page 149). You might be asked to demonstrate the partiality for paradox in metaphysical poetry. Or you might be asked to show how Lamb blends fact and fiction in "Dream Children: A Reverie" (page 466).

Interpretation. The word *interpret* in a question asks that you give the meaning or significance of something. You might, for example, be asked to offer an interpretation for a symbol, such as the mirror in "The Lady of Shalott" (page 557). You might be asked to interpret the final lines of a work such as "A Slumber Did My Spirit Seal" (page 436). Sometimes you will be asked to agree or disagree with a stated interpretation of a work, giving specific evidence to support your opinion.

You will find that there is frequent overlapping of approaches. In discussing a subject, you may draw upon illustration, explanation, analysis, or any other approach that is useful. In comparing or contrasting two works, you may rely on description or interpretation. However, an examination question generally will have a central purpose, and it is important that you focus on this purpose in preparing your answer.

On the following pages you will find some sample examination questions and answers for study and discussion. Note that the assignments (shown in italics) may be phrased as essay topics.

I

QUESTION   *One important aspect of Anglo-Saxon society was the relationship between the lord and his retainers, an arrangement that depended on mutual trust and esteem. How does the* Beowulf *poet illustrate this relationship?*

METHOD OF ATTACK   Note that a number of clues for handling this question are built into its language. The exercise asks you to present evidence that will throw light on the relationship between the warrior and his leader. The phrase "an arrangement that depended on mutual trust and esteem" provides you with a focus for your answer. Naturally, you must demonstrate close reading of the excerpt in your textbook.

Students are sometimes surprised to discover how much evidence they can supply if they examine a text closely. Here, for example, is a plan showing how details might be selected and organized.

Paragraph 1   *Statement of Intent:* Understanding the relationship between the lord and his followers in Anglo-Saxon society helps us understand the events in the poem.

BODY

Paragraph 2	*Warrior's Role*	*Evidence*
	Offer allegiance	Beowulf called "Higlac's follower"
	Demonstrate valor in battle	Beowulf fights Grendel without sword or shield lest he sully his reputation and lose Higlac's respect.
	Defend lord's honor	Praise of Beowulf not intended to belittle Hrothgar
	Protect lord	Beowulf's followers come to his aid against Grendel.

Paragraph 3	*Lord's Role*	*Evidence*
	Protect followers	Hrothgar called "Lord and protector" and "shelterer of warriors"
	Reward them with treasure	Beowulf's armor very likely a gift
	Provide hospitality	Herot, mead-hall, where they are feasted
		Queen toasts warriors and fills mead cups
	Show them honor	Hrothgar mourns "his lost friends and companions."

CONCLUSION

Paragraph 4   *Summing Up:* The loyalty and interdependence of the lord and his followers offered a stable, emotionally gratifying relationship.

Evidence

Herot a symbol of community of fellowship, providing order and harmony
Feasting and rejoicing within mead-hall represent contrast to bleak surroundings
Grendel an enemy of this community

Even if you have a great deal to say, you may sometimes find it difficult to get started. One way to begin an essay is to restate the examiner's question.

**ANSWER
INTRODUCTION**

Restate question.
State intent.

One important aspect of Anglo-Saxon society emphasized by the *Beowulf* poet is the relationship between the lord and his retainers, an arrangement based on mutual trust and esteem. The events of the poem take on added significance once we understand the code by which the lord and his followers were governed.

The warrior was obligated to show allegiance to his lord, to defend the honor and person of his lord, and to demonstrate his own valor in battle. Beowulf alludes on several occasions to his feudal lord Higlac, and refers to himself as "Higlac's follower." He boasts that he will fight Grendel without sword or shield lest he lose Higlac's respect. Similarly, Hrothgar's followers guard the honor of their lord: their praise of Beowulf is not intended to belittle Hrothgar. Beowulf's band of followers is governed by the same code of allegiance. They come to Beowulf's defense when he is attacked by Grendel.

In return for their loyalty, the lord was obligated to protect his warriors, to reward them with treasure, to provide hospitality, and to honor them. Hrothgar is called the "lord and protector" of Herot, and he is also referred to as the "shelterer of warriors." Very likely, the treasures that were dispensed included richly prized armor, such as the coat of mail Beowulf pledges to return to Higlac, should he meet death in battle. The lord offered hospitality to his followers by feasting them at lengthy banquets. To celebrate Beowulf's arrival, Hrothgar's queen toasts the warriors and fills their mead cups. Slain warriors were honored. Hrothgar mourns his dead followers as "lost friends and companions."

The loyalty and interdependence of the lord and his followers offered a stable, emotionally gratifying relationship. These ties must have been essential in a warrior society. Herot, the mead-hall where the Danes meet in peaceful times to feast and celebrate their victories, is a symbol of their community of fellowship, offering order and harmony in a somber world. When we realize how vital this union was in Anglo-Saxon times, then we see Grendel's raids as more than murderous assaults on Hrothgar's men. By undermining this relationship, he endangers the moral order of their society.

Length: 362 words

II

It is often noted that each of Chaucer's portraits in the Prologue *to* The Canterbury Tales *not only presents a convincingly lifelike image of an individual, but also reveals Chaucer's attitude toward his character. Select one of the characters presented in the* Prologue *and in a paragraph discuss Chaucer's attitude toward that character. You may use your textbook for reference.*

In preparing your answer to this question, take full advantage of the opportunity to consult your textbook. Assume that you have chosen the Pardoner as the subject of your essay. This is one approach you might use.

Chaucer's Attitude Toward the Pardoner

1 Emphasizes unattractive physical features
   long, lank locks of yellow hair that fall like "rat-tails" (662–666)
   "bulging eyeballs, like a hare" (671)
   voice like that of a goat (675)
   no beard (676–677)

2 Unmasks deception in abuse of church
   dispenses fraudulent "pardons come from Rome all hot" (674)
   sells fraudulent relics: a pillowcase as a holy veil (681–682)
   cheats honest parsons and makes "monkeys of the priest and congregation" (693)
   uses skill as an orator—"his honey-tongue"—to preach in order to "win silver from the crowd" (699–700)
   sings profane love songs with the Summoner (659–660)
   sings piously in church (the Offertory) when collection plate is passed (697)

3 Praises him ironically
   calls him a "noble ecclesiast" (695)
   says there is no pardoner of "equal grace" (680)

4 Aligns him with the Summoner, another rogue

> He satirizes the Pardoner as a swindler and hypocrite who deceives and cheats others under the pretense of piety.

Note that the statement at the right shows the conclusion that has been drawn from the evidence. This statement is called a *thesis statement*. A thesis statement is a sentence that expresses the *thesis*, or the central idea that gives focus to a paper.

In an essay consisting of several paragraphs, the thesis statement normally appears in the first paragraph. In a single-paragraph essay, the thesis statement will often be the topic sentence.

ANSWER

Thesis Statement

Point 1

Supporting Evidence

Point 2

Supporting Evidence

Chaucer satirizes the Pardoner as a swindler and hypocrite who deceives and cheats others under the pretense of piety. *One clue to Chaucer's attitude is found in his unflattering description of the Pardoner's appearance.* His long, lank locks of yellow hair suggest "rat-tails." He has "bulging eyeballs, like a hare." He has an unmanly face and an unpleasant voice. *Chaucer's critical attitude is also apparent in revealing how the Pardoner abuses the church for his own profit.* It is likely that the "pardons come from Rome all hot" are fraudulent and that the Pardoner is not licensed to distribute them. He also sells fraudulent relics, such as a pillowcase he claims to be a holy veil. In addition to these abuses, he cheats honest parsons and makes "monkeys of the priest and congregation." He uses his skill as an orator—"his honey-tongue"—to preach so that he can "win silver from the crowd." His fondness for singing, first noted when he joins the Summoner in singing love songs, is put to advantage in singing the Offertory in church, when the collection

Point 3

plate is passed. *In praising the Pardoner ironically, Chaucer cautions us that what appears on the surface is false.* He says there is no

Supporting Evidence

pardoner of "equal grace" and calls him a "noble ecclesiast" by way of stressing his talents as a liar and imposter. *It is no accident that*

Conclusion

Chaucer aligns him with the Summoner, another scoundrel who takes advantage of the church.

Length: 245 words

III

QUESTION   *In a paragraph, give your interpretation of the following lines from Macbeth, making clear their dramatic significance.*

> *I have lived long enough. My way of life*
> *Is fall'n into the sear, the yellow leaf;*
> *And that which should accompany old age,*
> *As honor, love, obedience, troops of friends,*
> *I must not look to have; but, in their stead,*
> *Curses, not loud but deep, mouth honor, breath,*
> *Which the poor heart would fain deny, and dare not.*
> *(V, 3, 22-28)*

This question asks you to interpret, or give the meaning of, a key passage in a selection. What you need to demonstrate in your answer is that you understand not only this passage but its importance in the play. Since you are instructed to write a single paragraph, the opening sentence should state the controlling idea of your essay.

ANSWER   This speech shows Macbeth's heartsick and remorseful state of mind before the crucial battle at Dunsinane. As he prepares for battle, Macbeth considers what his life will be like if he should be victorious. He feels that for him life is over: "I have lived long enough." All the comforts one looks forward to in old age will be denied to him. When he likens his stage of life to a yellow leaf, we see that all his hopes, once ripe, have withered. Instead of respect and love, he will receive curses. In place of loyal subjects and friends, he will have the empty vows—"mouth honor"—of cowards who serve him because they are poor in heart and are afraid to speak openly. Macbeth realizes the terrible irony of his life—all he had done to obtain and keep the throne has been for nought.

Length: 146 words

IV

QUESTION *What single poem included in your anthology would you choose to introduce a reader to English Romanticism? Analyze the poem, focusing on those characteristics of Romantic literature that you wish to emphasize. Use your textbook for reference.*

METHOD OF ATTACK This question allows you considerable freedom, and there are many choices open to you in handling the assignment. The word *characteristics* has a broad meaning and may be taken to include matters of form as well as subject matter. Some students will undoubtedly choose the poem first. Other students will be more comfortable first determining the characteristics to be emphasized and then using these as criteria for selecting a poem.

Assume that the poem chosen for this assignment is Shelley's "Ode to the West Wind" (page 493). The following outline divides the analysis into subject matter and form. The characteristics of Romanticism are listed in the left-hand column, specific evidence in the right-hand column.

Note that the writer does not attempt to cover every aspect of Romanticism, but focuses on a few important characteristics. Note also how the writer makes connections between the characteristics of Romanticism and their appearance in Shelley's poem.

Subject Matter

Characteristics of Romanticism	*Evidence in Poem*
Use of natural landscape in imagery	Dominant imagery drawn from nature—earth, sky, sea Central image of wind—"destroyer and preserver"—linked with cycle of seasons
Interest in relationship between mind and natural world	Explores relationship between his own imagination and the power of the wind
Continually reading meanings in nature	As agent of destruction and regeneration, wind corresponds to inner change from spiritual dejection to spiritual vitality: "Be thou, Spirit fierce, / My spirit!"
Emphasis on "spontaneous overflow of powerful feelings"	Poet confesses to a crisis of imaginative powers: "I fall upon the thorns of life! I bleed!"
Emotion and subjective experience	Seeks renewal of creative powers, calls on wind to inspire him: "Make me thy lyre."

Lyric, written in first person, preferred form for subjective experience	Ode suitable for expression of intense, personal experience
Elaborate structure, dignified style	Poet invokes West Wind
	Displays technical skill
Experiments in form widespread	Shelley's stanza a fusion of sonnet and *terza rima*: 4 tercets and couplet
	Individual experiment successful in conveying driving force of wind tossing leaves, clouds, waves
	Imposes order on disorder

ANSWER

INTRODUCTION
Restate question.

State intent.

In subject matter and in form, Shelley's "Ode to the West Wind" is an ideal introduction to English Romanticism. In this poem we can identify Romanticism's most characteristic subject: the poet's thoughts and feelings set in motion in response to the natural world. In the stanza Shelley invented for this ode, we have an example of the experimental boldness that led to new and distinctive forms.

BODY
Topic Sentence

The intense love of the physical universe, so pervasive in Romantic writing, is reflected in the imagery of Shelley's poem. Shelley draws his dominant images from nature — the leaves of the earth, the clouds in the sky, the waves in the sea. His central image of the

Supporting Evidence

wind, "destroyer and preserver," is linked with the cycle of the seasons. In autumn the wind destroys in order that there may be regeneration in the spring.

Topic Sentence

Like other Romantic writers, who read meanings in the natural world, Shelley is concerned with exploring the relationship between his own imagination and the power of nature. The wind is not only a feature of the landscape, but an instrument for change in the

Supporting Evidence

poet's mind. As the agent of destruction and rebirth, the wind corresponds to the change within the poet from spiritual dejection to spiritual vitality. It is transformed from a literal wind to a metaphorical wind of inspiration: "Be thou, Spirit fierce,/My spirit!"

Topic Sentence

Another important aspect of Romantic subject matter, the concern with emotion and subjective experience, is evident in Shelley's ode. The poet confesses to a crisis of his imaginative powers. He has lost the confidence and spontaneity of his boyhood and is chained

Supporting Evidence

by a "heavy weight of hours." Shelley's most direct and "spontaneous overflow of powerful feelings" is expressed in the line "I fall upon the thorns of life! I bleed!" He calls on the wind to inspire him: "Make me thy lyre."

Topic Sentence

In his choice of the ode as a poetic form, Shelley follows the Romantic preference for lyrics, the type of poetry best suited to expressing a range of emotions and reflections. The ode gives Shelley

	an effective vehicle for addressing the West Wind directly in the first person and for treating his subject in a dignified, stately style. Because it has a more elaborate structure than most lyrics, the ode also gives Shelley an opportunity to display his technical gifts.

Supporting Evidence

Topic Sentence

Shelley's ode should also be viewed as an outstanding example of the widespread practice among Romantic poets of experimenting with traditional forms. Shelley invents a stanza that is a highly complicated fusion of the sonnet and *terza rima.* It consists of four tercets, or triplets, and a couplet. The interlocking rhyme scheme of each stanza, in which the middle rhyme of each triplet becomes the first and third rhyme of the next triplet, is particularly effective in conveying the dramatic movement of the wind tossing the leaves, clouds, and waves. Yet, the sense of disorder and confusion associated with the wind is held in check by the regularity and control of the stanzaic pattern. The effect is that of the poet's imagination giving shape and meaning to the power of nature.

Supporting Evidence

CONCLUSION

Although no single work in the Romantic period can embrace the creative energy and genius of all its writers, Shelley's "Ode to the West Wind" is a good point of departure for further study. The reader of Shelley's poem will have a reasonably valid impression of Romanticism's concerns and one of its most magnificent achievements.

Summing Up

Length: 576 words

Writing on a Topic of Your Own

Choosing a Topic

In writing about literature, the object is to say something meaningful about the work under consideration. Some topics lend themselves to more useful investigation than others. A plot summary of *Macbeth*, for example, is not likely to lead readers to a greater understanding and appreciation of the play. An analysis of Macbeth's imagination, on the other hand, might give readers new insights into Macbeth's character. Choosing a topic is, in the first place, a matter of pursuing a worthwhile line of inquiry.

Choosing a topic is also a matter of making use of special abilities, experiences, and background. A writer with a strong interest in English history might profitably compare Shakespeare's play with its source in Holinshed's *Chronicles*. A writer who had studied other tragedies by Shakespeare might have sufficient skill to compare *Macbeth* with *Richard III*. These plays have many elements in common.

The choice of a topic, moreover, depends on the amount of time and space available.

A writer who is asked for a 500-word paper would not choose a subject that calls for exhaustive treatment. A three-paragraph essay might be just enough room to say something about one of Macbeth's soliloquies. A 1500-word essay might give a writer enough room to discuss some dominant images in the play.

Sometimes a topic will suggest itself while you are reading a work. You may find yourself puzzled or fascinated by some idea or technique. It may take several readings before you hit on a subject for analysis. While you were reading Galsworthy's story "The Japanese Quince" (page 920), you noted that the little tree plays an important role in the story. On rereading the story you might conclude that the tree functions as a symbol. Your topic might then become a study of the Japanese quince as a symbol in Galsworthy's story.

A topic may focus on one element or technique in a work. If you are writing about fiction (short story or novel), you might concentrate on some aspect of plot, character, setting, point of view, or theme; or you might examine an author's use of symbolism, irony, imagery, allusion, and so on. The composition exercise on page 743 of this textbook calls for discussing the dill pickle as a symbol in Katherine Mansfield's story. The exercise on page 727 calls for analysis of the images of light and shadow in Joyce's "Araby." Another exercise, on page 611, calls for analysis of Dickens' use of caricature in a chapter of *Hard Times*.

If you are writing about poetry, you might choose to analyze any rhetorical device (such as figurative language), patterns of sound, mood, structure, and so on. The composition exercise on page 143 calls for discussing the mood of five of Shakespeare's songs. The exercise on page 496 calls for explaining how figures of speech enrich the meaning of Shelley's "Ode to the West Wind." Still another exercise, on page 838, calls for analyzing the use and effect of sound patterns in Dylan Thomas' "Fern Hill."

In addition to the types of topics listed above, topics for drama may focus on the characteristics of a specific genre, such as tragedy or comedy.

A topic may deal with a specific problem in a work. One example of this kind is interpreting the final lines of Keats's "Ode on a Grecian Urn" (page 523).

A topic may deal with multiple aspects of a work. Such a topic calls for describing the means Coleridge employs to induce a "willing suspension of disbelief" in *The Rime of the Ancient Mariner* (page 461).

Especially frutiful for literary study are topics calling for comparison and contrast. Some aspect of two works may be compared. Some possible topics are comparing the elegiac tone of "The Seafarer" with the heroic tone of *Beowulf* (page 28); comparing ideas of retreat in Marvell's "The Garden" and Vaughan's "The Retreat" (page 251); comparing the use of setting in "The Train from Rhodesia" with its use in "Across the Bridge" (page 784).

A topic provides you with a focus for analysis. It is a point of departure for further study. Once you have a topic in mind, your object is to form it into a *thesis*, an idea that represents the conclusion of your findings. For example, if your purpose is to examine the Japanese quince as a symbol in Galsworthy's story, you might conclude after studying the evidence that the tree stands for certain qualities—joy, beauty, and spontaneity—that are a dramatic contrast to those qualities that characterize the figures in the story, namely order, convention, and material well-being. You would then need to present the evidence supporting your position.

It may be necessary to read a work several times before you can formulate a thesis. Do not be overly concerned if an idea comes slowly. This is a common experience.

Often a paper is unsatisfactory because it does not present a thesis clearly or forcefully. A paper that rambles on about Lady Macbeth's character may contain a great deal of information, but without a controlling idea, it will remain inconclusive. A paper that sets out to show how Lady Macbeth's character disintegrates has a clear purpose and focus.

You may find it helpful to phrase the problem or topic as a question. For example, if you have decided to compare the characters of Macbeth and Lady Macbeth, you might phrase your assignment as: "How are the characters alike, and how are they different?"

Gathering Evidence

It is a good idea to take notes as you read, even if you do not yet have a topic in mind. Later on, when you have settled on a topic, you can discard any notes that are not relevant. Some people prefer a worksheet, others index cards. Initially you should record all your reactions.

A topic may emerge during this early stage. As you continue to read, you will shape your topic into a rough thesis.

Let us suppose that you have chosen to compare Housman's "On Wenlock Edge" (page 928) with this poem:

Loveliest of Trees   *A. E. Housman*

Loveliest of trees, the cherry now
Is hung with bloom along the bough,
And stands about the woodland ride°
Wearing white for Eastertide.

Now, of my threescore years and ten,°   5
Twenty will not come again,
And take from seventy springs a score,
It only leaves me fifty more.

And since to look at things in bloom
Fifty springs are little room,   10
About the woodlands I will go
To see the cherry hung with snow.

---

3. **woodland ride:** a forest path, usually for riding horses.   5. **threescore years and ten:** seventy years, a Biblical allusion to the average life span. See Psalm 90:10.

Even a superficial reading shows that there is common ground for comparison and contrast. You might work out a chart of this kind for taking notes, letting the letter A stand for "Loveliest of Trees" and B for "On Wenlock Edge":

POINTS OF COMPARISON	SIMILARITIES	DIFFERENCES
Subject	In each poem, the speaker is looking at a woodland scene.	In A he views a tranquil scene of natural beauty: the cherry trees in bloom in spring ("Eastertide"). In B he views the turbulence of nature; the trees are being whipped by a strong wind.
	The natural scene in each poem leads the speaker to reflect on the brevity of life.	In Stanza 2 of A, the speaker reflects on how little time there is to enjoy the natural beauty of the world. He is twenty (line 6) and may have fifty more years of life (line 5) but "only" fifty more years seems "little room" to "look at things in bloom." In B the speaker does not regret the brevity of life. On the contrary, it puts an end to the tragedy and pain of life (lines 18–20).
Imagery, Figurative Language, etc.	Both poems use personification to endow nature with human qualities.	In A the trees are in holiday spirit, dressed up, "Wearing white for Eastertide." In B the trees, the wind, the hill are given human attributes stressing pain: the wood's "in trouble"; the Wrekin throws off *his* leaves; the wind shows its "old anger" by thrashing the trees.
	Both poems use metaphor to add emotional intensity.	Metaphor emphasizes beauty and delight in nature in A. In line 12, "the cherry hung with snow," snow may be a metaphor for the blooming trees, which are white like snow, or the snow on the trees may look like white blossoms. In B, metaphor emphasizes desolation and pain. See entire first stanza and lines 13–14.
Devices of Sound	In each poem lyrical quality reflects mood. Both make use of alliteration, rhyme, and repetition.	In A the poet uses alliteration for both emphasis and beauty of sound: "*b*loom" and "*b*ough" (line 2); "*w*oodland," "*W*earing *w*hite" (lines 3–4); "*s*eventy *s*prings" and "*s*core" (line 7). Also notable is the use of assonance: "*A*nd," "st*a*nds," "wood-l*a*nd" (line 3); "wh*i*te," "E*a*ster-t*i*de" (line 4); "s*i*nce," "th*i*ngs,"

POINTS OF COMPARISON	SIMILARITIES	DIFFERENCES
		"*in*," "F*i*fty," "spr*i*ngs," "l*i*ttle" (lines 9–10). There is consonance as well: "hu*ng*," "alo*ng*" (line 2), and subtle internal rhyme: "thing*s*"/"spring*s*" (lines 9–10). The end rhymes, simple and pleasurable, add a dimension to the meaning of the lines. The music in B is of a darker sort. Rhyme words tend to link pain or strife: "trouble"/"double"; "heaves"/"leaves"; "hanger"/"anger"; "riot"/"quiet"; "double"/"trouble"; "gone"/"Uricon." Devices of repetition emphasize feelings of distress: the alliteration of "*h*eaving," "*h*ill," and "*h*urt" in stanza 3; the assonance of "fl*ee*ce," "Wr*e*kin," and "h*ea*ves" in line 2; the consonance of stanza 2 in "stoo*d*," "ol*d*," "win*d*," "threshe*d*," "woo*d*"; as well as the repetition of the word *old* in line 7.
Theme	In both poems nature causes the speaker to reflect upon the human condition. In each poem there is a tension between permanence and impermanence—the eternal, unchanging patterns of nature and of human experience and the impermanence of the individual life.	In A the speaker makes us constantly aware of his mortality. The span of life is measured and seasons marked off. The time given is too little "room" to enjoy natural beauty. The word *now* (lines 1, 5) has an urgency—time is running out and we need to seize pleasure while we can. In B there is no respite from the sadness of life and no interruption in the tragic cycle. The speaker identifies his own disconsolate mood with the turbulence of nature, and takes comfort in the thought that human life is short.

You might find at this point that a thesis statement has begun to emerge: *Although the poems are quite different in thought and tone, they share an underlying concern with the transience of the individual life in contrast to the unchanging character of nature and of human experience.* You would continue to study the poems, gathering additional evidence to develop your thesis statement. The next step is organizing the material.

Organizing the Material

Before you begin writing, organize your main ideas into an outline. Your outline should provide for an introduction, a body, and a conclusion. The introduction should identify the authors, the works, or the problem that is under study. It should contain a statement of your thesis as well. The body of your paper should present the evidence supporting your thesis. If you are writing about the two Housman poems, you might relate setting, imagery and figurative language, and devices of sound to thematic development. The conclusion should bring together your main ideas or suggest additional ideas for study.

The outline will grow out of the notes you have compiled. Remember that you need not use *all* the evidence you have collected. You should include material that has bearing on your topic.

Outlining is the last important stage before writing your paper. An outline shows your major ideas and the order in which you will present them. If you plan your outline carefully, you will have a valuable guide to writing a coherent and effective essay.

Although many writers use the topic outline with success, you may prefer to use the sentence outline, which is more detailed. By phrasing your main ideas as complete sentences, you may arrive at the key statements of your paper.

This is one kind of outline you might use for a short paper. It indicates the main idea of each paragraph.

INTRODUCTION

Paragraph 1   *Thesis*   Although the two poems are obviously different in thought and tone, they share an underlying theme—a preoccupation with the transience of human life.

BODY

Paragraph 2   The setting in both poems is the woods, but the mood is contrasting.

Paragraph 3   In "Loveliest of Trees" the speaker reflects on the brevity of life's pleasures.

Paragraph 4   In "On Wenlock Edge" the speaker reflects on the brevity of life in terms of its pain.

Paragraph 5   The musical devices in each poem reflect the speaker's mood.

CONCLUSION

Paragraph 6   Housman contrasts the transience of the individual life with the eternal patterns of nature and human experience.

Writing the Essay

A good introduction is critical. In a short paper, be sure that your opening paragraph states your purpose (here, a comparison of two poems) and makes clear your thesis. Compare the following paragraphs for content and style:

Weak Introduction	Better Introduction
In this paper I will discuss "Loveliest of Trees" and "On Wenlock Edge" by A. E. Housman. I will point out similarities and differences in the two poems. I will show that the poems are linked by a common theme.	Because the lyrics "Loveliest of Trees" and "On Wenlock Edge" are quite different in thought and tone, we might assume that they represent contrasting or conflicting aspects of Housman's philosophy. If we look beyond the obvious differences, however, we find that the poems share an underlying theme. Both show Housman's preoccupation with the transience of human life, the ephemeral qualities of its pleasures, and an awareness of its pain.

Here is a model essay developing the thesis statement.

TITLE A COMPARISON OF "LOVELIEST OF TREES" AND "ON WENLOCK EDGE"

INTRODUCTION
Identify subject of paper.

Because the lyrics "Loveliest of Trees" and "On Wenlock Edge" are quite different in thought and tone, we might assume that they represent contrasting or conflicting aspects of Housman's philosophy. If we look beyond the obvious differences, however, we find that the poems share an underlying theme. Both show Housman's preoccupation with the transience of human life, the ephemeral qualities of its pleasures, and an awareness of its pain.

State thesis.

BODY
Topic Sentence

In each poem the speaker is communicating the character of a woodland scene. In "Loveliest of Trees," the setting is tranquil. It is spring ("Eastertide"); the speaker is in the woods, taking pleasure in looking at the cherry trees in bloom. The scene in "On Wenlock Edge," by contrast, is turbulent. The season is probably late fall or winter, and the wood is "in trouble." A powerful wind is whipping leaves off the trees and causing the saplings to bend.

Topic Sentence

Demonstrate close reading of text.
Use direct quotations where apt.

In each poem the setting causes the speaker to reflect on the brevity of life. In the second stanza of "Loveliest of Trees," the speaker works out the arithmetic of his life. He is twenty. In an expected life span of seventy (line 5), he can look forward to fifty more springs. Yet, fifty more springs are not enough ("little room") for the pleasures of nature: "to look at things in bloom." The speaker makes us aware throughout the poem that pleasures are ephemeral:

the repetition of *now* in lines 1 and 5 suggests that the moment is of short duration. Youth is fleeting: "Twenty will not come again." There is precious little time to enjoy life: There are *only* fifty springs remaining. This lyric carries a sad message. The speaker, knowing that his days are numbered, is determined to enjoy the beauty of the world while he can.

Topic Sentence — In "On Wenlock Edge," the speaker examines the brevity of human life in terms of its pains rather than its pleasures. During their brief stay on earth, human beings are subject to frustration and heartache. This was true for earlier civilizations as well as for his own. The Roman who once occupied this site was visited by the same passions ("blood") and the same frustrations ("thoughts that hurt him"). Like the wind that thrashes the trees, the "gale of life" brings suffering. The speaker finds only one consolation; life's anguish is resolved in death:

> Today the Roman and his trouble
> Are ashes under Uricon.

Topic Sentence — The lyrical quality of each poem reflects its mood. In "Loveliest of Trees," sound complements the loveliness of the woodland scene. Housman uses alliteration for both emphasis and beauty of sound: "*b*loom" and "*b*ough" (line 2); "*w*oodland," "*W*earing *w*hite" (lines 3–4); "*s*eventy *s*prings" and "*s*core" (line 7). Also notable is the use of assonance, markedly in lines 9–10: "s*i*nce," th*i*ngs," "*i*n," "F*i*fty," "spr*i*ngs," and "l*i*ttle." There is consonance as well: "hu*ng*," "alo*ng*" (line 2), and subtle internal rhyme: "things"/"springs" (lines 9–10). The end rhymes, simple and pleasurable, emphasize the speaker's awareness of the passing of time: *now, ten, again, score, more.* The music of "On Wenlock Edge" is of a darker sort. **Transition** — Rhyme words tend to link pain or strife: "trouble"/"double" (used twice); "heaves"/"leaves"; "hanger"/"anger"; "gone"/"Uricon." Devices of repetition emphasize feelings of distress: the alliteration of "*h*eaving," "*h*ill," and "*h*urt" in stanza 3; the assonance of "fl*ee*ce," Wr*e*kin," and "h*ea*ves" in line 2; the consonance of "stoo*d*," "ol*d*," "win*d*," "threshe*d*," and "woo*d*" in stanza 2; and the repetition of "old" in line 7.

CONCLUSION
Topic Sentence — Against the transience of the individual life, Housman sets the eternal, unchanging patterns of nature and of the human condition. Nature's cycle is unending. The cherry trees will bloom every spring; the wind that thrashes the trees on Wenlock Edge will do so again and again. Similarly, the joys and sorrows of human life will be renewed in every generation. This contrast underscores the unity of human beings and nature. The individual life is mortal; the characteristics of nature and of human experience are immortal.

Relate ideas to thesis.

Length: 667 words

Revising Papers

When you write an essay in class, you have a limited amount of time to plan and develop your essay Nevertheless, you should save a few minutes to proofread your work.

When an essay is assigned as homework, you have more time to prepare it carefully Get into the habit of revising your work. A first draft of an essay should be treated as a rough copy of your manuscript. Chances are that reworking your first draft will result in a clearer and stronger paper.

When you revise your paper, examine it critically for awkward sentences, inexact language, errors in capitalization, punctuation, and spelling. Rewrite any passages that are unclear or incomplete.

On pages 954–957 you will find an early draft of the essay that appears on pages 951–952. You might profitably compare the two versions of this paper. Notice how often the writer has edited sentences to make vague or general statements more specific.

Guidelines for Revising a Paper

1. *Check to see that your major point, a thesis, is clearly stated.* In a short essay, the thesis should be stated in the first sentence. In a longer paper, the thesis should appear in the introduction.

2. *Follow a logical organization.* A long composition should have an introduction, a body, and a conclusion. Each part of the essay should be clearly related to the thesis.

3. *Make sure that ideas are adequately developed.* Support any generalization with specific evidence.

4. *Check for errors in capitalization, punctuation, spelling, and sentence structure.*

Here is a first draft of the model essay on pages 951–952, showing
how it was revised for greater clarity, accuracy, and conciseness.

~~Housman's~~ *Because the* lyrics "Loveliest of Trees" and "On Wenlock Edge" are

~~obviously~~ quite different in tone and ~~in subject~~, *thought* ~~and~~ we might assume

represent contrasting or conflicting aspects of Housman's philosophy.

that they ~~express different philosophies of life. The reverse is true.~~

If we look beyond the obvious differences, however, we find that

The poems ~~actually~~ share an underlying theme. Both show Housman's

preoccupation with the transience of human life, the ephemeral

qualities of its pleasures, and an awareness of its pain.

Communicating the character of a woodland scene.

In each poem the speaker is ~~looking at trees~~. In "Loveliest of Trees,"

the setting is tranquil. The scene in "On Wenlock Edge," by contrast,

is turbulent. ~~In the first poem,~~ it is spring ("Eastertide"); the speaker

is in the woods, taking pleasure in looking at the cherry trees in bloom.

The season ~~in the second poem~~ is probably late fall or winter, and the

wood is "in trouble." ~~We know this because~~ a powerful wind is whipping

leaves off the trees and causing the saplings to bend.

the brevity of

In each poem the setting causes the speaker to reflect on ~~how short~~

the second stanza of   *the speaker*

life. ~~is / The speaker~~ in "Loveliest of Trees" works out the arithmetic

He is twenty. In   *(lines 5)*

of his life. ~~Given~~ an expected life span of seventy, he can look forward to fifty more springs. Yet, fifty more springs are not enough ("little

room") for the pleasures of nature: "to look at things in bloom."

The speaker makes us aware throughout the poem that pleasures are ephemeral:
the repetition of ~~The word~~ now, in lines 1 and 5 ~~which appears twice,~~ suggests that the moment is of

short duration. Youth is fleeting: "Twenty will not come again."

There is precious little time to enjoy life: There are only fifty

springs remaining. This lyric carries a sad message. The speaker,
knowing that his days are numbered,
is determined to enjoy the beauty of the world while he can.

In "On Wenlock Edge," the speaker examines the brevity of human life,
During their brief stay on earth, human beings are subject to
in terms of its pains rather than its pleasures. Frustration and

heartache ~~are the lot of all human beings~~. This was true for

his own.
earlier civilizations as well as for ~~the speaker's~~. ~~The speaker imagines~~

the Roman who once occupied this site, ~~He~~ was visited by the same
("flood")   ("thoughts that hurt him")   Like the wind that thrashes the
passions and the same frustrations. ~~Life, like nature, brings~~
trees, the "gale of life" brings suffering. The speaker finds only one consolation;
~~suffering. The only consolation for the speaker is that there is an~~

life's anguish is resolved in death:
~~end to life's anguish:~~

Today the Roman and his trouble

Are ashes under Uricon.

The lyrical quality of each poem reflects its mood. In ~~the first~~ "Loveliest of Trees,"

~~poem,~~ sound complements the loveliness of the woodland scene. ~~The poem~~

~~contains alliteration, assonance, consonance, and rhyme.~~ Housman uses

both

alliteration for ∧ emphasis and beauty of sound: "<u>b</u>loom" and "<u>b</u>ough" (line 2);

S 3-4

"<u>w</u>oodland," "<u>W</u>earing <u>w</u>hite" (line ∧ 3); "<u>s</u>eventy <u>s</u>prings" and "<u>s</u>core" (line 7).

Also notable is the use of assonance, markedly in lines 9-10: "s<u>i</u>nce,"

"th<u>i</u>ngs," "<u>i</u>n," "F<u>i</u>fty," "spr<u>i</u>ngs," and "l<u>i</u>ttle." There is consonance

as well: "hu<u>ng</u>," "alo<u>ng</u>" (line 2), and subtle internal rhyme: "things"/

emphasize the

"springs" (lines 9-10). The end rhymes, simple and pleasurable, ~~add a~~

speaker's awareness of the passing of time):

~~dimension to the meaning of the lines~~: <u>now</u>, <u>ten</u>, <u>again</u>, <u>score</u>, <u>more</u>.

The music of "On Wenlock Edge" is of a darker sort. Rhyme words tend

(used twice)

to link pain or strife: "trouble"/"double"/; "heaves"/"leaves"; "hanger"/
                                         ∧
"anger"; ~~"double"/"trouble"~~; "gone"/"Uricon." Devices of repetition

emphasize feelings of distress: the alliteration of "<u>h</u>eaving," "<u>h</u>ill,"

and "<u>h</u>urt" in stanza 3; the assonance of "fl<u>ee</u>ce," "Wr<u>e</u>kin," and

"h<u>ea</u>ves" in line 2; the consonance of "stoo<u>d</u>," "ol<u>d</u>," "win<u>d</u>," "threshe<u>d</u>,"

and "woo<u>d</u>" in stanza 2; and the repetition of "old" in line 7.

~~Housman shows us that~~ nature's cycle is unending. The cherry trees

will bloom every spring; the wind that thrashes the trees on Wenlock

Edge will do so again and again. Similarly, the joys and sorrows of

This contrast underscores the unity of human beings and nature.

human life will be renewed in every generation. The individual life

is mortal; the characteristics of nature and of human experience are

immortal. Against the transience of the individual life, Housman

sets the eternal, unchanging patterns of nature and of the human

condition.

ADDITIONAL SELECTIONS

Miss Brill   *Katherine Mansfield*

Although it was so brilliantly fine—the blue sky powdered with gold and great spots of light like white wine splashed over the Jardins Publiques[1]—Miss Brill was glad that she had decided on her fur. The air was motionless, but when you opened your mouth, there was just a faint chill, like a chill from a glass of iced water before you sip, and now and again a leaf came drifting—from nowhere, from the sky. Miss Brill put up her hand and touched her fur. Dear little thing! It was nice to feel it again. She had taken it out of its box that afternoon, shaken out the moth powder, given it a good brush, and rubbed the life back into the dim little eyes. "What has been happening to me?" said the sad little eyes. Oh, how sweet it was to see them snap at her again from the red eiderdown![2] . . . But the nose, which was of some black composition, wasn't at all firm. It must have had a knock, somehow. Never mind—a little dab of black sealing wax when the time came—when it was absolutely necessary . . . Little rogue! Yes, she really felt like that about it. Little rogue biting its tail just by her left ear. She could have taken it off and laid it on her lap and stroked it. She felt a tingling in her hands and arms, but that came from walking, she supposed. And when she breathed, something light and sad—no, not sad, exactly—something gentle seemed to move in her bosom.

There were a number of people out this afternoon, far more than last Sunday. And the band sounded louder and gayer. That was because the Season had begun. For although the band played all the year round on Sundays, out of season it was never the same. It was like someone playing with only the family to listen; it didn't care how it played if there weren't any strangers present. Wasn't the conductor wearing a new coat, too? She was sure it was new. He scraped with his foot and flapped his arms like a rooster about to crow, and the bandsmen sitting in the green rotunda[3] blew out their cheeks and glared at the music. Now there came a little "flutey" bit—very pretty—a little chain of bright drops. She was sure it would be repeated. It was; she lifted her head and smiled.

Only two people shared her "special" seat: a fine old man in a velvet coat, his hands clasped over a huge carved walking stick, and a big old woman, sitting upright, with a roll of knitting on her embroidered apron. They did not speak. This was disappointing, for Miss Brill always looked forward to the conversation. She had become really quite expert, she thought, at listening as though she didn't listen, at sitting in other people's lives just for a minute while they talked round her.

She glanced, sideways, at the old couple. Perhaps they would go soon. Last Sunday, too,

---

1. **Jardins Publiques** (zhär-dăɴʹ pōō-blēkʹ): French for "Public Gardens."
2. **eiderdown:** bed quilt stuffed with down from an eider duck.

3. **rotunda** (rō-tŭnʹdə): a circular structure, usually covered by a dome.

hadn't been as interesting as usual. An Englishman and his wife, he wearing a dreadful Panama hat and she button boots. And she'd gone on the whole time about how she ought to wear spectacles; she knew she needed them; but that it was no good getting any; they'd be sure to break and they'd never keep on. And he'd been so patient. He'd suggested everything—gold rims, the kind that curved round your ears, little pads inside the bridge. No, nothing would please her. "They'll always be sliding down my nose!" Miss Brill had wanted to shake her.

The old people sat on the bench, still as statues. Never mind, there was always the crowd to watch. To and fro, in front of the flower beds and the band rotunda, the couples and groups paraded, stopped to talk, to greet, to buy a handful of flowers from the old beggar who had his tray fixed to the railings. Little children ran among them, swooping and laughing; little boys with big white silk bows under their chins, little girls, little French dolls, dressed up in velvet and lace. And sometimes a tiny staggerer came suddenly rocking into the open from under the trees, stopped, stared, as suddenly sat down "flop," until its small high-stepping mother, like a young hen, rushed scolding to its rescue. Other people sat on the benches and green chairs, but they were nearly always the same, Sunday after Sunday, and—Miss Brill had often noticed—there was something funny about nearly all of them. They were odd, silent, nearly all old, and from the way they stared they looked as though they'd just come from dark little rooms or even—even cupboards!

Behind the rotunda the slender trees with yellow leaves down drooping, and through them just a line of sea, and beyond the blue sky with gold-veined clouds.

Tum-tum-tum tiddle-um! tiddle-um! tum tiddley-um tum ta! blew the band.

Two young girls in red came by and two young soldiers in blue met them, and they laughed and paired and went off arm in arm. Two peasant women with funny straw hats passed, gravely, leading beautiful smoke-colored donkeys. A cold, pale nun hurried by. A beautiful woman came along and dropped her bunch of violets, and a little boy ran after to hand them to her, and she took them and threw them away as if they'd been poisoned. Dear me! Miss Brill didn't know whether to admire that or not! And now an ermine toque⁴ and a gentleman in gray met just in front of her. He was tall, stiff, dignified, and she was wearing the ermine toque she'd bought when her hair was yellow. Now everything, her hair, her face, even her eyes, was the same color as the shabby ermine, and her hand, in its cleaned glove, lifted to dab her lips, was a tiny yellowish paw. Oh, she was so pleased to see him—delighted! She rather thought they were going to meet that afternoon. She described where she'd been—everywhere, here, there, along by the sea. The day was so charming—didn't he agree? And wouldn't he, perhaps? . . . But he shook his head, lighted a cigarette, slowly breathed a great deep puff into her face, and, even while she was still talking and laughing, flicked the match away and walked on. The ermine toque was alone; she smiled more brightly than ever. But even the band seemed to know what she was feeling and played more softly, played tenderly, and the drum beat, "The Brute! The Brute!" over and over. What would she do? What was going to happen now? But as Miss Brill wondered, the ermine toque turned, raised her hand as though she'd seen someone else, much nicer, just over there, and pattered away. And the band changed again and played more quickly, more gayly than ever, and the old couple on Miss Brill's seat got up and marched away, and such a funny old man with long whiskers hobbled along in time to the music and was

---

4. **toque** (tōk): a close-fitting hat.

nearly knocked over by four girls walking abreast.

Oh, how fascinating it was! How she enjoyed it! How she loved sitting here, watching it all! It was like a play. It was exactly like a play. Who could believe the sky at the back wasn't painted? But it wasn't till a little brown dog trotted on solemn and then slowly trotted off, like a little "theater" dog, a little dog that had been drugged, that Miss Brill discovered what it was that made it so exciting. They were all on the stage. They weren't only the audience, not only looking on; they were acting. Even she had a part and came every Sunday. No doubt somebody would have noticed if she hadn't been there; she was part of the performance after all. How strange she'd never thought of it like that before! And yet it explained why she made such a point of starting from home at just the same time each week—so as not to be late for the performance—and it also explained why she had quite a queer, shy feeling at telling her English pupils how she spent her Sunday afternoons. No wonder! Miss Brill nearly laughed out loud. She was on the stage. She thought of the old invalid gentleman to whom she read the newspaper four afternoons a week while he slept in the garden. She had got quite used to the frail head on the cotton pillow, the hollowed eyes, the open mouth and the high pinched nose. If he'd been dead she mightn't have noticed for weeks; she wouldn't have minded. But suddenly he knew he was having the paper read to him by an actress! "An actress!" The old head lifted; two points of light quivered in the old eyes. "An actress—are ye?" And Miss Brill smoothed the newspaper as though it were the manuscript of her part and said gently: "Yes, I have been an actress for a long time."

The band had been having a rest. Now they started again. And what they played was warm, sunny, yet there was just a faint chill—a something, what was it?—not sadness—no, not sadness—a something that made you want to sing. The tune lifted, lifted, the light shone; and it seemed to Miss Brill that in another moment all of them, all the whole company, would begin singing. The young ones, the laughing ones who were moving together, they would begin, and the men's voices, very resolute and brave, would join them. And then she too, she too, and the others on the benches—they would come in with a kind of accompaniment—something low, that scarcely rose or fell, something so beautiful—moving . . . And Miss Brill's eyes filled with tears and she looked smiling at all the other members of the company. Yes, we understand, we understand, she thought—though what they understood she didn't know.

Just at that moment a boy and a girl came and sat down where the old couple had been. They were beautifully dressed; they were in love. The hero and heroine, of course, just arrived from his father's yacht. And still soundlessly singing, still with that trembling smile, Miss Brill prepared to listen.

"No, not now," said the girl. "Not here, I can't."

"But why? Because of that stupid old thing at the end there?" asked the boy. "Why does she come here at all—who wants her? Why doesn't she keep her silly old mug at home?"

"It's her fu-fur which is so funny," giggled the girl. "It's exactly like a fried whiting."[5]

"Ah, be off with you!" said the boy in an angry whisper. Then: "Tell me, ma petite chérie—"[6]

"No, not here," said the girl. "Not yet."

On her way home she usually bought a slice of honeycake at the baker's. It was her Sunday treat. Sometimes there was an almond in her slice, sometimes not. It made a great

---

5. **whiting:** a fish.
6. **ma petite chérie** (må pə-tēt′ shâ-rē′): French for "my little darling."

difference. If there was an almond it was like carrying home a tiny present — a surprise — something that might very well not have been there. She hurried on the almond Sundays and struck the match for the kettle in quite a dashing way.

But today she passed the baker's by, climbed the stairs, went into the little dark room — her room like a cupboard — and sat down on the red eiderdown. She sat there for a long time. The box that the fur came out of was on the bed. She unclasped the necklet quickly; quickly, without looking, laid it inside. But when she put the lid on she thought she heard something crying.

FOR STUDY AND DISCUSSION

1. It is often said that in Katherine Mansfield's stories a single episode illuminates the whole lifetime of a character. What do the events on this Sunday afternoon reveal about Miss Brill's life?
2. In what way does Miss Brill's fur wrap function as a symbol in the story?
3. In what way is the tone of this story both sympathetic and ironic?

SUGGESTIONS FOR WRITING

1. Analyze the character of Miss Brill.
2. Compare "Miss Brill" with "A Dill Pickle" (page 740). Indicate how Mansfield treats the subject of loneliness in both stories.

The Sniper   *Liam O'Flaherty*

The long June twilight faded into night. Dublin lay enveloped in darkness but for the dim light of the moon that shone through fleecy clouds, casting a pale light as of approaching dawn over the streets and the dark waters of the Liffey.[1] Around the beleaguered Four Courts the heavy guns roared. Here and there through the city machine guns and rifles broke the silence of the night, spasmodically, like dogs barking on lone farms. Republicans and Free Staters were waging civil war.[2]

On a rooftop near O'Connell Bridge, a Republican sniper lay watching. Beside him lay his rifle and over his shoulders were slung a pair of field glasses. His face was the face of a student — thin and ascetic, but his eyes had the cold gleam of the fanatic. They were

deep and thoughtful, the eyes of a man who is used to looking at death.

He was eating a sandwich hungrily. He had eaten nothing since morning. He had been too excited to eat. He finished the sandwich, and taking a flask of whiskey from his pocket, he took a short draft. Then he returned the flask to his pocket. He paused for a moment, considering whether he should risk a smoke. It was dangerous. The flash might be seen in the darkness and there were enemies watching. He decided to take the risk. Placing a cigarette between his lips, he struck a match, inhaled the smoke hurriedly and put out the light. Almost immediately, a bullet flattened itself against the parapet of the roof. The sniper took another whiff and put out the cigarette. Then he swore softly and crawled away to the left.

Cautiously he raised himself and peered over the parapet. There was a flash and a bullet whizzed over his head. He dropped immediately. He had seen the flash. It came from the opposite side of the street.

---

1. **Liffey:** a river that flows into Dublin Bay, an inlet of the Irish Sea.
2. **civil war:** Civil war followed the founding of the Irish Free State in 1921. Free Staters fought to defend the new nation; Republicans fought for independence.

He rolled over the roof to a chimney stack in the rear, and slowly drew himself up behind it, until his eyes were level with the top of the parapet. There was nothing to be seen— just the dim outline of the opposite house-top against the blue sky. His enemy was under cover.

Just then an armored car came across the bridge and advanced slowly up the street. It stopped on the opposite side of the street fifty yards ahead. The sniper could hear the dull panting of the motor. His heart beat faster. It was an enemy car. He wanted to fire, but knew it was useless. His bullets would never pierce the steel that covered the gray monster.

Then around the corner of a side street came an old woman, her head covered by a tattered shawl. She began to talk to the man in the turret of the car. She was pointing to the roof where the sniper lay. An informer.

The turret opened. A man's head and shoulders appeared, looking towards the sniper. The sniper raised his rifle and fired. The head fell heavily on the turret wall. The woman darted toward the side street. The sniper fired again. The woman whirled round and fell with a shriek into the gutter.

Suddenly from the opposite roof a shot rang out and the sniper dropped his rifle with a curse. The rifle clattered to the roof. The sniper thought the noise would wake the dead. He stopped to pick the rifle up. He couldn't lift it. His forearm was dead.

"I'm hit," he muttered.

Dropping flat onto the roof, he crawled back to the parapet. With his left hand he felt the injured right forearm. The blood was oozing through the sleeve of his coat. There was no pain—just a deadened sensation, as if the arm had been cut off.

Quickly he drew his knife from his pocket, opened it on the breastwork of the parapet and ripped open the sleeve. There was a small hole where the bullet had entered. On the other side there was no hole. The bullet had lodged in the bone. It must have fractured it.

He bent the arm below the wound. The arm bent back easily. He ground his teeth to overcome the pain.

Then taking out his field dressing, he ripped open the packet with his knife. He broke the neck of the iodine bottle and let the bitter fluid drip into the wound. A paroxysm[3] of pain swept through him. He placed the cotton wadding over the wound and wrapped the dressing over it. He tied the end with his teeth.

Then he lay still against the parapet, and closing his eyes, he made an effort of will to overcome the pain.

In the street beneath all was still. The armored car had retired speedily over the bridge, with the machine gunner's head hanging lifeless over the turret. The woman's corpse lay still in the gutter.

The sniper lay still for a long time nursing his wounded arm and planning escape. Morning must not find him wounded on the roof. The enemy on the opposite roof covered his escape. He must kill that enemy and he could not use his rifle. He had only a revolver to do it. Then he thought of a plan.

Taking off his cap, he placed it over the muzzle of his rifle. Then he pushed the rifle slowly upwards over the parapet, until the cap was visible from the opposite side of the street. Almost immediately there was a report, and a bullet pierced the center of the cap. The sniper slanted the rifle forward. The cap slipped down into the street. Then catching the rifle in the middle, the sniper dropped his left hand over the roof and let it hang, lifelessly. After a few moments he let the rifle drop to the street. Then he sank to the roof, dragging his hand with him.

Crawling quickly to the left, he peered up at the corner of the roof. His ruse had succeeded. The other sniper, seeing the cap and rifle fall, thought he had killed his man. He was now standing before a row of chimney

---

3. **paroxysm** (păr'ək-sĭz'əm): a sudden spasm.

pots, looking across, with his head clearly silhouetted against the western sky.

The Republican sniper smiled and lifted his revolver above the edge of the parapet. The distance was about fifty yards—a hard shot in the dim light, and his right arm was paining him like a thousand devils. He took a steady aim. His hand trembled with eagerness. Pressing his lips together, he took a deep breath through his nostrils and fired. He was almost deafened with the report and his arm shook with the recoil.

Then, when the smoke cleared, he peered across and uttered a cry of joy. His enemy had been hit. He was reeling over the parapet in his death agony. He struggled to keep his feet, but he was slowly falling forward, as if in a dream. The rifle fell from his grasp, hit the parapet, fell over, bounded off the pole of a barber's shop beneath and then cluttered[4] onto the pavement.

Then the dying man on the roof crumpled up and fell forward. The body turned over and over in space and hit the ground with a dull thud. Then it lay still.

The sniper looked at his enemy falling and he shuddered. The lust of battle died in him. He became bitten by remorse. The sweat stood out in beads on his forehead. Weakened by his wound and the long summer day of fasting and watching on the roof, he revolted from the sight of the shattered mass of his dead enemy. His teeth chattered. He began to gibber to himself, cursing the war, cursing himself, cursing everybody.

---

4. **cluttered:** a variant of *clattered.*

He looked at the smoking revolver in his hand and with an oath he hurled it to the roof at his feet. The revolver went off with the concussion, and the bullet whizzed past the sniper's head. He was frightened back to his senses by the shock. His nerves steadied. The cloud of fear scattered from his mind and he laughed.

Taking the whiskey flask from his pocket, he emptied it at a draft. He felt reckless under the influence of the spirits. He decided to leave the roof and look for his company commander to report. Everywhere around was quiet. There was not much danger in going through the streets. He picked up his revolver and put it in his pocket. Then he crawled down through the skylight to the house underneath.

When the sniper reached the laneway on the street level, he felt a sudden curiosity as to the identity of the enemy sniper whom he had killed. He decided that he was a good shot whoever he was. He wondered if he knew him. Perhaps he had been in his own company before the split in the army. He decided to risk going over to have a look at him. He peered around the corner into O'Connell Street. In the upper part of the street there was heavy firing, but around here all was quiet.

The sniper darted across the street. A machine gun tore up the ground around him with a hail of bullets, but he escaped. He threw himself face downwards beside the corpse. The machine gun stopped.

Then the sniper turned over the dead body and looked into his brother's face.

1. The Irish Civil War was fought chiefly in small skirmishes. Often members of the same family were sharply divided in their loyalties. How does the story make use of both situations?
2. The central figure in the story is a Republican sniper, who is described as having the eyes of a fanatic. What is his obsession and how is it shown in the story?

3. What comment on war is made by the ironic ending of this story?

SUGGESTIONS FOR WRITING

1. Show how O'Flaherty prepares the reader for the ironic ending of "The Sniper."
2. Analyze the character of the sniper. Show how O'Flaherty gives us a psychological portrait of a fanatic.

The Open Window   *Saki*

"My aunt will be down presently, Mr. Nuttel," said a very self-possessed young lady of fifteen; "in the meantime you must try and put up with me."

Framton Nuttel endeavored to say the correct something which should duly flatter the niece of the moment without unduly discounting the aunt that was to come. Privately he doubted more than ever whether these formal visits on a succession of total strangers would do much towards helping the nerve cure which he was supposed to be undergoing.

"I know how it will be," his sister had said when he was preparing to migrate to this rural retreat; "you will bury yourself down there and not speak to a living soul, and your nerves will be worse than ever from moping. I shall just give you letters of introduction to all the people I know there. Some of them, as far as I can remember, were quite nice."

Framton wondered whether Mrs. Sappleton, the lady to whom he was presenting one of the letters of introduction, came into the nice division.

"Do you know many of the people round here?" asked the niece, when she judged that they had had sufficient silent communion.

"Hardly a soul," said Framton. "My sister was staying here, at the rectory, you know, some four years ago, and she gave me letters of introduction to some of the people here."

He made the last statement in a tone of distinct regret.

"Then you know practically nothing about my aunt?" pursued the self-possessed young lady.

"Only her name and address," admitted the caller. He was wondering whether Mrs. Sappleton was in the married or widowed state. An undefinable something about the room seemed to suggest masculine habitation.

"Her great tragedy happened just three years ago," said the child; "that would be since your sister's time."

"Her tragedy?" asked Framton; somehow in this restful country spot tragedies seemed out of place.

"You may wonder why we keep that window wide open on an October afternoon," said the niece, indicating a large French window that opened on to a lawn.

"It is quite warm for the time of the year," said Framton; "but has that window got anything to do with the tragedy?"

"Out through that window, three years ago to a day, her husband and her two young brothers went off for their day's shooting. They never came back. In crossing the moor to their favorite snipe-shooting ground they were all three engulfed in a treacherous piece of bog. It had been that dreadful wet summer, you know, and places that were safe in other years gave way suddenly without warning. Their bodies were never recovered. That was the dreadful part of it." Here the child's voice lost its self-possessed note and became falteringly human. "Poor aunt always thinks that they will come back some day, they and the little brown spaniel that was lost with them, and walk in at that window just as they used to do. That is why the window is kept open every evening till it is quite dusk. Poor dear aunt, she has often told me how they went out, her husband with his white waterproof coat over his arm, and Ronnie, her youngest brother, singing, 'Bertie, why do you bound?' as he always did to tease her, because she said it got on her nerves. Do you know, sometimes on still, quiet evenings like this, I almost get a creepy feeling that they will all walk in through that window — "

She broke off with a little shudder. It was a relief to Framton when the aunt bustled into the room with a whirl of apologies for being late in making her appearance.

"I hope Vera has been amusing you?" she said.

"She has been very interesting," said Framton.

"I hope you don't mind the open window," said Mrs. Sappleton briskly; "my husband and brothers will be home directly from shooting, and they always come in this way. They've been out for snipe in the marshes today, so they'll make a fine mess over my poor carpets. So like you menfolk, isn't it?"

She rattled on cheerfully about the shooting and the scarcity of birds, and the prospects for duck in the winter. To Framton it was all purely horrible. He made a desperate but only partially successful effort to turn the talk on to a less ghastly topic; he was conscious that his hostess was giving him only a fragment of her attention, and her eyes were constantly straying past him to the open window and the lawn beyond. It was certainly an unfortunate coincidence that he should have paid his visit on this tragic anniversary.

"The doctors agree in ordering me complete rest, an absence of mental excitement, and avoidance of anything in the nature of violent physical exercise," announced Framton, who labored under the tolerably widespread delusion that total strangers and chance acquaintances are hungry for the least detail of one's ailments and infirmities, their cause and cure. "On the matter of diet they are not so much in agreement," he continued.

"No?" said Mrs. Sappleton, in a voice which only replaced a yawn at the last moment. Then she suddenly brightened into alert attention—but not to what Framton was saying.

"Here they are at last!" she cried. "Just in time for tea, and don't they look as if they were muddy up to the eyes!"

Framton shivered slightly and turned towards the niece with a look intended to convey sympathetic comprehension. The child was staring out through the open window with dazed horror in her eyes. In a chill shock of nameless fear Framton swung round in his seat and looked in the same direction.

In the deepening twilight three figures were walking across the lawn towards the window; they all carried guns under their arms, and one of them was additionally burdened with a white coat hung over his shoulders. A tired brown spaniel kept close at their heels. Noiselessly they neared the house, and then a hoarse young voice chanted out of the dusk: "I said, Bertie, why do you bound?"

Framton grabbed wildly at his stick and hat; the hall door, the gravel drive, and the front gate were dimly noted stages in his headlong retreat. A cyclist coming along the road had to run into the hedge to avoid imminent collision.

"Here we are, my dear," said the bearer of the white mackintosh, coming in through the window; "fairly muddy, but most of it's dry. Who was that who bolted out as we came up?"

"A most extraordinary man, a Mr. Nuttel,"

said Mrs. Sappleton; "could only talk about his illnesses, and dashed off without a word of goodbye or apology when you arrived. One would think he had seen a ghost."

"I expect it was the spaniel," said the niece calmly; "he told me he had a horror of dogs. He was once hunted into a cemetery somewhere on the banks of the Ganges[1] by a pack of pariah[2] dogs, and had to spend the night in a newly dug grave with the creatures snarling and grinning and foaming just above him. Enough to make anyone lose their nerve."

Romance at short notice was her specialty.

---

1. **Ganges** (găn'jēz): a river in northern India and Bangladesh, sacred to Hindus.
2. **pariah** (pǝ-rī'ǝ) **dogs:** mongrel dogs important as scavengers.

FOR STUDY AND DISCUSSION

1. What contrasting impression does Saki create of Mr. Nuttel and Vera in the opening paragraphs of the story? How is this difference in temperament essential to the story?
2. Saki says of Vera: "Romance at short notice was her specialty." In what sense is he using the word *romance*?
3. How would you describe the tone of this story?

SUGGESTIONS FOR WRITING

1. The conversation between Framton Nuttel and Vera deals with a "great tragedy" in Mrs. Sappleton's life. Discuss the clues Saki uses to alert readers that this is a humorous story.
2. Compare the characters of Vera and Lady Carlotta in "The Schartz-Metterklume Method" (page 700). Show how both characters reveal a mischievous, witty, and imaginative nature.

W. Somerset Maugham (1874–1965) was born in Paris, where his father worked for the British Embassy. After he was orphaned at the age of ten, he went to live with his uncle, a clergyman in Kent. Maugham studied medicine but decided to pursue a career as a writer. He left for Paris in 1898. Eventually he became successful and was able to support himself comfortably as an author. Maugham is a compelling storyteller. His novels include *Of Human Bondage* (1915), which contains autobiographical elements; *The Moon and Sixpence* (1919), based on the life of the French painter Paul Gauguin; and *Cakes and Ale* (1930), Maugham's own favorite. His most famous story, "Rain" (1921), is set in the South Seas. Many of Maugham's stories and novels have been adapted for film.

The Verger°   *W. Somerset Maugham*

There had been a christening that afternoon at St. Peter's, Neville Square, and Albert Edward Foreman still wore his verger's gown. He kept his new one, its folds as full and

---

° **verger:** a person who takes care of the interior of a church.

stiff as though it were made not of alpaca but of perennial bronze, for funerals and weddings (St. Peter's, Neville Square, was a church much favored by the fashionable for these ceremonies) and now he wore only his second-best. He wore it with complacence, for it was the dignified symbol of his office, and without it (when he took it off to go home) he had the disconcerting sensation of being somewhat insufficiently clad. He took pains with it; he pressed it and ironed it himself. During the sixteen years he had been verger of this church he had had a succession of such gowns, but he had never been able to throw them away when they were worn out and the complete series, neatly wrapped up in brown paper, lay in the bottom drawers of the wardrobe in his bedroom.

The verger busied himself quietly, replacing the painted wooden cover on the marble font, taking away a chair that had been brought for an infirm old lady, and waited for the vicar to have finished in the vestry so that he could tidy up in there and go home. Presently he saw him walk across the chancel, genuflect in front of the high altar, and come down the aisle; but he still wore his cassock.

"What's he 'anging about for?" the verger said to himself. "Don't 'e know I want my tea?"

The vicar had been but recently appointed, a red-faced energetic man in the early forties, and Albert Edward still regretted his predecessor, a clergyman of the old school who preached leisurely sermons in a silvery voice and dined out a great deal with his more aristocratic parishioners. He liked things in church to be just so, but he never fussed; he was not like this new man who wanted to have his finger in every pie. But Albert Edward was tolerant. St. Peter's was in a very good neighborhood and the parishioners were a very nice class of people. The new vicar had come from the East End[1] and he couldn't be expected to fall in all at once with the discreet ways of his fashionable congregation.

"All this 'ustle," said Albert Edward. "But give 'im time, he'll learn."

When the vicar had walked down the aisle so far that he could address the verger with-

out raising his voice more than was becoming in a place of worship he stopped.

"Foreman, will you come into the vestry for a minute. I have something to say to you."

"Very good, sir."

The vicar waited for him to come up and they walked up the church together.

"A very nice christening, I thought, sir. Funny 'ow the baby stopped cryin' the moment you took him."

"I've noticed they very often do," said the vicar, with a little smile. "After all I've had a good deal of practice with them."

It was a source of subdued pride to him that he could nearly always quiet a whimpering infant by the manner in which he held it and he was not unconscious of the amused admiration with which mothers and nurses watched him settle the baby in the crook of his surpliced arm. The verger knew that it pleased him to be complimented on his talent.

The vicar preceded Albert Edward into the vestry. Albert Edward was a trifle surprised to find the two churchwardens there. He had not seen them come in. They gave him pleasant nods.

"Good afternoon, my lord. Good afternoon, sir," he said to one after the other.

They were elderly men, both of them, and they had been churchwardens almost as long as Albert Edward had been verger. They were sitting now at a handsome refectory table that the old vicar had brought many years before from Italy and the vicar sat down in the vacant chair between them. Albert Edward faced them, the table between him and them, and wondered with slight uneasiness what was the matter. He remembered still the occasion on which the organist had got into trouble and the bother they had all had to hush things up. In a church like St. Peter's, Neville Square, they couldn't afford a scandal. On the vicar's red face was a look of resolute benignity, but the others bore an expression that was slightly troubled.

"He's been naggin' them, he 'as," said the

---

1. **East End:** a crowded section of London containing industrial areas and slums.

verger to himself. "He's jockeyed[2] them into doin' something, but they don't 'alf like it. That's what it is, you mark my words."

But his thoughts did not appear on Albert Edward's clean-cut and distinguished features. He stood in a respectful but not obsequious attitude. He had been in service before he was appointed to his ecclesiastical office, but only in very good houses, and his deportment was irreproachable. Starting as a page boy in the household of a merchant prince,[3] he had risen by due degrees from the position of fourth to first footman, for a year he had been single-handed butler to a widowed peeress, and, till the vacancy occurred at St. Peter's, butler with two men under him in the house of a retired ambassador. He was tall, spare, grave, and dignified. He looked, if not like a duke, at least like an actor of the old school who specialized in dukes' parts. He had tact, firmness, and self-assurance. His character was unimpeachable.

The vicar began briskly.

"Foreman, we've got something rather unpleasant to say to you. You've been here a great many years and I think his lordship and the general agree with me that you've fulfilled the duties of your office to the satisfaction of everybody concerned."

The two churchwardens nodded.

"But a most extraordinary circumstance came to my knowledge the other day and I felt it my duty to impart it to the churchwardens. I discovered to my astonishment that you could neither read nor write."

The verger's face betrayed no sign of embarrassment.

"The last vicar knew that, sir," he replied. "He said it didn't make no difference. He always said there was a great deal too much education in the world for 'is taste."

"It's the most amazing thing I ever heard," cried the general. "Do you mean to say that you've been verger of this church for sixteen years and never learned to read or write?"

"I went into service when I was twelve, sir. The cook in the first place tried to teach me once, but I didn't seem to 'ave the knack for it, and then what with one thing and another I never seemed to 'ave the time. I've never really found the want of it. I think a lot of these young fellows waste a rare lot of time readin' when they might be doin' something useful."

"But don't you want to know the news?" said the other churchwarden. "Don't you ever want to write a letter?"

"No, me lord, I seem to manage very well without. And of late years now they've all these pictures in the papers I get to know what's goin' on pretty well. Me wife's quite a scholar and if I want to write a letter she writes it for me. It's not as if I was a bettin' man."

The two churchwardens gave the vicar a troubled glance and then looked down at the table.

"Well, Foreman, I've talked the matter over with these gentlemen and they quite agree with me that the situation is impossible. At a church like St. Peter's, Neville Square, we cannot have a verger who can neither read nor write."

Albert Edward's thin, sallow face reddened and he moved uneasily on his feet, but he made no reply.

"Understand me, Foreman, I have no complaint to make against you. You do your work quite satisfactorily; I have the highest opinion both of your character and of your capacity; but we haven't the right to take the risk of some accident that might happen owing to your lamentable ignorance. It's a matter of prudence as well as of principle."

"But couldn't you learn, Foreman?" asked the general.

"No, sir, I'm afraid I couldn't, not now. You see, I'm not as young as I was and if I couldn't seem able to get the letters in me 'ead when

---

2. **jockeyed** (jŏk'ēd): directed or maneuvered cleverly.
3. **merchant prince:** a lavishly wealthy merchant.

I was a nipper I don't think there's much chance of it now."

"We don't want to be harsh with you, Foreman," said the vicar. "But the church-wardens and I have quite made up our minds. We'll give you three months and if at the end of that time you cannot read and write I'm afraid you'll have to go."

Albert Edward had never liked the new vicar. He'd said from the beginning that they'd made a mistake when they gave him St. Peter's. He wasn't the type of man they wanted with a classy congregation like that. And now he straightened himself a little. He knew his value and he wasn't going to allow himself to be put upon.

"I'm very sorry, sir. I'm afraid it's no good. I'm too old a dog to learn new tricks. I've lived a good many years without knowin' 'ow to read and write, and without wishin' to praise myself, self-praise is no recommendation, I don't mind sayin' I've done my duty in that state of life in which it 'as pleased a merciful providence to place me, and if I *could* learn now I don't know as I'd want to."

"In that case, Foreman, I'm afraid you must go."

"Yes, sir, I quite understand. I shall be 'appy to 'and in my resignation as soon as you've found somebody to take my place."

But when Albert Edward with his usual politeness had closed the church door behind the vicar and the two churchwardens he could not sustain the air of unruffled dignity with which he had borne the blow inflicted upon him and his lips quivered. He walked slowly back to the vestry and hung up on its proper peg his verger's gown. He sighed as he thought of all the grand funerals and smart weddings it had seen. He tidied everything up, put on his coat, and hat in hand walked down the aisle. He locked the church door behind him. He strolled across the square, but deep in his sad thoughts he did not take the street that led him home, where a nice strong cup of tea awaited him; he took the wrong turning.

He walked slowly along. His heart was heavy. He did not know what he should do with himself. He did not fancy the notion of going back to domestic service; after being his own master for so many years, for the vicar and churchwardens could say what they liked, it was he that had run St. Peter's, Neville Square, he could scarcely demean himself by accepting a situation.[4] He had saved a tidy sum, but not enough to live on without doing something, and life seemed to cost more every year. He had never thought to be troubled with such questions. The vergers of St. Peter's, like the popes of Rome, were there for life. He had often thought of the pleasant reference the vicar would make in his sermon at evensong[5] the first Sunday after his death to the long and faithful service, and the exemplary character of their late verger, Albert Edward Foreman. He sighed deeply. Albert Edward was a non-smoker and a total abstainer, but with a certain latitude; that is to say he liked a glass of beer with his dinner and when he was tired he enjoyed a cigarette. It occurred to him now that one would comfort him and since he did not carry them he looked about him for a shop where he could buy a packet of Gold Flakes. He did not at once see one and walked on a little. It was a long street, with all sorts of shops in it, but there was not a single one where you could buy cigarettes.

"That's strange," said Albert Edward.

To make sure he walked right up the street again. No, there was no doubt about it. He stopped and looked reflectively up and down.

"I can't be the only man as walks along this street and wants a fag,"[6] he said. "I shouldn't wonder but what a fellow might do very well with a little shop here. Tobacco and sweets, you know."

He gave a sudden start.

---

4. **situation:** a position as servant.
5. **evensong:** evening church service.
6. **fag:** British slang for "cigarette."

"That's an idea," he said. "Strange 'ow things come to you when you least expect it."

He turned, walked home, and had his tea.

"You're very silent this afternoon, Albert," his wife remarked.

"I'm thinkin'," he said.

He considered the matter from every point of view and next day he went along the street and by good luck found a little shop to let that looked as though it would exactly suit him. Twenty-four hours later he had taken it, and when a month after that he left St. Peter's, Neville Square, forever, Albert Edward Foreman set up in business as a tobacconist and news agent. His wife said it was a dreadful comedown after being verger of St. Peter's, but he answered that you had to move with the times, the church wasn't what it was, and 'enceforward he was going to render unto Caesar what was Caesar's.[7] Albert Edward did very well. He did so well that in a year or so it struck him that he might take a second shop and put a manager in. He looked for another long street that hadn't got a tobacconist in it and when he found it, and a shop to let, took it and stocked it. This was a success too. Then it occurred to him that if he could run two he could run half a dozen, so he began walking about London, and whenever he found a long street that had no tobacconist and a shop to let he took it. In the course of ten years he had acquired no less than ten shops and he was making money hand over fist. He went round to all of them himself every Monday, collected the week's takings, and took them to the bank.

One morning when he was there paying in a bundle of notes and a heavy bag of silver the cashier told him that the manager would like to see him. He was shown into an office and the manager shook hands with him.

"Mr. Foreman, I wanted to have a talk to you about the money you've got on deposit with us. D'you know exactly how much it is?"

"Not within a pound or two, sir; but I've got a pretty rough idea."

"Apart from what you paid in this morning it's a little over thirty thousand pounds. That's a very large sum to have on deposit and I should have thought you'd do better to invest it."

"I wouldn't want to take no risk, sir. I know it's safe in the bank."

"You needn't have the least anxiety. We'll make you out a list of absolutely gilt-edged[8] securities. They'll bring you in a better rate of interest than we can possibly afford to give you."

A troubled look settled on Mr. Foreman's distinguished face. "I've never 'ad anything to do with stocks and shares and I'd 'ave to leave it all in your 'ands," he said.

The manager smiled. "We'll do everything. All you'll have to do next time you come in is just to sign the transfers."

"I could do that all right," said Albert uncertainly. "But 'ow should I know what I was signin'?"

"I suppose you can read," said the manager a trifle sharply.

Mr. Foreman gave him a disarming smile.

"Well, sir, that's just it. I can't. I know it sounds funny-like, but there it is. I can't read or write, only me name, an' I only learnt to do that when I went into business."

The manager was so surprised that he jumped up from his chair.

"That's the most extraordinary thing I ever heard."

"You see, it's like this, sir, I never 'ad the opportunity until it was too late and then

---

7. **render unto Caesar . . . Caesar's:** an allusion to Matthew 22:21. "Render therefore unto Caesar the things which are Caesar's; and unto God the things that are God's." To Albert, making a living as a businessman is not incompatible with having been verger of St. Peter's.

8. **gilt-edged:** of the highest quality.

some 'ow I wouldn't. I got obstinate-like."

The manager stared at him as though he were a prehistoric monster.

"And do you mean to say that you've built up this important business and amassed a fortune of thirty thousand pounds without being able to read or write? Good God, man, what would you be now if you had been able to?"

"I can tell you that, sir," said Mr. Foreman, a little smile on his still aristocratic features. "I'd be verger of St. Peter's, Neville Square."

FOR STUDY AND DISCUSSION

1. At the opening of the story, both the vicar and Albert Edward reveal their social prejudices. Why does the vicar believe Albert Edward is unsuited to the office of verger? Why does Albert Edward believe that the vicar is the wrong person for St. Peter's congregation?
2. In what way does Albert Edward show that he attaches great importance to social rank? What is his attitude toward his position at St. Peter's?
3. Maugham says that Albert Edward "knew his value and he wasn't going to allow himself to be put upon." How does he maintain his dignity with the vicar and the churchwardens? with the bank manager?
4. How is Albert Edward's character responsible for his success in business?
5. Point out the central irony of this story.
6. What comment do the events of the story make regarding the values of the vicar, the church-wardens, and the bank manager?
7. State the theme of "The Verger."

SUGGESTIONS FOR WRITING

1. Show how Maugham develops the character of Albert Edward through direct and indirect methods of characterization.
2. Discuss Maugham's use of irony in "The Verger."

There Is a Garden in Her Face   *Thomas Campion*

There is a garden in her face
Where roses and white lilies grow;
  A heav'nly paradise is that place
Wherein all pleasant fruits do flow.
    There cherries grow which none may buy   5
    Till "Cherry-ripe"° themselves do cry.

  Those cherries fairly do enclose
Of orient pearl a double row,
  Which when her lovely laughter shows,
They look like rose-buds filled with snow;   10
    Yet them nor° peer nor prince can buy,
    Till "Cherry-ripe" themselves do cry.

  Her eyes like angels watch them still;
Her brows like bended bows do stand,
  Threat'ning with piercing frowns to kill   15
All that attempt, with eye or hand
    Those sacred cherries to come nigh
    Till "Cherry-ripe" themselves do cry.

---

6. **"Cherry-ripe"**: cry of peddlars selling fruit. 11. **nor**: neither.

FOR STUDY AND DISCUSSION

1. Explain how the garden is used as a metaphor for a woman's beauty in this poem.
2. What is the meaning of the refrain in each stanza?
3. How does the woman in this poem correspond to the conventional mistress in Elizabethan sonnets? (See pages 121–123.)

SUGGESTION FOR WRITING

Compare Campion's lady with the lady in Shakespeare's Sonnet 130 (page 139).

The medieval morality plays used allegory in order to present a lesson concerning the soul's salvation. The characters have names that indicate their allegorical significance. Some are personified as abstract qualities, such as Truth or Gluttony; others represent classes, such as King or Mankind. A characteristic theme of morality plays is the summoning of Death.

The most famous of all medieval morality plays is *Everyman*, which was written at the end of the fifteenth century. It was popular in its own day and is still regarded as one of the milestones of the drama. The play is presented here in abridged form.

Everyman

Here beginneth a treatise how the High Father of Heaven sendeth Death to summon every creature to come and give account of their lives in this world, and is in manner of a moral play.

[*Enter* Messenger.]

Messenger. I pray you all give your audience,
And hear this matter with reverence,
By figure° a moral play,
The *Summoning of Everyman* called it is,
That of our lives and ending shows   5
How transitory we be all day.°
This matter is wondrous precious,
But the intent of it is more gracious,
And sweet to bear away.
The story saith: Man, in the beginning,   10
Look well, and take good heed to the ending,
Be you never so gay!
Ye think sin in the beginning full sweet,
Which in the end causeth the soul to weep,
When the body lieth in clay.   15

Here shall you see how Fellowship and Jollity,
Both Strength, Pleasure, and Beauty,
Will fade from thee as flower in May.
For ye shall hear how our Heaven King
Calleth Everyman to a general reckoning.   20
Give audience and hear what he doth say.   [*Exit.*]

[*Enter* God.]

God. I perceive, here in my majesty,
How that all creatures be to me unkind,°
Living without dread in worldly prosperity.
Of ghostly° sight the people be so blind,   25
Drowned in sin, they know me not for their God,
In worldly riches is all their mind,
They fear not my rightwiseness,° the sharp rod.
They use the seven deadly sins damnable,
As pride, covetise,° wrath, and lechery°   30
Now in the world be made commendable;

---

3. **By figure:** in form.   6. **all day:** every day.

23. **unkind:** ungrateful.   25. **ghostly:** spiritual.
28. **rightwiseness:** righteousness.   30. **covetise:** avarice.
lechery: The three additional deadly sins are envy, gluttony, and sloth.

And thus they leave of angels the heav-
enly company.
Every man liveth so after his own
pleasure,
And yet of their life they be nothing
sure.°
I see the more that I them forbear,   35
The worse they be from year to year:
All that liveth appaireth° fast.
Therefore I will, in all the haste,
Have a reckoning of every man's person.
They be so cumbered° with worldly
riches,   40
That needs on them I must do justice,
On every man living without fear.
Where art thou, Death, thou mighty
messenger?

[Enter Death.]

Death. Almighty God, I am here at your
will,
Your commandment to fulfill.   45
God. Go thou to Everyman,
And show him, in my name,
A pilgrimage he must on him take,
Which he in no wise may escape;
And that he bring with him a sure reck-
oning   50
Without delay or any tarrying.
Death. Lord, I will in the world go run
over all,°
And cruelly outsearch both great and
small.   [Exit God.]
Every man will I beset that liveth
beastly
Out of God's laws, and dreadeth not
folly.   55
He that loveth riches I will strike with
my dart,
His sight to blind, and from heaven to
depart,°
Except that alms be his good friend,

In hell for to dwell, world without end.
Lo, yonder I see Everyman walking;   60
Full little he thinketh on my coming;
His mind is on fleshly lusts and his
treasure,
And great pain it shall cause him to
endure
Before the Lord, Heaven King.

[Enter Everyman.]

Everyman, stand still! Whither art thou
going   65
Thus gaily? Hast thou thy Maker for-
geet?°
Everyman. Why askest thou?
Wouldest thou wete?°
Death. Yea, sir, I will show you:
In great haste I am sent to thee   70
From God out of his majesty.
Everyman. What, sent to me?
Death. Yea, certainly.
Though thou have forgot him here,
He thinketh on thee in the heavenly
sphere,   75
As, ere we depart, thou shalt know.
Everyman. What desireth God of me?
Death. That shall I show thee:
A reckoning he will needs have
Without any longer respite.°   80
Everyman. To give a reckoning longer
leisure I crave;
This blind° matter troubleth my wit.°
Death. On thee thou must take a long
journey:
Therefore thy book of count° with thee
thou bring;
For turn again thou cannot by no way.   85
And look thou be sure of thy reckoning,
For before God thou shalt answer, and
show
Thy many bad deeds and good but a few,

---

34. **sure:** secure.   37. **appaireth:** degenerates.
40. **cumbered:** encumbered.   52. **over all:** everywhere.
57. **depart:** part.

66. **forgeet:** forgotten.   68. **wete:** know.   80. **respite**
(rĕs′pĭt): delay.   82. **blind:** obscure.   **wit:** mind.
84. **count:** accounts.

How thou hast spent thy life, and in what wise,
Before the Chief Lord of Paradise.   90
Everyman. Full unready I am such reckoning to give.
I know thee not. What messenger art thou?
Death. I am Death, that no man dreadeth.°
For every man I 'rest° and no man spareth;
For it is God's commandment   95
That all to me should be obedient.
Everyman. O Death, thou comest when I had thee least in mind!
In thy power it lieth me to save.
Yet of my good° will I give thee, if thou will be kind,
Yea, a thousand pound shalt thou have,   100
And defer this matter till another day.
Death. Everyman, it may not be by no way.
I set not by° gold, silver, nor riches,
Nor by pope, emperor, king, duke, nor princes.
For and° I would receive gifts great,   105
All the world I might get;
But my custom is clean contrary.
I give thee no respite. Come hence, and not tarry.
Everyman. Alas, shall I have no longer respite?
I may say Death giveth no warning.   110
To think on thee, it maketh my heart sick,
For all unready is my book of reckoning.
But twelve year and I might have abiding°
My counting-book I would make so clear,
That my reckoning I should not need to fear.   115

Wherefore, Death, I pray thee, for God's mercy,
Spare me till I be provided of remedy.
Death. Thee availeth not to cry, weep, and pray;
But haste thee lightly° that thou were gone that journey,
And prove° thy friends if thou can.   120
For, wete thou well, the tide° abideth no man,
And in the world each living creature
For Adam's sin must die of nature.°
Everyman. Death, if I should this pilgrimage take,
And my reckoning surely make,   125
Show me, for saint° charity,
Should I not come again shortly?
Death. No, Everyman. And thou be once there,
Thou mayst never more come here,
Trust me verily.   130
Everyman. O gracious God, in the high seat celestial,
Have mercy on me in this most need.
Shall I have no company from this vale terrestrial
Of mine acquaintance that way me to lead?
Death. Yea, if any be so hardy,   135
That would go with thee and bear thee company.
Hie° thee that thou were gone to God's magnificence,
Thy reckoning to give before his presence.
What, weenest° thou thy life is given thee,
And thy worldly goods also?   140
Everyman. I had weened so, verily.
Death. Nay, nay; it was but lent thee.
And now out of thy sight I will me hie;

---

93. **no man dreadeth:** dreads no man.   94. **'rest:** arrest.
99. **good:** goods.   103. **I set not by:** I do not attach value to.   105. **and:** if.   113. **abiding:** delay.

119. **lightly:** quickly.   120. **prove:** test.
121. **tide:** time.   123. **of nature:** naturally.
126. **saint:** holy.   137. **Hie:** hasten.
139. **weenest:** think.

See thou make thee ready shortly,
For thou mayst say this is the day   145
That no man living may 'scape° away.
                                    [*Exit.*]
Everyman. Alas, I may well weep with
    sighs deep;
Now have I no manner of company
To help me in my journey and me to
    keep.
And also my writing° is full unready.   150
How shall I do now for to excuse me?
I would to God I had never be gete!°
To my soul a full great profit it had be,
For now I fear pains huge and great.
The time passeth; Lord, help, that all
    wrought.
                                            155
For though I mourn it availeth nought.
The day passeth, and is almost a-go;°
I wot° not well what for to do.
To whom were I best my complaint to
    make?
What and I to Fellowship thereof spake,   160
And showed him of this sudden chance?
For in him is all mine affiance;°
We have in the world so many a day
Be good friends in sport and play.
I see him yonder, certainly;   165
I trust that he will bear me company;
Therefore to him will I speak to ease
    my sorrow.

[*Enter* Fellowship.]

Well met, good Fellowship, and good
    morrow!
Fellowship. Everyman, good morrow,
    by this day!
Sir, why lookest thou so piteously?   170
If any thing be amiss, I pray thee me
    say,
That I may help to remedy.
Everyman. Yea, good Fellowship, yea,

I am in great jeopardy.
Fellowship. My true friend, show to me
    your mind;   175
I will not forsake thee to my life's
    end,
In the way of good company.
Everyman. That was well spoken, and
    lovingly.
Fellowship. Sir, I must needs know your
    heaviness.°
I have pity to see you in any distress.   180
If any have you wronged, ye shall re-
    venged be,
Though I on the ground be slain for
    thee,
Though that I know before that I should
    die.
Everyman. Verily, Fellowship, gra-
    mercy.°
Fellowship. Tush! By thy thanks I set
    not a straw.   185
Show me your grief, and say no more.
Everyman. If I my heart should to you
    break,°
And then you to turn your mind from
    me,
And would not me comfort when ye
    hear me speak,
Then should I ten times sorrier be.   190
Fellowship. Sir, I say as I will do indeed.
Everyman. Then be you a good friend at
    need.
I have found you true herebefore.
Fellowship. And so ye shall evermore;
For, in faith, and thou go to hell,   195
I will not forsake thee by the way!
Everyman. Ye speak like a good friend; I
    believe you well.
I shall deserve° it, and I may.
Fellowship. I speak of no deserving, by
    this day!

---

146. **'scape:** escape. 150. **writing:** a reference to the
book of accounts. 152. **be gete:** been born.
157. **a-go:** gone by. 158. **wot:** know. 162. **affiance**
(ă'fē-ăns'): trust.

179. **heaviness:** sorrow. 184. **gramercy:** I thank you.
187. **break:** disclose. 198. **deserve:** repay.

For he that will say and nothing do   200
Is not worthy with good company to go;
Therefore show me the grief of your
    mind,
As to your friend most loving and kind.
Everyman. I shall show you how it is:
Commanded I am to go a journey,   205
A long way, hard and dangerous,
And give a strait count° without delay,
Before the high judge Adonai.°
Wherefore, I pray you, bear me com-
    pany,
As ye have promised, in this journey.   210
Fellowship. That is matter indeed!
    Promise is duty,
But, and I should take such a voyage on
    me,
I know it well, it should be to my pain.
Also it makes me afeard, certain.
But let us take counsel here as well as   215
    we can,
For your words would fear° a strong
    man.
Everyman. Why, ye said, if I had need,
Ye would me never forsake, quick ne°
    dead,
Though it were to hell, truly.
Fellowship. So I said, certainly,   220
But such pleasures° be set aside, the
    sooth° to say.
And also, if we took such a journey,
When should we again come?
Everyman. Nay, never again till the day
    of doom.°
Fellowship. In faith, then will not I
    come there!   225
Everyman. Whither away, Fellowship?
    Will thou forsake me?
Fellowship. Yea, by my fay,° to God I
    betake° thee.   [*Exit.*]

Everyman appeals to Kindred and Cousin to accompany him, but they refuse. He then turns to
Goods.

Everyman. What friend were best me
    of to provide?
I lose my time here longer to abide.
Yet in my mind a thing there is: 230
All my life I have loved riches;
If that my Good° now help me might,
He would make my heart full light.
I will speak to him in this distress.
Where art thou, my Goods and riches?   235

[Goods *speaks from within.*]

Goods. Who calleth me? Everyman?
    What, hast thou haste?
I lie here in corners, trussed and piled
    so high,
And in chests I am locked so fast,
Also sacked in bags—thou mayest see
    with thine eye—
I cannot stir; in packs low I lie.   240
What would ye have? Lightly me say.°
Everyman. Come hither, Good, in all
    the haste thou may.
For of counsel I must desire thee.

[*Enter* Goods.]

Goods. Sir, and ye in the world have
    sorrow or adversity,
That can I help you to remedy shortly.   245
Everyman. It is another disease° that
    grieveth me;
In this world it is not, I tell thee so.
I am sent for another way to go,
To give a strait count general
Before the highest Jupiter of all;   250
And all my life I have had joy and pleas-
    ure in thee,

---

207. **strait count:** strict account.   208. **Adonai**
(ăd′ō-nī′): a Hebrew name for God.   216. **fear:** frighten.
218. **quick ne:** alive nor.   221. **pleasures:** jokes. **sooth:**
truth.   224. **day of doom:** Judgment Day.
227. **fay:** faith. **betake:** commend.

232. **Good:** Goods.   241. **Lightly me say:** tell me
quickly.   246. **disease:** trouble.

Therefore I pray thee go with me,
For, peradventure,° thou mayst before
   God Almighty
My reckoning help to clean and purify;
For it is said ever among   255
That "money maketh all right that is
   wrong."
Goods. Nay, Everyman; I sing another
   song,
I follow no man in such voyages;
For, and I went with thee,
Thou shouldst fare much the worse for
   me;   260
For because on me thou did set thy
   mind,
Thy reckoning I have made blotted and
   blind,
That thine account thou cannot make
   truly;
And that hast thou for the love of me.
Everyman. That would grieve me full
   sore,   265
When I should come to that fearful
   answer.
Up, let us go thither together.
Goods. Nay, not so! I am too brittle, I
   may not endure;
I will follow no man one foot, be ye
   sure.
Everyman. Alas! I have thee loved, and
   had great pleasure   270
All my life-days on goods and treasure.
Goods. That is to thy damnation, with-
   out lesing!°
For my love is contrary to the love ever-
   lasting.
But if thou had me loved moderately
   during,°
As to the poor to give part of me,   275
Then shouldst thou not in this dolor be,
Nor in this great sorrow and care.

Everyman. Lo, now was I deceived ere I
   was ware,
And all I may wyte° misspending of
   time.
Goods. What, weenest thou that I am
   thine?   280
Everyman. I had weened so.
Goods. Nay, Everyman, I say no;
As for a while I was lent thee,
A season thou hast had me in pros-
   perity.
My condition is man's soul to kill;   285
If I save one, a thousand I do spill;
Weenest thou that I will follow thee
From this world? Nay, verily.
Everyman. I had weened otherwise.
Goods. Therefore to thy soul Good is
   a thief;   290
For when thou art dead, this is my
   guise,°
Another to deceive in the same wise
As I have done thee, and all to his soul's
   reprief.°
Everyman. O false Good! cursed may
   thou be,
Thou traitor to God, that hast deceived
   me   295
And caught me in thy snare.
Ah, Good! thou hast had long my heartly
   love;
I gave thee that which should be the
   Lord's above.
But wilt thou not go with me indeed?
I pray thee truth to say.   300
Goods. No, so God me speed!
Therefore farewell, and have good day.
                              [Exit.]

In his despair, Everyman remembers Good Deeds.

Everyman. Of whom shall I now counsel take?

---

253. **peradventure:** perhaps.   272. **lesing:** lying.
274. **during:** during life.

279. **wyte:** blame on.   291. **guise:** method, custom.
293. **reprief:** reproach.

I think that I shall never speed°
Till that I go to my Good Deed.   305
But alas, she is so weak
That she can neither go° nor speak.
Yet will I venture° on her now.
My Good Deeds, where be you?

[Good Deeds *speaks from the ground.*]

Good Deeds. Here I lie, cold in the
    ground.   310
Thy sins hath me sore bound
That I cannot stear.°
Everyman. O Good Deeds, I stand in
    fear!
I must you pray of counsel,
For help now should come right well.°   315
Good Deeds. Everyman, I have under-
    standing
That ye be summoned, account to
    make,
Before Messiah, of Jerusalem King.
And you do by me,° that journey with
    you will I take.
Everyman. Therefore I come to you my
    moan to make.   320
I pray you that ye will go with me.
Good Deeds. I would full fain,° but I
    cannot stand, verily.
Everyman. Why, is there anything on
    you fall?°
Good Deeds. Yea, sir, I may thank you
    of all.°
If ye had perfectly cheered° me,   325
Your book of count full ready had be.
Look, the books of your works and
    deeds eke,°
Ah, see how they lie under the feet,
To your soul's heaviness.°
Everyman. Our Lord Jesus help me!   330

For one letter here I cannot see.
Good Deeds. There is a blind°reckoning
    in time of distress!
Everyman. Good Deeds, your counsel I
    pray you give me.
Good Deeds. That shall I do verily,
Though that on my feet I may not go;   335
I have a sister that shall with you also,
Called Knowledge, which shall with
    you abide
To help you make that dreadful reck-
    oning.

[*Enter* Knowledge.]

Knowledge. Everyman, I will go with
    thee and be thy guide,
In thy most need to go by thy side.   340
Everyman. In good condition I am now
    in everything,
And am whole content with this good
    thing,
Thanked be God my Creator.

Knowledge leads Everyman to Confession. Everyman does penance. Good Deeds, delivered from
her sickness, now rises and joins Everyman on
his journey. Knowledge gives Everyman the garment of contrition. Everyman is advised to summon Discretion, Strength, Beauty, and Five Wits
(senses) to help him on his pilgrimage. After receiving the last rites of the church, he approaches
the grave.

Everyman. And now, friends, let us go
    without longer respite.
I thank God that ye have tarried so long.   345
Now set each of you on this rood° your
    hand
And shortly° follow me.
I go before there° I would be. God be our
    guide.

---

304. **speed:** prosper. 307. **go:** walk. 308. **venture:**
gamble. 312. **stear:** stir. 315. **should . . . well:**
would be welcome. 319. **And . . . me:** if you do as I
say. 322. **full fain:** gladly. 323. **fall:** fallen. 324. **of
all:** for all. 325. **cheered:** cherished. 327. **eke:** also.
329. **heaviness:** sorrow.

332. **blind:** not legible. 346. **rood:** cross.
347. **shortly:** quickly. 348. **there:** where.

Strength. Everyman, we will not from you go

Till ye have done this voyage long. 350

Discretion. I, Discretion, will bide by you also.

Knowledge. And though this pilgrimage be never so strong,°

I will never part you fro.°

Strength. Everyman, I will be as sure by thee

As ever I did by Judas Maccabee.° 355

Everyman. Alas, I am so faint I may not stand,

My limbs under me doth fold.

Friends, let us not turn again to this land,

Not for all the world's gold.

For into this cave must I creep 360

And turn° to earth, and there to sleep.

Beauty. What, into this grave? Alas!

Everyman. Yea, there shall ye consume,° more and lass.°

Beauty. And what, should I smother here?

Everyman. Yea, by my faith, and nevermore appear. 365

In this world live no more we shall,

But in heaven before the highest Lord of all.

Beauty. I cross out all this! Adieu, by Saint John!

I take my tap in my lap° and am gone.

Everyman. What, Beauty, whither will ye? 370

Beauty. Peace, I am deaf. I look not behind me,

Not and thou wouldest give me all the gold in thy chest. [*Exit.*]

Everyman. Alas, whereto may I trust?

Beauty goeth fast away fro me;

She promised with me to live and die. 375

Strength: Everyman, I will thee also forsake and deny.

Thy game liketh° me not at all.

Everyman. Why then, ye will forsake me all?

Sweet Strength, tarry a little space.°

Strength. Nay, sir, by the rood of grace, 380

I will hie me from thee fast,

Though thou weep till thy heart tobrast.°

Everyman. Ye would ever bide by me, ye said.

Strength. Yea, I have you far enough conveyed.°

Ye be old enough, I understand, 385

Your pilgrimage to take on° hand.

I repent me that I hither came.

Everyman. Strength, you to displease I am to blame,°

Yet promise is debt, this ye well wot.°

Strength. In faith, I care not! 390

Thou art but a fool to complain;

You spend your speech and waste your brain.

Go, thrust thee into the ground. [*Exit.*]

Everyman. I had weened° surer I should you have found.

He that trusteth in his Strength 395

She him deceiveth at the length.

Both Strength and Beauty forsaketh me,

Yet they promised me fair and lovingly.

Discretion. Everyman, I will after Strength be gone;

As for me, I will leave you alone. 400

Everyman. Why Discretion, will ye forsake me?

Discretion. Yea, in faith, I will go from thee.

For when Strength goeth before,

---

352. **strong:** hard.   353. **you fro:** from you.
355. **Judas Maccabee:** Judas Maccabeus (măk′ə-bē′əs), a leader of the Jews against the Syrians in the second century B.C.   361. **turn:** return.   363. **consume:** decay. **more and lass:** completely.   369. **I take . . . lap:** I tuck my skirts up. Another reading of this line has "cap" for *tap.*

377. **liketh:** pleases.   379. **space:** while.
382. **tobrast:** break.   384. **conveyed:** escorted.
386. **on:** in.   388. **you to displease . . . blame:** I am to blame for displeasing you.   389. **wot:** know.
394. **weened:** supposed.

I follow after evermore.

Everyman. Yet I pray thee, for the love of the Trinity,   405
Look in my grave once piteously.

Discretion. Nay, so nigh will I not come.
Farewell everyone!   [*Exit.*]

Everyman. O all thing faileth save God alone—
Beauty, Strength, and Discretion.   410
For when Death bloweth his blast
They all run fro me full fast.

Five Wits. Everyman, my leave now of thee I take.
I will follow the other, for here I thee forsake.

Everyman. Alas, then may I wail and weep,   415
For I took you for my best friend.

Five Wits. I will no longer thee keep.°
Now farewell, and there an end! [*Exit.*]

Everyman. O Jesu, help, all hath forsaken me!

Good Deeds. Nay, Everyman, I will bide with thee: 420
I will not forsake thee indeed;
Thou shalt find me a good friend at need.

Everyman. Gramercy, Good Deeds! Now may I true friends see.
They have forsaken me every one;
I loved them better than my Good Deeds alone.   425
Knowledge, will ye forsake me also?

Knowledge. Yea, Everyman, when ye to Death shall go,
But not yet, for no manner of danger.

Everyman. Gramercy, Knowledge, with all my heart.

Knowledge. Nay, yet will I not from hence depart   430

Till I see where ye shall become.°

Everyman. Methink, alas, that I must be gone
To make my reckoning and my debts pay,
For I see my time is nigh spent away.
Take example, all ye that this do hear or see,   435
How they that I best loved do forsake me,
Except my Good Deeds that bideth truly.

Good Deeds. All earthly things is but vanity.
Beauty, Strength, and Discretion do man forsake,
Foolish friends and kinsmen that fair spake—   440
All fleeth save Good Deeds, and that am I.

Everyman. Have mercy on me, God most mighty,
And stand by me, thou mother and maid, holy Mary!

Good Deeds. Fear not: I will speak for thee.

Everyman. Here I cry God mercy!   445

Good Deeds. Short° our end, and 'minish° our pain.
Let us go and never come again.

Everyman. Into thy hands, Lord, my soul I commend.
Receive it, Lord, that it be not lost.
As thou me boughtest,° so me defend,   450
And save me from the fiend's boast,
That I may appear with that blessed host
That shall be saved at the day of doom.
In manus tuas,° of mights most,
Forever *commendo spiritum meum.°*   455

---

417. **keep:** watch over.

431. **where . . . become:** what shall become of you.
446. **Short:** shorten. **'minish:** diminish. 450. **boughtest:** redeemed. 454-455. *In manus tuas . . . commendo spiritum meum:* Latin for "Into your hands I commend my spirit."

[Everyman *and* Good Deeds *descend into the grave.*]

Knowledge. Now hath he suffered that
  we all shall endure,
The Good Deeds shall make all sure.
Now hath he made ending,
Methinketh that I hear angels sing

And make great joy and melody   460
Where Everyman's soul received shall
  be.

Everyman's soul is welcomed into heaven by an Angel. The Epilogue, spoken by the Doctor, a learned theologian, emphasizes the grim lesson of the play: we take nothing with us when we die except our good deeds.

FOR STUDY AND DISCUSSION

1. At the heart of every morality play there is a dramatic conflict. What is the central struggle in *Everyman?*
2. How does the author make Death an effective messenger?
3. How is the allegorical figure Fellowship endowed with human qualities? Cite specific lines in your answer.
4. The scene with Goods is one of the most dramatically effective episodes in the play. Show how Goods functions as both an abstraction and an individual.
5. Chart the stages in Everyman's progress from the instance of his dialogue with Death to his descent into the grave. What changes does he undergo?

SUGGESTIONS FOR WRITING

1. Discuss *Everyman* as a serious sermon on morality. What lesson in conduct does it teach?
2. Compare the allegorical figures in *Everyman* with those in the excerpt from *The Pilgrim's Progress* (page 283). How do the characters in both works maintain a dual focus, as persons in a narrative and as abstractions intended to convey moral meaning?

Guide to Literary Terms and Techniques

ALEXANDRINE *An iambic hexameter line—that is, a poetic line consisting of six iambic feet.* The last line of a *Spenserian stanza* is an alexandrine. The following alexandrine is from a stanza of John Keats's "The Eve of St. Agnes":

She sighed for Agnes' dreams, the sweetest of the year.

> See **Scansion, Spenserian Stanza.** See also page 125.

ALLEGORY *A tale in verse or prose in which characters, actions, or settings represent abstract ideas or moral qualities.* Thus, an allegory is a story with two meanings, a literal meaning and a symbolic meaning. The most famous allegory in English literature is John Bunyan's *The Pilgrim's Progress.* Bunyan's hero, Christian, makes a journey to the Celestial City, during which he meets such characters as Hope, Shame, and Despair.

> See pages 282, 973.

ALLITERATION *The repetition of similar sounds, usually consonants or consonant clusters, in a group of words.* Sometimes the term is limited to the repetition of initial consonant sounds. When alliteration occurs at the beginning of words, it is called *initial alliteration;* when it occurs within words, it is called *internal* or *hidden alliteration.* It usually occurs on stressed syllables.

Although alliteration sometimes appears in prose, it is mainly a poetic device. Like other forms of sound repetition, alliteration in poetry serves two important purposes: it is pleasing to the ear, and it emphasizes the words in which it occurs. A well-known example of alliteration is this line from Samuel Taylor Coleridge's "Kubla Khan": "Five miles *m*eandering with a *m*azy *m*otion."

Alliteration is an important poetic device in Anglo-Saxon poetry where it generally occurs on three of the four stressed syllables in a line. Something of the alliterative effect can be seen in this line from *Beowulf:* "And the *h*eathen's only *h*ope, *H*ell."

> See pages 21, 280, 796, 821.

ALLUSION *A reference to a person, a place, an event, or a literary work that a writer expects the reader to recognize and respond to.* An allusion may be drawn from history, geography, literature, or religion. In Act One of *Macbeth,* Ross praises Macbeth's valor and skill in battle by referring to him as "Bellona's bridegroom." In Roman mythology Bellona was the goddess of war.

The title of Elizabeth Bowen's story "Tears, Idle Tears" alludes to a poem of the same title by Alfred, Lord Tennyson.

> See page 754.

ANALOGY *A comparison made between two things to show the similarities between them.* Analogies are often used for illustration (to explain something unfamiliar by comparing it to something familiar) or for argument (to persuade that what holds true for one thing holds true for the thing to which it is compared). Samuel Johnson draws an analogy for the sake of argument in his *Preface to Shakespeare* when he compares a work of art to a work of nature:

> As among the works of nature no man can properly call a river deep or a mountain high, without the knowledge of many mountains and many rivers; so in the productions of genius, nothing can be styled excellent till it has been compared with other works of the same kind.

In "Notes on the English Character," E. M. Forster develops an analogy between the sea and the English character.

> See pages 709, 713.

ANTAGONIST *A person or force opposing the protagonist in a narrative; a rival of the hero or heroine.* Famous antagonists in literature include Professor Moriarty, Sherlock Holmes's antagonist in Arthur Conan Doyle's detective stories, and the monster Grendel, Beowulf's antagonist in the Anglo-Saxon epic poem *Beowulf.*

> See **Protagonist.**

ANTIPASTORAL See **Pastoral.**

ANTI-PETRARCHAN See **Sonnet.**

ANTISTROPHE See **Ode.**

ANTITHESIS *The balancing of two contrasting ideas, words, phrases, or sentences.* An antithesis is often expressed in a balanced sentence, that is, a sentence in which identical or similar grammatical structure is used to express contrasting ideas. A famous example of antithesis is this line from Alexander Pope's *Essay on Criticism:* "To err is human, to forgive divine."

> See pages 317, 360.

APHORISM *A concise, pointed statement expressing a wise or clever observation about life.*

For example:

> Silence is the virtue of fools.
> — Francis Bacon

> For fools rush in where angels fear to tread.
> — Alexander Pope

See pages 277, 349, 360.

APOSTROPHE *A figure of speech in which an absent or a dead person, an abstract quality, or something nonhuman is addressed directly.* George Gordon, Lord Byron uses apostrophe in *Childe Harold's Pilgrimage* when he addresses the ocean: "Roll on, thou deep and dark blue Ocean — roll!"

See pages 130, 392, 479, 488.

ASIDE *In drama, lines spoken by a character in an undertone or directly to the audience.* An aside is meant to be heard by the audience, but it is supposedly not heard by the other characters onstage. Here is an aside from *Macbeth*:

> Macbeth. [*Aside*] If chance will have me king,
>   why, chance may crown me,
> Without my stir.

(I, 3, 143–144)

ASSONANCE *The repetition of similar vowel sounds, especially in poetry.* Here is an example of assonance from John Keats's "Ode on a Grecian Urn": "Thou foster child of silence and slow time."

See pages 464, 796, 821.

ATMOSPHERE *The prevailing mood or feeling of a literary work.* Atmosphere is often developed, at least in part, through descriptions of *setting*. Such descriptions help to create an emotional climate for the work that serves to establish the reader's expectations and attitudes. For example, in "Across the Bridge," Graham Greene develops an atmosphere of decay and boredom with descriptions of the dusty, shabby town in which the story is set.

See **Setting.**
See also pages 219, 769.

AUTOBIOGRAPHY *A person's account of his or her own life.* An autobiography is generally written in narrative form and includes some introspection. Autobiographies are distinct from diaries, journals, and letters, which are not unified life stories written for publication. Autobiographies are also different from memoirs, which often deal, at least in part, with public events and important persons other than the author. An example of an autobiographical essay is George Orwell's "Shooting an Elephant."

See pages 380, 763.

BALLAD *A story told in verse and usually meant to be sung.* In many countries, the *folk ballad* was one of the earliest forms of literature. Folk ballads have no known authors. They were transmitted orally from generation to generation and were not set down in writing until centuries after they were first sung. The subject matter of folk ballads stems from the everyday life of the common people. The most popular subjects, often tragic, are disappointed love, jealousy, revenge, sudden disaster, and deeds of adventure and daring. Devices commonly used in ballads are the *refrain, incremental repetition,* and *code language.* A later form of ballad is the *literary ballad,* which imitates the style of the folk ballad. The most famous English literary ballad is Samuel Taylor Coleridge's *The Rime of the Ancient Mariner.*

See **Incremental Repetition, Refrain.**
See also pages 43, 48.

BALLAD STANZA *A type of four-line stanza.* The first and third lines have four stressed words or syllables; the second and fourth lines have three stresses. *Ballad meter* is usually iambic. The number of unstressed syllables in each line may vary. The second and fourth lines rhyme. Here is a ballad stanza from the Scottish folk ballad "Get Up and Bar the Door":

> Then by there came two gentlemen,
>   At twelve o'clock at night,
> And they could neither see house nor hall,
>   Nor coal nor candlelight.

See pages 48, 823.

BIOGRAPHY *A detailed account of a person's life written by another person.* Biographies in English have taken many different forms since they were first written in medieval times to praise the virtue of saints and to celebrate the feats of heroes. The modern biographer aims at accuracy and usually makes an attempt to interpret the personality of the subject. Details of the social and historical circumstances in which the subject lived are often included. A famous example of English biography is James Boswell's *The Life of Samuel Johnson.*

See pages 374, 380.

BLANK VERSE *Verse written in unrhymed iambic pentameter.* Blank verse is the verse form used in some of the greatest English poetry, including that of William Shakespeare and John Milton. Here is an example from Shakespeare's *Macbeth:*

> If you can look into the seeds of time,
> And say which grain will grow and which will not,

Speak then to me, who neither beg nor fear
Your favors nor your hate.

(I, 3, 58–61)

See pages 165, 217.

CAESURA   *A break or pause in a line of poetry.* In these lines from Robert Herrick's "To the Virgins, to Make Much of Time," the caesuras are indicated by double lines (‖):

Then be not coy, ‖ but use your time;
And while ye may, ‖ go marry . . .

See pages 21, 814.

CANTO   *A section or division of a long poem.* The most famous cantos in literature are those that make up Dante's *Divine Comedy*, a fourteenth-century epic. In English poetry, Alexander Pope's *The Rape of the Lock* and George Gordon, Lord Byron's *Don Juan* are divided into cantos.

See pages 351, 481.

CARICATURE   *The use of exaggeration or distortion to make a figure appear comic or ridiculous.* A physical characteristic, an eccentricity, a personality trait, or an act may be exaggerated. Thomas Gradgrind, in Charles Dickens' *Hard Times*, is such a figure.

See page 611.

***CARPE DIEM* TRADITION**   *A tradition dating back to classical Greek and Latin poetry and particularly popular among English Cavalier poets.* Carpe diem means, literally, "seize the day"—that is, "live for today." The *carpe diem* theme is epitomized in a line from Robert Herrick's "To the Virgins, to Make Much of Time": "Gather ye rosebuds while ye may."

See page 260.

CHARACTERIZATION   *The personality a character displays; also, the means by which a writer reveals that personality.* Generally, a writer develops a character in one or more of the following ways: (1) through the character's actions; (2) through the character's thoughts and speeches; (3) through a physical description of the character; (4) through the opinions others have about the character; (5) through a direct statement about the character telling what the writer thinks of him or her.

CLASSICISM   *A movement or tendency in art, literature, or music that reflects the principles manifested in the art of ancient Greece and Rome.* Classicism emphasizes the traditional and the universal, and places value on reason, clarity, balance, and order. Classicism, with its concern for reason and universal themes, is traditionally opposed to Romanticism, which is concerned with emotions and personal themes.

See pages 116, 252.

CLIMAX   *The point of greatest intensity, interest, or suspense in a narrative.* The climax usually marks a story's turning point. The action leading to the climax and the simultaneous increase of tension in the plot are known as the *rising action.* In William Shakespeare's *Macbeth*, the climax occurs during the banquet scene in Act Three. Macbeth, overcome by guilt and nervousness over the murders of Duncan and Banquo, sees the ghost of Banquo in the banquet hall. This tense moment is the play's *turning point.* After this moment, events turn against Macbeth and lead to his final downfall. All action after the climax is referred to as the *falling action,* or *resolution.* The term *crisis* is sometimes used interchangeably with *climax.*

See **Plot.**
See also page 190.

COMEDY   *In general, a literary work that ends happily with a healthy, amicable armistice between the protagonist and society.* Comedy is distinct from *tragedy,* which is generally concerned with a protagonist who meets an unhappy or disastrous end. Also, the comic protagonist may be a person of ordinary character and ability, and need not achieve the heroic stature of the protagonist in a tragedy. Comedies are often concerned, at least in part, with exposing human folly, and frequently depict the overthrow of rigid social fashions and customs. Wit, humor, and a sense of festivity are found in many comedies.

See **Farce, Satire.**
See also pages 304, 631, 644, 659, 668, 934.

CONCEIT   *A kind of metaphor that makes a comparison between two startlingly different things.* A conceit may be a brief metaphor, but it usually provides the framework for an entire poem. An especially unusual and intellectual kind of conceit is the *metaphysical conceit,* used by certain seventeenth-century poets, such as John Donne. In "A Valediction: Forbidding Mourning," Donne compares the souls of lovers to compasses in an *extended simile* that begins with these lines:

If they be two, they are two so
As stiff twin compasses are two,
Thy soul the fixed foot, makes no show
To move, but doth, if th'other do.

(lines 25–28)

See pages 235, 242, 363.

CONFLICT   *A struggle between two opposing forces or characters in a short story, novel, play, or narrative poem.* Conflict can be external or internal, and it can take one of these forms: (1) a person against another person; (2) a person against society; (3) a person against nature; (4) two elements within a person struggling for mastery. Many works contain more than one form of conflict. In William Shakespeare's *Macbeth*, for example, there is a conflict within Macbeth (his wish to murder Duncan and become king versus his loyalty to Duncan), and conflicts between Macbeth and other individuals in the play (Lady Macbeth, Banquo, Macduff). Conflict is often an important element in plot development and provides, among other things, the basis for *suspense*.

CONNOTATION *All the emotions and associations that a word or phrase may arouse.* Connotation is distinct from *denotation*, which is the literal or "dictionary" meaning of a word or phrase. For example, the word *springtime* literally means the season between the vernal equinox and the summer solstice, but the word usually makes most people think of such things as youth, rebirth, and romance. The word *shroud* literally means a cloth used for burial purposes, or anything that covers or protects. However, most people associate the word with death, gloom, darkness, and other shadowy, mysterious things.

CONSONANCE *The repetition of similar consonant sounds in a group of words.* Sometimes the term refers to the repetition of consonant sounds in the middle or at the end of words, as in this line from Thomas Gray's "Elegy Written in a Country Churchyard": "And a*ll* the air a so*l*emn sti*ll*ness ho*l*ds." Sometimes the term is used for *slant rhyme* (or *partial rhyme*) in which initial and final consonants are the same but the vowels different: li*tt*er/le*tt*er, *gr*een/*gr*oan.

> See **Alliteration.**
> See also page 814.

COUPLET *Two consecutive lines of poetry that rhyme.* Shakespeare frequently closes a scene with a couplet. Here are some examples from *Macbeth:*

Away, and mock the time with fairest *show;*
False face must hide what the false heart doth *know.*
(I, 7)

Hear it not, Duncan; for it is a *knell*
That summons thee to heaven or to *hell.*
(II, 1)

Make all our trumpets speak; give them all *breath.*
Those clamorous harbingers of blood and *death.*
(V, 6)

A *heroic couplet* is an iambic pentameter couplet. During the Restoration period and the eighteenth century it was a popular verse form. Alexander Pope perfected the *closed couplet*—that is, a couplet in which the two lines form a complete unit of

thought. Here is an example from *The Rape of the Lock:*

But when to mischief mortals bend their will,
How soon they find fit instruments of ill!
(III, 125–126)

> See pages 50, 122, 311, 359, 363.

DACTYL   See **Scansion.**

DENOTATION *The literal or "dictionary" meaning of a word.* For example, a denotation, or dictionary definition, of the word *star* (as in "movie star") is "an eminent actor or actress," but the *connotation* is that of an actor or actress who is adored by fans and who leads a fascinating and glamorous life.

DÉNOUEMENT (dā-nōō-män′)   *The outcome of a plot.* The dénouement is that part of a play, short story, novel, or narrative poem in which conflicts are resolved, or unraveled, and mysteries and secrets connected with the plot are explained.

DICTION *A writer's choice of words, particularly for clarity, effectiveness, and precision.* A writer's diction can be formal or informal, abstract or concrete, simple or ornate. In choosing "the right word," writers must think of their subject and their audience. Words that are appropriate in informal dialogue would not always be appropriate in a piece of formal writing.

> See pages 218, 306, 359.

DISSONANCE *A harsh or disagreeable combination of sounds; discord.*

> See page 814.

DRAMATIC MONOLOGUE *A kind of narrative poem in which one character speaks to one or more listeners whose replies are not given in the poem.* The occasion is usually a crucial one in the speaker's life, and the dramatic monologue reveals the speaker's personality as well as the incident that is the subject of the poem. An example of a dramatic monologue is "My Last Duchess" by Robert Browning.

> See pages 563, 571, 572, 574.

ELEGY *A poem of mourning, usually over the death of an individual.* It may also be a lament over the passing of life and beauty or a meditation on the nature of death. An elegy is a type of *lyric* poem, usually formal in language and structure, and solemn or even melancholy in tone. One of the greatest elegies in English is Alfred, Lord Tennyson's *In Memoriam.*

> See pages 7, 25, 381, 567.

EMBLEMATIC IMAGE *A verbal picture or figure with a long tradition of moral or religious meaning attached to it.* George Herbert's "Easter Wings" is an emblematic poem in which the verse takes the shape of wings.

See page 245.

EPIC *A long narrative poem telling about the deeds of a great hero and reflecting the values of the society from which it originated.* Many epics were drawn from an oral tradition and were transmitted by song and recitation before they were written down. Two of the most famous epics of Western civilization are Homer's *Iliad* and *Odyssey*. The great epic of the Middle Ages is the *Divine Comedy* by the Italian poet Dante. The two most famous English epics are the Anglo-Saxon *Beowulf* and John Milton's *Paradise Lost*, which employs some of the conventions of the classical epic.

See **Mock Epic**.
See also pages 7, 10, 124, 268, 349, 361.

EPIGRAM *A short, witty, pointed statement often in the form of a poem.* Here is an example from Alexander Pope's *Essay on Criticism*:

Be not the first by whom the new are tried,
Nor yet the last to lay the old aside.
(II, 135–136)

See page 360.

EPIGRAPH *A quotation or motto at the beginning of a chapter, book, short story, or poem that makes some point about the work.* One of the epigraphs preceding T. S. Eliot's "The Hollow Men" is a reference to Guy Fawkes Day, when English children carry stuffed effigies, or likenesses, of the traitor Fawkes. The epigraph serves as a motif throughout the poem for the ineffectuality Eliot identifies with his generation of "stuffed men."

See page 810.

EPILOGUE *A short addition or conclusion at the end of a literary work.* In the Epilogue to *Pygmalion*, Bernard Shaw tells his readers what happened to his characters after the conclusion of the play.

See page 906.

EPIPHANY *A moment of illumination, usually occurring at or near the end of a work.* In James Joyce's story "Araby," the epiphany occurs when the narrator realizes, with sudden clarity, that his dream of visiting the splendid bazaar has resulted only in frustration and disillusion.

EPITAPH *An inscription on a gravestone or a short poem written in memory of someone who has died.* Many epitaphs are actually epigrams, or short witty sayings, and are not intended for serious use as monument inscriptions. Here is an example:

Life is a jest, and all things show it.
I thought so once; but now I know it.
—John Gay, "My Own Epitaph"

See pages 381, 385, 606.

EPITHET *A descriptive name or phrase used to characterize someone or something, such as "America the Beautiful" or "Catherine the Great."* The *Odyssey*, Homer's epic, contains many epithets, such as "wine-dark sea" and "keen-edged sword."

See **Kenning**.

EPODE See **Ode**.

ESSAY *A piece of prose writing, usually short, that deals with a subject in a limited way and expresses a particular point of view.* An essay is never a comprehensive treatment of a subject (the word comes from a French word, *essai*, meaning "attempt" or "try"). An essay may be serious or humorous, tightly organized or rambling, restrained or emotional.

The two general classifications of essay are the *informal essay* (also called the *familiar* or *personal essay*) and the *formal essay*. An informal essay is usually brief and is written as if the writer is talking informally to the reader about some topic, using a conversational style and a personal or humorous tone. In an informal essay, the writer might digress from the topic at hand, or express some amusing, startling, or absurd opinions. In general, an informal essay reveals as much about the personality of its author as it does about its subject. By contrast, a formal essay is tightly organized, dignified in style, and serious in tone. Francis Bacon's "Of Studies" is an example of a formal essay.

See pages 225, 341, 348, 468.

EXEMPLUM *A tale, usually inserted into the text of a sermon, that illustrates a moral principle.* "The Pardoner's Tale" from Chaucer's *Canterbury Tales* is an exemplum; its moral is "Greed is the root of all evil."

See pages 74, 80.

EXPOSITION *That part of a narrative or drama in which important background information is revealed.*

FABLE *A brief story that is told to present a moral, or practical lesson.* The characters of fables are often animals who speak and act like human beings.

FALLING ACTION See **Plot**.

FARCE *A type of comedy based on a ridiculous situation, often with stereotyped characters.* The humor in a farce is largely slapstick—that is, it often involves crude physical action. The characters in a farce are often the butts of practical jokes: flying cream-pies hit them in the face and beds cave in on them.

FIGURATIVE LANGUAGE *Language that is not intended to be interpreted in a literal sense.* William Shakespeare uses figurative language in these lines from Macbeth's famous soliloquy at the end of *Macbeth*:

> Out, out, brief candle!
> Life's but a walking shadow, a poor player
> That struts and frets his hour upon the stage
> And then is heard no more.
>
> (V, 5, 23–26)

Shakespeare is not saying that life is actually a flickering candle, a shadow, or a nervous actor moving about on a stage. Rather, he is making comparisons between life and these other things, pointing out special similarities between them. By appealing to the imagination, figurative language provides new ways of looking at the world. Figurative language consists of such figures of speech as *hyperbole, metaphor, metonymy, oxymoron, personification, simile,* and *synecdoche.*

See terms noted above.
See also page 219.

FIGURE OF SPEECH *A word or an expression that is not meant to be interpreted in a literal sense.* The most common kinds of figures of speech—*simile, metaphor, personification,* and *metonymy*—involve a comparison between unlike things. Figures of speech are found in many familiar expressions, such as "It's raining cats and dogs" and "You're the apple of my eye."

FLASHBACK *A scene in a short story, novel, play, or narrative poem that interrupts the action to show an event that happened earlier.* Most narratives present events in chronological order—that is, as they occur in time. Sometimes, however, a writer interrupts this natural sequence of events and "flashes back" to tell the reader what happened earlier in the story or in a character's life. Often a flashback takes the form of a character's recollection. Katherine Mansfield, in "A Dill Pickle," and Elizabeth Bowen, in "Tears, Idle Tears," both use this technique.

See pages 740, 749.

FOIL *A character who sets off another character by contrast.* In *Macbeth* Banquo is a foil for Macbeth. Banquo is present when the Witches deliver their prophecy to Macbeth, and he is told that his descendants will be kings. Yet, unlike Macbeth, his ambitions are not stirred and he remains loyal to the king.

FOOT See **Scansion.**

FORESHADOWING *The use of hints or clues in a narrative to suggest what will happen later.* Writers use foreshadowing to create interest and to build *suspense.* Sometimes foreshadowing also prepares the reader for the ending of the story. In Graham Greene's "Across the Bridge," the ending of the story is foreshadowed in the fifth paragraph when the narrator refers to Mr. Calloway's story as a tragedy.

See page 769.

FREE VERSE *Verse that has either no metrical pattern or an irregular pattern.* Although most free verse belongs to the nineteenth and twentieth centuries, it can be found in earlier literature, particularly in the Psalms of the Bible.

HEROIC COUPLET See **Couplet.**

HYPERBOLE *A figure of speech using exaggeration, or overstatement, for special effect.* Shakespeare uses hyperbole in these lines from *Macbeth*:

> Will all great Neptune's ocean wash this blood
> Clean from my hand?
>
> (II, 6, 60–61)
>
> See page 501.

IAMB See **Scansion.**

IAMBIC PENTAMETER *A poetic line consisting of five verse feet* (*penta-* is from a Greek word meaning "five"), *with each foot an iamb—that is, an unstressed syllable followed by a stressed syllable.* Iambic pentameter is the most common verse line in English poetry. The following lines from *Paradise Lost* are written in *blank verse*—unrhymed iambic pentameter:

> At once as far as angels ken he views
> The dismal situation waste and wild:
> A dungeon horrible on all sides round
> As one great furnace flamed, yet from those flames
> No light, but rather darkness visible . . .
>
> (lines 59–63)
>
> See **Scansion.**
> See also pages 165, 574.

IMAGERY *Words or phrases that create pictures, or images, in the reader's mind.* Images are primarily visual, as in these lines from William Wordsworth's "Lines Composed a Few Miles Above Tintern Abbey":

> Once again I see
> These hedgerows, hardly hedgerows, little lines

of sportive wood run wild: these pastoral farms,
Green to the very door; and wreaths of smoke
Sent up, in silence, from among the trees!

(lines 14–18)

Images can appeal to other senses as well: touch, taste, smell, and hearing.

See pages 219–222, 230, 517.

INCREMENTAL REPETITION *The repetition of a previous line, or lines, but with a slight variation each time, that advances the narrative stanza by stanza.* This device is commonly used in ballads.

See page 43.

IN MEDIAS RES *A technique of plunging into the middle of a story and only later using a flashback to tell what has happened previously. In medias res is Latin for "in the middle of things."* Some famous examples of this technique are found in epics. Book I of Homer's *Odyssey,* for example, opens ten years after the Trojan War has ended. The goddess Athena instructs Odysseus' son to go to Sparta to inquire about his father, who should have returned home from the war ten years before. Only later, in Book IX, do we hear Odysseus tell about his adventures of the previous ten years. An English epic that begins *in medias res* is John Milton's *Paradise Lost.*

See page 268.

INTERLOCKING RHYME See **Rhyme.**

INTERLUDE In the late fifteenth century, a play with a nonreligious plot and characters.

See page 108.

INTERNAL RHYME See **Rhyme.**

INVERSION *The technique of reversing, or inverting, the normal word order (subject, verb, object) of a sentence.* For example, an inversion of "I went to the park" is "To the park went I." Writers may use inversion to create a certain tone or to emphasize a particular word or idea. A poet may invert a line so that it fits into a particular meter or rhyme scheme.

See page 386.

INVOCATION *At the beginning of an epic (or other poem) a call to a muse, god, or spirit for inspiration.* At the opening of *Paradise Lost,* Milton invokes Urania, the muse of sacred poetry, to inspire him.

See page 268.

IRONY *A contrast or an incongruity between what is stated and what is really meant, or between what is expected to happen and what actu-* *ally happens.* Three kinds of irony are (1) *verbal irony,* in which a writer or speaker says one thing and means something entirely different; (2) *dramatic irony,* in which a reader or an audience perceives something that a character in the story or play does not know; (3) *irony of situation,* in which the writer shows a discrepancy between the expected results of some action or situation and its actual results.

An example of *verbal irony* occurs in this speech from *Macbeth.* Lennox, a Scottish nobleman, tells another Lord how Macbeth responded to Duncan's murder by killing the two grooms:

How it did grieve Macbeth! Did he not straight
In pious rage the two delinquents tear,
That were the slaves of drink and thralls of sleep?
Was not that nobly done?

(III, 6, 11–14)

The real meaning of this speech, of course, is that Macbeth acted to cover his own crimes.

An example of *dramatic irony* can be found in Scene 6 of Act One. We know that Macbeth and Lady Macbeth are plotting to murder Duncan, but Duncan does not know that he is walking into a trap. The irony is intensified by the opening lines of the scene in which Duncan and Banquo remark on the serenity and loveliness of the setting.

In Thomas Hardy's "The Three Strangers," an *irony of situation* occurs when the two strangers at the chimney corner turn out to be the hangman and his intended victim.

See pages 176, 190, 332.

KENNING *In Old English poetry, an elaborate phrase that describes persons, things, or events in a metaphorical and indirect way.* The Anglo-Saxon poem "The Seafarer" contains kennings, such as "whales' home" for the sea.

See page 21.

LYRIC *A poem, usually a short one, that expresses a speaker's personal thoughts or feelings.* The *elegy, ode,* and *sonnet* are all forms of the lyric. As its Greek name indicates, a lyric was originally a poem sung to the accompaniment of a lyre, and lyrics to this day have retained a melodic quality. Lyrics may express a range of emotions and reflections: Robert Herrick's "To the Virgins, to Make Much of Time" reflects on the brevity of life and the need to live for the moment, while T. S. Eliot's "Preludes" observes the sordidness and depression of modern life.

See page 500.

MASQUE *An elaborate and spectacular dramatic entertainment that was popular among the English aristocracy in the late sixteenth and early seventeenth centuries.* Masques were written as dramatic poems and made use of songs, dances, colorful costumes, and startling stage effects.

See pages 115, 253.

MAXIM *A concise statement expressing a principle or rule of conduct.*

See page 380.

MELODRAMA *A drama that has stereotyped characters, exaggerated emotions, and a conflict that pits an all-good hero or heroine against an all-evil villain.* The good characters always win and the evil ones are always punished. Originally, melodramas were so called because melodies accompanied certain actions (*melos* means "song" in Greek). Also, each character in a melodrama had a theme melody, which was played each time he or she made an appearance on stage.

METAPHOR *A figure of speech that makes a comparison between two things that are basically dissimilar.* "Life is a dream," "Life is a vale of tears," and "Life is a hard road" are all examples of metaphor. Unlike a *simile,* a metaphor does not use a connective word such as *like, as,* or *resembles* in making the comparison.

Many metaphors are implied, or suggested. An *implied metaphor* does not directly state that one thing is another, different thing. Alfred, Lord Tennyson uses an implied metaphor in these lines from "Crossing the Bar":

I hope to see my Pilot face to face
When I have crossed the bar.

By capitalizing the word *Pilot,* the poet implies a comparison between God and the pilot of his ship.

An *extended metaphor* is a metaphor that is extended throughout a poem. In "Crossing the Bar," Tennyson compares death to a voyage at sea, at the end of which he will meet the "Pilot," or God.

A *dead metaphor* is a metaphor that has become so commonplace that it seems literal rather than figurative. Some examples are the *foot* of a hill, the *head* of the class, a *point* in time, and the *leg* of a chair.

A *mixed metaphor* is the use of two or more inconsistent metaphors in one expression. When they are examined, mixed metaphors make no sense. Mixed metaphors are often unintentionally humorous: "The storm of protest was nipped in the bud" or "To hold the fort, he'd have to shake a leg."

See page 569.

METAPHYSICAL CONCEIT See **Conceit.**

METAPHYSICAL POETRY *The poetry of John Donne and other seventeenth-century poets who wrote in a similar style.* Metaphysical poetry is characterized by verbal wit and excess, ingenious structure, irregular meter, colloquial language, elaborate imagery, and a drawing together of dissimilar ideas.

See pages 116, 235.

METER *A generally regular pattern of stressed and unstressed syllables in poetry.* In these lines from Robert Burns's poem "O, My Luve's like a Red, Red, Rose," the stressed syllables are marked (´) and the unstressed syllables are marked (˘):

As fair art thou, my bonnie lass,
So deep in luve am I;
And I will luve thee still, my dear,
Till a' the seas gang dry.

See **Scansion.**

METONYMY (mə-tŏn′ə-mē) *A figure of speech in which something very closely associated with a thing is used to stand for or suggest the thing itself.* "Three sails came into the harbor" is an example of metonymy; the word *sails* stands for the ships themselves. Other common examples of metonymy are *crown* to mean a king, *hardhat* to mean a construction worker, and *White House* to mean the President. William Shakespeare uses metonymy in the following lines from his play *Cymbeline:*

The scepter, learning, and physic, must
All follow this, and come to dust.

The words *scepter, learning,* and *physic* stand for the king, the scholar, and the doctor.

MIRACLE PLAY *A popular religious drama of medieval England.* Miracle plays were based on stories of the saints or on sacred history.

See page 108.

MOCK EPIC *A comic literary form that treats a trivial subject in the grand, heroic style of the epic.* A mock epic is also referred to as a *mock-heroic* poem. Perhaps the greatest mock epic in English is Alexander Pope's *The Rape of the Lock.*

See pages 350–351, 481.

MORALITY PLAY *An outgrowth of miracle plays.* Morality plays were popular in the fifteenth and sixteenth centuries. In them, virtues and vices were personified.

See pages 108, 973.

MOTIF *A recurring feature (such as a name, an image, or a phrase) in a work of literature.* A motif generally contributes in some way to the *theme* of a short story, novel, poem, or play. For example, a motif used by D. H. Lawrence in his story "The Rocking-Horse Winner" is the word *luck*. The main character of the story, a boy named Paul, discovers that he has the power to predict the winner in a horse race. However, this becomes an ironic kind of luck, for Paul grows obsessed with his power and is finally destroyed by it.

At times, *motif* is used to refer to some commonly used plot or character type in literature. The "ugly duckling motif" refers to a plot that involves the transformation of a plain-looking person into a beauty. Two other commonly used motifs are the "Romeo and Juliet motif" (about doomed lovers) and the "Horatio Alger motif" (about the office clerk who becomes the corporation president).

See page 729.

MOTIVATION *The reasons, either stated or implied, for a character's behavior.* To make a story believable, a writer must provide characters with motivation sufficient to explain what they do. Characters may be motivated by outside events, or they may be motivated by inner needs or fears.

MYSTERY PLAY See **Miracle Play.**

MYTH *A story, often about immortals and sometimes connected with religious rituals, that is intended to give meaning to the mysteries of the world.* In myths, gods and goddesses are usually identified with the immense powers of the universe: in the Greek myths, Zeus is associated with the sky, Hades with the underworld, Poseidon with the sea, Apollo with the sun, Athena with wisdom, Ares with war. But the gods are also given the forms and feelings of human beings. Thus, myths make it possible for people to understand and deal with things that they cannot control and often cannot see.

A body of related myths that is accepted by a people is known as its *mythology*. A mythology tells a people what it is most concerned about: where it came from, who its gods are, what its most sacred rituals are, and what its destiny is.

See pages 823, 847.

NARRATIVE POEM *A poem that tells a story.* One kind of narrative poem is the *epic*, a long poem that sets forth the heroic ideals of a particular society. *Beowulf* is an epic. The *ballad* is another kind of narrative poem. "Bonny Barbara Allan" is an example of a ballad.

NARRATOR *One who narrates, or tells, a story.* A story may be told by a *first-person* narrator, someone who is either a major or minor character in the story. Or a story may be told by a *third-person* narrator, someone who is not in the story at all.

The word *narrator* can also refer to a character in a drama who guides the audience through the play, often commenting on the action and sometimes participating in it. In Thornton Wilder's play *Our Town*, the Stage Manager serves as the narrator.

See **Point of View.**

NATURALISM *An extreme form of realism.* Naturalistic writers usually depict the sordid side of life and show characters who are severely, if not hopelessly, limited by their environment or heredity.

NEOCLASSICISM *A revival in the seventeenth and eighteenth centuries of classical standards of order, balance, and harmony in literature.* John Dryden and Alexander Pope were major exponents of the neoclassical school.

See pages 253, 304–308, 311, 362–363.

NOVEL *A book-length fictional prose narrative, having many characters and often a complex plot.* Some important English novels are *Tom Jones* by Henry Fielding, *Pride and Prejudice* by Jane Austen, *Great Expectations* by Charles Dickens, and *Ulysses* by James Joyce.

See pages 401, 423, 552, 554, 608, 914–915.

OCTAVE *An eight-line poem or stanza.* Usually the term *octave* refers to the first eight lines of an Italian sonnet. The remaining six lines form a sestet.

See **Sonnet.**

ODE *A complex and often lengthy lyric poem, written in a dignified formal style on some lofty or serious subject.* Odes are often written for a special occasion, to honor a person or a season or to commemorate an event. Two famous odes are Percy Bysshe Shelley's "Ode to the West Wind" and John Keats's "Ode on a Grecian Urn."

The *Pindaric ode*, named for the Greek poet Pindar, was a choral poem containing several stanzas. Each stanza had three sections: a *strophe*, an *antistrophe*, and an *epode*, which were sung by the chorus.

See pages 317, 493, 496, 518, 521, 524, 525.

ONOMATOPOEIA *The use of a word whose sound in some degree imitates or suggests its meaning.* The names of some birds are onomatopoetic, imitating the cry of the bird named: *cuckoo, whippoorwill, owl, crow, towhee, bobwhite.* Some onomatopoetic words are *hiss, clang, rustle,* and *snap.* In these lines from *The Rime of the Ancient Mariner*, Coleridge reproduces the fearful sounds of the land of ice:

It cracked and growled, and roared and howled
Like noises in a swound!

(lines 61–62)

OTTAVA RIMA   *A form of eight-line stanza.* The rhyme scheme is *abababcc. Don Juan* by George Gordon, Lord Byron is written in ottava rima.

See page 481.

OXYMORON   *A figure of speech that combines opposite or contradictory ideas or terms.* An oxymoron suggests a paradox, but it does so very briefly, usually in two or three words, such as "living death," "dear enemy," "sweet sorrow," and "wise fool."

See pages 242, 838.

PARADOX   *A statement that reveals a kind of truth, although it seems at first to be self-contradictory and untrue.* Richard Lovelace included a famous paradox in his poem "To Althea, from Prison":

Stone walls do not a prison make;
　Nor iron bars a cage;
Minds innocent and quiet take
　That for an hermitage . . .

See pages 237, 242, 262, 436, 930.

PARALLELISM   *The use of phrases, clauses, or sentences that are similar or complementary in structure or in meaning.* Parallelism is a form of repetition. In Alfred, Lord Tennyson's poem "Sweet and Low," the first and third lines of the first stanza are parallel in structure:

Sweet and low, sweet and low
Wind of the western sea,
Low, low, breathe and blow,
Wind of the western sea.

Parallelism is used extensively in Bible psalms, where the thought of one line is often repeated with some variation in the next line:

I will sing unto the Lord as long as I live:
I will sing praise to my God while I have my being.
Psalm 104

See pages 227, 230.

PARODY   *The humorous imitation of a work of literature, art, or music.* A parody often achieves its humorous effect through the use of exaggeration or mockery. In literature, parody can be made of a plot, a character, a writing style, or a sentiment or theme. The poet Algernon Charles Swinburne parodies his own verse in a humorous poem called "Nephelidia." In these lines, Swinburne is mocking a kind of lush verse that makes excessive use of *alliteration:*

Pallid and pink as the palm of the flag flower that flickers with fear of the flies as they float,
Are the looks of our lovers that lustrously lean from a marvel of mystic, miraculous moonshine.

PASTORAL   *A type of poem that deals in an idealized way with shepherds and rustic life (the word* pastoral *comes from the Latin word for shepherd,* pastor*).* Two pastoral poems are Christopher Marlowe's "The Passionate Shepherd to His Love" and Sir Walter Raleigh's "The Nymph's Reply to the Shepherd." Raleigh's poem might be called *antipastoral* because of its realistic tone.

See pages 131, 132, 249.

PATHOS   *The quality in a work of literature or art that arouses the reader's feelings of pity, sorrow, or compassion for a character.* The term is usually used to refer to situations in which innocent characters suffer through no fault of their own. An example of a scene with pathos is Scene 2 in Act Four of *Macbeth* in which Lady Macduff and her son are ruthlessly murdered by Macbeth's assassins.

PERSONIFICATION   *A figure of speech in which something nonhuman is given human qualities.* In these lines from "Blow, Blow, Thou Winter Wind," William Shakespeare personifies the wind. He addresses it as if it were a person who could consciously act with kindness or unkindness. He also gives it teeth and breath.

Blow, blow, thou winter wind,
Thou art not so unkind
　As man's ingratitude.
Thy tooth is not so keen,
Because thou are not seen,
　Although thy breath be rude.

See pages 130, 141.

PETRARCHAN SONNET   See **Sonnet.**

PLOT   *The sequence of events or actions in a short story, novel, play, or narrative poem.* Plots may be simple or complicated, loosely constructed or close-knit. But every plot is made up of a series of incidents that are related to one another.

Conflict, a struggle of some kind, is the most important element of plot. Conflict may be *external* or *internal,* and there may be more than one form of conflict in a work. As the plot advances, we learn how the conflict is resolved, either through the action or through major changes in the attitudes or personalities of the characters.

Action is generally introduced by the *exposition,* information essential to understanding the situation. The action rises to a *crisis,* or *climax.* This movement is called the *rising action.* The *falling action,* which follows the crisis, shows a reversal of fortune for the protagonist. In a tragedy this reversal leads to disaster; in a comedy, it leads to a happy ending.

The *dénouement* or *resolution* is the moment when the conflict ends and the outcome of the action is clear.

See pages 190, 218.

POINT OF VIEW *The vantage point from which a narrative is told.* There are two basic points of view: *first-person* and *third-person.* In the *first-person* point of view, the story is told by one of the characters in his or her own words. The first-person point of view is limited, since the reader is told only what this character knows and observes. Here is an example of first-person point of view from Jonathan Swift's *Gulliver's Travels:*

> The King was struck with horror at the description I had given of those terrible engines, and the proposal I had made. He was amazed how so impotent and groveling an insect as I (these were his expressions) could entertain such inhuman ideas . . .

In the *third-person* point of view, the narrator is not a character in the story. The narrator may be an *omniscient,* or "all-knowing," observer who can describe and comment on all the characters and actions in the story. Thomas Hardy's "The Three Strangers" is written from a third-person omniscient point of view:

> Shepherdess Fennel fell back upon the intermediate plan of mingling short dances with short periods of talk and singing, so as to hinder any ungovernable rage in either.

On the other hand, the third-person narrator might tell a story from the point of view of only one character in the story, as Virginia Woolf does in "The New Dress." All the action in that story is told by the third-person narrator, from the *limited* point of view of Mabel Waring.

See pages 333, 612, 715, 774.

PROTAGONIST *The central character of a drama, novel, short story, or narrative poem.* The protagonist is the character on whom the action centers and with whom the reader sympathizes most. Usually the protagonist strives against an opposing force, or *antagonist,* to accomplish something. The protagonist can be either heroic or ordinary, good or bad. For example, Beowulf is brave and good. Macbeth is noble and honorable at first, but becomes increasingly hateful.

PSALM *A song or lyric poem in praise of God.* The term usually refers to the one hundred and fifty sacred lyrics in the Book of Psalms in the Bible.

See page 229.

PUN *The use of a word or phrase to suggest two or more meanings at the same time.* Puns are generally humorous. In Act Two, Scene 3 of *Macbeth,* the Porter plays on the two meanings of the word *goose* in this line: "Come in tailor, here you may roast your goose." The goose was a tailor's pressing iron.

QUATRAIN *Usually a stanza or poem of four lines.* A quatrain may also be any group of four lines unified by a rhyme scheme. Quatrains usually follow an *abab, abba,* or *abcb* rhyme scheme. Here is a quatrain from William Wordsworth's "A Slumber Did My Spirit Seal":

> a A slumber did my spirit seal;
> b I had no human fears:
> a She seemed a thing that could not feel
> b The touch of earthly years.

See pages 48, 122.

REALISM *The attempt in literature and art to represent life as it really is, without sentimentalizing or idealizing it.* Realistic writing often depicts the everyday life and speech of ordinary people. This has led, sometimes, to an emphasis on sordid details.

See **Naturalism.**

REFRAIN *A word, phrase, line, or group of lines repeated regularly in a poem, usually at the end of each stanza.* Refrains are often used in ballads and narrative poems to create a songlike rhythm and to help build suspense. Refrains can also serve to emphasize a particular idea. A modern example of the use of refrain appears in Dylan Thomas' "Do Not Go Gentle into That Good Night."

See pages 43, 143, 837.

RESOLUTION See **Plot.**

RHYME *The repetition of sounds in two or more words or phrases that appear close to each other in a poem.* For example: *river/shiver, song/long, leap/deep.* If the rhyme occurs at the ends of lines, it is called *end rhyme.* Here is an example from William Blake's "The Tiger":

> In what distant deeps or *skies*
> Burnt the fire of thine *eyes?*
> On what wings dare he *aspire?*
> What the hand, dare seize the *fire?*

If the rhyme occurs within a line, it is called *internal rhyme.* Here is an example of internal rhyme from *The Rime of the Ancient Mariner:*

> The wedding *Guest* he beat his *breast* . . .

Approximate rhyme is rhyme in which only the final consonant sounds of the words are identical (as opposed to *exact rhyme*). *Cook/look* is an exact rhyme; *cook/lack* is an approximate rhyme.

A *rhyme scheme* is the pattern of rhymes in a poem. *Interlocking rhyme* is a rhyme scheme in which an unrhymed line in one stanza rhymes with a line in the following stanza. Interlocking rhyme occurs in an Italian verse form called *terza rima*.

See pages 464, 496, 814.

RHYTHM *The arrangement of stressed and unstressed syllables into a pattern.* Rhythm is most apparent in poetry, though it is part of all good writing. Rhythm often gives a poem a distinct musical quality, as in Samuel Taylor Coleridge's "Kubla Khan":

Ĭn Xánădŭ dĭd Kúblă Khán
Ă státelў pléasŭre dŏme děcrée,
Whĕre Álph, thĕ sácred rívĕr, rán
Thrŏugh cávĕrns méasŭrĕless tŏ mán . . .

Poets also use rhythm to echo meaning. In these lines from Alfred, Lord Tennyson's "Break, Break, Break," the pounding rhythm reinforces the image of waves crashing against the land:

Bréak, bréak, bréak,
Ŏn thў cóld grăy stónes, Ŏ Séa.

See pages 21, 165, 462, 564.

RISING ACTION See **Plot**.

ROMANCE *Any imaginative literature that is set in an idealized world and that deals with heroic adventures and battles between good characters and villains or monsters.* Originally, the term referred to a medieval tale dealing with the loves and adventures of kings, queens, knights, and ladies, and including unlikely or supernatural happenings. *Sir Gawain and the Green Knight* is the best of the medieval romances. John Keats's "The Eve of St. Agnes" is one of the greatest metrical romances ever written.

See pages 40, 81, 407, 507.

ROMANTICISM *A movement that flourished in literature, philosophy, music, and art in Western culture during most of the nineteenth century, beginning as a revolt against classicism.* There have been many varieties of Romanticism in many different times and places. Many of the ideas of English Romanticism were first expressed by the poets William Wordsworth and Samuel Taylor Coleridge.

See pages 406–410.

SATIRE *A kind of writing that holds up to ridicule or contempt the weaknesses and wrong-*

doings of individuals, groups, institutions, or humanity in general. The aim of satirists is to set a moral standard for society, and they attempt to persuade the reader to see their point of view through the force of laughter. The most famous satirical work in English literature is Jonathan Swift's *Gulliver's Travels*. In the distant land of Brobdingnag, where the people are twelve times as tall as a normal human being, Gulliver is brought before the King to describe the English people. Swift satirizes the English people through the King's response:

He was perfectly astonished with the historical account I gave him of our affairs during the last century, protesting it was only a heap of conspiracies, rebellions, murders, massacres, revolutions, banishments; the very worst effects that avarice, faction, hypocrisy, perfidiousness, cruelty, rage, madness, hatred, envy, lust, malice, and ambition could produce.

See pages 333, 340, 363, 913.

SCANSION *The analysis of verse in terms of meter.* Meter is measured in units called *feet*. A foot consists of one stressed syllable and, usually, one or two unstressed syllables. A line of poetry has as many feet as it has stressed syllables. Standard poetic feet include: *iamb*, one unstressed syllable followed by one stressed syllable (˘′) as in rePORT; *trochee*, one stressed syllable followed by one unstressed syllable (′˘) as in PATtern; *dactyl*, one stressed syllable followed by two unstressed syllables (′˘˘) as in SIlently; and *anapest*, two unstressed syllables followed by a stressed syllable (˘˘′) as in underTAKE.

A metrical line is named for its pattern and number of feet: *iambic pentameter* (5 iambs), *trochaic tetrameter* (4 trochees), *dactylic hexameter* (6 dactyls), *anapestic trimeter* (3 anapests), and so on.

Diagonal lines are often used to separate the poetic feet in a line:

Whў sŏ/pále ănd/wán, fŏnd/lóvĕr?

"Ĭs thĭs/thĕ ré/gĭŏn, thĭs/thĕ sóil,/thĕ clíme . . ."

Bréak,/bréak,/bréak,

Ăt thĕ fóot/ŏf thў crágs,/Ŏ Séa!/

See pages 21, 48, 165, 595.

SESTET *A six-line poem or stanza.* Usually the term sestet refers to the last six lines of an Italian sonnet. The first eight lines of an Italian sonnet form an *octave*.

See **Sonnet**.

SETTING *The time and place in which the events in a short story, novel, play or narrative poem occur.* A setting may serve simply as the physical background of a story, or a skillful writer may use setting to establish a particular *atmosphere*, which in turn contributes to the plot and theme of the story.

SIMILE *A comparison made between two things through the use of a specific word of comparison, such as* like, as, than, *or* resembles. The comparison must be between two essentially unlike things. To say "Susan is like her grandmother" is not to use a simile. But to say "Susan is like a golden flower" is to use a simile. In "To a Skylark," Percy Bysshe Shelley uses a simile to describe the flight of the bird:

> Higher still and higher
> From the earth thou springest
> Like a cloud of fire . . .

See **Figurative Language.**
See also pages 73, 497.

SOLILOQUY *In drama, an extended speech delivered by a character alone onstage.* The character reveals his or her innermost thoughts and feelings directly to the audience, as if thinking aloud. One of the most famous soliloquies in literature occurs at the end of Shakespeare's *Macbeth*, when Macbeth, near defeat, expresses a bleak and bitter vision of life:

> Tomorrow, and tomorrow, and tomorrow,
> Creeps in this petty pace from day to day
> To the last syllable of recorded time,
> And all our yesterdays have lighted fools
> The way to dusty death. Out, out, brief candle!
> Life's but a walking shadow, a poor player
> That struts and frets his hour upon the stage
> And then is heard no more. It is a tale
> Told by an idiot, full of sound and fury,
> Signifying nothing.

(V, 5, 19–28)

See page 212.

SONG *A short lyric poem with distinct musical qualities, normally written to be set to music.* It expresses a simple but intense emotion. "She Walks in Beauty" by George Gordon, Lord Byron is a song.

See pages 140, 477.

SONNET *A fourteen-line lyric poem, usually written in rhymed iambic pentameter.* A sonnet generally expresses a single theme or idea. Sonnets vary in structure and rhyme scheme, but are generally of two types: the *Petrarchan* or *Italian sonnet* and the *Elizabethan* or *Shakespearean sonnet*.

The Italian sonnet is a form that originated in Italy in the thirteenth century. The Italian sonnet has two parts, an *octave* (eight lines) and a *sestet* (six lines). Its rhyme scheme is usually *abbaabba cdecde*. The two parts of the Italian sonnet play off each other in a variety of ways. Sometimes the octave raises a question that the sestet answers. Sometimes the sestet opposes what the octave says, or extends it. The Italian sonnet is often called the Petrarchan sonnet, because the Italian poet Francesco Petrarch used it so extensively. He dedicated more than three hundred sonnets to a woman named Laura.

Petrarch inspired the vogue of sonnet writing in Elizabethan England. It became conventional for English poets to address sonnets to a beautiful but cruel mistress whose eyes were stars, whose lips were cherries, and whose cheeks were roses. Shakespeare's "Sonnet 130" has been called anti-Petrarchan because he inverts the conventions, describing his mistress in realistic terms.

The *Shakespearean* sonnet consists of three quatrains and a concluding couplet, with the rhyme scheme *abab cdcd efef gg*.

A less important sonnet form is the *Spenserian* sonnet. Its rhyme scheme is *ababbcbccdcdee*.

A group of sonnets related in some way—loosely or closely—is called a *sonnet sequence*. Examples are Edmund Spenser's *Amoretti*, Sir Philip Sidney's *Astrophel and Stella*, and Elizabeth Barrett Browning's *Sonnets from the Portuguese*.

See pages 121–123, 124, 128, 136, 139, 240, 267, 437, 506, 600.

SPENSERIAN STANZA *A nine-line stanza with the following rhyme scheme: ababbcbcc.* The first eight lines are written in iambic pentameter. The ninth line is written in iambic hexameter and is called an *alexandrine*. The Spenserian stanza was invented by Edmund Spenser for his epic poem *The Faerie Queene*. The Spenserian stanza was also used by Robert Burns, John Keats, and Percy Bysshe Shelley.

See page 125.

SPRUNG RHYTHM *A term created by the poet Gerard Manley Hopkins to designate a variable kind of poetic meter in which a stressed syllable may be combined with any number of unstressed syllables.* Poems with sprung rhythm have an irregular meter and are meant to sound like natural speech.

See pages 591, 595.

STEREOTYPE *A commonplace type or character that appears so often in literature that his or her nature is immediately familiar to the reader.* Stereotypes, also called *stock characters*, always look and act the same way and reveal the same traits of character. Examples of stereotypes are the temperamental movie star, the talkative cab driver, the mad scientist, the villain with a waxed mustache, and the wisecracking, hard-boiled private detective.

STREAM OF CONSCIOUSNESS *The style of writing that attempts to imitate the natural flow of a character's thoughts, feelings, reflections, memories, and mental images as the character experiences them.*

See pages 714, 715, 720.

STROPHE See **Ode.**

STYLE *An author's characteristic way of writing, determined by the choice of words, the arrangement of words in sentences, and the relationship of the sentences to one another.* Thus, one author may write long, complex sentences, while another writes short, terse ones. One author may use few adjectives, while another uses many. Style also refers to the particular way in which an author uses *imagery, figurative language,* and *rhythm.* Style is the sum total of qualities and characteristics that distinguish the writings of one writer from those of another.

See pages 242, 307, 342.

SUSPENSE *The quality of a story, novel, or drama that makes the reader or audience uncertain or tense about the outcome of events.* Suspense makes readers ask, "What will happen next?" or "How will this work out?" and impels them to read on. Suspense is greatest when it focuses attention on a sympathetic character. Thus, the most familiar kind of suspense involves a character in mortal danger: hanging from the ledge of a tall building; tied to railroad tracks as a train approaches; or alone in an old house, ascending a staircase to open the attic door. But suspense may simply arise from curiosity, as when a character must make a decision, or seek an explanation for something.

SYMBOL *Any object, person, place, or action that has a meaning in itself and that also stands for something larger than itself, such as a quality, an attitude, a belief, or a value.* A rose is often a symbol of love and beauty; a skull is often a symbol of death; spring and winter often symbolize youth and old age.

See page 794.

SYMBOLISM *A literary movement that arose in France in the last half of the nineteenth century and that greatly influenced many English writers, particularly poets, of the twentieth century.* To the Symbolist poets, an emotion is indefinite and therefore difficult to communicate. Symbolist poets tend to avoid any direct statement of meaning. Instead, they work through emotionally powerful symbols that suggest meaning and mood.

See pages 400, 678, 794.

SYNECDOCHE *A figure of speech that substitutes a part for a whole.* An example is T. S. Eliot's use of "feet" and "hands" to stand for "people" in the poem "Preludes."

See page 809.

TERZA RIMA *An Italian verse form consisting of a series of three-line stanzas in which the middle line of each stanza rhymes with the first and third lines of the following stanza, as follows:* aba bcb cdc, etc. Percy Bysshe Shelley's "Ode to The West Wind" is written in *terza rima.* Here are the first two stanzas:

a O wild West Wind, thou breath of Autumn's *being,*
b Thou, from whose unseen presence the leaves *dead*
a Are driven, like ghosts from an enchanter *fleeing.*

b Yellow, and black, and pale, and hectic *red,*
c Pestilence-stricken multitudes: O *thou,*
b Who chariotest to their dark wintry *bed* . . .

See pages 493, 496.

THEME *The general idea or insight about life that a writer wishes to express in a literary work.* All the elements of a literary work—plot, setting, characterization, and figurative language—contribute to the development of its theme. A simple theme can often be stated in a single sentence. But sometimes a literary work is rich and complex, and a paragraph or even an essay is needed to state the theme. Not all literary works have a controlling theme. For example, the purpose of some simple ghost stories is to frighten the reader, and some detective stories seek only to thrill.

See pages 218, 221.

TONE *The attitude a writer takes toward his or her subject, characters, or audience.* In writing about his childhood in his poem "Fern Hill," Dylan Thomas' tone is nostalgic. In *Preface to Shakespeare,* Samuel Johnson's tone is serious and admiring. Tone is found in every kind of writing. It is created through the choice of words and details.

See pages 370, 835.

TRAGEDY *In general, a literary work in which the protagonist meets an unhappy or disastrous end.* Unlike *comedy,* tragedy depicts the actions of a central character who is usually dignified or heroic. Through a series of events, this main character, or *tragic hero,* is brought to a final downfall. The causes of a tragic hero's downfall vary. In traditional dramas, the cause can be fate, a flaw in character, or an error in judgment. In modern dramas, where the tragic hero is often an ordinary individual, the causes range from moral or psychological weakness to the evils of society. The tragic hero, though defeated, usually gains a measure of wisdom or self-awareness.

See pages 148, 217.

TROCHEE See **Scansion.**

VILLANELLE *An intricate verse form of French origin, consisting of several three-line stanzas and a concluding four-line stanza.* The first and third lines of the first stanza are used as refrains in the succeeding stanzas and as the last two lines of the concluding stanza. Only two rhymes are allowed in a villanelle. A famous modern villanelle is Dylan Thomas' "Do Not Go Gentle into That Good Night."

See pages 837, 838.

WIT *A brilliance and quickness of perception combined with a cleverness of expression.* In the eighteenth century, *wit* and *nature* were related—nature provided the rules of the universe; wit allowed these rules to be interpreted and expressed.

See pages 306, 326, 362–363.

Glossary

Strictly speaking, the word *glossary* means a collection of technical, obscure, or foreign words found in a certain field of work. Of course, the words in this glossary are not "technical, obscure, or foreign," but are those that might present difficulty as you read the selections in this textbook.

Many words in the English language have several meanings. In this glossary, the meanings given are the ones that apply to the words as they are used in the selections in the textbook. Words closely related in form and meaning are generally listed together in one entry (**elucidate** and **elucidation**), and the definition is given for the first form. Related words that generally appear as separate entries in dictionaries are listed separately (**immerse** and **immersion**). Regular adverbs (ending in *-ly*) are defined in their adjective form, with the adverb form shown at the end of the definition.

The following abbreviations are used:

adj. adjective	*n.* noun	*v.* verb
adv. adverb	*prep.* preposition	

A

abase (ə-bās′) *v.* To humiliate; humble. — **abasement** *n.*
abhor (ăb-hôr′) *v.* To hate intensely.
abide (ə-bīd′) *v.* To await.
abiding (ə-bī′ding) *adj.* Lasting.
abject (ăb′jĕkt′, ăb-jĕkt′) *adj.* Miserable; wretched.
abjure (ăb-jŏŏr′) *v.* To renounce or give up.
abominable (ə-bŏm′ə-nə-bəl) *adj.* Loathsome.
abound (ə-bound′) *v.* To be plentiful.
absolution (ăb-sə-lōō′-shən) *n.* Forgiveness.
abstruse (ăb-strōōs′) *adj.* Hard to understand.
absurd (ăb-sûrd′, -zûrd′) *adj.* Ridiculous; laughable.
abysmal (ə-bĭz′məl) *adj.* Extreme; wretched.
abyss (ə-bĭs′) *n.* A bottomless depth or empty space.
access (ăk′sĕs) *n.* A means of nearing or getting.
accessible (ăk-sĕs′ə-bəl) *adj.* Approached or entered easily.
accrue (ə-krōō′) *v.* To increase or accumulate.
adage (ăd′ĭj) *n.* An old saying accepted as true.
adjacent (ə-jā′sənt) *adj.* Adjoining; near or close to.
admonish (ăd-mŏn′ĭsh) *v.* **1.** To warn. **2.** To speak disapprovingly.
admonition (ăd′mə-nĭsh′ən) *n.* **1.** A warning to avoid or correct something. **2.** A mild reproval.
advent (ăd′vĕnt) *n.* A coming or arrival.

adversary (ăd′vər-sĕr′ē) *n.* An opponent.
adversity (ăd-vûr′sə-tē) *n.* A state of misfortune.
afflict (ə-flĭkt′) *v.* To cause distress or suffering. — **afflicter** *n.*
affliction (ə-flĭk′shən) *n.* That which causes pain or suffering.
agility (ə-jĭl′ə-tē) *n.* The ability to move quickly and easily.
agitate (ăj′ə-tāt′) *v.* To upset or excite.
alacrity (ə-lăk′rə-tē) *n.* Eagerness or readiness.
alienate (āl′yən-āt′, ā′lē-ən-) *v.* To estrange.
alleged (ə-lĕjd′, ə-lĕj′ĭd) *adj.* Supposed.
alliteration (ə-lĭt′ə-rā′shən) *n.* The repetition of similar sounds, usually initial consonant sounds.
allude (ə-lōōd′) *v.* To make a casual or indirect reference.
amber (ăm′bər) *n.* A fossil resin, of a yellow or brownish-yellow color, used for ornaments.
amble (ăm′bəl) *v.* To walk in a slow, relaxed way.
amend (ə-mĕnd′) *v.* To change in order to correct.
amiable (ā′mē-ə-bəl) *adj.* Friendly; pleasant. — **amiability** *n.*
amorous (ăm′ər-əs) *adj.* Loving.
amphibious (ăm-fĭb′ē-əs) *adj.* Able to live on land and in water.
ample (ăm′pəl) *adj.* Abundant.
anarchy (ăn′ər-kē) *n.* Disorder and lawlessness.
anguish (ăng′gwĭsh) *n.* Great mental or physical suffering.
annals (ăn′əlz) *n. pl.* History or records in general.
annihilate (ə-nī′ə-lāt′) *v.* To destroy completely.
annul (ə-nŭl′) *v.* To cancel.
anoint (ə-noint′) *v.* To put oil on (in a ceremony).
anon (ə-nŏn′) *adv. Archaic.* Soon.
anthem (ăn′thəm) *n.* A song of praise or loyalty.
antidote (ăn′tĭ-dōt′) *n.* Something to counteract a poison.
antiquity (ăn-tĭk′wə-tē) *n.* The early period of history.
apathetic (ăp′ə-thĕt′ĭk) *adj.* Indifferent; uninterested.
apostate (ə-pŏs′tāt′, -tĭt) *adj.* Guilty of forsaking one's faith.
apothecary (ə-pŏth′ə-kĕr′ē) *n.* A person who prepares and sells drugs.
appall (ə-pôl′) *v.* To horrify, shock.
apparition (ăp′ə-rĭsh′ən) *n.* A ghost; a strange sight.
apprehend (ăp′rĭ-hĕnd′) *v.* To understand.
apprehension (ăp′rĭ-hĕn′shən) *n.* Understanding.
apprehensive (ăp′rĭ-hĕn′sĭv) *adj.* Fearful.
approbation (ăp′rə-bā′shən) *n.* Approval.
arbitrary (är′bə-trĕr′ē) *adj.* Determined by individual preference or whim.

ă pat/ā pay/âr care/ä father/b bib/ch church/d deed/ē pet/ē be/f fife/g gag/h hat/hw which/ĭ pit/ī pie/îr pier/j judge/k kick/l lid, needle/m mum/ n no, sudden/ng thing/ŏ pot/ō toe/ô paw, for/oi noise/ou out/ŏŏ took/ōō boot/p pop/r roar/s sauce/sh ship, dish/t tight/th thin, path/*th* this, bathe/ ŭ cut/ûr urge/v valve/w with/y yes/z zebra, size/zh vision/ə about, item, edible, gallop, circus/ä *Fr.* ami/œ *Fr.* feu, *Ger.* schön/ü *Fr.* tu, *Ger.* über/ KH *Ger.* ich, *Scot.* loch/N *Fr.* bon.

arbitrate (är′bə-trāt′) v. To settle a dispute as an impartial judge.

arduous (är′jōō-əs) adj. Difficult; laborious; taxing.

armistice (är′mə-stĭs) n. A truce.

arrears (ə-rîrz′) n. pl. Debts that are unpaid and overdue. —in arrears.

ascent (ə-sĕnt′) n. The act of rising or climbing.

aspirant (ăs′pər-ənt, ə-spīr′ənt) n. A person who seeks after honors or distinction.

aspire (ə-spīr′) v. To have some ambitious goal.

assay (ă-sā′, ăs′ā) v. To try; attempt.

assent (ə-sĕnt′) v. To agree. n. Agreement.

asunder (ə-sŭn′dər) adv. Apart.

athwart (ə-thwôrt′) adv. At a slant.

atone (ə-tōn′) v. To make amends.

atrophy (ăt′rə-fē) v. To waste away.

audacity (ô-dăs′ə-tē) n. Boldness; daring.

audible (ô′də-bəl) adj. Loud enough to be heard.—**audibly** adv.

auditor (ô′də-tər) n. One who hears or listens.

augment (ôg-mĕnt′) v. To make greater; increase.

autocrat (ô′tə-krăt′) n. Ruler with unlimited power. —**autocratic** adj.

avarice (ăv′ə-rĭs) n. Greed for wealth.

aver (ə-vûr′) v. To affirm.

avert (ə-vûrt′) v. To turn away.

avowed (ə-voud′) adj. Openly acknowledged.

awful (ô′fəl) adj. Awe-inspiring.

azure (ăzh′ər) adj. Sky-blue.

B

bailiff (bā′lĭf) n. A district official who has the power to collect taxes, keep the peace, etc.

baleful (bāl′fəl) adj. Threatening; evil.

balm (bäm) n. Anything healing or soothing.

balustrade (băl′ə-strād′) n. A railing supported by small posts.

barge (bärj) n. A large boat, generally flat-bottomed.

bark (bärk) n. A sailing boat.

barrister (băr′ĭ-stər) n. A lawyer.

battlement (băt′l-mənt) n. A wall with open spaces to shoot through, usually on top of a tower.

beacon (bē′kən) n. A light for warning or guiding.

beguile (bĭ-gīl′) v. To trick or cheat.

bellow (bĕl′ō) v. To cry out in a loud voice, as in rage or pain.

benediction (bĕn′ə-dĭk′shən) n. A blessing.

benevolence (bə-nĕv′ə-ləns) n. Kindliness.

benighted (bĭ-nī′tĭd) adj. Surrounded by darkness.

benign (bĭ-nīn′) adj. Good-natured; gentle.

beseech (bĭ-sēch′) v. To appeal earnestly.

besiege (bĭ-sēj′) v. To hem in.

besought v. Past tense of beseech.

bestow (bĭ-stō′) v. To give; grant.

bide (bīd) v. To stay; wait.

bine (bīn) n. A climbing, twining stem.

blanch (blănch, blänch) v. To become pale or white.

blaspheme (blăs-fēm′) v. To speak in an irreverent way (of God or sacred things).

blighter (blīt′ər) n. Slang. A contemptible or mean person.

blithe (blīth, blīth) adj. Carefree.

bloke (blōk) n. Slang. A man; fellow; chap.

boisterous (boi′stər-əs, -strəs) adj. Stormy; violent.

bole (bōl) n. A tree trunk.

bombast (bŏm′băst) n. Inflated language.

boorish (boor′ĭsh) adj. Awkward; clumsy; coarse in manners.

boracic (bôr-ăs′ĭk) n. Boric acid.

bounteous (boun′tē-əs) adj. Plentiful.

brandish (brăn′dĭsh) v. To wave or flourish in a menacing way.

brawn (brôn) n. Powerful, muscular strength.

breech (brēch) n. The part of a rifle located behind the barrel.

brethren (brĕth′rən) n. Brothers.

bridle (brīd′l) n. A head harness for a horse. — v. To draw one's head back quickly in anger, pride, etc.

brier (brī′ər) n. Also briar. A prickly or thorny bush. — **briery** adj.

brimstone (brĭm′stōn) n. Sulfur.

brougham (brōōm, brōō′əm, brō′əm) n. A closed carriage with the driver's seat outside in front.

bruiser (brōō′zər) n. A powerful man.

brusque (brŭsk) adj. Abrupt; discourteous — **brusquely** adv.

buckler (bŭk′lər) n. A small round shield held or worn on the arm.

buffet (bŭf′ĭt) v. To punch with the fist.

buffoon (bə-fōōn′) n. A person given to clowning.

bullion (bŏŏl′yən) n. Uncoined gold and silver.

buoyancy (boi′ən-sē, bōō′yən-) n. The ability to float in liquid or rise in air.

burgess (bûr′jĭs) n. Formerly a member of the British Parliament.

burrow (bûr′ō) n. A hole or tunnel made in the ground by an animal.

buttress (bŭt′rĭs) n. A projecting structure built against a wall for support.

byre (bīr) n. A cow barn.

C

cadet (kə-dĕt′) n. A younger son or brother.

calamity (kə-lăm′ə-tē) n. A disaster; misfortune.

calculation (kăl′kyə-lā′shən) n. Mathematical determination of quantity, amount, etc.

caldron (kôl′drən) n. A large kettle or boiler.

candid (kăn′dĭd) adj. Free from prejudice; honest; frank.

canopy (kăn′ə-pē) n. **1.** Something that forms a cover. **2.** The sky.

cant (kănt) n. Insincere moralistic talk.

carcass (kär′kəs) n. The human body (used scornfully or humorously).

careen (kə-rēn′) v. To lean on one side.

career (kə-rîr′) v. To go at full speed; rush wildly.

caricature (kăr′ĭ-kə-chŏŏr′) v. To make an absurd likeness of.

carter (kär′tər) n. A person who drives a cart.

casement (kās′mənt) n. A window frame that opens outward on hinges.

castigate (kăs′tə-gāt′) v. To punish or reprimand sharply. —**castigation** n.

cataract (kăt′ə-răkt′) n. A large waterfall.

cavalcade (kăv′əl-kād′, kăv′əl-kād′) n. A procession, generally of horsemen or carriages.

caviar (kăv′ē-är′) *n.* The eggs of sturgeon, salmon, etc., seasoned and usually served as an appetizer.

celestial (sə-lĕs′chəl) *adj.* Of the heavens; of the sky.

celibacy (sĕl′ə-bə-sē) *n.* The state of being unmarried.

cellarage (sĕl′ər-ĭj) *n.* A cellar; the space in a cellar.

censure (sĕn′shər) *v.* To criticize or disapprove of severely.

certes (sûr′tēz) *adv. Archaic.* Certainly.

certitude (sûr′tə-tōōd, -tyōōd) *n.* Sureness.

cessation (sĕ-sā′shən) *n.* A stopping or ceasing.

chafe (chāf) *v.* To make sore; irritate.

chaffy (chăf′ē) *adj.* Full of chaff; worthless.

chalet (shă-lā′) *n.* A type of Swiss dwelling, built of wood with an overhanging roof.

chalice (chăl′ĭs) *n.* A cup; goblet.

chamberlain (chām′bər-lĭn) *n.* A person who manages the household of a ruler or nobleman.

champ (chămp) *v.* To chew or grind noisily.

chaplain (chăp′lĭn) *n.* A member of the clergy attached to a chapel, as of a royal court.

chasm (kăz′əm) *n.* A deep crack in the earth's surface.

chaste (chāst) *adj.* Virtuous.

chastise (chăs-tīz′) *v.* To punish; scold severely.

cherubim (chĕr′ə-bĭm′, -yə-bĭm′) *n. pl.* Angels. Plural of *cherub.*

chide (chīd) *v.* To scold in a mild way.

chimerical (kī-mĕr′ĭ-kəl, -mîr′ĭ-kəl, kə-) *adj.* Imaginary; fantastic.

chivalry (shĭv′əl-rē) *n.* The noble qualities of courage and honor associated with medieval knights.

chronic (krŏn′ĭk) *adj.* Continuing; recurring.

chronicle (krŏn′ĭ-kəl) *v.* A record of events in the order in which they happened.

churn (chûrn) *n.* A container in which milk or cream is formed into butter.

cipher (sī′fər) *n.* Someone or something of no importance or value.

circumscribe (sûr′kəm-skrīb′) *v.* To encircle.

circumstantial (sûr′kəm-stăn′shal) *adj.* Accidental.

cistern (sĭs′tərn) *n.* A large receptacle used to hold water.

civil (sĭv′əl) *adj.* Polite; courteous. – **civilly** *adv.*

civility (sə-vĭl′ə-tē) *n.* Politeness.

clangor (klăng′ər, klăng′gər) *n.* A loud, ringing sound.

cleave (klēv) *v.* To stick to; cling.

clod (klŏd) *n.* A lump of earth or clay.

cloister (klois′tər) *n.* A place of religious seclusion. *v.* To seclude.

cloven (klō′vən) *adj.* Divided; split.

cob (kŏb) *n.* A short-legged, thickset horse.

colloquial (kə-lō′kwē-əl) *adj.* Informal.

combustible (kəm-bŭs′tə-bəl) *adj.* Catching fire and burning easily.

combustion (kəm-bŭs′chən) *n.* Burning.

commend (kə-mĕnd′) *v.* To praise.

commendation (kŏm′ən-dā′shən) *n.* Approval; recommendation.

commiseration (kə-mĭz′ə-rā′shən) *n.* Pity; compassion.

commission (kə-mĭsh′ən) *n.* Authorization to carry out certain duties.

commissioner (kə-mĭsh′ən-ər) *n.* An official authorized to carry out certain duties.

compass (kŭm′pəs, kŏm′) *v.* To go round.

compassion (kəm-păsh′ən) *n.* Pity.

complexity (kəm-plĕk′sə-tē) *n.* The state or condition of being involved or complicated.

compliance (kəm-plī′əns) *n.* A giving in to a request, demand, etc.

compositor (kəm-pŏz′ə-tər) *n.* A person who sets type.

compunction (kəm-pŭngk′shən) *n.* A strong feeling of uneasiness caused by a sense of guilt.

conceive (kən-sēv′) *v.* To imagine.

concierge (kŏn′sē-ûrzh) *n.* A custodian or janitor of a building such as an apartment house or hotel.

conciliate (kən-sĭl′ē-āt′) *v.* To win over; appease.

concourse (kŏn′kôrs, -kōrs, kŏng′-) *n.* A crowd; gathering.

condone (kən-dōn′) *v.* To excuse; overlook.

conduce (kən-dōōs′, dyōōs′) *v.* To tend or contribute (to something).

confound (kən-found′, kŏn-) *v.* To mix up; confuse.

confute (kən-fyōōt′) *v.* To prove someone or something to be mistaken or false.

conjecture (kən-jĕk′chər) *v.* To guess.

conjunction (kən-jŭngk′shən) *n.* A joining together; union.

conjure (kŏn′jər, kən-jōor′) *v.* To call upon or entreat.

connivance (kə-nī′vəns) *n.* The act of cooperating secretly with someone in wrongdoing.

consecrate (kŏn′sə-krāt′) *v.* To set apart as holy.

consequential (kŏn′sə-kwĕn′shəl) *adj.* Important.

consign (kən-sīn′) *v.* To hand over or deliver.

conspire (kən-spīr′) *v.* To plot or plan something.

constable (kŏn′stə-bəl, kŭn′) *n.* A peace officer.

consternation (kŏn′stər-nā′shən) *n.* Amazement; bewilderment.

contemn (kən-tĕm′) *v.* To scorn.

contemplation (kŏn′təm-plā′shən) *n.* Careful thought.

contempt (kən-tĕmpt′) *n.* Scorn.

contemptible (kən-tĕmp′tə-bəl) *adj.* Deserving of scorn; worthless.

contemptuous (kən-tĕmp′chōō-əs) *adj.* Scornful.

contend (kən-tĕnd′) *v.* To struggle against in combat or competition.

contention (kən-tĕn′shən) *n.* Strife; struggle; controversy.

contradiction (kŏn′trə-dĭk′shən) *n.* A statement that is contrary to another; denial.

contrive (kən-trīv′) *v.* To plan cleverly; scheme.

conventional (kən-vĕn′shən-əl) *adj.* Conforming to accepted standards or practices.

converge (kən-vûrj′) *v.* To come together at a point.

conversant (kŏn′vər-sənt, kən-vûr′-) *adj.* Well acquainted or familiar, as by study.

convulse (kən-vŭls′) *v.* To shake violently; agitate.

convulsive (kən-vŭl′sĭv) *adj.* Violently disturbing.

coomb (kōōm) *n.* A deep, narrow valley.

cope (kōp) *n.* A long capelike vestment.

copious (kō′pē-əs) *adj.* Plentiful.

copper (kŏp′ər) *n.* A large metal container or boiler.

coppice (kŏp′ĭs) *n.* See *copse.*

copse (kŏps) *n.* A thicket of small trees or shrubs.

corporeal (kôr-pôr′ē-əl, -pō′rē-əl) *adj.* Bodily; tangible.

corpulent (kôr′pyə-lənt) *adj.* Fat and fleshy.

corroborate (kə-rŏb′ə-rāt′) *v.* To confirm.

corruption (kə-rŭp′shən) *n.* Evil or wicked behavior.

cosmopolitanism (kŏz'mə-pŏl'ə-tən-īz-əm') *n.* Worldliness.

council (koun'səl) *n.* A serious discussion among a group of people.

counsel (koun'səl) *n.* Ideas; opinions.

countenance (koun'tə-nəns) *n.* **1.** The face. **2.** The look on a person's face.

counterfeit (koun'tər-fĭt) *n.* Imitation; sham.

courser (kôr'sər, kōr', koor'-) *n.* A graceful or swift horse.

courtliness (kôrt'lē-nəs, kōrt') *n.* Elegance of manners.

covenant (kŭv'ə-nənt) *n.* A binding agreement made by two or more individuals.

covet (kŭv'ĭt) *v.* To have a strong desire for something.

covetous (kŭv'ə-təs) *adj.* Excessively eager for something; greedy. — **covetousness** *n.*

crafty (krăf'tē, kräf'-) *adj.* Sly; cunning.

crag (krăg) *n.* A steep, rugged rock.

credulity (krĭ-doo'lə-tē, -dyoo'lə-tē) *n.* A tendency to believe something too quickly.

credulous (krĕj'oo-ləs, krĕd'yoo-) *adj.* Too easily convinced.

crevice (krĕv'ĭs) *n.* A narrow opening caused by a crack or split.

crockery (krŏk'ə-rē) *n.* Earthenware dishes, pots, etc.

crucify (kroo'sə-fī') *v.* To torment; torture.

crypt (krĭpt) *n.* An underground chamber used as a burial place.

cryptogram (krĭp'tə-grăm') *n.* Something written in code.

cud (kŭd) *n.* Something held in the mouth and chewed or rechewed.

cumulative (kyoom'yə-lā'tĭv, yə-lə-tĭv) *adj.* Increasing in size, volume, etc., by successive additions.

curfew (kûr'fyoo) *n.* The ringing of a bell to signal a certain time — the end of day, etc.

curtailing (kər-tāl'ĭng) *n.* An abridgement.

cynical (sĭn'ĭ-kəl) *adj.* Believing that there is no true goodness in anyone; scornful. — **cynically** *adv.*

D

dale (dāl) *n.* A valley.

dappled (dăp'ld) *adj.* Spotted.

darkling (därk'lĭng) *adj.* In the dark; dim.

dauntless (dônt'lĭs, dänt'-) *adj.* Fearless.

dauphin (dô'fĭn) *n.* Title of the eldest son of the French King, heir to the throne.

dearth (dûrth) *n.* Scarcity; lack.

debauchery (dĭ-bô'chə-rē) *n.* Indulgence of one's sensual appetites.

deceitful (dĭ-sēt'fəl) *adj.* Apt to cheat or lie; false.

decipher (dĭ-sī'fər) *v.* To translate into understandable language.

declamation (dĕk'lə-mā'shən) *n.* The act of speaking in a dramatic manner.

decorum (dĭ'kôr'əm, dĭ'kōr'əm) *n.* Good taste in speech, behavior, etc.

decrepit (dĭ-krĕp'ĭt) *adj.* Worn out; broken down.

deduction (dĭ-dŭk'shən) *n.* A sum or amount that is subtracted.

deface (dĭ-fās') *v.* To disfigure.

defer (dĭ-fûr') *v.* To put off to a future time.

deferential (dĕf'ə-rĕn'shəl) *adj.* Very respectful. — **deferentially** *adv.*

defile (dĭ-fīl') *v.* To make dirty.

deft (dĕft) *adj.* Skillful; quick. — **deftly** *adv.*

deify (dē-ə-fī') *v.* To make a god of.

delinquent (dĭ-lĭng'kwənt) *adj.* Not doing what duty or law requires.

delirious (dĭ-lĭr'ē-əs) *adj.* In a state of wild excitement.

deluge (dĕl'yooj) *n.* A great flood.

delusion (dĭ-loo'zhən, dĭ-lyoo'-) *n.* A false belief or opinion.

demean (dĭ-mēn') *v.* To lower in character or status.

demeanor (dĭ-mē'nər) *n.* Behavior; conduct.

demerit (dĭ-mĕr'ĭt) *n.* Defect; fault.

denominate (dĭ-nŏm'ə-nāt) *v.* To give a name to; call.

denote (dĭ-nōt') *v.* To be a sign of.

deplorable (dĭ-plôr'ə-bəl, dĭ-plōr'ə-) *adj.* Regrettable.

deprecate (dĕp'rĭ-kāt') *v.* To belittle. — **deprecation** *n.*

deprecatory (dĕp'rə-kə-tôr'ē, -tōr'ē) *adj.* Apologetic or downgrading.

deputation (dĕp'yə-tā'shən) *n.* An individual or group appointed to represent others.

depute (dĭ-pyoot') *v.* To make someone a deputy or substitute.

deputy (dĕp'yə-tē) *n.* A person appointed to act for another.

derisive (dĭ-rī'sĭv) *adj.* Mocking.

derive (dĭ-rīv') *v.* To receive or get (from a source).

desolate (dĕs'ə-lĭt) *adj.* Miserable; lonely.

despondent (dĭ-spŏn'dənt) *adj.* Discouraged; hopeless. — **despondently** *adv.*

desultory (dĕs'əl-tôr'ē, -tōr'ə) *adj.* Aimless; disconnected.

deviation (dē'vē-ā'shən) *n.* A departure from accepted norm, behavior, etc.

dexterity (dĕk-stĕr'ə-tē) *n.* Skill; cleverness.

diaphanous (dī-ăf'ə-nəs) *adj.* Transparent.

didactic (dī-dăk'tĭk) *adj.* Intended for instruction.

diffusive (dĭ-fyoo'sĭv, -zĭv) *adj.* Tending to spread out in all directions.

dignity (dĭg'nə-tē) *n.* Honor; worthiness; stateliness of manner.

diligence (dĭl'ə-jəns) *n.* Constant, careful effort.

diligent (dĭl'ə-jənt) *adj.* Hardworking; industrious.

diminish (dĭ-mĭn'ĭsh) *v.* To reduce in size, importance, etc.

diminutive (dĭ-mĭn'yə-tĭv) *adj.* Very small.

dire (dīr) *adj.* Dreadful.

direful (dīr'fəl) *adj.* Frightful.

dirge (dûrj) *n.* A funeral hymn.

discern (dĭ-sûrn', -zûrn') *v.* To see clearly.

discernible (dĭ-sûr'nə-bəl, dĭ-zûr'-) *adj.* Recognizable; distinguishable.

discomfit (dĭs-kŭm'fĭt) *v.* To make uneasy; embarrass.

ă pat/ā pay/âr care/ä father/b bib/ch church/d deed/ĕ pet/ē be/f fife/g gag/h hat/hw which/ĭ pit/ī pie/îr pier/j judge/k kick/l lid, needle/m mum/ n no, sudden/ng thing/ŏ pot/ō toe/ô paw, for/oi noise/ou out/oo took/oo boot/p pop/r roar/s sauce/sh ship, dish/t tight/th thin, path/*th* this, bathe/ ū cut/ûr urge/v valve/w with/y yes/z zebra, size/zh vision/ə about, item, edible, gallop, circus/ à *Fr.* ami/œ *Fr.* feu, *Ger.* schön/ü *Fr.* tu, *Ger.* über/ KH *Ger.* ich, *Scot.* loch/N *Fr.* bon.

discordant (dĭs-kôr′dənt) *adj.* Not in agreement; conflicting.

discourse (dĭs′kôrs′, -kōrs′) *n.* A long speech or written piece about a particular subject.

discreet (dĭs-krēt′) *adj.* Careful.

disdainful (dĭs-dān′fəl) *adj.* Scornful.

disposition (dĭs′pə-zĭsh′ən) *n.* Arrangement; order; plan.

dissemble (dĭ-sĕm′bəl) *v.* To pretend.

dissever (dĭ-sĕv′ər) *v.* To break up; separate.

dissipate (dĭs′ə-pāt′) *v.* To scatter.

distemper (dĭs-tĕm′pər) *n.* A mental or physical disorder.

distill (dĭs-tĭl′) *v.* To extract the essence of.

diverge (dĭ-vûrj′, dī-) *v.* To branch off.

divers (dī′vərz) *adj.* Various.

diversion (dĭ-vûr′zhən, -shən, dī-) *n.* A distraction.

divert (dĭ-vûrt′, dī-) *v.* To entertain.

dock (dŏk) *v.* To cut short.

doctrine (dŏk′trĭn) *n.* Teachings such as the principles of a religion; belief.

doleful (dōl′fəl) *adj.* Mournful.

dominant (dŏm′ə-nənt) *adj.* Prevailing; ruling; controlling.

dominion (də-mĭn′yən) *n.* Sovereign authority.

dotage (dō′tĭj) *n.* Feebleness and childishness due to old age.

dower (dou′ər) *n.* A dowry.

draught (drăft) *n.* A portion of liquid for drinking. British spelling of *draft*.

dregs (drĕgz) *n.* The most worthless part.

driblet (drĭb′lĭt) *n.* A small amount.

dubious (dōō′bē-əs, dyōō′) *adj.* Vague; doubtful.

dudgeon (dŭj′ən) *n.* Anger; resentment.

E

eccentric (ĕk-sĕn′trĭk, ĭk-) *adj.* Unusual in behavior.

ecclesiast (ĭ-klē′zē-ăst) *n.* A clergyman.

eclipse (ĭ-klĭps′) *v.* To darken or obscure.

ecstasy (ĕk′stə-sē) *n.* Great delight; rapture.

eddy (ĕd′ē) *v.* To move with a circular motion against the main current.

efface (ĭ-fās′) *v.* To erase; wipe out.

elocution (ĕl′ə-kyōō′shən) *n.* The art of public speaking. — **elocutionary** *adj.*

eloquent (ĕl′ə-kwənt) *adj.* Vividly expressive.

elucidate (ĭ-lōō′sə-dāt′) *v.* To explain; make clear. — **elucidation** *n.*

elude (ĭ-lōōd′) *v.* To avoid being caught; escape understanding.

embellish (ĕm-bĕl′ĭsh, ĭm-) *v.* To improve by adding detail to.

eminence (ĕm′ə-nəns) *n.* Greatness; celebrity.

enamor (ĭ-năm′ər) *v.* To fill with love. Usually occurs in the passive with *of: enamored* of his partner.

encumber (ĕn-kŭm′bər, ĭn-) *v.* To hinder; hamper.

endeavor (ĕn-dĕv′ər, ĭn-) *n.* An earnest effort. — *v.* To try to achieve.

engender (ĕn-jĕn′dər, ĭn-) *v.* To bring about.

enigma (ĭ-nĭg′mə) *n.* A perplexing statement or matter, seemingly unexplainable.

enisle (ĕn-īl′, ĭn-) *v.* To make into or like an island.

enjoin (ĕn-join′, ĭn-) *v.* To order someone to do something; urge.

enmity (ĕn′mə-tē) *n.* Deep hatred or antagonism.

enow (ĭ-nou′) *adj.* Enough.

ensconce (ĕn-skŏns′, ĭn-) *v.* To fix or settle snugly or securely.

entrails (ĕn′trālz′, -trəlz) *n.* The internal organs of human beings or animals.

entrance (ĕn-trăns′, -träns′, ĭn-) *v.* To fill with delight; enchant.

entreat (ĕn-trēt′, ĭn-) *v.* To beg.

equanimity (ē′kwə-nĭm′ə-tē, ĕk′wə) *n.* Evenness of mind or temper.

equipage (ĕk′wə-pĭj) *n.* Equipment.

espial (ĕ-spī′əl, ĭ-spī′-) *n.* Observation.

essence (ĕs′əns) *n.* That which gives something its identity.

esteem (ē-stēm′, ĭ-stēm′) *v.* To value highly; respect.

estimable (ĕs′tə-mə-bəl) *adj.* Worthy of esteem.

eternize (ĭ-tûr′nīz′) *v.* To immortalize.

ethereal (ĭ-thîr′ē-əl) *adj.* Not of the earth; spiritual.

ethical (ĕth′ĭ-kəl) *adj.* Having to do with what is considered to be right or wrong behavior.

evensong (ē′vən-sông′, -sŏng′) *n.* Evening worship service.

exaltation (ĕg′zôl-tā′shən) *n.* A feeling of great joy, power, etc.

exceeding (ĕk-sē′dĭng, ĭk-) *adj.* Extreme.

excel (ĕk-sĕl′, ĭk-) *v.* To be better than or superior to others.

execration (ĕk′sĭ-krā′shən) *n.* A violent denouncement.

execution (ĕk′sĭ-kyōō′shən) *n.* A carrying out, doing, etc.

exert (ĕg-zûrt′, ĭg-) *v.* To use energetically.

exigency (ĕk′sə-jən-sē) *n.* An urgent need.

exorbitant (ĕg-zôr′bə-tənt, ĭg-) *adj.* Excessive.

expedient (ĕk-spē′dē-ənt) *adj.* Advantageous; convenient. — *n.* A means to an end.

expenditure (ĕk-spĕn′də-chər, ĭk-) *n.* A using up of money, time, etc.

expiate (ĕk′spē-āt′) *v.* To make amends for.

exploit (ĕks′ploit′) *n.* A bold deed.

exponent (ĕk-spō′nənt, ĭk-) *n.* A person or thing that represents or symbolizes something.

expurgate (ĕks′pər-gāt′, -pûr-gāt′) *v.* To remove objectionable passages from a book, play, etc. — **expurgation** *n.*

extemporize (ĕk-stĕm′pə-rīz′, ĭk-) *v.* To do with little or no preparation.

extinguish (ĕk-stĭng′gwĭsh, ĭk-) *v.* To put out (a fire, etc.); destroy.

extort (ĕk-stôrt′, ĭk-) *v.* To get money, etc., from someone by threats.

extract (ĕk-străkt′, ĭk-) *v.* To draw out by effort.

extradition (ĕk′strə-dĭsh′ən) *n.* The turning over of an alleged criminal by one country, state, etc., to another.

exult (ĕg-zŭlt′, ĭg-) *v.* To rejoice greatly.

exultation (ĕg′zŭl-tā′shən) *n.* Rejoicing.

F

facile (făs′əl, -īl) *adj.* Easy; effortless.

faction (făk′shən) *n.* A group forming a minority within a larger group and generally working in opposition to the majority.

faculty (făk'əl-tē) *n.* An ability to do some particular thing.

fain (fān) *adv.* Gladly.

fallow (făl'ō) *adj.* Left uncultivated or unplanted.

fancy (făn'sē) *n.* Imagination; creativeness.

farrier (făr'ē-ər) *n. British.* A person who shoes horses.

farthing (fär'thĭng) *n.* A small British coin.

fastidious (fă-stĭd'ē-əs, fə-) *adj.* Extremely fussy about personal cleanliness and appearance.

fathomless (făth'əm-lĭs) *adj.* Too deep to be measured.

fealty (fē'əl-tē) *n.* Loyalty.

feat (fēt) *n.* A remarkable accomplishment.

feign (fān) *v.* To put on a deceptive appearance.

feigned (fānd) *adj.* Pretended.

fen (fĕn) *n.* A swamp; bog.

fervent (fûr'vənt) *adj.* Having or showing intense feeling.

fetch (fĕch) *v.* To go after and come back with.

fetter (fĕt'ər) *v.* To chain.

fidelity (fĭ-dĕl'ə-tē, fī-) *n.* Loyalty; faithfulness.

firstling (fûrst'lĭng) *n.* The first of a kind.

fissure (fĭsh'ər) *n.* A long, narrow, deep crack or crevice.

florin (flôr'ĭn, flŏr'-) *n.* A British coin worth two shillings.

folly (fŏl'ē) *n.* Foolishness.

forbear (fôr-bâr') *v.* To refrain from.

forte (fôrt, fōrt, fôr'tā) *n.* A special accomplishment or strong point.

fortissimo (fôr-tĭs'ə-mō') *adv.* Very loud.

frailty (frāl'tē) *n.* Weakness.

fraught (frôt) *adj.* Filled or loaded with.

friar (frī'ər) *n.* A member of a begging religious order.

frieze (frēz) *n.* A decorative band, as along the top of a wall in a room.

frivolous (frĭv'ə-ləs) *adj.* Of little value or importance; trifling.

frowzy (frou'zē) *adj.* Dirty and untidy.

fructify (frŭk'tə-fī', frŏŏk'-) *v.* To bear fruit.

frugal (frōō'gəl) *adj.* Thrifty.

furbish (fûr'bĭsh) *v.* To brighten by rubbing; polish.

furrow (fûr'ō) *n.* A narrow groove or rut made in the earth by a plow.

G

gall (gôl) *v.* To irritate; annoy.

galvanize (găl'və-nīz') *v.* To stimulate as if by electric shock.

gambol (găm'bəl) *v.* To jump and skip about in play.

gamester (gām'stər) *n.* A gambler.

garish (gâr'ĭsh) *adj.* Too bright or gaudy.

garland (gär'lənd) *n.* A circlet or string of flowers.

garner (gär'nər) *n.* A place for storing grain.

garnish (gär'nĭsh) *v.* To decorate; trim.

garrulous (găr'ə-ləs, -yə-ləs) *adj.* Habitually talkative.

gauge (gāj) *n.* A scale of measurement or a standard measure.

gauntness (gônt'nəs) *n.* Extreme thinness and boniness.

gear (gîr) *n.* Movable property.

genial (jēn'yəl, jē'nē-əl) *adj.* Pleasant; friendly. — **genially** *adv.*

gesticulate (jĕ-stĭk'yə-lāt') *v.* To move part of the body to express something.

glade (glād) *n.* An open area in a forest.

glean (glēn) *v.* To collect (facts, etc.) by patient effort.

glen (glĕn) *n.* A mountain valley.

gloss (glôs, glŏs) *n.* Brightness; sheen.

gnarled (närld) *adj.* Lumpy and twisted.

goodman (gŏŏd'mən) *n.* A husband or master of a household.

goodwife (gŏŏd'wīf') *n.* A wife or mistress of a household.

gorge (gôrj) *n.* A deep, narrow pass between steep heights. — *v.* To eat greedily.

gory (gôr'ē, gōr'ē) *adj.* Bloody.

gospel (gŏs'pəl) *n.* The teachings of Jesus and the Apostles.

grace (grās) *n.* **1.** Attractive quality. **2.** Favor; goodwill. **3.** Divine love given freely to human beings.

gradation (grā-dā'shən) *n.* A gradual change by steps from one stage to another.

gramophone (grăm'ə-fōn') *n.* A phonograph.

grandam (grăn'dăm', -dəm) *n.* An old woman.

grapple (grăp'əl) *v.* To grip and hold.

grave (grāv) *v.* To carve out; sculpture.

gridiron (grĭd'ī-ərn) *n.* A grill.

grievous (grē'vəs) *adj.* Causing grief.

grinder (grīn'dər) *n.* A tooth.

grisly (grĭz'lē) *adj.* Horrible; terrifying.

groat (grōt) *n.* An English silver coin.

grot (grŏt) *n.* A grotto.

grove (grōv) *n.* A small wood or group of trees.

grovel (grŭv'əl, grŏv'-) *v.* To cringe.

guile (gīl) *n.* Cunning; slyness.

gumption (gŭmp'shən) *n.* Courage and initiative.

H

hallowed (hăl'ōd) *adj.* Honored as holy.

harbinger (här'bən-jər) *n.* A person or thing that signals or announces what is to come.

harrowing (hăr'ō-ĭng) *adj.* Causing mental distress.

heath (hēth) *n.* An area of open wasteland overgrown with heather, low shrubs, etc.

heave (hēv) *v.* To raise with effort. — *n.* Rise and fall.

helm (hĕlm) *n.* A helmet.

hence (hĕns) *adv.* Away; from this place.

herald (hĕr'əld) *n.* A person or thing that announces important news or events to come.

hew (hyōō) *v.* To make or shape by cutting with an ax.

highwayman (hī'wā'mən) *n.* A man on horseback who robbed travelers on a highway.

hoary (hôr'ē, hōr'ē) *adj.* White or gray.

hollow (hŏl'ō) *n.* A hole.

homage (hŏm'ĭj, ŏm'-) *n.* Anything done to show honor or respect.

horizon (hə-rī'zən) *n.* The line where the sky seems to meet the earth.

ă pat/ā pay/âr care/ä father/b bib/ch church/d deed/ē pet/ē be/f fife/g gag/h hat/hw which/ĭ pit/ī pie/îr pier/j judge/k kick/l lid, needle/m mum/ n no, sudden/ng thing/ŏ pot/ō toe/ô paw, for/oi noise/ou out/ŏŏ took/ōō boot/p pop/r roar/s sauce/sh ship, dish/t tight/th thin, path/*th* this, bathe/ ŭ cut/ûr urge/v valve/w with/y yes/z zebra, size/zh vision/ə about, item, edible, gallop, circus/ à *Fr.* ami/œ *Fr.* feu, *Ger.* schön/ü *Fr.* tu, *Ger.* über/ ᴋʜ *Ger.* ich, *Scot.* loch/ɴ *Fr.* bon.

hostelry (hŏs′təl-rē) *n.* A lodging place.

hover (hŭv′ər, hŏv′-) *v.* To float in the air or move back and forth near a particular place.

husband (hŭz′bənd) *v.* To manage economically.

hyperbolic (hī′pər-bŏl′ik) *adj.* Exaggerated. — **hyperbolical** *adj.*

hypocrisy (hĭ-pŏk′rə-sē) *n.* A pretense of sincerity, virtue, etc.

I

ignoble (ĭg-nō′bəl) *adj.* Base; mean.

ignominy (ĭg′nə-mĭn′-ē, ma-nē) *n.* Disgrace or shame.

illumine (ĭ-lōō′mĭn) *v.* To light up.

immerse (ĭ-mûrs′) *v.* To submerge.

immersion (ĭ-mûr′zhən, -shən) *n.* Baptism in which the whole body is dipped in water.

immobility (ĭ-mō-bĭl′ə-tē) *n.* An inability to move.

immortalize (ĭ-môrt′l-īz′) *v.* To give lasting fame to.

impalpable (ĭm-păl′pə-bəl) *adj.* Not capable of being perceived by touch; intangible.

impart (ĭm-pärt′) *v.* **1.** To give. **2.** To make known.

impecunious (ĭm′pĭ-kyōō′nē-əs) *adj.* Without money; poor.

impede (ĭm-pēd′) *v.* To hinder or obstruct.

impediment (ĭm-pēd′ə-mənt) *n.* An obstruction; a hindrance.

impenetrable (ĭm-pĕn′ə-trə-bəl) *adj.* Unable to be passed through.

imperial (ĭm-pîr′ē-əl) *adj.* Having supreme authority.

imperialism (ĭm-pîr′ē-ə-līz′əm) *n.* The policy of extending a country's power by conquest and domination of other countries' economic and political affairs.

imperturbable (ĭm′pər-tûr′bə-bəl) *adj.* Serene, calm. — **imperturbably** *adv.*

impetuous (ĭm-pĕch′ōō-əs) *adj.* Acting suddenly without much thought.

impinge (ĭm-pĭnj′) *v.* To make an impression on.

impious (ĭm′pē-əs, ĭm-pī′-) *adj.* Without reverence for God; profane.

implacable (ĭm-plā′kə-bəl, -plăk′ə-bəl) *adj.* Unforgiving.

impostor (ĭm-pŏs′tər) *n.* A person who pretends to be something he or she is not.

imposture (ĭm-pŏs′chər) *n.* Fraud; deception.

impotence (ĭm′pə-təns) *n.* Powerlessness; helplessness.

impotent (ĭm′pə-tənt) *adj.* Powerless; helpless.

improvise (ĭm′prə-vīz′) *v.* To do on the spur of the moment without preparation.

impute (ĭm-pyōōt′) *v.* To charge with.

inaugurate (ĭn-ô′gyə-rāt) *v.* To start.

incantation (ĭn′kăn-tā′shən) *n.* The chanting of magical words to cast a spell.

incarnation (ĭn′kär-nā′shən) *n.* Appearance in human form.

incense (ĭn-sĕns′) *v.* To make very angry.

incessant (ĭn-sĕs′ənt) *adj.* Continuous.

incisive (ĭn-sī′sĭv) *adj.* Sharp; clear-cut.

inclination (ĭn′klə-nā′shən) *n.* A general disposition toward something.

incomprehensible (ĭn′kŏm-prĭ-hĕn′sə-bəl, ĭn-kŏm′-) *adj.* Not understandable.

inculcate (ĭn-kŭl′kāt) *v.* To impress on the mind by urging or repetition.

indictment (ĭn-dīt′mənt) *n.* A charge or accusation.

indignation (ĭn′dĭg-nā′shən) *n.* Anger.

indissoluble (ĭn′dĭ-sŏl′yə-bəl) *adj.* Lasting or permanent.

indubitable (ĭn-dōō′bə-tə-bəl, ĭn-dyōō′-) *adj.* Without doubt.

induce (ĭn-dōōs′, -dyōōs′) *v.* To cause; bring about.

infallible (ĭn-făl′ə-bəl) *adj.* Incapable of error. — **infallibly** *adv.*

infamous (ĭn′fə-məs) *adj.* Notorious.

infantry (ĭn′fən-trē) *n.* Foot soldiers as a group.

infectious (ĭn-fĕk′shəs) *adj.* Tending to spread or infect others.

infidel (ĭn′fə-dəl, -dĕl′) *n.* A nonbeliever regarding some religion.

infinite (ĭn′fə-nĭt) *adj.* Without beginning or end. — **infinitely** *adv.*

infirmity (ĭn-fûr′mə-tē) *n.* Weakness; feebleness.

infliction (ĭn-flĭk′shən) *n.* The act of punishing.

ingenious (ĭn-jēn′yəs) *adj.* Clever; inventive.

ingenuity (ĭn′jə-nōō′ə-tē, nyōō′ə-tē) *n.* Cleverness; inventiveness.

ingratiate (ĭn-grā′shē-āt′) *v.* To bring oneself into another's favor by conscious effort.

inherent (ĭn-hîr′ənt, -hĕr′ənt) *adj.* Basic; inborn.

injunction (ĭn-jŭngk′shən) *n.* A command.

inquisitive (ĭn-kwĭz′ə-tĭv) *adj.* Prying; curious.

inscribe (ĭn-skrīb′) *v.* To write on some surface.

inscrutable (ĭn-skrōō′tə-bəl) *adj.* Mysterious; not easily understood.

insensible (ĭn-sĕn′sə-bəl) *adj.* Unaware; indifferent. — **insensibly** *adv.*

insidious (ĭn-sĭd′ē-əs) *adj.* Progressing unnoticeably, but harmfully.

insipid (ĭn-sĭp′ĭd) *adj.* Dull; uninteresting; lifeless.

insolence (ĭn′sə-ləns) *n.* Bold disrespect in behavior or speech.

insuperable (ĭn-sōō′pər-ə-bəl) *adj.* Unconquerable.

integrity (ĭn-tĕg′rə-tē) *n.* The state of being of sound moral principle.

intemperance (ĭn-tĕm′pər-əns) *n.* Lack of restraint.

intercept (ĭn′tər-sĕpt′) *v.* To stop or interrupt the course of.

intercourse (ĭn′tər-kôrs′, -kōrs′) *n.* Dealings between or among people, countries, etc.

intermit (ĭn′tər-mĭt′) *v.* To stop temporarily; interrupt.

interpose (ĭn′tər-pōz′) *v.* **1.** To introduce an interrupting remark in a conversation. **2.** To come between.

interval (ĭn′tər-vəl) *n.* A space between two things.

intervene (ĭn′tər-vēn′) *v.* To come in as an influencing force.

intimidate (ĭn-tĭm′ə-dāt) *v.* To make afraid.

invariable (ĭn-vâr′ē-ə-bəl) *adj.* Constant. — **invariably** *adv.*

invincible (ĭn-vĭn′sə-bəl) *adj.* Unconquerable.

invoke (ĭn-vōk′) *v.* To call on.

invulnerable (ĭn-vŭl′nər-ə-bəl) *adj.* Incapable of being injured or damaged.

ire (īr) *n.* Anger.

irreconcilable (ĭ-rĕk′ən-sī′lə-bəl, ĭ-rĕk′ən-sī′-) *adj.* Incapable of being brought into agreement.

irretrievable (ĭr′ĭ-trē′və-bəl) *adj.* Incapable of being restored or recovered. — **irretrievably** *adv.*

irrevocable (ĭ-rĕv'ə-kə-bəl) *adj.* Incapable of being undone.

J

jaunt (jônt, jänt) *n.* A short trip for pleasure.

jest (jĕst) *n.* A joke or light remark.

jocund (jŏk'ənd, jō'kənd) *adj.* Jovial; cheerful.

jollity (jŏl'ə-tē) *n.* Fun; gaiety.

joust (jŭst, joust, jōost) *v.* To fight against another person with lances on horseback.

jovial (jō'vē-əl) *adj.* Playfully good-humored.

judicial (jōo-dĭsh'əl) *adj.* Showing careful consideration of all sides of a problem when making a decision. — **judicially** *adv.*

judicious (jōo-dĭsh'əs) *adj.* Showing good judgment.

jutty (jŭt'ē) *n.* A projecting part of a building.

K

kindle (kĭnd'l) *v.* To set on fire.

knave (nāv) *n.* A dishonest person.

knell (nĕl) *n.* **1.** The tolling of a bell. **2.** A signal of death or sorrow.

knickerbockers (nĭk'ər-bŏk'ərz) *n.* Short trousers gathered at or below the knee.

knoll (nōl) *n.* A small hill; mound.

L

laden (lād'n) *adj.* Burdened; afflicted.

laity (lā'ə-tē) *n.* All those people not counted among the clergy.

lament (lə-mĕnt') *v.* To grieve for.

lamentable (lăm'ən-tə-bəl, lə-mĕn'-) *adj.* Distressing. — **lamentably** *adv.*

lamentation (lăm'ən-ta'shən) *n.* Outward expression of grief.

lampoon (lăm-pōon') *n.* A piece of writing ridiculing or attacking someone.

lance (lăns, läns) *v.* To cut open.

languish (lăng'gwĭsh) *v.* To long or pine for something.

lapse (lăps) *n.* A minor fault or error.

largess (lär-jĕs', lär'jĭs, jĕs') *n.* Generous gifts.

laryngoscope (lə-rĭng'gə-skōp') *n.* An instrument for examining the inside of the larynx.

latitude (lăt'ə-tōod', tyōod) *n.* **1.** Freedom from narrow restrictions. **2.** A region or place.

laudable (lô'də-bəl) *adj.* Praiseworthy.

lea (lē, lā) *n.* A grassy meadow.

leech (lēch) *n.* A kind of bloodsucking worm.

legible (lĕj'ə-bəl) *adj.* Easily read or deciphered.

legislator (lĕj'ĭs-lā'tər) *n.* A lawmaker.

levy (lĕv'ē) *n.* The imposing or collecting of taxes or other payments.

libelous (lī'bə-ləs) *adj.* Damaging to reputation.

libertine (lĭb'ər-tēn') *n.* A morally unrestrained person.

lief (lēf') *adv.* gladly. *Had liefer* means "would rather."

liege (lēj) *n.* A lord or sovereign.

linnet (lĭn'ĭt) *n.* A small songbird.

lintel (lĭnt'l) *n.* The crosspiece over a door or window.

listless (lĭst'lĭs) *adj.* Spiritless. — **listlessly** *adv.*

literal (lĭt'ər-əl) *adj.* Real. — **literally** *adv.*

lithograph (lĭth'ə-grăf') *v.* To print using a process that involves the repulsion between grease and water.

livid (lĭv'ĭd) *adj.* Pale.

lope (lōp) *v.* To move with a steady, easy stride.

lore (lôr, lōr) *n.* The accumulated information on a particular subject.

loth (lōth, lōth) *adj.* Unwilling.

low (lō) *v.* To moo.

lucid (lōo'sĭd) *adj.* Clear to the mind.

luminous (lōo'mə-nəs) *adj.* Giving off light.

lustrous (lŭs'trəs) *adj.* Shining; bright.

lyre (līr) *n.* An instrument of the harp family.

lyric (lĭr'ĭk) *adj.* Expressing great enthusiasm or rapture.

M

magnitude (măg'nĭ-tōod', -tyōod') *n.* Size or extent.

mahout (mə-hout') *n.* An elephant driver or keeper.

malice (măl'ĭs) *n.* A desire to be hurtful to others.

malicious (mə-lĭsh'əs) *adj.* Spiteful; intentionally hurtful.

malignity (mə-lĭg'nə-tē) *n.* Intense ill will.

maneuver (mə-nōo'vər, -nyōo') *n.* A planned movement. — *v.* To move in a purposeful and skilled way for a particular reason.

manifold (măn'ə-fōld) *adj.* Varied.

manure (mə-nōor', -nyōor') *v.* To fertilize soil.

marge (märj) *n.* A border; margin.

marshal (mär'shəl) *n.* A high official of a royal household — *v.* To put in order.

marvel (mär'vəl) *n.* A wonderful thing; a miracle.

matins (măt'ĭnz) *n.* Morning prayers.

maxim (măk'sĭm) *n.* A general truth briefly expressed.

mead (mēd) *n.* A drink made from fermented honey and water, often with malt, spices, etc., added.

meddle (mĕd'l) *v.* To interfere in.

melodramatic (mĕl'ə-drə-măt'ĭk) *adj.* Sensational; exaggeratedly emotional.

mendacity (mĕn-dăs'ə-tē) *n.* lying.

mercenary (mûr'sə-nĕr'ē) *adj.* Greedy; working for payment only.

metropolis (mə-trŏp'ə-lĭs) *n.* A large city.

mettle (mĕt'l) *n.* Courage.

mezzotint (mĕt'sō-tĭnt, mĕd'zō-, mĕz'ō-) *n.* A print produced by a method that involves engraving on a copper or steel plate.

militant (mĭl'ə-tənt) *adj.* Ready and willing to fight.

millennium (mə-lĕn'ē-əm) *n.* An imagined golden age.

minion (mĭn'yən) *n.* A favorite.

minister (mĭn'ĭ-stər) *n.* A person acting as another's agent.

minstrelsy (mĭn'strəl-sē) *n.* A group of singers and poets who traveled from place to place singing and reciting.

mire (mīr) *n.* Wet, soggy ground; deep mud.

misanthrope (mĭs'an-thrōp, mĭz'-) *n.* A person who hates people.

ă pat/ā pay/âr care/ä father/b bib/ch church/d deed/ĕ pet/ē be/f fife/g gag/h hat/hw which/ĭ pit/ī pie/îr pier/j judge/k kick/l lid, needle/m mum/ n no, sudden/ng thing/ŏ pot/ō toe/ô paw, for/oi noise/ou out/ŏŏ took/ōō boot/p pop/r roar/s sauce/sh ship, dish/t tight/th thin, path/*th* this, bathe/ ū cut/ûr urge/v valve/w with/y yes/z zebra, size/zh vision/ə about, item, edible, gallop, circus/ à *Fr.* ami/œ *Fr.* feu, *Ger.* schön/ü *Fr.* tu, *Ger.* über/ KH *Ger.* ich, *Scot.* loch/N *Fr.* bon.

modify (mŏd'ə-fī) v. To change or alter.

molt (mōlt) v. To shed.

moor (mŏŏr) n. A tract of wasteland, often marshy.

mortal (môrt'l) adj. Destined to eventually die.

mortification (môr'tə-fĭ-kā'shən) n. Humiliation.

motley (mŏt'lē) adj. Composed of many different and unrelated elements or colors.

multifoliate (mŭl'tə-fō'lē-ĭt, -āt') adj. Having many leaves.

multitudinous (mŭl'tə-tŏŏd'n-əs, -tyŏŏd'n-əs) adj. Consisting of many elements, parts, etc.

municipal (myŏŏ-nĭs'ə-pəl) adj. Having to do with a city or town or its local government.

munificence (myŏŏ-nĭf'ə-səns) n. Generosity; liberality.

murky (mûr'kē) adj. Dark or gloomy.

muse (myŏŏz) v. To think deeply and at length.

mute (myŏŏt) adj. Unable to speak; silent.

N

naive (nä-ēv') adj. Not worldly-wise.

newt (nŏŏt, nyŏŏt) n. A small salamander that can live on land and in water.

niggard (nĭg'ərd) n. A stingy person.

noncommittal (nŏn'kə-mĭt'l) adj. Not committed to any particular opinion or position.

nutritive (nŏŏ'trə-tĭv, nyŏŏ'-) adj. Of value as food.

nymph (nĭmf) n. A nature goddess.

O

obdurate (ŏb'dyŏŏ-rĭt, ŏb'dŏŏ) adj. Hardhearted.

obligation (ŏb'lə-gā'shən) n. A responsibility—moral legal, or social.

oblique (ō-blēk') adj. Slanting; sloping.—**obliquely** adv.

oblivious (ə-blĭv'ē-əs) adj. Unaware.

obscene (ŏb-sēn', əb-) adj. Disgusting; repulsive.

obtrusive (ŏb-trŏŏ'sĭv, -zĭv, əb-) adj. Calling attention to itself in an unpleasant way.

odious (ō'dē-əs) adj. Disgusting; offensive.

offertory (ô'fər-tôr'ē, -tōr'ē, ŏf'ər-) n. The collection of money at a church service.

officious (ə-fĭsh'əs) adj. Meddlesome in a highhanded way.

ogle (ō'gəl, ô-) v. To make eyes at.

opacity (ō-păs'ə-tē) n. Obscurity.

opiate (ō'pē-ĭt, -āt) n. Something that soothes or quiets.

oracle (ôr'ə-kəl, ŏr'-) n. Something or someone believed to be a source of wisdom.

oratory (ôr'ə-tôr'ē, -tōr'ē, ŏr'-) n. Skill in public speaking.

orchestrate (ôr'kĭ-strāt') v. To combine in a harmonious way.

ordain (ôr-dān') v. To order; decree.

overcredulous (ō'vər-krĕj'ŏŏ-ləs, -krĕd'yŏŏ-) adj. Too easily convinced.

P

pallid (păl'ĭd) adj. Pale; wan.

pallor (păl'ər) n. Lack of color.

palsy (pôl'zē) n. Muscle paralysis.

paltry (pôl'trē) adj. Of little or no worth; insignificant.

panegyric (păn'ə-jĭr'ĭk, jī'rĭk) n. Elaborate praise.

paragon (păr'ə-gŏn') n. A model of perfection.

parallel (păr'ə-lĕl) adj. Being equidistant at every point; never meeting.

parish (păr'ĭsh) n. A district of British local civil government.

parishioner (pə-rĭsh'ən-ər) n. A member of a parish.

parricide (păr'ə-sīd') n. The murder of a parent.

parry (păr'ē) v. To turn aside a question or criticism with a clever or evasive reply.

partiality (păr'shē-ăl'ə-tē, pär-shăl'-) n. Particular fondness or liking.

passionate (păsh'ən-ĭt) adj. Having strong feelings.

pastoral (păs'tər-əl, päs'-) adj. Having to do with shepherds, rustics, or rural life.

pathos (pā'thŏs', -thôs') n. The quality in someone or something that arouses feelings of pity, sorrow, etc.

patron (pā'trən) n. A benefactor; sponsor.

pedantic (pə-dăn'tĭk) adj. Unduly adhering to forms or rules.

pedestrian (pə-dĕs'trē-ən) n. One who goes on foot.

peer (pîr) n. A noble, especially a member of a hereditary legislative body.

penal (pē'nəl) adj. Punishing.

penitent (pĕn'ə-tənt) adj. Feeling and expressing shame for having done something wrong.

pensive (pĕn'sĭv) adj. Thoughtful.

perceive (pər-sēv') v. To become aware of something.

perception (pər-sĕp'shən) n. Awareness; comprehension.

perchance (pər-chăns', chäns') adv. Perhaps.

perdition (pər-dĭsh'ən) n. Eternal damnation; hell.

peremptory (pə-rĕmp'tə-rē) adj. Not admitting denial; determined.—**peremptorily** adv.

perfidious (pər-fĭd'ē-əs) adj. Treacherous; deceitful.—**perfidiousness** n.

pernicious (pər-nĭsh'əs) adj. Destructive; deadly.

perpetual (pər-pĕch'ŏŏ-əl) adj. Lasting forever or for a long time.—**perpetually** adv.

perplex (pər-plĕks') v. To puzzle; confuse.

perplexity (pər-plĕk'sə-tē) n. Bewilderment.

perspective (pər-spĕk'tĭv) n. A point of view that shows things in their true relation to each other.

perturbation (pûr'tər-bā'shən) n. Disturbance.

perusal (pə-rŏŏ'zəl) n. A careful examination or study.

pervade (pər-vād') v. To be spread throughout.

perversity (pər-vûr'sə-tē) n. Deviation from what is considered right or good.

pervert (pər-vûrt') v. To lead astray; corrupt.

pestilence (pĕs'tə-ləns) n. A highly contagious disease, usually fatal.

petition (pə-tĭsh'ən) n. A formal request to a person or group in authority.

petulance (pĕch'ŏŏ-ləns) n. Peevishness.

philanthropic (fĭl'ən-thrŏp'ĭk) adj. Charitable; humane.

phlegm (flĕm) n. Mucous discharge.

phonetician (fō'nə-tĭsh'ən) n. An expert in the study of speech sounds.

phraseology (frā'zē-ŏl'ə-jē) n. Choice and pattern of words.

piety (pī'ə-tē) n. Devotion to religious practices or to family, parents, etc.

pilgrimage (pĭl'grə-mĭj) n. A long journey for a particular purpose.

piling (pī'lĭng) n. A structure of timbers or beams.

pillar (pĭl'ər) n. A person who is the main support of an institution, group, etc.

pious (pī′əs) *adj.* Showing religious devotion.

piston (pĭs′tən) *n.* A cylinder or disk that fits into a larger cylinder and moves back and forth under fluid pressure.

plenteous (plĕn′tē-əs) *adj.* Plentiful; abundant.

plutocracy (plōō-tŏk′rə-sē) *n.* Government by the wealthy.

ponderous (pŏn′dər-əs) *adj.* Extremely heavy; clumsy.

portico (pôr′tĭ-kō′, pōr′-) *n.* A porch or covered walk.

posterity (pŏ-stĕr′ə-tē) *n.* All succeeding generations.

potent (pōt′nt) *adj.* Powerful; mighty.

pram (prăm) *n.* A baby carriage.

prance (prăns, präns) *v.* To move in a lively way.

prate (prāt) *v.* To chatter.

precept (prē′sĕpt′) *n.* A rule setting a standard for conduct or action.

precinct (prē′sĭngkt) *n.* Neighborhood; environs.

precipice (prĕs′ə-pĭs) *n.* A steep or overhanging rock.

precipitate (prĭ-sĭp′ə-tāt′) *v.* To cause to happen prematurely.

predecessor (prĕd′ə-sĕs′ər, prē′də-) *n.* A person who comes before another in time—in a position, office, etc.

predominance (prĭ-dŏm′ə-nəns) *n.* Superiority in effectiveness, degree, quality, etc.

preface (prĕf′ĭs) *n.* An introduction to a play, book, etc.

prejudice (prĕj′ə-dĭs) *n.* An opinion, usually unfavorable, formed before knowing all the facts about a person or thing.

prelate (prĕl′ĭt) *n.* A high-ranking cleric, such as bishop or archbishop.

premises (prĕm′ĭs-əz) *n. pl.* A building and the area surrounding it.

preoccupation (prē-ŏk′yə-pā′shən) *n.* Absorption with one's thoughts.

prepossession (prē′pə-zĕsh′ən) *n.* Prejudice, especially favorable.

presumptuous (prĭ-zŭmp′chōō-əs) *adj.* Taking too much for granted.

pretense (prē′tĕns′, prĭ-tĕns′) *n.* An excuse; false reason.

pretension (prĭ-tĕn′shən) *n.* A claim to some distinction.

preternatural (prē′tər-năch′ər-əl) *adj.* Beyond the natural; abnormal.

pretext (prē′tĕkst′) *n.* An excuse.

prevail (prĭ-vāl′) *v.* To remain in force.

prevalent (prĕv′ə-lənt) *adj.* Of wide occurrence. —**prevalence** *n.*

prevaricate (prĭ-văr′ə-kāt′) *v.* To lie. —**prevarication** *n.*

prime (prīm) *n.* Youth; springtime.—*v.* to prepare.

prior (prī′ər) *n.* The head of a religious house.

prioress (prī′ər-ĕs) *n.* The woman in charge of a priory of nuns.

privy (prĭv′ē) *adj.* Secret; hidden.

proclaim (prō-klām′, prə-) *v.* To announce publicly.

procure (prō-kyŏor′) *v.* To acquire or obtain.— **procurement** *n.*

prod (prŏd) *v.* To poke.

prodigious (prə-dĭj′əs) *adj.* Enormous.

profane (prō-fān′, prə-) *adj.* Not connected with religious matters.

profess (prə-fĕs′, prō-) *v.* To declare openly.

proffer (prŏf′ər) *v.* To offer.

proficiency (prə-fĭsh′ən-sē) *n.* Skill; competence.

profligate (prŏf′lĭ-gĭt, -gāt′) *adj.* Wasteful; extravagant.

profound (prə-found′, prō-) *adj.* Complete; deep.

profuse (prə-fyōos′, prō-) *adj.* Generous.

progeny (prŏj′ə-nē) *n.* Offspring.

promontory (prŏm′ən-tôr′ē, -tōr′ē) *n.* A high point of land jutting out into a body of water.

prone (prōn) *adj.* Lying flat.

prophetic (prə-fĕt′ĭk) *adj.* Predicting or foreshadowing.

propound (prə-pound′) *v.* To propose.

providence (prŏv′ə-dəns, -dĕns′) *n.* Divine care or guidance.

provocation (prŏv′ə-kā′shən) *n.* A stimulus to action.

proximity (prŏk-sĭm′ə-tē) *n.* Nearness.

prudence (prōod′əns) *n.* Cautious behavior.

prudent (prōod′ənt) *adj.* Exercising sound judgment; cautious.—**prudently** *adv.*

publican (pŭb′lĭ-kən) *n.* An innkeeper.

pugilist (pyōo′jə-lĭst) *n.* A boxer or fighter.

purblind (pûr′blīnd) *adj.* Nearly blind.

purgative (pûr′gə-tĭv) *adj.* Cleansing.

purgatory (pûr′gə-tôr′ē, -tōr′ē) *n.* A place of punishment or suffering.

purport (pûr′pôrt′, -pōrt′) *n.* Intent.

pyre (pīr) *n.* A pile of wood on which a dead body is burned.

Q

quadrangle (kwŏd′răng′gəl) *n.* A figure having four angles—a square or rectangle.—**quadrangular** *adj.*

quadruped (kwŏd′rōo-pĕd′) *n.* A four-footed animal.

quaint (kwānt) *adj.* Agreeably old-fashioned.

quaver (kwā′vər) *v.* To tremble.

quell (kwĕl) *v.* To quiet; relieve, as pain.

quench (kwĕnch) *v.* To put an end to.

quicksilver (kwĭk′sĭl′vər) *n.* Mercury.

R

rack (răk) *v.* To torment.

raiment (rā′mənt) *n.* Clothing.

rancor (răng′kər) *n.* Malice; spitefulness.

rapier (rā′pē-ər, răp′yər) *n.* A long, slender two-edged sword.

rapture (răp′chər) *n.* Joy; great pleasure.

rash (răsh) *adj.* Reckless.

ratify (răt′ə-fī′) *v.* To approve.

raven (rā′vən) *adj.* Black and shiny.

ravenous (răv′ən-əs) *adj.* Very hungry.—**ravenously** *adv.*

ravish (răv′ĭsh) *v.* To seize and carry away by force.

rebuke (rĭ-byōok′) *v.* To scold sharply.

recalcitrant (rĭ-kăl′sə-trənt) *adj.* Difficult to control.

recapitulate (rē′kə-pĭch′ōo-lāt′) *v.* To review briefly; sum up.

reciprocate (rĭ-sĭp′rə-kāt′) *v.* To give in return.

ă pat/ā pay/âr care/ä father/b bib/ch church/d deed/ĕ pet/ē be/f fife/g gag/h hat/hw which/ĭ pit/ī pie/îr pier/j judge/k kick/l lid, needle/m mum/ n no, sudden/ng thing/ŏ pot/ō toe/ô paw, for/oi noise/ou out/ŏŏ took/ōō boot/p pop/r roar/s sauce/sh ship, dish/t tight/th thin, path/*th* this, bathe/ ŭ cut/ûr urge/v valve/w with/y yes/z zebra, size/zh vision/ə about, item, edible, gallop, circus/ à *Fr.* ami/œ *Fr.* feu, *Ger.* schön/ü *Fr.* tu, *Ger.* über/ KH *Ger.* ich, *Scot.* loch/N *Fr.* bon.

reck (rĕk) *v. Archaic.* To heed.

reckon (rĕk'ən) *v.* To count; consider.

reckoning (rĕk'ən-ĭng) *n.* A calculation.

recompense (rĕk'əm-pĕns') *v.* To pay; reward.

reconcile (rĕk'ən-sīl') *v.* To accept or agree to something.

recourse (rē'kôrs', -kōrs', rĭ-kôrs', -kōrs') *n.* A turning to someone or something for help.

recreant (rĕk'rē-ənt) *n.* A coward.

recumbent (rĭ-kŭm'bənt) *adj.* Reclining.

redeem (rĭ-dēm') *v.* To deliver from sin.

reek (rēk) *v.* To give off smoke, steam, or odors.

reflection (rĭ-flĕk'shən) *n.* Careful thought.

reflux (rē'flŭks') *n.* A flowing back.

reft (rĕft) *v.* Past participle of *reave,* to seize.

refute (rĭ-fyōōt') *v.* To prove to be wrong or false.

reiterate (rē-ĭt'ə-rāt) *v.* To say over and over again.

relish (rĕl'ĭsh) *v.* To enjoy the taste of; like.

remand (rĭ-mănd') *v.* To send back.

remnant (rĕm'nənt) *n.* A trace.

remonstrance (rĭ-mŏn'strəns) *n.* A protest.

remonstrate (rĭ-mŏn'strāt) *v.* To protest.

remorse (rĭ-môrs') *n.* A feeling of guilt for having done something wrong.

remote (rĭ-mōt') *adj.* Distant; slight.

render (rĕn'dər) *v.* To express in one's own way.

rendering (rĕn'dər-ĭng) *n.* An interpretation; drawing; translation.

repellent (rĭ-pĕl'ənt) *adj.* Repulsive.

repent (rĭ-pĕnt') *v.* To feel guilt for an action, thought, etc.

repentance (rĭ-pĕn'təns) *n.* Feelings of regret for wrong-doing.

repine (rĭ-pīn') *v.* To feel discontented.

repose (rĭ-pōz') *v.* To lie at rest.

reprisal (rĭ-prī'zəl) *n.* A paying back in kind.

reproachful (rĭ-prōch'fəl) *adj.* Full of blame.—**reproachfully** *adv.*

repudiation (rĭ-pyōō'dē-ā'shən) *n.* A refusal to accept or support.

repulse (rĭ-pŭls') *v.* To reject; repel.

requiem (rĕk'wē-əm, rē'kwē-) *n.* A song for the repose of the dead.

resound (rĭ-zound') *v.* To sound loudly.

respite (rĕs'pĭt) *n.* An interval of relief or rest.

resplendent (rĭ-splĕn'dənt) *adj.* Shining brightly; brilliant.—**resplendently** *adv.*

retch (rĕch) *v.* To try to vomit.

retrench (rĭ-trĕnch') *v.* To cut down or reduce; curtail.

retrograde (rĕt'rə-grād') *adj.* Moving backward; retreating.

revelation (rĕv'ə-lā'shən) *n.* The act of making something known.

reverberate (rĭ-vûr'bə-rāt') *v.* To make a loud, reechoing sound.

rhetoric (rĕt'ər-ĭk) *n.* **1.** Showy, inflated language. **2.** The art of using words effectively.

rigorous (rĭg'ər-əs) *adj.* Strict; harsh.

rill (rĭl) *n.* A small brook.

rote (rōt) *n.* **1.** Memory. **2.** A mechanical or routine process. Often with *by.*

rout (rout) *n.* A disorderly defeat or flight.

rue (rōō) *n.* **1.** Sorrowful remembrance. **2.** A strong-scented plant with yellow flowers.

ruminate (rōō'mə-nāt') *v.* To meditate.—**ruminative** *adj.*

rustic (rŭs'tĭk) *adj.* Pertaining to country life.

S

sack (săk) *v.* To fire from a job.

sacrilegious (săk'rə-lē'jəs) *adj.* Violating something sacred.

sage (sāj) *adj.* Wise—**sagely** *adv.*

salient (sā'lē-ənt) *adj.* Striking; prominent.

sally (săl'ē) *n.* A sudden rushing forth.

salvation (săl-vā'shən) *n.* A rescue from evil or danger.

salver (săl'vər) *n.* A tray.

sanction (săngk'shən) *n.* Authorized approval.

sanctity (săngk'tə-tē) *n.* Holiness; saintliness.

satiety (sə-tī'ə-tē) *n.* Surfeit; repletion.

saturnine (săt'ər-nīn') *adj.* Gloomy; morose.

saunter (sôn'tər) *v.* To stroll.

scabbard (skăb'ərd) *n.* A sheath for a sword or other weapon.

scant (skănt) *adj.* Meager.

scepter (sĕp'tər) *n.* A staff used by royalty on ceremonial occasions.

schism (sĭz'əm, skĭz'-) *n.* A split; rift.

scriptural (skrĭp'chər-əl) *adj.* Biblical.

scruple (skrōō'pəl) *n.* A feeling of uneasiness about doing things that one thinks are wrong.

scrupulosity (skrōō'pyə-lŏs'ə-tē) *n.* Conscientious honesty.

scullery (skŭl'ə-rē) *n.* A room next to the kitchen where chores are done.

scum (skŭm) *n.* Worthless matter or people regarded as worthless.

scutcheon (skŭch'ən) *n.* A shield.

scythe (sīth) *n.* A tool for cutting long grass, grain, etc.

sear (sîr) *v.* To burn or scorch.

secluded (sĭ-klōō'dĭd) *adj.* Isolated; private.

seclusion (sĭ-klōō'zhən) *n.* Isolation; privacy.

secular (sĕk'yə-lər) *adj.* Worldly, as opposed to religious.

seduce (sĭ-dōōs', -dyōōs') *v.* To tempt to wrongdoing.

self-complacency (sĕlf-kəm-plā'sən-sē) *n.* Self-satisfaction.

senility (sĭ-nĭl'ə-tē) *n.* Mental deterioration, usually in old age.

sensibility (sĕn'sə-bĭl'ə-tē) *n.* Emotional or intellectual responsiveness.

sentinel (sĕnt'n-əl) *n.* A guard.

sepulcher (sĕp'əl-kər) *n.* A burial chamber; tomb.

sequel (sē'kwĕl) *n.* Something that follows; a continuation.

seraph (sĕr'əf) *n.* An angel.

sere (sîr) *adj.* Dried up.

serenity (sĭ-rĕn'ə-tē) *n.* Calmness.

serf (sûrf) *n.* A person bound to a master.

servile (sûr'vəl, -vīl') *adj.* Slavelike.—**servilely** *adv.*

severance (sĕv'ər-əns) *n.* Separation.

sheathe (shēth) *v.* To enclose in a casing.

shire (shīr) *n.* A county.

shoal (shōl) *n.* A shallow place in a body of water.

siege (sēj) *n.* An attempt to capture a place by surrounding and blockading it.

signification (sĭg'nə-fĭ-kā'shən) *n.* Meaning.

sinew (sĭn'yōō) *n.* A tendon.

singular (sĭng′gyə-lər) *adj.* Extraordinary; strange —
singularly *adv.*

sinuous (sĭn′yōō-əs) *adj.* Winding and twisting.

skirmish (skûr′mĭsh) *n.* A brief conflict.

slack (slăk) *adj.* Loose. — **slackness** *n.*

sledge (slĕdj) *n.* A long, heavy hammer.

sloth (slôth, slŏth, slōth) *n.* Laziness.

slovenly (slŭv′ən-lē) *adj.* Sloppy in appearance, habits, etc.

slough (slŭf) *v.* To cast off; discard.

sludge (slŭj) *n.* Mud or ooze covering the ground.

slut (slŭt) *n.* A dirty, sloppy woman.

smart (smärt) *v.* To sting painfully.

smite (smīt) *v.* To strike forcefully.

sodden (sŏd′n) *adj.* Soaked through.

solace (sŏl′ĭs) *n.* Comfort; consolation.

solicitor (sə-lĭs′ə-tər) *n.* A lawyer.

solicitous (sə-lĭs′ə-təs) *adj.* Showing concern. — **solicitously** *adv.*

sordid (sôr′dĭd) *adj.* Dirty.

sovereign (sŏv′ər-ən) *adj.* Supreme; above all others.

sovereignty (sŏv′ər-ən-tē) *n.* Royal authority or power.

spawn (spôn) *v.* To produce; give birth to.

species (spē′shēz, -sēz) *n.* Kind; type; variety.

specter (spĕk′tər) *n.* A ghost.

speculation (spĕk′yə-lā′shən) *n.* A theory or conclusion based on guesswork.

speculative (spĕk′yə-lə-tĭv, -lā′tĭv) *adj.* Theoretical.

spew (spyōō) *v.* To gush out.

splay (splā) *v.* To spread out; expand.

sportive (spôr′tĭv, spōr′-) *adj.* Playful.

spraddle (sprăd′l) *v.* To spread the legs in a sprawling way.

sprite (sprīt) *n.* A fairy.

squeamish (skwē′mĭsh) *adj.* Easily made sick.

squire (skwīr) *n.* A young man of good birth who attends a knight.

staid (stād) *adj.* Sedate; sober.

stance (stăns) *n.* The standing posture of a person or animal.

stark (stärk) *adv.* Utterly; entirely.

stave (stāv) *n.* A stick or staff.

stealth (stĕlth) *n.* Furtiveness.

stench (stĕnch) *n.* A bad smell.

steward (stōō′ərd, styōō′-) *n.* A manager of a large household or estate.

stile (stīl) *n.* A set of steps used for getting over a fence or wall.

stipulate (stĭp′yə-lāt′) *v.* To specify a condition or term, as in a contract.

strait (strāt) *n.* A narrow waterway connecting two larger bodies of water.

strand (strănd) *n.* A foreign country (*poetic*).

stratagem (străt′ə-jəm) *n.* A deceptive maneuver.

subaltern (sŭb-ôl′tərn, *British* sŭb′əl-tûrn′) *adj.* Describing an officer holding a rank below captain.

subjective (səb-jĕk′tĭv) *adj.* Personal.

subserve (səb-sûrv′) *v.* To aid; be useful to.

subtile (sŭt′l) *adj.* Subtle.

subtle (sŭt′l) *adj.* Not obvious.

suckling (sŭk′lĭng) *n.* An unweaned child.

sufferance (sŭf′ər-əns, sŭf′rəns) *n.* The ability to endure pain.

sufficiency (sə-fĭsh′ən-sē) *n.* An adequate amount.

suffuse (sə-fyōōz′) *v.* To spread through or fill.

sullen (sŭl′ən) *adj.* Gloomy; sulky.

summarily (sə-măr′ə-lē, sŭm′ər-ə-lē) *adv.* Speedily.

sundry (sŭn′drē) *adj.* Miscellaneous; of an indefinite small number.

sup (sŭp) *n.* A sip.

supercilious (sōō′pər-sĭl′ē-əs) *adj.* Haughty; scornful. — **superciliously** *adv.*

superfluity (sōō′pər-flōō′ə-tē) *n.* An excess.

supine (sōō-pīn′, sōō′pīn′) *adj.* Lying down. — **supinely** *adv.*

supple (sŭp′əl) *adj.* Able to move and bend easily.

supplicant (sŭp′lĭ-kənt) *n.* A person who asks for something humbly.

supplication (sŭp′lĭ-kā′shən) *n.* A humble prayer or request.

surf (sûrf) *n.* Waves breaking on the shore.

surfeit (sûr′fĭt) *v.* To overindulge.

surmise (sər-mīz′) *v.* To guess.

sward (swôrd) *n.* Grass-covered earth.

swathe (swăth) *n.* A wrapping.

swivel (swĭv′əl) *n.* A device that lets the parts attached to it move freely.

symmetry (sĭm′ə-trē) *n.* Correspondence in shape, size, and arrangement of elements.

syndicate (sĭn′dĭ-kĭt) *n.* A group of people formed to carry out some undertaking.

T

taciturn (tăs′ə-tərn) *adj.* Untalkative; reserved. — **taciturnity** (tăs′ə-tûr′nə-tē) *n.*

tag (tăg) *n.* A short, familiar quotation.

taint (tānt) *v.* To infect; spoil.

talon (tăl′ən) *n.* A claw.

tarnish (tär′nĭsh) *v.* To dull.

tarry (tăr′ē) *v.* To linger.

tartar (tär′tər) *n.* A white substance used in laxatives.

taunt (tônt) *v.* To mock.

taut (tôt) *adj.* Pulled tight.

tedious (tē′dē-əs) *adj.* Tiresome.

temperance (tĕm′pər-əns, tĕm′prəns) *n.* Abstinence from alcoholic beverages.

temperate (tĕm′pər-ĭt, tĕm′prĭt) *adj.* Moderate.

tendance (tĕnd′əns) *n.* Attendance; attention.

tern (tûrn) *n.* A sea bird.

terrestrial (tə-rĕs′trē-əl) *adj.* Belonging to the earth.

thane (thān) *n.* In Scotland, a feudal lord.

thrash (thrăsh) *v.* To move wildly about.

tolerable (tŏl′ər-ə-bəl) *adj.* Bearable.

tongs (tôngz, tŏngz) *n. pl.* A device for grasping objects.

toper (tō′pər) *n.* A drunkard.

tortuosity (tôr′chōō-ŏs′ə-tē) *n.* A twisting or winding.

ă pat/ā pay/âr care/ä father/b bib/ch church/d deed/ĕ pet/ē be/f fife/g gag/h hat/hw which/ĭ pit/ī pie/îr pier/j judge/k kick/l lid, needle/m mum/ n no, sudden/ng thing/ŏ pot/ō toe/ô paw, for/oi noise/ou out/ōō took/ōō boot/p pop/r roar/s sauce/sh ship, dish/t tight/th thin, path/*th* this, bathe/ ū cut/ûr urge/v valve/w with/y yes/z zebra, size/zh vision/ə about, item, edible, gallop, circus/à *Fr.* ami/œ *Fr.* feu, *Ger.* schön/ü *Fr.* tu, *Ger.* über/ KH *Ger.* ich, *Scot.* loch/N *Fr.* bon.

trajectory (trə-jĕk′tə-rē) *n.* The path of something as it moves through space.

trammel (trăm′əl) *v.* To entrap or confine. Sometimes used with *up.*

transcend (trăn-sĕnd′) *v.* To go beyond a limit.

transcendent (trăn-sĕn′dənt) *adj.* Surpassing; excelling.

transcribe (trăn-skrīb′) *v.* To write out in full.

transfigure (trăns-fĭg′yər) *v.* To change the form of.

transformation (trăns′for-mā′shən) *n.* A change in form or appearance.

transgress (trăns-grĕs′, trănz-) *v.* **1.** To break a law; go beyond certain limits. **2.** To sin.

transgression (trăns-grĕsh′ən, trănz-) *n.* The breaking of a law.

travail (trə-vāl′, trăv′āl′) *n.* Agony.

treachery (trĕch′ə-rē) *n.* Betrayal.

treasonous (trē′zən-əs) *adj.* Traitorous.

tremulous (trĕm′yə-ləs) *adj.* Trembling.

trepidation (trĕp′ə-dā′shən) *n.* Fearfulness.

tress (trĕs) *n.* A lock of hair.

tribulation (trĭb′yə-lā-shən) *n.* Misery; suffering.

trivet (trĭv′ĭt) *n.* A three-legged stand or support for pots, hot dishes, etc.

triviality (trĭv′ē-ăl′ə-tē) *n.* A trifle.

truculent (trŭk′yə-lənt) *adj.* Eager to fight.

tumid (tōō′mĭd, tyōō-) *adj.* Swollen.

tumult (tōō′məlt, tyōō′-) *n.* **1.** Great noise and confusion. **2.** Emotional disturbance.

tumultuous (tə-mŭl′chōō-əs) *adj.* Confused and excited.

turbid (tûr′bĭd) *adj.* Thick and dense.

tyrannical (tĭ-răn′ĭ-kəl, tī-) *adj.* Unjust; cruel.

U

ulcerous (ŭl′sər-əs) *adj.* Infected, as an ulcer.

unanimous (yōō-năn′ə-məs) *adj.* Being in complete agreement.

unassuageable (ŭn′ə-swāj′ə-bəl) *adj.* Beyond relief.

unburnished (ŭn′bûr′nĭshd) *adj.* Unpolished.

uncanny (ŭn′kăn′e) *adj.* Weird; mysterious.

undivulged (ŭn′dĭ-vŭljd′) *adj.* Not revealed.

unintelligible (ŭn′ĭn-tĕl′ə-jə-bəl) *adj.* Not capable of being understood.

unlineal (ŭn′lĭn′ē-əl) *adj.* Not hereditary.

unplumbed (ŭn′plŭmd′) *adj.* Not explored.

unpremeditated (ŭn′prī-mĕd′ə-tā′tĭd) *adj.* Not planned beforehand.

unsanctified (ŭn′săngk′tə-fīd) *adj.* Not made holy.

unsavory (ŭn′sā′və-rē) *adj.* Offensive.

unslaked (ŭn′slākt′) *adj.* Unsatisfied.

upbraid (ŭp′brād′) *v.* To scold or rebuke.

usurp (yōō-sûrp′, -zûrp′) *v.* To seize power or possessions illegally.

utilitarian (yōō-tĭl′ə-târ′ē-ən) *adj.* Useful; practical.

V

vacillate (văs′ə-lāt′) *v.* To waver.

vain (vān) *adj.* Fruitless.

valance (văl′əns) *n.* A short curtain or drapery at the top of a window, bed, etc.

vale (vāl) *n.* A valley.

valediction (văl′ə-dĭk′shən) *n.* A farewell.

valiant (văl′yənt) *adj.* Brave.

valor (văl′ər) *n.* Bravery.

vanquish (văng′kwĭsh, văn′-) *v.* To defeat in battle or in an argument.

vantage (văn′tĭj) *n.* A position that provides a broad view of a place or an idea.

vaunt (vônt, vänt) *v.* To boast.

vehement (vē′ə-mənt) *adj.* Expressing intense emotion.

veneration (vĕn′ə-rā′shən) *n.* Reverence; deep respect.

vengeance (vĕn′jəns) *n.* The act of punishing another (or desire to do so) in return for an injury or wrong.

vengeful (vĕnj′fəl) *adj.* Wanting vengeance.

venom (vĕn′əm) *n.* Spite; malice.

venomous (vĕn′ə-məs) *adj.* Spiteful; malicious.

venture (vĕn′chər) *n.* An undertaking, sometimes risky.

verbatim (vûr-bā′tĭm) *adj.* Word for word.

verity (vĕr′ə-tē) *n.* A statement or belief acknowledged to be an established truth.

vermilion (vər-mĭl′yən) *n.* Bright red.

vermin (vûr′mĭn) *n.* Disease-carrying or destructive small animals or insects.

vernal (vûr′nəl) *adj.* Springlike.

vex (vĕks) *v.* To irritate.

victuals (vĭt′lz) *n.* Food.

vigilant (vĭj′ə-lənt) *adj.* Watchful and alert.

villainy (vĭl′ə-nē) *n.* Wickedness.

vindication (vĭn′dĭ-kā′shən) *n.* Justification; defense.

vintage (vĭn′tĭj) *n.* Wine of a particular year and place.

virtuous (vûr′chōō-əs) *adj.* Morally upright.

vivacity (vĭ-văs′ə-tē, vī-) *n.* Sprightliness.

voluble (vŏl′yə-bəl) *adj.* Talkative.

voluptuous (və-lŭp′chōō-əs) *adj.* Sensuous. —**voluptuousness** *n.*

votary (vō′tə-rē) *n.* Someone devoted to an ideal or faith.

W

wallop (wŏl′əp) *n. Obsolete.* A gallop.

wan (wŏn) *adj.* Pale; sickly; weak.

wanton (wŏn′tən) *adj.* Unrestrained; running to excess; extravagant.

warble (wôr′bəl) *v.* To sing.

ware (wâr) *adj.* Aware.

warrant (wôr′ənt, wŏr′-) *n.* Guarantee.

wary (wâr′ē) *adj.* Cautious.

wayward (wā′wərd) *adj.* Unpredictable.

wheelwright (hwēl′rīt′) *n.* A person who makes and repairs wheels.

whetstone (hwĕt′stōn) *n.* A stone for sharpening knives and tools.

wile (wīl) *n.* A trick.

wiseacre (wīz′ā′kər) *n.* A know-it-all.

withal (wĭth-ôl′) *adv.* Besides.

wrangler (răng′glər) *n.* A quarrelsome person.

wrath (răth, räth) *n.* Anger; rage.

wreathe (rēth) *v.* To encircle.

writ (rĭt) *n.* Something written; a document.

wroth (rôth) *adj.* Angry.

wrought (rôt) *adj.* Formed.

Y

yeoman (yō′mən) *n.* A servant in a noble household.

Z

zest (zĕst) *n.* Relish; wholehearted enjoyment.

Outline of Skills

Page numbers in italics refer to entries in the Guide to Literary Terms and Techniques.

LANGUAGE AND VOCABULARY

The following exercises appear in the textbook under the heads **Language and Vocabulary** or **The Growth of the English Language.**

COMPOSITION
The following exercises appear in the textook under the heading **For Composition**.

Writing About Literature
Writing an essay on characteristics of the epic hero, 21

Discussing concept of the hero in Anglo-Saxon times and today, 21

Comparing elegiac tone of "The Seafarer" with the heroic tone of *Beowulf*, 28

Comparing different versions of "Bonny Barbara Allan," 48

Comparing the Monk and the Parson in the *Prologue to The Canterbury Tales*, 73

Synthesizing a view of literature, customs, society, ideals, and beliefs of the Middle Ages, 95

Comparing the metaphorical idea in Wyatt's "Whoso List to Hunt" with that in Spenser's "Sonnet 67," 127

Comparing sonnets of Spenser and Sidney with regard to imagery, personification, and tone, 130

Comparing the sonnets of Shakespeare with sonnets by other Elizabethans, 139

Writing an essay on Shakespeare's "Tell Me Where Is Fancy Bred," 143

Discussing mood of Shakespeare's songs, 143

Analyzing character of Macbeth and Lady Macbeth, 217

Analyzing character flaws in *Macbeth*, 217

Relating clothing imagery in *Macbeth* to character, mood, and theme, 222

Showing how images of darkness, blood, nature, and the supernatural contribute to atmosphere in *Macbeth*, 222

Analyzing the argument of DeQuincey's essay, 224

Contrasting poems by an Elizabethan poet and Donne in terms of attitude, content, and language, 242

Analyzing Donne's major theme and variations in "Meditation 17," 244

Comparing Marvell's "The Garden" with Marlowe's "The Passionate Shepherd to His Love," 249

Comparing ideas of retreat in Marvell's "The Garden" and Vaughan's "The Retreat," 251

Comparing the advice given in "It Is Not Growing like a Tree" with that in "Virtue," 258

Analyzing the variety of Jonson's work, using direct quotations as illustrations, 258

Contrasting the philosophies of Lovelace and Suckling in "Why So Pale and Wan" and "To Lucasta, on Going to the Wars," 263

Writing an essay agreeing or disagreeing with Steele's point of view, 345

Explaining use of techniques of ridicule in the work of Pope and Swift, 361

Comparing satire of Pope with that of Addison and Steele, citing references to specific selections, 361

Demonstrating how Burns's use of dialect reflects the rural landscape of Scotland, 392

Defining the terms *innocence* and *experience* as Blake intended them, 400

Discussing Blake's contrary states with specific references to selections, 400

Interpreting final lines of "A Slumber Did My Spirit Seal," 436

Describing the means Coleridge employs to induce a "willing suspension of disbelief" in *The Rime of the Ancient Mariner*, 461

Writing an essay comparing Byron's view of nature with Wordsworth's, 488

Explaining how figures of speech enrich the meaning of Shelley's "Ode to the West Wind," 496

Comparing Keats's sonnet "When I Have Fears That I May Cease to Be" with Milton's sonnet "On His Blindness," 505

Interpreting the final lines of Keats's "Ode on a Grecian Urn," 523

Comparing Tennyson's "Ulysses" with Browning's "My Last Duchess," 580

Comparing and contrasting the seaside settings in Arnold's "To Marguerite—Continued" and "Dover Beach," 585

Writing an essay analyzing the philosophy of Housman's poetry, 598

Analyzing Dickens' use of caricature, 611

Writing an essay on Hardy's view of fate, using the incident of the escaped prisoner in "The Three Strangers," 625

Tracing the images of light and shadow in "Araby," 727

Showing how the contrast between reality and the boy's romantic impressions of objects helps develop the theme of "Araby," 727

Discussing significance of the words *luck* and *lucky* in "The Rocking-Horse Winner," 738

Discussing the dill pickle as a symbol in Katherine Mansfield's story, 743

Comparing techniques used by O'Flaherty and Conrad to create mood and atmosphere, 748

Writing an essay relating Tennyson's poem to events in "Tears, Idle Tears," 754

Selecting one sentence in "Shooting an Elephant" that best expresses Orwell's basic point and explaining why it does so, 767

Discussing the narrator's role in "Across the Bridge," 774

Comparing the view of nature developed in "A Sunrise on the Veld" with the view developed in O'Flaherty's "The Wild Goat's Kid," 780

Comparing use of setting in "The Train from Rhodesia" with its use in "Across the Bridge," 784

Discussing the use of symbols in poetry, using poems by Yeats, Shelley, and Blake, 794

Comparing the theme of Yeats's "Sailing to Byzantium" with that of Keats's "Ode on a Grecian Urn," 794

Comparing and contrasting Muir's "The Horses" with Brooke's "The Soldier," 804

Demonstrating how Eliot's poem "The Hollow Men" illustrates his poetic principle, 813

Selecting a theme in Thomas' poems and discussing its treatment in two of his poems, 838

Analyzing use and effect of sound patterns in "Fern Hill," 838

Discussing the plausibility of romantic promise at the end of *Pygmalion*, 913

Analyzing the character of Miss Brill, 961

Comparing "Miss Brill" with "A Dill Pickle," focusing on the subject of loneliness, 961

Showing how O'Flaherty prepares the reader for the ironic ending of "The Sniper," 964

Analyzing the character of the sniper, 964

Discussing humorous clues to the tone of "The Open Window," 966

Comparing characters in two of Saki's stories, 966

Showing how Maugham uses direct and indirect characterization in "The Verger," 971

Discussing Maugham's use of irony, 971

Comparing the lady in Campion's poem with the lady in Shakespeare's Sonnet 130, 972

Discussing *Everyman* as a sermon on morality, 982

Comparing allegorical figures in *Everyman* with those in *The Pilgrim's Progress*, 982

Other Writing Exercises

Writing a newspaper account of the story of Sir Patrick Spens and comparing it with the ballad, 48

Writing a character sketch, using Chaucer's *Prologue* as a model, 73

Writing an exemplum, 80

Writing an original sonnet in the Shakespearean pattern, 139

Rewriting two passages of Bacon's essay in Modern English, 227

Writing an essay telling whether the idea of "living for today" (*carpe diem*) would have been popular during the Middle Ages, 260

Writing a letter of exaggerated compliment imitating a poetic model, 260

Presenting arguments for and against a proposition, 278

Choosing a subject for an ode and listing the images, metaphors, and similes that might be used in praise of that subject, 317

Writing a diary entry for some event witnessed at first hand, 325

Writing a first-person account of an event from the past, choosing an identity and a clearly established viewpoint, 331

Writing an imaginary scene for a modern Gulliver, 340

Attacking a custom in the manner of Steele by discussing the motives of those who adhere to the custom, 345

Developing a modern mock-epic in an essay, 361

Writing a letter, using Johnson's letter to Lord Chesterfield as a model, 372

Writing a journal entry from Johnson's point of view, 380

Writing an epitaph, 386

Describing a familiar scene from memory, 432

Composing a sonnet commemorating an event of historical importance, 440

Describing a dream, 464

Writing a monologue expressing the thoughts and feelings of some heroic figure from literature, 563

Relating an experience of or inventing a comic sketch about Bunburying, 668

Writing an essay on the characteristics of Americans, 713

Viewing "Masculine Protest" from a different point of view, 761

Writing about a childhood experience, evoking its special qualities through images and concrete details, 838

Relating an imaginary story of transformation, 913

Index of Titles by Themes

Perceptions

Commentaries and Special Essays

Index of Fine Art

Credits

Kings and Queens of England

Important Kings Before the Norman Conquest

Bretwealdas

c.	477–491	Aelle, King of the West Saxons
c.	560–584	Caelwin, King of the West Saxons
	584–616	Aethelbert, King of Kent
c.	600–616	Raedwald, King of East Anglia
	616–632	Edwin, King of Northumbria
	633–641	Oswald, King of Northumbria
	654–670	Oswiu, King of Northumbria

King of Mercia

758–796	Offa

Kings of the West Saxons

802–839	Egbert
866–871	Aethelraed
871–899	Alfred
899–925	Edward the Elder
959–975	Edgar the Peaceable
979–1016	Aethelraed the Redeless
1016–1035	Cnut
1042–1066	Edward the Confessor
1066	Harold Godwinson

Normans

1066–1087	William I
1087–1100	William II
1100–1135	Henry I
1135–1154	Stephen

Angevins-Plantagenets

1154–1189	Henry II
1189–1199	Richard I
1199–1216	John
1216–1272	Henry III
1272–1307	Edward I
1307–1327	Edward II
1327–1377	Edward III
1377–1399	Richard II

Lancastrians

1399–1413	Henry IV
1413–1422	Henry V
1422–1461	Henry VI

Yorkists

1461–1483	Edward IV
1483	Edward V
1483–1485	Richard III

Tudors

1485–1509	Henry VII
1509–1547	Henry VIII
1547–1553	Edward VI
1553–1558	Mary (I)
1558–1603	Elizabeth I

Stuarts

1603–1625	James I
1625–1649	Charles I
1649–1660	Commonwealth and Protectorate
1660–1685	Charles II
1685–1688	James II
1688–1702	William III and Mary (II)
1702–1714	Anne

Hanoverians

1714–1727	George I
1727–1760	George II
1760–1820	George III
1820–1830	George IV
1830–1837	William IV
1837–1901	Victoria
1901–1910	Edward VII
1910–1936	George V
1936	Edward VIII
1936–1952	George VI
1952–	Elizabeth II

General Index

Titles of selections presented in the textbook are shown in italics. Numbers in italics refer to the pages on which author biographies appear. Names of authors represented in the textbook and other references are shown in regular type.

B 5
C 6
D 7
E 8
F 9
G 0
H 1
I 2
J 3